OLD TIMES IN
OLD MONMOUTH

OLD TIMES IN OLD MONMOUTH

Historical Reminiscences of
Old Monmouth County, New Jersey:
Being a Series of Historical Sketches
Relating to Old Monmouth County
(now Monmouth and Ocean),
New Jersey

To Which Is Appended the
History and the Centennial of
THE BATTLE OF MONMOUTH

*Edwin Salter and
George C. Beekman*

HERITAGE BOOKS
2010

HERITAGE BOOKS
AN IMPRINT OF HERITAGE BOOKS, INC.

Books, CDs, and more—Worldwide

For our listing of thousands of titles see our website
at
www.HeritageBooks.com

A Facsimile Reprint
Published 2010 by
HERITAGE BOOKS, INC.
Publishing Division
100 Railroad Ave. #104
Westminster, Maryland 21157

Originally published:
Freehold, New Jersey, 1887
Reprinted from a volume in the
Library of the Monmouth County Historical Association

— Publisher's Notice —
In reprints such as this, it is often not possible to remove blemishes from the original. We feel the contents of this book warrant its reissue despite these blemishes and hope you will agree and read it with pleasure.

International Standard Book Numbers
Paperbound: 978-0-7884-1228-8
Clothbound: 978-0-7884-8400-1

PREFACE.

The matter in this volume under the title of "*Old Times in Old Monmouth*" was originally contributed by the author, Hon. EDWIN SALTER, to the *Monmouth Democrat*, and was printed in that newspaper during the years 1873 and '74. At the suggestion of friends who desired to preserve these articles in a more convenient shape for reference the matter, after it was used in the newspaper, was made up into pages and one hundred copies only were printed from the forms, that being deemed at the time sufficient to supply all probable demands for it. Subsequently Judge BEEKMAN contributed to the columns of the *Democrat* the result of his researches into the history of the Boundaries and Townships of the County, and it was determined to add that contributition to the volume. The Centennial year followed, and it was proposed to still further enlarge the volume by adding to it the matter relating to that event, and also two interesting and valuable original articles by Gen. J. WATTS DE PEYSTER, of New York city, "*The Consideration of the Case of Gen. Charles Lee*," and "*The Affair at Freehold*."

The work of printing these pages was necessarily hurried and fragmentary, and at intervals. No effort was made at typographical nicety of execution ; the sole object being to preserve the articles in a convenient shape at the minimum of cost.

The index of names referred to in the book, which will be found in the end of the volume, was prepared as a labor of love by Rev. R. R. HOES, Chaplain in the U. S. Navy. It contains the names of over twenty-one hundred different persons, and to many of them reference is made a number of times. Besides there is an index prepared by the publisher to each article and subject treated of in the book.

A number of the volumes were distributed before the index was prepared. Only eighty-five perfect copies are remaining. These will be numbered in the order in which they are disposed of, and will be accompanied with a certificate showing the number. Parties in possession of the other volumes will be furnished with copies of the Index upon application, and certificates numbered from eighty-six to one hundred. THE PUBLISHER.

FREEHOLD, April, 1887.

NOTE.—Mr. SALTER says that the name GERRARD BOWNE, on p. 207, should be GERRARD BOURNE, who was a Rhode Islander and did not come to Monmouth. Also, on same page, that the copyist omitted the name of "JOHN TILLTON, 2 shares," which in the original record stands the sixth name on the list.

GENERAL INDEX.

A

American Prisoners, how treated by the British...... 15
Ancestors, our—of English Origin..........................162
Ancient Journal, an...107
Ancient Writer—Old Monmouth Described by an 3
Asbury, Bishop, in Old Monmouth, extracts from his journal...101
Assemblymen's Salaries, how paid.........................105
Assembly, Provincial, List of Members of............. 92
Asgill and His Companions..................................... 90
Asgill's Story, a Nobleman Tells............................. 84
Atlantic Township set off.......................................182

B

Bacon, John, refugee leader..................................... 43
" " capture and death of.......................122
Baptist Church, first one in New Jersey............105
" " Middletown, organization of......305
" " reference to..........................note 264
Baptists arrested and sent to Boston for preaching.187
Baptists, the Rogerine..147
Barclay of Ury, poem..237
Barkalow of Old Monmouth at Germantown......... 24
Barnegat Inlet, history of.......................................144
Battle Ground, visitors at the................................160
Battle of Monmouth—Appendix. (See Index of Appendices).
Berkeley and Carteret, their claims......................216
Bird, Richard, the Potter's Creek outlaw............... 39
Boston, Relief for Poor of.. 32
Boundaries and Townships....................................165
Boundary between Middlesex established............181
Bowne, Capt. John, Address of to his Children......222
Boy Tried for Murder...142
Brainerd, David, Missionary to the Indians, extract from his memoirs.....................................248
Brave Youth, a.. 23
Bridge Company, the Navesinck............................195
British Spy, Execution of a..................................... 66
Brown, John, (A. D. 1677,) martyrdom of, poem......248
Burying Ground of the Crawfords.........................317

C

Calendar, The—changed..........................103, note 222
Centennial Celebration—see Centennial Appendix.
Chief Ranger of Monmouth....................................105
Colman's Point, why so Named.............................. 7
Confiscation in the Revolution............................... 14
Congressional Representatives—list of.................162
County Judge, Indictment of a..............................256
" officials, the first.....................................166
Court House, first one built at Freehold..........note 248
Court Officials at Middletown seized and held as prisoners...264
Courts, authority of resisted by citizens of Middletown......................................169, 260, 263
Courts, extracts from ancient minutes of........248, 302
Courts, ancient modes of proceedings of..............240
" in A. D. 1694..169
Covenanters, Scotch, in Monmouth......................248
Coward, Capt. Joseph, sketch of............................ 24
Cranbury Inlet, history of......................................143
Crosswicks, Indian Conference at........................152

D

"Dark and Bloody Ground," Monmouth the........174
Davenport, Refugee leader..................................... 39

DeVries, David Peterson, voyages of......................227
Dog, a valuable 145
Dover township set off..173
Dutch Conquest the...223
" discover the western passage to India........299
" influence of the in Monmouth....................299
" Old Monmouth under the........................ 4
" their houses and furniture described..........300
Dutchman, first one holding a judicial position...note 269

E

East Jersey, extracts from the records of the Governor and Council..220
Eatontown township set off...................................196
Episcopalianism in Old Monmouth.......55, 95, note 264
" first converts to........................... 55
Essex, citizens of endorse Freehold resolutions...... 28
Executions of murderers and refugees at Freehold. 38
" first in the county...............................note 254

F

Fagan, Jacob, outlaw, killed and hung in chains... 36
Family Names, origin of..117
Farr, Thomas, and wife, murder of......................... 35
Fenton, Lewis, outlaw, killed................................. 35
Fire-Water, its first Indian victim.......................... 9
Fishing Point, location of................................note 176
Fish, swarming in New York Bay.........................231
Fontaine, John, extracts from Journal of..............232
Forked River, Refugee raid at................................ 45
Forman, Col. Jonathan and daughter....................145
Forman, Samuel, captures two British soldiers..... 23
Four-County Bridge, the..176
Fox, George, visits Middletown and Shrewsbury... 12
Freehold, answer to questions of Committee of as to arming the militia....................................301
Freehold, citizens of first to denounce Great Britain 28
" described by an ancient writer............... 3
" first Court House built in.....................248
" first County Court held at............note 269
" incorporation of town of......................195
" patriots tar and feather and burn a Tory pamphlet... 33
" the founder of....................................... 19
" the town of—date of its origin..........note 248
" township, original boundaries of............168
Freneau, Philip, Poet of the Revolution, sketch of..107
Friends. (See Quakers).

G

Goodluck, origin of the name................................. 68
" refugee raid at.. 45
Grain, prices of in 1683..105
Grand Jury, an Independent..................................256
Grandmothers, our Good-Looking.........................161
"Greens," The (Refugee Raiders)..........................113
Grenadiers, Charge of at Battle of Monmouth......159
Grenadier flag captured at Battle of Monmouth....158

H

Half Moon, extract from log-book of the............... 6
Hendricks, Vice Prest., U. S., ancestors from Monmouth...note 264
Hendricksons, The..150
Highways of Monmouth..................................165, 265
Holland neighborhood......................................note 183
Holmdel township set off.......................................185

GENERAL INDEX.

Holmes, Obadiah, narrative of..............................188
Horse-Pound, tradition of.........................note 180
Horrible Confession by British Provost Marshal....15
Horse Railroads chartered.................................195
Howell township set off.....................................180
Huddy, Capt. Joshua, attack on at Colts Neck........72
   "   "   "   capture of.............................16
   "   "   "   who responsible for his murder.......................................135
   "   "   "   the hero martyr.......................74
Hudson, Sir Henry, arrival of...................................6
   "   "   "   visit to Old Monmouth...........10
Hugenot Element, family names of..............note 231
Hyler, Capt. Adam, the Daring Privateer..............124

I

Imlaystown, an Indian tradition of........................22
Incorporated town, the first................................195
Indian Claims in Old Monmouth and vicinity.....53
   "   "   purchased by New Jersey..............21
   "   "   singular...21
Indian Claimants, the last....................................21
Indian Dinner, an..152
Indian Peter, a tradition of Imlaystown................22
Indian Queen, Bathsheba......................................22
Indian Will, an eccentric aboriginal....................22
Indians astonished at arrival of white men...........8
   "   deeds executed by..251
   "   first white man killed by.................................7
   "   hotels and hospitality of the..........................11
   "   Richard Hartshorne's agreement with...........21
   "   persons presented for selling rum to............250
   "   the first drunken..8
   "   the Raritan...22
Inlets of Old Monmouth.....................................143

J

Jackson township set off.....................................181
Jail Limits established..306
Jersies, the origin of the term............................166

K

Keith, George, a Quaker preacher.................note 166
   "   "   founder of Freehold..............................19
   "   "   converts Quakers to Episcopalianism....56
Keyport, incorporation of.....................................56
   "   Refugee raid at...113
King's Highway, a......................................note 178
King's Highways..251, 252

L

Lawrence Family, The...150
Laws of 1713, observations on the........................270
Lawyer, first practicing in Monmouth..........note 254
Lee, Gen. Charles, curious incident in life of, (Bat. of Monmouth Appendix, p. 60).
"Lee's, Plan, (Mr.)" for subjugating the Colonies. (Bat. of Monmouth Appendix, p. 4.)
Light House, Sandy Hook, first lighted.........note 180
Lincoln township set off......................................195
   "   "   act repealed..196
Long Branch, founder of as a watering place.....152
   "   "   great wrestling match at.......................154
   "   "   history and traditions of.......................152
   "   "   in 1819...144
   "   "   origin of name of.....................................152
   "   "   who first brought it into notice............152
Loyalists, American...55
   "   of Freehold, Middletown, Shrewsbury, Upper Freehold and Dover......................14
   "   of Old Monmouth..47

M

Manalapan, township set off...............................183
Mannahawkin, skirmish at....................................44
Marlborough township set off.............................182
Matawan township set off...................................186
Methodism expounded by Rev. Benjamin Abbott..70
   "   in Old Monmouth..100

Middletown, Baptist church of..........................105
   "   citizens of resist authority of the courts...260, 263
   "   described by an ancient writer...................3
   "   estimate of the morals of........................264
   "   extracts from the Town Book of.............216
   "   original boundaries of..............................168
   "   Refugee raid at..113
Militia, first act establishing the........................105
   "   first officers of the.....................................105
   "   of Monmouth in the Revolution..................71
Millstone township set off...................................180
Mills, William, an Old Monmouth preacher.......102
Monckton, Col., at Battle of Monmouth............157
Monmouth, contributions of to Poor of Boston....32
   "   county established......................................103
   "   described by an ancient writer..................3
   "   Fight. Henry Morford's story of—(Bat. of Monmouth Appendix, p. 30.)
   "   original boundaries of..............................103
   "   "   "   corrected............171
   "   "   township boundaries............168
   "   origin of the name......................................103
   "   resolutions against Great Britain..............29
   "   Patent, copy of the..1
Moody, the Refugee Partisan.................................58
   "   capture and escape of..................................59
Murray, Joseph, killed by Refugees....................304

N

Negro Cesar's indictment...................................253
   "   "   sentence..254
New England, our ancestors of the best blood of..162
News, how obtained in A. D. 1700.......................177
Nicolls, Gov., letters of......................................197

O

Ocean county set off..184
Ocean Grove, incorporation of............................196
Ocean township set off..183
Old Monmouth described.......................................3
   "   "   during the Revolution..............................113
   "   "   early history of..6
   "   "   under the Dutch..4
Old papers found by Judge Forman....................301
   "   "   of James G. Crawford...............................274
   "   "   of George W. and Richard Crawford....313
   "   "   of Ruliff E. Conover..................................308
Old Records—extracts from Book A, county records..200
Outlaws of the Pines......................................34, 37
Oyster laws, infringements of the......................157
   "   the, is it a wild or tame animal—a singular law suit...156

P

Peace, how the news was received.........................18
Peden at the grave of Cameron, poem.................246
Phalanx, North American, the............................177
Pine Robbers—see Outlaws of the Pines.
Pirates harbor in Raritan Bay......................note 259
   "   one of Kidd's rescued from the sheriff.....263
Pitcher, Capt. Molly, her bravery, sad end, &c....155
Plank Roads of Monmouth..................................192
Population of Monmouth in 1850........................184
Potter Church, the..128
Potter's Creek Outlaw, the....................................39
Presbyterians in Monmouth. (Also see Scotch Immigration)..
Prisoners, American, how treated by the British...15
Privateer, the Daring..124
Privateering on the Coast.....................................67
Privateers, list of captures by.............................125
   "   other..127
Profane swearing, indictment for.......................256
Public Conveyances in 1723................................178
Purgatory in Monmouth..12

Q

Quaker meetings in Middletown and Shrewsbury.11
Quakers, American sympathizers........................123

GENERAL INDEX.

Quakers, converted to Episcopalianism............ 55
"   erect Topanemus meeting house............238
"   George Keith and the immigration of Scotch............................244, 19
"   of the olden time, poem........................234
"   the Monmouth.....................................234
"   visit of distinguished to Monmouth........ 11
Queen Bathsheba... 22

R

Raids of the Refugees..................................71, 113
Railroads of Monmouth....................................193
Randolph Family, the.......................................151
Ranger, Chief, of Monmouth............................105
Raritan township set off...................................183
Records, extracts from ancient of Monmouth....239
Red Bank, incorporation of...............................195
"   Refugee raid at......................................113
Redstone Country, emigration to the................ 24
Refugees, a terrible day for the........................ 18
"   and murderers executed at Freehold.... 38
"   kill Joseph Murray..................................304
"   leader of in Dover.................................. 39
"   leader of in Monmouth and Burlington.. 43
"   Monmouth, in New York........................135
"   raid of the at Goodluck........................... 45
"   "   "   "   Mannahawkin..................... 44
"   "   "   "   Tinton Falls.......................113
"   "   "   "   Waretown.......................... 45
"   raids of the...................................71, 113
"   the.. 70
Refugee, Moody the Partisan............................ 58
Religious History of Old Monmouth, passages in..128
Religious toleration, Monmouth the pioneer of.....147
Rensselaer's Point, Hook, Pier.................note 229
Representatives, Congressional.........................162
Revolution causes of the War of the.................. 27
Royal Grenadiers at Battle of Monmouth...........157
Royal Volunteers, the of New Jersey...........50, 113
Ruse of Major Kearney.....................................115
Russell Family, attack on the.......................65, 115

S

Sandy Hook, ceded to the U. S..........................180
"   "   Inlet..note 168
"   "   light house first lighted............note 180
"   "   first white men enter A. D. 1524......... 6
Sandy New..note 183
Scotch Immigration...244
Settlers, the first in Monmouth........................ 51
Shrewsbury, notice for meeting at to support the King.. 32
"   described by an ancient writer............... 3
"   falls into line with the patriots............... 33
"   Inlet, history of.....................................144
"   township, original boundaries of...........168
"   Refugee raid at......................................113
Singular religious society, a.............................147
Slaves, record of manumission of.....................305
Southwick, Cassandra, poem............................234
Spy British, execution of a................................ 66
Stafford township set off..................................172
Steamboat, where first one landed............note 176
Story of Monmouth Fight, (Henry Morford)—Battle of Monmouth Appendix, p. 30.
Stout Family, the... 51
Surnames, list, origin and derivation of...........119
Swimming River, origin of the name..........note 177

T

Taxes, how levied..105
Temperance Society, the first in the U. S..........145
Tennent, Rev. William, his remarkable trial for perjury.. 90
Throg's Neck, origin of the name..............note 176
Tilton Family, the..145
Tinton Falls, origin of the name.................note 169
"   "   Refugee raid at..............................113
Tom, Capt. William, sketch of........................... 40
Toms River, discovery of, &c............................ 40
"   "   during the Revolution................18, 67
"   "   the attack on.................................. 16
Topanemus meeting house...............................238

Tories, how rewarded by the British................ 54
Townships in 1800..180
"   when established..............................145
"   resolutions of to raise money for ammunition, &c... 34
Travelling in 1723 and 1753................178, 179
"   two hundred years ago....................... 11
Turnpikes..194
Tye, Colonel, noted colored refugee leader......114

U

Union City, founder of....................................193
Universalists, origin of the Society in America....128
"   centenary of the................................133
Upper Freehold, portion of set off to Plumsted....184
"   "   resolutions of to raise money for ammunition, &c... 34
"   "   township set off................................172

W

Wall township set off.......................................185
Waretown, refugee raid at................................ 45
War of 1812, an amusing stratagem................149
"   scenes on the Coast............................148
Washington and Lee at Monmouth.................... 93
Watering Places in New Jersey—their origin....176
Waykake Landing... 8
White Men, astonishment of Indians at arrival of. 8
"   "   coming of the................................. 8
"   "   entering Sandy Hook...................... 6
"   "   first landing of............................... 7
"   "   first one killed by Indians............... 7
"   "   their first opinion of Monmouth.....162
White, Phil, capture and death of................60, 116
Wrecks and prizes......................................68, 69

Y

Year, the, legal and historical discrepancies explained.......................................103, note 222

INDEX TO THE APPENDICES.

BATTLE OF MONMOUTH APPENDIX.

Events preceding the... 2
"Mr. Lee's Plan" for subjugating the Colonies...... 4
Thomas F. Gordon's history of.......................... 6
British account of the......................................12
American account of the..................................19
Story of Monmouth Fight..................................30
Lossings history of..35
From Marshall's Life of Washington.................41
"   Col. Willetts' Narrative...........................50
"   Life of Gen. Knox....................................52
"   Moore's Diary of the Revolution.............54
Col. John Laurens' account of...........................56
Letters of Gen's. Wayne and Scott....................58
Washington's marching orders.........................59
Washington's letters of Instruction...................61
From Dawson's Battles of the U. S....................61
Letters of Washington, Lafayette, and others....71

CENTENNIAL APPENDIX.

Centennial Celebration, procession, exercises, orations, &c... 1 to 19
Centennial Poems by Henry Morford, Thomas Dunn English, F. P. Holmes, and Capt. Enoch Cowart...................................19 to 22
Comments of the Press............................23 to 30
S. S. Cox's Oration, full text of, corrected by the author..31 to 42
Consideration of the Case of Gen. Charles Lee, by Gen. J. W. DePeyster.........................43 to 50
List of Representatives from Monmouth in the Provincial Assembly, Legislative Council and State Legislature from 1703 to 1878...51 to 54
The Affair of Freehold; an exhaustive review of the History of the Battle of Monmouth, with copious notes, by Gen. DePeyster....55 to 74

OLD TIMES IN OLD MONMOUTH.

THE MONMOUTH PATENT.

As this noted instrument, though familiar to those who have made the early history of our State a special study, is not readily accessible to some of our readers, we copy it here for convenient reference to all interested in the history of Old Monmouth:

"To all whom these presents shall come: I Richard Nicolls Esq, Governor under his Royal Highness the Duke of York of all his Territories in America, send greeting.

"Whereas there is a certain tract or parcel of land within this government, lying and being near Sandy Point, upon the Main; which said parcel of land hath been with my consent and approbation bought by some of the inhabitants of Gravesend upon Long Island of the Sachems (chief proprietors thereof) who before me have acknowledged to have received satisfaction for the same, to the end that the said land may be planted, manured and inhabited, and for divers other good causes and considerations, I have thought fit to give confirm and grant and by these presents do give confirm and grant unto WILLIAM GOULDING, SAMUEL SPICER, RICHARD GIBBONS, RICHARD STOUT, JAMES GROVER, JOHN BOWN, JOHN TILTON, NATHANIEL SYLVESTER, WILLIAM REAPE, WALTER CLARKE, NICHOLAS DAVIS, OBADIAH HOLMES, patentees, and their associates, their heirs, successors and assigns, all that tract and part of the main land, beginning at a certain place commonly called or known by the name of Sandy Point and so running along the bay West North West, till it comes to the mouth of the Raritan River, from thence going along the said river to the westermost part of the certain marsh land, which divides the river into two parts, and from that part to run in a direct Southwest line into the woods twelve miles, and thence to turn away south east and by south, until it falls into the main ocean; together with all lands, soils, rivers, creeks, harbors, mines, minerals (Royal mines excepted) quarries, woods, meadows, pastures marshes, waters, lakes, fishings, hawkings, huntings and fowling, and all other profits, commodities and hereditaments to the said lands and premises belonging and appertaining, with their and every of their appurtenances and of every part and parcel thereof, TO HAVE AND TO HOLD all and singular the said lands, hereditaments and premises with their and every of their appurtenances hereby given and granted, or herein before mentioned to be given and granted to the only proper use and behoof of the said patentees and their associates, their heirs successors and assigns forever, upon such terms and conditions as hereafter are expressed, that is to say, that the said patentees and their associates, their heirs or assigns shall within the space of three years, beginning from the day of the date hereof, manure and plant the aforesaid land and premises and settle there one hundred families at the least; in consideration whereof I do promise and grant that the said patentees and their associates, their heirs, successors and assigns, shall enjoy the said land and premises, with their appurtenances, for the term of seven years next to come after the date of these presents, free from payment of any rents, customs, excise, tax or levy whatsoever. But after the expiration of the said term of seven years, the persons who shall be in possession thereof, shall pay after, the same rate which others within this his Royal Highness' territories shall be obliged unto. And the said patentees and their associates, their heirs successors and assigns shall have free leave and liberty to erect and build their towns and villages in such places, as they in their discretions shall think most convenient, provided that they associate themselves, and that the houses of their towns and villages be not too far distant and scattering one from another; and also that they make such fortifications for their defence against an enemy as may be needful.

"And I do likewise grant unto the said patentees and their associates, their heirs successors and assigns, and unto any and all other persons, who shall plant and inhabit in any of the land aforesaid that they shall have free liberty of conscience, without any molestation or disturbance whatsoever in their way of worship.

"And I do further grant unto the aforesaid patentees, their heirs, successors and assigns, that they shall have liberty to elect by the vote of the major part of the inhabitants, five or seven other persons of the ablest and discreetest of the said inhabitants, or a greater number of them (if the patentees, their heirs, successors or assigns shall see cause) to join with them, and they together, or the major part of them, shall have full power and authority, to make such peculiar and prudential laws and constitutions amongst the inhabitants for the better and more orderly governing of them, as to them shall seem meet; provided they be not repugnant to the public laws of the government; and they shall also have liberty to try all causes and actions of debts and trespasses arising amongst themselves to the value of *ten pounds*, without appeal, but they may remit the hearing of all criminal matters to the assizes of New York.

"And furthermore I do promise and grant unto the said patentees and, their associates aforementioned their heirs, successors and assigns that they shall in all things have equal privileges, freedom and immunities with any of his majesty's subjects within this government, these patentees and their associates, their heirs, successors and assigns rendering and paying such duties and acknowledgments as now are, or hereafter shall be constituted and established by the laws of this government, under obedience of his Royal Highness. his heirs and successors, provided they do no way enfringe the privileges above specified.

"Given under my hand and seal at Fort James in New York in Manhattan Island the 8th day of April, in the 17th year of the reign of our sovereign lord Charles the Second by the grace of God, of England, Scotland, France and Ireland, King, Defender of the Faith &c., and in the year of our Lord God 1665.

RICHARD NICOLLS.

"*Entered in the office of record in New York, the day and year above written.*

MATTHIAS NICOLLS, Secretary."

About seven years after the date of the above instrument, the following confirmations to portions of it were agreed 'o by Governor Carteret and Council:

NEW JERSEY May 28th 1672.

Upon the address of James Grover, John Bowne, Richard Hartshorne, Jonathan Holmes, patentees, and James Ashon and John Hanse, associates, impowered by the patentees and associates of the towns of Middletown and Shrewsbury. unto the Governor and Council for confirmation of certain privileges granted unto them by Colonel Richard Nicolls, as by patent under his hand and seal bearing date the 8th day of April Anno Domini One thousand six hundred sixty-five, the Governor and Council do confirm unto the said patentees and associates, these particulars following, being their rights, contained in the aforesaid patent, viz:

Imprimis: That the said patentees and associates have full power, license and authority to dispose of the said lands expressed in the said patent, as to them shall seem meet.

II. That no ministerial power or clergyman shall be imposed on among the inhabitants of the said land, so as to enforce any that are contrary minded to contribute to their maintenance.

OLD TIMES IN OLD MONMOUTH.

III. That all causes whatsoever (criminals excepted) shall first have a hearing within their cognizance, and that no appeals unto higher courts where sentence has been passed amongst them under the value of ten pounds be admitted.

IV. That all criminals and appeals above the value of ten pounds, which are to be referred unto the aforesaid higher courts, shall receive their determination upon appeals to his Majesty, not to be hindered.

V. That for all commission officers both civil and military, the patentees, as sociates and Freeholders, have liberty to present two for each office to the Governor when they shall think fit, one of which the Governor is to *Commissionate* to execute the said office, and that they have liberty to make peculiar prudential laws and constitutions amongst themselves according to the tenor of the said patent.

PH. CARTERET.

John Kenney, Lordue Andress, Samuel Edsall, John Pike, John Bishop, *Council*.

The causes which induced the following very material modification in the grants and privileges to the Monmouth patentees and their associates will be referred to hereafter.

"Directions, instructions and orders made by the late Lords Proprietors of the province of East New Jersey, to be observed by the Governor, Council and inhabitants of the said province, bearing date the 31st day of July, Anno Domini, 1674, amongst which there is as followeth, viz: as to inhabitants of Nevisinks, considering their faithfulness to the Lords Proprietors that upon their petition, their township shall be surveyed and shall be incorporated, and to have equal privileges with other the inhabitants of the Province, and that such of them who were the pretended patentees and laid out money in purchasing land from the Indians, shall have in consideration thereof five hundred acres of land to each of them to be alloted by the Governor and Council, in such places that it may not be prejudicial to the rest of the inhabitants, and because there is much barren land, after survey taken, the Governor and Council may give them allowance."

OLD MONMOUTH DESCRIBED BY AN ANCIENT WRITER.

MIDDLETOWN, SHREWSBURY AND FREEHOLD IN 1708.—NEW JERSEY A PARADISE.

We copy the following from the celebrated but quite rare work of Oldmixon, published in 1708. The Capitals, orthography and italics are about as in the original.

After describing Middlesex county, he says: "We cross over the river from Middlesex into

Monmouth County; Where we first meet with *Middleton* a pretty Good Town consisting of 100 Families and 30,000 Acres of Ground on what they call here *Out* Plantations. 'Tis about 10 or 12 miles over Land, to the Northward of Shrewsbury and 26 miles to the Southward of Piscattaway. Not far off, the Shoar winds itself about like a Hook and being sandy gives Name to all the Bay.

Shrewsbury is the most Southern Town of the Province and reckon'd the chief Town of the Shire. It contains about 160 Families and 30,000 Acres of *Out* Plantations, belonging to its Division. 'Tis situated on the Side of a fresh Water Stream, thence called Shrewsbury River, not far from its Mouth. Between this Town and *Middleton* is an Iron Work but we do not understand it has been any great Benefit to the Proprietors. Col. *Morris* is building a Church at the Falls. There's a new town in the County called

Freehold, which has not been laid out and inhabited long. It does not contain as yet above 40 Families and as to its *Out* Plantations we suppose they are much the same in number with the rest and may count it about 30,000 acres.

We have not divided the counties into Parishes and that for a good reason, there being none, nor indeed a Church in the whole Province worth that Name. But there are several Congregations of Church of *England* men as at *Shrewsbury, Amboy, Elizabeth* Town and *Freehold* whose Minister is Mr. *John Beak*; his Income is 65l. a year; and a Church is building at Salem.

In another place Oldmixon in speaking of the first settlers of New Jersey says:

"We must note that most of the first English Inhabitants in this country (East and West Jersey) were Dessenters, and most of them Quakers and Anabaptists. These people are generally industrious; Be their Hypocrisy to themselves if they are Hypocrites; but we must do them the Justice to own that they are the fittest to inhabit a new discovered Country, as posessing Industry, and shunning those publick Vices which beget Idleness and Want. Their enemies drove great numbers of them out of England, and the Jerseys had their share of them. The People here are for this Reason Dissenters to this Day, their being but two Church of England Ministers in both Provinces; and this may be one reason why there are no Parish Churches, which the Inhabitants may be afraid to build, least it might be a temptation for more Orthodox Divines to come among them.

"A gentleman asking one of the Proprietaries ' If there were no Lawyers in the Jerseys?' Was answered 'No.' And then 'If there were no Physicians?' The Proprietor replied 'No' 'Nor Parsons?' adds the Gentleman. 'No,' says the Proprietor. Upon which the other cry'd 'What a happy place must this be and how worthy the name of Paradice!" We do not perhaps differ more from this gentleman than we agree with him."

Oldmixon derived his information of New Jersey from two of the Proprietors as will be seen by the following extract from his preface:

"Mr *Dockwra* and Dr *Cox* were both so kind as to inform him fully of the JERSEYS and Mr. *Pen* did him the same Favor for *Pennsylvania*; these three Gentlemen doing him the Honor to admit him into their Friendship."

OLD MONMOUTH UNDER THE DUTCH.

Governor Parker, in his valuable address before the New Jersey Historical Society, produced the old town book of Middletown township, which gives the history of this section of East Jersey from 1667, to 1702. After the Dutch conquest in 1673, it was stated that little or nothing is recorded in the town book during their brief rule of less than a year.

Your readers may remember that the Dutch had the supremacy in New York and New Jersey until 1664, when the English conquered the Dutch. In 1673, a war having again broken out between England and Holland, a small Dutch squadron was sent over and arrived at Staten Island, July 30th. Captain Manning, the English officer temporarily in command at New York, surrendered at once without any effort to defend the place and the Dutch again resumed sway over New York, New Jersey and settlements along the Delaware. They retained it however only a few months, as by a treaty made in February following, these places were ceded back to England, though the English appear not to have taken formal possession until November following.. During this short time while the Dutch were again in authority, embracing the time that Governor Parker says the Middletown township book records but little or nothing, the following items relating to Old Monmouth, are found among the official records of the Dutch at New York. The first is an order issued shortly after their arrival; the orthography is given as we find it:

"The inhabitants of Middletown and Shrewsbury, are hereby charged and required to send their deputies unto us on Tuesday morning next, for to treat with us upon articles of surrendering their said towns under the obedience of their High and Mighty Lords, the States General of the said United Provinces, and his serene Highness, the Prince of Orange, or by refusall we shall be necessitated to subdue the places thereunto by force of arms.

"Dated at New Orange this 12th day of August. A. D. 1673. .

"CORNELIS EVERTSE, Jr."
"JACOB BENCKES."

In compliance with the above order, deputies from Shrewsbury, Middletown and other places in East Jersey, appeared in court on the 18th of August, and upon their verbal request the same privileges were granted to them as to Dutch citizens.

"August 19th 1673. Middletown, Shrewsbury and other towns in Achter Coll, to name two deputies each, who shall nominate three persons for Schout and three for Secretarys, out of whice said nominated persons by us shall be elected for each town, three magestrates and for the six towns, one Schout, and one Secretary.

"JACOB BENCKES."
"CORNELIS EVERTSE, Jr."

Achter Coll above mentioned, is said to mean "beyond the hills," that is, beyond Bergen Hills. The Dutch in New York it is stated sometimes called Old Monmouth and other parts of East Jersey, beyond Bergen Hills, by this name.

"August 23d, 1673. Middletown and Shrewsbury, reported that they had nominated double the number of magistrates.

"August 24th, from the nominations made by the inhabitants, the following were selected and sworn, viz:

"John Hance (Hance?), Eliakim Wardel, Hugh Dyckman.

"Sept. 6th, 1673. Captain Knyff and Captain Snell were sent to administer the oath of allegiance to the citizens of the various towns in East Jersey to the Dutch.

"14th of 7 ber, Captain Knyff and Lieut. Snell having returned yesterday from Aghter Coll, report that, pursuant to their commission, they have administered the oath of allegiance in the form herein before set forth, under date of ———— to the inhabitants of the undersigned towns, who are found to number as in the lists delivered to Council.

"Elizabethtown 80 men; 76 took oath, rest absent.
Newark........... 86 "   75   "   "
Woodbridge..... 54 "   53   "   "
Piscataway...... 43 "   43   "   "
Middletown...... 60 "   52   "   "
Shrewsbury...... 68 "   38   "   18 Quakers promised allegiance, the rest absent."

The following officers of the militia, elected, were sworn in by Captain Knyff and Lieut. Snell, by order of the Council of War, viz:

Middletown, Jonathan Hulmes, Captain; John Smith, Lieutenant; Thomas Whitlock, Ensign.

Shrewsbury, William Newman, Captain, John Williamson, Lieutenant; Nicles Brown, Ensign.

"29th, 7 ber, 1673, Notice is this day sent to the Magistrates of the towns, situated at the Nevesings, near the sea coast, which they are ordered to publish to their inhabitants, that on the first arrival of any ship from sea, they shall give the Governor the earliest possible information thereof.

"Sept. 7th, 1673, Whereas, the late chosen Magistrates of Shoursbury, are found to be Persons whose religion Will Not Suffer them to take on any oath, or administer the same to others, whereof they Can Not be fit Persons for that office, I have therefore though fit to order that by ye sd inhabitants of ye sd towne a New Nomination, shall be made of four persons of true Protestant Christian religion, out of which I shall Elect two, and Continue one of ye former for Magestrates off ye sd towne."

"Dated att ffort William hendrick, this 29th, 7 ber, 1673.   A. COLVE."

The date 7th ber, in the above extracts, means September, and the persons in Shoursbury [Shrewsbury] who could not take the oath were Quakers.)

"March 8th, 1674, In council at fort William Hendrick:

"Read and considered the petition of Bartholomew Appelgadt, Thomas Appelgadt and Richard Saddler, requesting in substance that they be allowed to purchase from the Indians, a tract of land, situated about two leagnes on this side of Middletown, near the Nevesings, fit for settlement of 6 or 8 families &c. Wherefore it was ordered:

"The Petitioners request is allowed and granted on condition, that after the land be purchased, they take out patents in form for it and actually settle it within the space of two years, after having effected the purchase, on pain of forfeiture.

"April 18th, 1674, John Bound (Bowne?), and Richard Hartshoerne, residing at Middletown, both for themselves and partners give notice that the land granted to Bartholomew Applegadt, Tho. Applegadt and Richard Sadler, in their petition is included in their, the Petitioners patent, requesting therefore that the said land may be again denied to said Appelgadt.

"Ordered, That the petitioners shall within six weeks from this date, prove, that the said land is included within their patent, when further order shall be made in the premises.

"April 19th, 1674, A certain proclamation being delivered into Council from the Magestrates of the Toune of Middletown, prohibiting all inhabitants from departing out of said toune, unless they give bail to return as soon as their business will have been performed, or they be employed in public service &c., requesting the Governers approval of the same, which being read and considered, it is resolved and ordered by the Governor General and Council, that no inhabitant can be hindered changing his domicile, within the Province unless arrested for lawful cause; however ordered that no one shall depart from the toune of Middletoune, unless he previously notifies the Magestrates of his intention."

RANDOM REMINISCENCES
OF THE
EARLY HISTORY OF OLD MONMOUTH.

THE WHITES ENTERING SANDY HOOK.

The earliest accounts we have of the whites being in the vicinity of Monmouth county is contained in a letter of John de Verazzano to Francis 1st, King of France. Verazzano entered Sandy Hook in the spring of 1524 in the ship Dolphin. On his return to Europe, he wrote a letter dated July 8th, 1524, to the King, giving an account of his voyage from Carolina to New Foundland. From this letter is extracted the following:

"After proceeding a hundred leagues, we found a very pleasant situation among some steep hills, through which a very large river, deep at its mouth, forces its way to the sea; from the sea to the estuary of the river any ship heavily laden might pass with the help of the tide, which rises eight feet. But as we were riding at good berth we would not venture up in our vessel without a knowledge of its mouth; therefore we took a boat, and entering the river we found the country on its banks well peopled, the inhabitants not differing much from the others, being dressed out with feathers of birds of various colors. They came towards us with evident delight, raising loud shouts of admiration and showing us where we could most securely land with our boat. We passed up this river about half a league when we found it formed a most beautiful lake three leagues in circuit, upon which they were rowing thirty or more of their small boats from one shore to the other, filled with multitudes who came to see us. All of a sudden, as is wont to happen in navigation, a violent contrary wind blew in from the sea and forced us to return to our ship, greatly regretting to leave this region which seemed so commodious and delightful, and which we supposed must also contain great riches, as the hills showed many indications of minerals."

Historians generally concede that the foregoing is the first notice we have of the whites entering Sandy Hook, visiting or being in the vicinity of old Monmouth.

ARRIVAL OF SIR HENRY HUDSON.

In the year 1609, Sir Henry Hudson visited our coast in the yacht or ship Half Moon, a vessel of about eighty tons burthen. About the last of August he entered the Delaware Bay, but finding the navigation dangerous he soon left without going ashore. After getting out to sea he stood northeastwardly and after awhile hauled in, and made the land probably not far distant from Great Egg Harbor.— The journal or log book of this vessel was kept by the mate, Alfred Juet, and as it contains the first notices of Monmouth county by the whites, remarks about the country, its inhabitants and productions, first landing, and other interesting matter, an extract is herewith given, commencing with September 2nd, 1609, when the Half Moon made land near Egg Harbor. The same day, it will be seen, the ship passed Barnegat Inlet, and at night anchored near the beach within sight of the Highlands.

Their first impression of old Monmouth, it will be seen, was "*that it is a very good land to fall in with, and a pleasant land to see;*" an opinion which in the minds of our people at the present day show that good sense and correct judgment were not lacking in Sir Henry Hudson and his fellow-voyagers!

Extract from the Log-Book of the Half Moon.

Sept. 2nd, 1609.—When the sun arose we steered nor h again and saw land from the west by north to the northwest, all alike, broken islands, and our soundings were eleven fathoms and ten fathoms.— The course along the land we found to be north east by north. From the land which we first had sight of until we came to a great lake of water, as we could judge it to be, (*Barnegat Bay,*) being drowned land which made it rise like islands, which was in length ten leagues. The mouth of the lake (*Barnegat Inlet*) had many shoals, and the sea breaks upon them as it is cast out of the mouth of it. And from that lake or bay the land lies north by east, and we had a great stream out of the bay; and from thence our soundings was ten fathoms two leagues from land. At five o'clock we anchored, being light wind, and rode in eight fathoms water; the night was fair. This night I found the land to haul the compass eight degrees. Far to the northward of us we saw high hills (*Highland?*):

for the day before we found not above two degrees of variation.

This is a very good laud to fall in with, and a pleasant land to see.

Sept. 3d—The morning misty until ten o'clock; then it cleared and the wind came to the south southeast, so we weighed and stood northward. The land is very pleasant and high and bold to fall withol. At three o'clock in the afternoon we came to three great rivers (*Narrows*, *Rockaway Inlet* and *the Raritan*); so we stood along the northward (*Rockaway Inlet*,) thinking to have gone in, but we found it to have a very shoal bar before it for we had but ten feet water. Then we cast about to the southward and found two fathoms, three fathoms and three and a quarter, till we came to the southern side of them; then we had five and six fathoms and returned in an hour and a half. So we weighed and went in and rode in five fathoms, ooze ground, and saw many salmons and mullets and rays very great. The height is 40° 30′ (*Latitude*.)

First Landing of the Whites in Old Monmouth.

Sept. 4th.—In the morning as soon as the day was light, we saw that it was good riding farther up; so we sent our boat to sound, and found that it was a very good harbor and four or five fathoms, two cable lengths from the shore. Then we weighed and went in with our ship. Then our boat went on land with our net to fish, and caught ten great mullets of a foot and a half long, a plaice and a ray as great as four men could haul into the ship. So we trimmed our boat and rode still all day.— At night the wind blew hard at the northwest, and our anchor came home, and we drove on shore, but took no hurt, and thank God, for the ground is soft sand and ooze. This day the people of the country came aboard of us and seemed very glad of our coming, and brought green tobacco leaves and gave us of it for knives and beads. They go in deer skins, loose and well dressed. They have yellow copper. They desire clothes and are very civil.— They have a great store of maize or Indian wheat, whereof they make good bread.— The country is full of great and tall oaks.

Sept. 5th.—In the morning, as soon as the day was light, the wind ceased and the flood came. So we heaved off the ship again into five fathoms and sent our boat to sound the bay, and we found that there was three fathoms hard by the southern shore. Our men went on land then and saw a great store of men, women and children, who gave them tobacco at their coming on land. So they went up into the woods and saw a great store of very goodly oaks and some currants, (*probably huckleberries*). For one of them came on board and brought some dried, and gave me some, which were sweet and good. This day many of the people came on board, some in mantles of feathers, and some in skins of divers sorts of good furs. Some women also came with hemp. They had red copper tobacco pipes, and other things of copper they did wear about their necks. At night they went on land again, so we rode very quiet but durst not trust them.

The First White Man Killed.

Sunday, Sept. 6th.— In the morning was fair weather, and our master sent John Colman, with four other men. in our boat over to the North side to sound the other river (*Narrows*), being four leagues from us. They found by the way shoal water, being two fathoms ; but at the north of the river, eighteen and twenty fathoms, and very good riding for ships, and a very narrow river to the westward between two islands (*Staten Island and Bergen Point.*)— The land they told us, was as pleasant with grass and flowers and goodly trees as ever they had seen, and here very sweet smells came from them. So they went in two leagues and saw an open sea (*Newark Bay*), and returned, and as they came back they were set upon by two canoes, the one having twelve men and the other fourteen men. The night came on and it began to rain, so that their match went out; and they had one man slain in the fight, which was an Englishman named John Colman, with an arrow shot in his throat, and two more hurt. It grew so dark that they could not find the ship that night, but labored to and fro on their oars. They had so great a strain that their grapnel would not hold them.

Sept. 7th.—Was fair, and by ten o'clock they returned aboard the ship and brought our dead men with them, whom we carried on land and buried and named the point after his name, Colman's Point. Then we hoisted in our boat and raised her side with waist boards, for defence of our men. So we rode still all night, having good regard for our watch.

Sept. 8th.— Was very fair weather ; we rode still very quietly. The people came aboard of us and brought tobacco and Indian wheat, to exchange for knives and beads and offered us no violence. So we fitting up our boat did mark them to see if they would make any show of the death of our man, which they did not.

Sept. 9th.—Fair weather. In the morning two great canoes came aboard full of men; the one with their bows and arrows, and the other in show of buying knives, to betray us; but we perceived their intent. We took two of them to have kept them, and put red coats on them, and would not suffer the others to come near us. So they went on land and two others came aboard in a canoe; we took the one and let the other go; but he which we had taken got up and leaped overboard. Then we weighed and went off into the channel of the river and anchored there all night.

The foregoing is all of the log-book of Juet that relates to Monmouth county.—The next morning the Half Moon proceeded up the North River, and on her return passed out to sea without stopping.

In the extract given above, the words in italics are not of course in the original, but are underscored as explanatory.

THE COMING OF THE WHITE MAN.

What the Indians thought of the Whites and their ships.—The Natives Astonished.—The Man in Red and the Red Man.—Fire Water and its First Indian Victim.—The First Indians Drunk, &c.

After Sir Henry Hudson's departure from the shores of Monmouth he proceeded towards Manhattan Island and thence up the river now bearing his name. The following traditionary account, the coming of the Whites according to Heckwelder, was handed down among both Delaware and Iroquois Indians. It is not often we meet in fact or fiction a more interesting story than this plain, simple Indian tradition. After explaining that the Indian chiefs of old Monmouth County, notified the chiefs on York or Manhattan Island, and that the chiefs of the surrounding country finally gathered at the last named place to give a formal reception, the tradition says:

A long time ago before men with a white skin had ever been seen, some Indians fishing at a place where the sea widens, espied something at a distance moving upon the water. They hurried ashore, collected their neighbors, who together returned and viewed intently this astonishing phenomenon. What it could be baffled conjecture. Some supposed it to be a large fish or other animal, others that it was a large house floating upon the sea. Perceiving it moving towards the land, the spectators concluded that it would be proper to send runners in different directions to carry the news to their scattered chiefs, that they might send off for the immediate attendance of their warriors.—These arrived in numbers to behold the sight, and perceiving that it was actually moving towards them, that it was coming into the river or bay, they conjectured that it must be a remarkably large house in which the *Manitto* or Great Spirit was coming to visit them. They were much afraid and yet under no apprehension that the Great Spirit would injure them. They worshipped him. The chiefs now assembled at New York Island and consulted in what manner they should receive their Manitto; meat was prepared for a sacrifice. The women were directed to prepare their best victuals. Idols or images were examined and put in order. A grand dance they thought would be pleasing, and in addition to the sacrifice might appease him if hungry. The conjurors were also set to work to determine what this phenomenon portended and what the result would be. To the conjurors, men, women and children looked for protection. Utterly at a loss what to do, and distracted alternately between hope and fear, in the confusion a grand dance commenced.—Meantime fresh runners arrived, declaring it to be a great house of various colors and full of living creatures. It now appeared that it was their Manitto, probably bringing some new kind of game. Others arriving declared it positively full of people of different color and dress from theirs, and that one appeared altogether in *red*. (This was supposed to be Sir Henry Hudson.) This then must be the Manitto.—They were lost in admiration, could not imagine what the vessel was, whence it came, or what all this portended. They are now hailed from the vessel in a language they could not understand. They answered by a shout or yell in their way. The house or large canoe as some call it, stops. A smaller canoe comes on shore with the red man in it; some stay by the canoe to guard it. The chief and wise men form a circle into which the red man and two attendants enter. He salutes them with friendly countenance, and they return the salute after their manner.—They are amazed at their color and dress, particularly with him, who glittering in red wore something, perhaps lace and buttons, they could not comprehend. He must be the great Manitto, they thought, but why should he have a white skin? A large elegant *Hockhack* (gourd, i. e. bottle, decanter, &c.,) is brought by one of the supposed Manitto's servants, from which a substance is placed into smaller cups or glasses and handed to the Manitto. He drinks, has the glasses refilled and handed to the chief near him. He takes it, smells it, and passes it to the next, who does the same. The glass in this manner is passed around the circle and is about to be returned to the red clothes man, when one of the Indians, a great warrior, harangues them on the impropriety of returning the cup unemptied. It was handed to them, he said, by the Manitto, to drink out of as he had. To follow his example would please him—to reject might provoke his wrath; and if no one else would he would drink it himself, let what would follow, for it were better for one man to die, than a whole nation to be destroyed. He then took the glass, smelled it, again addressed them, bidding adieu, and drank its contents. All eyes are now fixed upon the first Indian in New York, who had tasted the poison, which has since effected so signal a revolution in the condition of the native Americans. He soon began to stagger. The women cried, supposing him in fits. He rolled on the ground; they bemoan his fate; they thought him dying; he fell asleep; they at first thought he had expired, but soon perceived he still breathed; he awoke, jumped up, and declared he never felt more happy. He asked for more, and the whole assembly imitating him became intoxicated. While this intoxication lasted, the whites confined themselves to their vessels; after it ceased, the man with the red clothes returned and distributed beads, axes, hoes and stockings. They soon became familiar, and conversed by signs. The whites made them understand that they would now return home, but the next year they would visit them again with presents, and stay with them awhile; but as that they could not live without eating, they should then want a little land to sow seeds, in order to raise herbs to put in their broth.

Accordingly a vessel arrived the season following, when they were much rejoiced to see each other; but the whites laughed when they saw axes and hoes hanging as ornaments to their breasts, and the stockings used as tobacco pouches. The whites now put handles in the axes and hoes and cut down trees before their eyes, dug the ground, and showed them the use of stockings. Here, say the Indians, a general laugh ensued—to think they had remained ignorant of the use of these things, and had borne so long such heavy metals suspended around their necks. Familiarity daily increasing between them and the whites—the latter prepared to stay with them—asking them only for so much land as the hide of a bullock spread before them would cover; they granted the request.— The whites then took a knife, and, beginning at a place on the hide, cut it up into a rope not thicker than the finger of a little child. They then took the rope and drew it gently along in a circular form, and took in a large piece of ground; the Indians were surprised at their superior wit, but they did not contend with them for a little ground, as they had enough.— They lived contentedly together for a long time, but the new comers from time to time asked for more land, which was readily obtained, and thus gradually proceeded higher up the *Mahicannittuck* (*Hudson River*), until they began to believe they would want all their country, which proved eventually to be the case.

The name which the Indians first gave to the whites was *Woapsiel Lennape*, which signified white people. But in process of time, when disagreeable events occurred between them, the Indians laid aside this name and called them *Schwonnack*—the salt people—because they came across the salt water; and this name was always after applied to the whites.

The foregoing traditions are said to have been handed down among both Delaware and Iroquois. It has also been said that the Indian name for the Island upon which New York is situated (Manhattan) is derived from a word signifying " the place where we all got drunk together.": Some New York writers take umbrage in this statement, and say the drunken scene occurred up the river ; but the exact place where it occurred is immaterial. Perhaps some may think the city has since that time fairly earned that name ! Ancient writers testify that the first Indians who drank liquor generally became intoxicated by one drink, by two at most.

The Delawares owned and were spread over the whole country, from New York Island to the Potomac. They say they had a great many towns, among other places a number on the Lennapewihittack or Delaware river, and a great many in *Sheyichbi* on that part of the country now named Jersey. That a place named *Chichohaci*, now Trenton, on the Lannapewihittuck a large Indian town had been for many years together, where their great chief resided. The Delawares say Chickohacki is a place on the east side of the Delaware river above Philadelphia, at or near a great bend where the white people have since built a town which they call Trenton. Their old town was on a high bluff, which was always tumbling down, wherefore the town was called Chiehohacki, which is *rumbling* banks, or *falling* banks.

When the Europeans first arrived at York Island the Great Unami, chief of the Turtle tribe, resided southward across a large stream or where Amboy now is.— That from this town a very long sand bar (Sandy Hook) extended far into the sea. That at Amboy and all the way up and down their large rivers and bays and on great islands they had towns when the Europeans first arrived, and that it was their forefathers who first discovered the Europeans on their travel, and who met them on York Island after they landed.

SIR HENRY HUDSON'S VISIT TO OLD MONMOUTH.

A celebrated historian, in speaking of Hudson's visit to Monmouth County and vicinity in September, 1609, says :

" For a week Hudson lingered in the lower bay, admiring the gobdly oaks which garnished the neighboring shores, and holding frequent intercourse with the native savages of Monmouth, N. J. The Half Moon visited in return by the wandering Indians, who flocked on board the strange vessel, clothed with mantles of feathers and robes of furs and adorned with rude copper necklaces. Meanwhile a boat's crew was sent to sound the river which opened to the northward. Passing through the Narrows they found a noble harbor with very good riding for ships ; a little further on they came to the Kills between Staten Island and Bergen Neck— a narrow river to the westward between two islands. The lands on both sides were as pleasant with grass and flowers and goodly trees as ever they had seen, and very sweet smells came from them. Six miles up the river they came to an open sea, now known as Newark Bay. In the evening, as the boat was returning to the ship, the exploring party was set upon by two canoes full of savages, and one of the English sailors, named John Colman, was killed by an arrow shot into his throat. The next day Hudson buried, upon an adjacent beach, the comrade who had shared the dangers of his polar adventures, to become the first European victim to an Indian weapon, in the placid waters he had now reached. To commemorate the event, Sandy Hook was named Colman's Point. The ship was soon visited by canoes full of native warriors ; but Hudson, suspecting their good faith, took two savages, put red coats on them, while the rest were not suffered to approach."

In regard to the place where Colman was buried, most writers have taken it for granted that it was Sandy Hook, and one that it was Coney Island. But there is much plausibility in the following, from a paper published many years ago in the Proceedings of the New Jersey Historical Society :

" Dr. Strong, in his History of Flatbush, supposes Colman's Point to be Coney Island, and that Colman had been corrupted into Coney, but (in the opinion of the writer of this paper), it is a point about seven miles west of Sandy Hook, called by the Indians Mones-conk, and on Gordon's map called Point Comfort. Hudson, on the fifth of September, removed from his anchorage in the Horse Shoe, not counting it safe to remain there. A strong northwest wind had the night previous brought home the anchor and driven them ashore. In the morning, having got off without injury, he sent the boat to sound the bay and found three fathoms *hard by the Southern shore*. If, then, he left the Horse Shoe, as it is probable, there is no such roadstead as that described, with three fathoms hard by the southern shore, until we reach the bay between Point Comfort and Brown's Point, where the steamboats now land. The waters and a part of the shore in this vicinity were called by the Indians Chingarora—pronounced Shingarora—a name which ought by all means to have distinguished the flourishing village adjacent, instead of the uncouth name of Keyport."

The paper from which the foregoing extract was made, was furnished to the N. J. Historical Society by the Rev. Mr. Mar-

OLD TIMES IN OLD MONMOUTH.

cellus, well known to the older citizens of Freehold, who took great interest in all matters pertaining to the early history of Old Monmouth, and whose decease was not only regretted by an extensive circle of personal friends, but by every person interested in the early history of our state, cognizant of his earnest efforts to rescue from oblivion the fading records of the pioneers of Old Monmouth.

In commenting upon Hudson's first landing, Mr. Marcellus says :

"The first interview with Hudson and his crew presented an interesting spectacle —a grand subject for a painter. The Indians had never before seen a ship. The complexion of the men, their dress, language and manners, the sails and tackling of the ship—the vastness of the vessel itself—all was wonderful."

The fourth of September, 1609, is a memorable day in the annals of our state, as on that day, on the soil of Monmouth, occurred the first landing of whites in New Jersey.

Two days before this—that is, on September 2nd—Sir Henry Hudson sailed near the inlet now known as Barnegat Inlet. The log book of his ship speaks of the sea breaking upon its shoals, and from this it derives its name. The first Dutch explorers named it on their chart "Barende-gat," meaning "breakers inlet," or an inlet with breakers. Barende-gat was gradually corrupted to Barndegat, Bardegut, and finally to Barnegat.

RANDOM REMINISCENCES
OF THE
EARLY HISTORY OF OLD MONMOUTH.

TRAVELLING TWO CENTURIES AGO.

DISTINGUISHED QUAKERS VISIT OLD MONMOUTH.

Crossing the State in Ancient Times—Perilous Travelling—Indian Hotels and Hospitalities—Singular Accident and Remarkable Recovery—Friends' Meeting, in Middletown and Shrewsbury—Purgatory in Old Monmouth—Where was it?—Novel Life Preservers, &c.

It is doubtful if any more ancient accounts of travelling across New Jersey can be found than the following, extracted from the journals of John Burnyeate and George Fox, distinguished members of the Society of Friends ; in company with them were Robert Withers, George Patison and others, some of whom returned by the same route a few months afterwards.—These noted Quaker preachers left Maryland in the latter part of February, 1672, and arrived at New Castle, Delaware, about the first of March. From thence Burnyeate gives the following account of their journey across the State to Middletown :

"We staid there (New Castle) that night, and the next day we got over the river (Delaware). When we got over we could not get an Indian for a guide, and the Dutchman we had hired would not go without an Indian, so we were forced to stay there that day. The next day we rode about to seek an Indian, but could get none to go ; but late in the evening there came some from the other side of the town, and we hired one, and so began our journeying early the next morning to travel through the country, which is now called New Jersey ; and we travelled we supposed nearly forty miles. In the evening we got to a few Indian wigwams, which are their houses ; we saw no man nor woman, house nor dwelling, that day, for there dwelt no English in that country then.

"We lodged that night in an Indian wigwam, and lay upon the ground as the Indians themselves did, and the next day we travelled through several of their towns, and they were kind to use, and helped us over the creeks with their canoes ; we made our horses swim at the sides of the canoes, and so travelled on. Towards evening we got to an Indian town, and when we had put our horses out to grass we went to the Indian King's house, who received us kindly, and showed us very civil respect. But alas ! he was so poorly provided, having got so little that day, that most of us could neither get to eat or drink in his wigwam ; but it was because he had it not—so we lay as well as he, upon the ground—only a mat under us, and a piece of wood or any such thing under our heads Next morning early we took horse and travelled through several Indian towns, and that night we lodged in the woods ; and the next morning got to an English plantation, a town called Middletown, in East Jersey, where there was a plantation of English and several Friends, and we came down with a Friend to his house near the water-side, and he carried us over in his boat and our horses to Long Island."

Though Burnyeate says "there dwelt no English in that country then" it must not be inferred that the Europeans at this time had no settlements in West Jersey. The settlements there were near the Delaware river ; Burnyeate, Fox and their companions had to travel inland some distance from the Delaware so as to be able the more easily to cross the head of streams which empty into that river.

These Friends were travelling in great haste to get to a half yearly meeting at Oyster Bay, L. I., " to settle some difficulties there, which was the cause of our hard travelling." Crossing the State then in three or four days was considered fast travelling.

GEORGE FOX VISITS MIDDLETOWN AND SHREWSBURY.

The following is George Fox's account of the same journey and also of his return trip.

"We departed thence from New Castle, Del., and got over the river not without great danger of some of our lives. When we were got over we were troubled to procure guides ; which were hard to get and very changeable. Then had we that wilderness to pass through since called West Jersey not then inhabited by English ; so that we have travelled a whole day together without seeing man or woman, house or dwelling place. Sometimes we lay in the woods by a fire and sometime in the Indians' wigwams or houses. We came one night to an Indian town and lay at the king's house, who was a very pretty man. Both he and his wife received us very lovingly and his attendants (such as they were) were very respectful to us. They laid us mats to lie on ; but provision was very short with them, having caught but little that day. At another Indian town where we staid the king came to us and he could speak some English. I spoke to him much and also to his people, and they were very loving to us. At length we came to Middletown, an English plantation in East Jersey, and there were friends there, but we could not stay to have a meeting at that time, being so earnestly pressed in our spirits to get to the half yearly meeting of Friends of Oyster Bay, Long Island, which was near at hand. We went with a friend, Richard Hartshorne, brother to Hugh Hartshorne, the upholster in London, who received us gladly to his house, where we refreshed ourselves and then he carried us and our horses in his own boat over a great water, which held us most part of the day in getting over, and set us upon Long Island."

From thence Fox proceeded to Gravesend, L. I. In June following he returned to New Jersey. Of his return trip he writes as follows :

" Being clear of this place we hired a sloop and the wind serving set out for the new country now called Jersey. Passing down the bay by Conny Island, Naton Island and Stratton Island we came to Richard Hartshorne at Middleton harbor about break of day on the 27th of sixth month. Next day we rode about thirty miles into that country through the woods and over very bad bogs, one worse than all the rest, the descent into which was so steep that we were fain to slide down with our horses and then let them lie and breathe themselves before they go on.— This place, the people of the place called Purgatory. We got at length to Shrewsbury in East Jersey, and on First day had a precious meeting there, to which Friends and other people came far, and the blessed presence of the Lord was with us. The same week we had a men and women's meeting out of most parts of New Jersey. They are building a meeting place in the midst of them, and there is a monthly and a general meeting set up, which will be of great service in those parts, in keeping up the gospel order and government of Christ Jesus, of the increase of which there is no end, that they who are faithful may see that all who profess the holy truth live in pure religion and walk as becometh the gospel. While we were at Shrewsbury an accident befel which for a time was a great exercise to us.

John Jay, a friend of Barbadoes who came with us from Rhode Island and intended to accompany us through the woods to Maryland, being to try a horse, got upon his back and the horse fell a running, cast him down upon his head and broke his neck as the people said. Those that were near him took him up as dead, carried him a good way and laid him on a tree. I got to him as soon I could and feeling him, concluded he was dead. As I stood pitying him and his family I took hold of his hair and his head turned any way, his neck was so limber. Whereupon I took his head in both my hands and setting my knees against the tree I raised his head and perceived there was nothing out or broken that way. Then I put one hand under his chin and the other behind his head and raised his head two or three times with all my strength and brought it in. I soon perceived his neck began to grow stiff again and then he began to rattle in his throat an quietly after to breathe. The people were amazed but I bade them have a good heart, be of good faith and carry him into the house. They did so and set him by the fire. I bid them get him something warm to drink and put him to bed. After he had been in the house a while he began to speak, but di.l not know where he had been. The next day we passed away and he with us, pretty well, about sixteen miles to a meeting at Middletown through woods and bogs and over a river where we swam our horses and got over ourselves upon a hollow tree. Many hundred miles did he travel with us after this.

To this meeting came most of the people of the town. A glorious meeting we had and the truth was over all, blessed be the gret Lord God forever. After the meeting we went to Middletown harbor about five miles, in order to take our long journey next morning through the woods towards Maryland, having hired Indians for our guides. I determined to pass through the woods on the other side of the Delaware that we might head the creeks and rivers as much as possible. The ninth of seventh month we set forward, passed through many Indian towns and over some rivers and bogs. When we had rid over forty miles we made a fire at night and lay by it. As we came among the Inians we declared the day of the Lord to them. Next day we travelled fifty miles as we computed, and at night finding an old house, which the Indians had forced the people to leave, we made a fire and lay there at the head of Delaware bay. The ext day we swam our horses over a river about a mile, at twice, first to an Island called *Upper Dinidock* and thence to the main land, having hired Indians to help us over in their canoes."

The island called by Fox Upper Dinidenk is now known as Burlington Island; it was formerly called Matinicunk, which name Fox has misunderstood. He also calls the Delaware river here Delaware bay as he does in other places. By his journal it would seem no whites at that time lived at Burlington though a few whites had lived there and in the vicinity many years before.

It is impossible to read the accounts of travelling at this early period without being forcibly reminded of the contrast in travelling then and now. Many of the Quaker preachers speak of crossing streams in frail Indian canoes, with their horses swimming by their side; and one, the fearless, zealous John Richardson, (so noted among among other things for his controversies with "the apostate George Keith") in substance recommends, in travelling across New Jersey, "for *safety*, travellers' horses should have long tails." The reason for this singular suggestion was that in crossing streams the frail canoes were often capsized, and if the traveller could not swim, he might probably preserve his life by grasping his horse's tail. Mr. Richardson describes how one man's life was preserved by this novel life preserver; in this case the life-preserver being the long tail of Mr. R.'s own horse; and in commenting upon it he quaintly observes "that he always approved horses' tails being long in crossing rivers."

Long before Fox and Burnyeate crossed the state the whites, part'cularly the Dutch, frequently crossed our state by Indian paths, in going to and fro between the settlements on the Delaware and New Amsterdam (New York), though they have left but meagre accounts of their journeyings, and their are strong probabilities that the Dutch from New Amsterdam, after furs and searching for minerals, crossed the state as far as Burlington Island, Trenton, and points far up the Delaware from forty to fifty years before the trip of these Quaker preachers.

That their journeyings were not always safe, is shown in the following extract of a letter written by Jacob Alricks, September 20th, 1669 :

"The Indians have again killed three or four Dutchmen, and no person can go through; one messenger who was eight

14 OLD TIMES IN OLD MONMOUTH.

days out returned without accomplishing his purpose."

The next day he writes:

I have sent off messenger after messenger to the Manhattans overland, but no one can get through, as the Indians there have again killed four Dutchmen.

At the time of writing these letters Alricks resided in Delaware, and they were addressed to the Dutch authorities at New York.

CONFISCATION IN THE REVOLUTION.

Loyalists of Freehold, Middletown, Shrewsbury, Upper Freehold and Dover.

The sales of property in New Jersey adjudged to be confiscated during the war, appear to have been in accordance with the act of the Legislature, April 18th, 1778, entitled "An Act for taking charge of or leasing the real estates and for forfeiting the personal estates of certain fugitives and offenders, &c."

We give below a copy of an official advertisement of property to be sold in old Monmouth under this act. While among the names are found some who were quite noted for their services under the British, of whom mention is made in another chapter, yet there are probably several, who, because of conscientious scruples against war and to avoid being drafted, left the county and sought refuge in the British lines on Long Island or New York. This was probably the case in the township of Shrewsbury where Quakers were quite numerous. How the Quakers fared who stayed at home and risked drafting may be inferred from an extract, which we propose to give hereafter, describing drafting in Burlington county.

'During the course of the war it would seem that almost every man in the county capable of bearing arms, except Quakers, took an active part in the fearful strife on one side or the other.

As an evidence of how not only neighbor was arrayed against neighbor but relative against relative, it is only necessary to compare the names in this advertisement, with the names given in the list of the Monmouth militia. Not only are old families represented on both sides, but in some cases persons of the same name are prominent on both sides; for instance, Elisha Laurence, mentioned below, was a Colonel in the Loyalists, while another Elisha Lawrence, was a Lieutenant Colonel on the American side.

Most of the persons mentioned below were of the most honorable class of tories, or loyalists, as they called themselves—persons of education, wealth and standing, and for that very reason their activities in and advocacy of the British cause was very injurious to the Americans, so much so that it is said that at one time in the early part of the war the Refugees gained the ascendancy and had possession of Freehold village for about a week or ten days and we find that about Nov., 1776, General Washington "found it necessary to detach Colonel Forman of the New Jersey militia to suppress an insurrection which threatened to break out in Monmouth county, where great numbers were well disposed to the Royal cause."

"*Monmouth County*, ss: Whereas inquisition have been found and final judgment entered thereon in favor of the State of New Jersey against persons herein mentioned—Notice is hereby given that the real and personal estates belonging to Samuel Osburn, Thomas Leonard, Hendrick Van Mater, John Throckmorton, Daniel Van Mater, John Longstreet jr, Alexander Clark, Joseph Clayton, Israel Britton, John Okeson, John Thompson, Thomas Bills and Benzeor Hinkson, all of the township of Freehold, will be sold at Freehold Court House, beginning on Wednesday the 17th day of March next and continue from day to day until all are sold.

"Thomas Crowel, George Taylor jr, James Stillwell, John Mount, boatman. Conrad Hendricks, Joseph Baley, John Cottrell, Richard Cole, Samuel Smith, John Bown, James Pew. Thomas Thorne, Ezekiel Tilton, Joseph Taylor, John Tilton, of Middletown and William Smith of Middlesex having lands in said town, will be sold at public vendue, beginning on Monday the 22nd day of March next at the house of Cornelius Swart and continue from day to day until sold.

"John Taylor and William Walton at New York but having property in Shrewsbury, John Williams, Christopher Talman, John Wardell, Michael Price, James Mount, John Williams, Jr., John Pintard, Clayton Tilton, Samuel Cook, James Boggs, James Curlis, Asael Chandler,

OLD TIMES IN OLD MONMOUTH.   15

John Morris, William Price, Robert Morris, Peter Vannote, James Price, John and Morford Taylor, John Hankinson, Timothy Scobey, William Laurence, Peter Wardel, Oliver Talman, Richard Lippencott, Josiah White, Benjamin Woolley, Ebenezer Wardell, Robert Stout, Nathaniel Parker, John Hampton, Samuel Layton, Jacob Harber, Samuel Layton, Jacob Emmons, Britton White, Tobias Kiker and Daniel Lafetter, (Lafetra?), late of the township of Shrewsbury, and Garnadus Beekman of New York, having property in said township, will be sold at public vendue, beginning on Monday the 29th of March at Tinton Falls and continue from day to day until all are sold.

"John Leonard, Gisbert Giberson, Samuel Stillwell, Barzilla, Joseph, Thomas, William and Samuel Grover, John Horner, Fuller Horner, John Perine, William Giberson, Jr., Mallakeath Giberson, John Polhemus, Jr., Benjamin Giberson, Samuel Oakerson, Elisha Laurence and John Laurence sons of John, late of Upper Freehold and Isaac Allen late of Trenton, will be sold at public vendue beginning on Monday the 5th day of April next at Walls Mills and continue until all are sold.

"John Irons and David Smith, of the township of Dover, will be sold at Freehold Court House at the time of sales there.

"The two emissions called in and bank notes will be taken in pay. No credit will be given. The sale will begin at 9 o'clock each day. Also deeds made to the purchasers agreeable to act of Assembly by

" SAMUEL FORMAN
" JOSEPH LAURENCE
" KENNETH HANKINSON
"Commissioners.
" February 17th, 1779."

CAPTAIN WILLIAM CUNNINGHAM.

How American prisoners were treated by the British at New York. Horrible confession by the British Provost Marshal.

The following is copied from the *American Apollo*, February 17th, 1792. In it will be found some startling confessions, showing how hellish was the treatment of our ancestors who were confined as prisoners in New York during the Revolution by this fiend in human shape. It furnishes another reason why our forefathers so detested the British. It will amply repay perusal. Captain Joshua Huddy, and many other old Monmouth patriots, were for a time in this villain's charge :

"The life, confession, and last dying words of Captain William Cunningham, formerly British provost marshal in the city of New York, who was executed in London the 10th of August, 1791.

"I, William Cunningham, was born in Dublin barracks in the year 1738. My father was trumpeter to the Blue Dragoons, and at the age of 8 years I was placed with an officer as his servant, in which station I continued until I was 16, and being a great proficient in horsemanship, was taken as an assistant to the riding master of the troop, and in the year 1761 was made sergeant of dragoons, but the peace coming the year following, I was disbanded.— Being bred to no profession, I took up with a woman who kept a gin shop in a blind alley near the Coal Quay; but the house being searched for stolen goods and my doxy taken to Newgate, I thought it most prudent to decamp; accordingly set off for the North and arrived at Drogheda, where in a few months after I married the daughter of an exciseman by whom I had three sons.

"About the year 1772 we removed to Newry where I commenced the profession of scowbanker, which is the enticing of mechanics and country people to ship themselves for America on promises of great advantage, and then artfully getting an indenture upon them ; in consequence of which, on their arrival in America, they are sold or obliged to serve a term of years for their passage. I embarked at Newry in the ship Needham, for New York, and arrived in that port the 4th day of August, 1774, with some indented servants I kidnapped in Ireland, but who were liberated in New York on account of the bad usage they received from me during the passage. In that city I used the profession of breaking horses and teaching ladies and gentlemen to ride, but rendering myself obnoxious to the citizens in their infant struggles for freedom, I was obliged to fly on board the *Asia* man of war, and from thence to Boston, where my own opposition to the measures pursued by the Americans in support of their rights, was the first thing that recommended me to General Gage ; and when the war commenced I was appointed provost marshal to the royal army, which placed me in a situation to wreak my vengeance on the Americans. I shudder to think of *the murders I have been accessory to, both with and without orders from government, especially while in New York, during which time there were more than two thousand prisoners starved in the different churches by stopping their rations, which I sold.*

"There were also two hundred and seventy-five American prisoners and obnoxious persons executed, out of which number there were only about one dozen public executions, which chiefly consisted of British and Hessian deserters. The mode of private executions was thus conducted: A guard was dispatched from the provost about half after twelve at night to the Barrack street, and the neighborhood of the upper barracks, to order the people to shut their window shutters and put out their lights, forbidding them at the same time to presume to look out of their windows and doors on pain of death, after which, the unfortunate prisoners were conducted, gagged, just behind the upper barracks and hung without ceremony and there buried by the black pioneer of the provost.

"At the end of the war I returned to England with the army and settled in Wales, as being a cheaper place of living than in any of the populous cities, but being at length persuaded to go to London, I entered so warmly into the dissipation of the capital, that I soon found my circumstances much embarrassed, to relieve which I mortgaged my half pay to an army agent, but that being soon expended, I forged a draft for three hundred pounds sterling on the board of ordnance, but being detected in presenting it for acceptance, I was apprehended, tried and convicted, and for that offence am here to suffer an ignominious death.

"I beg the prayers of all good christians, and also pardon and forgivness of God for the many horrid murders I have been accessory to.

"WILLIAM CUNNINGHAM."

THE ATTACK ON TOMS RIVER.

Burning of the village. Capture of Captain Joshua Huddy. A day of horrors.

In giving an account of this affair we shall first copy a brief statement from Have's Collections, the editor of which visited the place in 1842 in search of historical information relating to olden times in Old Monmouth:

"In the American Revolution, a rude fort or blockhouse was erected a short distance north of the bridge, at the village of Toms River, on a hill about a hundred yards east of the road to Freehold, on land now belonging to the heirs of Elijah Robbins, deceased. In the latter part of the war, this blockhouse was attacked by a superior force of the enemy. Its commander, Captain Joshua Huddy, most gallantly defended it until his ammunition was expended and no alternative but surrender left. After the little brave garrison was in their power, it is said they deliberately murdered five men asking for quarters. From thence Captain Huddy, Justice Randolph, and the remaining prisoners were taken to New York, where, suffering the various progressions of barbarity inflicted upon those destined to a violent or lingering death, those two gentlemen, with a Mr. Fleming, were put into the hold of a vessel. Captain Huddy was ironed hand and foot, and shortly after barbarously hanged on the shore of the Highlands of Navesink."

During the war of the Revolution the chief organ of the tories and British in America was "Rivington's Royal Gazette," published in New York, of which paper and its editor we may have occasion to speak hereafter. Quite complete files of this paper are preserved in the library of the New York Historical Society. The following is its version of the attack on Toms River:

"The authentic account of the expedition against the rebel post on Toms River, New Jersey, under the Honorable Board of Associated Loyalists:

"On Wednesday the 20th inst (March 1782,) Lieutenant Blanchard of the armed whale boats, and about eighty men belonging to them, with Captain Thomas and Lieutenant Roberts, both of the late Bucks county volunteers, and between thirty and forty other refugee loyalists, the whole under the command of Lieutenant Blanchard, proceeded to Sandy Hook under the convoy of Captain Stewart Ross, in the armed brig Arrogant, where they were detained by unfavorable winds until the 23d. About 12 o'clock on that night, the party landed near the mouth of Toms River and marched to the blockhouse at the town of Dover (now Toms River) and reached it just at daylight. On their way they were challenged and fired upon, and when they came to the works they found the rebels, consisting of twenty-five or twenty-six twelve months men and militia, apprized of their coming and prepared for defence.

"The post into which they had thrown themselves was six or seven feet high, made with large logs with loop holes between and a number of brass swivels on the top, which was entirely open, nor was there any way of entering but by climbing over. They had, besides swivels, muskets with bayonets and long pikes for their defence. Lieutenant Blanchard summoned them to surrender, which they not only refused, but bid the party defiance ; on which he immediately ordered the place to be stormed, which was accordingly done, and though defended with obstinacy, was soon carried. The rebels had nine men killed in the assault, and twelve made prisoners, two of whom are wounded. The rest made their escape in the confusion.— Among the killed was a major of the militia, two captains and one lieutenant. The captain of the twelve months men stationed there, is amongst the prisoners, who are all brought safe to town. On our side, two were killed—Lieutenant Iredell of the armed boatmen and Lieutenant Inslee of the loyalists, both very brave officers, who distinguished themselves on the attack and whose loss is much lamented. Lieutenant Roberts and five others are wounded, but it is thought none of them are in a dangerous way.

"The Town, as it is called, consisting of about a dozen houses, in which none but a piratical set of banditti resided, together with a grist and saw mill, were, with the blockhouse burned to the ground, and an iron cannon spiked and thrown into the river. A fine large barge (called Hyler's barge,) and another boat in which the rebels used to make their excursions on the coast, were brought off. Some other attempts were intended to have been made, but the appearance of bad weather, and the situation of the wounded, being without either surgeon or medicines, induced the party to return to New York, where they arrived on the twenty-fifth."

The attack on Toms River was made on Sunday morning, March 24th, 1782. Captain Huddy received notice of the expected attack on the previous evening, and at once notified the inhabitants; sentinels were carefully stationed, and towards morning Captain Huddy sent a scouting party to reconnoitre. This party missed the British ; it is probable they went down along the river, while the enemy, guided by a refugee named William Dillon, came up the road near where the Court House now stands. The sentinels stationed some distance outside of the fort, on the enemy's approach, fired their guns to notify the little garrison. Before reaching the fort, the British were joined by a band of refugees under Davenport, whose stamping ground was in old Dover township ; himself and men had cabins and caves in the woods, by the head waters of Cedar Creek, Toms River and other streams. No Tory or Tory sympathizer was tolerated in the village of Toms River, which was the only reason that caused Rivington's Royal *Gazette* to call its people " banditti."

Upon the approach of the British, the Americans opened fire so effectually that the British account acknowledges that seven were killed or wounded, though the damage inflicted upon them must have been greater. A negro refugee killed, was left by them outside of the fort for the Americans to bury. On the side of the Americans, among the casualities, were Major John Cook, John Farr and James Kinsley, killed ; Moses Robbins wounded in the face ; John Wainwright fought until shot down with six or seven bullets in him. From circumstantial evidence it is probable that Captain Ephraim Jenkins was among the killed. Among the prisoners taken were Captain Joshua Huddy, Daniel Randolph, Esq., and Jacob Fleming. One of the guards named David im lay, escaped and hid in a swamp until the British left. Major Cooke (at one time of the 2nd regiment, Monmouth militia), it is said was killed outside the fort by a negro.

All the houses in the village were burned except two, one belonging to Aaron Buck and the other to Mrs. Studson. Aaron Buck was an active Whig, and one reason why his house was spared was owing, it is supposed, to the fact that his wife was a neice of William Dillen, the refugee guide. Mrs. Studson's husband, Lieutenant Joshua Studson, had been murdered by the refugee Captain John Bacon, a short time before, and the British probably thought injury enough had already been done to her. Among the houses burned was one belonging to Captain Ephraim Jenkins, and also one in which Abiel Aikens lived in which the first Methodist sermon at Toms River was preached, by Rev Benjamin Abbott, in 1778.

What a terrible day to the inhabitants of Toms River was that memorable Sabbath! Probably not less than a hundred women and children were rendered homeless; the killed and wounded demanded immediate attention; husbands and fathers were carried away captive, their household goods, provisions—their all destroyed. Some families were entirely broken up, the heads killed, mothers and chilren scattered, never as families meeting again.

MEMORANDA RELATING TO PERSONS MENTIONED IN THE FOREGOING.

William Dillon, the refugee guide, had once been tried and sentenced to death at Freehold, but subsequently pardoned, and the first we hear of him afterwards was as pilot of a British Expendition, which came from New York into old Cranberry inlet, then open, opposite Toms River, to recapture the ship "Love and Unity," which a short time previous had been captured by the Americans.

Aaron Buck was an active member of the militia. The Dillon whose daughter he married was a much better man than his brother, who acted as guide to the refugees. Aaron Buck left two daughters from whom have descended several respectable shore families. One married Judge Ebenezer Tucker, formerly member of Congress, after whom Tuckerton, in Burlington county, was named. The other married John Rogers, of Dover township, ancester of many persons now residing in Ocean county. It is said that after the war Mr. Buck in a temporary fit of insanity, committed suicide by hanging himself on board his vessel at Toms River.

Daniel Randolph, who then resided at Toms River, was well known throughout old Monmouth. A tory witness on the trial of Captain Richard Lippencott, in New York, testified that " Esquire Daniel Randolph, was a man of prominence and influence among the Whigs." He was soon afterwards exchanged for Captain Clayton Tilton.

Captain Ephraim Jenkins was in command of a militia company during the war. After the fight at the Block House, his family was scattered and his children cared for by strangers.

Abiel Aikens suffered severely during the war. In his old age (1808), the Legislature passed a law for his relief. He was the earliest friend of Methodism in that vicinity.

TOMS RIVER DURING THE REVOLUTION.

Toms River during the Revolution, was a place of considerable importance owing chieffly to the fact that old Cranberry Inlet, nearly opposite, was then open and perhaps the best inlet on our coast, except Little Egg Harbor. On this account it was a favorite base of operations for American privateers on the lookout for British merchant vessels carrying supplies to the enemy at New York. In another chapter are given some extracts from ancient authorities, showing that Toms River and vicinity was the scene of many stirring incidents during the war. The village was occupied by the Americans as a military post probably during the greater part of the Revolution. The soldiers stationed here were sometimes twelve months men, commanded by different officers, among whom it is supposed were Captains Bigelow. Ephraim Jenkins, James Mott, John Stout and Joshua Huddy. The duties of the militia stationed at Toms River, appear to have been to guard the inhabitants against depredations from the refugees; to check contraband trade by way of Cranberry Inlet to New York, and to aid our privateers who brought vessels into old Cranberry Inlet.

A TERRIBLE DAY FOR THE REFUGEES.

Peace Declared—How the news was received by the friends of the "Lost Cause"—Confiscation, Banishment, Despair.

Civil wars have ever been noted for being more terrible than those where one nation was against another; as in the last named case stranger meets stranger on the battle field, while in civil wars oftimes neighbor is arrayed against neighbor father against son, brother against brother In the war of the Revolution it was the lot of our ancestors to be compelled to undergo the hardships of both at the same time. They had not only to face the armies which England landed upon our soil but also thousands of native born Americans, who from what they thought sense of duty, or for plunder or revenge

OLD TIMES IN OLD MONMOUTH. 19

rallied to the cause of King and crown.— The number of Loyalists, that is, Americans, who aided the British, was much larger than is generally supposed. Sabine in his history of the Loyalists estimates the number who took up arms to aid the enemy at 25,000. The Loyalists themselves, in an address to the King, 1779, claimed that "*the Americans then in his Majesty's service exceeded in number the troops enlisted by Congress to oppose them*, exclusive of those who were in private ships of war." In 1782 they stated that there were *many* more Loyalists in the King's service than troops in the Continental army. At the close of the war they claimed that their losses were £7,046,178, besides debts to the amount of £2,354,135. Of their claims the British Government in 1788 had liquidated about £2,000,000.

Old Monmouth suffered during the war to an extent hardly equalled, certainly not surpassed by any other section of the country, and when the welcome news of peace was announced the patriots of this as well of every other section of the Union were overjoyed beyond expression. But the news which brought gladness to their hearts, was a terrible blow to the Refugees. It was not only the announcement to them that the cause for which they had so long fought was irretrievably lost, but also that they must forsake the land of their birth and seek homes elsewhere, that there property here would be confiscated and that without money or friends they must commence life anew on the cold shores of Nova Scotia or elsewhere. The following from an ancient authority, describes how the news of peace was received by the Refugees in New York :

"When the news of peace was known, the city of New York presented a scene of distress not easily described; adherents to the Crown who were in the army tore the lappels from their coats and stamped them under their feet and exclaimed that they were ruined ; others cried out that they had sacrificed everything to prove their loyalty and were now left to shift for themselves without the friendship of their King or country."

In September, previous to the final evacuation of New York by the British, upwards of 12,000 men, women and children embarked at the city and at Long and Staten Islands for Nova Scotia and the Bahamas.

Some of these victims to civil war tried to make merry at their doom by saying that they were bound to a lovely country where there are nine months winter and three months cold weather every year ! While others in their desperation would have torn down their houses, and had they not been prevented would have carried off the bricks of which they were built.

Those who went north landed at Port Roseway (now Shelburne) Nova Scotia and at St. Johns, where many, utterly destitute, were supplied with food at public charge and were obliged to live in huts built of bark and rough boards. Among the banished ones were persons whose hearts and hopes had been as true as Washington's, for in the division of families, which every where occurred and which formed one of the most distressing circumstances of the conflict, their wives and daughters, who although bound by the holiest ties to Loyalists, had given their sympathy to the right from the beginning, and who now in the triumph of the cause which had their prayers, went meekly—as woman ever meets a sorrowful lot—in hopeless, interminable exile.

GEORGE KEITH, THE FOUNDER OF FREEHOLD.

The following outline of the life of Rev. George Keith is by William A. Whitehead Esq. author of the History of East Jersey.

Among those selected by the Proprietaries in England to serve them in East Jersey was George Keith, a native of Aberdeen, an eminent Quaker, although originally a Scotch Presbyterian ; and among all whose names subsequently became widely known, his was one of those which obtained the greatest renown. Those who first welcomed him to the province as a fellow helper in subduing the wilderness could hardly have prefigured for him the course which events opened to him in this and the adjoining province of Pennsylvania. The circumstances which probably led to his acquaintance with the leading Scotch Proprietaries was his having under his charge in 1683 at a school which he taught in Theobalds, a son of Robert Barclay. He was appointed Surveyor General on the 31st of July, 1684, but did not reach the province until the spring of the following year. On the 9th of April he presented his credentials to the Council of Proprietors, but as the office to which he was appointed was already filled by William

Haige, under a commission emanating from Deputy Governor Rudyard, they found themselves delicately situated, and postponed the consideration of Mr. Keith's commission until their next meeting. It was unanimously agreed, however, that he should have one of their houses as directed by the Proprietors. (Thomas Warne was directed to "clear out" the one he inhabited to make room for him.) The Council at the appointed time were urged by Keith to decide in his favor, and they finally desired both of the applicants to appear before them on the 12th of June, when the office, in consequence of the absence of Mr. Haige and the inability, from some cause of his deputy, Miles Forster, was declared vacant and Mr. Keith authorized to take the oaths and assume the duties.

Besides performing the general duties of his office, for which he was well qualified, being " an excellent surveyor," he ran the division line between East and West Jersey in 1687; but in 1689 he left the province for Pennsylvania. Then residing at Freehold, of which settlement he was the founder, and where at the time of his removal he had " a fine plantation," he was induced by the solicitations of the Quakers of Philadelphia to accept the superintendence of a school in that city for fifty pounds, a house for his family, and whatever profits might accrue, with the promise of an increase to one hundred and twenty pounds after the first year, the poor to be taught gratis. This is the first and only allusion to his family I have noticed. He did not remain long in this humble situation (vacating it the next year) and we are warranted in attributing its acceptance to other inducements more likely to affect a man of his character than the pecuniary remuneration named. Having been eminent as a preacher and writer among the Quakers for several years, he became a public speaker in their religious assemblies in Philadelphia. Possessing quick natural talents, improved by considerable literary attainments, he was acute in argument and able in logical disputations and discussions of nice distinction in theological matters ; but having great confidence in his own superior capacity he was apt to indulge in an overbearing disposition, not altogether in accordance with christian moderation and charity.

These peculiarities of mind and temperament naturally impelled him to assume the part of a leader, and he soon, through his talents and energy, gathered a party inculcating plainness of garb and language and other points of discipline ; there being in his opinion " too great slackness therein." Connected with these religious tenets were the political doctrines of the abandonment of all forcible measures to uphold secular or worldly government and the emancipation of the negroes after a reasonable term of service.

Although his opinions and views met the approval of a large number of Friends, occasioning a serious division in that before united body—father and son, husband and wife, friends and relatives who had usually worshiped together, though still professors of the same faith in the main, being seen going to different places of worship, " heats and bitterness " being engendered, occasioning "many labors and watching, great circumspection and patience;" yet as they did not meet with the general acceptation he expected, Keith became captious and indulged in censure and reproach, accusing some of the most esteemed and approved ministers with promulgating false doctrines—although it is said the points he now condemned had been strongly advocated in his writings—and declaring those only who were associated with him true Quakers.

He was charged with exercising an overbearing temper and an unchristian disposition of mind in disparaging many of the society, and at a meeting of ministers in Philadelphia in June, 1692, "a declaration or testimony of denial " was drawn up, in which both he and his conduct were publicly denounced.

From this decision Keith appealed to the general meeting of Friends, at Burlington, and in the meanwhile wrote an address to the Quakers in which, as on different occasions verbally, he spoke in such disparaging, if not calumnious manner of the Deputy Governor and other functionaries, as to bring upon him the ire of the civil magistrates (themselves Quakers) and he was in consequence proclaimed in the market place, by the common crier, a seditious person and an enemy to the King and Queen's government. The general meeting confirming the declaration of the ministers, the separation became complete, but Keith continued preaching and writing in support of his views and for the establishment of his followers until early in 1694, when he appealed to the yearly meeting in London and appeared there in person ; but his behavior was such as led to the approval of the proceedings against him and his authority and influence were at an end.

This controversy occasioned much disturbance in the province of Pennsylvania and many of the pamphlets to which it gave birth are yet extant.

Excited it would seem by the opposition he had met with, although for a time he retained a considerable number of adherents in England, and disgusted with the society from which he had received so little sympathy while aiming for its advancement in what he conceived the essentials of true religion, Keith abjured the doctrines of the Quakers and became a zealous clergyman of the established Church of England.

He officiated for some time in his mother country, and in 1702 returned to America as a Missionary of the "Society for the Propagation of the Gospel in Foreign Parts ; sent out to travel through the different provinces for the purpose of inquiring into their true condition, their wants in regard to their spiritual interests and to arouse in the people a sense of the duties of religion."

His labors are said to have been very successful, particularly in Pennsylvania, New Jersey and New York to which he devoted more of his time than he did to the other provinces—from his previous acquaintance with the people. In the first two especially a large number of those Quakers who had adopted his views in the dissensions of 1691 and 1692, became converts to the doctrines and discipline of the Church of England.

He returned to England by way of Virginia and received a benefice in Sussex, worth one hundred and twenty pounds per annum, where he continued until his death to write against the doctrines of the Quakers. Prund's History of Pennsylvania says from well authenticated account it is asserted that he thus expressed himself on his death bed : "I wish I had died when I was a Quaker for then I am sure it would have been well for my soul."

SINGULAR INDIAN CLAIMS.

About the last remnant of Indians remaining in our state, sold their lands to the whites about 1801, and the year following removed to New Stockbridge, near Oneida Lake, New York, from whence, about 1824, they removed to Michigan, where they purchased a tract of land of the Menomonie Indians, on both sides of the Fox river near Green Bay.

In 1832, the New Jersey tribe, reduced to less than forty souls, delegated one of their number named Bartholomew S. Calvin, to visit Trenton and apply to our Legislature for remuneration for hunting and fishing privileges on unenclosed lands, which they alleged had not been sold with the land. Calvin was an aged man who had been educated at Princeton, where he was at the breaking out of the Revolution when he joined the American army. The claim, so unusual, was met in a spirit of kindness by our Legislature, who directed the State Treasurer to pay to the agent of the Indians, the sum of two thousand dollars, thus satisfactorily and honorably extinguishing the last claim the Indians brought against our state. Hon. Samuel L. Southard, at the close of a speech made at the time, said : "It was a proud fact in the history of New Jersey, that every foot of her soil had been obtained from the Indians by fair and voluntary purchase and transfer, a fact that no other state of the Union, not even the land which bears the name of Penn, can boast."

In 1678, a somewhat similar claim was brought by the Indians, against Richard Hartshorne, an early settler of old Monmouth, who had previously bought of them Sandy Hook, and lands around the Highlands. In that year, to prevent their trespassing upon his lands, he had to pay them to relinquish their claims to hunt, fish, fowl, and gather beach plums. The following it a copy of the agreement :

"The 8th of August, 1678. Whereas the Indians pretend that formerly, when they sold all the land upon Sandy Hook, they did not sell, or did except liberty to plumbs, or to say the Indians should have liberty to go on Sandy Hook, to get plumbs when they please, and to hunt upon the land, and fish, and to take dry trees that suited them for cannows. Now know all men by these presents, that I, Richard Hartshorne, of Portland, in the county of Monmouth, in East Jersey, for peace and quietness sake, and to the end there may be no cause of trouble with the Indians and that I may not for the future have any trouble with them as formerly I had, in their dogs killing my sheep, and their hunting on my lands, and their fishing, I have agreed as followeth:

"These presents witnesseth, that I, Vowavapon, Hendricks, the Indians sonn, having all the liberty and privileges of pluming on Sandy Hook, hunting, fishing, fowling, getting cannows &c., by these presents, give, grant, bargain, sell, unto Richard Hartshorne, his heirs and assigns forever, all the liberty and privilege of pluming, fishing, fowling, and hunting, and howsoever reserved and excepted by the Indians for him, the said Richard Hartshorne, his heirs and assigns, to have hould, possess, and injoy forever, to say that no Indian, or Indians, shall or hath no pretense to lands or timber, or liberty, privileges on no pretense whatsoever on any part a parcell of land, belonging to the said Richard Hartshorne, to say Sandy Hook or land adjoining to it, in consideration the said Hartshorne, hath paid unto the said Vowavapon, thirteen shillings money; and I the said Vowavapon, do acknowledge to have received thirteen shillings by these presents. Witness my hand and seal.

"VOWAVAPON X his mark.
"TOCUS X his mark.
" Signed, sealed and delivered in the presence of JOHN STOUT."

THE RARITAN INDIANS.

An ancient work says that when the whites first came to this country, the Raritans lived on the south side of Raritan bay and river, but they were flooded out by a storm, previous to 1650, and then removed to the north side. They afterwards it is supposed mingled with the Sanhicans or Wapingas, who finally left the state and located on the east side of the Hudson river, in New York state, near Anthony's Nose.

AN INDIAN DINNER—A SAVORY DISH.

BETHSHEBA, THE INDIAN QUEEN.

The last remnant of the Indians who frequented the lower part of old Monmouth, had their principal settlement at a place called Edgepelick or Edge Pillock about three miles from Atsion in Burlington county, from whence they removed to Oneida Lake, New York, in 1802. Before their removal, members of this tribe with their families would visit the shore once a year and spend some time fishing, oyster-ing, making baskets, &c. The most noted among the last Indians who regularly visited the shore were Charles Moluss, his wife, and wife's sister, who bore the euphonious names of Bash and Suke, among the ancient residents of old Stafford township, but in Little Egg Harbor, Burlington county, where they also were frequent visitors, Moluss' wife was known as Bathsheba, and considered as a kind of Indian Queen, on account of the great respect shown to her by her people and by the Quakers of Burlington, because of her possessing more intelligence, and having a more prepossessing personal appearance than the rest of her tribe. At Tuckerton, when her company visited there and put up their tents, Bathsheba was generally invited to make her home with some one of the principal inhabitants of the place. At Barnegat, her company generally camped on the place now owned by Captain Timothy Falkinburgh, where they were on friendly terms with the whites and quite disposed to be hospitable, but Bathsheba, Indian Queen though she may have been, occasionally prepared Indian delicacies for the table which the whites seldom appreciated. Some twenty years ago Eli Collins, a well remembered aged citizen of Barnegat, told the writer of this, that when he was a young man, one time he had been out from home all day, and on his way back, stopped at the hut of Moluss. His wife Bash, or Bathsheba, was boiling something in a pot which sent forth a most delightful odor to a hungry man, and he was cordially invited to dine. As he had been without anything to eat all day he willingly accepted the invitation; but he soon changed his determination when he found the savory smelling dish was *hop toad soup!*

INDIAN PETER.

A TRADITION OF IMLAYSTOWN.

About a century ago an Indian named Peter, said to have been connected by relationship and in business with the noted Indian Tom, after whom some, we think erroneously, considered Toms River to be named, resided at Toms River, but owing to an unfortunate habit of mixing too much whisky with his water, he became unfortunate, and about the time of the war removed with his family to the vicinity of Imlaystown, where he built a wigwam by a pond not far from the village.

Shortly after he located here his wife sickened and died. Peter dearly loved his squaw, and was almost heart-broken on account of the unlucky event. He could not bear the idea of parting with his wife, of putting her under ground out of sight. For a day or two he was inconsolable and knew not what to do; at length a lucky idea occurred to him; instead of burying her where he never more could see her, he would put a rope about her neck and place her in the pond and daily visit her. This idea he at once put into execution, and as he daily visited her, it somewhat assuaged his poignant grief.—
On one of his melancholy visits to the departed partner of his bosom, he noticed in the water around her a large number of eels. To turn these eels to account was a matter of importance to Peter, for though he loved his wife yet he loved money too. So he caught the eels daily, and for a week or so visited the village regularly and found a ready sale for them among the villagers.

But at length the supply failed—his novel eel trap gave out. A few days thereafter he was in the village and numerous were the inquiries why he did not bring any more of those good eels.

"Ah," said Peter very innocently, drawing a long sigh, "me catch no more eels—me squaw all gone—boo—hoo!"

His grief and singular reply called for an explanation, and he, thinking nothing wrong, gave it.

The result was a general casting up of accounts among the villagers, terrible anathemas upon the Indian, and a holy horror of eels among that generation of Imlaystown citizens, and even to this day it is said some of their descendants would as soon eat a snake as an eel.

(The above tradition we have no doubt is substantially correct; we derived it from Hon. Charles Parker, for many years State Treasurer, father of Gov. Parker, who some sixty years ago, while at Toms River, met with some of the disgusted purchasers of Indian Peter's eels.)

A BRAVE YOUTH.

One fine morning in May, 1780, as the family of David Forman, Sheriff of Monmouth County, were at breakfast, a soldier almost out of breath suddenly burst into the room and stated, that as he and another soldier were conducting to the Court House two men taken up on suspicion at Colt's Neck, they had knocked down his comrade, seized his musket and escaped. The Sheriff, on hearing this relation, immediately mounted his horse and galloped to the Court House to alarm the guard.—
His son Tunis Forman, a lad of about 17, and small of his age, seized a musket loaded only with small shot to kill blackbirds in the cornfields, and putting on a cartridge box, dispatched his brother Samuel (the late Dr. Samuel Forman of Freehold,) upstairs for a bayonet, and then without waiting for it, hurried off alone in the pursuit.

After running in a westerly direction about a mile, he discovered the men sitting on a fence, who on perceiving him ran into a swamp. As the morning was warm, he hastily pulled off his coat and shoes and dashed in after them, keeping close upon them for over a mile, when they got out of the swamp and each climbed into separate trees. As he came up they discharged at him the musket taken from the guard. The ball whistled over his head. He felt for his bayonet, and at that moment perceived that in his haste it was left behind. He then pointed his gun at the man with the musket, but deemed it imprudent to fire, reflecting even if he killed him, his comrade could easily master such a stripling as himself. He compelled the man to throw down his musket by threatening him with death if he did not instantly comply. Then loading the prize from his cartridge he forced his prisoners down from the trees and armed with his two loaded muskets, he drove them toward the Court House, careful however, to keep them far apart, to prevent conversation. Passing by a spring they requested permission to drink.

"No" replied the intrepid boy, understanding their design. "You can do as well without it as myself; you shall have some by and by."

Soon after, his father, at the head of a party of soldiers in the pursuit, galloped past in the road within a short distance.— Tunis hallooed, but the clattering of their horses hoofs drowned his voice. At length he reached the village, and lodged his prisoners in the county prison.

It was subsequently discovered that these men, whose name was John and Robert Smith, were brothers from near

Philadelphia, that they had robbed and murdered a Mr. Boyd, a collector of taxes in Chester county, and when taken, were on their way to join the British. As they had been apprehended on suspicion merely of being refugees, no definite charge could be brought against them. A few days after, Sheriff Forman saw an advertisement in a Pennsylvania paper describing them, with the facts above mentioned, and a reward of $20,000 Continental money offered for their apprehension. He, accompanied by his son, took them there, where they were tried and executed. On entering Philadelphia young Tunis was carried through the streets in triumph upon the shoulders of the military. In the latter part of the war this young man became very active. and was a peculiar favorite of General David Forman. He died not far from 1835. (The foregoing account is as related by the late Dr. Samuel Forman to Henry Howe, Esq.)

CAPTAIN JOSEPH COWARD.

In a Philadelphia work containing Sketches of Revolutionary Heroes is found the following notice of one of the patriots of old Monmouth :

" Joseph Coward was a native of Monmouth county, N. J. In view of his cognomen we may well exclaim, " What's in a name, my Lord?" He was a Coward, and yet one of the bravest of the Revolutionary Captains. He was a great terror to the Refugees *alias* Tories. At the Battle of Monmouth and at several other places, his undaunted courage was conspicuous.— When the British fleet lay off Sandy Hook, one of the supply ships ran too near the shore and stuck fast. With a few, Captain Coward captured her in defiance of two barges manned with superior numbers that were sent to the rescue. At the close of the war he returned to his farm, became the esteemed citizen and fully exemplified the noble attributes of an honest man."

From his name we should not be surprised if the above named hero was a relative of the late Captain Joseph Coward of Toms River, formerly a member of the Legislature, a gentleman much esteemed and popular among his political opponents, as well as friends.

A JERSEY BLUE AT THE BATTLE OF GERMANTOWN.

BARKALOW, OF OLD MONMOUTH.

The following story which we find in an old work is worth repeating:

" *A Brave Fellow.*—Among numerous feats of valor performed by individuals of the American Revolutionary army, none has pleased me more than the following, related by an eye witness.

" During the heat of the battle at Germantown, while bullets flew thick as hailstones, one Barkalow, of Monmouth, N. J., was levelling his musket at the enemy when the lock was carried away by a ball. Undismayed, he caught up the gun of a comrade, just killed by his side, and taking aim, a bullet entered the muzzle and twisted the barrel round like a corkscrew! Still undaunted, our hero immediately kneel'd down, unscrewed the whole lock from the twisted barrel, screwed it on the barrel from which the lock had been torn, and blazed away at the enemy.

" Can ancient Sparta or modern Britian boast a more brilliant display of cool, deliberate, unshaken courage ? This hero is still living."—*Niles Prin. Revolution*, 1822

THE REDSTONE COUNTRY.

OLD MONMOUTH CITIZENS EMIGRATING WEST.

At different times between fifty and a hundred years ago, a large number of the citizens of old Monmouth emigrated to what then was termed "the Redstone country." These emigrants left behind numerous relatives, and among their descendants are often heard inquiries as to the precise locality of this "Redstone country." The origin of the name at the present day seems somewhat singular.

The term "Redstone settlements" or "Redstone country," was employed to denote most f the country in Pennsylvania and Virginia west of the mountains. The name Redstone was applied to a creek which enters the Monongahela below Brownsville, Pa., upon which was a settlement called " Redstone Old Fort."

In that day coal, as an article of fuel, was unknown. It is stated that "the hills abounded with bituminous coal; and along water courses where the earth had been washed off, the coal was left exposed which often caught fire ; these fires came in contact with the surrounding earth and stones and gave them a red appearance—indeed so much so that when pulverized they were used in painting a Spanish brown color. Hence the name. Many of these red banks are now visible, the most prominent of which are in Redstone Creek, Fayette county, Pa."

The last considerable exodus of citizens of old Monmouth bound for the Redstone country, occurred some fifty odd years ago. Some of the emigrants from the county who went previous to this time, experienced great hardships, and at one time were so seriously annoyed by the Indians that they had to return until the troubles were over. One native of old Monmouth named Conover during the Indian troubles, became quite noted for his skill and bravery in meeting the savages, and his adventures were so thrilling that we shall try to find place for them hereafter; it will be seen that he did no discredit to the county that gave him birth.

INDIAN WILL.

AN ECCENTRIC ABORIGINAL OF OLD MONMOUTH.

In days gone by the singular character and eccentric acts of the noted Indian Will, formed the theme of many a fireside story among our ancestors, many of which are still well remembered by our older citizens, especially those belonging to the Society of Friends. Some of the incidents given below, derived many years ago from aged Friends, differ in some particulars, but we give them as related to us now, in hopes some of our readers can furnish corrections and additions. The first story given below, was published some thirty years ago, and as will be seen differs from other versions.

"About the year 1670, the Indians sold out the section of country near Eatontown to Lewis Morris for a barrel of cider, and emigrated to Crosswicks and Cranbury.— One of them, called Indian Will, remained and dwelt in a wigwam between Tinton Falls and Swimming river. His tribe were in consequence exasperated, and at various times sent messengers to kill him in single combat; but being a brave, athletic man, he always came off conqueror. On a certain occasion, while partaking of a breakfast of suppawn and milk at Mr. Eaton's with a silver spoon, he casually remarked that he knew where there were plenty of such. They promised if he would bring them they would give him a red coat and a cocked hat. In a short time he was arrayed in that dress; and it is said that the Eatons suddenly became wealthy. About 80 years since, in pulling down an old mansion in Shrewsbury, in which a maiden member of this family in her lifetime had resided, a quantity of *cob* dollars, supposed by the superstitious to have been Kidd's money, were found concealed in the cellar wall. This coin was generally of a square or oblong shape, the corners of which wore out the pockets."— (*Howe's Hist. Coll.*)

A somewhat similar or a variation of the above tradition, we have frequently heard as follows:

"India. Will often visited the family of Derrick Longstreet at Manasquan, and one time showed them some silver money which excited their surprise; they wished to know where he got it, and wanted Will to let them have it. Will refused to part with it, but told them he had found it in a trunk along the beach, and there was plenty of yellow money beside; but as the yellow money was not as pretty as the white, he didn't want that, and Longstreet might have it. So Longstreet went with him, and found the money in a trunk covered over with tarpaulin buried in the sand; Will kept the white money and Longstreet the yellow (gold,) and this satisfactory division, made the Longstreets quite wealthy."

It is very probable that Will found money along the beach, but whether it was from some shipwrecked vessel, or had been buried by pirates, is another question.— However, the connection of Kidd's name with the finding of the money would indicate that Will lived long after the year mentioned in the first quoted tradition, (1670.) Kidd did not sail on his piratical cruise until 1696. And from the traditionary information the writer of this has been able to obtain, Will must have lived many years subsequent.

In personal appearance, Will is described as having been stout, broad shouldered, with prominent Indian cast of features and rings in his ears, and a good sized one in his nose. The following are some of the additional traditions related of him:

Among other things which Will had done to excite the ill will of other Indians he was charged with killing his wife. Her brother named Jacob, determined on revenge; so he pursued him and finding Will unarmed, undertook to march him off captive. As they were going along, Will espied a pine knot on the ground, and managed to pick it up and suddenly dealt Jacob a fatal blow, and as he dropped to the ground, Will tauntingly exclaimed, "Jacob, look up at the sun—you'll never see it again." Most of the old residents who relate stories of Will, speak of his finding honey at one time on the dead body of an Indian he had previously killed, but whether it was Jacob or some other is not mentioned.

At one time, to make sure work of killing Will, four or five Indians started in pursuit of him., and they succeeded in surprising him so suddenly that he had no chance for defence or fight. His captors told him they were about to kill him and he must at once prepare to die. He heard his doom with Indian stoicism, and he had only one favor to ask before he died, and that was to be allowed to take a drink out of his jug of liquor which had just been filled. So small a favor the captors could not refuse. As Will's jug was full, it was only common politeness to ask them to drink also. Now if his captors had any weakness it was for rum; so they gratefully accepted his invitation. The drink rendered them talkative, and they commenced reasoning with him upon the enormity of his offences. The condemned man admitted the justness of their reproaches, and begged to be allowed to take another drink to drown the stings of conscience; the captors condescendingly joined him again—indeed it would have been cruel to refuse to drink with a man so soon to die. This gone through with, they persuaded Will to make a full confession of his misdeeds, and their magnitude so aroused the indignation of his captors, that they had to take another drink to enable them to do their duty becomingly. Indeed, they took divers drinks, so overcome were they by his harrowing tale; and then they become so unmanned, that they had to try to recuperate by sleep. Then crafty Will, who had really drank but little, softly arose, found his hatchet, and soon despatched his would-be captors.

It was a rule with Will not to waste any ammunition, and therefore he was bound to eat all the game he killed, but a buzzard which he once shot sorely tried him, and it took two or three days starving, before he could stomach it. One time when alone upon the beach he was seized with a fit of sickness and thought he was about to die; and not wishing his dead body to lie exposed, he succeeded in digging a shallow grave in which he lay for awhile; but his sickness passed off and he crept out and went on his way rejoicing. He would never, in the latter years of his life, kill a willet, as he said a willet once saved his life. He said he was in a canoe one dark night crossing the bay, somewhat the worse for liquor, and unconsciously about to drift out the inlet into the ocean, when a willet screamed, and the peculiar cry of this bird seemed to him to sound, "this way, Will; this way, Will!" and *that* way Will went and reached the beach just in time to save himself from certain death in the breakers.

When after wild fowl he had a singular way of talking to them in a low tone:— "Come this way, my nice bird, Will won't hurt you; Will won't hurt you!" If he succeeded in killing one he would say: "You fool, you believe me eh? Ah, Will been so much with the whites he *learned to lie like a white man!"*

An old resident of the present county of Ocean, says that "Indian Will sometimes travelled down along shore as far as Barnegat Inlet and always attended by a lot of big, lean, hungry looking dogs, to help him fight off other Indians."

Near the mouth of Squan River is a place known as "Will's Hole." There are two versions of the origin of the name.—One old gentleman living in the vicinity, says it was so called because Will was drowned in it. The other version is that Will drowned his wife here.

The following traditions of Indian Will were told last summer by the venerable Thomas Cook of Point Pleasant, recently deceased, to a correspondent of the New York *World*. Though copied in this paper at that time, yet in this connection they will bear republishing:

Along the shore of Squan river a small inlet was pointed out to me which is known as "Indian Will's Hole." Some three quarters of a century ago, an old Indian chief made his home in the woods attached to the Cook farm. He was a brawny, muscular savage, peaceably inclined towards the whites and suffered no molestation from them. Many of his people lived around him, but he preferred to occupy his cabin alone with his wife, while he spent most of his time in hunting and fishing.

But one day Indian Will brought home

a muskrat, which he ordered his spouse to prepare for dinner. She obeyed, but when it was placed upon the table, refused to partake of it. "Very well," grunted the noble red man, "if you are too good to eat muskrat you are too good to live with me." And thereupon took her down to the little bay spoken of, and caused her to sink so effectually that she has not yet come to the surface.

Indian Will had three brothers-in-law, two of whom resided on Long Island, and when in course of time word reached them of the manner in which the chief had "put away" their sister, they went down to Jersey to avenge her death. When they reached Will's cabin he sat inside eating clam soup. Knowing their errand, he invited them in to dinner, telling them that he would fight it out with them as soon as the meal was concluded. "Barkis was willin'" and they gathered around the aboriginal board, complimenting the steaming soup which was placed before them, and scooped it into their capacious jaws in the very felicity of sensuous enjoyment.

Before dinner was over Indian Will pretended that he heard some one approaching, and springing up hurried out of his cabin as if to meet him. But the instant he was out of sight of the two visitors, he caught up their two guns, which they had left leaning up against the cabin in full trust of his honor, and through the open door shot both, the last redskin falling dead as he was rushing out to close in with his treacherous host.

In those days it was the custom of the Indians to hold a yearly meeting or council at a place now known as Burrsville, somewhat like a dozen miles from this point. It was here that Indian Will encountered the third brother-in-law, and they started homeward together having no weapons with them, but carrying a jug of whiskey. Deep in the gloomy recesses of the pine woods, when his blood was inflamed with fire-water, this Indian told the chief that he must die as the death of his relatives must be avenged.

They halted and closed in the deadly struggle. Both were active and powerful men and it was a fight unto death; but late in the evening Indian Will appeared at his cabin with no companion but his whiskey jug. The next day he received several visitors from his race who had been at the Council the day before, and who had seen the two depart together. In quiring as to what had become of his comrade, he told them to search and they would probably find out.

They took the back trail of the chief and after an hour's tramping found the dead body. The crushed skull and a bloody pine knot near told the tale. Henceforth Indian Will was let alone and quietly died in his own cabin many years after. I find that in the deed of the Cook farm, this "Indian Will's Hole" is recognized, and its margin is given as one of the landmarks."

CAUSES OF THE REVOLUTION—PRINCIPLES INVOLVED.

Early Stand taken by the Citizens of Monmouth.—Proceedings of Meetings in Different Townships in 1774-5.—Freehold leads the State.—County Resolutions.—An Admirable Document.—Patriots Appeal to their Descendants.—"A Faithful Record" of 1774, and its Message to 1873.

Historians of other States have always conceded that the citizens of New Jersey were among the earliest and most active opponents of those tyrannical acts of Great Britain which brought on the war, and finally resulted in separation. Large and spirited public meetings were held in various parts of the State in 1774-5, to denounce the obnoxious laws, and to organize for counsel and defence.

At this stage of affairs, separation from England had not been proposed, and most of these meetings, while condemning the acts of the British Ministry and Parliament, still expressed decided loyalty to the King. Our ancestors warmly seconded the stand taken by the people of Boston, and freely forwarded contributions to the suffering inhabitants of that city.

We annex extracts from the proceedings of some of these meetings in Old Monmouth, as they exhibit the timely zeal and firm and decided spirit of its citizens, and also furnish the names of some of the leading spirits who were prominent in the early stages of political movements which brought on the Revolution. The several counties of the State were requested to send delegates to meet at New Brunswick, July 21st, 1774, to consider what action should be taken by the citizens of the Province of New Jersey. This convention was generally spoken of as the "Provincial Congress of New Jersey," and was a different body from the Legislature; in several instances, however, the same persons were members of both bodies. A number of persons named in these proceedings were afterwards, during the war, conspicuous in military or civil life, for their services in behalf of their country in legislative halls and on the field of battle.

For a year or two the citizens of the county appear to have been about unanimous in their sentiments, but when finally the subject of a separation from the mother country was boldly advocated, there was found to be a diversity of opinion, and some who were among the most active in the meetings of 1774-5, earnestly opposed the proposition, and eventually sided with England in the later years of that memorable struggle. The fearful consequences of this division, in which it would seem almost every man capable of bearing arms was compelled to take sides, we have endeavored to give in other chapters.

The citizens of Freehold had the honor, we believe, of holding the first meeting in New Jersey to denounce the tyrannical acts of Great Britain—of inaugurating the movements in our State which finally resulted in Independence. The date of their first meeting is June 6th, 1774: the earliest date of a meeting in any other place that we have met with, is of a meeting at Newark, June 11th, 1774.

The following is a copy of the Freehold Proceedings:

LOWER FREEHOLD RESOLUTIONS.

"FREEHOLD June 6th 1774.

"At a meeting of the Freeholders and Inhabitants of the Township of Lower Freehold in the county of Monmouth in New Jersey, on Monday the 6th day of June 1774 after notice given of the time place and occasion of this meeting

"*Resolved* That it is the unanimous opinion of this meeting, that the cause in which the inhabitants of the town of *Boston* are now suffering is the common cause of the whole Continent of North America; and that unless some general spirited measures, for the public safety be speedily entered into there is just reason to fear that every Province may in turn share the same fate with them; and that therefore, it is highly incumbent on them all to unite in some effectual means to obtain a repeal of the Boston Port Bill and any other that may follow it, which shall be deemed subversive of the rights and privileges of free born Americans.

"And that it is the opinion of this meeting that in case it shall hereafter appear to be consistent with the general opinion of the trading towns and the commercial part of our countrymen, that an entire stoppage of importation and exportation from and to Great Britain and the West Indies, until the said Port Bill and other Acts be repealed, will be conducive to the safety and preservation of North America and her liberties, they will yield a cheerful acquiescence in the measure and earnestly reccommend the same to all their brethren in this Province.

"*Resolved, moreover* That the inhabitants of this township will join in an Association with the several towns in the county and in conjuction with them, with the several counties in the Province (if, as we doubt not they see fit to accede to the proposal) in any measures that may appear best adapted to the weal and safety of North America and all her loyal sons.

" *Ordered* That

JOHN ANDERSON Esq   PETER FORMAN
HENDRICK SMOCK   JOHN FORMAN
ASHER HOLMES   Capt JNO COVENHOVEN
   and Dr. NATHANIEL SCUDDER

be a committee for the township to join those who may be elected for the neighboring townships or counties to constitute a General Committee for any purposes similar to those above mentioned; and that the gentlemen so appointed do immediately solicit a correspondence with the adjacent towns."

(Dr. Scudder subsequently was a Colonel in the First Regiment Monmouth Militia, and killed October 15th, 1781, as described elsewhere.)

The following week the citizens of Essex sent the following to the patriots of Monmouth:

ESSEX TO MONMOUTH.

" ELIZABETHTOWN June 13th 1774.

"Gentlemen: The alarming Measures which have been lately taken to deprive the Inhabitants of the American Colonies of their constitutional Rights and Privileges, together with the late violent attacks made upon the rights and liberties of the Colony of the Massachusetts Bay (for asserting and endeavoring to maintain their rights) manifestly intended to crush them without Mercy and thereby disunite and weaken the Colonies, and at the same time dare them to assert or own their Constitutional Rights, Liberties or Properties, under the Penalty of the like, and if possible, worse treatment; and as the Assembly of New Jersey are not like to meet in time to answer the Design proposed, and the neighboring Colonies are devising and expecting the immediate union of this Colony with them.

"Sundry of the Inhabitants of the County of Essex by Advertisements, convened a general Meeting of said County at Newark on Saturday last, when the said inhabitants unanimously entered into certain Resolves and Declarations upon that occasion, a copy of which you have enclosed. We the Committee appointed by the said Meeting, do earnestly request that You will immediately by Advertisements or otherwise, call a general Meeting of your County for the purposes aforesaid as soon as possible, as we have intelligence that it is most probable the General Congress of the Colonies will be held the latter end of July next. We think New Brunswick the most suitable place for the committee to meet, and with submission to them desire they will meet us at New Brunswick on Thursday July 21st next at 10 o'clock in the morning, unless some other time and place more suitable shall in the meantime be agreed upon.

"We earnestly request your answer as soon as possible.

"Letters of this Tenor and Date we now despatch to the other Counties in this Colony. We are, Gentlemen,
"your most ob't servants
"STEPHEN CRANE Chairman
"By order :
"To Messrs Edward Taylor, Richard Lawrence Elisha Lawrence, John Taylor and Henry Waddell, and other Inhabitants of the County of Monmouth, Friends to the Liberties and Privileges of the American Colonies."

(The above letter was directed to the above named gentlemen " or to any body else in Monmouth County.")

Delegates from the different townships in the county assembled at Freehold, July 19th, and the result of their decision is found in the following admirable document. It is lengthy but will well repay perusal. In the closing paragraph they trust that some faithful record will transmit the reasons which actuated them, to their posterity to whom they make a brief but eloquent appeal. As they desired, this record has been preserved, and as they desired, we do what we can to place it before their descendants:

MONMOUTH COUNTY RESOLUTIONS.

"On Tuesday July 19th 1774, a majority of the Committees from the several townships in the county of Monmouth of the Colony of New Jersey met according to appointment at the Court House at Freehold in said county; and appearing to have been regularly chosen and constituted by their respective townships, they unanimously agreed upon the propriety and expediency of electing a committee to represent the whole county at the approaching Provincial Convention to be held at the city of New Brunswick, for the necessary purpose of constituting delegates from this Province to the general Congress of the Colonies and for all other such important purposes as shall hereafter be found necessary.

"They at the same time also recorded the following Resolutions, Determinations and Opinions, which they wish to be transmitted to posterity as an ample testimony to their loyalty to his British Majesty, of their firm attacement to the principles of the glorious Revolution and their fixed and unalterable purpose, by every lawful means in their power, to maintain and defend themselves in the possession and enjoyment of those inestimable civil and religious privileges which their forefathers, at the expense of so much blood and treasure, have established and handed down to them.

"1st. In the names and behalf of their constituents, the good and loyal inhabitants of the county of Monmouth, in the colony of New Jersey, they do cheerfully and publicly proclaim their unshaken allegiance to the person and government of his most gracious Majesty King George the Third now on the British throne, and do acknowledge themselves bound at all times, and to the utmost exertion of their power to maintain his dignity and lawful sovereignty in and over all his colonies in America; and that it is their most fervent desire and constant prayer that in a Protestant succession, the descendants of the illustrious House of Hanover, may continue to sway the British sceptre to the latest posterity.

"2d. They do highly esteem and prize the happiness of being governed and having their liberty and property secured to them by so excellent a system of laws as that of Great Britain, the best doubtless in the universe; and they will at all times cheerfully obey and render every degree of assistance in their power to the full and just execution of them. But at the same time will, with the greatest alacrity and resolution oppose any unwarrantable innovations in them or any additions to or alterations in the grand system which may appear unconstitutional, and consequently inconsistent with the liberties and privileges of the descendants of free born American Britons.

"3d. As there has been for ages past, a most happy union and uninterrupted connection between Great Britain and her colonies in America, they conceive their interests are now become so intimately blended together and their mutual dependence upon each other to be at this time so delicately great that they esteem everything which has a tendency to alienate affection or disunite them in any degree, highly injurious to their common happiness and directly calculated to produce a Revolution, likely in the end to prove destructive to both; they do therefore heartily disclaim every idea of that spirit of independence which has, of late, by some of our mistaken brethren on each side of the Atlantic, been so groundlessly and injuriously held up to the attention of the nation, as having through ambition, possessed the breasts of the Americans.— And moreover they do devoutly beseech the Supreme Disposer of all events, graciously to incline the heart of our Sovereign and all his Ministers, to a kind and impartial investigation of the real sentiments and disposition of his truly loyal American subjects.

"4th. Notwithstanding many great men and able writers have employed their talents and pens in favor of the newly adopted mode of taxation in America, they are yet sensible of no convictive light being thrown upon the subject; and therefore, although so august a body as that of the British Parliament is now actually endeavoring to enforce in a military way, the execution of some distressing edicts upon the capital of the Massachusetts colony, they do freely and solemnly declare that in conscience they deem them, and all others that are, or ever may be framed upon the same principles, altogether unprecedented and unconstitutional, utterly inconsistent with the true original intention of Magna Charta, subversive of the just rights of free born Englishmen, agreeable and satisfactory only to the domestic and foreign enemies of our nation, and consequently pregnant with complicated ruin, and tending directly to the dissolution and destruction of the British Empire.

"5th. As they, on the one hand firmly believe that the inhabitants of the Massachusetts colony in general, and those of the town of Boston in particular, are to all intents and purposes as loyal subjects as any in all his Majesty's widely extended dominions; and on the other, that (although the present coercive and oppressive measures against them may have taken rise in some part from the grossest and most cruel misrepresentation both of their disposition and conduct) the blockade of that town is principally designed to lead the way in an attempt to execute a dreadful deep laid plan for enslaving all America. They are therefore clearly of opinion, that the Bostonians are now eminently suffering in the common cause of American freedom, and that their fate may probably prove decisive to this very extensive continent and even to the whole British nation; and they do verily expect that unless some generous spirited measures for the public safety be speedily entered into and steadily prosecuted, every other colony will soon in turn feel the pernicious effects of the same detestable restrictions. Whence they earnestly entreat every rank, denomination, society and profession of their brethren, that, laying aside all bigotry and every party disposition, they do now universally concur in one generous and vigorous effort for the encouragement and support of their suffering friends, and in a resolute assertion of their birth right, liberties and privileges. In consequence of which they may reasonably expect a speedy repeal of all the arbitrary edicts respecting the Massachusetts government, and at the same time an effectual preclusion of any future attempts of the kind from the enemies of our happy Constitution, either upon them or any of their American brethren.

"6th In case it shall hereafter appear to be consistent with the result of the deliberation of the general Congress, that an interruption or entire cessation of commercial intercourse with Great Britain and even (painful as it may be) with the West Indies, until such oppressive Acts be repealed and the liberties of America fully restored, stated and asserted, will on this deplorable emergency be really necessary and conducive to the public good, they promise a ready acquiesence in every measure and will recommend the same as far as their influence extends.

"7th. As a general Congress of Deputies from the several American Colonies is proposed to be held at Philadelphia soon in September next, they declare their entire approbation of the design and think it is the only rational method of evading those aggravated evils which threaten to involve the whole continent in one general calamitous catastrophe. They are therefore met this day, vested with due authority from their respective constituents, to elect a committee to represent this county of Monmouth in any future necessary trans actions respecting the cause of liberty and especially to join the Provincial Convention soon to be held at New Brunswick, for the purpose of nominating and constituting a number of Delegates, who in behalf of this Colony may steadily attend to said general Congress and faithfully serve the laboring cause of freedom and they have consequently chosen and deputed the following gentlemen to that important trust viz;

Edward Taylor   John Anderson
John Taylor   Dr Nathaniel Scudder
John Burrowes   John Covenhoven
Joseph Holmes   Josiah Holmes
Edward Williams   James Grover
John Lawrence.

' Edward Taylor being constituted chairman and any five of them a sufficient number to transact business. And they do beseech, entreat, instruct and enjoin them to give their voice at said Provincial Convention, for no persons but such as they in good conscience and from the best information shall verily believe to be amply qualified for so interesting a department; particularly that they be men highly approved for integrity, honesty and uprightness, faithfully attached to his Majesty's person and lawful government, well skilled in the principles of our excellent constitution and steady assertors of all our civil and religious liberties.

"8th. As under the present operation of the Boston Port Bill, thousands of our respected brethren in that town must necessarily be reduced to great distress, they feel themselves affected with the sincerest sympathy and most cordial commiseration; and as they expect, under God, that the final deliverance of America will be owing, in a great degree, to a continuance of their virtuous struggle, they esteem themselves bound in duty and in interest to afford them every assistance and alleviation in their power; and they do now in behalf of their constituents, declare their readiness to contribute to the relief of the suffering poor in that town; therefore they request the several committees of the country, when met, to take into serious consideration the necessity and expediency of forwarding under a sanction from them, subscriptions through every part of the Colony, for that truly humane and laudable purpose; and that a proper plan be concerted for laying out the product of such subscriptions to the best andvantage, and afterwards transmitting it to Boston in the safest and least expensive way.

"9th. As we are now by our Committees in this, in conjunction with those of other colonies, about to delegate to a number of our countrymen a power equal to any wherewith human nature alone was ever invested; and as we firmly resolve to acquiesce in their deliberations, we do therefore earnestly entreat them, seriously and conscientiously to weigh the inexpressible importance of their arduous department, and fervently to solicit that direction and assistance in the discoarge of their trust, which all the powers of humanity cannot afford them; and we do humbly and earnestly beseech that God, in whose hand are the hearts of all flesh and who ruleth them at his pleasure, graciously to infuse into the whole Congress a spirit of true wisdom, prudence and just moderation; and to direct them to such unanimous and happy conclusion as shall terminate in His own honor and glory, the establishment of the Protestant succession of the illustrious House of Hanover, the mutual weal and advantage of Great Britain and all her Dominions and a just and permanent confirmation of all the civil and religious liberties of America. And now lastly, under the consideration of the bare possibility that the enemies of our constitution may yet succeed in a desperate triumph over us in this age, we do earnestly (should this prove the case) call upon all future generations to renew the glorious struggle for liberty as often as Heaven shall afford them any probable means of success.

"May this notification, by some faithful record, be handed down to the yet unborn descendants of Americans, that nothing but the most fatal necessity could have wrested the present inestimable enjoyments from their ancestors. Let them universally inculcate upon their beloved offspring an investigation of those truths, respecting both civil and religious liberty, which have been so clearly and fully stated in this generation. May they be carefully taught in all their schools; and may they never rest until, through Divine blessing upon their efforts, true freedom and liberty shall reign triumphant over the whole Globe.

"Signed by order of the Committes,
"EDWARD TAYLOR Chairman"

BOSTON GRATEFULLY ACKNOWLEDGES MONMOUTH CONTRIBUTIONS.

The patriots of Monmouth promptly and freely contributed to the suffering inhabitants of Boston. In forwarding their first contribution " they entreated their brethren not to give up, and if they should want a further supply of bread to let them know it."

On the 21st of October, 1774, a letter was written on behalf of the Bostonians, to the citizens of Monmouth, in which they say :

"The kind and generous donations of the County of Monmouth in the Jersies we are now to acknowledge and with grateful hearts to thank you therefore, having received from the Committee of said county, per Captain Brown, eleven hundred and forty (1140) bushels of rye and fifty barrels of rye meal, for the suffering poor of this town which shall be applied to the purpose intended by the donors ; and what further cheers our hearts, is your kind assurances of a further supply, if necessary, to enable us to oppose the cruel Parliamentary Acts, levelled not only against this town, but our whole Constitution."

"COMMITTEES OF OBSERVATION AND INSPECTION."

"FREEHOLD December 10th 1774.

"In pursuance of the recommendation of the Continental Congress and for the preservation of American Freedom, a respectable body of the freeholders of Freehold township met at the Court House and unanimously elected the following gentlemen to act as a Committee of Observation and Inspection for said township :

John Anderson   Hendrick Smock
John Forman   John Covenhoven
Asher Holmes   Dr. Nath'l Scudder
Peter Forman   David Forman
          Dr. T. Henderson.

"The committee were instructed by their constituents to carry into execution the several important and salutary measures pointed out to them by the Continental Congress and without favor or affection to make all such diligent inquiry as shall be found conducive to the accomplishment of the great necessary purposes held up to the attention of Americans."

Upper Freehold, Dover and Middletown formed similar committees, and notified the Freehold committee.

Shrewsbury however failed to appoint a committee. This may have been owing to the prevalence of Quaker principles in the township. An attempt by the patriots of Shrewsbury was made to have a Committee appointed, as will be seen by the following copy of an advertisement put up in this township :

"ADVERTISEMENT.

"SHREWSBURY January 2nd 1775.

"Agreeable to the Resolutions of the late General Continental Congress—The Inhabitants of the town of Shrewsbury, more especially such as are properly qualified for choosing Representatives to serve in the General Assembly are hereby warned to meet at the house of Josiah Halstead, in said Shrewsbury, on Tuesday the 17th of this instant January at noon, in order to choose a Committee for the several purposes as directed by the said Congress.

"As the method ordered by the Congress seems to be the only peaceable method the case will admit of, on failure of which either confirmed Slavery or a civil war of course succeeds ; the bare mention of either of the two last is shocking to human nature, more particularly so to all true friends of the English Constitution.

"Therefore it becomes the indispensable duty of all such to use their utmost endeavors in favor of the first 'or peaceable method. and suffer it not to miscarry or fail of its salutary and much desired effects by means of any sinister views or indolence of theirs. Surely expecting on the one hand to be loaded with the curses arising from slavery to the latest posterity, or on the other hand the guilt of blood of thousand of their brethren and fellow Christians to lay at their door and to be justly required at their hands.

"Think well of this before it be too late and let not the precious moments pass."

A number of the citizens of Shrewsbury assembled at the time and place mentioned in the advertisement but they failed to appoint a committee. The following shows the conclusion to which the meeting came. It concludes more like a Quaker Meeting epistle than a town meeting resolve :

" Extract from a letter to a gentleman in New York dated Shrewsbury N. J. January 18th 1775.

" In consequence of an anonymous advertisement fixed up in this place, giving notice to freeholders and others, to meet on Tuesday the 17th inst in order to choose a Committee of Inspection etc, between thirty and forty of the most respect able freeholders accordingly met and after a few debates on the business of the day, which were carried on with great decency and moderation it was generally agreed (there being only four or five dissenting votes) that the appointment of a committee was not only useless, but they were apprehensive would prove a means of disturbing the peace and quietness which had hitherto existed in the township, and would continue to use their utmost endeavors to preserve and to gaurd against running upon that rock on which, with much concern, they beheld others, through an inattentive rashness, daily splitting "

The Freehold Committee of Observation and Inspection at a meeting held March 17th, 1775, took up the case of Shrewsbury township, and after stating the subject in a preamble they resolved that from and after that day they would esteem and treat the citizens of Shrewsbury as enemies to their King and country and deserters of the common cause of Freedom ; and would break off all dealings and connections with them " unless they shall turn from the evil of their ways and testify their repentance by adopting the measures of Congress."

The New Jersey Provincial Legislature, in May following, authorized other townships to appoint delegates for Shrewsbury, but the same month the refractory township, as will be seen by the following, chose delegates and also a committee of Observation, and so the unpleasantness ended.

SHREWSBURY FALLS INTO LINE.

"At a meeting of Freeholders and Inhabitants of the township of Shrewsbury this 27th day of May 1775, the following persons were by a great majority, chosen a committee of observation for the said town agreeable to the direction of the General Continental Congress held at Philadelphia September 5th 1774 viz.

Josiah Holmes   John Little
Jos. Throckmorton Samuel Longstreet
Nicholas Van Brunt David Knott
Cor, Vanderveer   Benjamin Dennis
Daniel Hendrickson Samuel Breese
Thomas Morford   Garret Longstreet
               Cornelius Lane.

" Ordered : That Daniel Hendrickson and Nicholas Van Brunt, or either of them, do attend the Provincial Congress now setting at Trenton, with full power to represent there, this town of Shrewsbury. And that Josiah Holmes, David Knott and Samuel Breese be a sub-committee to prepare instructions for the Deputy or Deputies who are to attend the Congress at Trenton.

" Josiah Holmes was unanimously chosen chairman.   JOSIAH HOLMES.
" Chairman and Town Clerk."

FREEHOLD PATRIOTS INDIGNANT.—NOVEL PROCEEDINGS.

March 6th, 1775.

A Tory pamphlet entitled " *Free Thoughts on the Resolves of Congress by A. W. Farmer* " was handed to the Freehold Committee of Observation and Inspection for their opinion. The committee declared it to be most pernicious and malignant in its tendencies and calculated to sap the foundation of American liberty. The pamphlet was handed back to their constituents who gave it a coat of tar and turkey buzzards feathers, one person remarking that " although the feathers were plucked from the most stinking of fowls, he thought it fell far short of being a proper emblem of the authors odiousness to the friends of freedom and he wished he had the pleasure of giving the author a coat of the same material."

The pamphlet in its gorgeous attire was then nailed to the pillory post.

The same committee severely denounced a Tory pamphlet written by James Rivington, editor of Rivington's Royal Gazette, the Tory paper, printed in New York.

By the following resolves it will be seen that the citizens of Upper Freehold favored arming the people if necessary, to oppose the tyrannical acts of Great Britain. A striking illustration of the stirring events of that perilous time is found in the fact that before a year had elapsed some of the prominent men in this meeting were aiding Great Britain to the best of their ability by voice, pen or sword :

UPPER FREEHOLD RESOLUTIONS.

"May 4th 1775. This day, agreeable to previous notice a very considerable number of the principal inhabitants of this township met at Imlaystown.

"John Lawrence Esq. in the chair: When the following resolves were unanimously agreed to :

"Resolved, That it is our first wish to live in unison with Great Britain, agreeable to the principles of the Constitution ; that we consider the unnatural civil war which we are about to be forced into, with anxiety and distress but that we are determined to oppose the novel claim of the Parliament of Great Britain to raise a revenue in America and risk every possible consequence rather than to submit to it.

"Resolved. That it appears to this meeting that there are a sufficient number of arms for the people.

"Resolved. That a sum of money be now raised to purchase what further quantity of Powder and Ball may be necessary ; and it is recommended that every man capable of bearing arms enter into Companies to train, and be prepared to march at a minutes warning ; and it is further recommended to the people that they do not waste their powder in fowling and hunting.

"A subscription was opened and one hundred and sixty pounds instantly paid into the hands of a person appointed for that purpose. The officers of four companies were then chosen and the meeting broke up in perfect unanimity.

"ELISHA LAWRENCE. Clerk."

THE OUTLAWS OF THE 1INES.

Among the most noted of these scoundrels may be mentioned Lewis Fenton, Jacob Fagan, Thomas and Stephen Burke alias Emmons, Ezekiel Williams, Richard Bird, John Bacon, John Giberson, John Wood, John Farnham, Jonathan and Stephen West, DeBow and Davenport.

Bird and Davenport appear to have operated principally in old Dover township. Giberson's head quarters appear to have been in the lower part of Burlington, from whence he made occasional raids into Stafford, then the southern township of Monmouth county.

In speaking of the Pine Robbers, Howe's Collections give several items derived chiefly from traditionary sources, relating to some of these notorious scoundrels. We give their substance below, appending occasional corrections and a large amount of additional matter., The compiler of 'the above named work derived his information from aged citizens of the country over three score years after the events referred to occurred. By comparing their traditionary accounts with letters written from Freehold and vicinity at the time, it will be seen that they differ only in minor details.

In speaking of Howell township, Howe says :

"Superadded to the other horrors of the Revolutionary war in this region, *the pines* were infested with numerous robbers, who had caves burrowed in the sides of sand hills, near the margin of swamps, in the most secluded situations, which were covered with brush so as to be almost undiscernable. At dead of night these miscreants would sally forth from their dens to plunder, burn and murder. The inhabitants, in constant terror, were obliged for safety to carry their muskets with them into the fields, and even to the house of worship. At length, so numerous and audacious had they become, that the state government offered large rewards for their destruction, and they were hunted and shot like wild beasts, when they were almost entirely extirpated."

The first of whom we shall speak is

LEWIS FENTON.

Fenton was originally a blacksmith, and learned his trade at Freehold. On one occasion he robbed a tailor's shop in that township. Word was sent him that if he did not restore the clothing within a week he should be hunted and shot. Intimidated by the threat, he returned the property accompanied by the following fiendish note :

"I have returned your d --- d rags. In a short time I am coming to burn your barns and houses, and roast you all like a pack of kittens."

In August, 1779, this villain, at the head of his gang, attacked, at midnight, the dwelling of Mr. Thomas Farr, in the vicinity of Imlaystown. The family, consisting of Mr. Farr and wife (both aged persons) and their daughter, barricaded the door with logs of wood. The assailants first attempted to beat in the door

OLD TIMES IN OLD MONMOUTH.

with rails, but being unsucessful, fired through a volley of ball, one of which broke the leg of Mr. Farr. Then forcing an entrance at the back door, they murdered his wife and dispatched him as he lay helpless on the floor. His daughter, though badly wounded, escaped, and the gang, fearing she would alarm the neighborhood, precipitately fled without waiting to plunder.

After perpetrating many enormiti, Fenton was shot, about two miles below Blue Ball, under the following circumstances:

Fenton and Burke beat and robbed a young man named VanMater of his meal, as he was going to mill. He escaped and conveyed the information to Lee's Legion, then at the Court House. A party started off in a wagon in pursuit, consisting of the Sergeant. VanMater and two soldiers. The soldiers lay on the bottom of the wagon concealed under the straw, while the sergeant, disguised as a countryman, sat with VanMater on the seat. To increase the deception, two or three empty barrels were put in the wagon. On passing a low groggery in the pines, Fenton came out with a pistol in hand and commanded them to stop. Addressing Van Mater he said:

"You d——d rascal! I gave you such a whipping I thought you would not dare to show your head;" then changing the subject inquired, "where are you going?"

"To the salt works," was the reply.

"Have you any brandy?" rejoined the robber

"Yes! will you have some?"

A bottle was given him; he put his foot on the hub of the wagon, and was in the act of drinking, when the sergeant touched the foot of one of the soldiers, who arose and shot him through the head. His brains were scattered over the side of the wagon. Burke, then in the woods, hearing the report and supposing it a signal from his companion, discharged his rifle in answer. The party went in pursuit, but he escaped.

Carelessly throwing the body into the wagon, they drove back furiously to the Court House, where, on their arrival, they jerked out the corpse by the heels, as though it had been that of some wild animal, with the ferocious exclamation: "Here is a cordial for your tories and wood robbers!"

In the above version it is stated that Fenton's companion was Burke, but ancient papers published during the war say it was DeBow. Of the two Burkes alias Emmons, Thomas and Stephen, we shall have occasion to speak before concluding.

By the following extract it will be seen that the brutal attack by Fenton and his gang on Thomas Farr and family, occurred in July, instead of August, as stated in the foregoing traditionary account from Howe:

"July 31st, 1779.—Thomas Farr and wife were murdered in the night near Crosswicks Baptist meeting house, and daughter badly wounded by a gang supposed to be under the lead of Lewis Fenton. About the same time Fenton broke into and robbed the house of one Andrews, in Monmouth County. Governor Livingston offered £500, reward for Fenton and £300, and £250 for persons assisting him."

The Pennsylvania Packet (1779) gives a notice of the attack on VanMater by Fenton, which corresponds with the following from another ancient paper, Sept. 29, 1779, probably written by a Freehold correspondent:

"On Thursday last (September 23d, 1779), a Mr. VanMater was knocked off his horse on the road near Longstreet's Mills, in Monmouth County, by Lewis Fenton and one De Bow, by whom he was stabbed in the arm and otherwise much abused, besides being robbed of his saddle. In the meantime another person coming up, which drew the attention of the robbers, gave VanMater an opportunity to escape. He went directly and informed a serjeant's gaurd of Major Lee's light dragoons, who were in the neighborhood, of what had happened. The serjeant immediately impresed a wagon and horses and ordered three of his men to secrete themselves in it under some hay. Having changed his clothes and procured a guide, he made haste, thus equipped, to the place where Fenton lay. On the approach of the wagon, Fenton (his companion being gone) rushed out to plunder it. Upon demanding what they had in it, he was answered a little wine and spirit. These articles he said he wanted, and while advancing toward the wagon to take possession of them, one of the soldiers, being previously informed who he was, shot him through the head, which killed him instantly on the spot. Thus did this villain end his days, which it is to be hoped will at least be a warning to others, if not to induce them to throw themselves on the mercy of their injured country."

In the early part of September, 1779, shortly before the VanMater affair, four of Fenton's gang were captured by the militia and lodged in Freehold jail.

JACOB FAGAN.

Fagan, also a monster in wickedness, was killed in Shrewsbury by a party of militia under Major Benjamin Dennis. The account here given is from Mrs. Amelia Coryel, a daughter of Mr. Dennis, living in January, 1843, in Philadelphia, and who, as will be seen in the narration, narrowly escaped death from the ruffians:

"On Monday in the autumn of 1778, Fagan, Burke and Smith came to the dwelling of Major Dennis, on the south side of Manasquan river, four miles below Howell Mills, to rob it of some plunder captured from a British vessel. Fragan had formerly been a near neighbor. Smith, an honest citizen, who had joined the other two, the most notorious robbers of their time, for the purpose of betraying them, prevailed upon them to remain in their lurking place while he entered the house to ascertain if the way was clear. On entering he apprized Mrs. Dennis of her danger. Her daughter Amelia (afterwards Mrs. Coryel), a girl of fourteen, hid a pocket book containing $80, in a bedtick, and with her little brother hastily retreated to a swamp near. She had scarcely left when they entered, searched the house and the bed, but without success.

"After threatening Mrs. Dennis, and ascertaining if she was unwilling to give information where the treasure was concealed, one of them proposed to murder her. "No," replied his comrade; "let the d——n rebel b——h live. The counsel of the first prevailed. They took her to a young cedar tree, and suspended her to it by the neck with a bed cord. In her struggles she got free and escaped. Amelia, observing them from her hiding place, just then descried John Holmes approaching in her father's wagon over a rise of ground two hundred yards distant, and ran towards him. The robbers fired at her; the ball whistled over her head and buried itself in an oak. Holmes abandoned the wagon and escaped to the woods. They then plundered the wagon and went off.

"The next day Major Dennis removed his family to Shrewsbury, under protection of the guard. Smith stole from his companions, and informed Dennis they were coming the next evening to more thoroughly search his dwelling, and proposed that he and his comrades should be waylaid at a place agreed upon. On Wednesday evening the Major, with a party of militia, lay in ambush at the appointed spot. After a while Smith drove by in a wagon intended for the plunder, and Fagan and Burke came behind on foot. At a given signal from Smith, which was something said to the horses, the militia fired and the robbers disappeared. On Saturday, some hunters in a groggery, made a bet that Fagan was killed. Search was made and his body was found and buried. On Sunday, the event becoming known, the people assembled, disinterred the remains, and after heaping indignities upon it, enveloped it in a tarred cloth and suspended it in chains, with iron bands around it, from a large chestnut tree about a mile from the Court House, on the road to Colts Neck. There hung the corpse in mid air, rocked to and fro by the winds, a horrible warning to his comrades, and a terror to travellers, until the birds of prey picked the flesh from its bones and the skeleton fell piecemeal to the ground. Tradition affirms that the skull was afterwards placed against the tree, with a pipe in its mouth, in derision.

"Mrs. Dennis, wife of Major Dennis, on another occasion came near being killed by a party of Hessians, who entered her dwelling, and after rudely accosting her, knocked her down with their muskets and left her for dead. In the July succeeding the death of Fagan, her husband was shot by the robbers Fenton and Emmons, as he was travelling from Coryel's Ferry to Shrewsbury. After the murder of her husband, she married John Lambert, acting Governor of New Jersey in 1802. She died in 1835."

Fagan's death above referred to occurred in September, 1778. An ancient paper has a communication dated October 1st, 1778, which says :

"About ten days ago Jacob Fagan, who having previously headed a number of villains in Monmouth county that have committed divers robberies and were the terror of travellers, was shot. Since which his body has been gibbeted on the public highway in that county, to deter others from perpetrating the like detestable crimes."

THE OUTLAWS OF THE PINES.

—

STEPHEN BURKE *alias* EMMONS, STEPHEN WEST AND EZEKIEL WILLIAMS.

The following is an extract from a letter dated at Monmouth Court House, January 29th, 1778 :

" The Tory pine robbers, who have their haunts and caves in the pines and have been for some time past a terror to the inhabitants of this county, have during the course of the present week, met with a very eminent disaster.

"On Tuesday evening last (January 26th) Captain Benjamin Dennis, who lately killed the infamous robber Fagan, with a party of his militia, went in pursuit of three of the most noted of the Pine Robbers and was so fortunate as to fall in with them and kill them on the spot. Their names are Stephen Burke alias Emmons, Stephen West and Ezekiel Williams. Yesterday they were brought up to this place and two of them it is said will be hanged in chains. This signal piece of service was effected through the instrumentality of one John VanKirk who was prevailed upon to associate with them on purpose to discover their practices and to lead them into our hands. He conducted himself with so much address that the robbers and especially the three above named, who were the leading villains, looked upon him as one of their body, kept him constantly with them and entrusted him with all their designs.

"VanKirk at proper seasons gave intelligence of their movements to Captain Dennis who conducted himself accordingly. They were on the eve of setting off for New York to make sale of their plunder, when VanKirk informed Captain Dennis of the time of their intended departure (which was to have been on Tuesday night last) and of course they would take to their boats. In consequence of which and agreeable to the directions of VanKirk, the captain and a small party of his militia planted themselves at Rock Pond, near the sea shore, and shot Burke, West and Williams in the manner above related.

"We were at first in hopes of keeping VanKirk under the rose, but the secret is out and of course he must fly the county, for the Tories are so highly exasperated against him that death will certainly be his fate if he does not leave Monmouth County. The Whigs are soliciting contributions in his favor, and from what I have already seen, have no doubt that they will present him with a very handsome sum. I question whether the destruction of the British fleet could diffuse more universal joy through the inhabitants of Monmouth than has the death of the above three most egregious villains."

REFUGEE VERSION OF THE DEATH OF BURKE *alias* EMMONS, WEST AND WILLIAMS.

William Courlies, of Shrewsbury, who joined the British about the last of 1778, testified before a British Court Martial in answer to the question as to what he knew respecting the deaths of Stephen West, Stephen Emmons alias Burke, and Ezekiel Williams, as follows :

" He (the deponent) was carried prisoner to Monmouth in January, 1779, on the night of the 24th of that month. He saw Captain Dennis of the rebel service bring to Freehold Court House three dead bodies ; that Captain Dennis being a neighbor of his (the deponent's) he asked where those men were killed. He replied, they were killed on the shore, where they were coming to join their regiments. Two of them, he said, belonged to Colonel Morris' corps, in General Skinner's brigade ; the other had been enlisted in their service by those two belonging to Colonel Morris' corps. He said, also, he (Capt. Dennis) had employed a man to assist them in making their escape at a place where he (Dennis) was to meet with them on the shore, at which place he did meet them ; that on coming to the spot he (Dennis) surrounded them with his party; that the men attempted to fire, and not being able to discharge their pieces, begged for quarters and claimed the benefit of being prisoners of war. He ordered them to be fired on, and one of them by the name of Williams fell ; that they were all bayonetted by the party and brought to Monmouth ; and that he (Dennis) received a sum of money for that action, either from the Governor or General Washington ; which of the two he does not recollect."

It is only necessary to say in connection with the above by Courlies's own statement, that at least two, if not all three, deserved death by the usual rule of warfare. They had evidently been noted for their marauding expeditions, as a reward was offered for them. They may have belonged to Skinner's " Greens " (the Loyalist organization of Jerseymen, so termed from their uniforms), but they had been noted for their frequent visits within the American lines, plundering, acting of course as spies, and endeavoring to enlist men for the British service within the patriot lines. The third man we infer remained in hiding places in the county, and when the others came over from the British lines would join them in their marauding expeditions, and he was shot while trying to join the enemy.

JONATHAN WEST.

" Jonathan West, another of this lawless crew, in an affray with some of the inhabitants of Monmouth, was taken prisoner to the Court House. His arm, being horribly mangled, was amputated. He soon after escaped to the pines and became more desperate than before. He used the stump of his arm to hold his gun. Sometime later he was again pursued, and on refusing to surrender, was shot."

FIVE MEN CONDEMNED.

The following item was published December, 1782:

" Five men were convicted at Monmouth Court House of burglary, felony, &c., and sentenced to be hanged—three on one Friday, the other two the next Friday."

Three refugees named Farnham, Burge and Patterson were executed at one time at Freehold. Our impression is that they are the three men referred to in the above paragraph, and that the other two were reprieved. We presume that Farnham is the same man who tried to shoot young Russell (as mentioned in speaking of the Russell outrage) while he was lying on the floor supposed to be mortally wounded but was prevented by Lippencott, who knocked up his musket.

EXECUTION OF THOMAS BURKE AND JOHN WOOD.

The following is from an ancient paper: " July 22nd 1778. We learn that the Court of Oyer and Terminer and General Jail delivery held in Monmouth in June last, the following persons were tried and found guilty of burglary viz : Thomas Emmons alias Bourke, John Wood, Michael Millery, William Dillon and Robert McMullen. The two former were executed on Friday last and the other three reprieved. At the same time Ezekiel Forman, John Polhemus and William Grover were tried and convicted of high treason and are to be executed on the 18th of August next."

William Dillon and Robert McMullen, mentioned above, were pardoned, but they showed no appreciation for the favor, for we find that shortly after, in September, Dillon piloted a British expedition into old Cranberry Inlet, opposite Toms River, to endeavor to recapture the ship " Love and Unity," which a short time before had been made a prize of by the Americans, the particulars of which will be given in speaking of privateering at Toms River and other places in old Monmouth during the war. When this expedition arrived at the Inlet, Robert McMullen, who seems to have been on shore waiting for them, siezed a small boat, hurrahed for the British, and rowed off to join their ships.

EXECUTIONS AT FREEHOLD.

The late Dr. Samuel Forman stated that no less than thirteen pine robbers, refugees and murderers were executed at different times on one gallows, which stood near the tree where Fagan was hung in the vicinity of the Court House, and that he assisted in the erection of the gallows. We are not certain who the thirteen were, but most of them are probably mentioned in the foregoing and other chapters, if those hung in chains after being shot are included.

Stephen Edwards was executed at Freehold for being a spy. Thomas Emmons alias Burke, John Wood, Farnham, Burge and Patterson were hung for burglary, felony, &c. Ezekiel Forman, John Polhemus and William Grover were sentenced to be executed, but we have found no mention of the sentence being carried into effect—but from circumstantial evidence it is probable that they were reprieved. Fagan was hung in chains after being shot, though not on the gallows. After Stephen Burke, West and Williams were shot and brought to Freehold, the American account says the bodies of two of the three were to be hung in chains.

In addition to executions, &c., above mentioned, a refugee named James Pew, formerly of Middletown township, joined the British and was taken prisoner by the Americans November 10th, 1779, and confined in Freehold jail, and five days after was shot by James Tilley, who was acting as sentry over him. It is probable that Pew was shot in attempting to escape. It is said that a coroner's jury condemned Tilley, but after two or three days confinement he was discharged.

DAVENPORT, THE REFUGEE LEADER OF DOVER.

The refugee leader Davenport appears to have confined most of his operations within the limits of the old township of Dover, then in Monmouth, now in Ocean. The militia stationed at Toms River were so active that Davenport and his band of desperadoes had but little chance to do serious mischief except by plundering dwellings at a distance from the principal settlements.

The most noted affair in which Davenport was concerned was in aiding the British expedition which captured the Block House at Toms River, and burned the village March 24th, 1782. One account of this affair says that Davenport was wounded when attacking the Block House, if so it must have been slightly ; as on the first of June following he landed at Forked River, ten miles below Toms River, with eighty men, half white and half black, in two barges. They first landed on the north side of Forked River and plundered, among others, the houses of Samuel Woodmansee and his brother who resided on what are now known as the Jones' and Holmes' places. They then proceeded across the south branch to the place in late years best known as "the Wright place" (formerly belonging to the father of Caleb Wright, the popular railroad conductor) in which at this time lived Samuel Brown, an active member of the old Monmouth militia.

They plundered Mr. Brown's dwelling, insulted his family, and burnt his salt works and came near capturing Mr. Brown himself, who had barely time to escape into the woods. They were particularly incensed against him for his activity in the patriot cause, he having, among other duties, served a year at the military post at Toms River.

After completing their work of destruction at Forked River, they proceeded down Forked River to the mouth, when one barge went up Barnegat bay, while the other, with Davenport himself, proceeded south to endeavor to destroy the important salt works of Newlin's at Waretown, and other salt works along the bay. Davenport expected to meet with no opposition, as he supposed there were no militia near enough to check him. But he had hardly got out of the mouth of Forked River into the open bay when he perceived a boat heading for him. His crew advised him to return as they told him the other boat must have some advantage or they would not venture to approach. Davenport told them that they could see the other boat was smaller and had fewer men and he ridiculed their fear. He soon found, however, why it was that the American boat ventured to attack them. Davenport's men had only muskets with which to defend themselves; the Americans had a cannon or swivel, and when within proper distance, they fired it with so effective an aim that Davenport himself was killed at the first discharge, and his boat damaged and upset by the frightened crew. It happened that the water where they were was only about four feet deep and his crew waded ashore, landing near the mouth of Oyster Creek, between Forked River and Waretown, and thus escaped, scattering themselves in various directions in the woods and swamps.

At Barnegat, some five miles south of where Davenport was killed, lived many Quakers who took no part in the war.

A day or so after Davenport's death some of his crew in a starved condition called on Ebenezer Collins and other Quakers at Barnegat, begging for food, which was given them, after which they left for parts unknown.

Thus ended the career of Davenport whose most noted exploit was in aiding a foreign foe to murder men who were once his neighbors and friends, burn their houses, and turn their families adrift upon the world.

Some distance back of Toms River is a little stream called "Davenport's Branch," which some suppose derives its name from Davenport's having places of concealment in the woods and swamps along its banks.

RICHARD BIRD, THE POTTERS CREEK OUTLAW.

This scoundrel, who was probably connected with Davenport's gang, was very obnoxious to the Americans on account of the many outrages in which he was concerned.

He was intimately acquainted with all the roads and bye paths in the woods and swamps in Dover township, and for a long time he managed to elude the vigilance of the militia. One day, however, he with a companion was seen along the road, a little south of Toms River, by some one, who at once notified the militia, two or three of whom immediately started in pursuit. Bird's comrade escaped by hiding under a bridge over which the pursuers passed, and Bird himself managed to elude them till after dark. His pursuers had heard that he occasionally visited a young woman of low character who lived in a lone cabin in the woods, and late in the evening they approached the cabin, and looking through the window saw Bird seated in the lap of a young woman. One of the militia fired through the window and Bird dropped off the girl's lap on the floor dead. The girl was so little affected by his death, that when the pursuers burst open the door and entered the room they found her busily engaged in rifling his pockets. Bird appears to have made his headquarters in the vicinity of the village of Bayville, formerly Potters Creek, in Dover township.

Bird was a married man, but when he joined the refugees, his wife forsook him and went to Toms River, where she resided many years after his death. While he was pursuing his wicked career, she bitterly denounced him, yet when she heard of his death, she greatly grieved, so much so that her neighbors expressed their surprise, knowing the disgrace he had been to her. The simple minded woman replied in substance, that it was not the man she so much cared but he often sent her a quarter of venison when he had more than he could use, and she should so miss such presents now!

A Bayville correspondent of the New Jersey *Courier* mentions the death of a relative of Dick Bird, a lady named Mrs. Mercy Worth, who lived to the remarkable age of 106 years, 6 months, and 24 days, who died March 5th, 1873. Her father was one of Washington's soldiers and served throughout the war. Her mother was a sister of the notorious Richard Bird, and moved away from Cedar Creek, Lacy township. for fear that Bird would be killed at her house, near which he had a cave where he stayed at night, which can still be seen.

CAPTAIN WILLIAM TOM.

A West Jersey Pioneer—After whom was Toms River named ?—The coming of the English—Indian Justice—Discovery of Toms River.

In regard to the origin of the name of Toms River, we have two distinct traditions ; one alleging that it was named after a somewhat noted Indian, who once lived in its vicinity ; the other attributes it to a certain Captain William Tom, who resided on the Delaware two hundred years ago, and who it is said penetrated through the wilderness to the seashore, on an exploring expedition, where he discovered the stream now known as Toms River ; upon his return he made such favorable representations of the land in its vicinity, that settlers were induced to come here and locate, and these settlers named it Toms River, after Mr. Tom, because he first brought it to the notice of the whites. While the writer of this, after patient investigation acknowledges that he can find nothing that *conclusively* settles the question, yet he is strong in the belief that the place derives its name from Mr. Tom, for the following reasons : First, Though there was a noted Indian residing at Toms River a century ago, known as "Indian Tom," yet the place is known to have borne the name of Toms River when he was quite a young man ; it is not reasonable to suppose the place was named after him when he was scarce out of his teens. Second, the position and business of Captain William Tom, was such as to render it extremely probably that the tradition relating to him is correct. Much difficulty has been found in making researches in this matter, as Capt. Tom was an active man among our first settlers before our West Jersey records begin, and information regarding him has to be sought for in the older records of New York and New Castle, Delaware. In his day Southern and Western Jersey were under control of officials, whose headquarters were at New Castle. Del. ; these officials were appointed by the authorities at New York. In his time Capt. John Carr appears to have been the highest official among the settlers on both sides of the Delaware, acting as Commissioner, &c. But at times it would seem that Capt. Tom was more relied upon in managing public affairs by both the Governors at New York, and the early settlers than any other man among them. In the various positions which he held, he appears to have unselfishly and untiringly exerted himself for the best interests of the settlers and the government.

He held at different times the positions of Commissary, Justice, Judge, Town Clerk and Keeper of Official Records relating to the settlements on both sides of the Delaware, collector of quit rents, &c. As collector of quit rents and agent to sell lands, his duties called him throughout

OLD TIMES IN OLD MONMOUTH. 41

the Southern half of our State, wherever settlers were found, and in search of eligible places for settlers to locate. And here his duties seem to have been somewhat similar to those performed for the Proprietors by the late Francis W. Brinley, so well remembered by our citizens. We find that Capt. Tom was continually traveling to and fro in the performance of his duties, was among the first white men to cross the State to New York, was on good terms with the Indians, with whom he continually must have mingled, and it is not at all unlikely in the performance of his duties, he crossed to the shore by Indian paths, so numerous and so frequented by the red men in his time, and thus visited the stream now known as Toms River.

As no outline of Capt. Tom's life and services has ever been published, we give the substance of the facts found relating to him, not only because of its probable bearing on the history of old Monmouth, and that our citizens may know who he was, but also because it gives an interesting chapter in the history of our State. It will be seen that he was a prominent, trusted and influential man before the founding of Philadelphia, Salem or Burlington, or before any considerable settlements existed in New Jersey. In looking back to the past, it seems a long while to Indian Tom's day, but Capt. William Tom lived nearly a century before him. The following items are collected from New York, Pennsylvania and Deloware records.

Capt. William Tom came to this country with the English expedition under Sir Robert Carre and Col. Richard Nicholls which conquered the Dutch at New Amsterdam, (New York) August. 1664. Immediately after the English had taken formal possession of New York, two vessels, the "Guinea" and the "William and Nicholas," under command of Sir Robert Carre were despatched to attack the Dutch settlements on the Delaware river. After a feeble resistance the Dutch surrendered about the first of October of the same year (1664). Capt. Tom accompanied this expedition, and that he rendered valuable service there is evidence by an order issued by Gov. Nicholls June 30, 1665, which states that for William Tom's " good services at Delaware," there shall be granted to him the lands of Peter Alricks, confiscated for hostility to the English. Capt. Tom remained in his majesty's service until August 27, 1668 ; during the last two years of this time he was Commissary on the Delaware. He was discharged from his majesty's service on the ground as is alleged " of good behaviour." In the early part of 1668, a servant of Mr. Tom's was killed by some evil disposed Indians, who it is said also killed one or more servants of Peter Alricks at the same time. The Indians generally were disposed to live on amicable terms with the whites, and these murders were the result it would seem of selling liquor to the Indians, the majority of whom seeing its evil effects, requested the white authorities to prohibit the sale of it among them. The perpetrators of these outrages were not apprehended, and because this was not done, Gov. Lovelace attributes another murder two years later ; he severely censured the authorities " for too much remissness in not avenging the previous murder on Mr. Tom's servant, &c."

On the 12th of August, 1669, Capt. Tom was appointed collector of quit rents, which were imposed on all persons taking up land along the Delaware river on both sides.

This office he held for three years when he resigned. Its duties must have been of considerable responsibility and labor, as it involved the necessity of visiting all places where settlers located from the Capes of the Delaware to the Falls of the Delaware (Trenton.) While engaged in this business it is probable that as he travelled from place to place he made it a point to search for eligible places for new settlers to locate, and acted as agent for the sale of lands At one time he acted as land agent for John Fenwick the noted Salem proprietor.

We find that Capt. Tom not only stood well in the estimation of Gov. Nicholls, but also in the opinion of his successor, Gov. Lovelace, who at the suggestion of Capt. T. issued several orders relating to affairs on the Delaware. Aug. 12, 1669, Gov. Lovelace at request of Wm. Tom, grants certain special favors to Finns and others removing near New Castle, Del. By his order " permission on request of Mr. Tom " was granted to families from Maryland to settle in the same vicinity " to the end that the said place may be inhabited and *manured*, it tending likewise to the increase of the inabitants." An order of the same date is preserved, which allows William Tom to kill and mark all wild hogs in the woods near his land.

In 1671 an extraordinary council was convened in New York on the occasion of the arrival of William Tom and Peter Alricks, just from the Delaware, with the particulars of the Indians murdering two Christians (Dutch) near Burlington. These murders were committed by two Indians who were known and who resided at "Suscunk," four miles east of Matiniconk or Burlington Island. Gov. Lovelace in a letter to Capt. Tom dated October 6, expresses great surpsise at what he has learned from Mr. Tom in regard to these murders. This letter gives stringent orders to guard against evil disposed Indians in the future, and from it we find that Burlington Island was then occupied as a kind of frontier military station. Gov. Lovelace "recommends a good work about Matiniconk house (on Burlington Island) which strengthened with a considerable guard would make an admirable frontier." Vigorous efforts were made to secure these Indian murderers, and the result is seen in the following letter written by Capt. Tom to Gov. Lovelace, Dec. 25th, 1671. He says "that about 11 days since, Peter Alricks came from New York, and the Indians desired to speak with us concerning the murders, whereupon they sent for me to Peter Rambo's, where coming they faithfully promised within six days to bring in the murderers dead or alive; whereupon they sent out two Indians to the stoutest, to bring him in. not doubting easily to take the other, he being an Indian of little courage ; but the least Indian getting knowledge of the design of the sachems, ran to advise his fellow, and advised him to run or else they would both be killed, who answered he was not ready, but in the morning would go with him to the *Maquas*, and advised him to go to the next house for fear of suspicion, which he did ; and the two Indians, coming to his house at night, the one being his great friend, he asked him if he would kill him, who answered " No, but the sachems have ordered you to die ;" whereupon he demanded " what his brothers said ;" who answered " they say the like." Then he. holding his hands before his eyes said " Kill me ;" whereupon the Indian that comes with Cocker shot him with two bullets in the breast, and gave him two or three cuts with a bill on the head and brought him down to Wicaco, from whence we shall carry him tomorrow to New Castle, there to hang him in chains for which we gave to the Sachems five match coats which Mr. Alricks paid them. When the other Indian heard the shot in the night, naked as he was, he ran into the woods ; but this sachem promised to bring the other alive, for which we promised three match coats. The sachems brought a good many of their young men with them, and there before us they openly told them " Now they saw a beginning, and all that did the like, should be served in the same manner." They promised if any other murders were committed to bring in the murderers. How to believe them we knew not, but the Sachems seem to desire no war."

What official position Capt. Tom held in these transactions is uncertain, but he appears to have been more relied upon than any other man to settle difficulties. at this time.

In 1673 Capt. Tom was appointed one of four appraisers to set a value on Tinicum Island in the Delaware. In 1674 he was appointed secretary or *clark* for the town of New Castle, and he appears to have had charge of the public records for several years. In 1673 the Dutch regained their power in New York, New Jersey and Delaware, but retained it only a few months ; after they were again displaced in 1674, Gov. Andross appointed Captains Cantwell and Tom to take possession for the King's use, of the fort at New Castle. with the public stores. They were authorized to provide for the settlement and repose of the inhabitants at New Castle. Whorekills (Lewes)and other places."

In 1675 some settlers complained against Capt. Tom for molesting them in the enjoyment of meadow lands which adjoined their plantations. The settlers probably supposed because they owned uplands, they should also have the use of meadow land without paying for the same. The Governor ordered a compromise. In 1676 he was appointed one of the Justices of the Peace and a Judge of the court. He sat as one of the Judges in an important suit in which the defendant was John Fenwick, the Salem Proprietor. Judgment was given against Fenwick, and a warrant issued to take him dead or alive. Fenwick finding it useless to resist, gave himself up, and was sent prisoner to New York.

Capt. Tom was reappointed justice and judge in 1677. Towards the latter part of this year complaint was made that the town records of New Castle were in confusion, and Mr. Tom was ordered to arrange and attest them. It is not improbable that ill health prevented him from completing this task, as we find his death announced January 12, 1678, coupled with the simple remark that, "his papers were in confusion."

From the foregoing and other facts that are preserved, it would appear that Wm. Tom was about the most prominent, useful and trustworthy man among the settlers from the time of the coming of the English to his decease, that he enjoyed the confidence of Governors Nicholls, Lovelace and Andross, that his varied duties were performed with general satisfaction to settlers, Indians and officials, and we may safely infer that he did as much or more than any other man in his day "towards the settlement and repose of the inhabitants" on both sides of the Delaware. It is no discredit to the name of Toms River that it should be derived from such a man.

In speaking of Capt. Tom's discovering Toms River, we do not refer to its original discovery, nor wish to convey the idea that he was the first white man who visited it. The stream was discovered by navigators fifty years before Capt. Tom came to America. They simply marked the stream on their charts without naming it. The particulars as far as is known of the original discovery of Toms River, and other places along our bay are too lengthy to be given here and may hereafter be furnished in another chapter. We will say, however, before concluding, that the fact that this river had been previously visited by the Dutch, was probably not known to Capt. Tom and the English in this day.

CAPTAIN JOHN BACON.

The Refugee Leader of Monmouth and Burlington—An Outlaw's Career and its Dreadful End.

This noted refugee leader, whose name is so well remembered by old residents of Monmouth, Ocean and Burlington, appears to have confined his operations chiefly to the lower part of old Monmouth county, between Cedar Creek in what is now Ocean county and Tuckerton in Burlington county. His efforts were mainly directed to plundering the dwellings of all well known, active members of the old Monmouth militia. Many old residents in the section where his operations were carried on, considered him one of the most honorable partizan leaders opposed to the patriot cause. Himself and men were well acquainted with the roads and paths through the forests of Burlington and old Monmouth, and had numerous hiding places, cabins, caves, &c., in the woods and swamps, where they could remain until some trustworthy spy informed them of a safe chance to venture out on what was then termed a *picarooning* expedition.

The following items, gleaned from various sources, give the most prominent events in which he was an actor. They aid to give a more vivid idea of the perils by which our ancestors were surrounded at home, and of the character of the man who, probably with the exception of Lieutenant James Moody, was about the most effective refugee leader in our state.

In ancient papers we have found notices of refugee raids in Burlington county, but they do not give the names of the leaders. It is probable that Bacon commanded some of these expeditions as he was well acquainted in Burlington, and his wife resided at Pemberton in the latter part of the war. About September, 1782, it is announced that a man, supposed to be a spy of Bacon's, was shot in the woods near Pemberton, by some of the inhabitants who went out to hunt him; and we find that the citizens of Burlington were so much exasperated against him that they organized expeditions to follow him in old Monmouth.

BACON KILLS LIEUTENANT JOSHUA STUDSON.

The *New Jersey Gazette*, published at Trenton during the later years of the Revolutionary war, has a brief item to the effect that "Lieutenant Joshua Studson was shot, December, 1780, by a refugee, near the inlet opposite Toms River."

Joshua Studson had been a lieutenant in the Monmouth militia, and was also appointed lieutenant in the State troops in Capt. Ephram Jenkins' company, Colonel Holmes' battalion, June 14, 1780. He resided at Toms River.

The following particulars of his death we believe to be substantially correct, though derived from traditionary sources:

Three men named Collins, Webster and Woodmansee, living in the lower part of old Monmouth, hearing that farming produce was bringing exorbitant prices in New York city among the British, loaded a whole boat with truck from farms along Barnegat bay, and proceeded to New York by way of old Cranberry inlet opposite Toms River, which inlet though now closed, was, during the war, the next best to Egg Harbor, as square rigged vessels (ships and brigs) occasionally entered it. These men were not known as refugees but undertook the trip merely to make money. They arrived safely in New York, sold out their produce, and were about returning home when Captain John Bacon called on them and insisted on taking passage back with them. Much against their will, they were forced to allow him to come on board. They arrived safely outside the beach near the inlet before sundown and lay there until after dark, being afraid to venture in the bay during daylight. In the meantime the patriotic citizens of Toms River had got wind of the proceedings of these men, and being determined to put a stop to the contraband trade, a small party under command of Lieutenant Studson took a boat and crossed over to the inlet and lay concealed behind a point inside, close to the inlet. After dark the whale boat came in, but no sooner had it rounded the point, than to the consternation of those in it, they saw the boat of the militia so close by, that there was no apparent chance of escape. Lieutenant Studson stood up in his boat and demanded their immediate surrender. The unfortunate speculators were unarmed and in favor of yielding, but Bacon, fearing that his life was already forfeited, refused, and having his musket loaded, suddenly fired it with so deadly an aim, that the brave lieutenant instantly dropped dead in the boat. The sudden, unexpected firing and the death of Studson, threw the militia into momentary confusion, and before they could decide how to act, the whale boat was out of sight in the darkness. The militia returned to Toms River the same night and delivered the body of the lieutenant to his wife, who was overwhelmed with sorrow at his sudden and unexpected death.

The crew of the whale boat, knowing it was not safe for them to remain at home, after this affair, fled to to the British army, and were forced into service, but were of little use as "they were sick with the small pox, and suffered everything but death," as one of them afterwards said, during their brief stay with the British. Taking advantage of one of General Washington's proclamations offering protection to deserters from the British army, they were afterwards allowed to return home.

SKIRMISH AT MANNAHAWKIN.

A Patriot Killed—Sylvester Tilton, an old Colts Neck citizen—His Wounding and Revenge.

Another affair, in which Bacon was a prominent actor, was the skirmish at Mannahawkin, in Ocean County, December 30th, 1781. The militia of this place, under command of Captain Reuben F. Randolph, having heard that Bacon, with his band, was on a raiding expedition and would probably try to plunder some of the patriots in that village, assembled at the inn of Captain Randolph's, prepared to give them a reception. After waiting until two or three o'clock in the morning, they concluded it was a false alarm, and so retired to rest, taking the precaution to put out sentinels. Just before daylight the Refugees came down the road from the north on their way to West Creek. The alarm was given and the militia hastily turned out but were compelled to retreat, as the refugees had a much larger force than they anticipated. As they were retreating, Bacon's party fired and killed one of the patriots named Lines Pangborn and wounded another named Sylvester Tilton. The refugees did not stop to pursue the Americans but passed on south towards West Creek.

In regard to the wounding of Sylvester Tilton, it is a well attested fact, that the ball went through him below one of his shoulders, and that the surgeon passed a silk handkerchief through his body, in search of the ball. He recovered his health and strength, much to the surprise of all who knew how seriously he had been wounded. He was convinced that a refugee named Brewer, one of Bacon's gang, was the man who had wounded him, and he always vowed to have satisfaction if he could ever find him. After the war he heard that Brewer was living in a cabin in some remote place near the shore, and he started on foot, one time, to find him. As he was on his way, he met a man named James Willetts, then quite a noted and highly esteemed Quaker, of old Stafford, who upon finding out Tilton's errand, vainly endeavored to persuade him to turn back. Finding he would not Willets asked permission to go along, hoping something would turn up to make a peaceable ending of the affair. Tilton consented to his going but plumply told the Quaker that if he interfered he would flog him too.

Arriving at the house where Brewer was Tilton suddenly opened the door and rushed in upon him before he could reach his musket, which he always kept in the room expecting such a visit

Tilton was a powerful man and he dragged Brewer to the door and gave him a most unmerciful pummelling, and then told him "You scoundrel! you tried to kill me once, and I have now settled with you for it, and I want you now to leave here and follow the rest of your gang." Most of the refugees had then gone to Nova Scotia.

After this affair Tilton removed to Colts Neck, near Freehold, where we believe his descendants yet live.

BACON AT GOODLUCK, FORKED RIVER AND WARETOWN.

On one of his picarooning or raiding expeditions, Bacon with fifteen or sixteen men plundered the dwelling house of John Holmes at Forked River, who then lived at the mill known in late years as Francis Cornelius' mill. The party camped in the woods, near the house, until daylight and then came and demanded money. Mr. Holmes was supposed to be somewhat forehanded and they hoped to have made a good haul. In the expectation of such a visit, he had buried many of his valuables in his garden. The refugees pointed a bayonet to his breast and threatened to kill him if the money was not forthcoming. Mr. Holmes' wife happened to have some money about her, which she delivered up and this seemed to satisfy them as far as money was concerned; they then ransacked the house and took provisions and such other things as they wanted.

An ancient paper says that about the last of April, 1780, "the refugees attacked the house of John Holmes, Upper Freehold, and robbed him of a large amount of Continental money, a silver watch, gold ring, silver buckles, pistols, clothing, &c." It is possible that this refers to the same affair—if so it occurred in old Dover township instead of Upper Freehold.

While a part of the gang remained at the mill a detachment went over to Goodluck, about a mile distant, to plunder the houses of two staunch patriots named John Price and William Price, two brothers who had lived in West Jersey during the first part of the war, but for the last two or three years of the struggle, had resided at Goodluck. These men had not only been active in the field during most of the war, but, to the extent of their abilities, aided the families of those who suffered at the hands of the enemy. When the dwelling of Capt. Ephraim Jenkins, at Toms River, was burned, and his family scattered, as described in a previous chapter, Lieut. John Price, (in after years, better known as Major Price,) took one of the children, a girl, and gave her a home. The activity of the Prices made them marked objects of refugee attentions.

Bacon's party, at this time, entered the houses of the Prices, and took whatever they could carry, though, we believe, these patriots, like others in those dark days, kept buried in gardens and fields many things they feared the refugees might covet. We have heard from an aged resident of Goodluck, a tradition of the visit of the refugees to the house of an American Lieutenant, at this village, and that the officer saw them just before they reached the house; he sprang up and grasped his lieutenant's commission, which he valued highly, from a high shelf, and sprang out of the back door just in time to escape. We presume this officer must have been Lieut. Price, as we know of no other officer then residing at Goodluck. Among other things found at Major Price's was a musket, fife and drum, the two last of which came near causing trouble among the tories themselves, for as they marched back to Holmes' Mill to rejoin Bacon, they used them for their amusements with such effect, that Bacon thought it was a party of Americans after him, and he arranged his men on the mill hill, prepared to fire as soon as the party emerged from the woods. Unfortunately for justice, he saw who the men were in time to stop firing. The Refugees then impressed Mr. Holmes' team to carry off the plunder they had gathered, and forced his son William Holmes to drive it; they went on to Waretown and took possession for a short time of a public house (of David Bennet's?) until they could find some safe way of getting their plunder to one of their secret rendezvous, one of which was supposed to be at this time in Mannahawkin swamp.

Among other zealous Americans for whom Bacon had strong antipathy were Joseph Soper and his son Reuben, both members of Captain Reuben F. Randolph's militia company. They lived about half way between Waretown and Barnegat at a place known as "Soper's Landing." His attentions to the Sopers were so frequent that they often had to sleep in the adjacent swamps along Lochiel brook.

Mr. Soper's son Reuben was murdered by Bacon on Long Beach about a mile south of Barnegat Inlet, the particulars of which will be given hereafter.

At this time there lived at Waretown an Englishman, named William Wilson, better known as "Bill Wilson," who seems to have acted as a kind of jackall for Bacon to scent out his prey for him. Mr. Soper was a vessel builder ; at one time he had received pay for building a small vessel. Wilson accidentally was a witness to his receiving the money, but he did not know the amount. After Wilson had left, Mr. Soper suspected he would inform Bacon, and so he divided his money into two parcels ; a small amount in one parcel, and the larger part in another, and then buried both lots in separate places not far from the house. Sure enough, in a very short time, Bacon and his gang visited the house, piloted by a man with a black silk handkerchief over his face that he should not be recognized. This man was generally believed to be Bill Wilson, though strong efforts were made to make the Sopers believe it was another man then residing at Waretown. Mr. Soper at this time, had taken refuge in the swamp, and the house was occupied only by women and young children. When the refugees entered they at once began behaving very rudely and boisterously, flourishing their weapons in a menacing manner, jambing bayonets in the ceiling, and other similar acts to frighten the women. Their threats compelled the women to lead them into the garden, to the spot where the smallest amount of money was buried, when they received which they seemed to be satisfied, thinking it was all they had ; they then returned to the house and made a clean sweep as they had done several times before, of provisions and clothing, and such other articles as they could carry. Among other things taken by Bacon at this time was one of Mr. Soper's shirts, which afterwards served Bacon's winding sheet, as he was subsequently killed with it on. Bill Wilson could never be fairly convicted of actual complicity in overt acts with the refugees, but all who knew him were convinced that he was a spy of Bacon's. It was alleged that he was with Bacon at Holmes' Mill's and at the Price's, at Goodluck. After the war closed he remained for some years in the vicinity of Waretown, but he found it a very uncomfortable place for him to live, for though no legal hold could be taken of him, yet occasionally some zealous whig, who had occasion to hate refugees, would take him in hand on a very slight pretext, and administer off-hand justice. At one time at Lochiel brook, below Waretown, Hezekiah Soper, whose brother was killed by Bacon, gave Wilson a sound thrashing and then nearly drowned him in the brook. At length, finding the place did not agree with him, he left Waretown, and moved over to the North beach, a few miles above the inlet, where he lived a lonesome, miserable life until his death, which occurred some sixty odd years ago.

THE MASSACRE ON LONG BEACH.

Bacon Kills Capt. Steelman, Reuben Soper and Others—Murder of Sleeping Men.

This was the most important affair in which Bacon was engaged. The inhuman massacre of sleeping men was in keeping with the memorable affair at Chestnut Neck, near Tuckerton, when Count Pulaski's guards were murdered by the British and Refugees.

The massacre at Long Beach took place about a mile south of Barnegat light house, and there were we think more men killed and wounded then than in any other action in that part of Old Monmouth now comprised within the limits of Ocean county.

A tory paper gives the following version of the affair ;

"A cutter from Ostend, bound to St. Thomas, ran aground on Barnegat Shoals, October 25, 1782. The American galley Alligator, Captain Steelman, from Cape May, with twenty-five men, plundered her on Saturday night last of a quantity of Hyson tea and other valuable articles, but was attacked the same night by Captain John Bacon with nine men, in a small boat called the Hero's Revenge, who killed Steelman and wounded the first lieutenant, and all the party except four or five were either killed or wounded."

In this account the number of Steelman's men is doubtless overestimated and Bacon's underestimated. When the cutter was stranded on the shoals, word was sent across the bay to the main land for help to aid in saving the cargo, in consequence of which a party of unarmed men, among which were Joseph Soper and two of his sons, proceeded to the beach to render what assistance they could. The party

OLD TIMES IN OLD MONMOUTH. 47

worked hard while there to get the goods through the surf on the beach. At night they were tired and wet, and built fires, around which they meant to sleep. It is supposed that as soon as they were all asleep that Bill Wilson who was there arose up slyly, got a boat and rowed off to the main land to inform Bacon how matters stood.

THE LOYALISTS OF OLD MONMOUTH.

To fairly comprehend the dangers by which our patriotic ancestors were surrounded during the early part of the Revolution, it is necessary to remember that those of its citizens who openly or secretly favored the enemy, were not a mere handful of men, but they were numbered by hundreds, and among them were men of all classes, from the highest to the lowest; clergymen, lawyers, physicians, merchants, farmers, mechanics and laboring men, and unprincipled men of no particular profession or business, who rejoiced at the opportunities given by the war for plunder, revenge and ofttimes murder. The best class of tories were too honorable to engage in midnight marauding expeditions against their former friends and neighbors, but cast their lot with the British, most of them in the military organization known as the "First Battalion New Jersey Royal Volunteers," commanded by an ex-Sheriff of Monmouth county. They rarely committed acts dishonorable as soldiers, yet their former high standing and influential positions served to exert a most injurious influence on the patriot cause among their former friends and acquaintances; the example of such men served to entice many to the ranks of the enemy and to cause others secretly to wish them well, or at least to strive to remain neutral at a time when their country most needed their services and in a county which suffered probably more severely during the war than did any other in the country. When we remember that our patriotic ancestors had to contend with such men, and with bands of marauding refugees, and also lawless robbers scattered through the pines—all in addition to a foreign foe, we cannot too highly extol the determined, vigilant, ceaseless efforts, the wisdom in planning, the skill and bravery in execution, shown by those noble patriots during the long, bloody and at times seemingly hopeless struggle. Though we may concede that some who deserted their country were in some respects wise and brave, yet they were no match for those left behind.

As was the case in the late war for the Union, the Revolution brought out from obscurity men whose abilities were never before known or suspected.

For the first year or two of the war our ancestors were seriously annoyed by Tory sympathizes who remained at home, some of whom had sons, brothers or other relatives in the British army. Some of these remained at home because age or other disability unfitted them for field service. These men for a time endeavored to injure the American cause by their insidious wiles wherever and whenever opportunity offered, when their acts came to the knowledge of the whigs, they were at once ordered to leave, while those who remained quiet, though closely watched were rarely molested.

Though the names Loyalist or Royalist would properly include all who favored the cause of the Crown, yet they were often limited to the more honorable class who joined the Royal Volunteer organization, to distinguish them from the small marauding bands commonly known as Refugees.— Among the most prominent of these loyalists, were some noticed below; it will be seen they numbered among them men of wealth, position, and learning; one succeeded in raising five hundred men to follow him over to the enemy, and it is not a little curious to find that from two of these tories, descended certain men who, in after years, nobly served our country in many a hard fought battle.

In this connection it is well to add, that as an offset to the Tories who left Monmouth and other parts of our state, to join the enemy, there were a large number of whigs, who came here and into other decided patriotic counties, from Long and Staten Islands, when the British took possession of those places.

Another fact should not be lost sight of, as it furnishes additional evidence of the peculiar troubles the patriots had to contend against, and that is, that many leading men who sided with them in this and other counties of the state, during the first year or two of the war eventually abandoned them and went over to the Royalists. Of some of these and their alleged reasons we shall endeavor to speak in another chapter.

For much of the following we are endebted to Sabine, but we have added many items from other sources which we deem reliable.

NOTICES OF PROMINENT LOYALISTS.

THOMAS CROWELL, of Middletown, joined the Loyalists and was commissioned Captain. His property was confiscated and advertised to be sold at the house of Cornelius Swart in Middletown, March 22d, 1779. During the war Governor Franklin, of the Refugee Board, ordered him to execute, without trial, a Monmouth officer, probably one of the Smocks, but the refugees who captured him protested so earnestly that the order was not executed.

LAWRENCE HARTSHORNE, of Shrewsbury, made himself so obnoxious as a Royalists, that he was compelled to fly to New York. He was a merchant and gave the British valuable information.

JOHN TAYLOR, formerly Sheriff of Monmouth County, a gentleman of great wealth, was born in 1716. When Lord Howe arrived in this country to offer terms of reconciliation, he appointed Mr. Taylor " His Majesty's Lord High Commissioner of New Jersey." This office, as well as the fact that all his children adhered to the Crown, and were in the British army, made him obnoxious to the whigs. He was indeed once tried for his life but acquitted. His property was applied to public use, but not confiscated, since he was paid for it in Continental money, yet such was the depreciation of that currency that payment was little better than confiscation. He died at Perth Amboy, in 1798, aged 82 years. His grandson was the celebrated Commodore Bainbridge, his daughter Mary having married Dr. Bainbridge, father of Commodore's William and Joseph Bainbridge. A Dr. Absalom Bainbridge was surgeon in " Skinner's Greens," the Royalist organization, elsewhere noticed.

WILLIAM TAYLOR, son of the above named John Taylor, had his estates confiscated, but after the war he purchased them again. He was a lawyer by profession and at one time Chief Justice of Jamaica.— He died at Amboy 1806.

COLONEL TAYLOR, of the New Jersey Royalists who sent Stephen Edwards as a spy into Monmouth, was from Middletown.— It is possible that he may have been one of the Taylors whose property was confiscated and advertised to be sold at Middletown, March 22d, 1779. He may have been a son of the John Taylor mentioned above, as it seems he had more than one son in the British service.

REV. SAMUEL COOKE, D.D., of Shrewsbury, Episcopal minister, was educated at Cain's College, Cambridge, England, and came to America as a missionary of the Society for the Propagation of the Gospel in Foreign Parts, in September, 1751, locating in Shrewsbury as successor of Rev. Thomas Thompson, in the care of the churches in Freehold, Middletown and Shrewsbury.— The Revolution divided and dispersed his flock. As a minister of the Church of England he thought it his duty to continue his allegiance to the Crown, and joined the British in New York. At the Court Martial trial of Captain Richard Lippencott, in New York, in June, 1782, he was a witness and styled " Reverend Samuel Cooke, clerk, deputy chaplain to the brigade of guards." His property we believe was confiscated and advertised to be sold at Tinton Falls, March 29th, 1779.

In 1785, he settled at Fredericktown, New Brunswick, as rector of a church there. In 1791, he was commissary to the Bishop of Nova Scotia. He was drowned in crossing the river St. John, in a birchen canoe, in 1795. His son who attempted to save his life perished with him.

THOMAS LEONARD, a prominent citizen of Freehold, was denounced by the patriot committee for his Tory principles and every friend of freedom advised to break off all connection with him on that account. He went to New York and after the war went to St. Johns, New Brunswick.

JOSEPH HOLMES, by adhering to the Tories, lost £900. After the war he went to Nova Scotia and settled at Shelburne.

ANDREW BELL, a name familiar to our older citizens on account of its frequent recurrence in deeds relating to Proprietor lands, joined the British army as secretary to Sir Henry Clinton. A diary kept by him up to the battle of Monmouth is preserved in the library of the New Jersey Historical Society. He died in 1843.— Though we believe he was not a resident of Monmouth yet he was well known and influential throughout the county.

JOHN LAWRENCE, of Monmouth county, was born in 1709. He was a justice of the court and a surveyor, and ran the division line known as " Lawrence's line," between East and West Jersey. Advanced in life at the beginning of the Revolution he did not bear arms, but accepted from the enemy the important duty of granting

OLD TIMES IN OLD MONMOUTH. 49

British protections to such Americans as he could induce to abjure the cause of their country and swear allegiance to Great Britain, for which he was arrested by the Americans and confined in Burlington jail for nine months. He died in 1794 aged 86 years. We propose to refer to John and Elisha Lawrence, in giving the proceedings of the patriot meetings in Upper Freehold and elsewhere in the county in 1774-5, and in other chapters.

ELISHA LAWRENCE, son of the above, was born in 1740. At the beginning of the Revolution he was Sheriff of Monmouth County; he soon joined the British, and raised by his own efforts chiefly, five hundred men whom he commanded, and was commissioned by the British, Colonel of the First Battalion, New Jersey Royal Volunteers. He was taken prisoner on Staten Island by Colonel Ogden under General Sullivan in 1777. His property was confiscated and advertised to be sold at Wall's Mills, April 5th, 1779. At the conclusion of the war he left with the British army, retained his rank as Colonel and retired on half pay. He was awarded by the British Government a large tract of land in Nova Scotia, to which he removed, but finally went back to England, and from thence to Cardigan, Wales, where he died. He married Mary Ashfield, of New York.

JOHN LAWRENCE, son of the above named John, and brother of Elisha, was born in 1747, graduated at Princeton College, studied medicine in the Philadelphia Medical College and became a physician of repute. In 1776 he was arrested by order of General Washington, and ordered by the Provincial Congress to remain at Trenton on parole, but leave was afterwards given him to remove to Morristown. As his father and brother held office under the British, he was narrowly watched. Fired at, after much annoyance (says one account—apparently a Tory one) by a party of militia, he retired to New York among the British, where he practiced medicine and commanded a company of volunteers for the defence of the city. After the war in 1783, he returned to Monmouth, where he lived unmolested. He died at Trenton, April 29th, 1830. In the list of names of persons in Upper Freehold whose property was confiscated and advertised to be sold at Wall's Mills, April 5th, 1779, are found the names of "Elisha and John Lawrence, son of John."

JOHN BROWN LAWRENCE was a member of Council and a lawyer. Because of his official relations to the Crown, he was arrested and imprisoned in Burlington jail for a long time on the charge of holding treasonable intercourse with the enemy but was tried and acquitted. He went to Canada after the war, where he received a large tract of land. His son was the celebrated Commodore Lawrence of "Don't give up the ship" fame, and Commodore Boggs, distinguished in the late rebellion, was a descendant.

CLAYTON TILTON, of Shrewsbury, joined the loyalists and was commissioned as Captain. He was captured by the Americans in the spring of 1782, about the same time that Phil White was, and confined in Freehold jail, but shortly exchanged for Daniel Randolph, Esq. He probably went to the British Provinces at the close of the war, as mention is made of a certain Clayton Tilton, a loyalist from New Jersey, marrying the widow of Thomas Green, at Musquash, New Brunswick, shortly after the war.

JOHN WARDELL, of Shrewsbury, an associate judge of Monmouth, on account of his tory proclivities, sought refuge within the British lines. His property was confiscated and advertised to be sold at Tinton Falls, March 29th, 1779. He was a neighbor and warm friend of Captain Richard Lippencott.

CAPTAIN RICHARD LIPPENCOTT, THE REFUGEE WHO HANGED CAPTAIN HUDDY.

This refugee who obtained such unenviable notoriety for hanging Captain Joshua Huddy, was born in New Jersey in 1745, and died at Toronto, Canada, in 1826, in his 82d year. At the breaking out of the war he was a resident of Shrewsbury township. Early in that memorable struggle he left Monmouth and went to New York and expressed to the Board of Associated Loyalists a desire for authority to raise a company, which was given him by the Board upon his signing the usual articles requiring him to obey the orders of Governor William Franklin, its President. On account of his activity in the Royal service, his property was confiscated and advertised to be sold at Tinton Falls, March 29th, 1779. He appears to have had many relatives among both the patriots and loyalists. The character he bore among the adherents of the Royal cause is shown by the following extracts During the British Court Martial trial held in New York in June, 1782, to try him for the murder of Captain Joshua Huddy, Colonel John Morris, commander of the second battalion of the brigade of New Jersey Royal Volunteers, testified as follows:

"He had known the prisoner (Lippencott) many years; he always supported a good character ever since deponent has known him; and he always endeavored to serve the Government all in his power, and that with propriety. Deponent has never known him guilty of plundering or any action of that kind."

John Wardell, late of Shrewsbury township, and formerly an associate judge of Monmouth, testified that "he had been acquainted with Lippencott more than 'en years; that he was his neighbor and was always looked upon as a peaceable, inoffensive man."

Rev. Dr. Samuel Cooke, the noted Episcopalian clergyman who settled in Shrewsbury in 1751, where he remained until the breaking out of the Revolution, and to whom reference is made in other chapters, at the time of Lippencott's trial was deputy chaplain to the brigade of guards in the British service; upon being sworn he said:

"He had not known Lippencott before the rebellion, but has been acquainted with him upwards of three years since Lippencott has been within his Majesty's lines. That he has been particularly acquainted with him, and has every reason to think his character stood as fair as that of any refugee within his Majesty's lines."

After the Revolution, Lippencott went to England to claim compensation for his losses and services. He obtained the half pay of captain for life, and the grant of 300 acres of land at York, (now Toronto) in Canada, upon which he settled about 1794. His only child, Esther Borden Lippencott, married George Taylor Dennison, and her son, George T. Dennison, some twenty odd years ago, was a member of the Canadian parliament. Sabine, in the first edition of his history of the loyalists, having made some remarks not very complimentary to Captain Lippencott, his grandson, George T. Dennison, addressed him a letter in which he endeavored to defend the acts and character of his grandfather. He says:

"Lippencott was naturally a person of the most harmless and quiet disposition. Philip White was half brother to his wife, and Lippencott was exasperated by the butchery of an innocent relative (*Stephen* *Edwards?*) who, found on a visit to his mother's house, was treated by Huddy as a spy. The old man (Lippencott) was respected by all who knew him in the country, rich and poor, and was so well known to all old loyalists who settled there, that persons came uninvited thirty or forty miles to pay tribute to his memory; hundreds still living will repudiate the unfavorable character as a man and a soldier given him by the American historian.— He was true to his Sovereign both in property and peril, and nobly maintained the Lippencott family motto, "*Secundus dubusque rectus.*" Indeed the truth is, as I have always heard it declared by himself and others, that he had the authority from Sir Henry Clinton himself to hang Huddy in retaliation for White."

As to what Mr. Dennison says in regard to the character of Lippencott after the war, it may be all quite true but it has but little to do with the hanging of Huddy during the war. Mr. Dennison is in error in saying that Sir Henry Clinton authorized the execution. On the contrary he was so indignant at the act that he at once ordered Lippencott to be Court Martialed, and Sparks, the historian, says that while in London, he saw original letters from Sir Henry Clinton and his successor, Sir Guy Carleton, expressing in the strongest terms their indignation at Huddy's murder. The fact probably is, that Mr. Dennison errs only in the name of the person; it is probable that his grandfather stated that he had the authority of his superior officer to hang Huddy, and from this Mr. D. inferred that this superior officer was Sir Henry Clinton. Who this superior officer really was will be seen by extracts we shall hereafter give from official British records, which show quite conclusively how far Lippencott was responsible for the murder of Huddy. It will be seen that Lippencott was not the only guilty party; as to whom the most guilt should be attached may be judged from the evidence produced on his trial.

THE NEW JERSEY ROYAL VOLUNTEERS.

The following are the names of some of the officers of this noted organization, composed mainly of Jerseymen, who aided the British during the Revolution.— The commanding officer was Cortland Skinner, and his brigade was often called "Skinner's Greens." The officers and men were from different counties, chiefly in East Jersey. Most of the Old Mon mouth Loyalists joined the First battalion of this brigade.

CORTLAND SKINNER, BRIGADIER GENERAL.
First Battalion.

Elisha Lawrence, Colonel.
B. G. Skinner,   "   1781.
Stephen Delancey, Lieut. Colonel.
Thomas Millidge, Major.
William Hutchinson, Captain.
Joseph Crowell,   "
James Moody, Lieutenant.
John Woodward,   "
James Brittain   "
Ozias Ausley, Ensign.
Joseph Brittain, "

Second Battalion.

John Morris, Colonel, Second battalion.
Isaac Allen, Lieut. Colonel "   "
Charles Harrison, Captain, "   "
Thomas Hunlock,   "   "   "
John Combs, Lieutenant "   "

Third Battalion.

Abraham Van Buskirk, Lieutenant Colonel, Third battalion.
Robert Timpany, Major,   "   "
Philip Cortland (N. Y.) "   "   "
Jacob Van Buskirk, Capt. "   "
James Servanier, Lieut.   "   "
Philip Cortland, Jr., Ensign "   "
John Van Orden,   "   "   "

The following named were also officers in this organization:
Elisha Skinner, Lieutenant Colonel, John Barnes, Major, R. V. Stockton, Major, Thomas Lawrence, Major, John Lee, Captain, Peter Campbell, ditto, John Barbara, ditto, Richard Cayford, ditto, William Chandler, ditto, Daniel Cozens, ditto, —— Keating, ditto. Lieutenants, Troup and Fitz Randolph. Absalom Bainbridge, Surgeon. Peter Myer, Ensign.

LIEUTENANT JAMES MOODY.

In the above list of Loyalist officers will be noticed the name of James Moody, Lieutenant in the First Battalion, in which were so many former residents of Monmouth. At the close of the war, Moody went to England, and shortly after his arrival there published a pamphlet entitled, "Lieutenant James Moody's Narrative of his Exertions and Sufferings in the cause of the Government since the year 1776 ; authenticated by proper certificates. London, 1783."

As this publication is rare, we propose hereafter to extract the substance which will be found to contain many things of value to the historian, and of much interest to the general reader. As a matter of course he strives to depreciate the Americans and their cause, and to exalt Tories and Toryism to the best of his ability, and on this particular account his narrative deserves a place in our local history, for to obtain a comprehensive view of life and times in the Revolution it is necessary to look at the causes and effects from a Tory stand-point. As during the war all who joined the Americans were not wholly good, so all who joined the British were not wholly bad, and to one who is curious to know what reasons were offered for their course by the more honorable Tories and what versions they gave to scenes in which they were actors, Lieutenant Moody's narrative will have peculiar value. His career, it will be seen, furnishes exciting incidents sufficient to form the ground work for half a dozen modern sensational novels. He made many raids into New Jersey, and on one expedition into Monmouth it was alleged that he caused the death of two Monmouth militia officers under circumstances so contrary to the usual rule of warfare, that when, afterward, he was captured, he was sentenced to be executed, but escaped almost miraculously.

THE FIRST SETTLERS IN OLD MONMOUTH.

—

THE STOUT FAMILY.

—

Indians on the War Path—Firm Stand of the Settlers—A League of Peace Never Broken.

Among the first whites who permanently settled in old Monmouth, was Richard Stout, who, with his own family and five other families, it is said, located in Middletown in 1648. The history of the Stout family, though familiar to those versed in the ancient history of our state, yet is so remarkable on account of the wonderful preservation of the life of Mrs. Stout, and of so much general interest because their descendants in our county and elsewhere are so numerous, and also because this family were among the first Baptists in New Jersey, that it will bear repeating, especially as it may prove new to many of our readers. The version of the remarkable history of Penelope Stout, as given in Benedict's History of the Baptists, is the one most familiar to our older citizens but believing that many of our readers may wish for preservation both this version and the one given in 1765, by Smith in his history of New Jersey, we append them with additional items from other sources.

The ship in which Penelope came to this country was wrecked on the coast of Monmouth, some two hundred and fifty years ago. The story of her remarkable preservation was handed down by tradition, in various parts of the state, for a century and a half with little variation except that some traditionary versions, at one time, located the place of the shipwreck on the Delaware.

The following version is the one published by Smith in 1765 :

"While New York was in the possession of the Dutch, about the time of the Indian war in New England, a Dutch ship, coming from Amsterdam, was stranded on Sandy Hook, but the passengers got ashore—among them was a young Dutchman who had been sick most of the voyage ; he was so bad after landing that he could not travel, and the other passengers, being afraid of the Indians, would not stay until he recovered ; his wife, however, would not leave him, and the rest promised to send for them as soon as they arrived at New Amsterdam (New York.) They had not been gone long before a company of Indians, coming to the water side, discovered them on the beach, and hastening to the spot, soon killed the man and cut and mangled the woman in such a manner that they left her for dead. She had strength enough to crawl to some logs not far distant, and getting into a hollow one lived within it for several days, subsisting in part by eating the excrescences that grew from it. The Indians had left some fire on the shore, which she kept together for the warmth. Having remained in that manner for some time, an old Indian and a young one coming down to the beach found her ; they were soon in high words, which she afterwards understood was a dispute ; the old Indian was for keeping her alive, the other for dispatching her.—After they had debated the point awhile, the oldest Indian hastily took her up and tossing her upon his shoulder, carried her to a place near where Middletown now stands, where he dressed her wounds and soon cured her. After some time the Dutch at New Amsterdam, hearing of a white woman among the Indians, concluded who it must be, and some of them came to her relief ; the old man, her preserver, gave her the choice to go or stay ; she chose to go. A while after, marrying one Stout, they lived together at Middletown among other Dutch inhabitants. The old Indian who saved her life used frequently to visit her ; at one of his visits she observed him to be more pensive than common, and sitting down, he gave three heavy sighs ; after the last, she thought herself at liberty to ask him what was the matter. He told her he had something to tell her in friendship, though at the risk of his own life, which was that the Indians were that night to kill all the whites, and he advised her to go to New Amsterdam ; she asked him how she could get off? He told her he had provided a canoe at a place which he named. Being gone from her she sent for her husband out of the field, and discovered the matter to him, who, not believing it, she told him the old man *never deceived her*, and that she with her children would go ; accordingly at the place appointed they found the canoe and paddled off. When they were gone, the husband began to consider the matter, and sending for five or six of his neighbors, they set upon their guard. About midnight they heard the dismal warwhoop; presently came up a company of Indians ; they first expostulated and then told the Indians if they persisted in their bloody designs, they would sell their lives very dear. Their arguments prevailed, the Indians desisted, and entered into a league of peace, which was kept without violati n. From this woman, thus remarkably saved, is descended a numerous posterity of the name of Stout, now inhabitants of New Jersey. At that time there were supposed to be about fifty families of white people, and five hundred Indians inhabiting those parts."

The account of Penelope Stout, as given in Benedict's History, is as follows :

"She was born in Amsterdam, in Holland, about the year 1602 ; her father's name was Vanprincis. She and her first husband (whose name is not known) sailed for New York (then New Amsterdam) about the year 1620; the vessel was stranded at Sandy Hook ; the crew got ashore and marched towards New York ; but Penelope's (for that was her name) husband being hurt in the wreck, could not march with them ; therefore, he and his wife tarried in the woods ; they had not been long in the place before the Indians killed them both (as they thought) and stripped them to the skin ; however, Pen-

OLD TIMES IN OLD MONMOUTH. 53

elope came to, though her skull was fractured and her left shoulder so hacked that she could never use that arm like the other; she was also cut across the abdomen so that her bowels appeared; these she kept in with her hand; she continued in this situation for seven days, taking shelter in a hollow tree, and eating the excrescence of it; the seventh day she saw a deer passing by with arrows sticking in it, and soon after two Indians appeared, whom she was glad to see, in hope they would put her out of her misery; accordingly, one made for her to knock her on the head; but the other, who was an elderly man, prevented him; and, throwing his match coat about her, carried her to his wigwam and cured her of her wounds and bruises; after that he took her to New York and made a present of her to her countrymen, viz: an *Indian* present, expecting ten times the value in return.— It was in New York that one Richard Stout married her; he was a native of England, and of good family: she was now in her 22nd year, and he in his 40th. She bore him seven sons and three daughters, viz: Jonathan, John, Richard, James, Peter, David, Benjamin, Mary, Sarah and Alice; the daughters married into the families of the Bounds, Pikes, Throckmortons and Skeltons, and so lost the name of Stout; the sons married into the families of Bullen, Crawford, Ashton, Truax, &c., and had many children. The mother lived to the age of 110, and saw her offspring multiplied into 502 in about 88 years."

Richard Stout, who married Penelope, was the son of John Stout, of Nottinghamshire, in England. His father interfered in a love affair with a young woman beneath his rank, so he got angry and went to sea in a man of war, and served seven years. He was discharged at New York (then New Amsterdam) and lived there some years, when he fell in with the Dutch widow, whom he afterwards married.

INDIAN CLAIMS IN OLD MONMOUTH AND VICINITY.

Conference of Whites and Indians—Description of last lands claimed by Indians—Names of leading Indians—Indians satisfactorily paid for all their land—Our ancestors as "doers of justice."

The last lands in Old Monmouth claimed by the Indians were described in certain papers, powers of attorney, &c., presented to a conference between the whites and Indians held at Crosswicks, N. J., in February, 1758. For several years previous the Indians had expressed much dissatisfaction because they had not received pay for several tracts of land, some of them of considerable extent in this and other counties. When the ill feeling of the Indians became apparent, the Legislature appointed commissioners to examine into the causes of dissatisfaction. Several conferences were held at Crosswicks, Burlington, Easton, Pa., &c. At the second conference at Crosswicks the commissioners on the part of the state were Andrew Johnson and Richard Salter, of the Council, and Charles Read, John Stevens, William Foster and Jacob Spicer.

The Indians were Teedyescunk, king of the Delawares; George Hopaycock, of the Susquehannas; Andrew Woolley, George Wheelwright, Peepy, Joseph Cuish, William Lonlax, Gabriel Mitop, Zeb Conchee, Bill News, John Pembolus, of the Crosswick Indians; Moses Totamy and Philip of the Mountain Indians; Tom Evans, of the Raritans; Robert Kekott, Jabob Mullis, Samuel Gosling of the Rancocus Indians; Thomas Store, Stephen Calviri, John Pompshire, Benjamin Claus, Joseph Woolley, Josiah Store, Isaac Still, James Calvin, Peter Calvin, Derrick Quaquay, Ebenezer Woolley, Sarah Store, widow of Quaquahela of the Cranbury Indians; Abraham Lacques, Isaac Swanelea, Southern Indians.

John Pompshire acted as interpreter.

The Indians informed the Commissioners that the lands they claimed could not by them be described by lines very intelligible to persons not on the spot, as they went to hollows and small brooks which had no certain names, but that they had described them as well as they could, and they delivered lists of the tracts they esteemed unpurshased as follows:

No. 1. A power of attorney from Capoose and Telamen, to Moses Totamy, dated January 30th, 1743-4, for lands on the south and southwest side of the south branch of the Raritan river, joining thereto, as explained by said power.

No. 2. A paper declaring the lands from the half way, from the mouth of Metetecunk to Toms River, from the heads of the rivers, belong to Captain John, Totamy Willockins; and from John Eastels (Estells?) to Hockanetcunk on Crosswicks; then on a straight course to Mount Holly and so up Rancocus creek

54 OLD TIMES IN OLD MONMOUTH.

and along the said creek to Jarvis Pharo's mill and so to the sea. Pompshire and Stephen Calvin say they are concerned in the tract.

No. 3. A power of attorney to Tetamy and Captain John, dated February 21st, 1747, from Tawlayenum, Tohokenum, Gooteleck, to sell lands in Egg Harbor between Mount Holly and Crosswicks.

They have a tract of land beginning at the Old Ford by John Fowler's; then in a line to Doctor's Creek, above but in sight of Allentown; then up the creek to the lower end of Imlaystown; then in a line to Crosswicks creek by Duke Horseman's; then along said creek to the place of beginning. Teedyscung and Totamy are concerned in the above lands.

Then they said that from the mouth of Squan to No. 2, belongs to Sarah Store, to whom it was given by her husband, to the heads of the branches, and so across from one branch to the other.

Tom Store and Andrew Woolley, claim a tract between Cranbury and Devil's Brook, possessed by Josiah Davidson's sons that has two new houses built thereon, in which is included the whole tract of the late President Hamilton *probably John Hamilton, governor from 1736 to 1738*); and also Mr. Alexander's surveys where Thomas Sowden lives; he has sold part of this aract to Hollinshead where McGee lives; also has sold some to Josiah Davidson, to Doore Marlet, John Wetherill and James Wilson. He claims lands from Cranbury brook to the cross roads lying on the right hand of the road, and is claimed by William Pidgeon; James Wall and John Story live upon one corner of it. They also claim from the mouth of Squan to the mouth of Shrewsbury, by the streams of each to their heads and across from one head to another. Also Vannote's place on the west side of Squan river. Also a piece at Topanemus bridge; in this piece Ben Ciaus is concerned.

Tom Store and Andrew Woolley, also claim a piece on the north side of South River—Polly Ritchies place.

Also a piece between Allentown and Millstone brook, where Hockan Gapee used to live, joining on the east side of the post road to Amboy, part of Dunstan's tract.

Also Vance's place, adjoining Millstone brook, on Amboy road, part of Fullerton's tract.

Also a swamp near Gawen Watson's place, belonging to the Johnston families and the Furmans.

Jacob Mullis claims pine lands on Edge Pillock Branch and Goshen Neck Branch, where Benjamin Springer and George Marpole's mills stands and all the lands between the head branches of those creeks to where the waters join or meet.

The Indians in general, claim their settlements near Cranbury on *Menolapan* river, near Falkner's tract, whereon many Indians now live. Also a few acres below the plantation of Robert Pearson's, on the North side of Crosswicks creek.

Having delivered these claims to the Commissioners, the Indians present executed a power of attorney to Tom Store, Moses Totamy, Stephen Calvin, Isaac Still and John Pompshire, or the major part of them, to transact all future business with the state government respecting lands.

In 1757 the government had appropriated £1,600 to purchase a release of Indian claims; one half to be laid out in purchasing a settlement for the Indians on the south side of the Raritan, whereon they might reside; the other half to purchase latent claims of back Indians not resident in the province. At the conference at Easton, in October, 1758, it was decided to purchase a tract of land in Evesham township, Burlington, containing over 3,000 acres, for the Indians to locate upon. There was there a saw mill and cedar swamp and satisfactory hunting ground. The Indians soon removed to this reservation, named Brotherton; in removing their buildings they were assisted by government. A house of worship and several dwellings were soon put up.

In 1765, it is said, there were about sixty persons settled there.

The remnant of these Indians sold out the tract and left the state in 1802, as elsewhere described. We believe they left behind a lot of half breeds, who also left the state some thirty years later.

HOW THE BRITISH REWARDED THE TORIES.

Dazzling Promises and how they were fulfilled—Loyalists die broken hearted.

The following is from the Albany Statesman, Sept. 1820:

By the following extract from the proceedings of the British House of Commons June 19th, 1820, it will be seen that the

Tories of the Revolution were but poorly rewarded for their loyalty to England and their base desertion of their own country. It seems the most fortunate of them received but *seven shillings in the pound*, of what had been promised them, as a remuneration for their losses and treasonable services. The conduct of the British government towards these miserable beings who were dazzled with promises and anticipations of princely wealth and princely honors, furnishes a monitory lesson of the wretched fate of the traitor. Many of them, it is said, *died of broken hearts* conscious of their own degradation, neglected and despised by those they had served, and treated with scorn and reproach by their own countrymen. How different was their lot from that of the revolutionary patriot and soldier, who was true to his country and whose motto was " Liberty or Death."

AMERICAN LOYALISTS.

A vote of £9,000 was proposed for American Loyylists.

Mr. Hume asked the Chancellor of the Exchequer whether government meant to take into consideration the claims of those loyalists who had been resident in America at the breaking out of the war, and who had been assured by their government that any losses they might sustain, would be made good by this country? Whereas in violation of the public faith they never had been remunerated.

The Chancellor of the Exchequer admitted that the people alluded to were a most *meritorious and unfortunate* class of men, but on the other hand, if the *claims of individuals were to be listened to* by his majesty's ministers, a dangerous precedent would be established and a door opened for their endless repetition.

Mr. Courtney observed that this claim stood on the *plighted faith of the country.* His conviction was, their case was quite different from that of all other claimants, and was, at least, entitled to the serious consideration of parliament—(*Hear.*)

Mr. Williams added his testimony to that of the last speaker. It was considerably more than thirty years since the claims accrued. Three fourths of the claimants were dead. and many of them of *broken hearts.*

Mr. Lockhart said that the American loyalists had never received any compensation for their losses. It was the merchants trading to America who consented to accept of £500,000 to be distributed amongst them by commissioners ; and when the resident loyalists applied to the courts in America, they were met with the plea of being *attainted persons* and *traitors to their country.*

The Chancellor of the Exchequer said the individuals in question had received their fair proportion of the £500,000 from the commissioners.

Mr. J. Smith said that they had received but *seven or eight shillings in the pound* of their reduced debt or claim.

The resolution was postponed to the following week.

EPISCOPALIANISM IN OLD MONMOUTH.

Pioneers of the Society.—Rev. Messrs. Keith, Talbot and Inness—First Converts to the Protestant Episcopal Church—One Hundred and Seventy Years Ago.

The most noted among the first clergymen of the Protestant Episcopal Church, who held services in the county, was the celebrated Rev. George Keith, an outline of whose life has been given in an other chapter. When he first located at Freehold he was an active member of the Society of Friends, as it would seem were others of the first settlers. He left Freehold in 1689 and went to reside in Philadelphia.— In 1694 he went to London and soon after abjured the doctrines of the Quakers, and became a zealous clergyman of the Church of England. He officiated some time in his mother country, and in 1702 he was sent to America as a missionary of the " Society for the Propagation of the Gospel in Foreign Parts." He sailed from England April 28, 1702, in the ship Centurian bound for Boston. After his arrival he travelled and preached in various parts of New England and New York, accompanied and assisted by the Rev. John Talbot, who had been chaplain of the ship, and who, a few years later, located at Burlington, N. J., in charge of the Protestant Episcopal Society there. Mr. Keith arrived at Amboy, and preached his first sermon in New Jersey in that place, October 3d, 1702. He says that among the audience were some old acquaintances, and some had been Quakers but were come over to the church, particularly Miles Forster and John Barclay (brother to Robert Barclay, who published the "Apology for Quakers.") After stopping a few days with Miles Forster, he left for Monmouth county, where he preached his first sermon, October 10, 1702. Of his travels and services in Monmouth we give his own account from his rare and curious little work entitled "A Journal of Travel from New Hampshire to Caratuck, on the Continent of America, by George Keith, A. M., late Missionary from the Society for the Propagation of the Gospel in Foreign Parts, and now Rector of Edburton, in Sussex. London: printed by Joseph Downing, for Brab. Aylmer at the Three Pigeons over against the Royal Exchange, Cornhill, 1706."

It will be noticed that he speaks of the Quakers at Freehold holding meetings separate from other Quakers. The cause of this separation is explained in the chapter giving an outline of his life.

Of his visit to Monmouth he says:

October 10, 1702.—We went to the meeting of the Quakers at *Toponemes* in Freehold in East Jersey, who used to keep a separate meeting from the other Quakers for their gross errors and joined with me and my friends in the separation about 1692 ; and it happened to be their yearly meeting where divers came from West Jersey and Pennsylvania. One of their preachers prayed and preached before I began. After he had done, I used some Church Collects I had by heart, in Prayer; and after that I preached on Heb. 5 : 9.—There was a considerable auditory of divers sorts, some of the Church, and some Presbyterians, besides Quakers. They heard me without interruption and the meeting ended peaceably. Their two speakers lodged in the same house with me that evening at the house of Thomas Boels, formerly a Quaker but now of the church. I had some free discourse with them about several weighty things. I told them so far as they used their gifts to instruct the ignorant and reclaim the vile errors of Quakerism, they were to be commended ; but that they had taken upon them to administer baptism and the Lord's Supper to any, they were greatly to be blamed, having no due call or ordination so to do.

We met again next day and after that I prayed, using the same Collects as the day before and preached on 1st Thes. 5 : 9 without any interruption, and the meeting peaceably ended. I could blame nothing in the matter of the second speaker, nor in the former, except where he said in his discourse "*That they who were in Christ, need not fear Hell.*" I endeavored to clear the matter in my discourse by distinguishing between an absolute fear of hell, such as wicked men ought to have and a conditional fear which good men, even such who are in Christ, ought to have ; and about this he and I had some private discourse also betwixt us, but he was dissatisfied and would not own *that any who were in Christ, ought to have any less of hell*, so much as conditional.

Sunday, October 17th, 1702. I preached at Middletown in East Jersey, where before sermon Mr. Talbot read the Church Prayers, and I preached on Matt. 28:19,20. One main part of my sermon being to prove Infant baptism to be included in the Apostle's commission as well as that of adult persons, their being several of the audience who were Anabaptists, who heard me civilly without interruption ; but most of the auditory were Church people or well affected to the Church.

October 24th, 1702. I preached at Shrewsbury at a house near the Quaker Meeting House, and it happened it was the time of the Quaker Yearly Meeting at Shrewsbury. My text was 2d Peter, 2 : 1, 2. The Church Prayers being read before sermon, we had a great congregation, generally well affected to the Church, and divers of them were of the Church, and that day I sent some lines in writing to the Quakers at their Yearly Meeting ; which Mr. Talbot did read to them in their meeting, wherein I desired them to give me a meeting with them some day of that week before their meeting was concluded; in which meeting I offered to detect great errors in their Author's books, and they should have full liberty to answer what they had to say in their vindication. But they altogether refused my proposition, and several papers passed betwixt us. In some of their papers they used gross reflections on the Church of England as much as on me.— We continued our meeting three days, as the Quakers did theirs. And the second day of our meeting at the same house, where we had formerly met, I detected Quaker errors out of their printed books, particularly out of the Folio Book of *Edward Burrough's Works*, collected and published by the Quakers after his death, and did read quotations to the Auditory, laying the pages open before such as were willing to read them for their better satisfaction, as some did read them.

(Mr. Keith here quotes what he considers some of their errors.)

October 26th. I preached again at Shrewsbury, on Matt. 7 : 13. In these

OLD TIMES IN OLD MONMOUTH. 57

meetings in Shrewsbury, Middletown and *Toponemes*, or where else in the Nethesinks (Nevisinks) Mr. Louis Morris and divers others of the best note in that county, frequented the congregations and places where we preached and did kindly entertain us at their houses where we lodged as we travelled too and again, particularly at Mr. Morris, Mr. Inness, Mr. Johnson, Mr. Boels and Mr. Read. Mr. Inness being in Priest's orders often preached among them and by preaching and conferences frequently with the Quakers and other sorts of people, as also by his pious conversation, has done much good among them and been very instrumental to draw them off from their errors and bring them over to the Church.

Mr. Keith left Monmouth about the last of October, 1702, for Burlington and elsewhere. He returned in December, and says:

December 20th, 1702. I preached at Dr. Johnston's at Nethersinks, on *Rev.* 22:14.

Dec. 25th, Friday, being Christmas. I preached at the house of Mr. Morris, on Luke 21.10, 11. And after sermon divers of the auditory received with us the Holy sacrament; both Mr. Morris and his wife, and divers others. Mr. Talbot did administer it.

December 27th, Sunday. I preached at Shrewsbury Town, near the Quaker Meeting House, at a Planter's house, and had a considerable auditory of Church people, lately converted from Quakerism, with divers others of the Church of best note in that part of the country. My text was Heb. 8.10, 11.

January 1st, 1703, Friday. I preached at the house of Thomas Boels, in Freehold, in East Jersey. My text was Isaiah 59.20, 21. Before sermon, after the Church Prayers, I baptized all his children, two sons and three daughters. He was formerly a Quaker, but is now come over to the Church; also a son of Samuel Dennis, a late convert from Quakerism.

Jan. 3d, 1703. I preached again at his house on the same text, and before sermon Mr. Talbot baptized two persons belonging to the family of John Read, formerly a Quaker, but was lately come over to the Church, with all his children, one son and two daughters. His two daughters were baptized by Mr. Talbot, October 20th, 1702; as also the same day was baptized William Leads (Leeds?), and his sister Mary Leads, late converts from Quakerism to the Church. And some days before at the house of John Read, Mr. Talbot baptized the wife of Alexander Neaper and his three children. Both he and his wife had been Quakers, but were come over to the Church.

January 4th, 1703. I came to the house of Robert Ray, in Freehold, in East Jersey, accompanied with Thomas Boels, and lodged at his house that night. At his and his wife's desire, I baptized all his children, some boys and some girls, in number five. His wife is come over to the Church, but he was not then come thoroughly out of Quakerism.

Mr. Keith after this proceeded to Burlington, Philadelphia, and so on to Maryland, Virginia, and elsewhere; in October, 1703, he returned to Monmouth, and of his services here he adds in his journal the following;

"October 10th, 1703, Sunday. I preached at *Toponemes*, in Freehold, in East Jersey, on Acts 24:12, and had considerable auditory, divers of them late converts from Quakerism to the Church. Mr. Inness above mentioned, did read the Prayers.— Mr. Talbot stayed to preach in several places in Pennsylvania and West Jersey for some time.

October 17th. I preached at Shrewsbury, near the Quaker Meeting House there, on Psalms 103:17, 18.

October 24th. I preached again there, on Heb. 8:10, 11, and Mr. Inness baptized two men and a child.

On the 31st of October, Mr. Keith preached at Amboy, after which he proceeded to New York and New England. On his return he says:

January 9th, 1704. I preached at the house of Dr. Johnston, in Neverthesinks, on Psalms 119:5, 113, and had considerable auditory.

January 16th. I preached at Mr. Morris's house at the Falls of Shrewsbury, in East Jersey, on 2 Cor. 5:17.

January 23d. I preached again at Mr. Morris's house, on 2 Peter 1:5.

January 30th. I preached at the house of Mr. Thomas Boels, in Freehold, in East Jersey, on 1 Cor. 15:58.

February 6th. I preached at the house of Mr. John Read, in Freehold, East Jersey, on Psalms 119:96.

After this Mr. Keith went to Burlington, Philadelphia, and shortly sailed for England.

LIEUT. JAMES MOODY, THE REFUGEE PARTISAN.

A Daring Renegade—Raid in Monmouth—Refugee Versions and Boasts—Death of Captain Chadwick and Lieutenant Hendrickson.

In the days of the Revolution, about the most shrewd and effective partisan leader in New Jersey, was James Moody. During the war we do not believe there was a single other Tory who was more noted througout the State for his daring operaations, than was he, and yet it is rare to find his name in any general or local history of New Jersey.

In Howe's Historical Collections of New Jersey, mention is made of a certain refugee, said to have been named *Bonnell* Moody, as having been active against the whigs in Sussex county. We very much doubt if ever there was a prominent refugee of that name in our State; we have no doubt but James Moody was the man referred to; certain it is that some of the deeds attributed to Bonnell Moody were performed by James Moody. An interesting account of James Moody's career in New Jersey, was published shortly after the war in London; though dictated by himself, and consequently more or less one sided, yet it contains many things of value to the historian and of interest to the general reader. At some future time we shall endeavor to give place to the substance of his narrative with the high British endorsements it obtained, but for the present we can only copy the substance of so much of it as relates to one of his raids in Monmouth. It will be seen that where he strives to depreciate Americans and laud the Tories to the best of his ability, yet he mentions some things worth recording in our local history.

"June 10th, 1779, Lieutenant James Moody requested a Tory friend named Hutchinson, with six men and some guides, to join him in a raid into Monmouth.— Moody had besides sixteen men. They started from Sandy Hook for Shrewsbury, and managed to elude the Rebel guard, and gained a place called *the Falls* (Tinton Falls.) There they surprised and took prisoners one Colonel, one Lieutenant Colonel, one Major and two Captains, with several other prisoners of lesser note, and without injury to private property, destroying a considerable magazine of powder and arms. With these prisoners and such public stores as they were able to bring off, Mr. Hutchinson was charged, whilst Moody brought up the rear with his sixteen men to defend them. They were as they expected, soon pursued by double their number and soon overtaken. Moody kept up a smart fire on his assailants, checking and retarding them till Hutchinson with his booty had got ahead to a considerable distance. He then also advanced for the next advantageous position, and thus proceeded from one good spot to another, still covering the prisoners till they gained a situation on the shore at Black Point where the enemy could not flank him. But just at this time the enemy was reinforced by ten men, so they were near forty strong. Hutchinson with one man crossed the inlet, behind which he had taken shelter, and came to Moody's assistance; and now a warm engagement ensued which lasted three quarters of an hour. By this time all their ammunition, amounting to 80 rounds was exhausted, and ten men, only three of whom were wounded, were in any capacity to follow a charge.

"The bayonet was Moody's only resource, and this the enemy could not withstand; they fled, leaving eleven of their number killed or wounded. Unfortunately for Moody, his small but gallant party could not follow up the blow, being in a manner utterly exhausted by a long harassed march in hot weather. They found the rebel Captain dead, and their Lieutenant also expiring on the field. There was something peculiarly shocking and awful in the death of the rebel captain. He was shot by Moody whilst with the most bitter oaths and threats of vengeance, after having missed fire once, he was again leveling his piece at him. Soon after the engagement, one of the rebels came forward with a handkerchief on a stick, and demanded a parley. His signal was returned and a truce agreed upon, the conditions of which were, that they should have leave to take care of their dead and wounded, while Moody and his party were permitted to return unmolested to the British lines.— None of Moody's men were mortally wounded. The public stores which they brought away, besides those destroyed, sold for upwards of £500, every shilling of which was given by Moody to his men, as a reward for meritorious."

From a subsequent paragraph in Moody's narrative, it appears that the names of the

OLD TIMES IN OLD MONMOUTH. 59

officers killed were Captain Chadwick and Lieutenant Hendrickson.

Moody was afterwards captured by the Americans, and was to have been hung for the murder of Captain Chadwick, but he managed almost miraculously to escape.

Some circumstances mentioned in different accounts of this raid, lead to a suspicion that Moody placed Captain Chadwick and Lieutenant Hendrickson in the rear of their company to prevent the firing of the Americans upon them, and that Chadwick and Hendrickson were shot in attempting to escape or after escaping.

The following is an American version of this raid from an ancient paper:

"A party of about fifty refugees landed in Monmouth and marched to Tinton Falls undiscovered, where they surprised and carried off Colonel Hendrickson, Colonel Wyckoff, Captain Chadwick and Captain McKnight, with several privates of the militia, and drove off sheep and horned cattle. About thirty of our militia hastily collected and made some resistance, but were repulsed with the loss of two men killed, and ten wounded, the loss of the enemy unknown."

Moody's Capture and Escape.

The following is Moody's own account of his capture, imprisonment for the killing of Captain Chadwick and Lieutenant Hendrickson, and escape. After referring to a raid in which he had been engaged, his narrative states that while he was retracing his steps with thirteen men towards New York, on the 21st of July, 1780, Moody and the greater part of his men fell into the hands of General Wayne, much to the joy of his captors, and to the whigs of New Jersey. "Moody is in the toils at last," was the word far and near. He was first sent to a place called the *Slote*, thence to Stony Point, thence to West Point, thence to Esopus, and thence back to West Point. Arnold who was then plotting to surrender the latter post, treated Moody with absolute barbarity, for by his order he was placed in a dungeon excavated in a rock, the bottom of which was ankle deep in water, mud and filth. In this dismal hole the wretched prisoner was fettered hand and foot, and compelled to sleep on a door raised on four stones above the disgusting mixture and proffered food at which he revolted which was brought to him in a wooden bowl that was never washed, and that was encrusted with dough, dirt and grease.—

The irons upon his wrists were ragged on the inner side and caused sores which gave him great pain, while his legs became irritated and swollen. He implored Arnold for relief, declaring that he preferred death to sufferings so intense. Some days after his second petition to be treated as a prisoner of war, an officer came into his prison and asked, "are you Moody, whose name is a terror to all good men?" When answered, the officer pointed to a gallows near by, and said: "A swing upon that you have long merited." Moody replied that he hoped to live to see him and a thousand other villains like him hanged for being rebels. The fetters were examined but not removed. His case was at last reported to General Washington, who ordered the irons to be taken off, and the serving of wholesome provisions, with leave to purchase milk, vegetables, &c.— Soon the prisoner was transferred to the Chief's own camp, where the Adjutant General examined his limbs and shocked at their condition, gave instant orders for humane treatment. While Moody was recovering he felt himself much at ease, expecting soon to be exchanged, when he was unexpectedly told that in two days, by order of Dr. Livingston, he was to be brought to trial; the court-martial was to be composed of picked men, and that Moody was sure of conviction—that he was charged with assassinating a Captain Chadwick, and a Lieut. Hendrickson.— These were the two officers who had fallen fairly in battle, near Black Point, in Monmouth county, as elsewhere related. The Ensign replied that he felt himself much at ease on that account, as it could be sufficiently cleared up by their own people who had been in and survived the action, as well as by some of their officers, who were at that time prisoners. He was told that this would be of little avail, as he had been so obnoxious to the whigs, and besides he had enlisted men in the State for the King's service, and this, by their laws, was death.

Moody says he affected an air of unconcern at this information, but at the same time he believed it was too serious and important to him to disregard. He resolved therefore, from that moment, to escape or perish in the attempt. His place of confinement was near the centre of the rebel camp. A sentinel was placed within the doors of his prison, and another without, besides four others close around and within a few yards of the place. The time now came on when he must either make his attempt or forever lose the opportunity. On the night of September 17th, busy in ruminating on his project, he had under pretence of being cold, got a watch coat thrown across his shoulders, that he might better conceal from his unpleasant companion the operations he meditated against his hand cuffs. While he was racking his invention to find some possible means of extricating himself from his fetters, he happened to cast his eye on a post fastened to the ground, through which a hole had been bored by an auger, and it occurred to him that it might be possible, with the aid of this hole, to break the bolt of his hand cuffs. Watching the opportunity therefore from time to time of the sentinel's looking another way, he thrust the point of the bolt into the above mentioned hole, and by cautiously exerting his strength and gradually bending the iron backwards and forwards he at length broke it. Let the reader imagine what his sensations were when he found the manacles drop from his hands. He sprang instantly past the inside sentinel, and rushing on the next, with one hand he seized his musket, and with the other struck him to the ground. The sentinel within and the four others who had been placed by the fence surrounding the place of his confinement, immediately gave the alarm, and in a moment the cry was general, "Moody is escaped from the provost!" It is impossible to describe the uproar which now took place throughout the camp. In a few minutes every man was in a bustle, every man was looking for Moody, and multitudes passed by him on all sides—little suspecting that the man they saw deliberately marching along with a musket on his shoulder, could be the fugitive they were in quest of. The darkness of the night which was also blustering and drizzly, prevented any discrimination of his person, and was indeed the great circumstance that rendered his escape possible. But no small difficulty still remained to be surmounted. To prevent desertion, which at that time was very frequent, Washington had surrounded his camp with a chain of sentinels, posted at about forty or fifty yards from each other; Moody was unacquainted with their stations; to pass there undiscovered would certainly be fatal. In this dilemna Providence again befriended him. He had gained their station without knowing it, when luckily he heard their watchword, "Look sharp to the chain—Moody is escaped from the Provost." From the sound of their voices he ascertained the respective situations of the sentinels, and throwing himself on his hands and knees, he was happy enough to crawl through the vacant space between two of them, unseen by either. Judging that their line of pursuit would be towards the British army, he made a detour into the woods on the opposite side. Through the woods he made his way with as much speed as the darkness of the night would permit, steering his course after the Indian manner by occasional groping and feeling the white oak; on the south side the bark of this tree is rough and unpleasant to the touch, but on the north side is smooth; hence it serves the sagacious traveller of the woods by night as well as by day, for his compass. Through the dismal woods and swamps he wandered until the night of the 21st, a space of 56 hours, during which time he had no other sustenance than a few beach leaves, (which of all the woods afforded, were the least unpleasant to the taste, and least pernicious to the health), which he chewed and swallowed to abate the cravings of hunger. In every inhabited district he knew there were friends of the British, and he had learned where and how to find them out, without endangering their safety, which was always the first object of his concern. From some of their *good* men he received minute information how the pursuit was directed, and where every guard was posted. Thus assisted he eluded their keenest vigilance, and at length by God's blessings, to his unspeakable joy, he arrived safe at Paulus Hook (Jersey City)."

PHIL WHITE, HIS CAPTURE AND DEATH.

A correct version of the affair—Refugee slanders refuted and vindicated—Affidavits of Aaron White and of Philip White, guards—Statement of General Forman, &c.

Though the death of the refugee Philip White, generally called Phil White, is occasionally referred to in modern historical works, there are none which give complete or correct accounts of the affair. In the brief statement given in Howe's Collections unjust imputations are cast upon his guard, as will hereafter be seen. When Captain Huddy was so brutally murdered by the Refugees near the Highlands, it

OLD TIMES IN OLD MONMOUTH.

will be remembered that a label was fastened to his breast, the last sentence of which was

Up goes Huddy for Philip White.

Though the Refugees at one time asserted that Captain Huddy had an agency in the death of Phil White, yet this preposterous charge was at once shown to be an infamous falsehood, as when White was killed, Captain Huddy was a prisoner, confined in New York in the old Sugar House (Duane's sugar house.) The British asserted that "he had taken a certain Philip White, cut off both his arms, broke his legs, pulled out one of his eyes, damned him and then bid him run."

How much of this was true will be seen by the conclusive evidence hereafter given, before quoting which we will copy the version of the affair given in Howe's Collections, derived in 1842, from a traditionary source:

"White, the Refugee, was a carpenter and served his time in Shrewsbury. Six days after Huddy was taken, he was surprised by a party of militia light-horse, near Snag Swamp, in the eastern part of the township. After laying down his arms in token of surrender, he took up his musket and killed a Mr. Hendrickson.— He was however, secured, and while being taken to Freehold, was killed at Pyle's Corner, three or four miles from there.— He was under a guard of three men, the father of one of whom was murdered at Shrewsbury the year previous, by a band of refugees, among whom was White, and he was therefore highly exasperated against the prisoner. Some accounts state that he was killed while attempting to escape; others with more probability that they pricked him with their swords and thus forcing him to run, cruelly murdered him."

There are several errors in the foregoing and it is to be regretted that the untrue charge of wanton cruelty, should have found its way into so useful a book. Correct versions of this affair are found in ancient papers, but for the present we will give several affidavits taken at the time as being the most conclusive evidence. These affidavits were forwarded to General Washington, and by him transmitted to Congress, April 20th, 1782.

These affidavits are of Aaron White, taken prisoner with Phil White, and of each of Phil White's guards. Before quoting them, we will say in regard to the statement in the extract from Howe's Collections that after Phil White had surrendered, "he took up his musket and killed a Mr. Hendrickson," that as no allusion is made to it in these affidavits, it may have occurred at some previous time, and this murder as well as his participation in the murder of John Russell, and in other outrages, undoubtedly caused the patriots to be anxious to capture him.

Deposition of Aaron White.

County of Monmouth, ss: Aaron White being duly sworn, deposeth:

That he was taken prisoner with Philip White; that the deponent left New York in company with Philip White, Jeremiah Bell, negro Moses, John Fennimore and Robert Howell, on Thursday night, the twenty-eighth of March last; that they sailed from New York to the Hook, where they remained till next morning, being Friday, the twenty-ninth; that Philip White and negro Moses were landed at Long Branch that morning; that the deponent understood that Captain Joshua Huddy was then a prisoner; that on the day following, being Saturday the thirtieth, the deponent being off in a boat with Fennimore, and having observed that the said Philip White and Moses had an engagement with some of the troops on shore, he (the deponent) went in a boat to their relief, meaning to take them off; that when he came on shore he joined the said Philip White and negro Moses, and pursued one Thomas Berkley, with whom they had been engaged; that in their pursuit, the light horse came down, and the deponent with the said Philip White were made prisoners; that they were put under guard to be sent to Freehold for confinement; that on the way from Colt's Neck to Freehold, between Daniel Grandin's and Samuel Leonard's, the deponent was told by one of his guard, that Philip White was running away; that the deponent looked back and saw the horsemen in pursuit of something, but being about half a mile distant, could not distinguish after whom or what the pursuit was; that the field in which they were pursuing was near the brook next to Mr. Leonard's, adjoining a wood; that Lieutenant Rhea and George Brindley left the deponent under guard of two men, and ran their horses back towards the place the other men were pursuing; that the deponent afterwards understood that it was Philip White they were pursuing, and that he was killed in the pursuit; that Captain

Joshua Huddy was not one of the guard or party, and the deponent understood and verily believes, that he was then a prisoner in New York ; and the deponent further and lastly declares, that the above is the truth as related without any fear, threats or compulsion whatever.

AARON WHITE.

Sworn before me this 15th day of April, 1782. DAVID FORMAN,
Justice of Peace, Monmouth County

That a clear idea of the order of the principal events referred to in these affidavits may be obtained, we will here state that Captain Joshua Huddy was taken prisoner at Toms River, on Sunday, March 24th, 1782; on Saturday, the 30th of March, six days after, Phil White and Aaron were taken prisoners by the Monmouth militia; the same day (March 30th), Philip White was killed, at which time Captain Huddy was confined in the sugar house prison in New York, where he had been put on Tuesday, March 26th, and remained here and in provost jail, until Monday, April 8th, when he was taken on board a sloop and put in irons, and four days later, April 12th, 1782, he was hanged near the Highlands; his body was delivered to the Americans, sent to Freehold and buried with the honors of war.— Three days after his death—on the 15th of April, these affidavits were taken while the recollections of all the circumstances referred to, were fresh in the minds of the witnesses.

STATEMENTS OF PHIL WHITE'S GUARDS.

Phil White's guards were William Borden, John North and John Russell. They were probably at the time attached to Captain John Walton's troop of light horse, but Russell and perhaps the other two had been in the regular Continental army previously. Their statement of the details of Phil White's death are undoubtedly correct. We shall hereafter, in the court martial trial at New York, of the Refugee captain, Richard Lippincott, give the Tory evidence, and it will be seen that there was nothing offered to invalidate the affidavits of the guards. The first statement we give is the

AFFIDAVIT OF WILLIAM BORDEN.

County of Monmouth, ss: William Borden, of full age, being duly sworn, deposeth:

That he with a certain John North, and John Russell, were ordered to guard a certain Philip White, mentioned in an address to his excellency, General Washington, to Freehold. That the guard was ordered to shoot him if he attempted to escape, of which the said Philip was informed ; that on their way the said Philip jumped off his horse, and on passing a fence next to the woods, the deponent fired and shot him through the body, the bullet entering his back and coming out of his right breast; that the said Philip at first fell, but recovered again, and attempted to get into the woods about two hundred yards distant ; that the deponent having leaped the fence on horseback, intercepted him in the way to the woods ; upon which he turned and threw himself into a bog, where the said John North met him and gave him a stroke with his sword ; that as the said Philip White turned, the deponent struck him with the butt end of his carbine, and he still continued to run till he was struck by the said John North as aforesaid ; that this deponent, three or four times called to him, " *White give up and you shall have quarters yet.*" That Captain Joshua Huddy was not one of the guard nor in company, but the deponent understood, and has no reason to doubt, that he was then a prisoner in New York. That the above happened between Daniel Grandin's and Samuel Leonard's in a field adjoining the woods, and through which the brook next to said Leonard's did run. On Saturday, the 30th of March last.

WILLIAM BORDEN.

Sworn before me this 15th day of April, 1782. DAVID FORMAN,
Judge of Court of Common Pleas Monmouth Co.

AFFIDAVIT OF JOHN NORTH.

County of Monmouth, ss : John North being duly sworn, deposeth and saith : That he, the deponent, was one of a certain guard that had custody of Philip White mentioned in the memorial to his excellency General Washington ; that the said guard was ordered to conduct the said Philip White from Long Branch (the place at which he with one Aaron White was taken prisoner,) to Freehold ; that the said guard was ordered, if he attempted to make his escape, to kill him ; that they were both informed that if they attempted to run they would be killed ; that on the way to Freehold, the said Philip White went sideways off his horse and ran to the fence next to the wood ; that the deponent fired at him but believes the ball did not take place upon him ; that William Borden, another of the guard, fired at him also, about the

same instant of time, and shot him through the body, the bullet entering his back and passing out under his right breast; that he fell upon his hands and knees, but recovered himself and arose and ran across a small field making for the woods; that the deponent left his horse and dropped his gun and pursued with his drawn sword ; that the deponent overtook him in a bog, and as he was passing, gave him a stroke across the face with his sword, upon which he fell and cried he was a dead man ; that the said William Borden several times called to him saying : " White, if you will give up you shall have good quarters yet;" that notwithstanding he continued to run to the last moment, when he was cut down by this deponent as aforesaid ; and was within three or four paces of a fence, which if he had passed, he would in all probability have effected his escape, provided the gunshot should not have proved fatal ; that Captain Joshua Huddy was not one of the guard, it being notoriously well known that he was then a prisoner with the enemy. That the above happened between Daniel Grandin's and Samuel Leonard's in a small field ; that the brook nearest Leonard's runs through the field ; that it was on Saturday the thirtieth day of March last.
JOHN NORTH.
Sworn before me this 15th April 1782.
DAVID FORMAN,
Justice C. C. Pleas Monmouth Co.

AFFIDAVIT OF JOHN RUSSELL.

County of Monmouth, ss : John Russell of full age, being duly sworn deposeth :
That he was one of the guard appointed to conduct Philip White and Aaron White to Freehold ; that the deponent was present at the time of the said Philip White's attempt to make his escape; that he has heard the affidavits of William Borden and John North and knows every circumstance therein mentioned to be true ; and in addition informs that in course of their pursuit after the said White, he passed the said deponent, and he, the deponent, gave him a slight wound in the forehead, but he still continued to run, although frequently desired to give up and he should have good quarters ; that this was the first blow he received ; that it was entirely his own fault ; that he received a single stroke with a sword, he running and refusing to submit to the last minute; that Joshua Huddy was then a prisoner in New York ; that this happened on Saturday the thirtieth of March last.
JOHN RUSSELL.
Sworn before me this 15th April, 1782.
DAVID FORMAN,
Justice of Peace Monmouth Co.

SECOND AFFIDAVIT OF WILLIAM BORDEN.

Four days after the foregoing affidavits were taken, it was thought advisable to take additional evidence, and William Borden was again sworn, and deposed as follows :
County of Monmouth, ss : William Borden, of full age, being duly sworn, saith :
That he, the deponent, was one of the guard appointed to conduct Philip White, a refugee prisoner, taken and killed as is at large set forth under oath of this deponent, taken the 15th of April instant; and farther this deponent saith that *the aforesaid Philip White received no other wounds* to the knowledge or belief of this deponent than those set forth and described in this deponent's oath as aforesaid ; that the report said to be circulated in New York, viz : that the said Philip White had his arms cut off, and one of his (the said White's) eyes pulled out and both his legs broken, is false and without any the least foundation ; for that he, the aforesaid Philip White, did not to this deponent's knowledge or belief receive any the least wound or hurt on either his (the aforesaid Philip White's) arms or legs neither was either of his (the aforesaid Philip White's) eyes pulled out.
Lastly, this deponent saith, that he this deponent was present at the time the aforesaid Philip White attempted to make his escape ; was in pursuit of him, the aforesaid Philip White, and was present at the time that the aforesaid Philip White was killed ; that this deponent saw John Russell and John North carry and put his (the aforesaid Philip White's) body in a wagon and attended the wagon up to the village of Freehold where his (the aforesaid Philip White's) body was the same evening buried ; and further this deponent saith not. WILLIAM BORDEN.
Sworn before me this 19th April, 1782.
DAVID FORMAN.

CERTIFICATE OF CAPTAIN JOHN WALTON.

This may certify that the within deponent, William Borden, has for several years last past, resided a near neighbor to me ; that he was at the time the within mentioned Philip White was killed, a soldier in my troop of horse ; and that during my acquaintance with him, the deponent, William Borden, he has on all occasions been reputed a man of strict veracity and humanity.

Given under my hand this 19th April, 1782. JOHN WALTON, Captain Light Dragoons.

CERTIFICATE OF JUDGE DAVID FORMAN.

This may certify that on Saturday the 30th of March, 1782, or thereabouts, I the subscriber, was present at the village of Freehold, when the body of Philip White was brought up ; that I went to the wagon and saw the corpse ; the guard attending showed me the gun shot wound on his breast, also the cuts of a sword on his face. At that time the corpse appeared to be laid with as much decency as could be, and without any appearance of wounds in either of his arms or legs ; neither did I ever hear that his (the aforesaid Philip White's) arms had been cut off or his legs broken, &c. until after the execution of Captain Joshua Huddy, viz.; on Saturday the 13th of April instant, and then I heard by a person from the British lines that a report prevailed there that the aforesaid Philip White had been most cruelly murdered by having his arms cut off, his legs broken, &c.

Given under my hand this 19th day of April, 1782. DAVID FORMAN.

The foregoing affidavits and certificates furnish a clear, satisfactory account of the cause and manner of Phil White's death, and completely exonerate his guard from the charge of wanton cruelty toward him. The probability is that Phil White supposed if he was taken to Freehold jail that he would be tried and hanged for his participation in the murder of the father of John Russel, one of his guards, and for other misdemeanors and so he determined to try to escape and he made the effort at a place where he thought the woods, marsh, and brook would favor him and impede the light horsemen.

The accounts published in ancient papers are substantially the same as given in these affidavits. A month or so afterward the British at New York made desperate efforts to trump up evidence of wanton cruelty against North, Borden and Russell, the three guards, but that it signally failed, will be seen by an abstract of the second affidavit of Aaron White, taken June 19th, about six weeks after Phil White's death. Aaron White, it will be remembered, was taken prisoner at the same time that Phil White was captured, and his affidavit while at Freehold, has already been given. It is probable that Aaron White was exchanged a few days after his first affidavit was taken, as we find by a copy of an order from the Board of Associated Loyalists that the officer in charge of prisoners at New York was ordered to deliver up Daniel Randolph and Jacob Fleming, two Americans captured at Toms River, with Captain Huddy, to be exchanged for the refugee, Captain Clayton Tilton and another refugee name not specified; but it is stated on the trial of Captain Richard Lippencott, that they were to be exchanged by Governor Franklin's order for Captain Clayton Tilton and Aaron White. A British military commission, of which Major General James Paterson was president, was organized in New York, to examine into the circumstances of Captain Huddy's death and Captain Richard Lippencott's responsibility therefore, and before this commission Aaron White testified substantially as follows :

" That he was taken prisoner by the rebels at Long Branch ; that one of the rebel militia named George Brindley told him if they did not take Phil White, that they would put him (deponent) to death ; that after Philip White was taken, he heard the said George Bridley swear by God that Phil White should not go alive to Freehold ; that the rebels stopped at Colts Neck and changed guard ; that while at Colts Neck, Philip White told him he was afraid the rebels would murder him before they got to Freehold ; that when they started from Colts Neck he (deponent) was taken on ahead and Philip White kept behind under a guard of three men ; that these three men were John Russell, John North and one Borden who he had heard called three of as bad persecuting fellows as any in the country ; that it was his opinion the rebels intended to murder Philip White ; that the sergeant of the guard that had charge of Philip White as far as Colts Neck, informed him in Freehold jail that if Phil White had not been removed from his care he would not have been killed ; that General David Forman with a lawyer came to him while he was in jail at Freehold and wanted him to make affidavit that Phil White was killed while endeavoring to escape ; that he told General Forman that he would die before he made such affidavit ;

that after he escaped (was exchanged?) from Freehold jail, his friends all unanimously told him that their opinion was that Philip White was most cruelly and inhumanly murdered ; that he did make an affidavit before General Forman, relating the circumstances of his leaving New York, of the skirmish, of a light horseman leaping over a fence and that the people of Freehold told him that Philip White was killed fairly ; that if General Forman sent in any other affidavit it must have been forged."

The foregoing was the strongest evidence the British and refugees could bring against Phil White's guard, and it will be seen that it amounts to but little and in no particular does it sustain the charge of wanton cruelty. It is a matter of pro found satisfaction that the evidence preserved is so conclusive not only because it exonerates the guards from the malicious charges made against them, but also because many descendants of these guards now live within the limits of old Monmouth, as do also multitudes of descendants of the four hundred citizens who assembled at Freehold, on the 14th of April, 1782, who inquired into and justified the acts of the guard.

The Refugees were very profuse at all times in their charges against the Monmouth patriots ; because the citizens of old Monmouth would not remain quiet and allow these precious scoundrels to roam at will throughout the county, robbing and murdering, they were denounced as guilty of inhumanity, wanton cruelty, persecution, &c.

The Refugees had a very simple way of avoiding trouble from Monmouth patriots —they had only to refrain from attempting to commit outrages among them.

ATTACK ON THE RUSSELL FAMILY.

As this outrage was an unusually aggravated one even for the Refugees, and as mention of some of the parties concerned in it is made in other chapters detailing other events during the Revolution, we give the particulars as derived from various sources. The first extract is from *Collin's New Jersey Gazette:*

"On the 30th of April, 1780, a party of negroes and refugees from Sandy Hook, landed at Shrewsbury in order to plunder. During their excursion, a Mr. Russell, who attempted some resistance to their depredations, was killed, and his grandchild had five balls shot through him, but is yet living. Captain Warner of the privateer brig Elizabeth, was made prisoner by these ruffians, but was released, by giving them two half joes. This banditti also took off several persons, among whom were Captain James Greene, and Ensign John Morris of the militia."

The following statement is from Howe's Collections: " Mr. Russell was an elderly man, aged about 60 years ; as the party entered his dwelling, which was in the night, he fired and missed. William Gilian, a native of Shrewsbury, their leader, seized the old gentleman by the collar, and was in the act of stabbing him in the face and eyes with a bayonet, when the fire blazed up and shedding a momentary light upon the scene, enabled the younger Russell who lay wounded on the floor, to shoot Gilian. John Farnham, a native of Middletown, thereupon aimed his musket at the young man, but it was knocked up by Lippincott who had married into the family. The party then went off. The child was accidentally wounded in the affray."

The Lippincott above referred to, we presume, was Captain Richard Lippincott, who had command of the party which executed Captain Joshua Huddy. An outline of his life will be given elsewhere. In regard to John Farnham, a refugee of this name was afterwards captured, tried and hung at Freehold—probably the same man.

In the extract from Howe's Collections, it will be noticed that a younger Russell is referred to as being wounded and lying on the floor. This was John Russell, at this time belonging to the Continental army, at home on a furlough to see his wife and parents. After the war, John Russell removed to Cedar Creek, in Ocean county, where he lived to quite an advanced age. His account of the affair was substantially as follows :

There were seven refugees, and he (John) saw them through the window, and at one time they got so that he told his father he was sure they could kill four of them, and he wished to fire, as he believed the other three would run. His father persuaded him not to fire, but to do so when they broke into the house. When they broke in, the father fired first, but missed his aim ; he was then fired upon and killed. John Russell then fired and killed the man (Gilian) who shot his father. During the affray young Russell was shot in the side, and the scars of the wound were visible until he died. After being wounded he fell on the floor and pretended to be dead. The refugees then went to plundering the house. The mother and wife of John were lying in a bed with the child; the child awoke and asked, "Grandmother, what's the matter?" A refugee pointed his gun at it and fired and said " that's what's the matter." Whether he really intended to wound the child, or only to frighten it, is uncertain, but the child, as before stated, was badly wounded but eventually recovered. As the refugees were preparing to leave, one of the number pointed his musket at young Russell as he lay on the floor, and was about firing, saying he didn't believe he was dead yet, whereupon another (Lippincott?) knocked up his musket, saying it was a shame to fire upon a dying man, and the load went into the ceiling. After the refugees were gone, John got up and had his wounds dressed and exclaimed to his wife, "Ducky! bring me a glass of whisky—I'll come out all right yet." He did come out all right and we have good reason to believe that before the war ended he aided in visiting merited retribution on the refugees for their doings at this time. Among the party was the notorious Phil White who was killed near two years later (March 30th, 1782.)

Of the seven refugees concerned in this outrage, at least three are known to have met with their just deserts, viz: Gilian, killed at the time, Farnham, hanged at Freehold, and Phil White, killed while attempting to escape from his guards between Colts Neck and Freehold.

EXECUTION OF A SPY.

One affair which caused the most intense excitement throughout old Monmouth, and elsewhere during the war of the Revolution, was the arrest, trial and execution of a young man named Stephen Edwards, on the charge of being a spy for the British. Though reference to it is rarely met with in our histories, yet there were but few events in the county during the Revolution, that created a greater sensation than did this.

One of the officers who tried Edwards, and assisted at his execution, was Captain Joshua Huddy, and this furnished one of the excuses the refugees gave for his inhuman murder near the Highlands some three years after. On the trial of the refugee leader, Captain Richard Lippincott, by a British Court Martial at New York, in the summer of 1782, for his participation in the hanging of Huddy, refugee witnesses testified that even while Huddy was a prisoner in their hands, and but a few days before his death, he boldly acknowledged his participation, and justified it on the ground that he was found with treasonable papers in his possession, which conclusively proved him to be a spy. On this trial, William Courlies, husbandman, late of Monmouth, then one of the Associated Loyalists (as the refugees called themselves,) testified—

"That in regard to the death of Stephen Edwards, he (Courlies) then resided at Shrewsbury, in Monmouth county. Edwards was taken out of his bed at his own house and carried to Freehold; the following day he was brought to some kind of a trial, and the day following executed.— The offense alleged against him was said to be his having some papers found in his pocket. Edwards bore an excellent good character. Deponent heard there was complaint made to General Washington or the Governor, about Edwards' death, but he cannot tell the result. General Forman was one of the Judges who presided at Edwards' trial; Huddy was another of the judges; he had the information from Huddy himself; did not recollect hearing who the other judges were; deponent was not present at the execution of Edwards, but was present at his burial.— Understood Edwards was tried for treason in consequence of papers found on his person."

Captain Wm. Cunningham, who then was the British Provost Marshal at New York, and who by his own confession, (which has been given,) just previous to his execution in London, in 1791, was as heartless a wretch as ever lived, testified on this trial that he (Cunningham) told Huddy while he was a prisoner in the provost, that he, the deponent, had heard that Huddy had hanged a refugee on a large oak near the Court House at Freehold, and deponent asked Huddy concerning this report. Huddy avowed, it saying: "By God he did, and he slushed the rope well, and that Colonel Forman assisted in pulling the rope hand over hand"—that was the very expression Huddy used.

John Tilton, carpenter, a refugee from Monmouth, testified that when the refugee party was putting Captain Huddy in irons on board the sloop which conveyed him to the Highlands, " he, the deponent, was present, and he asked Huddy if he thought it was good usage to iron him.— Huddy replied that he did not think it was ; but as he expected to be exchanged in a day or two, he did not mind the irons; and Huddy also said he expected to have the killing of deponent and many more yet. Deponent then asked Huddy if he expected to hang deponent as he had done poor Stephen Edwards? Huddy replied that he did not hang Stephen Edwards, he only tied the knot and greased the rope that it might slip easily."

The foregoing give the strongest points that we have been enabled to find against Captain Huddy for his participation in the trial and execution of Edwards. It will be seen that there was no attempt to disprove the charge that Edwards was a spy.

From all the information that we have been enabled to obtain, we are satisfied that the following account of Stephen Edwards arrest, trial and execution, from " Howe's Collections " is substantially correct :

Stephen Edwards, a young man, in the latter part of the war, left his home in Shrewsbury and joined the loyalists (refugees) in New York. From thence he was sent by Colonel Taylor of the refugees, a former resident of Middletown, back to Monmouth county, with written instructions to ascertain the force of the Americans there. Information having been conveyed to the latter, Captain Jonathan Forman of the cavalry, was ordered to search for him. Suspecting he might be at his father's residence half a mile below Eatontown, he entered at midnight with a party of men, and found him in bed with his wife, disguised in the night cap of a female.

" Who have you here ?" said Forman.

" A laboring woman," replied Mrs. Edwards.

The captain detected the disguise, and on looking under the bed, saw Edwards' clothing, which he examined, and in which he found the papers given him by Colonel Taylor.

He then said " Edwards, I am sorry to find you ! You see these papers ? You have brought yourself into a very disagreeable situation—you know the fate of spies!"

Edwards denied the allegation, remarking that he was not such and could not so be considered.

This occurred on Saturday night. The prisoner was taken to the Court House, tried by a Court Martial next day, and executed at 10 o'clock on Monday morning. Edwards' father and mother had come up that morning to ascertain the fate of their son, and returned with the corpse. Edwards was an amiable young man. The Forman and Edwards families had been on terms of intimate friendship, and the agency of the members of the former in the transaction, excited their deepest sympathies for the fate of the unfortunate prisoner.

The guilt of Edwards was conclusively proven ; deep sympathy was felt for his parents and wife, but the perils of the patriots at this time were so great that prompt and decisive action was necessary for their own preservation.

The foolhardiness of Edwards in keeping treasonable papers about him was remarkable. Some features of this affair will remind the reader of the unfortunate Major Andre. It is probable that Edwards was executed about September, 1778.

PRIVATEERING ON OUR COAST.

Toms River During the Revolution.

Prizes taken—Americans captured—An enemy searching for water loses his rum —Old Cranberry Inlet, &c.

Toms River appears to have been occupied by the Americans as a. military post during the greater part of the Revolution. The soldiers stationed here were generally twelve months men, commanded by different officers, among whom may be mentioned, Captains Bigelow, Ephraim Jenkins, James Mott, John Stout and Joshua Huddy. Captain Mott had command of a company called the " Sixth company " of Dover, and Captain Stout of the Seventh company. The Fifth company was from Stafford, and commanded by Capt. Reuben F. Randolph. These companies all belonged to the militia organization of old Monmouth.

The duties of the militia stationed at Toms River, appear to have been to guard the inhabitants against depredations from the refugees ; to check contraband trade by way of old Cranberry Inlet to New York, and to aid our privateers who brought prizes into the Inlet, which was a favorite resort for New Jersey, New England and other American privateers.

By the following extracts, it will be seen that old Dover township was the scene of many stirring incidents during the war.

About the 1st of April, 1778, the government salt works near Toms River, were destroyed by a detachment of British under Captain Robertson. One building they alleged belonged to Congress and cost £6,000 The salt works on our coast at Manasquan, Shark River, Toms River, Barnegat and other places, were so important to the Americans during the war that we propose to notice them in a separate article.

May 22d, 1778, it is announced that a British vessel with a cargo of fresh beef and pork, was taken by Captain Anderson and sixteen men in an armed boat, and brought into Toms River.

In the early part of August following, the British ship "Love and Unity," with a valuable cargo was brought into the Inlet; the cargo was saved but the ship was subsequently retaken by a large British force; the particulars of the capture and recapture are as follows from ancient letters:

"August 12th, 1778. We learn that on Thursday night, the British ship "Love and Unity" from Bristol, with 80 hhds of loaf sugar, several thousand bottles London porter, and a large quantity of Bristol beer and ale, besides many other valuable articles, was designedly run ashore near Toms River. Since which, by the assistance of some of our militia, she has been brought into a safe port and her cargo properly taken care of."

The cargo of this ship was advertised to be sold at Manasquan, on the 26th of August, by John Stokes, U. S. Marshal. The articles enumerated in the advertisement show that the cargo must have been a very valuable one. The Americans were not quite so lucky with the ship as with the cargo, as will be seen by the following extract.

"Friday, September 18th, 1778. Two British armed ships and two brigs, came close to the bar off Toms River (Cranbury) Inlet, where they lay all night. Next morning between seven and eight o'clock, they sent seven armed boats into the Inlet, and re-took the ship Washington formerly "Love and Unity" which had been taken by the Americans; they also took two sloops near the bar and captured most of the crews.

The captain of the ship and most of his officers escaped to the main land in one of the ship's boats. After they got ashore a man named Robert McMullen, who had been condemned to death at Freehold but afterwards pardoned, jumped into the boat, hurrahing for the British, and rowed off and joined them. Another refugee named William Dillon, who had also been sentenced to death at Freehold and pardoned, joined this party of British as pilot."

By the following extract it will be seen that the regenades McMullen and Dillon, had been out of jail but a very few weeks, when they aided the British in this expedition:

"July 22d, 1778. We learn that at the Court of Oyer and Terminer, held at Monmouth in June last, the following parties were tried and found guilty of burglary, viz: Thomas Emmons alias Burke, John Wood, Michael Millery, William Dillon and Robert McMullen. The two former were executed on Friday last, and the other three reprieved."

McMullen probably had some connection with the expedition—perhaps to spy out the whereabouts of the captured cargo, as he would not have been in that vicinity unless assured that a British force was at hand.

One tradition states that when he jumped into the boat he was flying for his life —" that he was pursued by the Americans and escaped by swimming his horse across the river near its mouth to a point which he called *Goodluck* Point to commemorate his escape."

Goodluck Point near the mouth of Toms River, undoubtedly received its name from some person flying for his life in the above manner, and it is possible that it might have been McMullen.

"On the 9th of December, 1778, it is announced that a British armed vessel. bound from Halifax to New York, and richly laden, came ashore near Barnegat. The crew, about sixty in number, surrendered themselves prisoners to our militia. Goods to the amount of five thousand pounds sterling were taken out of her by our citizens, and a number of prisoners sent to Bordentown, at which place the balance of prisoners were expected. About March, 1779, the sloop Success, came ashore in a snow storm, at Barnegat. She had been taken by the British brig Diligence, and was on her way to New York. She had a valuable cargo of rum, molasses, coffee, cocoa, &c., on board. The Prize master and three hands were made prisoners and sent to Princeton. In the case of this vessel and the one previously mentioned it is probable the Toms River militia aided, as the name of Barnegat was frequently applied to the shore north of the inlet, both on the beach and on the main land.

Feb. 8th, 1779, the sloop Fancy and schooner Hope, with cargoes of pitch, tar and salt are advertised for sale at Toms River by the U. S. Marshal. They were probably prizes. The Major Van Emburg mentioned in the following, belonged to the 2d Reg. Middlesex militia; he was taken May 14, 1780.

On the 5th of June, 1780, an ancient paper says: "On Sunday morning, Major Van Emburg and eight or nine men from West Jersey, on a fishing party, were surprised in bed at Toms River by the Refugees, and put on board a vessel to be sent prisoners to New York, but before the vessel sailed they fortunately managed to escape."

Toms River then did not seem quite as desirable place for pleasure resort as it is in the present day. History does not tell us whether the Major was successful in catching fish; all we know is that he got caught himself.

About the middle of December, 1780, a British brig in the West India trade, was captured and brought into Toms River.— This brig was short of water and provisions and mistaking the land for Long Island, sent a boat and four men ashore to obtain supplies. The militia hearing of it manned two boats and went out and took her. She had on board 150 hhds of rum and spirits, which our ancestors pronounced "excellent," by which we conclude they must have considered themselves competent judges of the article! With the British, rum must have been a necessity, as in every prize taken from them rum was an important part of the cargo.

The British brig Molly, was driven ashore in a snow storm near Barnegat; her prize crew were taken prisoners by the militia and sent to Philadelphia.

In December, 1780, Lieut. Joshua Studson of Toms River, was shot by the refugee Bacon, inside of Cranberry inlet. The particulars of this affair are given in a notice of Bacon's career, and therefor it is unnecessary to repeat them.

March 19, 1782. The privateer Dart, Capt. Wm. Gray, of Salem, Mass., arrived at Toms River with a prize sloop, taken from the British galley Black Jack. The next day he went with his boat and seven men in pursuit of a British brig near the bar. Unfortunately for Capt. Gray, instead of taking a prize he was taken himself. For a long time after, the Toms River people wondered what had become of him. In August following they heard from him. After getting outside the bar he was taken prisoner, and carried to Halifax, and subsequently released on parole. He stated he was well treated while a prisoner.

A few days after Capt. Gray was taken, the British attacked and burned Toms River. This was the last affair of any importance occuring in the immediate vicinity of Toms River during the war. But south of Toms River several noted affairs afterwards occurred. Davenport burned the salt works at Forked River, and was himself killed in June; in October, Bacon attacked and killed several men on the beach south of Barnegat lighthouse; in December, occurred the skirmish at Cedar Creek, where young Cooke was killed; on the 3d of April following, (1783,) Bacon was killed near West Creek.

A RHODE ISLAND PRIZE.

The original and following certificate is in pressession of Ephraim P. Empson, Esq., of Colliers Mills:

PROVIDENCE, Feb. 21, 1777.

This may certify that Messrs. Clark and Nightingale and Captain William Rhodes have purchased here at vendue, the schooner *Pope's Head*, which was taken by the privateers Sally and Joseph (under our command) and carried into Cranberry Inlet, in the Jersies, and there delivered to the care of Mr. James Randolph by our prize masters. JAMES MARO.
JOHN FISH.

MISCELLANEOUS ITEMS.

During the war there were interesting events occurring at Toms River, outside of military and naval matters.

In January, 1778, the sloop Two Friends, Capt. Alex. Bonnett of Hispaniola, was cast away near Barnegat, with 1,600 bags of salt, 49 hhds molasses, also a lot of rum, sugar, &c. Only 160 galls. rum saved. The shore people went to their assistance but one man was lost. The Capt. of the Two Friends, Alex. Bonnett, then shipped as a passenger in the sloop Endeavor of Toms River, for New York, but sad to relate, while she lay at anchor in the inlet, a storm at night parted the cable and all on board were drowned in the bay.

In December, 1778, Capt. Alexander of the sloop Elizabeth of Baltimore, was taken by the British, but he was permitted to leave in his small boat, and landed in Toms River inlet.

It was during the war, in the year 1777, that Rev. Benjamin Abbott, expounded the then new principles of Methodism, to the people of Toms River, first at the house of Esquire Abiel Aikens, and then at another place when "a Frenchman fell to the floor, and never rose until the Lord converted his soul. Here (at Toms River), we had a happy time," so says Abbott in his journal.

During the war there was of course no communication with New York, but the people of Toms River had considerable overland intercourse with West Jersey, Philadelphia and Freehold.

THE REFUGEES.

Historians generally concede that no state among the old thirteen suffered during the war of the revolution more than did New Jersey ; and it is generally admitted that no county in our State suffered more than did old Monmouth. In addition to the outrages to which the citizens were subjected from the regular British army, they were continually harassed by depredations committed by regularly organized bands of Refugees and also by the lawless acts of a set of outcasts known as "the Pine Woods Robbers," who though pretending to be Royalists yet if opportunity offered, robbed Royalists as well as Americans.

The Refugees or Loyalists, as they called themselves, were renegade Americans, regularly organized with officers commissioned by the "Board of Associated Loyalists" at New York. Of this body the first president was Daniel Coxe, a Jerseyman. It was organized in 1779, and its objects were the examination of captured Americans and suspected persons, and the planning of measures for procuring intelligence, and otherwise aiding the Royal cause. Coxe was appointed President (said a Refugee) to deprive him of the opportunity of speaking, as "he had the gift of saying little with many words." Another President of the Board was William Franklin, a natural son of Benjamin Franklin, and the last Tory Governor of New Jersey.

It is not probable that all who were called Jersey Refugees where natives of the state ; too many were it is true: but the thrift and industry of the inhabitants of old Modmouth, once the richest county in the state, the advantage of deep swamps for hiding, the proximity of Raritan Bay and the seaboard rendering it convenient to send plunder to New York, all formed attractions to draw here villains from other parts whose chief object was plunder, who scrupled at no crime to obtain booty or to gratify revenge.

The character of some of these men is clearly set forth in the following extracts, the first from Whig and the other from Tory authority.

Gov. Livingston, the able, fearless and eloquent first patriot Governor of New Jersey, in a message to the Legislature in 1777, says :

"The Royalists (Refugees) have plundered friends as well as foes : effects capable of division they have divided ; such as were not they have destroyed. They have warred on decrepid old age and upon defenceless youth ; they have committed hostilities against the professors of literature and against the ministers of religion; against public records and private monuments, books of improvements and papers of curiosity, and against the arts and sciences. They have butchered the wounded when asking for quarter, mangled the dead while weltering in their blood ; refused to the dead their right of sepulture, suffered prisoners to perish for want of sustenance, violated the chastity of wo men, disfigured private dwellings of taste and elegance, and in their rage of impiety and barbarism, profaned edifices dedicated to Almighty God."

Strong and emphatic as is the foregoing language of the patriotic Livingston, yet it fails to portray the brutality of some wretches who pretended to be Refugee Loyalists as clearly as the following brief extract from the evidence of a Tory named Galloway, of Pennsylvania, given under oath before Parliament. At the breaking out of the Revolution, Galloway, a Pennsylvanian of wealth and standing, sided with the Whigs, but soon turned Tory, and his property to the amount of £40,000 was confiscated. Speaking of Refugee outrages, he said :

"Respecting indiscriminate plunder it is known to thousands. In respect to rapes, a solemn inquiry was made and affidavit taken by which it appears that no less than twenty-three were committed in one neighborhood in New Jersey, some of them on married women, in presence of their helpless husbands, and others on daughters while their unhappy parents with unavailing tears and cries could only deplore their savage brutality."

OLD TIMES IN OLD MONMOUTH. 71

This was the evidence of as reliable a man as ever sided with the Tories. In corroboration of the foregoing we might instance, among other things, the burning of churches in Essex county, of ravishment of women (one of them nearly seventy years old), &c. And Jerseymen have the mortification of knowing that wretches pretending to be natives of this state disgraced the soil that gave them birth by acts of brutality elsewhere, among which may be mentioned the cold blooded murder of the brave Col. Ledyard at Fort Griswold, Conn., by a wretch known as the "Jersey Refugee, Bromfield." After the Americans had surrendered the fort, Bromfield asked who commanded it. The heroic Ledyard replied "I did, but you do now," and he delivered his sword to Bromfield. The cold blooded villain took it and immediately stabbed Ledyard to the heart.

That all the regularly organized Refugees or Loyalists as they called themselves were not as hardened villains as above described we shall endeavor to show hereafter. The best class of them were too honorable to engage in midnight marauding expeditions against their former friends and neighbors, but cast their lot with the regular British army, most of them in a military organization known as the "First Battalion New Jersey Royal Volunteers," of which a prominent officer was an ex-sheriff of old Monmouth. These New Jersey Royalists were sometimes termed "the Greens" and "General Skinner's Greens." General Skinner was their most noted commander, of whom a notice will be given hereafter, as also of other prominent officers.

To give an idea of the troublous times in which lived the citizens of old Monmouth, the following extracts from various sources are furnished, before which, we give the names of some of the officers of

THE MONMOUTH MILITIA IN THE REVOLUTION.

The following are some of the officers of the militia of old Monmouth during the war:

First Regiment.

George Taylor, Colonel. (Deserted to the enemy.)
Nathaniel Scudder, Lieutenant Colonel, Colonel.
Asher Holmes, First Major, Colonel.
John Smock, Captain, Major, Lieutenant Colonel, Colonel.

Thomas Seabrook, First Major, Lieutenant Colonel.
Elisha Walton, Ensign, Captain, Second Major, First Major.
Thomas Hunn, Captain, Second Major.
Kenneth Anderson, Adjutant.
David Rhea, jr., Adjutant.
John Stilwell, Quartermaster.
John Campbell, Quartermaster.
Richard Hartshorne, Quartermaster.
Thomas Barber, Surgeon.
Jacob Hubbard, Surgeon.
John Scudder, Surgeon's Mate.

Second Regiment.

David Brearley, Colonel.
Joseph Salter, Lieutenant Colonel.
Samuel Forman, Captain, Lieutenant Colonel, Colonel.
Elisha Lawrence, jr., First Major, Lieutenant Colonel.
William Montgomery, Captain, First Major.
James Mott, Second Major.
John Cook, Captain, Second Major.

Third Regiment.

Samuel Breese, Colonel.
Daniel Hendrickson, Colonel.
Auke Wikoff, Lieutenant Colonel, Colonel.
Dennis Denise, First Major.
Hendrick VanBrunt, Lieutenant, Captain, Second Major.

Of the First Regiment the first Colonel (Taylor) went over to the enemy; its next Colonel, Nathaniel Scudder, was killed at Black Point, Oct. 15th, 1781. Asher Holmes appears to have been transferred to a State Regiment.

A more extended list of officers and privates in these and other organizations will be furnished hereafter.

REFUGEE RAIDS IN OLD MONMOUTH.

"June 3d, 1778. We are informed that on Wednesday morning last, a party of about seventy of the Greens from Sandy Hook, landed near Major Kearney's (near Keyport) headed the Mill Creek, Middletown Point, and marched to Mr. John Burrows, made him prisoner, burnt his mills and both his store houses, all valuable buildings, besides a great deal of furniture. They also took prisoners Lieutenant Colonel Smock, Captain Christopher Little, Mr. Joseph Wall, Capt. Joseph Covenhoven (Conover) and several other persons, and killed Messrs. Pearce and

Van Brockle, and wounded another man mortally. Having completed this and several other barbarities, they precipitately returned the same morning to give an account of their abominable deeds to their bloody employers. A number of these gentry, we learn, were formerly inhabitants of that neighborhood."

April 26th, 1779. An expedition consisting of seven or eight hundred men under Colonel Hyde, went to Middletown, Red Bank, Tinton Falls, Shrewsbury and other places, robbing and burning as they went. They took Justice Coyenhoven and others, prisoners. Capt. Burrows and Col. Holmes assembled our militia and killed three and wounded fifteen of the enemy. The enemy, however, succeeded in carrying off horses, cattle and other plunder.

In May, two or three weeks after the above affair, some two or three hundred Tories landed at Middletown on a "pica rooning" (plundering) expedition, but were repulsed before doing much harm.

June 9th, 1779. A party of about fifty Refugees landed in Monmouth and marched to Tinton Falls undiscovered, where they surprised and carried off Col. Hendrickson, Col. Wyckoff, Capt. Chadwick and Capt. McKnight, and several privates of the militia, and drove off sheep and horned cattle. About thirty of our militia hastily collected, made some resistance, but were repulsed with the loss of two men killed and ten wounded, the enemy's loss unknown.

April 1st, 1780. About this time the Tories made another raid to Tinton Falls, and took seven prisoners. Another party took Mr. Bowne prisoner at Middletown, who but three days before had been exchanged and had just got home.

About the last of April the Refugees attacked the house of John Holmes, Upper Freehold, and robbed him of a large amount of continental money, a silver watch, gold ring, silver buckles, pistols, clothing, &c.

June 1st, 1780. The noted Colonel Tye, a mulatto, and formerly a slave in Monmouth county, with his motley company of about twenty blacks and whites carried off prisoners Captain Barney Smock and Gilbert Van Mater, spiked an iron cannon and took four horses. Their rendezvous was at Sandy Hook.

THE ATTACK ON CAPTAIN HUDDY AT COLTS NECK.

Sept. 1780. It is perhaps proper to give first the version of this affair as found in Howe's Historical Collectious of New Jersey, as the compiler of that work probably obtained his information from aged persons living in 1842, when he visited the locality.

After mentioning that the dwelling in which Captain Huddy resided during the war, was then owned by Thomas G. Haight, Esq., and standing in a central part of Colts Neck, he says:

Huddy distinguished himself on various occasions during the war, and became an object of terror to the Tories. In the summer of 1780, a party of about 60 refugees, commanded by Tye, a mulatto, one evening attacked this dwelling. Huddy, assisted only by a servant girl aged about twenty years, defended it for some length of time. Several muskets were fortunately left in the house by the guard generally stationed there, but at this time absent.—These she loaded, while Huddy by appearing at different windows and discharging them, gave the impression that there were many defenders. He wounded several and at last, while setting fire to the house, he shot their leader, Tye, in the wrist.—Huddy finding the flames fast increasing, agreed to surrender, provided they would extinguish the fire.

It is said that the enemy on entering were much exasperated at the feebleness of the defenders, and could with difficulty be restrained by their leader from butchering them on the spot. They were obliged to leave, as the militia soon collected and killed six on their retreat. They carried off with Huddy several cattle and sheep from the neighborhood, but lost them fording the creeks. They embarked on board their boats near Black Point between Shrewsbury and Navisink rivers. As the boats pushed off from shore, Huddy jumped overboard and was shot in the thigh as was supposed by the militia, then in close pursuit. He held up one of his hands towards them exclaiming, " *I am Huddy! I am Huddy!*" swam to the shore and escaped.

The name of the heroine who loaded the muskets for Huddy, says the above writer, was Lucretia Emmons, afterwards Mrs. Chambers, and she died at Freehold about 20 years before his visit.

Titus or Col. Tye as he was commonly called, usually commanded a mongrel crew of negroes and tories. He died of lockjaw, occasioned by the wound in his wrist. He was a slave of John Corlies, and was born and bred in the south part of this township. He was an honorable, brave, but headstrong man. Several acts of generosity are remembered of him, and he was justly more respected as an enemy than many of his brethren of a fairer complexion.

Marks of the fire were plainly discernable when the above writer visited the house in June, 1842, and on the eastern end of the house were several bullet holes.

In a Philadelphia paper published at the time, is a letter from Monmouth county dated Sept. 9th, 1780, which gives a version of this affair, stated to have been on the authority of Captain Huddy himself. The following is the substance of the letter:

"There were 72 men attacked him at his residence at Colts Neck. They were under the command of Lieutenant Joseph Parker and William Hewlett, and commenced the attack about an hour before day. They commenced staving a window to pieces, which aroused Huddy; the girl helped him to defend himself. Mrs. Huddy and another woman tried to persuade him to surrender, as defense was useless. Tye, "one of Lord Dunmore's crew," received a severe wound. After Huddy surrendered, they plundered the house. The fight lasted two hours. Six militia men came near and fired and killed their commander. Ensign Vincent and sixteen of the State Regiment attacked the refugees as they embarked, and wounded Huddy. The firing made confusion in the boats, and one overset and Huddy swam ashore."

The letter adds that the refugees made a silent, shameful retreat, loaded with disgrace, and the Americans made quite merry over the fact that it took seventy-two of the enemy two hours to take one man.

Oct. 15th, 1781. A party of refugees from Sandy Hook, landed at night at Shrewsbury and marched undiscovered to Colts Neck and took six prisoners. The alarm reached the Court House about four or five o'clock, P. M., and a number of inhabitants, among whom was Dr. Nathaniel Scudder, went in pursuit. They rode to Black Point to try to recapture the six Americans, and while firing from the bank Dr. Scudder was killed.

Dr. Scudder was Colonel of the First Regiment Monmouth Militia, and one of the most prominent, active and useful patriots of Monmouth, and his death was a severe loss to the Americans. He was buried with all the honors of war. General Forman's original order to Captain Walton to bury Dr. Scudder with all the honors of war, was presented to the New Jersey Historical Society in May, 1847, by Mrs. Forman.

About the beginning of August, 1782, Richard Wilgus, an American, was shot below Allentown, while on guard to prevent contraband trade with the British.

February 8th, 1782. About forty refugees under Lieutenant Steelman, came over Sandy Hook to Pleasant Valley.— They took twenty horses and five sleighs which they loaded with plunder; they also took several prisoners, viz: Hendrick Henderson and his two sons, Peter Covenhoven, Esq., (Esq. Covenhoven or Conover as the name is now called, was made prisoner once before, in 1779, as before related,) Garret Hendrickson, Samuel B Wife and son and Jaques Denise. At Garret Hendrickson's a young man named William Thompson got up slyly and went and informed Captain John Schenck, of Colonel Holmes' regiment, who collected all the men he could to pursue. They overtook and attacked the refugees, and the before mentioned William Thompson was killed and William Cottrell wounded.— They however took twelve refugee prisoners, three of whom were wounded. But in returning, they unexpectedly fell in with a party of sixteen men under Stevenson, and a sudden firing caused eight of the prisoners to escape. But Captain Schenck ordered his men to charge bayonet and the tories surrendered. Captain Schenck retook nineteen horses and five sheep, and took twenty-one prisoners.

The first of the foregoing extracts relating to the raid of the British in Middletown township in 1778, and then landing near Major Kearney's in the vicinity of Keyport, is probably the affair referred to in a tradition given in Howe's Historical Collections, which we append, as it explains why the refugees fled so precipitately. It will be noticed, however, that it does not agree with the extract quoted as to damage done, but we are inclined to believe that the extract copied from the ancient paper (Collins' Gazette) is correct, as it was written but a few days after the affair took place.

"The proximity of this part of Monmouth county to New York, rendered it, in the war of the Revolution, peculiarly liable to the incursions of the British troops. Many of the inhabitants, although secretly favorable to the American cause, were obliged to feign allegiance to the crown or lose their property by marauding parties of refugees from vessels lying off Sandy Hook. Among those of this description was Major Kearney, a resident near the present site of Keyport. On one occasion, a party of thirty or forty refugees stopped at his dwelling on their way to Middletown Point, where they intended to burn a dwelling and some mills. Kearney feigned gratification at their visit, and falsely informed them that there were probably some rebel troops at the Point, in which case it would be dangerous to march thither. He ordered his negro servant Jube thither to make inquiry, at the same time giving him secretly the cue to act. In due length of time, Jube, who had gone but a short distance, returned and hastily entered the room where Kearney and the refugees were, and exclaimed, " Oh, Massa! Massa! the rebels are at the Point thick as blackberries! They have just come down from the Court House and say they are going to march down here to-night." The ruse succeeded ; the refugees, alarmed, precipitately fled, retreated to their boats, leaving the Major to rejoice at the success of the stratagem which had saved the property of his friends from destruction."

The probability is that the ruse prevented the refugees from doing as much damage as they had intended, although they remained long enough to inflict considerable injury as has been related.

CAPTAIN JOSHUA HUDDY, THE HERO MARTYR OF OLD MONMOUTH.

Among the multitude of heroic men furnished by our State in aid of the struggle for independence, the name of Captain Joshua Huddy should ever occupy a conspicuous place in the memory of Jerseymen. Yet when we recall his daring deeds, his patriotic efforts and sacrifices and his unfortunate end, it is doubtful if less justice has been done to the services and memory of any other hero of his day.— Though the Continental Congress, as well as General Washington and other noted men testified their warm appreciation of his services ; though his name at one time was a household word, not only throughout this country but at the courts of England and France ; and though his unfortunate death and its consequences, for a time, caused the most intense excitement on both sides of the Atlantic, yet in the substance of the language of a report adopted by Congress in 1837, " It is fearful to state that after a lapse of fifty years, while the services of others of so much less merit have been made the theme of the biographer and the poet, the memory of Huddy has not been honored with an epitaph. His country, it would seem, has outlived the recollection of his services, and forgotten that such a victim was sacrificed for American liberty."

OUTLINE OF CAPTAIN HUDDY'S LIFE.

The following extracts from the archives of the State Department of New Jersey, were furnished in 1837 to a Congressional committee at the request of the chairman, by the late Governor Philemon Dickenson:

" Joshua Huddy signs his name as *Captain*, to a petition from the militia officers of the county of Monmouth, to the Legislature, which is dated the 12th of May, 1777.

"Captain Joshua Huddy is appointed by 'an act of the Legislature, passed September 24th, 1777, to the command of a company of artillery, to be raised from the militia of the State, and to continue in service not exceeding one year.

"In the accounts of the paymaster of the militia there is an entry of a payment made on the 30th of July, 1778, to Captain Joshua Huddy, of the artillery regiment for services at Haddonfield, under Colonel Holmes. In the same accounts a payment is also made to Captain Huddy on the 1st July, 1779, for the use of his horses in the artillery.

"I find a petition to the Legislature from the people of Monmouth, dated December 10th, 1781, recommending Captain Joshua Huddy as a proper person to command a guard, to be stationed at Toms River. On examining the minutes of both houses of the Legislature, I find no action had on this petition ; in fact there is no mention of its being presented. The Legislature adjourned on the 29th of December, and did not meet again until May 15th, 1782. Huddy was taken by the tories at Toms River, Sunday, March 24th, 1782, and it is not unlikely (as the Legislature had no action on this petition) he was ordered to that post by the Council of Safety, which exercised legislative powers during the recess of the Legislature. The minutes of the Council of Safety must be either lost or destroyed, as they cannot be found."

The above extracts were made and furnished to Governor Dickenson by George C. Westcott, then secretary of State. (In the original is an error corrected above ;

OLD TIMES IN OLD MONMOUTH.

it says that Captain Huddy was taken prisoner April 2d; it should be March 24th.)

The details of the attack on Toms River have been given.

Captain Huddy, with other prisoners, was taken to New York and lodged in the noted Sugar House prison, from whence he was taken on Monday, April 1st, 1782, to the prison of the Provost Guard in New York, where he was closely confined until Monday, April 8th, when he, with Daniel Randolph and Jacob Fleming, (both of whom were taken prisoners with Huddy at Toms River, but soon exchanged for two tories, named Captain Clayton Tilton and Aaron White,) were taken on board a sloop and ironed.

The following is a copy of the order to the Commissary of Prison at New York, to deliver him to the care of Captain Richard Lippincott, of the Refugees, to be taken on board the sloop:

NEW YORK, April 8th, 1782.

SIR:—Deliver to Capt. Richard Lippencott the three following prisoners : Lieutenant Joshua Huddy, Daniel Randolph and Jacob Fleming, to take down to the Hook, to procure the exchange of Captain Clayton Tilton and two other associated loyalists.

By order of the Board of Directors of Associated Loyalists.

S. S. BLOWERS, Secretary.

To Mr. Commissary Challoner.

Huddy, Randolph and Fleming were kept in irons in the hold of the sloop, until Tuesday evening, April 9th, when they were transferred to the guardship at Sandy Hook, where they were confined between decks until Tuesday, April 12th, on the morning of which day, Huddy was taken on shore by a party of refugees under command of Captain Richard Lippencott, and at about ten o'clock executed. One refugee account says the hangman was a negro. Captain Huddy executed his will under the gallows, signing it on the barrel from which he was a few moments after launched into another world.

CAPTAIN HUDDY'S WILL.

The following is a copy of the will of Captain Huddy, signed by him under the gallows:

" In the name of God, amen : I, Joshua Huddy, of Middletown, in the county of Monmouth, being of sound mind and memory, but expecting shortly to depart this life, do declare this my last will and testament:

"First : I commit my soul into the hands of Almighty God, hoping he may receive it in mercy ; and next I commit my body to the earth. I do also appoint my trusty friend, Samuel Forman, to be my lawful executor, and after all my just debts are paid, I desire that he do divide the rest of my substance whether by book, debts, notes or any effects whatever belonging to me, equally between my two children, Elizabeth and Martha Huddy.

"In witness whereof I have hereunto signed my name this twelfth day of April, in the year of our Lord one thousand seven hundred and eighty-two.

"JOSHUA HUDDY."

The will was written on half a sheet of foolscap paper, on the back of which was the following endorsement, evidently written shortly after the will was executed :

" The will of Captain Joshua Huddy, made and executed the same day the refugees murdered him, April 12th, 1782."

The will was found some years ago among the papers of his executor, the late Colonel Samuel Forman. It was signed by Captain Huddy, but was apparently written by another person. Captain Huddy's daughters subsequently became Elizabeth Green and Martha Piatt—the last named lived to an advanced age. In early life she removed to Cincinnati, Ohio; both daughters we believe left descendants.

After Captain Huddy's inhuman murder his body was left hanging until afternoon, when the Americans came and took it to Freehold, to the house of Captain James Greene, where it was April 15th. He was buried with the honors of war. His funeral sermon was preached by the well remembered Rev. Dr. John Woodhull, pastor of the First Presbyterian Church, Freehold.

CAPTAIN JOSHUA HUDDY, THE HERO MARTYR OF OLD MONMOUTH.

MEASURES FOR RETALIATION.

The execution of Huddy was regarded by General Washington as a matter of so much importance, that he directed that a number of general officers of the army should meet at West Point to decide on what measures should be adopted. At this council it was unanimously decided that retaliation should be made, and that it should be inflicted on an officer of equal rank, and the designation should be made by lot from among prisoners of war, unless the British surrendered Captain Richard Lippincott. A formal demand was made for the surrender of Lippincott and refused, and in consequence on the 13th of May, lots were cast among the British officers held as prisoners, (at this time confined at Lancaster, Pa.,) and the unfortunate victim was Captain Charles Asgill, (afterwards Sir Charles Asgill) of a noble family, at this time but nineteen years old. He was among the prisoners captured at Yorktown, Va.

The particulars of the casting of lots and the events consequent upon the selection of Captain Asgill, are of thrilling interest, and excited so much attention at the time that the celebrated Baron de Grimm speaking of the affair being made the ground work of a tragedy brought out in Paris, in 1789, says:

"The public prints all over Europe resounded with the unhappy catastrophe which for near eight months impended over the life of this young officer. The general curiosity in regard to the events of the war yielded, if I may say so, to the interest which young Asgill inspired, and the first question asked of all vessels from any port in North America, was always an inquiry as to the fate of that young man. It is known that Asgill was thrice conducted to the foot of the gibbet, and that thrice General Washington, who could not bring himself to commit the crime of policy without a struggle, suspended his punishment; his humanity and justice made him hope that the English general would deliver over to him the author of the crime Asgill was condemned to expiate.— Sir Henry Clinton, either ill-advised or insensible to the fate of young Asgill, persisted in refusing to deliver up the barbarous Lippincott. In vain the King of England, at whose feet the unfortunate family of Asgills fell down, had given orders to surrender up to the Americans the author of a crime which dishonored the British nation; George the Third was not obeyed.

"In vain the States of Holland entreated the United States of America the pardon of the unhappy Asgill. The gibbet erected in front of his prison did not cease to offer to his eyes those dreadful preparations more awful than death itself. In these circumstances, and almost reduced to despair, the mother of the unfortunate victim bethought herself that the Minister of a King armed against her own nation, might succeed in obtaining that which was refused her own King. Madam Asgill wrote to the French Minister, Count de Vergennes, a letter, the eloquence of which, independent of oratorical forms. is that of all people and languages, because it derives its power from the first and noblest sentiment of our nature."

Before giving farther details of Captain Asgills' case, his mother's letters, and the course of the French court, of Gen. Washington and of the Continental Congress relating to the affair, it would perhaps be proper to return to Captain Huddy and recall the particulars of such of the events of his life as have been preserved. The following, a part of which at least will be familiar to most of our readers, comes first in order:

HUDDY'S CAPTURE AND EXECUTION.

The next important affair in which we find Captain Huddy engaged, was in the defence of the military post at Toms River. As we gave elsewhere a detailed account of the attack of the British on this post, burning of the village, massacre of the men after asking for quarters, and other particulars relating to this affair, it is not now necessary to repeat them, except as they are incidentally given in some important papers, which will be copied hereafter. These papers contain many authentic, interesting particulars which should be preserved by the citizens of Old Monmouth. Before copying these, we quote the following extracts from "Howe's Collections:"

While Huddy was confined on board the guardship, he was told by one of the refugees, that he was to be hanged, "for he had taken a certain Philip White, a refugee in Monmouth county, cut off both his arms, broke his legs, pulled out one of his eyes, damned him and bid him run." He answered, "It was impossible I could have taken Philip White, I being a prisoner in New York, closely confined, and for many days before he was made a prisoner." One or two of his comrades corroborated this statement. Four days after (April 12th,) Huddy was taken by 16 refugees under Capt. Lippencott, to Gravelly Point, on the seashore at the foot of Navisink hills, about a mile north of the Highland lighthouse where he was deliberately executed. He met his fate with an extraordinary degree of firmness and serenity. It is said he even executed his will under the gallows, upon the head of that barrel from which he was to make his exit, and in a hand writing fairer than usual.—

The following label was attached to his breast:

"We, the refugees having long with grief, beheld the cruel murders of our brethren, and finding nothing but such measures daily carrying into execution; we therefore determined not to suffer without taking vengeance for the numerous cruelties; and thus begin, having made use of Capt. Huddy as the first object to present to your view; and further determine to hang man for man while there is a refugee living.

"Up Goes Huddy for Philip White."

The gallows was formed of three rails, and stood on the beach, close to the sea. Tradition states that Capt. Lippincott, observing reluctance in some of his men to take hold the rope, drew his sword and swore he would run the first through, who disobeyed orders. Three of the party, bringing their bayonets to the charge, declared their determination to defend themselves—that Huddy was innocent of the death of White, and that they would not be concerned in the murder of an innocent man.

The British version of the execution of Huddy will be given in the account of the trial of the refugee Captain Richard Lippincott.

CAPT. JOSHUA HUDDY, THE HERO MARTYR OF OLD MONMOUTH.

MEETING AT FREEHOLD.

As soon as the citizens of Old Monmouth received information of the barbarous murder of Capt. Huddy, a large meeting numbering some four hundred of the most respectable citizens of the county, assembled at Freehold to take appropriate action.—This meeting was held on the 14th of April, one day before Huddy's burial, and while his corpse was lying at the house of Capt. James Greene. This meeting considered and approved the following address:

To his Excellency George Washington, Esq., Commander in Chief of the combined Armies of America and France, acting in North America, &c., &c., &c.

The inhabitants of the county of Monmouth, being assembled on account of the horrid and almost unparalleled murder of Capt. Joshua Huddy, by the refugees from New York, and as we presume by approbation, if not by the express command of the British commander in chief, Sir Henry Clinton; hold it as our indispensable duty, as well to the United States in general, as ourselves in particular, to show to your excellency, that the aforesaid Captain Joshua Huddy, late commanding the post at Toms River, was after a brave and gallant defence made a prisoner of war, together with fifteen of his men, by a party of refugees from New York, on Sunday, the 24th of March, last past. That five of the said Huddy's men were most inhumanly murdered after the surrender; that the next day at night, to wit, on Monday, the 25th of March, aforesaid, the said Capt. Huddy and the other prisoners who had been spared from the bayonet, arrived at New York, and were lodged in the main guard, during that night; that on Tuesday morning, the 26th of the same month, the said Huddy was removed from the main guard to the sugar house, where he was kept closely confined, until removed from thence to the provost guard, on Monday, April 1st, where he, the said Captain Huddy, was closely confined, until Monday, the 8th of April, instant; when the said Captain Huddy, with two other prisoners, was removed from the provost jail at New York, on board of a sloop, then lying at New York dock, was put in the hold of said sloop in irons; and then the said Captain Huddy was told he was ordered to be hanged, although the said Captain Huddy *had never been charged, or brought to any kind of trial.* That the said Captain Huddy demanded to know upon what charge he was to be hanged; that a refugee by the name of John Tilton, then told him that he, (the said Captain Huddy meaning,) was to be hanged for that he had taken a certain refugee by the name of Philip White, and that he, (the said Captain Huddy, meaning,) had, after carrying him, the aforesaid Philip White, five or six miles, cut off his (the aforesaid Philip White's) arms, broke both his legs, pulled out one of his eyes, and most cruelly murdered him, the aforesaid Philip White; and further said, that he, the aforesaid Captain Huddy, was ordered to be hanged for the murder aforesaid; that Capt. Huddy replied that he had never taken the aforesaid Philip White prisoner; and further said, that he, the aforesaid Philip White was killed after he, the said Captain Huddy, was taken prisoner himself, and was closely confined at New York at the time the said Philip White was killed. Which in fact, and in truth, was exactly as the said Captain Huddy had related; for he, the aforesaid Philip White, was in New York, on Wednesday, the 27th of March, last past, and did on the night of that day, sail from New York to Sandy Hook, where he lay until Friday, the 29th of March; that late the same night, he in company with Aaron White, John Fennimore, negro Moses, John Worthley, and one Isaac, all refugees, weighed anchor for Sandy Hook, and ran down to Long Branch, in the township of Shrewsbury; that the said Philip White, (so as aforesaid mentioned to have been killed by the said Captain Huddy,) and the said negro Moses, landed on Long Branch, in Shrewsbury aforesaid, on Saturday morning, the 30th of March ; he, the said Joshua Huddy, being then a close prisoner in the sugar house at New York.

That he, the said Philip White, was taken prisoner on the same 30th of March, in the afternoon, and as a guard was conducting him, the said Philip White to jail, the said Philip in attempting to escape, was killed by his guard. That on Friday, the twelfth instant, a party of refugees, said to have been commanded by a Capt. Richard Lippencott, brought the said Capt. Huddy over to the Highlands of Middletown, hanged him at ten o'clock in the forenoon of the same day, and left him hanging until four o'clock in the afternoon, with the paper herewith annexed pinned upon his breast; at which time a party of the inhabitants having been informed of the cruel murder, went to the place of his execution, and cut the unhappy victim from the gallows.

These being a state of indutiable facts, fully proven, we do, as of right we may, look up to your excellency, as the person in whom the sole power of avenging our wrongs is lodged, and who has full and ample authority to bring a British officer of the same rank to a similar end ; for what man after this instance of the most unjust and cruel murder, will presume to say that any officer or citizen, whom the chance of war may put into the hands of the enemy, will not suffer the same ignominious death, on some such groundless and similar pretence.

And we do with the fullest assurance rely upon receiving effectual support from your excellency, because,

First, the act of hanging any person without any (even a pretended) trial, is in itself not only disallowed by all civilized people, but is considered as barbarous in the extreme, and most certainly demands redress.

Secondly, because the law of nature and of nations, points to retaliation as the only measure which can, in such cases, give any degree of security, that the practice shall not become general.

Thirdly, because the honorable, the Continental Congress, did on the 30th day of October, 1778, resolve in the following words :

" We, therefore, the Congress of the United States of America, do solemnly declare and proclaim, that if our enemies presume to execute their threats, or persist in their present career of barbarity, we will take such exemplary vengeance as shall deter others from a like conduct.— We appeal to that God who searcheth the hearts of men, for the rectitude of our intentions, and in his holy presence declare, that as we are not moved by any light and hasty suggestions of anger or revenge, so through every possible change of fortune, we will adhere to this, our determination."

Fourthly, because the minds of the people are justly irritated, and if they have not compensation through a public channel, they may, in vindicating themselves, open to view a scene at which humanity itself may shudder.

The above and within, was read to, considered of, and approved, by upwards of four hundred respectable citizens.

Ordered by them, that the Committee by us appointed, do in our names sign it.

Ordered, That General Forman and Col. Holmes be requested to wait on his excellency, General Washington, with it, and that they do wait his excellency's final determination.

MONMOUTH, April 14, 1782.

John Covenhoven,	Samuel Forman,
Thomas Seabrook,	William Wilcocks,
Peter Forman,	Asher Holmes,
Richard Cox,	Elisha Walton,
Joseph Stillwell,	Stephen Fleming,
Barnes Smock,	John Smock,
John Schanck,	Thomas Chadwick.

Accompanying the address is a copy of the label (elsewhere given) fastened to Huddy's breast. The committee appointed to wait on General Washington, in addition to the foregoing address, furnished him with the affidavits of Aaron White, John North, William Borden and John Russell, in relation to Philip White's case. These have been given in speaking of Philip White. They also furnished the affidavit of Daniel Randolph, a copy of which will begiven hereafter. When General Washington received their papers, he at once transmitted them to the President of Congress, with the following letter:

HEAD QUARTERS,
NEWBURGH, April 20, 1782.

SIR:—The enclosed papers, which I have the honor to transmit to your excellency, contain a state of facts, with their testimonials, respecting the death of Captain Joshua Huddy; who after being a prisoner some days, with the enemy at New York, was sent out with a party of refugees, and most cruelly and wantonly hanged on the heights of Middletown.

This instance of barbarity, in my opinion, calls loudly for retaliation; previous however, to adopting that measure, and for my own justification, in the judgment of an impartial world, I have made a representation by letter, (a copy of which is herein transmitted,) to Sir Henry Clinton, and have demanded from him, the actual perpetrators of this horrid act.

If, by Sir Henry's refusal, I should be driven to an act of retaliation, a British officer of equal rank must atone for the death of the unfortunate Huddy.

Happy, if I find that my resolutions meet the approbation of Congress, I have the honor to be, with the sentiments of sincere respect and esteem, Your Excellency's most obedient, and most humble servant, GEO. WASHINGTON.

His Excellency, the President of Congress.

CAPT. JOSHUA HUDDY, THE HERO MARTYR OF OLD MONMOUTH.

AFFIDAVIT OF DANIEL RANDOLPH ESQ., OF TOMS RIVER.

STATE OF NEW JERSEY, } ss.
  Monmouth County,

Personally appeared before me, David Forman, Esq., Judge of the Court of Common Pleas, of the county aforesaid, Daniel Randolph, Esq., of full age, who, being duly sworn according to law, deposeth and saith, that he, this deponent, did reside at Toms River, in the county aforesaid; that on Saturday night of the 23d of March, they, the inhabitants of Toms River, aforesaid, were informed by Captain Joshua Huddy, then commanding the guard at that post, that he, the aforesaid Captain Joshua Huddy, had information that a body of refugees were approaching to attack that post; that this deponent did join himself to the guard; that just as day began to appear on Sunday morning, Captain Huddy detached a party of his guard to make a discovery, where the enemy were, and to bring him accounts; that as this deponent expects, and believes the guard so sent out, as aforesaid, entirely missed the enemy, for that soon after, viz: before it was yet broad daylight, the enemy appeared in front of their small and unfinished blockhouse, and immediately commenced an attack, without any previous demand of a surrender; that Capt. Huddy, aforesaid, did all that a brave man could do, to defend himself against so superior a number; that after quarters were called for, and the blockhouse surrendered, this deponent saw a negro, one of the refugee party, bayonet Major John Cooke, and he also saw a number of the refugees, as aforesaid, jump into the blockhouse, and heard them say that they would bayonet them, but this deponent did not see the deed done to any other person but Major John Cooke. This deponent further saith, that the same day, viz: Sunday, the 24th day of March, they were carried on board the refugees' boats, and arrived at New York the evening of the same day; that he, this deponent, Capt. Huddy, and the other prisoners, were that night lodged in the main guard at New York; that on Monday morning, the 25th of March, aforesaid, Captain Huddy, this deponent, and the other prisoners, were carried and confined in the sugar house, where they remained close confined, until Monday, the 1st day of April; that on Monday, the 1st day of April, instant, aforesaid, Capt. Huddy, this deponent, and the other prisoners, aforesaid, were removed from the sugar house, aforesaid, to the provost guard at New York, aforesaid, and were there closely confined, until Monday, the 8th of April, instant, when this deponent, Capt. Joshua Huddy, and a certain Jacob Fleming, were taken out of the provost guard, aforesaid, and carried immediately on board a sloop, put down in her hold, and ironed; the aforesaid Joshua Huddy having irons on both feet and both hands And further, this deponent saith, that a certain refugee, called John Tilton, told the aforesaid Capt. Joshua Huddy, that he, the aforesaid Joshua Huddy, was ordered to be hanged; that the aforesaid

Capt. Huddy, then asked the aforesaid John Tilton, what charge was brought against him; that the aforesaid Tilton replied, for that he, the aforesaid Capt. Huddy, had taken a certain Philip White prisoner, and after carrying him, the aforesaid Philip White, six miles up in the country, that he, the aforesaid Capt. Huddy, had cut off both his, (the aforesaid Philip White's,) arms, broke both his, (the aforesaid Philip White's,) legs, pulled out one of the aforesaid Philip White's eyes, and then had damned him, the aforesaid Philip White, and bade him run; that he, the aforesaid Captain Huddy replied, and said, he never had taken Philip White; and moreover said, that it was impossible that he could have taken him, for that he, the aforesaid White was taken and killed, while he, the aforesaid Huddy, was a prisoner closely confined in New York. This deponent further saith, that he, this deponent, so said that the aforesaid White, was taken and killed, while Capt. Huddy was a prisoner, and therefore could not possibly be chargeable; upon which this deponent was told that he, this deponent should be hanged next; further this deponent saith that the aforesaid Capt. Huddy, was frequently charged with the murder of the aforesaid Philip White, in manner and form aforesaid. This deponent saith that he and Capt. Huddy were kept in irons, on board the sloop aforesaid, until they were put on board the guard ship at Sandy Hook, which was done on Tuesday evening, the 9th instant; that on board this guard ship, this deponent, Captain Huddy, and Jacob Fleming, were confined between decks until Friday, the 12th instant; that on Friday, the 12th inst., some men, strangers to this deponent, came between decks and told him, the said Capt. Huddy, to be prepared to be hanged immediately, for having murdered Philip White, as aforesaid, and took off the said Capt. Huddy's irons; that Capt. Huddy again said he was not guilty of having killed the aforesaid White, and should die innocent, and in a good cause; and with uncommon composure of mind and fortitude, prepared himself for his end; that they, then for the first time since the capture of this deponent, and the said Capt. Huddy, took the aforesaid Capt. Huddy from this deponent. That about noon of the same day, the aforesaid John Tilton told this deponent, that he, the aforesaid Capt. Joshua Huddy was hanged, and further said he, that Capt. Hud-

dy died *with the firmness of a lion.* Further, this deponent saith, that the aforesaid Capt. Joshua Huddy was never taken from him, this deponent, until he was taken off to be executed, and that he, the aforesaid Captain Huddy, never was called to any kind of trial, or allowed to make any defence; and lastly, this deponent saith, the corpse of the said Captain Joshua Huddy is now at the house of Capt. James Greene, and that he verily believes he came to his death by being hanged.

DANIEL RANDOLPH.

Sworn before me, this 15th of April, 1782, DAVID FORMAN, Judge of the C't of C. P.

A COUNCIL OF WAR.

The execution of Huddy was regarded by the Commander-in-Chief as a matter of such high import, that, in anticipation of the action of Congress upon his letter, he had directed that the general officers of the army, and the officers commanding brigades and regiments, should assemble at West Point, and decide on what measures should be adopted. On the 19th day of April, the meeting was held at the quarters of General Heath, when the following questions propounded by Washington were stated:

"Shall there be retaliation for the murder of Huddy?"

"On whom shall it be inflicted?"

"How shall the victim be designated!"

General Heath in his Memoirs describes the deliberations of the officers as independent of each other; no conversation was permitted between them on the question submitted, but each one was to write his own opinion, seal it up, and address it to the Commander-in-Chief. By this process, it was found the decision was unanimous that retaliation should take place; that it should be inflicted on an officer of equal rank; and the designation should be made by lot from among the prisoners of war who had surrendered at discretion, and not under convention or capitulation

This decision was approved by Washington, who gave immediate information of his intention to retaliate, to the British Cammander, unless the perpetrator of the bloody deed should be given up for execution.

No farther action for a time was taken, that Sir Henry Clinton might have opportunity to decide upon Washington's demand.

In the meantime occurred the following proceedings in Congress.

PROCEEDINGS IN CONGRESS, April, 1782.

The letter of General Washington to Congress, when received, was referred to a Committee consisting of Mr. Boudinot, Mr. Scott and Mr. Bee. The committee reported on the 20th day of April, 1782, and the following proceedings were then had:

A letter of the 20th, from the Commander-in-Chief, was read together with a memorial from the inhabitants of the county of Monmouth, in the State of New Jersey, and sundry affidavits, respecting the death of Capt. Joshua Huddy, who after being a prisoner some days with the enemy in New York, was sent out by a party of refugees, and was most cruelly and wantonly hanged on the heights of Middletown.

These papers being committed, and the committee having reported thereon:

Resolved, That Congress having deliberately considered the matter and the paper attending it, and being deeply impressed with the necessity of convincing the enemies of these United States, by the most decided conduct, that the repetition of their unprecedented and inhuman cruelties, so contrary to the laws of nations and of war, will no longer be suffered with impunity, do unanimously approve of the firm and judicious conduct of the Commander-in-Chief in his application to the British Gen. of New York; and do hereby assure him, of their firmest support in his fixed purpose of exemplary retaliation.

GENERAL WASHINGTON to SIR HENRY CLINTON.

HEAD-QUARTERS,
April 21st, 1782.

SIR:—The enclosed representation from the inhabitants of the county of Monmouth, with testimonials to the facts, (which can be corroborated by other unquestionable evidence,) will bring before your excellency, the most wanton, unprecedented, and inhuman murder that ever disgraced the arms of a civilized people.

I shall not, because I conceive it altogether unnecessary, trouble your excellency with any animadversions upon this transaction. Candor obliges me to be explicit. To save the innocent, I demand the guilty. Capt. Lippencott therefore, or the officer who commanded, at the execution of Captain Huddy, must be given up; or if that officer was of inferior rank to him, so many of the perpetrators as will, according to the tariff of exchange, be equivalent.

To do this, will mark the justice of your excellency's character; on the failure of it I shall feel myself justifiable in the eyes of God and man, for the measure to which I shall resort.

I beg your excellency to be persuaded, that it cannot be more disagreeable to you to be addressed in this language, than it is for me to offer it; but the subject requires frankness and decision.

I have to request your speedy determination, as my resolution is suspended but for your answer.

I have the honor to be, sir, your excellency's most obedient servant.

GEO. WASHINGTON.

His Excellency, SIR HENRY CLINTON.

Sir Henry Clinton replied to Gen. Washington on the 25th of April. He expressed surprise at the strong language which had been used. He refused to give up the perpetrator of the murder, but informed the American commander, that he had ordered a court martial to examine the charge against Capt. Lippencott before he received the letter. He did not pretend to justify the conduct of the loyalists, and expressed his regret for the fate of the sufferer. On the 1st of May, General Robertson, who had succeeded Clinton, reiterated the same sentiments which had been previously expressed by his predecessor, but still the culprit was protected in New York; and the American commander replied, in the strongest terms, that he had resolved upon retaliation, and given orders that a British officer should be designated to suffer. When Sir Guy Carleton took command of the British forces, in May, he communicated to General Washington his intention to preserve " the name of every Englishman from reproach, and to pursue every measure that might tend to prevent these criminal excesses in individuals." He did not hesitate " to condemn the many unauthorized acts of violence, which had been committed," and concluded that he should do every thing to mitigate the evils of war.— From these extracts, as well as the history of that day, it is evident that the British commander disavowed any participation in the death of Huddy, on the part of the British authorities. And it is said, by Dr. Thatcher, that the British Government were inclined to direct that Lippencott should be given up to Gen. Washington, but were finally prevented by the influence of the American loyalists, (or refugees.)

Baron de Grimm, in his celebrated Memoris, states, without any qualifications, that *George III gave orders " that the author of a crime which dishonored the English nation, should be given up for punishment,"* but he was not obeyed. It is highly probably that this statement is true ; the writer recorded it in 1775, and from the advantageous position he occupied, must be presumed to have known the fact. (vol. iv. p. 272.)

The people of New Jersey were exasperated beyond measure at the bloody catastrophe ; but when it was ascertained that the murderer would not be surrendered or punished, their indignation prompted the bold attempt to seize the miscreant by force. To effect this purpose, Capt. Adam Hyler, of New Brunswick, having ascertained that Lippencott resided in Broad street, New York, with a crew disguised as a British press gang, left the Kills at dark, in a single boat, and arrived at White Hill about nine o'clok. Here he left the boat in charge of a few men, and passed directly to Lippencott's house, where, on inquiry, it was ascertained he had gone to Cock Pit. (Naval Mag. Nov., 1839.) The expedition of course failed ; but the promptness with which it was conducted, proves the devotion of the brave men who were engaged to the common cause, and their execration of Huddy's assassin.

(Capt. Adam Hyler, above referred to, is the one who commanded the barge taken by the British at Toms River. In their accounts they boasted, it will be remembered, of capturing " one of Hyler's barges." We have accounts of a large number of the exploits of Hyler, in the waters around Old Monmouth, which we trust to find room for at some time, for it is rare to find, in fact or fiction, more skilfully planned and fearlessly executed deeds than those performed by Capt. Adam Hyler and his heroic companions.)

CASTING LOTS.

Exciting Scene—Captain Asgill the Victim—Affecting Incidents—Courts of Europe Excited.

The demand for Lippencott having been refused, General Washington, on the 4th of May, directed Brigadier General Hogan to designate by lot, from among the prisoners at either of the posts in Pennsylvania or Maryland, a British Captain who had been unconditionally surrendered ; as it was ascertained that no such officer was in his power, a second order was issued on the thirteenth of May, extending the selection to the officers who had been made prisoners by convention or capitulation.— Under this last despatch, the British Captains, who had been captured at Yorktown, were assembled at Lancaster, Pennsylvania, and the lot fell upon Captain Asgill.

Charles Asgill was a Captain of the guards, of a noble family, and at the time he was designated to suffer, but nineteen years of age. He was captured at Yorktown, confined during the winter of 1781-82 at Winchester, in Virginia, and had been removed but a short time to York, Pennsylvania, when the lot was cast against him. The officers from whom the victim was to be selected, were ordered to Lancaster, and were there informed by General Hogan the object for which they were assembled. Major Morgan, who was the senior British officer at that place, remonstrated, and used the following language :

"These gentlemen form but a small proportion, out of the total number of Captains who became prisoners at Yorktown, and I am sure, if time be afforded, there is not one of their comrades who will not hasten, even from England, for the purpose of placing himself by their side, in so trying an emergency, and staking his life with theirs."

The General, however, replied his orders were peremptory, but feelingly remarked, "when the lot has been declared on whom this blow shall fall, then you may rely upon it that every indulgence shall be shown which you could expect, or my own feelings dictate." The ceremony is minutely described by an eye witness, the late Gen. Graham, Lieutenant Governor of Sterling Castle, whose manuscript is published in the *United Service Journal*, November, 1834. To use his language :

"The excitement of the scene was now over, and we gazed upon poor Asgill with a bitterness and intensity of feeling, such as defied control. He was barely nineteen years of age ; lively, brave, handsome;

an only son, as we all knew, and an especial favorite with his comrades. To see him as we did, at that moment, in the full bloom of youth and beauty, and to know that his days, nay, his hours, were numbered—that was a demand upon the fortitude of those who loved him, such as they could not meet. We lifted up our voices and wept; and while a warm pressure of the hand was exchanged with each in his turn, the object of so much commiseration found it no easy matter, himself, to restrain his tears. Nor, to do them justice, were the Americans, either within or without the house, indifferent spectators to the drama. The Brigadier at once consented to delay the removal of the victim till the following morning; and readily granted a passport to enable an officer to set out on the instant for New York."

Captain Asgill was conducted to Philadelphia, and from thence was removed to Chatham. He was accompanied by his friend, Major Gordon, who attended him with the devotion of a parent to a child.

In the meanwhile the execution was suspended, but every effort was exerted, every plan that ingenuity could devise or sympathy suggest, adopted to save the innocent sufferer. Major Gordon appealed to the French Minister, then in Philadelphia; he wrote to the Count de Rochembeau, and despatched messengers to numerous influential Whigs throughout the Colonies, to interest them in behalf of his friend; and so eloquent and importunate were his appeals, that it is said by General Graham, " that even the family of Captain Huddy became themselves suppliants in Asgill's favor." These untiring exertions, unquestionably contributed to postpone the fate of the victim, until the final and successful intercession of the French Court obtained his release.

When Lady Asgill heard of the peril which impended over her son, her husband was exhausted by disease, and while the effect of the intelligence was pent powerfully up in her mind, it produced delirium in that of her daughter; under all these embarrassments she applied to King George the III, who, it is said, ordered the cause of this measure of retaliation, the wretched Lippencott. to be delivered up, which Clinton contrived to avoid. She did not cease her importunities, until she had dictated the following letter to the Count de Vergennes, who laid it before the King and Queen of France, and was immediately directed to communicate with General Washington, and implore the release of the sufferer. A letter, says the Baron de Grimm, "the eloquence of which, independent of oratorical forms, is that of all people, and all languages, because it derives its power from the first and noblest sentiment of our nature."

LADY ASGILL TO COUNT DE VERGENNES.

Eloquent Pleadings of a Mother for the Life of an only Son.

SIR :—If the politeness of the French court will permit a stranger to address it, it cannot be doubted but that she who unites in herself all the more delicate sensations with which an individual can be penetrated, will be received favorably by a nobleman who reflects honor not only on his nation, but on human nature. The subject on which I implore your assistance is too heart-rending to be dwelt upon; most probably the public report has already reached you. This relieves me from the burden of so mournful a duty. My son, my only son, dear to me as he is brave, amiable as he is beloved, only nineteen years of age, a prisoner of war, in consequence of the capitulation of Yorktown, is at present confined in America as an object of reprisals.

Shall the innocent suffer the fate of the guilty ? Figure to yourself, sir, the situation of a family in these circumstances.—Surrounded as I am with objects of distress, bowed down by fear and grief, words are wanting to express what I feel, and to paint such a scene of misery ; my husband given over by his physicians some hours before the arrival of this news, not in a condition to be informed of it; my daughter attacked by a fever, accompanied with delirium ; speaking of her brother in tones of wildness and without an interval of reason, unless it be to listen to some circumstances which may console her heart. Let your sensibility, sir, paint to you my profound, my inexpressible misery, and plead in my favor. A word—a word from you, like a voice from heaven, would liberate us from desolation, from the last degree of misfortune. I know how far General Washington reverences your character.—Tell him only that you wish my son restored to liberty, and he will restore him to his desponding family; he will restore him to happiness. The virtue and courage of my son will justify this act of clemency. His honor, sir, led him to America; he was born to abundance, to independence, and to the happiest prospects. Permit me once more to entreat the interference of your high influence in favor of innocence, and in the cause of justice, of humanity. Despatch, sir, a letter from France to General Washington, and favor me with a copy of it, that it may be transmitted from hence. I feel the whole weight of the liberty taken in presenting this request; but I feel confident, whether granted or not, that you will pity the distress by which it is suggested; your humanity will drop a tear on my fault and blot it out forever.

May that heaven which I implore, grant that you may never need the consolation which you have it in your power to bestow on THERESA ASGILL.

A NOBLEMAN TELLS ASGILL'S STORY.

Excitement in Holland and throughout Europe—The Gibbet—Asgill thrice conduced to it—Intense anxiety in Europe to hear of his fate, &c.

The statement of Captain Asgill's case would not be complete without the following extract, which contains some interesting facts not elsewhere given. It is from Baron de Grimm, who was led to notice the case on account of its being made the ground work of a tragedy called "Abdir," by de Sauvigny, represented in Paris in January, 1780.

"You can well remember the general interest which Sir —— Asgill inspired, a young officer in the English guards, who was made prisoner and condemned to death by the Americans, in reprisal for the death of Capt. Huddy, who was hanged by order of Capt. Lippencott. The public prints all over Europe resounded with the unhappy catastrophe, which for eight months impended over the life of this young officer. The extreme grief of his mother, the sort of delirium which clouded the mind of his sister, at hearing the dredful fate which menaced the life of her brother, interested every feeling mind in the fate of that unfortunate family. The general curiosity in regard to the events of the war, yielded, if I may say so, to the interest which young Asgill inspired, and the first question asked of all vessels that arrived from any port in North America, was always an inquiry into the fate of that young man. It is known that Asgill was thrice conducted to the foot of the gibbet, and that thrice Gen. Washington, who could not bring himself to commit this crime of policy without a great struggle, suspended his punishment; his humanity and justice made him hope that the English general would deliver over to him the author of the crime Asgil was condemned to expiate. Sir Henry Clinton, either ill advised or insensible to the fate of young Asgill, persisted in refusing to deliver up the barbarous Lippencott. In vain the King of England, at whose feet the unfortunate family fell down, had given orders to surrender up to the Americans the author of a crime which dishonored the English nation : George the 3d, was not obeyed. In vain the State of Holland entreated the United States of America the pardon of the unhappy Asgill. The gibbet, erected in front of his prison, did not cease to offer to his eyes those dreadful preparatives, more awful than death itself. In these circumstances, and almost reduced to despair, the mother of the unfortunate victim bethought herself that the Minister of a King, armed against her own nation, might succeed in obtaining that which was refused to her King. Madam Asgill wrote to the Count de Vergennes a letter, the eloquence of which, independent of oratorical forms, is that of all people and languages, because it derives its power from the first and noblest sentiment of our nature."

For seven months, the fate of this interesting young officer remained suspended, when, cheiefly through the intercession of the French Court, he was set at liberty.— The following are the proceedings of Congress directing his discharge :

THURSDAY, November 7th, 1782.

On the report of the Committee, consisting of Mr. Rutledge, Mr. Osgood, Mr. Montgomery, Mr. Boudinot, and Mr. Duane, to whom were referred the letter of the 19th of August last, from the Commander-in-Chief, the report of a committee thereon, and the motives of Mr. Williamson and Mr. Rutledge; and also, another letter, from the Commander-in-Chief, with a copy of a letter to him from the Count de Vergennes, dated July 29th last, interceeding for Capt. Asgill :

Resolved. That the Commander in-Chief

OLD TIMES IN OLD MONMOUTH.

be, and he hereby is directed, to set Captain Asgill at liberty?"

A copy of the foregoing proceedings and resolutions was forwarded by Gen. Washington to Capt. Asgill, together with a letter, given below, which exhibits the moral excellence, the great and commanding attributes that always distinguished the Father of his Country. "The decision of Gen. Washington in this delicate affair, the deep interest felt by the American people for the youthful sufferer, the pathetic appeals of Lady Asgill to the Count de Vergennes in behalf of her son,*(in the language of Congress, in 1837,) forms one of the most important and instructive portions of revolutionary history."

GENERAL WASHINGTON TO CAPTAIN ASGILL.

SIR:—It affords me singular satisfaction to have it in my power to transmit to you the enclosed copy of an act of Congress of the 7th inst., by which you are relieved from the disagreeable circumstances in which you have been so long. Supposing that you would wish to go to New York as soon as possible, I also enclose a passport for that purpose. Your letter of the 18th came regularly to my hands. I beg of you to believe that my not answering it sooner did not proceed from inattention to you, or a want of feeling for your situation; but I daily expected a determination of your case and I thought it better to await that, than to feed you with hopes that might in the end prove fruitless. You will attribute my detention of the enclosed letters, which have been in my possession a fortnight, to the same cause. I cannot take leave of you, sir, without assuring you that, in whatever light my agency in this unpleasant affair may be viewed, I was never influenced throughout the whole of it by sanguinary motives, but what I conceived to be a sense of duty, which loudly called upon me to use measures, however disagreeable, to prevent a repetition of those enormities which have been the subject of discussion; and that this important end is likely to be answered without the effusion of the blood of an innocent person, is not a greater relief to you that it is to me.

Sir, &c.   GEORGE WASHINGTON.

Immediately after this letter released him, Captain Asgill prepared himself to return to England, and in a short time embarked. The following letters from his mother exhibit a tone of high-wrought gratitude that was worthy of her exalted spirit:

Second Letter of Lady Asgill to Count de Vergennes—Outpourings of a Grateful Heart.

Exhausted by long suffering, overpowered by an excess of unexpected happiness, confined to my bed by weakness and languor, bent to the earth by what I have undergone, my sensibility alone could supply me with strength sufficient to address you.

Condescend, sir, to accept this feeble effort of my gratitude. It has been laid at the feet of the Almighty; and believe me, it has been presented with the same sincerity to you, sir, and to your illustrious sovereigns. By their august and salutary intervention, as by your own, a son is restored to me, to whom my whole life was attached. I have the sweet assurance that my vows for my protectors are heard by the Heaven to whom they are ardently offered. Yes, sir; they will produce their effect before the dreadful and last tribunal, where I indulge in the hope that we shall both meet together—you to receive the recompense of your virtues; myself, that of my sufferings. I will raise my voice to that imposing tribunal; I will call for those sacred registers in which your humanity will be found recorded—I will pray that blessings may be showered on your head—upon him, who, availing himself of the noblest privileges received from God—a privilege no other than divine—has changed misery into happiness, has withdrawn the sword from the innocent head, and restored the worthiest of sons to the most tender and unfortunate of mothers.

Condescend, sir, to accept this just tribute of gratitude due to your virtuous sentiments. Preserve this tribute, and may it go down to your posterity as a testimony of your sublime and exemplary beneficence to a stranger, whose nation was at war with your own, but whose tender affections had not been destroyed by war. May this tribute bear testimony to my gratitude, long after the hand which expresses it with the heart, which at this moment only vibrates with the vivacity of grateful sentiments, shall be reduced to dust; even to the last day of my existence, it shall beat but to offer you all the respect and all the gratitude with which it is penetrated.   THERESA ASGILL.

LADY ASGILL TO MAJOR GORDON.

A Grateful Mother to a True and Tried Friend of her Son.

Sir :—If distress like mine has left any expression but for grief, I should long since addressed myself to you, for whom my sense of gratitude makes all acknowledgments poor indeed. Nor is this the first attempt; but you were too near the object of my anguish to enter into the heart-piercing subject. I constantly prayed to Heaven that he might not add to his sufferings the knowledge of ours. He had too much to feel on his own account, and I could not have concealed the direful effect of his misfortune on his family, to whom he is as dear as he is worthy to be so. Unfit as I am at this time, by joy almost as insupportable as the agony before, yet sir, accept this weak effort from a heart deeply affected by your humanity and exalted conduct, as Heaven knows it has been torn by affliction. Believe me, sir, it will only cease to think in the last moments of life, with the most grateful, affectionate, and respectful sentiments to you. But a fortnight since, I was sinking under a wretchedness I could no longer struggle with. Hope, resignation, had almost forsaken me. I began to experience the greatest of all misfortunes—that of being no longer able to bear them.—Judge, sir, the transition the day after the blessed change takes place. My son is released; recovered; returned; arrived at my gate; in my arms. I see him unsubdued in spirits, in health; unreproached by himself, approved by his country in; the bosom of his family, and without anxiety, but for the happiness of his friend; without regret, but for having left him behind. Your humane feelings that have dictated your conduct to him, injured and innocent as he was, surely will participate in our relief and joy. Be that pleasure yours, sir, as well as every other blessing that virtue like yours and Heaven can bestow. This prayer is offered up for you in the heart of transport, as it was in the bitterness of my anguish. My gratitude has been soothed by the energy it has been offered with. It has ascended to the throne of mercy and is, I trust, accepted. Unfit as I am, for nothing but susceptibility so awakened as mine could enable me to write; and exhausted by too long anxiety; confined at this time to a bed of sickness and languor—yet I could not suffer another interval to pass, without this weak effort. Let it convey to you sir, the most heartfelt gratitude of my husband and daughters. You have the respect and esteem of all Europe, as an honor to your country and to human nature, and the most zealous friendship of, my dear and worthy Major Gordon,

Your affectionate and obliged servant,
Theresa Asgill.

The fate of Captain Asgill, while it was suspended in doubt, "filled the public prints all over Europe with anxious wishes for his release;" and in the year 1785, when the excitement of a former period had subsided, the story of this intended reprisal was made the groundwork of a tragic drama by the celebrated French writer, M. de Sauvigny; while in Anderson's History of the American War, published immediately after the peace, the author has deemed the incidents so memorable, that he has given a portrait of the young Asgill in the costume of the day.

While Captain Asgill's fate was in doubt, the British instituted a court martial to try Captain Lippencott, who was supposed to be the principal agent in the murder of Huddy. It will be seen, by extracts from the evidence of witnesses, hereafter given, that Governor Franklin, the President of the Board of Associated Royalists, gave verbal orders for the execution of Huddy, and that he afterwards basely endeavored to throw the whole blame on Lippencott. When Franklin gave the verbal orders, he designated Huddy as a proper subject for retaliation, as he said Huddy had been a chief prosecutor of refugees, and particularly instrumental in hanging Stephen Edwards, the refugee spy. The decision of the court will be given hereafter. It cleared Lippencott—perhaps justly. If so, Gov. William Franklin should have been hanged for Huddy's murder. Sir Guy Carleton, who was the British commander at New York, when Lippencott was acquitted, appeared disposed to do justly, and assured Washington, " that notwithstanding the acquittal of Lippencott, he reprobated the measure, and gave assurance of prosecuting a further inquiry."—Thanks to Sir Guy, he broke up this Board of Associated Royalists The war was about closing, and the necessities for retaliation about over ; and hence the request of the King and Queen of France, through Count Vergennes, for the release of Asgill, were favorably received.

OLD TIMES IN OLD MONMOUTH. 87

PETITION TO CONGRESS OF MARTHA PIATT, DAUGHTER OF CAPTAIN JOSHUA HUDDY, PRESENTED DECEMBER 21ST, 1836.

To the Congress of the United States :— Your Momorialist, Martha Piatt, now residing in Cincinnati, State of Ohio, Respectfully represents :

That she is the only surviving child of Captain Joshua Huddy, who was inhumanly put to death by a party of tories under the immediate command of Captain Lipencott, in the month of April, 1782.

Her deceased father, ever ready at the call of his country, had for from the commencement of the revolutionary war, from his devotion to the cause of liberty, become obnoxious to the enemy. He was made a prisoner of war by the refugees, in March, 1872, while he commanded a blockhouse in Monmouth county. N. J.: having defended that post with great bravery, until his ammunition was entirely expended. He was then taken to New York, and detained in close confinement for two or three weeks, when, without form of trial, he was told that he was ordered to be hanged. In pursuance of this resolution, he was carried over to the New Jersey shore, and executed, in a manner so barbarous, that the annals of savage warfare do not present an instance of human sacrifice more wantonly cruel.

This act, so dishonorable to the British character, (for Sir Henry Clinton, the Commander-in-Chief, refused to give up the perpetrator of the crime), was not less disastrous to the family of the lamented patriot, who was not permitted to die a soldiers' death, much less to enjoy the last kind offices of those dear to him by the strongest earthly ties. The first intelligence they received of his decease, was that he had perished on the scaffold. His widow left desolate, with two daughters of tender age, in common with the high-souled females of the revolution, trusted in Providence, and hoped that the country for which her husband's life had been sacrificed, would not forget her or her children.

The subject of Captain Huddy's murder, (for such is the appropriate name it deserves,) was referred to the American Congress by Gen. Washington, and the mode of retaliation he adopted unanimously approved by that body ; and the people of New Jersey, roused by the bloody deed to vengeance, addressed a spirit-stirring memorial to the Commander-in-Chief, detailing the facts, and requiring exemplary as well as summary retribution at his hand. While in obedience to these claims, a British officer was selected by lot, as the victim of retaliation, and while the melancholy interest which youth and innocence associated with the name of Captain Asgill, excited the deep sympathy of the American people ; while the heart-rending appeal of his noble mother to the Count de Vergennes in behalf of her devoted son, induced the mediation of the French Court to effect his release ; the name and fate of Capt. Huddy are only remembered as among the many instances of cruelty incident to a state of war. And the widow and the children of that martyred hero, have been left hitherto without the least token of the gratitude of their country.

Your petitioner appeals to the Justice of Congress. She is now seventy years of age: her mother is dead, and her sister also; she alone survives to feel anew the horrors of that dreadful moment, when she was told that she was fatherless, and that her gallant sire met the death of a malefactor ; while his only crime was his ardent attachment to the cause of American liberty. The gratitude of the country has been long deferred, and though late, your petitioner asks, that in common with the representatives of her deceased sister, she may be allowed such sum in money, and such quantities of land as her father would have been entitled to, had he served until the conclusion of the revolutionary war.

She commits her appeal to Congress in the full assurance that her claim will not be disregarded. And as in duty bound, &c.
MARTHA PIATT.

This petition was presented to Congress December 21st, 1836, and referred to a special committee, consisting of Mr. Storer, of Ohio; Mr. Buchanan, of Penn.; Mr. Hardan, of Ky.; Mr. Elmore, of S. C.; and Mr. Schenck, of N. J., in February following, reported a bill extending to the heirs of Captain Huddy the benefits of existing pension laws, the same as if he had been in the regular army, and also granting them six hundred acres of land, and also paying the sum of twelve hundred dollars, being the sum due Captain Huddy for seven years' service as Captain of Artillery.

The report of this committee, adopted by Congress February 14, 1837, is so ably written, and contains such vivid pictures of Old Monmouth during the war, and of Captain Huddy's services and sacrifices that it is well worth perusal and preservation, and we therefore append so much of it as has not already been quoted.

REPORT ADOPTED BY CONGRESS, IN RELATION TO PETITION OF MARTHA PIATT.

Huddy's services appreciated by Congress—Graphic picture of affairs in Old Monmouth ;—Is the nation grateful ?—Eloquent extracts.

The memorialist is the only surviving daughter of Captain Jushua Huddy of New Jersey, who was a soldier of the war of the revolution. Her father in 1776, was an officer in the militia of his native state, and in the autumn of 1777, was appointed by the Legislature to command a company of artillery, who were enlisted for twelve months. In 1779, he was engaged in the same duty; and in 1781, the people of Monmouth County, having recommeded him for the purpose, he was selected to command the post at Toms River. While gallantly defending himself against a superior force, he was there taken prisoner in 1782. and reserved for an ign minious death on the scaffold.

The tours of duty thus detailed, are extracted from official records, as will appear by papers attached to this report; but the history of the whole war in that region, if it should be minutely described, was a series of bold and hazardous efforts to sustain the cause of liberty ; in all which Capt. Huddy was eminently conspicuous. Brave, patriotic and persevering, he perilled his property and his life for his country, and at last perished in her defence.

Perhaps the annals of the civilized world do not present a more melancholy spectacle than was exhibited in New Jersey, while the British army occupied the city of New York. The people were all a arms, their substance wasted by the enemy, their farms untilled their families, dispersed. In addition to the constant and harassing inroads of the British, there was a fhe within her very borders more watchful and more relentless than the common enemy. Traitors to American liberty filled the land, willing to sacrifice their former friends to gratify their malignant passions, or to prove their loyalty to their King.— These men combined together for the avowed object of murder and plunder, were to be met at all points ; and it required the utmost energy, activity and address to oppose them. Their movements were sudden, and from their intimate knowledge of the country their march was often unknown until their object had been effected. Hence, the most untiring vigilance was required to counteract their plans ; and Capt. Huddy became so zealously engaged as a partizan leader, that he was more obnoxious to the tories that any individual in the American service. To these desperate men, it was then all important that one whom they so much dreaded should be deprived of power to oppose them and no means were left unattempted to effect their purpose.

(The report here proceeds to give an account of Capt. Huddy's capture, imprisonment and execution, which we have given elsewhere, after which it says:)

The documents which the committee have annexed to the report, minutely describe the horrid tragedy, and they forbear to sta e here the incidents which are there recorded in the language of eye witnesses. There is something so 'revolting in the mode a brave soldier was doomed to die : something so fiendlike in the haste to sacrifice him without the parting farewell of his friends and the consolations of religion that no age however barbarous can furnish a stronger instance of refined, deliberate cruelty. Yet, even here, the devoted sufferer sustained his high reputation for moral firmness and heroic devotion to liberty. Mr. Randolph testifies that when the refugees were taking the irons from Capt. Huddy, to conduct him to the gallows, the brave man said that he should die innocent, and in a good cause ; and with uncommon composure and fortitude, prepared himself for his end.' And to use the language of one who assisted at the execution, 'he met his fate with all the firmness of a lion.' His executioner was a negro.

The immediate agent in this deed of blood, was Richard Lippencott, a native of New Jersey, and then a Captain in the British service ; he was the instrument of a board of associated loyalists in New York, at the head of which was William Franklin, once the royal Governor of New Jersey, and Sampson S. Blowers, formerly of Boston, Secretary. The members of this board, after the murder had taken place, endeavored for a time to deny that they had directed it; but the evidence adduced on the trial of the perpetrator as well as on the subsequent publications of the loyalists themselves, abundantly prove that without the courage to act themselves they had the baseness to authorize the deed to be committed and the meanness to attempt the concealment of their privity to its perpetration.

Immediately after the murder, the people of Monmouth assembled and addressed to General Washington the spirit-stirring and eloquent memorial which he afterwards communicated to Congress, with the memorable correspondence which he held on the same subject with Sir Henry Clinton. These documents the committee annex, and would recommend their persual, not only as an authentic narrative of facts, (which are but little known at the present day,) but as proud examples of the lofty patriotism which distinguished the men of the revolution.

(The committee here recite Washington's measures for retaliation, and the action of the Congress of 1782, given else where, and then continue as follows :)

It is painful to state that after a lapse of fifty years, while the story of Asgill's captivity has been made the theme of the biographer and poet, the memory of the murdered Huddy has not been honored with an epitaph. His country it would seem, has outlived the recollection of his services and forgotten that such a victim was sacrificed for American liberty. The resolution of Congress, adopted on the day subsequent to the discharge of Asgill, and which required that, "the British commander should be called to fulfil his engagement to make further inquisition into the murder of Capt. Huddy and to pursue it with all the effect that a due regard of justice will admit," is yet unfulfilled and unrequited; and the only memorial in the public journals of America, gratitude for the services of the living and the character of the dead are resolutions of retaliation—none of sympathy or condolence.

The committee in the consideration of the case, cannot account for the silence of an American Congress upon a claim like this present which the history of the revolution so amply established. It is true, his representatives have made no appeal until they offered their memorial at this session, but it is believed the principles of natural justice are independent of all such agency. If their modesty has hitherto deterred them, it is at least the gratifying evidence that there is an American family who have forborne to remind the Legislature of the nation of its high duties and are contended to await the judgment of their countrymen, however tardy may have been its annoucement.

The children of Captain Huddy were both females, and were left at an early age to their mother's protection. She struggled as did the highsouled women of the revolution with the ordinary vicissitudes of war, and sustained herself by the prospect of future independence. When her gallant husband was in the field, she knew he was engaged in a holy cause and prepared herself for whatever result might occur; bus when she found that she was left desoente and the father of her children had been cruelly and wantonly murdered, she thenceforward lived but for them.— These orphans after the return of peace were married: one of them with her mother is dead; the survivor, who is the memorialist, at the advanced age of seventy years, now resides in the west and asks, ere she joins those who have already departed, that the sufferings of her father might be remembered and his services, even at this late day, requited by some token of national gratitude.

As Captain Huddy was not in the regular army there is no one of the resolutions of the old Congress that would include this case, were it a claim for military service merely. But when it is considered that he was actively engaged from 1776 until 1782 in a most hazardous and important duty, at a time when ordinary zeal would have become cold and ordinary courage crushed, when they regard his expose, his position and his untimely death, the committee can not but conclude that the spirit of these resolutions should be extended to your memorialist; and if there is such an attribute as national gratitude, it should now be exerted.

The committee report the following resolutions for the consideration of the House :

Resolved, That the Congress of the United States hold in high estimation and grateful remembrance the service of Captain Joshua Huddy, of New Jersey, in the war of the revolution, and unites in the opinion of the Continental Congress of 1782, that he was wantonly and inhumanly sacrificed by the enemy while in the heroic discharge of his duty.

Resolved, That in consideration of the services rendered to his country by Captain Joshua Huddy, and in the performance of which he was taken prisoner and afteawards executed for no other crime than his devotion to liberty, it is the duty of Congress to appropriate to his children the same sums they would have received had their father been a continental officer and had continued in the service until the close of the war; and the whole benefit of the resolutions of September 19th, 1777, and August 24th, 1780, be extended to them.

To carry which resolutions into effect, your committee report a bill.

(The substance of this bill has already been given.)

CAPTAIN ASGILL AND HIS COMPANIONS.

Humorous Account of a Serious Affair.

In speaking of casting lots among British officers for the purpose of retaliation for the murder of Captain Joshua Huddy, extracts were quoted from British writers who endeavored to make out that Captain Asgill's companions acted very unselfishly and generously towards him, but by the following extract it will be seen that their conduct was nothing to boast of. It is from James Smith, one of the authors of that celebrated work "Rejected Address." Smith occasionally used to visit Colonel Greville, once a somewhat noted character in connection with several literary journals. On one visit the Colonel related the particulars of what he termed the most curious circumstance of his life. He was taken prisoner during the American Revolution along with three other officers of the same rank; one evening they were summoned into the presence of General Washington, who announced to them that the conduct of the British government in condemning one of his officers (Cap'ain Huddy) to death as a rebel compelled him to make reprisals; and that much to his regret he was under the necessity of requiring them to cast lots without delay, to decide which of them should be hanged. They were then bowed out and returned to their quarters. Four slips of paper were put into a hat and the shortest was drawn by Captain Asgill, who exclaimed "I knew how it would be, I never won so much as a hit at backgammon in my life." Greville said he then was selected to set up with Captain Asgill, under pretext of companionship, but in reality to prevent Asgill from escaping and leaving the honor of being hang'd to be settled between the remaining three!

"And what," said Smith, "d d you say to comfort him?"

"Why I remember saying to him, when he left us, D—n it, old fellow, never mind;" but it may be doubted, added Smith, whether Asgill drew much comfort from the exhortation

This Colonel Greville was the one upon whom Lord Byron has conferred a not very enviable notoriety in the following lines:

"Or had at once the patron and the pile
Of vice and folly, Greville and Argyle."
—Law Quarterly Magazine London.

THE REMARKABLE TRIAL OF REV. WILLIAM TENNENT FOR PERJURY.

The remarkable trial of Rev. William Tennent, of the old Tennent church, for perjury, took place at Trenton in 1742 before Chief Justice Robert Hunter Morris.

The indictment upon which Mr. Tennent was tried was one of a series of indictments all growing out of the same transaction—the alleged stealing of a horse by the Rev Mr. Rowland; and the individual who was the cause of all the woes and perils which befel the unfortunate gentlemen who were supposed to be implicated, was a notorious scoundrel named Tom Bell, whose exploits would not suff r by a comparison with those of Jonathan Wild or Jack Sheppard. He was an adept in all the arts of fraud, theft, robbery and forgery. But his chief amusement consisted in travelling from one part of the country to another personating different individuals and assuming a variety of characters.— By turns he was a sailor, a merchant, a lawyer, a doctor, a preacher, and sustained each cha act r in such a way for a time as to impose on the public. The late Judge Richard S. Field, in a paper read before the N. J. Historical Society in 1851, reviewing the reports of this remarkable trial, furnished qu te a list of the misdeeds o this villain.

By far the most briliant of all Tom Bell's achievements was unquestionably that out of which grew the indictment of Rev. William Tennent for perjury. It so happened that Bell bore a striking resemblance to the Rev. Mr. Rowland, a popular preacher of the day, and a friend and associate of Whitfield and the Tennents.

OLD TIMES IN OLD MONMOUTH.

One evening Bell made his appearance at a tavern in Princeton dressed in a dark grey coat. He there met John Stockton, Esq., father of Richard Stockton, a signer of the Declaration of Independence, who coming up to him at one accosted him as the Rev. Mr. Rowland and invited him to his house. Bell assured him that he was mistaken—that his name was not Rowland. Mr. Stockton acknowledged his error and told him it proceeded from the very close resemblance he bore to that gentleman. This link was enough for Tom Bell. It at once occurred to him that here was a chance for playing one of his tricks. The very next day he went into what was then the county of Hunterdon and stopped at a place where the Rev. Mr. Rowland had occasionally preached, but where he was not well known. Here he introduced himself as Mr. Rowland, was invited to the house of a gentleman in the neighborhood, and asked to preach on the following Sabbath. He consented to do so, and notice to that effect was accordingly given. When the day arrived he accompanied the ladies to church in the family wagon while the master rode alongside, on a very fine horse. As they approached the church, Bell suddenly discovered that he had left his notes behind him and proposed riding back after them on the fine horse. This was at once agreed to and Bell mounted the horse, rode back to the house, rifled the desk of his host and took his departure, leaving the assembled congregation to wonder what had become of the Rev. Mr. Rowland.

We may imagine the satisfaction which Bell must have derived from this exploit. Mr. Rowland was a noted preacher of great pungency and power, and thundered the terrors of the law against all impenitent sinners. He was called by the professed wits of the day "Hell Fire Rowland." He was literally a terror to evil doers, and therefore it may be presumed an object of peculiar aversion to Tom Bell. The idea then of bringing such a man into disgrace and at the same time of pursuing his favorite occupation must have been doubly pleasing to him.

Rev. Mr. Rowland was at this time absent from New Jersey. He had gone for the purpose of preaching in Pennsylvania or Maryland in company with Rev. Wm. Tennent and two pious laymen of the county of Hunterdon by the names of Joshua Anderson and Benjamin Stevens, members of a church contiguous to the one at which Tom Bell proposed to officiate. As soon as they returned Mr. Rowladd was charged with the robbery of the horse. At the next term of Oyer and Terminer for Hunterdon county an indictment was preferred against him.

Great was the excitement produced by this event, owing in part to the peculiar state of the Colony at the time. Through the labors of Mr. Whitfield and his associates, among whom were Messrs. Tennent and Rowland, a great revival of religion had taken place in the Provinces. But there was a party in the Colony who were very hostile to this religious movement, who denounced its authors as fanatics and enthusiasts, and some of whom did not hesitate to brand them as hypocrites and imposters. Conspicuous among this party was the Chief Justice, Robert H. Morris, who whatever claim he may have had to respect, was certainly not distinguished either for religion or morality. To such men this charge against Mr. Rowland, one of the preachers who were turning everything upside down, was of course occasion of great triumph and rejoicing, and the most strenuous efforts made to procure his conviction. The grand jury at first refused to find a bill against him, but they were reproved by the Court and sent out again. They again returned without an indictment but the Court sent them out a second time with threats of punishment if they persisted in their refusal, and then they consented to find a true bill.

Thus Mr. Rowland was subjected to the ignominy of a trial. A clear case was made out on the part of the prosecution. A large number of witnesses swore positively that he was the identical person who had committed the robbery. On the other hand, the defendants called as witnesses, Messrs. Tennent, Anderson and Stevens, who testified that on the very day on which the robbery was committed they were in company with Mr. Rowland at some place in Pennsylvania or Maryland, and heard him preach. An alibi being thus clearly proved, the jury without hesitation acquitted him.

But still the public mind was not satisfied. The person whose horse had been stolen and whose house had been robbed was so convinced that Mr. Rowland was the robber, and so many individuals had, as they supposed, seen him in possession of the horse that it was resolved not to let the matter drop. Messrs. Tennent, Anderson and Stevens were therefore arraigned before the Court of Quarter Sessions, of Hunterdon, upon the charge of having sworn falsely upon the trial of Mr. Rowland, and indictments were found against each of them for perjury. These indictments were all removed to the Supreme Court. Anderson, conscious of his innocence and unwilling to be under the imputation of such a crime, demanded his trial at the next term of Oyer and Terminer. What evidence he offered in his defence does not appear, but he was convicted and condemned to stand one hour on the Court House steps with a paper on his breast whereon was written in large letters, " *This is for wilful and corrupt perjury.*" The trials of Tennent and Stevens were postponed.

Tennent, we are told, being entirely unused to legal matters and knowing no person by whom he could prove his innocence, had no other resource but to submit himself to Divine will, and thinking it not unlikely that he might be convicted, had prepared a sermon to preach from the pillory. True he employed Mr. John Coxe, an eminent lawyer of the Province to assist, and when he arrived at Trenton he found that William Smith one of the most distinguished members of the New York bar, who had voluntarily attended on his behalf; and Mr. Tennent's brother Gilbert who was then pastor of a church in Philadelphia, had brought with him Mr. John Kinsey, an eminent lawyer of that city, to aid in his defence. But what could they do without evidence? When Mr. Tennent was desired by his counsel to call on his witnesses that they might examine them before going into Court, he declared he knew no witnesses but God and his conscience. His counsel assured him, that however well founded this confidence might be, and however important before a heavenly tribunal, it would not avail him in an earthly court. And they therefore urged that an application should be made to postpone the trial. But this he would by no means consent to. They then informed him they had discovered a flaw in the indictment and proposed that advantage should be taken of it. (Mr. Stevens took advantage of this flaw and was cleared.) Mr. Tennent resisted with great vehemence saying it was another snare of the devil, and before he would consent to it he would suffer death. In the meantime the bell summoned them to the Court. While on the way to the Court House Mr. Tennent is said to have met a man and his wife who stopped and asked if his name was Tennent. He said it was and begged to know if they had any business with him. They replied " You know best." They then informed him that they resided in a certain place in Pennsylvania or Maryland, and that upon one occasion he in company with Rowland, Anderson and Stevens, had lodged at their house; that on the following day they had heard him and Rowland preach; that some nights before they left home, they had each of them dreamed that Mr. Tennent was at Trenton in the greatest possible distress, and that it was in their power, and in theirs alone to relieve him; that this dream was twice repeated and in precisely the same manner to each of them, and that it made so deep an impression on their minds that they had at once set off upon a journey to Trenton, and were there to know of him what they were to do. Mr. Tennent handed them over to his counsel, who to their astonishment found that their testimony was entirely satisfactory. Soon after, Mr. John Stockton, who mistook Tom Bell for Rev. Mr. Rowland, also appeared and was examined as a witness for Mr. Tennent. In short the evidence was so clear and conclusive, that notwithstanding the most strenuous exertion of the Attorney General to procure a conviction, the jury without hesitation acquitted Mr. Tennent.

MEMBERS OF THE NEW JERSEY PROVINCIAL ASSEMBLY FROM MONMOUTH COUNTY.

FROM THEIR FIRST SESSION BEGAN NOVEMBER 10th, 1703, AT PERTH AMBOY, TO THE REVOLUTION.

In the list of members of the Assembly, or " House of Representatives of the Province of Nova Cesarea or New Jersey," from 1703 to 1709, during which time there were four sessions, the names of the counties to which they severally belonged are not given. The records simply mention that they are from East or West Jersey as the case may be. Among the members from East Jersey it is probable that the following are from Monmouth County:

1st Assembly,	1703,	Obadiah Bowne, Rich'd Hartshorne,	
2d	"	1704,	{ Richard Hartshorne, John Bowne. { Richard Salter, Obadiah Bowne.
3d	"	1707,	{ John Bowne, William Lawrence, { Lewis Morris.
4th	"	1708-9, Gershom Mott, Elisha Lawrence.	

After this session the names of the counties to which the members belonged are given.

5th Assembly, 1709, Elisha Lawrence, Gershom Mott.
6th " 1710, Gershom Mott, William Lawrence.
7th " 1716, William Lawrence, Elisha Lawrence.
8th " 1721, William Lawrence, Garret Schenck.
9th " 1727, John Eaton, James Grover.
10th " 1730, John Eaton, James Grover.
11th " 1738, John Eaton, Cornelius Vandervere.
12th " 1740, John Eaton, Cornelius Vandervere.
13th " 1743, John Eaton, Robert Lawrence.
14th " 1744, John Eaton, Robert Lawrence.
15th " 1745, John Eaton, Robert Lawrence.
16th " 1746, John Eaton, Robert Lawrence.
17th " 1749, John Eaton, Robert Lawrence.
18th " 1751, Robert Lawrence, James Holmes.
19th " 1754, Robert Lawrence, James Holmes.
20th " 1761, James Holmef,* Richard Lawrence.
21st " 1769, Robert Hartshorne, Edward Taylor.
23d " 1772, Edward Taylor, Richard Lawrence.

Robert Lawrence was speaker of the Assembly in 1746-7, and again from 1754-1758.

THE PROVINCIAL CONGRESS OF NEW JERSEY.

The delegates appointed by the several counties to take action in regard to the tyrannical acts of Great Britain, assembled at New Brunswick, July 21st, 1774, and continued in session three days. Seventy-two delegates were present. The following had been elected from Monmouth county by a meeting held at Freehold Court House, July 19th, viz:

Edward Taylor, John Anderson, John Taylor.
James Grover, John Lawrence, Dr. Nath'l Scudder.
John Burrowes, Joseph Holmes, Josiah Holmes
Edward Willlams.

Edward Taylor was appointed chairman of the delegation. The Provincial Congress elected Stephen Crane, of Essex, Chairman, and Jonathian D. Sargent, of Somerset, clerk. Resolutions were passed similar in character to those adopted by the Monmouth meeting, recently published.

* James Holmes died and John Arderson was chosen in his place.

WASHINGTON AND LEE AT THE BATTLE OF MONMOUTH.

In the battle of Monmouth when Major General Charles Lee had very nearly lost the day by ordering a retreat, it is related by Irving that Washington "galloped forward to stop the retreat, his indignation kindling as he rode." "The commander-in-chief soon encountered Lee approaching with the body of his command in full retreat." "By this time" says Irving he was thoroughly exasperated.

" What is the meaning of this sir?' demanded he, in the sternest and even fiercest tone as Lee rode up to him. Lee, stung by the manner more than by the words of demand, made an angry reply and provoked still sharper expressions which are variously reported.

The "variously reported" expressions are the swearing, concerning the quality of which all the great historians including Irving are silent.

WHAT LAFAYETTE SAID

But the Marquis de Lafayette, when relating the circumstance to Governor Tompkins, of New York, in 1824, said that" this was the only time I ever heard General Washington swear. He called Lee a damned poltroon, and was in a towering rage. Another witness said that Washington cried to Lee " In the devil's name, sir, go back to the front or go to hell."

A PROFANE VIRGINIAN'S VERSION.

The late General Charles Scott, of Virginia, who had himself a most inveterate habit of swearing, being asked, after the Revolutionary war, whether it was possible that the beloved and admired Washington ever swore, replied in his inimitable way:

"Yes sir, he did once. It was at Monmouth and on a day that would have made any man swear. Yes sir, he swore that day Till the leaves shook in the trees, charming, delightful. Never have I enjoyed such swearing before or since. Sir, on that memorable day he swore like an angel from heaven!"

The foregoing would seem to justify General Lee's statement on his Court Martial trial, that he was " disconcerted, astonished and confounded " by Washington's words and manner.

WEEMS' ACCOUNT OF THE AFFAIR.

Says Weems, in his life of Washington:
" As Washington was advancing, to his infinite astonishment he met Lee retreating and the enemy pursuing.
' For God's sake, General Lee,' said Washington, in great warmth, 'what is the cause of this ill timed prudence?'
' No man sir,' replied Lee, ' can boast a larger portion of that rascally virtue than your Excellency.'
Darting along like a madman, Washington rode up to his troops, who at sight of him rent the air with " God save great Washington."

"My brave fellows can you fight?" said he.

They answered with three cheers.

"Then face about, my heroes, and charge!"

This order was executed with infinite spirit.

REV. C. W. UPHAM'S ACCOUNT.

Upham in his life of Washington says: "When General Washington met Lee retreating at the battle of Monmouth he was so exasperated as to lose control of his feelings for a moment and in his anger and indignation burst forth in violent expressions of language and manner.— Very harsh words were exchanged between him and Lee and a sharp correspondence ensued, which resulted in Washington's putting Lee under arrest. He was tried by Court Martial, convicted of disobedience of orders, of misbehavior before the enemy in making an unnecessary and disorderly retreat, and of disrespect to the Commander-in-Chief in the letters subsequently addressed to him, and sentenced to be suspended for one year,"

AN OLD CITIZEN OF MONMOUTH TELLS THE STORY.

The late Dr. Samuel Forman, whose father, David Forman and Peter Wikoff, acted as guides to General Washington, gave in 1842 the following version of what transpired on this memorable occasion.

"The action commenced in the morning after breakfast, in the vicinity of Briar Hill, distant a half or three quarters of a mile beyond the Court House. From thence the Americans under Lee slowly retreated before the enemy about three miles to the vicinity of the Parsonage, where a final stand was made and the principal action fought. Here Washington met Lee in the field immediately north of the dwelling, and riding up to him, with astonishment asked "What is the meaning of this?" Lee being somewhat confused and not distinctly understanding the question, replied: "Sir! sir!" Washington the second time said "What is all that confusion for and retreat?"— Lee replied "He saw no confusion but arose from his orders not being properly obeyed." Washington mentioned that "he had certain information that it was but a strong covering party of the enemy." Lee replied that "It might be so, but they were rather stronger than he was and that he did not think it proper to risk so much," or words to that effect. Washing-

ton said "You should not have undertaken it," and passed by him. Shortly after Washington again met him and asked "if he would take command there; if not, he (Washington) would; if General Lee would take command there, he would return to the main army and arrange it."— Lee replied that "his Exellency had before given him the command there."— Washington told him he expected he would take proper measures for checking the enemy there. Lee replied that his orders should be obeyed and that he would not be the first to leave the field; and Washington then rode away. Immediately after this General Hamilton, in a great heat, rode up to Lee and said "I will stay here with you, my dear General, and die with you; let us all die here rather than retreat."

OTHER HISTORIANS.

Marshall, Bancroft and Sparks in their lives of Washington merely state in substance that "Washington spoke in terms of warmth, implying disapprobation of Lee's conduct."

Mr. George H. Moore, librarian of the New York Historical Society published in 1860 a small volume entitled "The Treason of Charles Lee, &c" which gives some important facts in General Lee's career to which we shall endeavor to refer hereafter, but his work stops short of the battle of Monmouth.

Gen. Washington rarely used profane language, but there is no doubt that he did on this occasion, being exasperated at Lee's conduct, which gave suspicion of treachery. The charge of treason against Lee we shall endeavor to examine hereafter.

Our older readers remember the story of the College Divinity Professor who always held up Washington as a model for his pupils in all things. One day he was laboring to convince his scholars of the wickedness of profanity when one of them rose up and said: "Professor you told us to take Washington as an example in all things and you know he swore terribly at the battle of Monmouth." The Professor was nonplussed, but finally stammered "Ahem? ah, well—if ever any body *did* have an excuse for swearing it was Washington at the battle of Monmouth!

GENERAL LEE'S OWN VERSION.

General Lee, in his defence before the Court Martial, said:

"When I arrived first in his (Washington's) presence, conscious of having done nothing which could draw on me the least censure, but rather flattering myself with his congratulation and applause. I confess I was disconcerted, astonished and confounded by the words and manner in which his Exellency accosted me. It was so novel and unexpected from a man whose discretion, humanity and decorum I had from the first of our acquaintance stood in admiration of, that I was for some time unable to make any coherent answer to questions so abrupt and in a great measure unintelligible. The terms I think were these: 'I desire to know, sir, what is the reason whence arises this disorder and confusion?" The manner in which he expressed them was much stronger and more severe than the expressions themselves. When I recovered myself sufficiently I answered that I saw or knew of no confusion but which naturally arose from disobedience of orders, contradictory intelligence and the impertinence and presumption of individuals who were invested with no authority, intruding themselves in matters above their sphere; *That the retreat in the first instance was contrary to my orders and wishes.*

Washington replied all this might be true but he ought not have undertaken the enterprise unless he intended to go through with it."

EPISCOPALIANISM IN OLD MONMOUTH.

Freehold, Middletown, Shrewsbury, Stafford, &c. Missionary Efforts from 1745 to to 1751. Freehold Presbyterians and Episcopalians—Strife in Good Works.—Heathens (?) in the Pines. Rogerine Baptists, &c.

The following account of the missionary efforts of Rev. Thomas Thompson in old Monmouth, some century and a quarter ago is worthy of preservation by all interested in the early religious history of the county. We have seen it stated that but two copies of Mr. Thompson's work were to be found in America, one in the Connecticut Historical library and the other in the Astor library at New York. In our visits to the latter library in past years we have been surprised to see the value placed upon this little old fashioned book by people versed in the history of olden times in America, and it is almost as well known among them as Gabriel Thomas' History of West Jersey, &c., published 1698, of which the only known copy of the original edition is in the Franklin Library, Philadelphia, a copy of which we hope to find room for, before concluding these sketches. Lately another copy of Mr. Thompson's little book was discovered in an Episcopal library in South Carolina, and placed in the Congressional Library, at Washington.

In Mr. Thompson's account of his visit it will be noticed that he speaks disparagingly of the early settlers in the lower part of the county. His zeal for the tenets of this society by which he was employed, seems to have led him to make animadversions against the people there, which it would appear were not entirely deserved according to the testimony of ministers of other denominations, which we may give hereafter in sketches of the early history of other societies. It will be noticed that while he accuses them of great ignorance, yet he acknowledges having many conferences and disputes on religious topics with them, which shows that they were considerably posted in scriptural matters, but undoubtedly opposed to the Church of England.

Mr. Thompson's little work gives an account of his visit to Monmouth and also to Africa. We give all that relates to Old Monmouth. His remarks about heathenism in the pines is rather severe, when it is remembered that it was made after his visit to the negroes in Guinea, Africa. The society he terms "Culvers" were Rogerine Baptists, who were located some eleven years at Waretown, Ocean county, and then left and went to Schooley's Mountains.

An Account of the Missionary Voyages by the Appointment of the Society for the Propagation of the Gospel in foreign parts. The one to New Jersey in North America, and then from America, to the coast of Guiney.

By REV. THOMAS THOMPSON, A. M., VICAR OF RECULVER, IN KENT.

London; printed for Benj. Dod at the Bible and Key, in Ave Mary Lane, near St. Pauls. MDCCLVIII.

In the spring of the year 1745 I embarked for America, being appointed Missionary of the Society for the Propagation of the Gospel in Foreign Parts upon recommendation of my Reverend Tutor Dr. Thomas Cartwright, late Archdeacon of Colchester and a member of the Society, myself then a Fellow of Christ's College Cambridge. I went in a ship called the Albany, belonging to New York which sailed from Gravesend on the 8th day of May and providentially escaping some instant dangers on the passage, arrived at New York on the 29th of August. The Sunday following I preached both Morning and Afternoon at the Episcopal Church in that city, whereof the Reverend Mr. Commissary Vesey had then been rector more than forty years. On the next Sunday I passed over to Elizabeth-town in New Jersey on my journey to Monmouth County in the Eastern Division where I was appointed to reside and have the care of Churches in that county, being also licensed thereto by the Right Reverend the late Lord Bishop of London.

Being come to the place of my mission I presented my credentials and was kindly received and took the first opportunity of waiting upon the governor Lewis Morris Esq., at his seat at Kingsbury which is in the Western Division, and took the oath of allegiance and supremacy and also the abjuration oath and subscribed the Declaration in presence of his Excellency.

Upon making inquiry into the state of the churches within my District, I found that the members were much disturbed and in a very unsettled state, insomuch, that some of them had thoughts of leaving our communion and turning to the Dissenters. The particular occasion of this I forbear to mention.

As I came to gather more information, it presented to me, that many of those who frequented the Church worship never had been baptized; some heads of families and several others of adult age, besides a number of young children and Infants.

I perceived that it was not altogether neglect, but there was something of principle in the cause, that so many persons had not received the sacred ordinance of baptism and others did not procure it to their children. That part of the country abounding in Quakers and Anabaptists, the intercourse with these sects was of so bad influence, as had produced among the Church people thus conforming with their tenets and example. However the main fault was rather carelessness of the baptism and a great deal was owing to prejudice respecting the matter of god fathers and god mothers.

I seriously declare that the reconciling this order of the Church to the minds of people in the American colonies, is of more difficulty and trouble to the Missionary than almost all their work and business besides. And I am well assured that many of the Sectaries dislike nothing in the Church so much as that; and some I am apt to think, do stand out from our Communion purely upon that account and for no other reason.

I had many tedious arguments with my people upon this head. I also made it the subject of some of my discourses in the pulpit, till by one means or other, I at length brought them to a better understanding thereof and to be in a good degree satisfied with it.

After sometime they began to bring their children to Baptism, and when some had led the way, the rest followed, and presented those of their children which were under years of maturity, to be received into the Church and I christened thirteen in one day. After this it went on regularly. Parents had their children baptized as soon after they were born as conveniently could be done and one whole family, the man (whose name was Joseph West) his wife and nine children were baptized all at one time.

By frequent exhortations to the elder sort and often calling upon them to consider how they deferred a thing of that consequence to their salvation, I prevailed with many to take upon themselves the baptismal engagement, to whom I gave all necessary instruction both to inform their understanding and prepare their minds thereto.

The Churches which I served were well filled every Sunday and divers families that lived out of the county came to Divine service from several miles distance and were very constant devout attendants.— Besides these some of the Dutch Church often made a considerable addition to the number of my hearers.

I had three churches immediately in my charge, each of them situated in a different township, which had regular duty in such proportion as were agreed upon and subscribed to at a general vestry meeting soon after my coming there. The names of the townships are Freehold, Shrewsbury and Middletown. I also officiated at Allentown in Upper Freehold while that church was destitute of a minister, which was afterwards supplied by Mr. Michael Houdin, a convert from the Church of Rome, and a worthy clergyman, now the Society's missionary. These four townships comprised the whole county although 40 or 50

OLD TIMES IN OLD MONMOUTH.

miles in length and in some parts of it considerably wide. 1 also did occasional duty at other places as will be farther mentioned.

This mission to Monmouth County had been very early recommended to the Society but was not presently established. Dr. Humphrey's in his Historical account makes mention "that Colonel Morris, a gentleman of character and considerable interest in New Jersey (the same who was afterwards governor of the province) did in a letter in the year 1703 very earnestly solicit Dr. Beveridge (late Bishop of St. Asaph, a member of the Society) to send a missionary to Monmouth county in East Jersey where a considerable body of Church people had formed themselves into a gathered church and had promised all the help their narrow circumstances could afford their minister. The Society were not then able to support a missionary there, but the Reverend Alexander Innis, happening to be in those parts took the care of that people upon him. After a worthy discharge of his functions he died ;" and by his last will and testament appointed ten acres of land lying in Middletown to the service of God, which is the ground whereon the church now stands. Since that Mr. William Leeds became a benefactor to the church by making over his house and plantation to the society for the use and habitation of a missionary to be appointed to preach the gospel to the inhabitants of Middletown and Shrewsbury.

As to the church buildings I have found them all much out of condition, especially the church at Middletown, which was begun to be built, but the year before I came there, and had nothing done on the inside, not even a floor laid. So that we had no place for the present to assemble in Divine worship, only an old house which had formerly been a meeting house.

I had now a great and very difficult task of it to bring people to the communion. They that were conformable to this sacred ordinance were in very small numbers. Many persons of 50 or 60 years of age and some older had never addressed themselves to it. In this case it appeared to me that their will was less in fault than their judgment, which hung so much on the side of fear, that it overbalanced the sense of duty. 1 took all possible pains to satisfy their scruples, gave them frequent opportunities of the communion, and by the blessing of God gained most of the ancient people, besides many others, who gave due and devout attention to it ever after.

That 1 might lay a good foundation for the children and build them up in sound christian principles I began to catechize ; at first only asking questions in the Church catechism, but after a while I changed the method with them, so as still to keep the words of the catechism but raised other questions to the several clauses and matters contained therein to try what they understood of it ; and by this means led them further into the sense and meaning of every part of it.

The number of my catechumens began now to increase and several of riper years presented themselves with a seeming earnestness to receive the benefit of this instruction. So I carried it further and put Lewis' Exposition into their hands and appointed them a day about once a month to come to the Court House and say the parts which I set them to get by heart, and this course I continued till some of them could recite it from end to end.

There were others willing and desirous to be put forward in the way of godly knowledge who had not so good memories. To these I propounded two or three questions at a time upon some point of doctrine which they were to prepare themselves to answer the next meeting and to have the Scripture proofs written down to be then also produced. To this they applied themselves with great industry and gave extraordinary instances of their good understanding as well as diligence.

When the others had no more of Lewis's catechism to learn 1 made them repeat the Thirty Nine Articles of religion and then taught them to divide these into questions and answers, and they gave me in monthly the texts they had collected in proof of them.

In the interim I was not unconcerned for the poor negroes who wanted enlightening more than any, and therefore spake to their Masters and Mistresses to be at the pains to teach them the Catechism. And thus was taken good care of in some pious families and I catechized them in the Church a certain Sunday, and sometimes at home and after due instruction, those whom I had good assurance of 1 received to baptism, and such afterwards as behaved well I admitted to the communion.

Speaking here of negroes I will mention the case of one in whom it pleased God to give an example of his influencing favor under circumstances of a condemned criminal. This man was a servant at a place called Crosswicks, to a Quaker and had been convicted of a rape. He after his apprehension, and also at his trial did seem to be a very hardened wretch. According to the strictness of the laws, a negro is to be executed immediately after sentence; but the Judges were pleased to be so far favorable as to allow him the space of a fortnight to be prepared for death; which Christian indulgence gave me an opportunity to perform those offices to him which by the blessing of God and with the assistance of a neighboring clergyman, worked upon him by degrees, and at length brought him to a true repentance. For some time he held in a very obstinate temper, but when it begun that I could get anything from him, I found he was not wholly ignorant in the principles of christianity; and as he became more disposed to seriousness, his readiness of apprehension and aptness to learn made it easy to supply to him the further knowledge of religion, which, if he had considered sooner, might have prevented his coming to that untimely end. One particular in my dealing with him I shall speak of, as it may suggest a useful hint to those whose office may call them upon a like occasion and which practice I can from other experience recommend.

I took out of the Psalms such verses as are proper to a penitent sinner; which I made him repeat verse by verse after me, every now and then bidding him raise up his mind and thoughts to Heaven and consider that he was speaking to Almighty God. By this means putting the best words of devotion into his mouth, the most pertinent to his use; also holding up his attention; calling him to awe and reverence the poor criminal was drawn out into a sort of involuntary confession of his guilt and the sense of his soul soon corresponded with what his tongue uttered and he felt in himself, those affections which worked duly and properly after they had thus been excited. Being thoroughly instructed and grounded in the christian faith and there being no room to doubt the sincerity of his repentance, three days before his execution I baptized him and on that day gave him the communion.

In the year 1746 the Church at Middletown which had stood useless, being, as I have before mentioned, only a shell of a building, had now a floor laid and was otherwise made fit to have divine worship performed in it. The congregation of this church was but small and as the service could not be oftener than once a month, it was morally impossible to increase the number much, especially as there was a weekly meeting of Anabaptists in that town, so that it was the most I could propose to prevent those that were of the church from being drawn away by dissenters.

After necessity had been answered its demand in the fitting up of one church, expediency came next to be consulted for the finishing another, viz: St. Peters in the township of Freehold, which had been built many years but was never quite completed. The ground on which the church stands was the gift of one Mr. Thomas Boel, who had been a Quaker, but was brought over with many others of that persuasion by Mr. George Keith, one of the Society's first Missionaries, who himself had been one of that people but became a very zealous member and diligent servant of the church and was a person well learned. After his return from abroad he had the living of Edburton in Sussex and published his journal of missionary travel.

The situation of St. Peters church at Toponcmes, which is distant from any town, is however convenient enough to the congregation and was resorted to by many families in Middlesex county living within the several districts of Cranberry, Macheponeck, and South River; their missionary, my friend and brother Mr. Skinner gladly remitting to me the care of them, which he could not well attend to by reason of a wide and often dangerous Ferry over the Raritan which divides Middlesex county. I was therefore willing to give them all possible attendance and did often meet them and baptize their children and appointed certain days to preach at those places and there also catechize.

At a town called Middletown Point I preached divers times, the place being remote and few of the settlers having any way for convenience of coming to church. The inhabitants of Freehold township, were at least half of them Presbyterian. The church people and these interspersed among each other, had lived less in charity and brotherly love than as becomes churches. But they began on both sides to think less of the things in which they differed in opinion than of those in which they agreed. And when bickering and disputing were laid down, which was done at last, with the full consent of both parties, another strife arose from a better spirit in the way of peace, to provoke love and to do good works, in which neither side was less forward than the other.

The Church of England worship had at Shrewsbury been provided for by the building of a church, before there was any other in the county; but this church was now too small for the numerous congregation. People of all sorts resorted thither and of the Quaker which are a great body in that township, there were several who made no scruple of being present at divine service and were not too precise to uncover their heads in the house of God.

I went sometimes to a place called Manasquan almost twenty miles distant from my habitation where, and at Shark River, which is in that neighborhood some church families were settled who were glad of all opportunities for the exercise of religion. I baptized at Manasquan two Negro brethren, both servants to Mr. Samuel Osborne an eminent and very worthy member of the church, in whose family they had been taught good christian principles. The honest men were so gratified that each of them offered me a *Spanish* dollar in acknowledgment and would have thought themselves more obliged if I had not refused their presents.

From Manasquan for twenty miles further on in the country, is all one pine forest. I traveled through this desert four times to a place called Barnegat, and thence to Mannahawkin, almost sixty miles from home and preached at places where no foot of minister had ever come. Only at Mannahawkin. one Mr. Neill, a dissenting minister, who is now a presbyter of the Church of England (then living at Great Egg Harbor) visited Mannahawkin.

In this section I had my views of heathenism just as thoroughly as I have ever since beheld it. The inhabitants are thinly scattered in regions of solid wood. Some are decent people who had lived in better places, but those who were born and bred here, have neither religion nor manners and do not know so much as a letter in a book.

As Quakerism is the name under which all those in America shade themselves that have been brought up to none. but would be thought to be of some religion; so these poor people call themselves Quakers, but they have no meetings and many of them make no distinction of days, neither observing Lords Day nor the Sabbath; only some New England families were then lately settled there who were called Culvers and had a form and manner of their own which they held too sacred (though perhaps rather it was too monstrous) to be communicated and did not admit others into their assemblies. As for those who had removed thither from other parts of the country, they seemed very sensible of the unhappiness of their situation, living where they had no opportunity for the worship of God nor for the christian education of their children. I would have taken this difficult journey oftener, finding that some good might be done among them but having too much duty to attend to in other parts of my mission I could not do it.

As people were desirous of having a Schoolmaster and spoke of making up among themselves a competency for one, I proposed it to Mr. Christopher Robert Reynolds, the Society's schoolmaster at Shrewsbury; and those parts being within that township, it was not inconsistent with his appointment. He was willing to go and set up school there, and accordingly went down and taught a year, employing his diligence to good effect.

But his employers living so far asunder that they could not send their children to school all at one place, he was obliged to be often shifting and to go from one house to another, which was such a fatigue and labor to him, being in years and an infirm man, that he was not able to continue it and returned to Shrewsbury his former station.

In my journeying through this part of the country I had many conferences and disputes with the people. Some of them were willing to see their errors and others were as obstinate in defending theirs. And though ignorant minds and prejudiced cannot easily be made to apprehend the nature and necessity of the christian ordinances yet it pleased God that I brought some to a true sense of them and I gained a few to the communion, and baptized, besides children seventeen grown persons, of which number was Nicholas Wainright nearly 80 years of age.

I had now seen a great change in the state of my mission within the space of three years, through the grace of God rendering my labors effectual to a good end; in particular as to the peace and unison which the church members, after having been much at variance among themselves, were now returned to, and the ceasing animosities betwixt them and those of other societies; for these I account the most valuable success that attended my ministry.

After this the churches continued to flourish and in the latter end of the year 1750, having then been above five years in America upon this mission, I wrote to the venerable and honorable society a letter requesting of them to grant me a mission to the coast of Guiney, that I might go to make a trial with the natives and see what hopes there would be of introducing among them the christian religion. The summer following I received an answer to that letter from the Rev. Dr. Bearcroft, acquainting me that the Society had concluded to support me in the design of that voyage and would appoint another missionary in my stead for Monmouth county. And the next September Mr Samuel Cook of Caius college arrived with his proper credentials and I delivered up my charge to him.

Having took my leave of the congregation I set out on the 13th of November 1751 for New York, from thence to go upon my voyage to Africa, and at Elizabethtown waited on Governor Jonathan Belcher Esq., who succeeded Colonel Morris, to pay my respects to him before I left the province.

November 24th 1751 I preached both in the morning and the afternoon in the English church in New York of which Reverend Mr. Barclay is the worthy Rector and the next day went on board a brigantine called the "Prince George," Captain William Williams, bound for the coast of Africa.

METHODISM IN OLD MONMOUTH.

The Pioneers of the Society—Bishop Asbury at Freehold, Allentown, Long Branch, Squan, Kettle Creek, Goodluck &c—Rev. Benjamin Abbott's visit during the Revolution.

We have reason to believe that the pioneers of Methodism visited the county within a very few years after the principles of the society were first proclaimed in America, and that occasionally some preacher would hold forth in some of our churches, school houses or private houses as early as 1774. Some uncertainty exists as to where the first preachers held services in the county, owing to the fact that the early heroes of Methodism were not always very precise in giving the names of places where they preached, dates and other particulars interesting to the historian of the present day. The most complete and satisfactory journal is that of the faithful, zealous, untiring Bishop Francis Asbury, which is the more remarkable as it is doubtful if any minister of any denomination ever performed as much labor as he did in travelling and preaching. We append extracts from his journal relating to his labors in Monmouth. But other preachers had preceeded him. Rev. William Watters the first Methodist travelling preacher of American birth was stationed in our state in 1774, and he may have visited our county, though he makes no mention of it in his journal. That earnest, self sacrificing minister of the gospel, Rev. Benjamin Abbott visited old Monmouth in 1778. Mr. Abbott in his journal speaks of preaching at various places in that part of old Monmouth now composed within the limits of Ocean county, among which were Mannahawkin, Waretown, Goodluck and Toms River. But after leaving Toms River, he omits to name places ; he merely uses such expressions as "at my next appointment, &c.," without naming where it was. He probably preached at Freehold and other places within the limits of the present county of Monmouth. At some future time we shall endeavor to find room for so much of his journal as may relate to old Monmouth.

Though it is somewhat uncertain who were the first Methodist preachers in the county, yet the probabilities are that some, if not all the following named persons preached here before Abbott's visit in 1778, viz: Captain Thomas Webb, Reverends Philip Gatch, Caleb B, Pedicord, William Watters, John King, Daniel Ruff and William Duke.

Rev. John Atkinson in his "Memorials of Methodism in New Jersey," says:

"The Methodist Society of Monmouth (Freehold ?) must have been formed at an early period, probably about 1780, as in that year Job Throckmorton of Freehold was converted under the ministry of Rev. Richard Garretson and became a member of the Society. He was one of the first members in that region. The Methodists were much persecuted there at that time. His house was a home for preachers, and very likely Asbury was entertained at his dwelling during his visits to Freehold.— Everitt, Freeborn Garretson, Ezekiel Cooper, Ware, and others were accustomed to stop at his house. He was accustomed to relate incidents of Rev. Benjamin Abbott's powerful ministry, one of which is as follows :

OLD TIMES IN OLD MONMOUTH. 101

"On one occasion meeting was held in the woods, and after Freeborn Garretson had preached, Abbott arose and looked around over the congregation very significantly, and exclaimed : " Lord, begin the work; Lord, begin the work *now!* Lord, begin the work just *there!* pointing at the same time towards a man who was standing beside a tree, and the man fell as suddenly as if he had been shot and cried aloud for mercy."

In 1786 Trenton circuit probably included Trenton, Pemberton, Mount Holly, Burlington and Monmouth, Reverends Robert Sparks and Robert Cann preachers. In 1787 Rev. Ezekiel Cooper and Rev. Nathaniel B. Mills were the preachers. In 1788 Rev's John Merrick, Thomas Morrell and Jettus Johnson were the preachers.

BISHOP ASBURY IN OLD MONMOUTH.—EXTRACTS FROM HIS JOURNAL.

September 14th 1782. I came to New Mills (now Pemberton in Burlington county). I passed through Monmouth in Upper and Lower Freehold ; here lived that old saint of God, William Tennent, who went to his reward a few years ago.

Friday September 9th 1785. Heard Mr. Woodhull preach a funeral discourse on " Lord thou hast made my days as a handbreadth." In my judgment he spoke well.

(The Mr. Woodhull above referred to by Mr. Asbury, was probably the Rev. John Woodhull, D. D., who succeeded Rev. Mr. Tennent at the old Tennent Church, and who died Nov. 22d, 1824, aged 80 years.)

Saturday September 10th, 1785. I had liberty in preaching to the people of Monmouth on Joshua 24-17 and felt much for the souls present. (Freehold then was often called Monmouth and Monmouth Court House.)

Friday September 22nd, 1786. We dined at Amboy and reached Monmouth at night.

September 23rd, 1786. I preached life and love at Leonards· The people here appear very lifeless. I had lately been much tried and much blessed.

Tuesday September 26th, 1786. I had many to hear me at Potter's Church, but the people were insensible and unfeeling. (This Potter's Church was at Goodluck in Ocean County, and built by a benevolent resident of that place named Thomas Potter. Its singular history will be given in speaking of the Universalists' society.)

From Goodluck, Bishop Asbury proceeded to Batsto, Burlington county. In October, 1790, he preached at Crosswicks, Allentown and Cranbury. Of his next visit to this county he says :

Monday September 5th, 1791. I rode through much rain to Monmouth, N. J., where I preached to a congregation on " The just shall live by faith ; but if any man draw back, my soul shall have no pleasure in him." There is some stir among the people ; at Long Branch within eighteen months, as I am informed, nearly fifty souls have professed conversion.

Sept. 6th, 1791. I found the Lord had not left himself without witnesses at Kettle Creek.

Sept. 7th, 1791. At P——s Church (Potter's Church?) I learn some were offended. Blessed be God, my soul was kept in great peace.

From there Mr. Asbury proceeded to Little Egg Harbor.

October 28th, 1795. We came to Monmouth ; we would have gone to Shrewsbury but time and our horses failed us. I learn that the ancient spirit of faith and prayer is taking place below. I was shocked at the brutality of some men who were fighting ; one gouged out the other's eye ; the father and son then both beset him again, cut off his ears and nose and beat him almost to death ; the father and son were tried for a breach of the peace and roundly fined ; and now the man that has lost his nose is come upon them for damage. I have often thought that there are some things practiced in the Jersie's which are more brutish and diabolical than in any other of the states ; there is nothing of this kind in New England ; they learn civility there at least

We rode twenty miles to Emley's Church where the great revival of religion was some years ago. I felt a little of the old good spirit there still.

May 30th, 1806. I preached at Lower Freehold. I came home with Simon Pyle. Ah! what a death there is in the Leonard family.

May 1st, 1806. I breakfasted with Throckmorton ; his loss is his gain—he has lost his birthright as a citizens of the state but he has the blessing of God on his soul.

Sunday April 23rd, 1809. I preached at Tuckerton ; my subject was 2 Cor. 4-2. In the afternoon I preached again. On Modday I preached at Waretown. I staid awhile with Samuel Brown and came to

Thomas Chamberlain's; I was compellen by uncomfortable feeling to go to rest at six o'clock. At David Woodmanse's (Goodluck?) on Tuesday I preached on 2nd Tim. 2--15. On Wednesday after a rain I set out for Polhemus' chapel (Polhemus Mills) where I preached. My friends were exceedingly kind and I was very sick. I rose unwell on Thursday and took medicine and set out for Squan river. My host here, Derrick Longstreet, has been married twenty-four years; his wife once had twins and she has made him the father of sixteen children all of whom are sound and well. I had a noble congregation here of women and children; the men were generally gone from the neighborhood, either to the waters or to work. I was seriously unwell. On Friday at Newman's at Shark river I had women not a few. I suited my subject to my hearers and preached from Luke 10. 44-42. Ah! how many Marthas' and how few Marys! In the afternoon I spoke again at P. White's. We have meetings twice a day and sometimes at night. and the prospects are pleasing. The weather is severely cold.

Sunday, September 30th, 1809. At Long Branch my subject was Acts 3--26. It was given me to speak in strong words, words of God and from God At 3 o'clock I preached in the Episcopal church at Shrewsbury. I came home with John Throckmorton.

Monday, May 10th 1813. I preached at Allentown, nearly two hours and had gracious access to God and to truth. We lodged with John Hughes. I am filled with God.

REV. WILLIAM MILLS—AN OLD MONMOUTH PREACHER; A HERO OF THE WAR AND A SOLDIER OF THE CROSS.

The following sketch of Mr. Mills is by Rev. George A. Raybold, author of Methodism in West Jersey, whose ministrations in Monmouth county some forty odd years ago are so favorably remembered by many of our older citizens.

"Mr. Mills was a native of Monmouth, of Quaker descent. The fire of patriotic feeling irduced him, Quaker as he was, in 1776, to enter the American army in which he became an officer. He was taken prisoner by the British and was sent, after being changed from one vessel to another, to the West Indies. At length he was carried to Europe, from whence at the close of the war, he returned home and again settled in New Jersey. About the year 1792 the Methodist preachers came into the region of country where he resided. His wife solicited him to hear them, but he resisted; stating his belief that he had been so wicked his day of grace was past. By a remarkable dream he was at length convinced that there was mercy for him. He then attended the means of grace, until as he sought the Lord with all his heart, he soon found mercy and peace through faith in Jesus. He became a member of the first class formed in the vicinity of Shrewsbury in Monmouth. Soon after he found the Lord, he began to exhort others and was appointed class leader; and in the spring of 1799 he was received into the travelling connexion. His labors as an itinerant began on Milford circuit, Delaware, from whence he was sent to various places and finally returned to Jersey. In 1813 he was sent to Freehold, the place of his nativity and the first field of his Christian efforts. The soldier who had faced death at the cannon's mouth on the land and on the sea, now, as his end approached in reality felt no fear. He had a presentiment of his death and told his wife that "death seemed to follow him everywhere." His zeal for God and labors for the salvation of souls increased. The last time he left home he gave his wife sundry directions and advices in case he should die. He started as well as usual, and filled all his appointments, preaching most fervently until a short time before his death. On the 4th of December he left Long Branch, met class, and then returned to Mr. Lippencott's at the Branch. On Sunday morning he went into a room in Mr. Lippencott's to prepare for the service in the church, which was to commence at half past ten o'clock. The congregation was then collecting and the family, thinking he stayed too long in the chamber sent in to know the cause and found him fallen in a fit of apoplexy, almost deprived of sense. After a time he revived a little and on being asked if they should send for medical aid, he replied, "The Lord is the best physician." At about twelve o'clock the stupor and other unfavorable symptoms returned; he lingered until about six the next morning and then peacefully departed for a world of rest. Thus suddenly fell into the arms of death another faithful minister of the gospel; a zealous, faithful and acceptable preacher; an Israelite, indeed, in whom there was no guile; long however has he lived in the affectionate remembrance of the people of West Jersey, who knew him well."

In the year 1812, the year previous to Mr. Mills being sent to preach in Freehold circuit, the number of members embraced in the charge was seven hundred and thirty-six.

MONMOUTH COUNTY—WHEN ESTABLISHED.

OFFICIALS ONE HUNDRED AND NINETY YEARS AGO.

The name Monmouth was officially given to the county March 7th, 1683, as will be seen by the following extracts:

"Att a Councill held the 7th day of the mo-1 called March 168⅔ * * * * *

"A bill sent downe from the Deputyes for devideing the p'vince into Countyes read and agreed vtno."—*Journal of Proceedings of Gov. & Council*, 1682—1703.

The following is an extract from the bill referred to:

"At a General Assembly begun and holden at Elizabethtown in this Province of East New Jersey, the first day of the Month called March Anno Domini 1682 and in the Five and Thirtieth year of the reign of King Charles the Second, over England &c, and there continued by several adjournments thereof until the twenty eight day of the said Month of March, for the public Weale of this Province was Enacted as follows:

* * * * * * * *

"IV. *An Act to divide the Province into Four Counties.*—Having taken into consideration the necessity of dividing the Province into respective Counties for the better governing and settling Courts in the same :—

"*Be it Enacted*, by this General Assembly, and the Authority thereof, that this Province be divided into four counties as followeth : (Here follows the bounds of Bergen, Essex, and Middlesex, after which the bounds of Monmouth are given as follows:)

"*Monmouth County* to begin at the Westward Bounds of Middlesex county, containing Middletown and Shrewsbury and so extend Westward, Southward, and Northward to the extream Bounds of the Province. Provided this distinction of the Province into Counties, do not extend to the infringement of any Liberty in any Charter already granted."—*Leaming and Spicer.*

THE LEGAL AND THE HISTORICAL YEAR—DISCREPANCIES EXPLAINED.

In the foregoing may be noticed an apparent discrepancy in giving the year when the act referred to was passed.—Some authorities give the date as March, 1683; the "Journal of the Proceedings of the Governor and Council of the Province of East New Jersey, from 1682 to 1703," gives the date as March 168⅔, which leaves the general reader in doubt as to which year is meant—1682 or 1683; and "Leaming & Spicer's Grants and Concessions," published in 1752, expressly says the act was passed in March, 1682. This apparent discrepancy is explained by the fact that at that time the English legal year commenced March 25th; hence the legal year 1682 began March 25th, 1682, and ended March 24th, 1683. (See Leaming and Spicer, p 74 ;) and all acts passed in 1683 previous to March 25th, would be dated the legal year 1682. In the Journal of the Proceedings of the Legislature from 1682 to 1703, before referred to, two dates are given in such a manner that it would seem quite puzzling were it not for this explanation. On page 32 the date of the meeting of the Co ncil is March 24th, 168⅔. As March 25th, was Sunday the next daily session was March 26th, when the year is given as 1683. In ancient records when a date is given with what seems a fraction at the righthand, as in the case above mentioned, 168⅔, the meaning is that the upper figure gives the legal year and the lower one the historical year.

ORIGIN OF THE NAME OF THE COUNTY.

The name Monmouth was given to the county through the influence of Col. Lewis Morris who at the beginning of this session (March 1st,) was said to have been "Elected for Shrewsbury" as a Deputy, but his place declared vacant, probably because he had been selected by the Governor as a member of the council at that time.

Colonel Morris had purchased a large tract of land, in what was afterwards known as Monmouth County, October 25th, 1676, said to contain 3540 acres, whereupon he located, as described in 1680, "his iron mills, his Manors, and divers other buildings for his servants and dependants; together with 60 or 70 negroes about the Mill and Husbandry. To this plantation he gave the name of Tintern (corrupted afterwards to Tinton) after

104 OLD TIMES IN OLD MONMOUTH.

an estate which had belonged to the family in Monmouthshire, England, and from h m Monmouth county received its name."

Col. Lewis Morris, Joseph Parker, Peter Tilton and John Hance of Shrewsbury; and John Bowne and John Throgmorton (Throckmorton?) of Middletown. Richard Gardner was elected Clerk of the County Courts, Richard Hartshorne High Sheriff, and Richard Lippencott coroner. Richard Hartshorne tendered his resignation as Sheriff the following May, but it was not accepted; he appears to have refused to serve still, and May 31st Eliakim Wardell of Shrewsbury was elected.

In the act erecting County Courts it is enacted that "the Judge or Justices of the respective sessions of the County Courts shall be the Justices of the Peace of the said respective counties or three of them at least." Col. Morris was probably presiding judge. The following year the same justices were reelected, with the addition of James Grover of Middletown.

Two or three days after the passage of the acts establishing the two Courts above referred to the General Assembly passed "A Bill to settle the Court of Common Right," which was "the Supream Court of this Province," to which actions or suits from lower Courts, the debts or damages of which were five pounds or upwards, could be removed, and which had power to "Correct Errors in Judgement and reverse the same if there be just cause for the same." Of this Court the first members from Monmouth were Col. Lewis Morris (The learned, indefatigable corresponding Secretary of the New Jersey Historical Society, Hon. Wm. A. Whitehead, to whom our state is indebted more than to any other person for efforts to preserve the fading records of the past history of New Jersey, and to whom we have been indebted for several items in these chapters, a few years ago published a sketch of Col. Morris's life to which we may refer hereafter.)

As to the probability of some of the prominent early settlers favoring Col. Morris's propositon to name the county Monmouth, because of a friendly feeling for the Duke of Monmouth, beheaded a few years later, we shall endeavor to speak hereafter.

COURTS ESTABLISHED AND OFFICERS APPOINTED.

On the 13th of March, 1683, two acts were passed under the following titles:

"An Act to erect a Court of small Causes" and "An Act to Erect County Courts."— The Court for the trial of small causes was to be held in every township the first Wednesday of every month, and to have jurisdiction for "determening small causes and debts under forty shillings."

The act establishing County Courts fixed the following times and places for sessions in Monmouth, viz:

"The County of Monmouth, their sessions to be the fourth Tuesday in March in the public meeting house at Middletown yearly. The fourth Tuesday in June in the public meeting house at Shrewsbury yearly. The fourth Tuesday in September in the public meeting house at Middletown, and the fourth Tuesday in December in the public meeting house in Shrewsbury."

The next day after the passage of the above acts (on March 14th, 1683,) Lewis Morris, jr., was elected by the Council "high Sheriff" for the succeeding yeare from the 25th of this Instant Month," which he probably declined, as Richard Hartshorne was confirmed for the same office some ten days subsequently.

The following were the first Justices of the Peace appointed for Monmouth County (March 24th, 1683), viz:
(by virtue of being a member of the Council) and John Bowne.

During the same session (March, 1683), the following persons were authorized "to make and settle highways, passages, landings, bridges and ferries" in the county, viz:

The Surveyor-General Samuel Groome, Col. Lewis Morris, Capt. John Bound, Richard Hartshorne, John Hance, Joseph Parker, Lewis Morris, jun.

Among the members of "The General Assembly of the Province of East New Jersey" which met at Elizabethtown March 1st, 1683, were, from Monmouth, Colonel Lewis Morris of the Council, and Richard Hartshorne, John Bowne, Joseph Parker and John Hance, Deputies.

When Monmouth County was established its population was supposed to be between nine hundred and one thousand.— Secretary Nicholls (of N. Y.) estimated the population in 1682 of Shrewsbury at four hundred inhabitants; and Middletown one hundred families which would probably be about five hundred inhabitants.

OLD TIMES IN OLD MONMOUTH. 105

AN ACT FOR THE MILITIA—FIRST OFFICERS IN MONMOUTH.

An act with the above title was passed December 1st, 1683, and December 3d it was ordered for the better settling and exercise of the Militia under its provisions "that there bee one Major, and so many Captaines Com'issionated in each County as there be inhabitants to make up Companyes." For the County of Monmouth Captain John Bound was commissioned Major, and for Middletown James Grover Lieutenant, Safety Grover Ensign. For Shrewsbury, John Slocomb Captain, Geo. Stowlett Lieutenant, and Lewis Morris Ensign.

The Act for the Militia ordered that every male person between the ages of sixteen and sixty should be provided with arms, equipments, ammunition, &c., at his own expense under penalty of prescribed fines for each article not provided. A serjeant and corporal were authorized "to view arms every quarter or as often as the officer shall see cause." It was enacted that there should be four training or mustering days in a year, "two in the Spring and two in the Fall of the Leaf," under prescribed penalties.

CHIEF RANGER OF MONMOUTH.

December 3d, 1683, Captain John Slocomb was appointed "Chief Ranger" for Monmouth County. The duty of this officer is thus described:

"Forasmuch as many abuses are and have been committed within this Province, in the taking up, marking, selling and disposing of horses, mares and geldings * * be it enacted that there shall be one person appointed for each County who shall take up and receive all strays, register the same &c." The Chief Ranger was authorized to employ as many deputies as he thought proper. The importers of all cattle and horses were required to furnish the Ranger with a description of each head imported, and all drovers were required to do the same. The fees and penalties under the act must have made the office of the Ranger of considerable importance.

HOW TAXES WERE LEVIED—ASSEMBLY MEN'S SALARIES.

The following persons were appointed to make assessment of taxes in Monmouth under an act passed Dec. 5th, 1683, viz:

Captain John Bound, John Throgmorton (Throckmorton?) Peter Tilton, John Hance, Judah Allen and Joseph Parker.

This act "for defraying the public charges of this Province," enacted that fifty pounds be raised to defray public charges as follows: Bergen eleven pounds, Essex fourteen pounds, Middlesex ten pounds, Monmouth fifteen pounds. By this it would seem that even at this early date Monmouth was considered the richest county in East Jersey.

The taxes were to be paid in wheat at four shillings and sixpence the bushel; summer wheat at four shillings the bushel; Indian corn at two shillings and sixpence the bushel; and good merchantable pork at fifty shillings the barrel. Henry Lyon of Essex was appointed Treasurer of the Province to whom the tax was to be handed for the purpose of paying the clerks of the Council and Deputies four shillings each per day and ten pounds for transcribing the laws.

In addition to the above tax each town was required to pay its own Deputy to the General Assembly at the rate of four shillings per day; the year previous the rate of pay for the Deputies had been three shillings each, and as many of the towns had failed to pay their representatives then, provisions were inserted in this act to enforce the assessing and collecting the arrearages.

A fair idea of how far a member of the Assembly's per diem would go then towards meeting his expenses is gained by noticing the prices fixed for grain in the bill. The first year his per diem would buy a little over a bushel of corn; the second year a bushel of summer wheat. If he expended it for pork it would buy sixteen pounds.

THE BAPTIST CHURCH AT MIDDLETOWN.

THE FIRST BAPTIST CHURCH IN NEW JERSEY. ITS MEMBERS, PASTORS, TRIALS AND TRIUMPHS.

The following sketch of the noted church is from "Morgan Edwards, Materials, &c., of the State," published in 1792, with additions by Rev. David Benedict of Rhode Island, and published in his History of the Baptists, sixty years ago, (1813.)

"This is the oldest Baptist church in the State; it is thus distinguished for the village where the meeting house stands in a township of the same name, and county of Monmouth, about seventy-nine miles E. N. E. from Philadelphia. The meeting house is forty-two feet by thirty-two, erected on the lot where the old place of worship stood."

For the origin of this church, we must look back to the year 1667, for that was the year when Middletown was purchased from the Indians by 12 men and 24 associates. Their names are in the town book. Of them the following were Baptists:—

Richard Stout, William Cheeseman, William Layton,
John Stout, John Wilson, Wm. Compton,
James Grover, Walter Hall, James Ashton,
Jon'than Brown, John Cox. John Brown,
Obadiah Holmes, Jonathan Holmes, Thos Whitlock,
John Buckman, George Mount, Jas. Grover, jr.

It is probable that some of the above had wives and children of their own way of thinking; however the forenamed 18 men appear to have been the constituents of the church at Middletown, and the winter of 1668 the time.

How matters went on among these people, for a period of twenty-four years, viz., from the constitution to 1712, cannot be known. But in the year 1711, a variance arose in the church, insomuch that one party excommunicated the other and imposed silence on two gifted brothers that preached to them, viz, John Bray and John Okison. Wearied with their situation, they agreed to refer matters to a council congregated from neighboring churches. The council met May 12th, 1712. It consisted of Rev. Messrs Timothy Brooks, of Cohansey ; Abel Morgan and Joseph Wood, of Pennepek ; and Elisha Thomas, of Welsh Tract; with six elders, viz : Nicholas Johnson, James James, Griffith Mills, Edward Church, William Bettridge and John Manners. Their advice was—"To bury the proceedings in oblivion and erase the records of them;" accordingly four leaves are torn out of the church book. "To continue the silence imposed on John Bray and John Okison, the preceding year." One would think by this that these two brethren were the cause of the disturbance. "To sign a covenant relative to their future conduct ;" accordingly 42 did sign and 26 refused; nevertheless most of the non-signers came in afterwards : but the first 42 were declared to be the church that should be owned by sister churches. "That Messrs. Abel Morgan, Sen., and John Burrows, should supply the pulpit till the next yearly meeting, and the members should keep their places and not wander to other societies," for at this time there was a Presbyterian congregation at Middletown, and mixed communion in vogue.

The first who preached at Middletown was Mr. John Bown, of whom we can learn no more than he was not ordained, and that it was he who gave the lot on which the first meeting house was built. Cotemporary with him was Mr. Ashton, of whom mention will be made hereafter, and after him rose the forementioned Bray and Okison, neither of whom were ordained and the latter disowned. Mr. George Eaglesfield was another unordained preacher; but the first that may be styled pastor was—

REV. JAMES ASHTON.—He probably was ordained by Rev. Thomas Killingsworth, at the time the church was constituted in 1688 ; for Killingsworth assisted at the constitution. which gave rise to the tradition that he was the first minister. Mr. Ashton's successor was—

REV. JOHN BARROWES.—He was born at Taunton, Somersetshire, England, and there ordained ; arrived at Philadelphia in the month of November, 1711, and from thence came to Middletown in 1713, where he died at a good old age. Mr. Barrowes is said to have been a happy compound of gravity and facetiousness ; the one made the people stand in awe of him, while the other produced familiarity. As he was travelling one day a young man passed by him at full speed, and in passing Mr. Barrowes : said " If you would consider where you are going you would slacken your pace." He went on but presently turned back to inquire into the meaning of that passing salute. Mr. Barrowes reasoned with him on the folly and dangers of horse-racing (to which the youth was hastening ;) he gave great attention to the reproof. This encouraged Mr. Barrowes to proceed to more serious matters. The issue was a serious conversation. Here was a bow drawn at venture and a sinner shot flying! Mr. Barrowes was succeeded by—

REV. ABEL MORGAN, A. M.—He was born in Welsh Tract, April 13th. 1713, had his learning at an academy kept by Rev. Thomas Evans in Pencader; ordained at Welsh Tract in 1734, became pastor in 1748 ; died there November 24th, 1785.— He was never married, the reason it is supposed that none of his attention and attendance might be taken off his mother, who lived with him and whom he honored to an uncommon degree. Mr. Morgan was a man of sound learning and solid

OLD TIMES IN OLD MONMOUTH.

judgement; he has given specimens of both in his public disputes and publications, for it appears that he held two public disputes on the subject of baptism.—The first was at Kingswood, to which he was challenged by Rev. Samuel Harker, a Presbyterian minister. The other was at Cape May in 1743, with the Rev. (afterwards) Dr. Samuel Finley, President of Princeton College. Mr. Morgan's successor was—

REV SAMUEL MORGAN.—He was born in Welsh Tract August 23d, 1750; called to the ministry in Virginia; ordained at Middletown November 29th, 1785, at which time he took on him the care of the church. No account of Mr. Morgan's death has been obtained. This ancient church has for its pastor (1813) Mr. Benjamin Bennett. It was once well endowed but a considerable part of its temporalities were sunk by that sacrilegious thing (as Edwards calls it) *Congress money*.— What are its present posessions I have not learned.

PHILIP FRENEAU, THE POPULAR POET OF THE REVOLUTION.

AN ANCIENT MONMOUTH JOURNAL.

In the library of the New York Historical Society is preserved a copy of an ancient journal published in Monmouth county, which presents quite a contrast with the papers published in the county at the present time. This journal was called " *The New Jersey Chronicle*," and was published at "Mount Pleasant, near Middletown Point." The first number was issued May 2nd, 1795 and continued weekly for a year when it suspended for want of support. This *Chronicle* was quite a curious affair. It was printed by the author, Philip Freneau himself, who had mustered a medley of types for the purpose. The first number was of the humble dimensions of eight small quarto pages of seven inches by eight. This spirited little paper was soon enlarged, but typographically, at least, it always appeared of a somewhat sickly constitution.

The office types however were well employed in printing, this year, 1795, a new and comprehensive edition of Freneau's poems, in an octavo volume of 456 pages to which we shall refer before concluding. Its typographical execution is admirable for its day and speaks well for the pioneer printing press of Monmouth county.

From one sketch of Freneau's we extract the following:

OUTLINE OF HIS LIFE.

Philip Freneau, the popular poet of the days of the Revolution, who cheered the hearts of the citizens by his ready rhymes in behalf of the good cause, and opposition to its foes, while patriots were struggling for independence, was born in Frankfort street, in New York city, January 2nd, 1752. The family was of French Hugenot descent. Pierre Freneau the father of Philip and of Peter Freneau, distinguished in the history of South Carolina, bought an estate of a thousand acres at Mount Pleasant, Monmouth county, New Jersey, a family inheritance which his son afterwards occupied, and where he wrote many of his poems. Both the father and grandfather of Philip Freneau are buried in a vault in Trinity Churchyard, New York, by the side of their family relations.

Of the boyhood of Philip Freneau we know little, but we may infer from the position of his family and his subsequent attainments, that he was well instructed at the schools of the city, for we find him, in 1767, a student at Princeton College, N. J., where he graduated with credit after the usual four years course, in 1771. He began early the practice of versification; for in his sophomore year, at the age of seventeen, he composed a rhymed poem of decided promise, entitled "The Poetical History of the Prophet Jonah," which appears at the head of his first general collection of poems. Other compositions in various metres, on classical and historical themes, preserved in the same volume, were written during his collegiate course.

It was a creditable year for the institution when he graduated, for in his class were James Madison, afterwards President, and other men of note.

The commencement exercises at Princeton, in 1771 were of unusual interest. It was in the Presidency of that eminent patriot John Witherspoon, who, though born in Scotland, was proving himself, by his enlightened sagacity and devotion to freedom, an "American of the Americans." The political independence of the country, though not yet formally proclaimed, was ripening in Massachusetts and elsewhere, to its great declaration and invincible resolve. The young patriots of Princeton, on a spot destined to become memorable in the struggle, were already animated by the kindling promise of the future. Hugh

Henry Brackenridge, a graduate with Freneau, afterwards a celebrated Judge and author, and Freneau, had already developed a taste for poetry, and they united, for their commencement exercise, in the composition of a dialogue : " A Poem on the Rising Glory of America," which they pronounced together, sounding in animated blank verse, the achievements of colonization in the past and the visionary grandeur of empire hereafter. This joint poem was published in Philadelphia, in 1772. The portion written by Freneau opens the collection of his poems published in 1865 by W. J. Middleton, New York.

The next information we have of Freneau is gathered from the dates of the poems which he contributed to the journals published by Hugh Gaine and Anderson, in New York, in 1775. They exhibit his interest in the important military affairs of the year in Boston and are found in the work above named.

In a poem of this year, " Mac Sniggen," a satire on some hostile poetaster, he expresses a desire to cross the Atlantic :

" Long have I sat on this disast'rous shore,
And sighing, sought to gain a passage o'er
To Europe's towns, where, as our travellers say,
Poets may flourish, or perhaps they may ;"

An inclination for foreign travel, which was gratified in 1776, by a voyage to the West Indies, where he appears to have remained some time in a mercantile capacity, visiting Jamaica and the Danish island of Santa Cruz. Several of his most striking poems, as the " House of Night," and the " Beauties of Santa Cruz," were written on these visits.

In 1779, Freneau was engaged as a leading contributor to " The United States Magazine : A Repository of History, Politics and Literature," edited by his college friend and fellow patriot, Hugh Henry Brackenridge, and published by Francis Bailey, Philadelphia. It was issued monthly from January to December, when its discontinuance was announced " until an established peace and a fixed value of the money shall render it convenient or possible to take it up again." The volume forms a most interesting memorial, in its literary as well as historical matter, of this important year of the war. Freneau wrote much for it in prose and verse and with equal spirit in both.

His poem on " Santa Cruz," in this magazine, is prefaced by an interesting prose pescription of the island. In it occurs a noticeable testimony of the author on the subject of negro slavery.

Freneau has also recorded his detestation of the cruelties of West India slavery in verse, in the poem, a terrific picture of slave life, addressed " To Sir Toby, a sugar planter in the interior parts of Jamaica:"

" If there exists a HELL—the case is clear—
Sir Toby's slaves enjoy that portion here."

In another poem " On the Emigration to America, and Peopling the Western Country," published in his volume of 1795, Freneau comes nearer home, in the declaration of his opinions on this subject, when he writes : —

" O come the time and haste the day,
When man shall man no longer crush,
When reason shall enforce her sway,
Nor these fair regions raise our blush,
Where still the African complains,
And mourns his yet unbroken chains."

In after life, when the poet himself, under the mild system of Northern servitude, became the owner of slaves in New Jersey, he uniformly treated them with kindness, manumitted them in advance of the Emancipation Act in the State, and supported on the farm those of them who were not able to take care of themselves. One of these, a veteran mammy, proud of having opened the door in her day to General Washington and been addressed by him in a word or two on that important occasion, long survived the poet.

In the year following the publication of the Magazine, Freneau, having embarked as passenger in a merchant vessel from Philadelphia, on another voyage to the West Indies, was captured by a British cruiser off the Capes of the Delaware and carried with the prize to New York. There he was confined, on his arrival, in the *Scorpion*, one of the hulks lying in the harbor used as prison-ships. The cruel treatment which he experienced on board, with the aggravated horrors of foul air and other privations, speedily threw him into a fever, when he was transferred to the hospital ship, *Hunter*, which proved simply an exchange of one species of suffering for another more aggravated. How long Freneau was confined in this hideous prison we are not informed, nor by what influences he gained his discharge. He carried with him, however, on his escape, a burning memory of the severities and indignities he had endured, which he gave expression to in one of the most characteristic of his poetical productions, " The British Prison Ship," which was published by Francis Bailey, Philadelphia, 1781.

Freneau now became a frequent contributor of patriotic odes and occasional poems, celebrating the incidents of the war, to "The Freeman's Journal" of Philadelphia. Literature was, however, not then a profitable occupation; and Government, which had exhausted its resources in keeping an army in the field, had scant opportunity of rewarding its champions. The poet, looking to other means of subsistence, returned to his seafaring and mercantile hab its and became known by his voyages to the West Indies as "Captain Freneau." He still however, kept up the use of the pen. In 1783, besides his poetical contributions to the newspapers, including several New Years Addresses, written for the carriers of the Philadelphia journals, a species of rhyming for which he had great facility, we find him publishing in that city a translation of the travels of M. Abbe Robin, the chaplain of Count Rochambeau, giving an account of the progress of the French army from Newport to Yorktown. In 1784 Freneau was at the island of Jamaica, writing a poetical description of Port Royal.

The first collection of his poetical writings which he made, entitled "The Poems of Philip Freneau, written chiefly during the late War," was published by Francis Bailey "at Yorrick's Head, in Market street," Philadelphia, in 1786. It is prefaced by a brief "Advertisement" signed by the publisher, in which he states the pieces now collected had been left in his hands by the author more than a year previously, with permission to publish them whenever he thought proper.

The success of this volume led to the publication, by Mr. Bailey, of another collection of Freneau's writings in 1788. It is entitled "The Miscellaneous Works of Mr. Philip Freneau, containing his Essays and Additional Poems." This volume, as not uncommon even with works of very limited extent in that early period of the nation, was published by subscription. Among the subscribers were DeWitt Clinton, Edward Livingston and other distinguished citizens of New York; Matthew Carey, David Rittenhouse, John Parke A. M., and others of Philadelphia; thirty copies were taken in Maryland; but the largest number was contributed by South Carolina, that State supplying two hundred and fifty, or more than half the entire list. Captain Freneau was well known and highly appreciated at Charleston, which he frequently visited in the course of his mercantile adventures to the West Indies, and where his younger brother, Peter, who subsequently edited a political journal in that city, and was in intimate correspondence with President Jefferson, was already established as an influential citizen.

After several years spent in voyaging, we find Freneau again in active literary employment in 1791, as editor of the "Daily Advertiser," a journal printed in New York, the superintendence of which he presently exchanged for that of the "National Gazette," at Philadelphia, the first number of which appeared under his direction in October of the same year. He was employed at the same time by Jefferson, the Secretary of State,—the seat of government being then at Philadelphia,—as translating clerk in the State Department, with a salary of two hundred and fifty dollars a year. It was a time of fierce political excitement, when the newly framed Constitution, not yet fully established in its working, was exposed to the fierce criticism of its adversaries; while popular opinion was greatly excited by the rising tumult of ideas generated in the French Revolution. In this strife of parties Freneau was an active partisan of the new French ideas, was a supporter of Genet, the minister who sought to entangle the country in the great European struggle, and, as might be expected, was an unsparing assailant of the policy of Washington, whose character he had heretofore eulogized. Washington was annoyed, and Hamilton attacked Jefferson for his official support of the troublesome editor. Jefferson replied that he had befriended Freneau as a man of genius; but that he had never written for his paper. It is unquestionably true, however, that Freneau's political writings, at this time, had Jefferson's warmest sympathy.

The "Gazette" came to an end with its second volume and second year, in 1793, after which Freneau became a resident of New Jersey. He had still, however, an inclination to editorial life, and we accordingly find him, in the spring of 1795, publishing at Mount Pleasant, near Middletown Point, a new journal entitled "The Jersey Chronicle," before alluded to.

The same year from his press at Mount Pleasant he issued a volume of his poems entitled "Poems, written between the years 1768 and 1794, by Philip Freneau, of New Jersey." There are other editions of his poems, but this one is so rare that it is highly prized by antiquarians. In a late catalogue of a London bookseller it is advertised for sale, price £ 3.10 s. The last copy we have heard of for sale in this country was one in a Washington antiquarian bookstore for which the dealer asked some forty odd dollars, and finally got down to thirty-five, for a small octavo volume of 456 pages!

In 1797 he edited and aided in printing and publishing in New York, a miscellaneous periodical entitled "The Time Piece and Literary Companion." It was printed in quarto form and appeared three times a week. In 1799 he published in Philadelphia a thin octavo volume of "Letters on various subjects, &c.." under the nom de plume of "Robert Slender, A M."

For some years after this we have no particular account of his occupation, but he appears to have resided still in New Jersey, penning occasional verses on topics suggested by the day. In 1809 he published the fourth collection of his writings entitled "Poems published during the American Revolution," &c.

(Remainder of the article on Freneau next week.)

Freneau lived to commemorate the incidents of the second war wi.h Great Britain in 1812. He wrote various poems celebrating the naval actions of Hull, Porter, Macdonough and others. His traditionary hatred of England survives in these and other compositions which he puolished in New York, in 1815, in two small volumes entitled " A Collection of Poems on American Affairs and a variety of other subjects, &c." A distinguished writer says in reviewing this volume: " He depicts land battles and naval fights with much animation and gay coloring ; and being himself an old sun of Neptune, he is never at a loss for appropriate circumstance and expressive diction, when the scene lies at sea."

After witnessing and chronicling in his verse the conflicts of two wars, Freneau had yet many years of life before him.— They were mostly passed in rural retirement at Mount Pleasant. He occasionally visited New York, keeping up acquaintance with the leaders of the Democratic party. H.s appearance and conservation at this time has been graphically described by the late Dr. John W. Francis, in whom the genius and history of Freneau excited the warmest interest, and which he was published in the "Cyclopedia of American Literature."

" I had, says Dr. Francis, when very young, read the poetry of Freneau, and as we instinctively became attached to the writers who first captivate our imaginations, it was with much zest that I formed a personal acquaintaince with the Revolutionary bard. He was at that time about seventy-six years old, when he first introduced himself to me in my library. I gave him an earnest welcome. He was somewhat below the ordinary height; in person thin yet muscular; with a firm step though a little inclined to stoop; his countenance wore traces of care, yet lightened with intelligence as he spoke ; he was mild in enunciation, neither rapid nor slow, but clear, distinct and emphatic. His forehead was rather beyond the medium elevation ; his eyes a dark gray, occupying a socket deeper than common ; his hair must have once been beautiful ; it was now thinned and of an iron gray. He was free of all ambitious displays; his habitual expression was pensive. His dress might have passed for that of a farmer. New York, the city of his birth was his most interesting theme ; his collegiate career with Madison, next. His story of many of his occasional poems was quite romantic. As he had at command types and a printing press, when an incident of moment in the Revolution occurred, he would retire for composition, or find shelter under the shade of some tree, indite his lyrics, repair to the press, set up his types and issue his productions. There was no difficulty in versification with him. I told him what I had heard Jeffrey, the Scotch reviewer, say of his writings, that the time would arrive when his poetry like that of Hudilras, would command a commentator like Grey. It is remarkable how tenaciously Freneau preserved the acquisitions of his early classical studies, notwithstanding he had for many years, in the after portion of his life, been occupied in pursuits so entirely alien to books. - There is no portrait of the patriot Freneau; he always firmly declined the painters art and would brook no "counterfeit presentment." (*Cyclopedia of Amer. Lit.*)

The aversion of Freneau to sitting for his portrait, noticed by Dr. Francis, was one of his peculiarities, for which it is not easy to suggest a sufficient explanation. As an author he was careful of the preservation of his fame. Certainly the cause was not to be found in any unfavorable impression his likeness might create, for he was, as accurately described by Dr. Francis, of an interesting appearance in

rge. In youth he was regarded as handsome. His brother Peter was renowned in South Carolina for his personal beauty. But whatever the motive, Freneau resolutely declined to have his portrait painted. He was once waited upon by the artist, Rembrandt Peale, with a request for this purpose, by a body of gentlemen in Philadelphia; but he was inexorable on the subject. On another occasion, the elder Jarvis, with a view of securing his likeness, was smuggled into a corner of the room at a dinner party at Dr. Hosack's, to which the poet had been invited; but the latter detected the design and arrested its accomplishment. In late years, the neglect has been in a measure repaired. The portrait prefixed to the volume of his "poems with a memoir by Evert A. Duyckinck," published in 1865, was sketched by an artist, at the suggestion and dictates of several members of the poet's family, who retained the most vivid recollection of his personal appearance. It was pronounced by them a fair representation of the man in the maturity of his physical powers, previous to the inroads of old age. His daughter, Mrs. Leadbeater, and his grandson and adopted son, Mr. Philip L. Freneau, of New York, were among those who pronounced it a satisfactory likeness.

The poems of Philip Freneau, if we may be allowed here to repeat an estimate of his powers from a sketch written some years ago, represent his times, the war of wit and verse no less than of sword and stratagem of the Revolution; and he superadds to this material a humorous, homely simplicity, peculiarly his own, in which he paints the life of village rustics, with their local manners fresh about them; of days when tavern delights were to be freely spoken of, before temperance societies and Maine laws were thought of; when men went to prison at the summons of inexorable creditors, and when Connecticut deacons rushed out of meeting to arrest and waylay the passing Sunday traveller. When these humors of the day were exhausted, and the impulses of patriotism were gratified in song; when he had paid his respects to Rivington and Hugh Gaine, he solaced himself with remoter themes; in the version of an ode of Horace, a visionary meditation on the antiquities of America or a sentimental effusion on the lives of Sappho. These show the fine tact and delicate handling of Freneau, who deserves much more consideration in this respect from critics than he has received. A writer from whom the fastidious Campbell in his best day thought it worth while to borrow an entire line, is worth looking into. It is from Freneau's *Indian Burying Ground*, the last image of that fine visionary stanza:

"By midnight moons, o'er moistening dews,
In vestments for the chase arrayed,
The hunter still the deer pursues,
The hunter and the deer—a shade."

Campbell has given the line a rich setting in the lovelorn fantasy of O'Conor's Child:

"Bright as the bow that spans he tstorm
In Erin's yellow vesture clad,
A son of light—a lovely form,
He comes and makes her glad;
Now on the grass green turf he sits,
His tassell'd horn beside him laid,
Now o'er the hills in chase he flits
The hunter and the deer a shade."

There is also a line of Sir Walter Scott which has its prototype in Freneau. In the introduction to the third canto of *Marmion*, in the apostrophe to the Duke of Brunswick, we read—

"Lamented chief!—not thine the power
To save in that presumptuous hour,
When Prussia hurried to the field,
And snatched the spear but left the shield."

In Freneau's poem on the heroes of Eutaw, we have this stanza:

"They saw their injured country's woe;
The flaming town, the wasted field;
Then rushed to meet the insulting foe
They took the spear—but left the shield."

An anecdote which the late Henry Brevoort was accustomed to relate of his visit to Scott, affords assurance that the poet was really indebted to Freneau, and that he would not on a proper occasion, have hesitated to acknowledge the obligation. Mr. Brevoort was asked by Scott respecting the authorship of certain verses in the battle of Eutaw, which he had seen in a magazine, and had by heart, and which he knew were American. He was told that they were by Freneau, when he remarked "The poem is as fine a thing as there is of the kind in the language." Scott also praised one of the Indian poems.

We might add to these instances that in 1790 Freneau, in his poetical correspondence between Nanny, the Philadelphia Housekeeper, and Nabby her friend, in New York, upon the subject of the removal of Congress to the former city, hit upon some of the peculiar pleasantry of Moore's Epistles in verse, of the present century.

"Freneau surprises us often by his neatness of execution and skill in versification.

He handles a triple-rhymed stanza in the octosyllabic measure particularly well. His appreciation of nature is tender and sympathetic,—one of the pure springs which fed the more boisterous current of his humor when he came out among men, to deal with quackery, pretence and injustice. But what is, perhaps, most worthy of notice in Freneau is his originality, the instinct with which his genius marked out a path for itself, in those days when most writers were languidly leaning upon the old foreign school of Pope and Darwin. He was not afraid of home things and incidents. Dealing with facts, realites, and the life around him, wherever he was, his writings have still an interest where the vague expressions of other poets are forgotten. It is not to be denied, however, that Freneau was sometimes careless. He thought and wrote with improvidence. His jests are sometimes misdirected; and his verses are unequal in execution. Yet it is not too much to predict, that, through the genuine nature of some of his productions and the historic incidents of others, all that he wrote will yet be called for and find favor in numerous editions"—*Cyclopedia of Amer. Literature.*

This prediction was ventured nearly twenty years ago. It is in a measure fulfilled, an edition of his poems having been published in 1865, the only publication of any of his poems since 1815.

FRENEAU'S FAMILY.

Philip Freneau left a family of four daughters, all of whom were living in 1865. The mother of Governor Seymour of New York (Mary, the daughter of General Jonathan Forman) was a niece of Mrs. Philip Freneau, the wife of the poet. The Freneaus, through the second marriage of the poet's mother, are connected with the Kearney family of New Jersey. Philip Freneau married at about the age of thirty Miss Eleanor Forman, daughter of Samuel Forman, a wealthy citizen of New Jersey. General Jonathan Forman and Denise Forman, who were much engaged in military affairs in the State during the Revolution, were her brothers. David Forman also in military life was her cousin. This lady, who shared her husband's talent for poetry, corresponding with him, for several years before their marriage, in verse, was of marked character ahd intelligence. She was devotedly attached to the Episcopal Church, which the family attended, having left the French Church in the lifetime of the poet's father. Mrs. Freneau survived her husband many years, retaining in her latter days much of the most interesting memories of the days of the Revolution.

The remains of Mrs. Freneau repose, with those of her husband, in the family burial ground at Mount Pleasant, N. J. A monument to the poet's memory, within a few years has been erected on the spot.

Freneau lived nearly to the completion of his eightieth year. He lost his life, December 18th, 1833, "by exposure and cold while going on foot in the night during a snow storm to his residence near Freehold."

The *Monmouth Inquirer* thus announced his death :

"Mr. Freneau was in the village and started, toward evening, to go home, about two miles. In attempting to go across he appears to have got lost and mired in a bog meadow, where his lifeless corpse was discovered yesterday morning. Captain Freneau was a staunch Whig in the time of the Revolution, a good soldier and a warm patriot. The productions of his pen animated his countrymen in the darkest days of '76 and the effusions of his muse cheered the desponding soldier as he fought the battles of freedom."

"The eulogy of the Monmouth journal," says one writer, "will remain Freneau's highest distinction. He was the popular poet of the Revolution."

The following extract from a brief notice by Anna Maria Woodhull, of Freneau, is from the MONMOUTH DEMOCRAT of May 29th, 1873 :

"He first saw the light in the city of New York and was graduated at New Jersey College. For some time a resident of Monmouth, he was frequently the guest of the late Col. Elias Conover, grandfather of William H. Conover, Sr., of Freehold. At the time of his death he owned and occupied the house now belonging to Mr. John Buck situated about two miles below the town. He was a great admirer of Shakespeare. I own an old copy, formerly in his possession (Theobolds, London, 1772.) which I prize highly ; also an autograph bold and free, dated 1781."

In his volume of poems before referred to, printed and published by himself at Mount Pleasant in this County, he gives vivid local descriptions of a Monmouth county printing office in the olden time, and of other local matters which deserve preservation in our local history, and in another chapter we purpose quoting them and also a few other pieces as specimens of his style and as giving his sentiments on politics, temperance and religion and other subjects.

The most recent volume of his poems was published in 1865 by W. J. Middleton, New York, with an introductory memoir by Evert A. Duyckinck, to which we are indebted for many of the facts in the foregoing outline of his life. Though this volume only gives his poems relating to the Revolution yet the fine likeness of the poet prefixed make it a work which would be highly prized by many of our readers.

In the collection of his poems published in 1809, we find the list of subscribers which he procured for it headed by the names of James Madison then President, and Thomas Jefferson; and in Monmouth County we find the following subscribers, viz: Middletown: Jehu Patterson, Esq., Capt Hendrick Hendrickson, James Mott, Esq., Col. Jarrett Stillwell, Capt. Isaac Van Dorn, Capt. Denise Hendrickson, B. Gen. Richard Poole. Middletown Point: Cornelius P. Vanderhoof, Esq., Dr. William Reynolds, Capt. John Hall. Near Middletown Point, John Van Pelt, Merchant. Peter Johnson, William Walton. Allentown, Richard Stout, Merchant, Freehold, John Quay, Esq., Mr. David Cook. Monmouth, Hon. James Cox.

OLD MONMOUTH DURING THE REVOLUTION

Historians generally concede that no state among the old thirteen suffered during the war more than did New Jersey; and it is generally admitted that no county in our state suffered more than did old Monmouth. In addition to the outrages to which the citizens were subjected from the regular British army, they were continually harassed by depredations committed by regularly organized bands of Refugees, and also by the still more lawless acts of a set of outcasts known as the Pine Woods Robbers, who, though pretending to be Tories, yet, if opportunity offered, robbed Tories as well as Whigs.

The Refugees, or Loyalists as they called themselves, were generally native born Americans who sided with the British, regularly organized, with officers commissioned by the Board of Associated Loyalists at New York, of which body the President was William Franklin, the last Tory governor of New Jersey, an illegitimate son of Dr. Benjamin Franklin. The Refugees had a strongly fortified settlement at Sandy Hook, the lighthouse there defended with cannon and British vessels of war always lying in the vicinity. From this settlement or "Refugees' town," as it was sometimes called, these marauders would sally forth to plunder and murder in the adjoining county. To show the perils by which the citizens of old Monmouth were surrounded and the outrages to which they were subjected, we append some extracts chiefly from ancient papers, which though plain and unvarnished yet will give a vivid idea of life and times in this county in the dark days of the Revolution.

REFUGEE RAIDS IN OLD MONMOUTH.—PROMINENT PATRIOTS ROBBED, CAPTURED AND MURDERED.

"June 3d 1778. We are informed that on Wednesday morning last, a party of about seventy of the Greens from Sandy Hook, landed near Major Kearney's (near Keyport,) headed the Mill Creek, Middletown Point, and marched to Mr. John Burrows, made him prisoner, burnt his mills and both his store houses—all valuable buildings, besides a great deal of his furniture. They also took prisoners, Lieutenant Colonel Smock, Captain Christopher Little, Mr. Joseph Wall, Captain Joseph Covenhoven (Conover) and several other persons, and killed Messrs Pearce and Van Brockle and wounded another man mortally. Having completed this and several other barbarities they precipitately returned the same morning to give an account of their abominable deeds to their bloody employers. A number of these gentry, we learn, were formerly inhabitants of that neighborhood."

The "Greens" above mentioned, it is said, were Refugee or Loyalist Jerseyman who joined the British. Their organization was sometimes called "the New Jersey Royal Volunteers" under command of General Cortlandt Skinner, of whom some farther particulars may be given hereafter.

"April 26th, 1779. An expedition consisting of seven or eight hundred men under Col. Hyde went to Middletown, Red Bank, Tinton Falls, Shrewsbury and other places, robbing and burning as they went. They took Justice Covenhoven and others prisoners, Captain Burrows and Colonel Holmes assembled our militia and killed three and wounded fifteen of the enemy. The enemy however succeeded in carrying off horses, cattle and other plunder."

In the above extract the name of Justice "Covenhoven" is mentioned. The names of different members of the Covenhoven family are frequently met with in ancient papers and records among those who favored the patriot cause. Since that time the name has gradually changed from Covenhoven to Conover.

In May, two or three weeks after the above affair, some two or three hundred Tories landed at Middletown, on what was then termed a "picarooning" expedition. The term "picaroon" originally meaning a plunderer or pirate, seems to have been used in that day to convey about the same idea that "raider" did in the late Rebellion.

"June 9th, 1779. A party of about fifty Refugees, landed in Monmouth and marched to Tinton Falls undiscovered, where they surprised and carried off Colonel Hendrickson, Colonel Wyckoff, Captain Chadwick and Captain McKnight, with several privates of the militia, and drove off sheep and horned cattle. About thirty of our militia hastily collected, made some resistance but were repulsed with the loss of two men killed and ten wounded, the enemy's loss unknown.

April 1st, 1780. About this time, the Tories made another raid to Tinton Falls, and took off seven prisoners. Another party took Mr. Bowne prisoner at Middletown, who, but three days before, had been exchanged, and had just got home.

About the last of April, the refugees attacked the house of John Holmes, Upper Freehold, and robbed him of a large amount of continental money, a silver watch, gold ring, silver buckles, pistols, clothing, &c.

June 1st, 1780. The noted Colonel Tye, (a mulatto formerly a slave in Monmouth Co.) with his motley company of about twenty blacks and whites, carried off prisoners Capt. Barney Smock, and Gilbert Van Mater, spiked an iron cannon and took four horses. Their rendezvous was at Sandy Hook.

Shortly after this Colonel Tye aided in the attack on Capt. Joshua Huddy, at his house at Colts Neck. The particulars of this affair, we purpose publishing in a sketch of Captain Huddy. Colonel Tye, (or Titus, formerly a slave belonging to John Corlies,) though guilty of having a skin darker than our own, yet was generally acknowledged to be about the most honorable, brave, generous and determined of the refugee leaders. Like our forefathers, he fought for his liberty, which our ancestors unfortunately refused to give him.

October 15, 1781. A party of refugees from Sandy Hook landed at night, at Shrewsbury, and marched undiscovered to Colt's Neck, and took six prisoners. The alarm reached the Court House about four or five o'clock, P. M., and a number of inhabitants, among whom was Dr. Nathaniel Scudder, went in pursuit. They rode to Black Point to try to recapture the six Americans, and while firing from the bank Dr. Scudder was killed. Dr. Scudder was one of the most prominent, active and useful patriots of Monmouth, and his death was a serious loss to the Americans.

About the beginning of August, 1782, Richard Wilgus, an American, was shot below Allentown, while on guard to prevent contraband trade with the British.

February 8th, 1782. About forty refugees under Lieut. Steelman, came via Sandy Hook to Pleasant Valley. They took twenty horses and five sleighs, which they loaded with plunder; they also took several prisoners, viz: Hendrick Hendrickson and his two sons, Peter Covenhoven, or Conover as the name is now called, was made prisoner once before in 1779, as before related,) Garret Hendrickson, Samuel Bowne and son, and James Denise. At Garret Hendrickson's a young man named William Thompson, got up slyly and went off and informed Capt. John Schenck, of Col. Holmes' regiment, who collected all the men he could to pursue. They overtook and attacked the refugees, and the before mentioned William Thompson was killed and Mr. Cottrel wounded. They however took twelve refugees prisoners, three of whom were wounded. But in returning, they unexpectedly fell in with a party of sixteen men under Stevenson, and a sudden firing caused eight of the prisoners to escape. But Capt. Schenck ordered his men to charge bayonet, and the tories surrendered. Capt. Schenck took nineteen horses and five sleighs, and took twenty-one prisoners.

The first of the foregoing extracts, relating to a raid of the British in Middletown township, in 1778, and landing near Major Kearneys, in the vicinity of Keyport, is probably the affair referred to in a tradition given in Howes collections, which we give below, as it explains why the Refugees fled so precipitately. It will be noticed, however, that the tradition does not agree with extract quoted as to damage done; but we have no doubt but that the statement copied from the ancient paper (Collins Gazette) is correct, as it was written but a few days after the affair took place.

"The proximity of this part of Monmouth county to New York rendered it, in the war of the Revolution, peculiarly liable to the incursions of the British troops. Many of the inhabitants, although secretly favorable to the American cause, were obliged to feign allegiance to the crown, or lose their property by marauding parties of the refugees, from vessels generally lying off Sandy Hook. Among those of this description was Major Kearney, a resident near the present site of Keyport. On one occasion a party of thirty or forty refugees stopped at his dwelling on their way to Middletown Point, where they intended to burn a dwelling and some mills. Kearney feigned gratification at their visit, and falsely informed them there were probably some rebel troops at the Point, in which case it would be dangerous for them to march thither. He ordered his negro servant, Jube, thither to make inquiry, at the same time secretly giving him the cue how to act. In due length of time Jube, who had gone but a short distance, returned and hastily entered the room where Kearney and the Refugees were, and exclaimed: "Oh Massa! Massa! the rebels are at the Point thick as blackberries!" They have just come down from the Court house and say they are going to march down here to night. The ruse succeeded; the Refugees, alarmed, precipitately retreated to their boats, leaving the Major to rejoice at the stratagem which had saved the property of his friends from destruction."

The probability is that the ruse prevented the Refugees from doing as much damage as they had intended, although they remained long enough to inflict considerable injury, as has been related.

ATTACK ON THE RUSSEL FAMILY.

As the outrage was an unusually aggravated one, even for Refugees, and as it will be necessary to refer to some of the parties concerned in it hereafter, to explain other events, we give the particulars as derived from various sources. The first extract is from Collin's New Jersey Gazette:—

"On the 30th of April, 1780, a party of negroes and refugees from Sandy Hook landed at Shrewsbury, in order to plunder. During their excursion a Mr. Russell, who attempted some resistance to their depredations, was killed, and his grandchild had five balls shot through him, but is yet living. Captain Warner, of the privateer brig Elizabeth, was made prisoner by these ruffians, but was released by giving them two half joes. This banditti also took off several persons, among whom were Capt. James Green and Ensign John Morris, of the Militia."

The annexed additional particulars are from Howe's collections—"Mr. Russell was an elderly man, aged about 60 years; as the party entered his dwelling, which was in the night, he fired and missed.— William Gilian, a native of Shrewsbury, their leader, seized the old gentleman by the collar, and was in the act of stabbing him in the face and eyes with a bayonet, when the fire blazed up, and shedding a momentary light upon the scene, enabled the younger Russell, who lay wounded on the floor, to shoot Gilian. John Farnham, (A Refugee named Farnham was afterwards captured, tried and hung at Freehold—we presume it was the same man,) a native of Middletown, thereupon aimed his musket at the young man, but it was knocked up by Lippincott, who had married into the family. The party then went off. The child was accidentally wounded in the affray."

The Lippencott above referred to was, during the late years of the war, quite a noted refugee leader—the same Captain Richard Lippencott who executed Captain Joshua Huddy. (A New York publication entitled "Tales and traditions of New York, says that Capt. Lippencott was among the Refugees who attacked and burned Toms River.) It will be noticed that a younger Russell is referred to as having been wounded and lying on the floor. This was John Russell, a very active member of the Militia, who at the time of this outrage was at home on a furlough with his parents and wife. This John Russell after the war removed to Cedar Creek, in Ocean County, where he lived to quite an advanced age. His account of the affair is as follows:

There were seven refugees and he (John) saw them through the window, and at one time they got so near that he told his father he was sure they could kill four of them and wished to fire, as he believed the other three would run. His father persuaded him not to fire, but to do so when they broke into the house.—

When they broke in the father fired first but missed his aim; he was then fired upon and killed. John Russell fired and killed the man who shot his father. John Russell was shot in the side (the scars of the wound were visible until he died)— After being wounded he fell on the floor and pretended that he was dead. The refugees then went to plundering the house. The mother and wife of John were lying in a bed with the child; the child awoke and asked: "Grandmother wnat's the matter?" A refugee pointed his gun at it and fired and said "that's what's the matter." Whether he really intended to wound the child, or only to frighten it, is uncertain, but the child was, as before stated, badly wounded, but eventually recovered.

As the refugees were preparing to leave, one of the number pointed his musket at young Russell, as he lay on the floor, and was about firing, saying he didn't believe he was dead yet; whereupon another knocked his musket up, saying it was a shame to fire upon a dying man, and the load went into the ceiling. After the refugees were gone, John got up, had his wounds attended to, and exclaimed to his wife: "Ducky! I'll come out all right yet." He did come out all right, and we have good reason to believe before the war ended he aided in visiting severe retribution on the Refugees, for their doings at this time. Among this party of Refugees was the notorious Phil White.

THE CAPTURE AND DEATH OF THE REFUGEE, PHIL WHITE.

A correct version of the Affair. Slanders refuted and Patriots Vindicated. Affidavits of Aaron White, of Philip White's guards; Statements of Gen. Forman, &c.

Though the death of the refugee Philip White, (commonly called Phil White) is occasionally referred to in modern works, there are none which give complete or correct accounts of the affair. In the brief statement given in Howe's collections, unjust imputations are cast upon his guard, as will hereafter be seen.

When Capt. Huddy was so brutally murdered by the Refugees near the Highlands, it will be remembered that a label was fastened to his breast, the last sentence of which was

"*Up goes Huddy for Philp White.*"

Though the refugees at one time asserted that Capt. Huddy had an agency in the death of Phil. White, yet this preposterous charge was at once shown to be an infamous falsehood, as when White was killed, Capt. Huddy was a prisoner, confined in the old sugar house, New York, (Duane's sugar house). The British asserted that "he had taken a certain Philip White, cut off both his arms, broke his legs, pulled out one of his eyes, damned him and then bid him run." How much of this was true will be seen by conclusive evidence given below, before quoting, which we will give a version of the affair as given in Howe's collection, from a traditionary source.

"White, the Refugee, was a carpenter, and served his time in Shrewsbury. Six days after Huddy was taken, he was surprised by a party of militia lighthorse, near Snag Swamp, in the eastern part of the township. After laying down his arms in token of surrender, he took up his musket and killed a Mr. Hendrickson. He was however secured, and while being taken to Freehold, was killed at Pyle's Corner, three miles from there. He was under a guard of three men, the father of whom was murdered at Shrewsbury the year previous, by a band of reufugees, among whom was White, and he was therefore highly exasperated against the prisoner. Some accounts state that he was killed while attempting to escape; others with more probability that they pricked him with their swords and thus to run and cruelly murdered.

There are several errors in the foregoing and it is to be especially regretted that the untrue charge of wanton cruelty, contained at the close of this extract, should have found a place in so useful a book as the one containing it. Correct versions of this affair are found in ancient papers, but for the present we will give several affidavits taken at the time as being the most conclusive evidence. These affidavits were forwarded to Gen. Washington, and by him transmitted to Congress, April 20th, 1782.

These affidavits are of Aaron White, who was taken prisoner with Phil. White, and of each of the three guards.

Deposition of Aaron White.

COUNTY OF MONMOUTH. ss:—Aaron White being duly sworn, deposeth:

That he was taken prisoner with Philip White, that the deponent left New York in company with Philip White, Jeremiah Bell, negro Moses, John Fennimore and Robert Howell, on Thursday night, the

OLD TIMES IN OLD MONMOUTH.

28th day of March last; that they sailed from New York to the Hook, where they remained until morning, being Friday; that the deponent understood that Capt. Huddy was then a prisoner; that on the day following, being Saturday, the 30th, the deponent being off in a boat with Fennimore, and having observed that the said Philip White and Moses had an engagement with some of the troops on shore, he, the deponent, went in a boat to their relief, meaning to take them off; that when he came on shore he joined the said Philip White and negro Moses, and pursued one Thomas Berkley, with whom they had been engaged; that in pursuit, the light horse came down, and the deponent with the said Philip White were made prisoners, that they were put under guard to be sent to Freehold for confinement; that on the way from Colt's Neck to Freehold, between Daniel Grandin's and Samuel Leonard's the deponent was told by one of his guards that Philip White was running away; that the deponent looked back and saw the horsemen in pursuit of something, but being about half a mile distant, could not distinguish after whom or what the pursuit was; that the field in which they were pursuing was near the brook next to Mr. Leonard's adjoining a wood; that Lieut. Rhea and George Brindley left the deponent under guard of two men and ran their horses back towards the place the other men were pursuing; that the deponent afterwards understood that it is was Philip White they were pursuing, and that he was killed in the pursuit; that Joshua Huddy was not one of the guard or party, and the deponent understood and verily believes that he was then a prisoner in New York; and the deponent further and lastly declares, that the above is the truth as related without any fear, threats or compulsion whatever.

AARON WHITE.

Sworn before me this 15th of April, 1782-
DAVID FORMAN,
Justice of the Peace, Monmouth County.

That a clear idea of the order of the principal events referred to in these affidavits may be obtained, we will here state that Capt. Joshua Huddy was taken prisoner by the British at Toms River, on Sunday, March 24th, 1782; on Saturday, the 30th of March, six days after, Phil. White and Aaron, were taken prisoners by the Monmouth militia the same day (March 30th,) Philip White was killed, at which time Capt. Huddy was confined in the sugar house prison at New York, where he had been put on Tuesday, March 27th, and remained until Monday, April 8th, when he was taken on board a sloop and put in irons, and four days later—on the 12th of April, 1782—he was hung near the Highlands; his body was delivered to the Americans, sent to Freehold, and buried with the honors of war. Three days after his death—on the 15th of April, these affidavits were taken, while the recollections of all the circumstances referred to were fresh in the minds of the witness.

ORIGIN OF FAMILY NAMES.

A surname is an additional name added to a proper or given name for the sake of distinction, and so called because originally written *over* the other name instead of after it, from the French *Surnom*, probably derived from the Latin "Super nomen," signifying above the name.

Surnames have originated in various ways. Some are derived from the names of places; others from offices and professions, from personal peculiarities; from the Christian or proper name of the father; from the performance of certain actions; from objects in the animal, mineral and vegetable world, and from accidental circumstances of every varied character.

According to Camden, surnames began to be taken up in France about the year 1000, and in England about the time of the Conquest (1066) or a very little before.

Local names form the largest class of our surnames. First among these are those which are national, expressing the country whence the person first bearing the name came, as English, Scott, French, Ireland, Britain, Fleming (from Flanders) Gaskin, (from Gascony), &c. Names were taken from almost every county, town and hamlet, as Cheshire, Chester, Hull, Ross, Kent, Cunningham, Huntingdon, Preston, Compton, etc., so that local names of this class may number many thousands. For instance, a person whose native place was Chester, might remove to another, place the inhabitants of which, to distinguish him, would give him the surname of Chester, originally prefixing it with "*of*," frequently shortened to "*O*" or "*A*," signifying *from* or *at*, as *John of Chester*, *John O'Chester*; John at Kirby, John A'Kirby.

The prefixes after a time were dropped and the names descended to children as simply Chester and Kirby.

Besides these we have a great number of local surnames which are general and descriptive of the nature or situation of the residence of the persons upon whom they were bestowed, as Hill, Wood, Dale, Park, &c. The prefix *At* or *Atte* was generally used before these names as *John At Hill*, meaning John at the hill or John who lived at the hill; *James At Well, John At Wood*, now Atwell and Atwood. In this way men took surnames from rivers and trees from residing at or near them, as Beck, Gill, Grant, Beach, Bush, Ash, Thorn.

Surnames derived from Christian or baptismal names are probably next in number to the local surnames; some of these are probably the most ancient of all surnames, many of them varied by prefixes and suffixes. Of this class we have first, the names terminating in *son*, which was added to the name of the father; John the son of William, was called John, William's son—John Williamson; *Johnson*, John's son; *Thompson*, Thomas' son; *Simpson*, Simon's son; *Wilson*, Will's son.

The Welsh merely appended "*s*," instead of son, as *Edwards*, son of Edward; *Davis*, son of David; *Jones*, son of John; *Hughes*, son of Hugh; *Williams*, son of William, &c.

Then we have surnames formed from abbreviated names, pet names and nicknames, as *Watson* the son of Wat or Walter; *Watts*, signifying the same; *Dobson*, son of Dob or Robert.

A great many surnames are formed of abbreviated and nurse names with the addition of the diminutive terminations *ette, kin, cock* or *cox*, all of which signify "little" or "child." From the termination *ette* we have such names as *Willet*, which means little Will, or son of Will; *Hallet*, Little Hal or Henry. From *kin* or *kin's* we have Wilkins, Simpkins, Atkins, Higgins, Hawkins, Dobbins. From *cock* or *cox* we have Wilcox, Simcox, &c.

Some surnames have the prefix *Fitz*, of Norman origin, signifying son. as *Fitz Clarence*, son of Clarence, *Fitzgerald*, son of Gerald. Fitz was applied to sons both legitimate and illegitimate.

The Welsh in like manner prefixed *Ap* to denote son, as *David Ap Howell*, David son of Howell; *Evan Ap Rhys*, Evan son of Rhys or Reese; *Richard Ap Evan*, Richard son of Evan; *John Ap Hugh*, John son of Hugh. These names are now abbreviated into Powell, Price, Bevan, Pugh.

The affix "Ing" is of Teutonic origin, denoting progeny; *Whiting* means fair offspring; *Browning*, the dark or brown child, etc. *Let* of Anglo Saxon origin means little, as *Bartlett*, little Bart or Bartholomew; *Willett*, little Will.

The prefixes "*Mac*" and "*O*" found in Irish names signify the first, son, the latter grandson or descendant. Donnell's son would be called Mac Donnell; the grandson or descendant would be called O'Donnell; Mac Neall, the son of Neal; O'Neal, the grandson of Neal.

Names of trades, occupations and pursuits are next in number, as Smith, Carpenter, Taylor, Barker, Barber, Brewer, Sherman (a shearman, one who shears cloth), Naylor (nailmaker), Tucker (a fuller), etc. John the Smith was shortened to John Smith, Peter the Carpenter, to Peter Carpenter, &c.

Many surnames are derived from official names, both civil and ecclesiastical. Among these may be mentioned King, Earl, Knight, Pope, Bishop, Bailey, Marshall, Chamberlain, Priest, etc.

Personal characteristics have given origin to another class of surnames descriptive of mental or bodily peculiarities.— Among these are the names of color and complexion, as Black, Brown, White, Gray, Dunn (brown); and from the color of the hair, Whitehead, Fairfax (fair hair), Swartz (black), Fairchild, Blackman, etc.

Among those which indicate the mental or moral qualities are such as Goodman, Wise, Wiley, Meek, Moody, Bliss, Gay, Sage, Joy.

Among those derived from bodily peculiarity and from feats of personal strength or courage are Strong, Mickle, Little, Long, Armstrong, Turnbull, etc.

A few surnames are derived from animals, fishes and birds, generally for the reason given hereafter.

Of surnames derived from animals may be mentioned Wolf, Lion, Fox, Hare, Roe, &c. From Wild boar comes Wilbur; from Little Wolf or *Lupellas* comes Lovel; Todd means fix in Scotch; and from *Eber* or *Eafer*, a boar, is derived Everard, Everitt, Everingham, Everton, &c. Oliphant is from elephant.

Among the names of fishes and birds taken as family names may be mentioned, Pike, Salmon, Burt, Bass, Fish, etc; Dove,

OLD TIMES IN OLD MONMOUTH. 119

Finch, Peacock, Swan, Jay, Wildgoose (Wilgus), Heron, &c.

The mineral and vegetable kingdom have contributed their full quota, as instance Garnett, Jewell, Steel, Irons, Stone, Flint, Pine, Rose, Thorn, Burch, etc.

One reason why persons received as surnames the names of animals, fishes, birds, flowers, &c, was because in ancient times in England, not only innkeepers but tradesmen and mechanics of all kinds put on the signs over their doors a representation of something to attract attention and as a distinguishing mark of their place of business, as Wild boars, Elephants, Bulls, Swans, Peacocks, Dolphins, Cranes, Griffins, Guns, Bells, Pots, Pitchers, &c., which gave rise to the surnames of those who put them up or to some of their employes.

Camden says "that he was told by them who said they spake of knowledge, that many names that seem unfitting for men, as of brutish beasts, etc., came from the very signs of the houses where they inhabited. That some, in late time, dwelling at the sign of the Dolphin, Bull, Whitehorse, Racket, Peacocke, etc., were commonly called *Thomas at the Dolphin, Will at the Bull, George at the Whitehorse, Robin at the Racket*, which names, as many others of the like sort, with omitting *at*, became afterward hereditary to their children."

A few surnames have originated in nicknames, epithets of contempt and ridicule, imposed for personal peculiarities, habits, qualities, incidents or accidents which happened to their original bearers, as Doolittle, Bragg, Trollope, Silliman, &c.

The foregoing gives the principal sources from which the greater part of our surnames are derived, but many names yet remain, the origin of which are not accounted for, *but all surnames must have been originally significant*. The best authorities as to the origin and meaning of surnames are Lover, Camden and Arthur, the work of the last named being the most convenient and accessible.

We give below the meaning and origin of many familiar surnames as accepted by some authorities. In a few instances there is a difference of opinion among those who have investigated the subject. At some future time we shall endeavor to find room for a more complete list of surnames and quote different authorities — In some cases where different opinions are given as to the origin of surnames each may be correct owing to the fact that many names now common may have had different origins.

SURNAMES—THEIR ORIGIN AND MEANING.

Acheson, Atcheson. (Cornish British). An inscription or memorial.

Ackerman. (Saxon). From *Acker*, oaken, made of oak, and man. Signifying the brave, firm, unyielding man.

Acton. (Saxon). Oak-town or oak-hill.

Agnew. (Norman French). From the town of Agneau, in Normandy, whence the family originated. Agneau, in Normandy French signifies lambs.

Ackers, Aikens, Akers, Akins &c. (Saxon). Signify *oaken* or *place* of *oaks*, or oak man, a man firm and unyielding as an oak.

Allen, Allan. This name is derived, by one authority from the Sclavonic *Aland*, a wolfdog or hound. Camden thinks it is a corruption of Aelianus, which signifies sunbright. In the Gaelic, *Aluinn* signifies exceedingly fair, handsome, elegant, lovely. Irish, *Alun*, fair beautiful. The Gaelic and Irish derivations are probably correct.

Anderson. Son of Andrew.

Armstrong. A name given for strength in battle.

Austin. (Latin) A contraction of Augustine, from *Augustinus*, imperial, royal, great, renowned.

Bailey. A name of office.

Barculo, Barkalow. From the town Borculo or Borkulo in Holland.

Barnes. A distinguished family of Sotterly, Suffolk county, England. *Bearn*, a city in France. *Barnyz*, (Cornish Br.) a judge.

Bartlett. A diminutive of Bartholomew, meaning little Bart, or son of Bartholomew.

Barton. (Saxon). Local. From a town in Lincolnshire, England, meaning a corn town or barley village, from *bere*, barley, and *ton* an inclosure, house or village. In Devonshire *Barton* is applied to any freehold estate not possessed of manorial privileges.

Bates. (Anglo Saxon) Contention.

Bauer. (German). Farmer.

Baxter. (Anglo Saxon). Baker. Sir Walter Scott says that in Scotland it also meant a baker's lad.

Beadle. A name of office; an officer belonging to a university or parish.

Bedell. The same as Beadle, of which it is a corruption.

Beers. From *Beer*, a town in Dorsetshire, England, so called from *bere*, grain, barley; a fruitful place.

Bell. A name taken from the sign of an inn or shop. "John at the Bell" became "John Bell."

Bennett. A contraction or corruption of Benedict, from *Benedictus*, blessed.

Blair. A cleared plain or battle field.

Blake. A corruption of *Ap Lake*, son of Lake.

Bogart (Dutch) From boomgard, an orchard.

Bond. The father or head of a family, whence husband, a contraction of *house bond*.

Bonnal. (Cornish British). The house on the cliff. (See Burnell).

Bowen. (Welsh). A corruption of *Ap Owen*, son of Owen.

Bowne. (Cornish Br.) Signifies ready, active, nimble.

Bowman. A military name; one who used a bow; an archer.

Bowers. A shady recess; a cottage. The German *Bauer* is sometimes corrupted to Bower.

Bowyer. One who used or made bows.

Bradshaw. A broad wood or grove. One who lived near a wide grove.

Breese. (Welsh). A contraction of *Ap Reese*, son of Reese.

Brewer, Brewster. A brewer of malt liquor.

Brick. A corruption of Breek, signifying *broken*, a gap.

Britton, Brittain. A native of Britain.

Brower. From the Dutch Brouer, a brewer.

Bryan, Brian Brien. Nobly descended; also one who is fair spoken, wordy, specious.

Bunnell. A corruption of *Bonhill*, a parish in the county of Dumbarton, Scotland.

Burden, Borden. Louver says the surname Burden is probably a corruption of *bourdon*, a pilgrim's staff. It may also be derived from two Saxon words *Bour* and *den* signifying a house in the valley.

Chadwich. Cottage by the harbor.

Clayton. The Clay hill.

Cole. An abbreviation of Nicholas, common among the Dutch.

Connell, Connelly. From Celtic and Gaelic, *conal*, love, friendship.

Conway. From a river of this name in Wales.

Coombs. (Cornish Br.) A place between hills, a valley; in the Welsh Coom.

Courtney. From a town in France, *Courtenay* fifty-six miles south of Paris.— The name signifies "The court near the river."

Cox. From *cock* or *cox*, little, a term of endearment. The word was sometimes used to denote a leader or chief man. In West Jersey, some two centuries ago, Peter, Lacey, and Laurence Cock were prominent settlers; their descendants generally now spell the name Cox.

Crawford. From Crawford in Lancashire, Scotland, which some say derived its name from *cru* bloody and *ford*, a pass—bloody ford.

Crowell. From a town in England by that name.

Curtis. An abbreviation of courteous.

Dennis. A corruption of the Greek name *Dionysius*, divine mind.

Dunn. *Gaelic*, a heap, hill, mount, fortress. *Saxon*, brown, of a dark color, swarthy.

Dunning. Brown offspring, Child of Dunn.

Errick, Herrick. "There is a tradition" says Dean Swift "that the ancient family of Ericks or Herricks derive their lineage from Erick the Forester, a great commander who raised an army to oppose the invasion of William the Conquerer."

Errickson. Son of Eric. The old settlers of Monmouth of this name were probably of Swedish descent and first settled in West Jersey. Eric Errickson came over with the first Swedish settlers (1638?) A census of Swedes taken in 1693 gives the names of Joran Ericson, one child, Mats Errickson, three children, Eric Errickson, one child. An old tradition says that the first of the family who came to New Jersey, descended from Eric, king of Sweden.

Erwin, Irwin. Welsh *Erwyn*, very fair, white beautiful.

Evans. The Welsh for John, same as Johns, meaning son of Evan or son of John.

French. One who came from France.

Goudy, Gowdy. From *Gouda*, a town in Holland.

Gordon. A strong man, a hero, a giant.

Harris, Harrison. Son of Henry.

Hartshorne. The horn of a hart or male deer; an emblem or sign over a shop or inn, whence the name "Will at the Hartshorn."

Havens. From haven, a harbor. One who lived near a haven.

Henderson, Hendrickson. Son of Henry or Hendrick.

Herbert. (Saxon) From *Here*, a soldier, and *beorht*, bright—meaning an expert soldier, famous in war.

Higgins. Little Hugh, or son of Hugh.

Hilyard. Anciently Hildheard, *Hild* in Saxon is a hero or heroine, and *heard*, a pastor or keeper.

Hodges. Hodge was a nickname of Roger, and Hodges mean son of Hodge.

Hoffman. (Dutch) From *Hoofdam*, a captain or head man, *Hofman*, from *Hof*, a court—the man of the court.

Holman. A corruption of *Allemand*, a German, that is a mixture of all men, *Alle mann*.

Holmes. From *Holm*, a river, island or meadow; also cultivated rising ground.

Hume, Hulmes. Same as above.

Hood. (Saxon) From *houd*, the wood.

Hooper. A cooper.

Hopkins. Little Robert or son of Robert.

Hunn. A native of Hungary.

Irving, Irvine. From a river and town of same name in Ayrshire, Scotland.

Jeffrey. Corrupted from Geoffrey or Godfrey, from the German, signifying God's peace or joyful peace. This name was borne by the chief of the royal house of Plantagenet.

Jenkins. From Jenks or John; son of John.

Jennings. Same as Jenkins.

Kemble, Kimble. A corruption of Campbell, which family claims to be able to trace its lineage to the fifth century. *Cam* meant crooked, and *beul*, mouth—the man whose mouth inclined a little on one side.

Laird. The same as Lord.

Lane. (Gaelic) A plain; a narrow way.

Lawrence. Flourishing, spreading, from *Laurus*, the laurel tree. Sir Robert Laurence of Ashton Hall, Lancashire, England, accompanied Richard I. to the Holy Land 1191.

Leonard. The disposition of a lion. Lion hearted.

Lippencot. German. A town on the coast; one who lived on the coast—from *leben* to dwell, and *cote* side or coast.

Lloyd. (Welsh) Grey or brown.

Lowe. A hill.

Martin. Warlike, a chief man, a warrior.

Moore. (Gaelic) Great, chief, tall, mighty, proud.

Morgan. One born by the sea.

Morris. (Welsh) A hero, a brave man.

Norris. A North king; the third king at arms.

Osborn. From *hus*, a house, and *bearn*, a child—a family child or adopted child.

Owen. The good offspring, good child.

Palmer. A pilgrim from the Holy Land; so called because he carried a palm branch as a pledge of his having been to Palestine.

Pancoast, Pancost. A corruption of *Pentecost*, a name probably given to a child born on Pentecost day.

Pangburn, Pangbourn. A town in Berkshire, England.

Parker. The keeper of a park.

Powell. The son of Howell, which is from Cornish British *Houl*, the sun.

Potter. One who makes earthen vessels.

Price. The son of Rice or Reese, from *Ap Rice*.

Quacker boss. A thicket, a grove, mountain ash.

Randolph, Randall. Fair help. Good help.

Reeves. From *Reeve*, a bailiff, provost, or steward.

Reynolds. Sincere or pure love; a strong, firm hold.

Rice, Reese. A brave, impetuous man.

Roger. One who keeps the peace; strong counsel.

Rogers. Son of Roger.

Russell. Red haired, or somewhat reddish.

Schenck. An inn or public house, from the German *schenke*.

Sherman. One who shears cloth.

Smith. The most common of all surnames. The name is derived from the Anglo Saxon *Smitan*, to strike or smite.

"From whence comes *Smith*, all be he knight or squire,
But from the *Smith* that *forgeth* at the fire?"
                                    Verstegan.

Among the Highland class, the smith ranked third in dignity to the chief, from his skill in fabricating military weapons and his dexterity in using them. In Wales there were three sciences which a tenant could not teach his son without consent of his lord, *Scholarship, Bardism* and *Smithcraft*. This last was considered one of the liberal sciences, and the term had a more comprehensive sense than we now give it. The smith was required to have different branches of knowledge which are now practiced separately, such as raising the ore, converting it into metal, etc. It originally applied to all mechanical workmen whether in metal, wood or other materials.

The name John Smith is so common that it almost ceases to be a distinctive name. One writer contends, in an amusing article, that the name Smith is not only common in Great Britain and America, but among all the nations of the earth. He insists that the Hebrew name of Shem (Noah's son) was thus corrupted: Shem, Shemit, Shmit, Smith. A Philadelphia humorous writer, after asserting that Shem in Hebrew is the origin of Smith, says the name John Smith is found in other nations one and indivisible. Thus, Latin, Johannes Smithius; Italian, Giovanni Smithi; Spanish, Juan Smithas; Dutch, Hans Schmidt; French, Jean Smeets; Russian, Jonloff Skmittowski; Polish, Ivan Schmittiweiski; Chinese, Jahon Shimmitt; Icelandis, Jahne Smithson; Welsh, Jihon Schmidd; Tuscarora, Ton Qu Smittiu; Mexican, Jontli F. Smitti.

Snyder. (German) Schneider, a tailor.

Stanton. From *stan* a stone and *ton*, a hill or town.

Stewart. Malcolm III, king of Scotland, created Walter, the son of Fleance and grandson of Banquo, Lord High Steward of Scotland, from which office his family afterwards took, and retained the name of Stewart, and from thence descended the royal family of Stuart.

Stockton. A town in Durham, England.

Stokes. A parish in Buckinghamshire, England.

Stryker. (Danish.) From *strige*, to strike, to roam, to travel; hence a worker at a trade, a traveller.

Sutphen. (Dutch.) Originally Van Zutphen, that is, from the city of Zutphen in Germany.

Taggart. (Welsh.) A meeting house.

Tunison. Probably son of Teunis or Tunis.

Throckmorton. A corruption of *At Rockmoor-town*, "a town on a rock in a moor," in the vale of Eversham, Warwickshire, England.

Thwaite. A piece of ground cleared of wood.

Tice. (Dutch.) A familiar abbreviation of Matthias.

Tilton. Derived from Tilton, a village in England, probably an ancient place of tilling or tents. *Tilt*, Saxon, a tent.

Todd. *Tod*, a Scotch word for fox.

Townsend. One who lived at the end of the town.

Truax. (Cornish Br.) The place on the waters.

Van Cleve. From the city of Cleve or Cleves in Westphalia, Germany.

Vanderveer. From the ferry.

Voorhees. (Dutch.) From *voorhius* the fore room or best room of a house, or from *voor Hess*, before the town of Hess.

Walton. The name of several villages in England, from *wald*, a wood, and *ton* a town or village.

Watson and Watts. Son of Walter.

Worden, Werden. From *Wehr*, a fortification and *den*, a hill; a town in Netherlands called Woerdon.

Westervelt. The west field.

Woodruff. The governor or keeper of a wood, a forester.

Woodward. Wood-ward, a forest keeper or officer who had charge of a park or forest, and took charge of all offences committed.

Woolley. From *Woldley*, uncultivated lands, hills without woods.

Worth. (Saxon.) A court, farm, place.

THE DEATH OF BACON.

"John Bacon was a notorious refugee who had committed many depredations along the shores of Monmouth and Burlington counties. After having been a terror to the people of this section for some time, John Stewart, of Arneytown, (afterwards Captain Stewart), resolved if possible to take him. There had been a reward of fifty pounds sterling offered by the Governor and Council for his capture, dead or alive. A short time previous, in an engagement at Cedar Creek Bridge, Bacon and his company had discomfited a considerable body of State troops, killing a brother of Joel Cook, of Cook's Mills, (now Cookstown), Burlington county, which excited much alarm and exasperated the whole country. On the occasion of his arrest, Captain Stewart took with him Joel Cook, John Brown, Thomas Smith, John Jones, and another person whose name is not recollected, and started in pursuit, well armed. They traversed the shore and found Bacon separated from his men at the public house or cabin of William Rose, between West Creek and Clamtown (now Tuckerton), in Burlington County. The night was very dark, and Smith being in advance of the party, approached the house, and discovered through the window a man sitting with a gun between his knees. He immediately informed his companions. On arriving at the house, Captain Stewart opened the door and presenting his musket demanded a surrender. The fellow sprang to his feet, and cocking his gun was in the act of bringing it round to the breast of Stewart, when the latter, instead of discharging his piece, closed in with him and succeeded after a scuffle in bringing him to the floor. He then avowed himself to be John Bacon, and asked for quarter, which was at once readily granted to him by Stewart. They arose from the floor, and Stewart (still retaining his hold on Bacon) called to Cook, who, when he discovered the supposed murderer of his brother, became exasperated, and stepping back gave Bacon a bayonet thrust unknown to Stewart or his companions. Bacon appeared faint and fell. After a short time he recovered and attempted to escape by the back door. Stewart pushed a table against it. Bacon hurled it away and struck Stewart to the floor, opened the door, and again attempted to pass out; but was shot by Stewart (who had regained his feet) while in the act. The ball passed through his body, through a part of the building, and struck the breast of Cook, who had taken a position at the back door to prevent egress. Cook's companions were ignorant of the fact that he had given Bacon the bayonet wound, and would scarcely credit him when he so informed them on their way home. They examined Bacon's body at Mount Misery, and the wounds made by both bayonet and ball were obvious. They brought his dead body to Jacobstown, Burlington county, and were in the act of burying it in the public highway, near the village in the presence of many citizens who had collected on the occasion, when Bacon's brother appeared among them and after much entreaty succeeded in obtaining his body for private burial."

This affair took place on Thursday evening, April 3rd, 1783.

As there have been some disputes in traditionary accounts as to the exact manner of Bacon's death, we have been at much trouble to get at the truth. Some old residents of the vicinity where he was killed are positive that he was shot down after asking for quarter. They say that Captain Stewart's party suddenly opened the door and pointed a musket at Bacon, who instantly rose up and held a table before him and begged for quarter, but the musket was fired, and the ball went through the table and killed him. But after much patient investigation and inquiry we believe this story is untrue, and that the correct version is about as Governor Fort has given it. We are sorry to add, however, that the party treated the body with unjustifiable indignity. As soon as Bacon was killed his body was thrown into a wagon with his head over the tail-board, and the party drove for home that same night. Young Cook seemed quite "carried away" to think he had avenged his brother's death, and at the inns at Mannahawkin and Mount Misery, insisted on treating Bacon with liquor, fastening open his mouth while he poured liquor into it. The descendants of British sympathisers have charged the party with much cruelty, but the only foundations are the indignities offered to his body; and even there we can find some palliation for it, when we consider the excitement bordering on frenzy, of young Cook.

In addition to what has been quoted from Governor Fort regarding Bacon's burial, we have heard it stated that in accordance with an ancient custom with great criminals, the intention was to bury Bacon at the forks of some public roads, with a stake driven through the body; but his brother's arrival changed their plan. This brother of Bacon's was generally respected where he was known.

The writer of this is under impression that before the war Bacon's home was in Burlington county, though he occasionally worked in Stafford township, in Ocean county, and he has been told that Bacon left a wife and two sons at Pemberton; that his widow married a man named Morris, and that the two sons emigrated West, and became respectable and useful citizens.

It is but just to add that among old residents, generally of the Society of Friends, who though sympathizing with the Americans, yet were non-combatants, that Bacon was held to be among the most honorable of the refugee leaders. They say that except calling for a meal's victuals for himself and men in passing, he never molested the persons or property of any but Americans in the militia service.

Before closing, we will say that, although our State Council of Safety had declared Bacon an outlaw, and offered a reward for him dead or alive, yet it is probable that if he had been taken alive and delivered to the civil authorities he would have been liberated in pursuance of the treaty with England.

Hetfield, a much worse man than Bacon, many years after the war, had the impudence to return to Essex county (to endeavor to secure some property there), when he was arrested for his misdeeds during the Revolution; but the judge decided he must be liberated in pursuance of the treaty with England. Most of the old residents in Essex well remember the intense excitement and indignation raised by the return and liberation of this scoundrel.

The refugee leaders in our State—Hetfield, Bacon, Lippincott, Davenport, Moody and others—all doubtless held commissions from the " Board of Associated Loyalists," of which the President was William Franklin, the last British Governor of New Jersey.

CAPT. ADAM HYLER,
THE DARING PRIVATEER OF THE WATERS IN AND AROUND—OLD MONMOUTH.

It is rare to find in fact or fiction, more daring exploits recorded than those performed chiefly in the waters around old Monmouth, by Captain Adam Hyler, who resided at New Brunswick during the latter part of the Revolutionary war. From some unaccountable cause, the heroic deeds of this man have received but little notice from historians; indeed, we remember of but one modere work that makes any allusion to them, and that gives only two or three of the items published below.

Capt. Hyler's operations were carried on in Raritan bay, and along our coast as far down as Egg Harbor—chiefly, however, in the first named place. Though he sometimes used sail craft, yet he generally depended upon whale boats or large barges, rowed by skillful crews. These barges were generally kept at New Brunswick, but some were at times concealed in small streams emptying into Raritan bay and river, which place was then reached by old Cranberry Inlet.

Though the Refugee band which had its headquarters at the settlement on Sandy Hook, around the lighthouse, gave great annoyance to the patriots of Monmouth, yet their operations were much circumscribed by the efforts of Capt. Hyler and his brave compatriots, who seriously interfered with the vessels of the refugees, as well as of the British, and when opportunity offered as will hereafter be seen, hesitated not to attack their settlement, and even the lighthouse fort itself. The refugees would sometimes boast of successful midnight marauding expeditions into the adjacent country, but the bold, skillful exploits of Hyler, far eclipsed their best planned efforts.

A clear idea of Capt. Hyler's manner of harassing the enemy is given in the following extracts, copied from various ancient papers published at the time. They serve to aid in completing the picture of life and times in and around Old Monmouth during the Revolution.

" October 7th, 1781. On Friday last, Capt. Adam Hyler, from New Brunswick, with one gun boat and two whale boats, within a quarter of a mile of the guard ship at Sandy Hook, attacked five vessels, and after a smart conflict of fifteen minutes carried them. Two of them were armed, one mounting four six pounders, and one six swivels, and one three pounder. The hands made their escape with their long boats, and took refuge in a small fort, in which were mounted twelve swivel guns, from which they kept up a constant firing; notwithstanding which he boarded them all without the loss of a man. On board one of them was 250 bushels of wheat and a quantity of cheese belonging to Capt. Lippencott, bound to New York. He took from them fifty bushels of wheat, a quantity of cheese several swivels, a number of fusees, one, cask of powder and some dry goods; and stripped them of their sails and rigging—not being able to bring the vessels into port, in consequence of a contrary wind and tide. After which he set fire to all save one, on board of which was a woman and four small children, which prevented her from sharing a similar fate."

On the 13th of October, a week or ten days after the above mentioned affair, Capt. Hyler with one gunboat and two whale boats, boarded a sloop and two schooners, which all hands, except two, had previously left, and which lay under the cover of the light house fort at Sandy Hook, and brought them all off; but the sloop being a dull sailor, and being much annoyed from a galley lying near Staten Island, she was set on fire about three miles from the fort. One of the schooners running aground by accident, was stripped and left; the other a remarkably fine fast sailing Virginia built pilot, mounted with one four pounder was brought, with two prisoners, safely off.

On the 24th of the same month, he started with one gunboat to surprise the " refugee town " at Sandy Hook. He landed within three quarters of a mile of the light house, but found the refugees were out in Monmouth County on a plundering expedition. He however fell in with six noted villains who he brought off and lodged in a safe place. A subsequent notice of Capt. Hyler, says that at one time he captured the Captain of the guard at the light house, with all his men, but whether it was at this or some other time, is not stated.

Nov. 14th, 1781. On Saturday night, Capt. Hyler, with a gunboat and a small party of men went to the Narrows, where he captured a ship with fourteen hands, and brought her off with the intention of running her up the Raritan river, but near the mouth she unluckily got aground, and as the enemy approached in force, he was obliged to set her on fire. She was loaded with rum and pork; several hogsheads of the former he got out and brought off with the prisoners."

This ship captured was probably "The Father's Desire," as twenty hogsheads of rum and thirty barrels of pork were advertised by the U. S. Marshal to be sold a few days after; which the advertisement states were taken from a ship of this name by Captain Hyler.

"On the 15th of December, Capt. Hyler, who commands seven or eight stout whale boats, manned with near one hundred men, at the Narrows, fell in with two refugee sloops trading to Shrewsbury, one of them commanded by the noted villain, 'Shore Stephens,' and had on board £600 in specie, besides a considerable quantity of dry goods; the other had similar articles, also sugar, rum, etc. They were taken to New Brunswick."

The many daring exploits of Capt. Hyler, following so close one after another, aroused the British at New York, and they fitted out an expedition with the determination of destroying his boats, and if possible, capturing him. The following account of this expedition is derived chiefly from Philadelphia papers, of the date of January 15th and 16th, 1782:

"A party of the British lately (about January 9th) made an incursion to New Brunswick with the design, it is said, of carrying off the boats of the celebrated partizan, Capt. Adam Hyler. They landed at New Brunswick and plundered two houses, but were gallantly opposed by the neighboring militia, and the enemy were driven off with some loss. Farther accounts say there were some 200 refugees and British, and that they succeeded in destroying the whale boats. No Americans were killed, but five were wounded and six taken prisoners. Several tories were killed—four known to be, and several were seen to be carried off. The British made the attack about 5 o'clock, A. M., just before daylight, and the American account says the expedition was well planned, and that the Tories held the town for about an hour. The British regulars were detachments from the 40th and 42d regiments, under command of Capt. Beckwith, in six boats, and they took away all of Hyler's boats. The British alleged that Captain Hyler was a deserter from the Royalists."

It is probable that at this time, besides his boats at New Brunswick, Capt, Hyler had others concealed elsewhere, as we find early in the following spring he was at work as usual, apparently, but little inconvenienced by the loss of the boats taken by the British, though he may have built some in the meantime. In March following, when the British attacked and burned Toms River, they boasted of having captured there a fine large barge, belonging to Capt. Hyler.

In April, 1782, Capt. Hyler, in an open boat, boarded and took a large cutter, almost ready for sea, lying near Sandy Hook, and near the Lion man-of-war, 64 guns. This cutter mounted twelve 18 pounders, and was commanded by one White, formerly of Philadelphia, but turned apostate. Hyler blew up the vessel, which was designed as a cruiser, and took forty prisoners. Another account says the number of prisoners was fifty, and the cutter's armament was six 18 pounders and ten 9 pounders. At the same time he took a sloop which was ransomed for £400. The Captain of the cutter gives an amusing account of the way Hyler captured his vessel, which will be found hereafter.

"On the 25th of May, 1782. Capt. Hyler, with his armed boats, being in Shrewsbury river, a party of British troops, consisting of twenty-five men, under Capt. Shaak, was detached to intercept him in the gut. Hyler discovered them, and landed thirteen men, with orders to charge; when four of the enemy were killed or wounded, and the Capt. and eight men taken prisoners. By the firing of a gun it was supposed others were killed, as they were seen to fall. Just before this affair, Capt. Hyler had met with a hurt, or otherwise he probably would not have let a man es cape."

On the 2d of July, Captain Hyler, assisted by Captain Story, another brave partizan, in New York bay, with two whale boats, boarded and took the schooner Skip

Jack, carrying six guns, besides swivels, and burned her at noon, in sight of the guard-ship, and took the captain and nine or ten men prisoners. About the same time he also took three or four trading vessels, loaded with calves, sheep, &c.

These were probably about the last exploits in which Captain Hyler was engaged, as we find no farther mention of his name in ancient papers until the announcement of his death, some two months after. He died at New Brunswick, on the 6th of September, 1782.

The following from an ancient paper gives a graphic account of his manner of conducting his operations. It was originally published June 19th, 1782 :

"The exertions of the celebrated water partizan, Captain Adam Hyler, have been a considerable annoyance to the wood shallops, trading vessels, and plundering pirates of the enemy about Sandy Hook, Long Island, and Staten Island, for several months past. You have heard that his effort to take an eighteen gun cutter was crowned with success. It was indeed a bold and hazardous attempt, considering how well she was provided against being boarded. He was, however, compelled to blow her up, after securing his prisoners and a few articles on board. His surprising a captain of the guard, at the lighthouse, with all his men, a short time ago, was a handsome affair, and gained him much credit. He has none but picked and tried men ; the person who discovers the least symptom of fear or diffidence, be he who he will, is immediately turned on shore, and never suffered to enter again.—

In the next place, they are taught to be particularly expert at the oar, and to row with such silence and dexerity as not to be heard at the smallest distance, even though three or four boats be together, and go at the rate of twelve miles an hour.

"Their captures are made chiefly by surprise or stratagem ; and most of the crews that have hitherto been take by these boats declare they never knew anything of an enemy being at hand till they saw the pistol or cutlass at their throats.

"There was a droll instance of this some weeks ago, as one of the prisoners, a shrewd, sensible fellow, and late captain of one of the captured vessels, relates it himself. Said he, ' I was on deck with three or four men, on a very pleasant evening, with our sentinel fixed. Our vessel was at anchor near Sandy Hook, and the Lion man-of war about one quarter of a mile distant. It was calm and clear, and we were all admiring the beautiful and splendid appearance of the full moon which was then three or four hours above the horizon. While we were thus attentively contemplating the serene luminary, we suddenly heard several pistols discharged into the cabin, and turning around, perceived at our elbows a number of armed people, fallen as it were from the clouds, who ordered us to ' surrender in a moment, or we were dead men !' Upon this we were turned into the hold and the hatches barred over us. The firing, however, had alarmed the man-of-war, who hailed us, and desired to know what was the matter. As we were not in a situation to answer, at least so far as to be heard, Captain Hyler was kind enough to do so for us, telling them through the speaking trumpet that ' all was well.'— After which, unfortunately for us, they made no farther inquiry.' "

After the notorious refugee, Lippencott, had barbarously murdered Captain Joshua Huddy, near the Highlands, General Washington was anxious to have the murderer secured. He had been demanded of the British General, and his surrender refused. Captain Hyler was determined to take Lippencott. On inquiry he found that he resided in a well known house, in Broad street, New York. Dressed and equipped like a man-of-war press gang, he left the Kills, with one boat, after dark, and arrived at Whitehall about nine o'clock. Here he left his boat in charge of three men, and passed to the residence of Lippencott, where he inquired for him and found that he was absent, having gone to a cock pit. Thus failing in his object he returned to his boat, with his *press gang*, and left Whitehall, but finding a sloop lying at anchor off the battery, from the West Indies, laden with rum, he took her, cut her cable, set her sails, and with a north-east wind sailed to Elizebethtown 1oint, and before daylight had landed from her and secured forty hogsheads of rum. He then burned the sloop to prevent her re-capture.—(This again furnishes the groundwork of a very interesting story, published originally in Major Noah's New York Sunday Times, and afterwards republished by the author, in a book entitled " Tales and Traditions of New York."— The writer however, occasionally blends fiction with facts, which, though perhaps serving to increase the interest of his sto-

ries, yet renders his work unreliable as a matter of history).
The writer of this has been unable to find any notice of Captain Hyler previous to 1771. The occasion of this probably is that he was in the British service in the early part of the war, but being convinced of the unjustness of the cause in which he was engaged, he left them and joined the Americans. The British at New Brunswick, as before stated, charged him with being a deserter, and the Tory paper published in New York (Rivington's Royal Gazette), Jan. 12, 1782, says : " This Hyler is a deserter from the royal service, and ever since his defection has proved too successful an enterprizer in his various descents upon our vicinities."
The fact of Captain Hyler's having been formerly in the British service, increases our admiration for his bold operations.— Had he been taken by the British, he probably would have received a deserter's punishment.
The writer of this has had occasion to make a thorough examination of the original pay rolls of all vessels of war in the service of our government in the war of 1812, and previous, which rolls are now preserved in the Treasury Department at Washington. In looking over the rolls containing the list of officers and men serving under Commodore Perry and other noted heroes on the lakes is to be found the name of an under officer named Adam Hyler, who faithfully served throughout that war, who was evidently named after and probably a near relative of the Captain Adam Hyler of Revolutionary fame.

OTHER PRIVATEERS.

CAPTAIN STORER.

The following is from an ancient paper published in 1782, just previous to the close of the war.
" We learn that the brave Captain Storer, commissioned as a private boat of-war under the State, and who promises to be the genuine successor of the late Captain Hyler. has given a recent instance of his valor and conduct in capturing one of the enemy's vessels. He went in two boats through the British fleet in the Narrows, and boarded a vessel under the flag staff battery. He captured the vessel without alarm. She was a sloop in the Engineers department of H. B. M. service, and was carried away safely."

CAPTAIN WILLIAM MARRINER.

Captain Marriner lived in New Brunswick during the war. From notice of him in ancient papers, we find he was another brave enterprising partizan, as the following extracts will show, The first is from a letter dated June 17th, 1778.
" William Marriner, a volunteer, with eleven men and Lieutenant John Schenck, of our militia, went last Saturday evening from Middletown Point to Long Island, in order to take a few prisoners from Flatbush, and returned with Major Moncrieff and Mr. Theophilus Bacho (the worshipful Mayor and Tormentor-General, David Matthews, Esq., who has inflicted on our prisoners the most unheard of cruelties, and who was the principal object of the expedition, being unfortunately in the city,) with four slaves, and brought them to Princeton, to be delivered to his excellency the Governor. Mr. Marriner with his party left Middletown Point on Saturday evening, and returned at six o'clock next morning, having traveled by land and water above fifty miles, and behaved with greatest prudence and bravery."
The following is from an official naval work in the Library of Congress :
" The privateer Blacksnake was captured by the British, but in April, 1780, Captain William Marriner, with nine men in a whale boat, retook her. Captain Marriner then put to sea in his prize, and captured the Morning Star, of 6 swivels and 33 men, after a sharp resistance, in which she lost three killed and five wounded ; he carried both prizes into Egg Harbor."
After the war Captain Marriner removed to Harlem, where he lived many years.
The Daniel Matthews alove spoken of was the Tory Mayor of New York, during the Revolution, and noted for his enmity to all favoring the Americans.

CAPTAIN JACKSON.

" December 18th, 1782.—Capt. Jackson of the Greyhound, in the evening of Sunday, last week, with much address, captured within the Hook, the Schooner Dolphin and sloop Diamond, bound from New York to Halifax, and brought them into Egg Harbor. These vessels were both condemned to the claimants, and the sale amounted to £10,200.

SUCCESSFUL EXPLOIT.

In the following item from the *Packet,* Jan. 1779, no names are mentioned.

"Some Jerseymen went in row boats to Sandy Hook and took four sloops, one of which was armed. They burned three and took one; also nineteen prisoners. The share of prize money per man, was £400."

PASSAGES IN THE RELIGIOUS HISTORY OF OLD MONMOUTH.

THE UNIVERSALISTS—ORIGIN OF THE SOCIETY IN AMERICA.

THE POTTER CHURCH.

A Free Church in the Olden Time—A Refuge for Methodism in its Dark Days—The Cradle of Universalism in America—Its Benevolent Founder and Remarkable Incidents in his Life.

A singular and interesting chapter in the religious history of our State, and one but little known outside of members of the Universalist society, relates to a church formerly called "the Potter church," built not far from 1760 to 1765, at Goodluck, in that part of old Monmouth now confined within the limits of Ocean county, by a benevolent resident of that village named Thomas Potter. Before building the church, Potter had been in the custom of opening his house to travelling preachers of all persuasions; and, after a while, to accommodate them, he built this church free for all denominations. His object is best expressed in his own words: "As I firmly believe that all mankind are equally dear to Almighty God, they shall all be equally welcome to preach in this house which I have built." After it was built, it was used by traveling ministers of the Presbyterian, Baptist, Quaker, Methodist and other societies, and in it was preached the first Universalist sermon ever delivered in America. The Methodist society in New Jersey owe a debt of gratitude to Thomas Potter for always opening his church to the noble pioneers of Methodism in the dark days of its history, when Methodism not only met with opposition from other societies on account of difference in religious sentiments, but also, when during the Revolution, their enemies most unwarrantably slandered them by charging them with being in sympathy with Great Britain. Though these slanders had the effect of rendering the heroes of Methodism so unpopular that they could hardly obtain a hearing in most parts of this State, as well as in other States, yet the Potter church was always open to them, and so often used by them, that some Methodist writers at the present day who have found the name of this church frequently mentioned in the journals of these pioneers, have concluded it must have been a Methodist church, though where it was situated, and why it was so called, they have been unable to divine. Among the preachers well known in the annals of Methodism who preached in it, were Benjamin Abbott and Bishop Asbury; and in it was married James Sterling, the most earnest, effective layman the society had in its early struggles in New Jersey.

The most satisfactory account of Thomas Potter and his church is given by Rev. John Murray, who preached in it the first Universalist sermon ever delivered in America, under circumstances so very singular that his narrative forms an interesting as well as important part of our church history. As *Murray's Journal* is rarely to be met with except occasionally among some of his own denomination, we give the substance of his account, though, before giving it, it is necessary to say a few words in regard to Mr. Murray himself.

The Rev. John Murray, the first preacher of Universalism in America, sailed from England for New York, July 21st, 1770.— When he left England though a warm advocate of the principles of that society, yet he was not a regular preacher and had but little idea then of becoming one in America. During a thick fog in the early part of the month of September, the brig "Hand in Hand," in which he was acting as supercargo, struck on the outer bar of old Cranberry Inlet (now closed) nearly opposite Toms River; she soon passed over and was held by her anchors from going on shore. Here she remained several days before she could be got off. While lying here the provisions of the brig were exhausted, and after locking up the vessel, all hands proceeded in a boat across the bay to the main in search of sustenance. Being unacquainted with the main, they spent a great part of the day before they could effectuate their purpose, after which, it being late, they proceeded to a tavern to stay all night. Mr. Murray's mind appears to have been much exercised by eventful scenes in his previous life and to have longed to get somewhere where the busy cares of the world would not disturb his meditations; and hence as soon as the boatmen arrived at the tavern he

OLD TIMES IN OLD MONMOUTH. 129

left them for a solitary walk through the dark pine grove. "Here," said he, I was as much alone as I could wish and my heart exclaimed, Oh that I had in this wilderness the lodging of a poor wayfaring man; some cave, some grot, some place where I might finish my days in calm repose." As he thus passed along musing, he unexpectedly reached a small log house where he saw a girl cleaning fish; he requested her to sell him some. She had none to spare, but told him he could get all he wanted at the next house. "What, this?" said Mr. Murray pointing to one he could just discern through the woods.— The girl told him no, that was a meeting house. He was much surprised to find a meeting house there in the woods. He was directed to pass on by the meeting house and at the next house he would find fish. He went on as directed and came to the door near which was a large pile of fish of various sorts, and standing by was a tall man, rough in appearance and evidently advanced in years. "Pray sir," said Mr Murray, "will you have the goodness to sell me one of those fish?"— "No sir," was the abrupt reply of the old gentleman. "That is strange," replied Mr. Murray, "when you have so many fish, to refuse me a single one!"

"I did not refuse you a fish, sir; you are welcome to as many as you please, but I do not sell the article; I do not sell fish, sir, I have them for taking up and you may obtain them the same way." Mr. Murray thanked him; the old man then inquired what he wanted of them, and was told he wished them for supper for the mariners at the tavern. The old man offered to send the fish over for him, and urged Mr. Murray to tarry with him that night. Mr. Murray consented to return after visiting the crew at the public house. This old gentleman was Thomas Potter.— Mr. Murray says he was astonished to see so much genuine politeness and hospitality under so rough an exterior, but his astonishment was greatly increased on his return. The old man's room was prepared, his fire bright and his heart opened.— "Come," said he, "my friend, I am glad you have returned, I have longed to see you, I have been expecting you a long time." Expecting him! Mr. Murray was amazed, and asked what he meant. Mr. Potter replied, "I must answer in my own way; I am a poor ignorant man, I know how neither to read or write; I was born in these woods and worked on these grounds until I became a man, when I went on coasting voyages from here to New York; I was then about getting married, but in going to New York once I was pressed on board of a man-of-war and taken in Admiral Warren's ship to Cape Breton. I never drank any rum, so they saved my allowance; but I would not bear an affront, so if any of the officers struck me I struck them again, but the admiral took my part and called me his new-light man. When I reached Louisburg I ran away and traveled barefooted through the country and almost naked to New York, where I was known and supplied with clothes and money, and soon returned home, when I found my girl married. This rendered me unhappy, but I recovered my tranquility and married her sister. I settled down to work and got forward quite fast; constructed a saw mill, possessed myself of this farm and five hundred acres of adjoining land. I entered into navigation, own a sloop and have now got together a fair estate. I am, as I said, unable to read or write, but I am capable of reflection; the sacred Scriptures have been often read to me, from which I gathered that there is a great and good Being who has preserved and protected me through innumerable dangers, and to whom we are all indebted for all we enjoy; and as He has given me a house of my own I conceived I could do no less than to open it to the stranger, let him be who he would; and especially if a traveling minister passed this way he always received an invitation to put up at my house and hold his meetings here.

"I continued in this practice for more than seven years, and illiterate as I was I used to converse with them, and was fond of asking them questions. They pronounced me an odd mortal, declaring themselves at a loss what to make of me; while I continued to affirm that I had but one hope; I believed that Jesus Christ suffered death for my transgressions, and this alone was sufficient for me. At length my wife grew weary of having meetings held in her house, and I determined to build a house for the worship of God. I had no children, and I knew that I was beholden to Almighty God for everything which I possessed, and it seemed right I should appropriate a part of what He bestowed for his service. My neighbors offered their assistance, 'But no,' said I, 'God has given me enough to do this work without your aid, and as he has put it in my heart to do so, so I will do.' 'And who,' it was asked, ' will be your preacher?' I answered, God will send me a preacher, and of a very different stamp from those who have heretofore preached in my house. The preachers we have heard are perpetually contradicting themselves; but that God who has put it into my heart to build this house, will send one who shall deliver unto me his own truth; who shall speak of Jesus Christ and his salvation. When the house was finished I received an application from the Baptists, and I told them if they could make it appear that God Almighty was a Baptist, I should give them the building at once. The Quakers and Presbyterians received similar answers. No, said I, as I firmly believe that all mankind are equally dear to Almighty God, they shall all be equally welcome to preach in this house which I have built. My neighbors assured me I should never see a preacher whose sentiments corresponded with my own, but I uniformly replied I assuredly would. I engaged for the first year with a man whom I greatly disliked; we parted, and for some years we have had no stated minister. My friends often asked me, ' where is the preacher of whom you spoke ?' and my constant reply, ' he will by and by make his appearance.' The moment, sir, I saw your vessel on shore it seemed as if a voice had audibly sounded in my ears, ' There, Potter, in that vessel, castaway on that shore, is the preacher you have so long been expecting.' I heard the voice and believed the report, and when you came up to my door and asked for the fish the same voice seemed to repeat, ' Potter, this is the man—this is the person whom I have sent to preach in your house !'"

As may be supposed Murray was immeasurably astonished at Mr. Potter's narrative, but yet had not the least idea that his wish could ever be realized. He asked him what he could discern in his appearance to lead him to mistake him for a preacher. ' What,' said Potter, ' could I discern when you were in the vessel that could induce this conclusion? Sir, it is not what I saw or see, but what I feel which produces in my mind full conviction.'— Murray replied that he must be deceived, as he should never preach in that place or anywhere else.

" Have you never preached—can you say you never preached ?"

" I cannot, but I never intend to preach again."

" Has not God lifted up the light of His countenance upon you ? Has he not shown you the truth ?"

" I trust he has."

" Then how dare you hide this truth ?— Do men light a candle and put it under a bushel. If God has shown you His salvation why should you not show it to your fellow men. But I know that you will, I am sure that God Almighty has sent you to us for this purpose. I am not deceived, sir, I am sure I am not deceived."

Murray was much agitated when this man thus spoke on, and began to wonder whether or no God who ordains all things, had not ordained that this should come to pass, but his heart trembled, he tells us, at the idea. He endeavored, he says, to quiet his own fears and to silence the warm hearted old man by informing him he was supercargo of the vessel, that property to a large amount was entrusted to his care, and that the moment the wind changed he was under solemn obligations to depart.

" The wind will never change," said Potter, " until you have delivered to us in that meeting house a message from God."

Murray still resolutely determined never to enter any pulpit as a preacher, but being much agitated in mind asked to be shown to bed after he had prayed with the family. When they parted for the night, his kind host solemnly requested him to think of what he said.

" Alas, says Murray, he need not have made this request ; it was impossible to banish it from my mind; when I entered my chamber and shut the door, I burst into tears ; I felt as if the hand of God was in the events which had brought me to this place, and I prayed most ardently that God would assist and direct me by his counsel."

So much exercised was he in mind that he spent the greater part of the night in praying and weeping, " dreading more than death, he says, supposing death to be an object of dread, the idea of engaging as a public character." In his writings he gives the substances of his meditations and prayers on that memorable night. In the morning his good friend renewed his solicitations : " Will you speak to me and my neighbors of the things which belong to our peace ?"

Murray seeing only thick woods, the tavern across the fields excepted, requested to know what he meant by neighbors.

"O, sir, we assemble a large congregation whenever the meeting house is opened; indeed when my father first settled here he was obliged to go twenty miles to grind a bushel of corn, but now there are more than seven hundred inhabitants within that distance."

Murray still could not be prevailed upon to yield, but Potter insisted and seemed positive the wind would not change until he had spoken to the people. Thus urged, Murray began to waver and at length he tells us he "implored God, who sometimes condescends to indulge individuals with tokens of his approbation, graciously to indulge me upon this important occasion, and that if it was His will that I should obtain my soul's desire by passing through life as a private individual, if such was not his will that I should engage as a preacher of the ministry, He would vouchsafe to grant me a wind as might bear me from this shore before another Sabbath. I determined to take the changing of the wind for an answer."

But the wind changed not, and towards the close of the Saturday afternoon he reluctantly gave his consent to preaching the next day, and Mr. Potter immediately despatched his men on horse back to notify the neighbors, which they were to continue to do until ten o'clock in the evening. Mr. Murray appears to have had but little rest that night, thinking over the responsibilities of the avocation he was so unexpectedly about to be engaged in, and of what he should say and how he should address the people; but the passage "Take no thought what ye shall say," etc., appears to have greatly relieved his mind. Sunday morning they proceeded to the church. Potter very joyful and Murray uneasy, distrusting his own abilities to realize the singularly high formed expectations of his kind host. The church at that day is described as being "neat and convenient, with a pulpit rather after the Quaker mode, with but one new pew and that a large square one just below the pulpit in which sat the venerable Potter and his family and visiting strangers; the rest of the seats were constructed with backs, roomy and even elegant." As Murray was preaching Potter looked up into the pulpit, his eyes sparkling with pleasure, seemingly completely happy at the fulfillment of what he firmly believed a promise long deferred. We have no record of the substance of this, the first Universalist sermon in America, nor of its impression upon any of the hearers save one—that one Thomas Potter himself, appears to have had all his expectations realized, and upon their return home overwhelmed Murray with his frank, warm-hearted congratulations; and soon visitors poured in.—Said Potter to them "This is the happiest day of my life; there, neighbors, there is the minister God has sent me," Murray was so overcome by the old man's enthusiastic demonstrations that he retired to his room and tells us he "prostrated himself at the throne of grace, and besought God to take him and do with him what he pleased."

After a while he returned to the company and found the boatmen with them, who wished him to go on board immediately, as the wind was fair. So he was compelled to leave. His host was loth to part with him and exacted a promise from him to return, which he soon did, and preached often in the Potter church and other villages. The first place he visited during this stay was Toms River. He relates two or three interesting scenes occurring here, in explaining to individuals his peculiar religious views. The next village he visited was probably Mannahawkin, for though he does not mention the name, yet he speaks of a Baptist preacher and church, of a family of Pangburns, &c., and there was then a Baptist church at that village, and the Pangburn family were then prominent members of it. (Lines Pangburn was a delegate from the Mannahawkin Baptist church to the Baptist General Association; in 1771. A man named Lines Pangburn was afterward killed by refugees at Mannahawkin—probably the same one.)

For many years, and though travelling in various parts of the United States, yet as long as Thomas Potter lived, his house at Goodluck was considered by Murray as his home. At length, after being away some time upon a religious mission, he returned and found that his good old friend was dead; his letter describing this visit, recounting some of the scenes of Potter's life, his traits of character, his own feelings, etc., is full of tender feeling and sincere grief, admirably expressed, and the substance of the discourse which he preached on that occasion, in that memorable old chapel, is a touching specimen of Murray's eloquence. A brief extract will serve to give an idea of Murray's style and of his feelings towards his departed friend. His text was "For ye are bought with a price; therefore glorify God in your body and in your spirit which are God's." Towards the close of his discourse, pointing towards Potter's grave which could be seen from where he stood, he says :

"Through yonder open casement I behold the grave of a man, the recollection of whom swells my heart with gratitude, and fills my eyes with tears. There sleeps the sacred dust of him who well understood the advantages resulting from the public worship of God. There rests the ashes of him who glorified God in his body, and in his spirit, which he well knew were the Lord's. He believed he was bought with a price, and therefore he declared that all that he had and all that he was, were righteously due to God, who created and purchased him with a price, all price beyond. There rests the precious dust of the friend of strangers, whose hospitable doors were ever open to the destitute, and him who had none to relieve his sufferings ; his dust reposes close to this edifice, itself a monument of his piety. Dear, faithful man, when last I stood in this place, he was present among the assembly of the people. I marked his glistening eye ; it always glistened at the emphatic name of Jesus. Even now, I behold in imagination, his venerable countenance, benignity is seated on his brow, his mind, apparently open and confiding, tranquility reposeth upon his features, every varying emotion evincing faith in that enduring peace which passeth understanding.— Let us, my friends, imitate his philanthropy, his charity, his piety. I may never meet you again until we unite to swell the loud hallelujahs before the throne of God. But to hear of your faith, of your perseverance, of your works of charity, of your brotherly love, will heighten my enjoyments and soothe my sorrows, even to the verge of mortal pilgrimage."

Potter in his will left the church to Murray. The clause in his will reads, as given in Murray's life, as follows :

"The house was built by me for the worship of God ; it is my will that God be worshipped in it still, and for this purpose I will that my ever dear friend, John Murray, preacher of the gospel, possess it, having the sole direction, disposal and management of said house and one acre of land upon which it stands and by which it is surrounded."

It was Mr. Murray's desire as well as Mr. Potter's, that the church should be kept free to all denominations for the worship of God. In his sermon just quoted he says : " Thomas Potter built this house that God might be worshipped without interruption, that he might be worshipped by all whom he should vouchsafe to send. This elegant house, my friends, the first friends who hailed my arrival in this country, this house with its adjoining grove is yours. The faithful founder bequeathed it to me that none of you may be deprived of it," and in Mr. Murray's will he expressly left it *free to all denominations.*

This church property is now under the control of the Methodists, the Universalists, though manifesting little or no disposition to dispute their claim, yet contend that its sale was through "the mismanagement of the executor to satisfy illegal claims, &c." The Universalists held an interesting conference at the church, May 15th, 1833, which was attended by many of their leading preachers and laymen, and while there erected the tombstone over Potter's grave, which yet marks the spot where he was buried. The ceremony was quite impressive. Rev. A. C. Thomas delivering an appropriate discourse, after which a hymn composed for the occasion, was sung among other exercises. This conference, while there, adopted a circular letter to their churches generally, in which, among other things they say : " We have been on a mission of love and gratitude, have assembled in the ancient house of our Fathers, have convened around the grave of the venerated Potter, and dropped a tear of grateful remembrance on the spot where repose his ashes, etc.," and then earnestly invite their brethren from the East and from the West, from the North and from the South to unite with them "in an annual pilgrimage to this sacred spot—this Holy Land, in order that we may all receive a little of the Godlike spirit of benevolence which warmed the soul of that man of God, and friend of man, Thomas Potter.

Their earnest and feeling appeal to their brethren to make this annual pilgrimage, however, has met with a very feeble response, though since the time that John Murray delivered his first sermon in September, 1770, the churches of his followers have increased to perhaps twelve hundred, yet only once in a long while does one of their members make this pilgrimage to this 'Holy Land ;' when they do and express a desire to preach, the doors are thrown open to them, and as long as the trustees are thus liberal to them as well as other denominations, they cer-

OLD TIMES IN OLD MONMOUTH. 133

tainly can have no occasion to question the title.

The substance of the foregoing account is derived from Everett's life of Murray and from writings of Murray himself. The warm unqualified endorsement of the character of Murray, as a man, by such noble hearted men as General Greene of Revolutionary fame, and others who knew him, well show that implicit reliance can be placed upon his statements. In 1832, the Rev. A. C. Thomas visited Toms River and Goodluck, and in both places found persons who had listened to Murray in their youth, and cherished the faith they heard from him, and he conversed with several who remember having heard the circumstances related by Murray of his first meeting with Potter, corroborating Murray's statements.

Before dismissing the subject it may not be amiss to add that one tradition of the origin of the name of Goodluck, as applied to this village, is that when Murray was looking for provisions on his first arrival, and finding Potter so kind and open hearted, and the magnificent groves of pine so suited to his meditative mind, he exclaimed : 'Good Luck !' that I have found such a place and such a man. (There is another tradition of the name of Goodluck Point, near Toms River, which is different from the origin of Goodluck village.)

An old gentleman brought up in the vicinity of the church, whose father was a neighbor and friend of Thomas Potter, stated that he often heard his father relate Potter's story of the naming of the place on this account; that in relation to Potter being carried off by a man of-war, he was gone so long the neighbors thought him dead, and the girl to whom he was to be married, thinking so also, she had married another man just before his return ; that Potter often told his neighbors, after he built the church, that God would send a minister after his own heart, and that in Murray he found fulfilled his long deferred expectations.

THE CENTENARY OF UNIVERSALISM.

The one hundredth anniversary of the introduction of Universalism into the United States was celebrated by a large con vocation of clergy and members of the Society at Gloucester Mass., in September, 1870; and the week following, on Sept. 28th, memorial exercises conducted by that father in the church, Rev. Abel C. Thomas, of Philadelphia, was held at the old Potter Church at Goodluck. The exercises consisted of praying, singing, address by Mr. Ballou, of Philadelphia, &c., after which the congregation were dismissed until one o'clock, when the grave of Mr. Potter the founder, of the church, was decorated with appropriate ceremonies. Forty years ago Rev. A. C. Thomas caused a wooden fence to be put around Potter's grave ; on the centenary occasion this was removed and a neat iron fence substituted.

The following letter from Rev. A. C. Thomas, to the Editor of the New Jersey *Courier,* giving some interesting details of the celebrations at Gloucester and Goodluck, and also items in the rise and progress of the Society, is worthy a place in the history of the church :

THOMAS POTTER AND JOHN MURRAY.

Mr. Editor:—In behalf of many Universalists, I thank you for your late fair and liberal article respecting Thomas Potter, of Good Luck, and the Rev. John Murray.— We expect no man to endorse the statements of the latter, as recorded in his autobiography ; nor the traditional accounts of his remarkable interview with the former ; but we are happy to know that the time has arrived for a truly catholic representation of our history as a people, as illustrated recently in your columns.

In one item you were misinformed. We had no expectations of large "delegations" of our members at the late celebration in Goodluck. Our centenary had been attended the week previously in Gloucester, Mass., the number present being variously estimated from ten thousand to fifteen thousand, including two hundred and fifty out of our six hundred and fifty clergymen. It was the date of the stated annual session of our General Convention, and was appointed to be held in Gloucester under the following circumstances.

In 1770 a Mr. Gregory, presumably a mariner, brought from London to Gloucester a book written by Rev. James Relly, in advocacy and defence of the doctrine of the restoration of all souls, in the Lord's own time and way. This book was passed from hand to hand, and made happy converts of a number of influential, religious people.

It would require no great stretch of the imagination to date the landing of that book on the 28th of September, of the year named ; and on that day Rev. John Murray, a disciple of Relly (in the sense that Relly was a disciple of Christ) landed on the coast of New Jersey, as narrated in your recent article.

After an extended missionary service in New Jersey, Pennsylvania, and New England, Murray was for the second time in Boston in 1774. Having heard of him as a disciple of Relly, the Gloucester people sent for him. He accepted the invitation, the visit being a meeting of the lines of providence in the case. Here he afterwards settled as pastor, his meetings for worship being held in private houses until 1788. In that year a meeting house was erected, and a more pretensious one in 1805. The old building was then sold and devoted to secular uses in the village. Ten years later it was removed to a farm about two miles distant, and since that time has been used as a hay-barn.

In 1804 Murray removed to Boston, and his successor in Gloucester, Rev. Thomas Jones, for forty-two years was minister of the parish, dying in 1846.

During the session of our General Convention last week, we had a memorial service at the old church barn, and also at the grave of Father Jones, the latter being marked by a huge granite obelisk in the Cemetery.

The late great convocation in Gloucester antedated the landing of Murray by the space of one week; and a few of us determined to spend the exact centenary at Goodluck. This was what took us there; and there, precisely one hundred years from the landing of Murray, we held a memorial service in the old church, and also at the grave of Thomas Potter—the order being substantially the same that we had used in Gloucester. The only change was in this : " We strew this evergreen and these flowers in memory and honor of Thomas Potter, the friend and patron of John Murray, our early preacher of Universalism in America."

After a brief address by the Rev. Abel C. Thomas, who conducted the services, the following hymn was sung, and the service proceeded in the order given below.

Whilst far and wide thy scattered sheep,
Great Shepherd, in the desert stray,
Thy love by some is thought to sleep,
Unheedful of the wanderer's way.

But truth declares they shall be found,
Wherever now they darkling roam,
Thy love shall through the desert sound,
And summon every wanderer home.

Upon the darkened ways of sin,
Instead of terror's sword and flame,
Shall love descend—for love can win
Far more than terror can reclaim

And they shall turn their wandering feet,
By grace redeemed, by love controlled,
Till all at last in Eden meet,
One happy, universal fold.

All the ends of the world shall remember and turn unto the Lord, and all the kindreds of the nations shall worship before thee :

For the kingdom is the Lord's and he is the Governor among the nations.

Send forth thy light and thy truth, O Lord ; let them lead us and bring us to thy holy hill, and to thy tabernacles, even unto God our exceeding joy.

Thou wilt show us the path of life : in thy presence is fulness of joy : at thy right hand there are pleasures for evermore.

How amiable are thy tabernacles, O Lord of Hosts ! My soul longeth, yea, even fain'eth for the courts of the Lord :

My heart and my flesh crieth out for the living God,

As the sparrow findeth a house, and the swallow a nest for herself where she may hide her young, so let me dwell at thine altars, O Lord of Hosts, my King and my God.

Blessed are they who dwell in thy house : they will be still praising thee.

A day in thy courts is better than a thousand elsewhere : I had rather be a door-keeper in the house of my God than to dwell in the tents of ungodliness.

O Lord of Hosts, blessed is the man that trusteth in thee.

Thy perfection is higher than heaven : what can we do to celebrate thy praise ? It is deeper than hell : what can we know of thy fathomless love ?

We praise thee, O God : we acknowledge thee to be the Lord.

All the earth doth worship thee, the Father everlasting. To thee all angels cry aloud, the heavens and all the powers therein. To thee, cherubim and seraphim continually do cry.

Holy, holy, holy Lord of Sabaoth ! heaven and earth are full of the majesty of thy glory !

The illustrious procession of the patriarchs praise thee :

The jubilant assembly of the prophets praise thee :

The glorious company of the apostles praise thee :

The noble army of martyrs praise thee :

The Holy Church throughout all the world doth acknowledge thee, the Father of an infinite majesty :

Also thy well-beloved and consecrated Son and the Holy Ghost the Comforter.

OLD TIMES IN OLD MONMOUTH.   135

O God, the King of Glory, help thy servants whom thou hast redeemed by the hand of thy mighty power:
Make them to be numbered with thy saints in glory everlasting.
O Lord, save thy people and bless thy heritage : govern and lift them up forever.
Day by day we manifest thee ; and we worship thy name ever ; world without end.
Vouchsafe, O Lord, to keep us evermore without sin. All our trust is in thee.
O Lord, in thee have I trusted: Let me never be confounded.

It is nothing wonderful that the occasion should have special attractions for me. After the final visit of Murray to Goodluck (it was I believe in 1790) no Universalist clergyman had been there until my first visit in 1832—being accompanied by Richard Norton and James Ely, of Hightstown. I was again there, accompanied by several friends, in May 1833—at which date we erected a plain headstone at the grave of Potter, and engaged Benjamin Stout (then owner of the Potter farm) to erect a paling fence. This was removed a few weeks since, and a beautiful and substantial iron one substituted, by an organization known as the Goodluck Association. This Association also recently bought an acre of wooded ground adjacent to the meeting house as a sort of perpetual memorial.

We have no present thought of establishing a worshiping assembly in that vicinity, and the courteous treatment received from all the neighbors, and from the Rev. Mr. Johnson, Methodist minister in charge, gives us assurance that the door of the old meeting house will not be closed against us for an occasional service in years to come.

Truly yours,   ABEL C. THOMAS.
PHILADELPHIA, Sept. 30, 1770.

WHO WAS RESPONSIBLE FOR CAPT HUDDY'S MURDER?

MONMOUTH REFUGEES IN NEW YORK AND BOARD OF ASSOCIATED LOYALISTS' ACTION.— CAPTAIN RICHARD LIPPENCOTT'S TRIAL, &c.

Captain Joshua Huddy, Daniel Randolph, Esq., and Jacob Fleming, it may be remembered, were made prisoners by the British, at Toms River, March 24th, 1782. While they were in the custody of the British at New York, the Americans on the 30th of the same month, captured Philip White, Aaron White and other refugees as elsewhere described, and also captured at or about the same time Captain Clayton Tilton. Aaron White, Tilton and probably the others, except Phil White killed in attempting to escape, were taken to Freehold and lodged in the jail. Tilton and Aaron White were subsequently exchanged for Randolph and Fleming, before which it will be seen, by the following extracts, that while the Board of Associated Loyalists, in their official capacity ordered Huddy to be delivered to the custody of Lippencott for the ostensible purpose of having him exchanged for Tilton, yet that this was only a pretext ; that the real object was to have him executed and that without any form of trial. The following is a copy of the order on the commissary of prisoners.

NEW YORK, April 8th, 1782.
SIR : Deliver to Captain Richard Lippencott the three following prisoners :— Lieutenant Joshua Huddy, Daniel Randolph, and Jacob Fleming to take them to the Hook (Sandy Hook) to procure the exchange of Captain Clayton Tilton and two other associated loyalists.
By order of the board of directors of associated loyalists.
S. S. BLOWERS, Secretary.
Mr. Commissary CHALLONER.

On the trial of Lippencott, Walter Challoner the commissary of business testified in substance as follows :

"He never knew anything of Joshua Huddy's being to be delivered to Lippencott, till Lippencott brought the order.— In going from deponent's house to the provost with Lippencott, he told deponent that the three prisoners, whom that order concerned, were intended to be exchanged for Philip White, Captain Tilton and another White. In their conversation in going to the provost, Capt. Lippencott told deponent that if White was murdered as reported, they intended to execute Huddy for him."

It will hereafter be seen that at this time Lippencott knew that Phil White was really dead.

The Secretary of the Board of Associated Loyalists, S. S. Blowers, gave his testimony which, as far as it goes seems to palliate the action of that body. His evidence refers to what transpired before the Board in its official capacity and it may be substantially true so far as his knowledge extended but that it did not give all the facts relating to the order for Huddy to be delivered to Lippencott will be seen by the testimony of other witnesses. This Secretary, Mr. Blowers, stood high among the loyalists.— He was a graduate of Harvard College.— After the war he went to Halifax and was appointed Attorney General, elected Speaker of the House of Assembly, and in 1797 appointed Chief Justice of the Supreme Court.

According to Mr. Blowers' testimony, Lippencott appeared before the Board on the 8th of April and stated that Captain Tilton was a prisoner at Freehold and he was afraid the Americans would hang him unless he could have some prisoner to hold for Tilton's security; he proposed to have Huddy delivered to him and also two others named Randolph and Fleming. He wished to take these three men to Sandy Hook and to offer Huddy for Tilton, and if that offer did not answer, to give all three to procure his exchange; but if the first offer was accepted, then to give Randolph and Fleming for two other Loyalists. The order was thereupon given him as the Commissary of prisoners for Huddy, Randolph and Fleming. The next day, April 9th, Lippencott again appeared before the Board and proposed to make an expedition into the Jerseys with a view to

FORCE FREEHOLD JAIL

with a party of about thirty loyalists and rescue Clayton Tilton, or if that was found impracticable, to seize General Forman, that he might by one of these means, procure the release of Tilton, and he requested a requisition for men, ammunition and provisions for the expedition. The proposal was agreed to. While the necessary orders were being made out, Lippencott took a paper from his pocket and went towards Governor Franklin and said, "this is the paper we mean to take down with us."— This paper it would seem, was the label afterwards fastened to Huddy's breast when he was hung. The secretary said that Governor Franklin only looked at the paper but did not read it, that Mr. Stewart, another member of the Board, tried to read it by looking over Franklin's shoulder and that Daniel Coxe, of N. J., also of the Board and its first president, hastily said "we have nothing to do with that paper; Captain Lippencott, keep your paper to yourself."

From the evidence of Mr. Blowers and more particularly from that of other witnesses it is plainly evident that the members of the Board were acquainted with the nature of the contents of the paper although they did not choose to recognize it in their official capacity.

Captain Thomas Crowell, a refugee from Middletown, testified in substance as follows:

"In consequence of several loyalists having been executed in Monmouth, deponent obtained from the commandant, through Governor Franklin, orders to receive three prisoners and follow such directions as deponent might give with respect to their confinement. That it was proposed to have executed one of them by way of retaliation, the Board of Directors having promised deponent that orders should be given for that purpose; but some dispute intervening among loyalists who had taken those prisoners, the order was not given, nor did the execution take place; but deponent in consequence of the declaration made by the Board, dated December 28th, 1780, should have thought himself justifiable in executing one of those prisoners, even had he received only a verbal order from the Board, having never seen any prohibition against the declaration alluded to."

HUDDY'S MURDER SUGGESTED.

Samuel Taylor, a refugee from New Jersey, probably from Shrewsbury, in his testimony said:

"Early in April he waited on Governor Franklin and informed him that the Americans had taken Captain Tilton and Philip White and had murdered the latter in a cruel manner, and requested the Governor to give an order for the delivery of Joshua Huddy and Randolph in order to exchange the latter for Tilton and execute Huddy in retaliation for White. The Governor replied that *he would give the necessary orders, if he thought the deponent would execute Huddy;* to which deponent replied 'he need not fear that.' After the prisoners were removed to the provost, deponent waited on Governor Franklin who told him he would give the desired orders; and as deponent was ordered on another service, the Governor asked what officer he thought should command the party to go out and execute Huddy. Deponent answered, he thought CAPTAIN LIPPENCOTT A PROPER PERSON TO

EXECUTE HUDDY,

and deponent believed he would undertake it. The Governor then told him he wished Captain Lippencott would call at the Board room next day at 2 P. M; in

OLD TIMES IN OLD MONMOUTH.

consequence of deponent's telling this to Lippencott, the latter accordingly attended at the appointed time and place ; but the directors would not give Captain Lippencott the order unless deponent was sent for by the Board ; that when he asked for the order to be given to Captain Lippencott, a member of the Board said he should have it ; that in the course of the conversation with Governor Franklin, *the governor told him that they were not only to hang Huddy*, but that if the rebels hanged any other in retaliation for him. they (the loyalists) should continue retaliating, by hanging man for man, and if necessary he would give up all the prisoners taken at Toms River for the purpose. Deponent said as to Governor Franklin's powers, *the Associated Loyalists looked upon him as their commanding officer and felt bound to obey his orders whether verbal or written ; that he considered Franklin's orders for executing Huddy, lawful orders*, which if not obeyed would have been censurable by a Court Martial, and if the orders had been given to deponent he would have thought himself answerable for disobeying them."

GOVERNOR FRANKLIN WANTS HUDDY HANGED.

At this point in the trial, the prisoner, Captain Lippencott, asked the witness Taylor " Did he ever hear Governor Franklin say that they should not have Huddy unless they would execute him ?" To which Taylor replied :

" On asking for Huddy, Governor Franklin said to deponent, 'Will you execute him when you take him out ?' He replied he would or would not have made application for him ; and Governor Franklin then said 'You shall have him.'

Another refugee from Monmouth, Moffat (Mortord?) Taylor of Shrewsbury in his testimony said :

" Deponent was with Governor Franklin on the subject of executing Huddy, that Governor Franklin said Randolph and Fleming were to be kept as hostages to be exchanged for Captain Tilton and Aaron White *and that Huddy was to be executed for Philip White*, and if Huddy was not executed, he had better be left in jail, as one prisoner by the name of Smock had been taken out of jail to be executed but was not, which occurrence gave cause to the rebels to think the loyalists were afraid of them and dared not hurt them. Deponent told Governor Franklin he had no commission, upon which Franklin said that Captain Lippencott had a commission and told deponent to go to him and he dared say that Lippencott would be fond of the job. Deponent then went to Lippencott and told him that Governor Franklin had appointed deponent to call on him and ask if he was willing to go. After that Lippencott went to Governor Franklin and deponent had nothing farther to do with it."

The above witness refers to a Smock having been taken out of jail to be executed. Captain Barnes Smock and Lieutenant Henry Smock of Monmouth, were cap; tured by the British in September 1870 the officer referred to was probably the first named and he may have been the officer referred to in the evidence of Captain Thomas Crowell already quoted.

THE HANGING OF HUDDY.

Captain Huddy, Randolph and Fleming were taken by Lippencott and his party on board a sloop on the 9th of April, and sailed for Sandy Hook, where they found the British man of war, *Brittania*, on board of which they lodged the prisoners a day or two after. Early on the 12th, Lippencott came for Huddy, and showed Captain Morris, of the *Brittania*, two papers, one being the label which was afterwards fastened to Huddy's breast. Captain Morris asked Lippencott what he intended to do with Huddy. Lippencott replied that he intended to put the orders of the Board of Refugees in execution which was to hang Huddy. Lippencott borrowed a rope from Captain Morris and then proceeded on his infamous mission.

Timothy Brooks, a Pennsylvania Refugee, who was one of Lippencott's party when Huddy was hanged, testified that he saw Huddy hanged and that he was executed by a negro, that Lippencott shook hands with Huddy as he (Huddy) was standing on the barrel, by Huddy's request; that on the 9th of April he heard that Governor Franklin had ordered Huddy to be hanged ; the party which hanged Huddy consisted of twenty-three, counting Captain Lippencott, exclusive of the prisoner. Among the number was a Mr. Tilton who some said was an officer. This Tilton was John Tilton, a refugee from Middletown, Monmouth, who testified that he called on Governor Franklin, before Huddy was delivered to Lippencott, and Franklin said Joshua Huddy must be executed or the loyalist prisoners would all be hanged ; that when the party was putting Huddy in irons on board the sloop, he was present and he asked him if he thought it good usage to iron him. Huddy replied "he did not think it was; but as he was about to be exchanged in a day or two he did not mind being in irons." This Tilton witnessed the hanging of Huddy and returned to the *Brittania* about noon and reported that " Huddy died with the firmness of a lion."

GENERAL WASHINGTON ENDORSES THE DECISION OF FREEHOLD PATRIOTS.

The Freehold patriots heard of the execution of Huddy the day that it occurred and that it was done without any form or pretense of a trial. They at once instituted a thorough investigation of the circumstances attending it, and of the pretexts plead in justification. The evidence produced, published in the chapter relating to Phil White, his capture, attempt to escape and manner of death, show that the alleged cruelties were absolute fabrications. General Forman and Colonel Holmes were requested to wait on and present the evidence to General Washington who considered it a matter of so much importance that on the 19th of April he convened a board of officers to take it into consideration; this board after mature deliberation decided that retaliation should be made by selecting an officer of equal rank unless Lippencott was given up. The next day General Washington wrote a letter to Congress informing them that he deemed the murder of Huddy so barbarous as to require retaliation and trusts that his decision will meet the approval of that body (which was subsequently given); and the day following (April 21st) he wrote to Sir Henry Clinton demanding that Lippencott should be given up.

Sir Henry Clinton replied to General Washington on the 25th of April. He refused to give up the perpetrator of the murder, but informed the American commander that he *had ordered a court martial to examine the charge against Lippencott before his letter was received.* He did not pretend to justify the conduct of the loyalists and expressed his regret for the fate of the sufferer.

On the trial of Lippencott, which took place in June, the main points at issue were: " Was the execution of Captain Huddy justifiable;" and " Did Captain Lippencott execute Huddy on his own responsibility or did he do it by orders of the Loyalist Board."

DECISION OF THE BRITISH COURT MARTIAL.

The following is a copy of the decision of the Court:

" The court having considered the evidence for and against the prisoner Captain Richard Lippencott, together with what he had to offer for defence; and it appearing that (although Joshua Huddy was executed without proper authority) what the prisoner did in the matter was not the effect of malice or ill will, but proceeded from a conviction that it was his duty to obey the orders of the Board of Directors of Associated Loyalists, and his not doubting their having full authority to give such orders, the court are of opinion that he, the prisoner, Captain Richard Lippencott is *not guilty* of the murder laid to his charge, and do therefore acquit him."

This decision not only virtually admits that the execution of Huddy was murder, but throws the blame on the Board of Associated Loyalists at the head of which was Governor William Franklin. The evidence we have already quoted will show the grounds upon which they based their decision. It is worthy of note that before the trial was concluded Governor Franklin left New York and sailed for England and so avoided any investigation of his conduct that might have been contemplated.

Sir Guy Carleton took command of the British forces in New York in May, and he evidently looked upon the Board with less favor than had Clinton. In a letter to General Washington, immediately after his assuming command, he expressed his intention to preserve " the name of Englishmen from reproach and to pursue every measure that might tend to prevent these criminal excesses in individuals."— He did not hesitate to condemn the many unauthorized acts of violence which had been committed, and concluded that he should do everything to mitigate the evils of war. As one proof of his sincerity he at once broke up the Board of Associated Loyalists.

On the 13th of May, the lot was ordered by General Washington which resulted in the selection of Captain Asgill to be held as hostage for Lippencott.

LIPPENCOTT'S OWN DEFENSE ON THE TRIAL.

After Lippencott was arrested and confined in the Provost jail he had frequent conversations with Captain William Cunningham, the Provost Marshal, about the execution of Huddy. Cunningham, expecting to be called upon as a witness at the trial, noted down Lippencott's statements and after submitting them to Lippencott, he made deposition on the 10th of May as follows:

"He heard Captain Lippencott say that Governor Franklin often said there was no way of stopping the rebels from massacreing the refugees but by retaliation, and he wanted one Mason to be the object. Captain Lippencott said he would be the man who would cause it to be done, if the Governor would give him an order in writing, so that he might stand fair in the eyes of his excellency the commander-in-chief.— Governor Franklin replied that he could give no written order, but would answer the consequences to the commander-in-chief, as it was the only way of putting a stop to the rebels hanging and murdering the loyal refugees. And he farther heard Captain Lippencott say that he had been told some time ago, by two refugees, that the honorable board would give up Captain Huddy and two other prisoners; and that Huddy should be executed for Philip White, and the other two should be executed for Captain Tilton and another for Aaron White (supposing Tilton and White had been executed by the rebels; if not they were to be offered in exchange for them. That Captain Lippencott waited on the honorable board with a label that was intended to be fixed on Huddy's breast, and gave it into the hands of the Governor and asked him if he thought that would do, or something to that effect. Mr. Cox, who was present, made answer, and said Captain Lippencott ought to have kept that to himself; Captain Lippencott answered, he never did anything but what was done above board. The Governor read it and then gave it to another of the board to read; and when Captain Lippencott was going, the Governor wished him luck or success, or words to that effect.— He further says Captain Lippencott seemed a little affected when deponent gave him a copy of his crime, and expressed a seeming surprise, by saying, "Ha! is this the way the board is going to leave me!" or words to that purpose.

He further saith, before Lippencott was made a prisoner, he (Lippencott) told him the board sent him near three sheets of paper written, the contents of which were to acquit the board of knowing anything of Huddy's death, and that he (Lippencott) should take it entirely on himself, and sign the paper and send it to the board; which he believed he should have done, but deponent making him prisoner at the time he was copying it had hindered him from so doing."

It will be noticed, that Lippencott asserted that Governor Franklin promised him if he would execute Huddy without a written order that he (Gov. Franklin) would answer the consequences to the British commander-in-chief, and this assertion is substantiated by the evidence of others. How Franklin performed his promise will be seen by the following.

COWARDLY ACT OF THE LOYALIST BOARD.

In the affidavit of Captain Cunningham, reference is made to a certain paper sent by the Board of Loyalists to Lippencott to sign; the purport of the paper being to exonerate the Board from all responsibility, for the murder of Huddy. Cunningham was such an unmitigated scoundrel, as proven by his own confession given in another chapter, that but little credence would be attached to his affidavit but for the fact that it is corroborated by other reliable evidence. The paper referred to was produced before the Court which tried Lippencott. It was written by Mr. Alexander, one of the Board, at the office of the Board, at the instigation of the members. We give the whole of this paper, remarkable as showing the cowardice and duplicity of the Board and their efforts to sacrifice the man they had used as a tool, to save themselves. It was to have been sent to Governor Franklin as the chief of the Board.

"SIR:—In compliance with the orders of the honorable board of directors, we beg leave to communicate to your excellency, for their information, an account of the proceedings of the loyalists from Monmouth on the late expedition for the relief of Captain Clayton Tilton and two other loyalists, then prisoners with the rebels in that county.

Being frustrated in the design of bringing off Captain Tilton by force and our offers for exchange rejected, we dreaded that he was reserved for a fate similar to that our associate Philip White had suffered, who was taken at the same time with Captain Tilton, and inhumanly and wantonly murdered by the guard who were conveying him to Monmouth jail. This recent instance of cruelty, added to the many daring acts of the same nature' which have been perpetrated with impunity by a set of vindictive rebels, well known by the name of the Monmouth Retaliators, associated and headed by one General Forman (whose horrid acts of cruelty have gained him universally the name of Black David,) fired our party with an indignation only to be felt by men who for a series of years have beheld many of their friends and neighbors butchered in cold blood under the usurped form of law, and often without that ceremony, for no other crime than that of maintaining their allegiance to their government under which they were born, and which the rebels audaciously call treason against the States.— We thought it high time to convince the rebels we would no longer tamely submit to such glaring acts of barbarity; and though we lament the necessity to which we have been driven, to begin a retaliation of intolerable cruelties long continued and often repeated, yet we are convinced that we could not have saved the life of Captain Tilton by any other means. We therefore pitched upon Joshua Huddy as a proper subject for retaliation, because he was not only well known to have been a very active and cruel persecutor of our friends, but had not been ashamed to boast of his having been instrumental in hanging Stephen Edwards, a worthy loyalist, and the first of our brethren who fell a martyr to republican fury in Monmouth County. Huddy was the man who tied the knot and put the rope about the neck of that inoffensive sufferer. This fact will appear by two affidavits which we have the honor to enclose.

It is true in this instance we have acted without the orders or knowledge of the honorable board; but we hope, when they are pleased to take into consideration the motives which induced us to take this step, and that Huddy was executed in the county where so many acts of cruelty have been committed on Refugees, they will not think our conduct reprehensible, more especially when your excellency peruses the following state of facts. (*The facts alluded to are not found in the originals.*) Many of the above facts are ascertained by affidavits; and such as are not are too notorious to be denied even by General Forman himself, the most persecuting rebel in the country. By a strange fatality, the loyalists are the only people that have been treated as rebels, during this unhappy war; and we are constrained by our sufferings to declare that no efforts have been made by the Government, under whose protection we wish to live, to save our brethren from ignominious deaths. It is our fixed determination, however repugnant to our feelings (having on all occasions treated our prisoners with tenderness, and often indulge them with paroles which they have frequently violated) that should the rebels, to answer their malignant purposes, continue to punish the loyalists, under their usual distinction of prisoners of state from prisoners of war, they shall feel a severe retaliation in every instance—the just vengeance due to such enormities. Blood shall flow for blood, or the loyalists will perish in the attempt.

We have the honor to be on behalf of the associated loyalists of Monmouth County, your excellency's most obedient servants."

This paper prepared by the Board for Lippencott to sign, it will be seen by reference to the evidence of different witnesses already quoted, was false in every essential particular. While it is true that the written order to get Huddy out of the Provost jail, into the charge of Lippencott makes the pretext that it was to have him exchanged for Tilton, yet the real object as expressed by verbal orders of Governor Franklin was to have him taken within the limits of Monmouth and there executed. They were not frustrated in any attempt to bring off Tilton by force, for if any such attempt had been made it would have been shown on the trial, nor was any attempt to have him exchanged mentioned. It was not Lippencott who suggested the hanging of Huddy—he was only a tool, perhaps too willing, of Governor Franklin and his associates. There was no reason to fear that "Tilton was reserved for a fate similar to Phil White's;" no evidence was produced to show that the Monmouth patriots considered him other than a prisoner of war captured under usual circumstances and to be held for exchange. General Forman, or Black David as they preferred calling him, and his associates never executed a refugee unless under circumstances justifiable by the rules of warfare, as has already been shown in other chapters. The Pine Robbers, Fagan, Fenton, Burke and others of that class met their fate for burglary, murder and other crimes, for committing what Sir Guy Carleton called "unauthorized acts of violence" and what he pointedly condemned. Stephen Edwards came into the American lines as a spy; treasonable papers were found in his possession; so positive was the proof against him that one of the warmest friends of his family, who would have been glad of any pretext to save him, was compelled to vote for his condemnation.

But the most noticeable falsehood which the Board asked Lippencott to sign was that he "had acted without the knowledge or consent of the Board!"

On this point, in addition to the evidence already quoted, we copy the testimony of Henry Stephensen, a surgeon in the British legion, relating a conversation between himself and two members of the Board that took place at the office of *Rivington's Royal Gazette*, the Tory paper at New York. Mr. Stephenson was asked:

"Did he recollect a conversation between himself and several other gentle men, at Mr Rivington's (soon after the confinement of the prisoner for the crime now charged against him) respecting a paper that was sent to the prisoner by some one of the honorable board of directors, to be signed by the prisoner, assigning reasons for the execution of the said Joshua Huddy; and was deponent then censuring a part of said paper which expressed the execution of Huddy to be without the knowledge of the Board? During the conversation, did Messrs. Stewart and Alexander, both members of the Board, come into Mr. Rivington's and what further conversation passed on the subject?"

Surgeon Stephenson deposed in answer as follows:

"Yes, he recollects a conversation. He was at Mr. Rivington's one evening, some little time after the prisoner was confined in the provost, and was mentioning to some gentlemen that a report had prevailed in town that the board of directors had drawn up an instrument in writing, which they wished Captain Lippencott to sign, purporting that Captain Huddy was executed without their knowledge or consent. Just at the time they were talking on the subject Mr. Alexander and Mr. Stewart, two of the board, came in; and after mentioning the above report, deponent put the following question to them: 'First, Did you gentlemen send such an instrument in writing to Captain Lippencott to sign or not? They replied, there had been a paper sent to him but that Captain Lippencott might alter it as he thought proper, or words to that effect.— Mr. Alexander particularly mentioned that he had objected to the words "without their knowledge or consent," being inserted. The second question was 'Though Huddy was executed, was it not done by your knowledge and consent or approbation.' They assented and said it was."

The office of Rivington's *Royal Gazette* was quite a noted resort for British officers and it is evident they criticised pretty freely the action of the Board. Both Alexander and Stewart had personal knowledge of the falsity of the statement "without knowledge or consent of the board," as when, on the 8th of April, Lippencott appeared before the Board in response to Gov. Franklin's request to consent to take command of a party to hang Huddy, both of these men were present and fully talked over the matter. Mr. Alexander objected to putting in the words but was overruled by the other members, who quieted his scruples by telling him Lippencott could alter it if he chose. They well knew the fearful predicament into which they had got Lippencott.

This paper was gotten up by the Board to shield themselves, because, to their surprise, no sooner was the news of Huddy's execution heard in New York than the regular British officers generally denounced it as "a reproach to the name of Englishmen," and a desire was expressed to have an investigation to find out the real author or authors to hold responsible. Alarmed at the threatening aspect of affairs they drew up this paper to be signed by Lippencott. It would seem as though they thought as Lippencott found his action so severely denounced by the regular British and that they were arrayed against him, that he would want to retain the active friendship of the Board to stand between him and the regular British authorities, and that to secure their active services in his behalf he would probably consent to sign this paper. And their calculation proved correct, for he had commenced copying it off when he was arrested. The truth then flashed upon him that the Board to save themselves wanted to sacrifice him, and then he determined to let matters take their course and simply look out for himself, and, as he expressed it, "to have the saddle put on the right horse."

An idea of the feeling among the regular British officers in regard to Huddy's death may be inferred from the testimony of Surgeon Stephenson, but it was most emphatically shown by the action of Sir Henry Clinton himself, who was so indignant at the barbarous murder of Huddy that he had ordered Lippencott's-trial by Court Martial before he received General Washington's letter demanding his surrender. There is good reason to believe that Sir Henry thought the really guilty party was the Board of Associated Loyalists, and especially its head, Governor Franklin, who so cowardly fled to England leaving both Lippencott and Asgill to their fates; and Clinton's successor, Sir Guy Carleton, was so satisfied of the disgraceful conduct of the Board that he broke it up.

As before stated, the decorum of the court martial virtually threw the blame of Huddy's murder on Governor Franklin and his associates, and this decision was subsequently endorsed by competent American authority, as will be seen by the following extract from a report made to Congress in 1837 by a select committee of that body which had thoroughly investigated the whole subject:

"The immediate agent in this deed of blood was Richard Lippencott, a native of New Jersey and then a captain in the British service. He was the instrument of a board of associated loyalists in New York, at the head of which was William Franklin, once Royal governor of New Jersey. The members of this body, after the murder had taken place, endeavored for a time to deny that they had directed it; but the evidence adduced on the trial of the perpetrator, as well as subsequent publications of the loyalists themselves, abundantly prove that, without the courage to act themselves, they had the baseness to authorize the deed to be committed, and the meanness to attempt the concealment of their privity to its perpetration."

A BOY TRIED FOR MURDER.

THE STATE AGAINST AARON, A SLAVE OF LEVI SOLOMON'S.

The defendant, Aaron, a black boy about eleven years of age, was indicted in the Court of Oyer and Terminer of Monmouth in October, 1817, for the murder of Stephen Connelly, a child little more than two years old. The indictment in the usual form charged the prisoner with the murder on the 26th of August, 1817, by throwing the child into a well. It appeared in evidence that the prisoner was born in July, 1806, was of ordinary size and in the opinion of some witnesses, possessed common capacity and intelligence; by the testimony of others he was more cunning and smarter in his play than usual for boys of his age. Stephen Connelly was a stout healthy child, and on the 26th of August, in the after part of the day, was found in a well about 18 or 19 feet deep, having a curb two and a half feet high, so that he could reach the top with his hands, and it was in such a state that all the witnesses thought it impossible for him to get over it. The well was in a cornfield and orchard about one hundred rods from two public roads and the same distance from the house in which Stephen lived. The corn was so high and thick that a person at the well could not be seen except by looking along the rows. It was in the neighborhood of a number of houses.

Stephen was seen playing in the road with the prisoner a short time before he was missed by the family; and when they were searching for him the prisoner was up in a cherry tree. Being asked if he had seen him, he said, "yes, he is gone up the road;" being told to come down and help look for him, he looked along the road and called aloud three or four times but did not get down. After the body was found and taken out of the well, he came up and seeing it lying there he said, "so you've found Stephen." There was yet nothing in his manner which excited attention or suspicion. That night he went to bed earlier than usual, and without his supper. The next morning he told a young lad, an apprentice to his master that he saw Stephen fall into the well; and that he was ten or twelve paces off; that he went up and saw Stephen splash the water and then went to pick apples which his master had directed him to do. Being asked why he did not tell it he gave no answer. On his trial (May, 1818) the prisoner was defended by Garret D. Wall, L. H. Stockton and Joseph W. Scott. For the state appeared R. Stockton, jr., Deputy Attorney General and R. Stockton.

His counsel objected to any evidence of his confessions as improper and incompetent, he being under the age of twelve years. After argument the court admitted the confessions in evidence. It then appeared that at the coroner's inquest the prisoner was summoned; at first he appeared terrified but soon became composed. He then repeated the story he had told before, adding that Stephen climbed over the curb and fell in; and that he did not tell anybody for fear they would think he

OLD TIMES IN OLD MONMOUTH. 143

did it. He was very closely pressed by the jury with questions as to his own guilt and told that he had better tell the whole truth to them. He steadily denied doing the act. After examining him some time, the jury went to the well that he might shew them how Stephen got over. He shewed them. His master and one of the jurors then took him aside and asked him about it. He then told them he had done it; that Stephen went to the well and put his hands on the curb and he took hold of his legs and threw him over; that he gasped and caught his breath and made the water splash as he fell; and that he (prisoner) being frightened, ran away to picking apples; that he denied it before because he was afraid they would send him to jail. He repeated the same thing to the whole jury. He was urged and questioned closely but all the witnesses denied that either promises or threats or improper contrivances were used to induce him to make the confession; but he was frequently and constantly told to tell the truth and that would be best for him. He seemed to understand what he was about and to understand his answers.

He continued for three or four weeks to make the same confession to the gaoler and many other persons; and then he began to deny the fact and continued the denial until the time of trial.—When he first denied, the gaoler asked him why he had owned it before; he said that one of the jurymen told him the devil would get him if he denied it, but if he confessed it he would not be sent to jail. This was explicitly denied by the juror referred to; he was further asked who had been to see him, and he replied his master but that he did not tell him to deny it.

At the time of his first confession, and frequently afterwards, he gave as a reason for the act that he did it to spite the father of Stephen because he had driven him out of the shop and threatened to whip him; at other times he said he said he had no reason for it.

The case was ably argued and the court gave a minute charge to the jury who found the prisoner guilty.

A motion was then made for a new trial, it being desired by the court that the opening of the Supreme Court of N. J., at bar upon several legal questions (given in 1st Southard reports) might be known.—The trial took place in May, 1818. In September following it was taken up by the Supreme Court and its decision on the various points was made by Chief Justice Kirkpatrick. In regard to the liability of minors under fourteen years of age to punishment, the Chief Justice quoted various authorities from which the Court decided that upon this naked confession of Aaron's he could not be convicted of a capital offence—"that the confession is a simple, naked confession, disclosing no fact, pregnant with no circumstances to give it authority or in any way to corroborate it. It did not even lead to the discovery of the body of the deceased, for it was found before; it opens no proof of malice or hatred or ill will against the child but rather to the contrary; it is a mere naked confession of an infant under the age of eleven years obtained by some degree of pressure, at least, after a firm denial and as such (I speak with great deference to the learning of the Court which tried the cause) I should incline to think it ought not to have been admitted as evidence; and if admitted that it ought not to have been the ground of conviction."

A new trial was granted at which the prisoner was discharged; and we have been told by an old gentleman, a regular attendant of the Freehold Courts in that day, that it was believed the boy was afterwards sold as a slave in the West Indies.

THE INLETS OF OLD MONMOUTH

OLD CRANBERRY INLET.

A century ago Cranberry Inlet, nearly opposite Toms River, was one of the best inlets on the Jersey coast. The question as to the exact year when it was opened was brought before one of our courts a few years ago in a suit involving title to land in the vicinity, but no decisive information was elicited upon the trial. It is probable, however, that it broke through about 1750. It is laid down on Lewis Evans's map, 1755, and Jeffrey's (English) map, same year, and on the latter and other maps it is called New Inlet. On Jeffrey's map Toms River is called Goose Creek, and Barnegat Bay is called Flat Bay Sound. Cranberry Inlet closed about the year 1812, though for several years previous it had commenced filling up, gradually shoaling more and more each year until it was finally closed up. During the Revolutionary war it was a place of considerable importance as it afforded conveniences to our privateers on the lookout for British vessels bound in and out of New York.— Though we have no exact account of the depth of water on the bar, yet in its best days it must have been equal to the best inlets now on our coast, as we find that loaded, square-rigged vessels occasionally entered it. David Mapes, the much esteemed and noted colored Quaker of Tuckerton, when a boy, resided in this vicinity, and was employed by Solomon Wardell to tend cattle on the beach when the inlet broke through. He slept in a cabin and one morning on awakening was surprised to see that the sea had broken across the beach during the night.

(In a previous article relating to Capt. Adam Hyler, by the accidentally omission of one line in the copy it was made to appear that Cranberry Inlet opened into Raritan Bay. Though most of our readers would infer it was from a typographical error yet it reminded us that a brief notice of this Inlet, so frequently referred to in Revolutionary times, but now among the things of the past, should be given to explain events related in previous chapters referring to it.)

ATTEMPTS TO OPEN NEW INLETS.

The closing of Cranberry Inlet caused great inconvenience to persons along Barnegat Bay engaged in the coasting trade as it compelled vessels from the upper part of the bay to sail several miles out of their way to Barnegat Inlet to get to sea. About the year 1821 an attempt to open a new inlet near the head of the bay was made by a man named Michael Ortley.— He worked at it off and on for several years and spent considerable money in the undertaking; at length, one day a large company of men volunteered to aid him in completing the enterprise. In the evening after finishing it, Mr. Ortley and his friends had quite a merry time in celebrating the completion of the work. But great was their disappointment the following morning to find that the running of the tide which they had supposed would work the inlet deeper, had on the contrary raised a bulkhead of sand sufficiently large to close it up, and the result was the inlet was closed much more expeditiously than it was opened.

Many supposed that if an effort was made to open an inlet farther down the bay in the vicinity of old Cranberry, it would prove more successful. Acting upon this supposition, another effort was made to open one about opposite Toms River. The work was completed July 4th, 1847, by some two or three hundred men under the direction of Anthony Ivins, jr. In this undertaking, care was taken to let in the water when it was high tide in the bay and low water outside; but this enterprise also proved a failure as it filled up about as soon as Ortley's.

SHREWSBURY INLET.

Shrewsbury Inlet was open in 1778; it closed again about 1800; again opened about 1830; and again closed about 1847. Just before the closing of the inlet at this time, the writer of this was engaged in the coasting trade and one time in sailing down the beach noticed a little steamer, called the *Cricket*, from New York, wrecked on the bar. This wreck seemed to hasten the closing of the inlet by gathering the sand around it as it washed in and out.

BARNEGAT INLET.

This inlet has always been open from our earliest accounts. It was first noticed by a Dutch navigator, probably Capt. Mey in the celebrated little yacht *Restless* in 1614, who on account of its dangerous bar called it "Barendegat," which means breakers inlet or an inlet with breakers.— The character of the inlet has always been the same as at present except during the few years when Cranberry was open when it was much shoaler than before or since. It has shifted up and down the beach two or three miles and is still shifting and changing. A few years ago it washed down the old lighthouse built in 1834 and now exhibits a decided inclination to wash down the new one.

LONG BRANCH IN 1819.—BATHERS AT FAULT.

The company at this salubrious retreat is represented to be very numerous and respectable this season. The New York *Advocate* says there is a kind of military or naval regulation there which strangers often contravene from ignorance; that is when the stipulated time for ladies bathing arrives, a white flag is hoisted upon the bank, when it is high treason for a gentlemen to be seen there; and when the established time for gentlemen arrives, the red flag is run up which is sometimes done by mistake and produces rather ludicrous misunderstandings A wag lately hoisted both flags together which created some awful squinting and no little confusion.— (Niles' *Register*, 1819. Sup., p. 159.)

OLD TIMES IN OLD MONMOUTH. 145

TOWNSHIPS IN MONMOUTH—WHEN ESTABLISHED.

When the county of Monmouth was established in 1683 it was divided into two townships, Middletown and Shrewsbury. Stafford was established in 1749. Upper Freehold, Freehold and Dover were defined by an act passed June 25, 1767, to take effect in March of the following year. Howell was established in 1801 and Millstone in 1844; Jackson, now in Ocean county in 1844; Plumsted, now in Ocean, in 1845, and Union, now also in Ocean, in 1847; Atlantic, in 1847; Raritan, Marlboro and Manalapan in 1848; Ocean, 1849; Wall, 1851; Holmdel and Matavan in 1857.

THE FIRST TEMPERANCE SOCIETY IN THE U. S.

Old Monmouth has the honor of organizing the first Temperance Society in the country, which was established at Allentown in 1805 and called "The Sober Society," and was composed of fifty-eight members. (Newark *Daily Adv. and Hist. Rec.* 1859).

A VALUABLE MONMOUTH DOG.

In the Journal of a Quaker named James Craft, published in Historical Record, Oct., 1851, it is said:
"1780, 2nd mo. 20th : Money very plenty. £300 given for a dog in Monmouth."

COL. JONATHAN FORMAN AND DAUGHTER.

The following is from the Utica N. Y. *Observer*, 1859.

"Died, at her residence in Utica, Sept. 16th, 1859, Mrs. Mary Ledyard Seymour, wife of the late Hon. Henry Seymour. She was the daughter of Col Jonathan Forman, and was born at Monmouth New Jersey, Feb. 18th, 1785. Her father at the age of 19, left Princeton College to join the American army. He entered it as a lieutenant, and served during the war, rising to the rank of colonel. The mother of Mrs. Seymour was a niece of Col. Ledyard who was in command of Fort Griswold, opposite New London, Conn., at the time of its capture by the British. She aided in taking care of the wounded of that massacre, by which nineteen of her relatives perished. When Mrs. Seymour was about twelve years old she removed to Cazenovid, in Madison county, at that time a "frontier settlement." There was then no carriage road west of Whitestown, and in many places they were obliged to use axes to make their way in that direction. It is said that the carriage of Col. Forman, was the first conveyance of the kind that passed beyond the site of Whitestown.— He drove to Chittenango and the family went thence to Cazenovia on horseback.— Her parents died many years ago, but her uncle, Major Samuel S. Forman, of Syracuse, still lives, in his 96th year. Miss Forman was married to Mr Seymour at Cazenovia on the 1st of January, 1807. Mr. Seymour was then a merchant in the town of Pompey, Onondago County. He continued in business there, exercising a wide and beneficial influence in that county until 1819, when he removed with his family to Utica. His subsequent honorable and useful career is known to the people of the State. He died in August, 1837, at his dwelling in Whitesboro street, in this city, where Mrs. Seymour has ever since resided."

Mrs. Seymour above mentioned, a native of Monmouth, was the mother of Gov. Horatio Seymour, of N. Y., and a niece of Philip Freneau, the poet of the Revolution. Col. Ledyard above referred to, was brutally murdered by a renegade New Jersey refugee, named Bromfield. After the Americans had surrendered the fort, Bromfield asked who commanded it. The brave Ledyard replied, "I did but you do now," and handed his sword to Bromfield. The villain took it and immediately stabbed Ledyard to the heart.

About the time Col. Forman left for New York, many families of old Monmouth emigrated to the western part of that state to what they then termed "the Genesee country."

THE TILTON FAMILY.

Among the twelve original patentees of old Monmouth is found the name of John Tilton, and members of this family were among the first English settlers who located here. The earliest mention we have found of the Tilton family is in the Lynn, Mass., records which speak of John Tilton and William Tilton as being there in 1640. About the time of their arrival the Puritans of New England were much exercised by the advent among them of the Baptists and strong efforts were made by the Puritans to get rid of them. At this time in Lynn the most noted, influential person among the Baptists was Lady Deborah Moodie, afterwards long and favorably known among the original settlers of Long Island. Among others who were inclined to adhere to the Baptists with Lady Moodie was Mrs. Tilton, as will be seen by the following extract from the Lynn records of the date of December 12th, 1642, which we give literally with its quaint wording and peculiar orthography:

The Lady Deborah Moodie, Mrs. King, and the wife of John Tilton were presented for *hooldinge* that the baptising of infants was *noe* ordinance of God."

The proceedings against them resulted in their leaving Lynn, and the next year, (1643,) we find mention of Lady Moodie, the Tiltons, William Goulding, Samuel Spicer, and others at Gravesend, Long Island, founding the settlement from which afterwards came many persons to Old Monmouth. For a long time, John Tilton was a prominent man at Gravesend, enjoying the respect of the English and the confidence of the Dutch authorities at New York or New Amsterdam as it was then called, and holding official positions until the appearance, in 1657, of the Quakers among the Gravesend settlers. No sooner did the Quakers begin to promulgate their views than the Dutch authorities issued severe edicts against them and all who harbored "those abominable impostors, runaways and strolling people called Quakers." The following year John Tilton was fined £12 Flemish money for harboring a Quaker woman. From that time forward both Tilton and his wife seem to have strongly sympathized with the persecuted sect and soon cast their lot among them altogether, which greatly excited the ire of the Dutch and especially of old Governor Peter Stuyvesant. On the 5th of October, 1662, John Tilton and Mary his wife were summoned before the Governor and his council, at New Amsterdam, (New York,) charged with having entertained Quakers and frequenting their conventicles. They were condemned and ordered to leave the province before the 20th of November following, under pain of corporal punishment. It is supposed that through the efforts of Lady Moodie, who had great influence with Governor Stuyvesant, that the sentence was either reversed or changed to the payment of a fine. The following derived from the record of their trial is a curiosity in these days of religious toleration, especially to Jerseymen whose state has the proud distinction of never having allowed religious persecution within its borders. From the record it appears that

"Goody Tilton, (Mrs. Tilton,) was not so much condemned for assisting at conventicles as for having, *like a sorceress, gone from door to door to lure and seduce the people, yea even young girls, to join the Quakers.*"

On the 19th of September, 1662, John Tilton was fined, as the record says, *for permitting Quakers to quake* at his house at Gravesend. Many other persons were prosecuted at this time by the Dutch on similar charges, among whom were the Bownes, Spicers, Townsends, Holmeses and others, ancestors of numerous Jersey families of these names. Some of these families had been persecuted by the Puritans of New England, to escape which they came to Long Island. Here, being again persecuted by the Dutch, they seem to have determined to seek some place where they could worship God as they pleased.—The lands in Monmouth county impressed them so favorably that the following year (1663) they made large purchases of the Indians, which greatly excited the indignation of the Dutch at New Amsterdam, who laid claim to the land asserting that they had bought the best of it of the Indians ten or twelve years before. The details of the controversy which ensued and the arguments advanced by both sides are too lengthy to introduce in this place.—Suffice it to say that some of the difficulties were ended by the conquest of the Dutch by the English the following year. In 1665 John Tilton and eleven associates obtained from Gov. Richard Nicholls the celebrated document known as "the Monmouth Patent," which has been published in another chapter, which guaranteed liberty of conscience to all settlers.

After the conquest of the Dutch by the English, though we have met with no positive information on the point, yet we are inclined to believe that John Tilton found, by the change, that he could remain at Long Island without molestation, he preferred in his days there and leave his share in his Monmouth purchases to his children. He died at Gravesend, L. I., in 1688; his wife died a few years before, in 1683. His will dated 15th of 7th month 1687 was recorded at Brooklyn, L. I., April 3d, 1688, in Book of Records Vol. 1, page 108. This will shows he left two sons named John and Thomas, and daughters named Sarah, who married John Painter, Abigail who married —— Scott, Esther, who married Samuel Spicer, and Mary, who married — Carman. In his will he left a lot of land at Gravesend to his executors, to be used as a graveyard for them and their successors, and "for all friends of the everlasting truth of the Gospel as occasion serves, forever, to bury there dead therein."

OLD MONMOUTH THE PIONEER OF RELIGIOUS TOLERATION.

Every citizen of old Monmouth has just cause to be proud of the fact that the original patentees were among the first in America to guarantee toleration to all settlers in religious matters. In Rhode Island while Roger Williams advocated "a free, full and absolute liberty of conscience" it is charged that Roman Catholics were excepted in the charter of 1663. The much vaunted toleration act of Maryland limited toleration to "all who believed in Jesus Christ." William Penn did not arrive in America until October, 1682, nearly eighteen years after the Monmouth patentees declared that every settler should have FREE LIBERTY OF CONSCIENCE WITHOUT ANY MOLESTATION OR DISTURBANCE WHATSOEVER IN THE WAY OE THEIR WORSHIP.

THE ROGERINE BAPTISTS.

A SINGULAR RELIGIOUS SOCIETY IN OLD MONMOUTH.

About the year 1737 a society of Rogerine Baptists, or Quaker Baptists as they were then called, located at Waretown, now in Ocean county. From various notices of the history of this singular sect and how a society came to be located in Old Monmouth, we extract the following: This society was founded by John Rogers, about 1674. His followers baptized by immersion; the Lord's supper they administered in the evening with its ancient appendages. They did not believe in the sanctity of the Sabbath; they believed that since the death of Christ all days were holy alike; they used no medicines nor employed doctors or surgeons; would not say grace at meals; all prayers to be said mentally except when the spirit of prayer compelled the use of voice; they said "all unscriptural parts of religious worship are idols," and all good christians should exert themselves against idols, &c. Among the idols they placed the observance of the Sabbath, Infant baptism, &c. The Sabbath they called the New England idol and the methods they took to demolish this idol were as follows: They would on Sundays try to be at some manual labor near meeting houses or in the way of people going to and from church. They would take work into meeting houses, the women knitting, the men whittling and making splints for baskets, and every now and then contradicting the preachers.— "This was seeking persecution," says one writer, * and they received plenty of it, insomuch that the New Englanders left some of them neither liberty, property nor whole skins."

John Rogers, the founder of the sect, who, it is said, was as churlish and contrary to all men as Diogenes, preached over forty years, and died in 1721. The occasion of his death was singular. The small pox was raging terribly in Boston and spread an alarm to all the country around. Rogers was confident that he could mingle with the diseased and that the strength of his faith would preserve him safe from the mortal contagion. Accordingly he was presumptuous enough to travel one hundred miles to Boston to bring his faith to the test: the result was that he caught the contagion, came home and died with it, the disease also spreading in his family and among his neighbors. This event one would think would have somewhat shaken the faith of his followers but on the contrary it seemed to increase their zeal.

In 1725, a company of Rogerines were taken up on the Sabbath in Norwich, Conn., while on their way from their place of residence to Lebanon; they were treated with much abuse and many of them whipped in a most unmerciful manner.— This occasioned Gov. Jenks, of Rhode Island, to write spiritedly against their persecutors, and also to condemn the Rogerines for their provoking, disorderly conduct.

One family of the Rogerines was named Colver or Culver, (Edward's History spells the name one way and Governor Jenks the other). This family consisted of John Colver and his wife, who were a part of the company which was treated so rudely at Norwich, and five sons and five daughters, who, with their families, made up the the number of twenty-one souls. In the year 1734, this large family removed from New London, Conn., and settled in New Jersey. The first place they pitched upon for a residence, was on the east side of

Schooley's Mountain, in Morris county.—They continued here about three years and then went in a body to Waretown, then in Monmouth but now in Ocean county. While here they had their meetings in a school house, and their peculiar manner of conducting services was quite a novelty to other settlers in the vicinity. As in England, during the meeting the women would be engaged in knitting or sewing, and the men in making axe handles, basket splints or engaged in other work, but we hear of no attempt to disturb other societies.

They continued at Waretown about eleven years, and then went back to Morris county and settled on the west side of the mountain from which they had removed. In 1790 they were reduced to two old persons whose names were Thomas Colver and Sarah Mann; but the posterity of John Colver, it is said, is yet quite numerous in Morris county. Abraham Waeir from whom the village of Waretown derives its name, tradition says was a member of the Rogerine Society. When the main body of the society left, he remained behind, and became quite a prominent business man, generally esteemed; he died in 1768, and his descendants removed to Squan and vicinity near the head of Barnegat bay.

Before concluding this notice of the Rogerines, it should be stated that another thing in their creed was that it was not necessary to have marriages performed by ministers or legal officers; they held that it was only necessary for the man and woman to exchange vows of marriage to make the ceremony binding, A zealous Rogerine once took to himself a wife in this simple manner, and then to tantalize Governor Saltonstall called on him to inform him they had married themselves without aid of church or state, and that they intended to live together as husband and wife without their sanction. "What," said the Governor, in apparent indignation, "do you take this woman for your wife?" "Yes, I most certainly do," replied the man. "And do you take this man for your husband?" said he to the woman. The woman replied in the affirmative. "Then," said the wily old governor, "in the name of the Commonwealth I pronounce you husband and wife—whom God hath joined together let no man put asunder? You are now married according to both law and gospel."

The couple retired much chagrined at the unexpected way the Governor had turned the tables upon them, despite their boasting.

THE WAR OF 1812.

Scenes on our Coast.

During the last war with England the vigilance of the British cruisers on our coast seriously injured the business of New Jersey coasting vessels. Commodore HARDY in his flag ship the "Ramillies," a 74 gun ship, had command of the British blockading vessels on our coast. Most accounts, written and traditional, concede that he was one of the most honorable, high-minded men in the British service, entirely different from the infamous Admiral Cockburn, who commanded the blockading squadron farther south. Commodore Hardy rarely took private property except contraband of war without offering compensation. Most of the coasters in the southern part of Old Monmouth, along Barnegat bay, were engaged in the lumber business and the stoppage of their trade was seriously felt. Occasionally some bold fortunate captain would manage to run the blockade and reach New York and be well repaid for his risk, but others who tried the experiment or were preparing to, were not quite so fortunate.

On the 31st of March, 1812, Commodore Hardy, in the Ramillies, came close to Barnegat Inlet and sent in two long barges loaded with armed men after two American vessels lying in the inlet waiting a chance to slip out. They first boarded the schooner Greyhound, Capt. Jesse Rogers, of Potters Creek, and attempted to take her out but she grounded and the enemy fired her and both vessel and cargo were burned up. They then set fire to a sloop belonging to Waretown, owned by Captain Jonathan Winner, Hezekiah Soper and Timothy Soper; this vessel was saved, however, as signals were unexpectedly fired from the ship which caused the barges hastily to leave for the ship that she might start in pursuit of some vessel seen at sea. As soon as the barges left, the Americans went on board the sloop and extinguished the fire. While the British were in the Inlet a party landed on the beach near the present lighthouse and killed some fourteen or fifteen head of cattle belonging to Jeremiah Spragg and John Allen. The owners were away but the British left word if they presented their bill to Commodore Hardy he would settle it, but they were too patriotic to do anything that savored of furnishing supplies to the enemy. In some instances on the New Jersey coast where cattle and other things had been taken by Hardy and word left that he would pay for them, the owners thought themselves justifiable in going off to his ship and getting the money, as the supplies were not furnished voluntarily but taken by force.

The appearance of the Ramillies at this time at Barnegat Inlet created much excitement in the villages along the bay.— At Waretown, for fear that the barges might land and commit excesses like those which disgraced the operations of Cockburn, the women and children, and valuables easily carried were sent to a hamlet in the woods a few miles west of the place. At Forked River the late Hon. Charles Parker (father of Gov Parker) had just completed a large building for a dwelling, store house, &c., at the upper landing. The roof of this building was crowded with spectators, who, though six or seven miles distant, had a fair view of the ship, burning vessel and movements of the enemy.

At another time the schooner President, Captain Amos Birdsall, of Waretown, bound to New York, was taken by Commodore Hardy, who at once commenced taking from the schooner her spars, deck plank, &c. Captain Birdsall had liberty to leave with his crew, in a yawl, whenever he pleased, but on account of high winds he was detained a day or two, when he succeeded in getting on board a fishing smack and thus got home. Before he left, his schooner's masts had been sawed into plank by the British.

The sloop Elizabeth, Captain Thomas Bunnell, of Forked River, was captured by barges sent in Barnegat Inlet; she was towed out to sea, but the British shortly after lost her on Long Island. She was owned by William Platt and Thomas Bunnell.— At another time Captain Bunnell was captured by the British and detained some time and then put on board a neutral (Spanish ?) ship and finally reached New York.

The sloop Traveller, Captain Asa Grant, was fired by the British but the fire was extinguished before much damage was done. The sloop Maria and another sloop not remembered were chased ashore near Squan Inlet.

An Amusing Stratagem.

The noted Commodore Percival, who died a few years ago, familiarly named " Mad Jack Percival," in the early part of his naval career was the hero of an adventure on the coast of Monmouth which is thus described by a paper published in New York at the time:

"On Sunday morning, July 4, 1813, the fishing smack Yankee was borrowed by Commodore Lewis, who has command of the American flotilla stationed at Sandy Hook, for the purpose of taking by stratagem the sloop Eagle, tender to the Poictiers 74, cruising off and on Sandy Hook, which succeeded to a charm. A calf, a sheep and a goose were purchased and secured on deck. Thirty men, well armed, were secreted in the cabin and forepeak. Thus prepared the Yankee stood out of Mosquito Cove as if going on a fishing trip to the Banks; three men only being on deck dressed in fisherman's apparel with buff caps on. The Eagle on perceiving the smack immediately gave chase, and after coming up with her and finding she had live stock on board ordered her to go down to the Commodore, then five miles distant. The helmsman of the smack answered " Ay ! ay, sir !" and apparently put up the helm for that purpose which brought him alongside the Eagle not three yards distant. The watchword *Lawrence* was then given when the armed men rushed on deck from their hiding places and poured into her a volley of musketry which struck the crew with dismay and drove them so precipitately into the hold that they had not time to strike the flag. Seeing the enemy's deck clear, Sailing-master Percival, who commanded the expedition, ordered the men to cease from firing ; upon which one of the men came out the hold and struck the Eagle's colors. They had on board a thirty-two pound brass howitzer loaded with canister shot, but so sudden was the surprise they had not time to discharge it. The crew of the Eagle consisted of H. Morris, master's mate of the Poictiers, W. Price, midshipman, and 11 seamen and marines. Mr. Morris was killed, Mr. Price mortally wounded, and one marine killed, and one wounded. The Eagle with the prisoners arrived off the Battery in the afternoon and landed the prisoners at Whitehall, amid the shouts and plaudits of thousands of spectators assembled at the Battery to celebrate the anniversary of independence.— Mr. Morris was buried at Sandy Hook with military honors. Mr. Price was carried to New York, where on Thursday he died; and was buried with military ceremonies in St. Paul's churchyard."

A traditionary version of this affair, which we have heard from old citizens, says that Percival wished to make his boat appear as a market boat, that he placed one of his men on a seat close to the bulwark disguised as an old Quakerish looking farmer, with broad brimmed hat and long staff in hand, while he looked like an ignorant boor at the wheel and by his answers made the British think he was half-witted. When ordered to drop along side under threat of being fired into, he made a silly reply to the effect " You had better not try it, for Dad's big molasses jug is on deck and if you broke that he would make you sorry for it."

THE LAWRENCE FAMILY.

The Lawrence family claim to be descended from Sir Robert Lawrence, of Ashton Hall, Lancastershire, England, who went to Palestine during the Crusades with Richard Cœur de Leon, and participated in the siege of St. Jean de Acre, in the year 1119, and was the first to plant the banner of the cross on the battlements of the town for which he was knighted. A grandson of Sir Robert Lawrence, named Sir James Lawrence, married into the Washington family, having been united to Matilda Washington in the reign of Henry III.— General George Washington's half brother Lawrence, was so named on account of his relationship to this family.

The first Lawrences who came to America were two brothers, John, aged 17 years, and William, aged 12 years, and also Mary Lawrence, aged nine years, who embarked in the barque *Planter*, April 2nd, 1635; her passengers were chiefly from St Albans, Hertfordshire, England. Another brother named Thomas, came over in 1655, twenty years later. The greater portion of the Lawrences in America are descended from William, the second brother.

The first Lawrence who settled within the limits of Old Monmouth, whose name the writer has met with, was Elisha, a son of William. Elisha commenced business as a merchant, in the latter part of the seventeenth century, at Cheesequakes, on the south side of the Raritan, but his store having been pillaged by the crew of a French privateer, he removed to Upper Freehold then a wilderness. He represented the county in the provincial Assembly in 1708—9. His residence was called Chestnut Grove. He was born in 1666, and died May 27th, 1724. He married Lucy Stout and had children as follows; sons, Joseph, Elisha and John, and daughters, Hannah, who married Richard Salter, Elizabeth, who married Joseph Salter, Sarah, who married John Ember and Rebecca, who married a New Yorker named Watson. The second son, Elisha, had a son named John Brown Lawrence, who was the father of the celebrated Commodore Lawrence of "Don't give up the ship" fame, and grandfather of Commodore Boggs, who so distinguished himself in the Varuna in passing the forts below New Orleans during the late rebellion.

The genealogy of the Lawrence family has been traced out and published with more or less completeness in several works, the most extensive of which is one devoted to giving the history and genealogy of the family, published by T. Lawrence, New York, in 1858. In the present article it is impracticable to give the genealogy of all the Lawrences in old Monmouth, but we append that of one branch, members of which were quite noted in the Revolutionary history of the county as will be seen by reference to sketches of them in chapters previously published.

As above stated, the first, named Elisha, had a son named John, who ran the noted Lawrence's line between East and West Jersey, who was born 1708. This John married Mary, daughter of William Hartshorne, and had children as follows; John, a physician, who died unmarried; Helena who married James Holmes, merchant, New York; Lucy, who married Rev. Henry Waddell, of New York, and who was installed pastor of the Episcopal church, at Shrewsbury, in 1788; Elizabeth, who married William LeCompte of Georgia; Mary and Sarah who died single, and Elisha, who married Mary Ashfield, of New York, and who was Sheriff of Monmouth county at the breaking out of the Revolution.

THE HENDRICKSONS.

This family is of Dutch origin, and members of it were among the first whites who came to New Amsterdam, (now New York). Captain Cornelis Hendrickson, (says our account,) was the first navigator who set foot on the soil of Pennsylvania and West Jersey, and probably the first white man who set foot in that part of old Monmouth now comprised within the limits of Ocean. About the latter part of 1614 he cruised along the New Jersey coast making explorations in the celebrated little yacht "Onrest" (Restless) the first vessel built in New York. He returned to Holland, in 1616, to give an account of his discoveries.

Of the Hendricksons who settled in this country among the first comers, were Rutger and Legar, who settled up the Hudson river at Rensaelters-wyck, 1630; Cornelis, who was there in 1642: another Cornelis came over in the ship Gilded Beaver and landed at New York in May, 1658.— Gerrit came from Scrool, in Holland, in the ship St. Jean Baptiste, and landed May, 1661 Alfred came from Maersen, in the ship "Fox" May, 1662. Hendrick came from Westphalia in the ship Rosetree, March, 1663.

Some of the family at a very early day settled in old Monmouth, and during the Revolution many of them were in the service of their country in various capacities, meeting with the usual vicissitudes of war. This family appear to be great sticklers for handing down old family names.— Among the first comers over two hundred years ago and from that time on down through the Revolution to the present wherever Hendricksons have been or may be, there are found the Cornelius's, Gerrits, Alberts and Hendricks or Henrys.

The Randolph Family.

The ancient name of this family, so numerous in New Jersey and elsewhere, was Fitz Randolph, for which reason members retain at the present day the letter F as the initial of a middle name. They are said to be descended from Edward Fitz Randolph who came when a lad with his parents to Barnstable, Massachusetts, in the year 1630. The following items relating to him are from New England authorities.

In a manuscript of the Rev. John Lothrop, the first pastor of the churches at Barnstable and Scituate, the names of owners of dwellings which were built when he arrived, and also those built shortly after are given. From his manuscript, copied in a modern New England work, the following items are extracted :

"The Houses in ye planta—(*manuscript obliterated.*)

Scituate.

Att my comeing hither, onely these wch was aboute the end of Sept. 1634."— After naming those which were already built on his arrival, he says the 36th one, built in 1636, was occupied by "the young Master Edward Fittsrandolfe."

From the church records of Barnstable and Scituate are derived the following items relating to the founder of this family in America.

"Married. Edward Fittsrandolfe to Elizabeth Blossome, May 10th, 1637."

Miss Blossome was a daughter of "Widow Blossome" whose name is frequently mentioned in Old Plymouth colony records as far back as 1632.

"Edward Fitts surrandolfe joyned (church) May 14th, 1637. Our Brother Fittsrandolfe's wife joyned August 27th, 1643.

Baptized: Nathaniell son of Edward Fittsrandolfe, Aug. 9th, 1640. Died Nathanniell son of Edward Fitts Randolfe, December 10th, 1640. Baptized Nathaniell son of Edward Fittsrandolfe, May 15th, 1642. Baptized Mary daughter of Edward Fittsrandolfe, October 6th, 1644. Baptized Hannah daughter of above, April 23d, 1648. Baptized Margaret, daughter of above, June 2nd, 1650. Baptized John, son of above, Jan. 2nd, 1652.

"Mary Fitzrandle, daughter above named married Samuel Hincley, 1668."

The last named Nathanniell became quite a conspicuous man in after years.— It is said that descendants of Edward Fitz Randolph went to Piscataqua, New Hampshire, and from thence removed to Piscataqua, New Jersey, and from thence descendants went to Monmouth and elsewhere. Bennington F. Randolph, Esq., formerly of Freehold, the late Judge Joseph F. Randolph, formerly M. C., and Senator Theodore F. Randolph, are, we believe, descendants of Edward Fitz Randolph.

By the extracts quoted above, it will be seen that the old Puritan pastor was sorely puzzled as to the proper mode of spelling the name Fitz Randolph, but we certainly must give him credit for noting down minute particulars.

We have been informed that quite a complete history of the Fitz Randolph family has been preserved by some descendants in Philadelphia, especially by Hon. Ross Snowden, a prominent member of the Pennsylvania Historical Society.

152   OLD TIMES IN OLD MONMOUTH.

LONG BRANCH.

WHO FIRST BROUGHT IT INTO NOTICE.

The earliest mention of Long Branch as a watering place in any historical work that the writer of this has found, is in Watson's Annals of Philadelphia, published in 1830, as follows :

"This place, before the Revolution, was owned by Colonel White, a British officer, and an inhabitant of New York. The small house which he occupied as a summer residence was existing among a clump of houses owned by Renshaw, in 1830.— In consequence of the war the place was confiscated. The house was first used as a boarding house by Elliston Perot of Philadelphia in 1788. At that time the whole premises were in charge of one old woman left to keep the place from injury. Of her Mr. Perot begged an asylum for himself and family, which was granted, provided he could get beds and bedding from others. Being pleased with the place he repeated his visit there three successive years, taking some friends with him. In 1790-1, Mr. McKnight, of Monmouth, noticing the liking shown for the place deemed it a good speculation to buy it.— He bought the whole premises containing one hundred acres for £700 and then got Mr. Perot and others to loan him two thousand dollars to improve it. He then opened it for a watering place and before his death it was supposed he had made forty thousand dollars by the investment. The estate was sold to Rehshaw for $13,000."

In the foregoing extract Watson says the property originally belonged to a British officer named White, whose property was confiscated during the Revolution.— We cannot now recall the name of but four loyalists of the name who belonged to or held property in old Monmouth, viz : Philip, who was killed by his guards in attempting to escape on the way to Freehold ; Aaron, (brother of Philip) and John, both of whom went to the British Provinces at the close of the war, and Josiah White, of old Shrewsbury township, whose property was confiscated and advertised to be sold at Tinton Falls. March 29th, 1779. The last named may be the one referred to as we have found no mention of the confiscation of property of others.

According to Watson it would seem that

ELLISTON PEROT WAS THE FOUNDER

of Long Branch as a watering place. The Perot family has been a prominent one in Philadelphia annals. During the Revolution the Perot mansion at Germantown was used by Lord Howe as a residence, and after the war, while General Washington was president, he also occupied it for a time during the prevalence of the yellow fever in the city in 1793. Members of this family have always been patrons of some of our New Jersey watering places.

THE LAST INDIAN CLAIMANTS.

At a conference between the whites and Indians held at Crosswicks, N. J., in February, 1758, two Indians known by the whites as Tom Store and Andrew Woolley claimed the land "from the mouth of Squan river to the mouth of Shrewsbury, by the streams of each to their heads and across from one head to another." This claim was satisfactorily settled at a subsequent conference held at Easton, Pa., in October of the same year. These Indians belonged to a band of the Delawares then known as the Cranbury Indians ; their principal settlement was about two miles northeast of the present village of Cranbury and was established through the instrumentality of the celebrated Rev. David Brainerd, and by him called Bethel. The Indians came here in 1746 from Crosswicks "to be away from bad whites." At the above mentioned Crosswicks conference, several delegates, beside Tom Store and Andrew Woolley, attended from the Cranbury Indians with papers, claims, powers of attorney, &c., for themselves and the rest of the band, all of which were settled to the satisfaction of the Indians.

HISTORY AND TRADITIONS OF LONG BRANCH.

The following extracts are from the New York *Gazette*, Morris' *Guide*, and other authorities, to which some comments are added :

" The nomenclature of popular resorts has become a matter of acknowledged interest. Various surmises—some of them absurd, all incorrect—have gone the rounds as to the origin of Long Branch, among them an hypothesis in a traveler's directory, that it was termed longest branch or route from that point on the seashore to Amboy."

From the best sources we find a tradition generally credited among the best informed descendants of old settlers, that a party of Indians whose grounds lay back of this portion of the coast, visited the shore in the fall of 1734. So well pleased were the red men with this inaugural visit to the seaside, that like many of their modern white brethren, they became *habitues* of the place, still adhering to the original camping ground, a location near the present Clarendon Hotel—the nearest to the depot. Here they made their annual pilgrimage for fishing, &c., and welcoming, after a long march, the termination of the land, called the place "Land's End;" this became a general term for the extent of waste which they gradually explored, and on which they established other camping grounds, such as Squan beach, &c., and the original spot was designated as "Land's End at the Long Branch," a small stream branching from the South Shrousbury (Shrewsbury) River and extending for a considerable distance nearly parallel with the coast. This stream still meanders through the vicinity of the depots and supplies an abundance of ice during the winter. The locality was thus designated by the abbreviated term Long Branch.

A few years thereafter settlers bought crown lands for twenty shillings per acre, and to protect their dwellings from the winter winds upon the coast, located them a short distance from the shore, pursuing the double calling of farmers and fishermen. They opened the Burlington pathway to Monmouth Court House and attracted other settlers, thus establishing old Long Branch village, one and a half miles from the beach, and within a radius of this distance embracing a population of over three thousand. A portion of this village just beyond the toll gate, is still quaintly termed "the pole"—from a liberty pole having been constantly renewed at this point with patriotic devotion since 1812. That portion which the wealthier citizens have erected for summer resorts is naturally termed "the shore," the nearest spot Branchville, the South Shrewsbury river landing Branchport, three quarters of a mile from the village, beside Rockville on the south and Loyalton on the west.—Guests at the beach still go over to "the Pole" for purchases, in which a greater variety is desirable than can be found at the shore. Here is the red post office, though for greater convenience a branch shore post office has been established.

When the old settlers at the "Pole" had opened the Burlington pathway to Monmouth Court House, intersecting a road to Burlington, communication was then opened with this point of the Atlantic coast, possessing advantages as a salubrious seaside resort far superior to any other. We are credibly informed that no other portion of this coast commands a bluff of more than from half a mile to a mile extent, while Long Branch has a continuous range of five miles of bluff, which extends over a rolling country of increasing elevations back to Monmouth Court House at Freehold, a distance of seventeen miles. At the early period indicated, Philadelphians availed themselves of the opportunity thus presented to drive over the new road and enjoy the luxuries of a sea bath, but there being no inns for many miles they were compelled to return a long distance on their way homeward for a nights entertainment. A Mr. BENNETT proved himself the man for the times by erecting a small building for the accommodations of these summer visitors, and upon a site a little east of the present Metropolitan Hotel; the exact ground has long since been confiscated by old Neptune and is now available only for bathing purposes. This, by the way, is in the vicinity of the Indians' first camping ground in 1734. The next man of enterprise of whom we have an account was named McKnight; he built a hotel about a mile down the beach beyond Pitman's. It was called Bath, or Green's hotel. This was destroyed by fire a few years ago.

To the above readable article, which we find credited to the New York *Gazette* a few years ago, and which was copied into many papers in our State, we take exceptions on one or two points. The writer evidently had not read the account of Watson, who had been familiar with the habitues of Long Branch forty or fifty years before. And we believe the Indians had visited the place long before 1734 ; in fact before the time the whites had any knowledge of the locality. Long before this the fierce, warlike Mohawks of New York, the terror of New Jersey Indians, occasionally made inroads into our State, conquering and plundering the red men within our borders, who were no match for them. When anticipating their raids, our West Jersey Indians would send their squaws and children to the sea shore for safety ; and it is probable that Squan received its name from this fact, being probably derived from the Indian words *Squaw,* or Squaw's place. The Indians who visited Long Branch in 1734 were probably from Crosswicks, and after 1746 the Cranbury Indians frequented this section and laid claim to it as elsewhere stated.

ORIGIN OF NAME—THE GREAT WRESTLING MATCH.

"Long Branch takes its name from a brook; a branch of the South Shrewsbury river, which runs in a direct line northward with the coast. It is of little use except for gathering ice for the hotels and cottages.

Tradition points to an Indian fishery, established in 1734, as the first occupation of this place, which was styled at that time 'Land's End.' A legend tells us that in those early times four men, named Slocum, Parker, Wardell and Hulett came from Rhode Island in quest of land. They found the Indians friendly but not disposed to sell. It was proposed by the Yankees that a wrestling match should be made up between one Indian and one of the whites, to be decided by the best in three rounds. If the champion of the white man won, they were to have as much land as a man could walk around in a day; if otherwise they were to leave peaceably. John Slocum was selected for the struggle—a man of great proportions, athletic and of great strength, courage and inflexibility of purpose. Great preparations were made to witness the encounter. The chosen Indian wrestler practiced continually for the event. The day long expected proved cloudless and auspicious. The spot chosen was the present Fish Landing. A circle was formed and the Indian champion, elated, confident and greased from head to foot, appeared. Slocum advanced cooly and the struggle began; it was long and doubtful; finally Slocum threw his antagonist but in an instant the Indian was again on his feet. A murmur ran through the circle.—Again the Indian made a violent effort and both fell. Another murmur was heard.—Silence prevailed as they came together again, broken only by the roaring of the surf. A long struggle. Slocum inured to toil, hardy and rugged, proved too much for the Indian and threw him, to the intense disappointment of the Indians and undisguised joy of the whites. The terms were then all arranged. John Slocum had two brothers and they located that part of Long Branch reaching from the shore to Turtle Mill brook, embracing all lands lying north of the main road, from the sea to Eatontown, between these two points, to the south of Shrewsbury, except Fresh Pond and Snag Swamp, which was located by one of the Wardell family. A considerable portion of these lands continued in the possession of the Slocums until thirty or forty years ago. All are now gone into other hands. The Parkers placed themselves on Rumson's Neck. Hulett lived for a time at Horse Neck but afterwards left this region. Indian warrants, it is said, still exist in the county conveying these lands to the white owners.

After some years a few hardy settlers from neighboring provinces purchased lands from the agents of the Crown at the rate of twenty shillings per acre, deeds for which, it is stated, are in existence over the signature of King George III or his agents."

A notice of Long Branch in 1819, from a paper published at the time, has been given in a previous article. Probably the most noted Indian in this section of Old Monmouth was the celebrated Indian Will, of whom a number of traditions were published in the DEMOCRAT, June 5th, 1873. He was well known at Eatontown, Long Branch and vicinity, at Squan and along the coast down as far as Barnegat. A tradition in Howe's Collections says the Indians in this section sold out their lands to Lewis Morris in 1670, but Indian Will refused to leave. The probability is that this tradition has confounded two transactions. Indian Will, according to the best traditionary authority, lived near a century later and the Indian sale of land with which his name has been connected was probably the one originating at a conference held at Crosswicks in February, 1758, and concluded at Eastern Pennsylvania in the same year, particulars of which were given in the article headed "Indian Claims in Old Monmouth," in the DEMOCRAT of July 24, 1873.

NEW JERSEY WATERING PLACES—THEIR ORIGIN.

The first seaside resorts in New Jersey in all probability were Long Beach in Monmouth, and Tuckers' Beach in Little Egg Harbor. The first named place, now in Ocean county, is opposite to the villages of Barnegat and Mannahawkin and the latter opposite Tuckerton. Of these places Watson's Annals of Philadelphia says:

"We think Long Beach and Tucker's Beach in point of earliest attraction as a seaside resort for Philadelphians must claim the precedence. They had their visitors and distant admirers long before Squan and Deal and even Long Branch itself had got their several fame. To those who chiefly desire to restore languid frames and to find their nerves braced and firmer strung, nothing can equal the invigorating surf and general air. * * * Long Branch—last but greatest in fame—because the fashionables who rule all things have made it so, is still inferior as a surf to those above named."

Before the Revolution, Philadelphians and others from a distance, who visited Long and Tucker beaches, went in old fashioned shore wagons on their return trips from the city and took with them their stoves, blankets, &c. Some people on the beaches began to make provisions to receive these transient boarders and so originated this business in New Jersey in which now annually is spent such an immense amount of money. The shore wagons carted fish and oysters to Philadelphia, Trenton and other places over a hundred years ago, and these primitive conveyances on their return trips were first used to convey health or pleasure seekers to our earliest seaside resorts. What a contrast between then and now—between an oyster wagon and a palace car!

Long Branch comes next in order being first known as a watering place about 1788.

Cape May began to be known as a watering place about 1813. Atlantic City was founded some forty years later, about the time of the completion of the Camden and Atlantic Railroad.

The foregoing watering places from Long Branch to Cape May, it is said, were all brought into notice by Philadelphians.

A Sea Shore correspondent says:

"The first seaside health or pleasure seekers from Philadelphia would present quite a contrast with the great majority of visitors at our watering places at the present day in their methods of enjoying themselves. At home, being citizens of property and standing they would of course conform to the customs of city life in dress and other matters, but at the seashore they often adopted the common fisherman clothes and enjoyed themselves by fishing, oystering, bathing, &c., unrestrained by fashionable conventionalities. From the shore villages, the inhabitants young and old would often get up "beach parties" to have a good time bathing in the surf during the day, and enjoying themselves by plays and dances in the evening, and it was no uncommon thing to see the visitors from the city mixing in with their sports, evidently enjoying and being benefitted by them. Some twenty years ago I frequently met, at one of our seaside resorts a prominent young Philadelphia merchant whom I especially noticed because an ancestor of his first brought Long Branch into notice and his method of enjoying himself was similar to our first shore visitors. He had his own fishing boat and pleasure yacht; at times in red flannel shirt and fisherman clothes he would engage in fishing, oystering, &c., and he was an expert in handling his yacht whether by himself, racing with other boats, or taking rural parties on pleasure excursions. He evidently enjoyed himself in these healthful methods of passing away his time, reminding me of the celebrated Prince MURAT's manner of spending his time in the same locality some forty or fifty years before."

CAPTAIN MOLLY PITCHER.
Her bravery at Fort Clinton and Monmouth—Her Sad End.

From various articles relating to this noted woman the following are selected:

"The story of a woman who rendered essential service to the Americans in the battle of Monmouth is founded on fact.— She was a female of masculine mould, and dressed in a mongrel suit, with the petticoats of her own sex and an artilleryman's coat, cocked hat and feathers. The anecdote usually related is as follows: Before the armies engaged in general action, two of the advanced batteries commenced a severe fire against each other. As the heat was excessive, Molly, who was the wife of a cannonier, constantly ran to bring her husband water from a neighboring spring. While passing to his post she saw him fall and on hastening to his assistance, found him dead. At the same moment she heard an officer order the cannon to be removed from its place, complaining he could not fill his post with as brave a man as had been killed. "No," said the intrepid Molly, fixing her eyes upon the officer, "the cannon shall not be removed for the want of someone to serve it; since my brave husband is no more, I will use my utmost exertions to avenge his death." The activity and courage with which she performed the office of cannonier during the action, attracted the attention of all who witnessed it, and finally of Washington himself, who afterward gave her the rank of lieutenant and granted her half-pay during life. She wore an epaulette and was called ever after Captain Molly. (*Howe's Collections.*)

LOSSING in his Field Book of the Revolution thus mentions MOLLY PITCHER:

"She was a sturdy young camp follower only twenty two years of age and in devotion to her husband, who was a cannonier, she illustrated the character of her countrywomen of the Emerald Isle. In the action (Battle of Monmouth) while her husband was managing one of the field pieces, she constantly brought him water from a spring near by. A shot from the enemy killed him at his post; and the officer in command, having no one competent to fill his place, ordered the piece to be withdrawn. MOLLY saw her husband fall as she came from the spring and also heard the order. She dropped her bucket, seized the rammer and vowed that she would fill the place of her husband at the gun and avenge his death. She performed the duty with a skill and courage which attracted the attention of all who saw her. On the following morning, covered with dirt and blood, General GREENE presented her to General WASHINGTON, who admiring her bravery, conferred upon her the commission of Sergeant. By his recommendation her name was placed upon the list of half pay officers for life. She left the army soon after the Battle of Monmouth and died near Fort Montgomery among the Hudson Highlands. She usually went by the name of Captain MOLLY. The venerable widow of General HAMILTON, who died in 1854, told me she had often seen Captain MOLLY. She described her as a stout, red-haired, freckled-faced young Irish woman with a handsome, piercing eye. The French officers, charmed by the story of her bravery, made her many presents. She would sometimes pass along the French lines with her cocked hat and get it almost filled with crowns."

The same writer visited the locality of Forts Montgomery and Clinton on the Hudson, where MOLLY PITCHER ended her days and there found old residents who "remembered the famous Irish woman called Captain MOLLY. the wife of a canonier who worked a field piece at the battle of Monmouth on the death of her husband. She generally dressed in the petticoats of her sex with an artilleryman's coat over. She was in Fort Clinton with her husband when it was attacked in 1877. When the Americans retreated from the fort, as the enemy scaled the ramparts her husband dropped his match and fled. MOLLEY caught it up, touched off the piece and then scampered off. It was the last gun the Americans fired in the fort. Mrs. ROSE remembered her as *Dirty Kate*, living between Fort Montgomery and Buttermilk Falls, at the close of the war, where she died a horrible death from syphilitic disease. WASHINGTON had honored her with a lieutenant's commission for her bravery in the field of Monmouth nearly nine months after the battle, when reviewing its events."

IS AN OYSTER A WILD ANIMAL OR A TAME ONE?

This question to many may appear absurd but it has been broached in lawsuits in our state involving business enterprises to the amount of some thousands of dollars yearly. It originated in the question whether or not a man had an exclusive right to oysters which he had planted.— The first case carried up to the New Jersey Supreme Court relating to planted oysters began in old Shrewsbury township about seventy years ago. A man named Leverson sued two men named Shepard and Layton for the larceny of 1,000 oysters which he had planted in North river, Shrewsbury township. The case came before Esquire Tiebout who gave judgment for the plaintiff, three dollars. The defendants' appealed to the Monmouth Common Pleas where the Justice's decision was confirmed. The case was then carried to the Supreme Court and tried in 1808. The decision, however, was confined to one point, that of planting where there is a natural growth: "Action does not lie for taking oysters claimed as planted by him in a common navigable stream, in which others were found." The court seemed to consider the throwing of oyster plants where there is a natural growth, as an abandonment, and compared it to a man "who should take a deer in a forest and be simpleton enough to let it go again in the same forest, saying, 'this is my deer and no man shall touch it;' it would never be asked by the next taker what was the intention of the simpleton; the very act of letting it go was an abandonment."

The question of the right to planted oysters was again brought before the Supreme

Court in 1821, in the noted case of Arnold *vs* Mundy, on an appeal in a case from Perth Amboy; but this suit hinged mainly on title to lands under water, the plaintiff having purchased from the East Jersey Proprietors some forty odd acres of land under water on which was the oyster bed.

Just fifty years after the laws relating to planted oysters had been first discussed in Monmouth, the subject was finally and clearly settled by the Supreme Court. On an appeal from Cape May, tried in 1858, it was charged that Thomas Taylor had stolen oysters to the value of eighteen dollars from George Hildreth. This time the question of the right to oysters planted where there was no natural growth was reached and decided. As regards the question whether an oyster is a wild animal or a tame one the inference from the trial is that an oyster from a natural growth bed is a wild animal and one from a bed planted where there was no natural growth, is a tame one! The counsel for the defendant (Taylor) plead that "oysters being animals *feræ naturæ* (of a wild nature—wild animals) there can be no property in them unless they be dead or reclaimed or tamed or in the actual power or possession of the claimant."

The Chief Justice in giving the opinion of the Court said :

"The principle (advanced by defendant's counsel) as applied to animals *feræ naturæ* is not questioned. But oysters, though usually included in that description of animals, do not come within the reason or operation of the rule. The owner has the same absolute property in them that he has in inanimate things or domestic animals. Like domestic animals they continue perpetually in his occupation and will not stray from his house or person. Unlike animals *feræ naturæ*, they do not require to be reclaimed and made tame by art, industry or education, nor to be confined in order to be within the immediate power of the owner. If at liberty, they have neither the inclination nor power to escape. For the purposes of the present inquiry they are obviously more nearly allied to tame animals than to wild ones, and perhaps more nearly allied to inanimate objects than to animals of either description. The indictment could not aver that the oysters were dead, for they would then be of no value ; nor that they were reclaimed or tamed for in this sense they were never wild and were not capable of domestication ; nor that they were confined for that would be absurd."

It was the decision of the court that "The owner has the same absolute property in oysters that he has in inanimate things or domestic animals, and the rule that applies to animals *feræ naturæ* does not apply to them," and that an indictment would lie for stealing oysters planted in a public or navigable river where oysters do not grow naturally, and the spot designated by stakes or otherwise.

ALLEGED INFRINGEMENTS OF OYSTER LAWS.

The Newark *Evening Courier* of December 21st, 1874, contained an interesting article relating to the oyster trade of Newark Bay, Staten Island Sound, Perth and South Amboy, &c., during the year 1874, from which we extract the following :

"The great beds at the mouth of the Raritan river, now retained and staked by private individuals for their own use, are one mile and a half long and one mile wide. They were what is termed a natural bed up to forty years ago, and were first taken possession of by a company from Perth Amboy. They were held by this company without color of law for about five years, when the people interested in the oyster business compelled this monopoly to relinquish their claims on the beds, but in return they severally staked them off for their own use, and still retain them to the exclusion of citizens of their own and other counties without the least shadow of law. It is thought that this question, together with a law looking to the better preservation of oysters in the beds, will receive the attention of the Legislature."

We should suppose the law in this case had been clearly settled by the Supreme Court, which those interested can find stated at length in 1st Halsted, case of Arnold vs Mundy, and 3d Dutcher, State vs Thomas Taylor.

COLONEL MONCKTON AND THE ROYAL GRENADIERS AT THE BATTLE OF MONMOUTH.

Lieutenant Colonel Honorable H. Monckton, generally called Colonel Monckton, according to both written and traditional accounts was one of the most honorable officers in the service of the British—accomplished, brave, of splendid personal appearance and of irreproachable moral character. He was in the battle of Long Island in August 1776, when he was shot through the body and lay for many weeks at the point of death. He recovered and for his gallantry on that occasion was promoted from the 5th Company, 2d Grenadiers, to be Lieutenant Colonel and was in command of the battalion at the battle of Monmouth, in which the 1st and 2nd Royal Grenadiers bore a conspicuous part and in a charge, the heroic Monckton and the greater part of the officers of the genadiers, the flower of the British army, fell from a terrible fire from the Americans under General Wayne. The spot where Colonel Monckton was killed is said to be about eight rods north-east of the old parsonage and he was buried about six feet from the west end of the church. About thirty years ago a board was set up to mark his grave by William R. Wilson, a native of Scotland, who will long and favorably be remembered by hundreds of citizens of Monmouth and Ocean as a successful teacher and for his many good qualities of head and heart. He died at Forked River, in Ocean county, about nineteen years ago, and the respect retained for him by his old scholars near the battle ground, and elsewhere in Monmouth, was evidenced by the fact of their sending for his body and giving it a suitable final resting place in the vicinity of his first labors in this county. Mr. Wilson, or "Dominie Wilson" as he was familiarly called on account of his once having been a clergyman, deserves a more extended notice than we have space for in the present article.

On the board prepared and set up by Mr. Wilson was inscribed

HIC JACET
COL. MONKTON
KILLED 28 June
1778
W. R. W.

Mr. W. may have been induced to put up the board by noticing that in the reminiscences of the battle published by Henry Howe, who visited the ground in 1842, attention was called to the fact that no monument marked the grave.

In 1850, Benson J. Lossing visited the battle ground and made a sketch of the head board which was given in his valuable work, the Field Book of the Revolution, and it is also given in a late number of the American Historical Record Mr. Lossing says that when he visited the grave " the only monument that marked the spot was a plain board painted red, much weather worn, on which was drawn in black letters the inscription seen in the picture given. The board had been set up some years before by a Scotch school master named William Wilson, who taught the young people in the school house upon the green near the old Meeting House." In speaking of Col. Monckton he says: " At the head of his grenadiers on the field of Monmouth, he kept them silent until they were within a few rods of the Americans, when waving his sword he shouted " Forward to the charge !" Our General Wayne was on his front. At the same moment " Mad Anthony " gave a signal to fire. A terrible volley poured destruction upon Monckton's grenadiers and almost every British officer fell. Amongst them was their brave leader.— Over his body the combatants fought desperately until the Americans secured it and bore it to the rear."

CAPTAIN WILSON AND DOMINIE WILSON.
THE GRENADIER FLAG.

A writer in the American Historical Record, June, 1874, referring to the above notice says it reminds him " of the relics of the Royal Grenadiers and of their gallant Colonel which are still in existence ; and I was struck with the coincidence in name of the Scotch schoolmaster, William Wilson, who set up the board that marks the Colonel's grave, with that of the Irish Captain, William Wilson, by the rifles of whose company Monckton fell. On the parlor table of Captain William Wilson Potter, of Bellefonte, Pennsylvania, a great grandson of General James Potter, of the Revolution, may be seen any day for the asking, the flag of the Royal Grenadiers, captured on the field of Monmouth, by his (maternal) grandfather, the late Judge William Wilson, of Chillisquaque Mills, Northumberland county, Pennsylvania. The ground or main surface is lemon or light-yellow heavy corded silk, five feet four inches by four feet eight inches. The device at the upper right corner is twenty inches square, and is that of the English Union which distinguishes the *Royal* standard of Great Britain. It is composed of the cross of St. George, to denote England, and St. Andrews cross in the form of an X to denote Scotland. The field of the device is blue, the central stripes (cross of St. George) red, the marginal ones white. The flag has the appearance of having been wrenched from its staff, and has a few blood stains on the device, otherwise it looks as bright and new as if it had just come from the gentle fingers that made it, although ninety-six years have rolled away since its golden folds drooped in the sultry air of that June day battle."

The following is an account of that part of the engagement relating to

THE CHARGE OF THE GRENADIERS.

After General LEE's retreat was checked by General WASHINGTON in person, the latter formed a new line for his advanced troops, and put LEE again in command General WASHINGTON then rode back to the main army and formed it on an eminence, with a road in the rear and a morass in front. The left was commanded by Lord STIRLING with a detachment of artillery; LAFAYETTE with WAYNE was posted in the centre, partly in an orchard and partly sheltered by a barn; General GREENE was on the right with his artillery under General KNOX, posted on commanding ground. General LEE maintained his advanced position as long as he could, himself coming off with his rear across a road which traversed the morass in front of STIRLING's troops. The British followed sharp, and meeting with a warm reception, endeavored to turn the left flank but were driven back; they then tried the right, but were met by General GREENE's forces and heavy discharges from KNOX's artillery, which not only checked them but raked the whole length of the columns in front of the left wing. Then came a determined effort to break the centre maintained by General WAYNE and the Pennsylvania regiments; and the Royal Grenadiers, the flower of the British army, were ordered to do it. They advanced several times, crossing a hedge-row in front of the morass and were driven back. Col. MONCTON, their commander, then made a speech to his men (the troops at the parsonage and those in the orchard heard his ringing voice above the storm of battle), and forming the Grenadiers in solid column, advanced to the charge like troops on parade; the men marching with such precision that a ball from Combs Hill enfilading a platoon isarmed every man.

WAYNE ordered his men to reserve their fire, and the British came on in silence within a few rods, when MONCTON waved his sword above his head and ordered his grenadiers to charge. Simultaneously WAYNE ordered his men to fire and a terrible volley laid low the first ranks and most of the officers. The colors were in advance to the right with the Colonel and they went down with him. Captain WILLIAM WILSON and his company who were on the right of the 1st Pennsylvania regiment, (Colonel JAMES CHAMBERS) made a rush for the colors and the body of the Colonel. The Grenadiers fought desperately and a hand to hand struggle ensued, but the Pennsylvanians secured his body and the colors; the Grenadiers gave way, and the whole British army fell back to LEE's position in the morning. They decamped so quietly in the night that General POOR, who lay near them with orders to recommence the battle in the morning, was not aware of their departure.

The following reminiscences, published by HOWE were mainly derived from the late venerable Dr. SAMUEL FORMAN, who was on the battle field the day after the action.

The advanced corps of Americans under WAYNE was on high ground close by a barn about twelve rods back of the parsonage, while a park of artillery were on Combs Hill, a height commanding that of the enemy. The British grenadiers several times crossed the fence and advanced toward the barn, but were as often driven back by the fire of the troops stationed there and the artillery from Combs Hill. At length Col. MONCTON made to them a spirited address which was distinctly heard by the Americans at the barn and parsonage, distant only twenty or thirty rods. They then advanced in beautiful order as though on parade. As they appeared within a few rods of the barn, WAYNE ordered his men to pick off the officers. * * * The spot near where Col. MONKTON was killed is (1842) marked by an oak stump about eight rods northeast of the parsonage. * * * The most desperate part of the conflict was in the vicinity of where MONKTON fell. There the British grenadiers lay in heaps like sheaves on a harvest field. Our informant states that they dragged the corpses by the heels to shallow pits dug for the purpose and slightly covered them with earth; he saw thirteen buried in one hole. For many years after, their graves were indicated by the luxuriance of the vegetation. Among the enemy's dead was a sergeant of the grenadiers, designated as the "high sergeant." He was the tallest man in the British army, measuring seven feet four inches in height.

The day was unusually hot even for the season and both armies suffered severely;

the British more than the Americans, because of their woollen uniforms and burdened with their knapsacks and accoutrements, while the latter where divested of their packs and superfluous clothing. The tongues of great numbers were so swollen as to render them incapable of speaking. Many of both armies perished solely from heat and after the battle were seen dead upon the field, without mark or wound, under trees and beside the rivulet, where they had crawled for shade and water. The countenances of the dead became so blackened as to render it impossible to recognize individuals. Several houses in Freehold were filled with the wounded of the enemy, left on their retreat in care of their surgeons and nurses. Every room in the Court House was filled. They lay on the floor on straw. and the supplication of the wounded and the moans of the dying presented a scene of woe. As fast as they died, their corpses were promiscuously thrown into a pit on the site of the present (1842) residence of Dr. THROCKMORTON, and slightly covered with earth.

In addition to the above statements of Dr. FORMAN regarding the heat of the day, we remember on our first visit to the battle ground forty odd years ago being told by an old gentleman residing in the vicinity, while describing the battle, that both the British and Americans were so overcome by the heat, and were suffering so much from thirst, that as they approached the stream, the troops of both armies, regardless of discipline, broke from their ranks and rushed to the brook to quench their thirst at the same time, and but a little distance apart. Many were unable to resume their places in the ranks and we.'e found dead as above related. Of the British it is stated that fifty nine perished from the heat.

VISITORS AT THE BATTLE GROUND.

" If there's a hole in all your coats
   I rede you tent it ;
A chield's among you taking notes,
   And faith he'll prent it."

So said the poet Burns in reference to Captain Grose, noted for his peregrinations through Scotland collecting antiquities of the kingdom, and we have been forcibly reminded of his lines in reading various comments made by visitors to the Monmouth battle ground. These comments are in the main very favorable to the citizens of old Monmouth, but occasionally we meet with an unpalatable note.

The author of the Field Book of the Revolution says :

"I visited the battle ground of Monmouth toward the close of September, 1850, and had the good fortune to be favored with the company of Doctor John Woodhull, of Freehold, in my ramble over that interesting locality. Dr. Woodhull is the son of the beloved minister of that name who succeeded Rev. William Tennent in the pastoral care of the congregation that worshipped in the Freehold meeting house, and who, for forty-six consecutive years, preached and prayed in that venerated chapel. Dr. Woodhull was born in the parsonage yet upon the battle ground, and is so familiar with every locality and event connected with the conflict, that I felt as if traversing the battle field with an actor in the scene."

Mr. Lossing next speaks of a heavy storm which compelled him to take shelter in the old Tennent church ; resting his portfolio on the high back of an old pew he sketched a picture of the neat monument erected to the memory of Rev. John Woodhull, D. D., who died Nov. 22nd, 1824, aged 80 years. He next refers to Rev. William Tennent who was pastor of that flock for forty-three years, and gives an outline of his life, and then says :

" When the storm abated we left the church and proceeded to the battle ground. The old parsonage is in the present possession of Mr. William T. Sutphen, who has allowed the parlor and study of Tennent and Woodhull to be used as a depository of giain and of agricultural implements! The careless neglect which permits a mansion so hallowed by religion and patriotic events to fall into ruin, is actual desecration and much to be reprehended and deplored. The windows are destroyed, the roof is falling into the chambers ; and in a few years not a vestige will be left of that venerable memento of the *field of Monmouth.*

" We visited the spot where Monckton fell ; the place of the causeway across the morass (now a small bridge upon the main road) ; and after taking a general view of the whole ground of conflict and sketching a picture, returned to Freehold.

" It had been to me a day of rarest interest and pleasure, notwithstanding the inclement weather ; for no battle field in our country has stronger claims to the rever-

OLD TIMES IN OLD MONMOUTH. 161

ence of the American heart than that of the plains of Monmouth. * * *

"The men and women of the Revolution but a few years since, numerous in the neighborhood of Freehold, have passed away, but the narrative of their trials during the war have left abiding records of patriotism upon the hearts of their descendants. I listened to many tales concerning the Pine Robbers and other desperadoes of the time, who kept the people of Monmouth county in a state of continual alarm. Many noble deeds of daring were achieved by the tillers of the soil, and their mothers, wives and sisters; and while the field of Monmouth attested the bravery and endurance of American soldiers, the inhabitants whose households were disturbed on that memorable Sabbath morning by the bugle and the cannon peal, exhibited in their daily course the loftiest patriotism and manly courage. We will leave the task of recording the acts of their heroism to the pen of the local historian."

The following item we find published in a magazine over a year ago: "Attention has lately been called to the condition of the grave of Col Monckton, in the burial ground of the Freehold Meeting House in Monmouth Co., N. J. It should be properly cared for, for Monckton, though a foeman to the Americans when he fell mortally wounded at the battle of Monmouth, was a gallant officer, and a man of irreproachable moral character."

OUR GOOD LOOKING GRANDMOTHERS.

WHY JERSEY LADIES ARE SO ATTRACTIVE.

All histories of Revolutionary times concede that in patriotism our forefathers were not excelled by the people of any other state. From the following extracts it will be seen that during the last century the women also of New Jersey were held in high repute by people in other states. Jerseymen of the present day very well know that the ladies of our state now are hard to excel in beauty, intelligence, amiability, industry and other deservable qualities. And it is gratifying to know that their maternal ancestors obtained such marked commendation from competent judges in other states.

Guthrie's Geography, published by the celebrated Matthew Carey in 1795, says:

"There is at least as great a number of industrious, discreet, amiable, genteel and handsome women in New Jersey in proportion to the number of its inhabitants as in any one of the thirteen states."

Winterbottom's Geography, published in New York the following year, quotes the above extract, but the author thinking such compliments unusual in such a work prefaces his quotation with the remark that "It is not the business of the geographer to compliment the ladies, nor would we be thought to do so when we say that there are in New Jersey as great a number of industrious, discreet, &c."

Morse's Geography, published in New York by the father of the celebrated Professor Morse, quotes and endorses the remarks of both of the above writers, and adds that "the ladies of New Jersey are as well educated and intelligent as the ladies of any other state." We will take the liberty here of expressing our gratification that Morse quoted the most of his complimentary remarks from other writers; had he expressed them in his own language we might reasonably fear as bungling work as he made in describing Albany and its inhabitants. In an early edition of his geography, which we found in the library of the New York Geographical and Statistical Society, he says:

"There are over six hundred houses in Albany and the population is over ten thousand mostly of the gothic style of architecture with their gable ends turned to the streets."

Ten thousand people of the gothic style of architecture with their gable ends turned to the street would have presented a remarkable spectacle. He probably meant this description to apply to the houses and not the people.

Among more ancient writers who described the people of New Jersey was Gabriel Thomas, who published a work in 1698, describing Pennsylvania and West Jersey, but one copy of which is known to be in existence. From this copy, in the Philadelphia Franklin Library, we extract the following, relating to the inhabitants of Pennsylvania and New Jersey:

"The men are all industrious and healthy, the children born here are beautiful, without spot or blemish, and every married lady has a baby in her lap, or one —" Ahem! well, these old writers have sometimes such a blunt way of expressing themselves, that a bashful man feels rather dubious about the propriety of quoting exactly the conclusion of the sentence, but it substantially means "that they present external evidence of soon being able to have one to tend."

From the foregoing it will be seen that it is perfectly natural that Jersey ladies should be fascinating; they take after their mothers and female ancestors; like them they are "industrious, discreet, amiable, genteel, handsome and intelligent." But these complimentary expressions are left out of modern geographies, not because they are inappropriate, but doubtless out of respect to ladies of other states and to the men of this; for if they were now published in our text books, men from other states might flock here for partners to the aggravation of the girls they left behind them, and of the young men of New Jersey, who would naturally object to such inroads for such a purpose.

OUR ANCESTORS OF ENGLISH ORIGIN.—THE BEST BLOOD OF NEW ENGLAND.

The following complimentary remarks about our first white settlers of English origin are from Watson's Annals of Philadelphia:

"The vicinity of Philadelphia to New Jersey has had the effect to contribute a great deal of Jersey population to the city and a good race of citizens they make.— They may be considered as a people much formed from the best Yankee blood. All along the seaboard, the first settlers there, as their names show, came from New England in colonial times. In the Revolution the Governor of Pennsylvania (Reed) was from New Jersey; so too Attorney General Sargent and Commissary General Boudinit. Not long since, all the officers of the Mayor's Court, Mayor, Recorder, prosecuting officers and even the crier were Jersey born."

THE FIRST WHITE OPINION OF OLD MONMOUTH.

On the 2nd day of September, 1609, Sir Henry Hudson in the ship *Half Moon*, cruised along the shore of the county, and at night anchored not far from Long Branch. His journal or log book was kept by his mate, Alfred Just. After describing the coast, &c., at the close of the day's record, he says:

"This is a very good land to fall in with, and a pleasant land to see."

This is the most ancient opinion of the county to be found expressed by a white person, and one in which all its citizens will agree as correct and applicable at the present day.

CONGRESSIONAL REPRESENTATIVES.

By an act of Congress approved June, 1842, all members of Congress were required to be elected by Congressional Districts. Under that law the following persons have been elected to Congress to represent the districts to which Monmouth has belonged.

SECOND CONGRESSIONAL DISTRICT.

28th Congress	1843-4	George Sykes of Burlington Co.
29	"	1845-6	"	"	"	"
30	"	1847-8	William A. Newell Monmouth "
31	"	1849-50	"	"	"	"
32	"	1851-2	Charles Skelton	Mercer "
33	"	1853-4	"	"	"	"
34	"	1855-6	George R. Robbins	"	"
35	"	1857-8	"	"	"	"
36	"	1859-60	J. L. N. Stratton, Burlington "
37	"	1861-2	"	"	"	"
38	"	1863-4	William A. Newell, Monmouth "
39	"	1865-6	George Middleton	"	"
40	"	1867-8	Charles Haight	"	"
41	"	1869-70	"	"	"	"
42	"	1871-2	Samuel C. Forker, Burlington '

THIRD CONGRESSIONAL DISTRICT.

| 43 | " | 1873-4 | Amos Clark, Jr., Middlesex | " |
| 44 | " | 1875-6 | Miles Ross | " | " |

It is a coincidence that since the District law of Congress passed, the Democrats have elected nine members and their opponents just nine including Samuel G. Wright elected, but who died before taking his seat.

CONGRESSIONAL MEMORANDA.

Among those who were natives of, or have represented Old Monmouth in the National councils, may be mentioned the following:

DR. NATHANIEL SCUDDER.

Dr. Scudder was a delegate to the Continental Congress from New Jersey from 1777 to 1779, and was one of the signers of the articles of Confederation. He was the son of Col. Jacob Scudder of Monmouth Court House, born May 10th, 1733. After graduating at Princeton College in 1751, he gave his attention to the practice of medicine. At the outbreak of the Revolution he was commissioned Lieutenant Colonel, First Regiment; Colonel same regiment Nov. 28th, 1776. Delegate to Congress 1777-9. He was killed by the Refugees, Oct 16th, 1781, at Black Point (Shark River?) He was at the time engaged in conversation with General David Forman and it is supposed the shot was aimed at the latter. General Forman attributed his marvelous escape to an involuntary step backward which became "the most *fortunate step* in all his life."

An interesting outline of Dr. Scudder's life was published in the MONMOUTH DEMOCRAT, May 29th, 1873, by Anna Maria Woodhull.

JOHN ANDERSON SCUDDER, M. D.,

Was a representative in Congress from New Jersey for the unexpired term of James Cox who died in 1810. He was the eldest son of Dr. Nathaniel Scudder, above mentioned. He was born March 22nd, 1759; served as Surgeon's mate in the Revolutionary army; was a member of the Assembly for several years and finally removed to Kentucky.

GENERAL JAMES COX.

James Cox was a native of Monmouth County, born in 1753; served several years as a member of the Legislature, and was Speaker of the Assembly; commanded a company of militia in the Revolution and was at the battles of Germantown and Monmouth; was subsequently a Brigadier General of militia. Was a representative in Congress 1809-10. Died September 12th, 1810.

REV. BENJAMIN BENNETT.

Born in 1762, was a Baptist minister and a Representative in Congress from 1815 to 1819. He died at Middletown, N. J., October 8th, 1840.

GARRET D. WALL

was born in Monmouth county, March 10th, 1783; licensed attorney in 1804 and as counsellor in 1807. Appointed clerk of the Supreme Court in 1812, holding the position for five years; commanded a volunteer company at the defence of Sandy Hook in the war of 1812, and was Quarter Master General of the State from 1815 to 1827. In 1827 he was elected to the General Assembly; in 1829 was appointed United States District Attorney for New Jersey and the same year was elected Governor of the State by the Legislature but he declined the appointment. General Wall was elected a member of the United States Senate to serve from 1835 to 1841. In 1843 his health was impaired by a stroke of paralysis, but in 1848 he was appointed Judge of the Court of Errors and Appeals, which office he occupied until his death at Burlington, N. J., Nov. 22, 1850.

His son, Colonel James W. Wall, born in Trenton, was elected Senator in 1863 to fill an unexpired term.

JOHN C. TEN EYCK,

was born at Freehold, March 12th, 1814.— In 1839 was appointed Prosecutor of the Pleas for Burlington county, holding the position for ten years; was a member of the Convention to frame a new state constitution in 1844, and was elected United States Senator in 1859 to serve six years.

DANIEL B. RYALL

was born at Trenton, Jan. 30th, 1798.— Came to Freehold to practice law in 1820, where he remained in practice 35 years.— He was a member of the State Legislature for three years, and Speaker of the House for the same time. He was Representative in Congress from 1839 to 1841. He died at Freehold, Dec. 17th, 1864.

SAMUEL G. WRIGHT was elected a member of Congress in the fall of 1844 but died July 30, 1845, before taking his seat. He was born in 1787, and died near Allentown (at Harrison's Hill?)

JAMES H. IMLAY was a representative in Congress from 1797 to 1801. We have found no record of his nativity but presume he was from Monmouth. He graduated at Princeton in 1786, and was for a time a tutor in that college.

WILLIAM L DAYTON was born at Baskenridge, Somerset County, February 17th, 1807; graduated at Princeton in 1825, practiced law in Freehold many years, was appointed Judge of the Supreme Court in 1838; and appointed in 1842 to fill vacancy caused by death of Samuel L. Southard, and again in 1845 serving to 1851 United States Senator. In 1857 was Attorney General of the State; appointed Minister to France by President Lincoln in 1861, and died in Paris at Hotel de Louvre Dec. 1st, 1864. The most laudatory notice of him published in the Paris papers was written by John Slidell, the Rebel Commissioner whom Judge Dayton for three years had earnestly opposed.

THE BOUNDARIES & TOWNSHIPS OF MONMOUTH.

WITH AN ACCOUNT OF SOME OF THE HIGHWAYS, TURNPIKES, AND RAILROADS THROUGH THE SAME.

BY HON. GEO. C. BEEKMAN.

FREEHOLD. N. J., January 25, 1877.

To the Editor of the Monmouth Democrat:

Having lately been obliged in a law case to search the old laws and records in reference to some of our township and county boundaries in connection with certain highways, I thought I would write out the results of my investigation, as it might save time and labor for others in the future. I herewith send it to you for publication, if you deem the information will prove of any interest or benefit to the public. Respectfully,

GEO. C. BEEKMAN.

The *Boundaries and Townships of Monmouth, with an account of some of the Highways, Turnpikes and Railroads in and through the same.*

Part of what is now Monmouth County began its political existence April 8th, A. D. 1665. Col. Richard Nicolls, then in command of the English piratical expedition at New York, confirmed and granted unto William Golding, Samuel Spicer, Richard Gibbons, Richard Stout, James Grover, John Bown, John Tilton, Nathaniel Silvester, William Reape, Walter Clark, Nichollas Davis, Obadiah Holmes, patentees, and their associates, their heirs, successors and assigns, all that tract of land "beginning at a certain place commonly called or known by the name of Sandy Point,* and so running along the bay, west northwest, till it comes to the mouth of Raritans River; from thence going along the said river to the westermost part of the certain marshland, which divides the river unto two parts, and from that part to run in a direct southwest line into the woods twelve miles and then to turn away southeast and by south until it falls into the main ocean." These rough boundaries would seem to include all the lands lying east of a straight line drawn from the crook in Raritan River, just below the mouth of South River, to where Monmouth Junction is now located, and all the lands northward and eastward of a straight line from Monmouth Junction to the mouth of Metedecunk Creek. Two settlements were at once begun on this territory; one at Middletown, the other at Shrewsbury. The Shrewsbury River, and its tributary, Swimming River, seem to have been the

* Now called Sandy Hook.

only dividing lines between these settlements. November 5th, 1675, an act was passed by the Assembly at Elizabethtown, establishing Courts of Sessions for each county. The following language is used: "The two towns of Nevysink to make a county; their sessions to be the last Tuesday in March and first Tuesday in September."† This is the first mention of a county. April 6th, 1676, the Assembly made the following order: "The Nevysinks lying so remote, and difficulty of passage by water sometimes so much, and upon request and desire of aforesaid deputies of Middletown and Shrewsbury, and for more certain and speedy passage of deputies in future, inhabitants of Middletown to choose two men, to join with two chosen out of Piscataqua, to make out the nearest and most convenient way that may be found between said towns, and upon county charge. This to be done between this and tenth of May next."‡ Before the Quintipartite deed was executed, July 1st, 1676, the proprietors owned the whole of New Jersey, as tenants in common. By this instrument, Sir George Carteret became the sole owner of one half of New Jersey. This deed § fixes the north partition station, at the most northerly point as boundary of New Jersey, which is in Latitude 41° 40′. And the south partition station, at the most southerly point of the east side of Little Egg Harbor. A *straight* and *direct* line between these stations to constitute the division line, or as sometimes called the "province line." All lands east of this line to be called East Jersey, and all west, West Jersey. Thus originated the term "Jersies" as applied to our State." "The County of Nevysink" fell in East Jersey. Many important acts were passed at an Assembly in Elizabethtown, in 1682. Among others an act dividing East Jersey into four counties, viz: Bergen, Essex, Middlesex and Monmouth. The bounds of Monmouth County are loosely fixed as follows: "Monmouth County to begin at westward bounds of Middlesex county, containing Middletown and Shrewsbury, and to extend westward, southward and northward to the extreme bounds of the Province." Thus a name and rude limits were given to this county. Prior to the act, this part of New Jersey was sometimes called the Towns of Middletown and Shrewsbury, and sometimes The inhabitants or towns of Navesink, Nevysink, Nevesincks, &c.‖ Colonel Lewis Morris, who was then a resident of Tinton Falls, in this county, and a member of the Governor's Council, is supposed to have selected the name. He was a native of Monmouth shire, in England, and naturally gave the name of his childhood's home to his new home in the wilds of America. This Assembly, in 1682, provided for appointments of High Sheriff, Justices of the Peace, Clerk of the Courts, and other county officers. Lewis Morris, Junior, was the first, and Richard Harts horne was the next, High Sheriff of Monmouth. Provision was made to build 'goals" or jails in each county; and commissioners were appointed to lay out highways, build bridges, arrange landings and ferries. The commissioners for Monmouth were the Surveyor General, Col. Lewis Morris, Capt. John Bown, Richard Hartshorne, James Hance, Joseph Parker, and Lewis Morris, Jr. In 1686 the Assembly appointed as Commissioners of Highways, etc., John Throckmorton, John Slocum, and Nicholas Brown, in the place of Col. Lewis Morris, John Bown, and Joseph Parker. In 1687 George Keith,¶ the Surveyor General, tried to run the partition line between East and West Jersey. He ran a line from Egg Harbour about sixty miles to Dobies Plantation, on Raritan River, and then finding his course too far south, he gave up the attempt. The West Jersey people accused him of trying to cheat them. This line has always been the southwest boundary line of Monmouth. In 1687 the Commissioners of Highways laid out following roads in the county, being the first of which we have any record in our county. Book A, B, C, of Deeds in Monmouth County Clerks's office, has the following entry:

"Records off ye highways in ye countie of Monmouth laid outt the second day of March, Anno Dom. one thousand six hundred and eighty seven. From Shrewsbury Falls to Swimming River Bridge as the road now lieth to two white oaks, girdled on ye south side, of ye same, at John Ruckman's hill: then by stakes to the barrs near his house

---

† Leaming & Spicer, page 96. ‡ Leaming and Spicer, page 118
§ Leaming and Spicer, page 61, &c.

‖ Book A, B, C, of Deeds in Monmouth County Clerk's Office.

¶ A Scotchman, who founded Freehold, where he lived some time. He was a Quaker preacher, afterward became an Episcopalian, and started Episcopal churches in Freehold and Shrewsbury, by turning Quakers over

all along ye Kings highway six rods broad,* through Middletown street as ye road now lyeth to the bridge, a little easterly from John Stouts house,† and into a drift-way three rods, following the old way through ye Poplar Field and out by James Grovers to the ——— of the lott that was Jonathan Holmes; thence following ye cartway, that now is to the east side of ye lott, which belonged to James Ashton; thence following ye old-way, laid out by James Grover, to the most easterly side of Stephen Arnold's poplar lot; and thence keeping ye old path to William Layton's; and thence up the hill along the path that goes toward Portland Point, and so along that way till it comes (as now it is) to Poorman's Plain; thence from the head of Poorman's Plain along through said Plain, by now mark't trees, till it comes to the way, that goes over ye Stony Runn, and so along the way, as it now goes to Richard Davis' most easterly lines, and then to turn down, by now mark't trees, to the mouth of ——— Creek at ——— river, and again from Richard Davis' most easterly lines, as the way now goes. to ——— Samuel ——— lands, so along through Jeremiah Bennett's land as the ——— went, and so through Richard Hartshorne's lands, as the way now goes, to his house, and thence to the most northerly part of Sandy Hook Point. A drift way, three rods wide running from John Stout's bridge and beginning at the way by William Laytons, as the road now lyeth, to James Grover's Mill and Mill brook and bog, at the south of Stephen Arnold's lott so called, as the way now goes to ye head of the old spring and ——— line, that parts James Ashton's land and Job Throckmorton's, and so along mark't trees, till it comes to Thomas ——— path, and thence as ye way now goeth, to ye bay side. Beginning at ye pond, by Richard Gardiner's meadow, and so through Thomas Harbert's path and house, as ye way goes to Benjamin Devill's house and so through Benjamin Devill's land, by mark't trees, till it comes in the way in Poorman's Plain to ye grave. And beginning att Thomas Morford's on Navesinoks River, going along, as the way now goes to the Middletown road, by John Stout's Bridge. And beginning at the King's highway in Middletown by the Indian ——— thirtie chains in length, the breadth of the way — Rod, lying betwixt Richard Hartshorne's lott and Sarah Reape's, and thence as the way now goes, a drift path to William Campton's; it a King's highway from James Grover's to the mouth of Waykick Creek ¿ as the way now goes, being six rods wide; it a drift way from Thomas Whitlock's, as the way now lyes to the King's highway in Middletown and a passage for people over Waykick meadow to cart their hay, as the way now lyeth into the King's highway. And beginning att King's highway in Middletown, by the Prisson, ‖ on the west by Robert Hamilton's lott, and east of Mary Pedler's or Thomas Cox's lott, in length ——— chains, and in breadth eighteen rods, and thence a drift way to Swimming River Bridge as the way lyeth, ¶ it beginning in the north side of ye Prisson, running northerly, two chains broad, and twenty chains long, bounded west by Robert Hamilton's, east by Samuel Spicer's, and it is to be noted that these three highways above mentioned are not to hemed in. First, that six rods broad and thirteen chains long, lying betwixt Richard Hartshorne's land and Sarah Reape's; their lott. The second, that of eighteen rods broad and thirteen chains long, bounded west by Robert Hamilton's lott, and east by Thomas Cox, lying from the Prisson, south, and the third eight rods broad and twenty chains long, bounded west by Robert Hamilton's, and east by Samuel Spicer's, running from the highway over against the Prisson, north. And it is to be noted that from the King's highway east of the Leonard's, a driftway as to go to ye Leonard's Sawmill, and thence as the cartway goeth to Peter Tilton's cartway, to Hop River, rounding the bank as the cartway goeth, and so westward of William Leed's new house, and so along as the old way now goeth to the King's highway. And Burlington path being the King's highway from Crosswicks Creek, by George Keith's Plantation** to John Hampton's, as ye way now goeth, and so to the Leonard's, and thence to the Falls as the way goeth, but it is to be made more straight at the Leonard's, and some other places betwixt that and the Falls.

---

* The front foundation walls of the tavern on one side and the front foundation wall of Dr. Taylor's house on the other side mark original bounds of this road. These and corner of Charles Dubois's lot are only landmarks to fix it.

† Stood where the residence of late G. C. Hendrickson now stands. [———] means illegible words.

¿ Landing at or near the mouth of Waykake Creek, called at a later day Tanner's Landing.
‖ Where Episcopal church now stands in Middletown. ¶ Road from Middletown to Nut Swamp.
** At Freehold.

And from John Hampton's plantation, the path being the King's highway, is to go as the path now goeth, to Hop River, at the usual crossing westerly of William Lawrence's field, and so northerly by mark't trees, through John Bray's land, and Eleizar Cottrell's, till it comes to a gullie, and thence along the said gullie, bounding the said Cottrell's, and thence by mark't trees to goe betwixt Eliezar Cottrell's and Jonathan Holmes, their bound lines that bound betwixt them, and so to the brook of Cheeseman's, and thence crossing the brook at the usual place, by mark't trees betwixt Cheeseman's and Morford's land, till it comes to the old path to Middletown. And from Middletown a King's highway is to goe by the side of John Ruckman's †† hill, as aforesaid, to old Richard Stout's, as the way now lieth, and from thence to the Widow Bound's,‡‡ and so along as the way now lieth to the head of Cheesequake's, and thence to the Ferry over against Perth Amboy.

And a way is to goe from Shrewsbury Falls, as the way now goeth, to Richard Stout's the younger, his plantation. And from the crossing of Hop River, at Burlington path, a way is to goe as now it goeth, by mark't trees to John Reid's, and thence as the way goeth to the King's highway, betwixt Middletown and Cheesequakes. And a driftway is to goe from a marked tree, a black oak standing by Burlington pathway, on the east side, betwixt John Hampton and Hop River, on a ridge of land, by marked trees, (the which ridge lieth betwixt the heads and branches of Hop River easterly, and South River westerly,) into the King's highway of Wickatoung, §§ by mark't trees till it comes to a black oak, by the south side of the highway, marked on four sides; thence by mark't trees to the east side of Baker's fence at Wickatoung, and along the hill by the old way that goeth to the landing-place at Matteawan Creek on the south side."

Some parts of this, the first record of a laid out road in Monmouth County, is hard to decipher, and some words so blurred, that their meaning must be guessed. Provision should be made to transcribe this record and keep it attached to the old one. The Widow Boune referred to in this record was the wife of Capt. John Bowne, original patentee. His house stood where the residence of the late William H. Crawford now stands, in Holmdel township. It came to the Crawfords by intermarriage with Bownes. She is also the same person referred to in a deed of August 10th, 1690, recorded in Book A B C of Deeds, from the Indian Sachems, Ilosechcote, Tapchalawug, and Talinguanecan. At a General Assembly held at Perth Amboy, begun Oct. 12th, and continued until Nov. 3d, 1693, an act was passed for dividing each county into townships. This gave definite limits to the the townships of Monmouth. The language is as follows:

"In the County of Monmouth, the township of Middletown includes all the land, from the mouth of Navesinks River,‡ and runs up said river, and Swimming River and Sawmill Brook, to Burlington Path; thence over to the upper end of William Lawrence's land, on Hop River; thence up the run, which divides said Lawrence and John Johnston, to the head thereof; thence to the lower end of Richard Saltars land on Hop Brook; thence up the said brook, to the head thereof; thence to the meeting of Gravel and Watson's Brook; thence to the head of Matawan; thence to the head of Cheesequake's Creek; thence down said Creek to the Bay; and thence round along the shore to where it began. The township of Shrewsbury includes all the land from the mouth of Neversink River, and runs up the said river, and Swimming River, and Saw Mill Brook, to Burlington Path; thence the nearest way to the Pines, and along the edge of the Pines to Burlington Path, and along Burlington Path to the Pine Brook; and along the edge of the Pines to the line of the Province, and along Province Line to the sea; and thence along the shore to where it began. The township of Freehold includes all the land from the head of Cheesequakes Creek, and runs along the lines of Middletown to Burlington Path; thence along the line of Shrewsbury to the line of the Province; thence along the Province line to the line of the Coun-

†† Residence of late Rev. J. Ten Broeck Beekman is on this hill.

‡‡ This road from Middletown to Holland and from there to William H. Crawford's, dec'd, late residence, and so to Cheesequakes.

§§ Sometimes spelled Wicatunk, near what is now Marlborough village.

‡ At this time the inlet through Sandy Hook was open. And Sandy Hook proper was part of the main land joining the Navesinck Hills, at the point now owned by E. Minturn, and one of the above laid out roads ran over it to the extreme point of the Hook.

OLD TIMES IN OLD MONMOUTH. 169

ty; thence northeast along the said county line to where it began."

Thus, for the first time, regular boundaries were fixed for the two old townships, and the new one of Freehold established. The Assembly passed an act which recited that some of the commissioners of highways, appointed by the act of 1682, are deceased, superannuated, or otherwise disabled, and then makes the following new appointments of such commissioners for Monmouth: The Governor, the Surveyor General, Lewis Morris, of Tinton,* Lewis Morris of Passage Point,† John Hance, John Stout, Nicholas Brown, William Lawrence, Jr., Benjamin Burden, John Havens, Richard Hartshorne, Thomas Boel. They or the majority are authorized to act.

In 1694 the county courts of Monmouth met twice a year, "on fourth Tuesday of March, in the Publick Meeting House of Middletown, on fourth Tuesday of September, in the Publick Meeting House of Shrewsbury." From this year up to the surrender to the English Government in 1702, confusion and great disorder prevailed, the people, especially those of Middletown, paying little or no regard to the courts or the constituted authorities. They went so far in their resistance as to break up a court in Middletown, and imprisoned the Judges, Attorney General, and officers. Our records show that no regular courts were held for some time, and lawlessness prevailed unchecked. After the surrender, public matters began to assume orderly and definite shape.

The following highways were laid out, which are given in full as they serve to fix locations and residences of those days. In Book "D" of Deeds, page 199, Monmouth Records, appears the following entries:

RECORD OF HIGHWAYS.

Also a road laid out in Freehold, beginning by Richard James, att ye Indian Path, and along ye s'd path to ye pine bridge; thence as ye old Indian Path goes to ye west side of David Stout's field; thence along ye marked trees to ye division line of the province, to lye and remain of ye breadth of two rods wide, allowing to David Stout one swinging gate, to Marmaduke Horsman one swinging gate, to John Kirby one swinging gate, and to Anthony Woodward two swinging gates, laid out by us this twenty-seventh day of October, Anno Domini 1708.

OBADIAH BOWNE,
ELISHA LAWRENCE,
Commissioners.

Laid out a road of two rods wide, beginning in ye road by David Johnston's house; thence along the path to ye old schoolhouse; thence along the partition line of Holmes and Cottrell, at ye pathway in ye pathway marked, to Cheesman Brook; thence as ye road now lyes to Middletown. Given under our hands this 22d day of September, 1708.

OBADIAH BOWNE,
JOHN LEONARD,
ELISHA LAWRENCE,
Commissioners.

September ye 22d, 1708. Also, a road laid out of two rods wide, beginning in ye road by James Grover's, in Middletown; thence along ye road as it goes to Shole Harbour, until it comes to ye head of ye bogge meadow; thence up ye barren hill, the most direct and convenient way along ye way as now marked, along the east side of Jonathan Ruckman's field till it comes to the old path.
ELISHA LAWRENCE,
OBADIAH BOWNE,
Commissioners.

September 22, 1708. Then laid out a road two rods wide, beginning att Swimming River Bridge; thence along ye old road on ye northeast side of ye orchard, by ye path to ye house that formerly William Hunt dwelt in; thence turning the corner as ye road now lies to ye bridge that now goes over ———— River, a road laid out by us beginning in ye road at Jumping Brook; thence as ye path now goes to the road by Skunks Hill. Given under our hands this 22d day of September, Anno Domini 1708.
ELISHA LAWRENCE,
OBADIAH BOWNE,
JOHN LEONARD,
Commissioners.

This seventh day of May, Anno Dom. 1709, laid out a bye way for Capt. Anderson, Thomas Mattage, ———— Mattison, from their plantations to fall into ye Landing Road. 'Tis to cross Manalapan River, at Joseph Allen's old bridge, a little below ye mouth of Clear Brook, the said way to run from ye walnut tree to ye

---

* He called his place Tintern manor, at what is now Tinton Falls, a corruption of Tintern.

† I do not know who this Lewis Morris was, or where Passage Point was situated. Our old Court records show that he was afterward killed by negroes, doubtless his own slaves, as there are evidences that he was a man of ungovernable temper.

point of upland, and is to cross Clear Brook to ye said point at ye maple tree in ye brook by a fallen old great tree, and so along ye marked trees to Manalapan brook, where Ben Allen built a bridge; thence following ye marked trees until it falls into the Landing Road, before it comes at William Davison's bridge, etc.

JOHN REID,
JOHN HEBRON,
Commissioners.

The highway to run from the rear of Richard Hartshorne's west ―― to John Hav is' land, two chains and a half to the southward of his house; thence ye most direct course to Rack Pond, above head of ye lott. Also a driftway to go partly on Richard Stout's land, and partly on John Lawrence's land, from ye aforesaid highway. Also a highway from ye highway that goeth along ye rear of Joseph Lawrence's land, as ye way now goeth, to Hochocson swamp; then to ye line that parts Morris and Thomas Leonards; thence along ye said line to ye brook; thence down ye brook to ye bridge; from thence to ye place where ye bridge was made over, below the Sawmill; thence as ye way goeth to William Lawrence's Mill. Also a highway to go from ye rear of Joseph Lawrence's land, where ye other ways meet, as ye way is now marked. Also a highway from ye way that runs along ye rear of ye lott along ye line that parts Goodbody's land and Brindley's land; thence along Brindley's line till it comes into ye aforesaid way to go ――. Also another highway laid out four rods broad, beginning at ye west side of ye Meeting House,* in Shrewsbury, betwixt Judah Allen and Restore Lippincott lives, as it was formerly laid out to ye North River. Given under our hands this first day of March, 1709

OBADIAH BOWNE,
JOIN LEONARD,
ELISHA LAWRENCE,
JOHN WOOLLEY,
Commissioners.

By order of said Commissioners,
JAMES BOLLEN, Clerk.

Book "D" of Deeds, page 202, Monmouth Records. Also another driftway or road laid out by and beginning upon the top of the hill where ye path now goes, up over ye part of Swimming River, that leads up to Henry Leonard's sawmill (1st) where ye road that comes from William Lawrence's to Shrewsbury crosses said river; thence running southwest to a small black oak tree, being ye corner tree of Johannes Polhemus and Ouka Leffers; and thence along ye line of ye said Polhemus and Leffers to lie and remain upon Polhemus's land, until it comes to where ye aforesaid road crosses said Polhemus' and Leffers' land or line; to lie and remain ye breadth of one rod, allowing one swinging gate, nearest to aforesaid corner tree, and another at or near to west end of Polhemus new cleared land. Given under our hand this 10th day of June, 1710.

OBADIAH BOWNE,
ELISHA LAWRENCE.

To Overseers of Freehold:

Wee do order you to order swinging gate in the road that is laid out by us, where it goes through Benjamin Borden, Jr's, field, at Crosswicks, where same now stands. Given under our hands this sixteenth day of April, 1711.

BENJAMIN BORDEN,
OBADIAH BOWNE,
Commissioners.

Laid† out in Shrewsbury, a highway of two rods wide, beginning at a white oak tree, a corner between ye land of John Eaton and that of William Hull by the highway that goes between ye meeting house and Long Branch, and running south, sixty five degrees west, fifty-one chains into ye way by Henry Allen's N. E. corner; thence as ye way goes, south, eighty-three degrees west, twenty-three chains; thence south, eighty-six degrees west, fourteen chains; thence south, sixty-one degrees west, seventeen chains; thence west, fifty-two chains and one rod to ye road that comes from Manasquan to ye Falls, about two chains to ye southward of John ――'s house.

JOHN REID,
JOHN LEONARD,
Commissioners.

Memorandum.‡ This 13th day of October, 1713, then laid out several driftways in Middletown bounds, (First): that part of the way from Middletown to Chinquerors,§ beginning at a white oak tree on the east side of Daniel Tilton's mill dam; thence to the east end of the dam and then over along upon the dam, to the other side thereof, and then along the way to Chinquerors, to be two rods wide, except on the dam, where 'tis to be

---

* Old Quaker meeting house.
† Book D of Deeds, page 202.
‡ Book D of Deeds, page 206. § Near Keyport.

OLD TIMES IN OLD MONMOUTH.

of a convenient breadth for strength and substance. Also another way of a rod and a half wide from Chinqueror's Road by the corners of the fences of James Hubbard and Cornelius Covenhoven, and running along by Dr. Hubbard's house; and thence to the bridge on Hop Brook; and thence over the brook along the line between Benjamin Stout and Hendrick Hendrickson, to a valley near the end of it; then to Joseph Golden's southwest corner of his new field, and following his and Obadiah Bowne's lines to the gulley; then rounding the hill to Mahoras Run, where the path from Daniel to Hendrick Hendrickson's pusses; and following the path to Daniel's line, and then through his field, as he shall apoint, to the line between him and John Wall, and along between 'em over the swamp and along by Walls fence and path, to the line between Thomas Smith and Cornelius Dorn, and then the best way to the mill dam of Thomas Tilton, and over along the dam to the path that goes to Wakick Landing||, and following the same path to the said landing. Also another way from the old path at the line between Daniel Hendrickson and Peter Wyckoff, and following the line between 'em and to the old Ford of Mahoras brook; and then along the southside of Andrew Wilson's to Samuel Ruckman's; and between him and Wilson to John Ruckman's, and along between John and Samuel Ruckman's to Middletown.
     JOHN REID,
     OBADIAH BOWNE,
     JOHN HEBRON,
     Commissioners.

Laid out a highway from Henry Leonard's sawmill to Barnegate; that is from said saw mill along John Hankins' path to Hay path; then to ye head of Sarah Reape's meadow and down ye side of ye said meadow as ye line of marked trees. to the Fish path; thence as that goes to Manasquan; thence along ye Fish Path to the Cedar Path, and along the Cedar Path as the marked trees that leads to Metetecunk and following the marked trees to Goose Creek, called Toms River, and over said river by marked trees to the line of land late Thomas Hart.
     JOHN REID,
     ELISHA LAWRENCE.
     OBADIAH BOWNE,
     Commissioners.

Laid* out a driftway from Burlington road to Thomas Melag's mill, beginning at a black oak tree marked by ye road which goes from Shrewsbury to Burlington, about ten chains eastward from Cornelius Thomson's house, and following ye line of marked trees to the said mill. This third day of April, Anno Dom'n 1714, 'tis two rods wide.
     JOHN REID,
     JOHN HEPBURN,
     Commissioners.

Memorandum,† this seventh of March, 1714. We the under-subscribers, surviving commissioners appointed by the act of the General Assembly for laying out highways in ye County of Monmouth, do appoint Capt. Richard Stout and Stoffel Longstreet in place of Benjamin Borden who is removed out of said county, above a year, and Capt. John Leonard, deceased, above a year.
     JOHN REID,
     OBADIAH BOWNE,
     ELISHA LAWRENCE,
     JOHN HEPBURN,
     JOHN WOOLLEY,
     Commissioners.

Memorandum this 29th day of November, 1714. Laid out a part of a driftway from ye way which crosses ye brook and dam of Daniel Tilton's, beginning at a chain westward of s'd Tilton's Mill House, and running down on ye tops of ye bank about four chains to a small red oak tree on the top of ye bank; thence right across the brook and the best and shortest way into ye way again, which was formerly laid out.
     JOHN REID,
     OBADIAH BOWNE,
     Commissioners.

The above seem to be the principal roads laid out in our county during early times. In 1709-10, an effort was made to fix more definitely the boundaries of the county. At a General Assembly held at Burlington, Col. Richard Ingoldsby, Lieut-Governor, an act was passed on the 21st of January, "for dividing and ascertaining the boundaries of all the counties in this Province." The preamble of the act shows that there existed such great uncertainty as to the county limits as seriously to interfere with the jurisdiction of courts, that the officers of many counties did not know their own boundaries. Section 5th of this act refers to Monmouth. "The county of Monmouth begins at the mouth of the creek aforesaid, that parts the land of Captain Andrew Bowne, deceased, and

---

|| Known afterwards as Tanner's Landing,
* Book D of Deeds, page 206.

† Book D of Deeds, page 211.

OLD TIMES IN OLD MONMOUTH.

George Willocks; thence following the line of Middlesex County, to the line of the eastern and western division aforesaid; thence southerly along the said division line to the sea; thence along the sea to the point of Sandy Hook; thence up the bay to the aforesaid creek where it first began." The boundaries thus fixed did not prove satisfactory, and another act was passed, March 15th. 1713-14, entitled "an act for settling the bounds between the counties of Somerset, Middlesex and Monmouth." Section Second provides that "the boundary line between Middlesex and Monmouth counties shall be and begin at the mouth of the creek that parts the land of George Willocks and the land that was formerly Capt. Andrew Bowne's line to the rear of the said land; thence upon a direct course to Warn's bridge on the brook where Thomas Smith did formerly live; thence upon a direct course to the southeast corner of Barclay's tract of land that lies near Machiponix; thence to the most southermost part of said tract of land, including the whole tract of land in Middlesex county; thence upon a direct line to Assanpink bridge, on the high road, including William Jones, William Story, Thomas Ruckman and John Guyberson in Monmouth county; thence along the said road to Aaron Robins's land; thence westerly along the said Aaron Robins's and James Lawrence's line to the line of the eastern and western division aforesaid, incluing the said Robins and Lawrence in Monmouth county." A supplement passed Nov. 28, 1822, speaks of "Whale Creek" as the beginning of the bounds of the counties of Middlesex and Monmouth. Section third of this supplement declares the northerly bounds of the county of Monmouth "to be the middle or midway of the waters of Raritan Bay, from the line of Middlesex to the main channel, which passes by Sandy Hook, and along the said channel to the sea." April 9, 1866, an act was passed to take immediate effect, "that the northerly bounds of Monmouth, from the line of Middlesex County are extended along the midway of the waters of Raritan Bay to the main sea. Pamphlet Laws, 1866, page 964. The southwestern boundaries of Monmouth, except where bounded by Middlesex, was fixed by the Province line as run by Keith, and the rest by the ocean and Raritan Bay, leaving only the boundaries on Middlesex to be determined.

When that was settled by the act of 1713-14 and its supplements the county had well defined boundaries. At a General Assembly held at Perth Amboy, from January 13th to March 28th, 1718-19, an act was passed March 27th to ascertain partition line between eastern and western division of Province of New Jersey. The preamble sets out that many doubts, debates and controversies have arisen, respecting the true location of this line; and to settle these difficulties, it is enacted that a straight and direct line from the most northerly part or boundary of the Province of New Jersey, on the nothermost branch of the River Delaware unto the most southerly point of a certain beach or island of sand, lying next and adjoining to the main sea, on the north side of the mouth or entrance of a certain Inlet, Bay, or Harbour, known by the name of Little Egg Harbour, is and shall forever hereafter remain and be the line of partition between the eastern and western divisions of this province. In 1743 John Lawrence ran the division line or province line. He ran his line from Latitude 41° 40′ in what he supposed a straight course to the south station point at little Egg Harbour. This has been said to be the true line. At all events generally acquiesced in down to the present time. Both East and West Jersey proprietors gave and received deeds in which Lawrence's line was assumed to be correct. This line, however, is not the boundary line of Monmouth county, but the line governing the land titles of East and West Jersey.

Upper Freehold was the next township established after Freehold; this was about 1745, and was by patent, but where that patent is recorded I have been unable to ascertain.

The township of Stafford was next created by patent, dated March 3d, 1749. The language is as follows: "George the Second, by the Grace of God, of Great Britian, France and Ireland, King, defender of the faith, &c., to all to whom these presents shall come Greeting: Know ye that we of our especial grace, certain knowledge and mere motion, have given, and granted, and by these presents do give and grant for us, our heirs and successors, to the inhabitants of the southwestern part of the township of Shrewsbury, in our County of Monmouth, in our Province of New Jersey, within the following boundaries, to wit: Beginning at old Barnegat Inlet, and from the north end of the beach, lying to the southward of the said Inlet, running over the Bay, north, forty six degrees west, five miles and thirty seven chains to the mouth of Oyster Creek; and then west, eleven miles and seventy chains to Pine tree in the southwest plain, in the old partition line of East and West Jersey, formerly run by George Keith; thence bounded by the old division line, north, nineteen degrees east, nineteen miles and sixty chains to the south stationary point of division between East and West Jersey, at the main sea northeasterly to the place of beginning, according the plan hereto annexed, to be and remain a perpetual township and community, in word and deed, to be called and known by the name of the township of Stafford. And we further grant to the said inhabitants of the township aforesaid, and their successors, to choose annually two Commissioners of the Highways, one Overseer of the Highway, one Overseer of the Poor, one Assessor, one Town Collector and one Constable for the town afore said; and to have, hold, and enjoy all other privileges, rights, liberties and immunities that any other township in our said province do or may of right enjoy. And the said inhabitants are hereby constituted and appointed a township by the name aforesaid, to have and enjoy the privileges aforesaid to them. In testimony whereof we have caused these, our letters, to be made patent, and the Great Seal of the Province of New Jersey to be hereunto affixed. Witness, our trusty and well beloved Jonathan Belcher, Esq., our Captain General and Governor in Chief in and over our Province of Nova Cæsarea or New Jersey, and territories therein depending, in America, Chancellor and Vice-Admiral in the same, &c., at Burlington, the third day of March, in the twenty-third year of our Reign, A. D. MDCCXLIX"

This patent was recorded in Secretary's office in Burlington, in Book A A A of Commissions, folio 305, etc.

At a general assembly held at Burlington in 1767, a number of the inhabitants of the Township of Shrewsbury, presented a petition setting forth that they had long labored, under many and great difficulties, "by reason of the large extent of said Town."* A glance at the map will show that they had good cause for this complaint, as Shrewsbury then included all of what are now, the shore townships of both Monmouth and Ocean Counties, excepting Middletown and Stafford. To remedy this inconvenience, an act was passed January 24, 1767, entitled "an act to divide the town of Shrewsbury, and annex parts thereof to the Towns of Freehold and Upper Freehold," "All that part of said Town of Shrewsbury, beginning at Cranberry Inlet, and running thence up the Bay to the mouth of Metetecunk River; thence up the said River to the first bridge, which now is over the said River; thence west, until it shall intersect a line to be run south, eighteen degrees east, from the place where Burlington Old Path, crosseth the north Branch, of Toms River, called Pine Brook; thence from the intersection of the said lines south, fifty six degrees west to the old division line, called Keith's line; thence along said Keith's line to the line of the Town of Stafford; thence along the same, to the main sea or ocean, and thence, bounded by the sea to the above mentioned beginning; shall be and is hereby, divided off from the said Township, and made a separate Town to be called by the name of the Town of Dover. All that part of the aforesaid Township of Shrewsbury, beginning at the mouth of Passaquanaqua Brook, where it empties into Manasquan River, and from thence running south, to the line of the before mentioned town of Dover; thence west, along the same line, to the line of that part of said township of Shrewsbury annexed to the Town of Upper Freehold; thence north, eighteen degrees west, to where Burlington Old Path crosseth the north branch of Toms River, alias Pine Brook; thence easterly along the bounds of Freehold to where it began, shall and is hereby divided, off from the said town of Shrewsbury, and annexed unto the town of Freehold, and forever hereafter. shall be accounted part thereof.

"All that part of the town of Shrewsbury, beginning, where Burlington Old Path crosseth the before mentioned, north branch of Toms River; thence running south, eighteen degrees east to the line of Dover aforesaid; thence south, fifty six degrees west, along said line of Dover to the before mentioned line called Keith's line; thence along the said line to the line of Upper Freehold; thence along the line of Upper Freehold, to where it began, shall be and hereby is, divided off, from the said town of Shrewsbury, and annexed unto the town of Upper Freehold,

---
* Allinson's Laws, page 299, etc.

and forever hereafter shall be accounted part thereof."

The "Keith line" mentioned in this act," "began at the most southerly part of a certain beach, or island, lying next and adjoining the main sea, to the northward of a certain Bay, Inlet, or Harbour, lying on the seacoast of this Province, and commonly called or known, by the name of Little Egg Harbor, and running thence according to natural position, on a north northwest, fifty minutes more westerly course, to the southwesterly corner, of a certain tract of land, lying to the westward of the south branch of Raritan River, heretofore granted, by the proprietors of the eastern division, of the Province, to John Dobie, and commonly called or known, by the name of Dobie's Plantation." This line, as said before, never gave satisfaction, and was never accepted by the western proprietors, so far as their individual titles to land, affected thereby, was concerned. Keith seems to have been an unscrupulous man, and very much disliked by the Quakers of West New Jersey. Soon after the establishment of Dover township the stirring times of the Revolution began. Monmouth was the "dark and bloody ground" during the war. Exposed all along our seacoast, with British fleets, anchored almost constantly, within Sandy Hook; with a large number of disaffected inhabitants in our midst, whose ravages and outrages shamed those of the hireling Hessians; traversed by the contending armies; and harrassed incessantly by prowling bands of British, tories, pine robbers and river pirates; all efforts to improve, and seemingly all legal proceedings, ceased to a great extent. In 1780, however, a record of highways, was commenced in Road Book B, which has been continued to the present time, in Books C, D, E, F, G and H of roads. Prior to this record, the roads laid out, were recorded, with deeds, court minutes, and other miscellaneous papers, and can be found in Books A, B, C, D, E, F, G, H, of deeds and Books No. 1 and No. 4 (also marked Roads 'A') of Common Pleas minutes, in Monmouth clerk's office. As it may gratify the curiosity of some, I give two of these road returns. On page 1 of road book B, is the following entry: "Surveyed and laid out by us, the subscribers, the third day of July, 1780, a road of two rods wide, agreeable to a petition of a number of the neighboring inhabitants, bearing date the 19th day of June, 1780, through the lands of John Truex and Isaiah Hoffmire, beginning at a whiteoak saplin, standing by the side of the highway, that goes from Skunks Hill to the Falls, in Shrewsbury. Said saplin being a corner, between the lands of the aforesaid John Truex and Isaiah Hoffmire; from thence running along the line between said Truex and Hoffmire, west, eleven chains and seventy four links; thence north, forty seven degrees and fifteen links west, three chains; thence north, seventy two degrees and a half west, twenty seven chains; thence north, eleven and a half degrees east, nine chains and fifty links; thence south, eighty eight degrees one chain; thence north, eleven degrees east, three chains; thence north, eighty degrees and fifteen minutes west, sixteen chains and seventeen links; thence north, five degrees and forty five minutes west, nine chains to the highway, that goes from Middletown to Freehold. Witness our hands the day and year above written.

JOHN STILLWELL.
CORN'S COVENHOVEN,
    Middletown.
GEORGE WALKER.
CORNELIUS COVENHOVEN,
    Freehold.
STOFFEL LONGSTREET,
THOMAS COX,
    Upper Freehold.

A comparison of this return, with those of nearly a century before, will show a great advance toward that accuracy which now characterizes the laying out of highways. The reason of this, will be found in the decisions, by our Supreme Court respecting roads. A great many returns of roads have been upset, by our courts, for inaccuracies, as to beginning and ending points, and other defects. An examination of returns, in the road book above mentioned, will show the particularity required, at the present time, a century later.

The following is another return recorded in Book B of Roads, pages 13-14 by J. Rhea, Clerk of Monmouth. on the 27th of July, 1785. "Application having been made to us, the subscribers, Surveyors of the roads, in the counties of Monmouth and Burlington, to lay out a road in said counties, leading from Joshua Gibbs, to the road, leading from Allentown to Crosswicks; and having met and viewed the ground, and heard the allegations of the parties, do agree to lay the same as follows: Beginning near Joshua Gibbs, in the road, leading from Crosswicks to Richard Waln's Mill, and at the corner of the lands of Nathan Wright and Joshua Gibbs; and runs thence, between the lands of Nathan Wright, on the eastwardly side, and Joshua Gibbs, Abner Stewart, and Alexander Howard, on the westwardly side; north, seventeen degrees and thirty five minutes west, twenty eight chains and eighty eight links, (and supposed to be on the line between the said counties); thence through the lands of the said Nathan Wright. north, nine degrees west, three chains and fifty five links; thence through the same, north, nineteen degrees east, four chains; thence through the same, north, nine degrees ten minutes east, two chains and thirty four links; thence north, thirty four degrees and ten minutes west, three chains and twenty links, to the northwardly side of Crosswicks Creek, crossing the same on the line between the aforesaid counties; thence through the lands of Michael Rogers, north, seven degrees and forty minutes east, seven chains to a line between said Rogers' and James Jackson's land; thence on the same north, thirty four degrees and forty minutes west, nineteen chains and thirty three links; thence on the same, north, thirty degrees and forty minutes west, ten chains and twenty nine links; thence through the lands of said Rogers, between the lands of said Rogers and George Woodward, south, seventy two degrees west, thirteen chains; thence through the land of late John Quicksel's, north, eighty nine degrees west, seventeen chains and thirty eight links; thence on the line between the same, and lands of Michael Rogers, north, two degrees and forty minutes west, thirty two chains and seventy five links; thence through the lands of said Quicksel, north, fifty one degrees and forty minutes east, three chains; thence through the same, north, thirty one degrees east, twelve chains and fifty links crossing a point of Abraham Tilton's land; thence on a line, between said Tilton and Benedict Dorsey's land, north, thirteen degrees west, three chains and nineteen links; thence between the same, north, thirty four degrees east, six chains and ninety five links, crossing the line of the aforesaid counties; thence on the line of said lands. north, thirty nine degrees west, one chain and sixteen links to the line of the aforesaid counties; thence along the same on a line between the lands of Abraham Tilton, on the westwardly side, and Benedict Dorsey, Samuel Kelly and Amos Middleton on the eastwardly side, north, twenty one degrees west, seventy two chains and seventy five links to the road leading from Allentown to Crosswicks; which road we do lay out, two rods wide. That is to say, one rod wide on each side of said lines; and we do direct the Overseers of the Roads, in the township of Upper Freehold, in the County of Monmouth, and the Overseers of the Roads of the townships of Nottingham† and Hanover, in the county of Burlington. to build a sufficient bridge over Crosswicks Creek in said road, and clear out and open the whole thereof, agreeable to law, on or before the twenty-fifth day of this instant, June. Witness our hands this tenth day of June, 1785.

  Jos. Lawrence,
  Edward Taylor,
  David Forman,
  Benj. Covenhoven,
  John Price,
  Gabriel Woodmansee,
  Joseph Lamb,
  Jonathan Branson,
  Isaac Cowgill,
  Thomas Thorne, Jr.,
  Thomas Thorne.

This return was also recorded in Clerk's office of Burlington County, in Road Book No. 1, page 127, June 20th, 1785, by John Phillips, Clerk of the County.

In 1821 certain parts of this road was straightened. These alterations are recorded in Book C of roads, page 107, in clerk's office, at Mount Holly. This road seems to have been laid out, for the mutual convenience and benefit of the Inhabitants of the three townships, of Hanover and Nottingham in Burlington, and Upper Freehold in Monmouth, and intended that two townships of Burlington, should be at one half, and township of Upper Freehold, at the other half, of the expenses of building and maintaining, the road and bridge over Crosswicks Creek.

---

† Nottingham township was taken from Burlington county, in 1838, to form a part of Mercer county. In 1842 Nottingham was divided, and only the tract between Delaware River and Delaware and Raritan Canal retained original name. The greater part was made into Hamilton township. What was left was afterwards absorbed into the City of Trenton, and the name is now extinct as a township in Mercer County. It is to be regretted that old names, so suggestive of places in the old world, from which first settlers came, should be lightly changed for names whose only merit, at most, seems to be "prettiness of sound."

The road was evidently intended to be laid on old Keith line; which was the division line between the two counties; but near the bridge, on account of a low marsh and a deep ravine, which would necessitate great expense to all the townships interested, if a straight line was followed; therefore, the line of the road was run off to go around this bog and ravine, and then turned back on the province line. This bend caused the road to cross Crosswicks Creek, entirely within the limits of Monmouth. We find, however, that Burlington county has lived up to the liabilities incurred down to the present time, and always paid her just proportion of expense of keeping up this bridge. When Nottingham was set off into Mercer, such legal liabilities as belonged to this portion of Burlington followed the territory, and were transferred to Mercer county; one of which was one-fourth of the expense of keeping up this bridge, generally known as Fowler's Bridge. Not until a very late date has any attempt been made by Mercer county to evade the payment of her just proportion of the costs of rebuilding Fowler's Bridge. The townships of Hamilton in Mercer, of Hanover in Burlington, and Upper Freehold in Monmouth, meet at or very near this bridge, and before a part of Plumstead township was annexed to Upper Freehold, the Ocean county line came up to same point, and Ocean County also contributed her share towards the rebuilding of this bridge. It was then sometimes called the "Four County Bridge."

During the first century of the existence of our county, many roads which appear on the records were never actually opened and made passable; or were partly opened, and from want of use soon grew up with trees. Others, again, degenerated into mere drift roads, winding through the woods, and were frequently changed by individuals, without legal authority, as clearings were made, and new farms and residences came into existence. The travel in early days was either on foot or horseback, following the Indian paths, which generally ran over high ground, avoiding steep hills and ravines, swamps, bogs, deep streams, and even shallow ones, with miry meadows on either side, or those apt to be swollen and rendered impassable by freshets. These paths, gradually, became cart roads and wagon roads. The vehicles of our first settlers were generally carts drawn by oxen. One of the principal roads, actually used, ran from Middletown to the Landing, near or at the mouth of Waykake Creek. It followed nearly the same course as the present road by Harmony school house.

Between 1665 and 1700, sailing vessels made occasional trips during the summer, from Grave-end, on Long Island, to this Landing, and between here and Perth Amboy and New York, and once in awhile to Rhode Island, by the ocean, when the weather was favorable. The parents or near relatives of many of our original settlers lived in Rhode Island, and some of the eastern towns of Long Island, and also in Westchester county, New York. A highway ran from Gravesand, across the Island to the Sound, opposite Throg's Neck.* Here they crossed into Westchester county, and reached the public road running from New York into the New England colonies. As the old settlers died off, and ties of consanguinity became weakened by time, this intercourse with the parent settlements in Rhode Island and Long Island gradually ceased. This landing at Waykake, however, continued to be the chief port of Monmouth, for passengers and freight, down to the year 1820; at all events down to a time within the memory of our old men.† On account of calms or storms a week was sometimes taken to make this trip to New York, and it was considered pretty near as great an undertaking as it now is to make a voyage to Europe.

Sometime between 1667 and 1690, one Christopher Allmy, who came from Rhode Island and settled in this county, made an occasional trip with a sailing vessel, in summer time, out of Shrewsbury River

---

* Named from the Throckmorton family, who settled there. From here two of the younger sons, John and Job, came over by Gravesend to Monmouth, among the first settlers, and were the ancestors of the Throckmortous now in this county.

† The first landing was some little way up Waykake Creek from the mouth. Afterward a dock was built out in the Bay, on the shore some distance below the mouth of the Creek. This was called Tanner's Landing. There was also a landing in Matawan Creek occasionally used prior to 1689, and afterwards for the convenience of settlers back in the region around Pleasant Valley, Marlborough, Mount Pleasant, etc. The first steamboat which ever ran to Monmouth County, ran up to the landing in Matawan Creek. This was a side wheel steamboat, commanded by a Captain Penyer. This was forty-five or fifty years ago. Keyport, prior to this time, had no existence, and the region there was common, y called Fishing Point, and was celebrated for its Chingarora oysters, which oysters were free to all who had a mind to take them. Nearly every farmer owned a clam rake and oyster tongs—and got part of his living out of the public waters.

OLD TIMES IN OLD MONMOUTH.

and Inlet to the Rhode Island Ports. He carried passengers and peltries and brought back settlers with their moveables and such goods as could be procured in the New England colonies, and were in demand here. He finally became involved in law suits, and returned to Rhode Island, where he continued to live until his death, as is supposed.

The usual route for travellers prior to 1700, was to Gravesend, and then by boat across the Bay to the Waykake Landing, then by the road to Middletown. Here was an inn or tavern,‡ where a "square meal," a pipe to smoke, and something strong to drink, with a good bed, could be had for a few shillings. Accommodations could also be had, with out charge, if the traveller wished, at nearly any private house. News from abroad was very welcome, and the hospitality which has always characterized the farmers of Monmouth, made every stranger a welcome guest. The warmest nook of the old fashioned hearth, and the best he could afford, was given to the visitor, with a cheerful heart. Nowadays, the teachings of New England economy, is apt to condemn such hospitality as the conduct of the Prodigal son.

From Middletown the usual way to get to Shrewsbury was by the road leading through "haunted" Balm Hollow,§ by what was the John Golden farm, to Ogden's corner, by the John Bowne Crawford farm; then through Morrisville past the old Hubbard House; then turning easterly by or near the present residence of Denise H. Smock, over, through or near the Middletown Episcopal Church farm, and from there to Swimming River,|| at or near the present bridge on Leedsville road, and then the general course of the present road to Tinton Falls, and from thence to Shrewsbury. This road avoided all the steep ravines and high hills to the south of Middletown, and all meadows, bogs and streams, except Swimming River. This was bridged at a very early day, as appears from the Monmouth Record. In Book "A" of Deeds is the following entry:

"Att a Court of Sessions, held at Shrewsbury, at ye house of Nicholas Browne, ye 2, 3, 4 of September, 1679. Present—Capt. John Bowne,¶ Mr. Joseph Parker, Justices of the Peace; Mr. Richard Gibbons, Mr. Jonathan Holmes, Assistants. Att this Court, John Higgs is ordered to be tyed to a whipping post, with a bunch of rods tied to his back, half an hour, and his wife by him, and pay a fine of ten pounds for fornication.

"This Court also directs the bridge over Swimming River to be made new at equal charge of the towns of Middletown and Shrewsbury, and Tinton Maner, and appoint as overseers, Richard Gardner, of Tinton Maner, James Grover, Jr., of Middletown, and John Slocum, of Shrewsbury."

From this record it is evident that a bridge had existed over this stream prior to 1679 sufficiently long to get old and out of repair. Probably, ten or twelve years, which would fix the road, and the thoroughfare between the two old settlements, as far back as 1667.

The highway from Middletown to Freehold, as actually used, followed the road to Shrewsbury, as far as the old Hubbard house, lately owned by R P. Smock; thence turning, southwesterly, crossing the stream near brick house built by David Williamson; then following pretty much the same direction as present road by the Barnes Smock farm, now owned and occupied by John J. Crawford; then across Hop Brook at present bridge; so up the hill, by the old Van Mater race track, and then over to the road now running to Phalanx*; thence turning southwesterly on the present course of the road past S. W. Jones's house; thence by

---

‡ This tavern stood on or near the site of the present residence of Mr. George Bowne, opposite to the Railroad Bridge, over which the Middletown Street now passes.

§ Between this place and Middletown Village, just east of Beekman's woods, stands the old house where Jonathan Tilton lived and died. He was the grandfather of Theodore Tilton, now so widely known on account of his law suit with Rev. Henry Ward Beecher.

|| Called Swimming River, because a certain traveller, who tried to cross during a spring freshet, was obliged to swim his horse over.

¶ This John Bowne was the patentee named in the Nicoll Patent, also Speaker of the Assembly in 1682-3. He died about 1684, leaving a son, John Bowne, who was a prominent man and Speaker of the Assembly in Cornbury's time. Capt. Andrew Bowne, who was a member of the council, and also Acting Governor just previous to the surrender to the English Government, 1702, was, as I believe, a brother of this Capt. John Bowne. I think Mr. James Crawford, at Crawford's Corner, has some of his original commissions and papers.

* This is where the disciples of Fourier, [a French writer on social science], established their Phalanstery. Horace Greeley, at one time, took a great interest in it. Fourier's idea of a common dwelling house with separate apartments, and the use of the skill, wisdom, and grace of each individual was visionary. The lazy ones eat up what the industrious ones earned, and the women would quarrel when only separated by a thin partition wall. The concern bursted up and the people of Monmouth were not sorry.

a road now closed to the south of Edinburgh; so over to the old Barrentown road now called Montrose; thence following general course of the present road and Dutch Lane road to Freehold. This road avoided all streams of any size except Hop Brook and the brook near Williamson's brick house, and nearly all hills, ravines and meadows, and was for the most part sandy, and therefore better in the winter than in the summer.

There was an important highway, and one greatly used prior to 1720, and perhaps for a long time afterward, running from Middletown over to Holland, by the old Luyster House, and Hendrickson House to the Crawford neighborhood; from thence to Mount Pleasant,† and then to what is now Jacksonville‡ in Middlesex county; and from there a path ran to the Indian Ford on the Raritan, three miles above its mouth, and also a road down to the mouth of the river, near where the railroad docks are now located.§ There was a ferry over to Perth Amboy for man and beast. From Perth Amboy the traveller could go by land to Woodbridge, Elizabethtown and Paulus Hook, (as Jersey City was then called), or he could cross over in a row boat to Staten Island, near the old Billop House, and then travelling by land to the Narrows, cross here in a row boat, to what is now Fort Hamilton, and then go down either to Gravesend or up to Flatbush, Brooklyn, and by the ferry over the East River to New York. This route was sometimes taken when a person wanted to make a certain journey to New York, and was also used in winter time, when the Bay was filled with ice. The usual way, however, was to go from Perth Amboy in a sailing vessel, which went by outside passage, through the Narrows, when the weather was good, and by inside passage when bad. An account is given by Benjamin Franklin in his Memoirs of this route. He was then a boy, and had run away from his parents in Boston to New York, and was on his way, in 1723, from New York to Philadelphia, in search of employment as a printer or type setter. Let the Doctor speak

for himself: "I set out, however, in a boat for Amboy, leaving my chest and things to follow me around by sea. In crossing the bay, we met with a squall that tore our rotten sails to pieces, prevented our getting into the Kill, and drove us upon Long Island. In our way, a drunken Dutchman, who was a passenger, too, fell overboard. When he was sinking, I reached through the water to his shock pate, and drew him up, so that we got him in again. His ducking sobered him a little, and he went to sleep, taking first out of his pocket, a book, which he desired I would dry for him. It proved to be my old favorite author, *Bunyan's Pilgrim's Progress* in Dutch, finely printed, on good paper, copper cuts, a dress better than I have ever seen it wear in its own language. I have since found that it has been translated into most of the languages of Europe, and suppose it has been more generally read than any other book, except the Bible. Honest John was the first that I know of, who mixed narratives and dialogues, a method of writing very engaging to the reader, who in the most interesting parts finds himself, as it were, admitted into the company present at the conversation. De Foe has imitated him successfully in his *Robinson Crusoe*, in his *Moll Flanders* and other pieces; and *Richardson* has done the same in his *Pamela*, &c.

"On approaching the island, we found it was in a place where there could be no landing, there being a great surf on the stony beach. So we dropt anchor and swung out our cable toward the shore. Some people came down to the shore and hallowed to us as we did to them, but the wind was so high, and the surf so loud, that we could not understand each other. There were some small boats near the shore, and we made signs and called to them to fetch us; but they either did not comprehend us, or it was impracticable, so they went off. Night approaching, we had no remedy but to have patience, till the wind abated, and in the meantime, the boatmen and myself concluded to sleep, if we could; and so we crowded into the hatches, where we joined the Dutchman who was still wet, and the spray breaking over the head of our boat, leaked through to us, so that we were soon almost as wet as he. In this manner we lay all night with very little rest; but the wind abating next day, we made a shift to reach Amboy before night, hav-

---

† Philip Freneau, the poet of the Revolution, had a residence here until his death.

‡ Formerly Cheesequakes.

§ This road from Raritan River to Middletown was what they called a King's Highway, that is six rods wide, without swinging gates, and free for all to travel without molestation. In early times, it was deemed a very serious offense to offer violence or malignity to a person on the King's Highway.

OLD TIMES IN OLD MONMOUTH. 179

ing been thirty hours on the water, without victuals or any drink but a bottle of filthy rum, the water we sailed on being salt. In the evening, I found myself very feverish, and went to bed, but having read, somewhere, that cold water drank plentifully was good for a fever, I followed the prescription, and sweat plentifully most of the night; my fever left me, and in the morning, crossing the Ferry,|| I proceeded on my journey on foot, having fifty miles to Burlington, where I was told, I should find a boat, that would carry me the rest of the way to Philadelphia. It rained very hard all the day. I was thorougly soaked, and by noon a good deal tired, so I stopped at a poor inn,¶ where I staid all night. Beginning, now, to wish I had never left home, I made so miserable a figure, too, that I found by the questions asked me, I was suspected to be some runaway indentured servant, and in danger of being taken up on that suspicion. However, I proceeded next day and got in the evening to an inn|| within eight or ten miles of Burlington, kept by one Dr. Brown. (Account of Dr. Brown omitted). At his house, I lay that night, and arrived the next morning at Burlington, but had the mortification to find that the regular boats had gone a little before, and no other expected to go before Tuesday, this being Saturday."

In appendix to Dunlap's History of New York, page 178-9, is the following account of the ways of travelling, in 1753, from New York to New Jersey, and through to Philadelphia: The improvements in travelling, was at this time, so great, that a man might, (wind, weather and other circumstances favoring), arrive at Philadelphia from New York, or *vice versa*, in three days, as the following notification specifies: "A commodious stage boat will attend at the city hall slip, near the Half Moon Battery to receive goods and passengers, on Saturdays and Wednesdays; and on Mondays and Thursdays will set out for Perth Amboy Ferry; there a stage wagon will receive them, and set out on Tuesdays and Fridays, in the morning, and carry them to Cranberry, and then the same day with fresh horses to Burlington, where a stage boat receives them and sets out for Philadelphia." These packet boats were small sloops navigated by a man and boy, or at most by two men, (a captain and mate,) and that by the 'outside passage,' that is, through the Narrows, and proceeding to Amboy Bay, the vessel might be driven, (as was the case several times), to sea; and when the weather discouraged the crew or captain from attempting the outside passage, they went by the "Kills" or Auther Kull Sound, between Staten Island and the main land, which passage, sometimes, occupied three days, though ordinarily performed in one.

"A second way to Philadelphia was by crossing the Bay to Staten Island in a perriauger,* or pettyauga, a boat without keel, with two masts and two large sails, the lack of keel supplied by lee boards, all these managed by one man, who was likewise helmsman and very frequently drunk. In a gale of wind, you confided to this man and, perhaps, an assistant boy all your worldly hopes, including that of reaching Staten Island, which if you arrived at, you crossed the Ferry at Arthur Kull Sound, and a scow carried you to the "Blazing Star" (the sign of the Ferry House being a comet) at Woodbridge; from thence, you proceeded, crossing the Raritan in a scow at New Brunswick, and the Delaware in another at Trenton; another river was crossed in a floating bridge of planks, and on the third or fourth day you might arrive at Penn's city."

"The third and most common route was to cross the North River to Paulus Hook in a boat, similar to the above, called a perryauger, with same protection and guidance, but a shorter distance and less time for suffering. You then were dragged through marshes to Hackensack River, and was ferried over in a scow, then to Passaick River, and as before with no haste, ferried over, and then as above said, over three more rivers, and in about three days you might be set down at the "Indian Queen" in Philadelphia."

The same author, on page 197 of his appendix, shows the difficulties sometimes incident to this way of travelling: "On January 28th, 1768, Colonel Kalb, (known afterwards in American history as Baron De Kalb, and killed at battle of Camden), with eight others in crossing from the Blazing Star, New Jersey, to Staten Island, was the only person who escaped unin-

---

|| Prior to this time, a road had been laid out, and opened from what is now South Amboy, through by Cranberry to Bordentown, and through to Burlington.
¶ Doubtless at Cranbury
|| Bordentown.

* The late Commodore Vanderbilt, in his boyhood, followed this business between Staten Island and New York with such a boat.

jured, the rest either dying from suffering all night on a sand bar, where the scow sunk, or being more or less frozen, some losing toes, others feet. But Kalb, after being with the rest rescued from their perishing condition, instead of sitting with them by the fire, put his feet and legs in cold water, and took some refreshments, then went to bed and got up unhurt by the frost. One gentleman, a Mr. George, died before succour arrived."

But now to return to the County and Township matters. Nov. 16th, 1790, the legislature of the State enacted the following :[†] "That jurisdiction of this State in and over a lot of land situate at point of Sandy Hook, in County of Monmouth, containing four acres, on which light house and other buildings are erected shall be and same is hereby ceded to and vested in the United States of America forever."[‡]

In 1800, Monmouth county had the following townships: Middletown, Shrewsbury, Freehold, Upper Freehold, Dover and Stafford. Six township with a population of nineteen thousand eight hundred and seventy two persons. Feb. 23d, 1801, an act was passed "to divide the the township of Shrewsbury." "All that part of the township of Shrewsbury, in the County of Monmouth, lying within the following boundaries, to wit: Beginning at the main sea or ocean, in the middle of Shark River Inlet, and from thence running up the main stream thereof up along its several windings to a place called and known by the name of the Horse Pound ;[§] and from thence from a certain pine tree standing by the edge of the brook in the Horse Pound, lettered I. P., said to be the beginning corner of a tract of land, surveyed and returned for Joseph Potter, deceased, on a straight line, to the head spring of Mingumehone Branch, at the foot of Manhomony Hill, near the widow Harvey's house ; and from thence, on a straight line, to the most southerly corner of a tract of land, belonging to the Reverend Samuel Pyle|| called the Mill tract; from thence along said Pyle's southerly bound lines, till it meets the easterly bound line of the township of Freehold, and from thence along said line, southerly, until it meets the northerly bound line of the township of Dover ; and from thence, eastwardly, along the line of said township until it comes to the main ocean, and from thence along the same, northerly, to the place of beginning, shall be and the same is hereby set off from township of Shrewsbury, and the same is hereby established a separate township to be called by the name of The Township of Howell."¶ So named in honor of Richard Howell, who was then Governor of the State.

Feb. 28, 1844, the the township of Millstone was created by an act of the Legislature, as follows : "That all that part of the townships of Upper Freehold and Freehold, in the County of Monmouth, and of the township of Monroe, in the County of Middlesex, lying within the boundaries and descriptions following to wit, Beginning in the middle of the Mount Holly road, near Asher Smith's tavern,** and where the road to Preston's factory strikes the same, in the township of Freehold ; thence running along the middle of the road leading from the said Smith's tavern to Hannah Clayton's Inn, to where the public roads cross near the said Inn ;†† thence following the middle of the public road, northerly to a point opposite the dwelling house of William Osborn ; thence north, twenty nine degrees west to the county line, between Monmouth and Middlesex ; thence westerly, in a direct line, through the township of Monroe, in the County of Middlesex, to the bridge over the Millstone brook, on the public road, near Daniel D. Reed's dwelling house ; thence down the middle of the said Millstone brook, until it reaches the County line, between Mercer and Middlesex, at or near the head of Peter Wikoff's mill pond ;

---

† See Laws of New Jersey, by William Paterson, printed by Abraham Blauvelt, at New Brunswick, A. D. 1800.

‡ The light house on Sandy Hook was lighted for the first time on the night of January 18th, 1764.

§ Horse Pound, called so according to tradition, because at this place the Indians caught the horses and cattle of the first settlers, which ran wild in the woods, distinguished only by certain marks, which were entered in Township and County records. The Indians are said to have built a brush fence, in shape of a triangle, the apex at this place which was a bad mire hole or bog. This fence ran off a mile, diverging until the two lines were nearly a mile apart. The horses and cattle were driven in at the base, and following the fences down, came to the bog, were they mired and were easily captured.

|| This should be Rev Simon Pyle. He was a Minister of the Methodist Episcopal Church Preached during the first part of his life through Virginia, Maryland and South Jersey. Afterwards settled here as a farmer. Was also a local preacher. He was the father of Simon F. Pyle, the well-known surveyor at Jerseyville.

¶ Bloomfield's Laws, page 17, etc.

** Now called Smithburg, formerly Smithville.

†† Now Manalapanville.

thence southerly, following the said County line to the Monmouth County line; thence southwesterly following the said Monmouth County line to the bridge over the Assanpink brook, on the York road; thence up the middle of the said brook easterly, till it strikes the bridge on the land of Joseph I. Ely, son of Isaac Ely, deceased, in the middle of the new road leading from Hightstown to Britton's tavern, sometimes called the stone tavern; thence southerly in a direct line, to a point in the public road, one rod west of said Britton tavern; thence running as the needle now points, south, six degrees and thirty minutes east, over Sugar Loaf Hill, to the Ivanhoe or north branch of Lahaway creek; thence up the middle of said Ivanhoe, to its head, at a spring near the late residence of Elisha Karr, deceased; thence a due east course to the Mount Holly Road; thence northeasterly, along the middle of the said Mount Holly road to the place of beginning, shall be and hereby is set off from the said townships of Upper Freehold and Freehold in the County of Monmouth, and Monroe in the County of Middlesex, and made a separate township to be called and known by the name of "The township of Millstone," and all that part of the said township of Monroe, in the county of Middlesex, which lies within the above mentioned boundaries, shall be and the same is hereby attached to and made a part of the County of Monmouth, and shall be subject to all the laws which the County of Monmouth now is or may be subject to; and the said line shall hereafter be the boundary line between the said County of Monmouth and the County of Middlesex."*

The people of Middlesex did not seem to like this summary annexation of a part of their territory; so the very next year they procured the passage of a law restoring to Monroe township all the territory taken, and establishing the old boundary line between the two counties.†

After this, in 1847, some of the inhabitants of a little triangular piece of Monroe, in Middlesex, ambitious to become citizens of Monmouth, or dissatisfied with their situation, had part of this same boundary again changed, "to begin at the point in the Middlesex and Mercer County line, where the middle of the public road leading from Milford, by way of Disbor-

ough's northwest corner to Perrineville, crosses the same; and shall run thence along the middle of the said road, an easterly course, till it strikes the present Middlesex and Monmouth County line; the residue of the northern boundary line of the Township of Millstone, remaining as heretofore." That all that part of the township of Monroe, in the County of Middlesex, lying southward of the aforesaid bounds is annexed to said township of Millstone; also that said line shall hereafter be the boundary line between Monmouth and Middlesex counties.‡

In 1844, the township of Jackson, (so named in honor of President Jackson, and because its inhabitants were his staunch supporters), was set off by the following enactment: "All that part of the township of Upper Freehold, Freehold and Dover, in the County of Monmouth, lying within the boundaries and descriptions following, to wit: Beginning at Arneytown, at the junction of the New Egypt and Hornerstown roads; and running thence along the middle of the Hornerstown road to the Crosswick's Creek; thence down the middle of said creek to the mouth of the Lahaway; thence along the middle of the Lahaway, following the course of the north branch thereof (commonly called Ivanhoe) to its head; thence eastwardly across the township of Freehold, to the point where the north branch of the Metetecunck River crosses the line between the townships of Howell and Freehold; thence southwardly along the line between Howell and Freehold to the township of Dover; thence in a direct course to the southwest angle of the township of Upper Freehold, where the Slab bridge branch crosses the old province line; thence along the said line to the place of beginning."* The boundaries between Jackson and Millstone were altered in 1846. The southern boundary line of township of Millstone to commence "in the public road, one rod west of Britton's tavern, and shall run thence south, six degrees and thirty minutes east, as the needle pointed in February, 1844, over Sugar Loaf Hill to the Ivanhoe; and thence continue the same course to the middle of the Mount Holly Road; thence northeasterly, along the middle of the same, to the point in said road where the line of Millstone, at its formation struck

---

* Pamphlet Laws of N. J., 1844, page 140-1.
† Pam. Laws of 1845, page 148, etc.

‡ Pam. Laws of 1847, page 86.
* Pam. Laws of 1844, page 167.

the said road. And all that part of the township of Jackson lying northward of said bounds, is annexed to Millstone.† In 1845 Plumsted was erected into a township. That part of the township of Jackson lying west of a line, "beginning in the middle of the Lahaway Creek, where the public road crosses the same, near Moses Ivin's Grist Mill, and in the line dividing the townships of Upper Freehold and Jackson, and running thence, along the middle of said public road to Monmouth road, near Moses Ivin's dwelling house; and from thence, along the middle of the Manahawkin road, in a southwardly direction, to where the same intersects the line of the township of Dover."‡ In 1846 the township of Union was set off from Stafford and Dover as follows: All that part of the townships of Stafford and Dover lying within the following boundaries: "Beginning at the sea and running first, a due west course to the southerly point of Harvest point; thence north forty five degrees west, crossing the Bay to the main meadows; thence northeasterly, along the edge of the same to the north of Gunning River; thence up said river, its various courses, to the north of Fresh Creek; thence up said creek, its various courses, to the north line of a tract of land, known as the Fresh Creek Lot, now owned by the heirs or devisees of Samuel G. Wright, deceased, and others; thence westerly, along said line to the westerly end thereof; thence north, fifty two degrees and fifty minutes west, along a line known as the Ogden line, to a stone, being the second corner of a tract of land known as the Ogden tract; standing on a course north, ten degrees and twenty one minutes east, eight chains and seventy five links, from a large stone standing on Par's cabin knoll; thence northwesterly to the northwest corner of a tract of land that Joseph W. Pharo, deceased, purchased of the executors of Samuel Pharo, deceased; thence north, fifty degrees west, one hundred and eight chains and twenty seven links to a stone in west line of Sunmans'§ Patent; thence north seventy degrees west, to the Burlington county line; thence up and along said county line, to intersect with a due west course from the head of the main southerly branch of Cedar Creek, known as Factory branch; thence a due east course to the head of said Factory branch; thence down and along said branch and creek to the Bay; thence southerly along the edge of the same to the beginning."‖

The Legislature of New Jersey, March 12th, 1846, ceded to the United States the jurisdiction over that part of Sandy Hook, "lying north of an east and west line, through the mouth of Youngs Creek, at low water, and extending across the Island or Cape of Sandy Hook, from shore to shore, and bounded on all sides by the sea, and Sandy Hook Bay." The United States to retain jurisdiction only so long as they use these lands for military or public purposes. The civil and criminal laws to operate within this tract, so far as not incompatable with the use and enjoyment of the premises by the United States.¶

In 1847 the township of Atlantic was formed from Shrewsbury, Freehold and Middletown. The beginning of the boundaries is at the southwest corner of the township of Shrewsbury, where the Freehold, Shrewsbury and Howell township lines meet; thence running northerly, until it comes to the mouth of the road that leads through Jacob Conover's farm; thence northerly, following the middle of said road until it comes to the road near —— Hulse's house, which road leads to John J. Ely's mills; thence easterly, following the middle of said road, until it strikes Middle Hop Brook; thence easterly, down said brook, its various course until it comes to Swimming River Bridge; thence southerly, along the middle of the main road leading to Tinton Falls, until it comes to Haggerty's corner; thence southerly, until it strikes the Tinton Falls mill-pond brook; thence up the said brook, its various courses, until it comes to Pine Brook; thence up the said Pine Brook, until it strikes the Howell township line; thence westerly, along the line dividing the townships of Howell and Shrewsbury, to the Freehold line. the place of beginning."**

In 1848 three new townships were created. Marlborough, (so called on account of its marl beds), was taken from Freehold, as follows: "Beginning at the northwest corner of the township of Freehold in the line between the counties of Mid-

† Pamphlets Laws of 1846, page 120.
‡ Pamphlet Laws of 1845, page 60.
§ Sonmans it ought to be. Peter Sonmans was son of Arent Sonmans, only Hollander among the twenty-four proprietors of East Jersey.

‖ Pamphlet Laws of 1846, page 10–11.
¶ Pamphlet Laws of 1846, page 124.
** Pamphlet Laws of 1847, page 66–67.

dlesex and Monmouth, and at the point where the line of the townships of Middletown and Freehold meet; thence running along the line between the said townships of Freehold and Middletown, in a southeasterly direction until it comes to the line of Atlantic township, in said county of Monmouth, at the point in said line where the lines of the townships of Freehold, Middletown and Atlantic meet; thence along the line of Atlantic township in a southwesterly direction till it comes to a point opposite the house of William I. Sickles; thence leaving the said Atlantic line, and running westwardly, in a straight line, to the brook, near John Griggs' distillery; thence down said brook, its various courses, 'till it comes to a point four hundred yards west of David R. Vanderveer's house; thence northerly in a straight line, to a point one chain north of John F. Barricklo's house; thence westerly in a straight line to a point in the line of Middlesex County, lying one chain south of Richard Magie's house; thence down said line to the beginning."†† Manalopan township (old Indian name, meaning good corn-land), was also taken from Freehold township, "beginning at Asher Smith's tavern, at the southeast corner of the township of Millstone, in the road leading from Mount Holly to Freehold, and from thence running along the middle of said road, northwardly to the mouth of the road leading to Blacks Mills; thence in a northwardly course, to a stone planted in the middle of the road, leading from Englishtown to Freehold, said stone being the corner of the farms now owned by William T. Sutphin (formerly the parsonage farm of the First Presbyterian church of Freehold), and that of John E. Gordon; thence north, forty degrees and thirty seconds east, till it strikes the line of the township of Marlborough; thence along the southerly line of Marlborough, until it strikes the boundary line between the counties of Monmouth and Middlesex; thence following said boundary line southwardly to the northeast corner of the township of Millstone; thence along the southern boundary line of said township to the place of beginning."*

The Township of Raritan was set off from Middletown as follows: " Beginning at Tanner's Landing, on the shore of Raritan Bay; thence running southerly along the new road, near Thomas Arrowsmith's*1 to the road leading from the village of Middletown to Keyport; thence along the road by Daniel D. Hendrickson's, to the corner of John P. Luyster's and William H. Hendrickson's land; thence westerly to the road running by Hendrick V. Luyster*2; thence along the said road to the road leading from Middletown to Holmdel*3; thence along the road by John Golden to the corner of Ann Ogborn, deceased; thence following the road through Morrisville to the road leading from Holmdel to Leedsville*4; thence southerly to the Atlantic township line, between the lands of Joseph Conover, and Aaron VanMater; thence along the line of said Atlantic township, in a westerly direction to the line of Freehold township; thence following the line between Freehold and Middletown Townships to the line between the counties of Monmouth and Middlesex; thence down the said county line to Raritan Bay; thence along the shore of said Bay to the place of Beginning*5."

Thus the old township of Middletown was cut down to her present limits. In 1849, Feb. 24, an act was passed " to divide the township of Shrewsbury " as follows: The township of Shrewsbury shall be and hereby is divided into two townships by a line running as follows, to-wit: " Beginning at the mouth of Shrewsbury South river, and running up said river to Eatontown Landing Creek, to the east line of Jacob White's land; thence northerly along the line of land between Jacob White and Peter Castler to Parker's Creek; thence up said creek to the Eatontown Mill Brook; thence up said brook to sai mill; thence up the pond to a point where a line south, ten degrees west, will strike the road west of Asel Spinning's; thence on a straight line to the road leading from Eatontown to Shark River, where said road crosses Cranberry Brook; thence along said road as it runs across Jumping Brook, to the northwest

---

* (1) A Judge of Court of Errors and Appeals and a prominent politician in Monmouth at one time. One of his sons, George, became Colonel of a New York regiment, and was killed at the Battle of Gettysburg, while bravely leading his regiment.
*(2) This neighborhood called Holland; several Dutch families came from the west end of Long Island and bought out the original English settlers or their descendants in this vicinity, between 1690 and 1720.
*(3) Formerly Baptisttown.
*(4) Formerly Sandy New, afterwards Leedsville, named after an old settler, William Leeds, who came from Burlington county.
*(5)Pamphlet Laws of 1848, page 95.

†† Pamphlet Laws of 1848, page 48.
* Pamphlets Laws of 1848, page 199.

corner of Skullthorp's farm; thence on a straight line running west of the school house near John P.L. Tilton's to the Howell line. The northwesterly part to be called the township of Shrewsbury, and the southeasterly part to be called the township of Ocean*6." During the same session, that part of Upper Freehold was annexed to the township of Plumsted, which begins at "the mouth of Lahaway, at its junction with Crosswicks Creek; thence down the middle of said Crosswicks Creek to the Burlington County line; thence southwardly along the division line between the counties of Burlington and Monmouth to the northwest corner of the township of Plumsted, at Arneytown; thence along the middle of the Hornorstown road to the Crosswicks Creek; thence down the middle of said creek to the place of beginning*7." In 1850, Monmouth was shorn of the larger part of her territory by the erection of Ocean county.

Five whole townships, viz.: Stafford, Union, Dover, Jackson and Plumsted, and a part of Howell, were taken off. The words of the first section of the act, passed Feb. 15, 1850,*8 are as follows: "All that part of the County of Monmouth, contained within the following boundaries, viz.: Beginning at Manasquan inlet and mouth of Manasquan river; thence up the middle of said river, to the first bridge over the same; thence westerly to a corner on the south side of said river, near the old bridge; thence southwesterly, to the road leading to Jackson's Mills; thence along said road till it strikes the line between Howell and Jackson townships; thence along said line to the northeast corner of Jackson township; thence along the line between Jackson and Freehold townships, till it strikes the road leading from Freehold to Mount Holly; thence up the middle of said road to the Plumsted line; thence down said line to Moses Ivin's flood gate bridge, over the Lahaway creek, being the beginning corner of Plumsted township; thence following the Plumsted line, the several courses thereof, to the line between Burlington and Monmouth counties; thence along said line to the sea shore; thence along the sea to the place of beginning, be and the same is hereby erected into a separate county, to be called the County of Ocean; and the said lines shall hereafter be the division lines between the counties of Monmouth, Burlington and Ocean." After Ocean County was formed, Monmouth consisted of Middletown, Shrewsbury, Atlantic, Raritan, Marlborough, Freehold, Howell, Ocean, Manalapan, Millstone and Upper Freehold, eleven townships, with a population of thirty thousand two hundred and thirty-eight free persons, and seventy-five slaves*9.—In 1851 an act was passed which recites, that by the erection of Ocean County, and making the Freehold and Mount Holly road part of the boundary line between the two counties, a portion of Jackson township, lying north of said road, was left outside of the boundaries of any county, and that "all that part of the township of Jackson, lying north of the road leading from Freehold to Mount Holly, is set off and annexed to the township of Upper Freehold†1." In 1854, John L. Corlies, of Monmouth, Stacy B. Read, of Burlington, and Joseph Woodward, of Ocean County, were appointed by act of the Legislature to ascertain and mark the lines of partition between the County of Ocean and the counties of Burlington and Monmouth, and when ascertained to file their certificate of the line fixed in Secretary of State's office†2.

A supplement to this last act was passed in 1857. The preamble recites: "Whereas it appears that the commissioners appointed by the act of the Legislature, approved March 17, 1854, to ascertain, run and mark the boundary line between the counties of Burlington and Ocean, have not run and marked that portion of said line, from Crosswicks Creek, near Shelltown, to the north branch of Rancocas Creek, usually called Hartshorne's mill branch, a distance of between eleven and twelve miles, and running through the most populous and thickly settled part of the whole tract; and that the line determined upon, in the report of said commissioners, is at variance and greatly differs from the ancient landmarks, old monuments, original chartered limits, long established, well known and undisputed boundary along this section, between said counties; and that in consequence thereof, divers disputes and controversies have arisen and are likely to arise, with respect to the collection of taxes, and so forth, to the great inconvenience and disadvantage of the inhabitants between those places; therefore be it en-

---

*(6) Pamphlet Laws of 1849, pages 115 and 116.
*(7) Pamphlet Laws of 1849, page 299.
*(8) Pamphlet Laws of 1850, page 73.

*(9) Abstract of population, and statistics of New Jersey, annexed to Pamphlet Laws of 1852, page 9.
†(1) Pamphlet Laws of 1851, page 323.
†(2) Pamphlet Laws of 1854, page 451.

acted by the Senate and General Assembly of the State of New Jersey, 'That the line of partition between the said County of Ocean and the said County of Burlington, between the beginning and ending points hereinafter mentioned, shall be as follows, that is to say: Beginning at a point in the middle of the channel or watercourse of Crosswick's Creek, opposite a stone placed by the said commissioners, on the southerly side of said Creek, lettered "B," on west side, and "O," on the east side; which stone is distant three chains and fifty-three links, on a course south, thirty-one degrees and forty-eight minutes west, from a birch tree, near the southeast corner of the bridge, over said creek, usually called Fowler's Bridge, near and northwardly from the village of Shelltown; and from said point to run in a straight or right line over said stone, according to the original metes and bounds and ancient monuments, the general course of the road usually called the old Province line, or County line road, laid in eighteen hundred and four, as the said road is now opened from Shelltown to the road from New Egypt to Jacobstown; and to continue the general course of the said Province line road, until it strikes the soldier Joe corner stone, on the north side of Hockomic pond, a branch of Crosswicks Creek; and from that stone in a direct line, southerly to the stone near Hartshorne's Mill, placed by said commissioners; next southerly of the stone placed at or near Crosswick Creek†3. Monmouth County is affected by this act, because in 1869 "all that part of the Township of Plumsted, in the County of Ocean, lying north of the middle of the Monmouth and Mount Holly road," was annexed to and made part of the Township of Upper Freehold. The middle of said road being made the boundary line between Ocean and Monmouth counties†4.

In 1851 the township of Wall *1 (so named in honor of Garret D. Wall) was set off from the township of Howell, "all that part of the township of Howell lying within the following boundaries, to wit: beginning at the sea or ocean in the middle of Shark River Inlet; and from thence running up the middle of the main stream thereof, along its general windings, to a place called and known by the name of the Horse Pond, *2, to a certain pine tree standing by the edge of the brook, in said Horse Pond, lettered "I. P.," said to be the beginning of a tract of land returned to Joseph Potter, deceased; thence westerly along the line between the townships of Howell and Atlantic, sixty-one chains; thence southerly on a straight line to the mouth of Squancum brook; where it empties into Manasquan River on the south side thereof; thence from the mouth of the aforesaid Squancum brook south, three degrees and thirty minutes east, to the north line of Ocean county; thence northerly along said line to Manasquan River, near old Squan Bridge; thence down the middle of said river to the ocean at Manasquan inlet; thence northerly along the ocean to the beginning."

In 1857 two townships were set off from Raritan by one act. First, "All that part of the township of Raritan, contained within the following boundaries and lines, that is to say: Beginning in the centre of the public road leading from Arrowsmith's Mills to Tanners' Landing, and in the line between the townships of Raritan and Middletown, at the northeast corner of lands of John P. Smith; and from thence running in a southwesterly direction, in a straight line, to the bridge near Murphy's *3 Tan Yard, in the public road leading from Middletown to Middletown Point; thence westerly along the middle of the said road to the intersection of said road with the road leading from Holmdel to Brown's Point; thence southerly along the middle of the last named road to the intersection of said road with the road leading from Beers' corner to Mount Pleasant, near the residence of Ann Van Brackle; and thence running in a straight line, on a southerly course to the northeast corner of the township of Marlboro', near the dwelling house of Samuel Beers; thence along the division line between the township of Raritan and the townships of Marlboro' and Atlantic to the Middletown line; thence northerly along the division line, between the town-

---

†(3) Pam. Laws of 1857, page 477 and 8.
†(4) Pam. Laws of 1869, page 151.
*(1) Pam. law of 1851, page 191.
*(2) Should be " Horse Pound."

*(3) Formerly owned by Francis Murphy, once Judge of the Monmouth Pleas, and by his father, Timothy Murphy, who was a Justice of the Peace many years, and who also was a Judge of the Monmouth Pleas. The last was a school teacher at one time. Garret D. Wall went to school to him when a boy, and is said to have received many a thrashing at his hands to correct mischievous propensities. There Judge Joseph Murphy, now of Freehold, was born and reared. His brother, John G Murphy, went to Brooklyn. He was the father of Hon Henry C. Murphy, formerly Minister to Holland. and now a prominent public man in the State of New York Also author and translator of several historical works

ships of Raritan and Middletown to the place of beginning. The same is set off from the township of Raritan and made a separate township to be called Holmdel· Also, all that part of the township of Raritan, contained within the following boundaries and lines, that is to say, beginning in the division line between the townships of Marlboro' and Raritan, at the northeast corner of said township, of Marlboro' near the house of Samuel Beers; from thence running in a northerly direction, in a straight line, to the intersection of the road leading from Beer's corner to Mount Pleasant, with the road leading from Brown's Point to Holmdel; thence northerly along the centre of the last named road, to the intersection of said road, with the road leading from Mechanicsville to the Middletown Point and Keyport Plank Road; thence in a northwesterly direction, in a straight line to the mouth of Mohingson Creek, where it empties into Matawan Creek, and in the centre of said Matawan creek; thence down the middle of said Matawan creek to the mouth of said Matawan creek, where it empties into the Raritan Bay; thence along the shore of said Raritan Bay, to the division line between the counties of Monmouth and Middlesex, (being the division line between the township of Raritan and the said county of Middlesex) to the line of the township of Marlboro; thence easterly along the division line between the townships of Marlboro and Raritan to the place of beginning, is set off from the township of Raritan, and made a separate township to be called Matawan.*4.

The township of Holmdel 'was named after the Holmes's, several of whom were, now are, and have been, for generations, large land owners and influential men in this region.

From the first settlement of the county, down to the present time, many offices of honor and trust, in Monmouth, have been held by members of this family. With but few exceptions, the Holmes's have led honorable lives. been good citizens, and prospered in business.

Much of the progress of our county in agriculture has been due to the industry, and strong common sense, which have characterized them. For two centuries, the old families of Monmouth have intermarried with the Holmes's. At this time, perhaps, one-fourth of our inhabitants,

*(4.) Pamphlet Laws of 1857, page 29-30.

who are descendants of the English Baptist and Quaker settlers, and the Dutch, French, Huguenot and Scotch settlers of this county, are connected by ties of blood with the Holmes's. The Rev. Obadiah Holmes, second pastor of the old Baptist Church, at Newport, Rhode Island, was the ancestor of this family.

In the History of the Baptists, Vol. 1st, page 208, etc., by Isaac Backus, published in 1777, is an account of Rev. Obadiah Holmes, written by himself. He was one of the patentees in Nicoll's Patent, but like some others, never actually settled here. He made occasional visits from Rhode Island, and helped organize the Baptist Church at Middletown, which was the first of this sect in New Jersey, and either the third or fourth in America. Many of the Rhode Island Baptists were among the purchasers of "Newasunk, Navarumsunk and Pootapeck" as the Indian names of the region, from Raritan Bay to Shark River. are spelled on our early records. A list of those purchasers is entered in Book "A" bound with Books "C and D" of Deeds, in Monmouth Clerk's office. Many of the names of prominent men in Rhode Island, from 1646 to 1700, appear on this list. For example, the names of the following Presidents or Governors of Rhode Island, who were elected each year:

John Coggshall, Governor of Rhode Island in 1647-68, Walter Clark, Governor in 1676-86-99.

William Codington, Governor in 1683-85. He died in 1688. Henry Bull, Governor in 1685-90.

Also names of following Assistant or Lieutenant Governors of Rhode Island:

Job Allmy, William Reape, Edward Thurston, Daniel Gould, Joshua Coggshall, Christopher Allmy, Stephen Arnold, Edward Smith, Francis Brindley.

In a memorandum made by Roger Williams, in 1638, and published in Vol. 1, page 92, of Backus' History, he speaks of John Throckmorton,* William Arnold,

* This John Throckmorton was with Anna Hutchinson, at Westchester, N. Y. After she was killed by the Indians he still held his land and possessions by his sons in Westchester; but he was at Providence, Rhode Island, the most of his time, holding his citizenship there. It was often the case, in those days, for the same person to be put down as a citizen of two or three different places. This was done to hold lands and secure patents, which like Nicolls' patent required a certain number to settle within a limited time. Population being scant the names of persons were often entered on record as actual settlers when they were not. There was considerable dodging back and forth of this kind, between the Long Island towns and Monmouth.
† Book A, B, C, of Deeds.

OLD TIMES IN OLD MONMOUTH. 187

Thomas James. Robert Cole and Ezekiel Holliman as his friends and associates. All of these persons had sons among the early settlers viz: Stephen Arnold, Job and John Throckmorton, William James, Edward Cole, and Samuel Holliman. There were also many others from Rhode Island, as Richard and Benjamin Borden, Thomas Potter, Robert Carr, John Smith, Zachary Gant or Gaunt, Robert Hazard, etc., etc.

All the persons entered as purchasers in Book A of Deeds, did not actually settle. Some sent their sons or near relatives and some sold out or abandoned their shares.

Two of Rev. Obadiah Holmes's sons came over, Obadiah and Jonathan; the first only remained a few years and then went back to Rhode Island. Jonathan Holmes remained and was one of the first officials elected at a meeting† of the inhabitants of Middletown on "Newasunk Neck," and of Shrewsbury on "Navarumsunk Neck," held Dec. 19, 1667. The name is sometimes spelled "Hullmes" in the old records.

The Rev. Obadiah Holmes was a trusted and faithful leader of the Baptists of Rhode Island. He was a staunch, conscientous man, of profound religious convictions. Like many others of the day he suffered persecution on account of his faith at the hands of the intolerant and tyrannical Puritans of New England.— When sentenced by them to pay a fine for preaching Baptist doctrines, or be whipt, he refused to pay, although able to do so. He deemed a payment of the fine to be an acknowledgement of error, and he chose rather to suffer than " deny his Lord." The Plymouth Records show that he, with others, were presented by a Puritan Grand Jury, because of preaching the Baptist faith. The following is a true copy of the Court Record.

"At a General Court holden at New Plymouth, the second of October, 1650, before William Bradford, *gentleman*, Governor, Thomas Prince, William Collyare, Capt. Miles Standish, Timothy Hetherly, William Thomas, John Allen, *gentlemen*. Assistants (and a house of Deputies.) "Presentment by the Grand Inquest.*
October, second, 1650.
"Wee whose names are here underwritten, being the Grand Inquest, doe present to this Court, John Hazell, Mr. Edward Smith† and his wife, Obadiah Holmes, Joseph Tory and his wife, and the wife of James Man, William Deuell‡ and his wife, of the town of Rehoboth, for the continuing of a meeting upon the Lord's day from house to house, contrary to the order of this Court, enacted June 12, 1650.

THOMAS ROBINSON,
HENRY TOMSON,
etc., to the number 14."

What was done with them under this indictment, does not appear on record.

The next year, on July 19, 1651,§ John Clarke, Obadiah Holmes and John Crandal, being the representatives of the Baptist Church in Newport, at the request of William Witter, went to his house in Lynn, he being an old man, unable to go a long journey. While holding service here, two constables came and arrested them under a warrant issued by Robert Bridges. They appeared to be somewhat of Quakers, as they insisted on keeping their hats on in Court when brought before Bridges. He committed them to prison at Boston. The words of the commitment were as follows.||

"To the Keeper of the Prison at Boston :
By virtue hereof, you are required to take into your custody, from the constable of Lynn, or his deputy, the bodies of John Clarke, Obadiah Holmes and John Crandal, and them to keep until the next County Court to be held at Boston, that they may then and there answer to such complaints as may be alledged against them; for being taken by a constable at a private meeting at Lynn, upon the Lord's day, exercising among themselves, to whom divers of the Town repaired and joined with them, and that in the time of the public exercise of the worship of God ; as also for offensively disturbing the peace of the congregation, at their coming into the public meeting, in the time of prayer in the afternoon, and for saying and manifesting that the church in Lynn was not constituted according to the order of our Lord, and for such other things as shall be alledged against them, concerning their seducing and drawing others after their erroneous

---

* These men had never exercised any power in the Old World, and when invested with power in the wilderness of America, they were somewhat like the "Beggar on Horseback."

† Edward Smith's name appears in Book A, B, C, of Deeds, Monmouth records, as a purchaser.
‡ Query. Is the name Deuell the same name which is spelled in Monmouth Records, as Devell or Devill? The " U " and "V" of the old writers in our records are sometimes very similar.
§ Backus History, Vol. 1, page 215, etc.
|| Backus History, Vol. 1, page 218-19.

judgments and practices, and for suspicion of having their hands in rebaptizing of one or more among us, as also for neglecting or refusing to put in sufficient security for their appearance at the said Court. Hereof, fail not at your peril.
ROBERT BRIDGES."
July 31, 1651. John Clarke and Obadiah Holmes were brought before the Court¶ and sentenced to pay a fine or be " well whipt." Clarke's fine was paid. "John Crandal was fined five pounds only for being with the rest. He was released upon promise of appearing at their next Court, (*though they did not let him know when it was till it was over, and they then exacted the fine of the keeper*), and he with Mr. Clark returned home. Mr. Holmes was kept in prison till their Court met in the beginning of September, and then, after a public lecture in Boston, the sentence of Court was executed upon him."*1

Rev. Obadiah Holmes wrote an account of this as follows.*2

" Unto the well beloved brethren, John Spilsbury, William Kiffen, and the rest that in London stand fast in the faith, and continue to walk stedfastly in that order of the gospel which was once delivered unto the saints by Jesus Christ; Obadiah Holmes, an unworthy witness that Jesus is the Lord, and of late a prisoner for Jesus sake at Boston, sendeth greeting.

Dearly beloved and longed after,

" My heart's desire is to hear from you, and to hear that you grow in grace, and in the knowledge of our Lord and Saviour Jesus Christ, and that your love to him, and one unto another, as he hath given commandment, aboundeth, would be the very joy and great rejoicing of my soul and spirit. Had I not been prevented by my beloved brethren of Providence, who have wrote unto you, wherein you have my mind at large; and also by our beloved brother Clarke, of Rhode Island, who may, if God permit, see you, and speak with you mouth to mouth, I had here declared myself in that matter. but now I forbear; and because I have an experimental knowledge in myself, that in members of the same body, while it stands in union with the head, there is a sympathizing spirit, which passeth through, and also remaineth in each particular, so that one member can neither mourn nor rejoice, but all the members are ready to mourn and rejoice with it; I shall the rather impart unto you some dealings which I have had therein from the sons of men, and the gracious supports which I have had from the Son of God, my Lord and yours, that so like members you might rejoice with me, and might be encouraged, by the same experiment of his tender mercies, to fear none of those things which you shall suffer for Jesus sake. It pleased the Father of lights, after a long continuance of mine in death and darkness, to cause life and immortality to be brought to light in my soul, and also to cause me to see that this life was by the death of his Son, in that hour and power of darkness procured, which wrought in my heart a restless desire to know what the Lord, who had so dearly bought me, would have me to do, and finding that it was his last will (to which none is to add, and from which none is to detract) that they which had faith in his death for life, should yield up themselves to hold forth a lively consimilitude or likeness unto his death, burial and resurrection, by that ordinance of baptism, I readily yielded thereto, being by love constrained to follow the Lamb, (that takes away the sins of the world), whithersover he goes. I had no sooner separated from their assemblies, and from communion with them in their worship of God, and thus visibly put on Christ, being resolved alone to attend upon him, and to submit to his will, but immediately the adversary cast out a flood against us, and stirred up the spirits of men to present myself and two more to Plymouth Court, where we met with four petitions against our whole company to take some speedy course to suppress us; one from our own plantation, with 35 hands to it; one from the church, as they call it, at Taunton; one from all the ministers in our colony, except two, if I mistake not, and one from the Court at Boston, in the Massachusetts, under their Secretary's hand; whereupon the Court straitly charged us to desist, and neither to ordain officers, nor to baptize, nor to break bread together, nor yet to meet upon the first day of the week; and having received these strait charges, one of the three discovers the sandy foundation upon which he stood, who, when the flood came and the wind blew, fell, yet it pleased the Frther of mercies (to whom be the praise) to give us strength to stand, and to tell them it was better to obey God than man; and such was the grace of our God to us-

¶ John Endicott, Governor, presided.
*1 Backus' Histery, Vol. 1, page 228.
*2 Backus' History, Vol. 1, page 229, etc.

OLD TIMES IN OLD MONMOUTH. 189

ward, that though we were had from Court to Court, yet were we firmly resolved to keep close to the rule, and to obey the voice of our Lord, come what will come.

" Not long after these troubles I came upon occasion of business into the colony of the Massachusetts, with two other brethren, as brother Clarke being one of the two can inform you, where we three were apprehended, carried to Boston, and so to the Court, and were all sentenced ; what they laid to my charge, you may here read in my sentence *1, upon the pronouncing of which, as I went from the bar, I expressed myself in these words : I bless God, I am counted worthy to suffer for the name of Jesus. Whereupon John Wilson (their pastor, as they call him) struck me before the judgment seat, and cursed me, saying, the curse of God or Jesus go with thee *2 ; so we were carried to the prison, where not long after I was deprived of my two loving friends, at whose departure the adversary stepped in, took hold of my spirit, and troubled me for the space of an hour, and then the Lord came in, and sweetly relieved me, causing me to look to himself, so was I stayed, and refreshed in the thoughts of my God ; and

---
*1 " The sentence of Obadiah Holmes, of Seaconk, the 31st of the 5th m. 1651.
" Forasmuch as you Obadiah Holmes. being come into this jurisdiction about the 21 of the 5 m. did meet at one Wm. Witter's house, at Lynn, and did here privately (and at other times, being an excommunicate person. did take upon you to preach and baptize) upon the Lord's day, or other's days, and being taken then by the constable, and coming afterward to the assembly at Lynn, did, in disrespect to the ordinance of God and his worship, keep on your hat, the pastor being in prayer, insomuch that you would not give reverence in vailing your hat, till it was forced off your head, to the disturbance of the congregation, and professsing against the institution of the church, as not being according to the gospel of Jesus Christ ; and that you, the said Obadiah Holmes. did, upon the day following, meet again at the said Wm. Witter's, in contempt to authority, you being then in the custody of the law, and did there receive the sacrament. being excommunicate, and that you did baptize such as were baptized before, and thereby did necessarily deny the baptism that was before administered to be baptism, the churches no churches, and also other ordinances, and ministers, as if all were a nullity ; and also did deny the lawfulness of baptizing of infants ; and all this tends to the dishonor of God, the despising the ordinances of God among us, the peace of the churches, and seducing the subjects of this commonwealth from the truth of the gospel of Jesus Christ, and perverting the strait ways of the Lord, the Court doth fine you 30 pounds, to be paid, or sufficient sureties that the said sum shall be paid by the first day of the next Court of Assistants, or else to be well whipt, and that you shall remain in prison till it be paid, or security given in for it. By the Court,
INCREASE NOWELL.
*2 " Mr Wilson is represented by his cotemporaries as one of the most humble, pious and benevolent men of the age." *Massachusetts History*, vol. 1, p. 258. But when that darling p int, *infant sprinkling*, was in danger, see how it makes the most benevolent act like cruel persecutors !"—Note by Isaac Backus.

---

although during the time of my imprisonment the tempter was busy, yet it pleased God so to stand at my right hand, that the motions were but sudden, and so vanished away ; and although there were that would have paid the money if I would ac cept it, yet I durst not accept of deliverance in such a way, and therefore my answer to them was, that although I would acknowledge their love to a cup of cold water, yet could I not thank them for their money, if they should pay it So the Court drew near, and the night before I should suffer according to my sentence, it pleased God I rested and slept quietly ; in the morning my friends come to visit me, desiring me to take the refreshment of wine, and other comforts ; but my resolution was not to drink wine, nor strong drink that day until my punishment was over; and the reason was, lest in case I had more strength, courage and boldness than ordinarily could be expected, the world should either say he is drunk with new wine, or else that the comfort and strength of the creature hath carried him through ; but my course was this : I desired brother John Hazel to bear my friend's company, and I betook myself to my chamber, where I might communicate with my God, commit myself to him, and beg strength from him. I had no sooner sequestered myself, and come into my chamber, but Satan lets fly at me, saying, Remember thyself, thy birth, breeding, and friends, thy wife, children, name and credit : but as this was sudden, so there came in sweetly from the Lord as sudden an answer 'Tis for my Lord, I must not deny him before the sons of men (for that were to set men above him) but rather loose all, yea wife, children, and mine own life also. To this the tempter replies, Oh but that is the question, is it for him ? and for him alone ? is it not rather for thy own, or some other's sake ? thou hast so professed and practiced. and now art loth to deny it ; is not pride and self in the bottom ? Surely this temptation was strong, and thereupon I made dilligent search after the matter, as formerly I had done. and after a while there was even as it had been a voice from heaven in my very soul bearing witness with my conscience, that it was not for any man's case or sake in this world, that so I had professed and practiced, but for my Lord's case and sake, and for him alone ; whereupon my spirit was much refreshed ; as also in the consideration of these three scriptures, which speak on this wise, Who shall lay any thing to the charge of God's elect? Although I walk through the valley and shadow of death I will fear no evil, thy rod and thy staff they shall comfort me. And he that continueth to the end, the same shall be saved.

But then came in the consideration of the weakness of the flesh to bear the strokes of a whip, though the spirit was willing, and thereupon I was caused to pray earnestly unto the Lord, that he would be pleased to give me a spirit of courage and boldness, a tongue to speak for him, and strength of body to suffer for his sake, and not to shrink or yield to the strokes, or shed tears, lest the adversaries of the truth should thereupon blaspheme and be hardened, and the weak and feeble-hearted discouraged, and for this I sought the Lord earnestly; at length he satisfied my spirit to give up, as my soul so my body to him, and quietly to leave the whole disposing of the matter to him; and so I addressed myself in as comely a manner as I could, having such a Lord and Master to serve in this business. And when I heard the voice of my keeper come for me, even chearfulness did come upon me, and taking my testament in my hand, I went along with him to the place of execution, and after common salutation there stood. There stood by also one of the magistrates, by name Increase Nowell, who for a while kept silent, and spoke not a word, and so did I, expecting the governor's presence, but he came not. But after a while Mr. Nowel bade the executioner do his office; then I desired to speak a few words, but Mr. Nowel answered, it is not now a time to speak.— Whereupon I took leave, and said, men, brethren, fathers and countrymen, I beseech you give me leave to speak a few words, and the rather because here are many spectators to see me punished, and I am to seal with my blood, if God give strength, that which I hold and practice in reference to the word of God, and the testimony of Jesus; that which I have to say in brief is this. Although I confess I am no disputant, yet seeing I am to seal what I hold with my blood, I am ready to defend it by the word, and to dispute that point with any that shall come forth to withstand it. Mr. Nowel answered me, now was no time to dispute. Then said I, then I desire to give an account of the faith and order I hold, and this I desired three times, but in comes Mr. Flint, and saith to the executioner, *Fellow, do thine office, for this fellow would but make a long speech to delude the people.*[3] So I being resolved to speak, told the people; that which I am to suffer for is the word of God, and testimony of Jesus Christ. No, saith Mr. Nowel, it is for your error, and going about to seduce the people. To which I replied, not for error, for in all the time of my imprisonment, wherein I was left alone (my brethren being gone) which of all your ministers in all that time came to convince me of an error; and when upon the governor's words r motion was made for a public dispute, and upon fair terms so often renewed, and desired by hundreds, what was the reason it was not granted? Mr. Nowel told me, it was his fault that went away, and would not dispute; but this the writings will clear at large. Still Mr. Flint calls to the man to do his office; so before, and in the time of his pulling off my cloaths I continued speaking, telling them, that I had so learned, that for all Boston I would not give my body into their hands thus to be bruised upon another account, yet upon this I would not give the hundredth part of a [4] *wampum peaque* to free it out of their hands, and that I made as much conscience of unbuttoning one button, as I did of paying the £30 in reference thereunto. I told them moreover, the Lord having manifested his love towards me, in giving me repentance towards God and faith in Jesus Christ, and so to be baptized in water by a messenger of Jesus into the name of the Father, Son and Holy Spirit, wherein I have fellowship with him in his death, burial and resurrection, I am now come to be baptized in afflictions by your hands, that so I may have further fellowship with my Lord, and am not ashamed of his sufferings, for by his stripes am I healed.

"And as the man began to lay the strokes upon my back, I said to the people, though my flesh should fail, and my spirit should fail, yet my God would not fail. So it pleased the Lord to come in, and so to fill my heart and tongue as a vessel full, and with an audible voice I broke forth, praying unto the Lord not to lay this sin to their charge; and telling the people, that now I found he did not fail me, and therefore now I should trust him forever who failed me not; for in

*[3] Thomas Flint was chosen one of their magistrates in 1643.
*[4] A *wampum peaque*, is the sixth part of a penny with us.—Notes by Isaac Backus.

truth, as the strokes fell upon me, I had such a spiritual manifestation of God's presence as the like thereof I never had nor felt, nor can with fleshly tongue express; and the outward pain was so removed from me, that indeed I am not able to declare it to you, it was so easy to me, that I could well bear it, yea, and in a manner felt it not, although it was grievous, as the spectators said, the man striking with all his strength, (yea, spitting in his hand three times, as many affirmed), with a three-corded whip, giving me therewith thirty strokes. When he had loosed me from the post, having joyfulness in my heart, and cheerfulness in my countenance, as the spectators observed, I told the magistrates, you have struck me as with roses; and said moreover, although the Lord hath made it easy to me, yet I pray God it may not be laid to your charge.

"After this many come to me rejoicing to see the power of the Lord manifested in weak flesh; but sinful flesh takes occasion hereby to bring others in trouble, informs the magistrates hereof, and so two more are apprehended as for contempt of authority; their names were John Hazel and John Spur, who came indeed and did shake me by the hand, but did use no words of contempt or reproach unto any; no man can prove that the first spoke anything, and for the second, he only said thus, blessed be the Lord; yet these two tor taking me by the hand, and thus saying after I had received my punishment, were sentenced to pay 40 shillings, or to be whipt. Both were resolved against paying their fine; nevertheless after one or two days imprisonment, one paid John Spur's fine, and he was released; and after six or seven days imprisonment of brother Hazel, even the day when he should have suffered, another paid his, and so he escaped, and the next day went to visit a friend about six miles from Boston, where the same day he fell sick, and within ten days ended his life. When I was come to the prison, it pleased God to stir up the heart of an old acquaintance of mine, who with much tenderness, like the good Samaritan, poured oil into my wounds, and plastered my sores;*2 but there was present information given what was done, and inquiry made who was the surgeon, and it was commonly reported he should be sent for, but what was done I yet know not. Now thus it hath pleased the Father of mercies so to dispose of the matter, that my bonds and imprisonments, have been no hindrance to the Gospel, for before my return, some submitted to the Lord, and were baptized, and divers were put upon the way of inquiry. And now being advised to make my escape by night, because it was reported that there were warrants forth for me, I departed; and the next day after, while I was on my journey, the constable came to search at the house where I lodged, and so I escaped their hands, and was by the good hand of my heavenly Father brought home again to my near relations, my wife and eight children. The brethren of our town, and Providence having taken pains to meet me four miles in the woods where we rejoiced together in the Lord. Thus have I given you as briefly as I can, a true relation of things; wherefore my brethren rejoice with me in the Lord, and give glory to him, for he is worthy, to whom be praise forevermore; to whom I commit you, and put up my earnest prayers for you, that by my late experience who have trusted in God and have not been deceived, you may trust in him perfectly. Wherefore my dearly beloved brethren, trust in the Lord, and you shall not be confounded; so I also rest, Yours in the bond of charity,
OBADIAH HOLMES."*3

Mr. John Spur, an eye-witness, gives also an account of the sentence.

"Mr. Cotton in his sermon immediately before the Court gave their sentence against Mr. Clarke, Obadiah Holmes, and John Crandall, affirmed, that denying infant baptism would overthrow all, and this was a capital offence; and therefore they were foul-murtherers. When therefore the governor, Mr. John Endicot, came into the Court to pass sentence against them, he said thus, you deserve to die, but this we agreed upon, that Mr. Clarke shall pay £20 fine, and Obadiah Holmes, £30 fine, and John Crandal £5 and to remain in prison until their fines be either paid or security given for them, or else they are all of them to be well whipped. When Obadiah Holmes was brought forth to receive his sentence, he desired of the magistrates, that he might hold forth the ground of his practice; but they refused to let him speak, and commanded the

---

*2 In a manuscript of Governor Joseph Jenck's, wrote near 50 years ago, he says; "Mr. Holmes was whipt thirty stripes, and in such an unmerciful manner, that in many days, if not some weeks, he could take no rest but as he lay upon his knee- and elbows, not being able to suffer any part of his body to touch the bed whereon he lay. But Mr. Clarke being a scholar bred, a friend of his, paid his fine."—Note of Isaac Backus.

*3 Clarke's narrative, p. 16—23.—Note of Isaac Backus.

whipper to do his office; then the whipper began to pull off his cloaths, upon which Obadiah Holmes said, Lord lay not this sin unto their charge; and so the whipper began to lay on with his whip; upon which Obadiah Holmes said, O Lord, I beseech thee to manifest thy power in the weakness of thy creature. He neither moving nor stirring at all for their strokes, brakes out in these expressions, blessed and praised be the Lord, and thus he carried it to the end, and went away rejoicingly; I John Spur being present, it did take such an impression in my spirit to trust in God, and to walk according to the light, that God had communicated to me, and not to fear what man could do unto me, that I went to the man (being inwardly affected with what I saw and heard) and with a joyful countenance took him by the hand when he was from the post, and said, praised be the Lord; and so I went along with him to the prison; and presently that day there was information given to the Court what I had said and done; and also a warrant*4 granted out that day to arrest both myself and John Hazel, which was executed on the morrow morning upon us, and so we were brought to the Court and examined. The governor, John Endicot, asked me concerning Obadiah Holmes, according as he was informed by old Mr. Cole, and Thomas Buttolph, of my taking him by the hand and smiling, and I did then freely declare what I did, and what I said, which was this: Obadiah Holmes, said I, I do look upon as a godly man; and do affirm that he carried himself as did become a Christian, under so sad an affliction; and his affliction did so affect my soul, that I went to him being from the post, and said, blessed be the Lord. But said the governor, what do you apprehend concerning the cause for which he suffered? my answer was, that I am not able to judge of it; then said the governor, we will deal with you as we have dealt with him. I said unto him again, I am in the hands of God. Then Mr. Symonds a magistrate said, you shall know that *you are in the hands of men.* The governor then said, keeper, take him, and so I was presently carried away to preson.

"The next day about one of the clock I was sent for again into the Court; the governor (being about to go out of the Court when I came in) delivered his speech to me; said he, you must pay 40 shillings or be whipped. I said then to those of the Court that remained, tnat if any man suffer as a Christian let him glorify God in this behalf. Then I desired to know what law I had broken, and what evil I had done? but they produced no law, only they produced what the two witnesses had sworn against me.*5 My speech thereto was this; My practice and carriage is allowed by the word of God, for it is written in Rom. 12. *Be like affectioned one towards another, rejoice with them that rejoice;* and it is contrary to my judgment and conscience to pay a penny. Then said Mr. Bendal, I will pay it for him, and there presented himself. I answered then and said, I thanked him for his love, but did believe it was no acceptable service for any man to pay a penny for me in this case; yet notwithstanding the Court accepted of his profer, and bid me be gone, then John Hazel to be examined. JOHN SPUR."*6

Rev. Obadiah Holmes died at Newport. Rhode Island, Oct. 15, 1682. aged 76 years. He was buried on a farm he owned at Middletown, Rhode Island.

The name of the Township of Holmdel, in Monmouth County, is, therefore, a lasting memorial of this "good and true man," who was a martyr of the Baptist faith.

To return to county affairs:

The period from 1850 to 1877 may be termed the era of turnpikes and railroads in the county.

From 1848 to 1856, a number of plankroad companies were incorporated, but only three were actually built.

" The Freehold and Howell," on the old highway from Freehold to a point this side of Blue Ball. This was chiefly for the benefit of the marl carters, from Squankum pits to Freehold. This traffic em-

---

*4 *To the keeper or his deputy.*
By virtue hereof you are to take into your custody, and safe keeping the body of John Spur for a heinous offence by him committed, hereof fail not. Dated the 5th of the 7th month, 1651. Take also into your safe keeping John Hazel.
By the Court. INCREASE NOWEL.

*5 J— Cole being in the market place, when Obadiah Holmes came from the whipping post, John Spur came and met him presently, laughing in his face saying, Blessed be God for thee brother, and so did go with him, laughing upon him up towards the prison, which was very grievous to me to see him harden the man in his sin, and shewing much contempt of authority by that carriage, as if he had been unjustly punished, and had suffered as a righteous man under a tyrannical government. Deposed before the Court, the 5th of the 7th month. INCREASE NOWEL.

I, Thomas Buttolph, did see John Spur come to Obadiah Holmes, so soon as he came from the whipping post, laughing in his face, and going along with him toward the prison to my great grief to see him harden him in his sin, and to shew such contempt of authority. Deposed the 5th of the 7th month, 1651, before the Court.
INCREASE NOWEL.

*6 Narrative p. 26—28—Note by Isaac Backus.

ployed a great many men and teams; long lines of wagons could be met almost at any time, between Freehold and Our House Tavern. The construction of the Freehold and Squankum railroad afterwards broke up the business.

The Monmouth County plank road company constructed a plank road on the highway from Freehold by way of Matawan, as now called, to Keyport. This was the first one built, and was considered a great enterprise; although some of the descendants of the old Dutch land owners along the route thought their liberties were greatly infringed when they were required to pay toll for riding on the old highways their fathers built, through their own lands. To assert their rights a number of them, armed with axes, publicly cut down the gates between Freehold and Keyport.

The third plank road was built from Port Monmouth (as that part of Shoal Harbor was then for the first time named,) through Chanceville, now New Monmouth, to Middletown village. William Morford, David Luyster, Samuel I. Taylor, Charles Morford and George C. Murray, were constituted a body corporate to build a plank road from the dock of the Port Monmouth Transportation Company to Middletown village.*1

A long dock was built out over the clam ming ground to deep water, a little east of the late railroad dock. The steamboat *Eagle* was built, and ran from this dock, carrying passengers and farming produce to New York City. The expenses and leakages were greater than the profits, and so the plank road and dock went down a number of years ago; scarcely a vestige is now left.

Before the days of the plank road and steamboat *Eagle*, Compton's Creek, on the Bay side, and Tylee Conover's dock on the river side, were the principal ports for the farmers of Middletown to send their produce, by sloops, to New York; and before this, Tanner's Landing, at Waykake, was the principal port.

There was also, in 1852, a plank road company incorporated to build a road from Florence, on the river Delaware, to Union, on the Raritan Bay, below Keyport. This was the work of a land speculator from New York, named Lloyd. He had become the owner of quite a large tract of the low meadow lands and sandy uplands in this vicinity. He put up a number of cheap houses, built a steam saw mill and basin, a dock, hotel, and some other flimsy but showy structures. The plank road was to be built to Delaware river and connect by steamboat with Philadelphia.—(About two miles of plank road from Union to Keyport was actually constructed). He also had a steamboat running from his dock at Union, to New York. It was given out that Union would be a great city, and all who bought lots would soon get rich.

Only a few hapless victims took the bait. The original Waykakers, noted for their "cuteness," did not invest.

Plank roads, by experience, were found to be unprofitable, and they soon gave way to our present turnpike roads.

In 1851 the act of incorporation was procured under which the first railroad in the county was built. This was the great event of the time.

John C. Cox, Henry Bennett, Joseph Combs, Aaron Gulick, Richard McDowell, and such other persons as thereafter might be associated with them, were constituted a body corporate, by the name of the Freehold and Jamesburg Agricultural Railroad Company, to build a "railroad from the village of Freehold, to the railroad running from New Brunswick to Trenton, crossing the Camden and Amboy railroad at Jamesburg, and intersecting the railroad running from New Brunswick to Trenton, at or near Dean's Pond."*2 This road was built as far as Jamesburg, and then the people of Freehold considered themselves the "Hub" of the county, as they could get to New York city, by way of South Amboy, in about three or four hours.

The next railroad built was authorized by an act of incorporation passed March 3d, 1854.

William Haight and Samuel W. Jones, of Monmouth; Washington McKean and William Torry, of Ocean county; Thomas H. Richards and George McHenry, of Burlington county; Jonathan Pitney and Edward Taylor, of Atlantic; Edmund L. B. Wales and Samuel S. Marcy, of Cape May county, were incorporated by the name of The Raritan and Delaware Bay Railroad Company, to construct a railroad from some point on the Raritan Bay, eastward of Keyport, to the village of Toms River in Ocean county, and thence to May's Landing, in Atlantic county; and thence

---

*1 Pam. Laws of 1854, page 195.   *2 Pam. Laws of 1851, page 201.

through the counties of Atlantic and Cape May to Cape Island on the Atlantic Ocean.*3

A very long dock of nearly a mile, or 4,800 feet, was by additions at different times finally built out over the Shoal Harbor flats just west of where the old dock, connected with the Port Monmouth and Middletown plank road, had stood. From the end of this dock the railroad ran through the township of Middletown, just east of Hedden's Corner, crossing Shrewsbury township, and a corner of Atlantic township, to Huckleberry Hill in Wall township; thence into Howell township to the village of Farmingdale, formerly Upper Squankum; thence through Howell township by Lower Squankum to Bricksburg, in Ocean county.

The Torrey family was mainly instrumental in building this road. They owned large tracts of pine barrens in Ocean county, which this road opened, and they were enabled to sell and did sell, chiefly to New Englanders.

Red Bank, Eatontown, Long Branch and all this section of Monmouth, was greatly helped by the railroad. The people of Red Bank especially, began to dispute the palm of being the "Hub" with Freehold, and wanted a Court House and Jail. A branch railroad was built from Eatontown Junction to Long Branch.

In 1870, the Raritan and Delaware Bay Railroad having been sold under a foreclosure, an act was passed, which, among other things, changed its name to the New Jersey Southern Railroad Company.*4— Jay Gould's manipulations with this road led to the appointment of a receiver by the Court of Chancery. Even the employees on the road were unpaid. The feeling was so bitter against Gould, that threats were openly made at one time, to burn down the East End Hotel at Long Branch, which he controlled, and his oceanside cottage near there.

In 1856 an act incorporating the Long Branch and Sandy Hook railroad company was passed. This road was afterwards constructed from near the point of Sandy Hook to Long Branch so close to the ocean beach in some places, that the surf blends with the rattle of the cars and the shriek of the locomotive whistle; and at times in high tides the waves have washed over the track.- When the road was built the people of Long Branch were jubilant, and fondly deemed their place the first in the county. They, too, began to ask for a Court House and Jail.

When the *Plymouth Rock*, enlivened by bands of music, and commanded by Col. James Fisk, of Black Friday and Stokes fame, ran from the terminus of the road at Sandy Hook to New York, this railroad company saw its best days.

In 1864 The Pemberton and Hightstown Railroad Company was incorporated, with authority to build a railroad from Pemberton in Burlington county, and passing through the villages of Wrightstown and Cooktown in Burlington county, the villages of New Egypt and Hornerstown in Ocean county, of Fillmore and Imlaystown in Monmouth, and ending at Hightstown. The construction of this railroad diverted a great deal of traffic and travel off towards Jamesburg and Hightstown, which ought to have been retained within the county.

A railroad ought long ago to have been built from Mount Holly through Upper Freehold, Millstone, by Freehold, to Matawan or Keyport. This is the natural route for the people of Monmouth, and would give easy access both to New York and Philadelphia.

The old Camden and Amboy lawyers and agents, formerly, and the Pennsylvania Central R. R's. lawyers and agents, since, have either, by open or secret means, prevented the construction of such a road. The monopoly did not want a rival or competing road through the State, and therefore crushed in the bud whatever looked like such an enterprise.

In 1857 two turnpike companies were incorporated. The first to build a 'pike from Red Bank to Shrewsburytown, and the second to build a 'pike from Shrewsburytown to Colts Neck, by way of Tinton Falls.*5

Only one of these roads was built under these charters; that from Red Bank to Shrewsburytown on the old highway.— This was about the beginning of a great many turnpike charters, obtained during different years, down to 1876. Under these charters turnpikes have been constructed, principally on the old highways, all around and in and through the county to all the towns and villages of any importance.

While these turnpikes are a great improvement, and should be encouraged and kept up, still they should be compelled to

---

*3 Pam. Laws of 1854, page 214.
*4 Pam. Laws of 1870, page 230.

*5 Pam. Laws of 1857, pages 272-345.

OLD TIMES IN OLD MONMOUTH. 195

live up to the requirements of their charters. Of late years many have been suffered to get out of order. That is, not kept up in the hard and solid condition the law compels and the people demand.

Bad roads are a great disadvantage, but when it comes to paying for the privilege of riding over miserable roads, the people ought not to submit for a moment to such imposition. At this time, either through carelessness, poverty or meanness, some of our turnpike roads are in no better condition than the old, free highways.— There is " neither rhyme nor reason " in paying toll on a poor turnpike.

In 1867 a charter for the first horse railroad company was obtained, to build such a road from Matawan to Keyport, along or on the Monmouth county plank road *6 Afterwards, a similar charter for such a road within the corporate limits of Long Branch, was procured.*7 Neither of these horse railroads have been built, but no doubt, in the future, we shall have a number of them in our county.

The next railroad built was the Freehold and Squankum, and then the Farmingdale and Squan Village, which railroads connected Wall, Howell, Freehold and Manalapan townships.

The Monmouth County Agricultural Railroad Company was incorporated in 1867, to build a railroad from Freehold by way of the village of Matawan to the village of Keyport.†1 This is the famous railroad which has wearily dragged its slow length through so many years. The road of strife, contention and intrigue.— Partly graded it has mocked the hopes and disappointed the people of all the western townships of Monmouth for many years. It is the road the people of Freehold, Marlborough, Manalapan, Millstone and Upper Freehold need. Of the last importance to their interests and future welfare. By ways that are dark the completion of this road has been delayed a long time. If this road is built, and then extended to Upper Freehold, the county will be fully supplied with railroad facilities. In 1867 the first municipality, or incorporated town, was established under the name of the " Long Branch Police, Sanitary and Improvement Commission." A very high sounding and pretentious title, which created great expectations. The limits in which this machine was to do its work was bounded north by the road running from Branchport to Atlanticville, south by Thompson's pond, east by the Atlantic ocean and west by a line running parallel with the coast and one third of a mile west from high water mark.†2

In 1869 the village of Freehold was incorporated; next in 1870 Keyport and Red Bank. The people of these towns must exercise " eternal vigilance " or their taxes some day will be a burden, which will equal the rents of half a century ago.

In 1872 the Navesinck Bridge Company was chartered to build a draw bridge, from a point at Highlands of Navesinck to the sea beach on Sandy Hook, across the Navesinck River.†3 After Shrewsbury and South Shrewbury unite, the stream is properly the Navesinck River, from there to the Bay.

In 1867 the township of Lincoln was erected, as follows: "That the township of Ocean, in the county of Monmouth, shall be hereby divided into two townships by a line running as follows, to wit :" Beginning at the mouth of Peter Reynold's Mill Brook, where it empties into Shark River, and running up said brook to said mill, thence a straight line northeasterly to the southwest corner of Elisha J. Morrison's farm, by a bridge over a stream which empties in Great Pond ; thence down the said stream, to the aforesaid Pond, and around the same to the north side thereof, to the southeast corner of Jeremiah White's farm, being also the southwest corner of the farm of Garret Vanderveer; thence along the line of said White and Vanderveer, due north to the Deal road leading from thence, to the Eatontown and Long Branch turnpike road, by Elisha Lippincott's store; thence along said Deal road to a cross road at the foot of Negro Hill, near the Methodist Episcopal Church, leading to Lane and Corlies' store; thence along the middle of said cross road to a stone planted for the northwest corner of John Levey's farm, being also the northeast corner of the farm of, late James T. Woolley, deceased; thence north nine degrees east to the Turtle Mill brook; thence down the said brook and creek to the southeast corner of George Hance's farm; thence along the east line of said farm to the northeast corner thereof, being a corner of lands belonging to William Morris; thence north, thirty-five and a half degrees west, of South Shrewsbury River,

---
*6 Pam. Laws of 1867, page 498.
*7 Pam Laws of 1874, page 743.
†1 Pam. Law of 1867, page 574.

†2 Pam. Laws of 1867, page 976.
†3 Pam. Laws of 1872, page 251.

being the Shrewsbury township line; the easterly part to be called the township of Ocean and the westerly part the township of Lincoln.†4 This division, as a glance at the map will show, made two long straggling townships, with a boundary line between as crooked as a worm fence.

This irregular line took in Republican voters and left out Democratic voters, for the object in the creation of this new township of Lincoln was purely partizan. It excited the Democrats to such an extent that at the first town meeting they made an extraordinary effort and elected the Democratic ticket. The next year the act making this division was repealed †5 and so the township of Lincoln perished in its infancy.

In 1868 the last and most important railroad charter was obtained, viz: The New York and Long Branch Railroad, to construct a railroad from a point at the village of South Amboy, in Middlesex County, to any point on the line of the Raritan and Delaware Bay, north of Eatontown, with the privilege of extending the same to Long Branch in the County of Monmouth.†6 The next year a supplement was passed, authorizing this company to extend this road across the Raritan River and connect with Woodbridge and Perth Amboy Railroad, or any others which may be built, and to cross the Raritan by a bridge or ferry. At the same session another supplement required the bridge to have a draw of at least one hundred feet.†7 Thus were taken the first steps which resulted in the construction of the railroad in 1876 as far as Sea Girt and Squan village, in Wall township.

This road gave the people of Monmouth their true and natural outlet, and promises to bring about a wonderful change in the future. Quick and sure connections with the Great City of this Continent, must prove of incalculable benefit to any county, but especially to a county with the natural advantages possessed by Monmouth. Mr. Henry S. Little, late Senator of Monmouth, and Gordon D. White, since deceased, deserve much credit for the accomplishment of this enterprize.— Here it may be remarked that about two hundred years ago the line of travel by land from Pootapeck as the region south of South Shrewsbury River was called, lay through Shrewsbury, Middletown, Perth Amboy, Woodbridge and Elizabeth, (the five old towns) to Jersey City, or Paulus Hook as then called. This railroad brings back the line of travel almost through the same towns.— Who, however, is able to appreciate the change between then and now? This railroad binds together all the eastern shore townships of the county. And in connection with the land improvement and seaside associations which have taken up so much land in Ocean and Wall townships along the rivers, inlets and adjoining the ocean, promise to make those sandy barrens "to bloom and blossom like the rose."

The Ocean Grove Camp Meeting Association of the Methodist Episcopal church, by an act of the Legislature passed in 1870, inaugurated these sea-side improvement companies. Remarkable success attended their efforts. What was a dreary stretch of sand and scrub pines only a few years ago, has become a thriving town, sometimes thronged by twenty thousand people, when the camp meetings are in progress. Many other associations have followed this, until the sea coasts of Wall and Ocean promise to be in the future the most populous part of the county.— Asbury Park, too, seems to have sprung up, like Aladdin's Palace, in a night. Great credit is due to James A. Bradley for his intelligent and energetic efforts to build up this part of the county. He has turned the pine barren into a pleasant and thriving town, making homes and a living for hundreds. Almost single handed, he has battled off those nuisances which have hitherto stopped the growth of several of our bay, river and ocean towns, which once had bright prospects.

In 1873 the last township of our county was erected by the name of the township of Eatontown. It was formed from all that portion of the townships of Ocean and Shrewsbury lying within the following boundaries, to wit: Beginning at Cranbury Brook, where it crosses the line of said townships of Ocean and Shrewsbury, and running easterly down said brook or stream, the several courses thereof to the Long Branch corporation line, the saw mill now standing upon or over said stream to be considered in the aforesaid township of Ocean and the Ocean Mills standing upon or over said stream, to be considered in the township of Eatontown; thence running along the westerly line of said corporation, to the railroad leading

†4 Pam. Laws of 1867, page 162.
†5 Pam. Laws of 1868, page 785.
†6 Pam. Laws of 1868, page 322.
†7 Pam. Laws 1869, see pages 807, and 1911.

OLD TIMES IN OLD MONMOUTH. 197

from Eatontown to Long Branch; thence northeasterly to the southeast corner of John E. Pye's land; thence north to the South Shrewsbury River, being the boundary line between said township of Ocean and Shrewsbury; thence westerly to the point of land known as Horse Neck, at the end of a new road; thence westerly along said new road or highway, to the turnpike leading from Red Bank to Eatontown; thence southerly along said turnpike to the junction of the road leading from Eatontown to Tinton Falls; thence westerly along said road towards Tinton Falls to the corner of the road leading from the northwest corner of John G. Vanderveer's farm to the Halfway House; thence southerly along said road or highway to the place of beginning.†8— This is the last division of the county, making at this time the beginning of the second century of our existence as a nation, fifteen townships in the county with a population of forty-eight thousand five hundred and nineteen persons.†9 Any further division into townships, or of the County, for many years to come, can be of no practical benefit to any one unless to the additional office holders created, or to some of the lot owners of the particular village which might secure a new county seat. There is less need of such a division now than at any other time in the past, as the railroads supply quick and cheap access to the county seat, while formerly it required all day to come and go, with expense of a team besides. If a railroad from Matawan is built to Freehold and extended on through the county to Mount Holly, all the townships of the county will be bound closely together, with quick and easy access into all the important parts, and with New York city and Philadelphia in close proximity on either side.

Thus an account of the boundaries and township divisions is brought down to the year 1877, the two hundred and twelfth year since the rough limits of what is now the greater part of Monmouth were laid down on Nicoll's Patent. A great deal of it is dry reading, but it serves to show the gradual changes in territorial limits and subdivisions of what is now one of the first agricultural counties in the United States. It would be vain to conjecture what will be the condition of things in our county a century hence.—

But one thing is sure, that if the population and improvement increase in the same ratio the next hundred years as they have the past twenty-five, Monmouth county must occupy one of the first places. At this time, none have a better promise of future prosperity, and none is more desirable, as a place of residence. If our people are just and true to themselves and others, under the blessing of Providence, our County of Monmouth will exercise a far-reaching influence and attain to a very great prosperity.

FREEHOLD, N. J., May 4th, 1877.

APPENDIX

TO

THE BOUNDARIES, &c., OF MONMOUTH.

COMPILED BY HON. G. C. BEEKMAN.

Whereas Richard Nicolls, Esq., formerly Governor of this Province of New Jersey, and that of New York, by commission under James (then) Duke of York and Albany, &c , and by virtue of the powers and authority vested in him, by the same Duke of York, did on or about the year of our Lord, one thousand six hundred and sixty-four, publish in print certain terms to the inhabitants of the Provinces aforesaid and others, by observing whereof, they might acquire property in lands in either of the said Provinces, which terms so published follows in these words, viz: The conditions for new planters in the Territories of his Royal Highness the Duke of York.

The purchases are to be made from the Indian Sachems, and to be recorded before the Governor. The purchasers are not to pay for their liberty of purchasing to the Governor.

The purchasers are to set out a town and inhabit together. No purchaser shall at any time contract for himself with any Sachem without consent of his associates or special warrant from the Governor.

The purchasers are free from all manner of assessments or rates for five years after their Town Plott is set out, and when the five years are expired they shall only be liable to the Publick Rates and payments according to the custom of other inhabitants, both English and Dutch.

All lands thus purchased and possessed,

---

†8 Pam. Laws of 1873, page 630.
†9 See last census.

shall remain to the purchasers and their heirs as free lands to dispose of as they please.

In all Territories of his Royal Highness liberty of conscience is allowed, provided such liberty is not converted to licentiousness, or the disturbance of others in the exercise of the Protestant Religion. The several townships have liberty to make their particular laws, and decide all small causes within themselves.

The lands which I intend shall be first planted are those upon the west side of Hudson's River, at or adjoining to the sopes, but if any number of men sufficient for two or three or more towns shall desire to plant upon any other lands they shall have all due encouragement proportionable to their quality and undertaking. Every township is obliged to pay their minister according to such agreement as they shall make with them, and no man to refuse his proportion, the minister being elected by the major part of the householders, inhabitant of the town. Every township hath the free choice of all their officers, both civil and military, and all men who shall take the oath of allegiance and are not servants or day laborers, but are admitted to enjoy a town lot, are esteemed free men of the jurisdiction, and cannot forfeit the same without due process in law. R. NICOLLS.

(Leaming and Spicer, Page 667-8.)

Such were the inducements offered by Col. Nicolls, to encourage people to settle the wild lands which were valueless without inhabitants.

The commission from James, Duke of York, to Richard Nicolls, a copy of which is published on pages 665 and 66 of Leaming & Spicer, gave him full power to offer such inducements. The language is, " I do hereby constitute and appoint him, the said Richard Nicolls, Esq., to be my Deputy Governor within the lands, islands and places aforesaid, to perform and execute all and every the powers which are by the said letters patent, granted unto me to be execute by my Deputy Agent or Assign." The Monmouth Patent (a copy of which appears on 661-2-3 of Leaming & Spicer), granted by him, was within the scope of his authority and would doubtless have been confirmed and ratified but for the management and intrigues of Berkeley and Carteret, who seemed to exercise a controlling influence over the Duke of York. The settlers of Monmouth, fully relying on the validity of Nicolls's promises and his Patent, proceeded to expend their means and devote their time and labor to the settlment of the County.

The old records in clerk's office and the Town Book of Middletown contain some account of their proceedings. These in connection with Leaming & Spicer will afford a correct idea of their claims and of the dispute between them and the proprietors.

The first entry in Book " A " of Deeds is a copy of the Nicolls's Patent from the Records in New York. As this has been frequently published, it is unnecessary to give it. Immediately following the " Patent," on page 4, is a copy of a letter from Richard Nicolls, the Governor, directed to the inhabitants of Middletown and Shrewsbury and dated August 10th, 1667.

" To Friends."

"Your address to me, bearing date ye 26th day of July, and your answer of ye 4th of August by the hands of James Grover is received. In answer to it I shall not deny you my advice. Now as I have contributed on my part to your first settlement, soe I think I must to remove such doubts and questions now remaining amongst you. In the first place you must rest satisfied with the assignment made by his Royal Highness, the Duke of York, unto Lord Berkeley and Sir G. Carteret of all the lands lying on the west side of Hudson River, wherein your tract is included. You must submit to ye Governor and government, established in ye Province of New Jersey. You may depend safely for your title to ye land upon the Patent granted unto you by me, and I am confident that when you speak with Capt. Carteret, he will assure you of the same, that your lands are lands to yourselves, paying only such moderate acknowledgement, as the rest of your naibours doe or may doe hereafter.

"Having briefly given you answer to the head of your questions, it remains only that I must not pass over your kind expressions toward me, without detaining you with my best assurances, that whenever I can at any tyme contribute more to your prosperity, you shall not fayle off further assistance. August 10th, at Fort James, in New York.

"Your loving Friend,
"R. NICOLLS.
"To the Inhabitants at Newasink."

OLD TIMES IN OLD MONMOUTH. 199

The next entry on page 5th is as follows:

Att a General Assembly of the inhabitants of Shrewsbury, on Narumsunk Neck, the 14th of December, A. D. 1667.

Officers chosen by the inhabitants off Middletown, on Newasunk Neck, and establisht by oath, at this present assembly or court, held the day and year above written.

Officers for Middletown.

Richard Gibbons, constable; Jonathan Holmes, Wm. Lawrence, overseers; Stephen Arnold, James Ashton, deputies.

Portland Poynt.

Henry Percy, Richard Richardson, overseers; James Bowne, deputy.

Officers for Shrewsbury on Narumsunk.

Peter Parker, constable; Christopher Allmy, Edward Pattison, overseers; Eliakim Wardell, Bartholemew West, deputies.

The several acts or orders enacted att this present assembly, upon the propositions presented by the Inhabitants to the Paterl ees and Deputies, are in order set down, viz:—

First, it is hereby ordered, that according to ye tenour off the first proposition, that the time and exact account of what sums of money and goods hath bin imployed by those persons who ware formerly made choice of to act in the behalf of themselves and others in the purchase of this whole tract of land from the Indians, shall be drawn up and presented to the next Court or Assembly of Deputies and others, the representatives of the inhabitants in general, or sooner if tyme or opportunity permits, with the account in particular of charges which hath —— therefrom.

Likewise it is hereby expressly ordered and commanded that every person who hath right to debate and determine off things pertaining to the orderly settlin' of the land, may upon all meet occasions exercise liberty by way of vote. That is to say, such men as shall be made choice off by the general vote off the inhabitants with the proper number of persons expressed in the charter or Grand Patent, and have full power and charge to make all publique laws and orders, authentique, or the major part of them soe chosen, which privilege is granted only to the number of purchasers.

The townsmen chosen inhabitants ——

— of shares of land are hereby restricted and confined to their own town affairs, according to the second proposition.

The tenour or substance of the third and fourth propositions is the number of those who have a right to vote in full and general meetings, viz, each full purchaser. How many are taken in witn such, who have already paid, and those which have not paid, together with ye number of inhabitants in general, ye account hereof is likewise referred to ye next General Assembly.

The effect of ye 5th proposition, as touching the choice of officers, hath already been put in practice.

As touching the 6th, it is ordered that three men out of each town, that is to say, two of them to be surveyors, shall in the first place, take a full view of each neck of land, commonly called Newasink and Narumsunk, and to give report of the same to the best of their judgment and observation, as to the quantity of upland and meadow, that soe a fair and equal division may proceed, whereby the lymits of each Town might bee appointed and set down, with all convenient expedition. That is to say between this and the last of February, and that good observation as well of quality as of quantity may be given in, that soe each neck might be peopled in such fitt proportion, as shall be thought most fitt and equall.

Concerning the 7th proposition, it is ordered that whereas certain inhabitants of Rhode Island and elsewhere, have bin ingadged to have —— their —— in the settlement of this land upon —— whereby their —— and privileges off full purchasers with others is forfeited or lost by their neglect or remiss dealings. It is hereby determined that all such persons aforesaid, which may happen to arrive here between this and the next springtide, with intent to settle here according to their former grant, it shall remain wholly in the choice of the officers here appointed and inhabitants, whether such shall be admitted in as purchasers, or else upon such other terms as may hereafter to them be propounded. And further, it is ordered, that none shall of himself with others, take upon him or them to take up or dispose off to his own or other men's use, without getting order from the constable and overseer of the town or towns, that is to say, such lotts or pieces of land as is not already settled, unless that a man or family from other —— bee settled thereon, and that by orderly choice off lotts as they lye now or shall be layd outt. None to leave or take without especial order as aforesaid.

The 9th proposition is likewise approved and wholly granted, as touching the conventions of town inhabitants and meetings together, to consult for the mutual commodity or good off each other as occasion shall require, and to make such orders as shall be thought expedient for the tyme present and future, and to appoint a clark to keep and register ——— their acts and proceeding, always provided, that they inact nothing contrary to the acts, laws or orders as well of the General Assembly of both towns, as off the public laws of the government.

The selling of strong liquor to Indians is likewise, by virtue of this act, forbidden, according to the forfeiture or penalty prescribed or set down by the laws of the country.

The admittance of townsmen is allowed soe far as to make up the number of one hundred with the inhabitants which are here already seated.

The money received for each township to remain in the seven men's hand, viz: Wm. Goulding, John Bown, John Tilton, James Grover, Richard Stout, Samuel Spicer, Richard Gibbons For the which they are to be accountable unto the inhabitants who are most concerned herein.

The aforesaid townsmen are to have equal privileges with the purchaser in the use of common meadows, as in proportion of upland assigned to each in lotts.

Portland Point to be reduced into ten divisions or lots and no more.

Richard Richardson chosen and appointed to record the acts, orders and deeds with ye register of the same ——— to the land as Recorder in General.

BOOK " A," PAGE 8-9.

Att a General Assembly of the Pattentees and Deputies, held the 4th of June att Portland Poynt, the actes and orders as followeth :

Whereas an order was made by the Patentees and Deputies of this Court, held the 14th day of December last, att Shrewsbury, on Narumsunk, for survey of these two Necks, viz: Newasink and Narumsunk, which for some pretence or cause alledged to this court, the business was neglected. After debate of which, it is hereby again ordered, that according to the tenour of the aforesaid order, three men out of each town, two of them to be surveyors, are to take a full view, both of the upland and meadow of each neck and to take good observation of the quantitie and qualitie of each, and to give report thereof, so as formerly was ordered, only one man to be chosen by the inhabitants, (upon choice made of the other six aforesaid), and he to stand as umpire between each town, and him to have timely notice given him by the constable of this order, for and in the name of the towns and this to be done by the latter end off November next at furtherest, and then no moor shares off land are to be layed out until this be done, nowhere in the lymetts of the whole tract or purchase of land.

Ordered, upon full debate hereof, that noe moor persons whatsoever, either purchasers, townsmen or others shall henceforth be admitted or taken in, there being in numbers about 100, as near as att present can be found, or if it be found there are not soe many, yet notwithstanding noe moor are to be from henceforth admitted as aforesaid.

Ordered, That at or before the time off ye survey of the two necks above mentioned, the whole tract of land pertaining to all the intire purchase is to be surrounded and marked out by those which are appointed for survey of the two Necks, in particular as aforesaid.

Ordered, That upon proposition and debate for another highway in Shrewsbury on Narumsunk, the breadth of the said highway to be ——— and not under the breadth, over it left to the discristion of the townsmen; likewise that those fences which are now made, which shall be found standing in the highway, are to remain in that place, until they be ———
——— And this highway to be understood and meant the common passage highway and street which goes from one end of the town to the qther.

Ordered, That upon all and every occasion off laying out of lands, that each town have their liberty to make choice of a man for laying out off land within the bounds of each town. And that none shall be laid out but by the major vote off the town, and according to the former order for lotts.

Ordered, That each town inhabitant shall have liberty to choose four men for assistants to the overseers and constable, for the managing of all affairs relating to each town, for preventing disorders or

OLD TIMES IN OLD MONMOUTH. 201

contemptuous behaviour in word or deed off any person or persons. And in case any order or act by them soe chosen, shall be neglected or left undone, the constable aforesaid with the overseers and the four assistants aforesaid have hereby power to see such act or order by them soe done or made, to be executed and performed accordingly. And this act to stand in full force until a more particular law or order be given forth by the Superior Court, etc.

Ordered, That in answer to the proposition concerning the giftland, the determinate Resolutions thereon, upon full debate was this, that ——— it is not yet ——— intended by this court and expected by the natives, and for other reasons it was thought fit to remit the consideration hereof, to the next General Assembly, then to be ended. In the meantime all things relating thereto are to stand as now they do, unalterable. Noe part or parcel of ye said land to be at all disposed of.

Ordered, That the former proceedings on acts of the Road Island men, in their laying out of land on Narumsunk, the consideration hereof be likewise referred to the next court whether to stand or noe.

Ordered, That the next General Assembly off the Pattentees and Deputies for the towns of Middletown and Shrewsbury be on the last Wednesday in November next.

Book "A," page 12.

The Overseers, thare Ingadgement, May ye 26, 1669.

We, whose names are hereunto subscribed, being chosen by the inhabitants off Middletown for overseers, we do hereby promise and ingadge to perform the office and place thereof, according to our best understanding in all cases on actions of debt and trespass, amounting to ye sum of ten pounds, according to the charter given and granted to the company of purchasers off Newasink, Narumsunk and Pootapeck. In witness whereoff we have hereunto subscribed this 26th of May, 1669. The mark of
RICHARD X STOUT,
JONATHAN HULLMES,
EDWARD SMITH,
JAMES BOWNE.

Subscribed in Court before the Pattentees and Deputies of the towns of Middletown and Shrewsbury, May 26th, 1669.
R. RICHARDSON,
Recorder.

PAGE 14.

I, underwritten, do hereby in sollom manner promise and ingadge, to perform ye place and office of a constable to the best of my understanding, as a conservator of the publique peace in the town of Shrewsbury, and in all things relating thereunto to the utmost of my power, unto the which I have hereunto subscribed the 26th of May, 1669.
ELIAKIM WARDELL.

Subscribed in Court before the Patentees and Deputies of the towns of Middletown and Shrewsbury, May ye 26th, 1669.
R. RICHARDSON,
RECORDER.

The same Ingadgement verbatum, the same day, being ye 26th off May was subscribed by James Ashton, constable of Middletown.
Witness: R. RICHARDSON.

PAGE 16.

May 27th, 1669.

Ordered, That if any person or persons in ye limits of ye towns of Middletown and Shrewsbury, shall contemptuously deny to assist ye constable upon his express command in ye King's name for the keeping of ye publique peace, suppressing of rioters, disorderly persons, he or they soe offending, shall be liable to pay ye sum off forty shillings, to be forthwith levied upon his or thare share after due process made, and complaint made by the constable to the overseer of each town of fact, or a greater sum according to ye nature or manner of fact or facts ——— further that all persons inhabiting in ye limits off ye towns aforesaid, are hereby required to give assistance upon all ——— occasions to ye constable or his lawfull deputy, upon pain of forfeiture aforesaid.

Ordered, That all publique charges incurred, is to be levied upon and paid out off ye estate off every person, inhabitant of those towns, and ye constable hath hereby power to see this order performed, when tyme and occasion shall require.

PAGE 19.

November 2, 1669.

At a court held this day, at the house of Randall Huet, on Portland Point.

Present—James Ashton, Constable; Richard Stout, James Grover, John Bowne, James Bowne, Pattentees; Jonathan Hullmes, Edward Smith, Deputies.

William Bowne and James Bowne off the Town of Middletown, on Newasink Neck, are appointed to act as Patentees in the room of John Tilton and Samuel Spicer, of Gravesend, according to an order under both their hands, as appears on record, bearing date the 26th day of May last.

Ordered, That the Court is adjourned to the last Wednesday in December next, and in the meantime Richard Richardson is to give notice to the constable off Shrewsbury, in some convenient tyme, hereof, and further that ye inhabitants off Portland Point have liberty to determine among themselves, whare to have thare principal lotts off land laid out, and to give in thare result thereof at the next Assembly.

PAGES 19-20-21.

Att a court held at Portland Point, 28th day of December, 1669:

Present—John Bowne, James Grover, Richard Gibbons, Richard Stout, Wm. Bowne, John Ruckman, Patentees; James Bowne, Jonathan Hulmes, Edward Smith, Richard Lippincott, John Hanse, Deputies and Overseers; James Ashton, Constable.

Ordered, That it is granted unto John Haunse, off Shrewsbury, for him to hold and enjoy two lotts of land, according to a former verbal grant, being already layd out and taken up by him, the said John Haunse, at or near Pootapeck, and that him, ye said John, shall hold the said two lots for and in the behalf of James Heard and Edward Wharton, purchasers. The said John having produced the orders tharefore from under the said Heard and Whartons hands to this present Court, and further it is ordered by the said court and authority aforesaid, that noe lotts of land more be granted to any other, which are or shall be laid out, until the payment thereof be first made clear and evident to this court, notwithstanding any pretence whatsoever.

Ordered. That upon the proposition made by the deputies for an assurance under hand in wrighting to every man interested in the title of land within this purchase. It is hereby reported to the Pattentees, viz: James Grover, John Bown, Richard Stout, and the rest here present of the Pattentees, upon a tyme convenient ———— draught off ye said assurance, and present the same to the Recorder, for to be delivered into his hands, unto whom the inhabitants may repair for a transcript thereof, or copy under his the said Recorder's hand, agreeing with the original, so to be given as aforesaid, which shall by virtue off this order be authentique as any assurance which can be made or given forth by ye aforesaid Patentees. The same assurance so to be given and made, as our the said Patentees proper did, and the same to be grounded or modeled according to the tenour off the Patent, given and granted to the Pattentees and thare associates, under the name and seal of Collonoll Richard Nicholes, late Governor of New York, and this to be done between this and the first of March next.

Ordered, That for the defraying of the charges and expenses about the publique business of these towns in court, that thare shall be allowed to each person so imployed, viz, the patentees, deputies and constables, and to each of them, three shillings per day, to be levied upon the publique account of these towns by the constable according to an order made the last court, on 27th of May.

Ordered, That whereas some disorders hath lately happened in ye unlawful killing of swine under ye pretence of running wild and unmarkt in ye woodes. For the prevention of which illegal practizes for the future, it is hereby expressly ordered, that noe person whatsoever within ye limits of these towns, shall from henceforth presume to kill any hogs unmarkt, notwithstanding any pretence off lawful ———— until he first acquaint the overseers of town, off his intent and purpose herein, and after which, if any person happen to kill any swine unmarkt ————, that then he shall bring the said swine or hogg un to the town, after opening or embowelling whole and entire, and present him to public view, and to the officers aforesaid, that soe an order may bee taken therein, as shall be thought fitt, but if any manner of person shall henceforth by any unlawful wayes or secret practizes ———— to kill and convey away swine, which are not markt as aforesaid, contrary to the true intent and meaning off this act or order here sett down the parties, he or they so offending shall be liable to forfeit five pounds and ye same to be forthwith levied up on the estate of ye offender, upon proof of the fact committed by the officers which shall be appointed hereto, and the same to be disposed of as the Court shall think fitt.

Ordered, That the lymitt or bound of this town off Middletown is to be set forth and bounded westward off the town for the further inlargement of the same, soe as shall be agreed upon after a full view taken of ye land which is to be done at or upon the 16th day of March next, and after this is so done, the return boundes thereof is to be taken and set down in wrighting, as exact as may be, and the same to be recorded in the Town Book.

Ordered, That the Inhabitants off Portland Point by virtue of this order, have full power and liberty to take up their principal lott of land on second division at or near a small creek within the limitts of this town of Middletown, called Manymind Spring, and thare to be layed out, that thare be not land enough conveniently to accommodate them, ye said inhabitants. They shall have liberty to take up what share be wanting upon Newasink River, in some convenient place, to make up ye full compliment of the number of acres of plantable land, together with meadow equal to ye rest of the inhabitants of the aforesaid town.

PAGE 22.

By order of the Pattentees, etc., a record off John Jenkins, of Sandwich, the Deed or Conveyance off Land unto George Allen, July the 5th, 1670.

Know all men by these presents that I, John Jenkins, off the Town of Saundwith, in the colony of New Plymouth, in New England, ———— for and in consideration of ye sum of ———— in hand payd by George Allen, off ye Town of Sandwich, in the colony aforesaid, planter, unto me ye aforesaid John Jenkins. The receipts of it, I, the sayed John Jenkins doe acknowledge myself fully satisfied and payd, and have bargained and sould from myself, my heirs and assigns, and by those presents doe hereby and absolutely bargain and sell unto ye said George Allen, his heirs and assigns, all my landes in ye county or colony of New Jersey, both upland and meadow land, containing one whole share or purchase which I, the said John Jenkins, have bought off William Reape off Newport, upon Rhode Island merchants, as may appear by letter under the hand of Walter Clarke off Newport, clerk for the company of purchasers, bearing date the seventeenth of the eleventh month, one thousand six hundred and sixty seven, and also by ————, under the hand of Henry Bull, of the same Island, bearing date the thirteenth of the fourth month, one thousand six hundred sixty and five.

The which share of land being a whole purchase or share off the whole tract of land purchased of the Indians. As also may further appear, I being inroled upon ye list at Rhode Island. The which share of land lying and in New Jersey aforesaid, and which land lyeth in three necks, with more land adjacent thereto, which necks are called Newasink, Narumsunk and Pootapeck, whether divided or undivided, both upland and meadow, with all the privileges and appurtenance thereunto belonging.

To have and to hold unto the aforesaid George Allen, his heirs and assigns, forever, and I the same John Jenkins, for myself, my heirs or assigns, doe covenant and grant to and with the said George Allen, his heirs and assigns, to warrent and save harmless the said George Allen, his heirs and assigns, from any manner of person or persons that shall lay any lawful claim upon the said bargained premises, from, by or under me, the aforesaid John Jenkins.

In witness whereof I have hereunto set my hand and seal this second of June, 1670. JOHN JENKINS.

In the presence cf us,
RICHARD HANDLEY,
JOHN JENING.

PAGE 23.

By order of ye Pattentees, July 7th, 1670.

This may certifi to all whom it may concern, that I, Daniel Gould, off Newport, on Rhode Island, having half a share off land in ye county of New Jersey, according to ye purchase and sharings off those lands which are commonly called, and known by ye Indian names of Newasink, Narumsunk and Pootapeck, have bargained and sould, and by these presents for myself, my heirs are freely, fully and firmly, make over and yield up all my whole right, title and interest, which I have or ever had in the aforesaid land unto George Allen, off Sandwich, in the colony of New Plymouth, in New England to him and his heirs forever, firmly to possess and enjoy to ye worlds end, from any molestation of me, my heirs, forever. In witness, whereoff, I have hereunto set my hand and seal the 12th day of ye fourth month, 1670.

DANIEL GOULD.

In the presence of us,
WM. RICHARDSON.
WALTER CLARK.

PAGE 23.

This may certify to all whom it may concern, that I, Joshua Coggshall, of Portsmouth, on Rhode Island, doe order and allow George Allen, of Saundwich, to divide and disporse of my half share of land which I have in ye county off New Jersey, in as full and ample manner as if I was thare, present myself. As witness my hand ye 14th day of ye 4th month 1670.

JOSHUA CAGGSHALL.

In ye presence of us,
DANIEL GOULD,
NICHOLAS EASTON, JUNIOR.

PAGE 24.

July 5th, A. D. 1670.

At a Court held the day and year above written, at Portland Poynt.

Present—William Reap, John Bowne, James Grover, William Goulding, Richard Gibbons, Richard Stout, Patentees; John Hance, Eliakim Wardell, James Bowne, Deputies.

Peter Tilton, William Shaddock, Eliakim Wardell and Richard Lippincott ware established overseers for the town of Shrewsbury, according to a certificate under the Town Clerk's hand, bearing date the 4th day of the 5th month, as likewise ingadged according to the former act, set down in this intitled, "the overseers' ingadgment," as also John Hance is ingadged constable, upon choice made by the major voat of the Inhabitants of Shrewsbury, according to the certificate under the Town Clerk's hand, who also ware . ppointed and chosen deputy as appears by the sayd certificate to act this present court in the Town's behalf.

The Pattentees aforesaid having given notice to ye overseers chosen and deputies of Middletown, to appear at this present meeting, to show and auditt all accompts pertaining to the purchase of the three necks of land. William Reap, of Rhode Island, merchant, being present to render his part of accounts with the rest interested herein, for the satisfaction of the purchasers who are herein concerned, this answer following, inserted on record, was received, viz:

Friends, the Pattentees at Portland Poynt:—This is to give you notice that ye town having formerly made choice of deputies for ye next court, which court hath formerly been fixt to be held about eight days hence, but now at present neeting it falls out that one of the deputies is at present disabled, by reason of sickness, to attend this day, and the town is not now in a —— to make choice of another, by reason of the short notice off ye warning, which otherwise may be had for new choice against the fixt day formerly published amongst us by the pattentees. As for William Reap being there to give in accompt, I consider that may bee done without the presence of ye deputies, they being not able to —— of them.

By me.
JOHN WILSON,
Town Deputy.

Dated the 4th of the 5th month, 1670.

PAGE 25.

Record of Intelligence given for a meeting to some nominated associates at Shrewsbury, February 15th, 1670.

Friends:—This is to give you notice that thare is a meeting intinded by the Patentees and thare associates, on Thursday next, the 22d day of this instant month, at James Grover's house, at ye mill, at eight of the clock. This meeting requiring the presence of every person who are nominated associates, thare and then to declare their willingness and assent, and your —— and propositions to be presented and put in practice without delay, which may tend to ye —— of others, in the —— purchasing and possessing of land comprehended in the Pattent. This warning requiring speedy compliance herein, or else to declare your mind either for the declining or otherwise prosecuting the business.

To Mr. Christopher Allmy, Eliakim Wardell, John Hance, R. Lippincott, Wm. Shaddock, Edward Pattison, Barth. West. Nich. Browne, Tho. Winterton, nominated associates.

This voat was directed to John Hance to communicate the contents thereof to ye persons above said.

Subscribed by
RICHARD HARTSHORNE,
JOHN BOWNE,
RICHARD GIBBONS,
RICHARD STOUT.

R. RICHARDSON, Clerk.

PAGE 27, etc.

Newasink, Narumsunk and Pootapeck, Dr. as followeth to William Reape.

	£.	s.	d.
To John Tilton & Company, in peagec,	24	5	0
In rum at tymes at 7-6 per gallon,	23	10	0
45 — duffels,	25	02	0

OLD TIMES IN OLD MONMOUTH. 205

	£	s.	d.		£	s.	d.
To the Sachim of ye gift land, and to Randal Huet in rum,	1	00	6	To 5 trading coats at 150 gilders is	6	5	0
To a sloop hire 10 days, with expences in provisions upon a voyage with the Patentees to Pootapeck Neck,	4	06	0	To a gun and pair of breeches, 46 gilders,	1	19	6
				To ditto in peaqec, 20 gilders, 1 anchor of brandy is 160 gilders, which reduced into English,	6	18	8
To the charge of three men sent from Rhode Island to sittle ye, the countery affairs here,	3	08	0	To tobacco at tymes 32, one shirt 10 gilders is 42,	1	15	0
To the use of Derrick Smith's sloope, for their transport,	4	11	6	To ditto in white and black peaqe, 310 g., and 1 pair breeches at 6 is 316 gilders in money,	13	07	6
To 21 days for myself on ye publique affairs with provision,	3	03	0	To 2 coats and 1 pair of breeches, 70 gila.,	2	19	0
To the forbearance of my money,	0	00	0	To boat hire at 3 times 323 gilders,	13	09	06
To my expense of now attending the publique service at the making of this account,	0	00	0	To Popamora and his men at times, in wine,	5	16	10
	89	07	0	To several men and wages for several voyages, made for the purchase of Newasunk,	66	17	06

The above accompt of disbursements of Wm. Reap, amounting to £89, 07s, 0d, is owned by us, the Pattentees and deputies now present at Portland Point.

Witness our hands this 5th day of July, 1670.

    WILL GOULDING,
    JAMES GROVER,
    JOHN BOWNE,
    RICHARD GIBBONS,
        his
    RICHARD X STOUT,
        mark.
        Pattentees.
    JOHN HANCE,
    ELIAKIM WARDELL,
    JAMES BOWNE,
        Deputies.

Testis: R. RICHARDSON.

PAGE 23.

Newasink, Narumsunk and Pootapeck, Dr., to several disbursements, by James Grover, John Tilton, Wm. Goulding & Company, as followeth:

	£	s.	d.
To Poppamora in black peaqec, 486 gilders, which is 20 to 5,	20	05	0
To him in white peaqec, 162 gilders, which is	6	15	0

To recording the deed of sale in New York 30 gilders paid to Popamora, 1 coat and breeches is 40 gilders, in all 70 gilders, — 2 19 0

                                  149 6 10

The accompt of the second purchase.

	£	s.	d.
To several sachims in peaqeu 1,320 gild. is	55	00	00
To 9 blankets, 360 gilders,	15	00	00
T 9 coats at 315 g., 9–240 is 555 g. is	23	07	06
To 4½ lbs of powder, 21 g., 15½ lbs. of lead, 11 ——, 27 g., in all 59 gilders, and in English,	02	09	06
To expenses on Indians at New York, 60 g. is	02	10	00
To expense on them at Gravesend, is 59 g.,	02	01	10

206   OLD TIMES IN OLD MONMOUTH.

	£	s.	d.
To recording the deed, 25 g., is	1	00	00
To tobacco to them all times 20 g., is	0	17	10
To our voyage in the purchase and marking out the 2 Necks, Narumsunk and Pootapeck, together with provisions the Indians had on voyage, 720 gilders is	29	11	08
To anchors of rum, 200 g.,	3	06	08
To treat with the Jersey Governor, expenses 350 g.,	13	11	08
To expenses at Narumsunk on ye county affairs, 480 g	20	00	00
To the sachims coates, 210 gilders,	8	15	00
To incidental charges, 600 gilders,	25	00	00
To Christopher Allmy, 50 gilders for himself and his boat at Narumsunk,	2	01	08
Sum total is	359	10	00

PAGES 29 & 30.

Newasink, Narumsunk and Pootapeck, Cr., by several moneys paid to James Grover & Company, as followeth :

	£	s.	d.
By Samuel Spicer	4	0	0
James Grover	4		
William Goulding	4		
John Bown	4		
Richard Gibbons	4		
Richard Stout	4		
John Tilton	4		
Nath. Silvester	6		
Thomas Moor	1	13	04
*John Cunklin	0	15	0

*NOTE.—The above are all Long Island people chiefly from Gravesend.

** NOTE.—The following are Rhode Island people.

**	£	s.	d.
By Walter Clark	3	0	0
Petter Esson	3		
Thomas Winterton	3		
Richard Lippincott	13	10	00
Emanuel Wooley	3		
Tom Shaddock	3		
Edward Wharton	3		
Richard Borden	9		
William James	1	05	0
Robert Carr	3	00	0
Thomas Potter	3		
George Webb	3		
John Coggshall	3		
William Codington	3		
Thomas Clifton	3		
Henry Bull	3		
Samuel Holliman	3		
Nicholas Browne	4		
Richard Richardson	4		
Christopher Allmey	4		
Jonathan Holmes	3		
John Cooke	3		
George Chutte	3		
M. Lucer	4		
Obadiah Holmes	4		
Steven Arnold	3		
Edward Smith	3		
Nicholas Davis	8		
Wm. Shaberly	4		
Roger Ellis and his son	6		
Eliakim Wardell	4		
Edward Tartt	3	17	6
Edward Pattison	4		
Barth. West	4		
Robert West	4		
Thomas Whitlock	3	17	6

NOTE.—The following from Rhode Island, Long Island and Weschester Co., N.Y.

	£	s.	d.
By John Horabin	2	01	8
James Bowne	1	14	6
John Wilson	4	00	0
John Ruckman	4		
Thomas Cox	3	10	0
Edmund Laphitra	3	10	
Francis Masters	3	10	
John Townsend	4		
Henry Lippet	4		
Tobias Haudson	4		
John Hannce	4		
Zachery Gaunt	1	10	0
Francis Brindley	3	10	
Ralph Gouldsmith	3	10	
Walter Wall	4		
John Wall	3	10	
Job Allmey	4		
Joseph Coleman	3		
John Thogmorton	1	06	8
John Bown of H. L	3		
Wm. Bown	1	06	8
Thomas Potter	1		
	253	17	6

Newasink, Narumsunk and Pootapeck, Cr, by several sums of money paid William Reape as followeth :

NOTE.—Nearly all ef these are Rhode Island people.

OLD TIMES IN OLD MONMOUTH. 207

	£.	s.	d.		
By Edward Thurston	3	0	0	Mark Lucer	1
John Allen and Robert				Obadiah Holmes	1
Taylor	3	0	0	Stephen Arnold	1
Nathan Tomkins	4			Edward Smith	1
Richard Lippencott	3			Nich. Davis	2
George Mount and Benjamin Bordin	6			Wm. Shaberly	1
				Rogers Ellis & Son	2
Richard Bordin	2	10		Eliakim Wardell	1
John Jenkins	3			Edward Tartt	1
Daniel Gould and Joshua				Edward Pattison	1
Coggshall	3	10		Bartholemew West	1
Richard ————	4	10		Robert West	1
John Wood	4	10		Thomas Whitlock	1
Gerrard Bowne	4	10		John Horabin	1
Robert Story	9			James Bowne	1
William Shaddock and				John Wilson	1
George Webb	1			John Ruckman	1
William Shaddock and				John Townsend	1
John Jenkins	2			Henry Lippitt	1
Thomas Clifton	0	10		Tobias Haudson	1
Robert Carr and Walter				John Haunce	1
Clark	1			Francis Brindly	1
				Walter Wall	1
	34	10	0	Job Allmey	1
				Joseph Coleman	1

Page 33–34.

A list off the names of the purchasers of Newasink, Narumsunk and Pootapeck.

Shares of Land.

Samuel Spicer	1	Wm. Bowne	1
James Grover	1	John Smith	1
John Bowne	1	Wm. Reape	2
Richard Gibbons	1	John Bown of F. L	1
Richard Stout	1	Edward Thurston	1
Nathaniel Sillvester	2	John Allen & Robt. Taylor	1
John Throckmorton	1	John Jenkins	1
Walter Clark	1	Zachary Gant	1
Peter Easson	1	Nathaniel Tomkins	1
Tho. Winterton	1	Benjamin Spicer	1
Richard Lippincott	4	Joseph Boyer	1
Emanuel Wooley	1	George Mount	1
Wm. Shaddock	1	Benj. Borden	1
Edward Wharton	1	Richard Sissell	1
Richard Borden	3	Daniel Gould & Joshua Coggshall	1
Wm James	1	Gerrard Bowne	1
Robert Carr	1	Gideon Freeborn and Robert Hazard	1
Thos. Potter	1	John Wood	1
George Webb	1	Thomas Hart	1
John Coggshall	1	John Tomson	1
Wm. Codington	1	Edward Cole	1
Thomas Clifton	1	Robert Story	2
Henry Bull	1	William Gifford	1
Samuel Holman	1	James Leonard	1
Nicholas Browne	1	Thomas Dungan	1
Richard Richardson	1	John Haundell	1
Christopher Allmey	1	Marmaduke Ward	1
Jonathan Holmes	1	Richard Moor	1
John Cooke	1	Ralph Gouldsmith	1
George Chute	1	James Ashton	1
			—
			97

The names of such who are entered as township men.

Townshippers.
Thomas Cox... 1
Edmund Laphitra... 1
Francis Masters... 1
John Hall... 1
Bashan... 1
James Grover, Junior... 1
Richard Sadler... 1
Daniel Estill... 1
Wm. Laurence... 1
Wm. Shearman... 1
——— Page ... 1
Wm. Layton... 1
Wm. Goulding... 1
John Stout... 1
Henry Percy ... 1
John Bird... 1
Randall Huet, Jr... 1
Randall Huet, Sr... 1
Samuel Spicer... 1
Barth' Lippincott... 1
Job Throckmorton... 1

PAGE 35.

An order made by the Pattentees and Deputies here present at Portland Point, the sixth of July, 1670, as followeth :

Whereas, It appears by the list of names of the purchasers and townsmen of these Necks of Newasink, Narumsunk and Pootapeck, that several have come short of payment, of their due sums of money equal with the rest, it is hereby expressly ordered by the Patentees and Deputies, that after due and timely notice given, to the parties aforesaid, for the payment and making up the several sums that is wanting, the parties aforesaid are to make payment of the same so far as is properly due, by the last of November next, otherwise in case of delay or fraudulent dealing, in the premises, the penalty for such default, after publication of this order, to forfeit their lands to those who are hereby impowered to sieze thareupon, namely, the pattentees whose names are hereto inserted, who, by virtue of an account given in of all disbursements pertaining to the whole intire purchase of these necks. It appears thereby that a certain sum of money is thereby due unto them, the aforesaid Pattentees, to ask demand, sue for ———, also to discharge the several persons which are found wanting in the making up of the full payment with the rest of the purchasers and townsmen. WILL GOULDING,
JAMES GROVER,
JOHN BOWNE,
RICHARD GIBBONS,

his
RICHARD X STOUT,
mark.
WILLIAM REAPE.
Testis: R. RICHARDSON.
PAGE 36.

July 8th, 1670.

It is thought meet by the Pattentees, that a convenient number of purchasers who were the first and principal in the purchase of these necks, viz : Newasink, Narumsunk and Pootapeck are hereby to be nominated, elected and chosen as associates with the Pattentees whose names are inserted and set down, who by virtue of this act or order shall henceforth have a full interest, right and claim in ye pattent given and granted to the Pattentees, by Richard Nicholls, Esq., late Governor off New York, to chose men who are tharein expressly nominated and ——— as may appear, who, together with their associates hereby declared to act together, for the settlement and purchase off lands, which at present lies void, according to title, tenour, grant and substance of the aforesaid Pattent. The which the said Pattentees and now received associates and combinates together, doe promise and hereby ingage one to the other to defend, justify and maintain the said Pattent, according to the true intent and meaning thareof, upon the penalty or forfeiture off each share of land to those, who from this time forward shall any way endeavor to overthrow, disannul or any way infringe the liberties thareof, as it is given and granted to all the pattentees and associates, whose names with those of the said Pattentees are here expressed, viz :

William Bowne, Thos. Whitlock, John Wilson, John Ruckman, Walter Wall, John Smith, Richard Richardson, John Horabin, James Bowne, Jonathan Holmes, Christopher Allmey Eliakim Wardell, Bartholemew West, John Haunce, James Ashton, Edward Pattison, Wm. Shaddock, Thomas Winterton, Edward Tartt, Benjamin Burdin.

Those above named, we the above said Pattentees, have chosen and selected to bee associates with us according to the premises aforesaid.

Witness our hands the day and year above said.

WILLIAM GOULDING,
JAMES GROVER,
RICHARD GIBBONS,

WILLIAM REAPE,
JOHN BOWNE,
his
RICHARD X STOUT.
mark.

Test: R. RICHARDSON.

NOTE.—The names of the patentees appear on this page, in their own hand writing. The hand writing of John Bowne is bold, plain and heavy, each letter is distinct and well formed. That of Wm. Reape is large and plain.

PAGE 38.

July 8, 1670.

Ordered, That no manner of persons whatsoever, shall presume to take upon him or them, to purchase or take up unto themselves, any part or parcell of land without the order, consent or approbation of the pattentees and associates, within the bounds or limitts of this Patent from the Indians or natives. The person so doing shall loose the value of the money so disposed of, and bee liable to such further fine or penalty as the pattentees and associates shall see cause, (or the major part of them shall fix.)

Ordered, That about November next the Lottes of land remaining in com non, —— of the full noumber of one hundred and eighteen, are to be layd out by James Grover. appointed hereunto.

Ordered, That upon the first Monday of the mouth of April, each town, viz, off Middletown and Shrewsbury, are to make choice of their overseers and constables, and after choice made the officers soe chosen. are to be establisht at the next General Court held at Portland Point.

PAGE 39.

At a meeting of sum inhabitants of Middletown and Shrewsbury, May 15, 1671, at James Grover's house, it was then and there concluded on, that after the exact laying out of both the towns aforesaid, and the townsmen made equal with the purchasers in the same towns. After this is soe done the next adjacent land to each town is to be layd out for the benefit of the purchasers, in equal plots to thare own proper use, in such convenient quantity as shall be hereafter agreed upon, by the nomber of purchasers aforesaid, herein concerned.

PAGE 40.

May 15, 1671.

At a meeting holden the 15th of this instant month, it was ordered and agreed upon by the pattentees present, viz: John Bowne. James Grover, Richard Stout, Richard Gibbons, with the rest of the inhabitants of Middletown and Shrewsbury, (whose names are extant in this Book), that at or upon the 29th day off September next, a meeting is appointed for the choice of a fitt number of men, to survey the two necks of Newasink and Navarumsunk, and for to give thare judgment touching the qualitie and quantitie, both of the upland and the meadow, according to ye substance of former orders and agreements. This being assented to and now again agreed unto by ye inhabitants. At the same time and day, Richard Richardson was appointed to stand as Recorder for both towns, according to an agreement expressed in this book for one whole year from the date hereof.

May 31, 1672.

Whereas, Richard Lippincott and Nicholas Browne, inhabitants of the town of Shrewsbury, was formerly nominated for associates according to an act made July 8th, 1670.

As is expressed in the 36th folio of this booke (the entry of whose names being then omitted   or forgotten) the said parties aforesaid, Richard and Nicholas, are likewise to be added to the number of associates therein expressed by order of the Pattentees.

This is the last entry of orders by the Patentees. The rest of Book "A" consists of deeds, bills of sale and agreements, with forms of court proceeding, and on page 66, Philip Carteret, Governor of New Jersey, appears as presiding judge, Sept. 6th, 1676, at a court in Shrewsbury. Between 1672 and 1676, the records of Monmouth county, show no court proceedings and no legislation by the Patentees, under the Nicolls Patent. Either the records of this time have been lost or the Patentees ceased to exercise judicial and legislative power under Nicoll Patent, after 1672.

PAGE 85 OF LEAMING & SPICER.

At a General Assembly begun the third of November, 1668, the deputies for Middletown and Shrewsbury were Jonothan Hulmes (Holmes), Edward Tart, Thomas Winterton and John Hans (Hance), but they refusing to take or subscribe to the oaths of allegiance and fidelity, but with provisoes and not submitting to the Laws and government, were dismissed.

PAGE 89–90.

An act to inforce the inhabitants of Middletown and Shrewsbury, to pay the rate passed November 7, 1668.

210 OLD TIMES IN OLD MONMOUTH.

Item. Whereas, there was an act of General Assembly, past the 30th day of May last for the rate of thirty pounds to be raised upon the country for the defraying of publick charge, and that equally to be levyed upon the towns that were then in being, (viz.), the town of Bergen, Elizabethtown, Newark upon Pishawack River, Woodbridge, Middletown and Shrewsbury, that is to say five pounds for each town.

Now the major part of the inhabitants of Middletown and Shrewsbury, refusing to pay the same, contrary to the consent and act of their own deputies, and likewise refuse to submit to the Laws of this Government. It is hereby inacted by this present General Assembly, that Mr. Luke Wattson and Mr. Samuel Moore, shall go and demand the aforesaid rate of five pounds from each town, together with forty shillings from each of the said towns, whichis their just proportion of a rate of twelve pounds, now made by this present General Assembly for the defraying of publick charges, which if they refuse to pay, the said Luke Watson and Samuel Moore, to take by way of distress, together with the charges and expenses of the country is and shall be at, for their obstinate refusal of paying their just dues according to Law, and for their so doing the General Assembly doth undertake to save them harmless.

It is further enacted by the authority aforesaid, that Luke Watson and Samuel Moore aforesaid, do demand the positive resolution of the inhabitants, or the major part of them, of the said towns, whether or no they will submit to the Laws and Government of the Province, under the Right Honorable John Lord Berkely and Sir George Cartaret, Knight and Baronet, the absolute Lord Proprietors of the same, according to His Royal Highness the Duke of York, grant, upon which answer the General Assembly will proceed accordingly.

LEAMING & SPICER.
PAGE 663-64.

New Jersey, May 28th, 1672.

Upon the address of James Grover, John Bowne, Richard Hartshorne, Jonathan Holmes, Patentees, and James Ashton, and John Hause, associates, impowered by the patentees and associates, of the Towns of Middletown and Shrewsbury, unto the Governor and Council for confirmation of certain privileges granted unto them by Col. Richard Nicolls, as by Patent under his hand and seal, bearing date the 8th day of April, Anno Domini one thousand six hundred and sixty-five, the Governor and Council do confirm unto the said Patentees and Associates, these Particulars following, being their Rights contained in the aforesaid Patent, viz:

Imprimis. That the said Patentees and Associates have full power, license and authority to dispose of the said lands expressed in the said Patent, as to them shall seem meet.

II. That no ministerial power or clergyman shall be imposed on among the inhabitants of the said land, so as to in force any that are contrary minded, to contribute to their maintenance.

III. That all causes whatsoever (criminals excepted) shall first have a hearing within their cognizance, and that no appeals unto higher courts, where sentence have been passed amongst them, under the value of ten pounds, be admitted.

IV. That all criminals and appeals, above the value of ten pounds which are to be referred unto the aforesaid higher courts, shall receive their determination upon appeals to his Majesty, not to be hindered.

V. That for all commission officers, both civil and military, the Patentees, Associates and Freeholders have liberty to present two for each office, to the Governor, whom they shall think fit, one of which the Governor is to commissionate to execute the said office, and that they have liberty to make peculiar prudential laws and constitutions amongst themselves according to the tenor of the said Patent.

PH. CARTARET.

JOHN KENNY,
LORDUE ANDRESS,
SAMUEL EDSALL,
JOHN PIKE,
JOHN BISHOP.

This compromise arrangement by Philip Carteret and his council, with the people of Monmouth, did not meet the approval of George Carteret, or subsequent proprietors. It had the effect of quieting the people of Monmouth, however, for some time. When opposition began again it was manifested through their deputies in General assembly, and not at town meetings.

The following extracts from Leaming and Spicer show the efforts of Lord Berkely and Sir George Carteret to deprive the settlers of Monmouth of their rights and privileges under the Nicolls Patent. They were friends and courtiers of the King of England, and could wield the whole power of the English Government, and of the colonial authorities, to advance and promote their own interests and suppress opposition. The Quaker and Baptist settlers of Monmouth protected by the wilderness their poverty, and that indomitable spirit which had enabled them to brave and survive persecutions, both in old and New England, cared but little for the Royal proclamations and edicts, requiring them to be submissive to the two courtiers, whose only object was to enrich themselves and increase their own individual power.

PAGE 31-32.

Copy of His Royal Highness, the Duke of York's letter, to Colonel Lovelace.

Colonel LOVELACE—I did in the year 1664 by Deed under my hand and seal, of the 24th of June, for the consideration therein mentioned, grant unto John Lord Berkely of Stratton, and Sir George Carteret, Knight and Baronet, their heirs and assigns, all that tract of land adjacent to New England to go westward of Long Island and Manhattan Island, as the same is bounded and set forth in and by the said deed, with all appurtenances whatsoever to the said lands and premises belonging, in as full and ample manner, as the same is granted unto me by His Majesty's Letters Patent, under the Great Seal of England, bearing date the 12th day of March, in the 15th year of His Majesty's Reign, of which said premises, they were actually possessed, by virtue of an indenture of lease by me made unto them, all of which has been sufficiently notified in those parts, both by the said grantees publickly pursuing the end of the said grant, and by my letters of the 28th of November, 1664, to Colonel Nicholls, then Governor of my Territories in America, signifying the same to him, and requiring him and all others therein concerned, to yield their best assistance in the quiet possession and enjoyment of the premises, to all such persons as my said grantees should at any time appoint and authorize to negotiate their affairs in those parts.

Nevertheless, I am informed that some contentious persons there, do lay claim to certain tracts of these lands, under color of pretended grants thereof, from the said Colonel Nicolls,* namely, one of the first of December, 1664, to John Baker and his associates, and another of the 8th of April to William Golding and his associates, * * both of which grants, (being posterior to my said grant of the 24th of June), as I am informed, are void in law, and therefore I would have you take notice yourself, and when occasion offers, make known to the said persons and to all others, if any be pretending from them that my intention is not at all to countenance their said Pretentions nor any others of that kind, tending to derogate in the least from any Grant above mentioned, to the said John Lord Berkeley and Sir George Carteret, their heirs and assigns; and they, my said Grantees, having promised to give effectual direction to their deputies and agents there to be assisting to you, I do desire you and all others herein concerned, in like manner, effectually to assist them in furthering the settlement and maintaining the quiet of these parts. Your loving friend,

JAMES * * *

WHITE-HALL, 25th November, 1672.

PAGE 35-36-37.

The Declaration of us, the Lords Proprietors of the Province of New Cæsarea or New Jersey. To all adventurers, planters, inhabitants, and all other persons, to whom it may concern, within any town and plantations in the said province.

We being made very sensible of the great disorders in the said Province, occasioned by several persons, to the great prejudice of ourselves, our Governor and council, and all other peaceable and well minded inhabitants within our said prov-

---

* The seizure of New York and New Jersey, or as then called, New Netherlands, by the expedition under command of Col. R. Nicolls, not only during time of peace and without declaration of war, but while a treaty of peace between England and Holland subsisted, led to a war between the two countries. Jan DeWitt, the Grand Pensionary of the Dutch Republic, was not the man to submit to such an outrage quietly. The Dutch fleets, under De Ruyter, penetrated River Thames, burnt the English shipping, threatened London and spread alarm and terror throughout Great Britain. After war of two years in which the advantage was with the Republic, it was concluded by the peace of Breda in July, 1667.

* * The Monmouth Patent.

* * * After the death of Charles II, his brother James, the Duke of York, became King, Feb. 6th, 1685, as James II. He was a bigoted scoundrel. In 1688 he was driven from his Throne and Kingdom by William of Orange, the Stadtholder of the Dutch Republic, who invaded England with an army of fifteen thousand Dutchmen. James II unjustly took New Yo k and New Jersey from the Dutch, and the Dutch took from him his Crown and Kingdom, and a Dutchman occupied his Throne. He died an exile in France, Sept. 2d, 1701.

ince, by claiming a Right of Propriety both of Land and Government.

(1) We do, therefore, hereby declare, that all lands granted by our Governor to the 28th of July, 1672, and confirmed in our names by Patents or charters, upon record in our secretary's office, and under our Province Seal, signed by him and the major part of his council, shall remain to the particular owners thereof, their heirs, etc., forever, with all the benefits, profits and privileges therein contained, they performing what they are obliged unto in every of the said respective Patents or charters.

II. For such as pretend to a right of Propriety to Land and Government, within our Province, by virtue of any Patent from Governor Colonel Richard Nicolls, as they ignorantly assert, we utterly disown any such thing. A Grant they had from him upon such conditions which they never performed.

For by the said Grant, they were obliged to do and perform such acts and things as should be appointed by his Royal Highness or his Deputies. The power whereof remains in us by virtue of a Patent from his said Royal Highness, bearing date long before these Grants, which hath been often declared by our Governor (and now ratified and owned under the sign manual of his said Royal Highness, to Colonel Lovelace, bearing date 25th of November, 1672), who demanded their submission to our authority, and to Patent their lands from us, and pay our Quit Rent according to our Concessions, which if they had done or shall yet do, we are content that they shall enjoy the tract or tracts of land they are settled upon, and to have such other privileges and immunities as our Governor and Council can agree upon; but without their speedy compliance as above said, we do hereby order our Governor and our Council to dispose thereof, in whole or in part, for our best advantage, to any other persons. And if any person or persons do think they have injustice or wrongs done by this our positive determination, they may address themselves to the King and Council, and if their Right to that land or government appears to be better than ours, we will readily submit thereunto.

III. Our order is, that those persons, that were the chief actors in attempting the making an alteration in our Government, be proceeded against, according to a declaration of our Governor and Council, bearing date the twenty-eighth day of May, 1672. except they shall immediately, upon publication hereof, make their addresses to our Governor and council for remission of their offences. And that all persons that have sustained any loss or damage by maintaining our just Right and Interest, since the 26th day of March, 1672, may have reparation in Law with their charges, they have and shall be at in any court or courts within our said Province, that are or shall be constituted and commissioned by special commission from our Governor, according to a declaration by our Governor and council, bearing date the third day of April, 1672.

IV. That all grants of land, conveyances, surveys or any other pretences for the Hold of land whatsoever, within our said Province, that are not derived from us according to the prescriptions in our Concessions and entered upon record in our Secretary's office in our said Province, we declare to be null and void in Law.

V. That the Constable of every respective town within our Province, shall have power by warrant from our Governor, to take by way of distress from every individual inhabitants within their respective jurisdictions, their just proportion of rent due to us yearly, beginning the 25th day of March, 1670, and for his charge and trouble about the same, if they refuse to deliver it in at some convenient place, which the said constable shall appoint, within their respective jurisdictions, by the 25th day of March, yearly, the constables only to be accountable to our Receiver General. And altho' our Concessions say it shall be paid in current or lawful money of England, yet at the request of our Governor and Council, we shall accept of it in such merchantable pay as the country doth produce at merchants' price to the value of money Stirling and if by this means we cannot obtain our rent, then the marshall of the Province shall be impowered as aforesaid, to collect the same at the charge of such the inhabitants, as do refuse to pay at the time and place aforesaid.

VI. That all matters and causes which have been tried in our Province, by special commission from our Governor, upon which judgment hath passed according to Law, be allowed by us and be forthwith put in execution.

Witness our our hands and seals the 6th day of December, 1672.

J. BERKELEY, (L. S.)
G. CARTERET, (L. S.)

On Page 38, John Berkeley and George Carteret, among other matters, promulgate the following order, for like the horse leeches daughter, their continual cry seemed to be give, give, give, viz :

"That the arrears of the quit rents of Elizabeth Town, Newark, Piscataquay and the two towns of Navesink,† and all others that have not paid since the year 1670, be paid to our Receiver General in three years from 1673, at the rate of one half penny a year for every acre, besides their growing rent, until their arrearages be satisfied and paid."

PAGE 38–39.

Proclamation form Charles II, King of England.
"Charles, R.††

Trusty and well beloved: We greet you well. Having been informed that some turbulent and disaffected persons, living and inhabiting within the Province of Cæsarea or New Jersey, (the Propriety whereof we have granted to our right, trusty and well beloved councellors, John Lord Berkeley of Stratton and Sir George Carteret, Knight and Baronet), do refuse to submit and be obedient to the authority derived from us to the said Lord Berkeley and Sir George Carteret, as absolute Proprietors of the same, to the great prejudice of the said Lords Proprietors, the disturbance of the inhabitants and hindrance of the whole Plantation there designed. We do therefore, hereby require you in our name, strictly to charge and command all persons whatsoever, inhabiting within the said Province, forthwith to yield obedience to the Laws and Government there settled and established by the Lords Proprietors, having the sole power under us to settle and dispose of the said country upon such terms and conditions as they shall think fit, and we shall expect a ready compliance with this, our will and pleasure, from all persons whatsoever dwelling or remaining within the aforesaid province, upon pain of incurring our high displeasure, and being proceeded against with due severity, according to law, whereof you are to give publick notice to all persons that are or may be concerned, and so we bid you farewell.

Given at our Court, at Whitehall, the 9th day of December, 1672, in the twenty-fourth year of our Reign.

By his Majesty's command,
HENRY COVENTRY."

PAGE 39–46.

Letter from Berkely and Carteret to the Deputy Governor and Council.
"Whitehall, the 10th December, 1672.

"We hope as soon as this comes to your hands, and that you have perused these papers, which we have sent by Mr. Moore, the turbulent spirits in that Province will not continue any longer in their obstinate and wonted extravagancies, but will be satisfied with His Royal Highness's letter to Colonel Lovelace, whom we desire you to assist on all occasions, the copy of which letter this Bearer brings with him to deliver unto you, and when received, we desire you to publish the same, with all other orders from us to the several inhabitants, that they may be informed of their mistakes, and how they have been mislead; for you will find his Royal Highness doth declare, that the Grants of Colonel Nicholls is posterior to our Patent, and therefore, both in law and equity, the right is solely in us, and upon that account we have sent over out determination concerning the Hold of Lands; as also our interpretation of some articles in our concessions, according to which we desire you to act, and not to recede from any of them. As for Mr. Bollen, we desire you to order our Receiver General to pay him out of our Quit Rents, the sum of ten pounds, yearly, for two years, from the date hereof. You will receive some Law Books to which you may apply yourself upon all occasions, and you shall not want any encouragement from us, that may contribute to your prosperity and welfare, not doubting that you will discharge the trust reposed in you, with as much candor and integrity for the maintenance of our just Rights and intent as we desire to remain

Your very loving Friends,
J. BERKELEY,
G. CARTERET."

PAGE 49.

Proclamation from Charles II, King of England.
Charles R.

Trusty and well beloved, we greet you well. Whereas, our right and well beloved Councellor, Sir George Carteret, Knight and Baronet by grant derived under us, is seized of the Province of New Cæsarea or New Jersey in America, and of the

---
† Middletown and Shrewsbury.
†† "R" stands for Rex, a Latin word meaning King.

jurisdiction thereof as Proprietors of the same, in the plantation of which said Province the said George Carteret has been at great charge and expense; and whereas, of late, great troubles and disorders have happened there by some ill affected persons, we being willing and desirous to encourage the inhabiting and planting of the said Provin' *, and to preserve the peace and welfare of all our loving subjects residing there, we do therefore, hereby require you in our name to use your most endeavours to prevent all troubles and disorders there, for the future and strictly to charge and command all persons whatsoever, inhabiting within the said Province forthwith, to yield obedience to the Laws and Government which are or shall be there established by the said Sir George Carteret, who hath the sole power under us, to settle and dispose of the said country upon such terms and conditions as he shall think fit; and we shall expect a ready complyance with this our will and pleasure, from all persons whatsoever dwelling or remaining within the same, upon pain of incurring our high displeasure, and being proceeded against according to law, whereof you are to give publick notice to all persons that are, or may be concerned. And so we bid you farewell. Given at our Court, at Windsor, the 13th day of June, 1674. In the 26th year of our Reign.

By his Majesty's command,

ARLINGTON.

Carteret seems to have determined to compromise the difficulties with the people of Monmouth, for in July, 1674, he made the following orders; page 53. As to the inhabitants of Navysink, considering their faithfulness to the Lords Proprietors, that upon their petition, their township shall be surveyed, and shall be incorporated, and to have equal privileges with other inhabitants of the Province, and that such of them who over the pretended Patentees, and laid out money in purchasing land from the Indians, shall have in consideration thereof, five hundred acres of Land, to each of them, to be alloted by the Governor and Council, in such places that it may not be predjudicial to the rest of the inhabitants, and because there is much Barren Land, after survey taken, the Governor and Council may give them allowance.

PAGE 93.

Capt. John Bound (Bowne), John Thog-morton (Throckmorton), for Middletown, have subscribed.

William Shatlock, John Slocum, for Shrewsbury; John Slocum hath subscribed, but the other refusing to swear or sub scribe, was dismissed.

This Assembly, among others, passed the following act:

PAGE 99.

XIII. Be it enacted by this present Assembly, that for the better maintaining and upholding of the lawful authority of the Province, and for the encouragement of the same, if any person or persons shall res'st the authority established by the Lord Proprietors, as namely, the Governor, Councelors, Justices of the Peace, either in words or action, either by wounds, blows or the like, or by speaking contemptuously, reproachfully or maliciously of any of them, as also to or of the Marshall or the respective constable, in or for the due execution of their respective offices, they, and either of them shall be liable to such fine, banishment or corporal' punishment, as the court before whom it shall come, shall Judge meet upon due exar nation thereof, from whose sentence no appeal to be allowed, the fines to be levied by way of distress according to the order of the said court for the use of the publick.

PAGE 123.

Acts made by the General Assembly, began at Woodbridge, the tenth day of October, 1677. We finding by constant experience for several years past, that the town of Shrewsbury hath been deficient, if not negligent and careless, in sending of their deputies, or sending such as will not conform to the order of the concessions respecting the Deputies, whereby the said Assembly is weakened, and the publick work hindered; and whereas, there is an Act of Assembly made for prescribing the same, and yet not redressed, it is therefore enacted by the present Assembly, that Richard Lippincott being chosen by the Town of Shrewsbu.y for this present year, to assemble with the rest of the Deputies, and not appearing a ording to order shall pay ten shillings for every day's absence during the time of the Assembly's sittings.

PAGE 151.

Proclamation from the King.

Charles, R.

Whereas, His Majesty for divers good

causes and considerations, him thereunto moving, by Letters Patents, bearing date the twenty-ninth day of June, Anno Dom ini 1674, in the twenty-sixth year of His Majesty's reign, was pleased to give and grant unto his dearest brother James, Duke of York, several Territories, Islands, and tracts of land in America, part of which were since called by the name of New Cæsarea, or New Jersey, and was vested in John Lord Berkely, of Stratton, and Sir George Carteret, Knight and Baronet, who were both of his Majesty's most Honorable Privy Council, and in their Heirs and Assigns; and the east part or portion of the said Province of New Jersey, by a certain deed of partition afterwards made, became the share of the said George Carteret, his heirs and assigns, and was agreed to be called East New Jersey, and was since assigned to the present proprietors.

And whereas, His Royal Highness James, Duke of York, by his indenture, bearing date the fourteenth day of March, Anno Dom. 1682, in the thirty-fifth year of his Majesty's Reign, (for the consideration therein mentioned), did grant and confirm the said Province of East New Jersey, (extending eastward and northward all along the Sea Coast and Hudson's River, from Little Egg Harbour to that part of Hudson's River, which is in forty-one degrees of northern latitude, and otherways bounded and limitted as in said grant and confirmation, relation being thereunto had, may more particularly and at large appear), unto James, Earl of Perth, John Drummond, of Lundie ; as also unto Robert Barclay, of Eury, Esq ; Robert Gordon, of Clunie, Esq ; and others, his Majesty's loving subjects in England, Scotland, and elsewhere, to the number of twenty-four grantees, and to their heirs and assigns forever, together with all powers and jurisdictions necessary for the good government of the said Province. His Majesty, therefore, doth hereby declare his Royal Will and Pleasure, and doth strictly charge and command the Planters and Inhabitants, and all other persons concerned in the said Province of East New Jersey, that they do submit and yield all due obedience to the Laws and Government of the said grantees, their heirs and assigns, as absolute Proprietors and Governors thereof, (who have the sole power and right derived under his Royal Highness from his said Majesty, to settle and dispose of the said Province upon such terms and conditions as to them shall seem good), as also to their Deputy or Deputies, Agents, Lieutenants, and officers, lawfully com nissionated, by them according to the powers and authorities granted to them. And of this, His Majesty's Royal Will and pleasure, the Governor and Council is required to give publick notice, his Majesty expecting and requiring forthwith, a due comliance with this his Royal will and pleasure, from all persons as well without the province as within the same, (who these presents do or may concern,) as they will answer the contrary thereof, at their peril. Given at the Court, at Whitehall, the twenty-third day of November, 1683, in the thirty-fifth year of his Majesty's Reign.

By his Majesty's command,

SUNDERLAND.

The new Proprietors seem to have overlooked or perfectly ignored the compromise effected by George Carteret, through his deputy, Philip Carteret, for in their instructions to their Deputy Governor, Gawen Lawrie, dated Nov. 13, 1684, occurs the following :

PAGE 198.

To end all controversies and differences with the men of Neversinks and Elizabeth town, or any other planters or persons whatsoever, concerning any pretended titles, or claim to land in the said Province. And we do hereby declare that we will not enter into any treaty on this side, with any of those people who claims by Colonel Nicholls Patent, nor with any others that challenge Land by Patents from the late Governor Carteret, as being both an affront to the Government there and of evil consequence, to make things to be put off by delays, and thereby hinder the settlement of our affairs in the Province.

Thus the old wounds were opened, and in spite of the Royal Proclamation the people of Monmouth did not shrink from the contest. Disorders soon began, which ended in the total loss to the Proprietors of the right of Government. They were unable to carry their points, and so voluntarily surrendered to the English Government, n 1702. And from that time, down to Revolution, the people of New Jersey, were ruled by Governors and councelors appointed by the British Government.

Extracts from the old Town Book of Middletown, showing the views and acts of the settlers of Monmouth in reference to the claims of Berkeley and Carteret, and their incessant efforts to squeeze money out of them under the name of quitrents and rates.

(Orthography corrected.)

October 28, 1668.—In a legal Town meeting, it was ordered that the following declaration shall be sent by the Deputies, to the General Assembly.

We freeholders, for the satisfaction of Governor and Council, declare,

That whereas, certain men, (by name) James Grover and John Bowne, appeared as deputies to act in the county's behalf ; we declare, that these men were not legally chosen according to summons. It was not published in any part of the connty until the night before, being the 24th of May. The Inhabitants being many and settled near twenty miles distant, could not be gathered together as above said. Yet it appears that some few, to whom the summons first came, made choice of them, unknown to the major part of the country, who had no hand in this choice, and knew not of their going as deputies, until they were gone. This we declare to the Governor and Council, conceiving under the circumstances, that we are not obliged to sustain their acts. The choice being so illegal, and being fearful to do any act which might infringe or violate any of the liber ties and privileges of our Patent†. This is our determination, which we desire our Deputies to present to the Governor and Council for their satisfaction, that it was neither contempt, obstinacy nor wilfulness on our part, but because the choice was not legal according to the summons.

Witness,
JAMES GROVER.
Town Clerk.

At the same town meeting held at Middletown village, the following resolution was adopted :

The inhabitants taking into consideration the liberties and privileges, granted by Patent, and fearing to have their Deputies involved by any oath, engagement or subscription, whereby any prejudice or infringement may come, upon the liberties and privileges thereof. do hereby order and enact, and by those present it is ordered and enacted, that the following Proviso shall be presented to the Governor and Council, to be inserted in the oath, engagement or subscription, viz : " Provided that no Law, Act or Command, which is, or may be made, enacted or commanded, shall in any way infringe the liberties and privileges of our Patent††. It is further ordered that if the Governor and Council please not to admit of this Proviso in the oath, engagement or subscription that then the Deputies shall refuse either to engage, promise or subscribe.

Nov. 1st, 1668.—Jonathan Holmes and Edward Tart were by pluralities of votes chosen Deputies from Middletown to the General Assembly at Elizabethtown.

February 1668-9.—The following resolution was passed at a town meeting in Middletown village.

In a legal Town Meeting for future security of the goods and chattels, which belong to the inhabitants of this Town, it is hereby ordered and agreed upon, that every inhabitant is jointly enjoined to give their assistance to secure the goods of every particular inhabitant against any one who shall attempt to take or carry anything out of the Town, under any pretence or colour whatsoever.

And it is further ordered, that every particular inhabitant shall make his appearance at demand or warning of the constable, or others authorized by him, to meet anywhere in the Town, under penalty of five pounds for non-appearance or non-assistance. And it is likewise ordered and agreed on by the inhabitants, that if any one who is an inhabitant, shall get into trouble about anything concerning the premises above specified, or shall be called, by virtue of any writ or warning to appear before any Governor or Court, on account of such appearance or assistance, that every such inhabitant shall have his time and expenses paid by the Town, and his private business go on during his absence.— These orders to stand in force until further orders. Ordered to be entered and subscribed by the major part of the Town.

At the same time, James Ashton, Jonathan Holmes, Richard Gibbons, Richard Stout, William Lawrence and Edward Tart were appointed, to answer the agents of the Proprietors in writing. The Clerk of the Town is authorized to receive the laws from Luke Watson and Samuel Moore the agents of the Proprietors. but to declare that the Town receives the laws, for their own security only.

---
†The Nicoll Patent of April 8, 1665.   ††Nicoll Patent.

OLD TIMES IN OLD MONMOUTH. 217

It was also determined at this Town Meeting, that no Inhabitant shall be seized upon or carried, by violence out of the Town, until the Town shall further determine.

The following entry is also made in Town Book, same day.

Forasmuch as Luke Watson and Samuel Moore, the Governor's messengers, do command us to aid and assist them, in distraining goods of the Inhabitants of Middletown, to discharge levies levied upon them. This we declare, that we own Captain Philip Carteret as our Governor, whose *lawful, good and just* commands, we shall and will obey in all things, not for wrath, but for conscience sake, toward God; the liberties and privileges of our Patent, however, to be maintained in a full and ample manner.

But forasmuch as the Governor has sent you to distrain the goods, from a people that have not as yet submitted to him.— (If the act of the General Assembly did not hold forth so much, *we would not say so,*)— though the same people will be ready to yield true submission to him, their Governor in all things good and lawful, the liberties and privileges of their Patent, however to be maintained.

We say, forasmuch as he has sent you to take distraint of their goods, as in our consciences we judge not to be just, *for how can anything be due from any man or people, who are not submitted ;* we shall be passive in refusing either aid or assistance to you, in this distraint.

March 17th, 1668-9.—In a legal town meeting, the major part being present, it was this day put to vote, concerning the answer to the demand of Luke Watson and Samuel Moore, who were authorized by the General Assembly, to demand our positive resolution of submission to the Government of the "absolute Lords Proprietors," as sayeth the Act bearing date November 7th.

It was unanimously resolved, that the following is our *positive resolution,* and shall be presented to the General Assembly viz:

That if the oath of allegiance to our Sovereign Lord the King, and fidelity to the Lords Proprietors interest, be the submission intended in the Act, this is our determination. That as true, loyal subjects to the King, we are ready, at all demands, either to engage, swear or subscribe all true allegiance to His Royal Majesty of England, as in duty bound, either before the Governor or any other Minister of Justice, authorized by him to administer the same, without any equivocation or mental reservation, as true, loyal subjects ought to do. This we will perform absolutely.

As to the "Lords Proprietors interest," this is a new and unheard of thing to us, and so obscure to us, that at present we are ignorant what it is. Yet as men not void of judgment, knowing right well that all oaths, engagements or subscriptions ought to be administered in truth, in righteousness and in judgment, upon which consideration, we are not willing to swear to we know not what. Yet by what has been presented and come to our hands from the Governor a several times, viz: An order or law came in the year 1666, prohibiting any from selling wine to the Indians, under great penalty, though it seems now that above the quantity of two gallons is tolerated by a law.

2d. Warrants coming to our hands, not in His Majesty's name, but in the Lords Proprietors name, being such a name as *we simple creatures* never heard of before.

3d. An account that our Deputies gave us, being returned from the General Assembly held in November last, who informed us that the Honored Governor told them (speaking concerning our Patent,) "That notwithstanding your Patent" said he, "yet new Lords must have new Laws." And further they declared to us, that the Governor told them "that Governor NICOLLS could not give away his Master's land ;" and further said, "that when your Patent was granted, Captain James Bollen, my Secretary, put in his caveat, and so put a stop to it." Captain Bollen then approved the same.

4th. An order coming from the Governor and Council, bearing date the first of March, 1668, prohibiting the Towns of Middletown and Shrewsbury from electing any officer, or any officer from executing any office, under penalty of being proceeded against as Mutineers.

6th. An act of the General Assembly styling the Right Honorable John Lord Berkley, and Sir George Carteret, the Absolute Lords Proprietors. By which we conceive, that the Lords Proprietors interests is not only the absolute sovereignty, from which all laws must originate, but also the absolute Propriety, from which all lands must be holden. We say, that if this is the interest specified in the Governor's late order, and intended as the oath, and in part the submission demanded by the Act, then this is our determination:

We have received a Patent from his Royal Highness, the Duke of York's Deputy, acknowledging that we had purchased our lands from the Chief Proprietors of the Country, and also impowering us to give prudential laws to ourselves, both for our own safety and our well being; should we submit our interests so far, as either engaging, swearing or submitting to the laws of the Government under the Lords Proprietors, how contrary and prejudicial it will be to our present safety, as witness a law made the last General Assembly, giving liberty to sell wine to the Indians, which liberty tends merely to our destruction, many sad former experiences have we had among us, witnessing the same; it being a liberty so contrary to the Laws of New York, from whence our Patent had its origin. Besides our Patent gives us such liberty as making laws for ourselves, how are we obliged to take laws from the government of the Lords Proprietors? (Criminal cases and appeals excepted.) By which it is manifest, that neither the Lords Proprietors, nor the General Assembly can in the least break our liberties and privileges. But we ourselves would be found to be self-violators of them, in submitting, by swearing to such an interest as we are not bound to do. Besides, at present no provision has been made by the Lords Proprietors Government for the conservation of the liberties and privileges of our Patent, they are liable to be infringed upon, by such acts as are passed by the majority vote of the General Assembly. Then how should we submit by swearing to the Laws of the Government, and not be guilty of violating our Patent ourselves.

And forasmuch as they are styled "Absolute Lords Proprietors," from thence it is also absolutely granted and necessarily follows, that all the Inhabitants who live in this Propriety, are the absolute tenants of the Lords Proprietors, and by virtue of their submission and oath to their interests, are irrevocably pledged to pay such Lords rent, and to sustain the interests to which they are sworn; should we submit to the interest so far as by swearing thereunto, having a propriety of land not only purchased from the Chief Proprietors of the Country, viz.: the Indians, but also granted unto us by the Deputy to His Royal Highness, the Duke of York (which appears under hand and seal,) it would be an act beneath the wisdom of the owners of such a Patent. And herein we should appear to be self-violators of our Patent ourselves.

And, forasmuch as the Lords Proprietors require rent from such Inhabitants as live upon this propriety, as appears in the concessions, viz.: a half penny an acre at least, should we submit so far to their interest by swearing, whose acknowledgments by virtue of a Patent to his Royal Highness; have their dependency upon such payments as others, his Majesty's subjects, do in the Government of New York to his Royal Highness. It would be be an act as we conceive, which would be a dishonor to him that gave it.

Therein we should appear to be self violators of our Patent ourselves; but, forasmuch, as there is an assignment made by His Royal Highness to the Lords Proprietors of such a tract of land, in which our Patent may be comprehended. We look at ourselves to be notoriously responsible to the Lords Proprietors, in all such acknowledgements as others, His Majesty subjects do, in the government of New York to His Royal Highness, but also to transmit all criminals from among ourselves, and such appeals as are proper to be transmitted, for the trial of the Lords Proprietors Government. These and no other, being the same injunctions which we once were subordinate to in the Government of New York, and not now in any way nullified, altered or changed, as we conceive, but only transferred by virtue of assignment to the said Lords Proprietors and their Government. Notwithstanding, for the future benefit and tranquility, and for the establishment of peace in the Province, we shall be willing to submit to the Lords Proprietors interest, according to the late order, provided that some secure way can be arranged or some provision made, by the Lords Proprietors government, which might secure us from destroying ourselves, by weakening our Patent, which we so highly prize, and which, indeed, is the very foundation of our livelihood. If no secure way or course can be thought of, or projected, to secure our interests, we are, at present, resolved not to entangle ourselves into any other interest appertaining to any man; but shall, *by the assistance of God, stick to our Patent.* The liberties and priviliges thereof are our interests, which were once committed to us, not to betray like treacherous men, who, for filthy lucre's sake, have been ready to betray themselves and others. But to deal faithfully with it, being a trust committed to us. In so doing, we conceive, we need not fear what any man or power can do unto us. And, forasmuch, as at present, we conceive that upon this, our interests, there has been, lately, an inroad made upon it, by virtue of an order coming from the Governor and Council, and by commission published in our town, prohibiting any officers that have been constituted by virtue of our Patent to excute any office, till they had sworn to the Lords Proprietors Interests, under penalty of being proceeded against as mutineers; to save which, we shall make our addresses unto the highest authority in the country, for remedy.— This is our positive resolution in answer to the Act, desiring further that this, our answer, may be presented to the General Assembly to prevent misinformation.

December 6, 1671.—In a legal Town Meeting, the major part being present, it was ordered that the folllowing writing shall be sent to the Governor and Council and Deputies of the Towns of this Province which are to assemble together, at Elizabeth town on the 12th of the present month.

Capt. Philip Carteret Honored Governor, the Council and Deputies of the General Assembly. We received by the hand of some of the men of Woodbridge, the late acts of the General Assembly, at their last adjournment, bearing date 22nd of November, and also a summons under hand and seal of the Province for choice of Burgesses for a further Assembly to be held on the 22th of the present month, both of which being enclosed in a paper sent unto us by the Honored Governor, desiring our compliance to answer the summons, and further requiring our positive answer by the bearer.

To which we say, that such is and has been our forwardness to comply at all times, that there has been and is no need of any occasion, either to instigate or augment our forwardness thereunto. Having not at any time wilfully omitted any opportunity, of appearing by our deputies to do such service, as has been requiied of us. Besides the sincerity of our desires being so well known to God and our own consciences herein. In point of true loyal submission to the Government of the Lords Proprietors so far forth as is proper to our condition, to the very utmost that can be claimed from us, whose just powers, we have formerly (as it is well known) with all plainness owned. But when we consider (having pondered we in our minds), the late act was presented to us, and being therein charged with no less than contempt of authority of Government; the charge being so general, viz.; the Towns of Middletown and Shrewsbury, the forcibleness of the charge so great, viz.; an Act of the General Assembly and withall, judging the charge, the whole ground of the Act, for what greater force can there be than a General Act.

We say, (weighing these things in the balance of equity), we judge ourselves at present, altogether incapable of answering the summons. Apprenending ourselves at present rather in need to be cleared publicly of so grave a charge, than to join with the Governor, Council and Deputies of the towns of the Province, in the exercise of any legislative power, for the settlement of any thing, needful and necessary for the well governing of this Province. And should now appear and answer to the charge, if that writ had appeared amongst us, which the late Assembly gave the Governor, the power to issue forth. Furthermore (conceiving under correction) that no such prerogative or privilege may be conferred upon contemners and despisers of government, much less, no such thing as either the dignity of a Freeholder to elect, or the dignity of a Deputy to act for the good and welfare of any State or Province; and therefore for the full clearing of ourselves, our desire is that the late Act (according to the current thereof), may be exactly prosecuted so that the power, (which the late Assembly of Deputies at their last adjournment, took upon them to give the Governor), may now be put in execution. For had that writ appeared now amongst us, we question not, but we should have showed our ready and willing obedience to have answered thereunto, being careful of incurring any attainder of rebellion. But that writ appearing not among us, we judge ourselves not obliged to come to answer; and thus in brief, have we given account of our present condition. Under favor, waiting only with all humility, (pro forma tantum), as to what is further required of us in the late act, viz: to show cause why we will not pay our just proportion of the expences of provisions expended at two Assemblies, in the year 1668. We answer, that what was expended at the Assembly, held May 25th, 1668, we had no deputies there to expend. Further what was expended at the adjournment in November following in the same year, our deputies who were there, were not suffered to act, but some of them have reported to us, that the Deputies of the Towns of the Province, invited them one night to supper, which before their departure thence they tendered them money for it, so that, as we abhor all such baseness of spirit as to eat any man's bread for naught, we came not by what we have *so lightly*, as to pay other men's expences, who we conceive rather show an evil mind in desiring it.

So that if anything by the Power of the Province be forced from us at any time, (upon this account), viz, for the discharge of expences of provisions for these two Assemblies, we hope we shall neither be ashamed or afraid to declare it to be an open and manifest wrong. Further, we give you to understand the cause and reason why our deputies appeared not, at the last adjournment. When the time came for them to go, our vessel was accidently drove away, by which means they were disabled from coming, and for the season of near fourteen days together, no vessel could be got in any capacity to transport them. This being the very ground and reason why they came not, and therefore we answer, that which providentially happens, men of reason and understanding will be well satisfied therewith.

It is further ordered, that the Clerk (at present) shall sign to above answer, in the name of the Town, and shall send it back by the Woodbridge men, with the directions running thus, viz: To the Honorable Governor and Council and Deputies of the Towns of this Province, assembled together at Elizabethtown.
Testis:

EDWARD TART, T. C.

SOME EXTRACTS FROM THE "RECORD OF THE GOVERNOR AND COUNCIL OF EAST NEW JERSEY, 1682—1703," RELATING TO MONMOUTH.

Page 60—61.

At a Council held 17th of May, 1683.

In the afternoon we entered into a debate, after some small summary of our forenoon's discourse, about the demand of Neversinkes, by colour or virtue of the Nicoll Patent. After a long debate of three or four hours, our discourse came to this result. That after the Duke of York and the King, by their letters, had required all persons to submit to the Government of Sir George Carteret, at and upon these terms. And this Province had knowledge thereof, viz: in the month of May, A. D. 1673, John Bowne and James Grover, for, and in behalf of the Towns of Neversinkes, petitioned the Governor and Council that no conclusion should be made of their Patent rights till they could make their address to the Proprietors; and that when they had made such address, they would acquiesce in the Lords Proprietors determination, To which the Governor and Council then agreed. That the said Petitioners, in pursuance thereof, sent a petition and remonstrance to the then Lords Proprietors, yielding all their pretensions up to the Lords Proprietors, which Petition was read by the Lords Proprietors September 5th, 1673.—After this resignation the Lords Proprietors, by their grant under their hands and seals, ordered and granted unto the Patentees 500 acres of land apiece. The Patentees accepted of the same and petitioned to have the same laid out. Warrants were granted for the same. Some were surveyed and patented, particularly that of Richard Hartshorne, which appeared to be a full conclusion of that affair, unless it was made to appear that such petitions and procedure, were not by consent or approbation of the Town.

They being done by approbation of some who subscribed to that purpose.—Richard Hartshorne declared, as for his own part, he believed that all persons would pay for their patented land in those two Towns, and for his own part he would. But the matters being transacted by John Bowne, now speaker of the House of Deputies, it was proposed that he and Joseph Parker, now deputies of those two Towns, should debate the premises further to-morrow, and so the debate with night concluded.

Adjourned to 7 o'clock to-morrow morning, at a Council held the 18th day of May, A. D. 1683.

Present—the Deputy Governor, Samuel Groome, Thomas Warne, Proprietors.—Capt. Berry, Capt. Sandford, Lawrence Andress, Benj. Price, of the Council.

PAGE 62—63.

John Bowne, Richard Hartshorne and Joseph Parker came here, and in open Council, a summary discourse was had

OLD TIMES IN OLD MONMOUTH.   221

with them of all matters passed yesterday.

And after a serious debate upon the agreement and settlement made by the late Lords Proprietors with the two towns of Neversinkes, debated yesterday. We inquired into the truth of those petitions and addresses, and the submission and resignation of their pretended rights to the late Lords Proprietors. And they all owned and agreed they were true, but alleged that the same was done for fear. It was answered that the like allegation may ever be made, but as an evidence to the contrary, the petitioners themselves demonstrated besides, that the patentees had after the Lords Proprietors grace and favors, granted them 500 acres of land apiece, they returned a letter of acknowledgement and thanks. And their Associates, in compliance therewith, all patented their land according to the Concessions, none excoepted, and continued ever after satisfied therewith. All contented with what was done, and made no demonstration of the least dissatisfaction, which proved a voluntary and satisfactory agreement.

Inspection was made of the Books, and therein was viewed their several warrants for lands to the patentees, several whereof enjoy them to this day.

The Patentees alleged they were to have their land free of rent. It was answered no, for that grants of that nature was no otherwise but by rent, as the late Governor and others, and as also Richard Hartshorne, who had his Patent and he declared he would pay his rent, and believed all the Inhabitants of these two towns would do the same. An authority under all the people hands was produced, and they left to the persons above and three more, which three others were not here, however they alleged they had full power in themselves to end all pretensions with us. Then was inspected the late Lords Proprietors resolve, wherein they give 500 acres of land apiece to the Patentees, and order allowance for Barrens to all others the Associates. Then it was offered that such allowance was given, as particularly to R. Hartshorne three acres for one in respect of Barrens, and others in proportion to the barrenness of the soil. But if any complained of due allowance, we were ready to make a resurvey for further allowance, which seemed to conclude the business without further difficulty. But Richard Hartshorne, Joseph Parker and John Bowne, consulting privately together, told us, they were limited by the Towns, what terms to make, notwithstanding under their hands they had given full power, which was to demand to have all their land, at half a bushel of wheat, for one hundred acres. Then we told them we hoped they would show us such limitation, as well as the other full authority.

Their limitation they alleged, they had not in writing, but by word of mouth. That we told them was unfair; to have one authority to produce in order to treat, and another secret, which they told not us of when we entered into the treaty. And such commissions and authorities, wise and honest men have frequently refused, as not fit for honest men to execute. So this being their terms, and now having their words for it, and nothing under-hand, besides the unreasonableness of the demand, we found cause to dissent from further debate. They then alleged, as for all quit rents for lands patented, they would pay, and other pretensions leave, until it could be otherwise composed. We then proposed to them that the case should be fairly from first to last, from the Patent of Governor Richard Nicolls to this day, be stated without a comment, and to leave the whole to any lawyers, judges, honest men, or king and council for a final end; or if they had any other ways to propose, we desired them to offer it. Upon which they, not seeming to incline to any friendly end, neither accepted nor rejected our proposition, nor offered any other ways or means, to end or determine the same, but left us, which is the sum of our conference.

It may be remarked that the Governor and Council represented the Proprietors and their interests. The House and Deputies represented the inhabitants of the different towns.

The people of Monmouth under the leadership of John Bowne, early learned that the best way to oppose the Proprietors, was through their representatives in the House of Deputies. And in this way their opposition was manifested, especially to obtain the management of their local affairs. The disputes between the Governor and Council, and the Deputies were many and bitter, and the men of Monmouth appeared to be the leading spirits in this opposition. The above extract shows how near the conflicting claim under Nicolls Patent, and those under grant to

Berkely and Carteret ever came to a settlement. The breach grew wider and wider, until the Proprietors were compelled to yield up their right of government to the English Crown, which happened in 1702.

PAGE 69.

Message from Deputies in writing.

Considering the season of the year and the necessity of the Representatives of this province to be at their habitations, the weather being so wet, by which reason their crops of corn may be in much danger, to their great damage and loss, which, possibly may be prevented by their speedy repairing home, wherefore, the Deputies move for an adjournment of this Assembly, until the third Tuesday of October next.

Order of the House.
JOHN BOWNE.

Elizabeth Town, May 22d, 1683.

The Governor and Council returned the message without any answer.

PAGE 107.

May 29th, 1684.

A petition from John Bowne setting forth that his father John Bowne, deceased, had an order to take up and purchase of the Indians 500 acres of land, granted by the late Lords Proprietors to him as a patentee of Neversinkes. That he had purchased the land of the Indians, and requests to have a warrant to survey the same to him. The matter being here fully debated and Capt. Bowne†, brother to the petitioners' father, and the petitioner being here present, and being inquired whether the widow Bowne had Nicoll's Patent, they answered they believed not, but they believed Richard Hartshorne had the same. The petitioner said his father some time past had it, that the last spring, 12 months, it was sent for to those parts, and his mother delivered the same to the Messenger. It appearing that the 500 acres granted to the deceased was for the surrender or resigning of Gov Nicolls' Patent, of which he was one of the patentees. It was ordered it be referred to the Governor to answer the Petitioners' request, who may grant the warrant for survey as he sees meet and just.

John Bowne, whose name appears so prominently on our early records, was a trusted leader of the first settlers, and whatever has a tendency to throw light on his character, must be of interest. The following is a copy of an old paper found among the private papers of an old Monmouth county family:

"Some words of Advice or Councell spoken by Capt. John Bowne to his children, as he lay on his death Bed, Jan'y ye 3rd, 168¾."*

"There is no way in the whole world for a man to obtain felicity, in this world or in the world to come, but to take heed to the ways of the Lord, and to put his trust in Him, who deals faithfully and truly with all men; for he knocks at the doors of your hearts, and calls you to come and buy, without money and without price. My desire is, that in all actions of Meum and Teum you deal not deceitfully, but plane hearted with all men, and remember that your dying Father left it with you for your instruction, that when trust is with your Honor to preserve it. And in all contracts and bargains that you make, violate not your promise, and you will have praise. Let your Mother be your counsellor in all matters of difference, and goe not to Lawyers, but ask her councell first. If at any time, any of you have an advantage of a poor man at law, O pursue it not, but rather forgive him if he hath done you wrongue, and if you do so, you will have help of the Law of God and of his people. Give not away to youthful jolities and sports, but improve your leisure time in the service of God. Let no good man be dealt churlishly by you, but entertain, when they come to your house. But if a vitious, wicked man come, give him meat and drink to refresh him, and let him pass by your doors. It has been many times in my thoughts, that for a man

---

† Capt. Andrew Bowne.

* Pope Gregory XIII, in 1582 changed the calendar of Julius Cæsar; this calendar gave each year about eleven minutes too much. This error in 1582, amounted to about ten days, and at this time, 1877, would be about twelve days. Pope Gregory deducted ten days from the year 1582, by ordering October 5th to be called the 15th. He also introduced the system of leap year. This Gregorian calendar was adopted by an act of the English Parliament in 1752, the 3d of the month of September, of that year, being called the 14th, making a deduction of eleven days from this year. From the 14th century to 1752, the legal and ecclesiastical year began on the 25th of March, although in ordinary usage, particularly among the Catholics, it was frequently the case to begin the year with January. Thus two styles of computing the year prevailed in England and the Colonies. The change by law in 1752, conformed to popular usage, and made January, February and March, the first three months of the new year, instead of the last three months of the old year. In Monmouth county old tombstones and old papers are often seen with the date written thus —170%. This was to cover both styles. Thus the date given above of 168¾ shows that according to old style and the legal year prior to 1752, Capt. Bowne died in the ninth month of 1683, but according to new style and legal year since 1752, he died in the first month of the year 1684.

OLD TIMES IN OLD MONMOUTH. 223

to marry a wife and have children, and never take any care to instruct them, but leave them worse than the Beasts of the Field, that if a man ask concerning the things of God, they know not what it means, O this is a very sad thing. But if we can season our hearts, so as to desire the Lord to assist us, he will help us and not fly from us."

Capt. John Bowne's wife survived him many years. Her name was Lydia. After his death she lived with one of his sons in Monmouth.

THE DUTCH CONQUEST.

In July, 1673, the two Dutch Admirals, Cornelis Evertsen and Jacob Binckes with their squadrons, appeared before New York City.

The English surrendered without resistance, and the three-colored ensign of the little Republic once more floated over New York and New Jersey. The city was called New Orange, and Fort James was called Fort William Hendrick. This conquest was not treacherously effected in time of peace, but during open war between England and Holland.

A Council of War was organized, consisting of the Admirals and Captains, for the government of the country. A watch was stationed on the Navesinck Hills, to send word of approaching ships to the authorities. The Netherlanders held sway, until under the treaty of peace between Holland and England, on the 9th of February, 1674, the New Netherlands were transferred to England, and on the 10th of November following, the Dutch Governor, Captain Colve, delivered the country over to Sir Edmund Andros, the English Governor. For the first time England obtained the lawful and just control of New York and New Jersey. Her right was now undisputable, but until this time she had no just right to the sovereignty of this territory, unless "might makes right."

The following extracts from Vol. 2 of Documents relating to the Colonial History of New York, comprise all therein contained relating to Monmouth County, with some notes by E. B. O'Callaghan, the Editor, which serve to explain this period of Dutch occupation.

PAGE 572.

Cornelis Evertsen was the oldest son of the renowned Admiral Cornelis Evertsen, who was killed in the naval fight with the English, June 11th, 1666. Being a Captain in the navy on the death of his father, the States of Zealand recommended that he be put in command of a ship of war, and on the 15th of December, 1672, he was promoted to the rank of Commander of a squadron of fifteen ships of the line, with which he proceeded to the West Indies, where he captured seven and burned five vessels, and obtained considerable booty. He afterwards destroyed sixty five French Newfoundland traders, and sailed to Martinico, where he met Capt. Jacob Binckes, in command of four men of war. Having joined forces, they visited all the English and French islands and took a ship bound to Galway. After inflicting much damage on the enemy in these islands, he sailed to New York, which he reduced, and changed the name of the country to New Netherlands, and of the city to New Orange. By this time, he had with him about twenty English prizes captured in the Virginia waters, and elsewhere and many prisoners. In December, 1673, he returned to Cadiz, after destroying more than eighty English and French ships, and capturing New York and St. Eustatius. In 1675 he was appointed Rear Admiral; in 1679 Vice Admiral; and in 1688 Admiral, in which last capacity he commanded a squadron, which accompanied William III to England.

On 30th of June, 1690, he engaged the French Fleet off Beachy Head, but through the treachery of Admiral Torrington, who commanded the English portion of the allied fleet, he was forced to retreat to Rye Bay. Torrington was committed to the Tower and the Dutch Admiral received the thanks of the King.

After a life of great activity in which he covered himself with glory, Admiral Evertsen died in November, 1706, and was buried at Middelburgh, in St. Peters Church, *Kok* XIV, 564.

E. B. O'CALLAGHAN.

PAGE 579.

At a meeting of the Commanders and Honorable Council of War of New Netherlands, holden in Fort William Hendrick, on Saturday, 19th of August, A. D. 1673.

Present, Commander Jacob Binckes, Commander Cornelis Evertsen, Captain Anthony Colve.

The Deputies from the Towns of Elizabethtown, Newark, Woodbridge, Piscataway, Middletown and Shrewsbury appearing, are ordered to call together the inhabitants of their respective towns; and have them nominate by plurality of votes, a double number for schepens or magistrates of said towns; also from each town to elect two Deputies, who shall meet together as one board, and there nominate by the greater number of votes, three persons for Schouts, and three for secretary, over the said six towns, to which end the following act is sent to each of them.

The Commanders in Chief and Council of War at Fort William Hendrick, do hereby order and strictly require the inhabitants of Elizabethtown to call a Town Meeting, and by a general vote to nominate six persons for magistrates of their said Town, also to appoint two Deputies, who are to meet with the rest of the Five neighboring towns, viz: Newark, Woodbridge, Piscataway, Middletown and Shrewsbury; which said Deputies shall be authorized to nominate three persons for schout and three for secretary, out of which nominated persons, we will select for each town three magistrates, and for the said six towns in general, one for schout and one for secretary. The said inhabitants and deputies are hereby required to make a return thereof to us within the next six days ensuing. Dated at Fort William Hendrick, the 19th of August, A. D. 1673.

JACOB BINCKES,
CORNELIS EVER'SEN, JR.

Jacob Binckes, after the reduction of New York, returned to Europe, and obtained considerable reputation in the war between France and Holland, in which he commanded a squadron of thirteen ships. With them he set sail on the 16th of March, 1676, against the French possessions in the West Indies, and arrived before the Island of Cayenne, on the 4th of May, attacked the place with great fury, and reduced it in a short time; after which he captured St. Martins and proceeded to the Island of Tobago, then in the possession of the Dutch, whether he was followed in February, 1677, by Count de'Estrees, the French Admiral, who demanded the surrender of the Fort. This being refused, the place was stormed, and the Dutch fleet attacked. After an engagement, which lasted from the break of day until night, the French were obliged to retire with considerable loss, leaving the victory to the Dutch.

M. de'Estrees returned to France, whence he was again despatched in October and arrived in December following, with sixteen sail of the line before Tobago. Then he landed 1,500 men with suitable artillery and summoned Commander Binckes, who refused to surrender. The place was soon after invested and the cannonading began on both sides. Towards noon, Commander Binckes, Captain de'Montigney of the marines, and other officers were about sitting down to dinner. Unfortunately the dining room was directly over the magazine or store, where the ammunition was kept. Along the pathway leading from the store to the battery, much powder was strewed by those supplying the gunners, and one of the enemy's fire balls falling in the path, set the train on fire, and in a moment the magazine exploded, instantly killing Vice Admiral Binckes and most of his officers. —*Kok* VI, 562; *History of the Buccaniers*, 3d edition, London, 8 vo., 1,704, pp. 177–180. Thus perished on the 12th December, 1677, in the height of a brilliant career, this brave seaman who identified himself with our history by the reduction of New York, thus vindicating the honor of Fatherland.

E. B. O'CALLAGHAN, ED.

PAGE 582.

August 23.—Middletown and Shrewsbury presented names of persons, nominated for Magistrates to the Council of War. From these on the next day, Cornelis Evertsen, Jacob Binckes and Anthony Colve selected as schepens of Shrewsbury, John Hance, Eliakim Wardell and Hugh Dyckman, who were ordered to come to Fort William Hendrick and be sworn in. This they did on the first of September.

PAGE 589.

At a meeting of the Council of War, August 29, the following oath was prescribed to the Inhabitants of English origin, to take—We do swear in the presence of Almighty God, that we will be true and faithful to the High and Mighty Lords, the States General, the United Provinces of his serene Highness, the Lord Prince of Orange, and to their Government here, for the time being, and to behave ourselves upon all occasions, as true and lawful subjects, provided only, that we be not forced to take up arms against our own nation, if they be sent hither by authority of His Majesty of England, except they be accompanied by the forces of other nations, then we oblige ourselves to take up arms against them, so help us God.

PAGE 598.

Sept. 6.—Captain Knyff of the Dutch infantry or marines, and Lieut. Snell, are ordered to proceed to Shrewsbury and Middletown and administer the oath of allegiance to the Inhabitants. These officers doubtless went over in a sloop, taking their company with them. It was an eventful day in Middletown, when these Dutch officers and soldiers marched into the village and exacted this oath, probably on a Dutch Bible. The English settlers had very little reverence for the Bibles of the Hollanders. They always insisted, that the devil's hoofs and horns stuck out of every Dutchman's Bible. Having such an opinion, an oath on such a Bible, would be of little force.

PAGE 607-8.

On the 13th of September, Capt. Knyff and Lieut. Snell returned and reported to the Council of War, That there were sixty men in Middletown, and fifty-two had sworn allegiance to the Republic of Holland, and eight were absent. In Shrewsbury there were sixty-eight men, thirty-eight of whom had taken the oath and eighteen who were Quakers, promised allegiance to the Dutch Government, and that twelve were absent. Capt. Knyff and Lieutenant Snell, swore in the following officers of militia.

Middletown.   JONATHAN HOLMES, Capt.
               JOHN SMITH, Lieut.
               JOHN LONGSTREET, Ens'n.
Shrewsbury   WILLIAM NEWMAN, Capt.
               JOHN WILLIAMS, Lieut.
               NICHOLAS BROWNE, Ens'n.

PAGE 617.

Free Pass for Walter Webly. Whereas, I am informed that Walter Webly, still scruples to come hither, through fear that he should be molested, on account of the effects, which he hath removed hence, for the benefit of the orphan child of the late Richard Morris, therefore have I thought proper on request to me made, in his behalf, to grant to said Walter Webly again, free conduct and passport, and at the same time to make known, that it was never intended to seize the effects of said child, but only those belonging in lawful propriety to Col. Lewis Morris. Dated Fort William Hendrick, 26th of Sept., 1673.
ANTHONY COLVE.

PAGE 619.

On request made on behalf of Col. Lewis Morris, pass and repass is granted to him to come into this government, on condition that he attempt nothing to its prejudice during his sojourn.

Notice is this day sent to the magistrates of the Town situate at the Nevesings, near the sea coast, which they are ordered to publish to their inhabitants, that they on the first arrival of any ships from sea, shall give the Governor the earliest possible information thereof.

Whereas, the late chosen Magistrates of Shrewsbury are found to be persons, whose religion will not suffer them to take any oath, or administer the same to others, therefore they cannot be fit persons for that office. I have thought fit to order that the Inhabitants of said Town, make a new nomination of four persons of the true Protestant church religion, out of which I shall select two and continue one of the former Magistrates of said Town. Dated at Fort William Hendrick, 29th of Sept. 1673.   ANTHONY COLVE.

"Lewis Morris was a native of Monmouthshire, Wales, and Commander of a troop of horse in the Parliament Army against Charles I. He afterward, went to the West Indies, purchssed "a lovely estate" on the Island of Barbadoes, and was member of the Council of that Island. In 1654, an expedition having been fitted out against the Spanish possessions in those parts, a commission of Colonel was sent to him by Protector Cromwell, but when the fleet arrived at Barbadoes in 1655, " he prized himself at so high a rate" that he demanded a present of one hundred thousand weight of sugar, to pay his debts, before he would consent to accompany the fleet. He finally, however, consented, and was present at the reduction of Jamaica, after which he returned to Barbadoes, and is said to have been interested in the purchase of St. Lucia in 1663. He now openly professed the principles of the Quakers, and as one of their prominent members entertained the celebrated George Fox, at his seat near Bridgetown, when he visited Barbadoes in 1671; he signed the addresses to the Governor and Legislature, complaining of the persecution to which the Friends were subjected. Mr. Morris himself had been mulcted in fines to the amount of 15.193 pounds of sugar, for refusing to pay church dues and ministers money, and to furnish men and horses for the militia. On receiving intelligence of the death of his brother Richard, he came to this country, whilst it was in possession of the Dutch in the year 1673 and not after the year of 1674, as erroneously stated by Dunlap and others. After visiting Barbadoes for the purpose of winding up his affairs, he returned to New York in 1675 and settled at Broncks land, Westchester county, for which he received a patent the 25th of March, 1676. He was afterwards a member of Governor Dongan's Council from 1683 to 1686 and died in the year 1691 at his "plantation over against Harlem." This property is called "his manor of Morrisania," by Mr. Whitehead, in the *Introductory Memoir* to the papers of Governor Morris, p. 3, but erroneously.— The Manor of Morrisania was not erected until the 6th of May, 1697, some six years after Colonel Morris' death. Granville Penn's Memorial, Admiral Penn. II, 41, 42, 46 ; Fox's Journal, folio 433.

Besse's Sufferings of the Quakers, II. 313, 314, 315, New York Council Minutes. V. 43, 78, 86, 93, 158, VII. 109.

E. B. O'CALLAGHAN, Editor.

PAGE 658.

Proclamation of a day of Humiliation and Thanksgiving. Trusty and well beloved :

Considering the manifold blessings and favors which the Bountiful and Merciful God, hath been pleased graciously to bestow on this province and the inhabitants thereof, among which is to be *esteemed beyond all others*, the free and pure worship of God, which blessing, together with all others ought not only to draw and oblige us to dutiful thankfulness, but also to meekness and repentance, because of our manifold sins and transgressions. To the end that said blessings and favors of our God, may be continued towards us, and that this people and country may be free from his well deserved wrath and indignation. Know ye therefore, that we have thought it necessary, and do by these presents order and proclaim, a universal day of fast, humiliation and thanksgiving, which shall be held in this province, on the first Wednesday of the ensuing month of December, being the second day of that month, and so also upon the every first Wednesday of the month ensuing. To the end that said day of Humiliation and Thanksgiving may be the better put in practice, and execution, we do strictly prohibit and forbid, on the said day of Humiliation and Thanksgiving, all manner of labor, and exercisings, of hunting, fishing, gaming, excess in drinking and the like. All innkeepers and ordinaries not to retail any liquor or drink, upon penalty of corporal punishment. To the true performance of which, we do hereby strictly order and command all magistrates, officers and justices of this Province to prosecute all transgressors, according to the tenour thereof, and to cause this Proclamation to be published in due time and place. So we recommend you to the protection of Almighty God. Trusty and well beloved,

Your loving friend,
ANTHONY COLVE.

In Fort Wm. Hendrick, the 15th of November.

By order of the Governor General of the New Netherlands.

NICHOLAS BAYARD,
Secretary.

This is the first record we have of Thanksgiving Proclamation in Monmouth. This was doubtless read at Middletown and Shrewsbury. The rough sea fighter and sailor, Capt. Colve, writes like a minister, but it was probably dictated by some Dutch clergyman.

PAGE 694.

At a council held March 8th, 1674, Bartholomew Applegate, Thomas Applegate and Richard Sadler, present a petition requesting, in substance, that they may be allowed to purchase from the Indians, a tract of land situate about two leagues on this side of Middletown, near Nevesings, fit for a settlement of six or eight families. This request was granted on condition, that after the land is purchased, they take out formal patents for it, and actually settle it within two years after purchase.

PAGE 706.

At a Council held April 18, 1674, John Bowne and Richard Hartshorne, residing at Middletown, both for themselves and partners, give notice that the land granted to Bartholomew Applegate, Thomas Applegate and Richard Sadler, in their petition, is included in their, the Petitioners Patent, and requested that said land may be denied to said Applegates.

The Council ordered Bowne and Hartshorne, within six weeks from date, to prove that land in question is included within their Patent, then further action will be taken.

A certain Proclamation being delivered to the council, from the Magistrates of the Town of Middletown, prohibiting and forbidding all inhabitants from departing out of said Town, unless they give bail to return, as soon as their business shall have been performed, or they be employed in public service, and requesting the Governor's approval of the same ; which proclamation, being read and considered, it is ordered by the Governor-General and Council, that no inhabitant can be hindered from changing his domicil within this Province, unless arrested for lawful cause. However, no one shall depart from the Town of Middletown, unless he previously notifies the Magistrates of his intention.

PAGE 707.

April 25, 1674.—We are this day informed that a ship or ships have come to anchor within Sandy Hook. Capt. Cornelis Ewoutse is hereby ordered instantly to sail with the Snow, under his command to Sandy Hook, to learn what ships they be, and give me notice thereof in the speediest manner, but at the same time take care not to imperil the Snow.

A. COLVE.

The above comprises all the record there is, so far as our County of Monmouth is concerned. The only record we have of this period in our County, is that contained in the Old Town Book of Middletown Township, as follows :

August 3d, 1673.—Upon receipt of a summons for choice of deputies, from the city of New Orange, by order of the Admirals and Commanders in Chief of the fleet, belonging to the States General and Prince of Orange; and also by order of Captain John Berry, late Deputy Governor, the Town this day convened together for election. And upon a perfect vote James Grover and John Bowne were, by the pluralities of votes, chosen deputies to treat with the said Admirals and Commanders in Chief. And unto whom full power, license and authority are hereby conferred, to make a full and plenary surrender, upon such articles as shall be agreed on. The summons or notice is ordered to be recorded as follows :

The 30th of July. Fort James and the city of New York, being this day reduced to the obedience of the States General and Prince of Orange, by certain ships of war. The Admirals and Commanders in Chief of said fleet sent a summons to this Town, to come and yield to certain articles of surrender the 5th of the present month, otherwise to expect to be subdued by force of arms. A true copy of which is as follows, viz: "The Inhabitants of Middletown and Shrewsbury, in the Province of New Jersey, are hereby forcibly charged and required, to send their deputies of the said Towns to this place, on Tuesday morning next, to treat with us upon certain articles of surrender. On refusal we shall be necessitated to subdue you by force of arms. Dated at the State House at the city of New Orange, the first day of August, 1673.

CORNELIS EVERSON DE JOYCE,
JACOB BEHELL, (BINCKES).
NICHOLAS BIARD, (BAYARD),
Secretary.

By order of the Admirals and Commanders in Chief of the Fleet riding in the North River.

You are hereby required to make choice of two deputies for your Town, and that they appear at the city of New York, on Tuesday ensuing next, being the fifth instant, to consider and advise of what conditions shall be thought best, to endeavor to obtain. Being required by the General to give you notice of the time appointed, for debating and determining the same. Given under my hand this first day of August, 1673. JOHN BERRY.

To John Bowne, Esq., to be published at a Town Meeting in Middletown. The said Deputies to be chosen by the Inhabitants.

August 26th, 1673.—Upon receipt of an order from the Commanders in Chief and Council of War, resident at Fort William Hendrick, at New Orange, for the choice of six persons, being inhabitants of the Town, to be presented to Commanders aforesaid, to take three for Town Magistrates, also for choice of two deputies to act at Woodbridge, according to the terms of the above order. The Towns this day convened together for election, and upon perfect vote the choice was as follows, etc., etc. :

Sept. 12, 1673.—An order from Council of War, at Fort Orange, to take a list of all males above sixteen years of age, and for choice of militia officers.

This was the last order from Dutch Authorities which appears on the Old Town Book of Middletown. The Shrewsbury record and general record of the county for this period, if any were kept, have been destroyed or lost.

VOYAGES OF DAVID PETERSON DE VRIES, TRANSLATED BY HON. HENRY C. MURPHY.

PAGE 61-2.

1633, May 21st. We arrived at noon, again, at our ship at Sandy Hook. Saw our ships' boat lying on the point where people were catching fish, with a seine. Went and told them to come aboard, as soon as they had made a haul or two.

PAGE 63.

The bay inside of Sandy Hook is a large one, where fifty or sixty ships can lie, well protected from the wind of the sea.

Sandy Hook stretches a full half a mile† from the hills, forming a flat sandy beach, about eight or nine paces wide, with small blue plum trees which there grow wild.

The Albany Records, Vol. xxi, page 401, give an account of the Monmouth shore near the Navesinck Highlands, in the year 1663. The following is the substantial translation from the Dutch.

1663. Voyage to Newesing (Navesinck) made in the company's sloop, with what happened during it. There were on the sloop, Captain Martin Cregier, Govert Loockermans, Jacques Cortelyou, Peter Zevel, with ten soldiers, two sailors, and the Sachem, with a savage from Staten Island.

6th December. We sailed from the Manhattans (New Amsterdam, now New York) about 3 o'clock, and arrived about evening at 6 o'clock at Staten Island, where the Sachem of said Island, with the savage went on shore. They remained there about an hour, and then returned. Hoisting again our sail, we sailed through the Kil Van Kol, arrived at the back of Shutters Island upon shallow water, cast our anchor, and stayed there until next ebb tide.

7th December. We raised our anchor again about three in the morning, and rowed down with the ebb the Creek behind Staten Island. Somewhat later in the morning, we hoisted our sail and tacked, until the ebb tide was over, and then again cast our anchor. The flood tide being gone about two o'clock in the afternoon, we raised the anchor and tacked again.

We discovered a sail towards evening, which we approached and spoke to them. It was Peter Lawrenson and Jacob Cowenhoven (now Conover) with a small sloop. They said they had been out to trade for venison. We both tacked together with our sloops, the same evening, towards the end of Staten Island, and cast there our anchors just opposite the Reritan River, where we saw two houses with Southern savages. Conover informed us, that the English in an open sloop, being nineteen strong, sailed the day before up Raritan River, where the Indians of the Navesinck* and Raritans were collected together, about three miles up on the River. The savages communicated the same. We remained that night before Raritan River, in order to sail up it the next morning and follow the English.

During the night there was a severe gale from the northwest, and we were compelled to remain all night.

December 8.—The wind continued to blow very severely from the north west, so that we could not proceed up the Raritan River, and were compelled to stay there that day. We determined then to send the Indian JOHN by land to the savages of Navesincks and Raritans, who were assembled about three miles up on the Raritan River. This was done at once, with verbal orders, that he should tell the Sachems of the Navesincks and Raritans, that we were laying with our sloop before the River, and we wished that they would come here and have a talk with us. We also told JOHN to tell the Sachems, if some English had arrived or were actually among them, with the view to purchase lands of them, that they should not sell it to the English, as they had not even asked it of the Dutch Sachems on the Manhattans, and came there secretly. That if the Sachems of the Navesincks wished to sell some land, that they should come to us, and we would talk it over with them. John, as soon as the sun rose, departed to tell the Indians, while we remained before the River.

December 9.—We saw in the morning, about 9 o'clock, the English vessel coming down, we immediately raised our anchor and sailed towards them. Arriving near them, we asked "From whence they came." On which the Captain, Christopher Elsworth answered " From the River." We asked " What he had done :" he answered " He brought the English there." We told him " This was wrong; it was against our government to act in this manner, and that he should answer for it," on which William Goulding cried

---

† See Danker and Sluyter, account in 1680. They state Sandy Hook is some three miles long. We know that Sandy Hook is gradually extending out towards Long Island, but this discrepancy in the two accounts cannot be reconciled in this way, as the time (40 years) would be too short, unless violent storms made the beach.

*Indians on the Raritan River were closely connected with those, in what is now Monmouth County. An Indian path ran from Raritan River over to what is now Middletown village, where it forked, one going to Bay shore, the other over to Clay Pit Creek on the Shrewsbury River.

out, "It is well. It is well." In the vessel were Charles Morgan, John Bowne, James Holbert, John Totman, (probably Tilton) Samuel Spicer, Thomas Whitlock, Sergeant Gybbings, (doubtless Richard Gibbons.) From the First Bay, a man named Kreupels-Bos, one from Flushing, two from Jamaica, and a few more whom we knew not, to twenty in number. On the same day in the afternoon, about 3 o'clock, John, the savage, returned, whom we had sent in the night to the Navesinck Sachems, who were encamped at a considerable distance from the Raritan River. John, the savage, brought to us six or seven savages, who told us "that the English, before John the savage came to them, had arrived there and presented the savages with some rum, and two fathoms of black wampum and one of white, after which they asked them, if they would sell to them some land. In the meantime John, our savage, came, when the whole arrangement terminated, and the English left.

December 10—We departed again from Raritan River, accompanied by two Indians, who were acquainted with the lands of the Navesincks. We went down the bay and arrived at the creek, which enters between Rensselear's Pier *1 and the said point; met here again Christopher Elsworth in his little sloop, and the English sitting on shore near the creek. We went with our boat on shore, and went towards them along the strand. When we approached them we saw everyone standing with their weapons. When the Sheriff, Charles Morgan, and John Bowne advanced towards us, I asked them "What their business was?" They answered "They were trading." We replied "If they went to trade, why then had they such a strong force with them?" They said " Indians were villains and could not be trusted, and therefore they went in such numbers." We told them "that we were informed they came to purchase lands from the Indians." They answered, " We went only there to see the lands." We again told them " that they ought not to undertake to purchase any land of the Indians, as the largest part was already purchased by the Dutch." John Bowne then asked me "under what government

I presumed that they resided." I answered "that they lived under that of the States General and under that of the Director General and Council here." To which he replied " Why then are we not permitted to trade and explore lands as well as you?" I answered him " that they ought not to undertake to purchase any lands from the Indians, except they had previously obtained the consent of Governor Stuyvesant and Council," to which John Bowne replied " It shall be well." Then said Christopher Elsworth, " I told them the same before, that they should not do it." Govert Loockermans told them then " Ye are a party of traitors and you act against the Government of the State." They said " the Kings patent was quite of another cast." Loockermans asked " from whom have you your pass." They answered " from the Manhattans." Loockermans retorted " Why do you act then against the State ?" To which Chas. Morgan answered, " Sek noty bey affet."*2

The English had their savage with them who was of the Navesincks, and had a hand in the murder *3 of Mispath's Kil, as our savage informed us, whom we had taken with us in our sloop, and carried hither, and his name was Quikems, living on the Navesinck River, at the land called Townsing. We left the English along shore, and went up the River about four miles, along the shore under the West Hills, where the country is very mountainous. On the opposite side, as the savages informed us, the soil was very poor, but some good land—old cornfields, and some planting ground, which I had before explored with Cortelyou. Then we crossed the hilly part about nine miles, *4 and perceived by a sign on board,

*1. In the old Dutch records the Navesinck Highlands are sometimes called Rensselear's Point, or Hook, and sometimes, Pier. This last name, no doubt, originated from the appearance of these hills to a vessel far out at sea. The adjoining lowlands lay below the horizon, the hills project boldly and squarely out, and resemble a pier or wharf to a vessel far out on the ocean.

*2. Probably Indian words.
*3. This murder was probably that of Aart Theunissen Van Patten, who, while on a trading expedition in Shrewsbury River, was killed by the Indians, October 1643, somewhere near what is now Port Washington.
*4. In this account of the region now embraced in Middletown township, there is no mention of any settlement by the Dutch. The general tone would warrant the inference, that the whole region was in the undisturbed occupation and control of the Indians. Besides there was plenty of unoccupied land in the vicinity of New York, and no reason why any of the Dutch should go to a region so isolated where they would be exposed to the attacks of the Raritans and other Indians, who had only a few years before (1655) devastated Staten Island. Monmouth County was doubtless visited by trading, hunting, and fishing expeditions of the Dutch from New York, and certain purchasers of land made from Indians and patents taken out, but there was no actual settlement by clearing lands, building houses and living in them with their families. The English from Long Island, Westchester and Rhode Island, were the first actual settlers in Monmouth county.

that Christopher Elsworth with his sloop and the English had entered the River. We remained before it during the night. DECEMBER 11.—The wind being south west, we resolved to sail towards the Manhattans, which we did.

Extracts relating to Monmouth, from "Journal of a Voyage to New York in 1679-80 by Jasper Danker's and Peter Sluyter of Weiwerd in Friesland." Translated by Hon. Henry C. Murphy, from the Dutch, pages 95, 96, 97, 98, 99 and 100.

1679, THURSDAY, SEPT. 21ST.—It however cleared away, and we wore over again, and immediately saw the land distinctly, which caused new rejoicing. We perceived clearly, that we had been sailing since yesterday, along the shore, although it was too far off to be seen. Rensselaer's Hook, which adjoins Sandy Hook, was in front or north of us; and we had sailed N. N. E. and N. by E. It was about one o'clock when we first saw land. It is not very high, but like a dome, only it is a little higher. Long Island is not very high. Rensselaer's Hook, which is the most westerly point of the bay, is the highest of all. Sandy Hook is low and stretches out about three miles eastwardly, from Rensselaer's Hook and makes the channel.— You must be close on Sandy Hook, before you can see Long Island. We intended to run in, but could not well do so this evening, in consequence of the mist continually intercepting the sight of the land. As the weather was calm and the sea smooth, we came to anchor in thirteen fathoms of water, and lay there quietly all night.

22D, FRIDAY.—When the day began to break, they were all in an uproar; but the weather continued misty, with a northeast wind, for which reason we judged we could not make the channel. All those who were so joyful and merry yesterday, were now more sober, as we were compelled to keep off land, so as not to be caught on a lee shore, from which it is very difficult to get away. The fog cleared up a little about ten o'clock, and we sailed again towards the shore, when we perceived we were approaching the west side. It rained part of the time and was misty, so that sometimes we could only see the land dimly, and for a moment, and Sandy Hook hardly at all. About noon we saw a ketch to the seaward of us, but we did not speak to her. She was laying her course to the west. This coast surely is not very easy to enter, especially in the autumn. Our captain had trouble enough, though our mate did not agree with him. Sailing inward. we had 13, 14, 15, 16 fathoms of water, but very uneven bottom as we approached the shore. We laid our course N. N. E. and N. E. by N., and from the shore S. S. W. and S. At four o'clock in the afternoon we determined to run in, if it were possible. We could see the land a little better and also Rensselaer's Hook. Everybody therefore was very industrious, tome in looking after the sails, ropes and tackle, so as to be able to turn and tack ship quickly. Others were constantly on the lookout for land, and specially to discover Sandy Hook in order to secure she best channel, which is next to that point; for not far from it, on the other side, are the east Banks, which are very dangerous. We did our best, first in a calm, and then with a little breeze to enter. We caught sight of Sandy Hook at last, but it was soon hid by the fog. We observed how the land lay by the compass, and so sailed accordingly, expecting a good flood tide, which would begin to make at six o'clock. The deep lead was thrown constantly, and we found five and four fathoms in the shallowest places near the channel. It was low water, and the wind was N. E. and E. N. E., which took us soon inside, short around the point of Sandy Hook into the Bay towards the Highlands of Rensselaer's Hook. Upon passing the Hook which was now east of us, we found deep water at 5, 6, 7, and 8 fathoms, and ran as I have said, immediately for the highlands and came to anchor in ten fathoms of water, praising the Lord again, and thankful for the many instances of his goodness towards us.— This is a very fine bay, where many ships can lie, protected from all winds except the S E, which however cannot do much damage, because the east banks lie before it, and at the worst the ships can only be driven in the wind. They determined this evening, to go up early in the morning, in the jolly boat to Staten Island or Long Island, for a pilot.

23D SATURDAY.—It rained the whole night. Our ship lay as quiet as if she were made fast to the piles at Amsterdam, which was very unusual for us. The wind being west in the morning, they changed their resolution of going up for a pilot, and as the wind was so favorable, determined to take her up themselves. The anchor was therefore raised and we sailed on, for the purpose of passing between Staten Island and Long Island, where there are two high points of land, for that reason called Hoofden (headland.†)

We turned gradually from Sandy Hook to the right, in order to avoid the shores of the east bank, and so sailed to the Hoofden. We had a good flood tide, and four or five fathoms of water at the shoalest part; but the wind shifted again to the north, and we were compelled to tack, which rendered our progress slow, for it was quite calm. Coming to the Hoofden and between them, you have 10, 11 and 12 fathoms of water. As soon as you begin to approach the land, you see not only wood, hills, dales, green fields and plantations, but also the houses and dwellings of the inhabitants, which affords a cheerful and sweet prospect, after having been so long upon the sea. When we came between the Hoofden, we saw some Indians on the beach with a canoe, and others coming down the hill. As we tacked about we came close to this shore, and called out to them to come on board the ship, for some of the passengers intended to go ashore with them. But the Captain would not permit it, as he wished, he said to carry them according to contract to the Manathans, though we understood well why it was. The Indians came on board, and we looked upon them with wonder. They are dull of comprehension, slow of speech, bashful, but otherwise bold of person and red of skin. They wear something in front over the thighs, and a piece of duffel like a blanket around the body, and this is all the clothing they have. Their hair hangs down from their heads in strings, well smeared with fat, and sometimes with quantities of little beads twisted in it out of pride. They have thick lips and thick noses, but not fallen in like the negroes; heavy eyebrows or eyelids, brown or black eyes, thick tongues, and all of them black hair. But we will speak of these things more particularly hereafter.

After they had obtained some biscuit, and had amused themselves a little, climbing and looking here and there, they also received some brandy to taste, of which they drank excessively, and threw it up again. They then went ashore in their canoe, and we having a little breeze, sailed ahead handsomely. As soon as you are through the Hoofden, you begin to see the city which presents a pretty sight. The fort, which lies upon the point between two rivers, is somewhat higher, and as soon as they see a ship coming up, they raise a flag on a high flagstaff, according to the colors of the sovereign, to whom they are subject, as accordingly they now flew the flag of the King of England.

We came up to the city about three o'clock, where our ship was quickly overrun with people, who came from the shore in all sorts of craft, each one inquiring and searching after his own, and his own profit. No custom house officers came on board as in England, and the ship was all the time free of such persons. We came to anchor there before the city at three o'clock. Every one wanted to go ashore immediately. We let those most in a hurry go before us, when, leaving our property in charge of Robyn, we also went in company with a passenger named Genet, who took us to the house of his father-in-law where we lodged. It is not possible to describe, how this bay swarms with fish both large and small, whales, tunnies, porpoises, whole schools of innumerable other fish and a sort like herring, called there marsbanckers, and other kind—which eagles and other birds of prey swiftly seize in their talons, when the fish come up to the surface, and hauling them out of the water, fly with them to the nearest woods or beach as we saw."

Page 140 to 150, Account of a trip to Staten Island. Went from Long Island over in a row boat. On page 142 he says: "There are now about a hundred families on the Island, of which the English constitute the least portion, and the Dutch and French§1 divide between them about equally the greater portion. They have neither church nor minister, and live rather far from each other, and inconveniently to meet together. The English are less disposed to religion and inquire little after; but in case there was a minister, would contribute to his support. The French and Dutch are very desirous and eager for one, for they spoke of it wherever we went, and in the event of not obtaining Dominie Tessemaker, they would send or had sent to France for another. The French are good reformed churchmen,

---

† "The name of the Hoofden" was derived as the journalist subsequently informs us, from resemblance of the shores to the Hoofden or headland of Dover and Calais. (Note by Henry C. Murphy.)

§1 From this French Huguenot element on the southern part of Staten Island, there has been, in the past, some accession to the population of Monmouth. From this source we derive such names as Micheau, Rezeau corrupted into Rezo, Crocheron, Hillyer or Hilliard, Journeay, Seguine or Segoine, Mersereau, Perine or Perrine, &c., &c.

and some of them are Walloons. The Dutch are also from different quarters.

PAGE 146.

Shortly before evening, we arrived at the plantation of a Frenchman, whom they called Le Chaüdronnier, (the coppersmith,) who was formerly a soldier under the Prince of Orange, and had served in Brazil. He was so delighted, and held on to us so hard, that we remained and spent the night with him.

13th, Friday.—We pursued our journey from plantation to plantation until we came to that of Pierre le Gardinier, who had been a gardener of the Prince of Orange, and had known him well. He had a large family of children and grand-children. He was about seventy years of age, and was still as fresh and active as a young person. He was so glad to see strangers, who conversed with him and his, in French language about the good, that he leaped for joy. After we breakfasted here, they told us that we had another large creek to pass, called the Fresh Kil, and that we could probably be set across the Kil Van Kol to the point of Mill creek, where we might wait for a boat to carry us to the Manathans. The road was long and difficult, and we asked for a guide, but he had no one, in consequence of several of his children being sick. At last he determined to go himself, and accordingly carried us in his canoe over to the point of Mill Creek in New Jersey, behind Kol, (Achter Kol§2). We learned immediately that there was a boat up this creek, and would leave that night for the city. After we had thanked and parted with Pierre le Gardinier, we determined to walk to Elizabethtown, a good half hour's distance, where the boat was. From the Point to this village, there is a fine wagon road, but nowhere in this country had we been so pestered with mosquitoes (muggen) as we were on this road. The land about here is very poor, and is not well peopled. We found the boat and spoke to the Captain, who left about two hours afterwards, but as the wind was going out of the creek, he lay by and waited for the tide. We returned by evening to the Point, where we were to stay until morning. There was a tavern on it kept by French papists, who at once took us to be priests, and so conducted themselves toward us, in every respect accordingly. Although we told them and protested otherwise. We slept there that night and at three o'clock in the morning set sail.

On page 278 and 9.—The journalist gives an account of an attempt, to make a voyage to "Neversinck" he says. We tacked about and reached Coney (Cony"nen) Island, a low sandy island lying on the east side of the entrance from the sea. We came to anchor under the outermost point, when we should have gone inside of Sandy Hook (Sant Hoeck§3) in a creek as we were able yet to do, but he said we must go outside of Sandy Hook, around by the sea, and then make for a creek there. I began now to have other thoughts. To put to sea in such a light, low, decayed and somewhat small boat, with rotten sails and an inexperienced skipper,§4 at that time of night, did not suit me very well." The attempt to reach Monmouth County was abandoned, but from this account it appears that the Shrewsbury inlet was open at this time, (1680) and that there was some intercourse by sailing vessels out of Shrewsbury river with New York and Long Island. Shrewsbury Inlet was called Beeregat by the Dutch.

FROM JOURNAL OF JOHN FONTAINE, A FRENCH HUGUENOT.

Oct. 22d, 1716.—In the morning about seven of the clock we raised our anchor, and set our sails, wind at N. W., a stiff gale and great sea, and about 12 of the clock we split our jib and foresail. At three we were up with Sandy Hook, which is the cape land of New York port. The land is low and sandy with few trees upon it. About sunset we came to an anchor under Sandy Hook, in seven fathoms water, and three miles from shore.

23d.—In the sloop at anchor under Sandy Hook. The weather was so foggy all day that we could not see the shore, nor landmarks, so we could not hoist our anchor, for this is a very dangerous bay to come up, without one has fair weather to see the landmarks. There are several banks and shoals of sand, which are very dangerous. There is a great deal of water

§2 The term Achter Kol, literally behind Kol, that is back of the Kol, a name giv n to the river or Kol between Staten Island and the main land, from its peculiar shape, was applied to all the territory west of the river Kol and the Hackensack.

Kol is here used as an abbreviation of Kil Van Kol.—Mill Creek seems to have been the stream now known as Elizabethtown creek—Note by Henry C. Murphy. Arthur Cull is a corruption of Achter Kol.

§3 Hoeck is a Dutch word, corrupted into Hook.
§4 Skipper is a Dutch word for a Captain of a ship or vessel.

fowl of all sorts on these shoals. I observe that the ducks and geese are sooner here, than with us in Virginia.

24th.—Calm weather, but such a fog that we could not see half a mile. We had a mind to go ashore, but the master and sailors were afraid that they could not find the sloop again with the boat, so we consented to remain on board. This fog is occasioned by the burning of the woods, for at this season, the inhabitants set the woods on fire, and the Indians also about this time of the year go a fire hunting.

25th.—We are still at anchor, weather very foggy, so that the master will not venture up with his sloop. About twelve it cleared, so that we could see the land, and we got out the boat, and the men landed us in Staten Island. We were obliged to walk about four miles, not being able to hire any horses. This island is mostly high land and rocky, and that part of the land which is good is mixed with small stones. There are some good improvements here; the inhabitants are mostly Dutch; the houses are all built with stone and lime; there are some hedges as in England. The chief increase is wheat and cattle, they breed large horses here.

About five of the clock we came to the Ferry, between Long Island and Staten Island, which is about one mile broad. The main body of New York River runs between these islands. We crossed the ferry and came upon Long Island, to a small sort of village, where, it being late, we put up at the house of a Dutchman, one Harris Hendrick. (Hendrick Hendrickson.) We were well lodged and had a good supper.

26th.—About eight of the clock in the morning, we hired two horses to go to New York. It is about eight miles from this ferry by land, but not near so much by water. Long Island is generally very plain ground, bears extraordinary good grass, and is an excellent place for cattle. It produceth wheat and all English grain in abundance. The chief part of the inhabitants are Dutch, but there are some few French. Amongst them there are several good improvements, and many fine villages, the woods are mostly destroyed. Besides the plentiful produce of the Island, there is every advantage for fishing and fowling that can be wished. About eleven o'clock we came to a fine village opposite New York, and we crossed the ferry. The river is about a quarter of a mile over, and runs very rapidly; there are good convenient landings on both sides.

Friday, 9th November, 1716.—At five of the clock in the morning, got all our things in the ferry-boat, and set out for Amboy; the wind was contrary, and it blew so hard that at nine we were forced back again. So, Mr. Kearney and I, we hired two horses, and went seven miles out of town to Colonel Morris's, where we dined, and returned at night to our lodgings in New York.

10th.—At eight in the morning, I bought a horse of Mr. Lancaster Sims, and paid him £8 for it. We crossed the ferry from New York to Long Island about ten, and mounted our horses. We passed by a fine village called Flatbush, and at twelve we reached Hans Hendrick's (Hendrickson's) house. The ferryman endeavored to cross the ferry from thence to Staten Island, but had to put back, so we dined at Hendrick's. At three, we saw a ship called the Cæsar Galley run aground upon White Bank. At five, we got into the boat again, and with much difficulty crossed to Staten Island, then we mounted our horses and came to one Stuart's, an inn on the road, about seven miles from the ferry, where we supped, and lay all night.

Sunday, 11th.—At seven in the morning we set out from Stuart's, and at twelve of the clock, we came to one Colonel Farrier's (Farmer) house, where the ferry is kept, and we got ferried over to Amboy, which is a small village, where the Governor hath a house and gardens. It is a very agreeable place, surrounded on two sides by the water. After dinner we went to church. The church is very small, and much out of repair. The wind blew so hard that we could not get our horses ferried over, so we were obliged to remain all night.

12th.—The wind continued blowing very hard at N. W., and we could by no means get over the ferry in the morning; so we took a walk abroad in the country about here, which is very agreeable. At two we returned to our inn and dined. We met with two gentlemen from New York, both lawyers, Justice Johnson and Mr. Bickley. We drank till ten, and to bed.

13th.—At ten we crossed the ferry, and mounted our horses; we dined at two, and continued on our way from three until seven. We made but thirty-two miles this day. We had bad entertainment.

14th.—At half an hour after seven we set out from our lodgings, and within one mile of Burlington I met with Mr. John Ballaguier. At eleven we came to Burlington, where we dined. It is a very pretty village, and there is a river passes through it navigable for sloops. At half an hour after twelve we set out for Philadelphia, the distance is twenty miles from Burlington. The roads are good here. At six we arrived at Philadelphia, and I waited on Mr. Samuel Perez and gave him Mr. Freneau's letter. He had no service for me.

The Monmouth Quakers.

The following poems, by the "Quaker Poet of America," illustrate certain characteristics of the Quaker settlers of Monmouth, and also show certain persecutions which the Quakers suffered in the Old and New World. The last poem is of especial interest, because Robert Barclay was one of the twenty-four proprietors of East Jersey, and their first Governor. He remained at Aberdeen, Scotland, but discharged the duties of the office here through a deputy. It was through his influence that several Scotchmen like George Keith, John Reid, Thomas Gordon, etc., were appointed to office here. Their names are closely identified with the early history of our county. He also used his influence to soften the persecutions of the Scotch Presbyterians, to effect their release from the tolbooths, or prisons, and direct their steps to the shores of New Jersey.

The Quaker of the Olden Time.

The Quaker of the olden time!—
How calm and firm and true,
Unspotted by its wrong and crime,
He walked the dark earth through.
The lust of power, the love of gain,
The thousand lures of sin
Around him, had no power to stain
The purity within.

With that deep insight which detects
All great things in the small,
And knows how each man's life affects
The spiritual life of all,
He walked by faith and not by sight,
By love and not by law;
The presence of the wrong or right
He rather felt than saw.

He felt that wrong with wrong partakes,
That nothing stands alone,
That whoso gives the motives, makes
His brother's sin his own.
And, pausing not for doubtful choice
Of evils great or small,
He listened to that inward voice
Which called away from all.

O Spirit of that early day,
So pure and strong and true,
Be with us in the narrow way
Our faithful fathers knew.
Give strength the evil to forsake,
The cross of Truth to bear,
And love and reverent fear to make
Our daily lives a prayer!

Cassandra Southwick.
1658.

To the God of all sure mercies let my blessing rise to-day,
From the scoffer and the cruel He hath plucked the spoil away,—
Yea, He who cooled the furnace around the faithful three,
And tamed the Chaldean lions, hath set His handmaid free!

Last night I saw the sunset melt through my prison bars,
Last night across my damp earth-floor fell the pale gleam of stars;
In the coldness and the darkness all through the long night-time,
My grated casement whitened with autumn's early rime.

Alone, in that dark sorrow, hour after hour crept by;
Star after star looked palely in and sank adown the sky;
No sound amid night's stillness, save that which seemed to be
The dull and heavy beating of the pulses of the sea;

All night I sat unsleeping, for I knew that on the morrow
The ruler and the cruel priest would mock me in my sorrow,
Dragged to their place of market, and bargained for and sold,
Like a lamb before the shambles, like a heifer from the fold!

O, the weakness of the flesh was there,—the shrinking and the shame;
And the low voice of the Tempter like whispers to me came:
"Why sit'st thou thus forlornly!" the wicked murmur said,
"Damp walls thy bower of beauty, cold earth thy maiden bed?

"Where be the smiling faces, and voices soft and sweet,
Seen in thy father's dwelling, heard in the pleasant street?
Where be the youths whose glances, the summer Sabbath through,
Turned tenderly and timidly unto thy father's pew?

"Why sit'st thou here, Cassandra?—Bethink thee with what mirth
Thy happy schoolmates gather around the warm bright hearth;
How the crimson shadows tremble on foreheads white and fair,
On eyes of merry girlhood, half hid in golden hair.

"Not for thee the hearth-fire brightens, not for thee kind words are spoken,
Not for thee the nuts of Wenham woods by laughing boys are broken,
No first-fruits of the orchard within thy lap are laid,
For thee no flowers of autumn the youthful hunters braid.

"O, weak, deluded maiden!—by crazy fancies led,
With wild and raving railers an evil path to tread;
To leave a wholesome worship, and teaching pure and sound;
And mate with maniac women, loose-haired and sackcloth bound.

"Mad scoffers of the priesthood, who mock at things divine,
Who rail against the pulpit, and holy bread and wine;
Sore from their cart-tail scourgings, and from the pillory lame,
Rejoicing in their wretchedness, and glorying in their shame.

"And what a fate awaits thee?—a sadly toiling slave,
Dragging the slowly lengthening chain of bondage to the grave!
Think of thy woman's nature, subdued in hopeless thrall,
The easy prey of any, the scoff and scorn of all!"

O, ever as the Tempter spoke, and feeble Nature's fears
Wrung drop by drop the scalding flow of unavailing tears,
I wrestled down the evil thoughts, and strove in silent prayer,
To feel, O Helper of the weak! that Thou indeed wert there!

I thought of Paul and Silas, within Philippi's cell,
And how from Peter's sleeping limbs the prison shackles fell,
Till I seemed to hear the trailing of an angel's robe of white,
And to feel a blessed presence invisible to sight.

Bless the Lord for all His mercies!—for the peace and love I felt,
Like the dew of Hermon's holy hill, upon my spirit melt;
When, "Get behind me, Satan!" was the language of my heart,
And I felt the Evil Tempter with all his doubts depart.

Slow broke the gray cold morning; again the sunshine fell,
Flecked with the shade of bar and grate within my lonely cell;
The hoar-frost melted on the wall, and upward from the street
Came careless laugh and idle word, and tread of passing feet.

At length the heavy bolts fell back, my door was open cast,
And slowly at the sheriff's side, up the long street I passed;
I heard the murmur round me, and felt, but dared not see,
How, from every door and window, the people gazed on me.

And doubt and fear fell on me, shame burned upon my cheek,
Swam earth and sky around me, my trembling limbs grew weak:
"O Lord! support Thy handmaid; and from her soul cast out
The fear of man, which brings a snare—the weakness and the doubt."

Then the dreary shadows scattered, like a cloud in morning's breeze,
And a low deep voice within me seemed whispering words like these:
"Though thy earth be as the iron, and thy Heaven a brazen wall,
Trust still His loving-kindness whose power is over all."

We paused at length, where at my feet the sunlit waters broke
On glaring reach of shining beach, and shingly wall of rock;
The merchant ships lay idly there, in hard clear lines on high,
Tracing with rope and slender spar their network on the sky.

And there were ancient citizens, cloak-wrapped and grave and cold,
And grim and stout sea-captains with faces bronzed and old,

And on his horse, with Rawson, his cruel clerk at hand,
Sat dark and haughty Endicott, the ruler of the land.

And poisoning with his evil words the ruler's ready 'ear,
The priest leaned o'er his saddle, with laugh and scoff and jeer;
It stirred my soul, and from my lips the seal of silence broke,
As if through woman's weakness a warning spirit spoke.

I cried, "The Lord rebuke thee, thou smiter of the meek !
Thou robber of the righteous, thou trampler of the weak !
Go light the dark, cold hearth-stones—go turn the prison lock
Of the poor hearts thou hast hunted, thou wolf amid the flock !"

Dark lowered the brows of Endicott, and with a deeper red
O'er Rawson's wine-empurpled cheek the flush of anger spread ;
" Good people," quoth the white-lipped priest, " heed not her words so wild,
Her Master speaks within her—the Devil owns his child !"

But gray heads shook, and young brows knit, the while the sheriff read
That law the wicked rulers against the poor have made,
Who to their house of Rimmon and idol priesthood bring
No bended knee of worship, nor gainful offering.

Then to the stout sea-captains the sheriff, turning, said—
" Which of ye, worthy seamen, will take this Quaker maid ?
In the Isle of fair Barbadoes, or on Virginia's shore,
You may hold her at a higher price than Indian girl or Moor."

Grim and silent stood the captains ; and when again he cried,
" Speak out, my worthy seamen !"—no voice, no sign replied ;
But I felt a hard hand press my own, and kind words met my ear—
" God bless thee, and preserve thee, my gentle girl and dear !"

A weight seemed lifted from my heart—a pitying friend was nigh,
I felt it in his hard, rough hand, and saw it in his eye ;
And when again the sheriff spoke, that voice, so kind to me,
Growled back its stormy answer like the roaring of the sea—

"Pile my ship with bars of silver—pack with coins of Spanish gold,
From keel-piece up to deck-plank, the roomage of her hold,
By the living God who made me !—I would sooner in your bay
Sink ship and crew and cargo, than bear this child away !"

" Well answered, worthy captain, shame on their cruel laws !"
Ran through the crowd in murmurs loud the people's just applause.
" Like the herdsman of Tekoa, in Israel of old,
Shall we see the poor and righteous again for silver sold ?"

I looked on haughty Endicott ; with weapon half-way drawn,
Swept round the throng his lion glare of bitter hate and scorn ;
Fiercely he drew his bridle-rein, and turned in silence back,
And sneering priest and baffled clerk rode murmuring in his track.

Hard after them the sheriff looked, in bitterness of soul ;
Thrice smote his staff upon the ground, and crushed his parchment roll.
" Good friends," he said, " since both have fled, the ruler and the priest,
Judge ye, if from their further work I be not well released."

Loud was the cheer which, full and clear, swept round the silent bay,
As, with kind words and kinder looks, he bade me go my way ;
For He who turns the courses of the streamlet of the glen,
And the river of great waters, had turned the hearts of men.

O, at that hour the very earth seemed changed beneath my eye,
A holier wonder round me rose the blue walls of the sky,
A lovelier light on rock and hill, and stream and woodland lay,
And softer lapsed on sunnier sands the waters of the bay.

Thanksgiving to the Lord of life !—to Him all praises be,
Who from the hands of evil men hath set his handmaid free ;
All praise to Him before whose power the mighty are afraid,
Who takes the crafty in the snare, which for the poor is laid !

Sing, O my soul, rejoicingly, on evening's twi-
light calm
Uplift the loud thanksgiving—pour forth the
grateful psalm ;
Let all the dear hearts with me rejoice, as did
the saints of old,
When of the Lord's good angel the rescued
Peter told.

And weep and howl, ye evil priests and mighty men of wrong,
The Lord shall smite the proud, and lay his
hand upon the strong.
Woe to the wicked rulers in his avenging hour!
Woe to the wolves who seek the flocks to rav-
en and devour!

But let the humble ones arise—the poor in
heart be glad,
And let the mourning ones again with robes
of praise be clad,
For He who cooled the furnace, and smoothed
the stormy wave,
And tamed the Chaldean lions, is mighty still
to save!

BARCLAY OF URY.

Among the earliest converts to the doctrines of Friends in Scotland was Barclay of Ury, an old and distinguished soldier, who had fought under Gustavus Adolphus, in Germany. As a Quaker, he became the object of persecution and abuse at the hands of the magistrates and the populace. None bore the indignities of the mob with greater patience and nobleness of soul than this once proud gentleman and soldier. One of his friends, on an occasion of uncommon rudeness, lamented that he should be treated so harshly in his old age who had been so honored before. "I find more satisfaction," said Barclay, "as well as honor, in being thus insulted for my religious principles, than when, a few years ago, it was usual for the magistrates, as I passed the city of Aberdeen, to meet me on the road and conduct me to public entertainment in their hall, and then escort me out again, to gain my favor."—*John G. Whittier.*

Up the streets of Aberdeen,
By the kirk and college green,
Rode the Laird of Ury ;
Close behind him, close beside,
Foul of mouth and evil-eyed,
Pressed the mob in fury.

Flouted him the drunken churl,
Jeered at him the serving-girl,
Prompt to please her master ;
And the begging carlin, late
Fed and clothed at Ury's gate,
Cursed him as he passed her.

Yet, with calm and stately mien,
Up the streets of Aberdeen
Came he slowly riding ;
And, to all he saw and heard,
Answering not with bitter word,
Turning not for chiding.

Came a troop with broadswords swinging,
Bits and bridles sharply ringing,
Loose and free and froward ;
Quoth the foremost, "Ride him down !
Push him ! prick him ! through the town
Drive the Quaker coward !"

But from out the thickening crowd
Cried a sudden voice and loud :
"Barclay ! Ho ! a Barclay !"
And the old man at his side
Saw a comrade, battle tried,
Scarred and sun-burned darkly ;

Who with ready weapon bare,
Fronting to the troopers there,
Cried aloud : "God save us,
Call ye coward him who stood
Ankle deep in Lutzen's blood,
With the brave Gustavus ?"

"Nay, I do not need thy sword,
Comrade mine," said Ury's lord ;
"Put it up, I pray thee ;
Passive to his holy will,
Trust I in my Master still,
Even though He slay me.

"Pledges of thy love and faith,
Proved on many a field of death,
Not by me are needed."
Marvelled much that henchman bold,
That his laird, so stout of old,
Now so meekly pleaded.

"Woe's the day !" he sadly said,
With a slowly-shaking head,
And a look of pity ;
"Ury's honest lord reviled,
Mock of knave and sport of child,
In his own good city !

"Speak the word, and master mine,
As we charged on Tilly's line,
And his Walloon lancers,
Smiting through their midst we'll teach
Civil look and decent speech
To these boyish prancers !"

"Marvel not mine ancient friend,
Like beginning, like the end ;"
Quoth the Laird of Ury,
"Is the sinful servant more
Than his gracious Lord who bore
Bonds and stripes in Jewry ?

"Give me joy that in His name
I can bear, with patient frame,
All these vain ones offer ;
While for them He suffereth long,
Shall I answer wrong with wrong,
Scoffing with the scoffer ?

"Happier I, with loss of all,
Hunted, outlawed, held in thrall,
With few friends to greet me,
Than when reeve and squire were seen,

Riding out from Aberdeen,
 With bared heads to meet me.

"When each goodwife, o'er and o'er,
 Blessed me as I passed her door;
 And the snooded daughter,
Through her casement glancing down,
 Smiled on him who bore renown
 From red fields of slaughter.

"Hard to feel the stranger's scoff,
Hard the old friend's falling off,
 Hard to learn forgiving;
But the Lord His own rewards,
And His love with theirs accords,
 Warm and fresh and living.

"Through this dark and stormy night
Faith beholds a feeble light
 Up the blackness streaking;
Knowing God's own time is best,
 In a patient hope I rest
 For the full day-breaking!"

So the Laird of Ury said,
Turning slow his horse's head
 Towards the Tolbooth prison,
Where, through iron grates, he heard
 Poor disciples of the Word
 Preach of Christ arisen!

Not in vain, Confessor old,
Unto us the tale is told
 Of thy day of trial;
Every age on him, who strays
From its broad and beaten ways,
 Pours its sevenfold vial.

Happy he whose inward ear
Angel comfortings can hear,
 O'er the rabble's laughter;
And, while Hatred's fagots burn,
Glimpses through the smoke discern
 Of the good hereafter.

Knowing this, that never yet
Share of Truth was vainly set
 In the world's wide fallow;
After hands shall sow the seed,
After hands from hill and mead
 Reap the harvests yellow.

Thus, with somewhat of the Seer,
Must the moral pioneer
 From the Future borrow;
Clothe the waste with dreams of grain,
And, on midnight's sky of rain,
 Paint the golden morrow!

Thomas Laurie, John Barclay the brother of the Governor, and perhaps Thomas Warne, with other Scotch and English Quakers, erected a meeting house at Topanemus as early as 1684. John Reid, a Scotch Quaker who lived first at Perth Amboy, and afterwards on a clearing on Hop Brook, near Topanemus, attended here while living at Amboy. He was deputy surveyor and also something of a lawyer. In 1702 he was appointed Surveyor-General. His tombstone may still be seen in the old Topanemus burying ground.— The inscription is rapidly being defaced by the weather:

"Here lies the body of John Reid,
 who came from Scotland
His native Country with his wife Margaret and three daughters to New Jersey, the 19th of Dec., A. D. 1683. He died 16th of Nov. 1723, aged 67 years."

Topanemus graveyard is about a mile west of the village of Marlborough. The lands of Hendrick E. Conover, of Freehold, bound it on the north, east and south, and the Barricklo farm on the west. It is on a high knoll overlooking the surrounding country on every side. The Quaker meeting house stood on the northeast end. After the Quakers were converted to Episcopacy by the renegade George Keith, it became the place of meeting for that sect, until their present church edifice in Freehold town was built. This was some time before the Revolution. "Topanemus burying ground" is now a lonely but very beautiful place. On the northwest side stands a gigantic white oak, some four feet in diameter. The Barricklo family still use a small plot on the west side enclosed by an iron fence, as a burial place. On the south side are the ancient graves of the Reids and Bairds. Near the centre is the grave of Thomas Warne, covered with a slab about six feet long by three feet wide, and this inscription thereon:

"Here is interred the body of Thomas Warne. He was born in Plymouth, in Devonshire, Great Britain. Lived some time in Ireland, and in the 31st year of his age came over as a Proprietor in East Jersey. Who died with the dead, May 15th, Anno 1722, aged seventy years."

Just southeast of Warne's grave is that of Col. John Anderson, covered with a similar slab. He was a judge at one time in Monmouth county, and a leading man.— The stone is inscribed:

"Col. John Anderson, once President of His Majesty's Council of the Province of New Jersey, who died 28th day of March, 1736, aged 71 years.
"His Country's true friend, obliging to neighbors,

Gave no man offence, paid each for their labors,
Was easie at home, abroad dare appear,
Gave each man his dues and no man did fear."
There is another line, but so covered with moss that I did not attempt to decipher it.
There are several other tombstones bearing Scotch names, and record the fact that those who there rest were natives of Scotland, as Clark, Doue, Rockhed, etc.
A great many persons have evidently been buried here without headstones, and nearly all traces, save very slight depressions in the ground, are obliterated.
The descendants of the Dutch, who now own all the lands around about here, have carefully guarded and preserved from ruin, this ancient burial place of the Quakers. Lewis Morris, in 1700, wrote to the Bishop of London, and gave a short account of the Quakers who here assembled from the surrounding region, now embraced in the counties of Monmouth and Middlesex. The Topanemus Meeting house appears to have been the centre of the different clearings and settlements of the Scotch Quakers in the western part of Monmouth, and the eastern part of Middlesex. Governor Barclay's influence gave them a prominent position in public matters at that time. As soon as Barclay's influence ended, the most of these Scotch Quakers became Episcopalians.

MONMOUTH RECORDS.
BOOK A OF DEEDS, PAGE 17.

In 1668, Zachary Gant of Rhode Island, sells his share of the tract of land, "of which Newasink in New Jersey is a part, and of which John Tilton of Gravesend, and Walter Clark of Rhode Island, are two of the Patentees" to his brother, Annias Gant.
The witnesses to the paper are John Easton and Israel Gant.

PAGE 18.
John Throckmorton, Jr., of Middletown, appoints his father, John Throgmorton, of Providence, Rhode Island, his attorney, Nov. 6, 1669. Witnesses to the instrument are Jonathan Holmes, (who describes himself as son of Obadiah Holmes of Rhode Island,) and Edward Smith, (who describes himself as son of Edward Smith of Rhode Island.)

PAGE 41.
Robert Story sells "his share of Newasink, Naverumsunk and Pootapeck, to John Jay, of the Island of Barbadoes, in 1671.

PAGE 44.
Randal Huet sells Oct. 8th, 1672, his house lot, and other lands, to "Derrick Tunison."

PAGE 49.
William Shaberly, of Island of Barbadoes, mariner, in 1672 sells his share to John Jay, of that Island.

PAGES 51-2.
Robert Carr, of Newport, R. I., Nov. 26, 1672, sells his whole share to Gyles Slocum of Portsmouth, Rhode Island, who then conveys it to his son, John Slocum.
This John Slocum was Ranger for the county, and quite prominent in our early history. He is often called Capt. John Slocum.

PAGE 56.
In 1671, Samuel Borden of Portsmouth, R. I., sells his share to Lewis Mattix, of same place.

PAGE 61.
Record of Thomas Moore. His deed of of sale to Christopher Allmey, for a share of land. Recorded Feb. 16th, 1674.
Know all men, by these presents that I, Thomas Moore of Southhold, Senior, on Long Island, have for myself, my haires, executors and administrators, sould and made over to Christopher Allmey, of Shrewsbury, in New Jersey, all my right, title and interest in a parcel of land, lying in a place commonly called Newasink, Narumsunk and Pootapeck, and the other adjacent lands, purchased or to be purchased, as to the Indian title to these lands, I being one of the first purchasers of the said lands. And I doe hereby warrant this my sale good in law, free from any person or persons, any way from me or my order. I, the said Thomas Moore, have for myself, my haires, executors and administrators, fully and absolutely sould and made over to the aforesaid Christopher Allmey, his haires, executors and administrators, all the aforesaid lands, meddows, commons, trees, timber, with all and singular the privileges, appurtenances, proffits and immunities that shall or may belong to the aforesaid lands. And doe hereby acknowledge to have received for the premises, a valuable consideration to my satisfaction. To the confirmation of the premises and every of them, I, the said Thomas Moore, have for myself, my haires and administrators, subscribed my

name and set my seal, the 24th day of August, 1674. THOMAS MOORE, [L. s.]
Signed, sealed and delivered }
in the presence of }
NATHANIEL CODDINGTON,
ANTHONY WALTERS.

BOOK B OF DEEDS, PAGE 19.

William West, attorney of Stephen West of Mackataugh Island, in New England, sells to Thomas Webly, of Shrewsbury, in 1690.

PAGE 48.

John Gibbonson (Giberson) and Daniel Hendrickson, of Flatbush, L. I., in 1693 sell a tract of land to William Whitlock. Daniel Hendrickson and his brother Hendrick, a few years after 1693, settled on a tract of land just west of Middletown Village. Hon. William H. Hendrickson, a lineal descendant of one of these brothers, resides on and now owns the original Hendrickson homestead. Hendrick and Daniel, the original settlers, were sons of Hendrick Hendrickson, who lived near what is now Fort Hamilton, on Long Island.—Nicholas VanBrunt married one of his daughters, and was sheriff of Monmouth county at one time.

This Hendrick Hendrickson was probably the same man who came to America in the ship *Rosetree*, in 1663, and was a native of Westphalia. See O'Callaghan's Doc. His. of N. Y., Vol. 3d, page 60.

BOOK A OF DEEDS, PAGES 64-65.

For the orderly settlement of a Court of Sessions, to be held in the Countie of Middletown, by the Justices of the Peace, and officers appointed according to the form here prescribed.

The tittle of the Courtt to bee entered thus:

"At a Court of Sessions held at ⸺ in the Province of New Jersey, by the Lords Proprietor's authoritie, in the year of the raigne of our Soveraign Lord, Charles Second, by the grace of God, King of Great Britain, France and Ireland, Defender of the Faith, and, in the year of ye Lord God, &c."

"Insert the names of the Justices."

SILLENCE COMMANDED.

Then lett the Cryer or Undersheriff make proclamation and say "O yes" thrice, and "Sillence commanded in ye Courtt upon paine of imprisonment."

SUTTERS TO APPEARE.

After sillence commanded let the Cryer make proclamation saying:

"All manner of Persons that have anie thing to doe at this Court, draw near and give your attendance; and if any one shall have anie plaintt to enter or sute to prosecute, let them come forth and they shall be heard."

Sillence then commanded and proclamation soe made, the Cryer shall call for the Plaintiff thus : " A. B. come forth and prosecute thy action against D. D., or els thou wilt bee nonsutted."

And the Plaintiff putting in his declaration, the Cryer shall call to the Defendant saying, " D. D. cume forth and save thee and thy Baile, or els thou wilt forfeit thy recognizance."

Thus much as touching the forme and maner of the Court proceedings, and according to ye custome and maner of New York government.

Richard Sadler, of Middletown, appointed Cryer and Marshall for the present year 1676. The place appointed for houlding the Court is to be at Shrewsbury, at Francis Borden's house. The form of an oath for the Jurato.

" You shall swear in the presence of Almighty God, that you will true triall make and just verdict give, to ye best of your understanding in the cause depending, or that shall cume before you the present Court, according to evidence."

Ye Cryer or Countie Marshal—His oath.

" You shall swear in the presence of Allmighty God, that you will dewly and truly, according to ye best of your ability and as occasion shall require, to serve and execute all such warrants, writts, orders and executions as shall be delivered unto your hands, by the authoritie of ye Court, as also to do and act all things, which properly belong to your place as Countie Marshall."

AUGUST 21ST, 1676.—Richard Sadler sworn and appointed Countie Marshall aforesaid.

The Clerk of the Sessions—His oath.

" You doe hereby sware in the presence of Allmighty God, that you will according to the best of your care and endeavor, keep a true and exact register of all acts, orders and determinations of ye Court of Sessions held for this Countie of Middletown."

Form of an oath for a Witness.

" You shall sware in the presence of Allmighty God, that you shall speak the truth, the whole truth, and nothing but the truth, in the case depending between A. B. and D. D., to the best of your knowledge and remembrance."

OLD TIMES IN OLD MONMOUTH. 241

PAGE 66.

SEPTEMBER 6TH, 1676.—At a Court of Sessions held at Shrewsbury, in the Countie of Middletown, the day and year above written, by the Lord Proprietor, Sir George Cartterett, his authoritie, in the 28th year of the raigne of our Soveraign Lord, Charles Second by the grace of God, King of Great Britain, France, Ireland, Defender of the Faith, and in the year of our Lord God, 1676.

Phillip Cartereit, Esq., Governor in the Province of New Jersey.

Present,
    Mr. John Bowne,   ⎫
    Mr. James Grover,   ⎬ Justices of the Peace.
    Mr. Joseph Parker,   ⎭

The names of the Jury appointed, sworn and impaneled for the present Court ware as followeth.

Middletown,
Mr. James Ashton,
Mr. John Williams,
Mr. James Bowne,
Mr. Thomas Cox,
Mr. James Dorsett,
Mr. John Stout.

Shrewsbury,
George Chute,
George Hulitt,
Randal Huett,
Thomas Barnes,
Thomas Applegate, Sr.,
Henry Dier (Dyer).

THE COURT ORDERS.

Upon the hearing of the businesse depending between Edmund Laphitra, plain tiff, and Francis Masters, defendant, and finding ye action by the said plaintiff wrong stated, the plaintiff is nonsutted and adjudged to pay costs and charges.

PAGE 68.

A COURT ORDER.

Wheseas we find a neglect in several persons, who have bin warned to appear and attend upon the bussinesse of this Court in the tyme of thare setting, as jurymen, for the preventing of such neglect for the future tyme, it is hereby ordered by the authoritie of this Court, that if any juryman, after lawful warning as aforesaid, shall refuse to attend the Court or wilfully be absent, during the time of the Court's setting, or until hee bee by ye Court dismissed, the party soe offending shall pay as a fine the sume of five shillings, to be levied as a fine for every days default, and for the time of his absence in the tyme of Courts setting, to be fined according to the pleasure or discretion of ye Court.

ATTACHMENT.

Record of an attachment for Thomas Applegate, Senior.

Nov. 20th, 1676.

To the constable, Marshall or his deputy.

These are in His Majestys name to command you to attach, the chattells of Major John Fenwick, which are now in the hands of Thomas Applegate, Senior.

Oct. 29th, 1876.   JAMES GROVER.

PAGES 69–70.

Nov. 21, 1676.—Nathaniel Lippitt, Plaintiff against Christopher Allmey Deft., in an action of the case for breach of contract to the damage of Plaintiff, ten pounds.

Nathaniel Lippitt, plaintiff against Christopher Allmey, Defendant in an action of detainure, for retaining of a Barrill of goods of Sondery sorts to the value of Ten Pounds.

JURY.

The names of the Jurymen impaniled the day and year above said:
Mr. Peter Parker, Foreman,
Jonathan Hulmes,
Edmund Laphitra,
Thomas Applegate, Jr.,
Thomas Barnes,
John Haunse,
George Mount,
John Smith,
Thomas Cox,
James Dorsett,
Richard Stout,
John Stout.

At a Court held at Middletown, in special manner called by the Plaintiff above said, the day and year above said in ye Province of New Jersey in the 28th yeare of ye raign of our Soveraign Lord Charles ye Second by ye grace of God, King of Great Brittain, France and Ireland and by authoritie of ye Lord Proprietor and in ye year of Lord God 1676, Phillip Carteret, Esq., Governor.

Present,
    Capt. John Bowne,   ⎫
    Mr. James Grover,   ⎬ Justices
    Mr. Joseph Parker.   ⎭

The verdict of the jury impaniled, delivered into Courtt in ye action depending between Nathaniel Lippett, Plaintiff, and Christopher Allmey, Defendant, is as followeth:

" For breach of covenant, wee find for the Plaintiff forty shillings with costs and charges of ye Court."

" We do oblige the Defendant to deliver unto ye Plaintiff, ye Barrill with all his goods in good condition."

"This second action is allowed concerning ye Barrill of goods, given in according to evidence and Jury Verdict, by the members of this Court."

"And likewise further ordered that the Plaintiff, Nathaniel Lippett forthwith address himself to the constable of Shrewsbury, and one man more chosen by him, ye constable, who shall by virtue of this order, have power to take into their custodie the afforesaid barrill of goods. The said Nathaniel Lippett pronouncing, by oath, the said barrill of goods, to be his own proper goods, if so it be required by Christopher Allmey Defendant, or any other in in his behalf."

The first action in the breach of covenant is allowed by the members of this Courtt, but forasmuch, as Christopher Allmey Defendant hath alleged to this Court, that he is, at present, improvided with sufficient testimony or witnesses in the cause allready debated, between him ye said Defendant and Nathaniel Lippitt, Plantiff upon such his request or allegation, ye Court hath thought fit to order ye aforesaid amercement of forty shilling, be at present suspended, until there be a rehearing thereof, at ye next Court or sooner, if occasion required. He the Defendant putting in sufficient Bonds to prosecute his action against said Lippett.

PAGE 71.

Upon ye complaint of Richard Sadler, constable, and Countie Marshall against Christopher Allmey for coutemptuous demeanor towards him, ye said Richard, in ye tyme of his officiating as a Countie Marshall, in the kings business, as likewise for ye detaining of certain writs or warrants granted by Mr. James Grover and Joseph Parker, justices. So far as is made apparent to this Court, by him the aforesaid Richard, ye Court taking ye same unto their consideration, and by virtue of an act of assembly provided in such cases, ye Court doth hereby order that ye said Christopher Allmey shall pay, as a fine for such contempt, ye sume of three pounds, by way of amercement to be, levied upon his estate for the use of ye Publique.

Upon ye Countie Marshalls information to ye Court of lawful warring to Joseph Hulitt, James Percy and Derrick Tunison, according to order for theire appearance, at the present Court, as witnesses, who fayling to appear, the Court hath thought fit for such theire contempt, to amerce the said parties, in like sum of thirty shillings —10 shillings each person—for this theire contempt, to be levied upon the estate of each person, by the Marshall, unless good and lawful excuse be made by the persons aforesaid.

PAGE 72.

March 13th, 1676,
Christopher Allmey
Plaintiff,
Against
Francis Masters,
Defendant

in an action of the case for Slaunder and Defamation, to ye sum of one hundred pounds, for the trouble, charge and wrong done to him, ye said Plaintiff, for which he craves judgment of this Court. The Court conclude they have no jurisdicion of this suit.

PAGE 74.

Province of New Jersey.
The oath of a constable.

Whereas, you A. B. are chosen by——— to be constable amung the Inhabitants, being in the place commonly called———

You doe sware by the ever-living God, that you will endeavor the preserving of ye peace and ye discovery and prevention of all attempts against ye same. You shall directly and truly publish all orders and proclamations that shall be directed to you, by ye authoritie in this Province established; and execute all warrants and commissions that in like manner, shall be imposed upon you, as aforesaid, you are to prevent with your best care and industry all unlawful assemblies and to assist all such officers, as shall bee imployed for the service of ye king and ye Lords Proprietors. And for performance of ye same you shall in His Majesties name command such strength of His Majesties subjects as necessitie of ye affayre requires. And in all other things to perform the duty of constable, according to ye best of your judgment and laws of our nation.— So help you God.

Thomas Huitt of Shrewsbury sworne constable, according to ye manner and form expressed in this Book. March 28 1677.

PAGE 76.

AN ATTACHMENT.

To the County Marshall or his Deputy.

These are in His Majestys name to will and require you, upon sight hereof, forthwith to attach the chattels of John Fenwick of New Salem, in the Province of New Caesarea or New Jersey, here in America, being one paire of oxen or steers and one black cow and calf, now running in the woods near Shrewsbury, or as many of them as can be found, to answer Walter Webly of the Citty of New York, factor, by his Attorney Richard Hartshorne, in an action of debt of twenty pounds ster ling, at the next Court of Sessions to be holden for the County of Newasinks, whereof you are not to fail as you will answer ye contempt and soe make a true return.

Dated ye 24th of August 1677, by me
JOHN BOWNE.

This atttachment is served according to the tenour hereof, that is to say, two steers or oxen and one cow by me
RICHARD SADLER.

Province of New Jersey
A copy of ye warrant of arrest on Christopher Allmey.   March 18th, 1677

Whereas, I am informed that Christopher Allmey of ye Towne of Shrewsbury in ye Countie of Newasinks, hath unlawfully seized into his own hands and converted to his own use a certain wrack of sea, being a vessel loaden with log wood and other commodities, without giving account thereof according to law. These are therefore, in His Majestys name to will and require you, on sight hereof to arrest ye body of ye said Christopher Allmey and him safly keep in your custedie, or convey to ye Common Geole, thare to be held, till he hath put in good securtie to answer to the action of William Sandford, Attorney for our Soveraigne Lord ye King, in an action upon ye case, at ye next Court to be holden for ye Countie aforesaid of five hundred pounds sterling, and to stand ye judgment of ye said Court. Hereof fail not at your perril. Given under my hand and seal at Elizabethtown in ye Province above mentioned the 2d day of March An Dom, 1677.

P. CARTERET.
To the Marshall of ye Countie aforesaid or his lawful Deputy.

The above and two other suits were instituted against Allmey, to be tried at the next Court. Two by Philip Carteret, Governor, in behalf of the Proprietor, Sir George Carteret, and one by William Sandford, the Attorney General, in behalf of the King.

The first suit was for taking possession of a vessel wrecked on the Jersey coast, laden with logwood and other goods. The second suit, for transporting on his vessel goods out of New Jersey, to other colonies, without paying custom. The specific charge is, "that he departed with his sloop, loaded with tobacco and other goods, out of the port of Shrewsbury to Rhode Island, without making any entry of the same."

The third suit was for taking a whale on the Jersey coast, and converting it to his own use.

The cases against Allmey were tried at Middletown Village, March 28th, 1678. William Sandford, the Attorney General, prosecuted the actions in behalf. of the Proprietor and the King.

The Jury rendered the following verdicts:

The Juries verdict for logwood wrack. The Hon. Governor, Phillip Carteret, Esq., plaintiff. Christopher Allmey, defendant.

We, whose names are under-written, having seriously discoursed and considered ye matter in difference, between ye plaintiff and defendant, find according to evidence and our best understanding in ye law, ye defendant, Allmey,

NOT GUILTY.

March, ye 26th. The Juries verdict for Whale Fish.

We, the jurors, whose names are subscribed, doe find ye defendant, Allmey, *guilty only in matter of fact* in taking and keeping one boat load of blubber, but matter of law and costs of suit we leave to ye Court.

James Ashton,
Robert Hamilton,
Henry Marsh,
William White,
Joseph Grover,
Joseph Huitt,
Thomas Cox,
Richard Stout, Sr.,
George Mount,
James Dorsett,
John Stout,
Charles Eccles.

Court's judgment upon ye Juries verdict, allowed, and ye defendant to pay costs of suit.

The last entry in Book A of Deeds, is a copy of one of Sir Edmund Andros' commissions.

"I, Edmund Andros, Kn't., Governor General, Vice Admiral, under His Royal Highness, James, Duke of York and Albany, and of New York, and territories in America, by virtue of His Majesties Letters Patent and the commission and authority, directed unto me, under His Royal Highness, I do, hereby, in His Majesty's name, constitute and appoint you, Capt. John Bown and Mr. Thomas Snozell, to be Justices of the Peace, for Middletown and Shrewsbury precincts, giving you full power and authority to act as Justices of the Peace ought or may do, according to law and practice. And all persons whom it may concern, are strictly charged and required to give you due respect and obedience, accordingly. This commission to be of force for the space of one whole year, or till further order.

Given under my hand and seal and the seal of the Province of New York, the 3d day of May, in the 32d year of His Majesties Reign, Anno Domini 1680.

                        ANDROSS.

Passed the office,
  MATHIAS NICOLLS, Sec'y.

A true copy of Governor Andross' commission, given unto Capt. John Bowne and Mr. Thomas Snozell, for Justices of the Peace of Middletown and Shrewsbury.

             JAMES BOWNE, Clerk.

James Bowne succeeded Richard Richardson as Clerk or Recorder of the County.

    BOOK C OF DEEDS, PAGE 1.

At a Court held at Shrewsbury, June 26, 1683. Court composed of President, Capt. John Bowne, John Hance, Joseph Parker, Peter Tilton, John Throgmorton, Assistants.

Isaac Oung was chosen Cryer of the Court, and his subscription taken as followeth:

"I doe hereby solemnly promise as in the presence of God, that I will bear true allegiance to the King of England, his heirs and successors. And that I will be faithful to the interests of the Lords Proprietors of this Province of New East Jersey, their heirs, executors and assigns.—And that I will perform the office of Cryer of the Court of Sessions for the County of Monmouth, and faithfully execute such commands of the Court as to my said office doth belong. Witness my hand this 26th of June, 1683.

                His
       ISAAC M OUNG.
             mark.

Subscribed before me,
  JOHN HANCE.

        PAGE 6.

A copy of the fees of a County Court:

	£.	s.	d.
To the members of the Court, each action	00	07	06
To the jury for the trial of each action	00	09	00
To the Clerk for summons and entering	00	02	00
For entering the judgment	00	00	09
For an execution	00	01	06
For an order in Court	00	01	06
For a copy of an order and judgment	00	01	06
For taking a deposition	00	00	09
For recording an attachment	00	01	06
For recording a petition	00	01	06

For recording any other writing, according to the judgment of the Court.

        PAGE 43.

At a Court held at Middletown, Sept., 1686. The Court being sett, Lewis Morris was called, having been arrested to appear at this Court by warrant from John Hance, John Throckmorton and Peter Tilton, to answer to what shall be alleged against him, in behalf of our Soveraign Lord the King, concerning an information brought in, about the oath of a Negro woman named Franck. The said Lewis Morris did appear with a Habeas Corpus from the Governor Gawen Laurie, to be removed to the next Court of Common Right to be holden at Amboy Port, the second "Tewsday" in October next, which we allowed of.

        PAGE 47.

At a Court of Sessions at Middletown, March 22d, 1686-7, Lewis Morris' commission as Justice of the Peace was read. The Commission of Robert Hamilton as Major and as Clerk of Peace, was read, and he "was engaged for clerk of the peace."

        PAGE 67.

The Grand Jurymens Ingagement.

You shall diligently enquire and true presentment make, of all such matters, articles and things as shall be given you in charge, and of all other matters and things as shall come to your knowledge touching this present service. The King's council your fellowes and your own you shall keep secret. You shall present no person for hatred or malice, neither shall you leave any unpresented for fear, favor or affection, or reward or gain, or any hope thereof, but in all things you shall present the truth and nothing but the truth, to the best of your knowledge, so help you God.

       THE SCOTCH.

About the year 1682, an emigration from Scotland by the way of Perth Amboy began to flow into Monmouth County.—Scotch Quakers like Thomas Lawrie, John

OLD TIMES IN OLD MONMOUTH

Barclay, etc., were actually settled in the old Township of Freehold or on the confines thereof, in Middlesex County, as early as 1684. These and the English Quakers, who were scattered on isolated clearings, through what are now the western townships of Monmouth, had their meeting house at Topanemus. Prior to 1682 we find only three or four Scotch names on our records. These had no doubt, come from the Barbadoes by way of Newport, R. I., or New York and Gravesend.

About 1682 the influence of the Great Quaker author and then Governor of East Jersey, Robert Barclay, together with the selfish interests of some of the other twenty-four Proprietors, directed quite a number of Scotch people to Perth Amboy.— From here they scattered out through the adjacent country. Monmouth county was desirable, and many crossed the Raritan River and took up their abode through what are now the western Townships of the County. They called what is now the village of Matawan, New Aberdeen, and as early as 1692, had built a house of worship at the place, now known as the old Scotch Burying Ground, on John Van Kirk's farm. The following extract from Vol II, (pages 479-80-81) of Chambers' Domestic Annals of Scotland, shows one of the causes which induced this emigration from Caledonia.

"George Scott of Pitlochie, had some claims upon the public in compensation for certain Manuscripts originally belonging to his father, Sir John Scott, of Scotstarvet, which he had surrendered to the Court of Sessions. Sir John had written a curious book entitled an " Account of the staggering state of Scotch statesmen," in which, with irrepressible marks of gusto, he detailed the misfortunes which had befallen, the persons and families of most of those, who had taken a lead in public affairs, or borne office during the preceding century.

Now the usual destiny had overtaken his own son, who was fallen into poverty, and somewhat at a shift for a living. For some time he besieged the Privy Council for help or patronage, and was at length gratiged with a very peculiar gift. About two hundred peasants had been taken up, for various acts of recusancy; and for safety, on the approach of Argyle, they were gathered out of the prisons, driven off like a flock of sheep to the east side of the Island, and huddled into a vault in Dunnottar Castle, where they lived a few weeks in circumstances of privation, as to food, air, water, and general accommodations, truly piteous. Hearing of their sad state, and relenting somewhat, the Council caused these poor people to be brought to Leith. It was hoped, perhaps, that they would now make such submissions, as might warrant their liberation; and some did thus work themselves free, but the greater number positively refused to take the oath of allegiance as " embodied with the supremacy," as they would be thus rejecting Christ from " the rule in his own house," as well as over their own consciences.

Pitlochie, who was himself a vexed Presbyterian, being now in contemplation of a settlement in the Colony of East Jersey, and in want of laborers or bondsmen for the culture of his lands, petitioned the Council for a consignment of these tender conscienced men, and nearly a hundred who had been condemned to banishment, were at once " gifted " to him. He freighted a Newcastle ship to carry them, and the vessel sailed from Leith Roads (September 5, 1685), carrying with her a number of " dyvours and broken men," besides the Covenanters. It was a most disastrous voyage. Partly perhaps, because of the reduced, sickly state of most of the prisoners at starting, but more through a deficiency of healthful food and the want of air and comfort, a violent fever broke out in the ship before she had cleared Lands End. It soon assumed a malignant type, and scarcely an individual on board escaped. The whole crew, except the Captain and Boatswain, died. Pitlochie himself, and his wife, died.

Three or four dead were thrown overboard every day. Notwithstanding this raging sickness, much severity was used towards the prisoners at sea, by the Master of the ship and others. Those under deck were not allowed to worship by themselves; and when they engaged in it, the Captain would throw down great planks of timber upon them, to disturb them, and sometimes to the danger of their lives.

Fifteen long weeks were spent by the Prison Ship, before she arrived at her destination; and in that time seventy had perished. The remainder were so reduced in strength, as to be scarcely able to go ashore. The people at the place where they landed (Perth Amboy), not having the gospel among them, " were indifferent to the fate of the Scottish Presbyterians, but at a place a few miles inland,† where there was a minister and congregation, they were received with great kindness. They then became the subject of a singular litigation ; a Mr. Johnston, the son-in-law and heir of Pitlochie, suing them for their value as bond-servants. A jury found that there was no indenture between Pitlochie and them, but that they were shipped against their will ; therefore, Mr. Johnston had no control over them." The author then goes on to say that these Scotchmen all died or removed.— Where he gets his authority for this statement does not appear. No doubt they all removed from Perth Amboy, and were glad to get away from this mosquito afflicted place, where their sufferings elicited so little sympathy. They may have removed over in Monmouth County, where they had found some good Samaritans among the Quakers. John Reid was at Amboy, and a Quaker, to direct them among his friends of Topanemus. At all events only a few years later, in 1692, we find Scotch Presbyterians building a church about two miles north of the Topanemus Quaker Meeting House, and they were doubtless, part of these same exiles. The graveyard adjoining this church still exists, and is called the old Scotch Burying Ground. The site of the old church can be plainly seen by the depression in the ground and the absence of graves. This shows that the church stood east of the centre, facing the old road leading to Englishtown. This Burying ground is in the Township of Marlborough, a short distance from the farm house where Ira Conover lived until his death, now owned and occupied by Gideon C. McDowell.

It was doubtless the kind treatment of the Scotch Quakers of Topanemus, as well as the attractiveness of the country hereabouts, which caused them to locate through this region. Some of our farmers in this vicinity, have lately caused this old grave yard to be cleared up, and built a new fence around it. The grave of Rev. John Tennant is in the centre and marked by a flat slab. The names on many of the old tombstones show their Scottish origin. For example—that of Michael Henderson, who died August 23d, 1722, and John Henderson, who died Jan. 1st, 1771, in his 74th year.

†This was probably at Topanemus. Several of the Quakers of this congregation were Scotchmen, and would naturally sympathize with their countrymen in affliction. John Reid was at Amboy to direct them here.

Samuel Crawford, who died July 8th, 1748, aged 35 years.

On an adjacent tombstone is this inscription :

"Here lies the body of William Crawford, late High Sheriff of Middlesex county, who departed this life the 22d day of March, 1760, in his 50th year.

Very near the last is a double tombstone, sculptured with a ghostly semblance of the human face, with the following inscription :

"Here lies the body of Margaret, wife of William Redford, who came from North Britain 1682, who died April 17, 1729, aged 84 years."

Here lies the body of William Redford, who came from North Britain 1682, and died March 1725-6, aged 84 years.

On this side of the yard is the grave of Richard Clark, whom the headstone shows was born in Scotland, 1663, and died May 16, 1733, aged 70 years.

Other tombstones record the names of Archibald Craig, who died January 19, 1758, aged 73 years ; of Mary his wife, Nov. 1, 1752, aged 69 years, of Anthony Ward, born in Great Britain and died in 1746, aged 76.

Elizabeth, wife of Jeremiah Reeder, who died 1735, aged 79. There are a great many graves without headstones, and only slight irregularities in the ground, to show they ever existed. Of late years only the Quackenbushes, the Boices and Probascos have buried here. The Dutch have followed the Scotch, and that sympathy which has existed between the people of these two countries in life, is here continued in death. The character of the persecutions in Scotland, which drove the Covenanters to Monmouth, is well shown in the following poems of Mrs. A. Stuart Menteath, in her "Lays of the Kirk and Covenant." The progenitors of several of our Monmouth county families of Scotch descent, were actors in like scenes.

PEDEN AT THE GRAVE OF CAMERON.

This poem (with the next) refers to the darkest period of Scotland's dark history—between the Restoration and the Revolution—a time, during the whole of which, her annals may be said to have been traced in blood. From the sending down of the Highland host, as it was called, in the end of the year 1677, to waste and depopulate the western counties, where the Presbyterian interest was strongest, to the day when indignant Britain hurled the tyrant James from his throne, the miserable peasantry, more especially of Ayrshire and Galloway, enjoyed not the breathing space of a day; and if the persecution appeared at any season to relax, it was simply because the agents of oppression found no more spoils to gather, and no more victims to destroy.

On the 20th of July 1680, Richard Cameron, with a handful of his followers, fell, not without a brave resistance, at Ai-smoss. The head and hands of Cameron were severed from his body, and with a cold-blooded ferocity, strongly characteristic of the times and of the men, they were carried by the dragoons of Earlshall to Edinburgh, and exposed before the eyes of his old father, who had long lain a prisoner there. With the very wantonness of cruelty, they taunted the bereaved parent by asking if he knew the ghastly relics? "I know, I know them!" said the poor old man, "they are my dear, dear son's. Good is the will of the Lord who cannot wrong me nor mine, but has made goodness and mercy to follow us all our days!" This anecdote affords as fair an illustration as can be given, of the spirit which respectively animated the two parties. Cameron's headless body was buried where he fell, and to that lone grave did Alexander Peden, a fellow-labourer in the gospel, repair; and, sitting down by the spot where his friend of many years had found at last the rest they had so often wearied for, he could not repress the heart-wrung ejaculation, "O to be wi' thee, Ritchie!"—*Note by the authoress.*

A sound of conflict in the moss! but that hath
   passed away,
And through a stormy noon and eve the dead unburied lay;
But when the sun a second time his fitful splendours gave,
One slant ray rested, like a hope, on Cameron's new-made grave!

There had been watchers in the night, strange
   watchers gaunt and grim!
And wearily, with faint lean hands, they toiled a
   grave for him;
But ere they laid the headless limbs unto their
   mangled rest,
As orphaned children sat they down and wept upon his breast!

O! dreary, dreary, was the lot of Scotland's true
   ones then—
A famine-stricken remnant, wearing scarce the
   guise of men,
They burrowed, few and lonely, 'mid the chill,
   dank mountain caves,
For those who once had sheltered them were in
   their martyr-graves!

A sword had rested on the land—it did not pass
   away;
Long had they watched and waited, but there
   dawned no brighter day;
And many had gone back from them who owned
   the truth of old,
Because of much iniquity their love was waxen
   cold!

—There came a worn and weary man to Cameron's place of rest,
He cast him down upon the sod, he smote upon
   his breast;
He wept, as only strong men weep, when weep
   they must or die,
And, "Oh! to be wi' thee, Ritchie!" was still his
   bitter cry!

"My brother! O my brother! thou hast passed
   before thy time,
And thy blood it cries for vengeance, from this
   purple land of crime;
Who now shall break the bread of life unto the
   faithful band—

Who now upraise the standard that is shattered
   in thine hand!

"Alas! alas! for Scotland! the once beloved of
   Heaven,
The crown is fallen from her head, her holy garment riven;
The ashes of her Covenant are scattered far and
   near,
And the voice speaks loud in judgment, which in
   love she would not hear!

"Alas! alas! for Scotland! for her mighty ones
   are gone:
Thou, brother, thou art taken—I am left almost
   alone;
And my heart is faint within me, and my strength
   is dried and lost,
A feeble and an aged man—alone against a host!

"O pleasant was it, Ritchie, when we two could
   counsel take,
And strengthen one another to be valiant for His
   sake;
Now seems it as the sap were dried from the old
   blasted tree,
And the homeless, and the friendless, would fain
   lie down with thee!"

It was an hour of weakness, as the old man bowed
   his head,
And a bitter anguish rent him, as he communed
   with the dead;
It was an hour of conflict, and he groaned beneath the rod,
But the burthen rolled from off him as he communed with his God!

"My Father! O my Father! shall I pray the
   Tishbite's prayer,
And weary in the wilderness while Thou wouldst
   keep me there?
And shall I fear the coward fear of standing all
   alone,
To testify for Zion's King, and the glory of his
   throne?

"O Jesus, blessed Jesus! I am poor, and frail,
   and weak,
Let me not utter of mine own—for idle words I
   speak;
But give me grace to wrestle now, and prompt my
   faltering tongue,
And breathe Thy name into my soul, and so I
   shall be strong!

—"I bless Thee for the quiet rest, thy servant
   taketh now,
I bless Thee for his blessedness, and for his crowned brow;
For every weary step he trod in faithful following
   Thee,
And for the good fight foughten well, and closed
   right valiantly!

"I bless Thee for the hidden ones, who yet uphold Thy name,
Who yet for Zion's King and Crown shall dare
   the death of shame;

I bless Thee for the light that dawns even now
    upon my soul,
And brightens all the narrow way with glory from
    the goal !*

"The hour and power of darkness, it is fleeting
    fast away—
Light shall rise on Scotland, a glorious gospel
    day ;
Woe! woe! to the opposers, they shall shrivel in
    His hand,
Thy King shall yet appear for thee, thou cove-
    nanted land !

"I see a time of respite, but the people will not
    bow ;
I see a time of judgment, even a darker time than
    now ;
Then Lord uphold thy faithful ones, as now Thou
    dost uphold,
And feed them, as Thou still hast fed, thy chosen
    flock of old !

"The glory ! O the glory ! it is bursting on my
    sight,
Lord ! thy poor vessel is too frail for all this
    blinding light !
Now let Thy good word be fulfilled, and let Thy
    kingdom come,
And Lord, even in Thine own best time, take Thy
    poor servant home !"

Upon the wild and lone Airsmoss, down sank the
    twilight grey,
In storm and cloud the evening closed upon that
    cheerless day ;
But Peden went his way refreshed, for peace and
    joy were given,
And Cameron's grave had proved to him the very
    gate of heaven !

The Martyrdom of John Brown.

Many of the stories of his prophetic powers that have come down to us, bear indeed the marks of a credulous age, and of that exaggeration with which all tradition seems, by the operation of some immutable law, to encrust itself in its progress down the stream of time, and the book entitled " Peden's Prophecies," has been fully proved not to be genuine. Still, enough remains after careful sifting, to remind us, that He who provided meat for Elijah, weary in the wilderness, in the strength of which he went forty days, yet lives to supply the need of His people according to their peculiar circumstances ; and who shall say what cordials He prepares for fainting seasons—what glimpses of futurity and of glory He lets in upon the soul of those, who, standing in jeopardy of their lives every hour, for the name of Jesus, look up, like Stephen, "steadfastly into heaven !"
Perhaps there never was another traditionary reputation so black, so well-earned, and so thoroughly authenticated in all its leading features, as that borne by John Graham of Claverhouse, the " bluidie Claver'se" of our shuddering peasantry ; the "gallant Dundee" of song worthy of a better theme ; and the forlorn hope for a hero, of certain of our modern Jacobite romancers upon history ! Truly they are much to be pitied for the materials they have to work upon ! and we might almost compare their self-imposed task, to that of som, poor artificer of images in a heathen or Popish country compelled to fashion an idol from a stock, and perpet-

*Peden was by many supposed to possess the spirit of prophecy.

ually thwarted in his attempted sculpturing of beauty, by theknots and distortions of an inveterately ungraceous crab ! All the waters of Helicon would, we suspect, be wasted, in the endeavour to wash the bloodstains from the memory of Graham of Claverhouse -The most palpable result of the encomiums of his recent admirers has been, to force from the obscurity to which they have for some time been suffered to remain, the too convincing proofs of his deficiency, even in those qualities for which he has so long usurped credit—personal courage, and loyalty to his ill-fated and evil-counselled,king !—*Note by the authoress.*

It is the cold grey morning,
    Slow creeping o'er the hill ;
But no wild bird giveth warning,
    All insect mirth is still !

In vain the sun would scatter
    The chill dank mists away ;
And the rain's unceasing patter
    Weeps in the cheerless day !

Forth o'er the dreary moorland,
    The preacher strains his eyes ;
Once more the staff is in his hand,
    Once more he turns to fly,

As the partridge on the mountains,
    His life is hunted still ;
And his bosom's troubled fountains,
    Reflect the coming ill.

He turned him to the mother,
    Low bending o'er her child ;
A groan he sought to smother,
    His voice was hoarse and wild.

" Poor wife ! poor wife !" he muttered,
    " A weary, dreary dawn—
Bethink the words I uttered,
    Upon thy marriage morn.

" I bade thee prize him highly,
    For a man of God was he ;
Yet keep the garment nigh thee,
    His winding sheet to be !

" Poor wife ! poor wife !" he mutters,
    " A dreary, weary dawn !"
Ere answering word she utters,
    The wanderer is gone !

And she is left all lonely,
    With the sickness at her heart,
That for him she loveth only,
    Those boding words impart.

Upon her babe she gazes,
    But comfort is not there—
Her eyes to heaven she raises,
    And meekly bows in prayer.

And, as her prayer ascended,
    Her faded eye grew bright,
As though a beam descended,
    And touched her soul with light !

And meekly now she goeth
    About her household care ;
Each homely task she doeth,
    Being sanctified by prayer !

—The evening meal awaits him,
  The wife hath done her part ;
What now—what now belates him,
  Oh ! the boding at her heart !

Forth o'er the dreary moorland,
  She strains her anxious eye ;
A tramp of horse !—a ruthless band
  Athwart the mist draw nigh !

With oaths and dreadful laughter,
  Athwart the mist they come ;
With shouts all breathing slaughter,
  They drag her husband home !

" Come forth ! come forth ! and greet him,
  Thou singer of sweet psalms "—
She goeth forth to meet him,
  Her infant in her arms !

" Now get thee to thy praying,"
  (The bloody Claver'se spake ;)
" My haste brooks no delaying,
  I've other dogs to take ! "

—Upon his native heather
  The martyr knelt him down ;
" 'Tis sudden, O my Father !
  But Thou wilt keep Thine own !

" And thou, my wife, my leal one !
  O ! grudge not o'er thy dead—
I told thee that this hour would come,
  When thou and I were wed ! "

His last farewell is spoken,
  He prays his latest prayer ;
In silence all unbroken
  His murderers gird him there !

In silence all unbroken—
  Save by that pleading tone,
Pleading for one last token,
  From the Eternal Throne !

Strong is the good man's weakness,
  Mighty the power of prayer ;
Almost the victim's meekness,
  Subdues the fierce ones there !

Awe-struck and conscience-haunted,
  Those rude, stern soldiers stand
A terror all unwonted,
  Palsies the ruffian band !

Visions of coming judgment,
  Flash on the startled brain—
A moment paused the dire intent,
  A moment—but in vain !

" What craven ! ho ! " the demon-shout
  Of laughter filled the air ;
And Claver'se drew his pistol out—
  And hushed the martyr's prayer !

A flash ! a sound ! a woman's scream—
  Earth ! thou hast borne these things !
And still, as in a maniac's dream,
  That demon-laughter rings !

" Ho, ho, gudewife ! our work speeds fast,
  What deem'st thou of him now ? "

'Twas strange, the sudden spasm that past,
  O'er that new widow's brow !

'Twas strange, the white cheeks flushing,
  The kindling of the eye :
" Aye thought I only gude of him,
  Now meikle mair than aye ! "

Grim smiled the bloody Claver'se—
  " And by my troth " he cried,
" Methinks the deed were none the worse,
  To lay thee by his side ! "

Stern in her spirit's sadness,
  She answered, " Even so—
Even to such height of madness,
  Thy cruel rage may go !

" Do with me as ye will and can "—
  (Here swelled her bosom's flood),
" Yet must thou answer God and man,
  For this day's work of blood !

" To man, my answer will I bear—
  For God "—he glanced on high,
The very troopers shrank to hear
  The oath of blasphemy !

Coldly he motioned on his train,
  And turned his charger's head ;
A moment checked his bridle rein,
  Then left her—with the dead !

Left her, the broken-hearted,
  Beside her dead to die ;
O surely, life hath parted
  In that sore agony !

No ! for her woman's spirit,
  Is strong to bow and bear ;
No ! For she doth inherit
  His faith who sleepeth there !

No ! for her infant's wailing,
  Forbids her to depart ;
And God's own peace prevailing,
  Binds up the broken heart !

—Warned by the tempest token,
  The wanderer seeks once more,
The shelter, oft bespoken,
  Of that lone cottage door.

Clouds o'er the wan moon fleeting,
  Shadow the starless night ;
Vainly he yearns for greeting,
  Of that quenched ingle-light

All dark—all dark and lonely,
  His hurrying footsteps found
And that sad widow only,
  Low seated on the ground !

Beside her dead she bideth—
  O prophet, sadly sooth !
He knows the grey plaid hideth,
  The husband of her youth !

" Poor wife ! poor wife ! *his* crown is won,
  But sore bereaved art *thou !*
Dear Saviour ! help the helpless one—
  Thou art her husband now ! "

It was from the resolute and staunch Scotch Covenanters, that part of the population of Monmouth has sprung, and we, therefore, may well feel a deep interest in the scenes amidst which they lived. From 1692, when the Presbyterian or Scotch church of Freehold Township was organized, down to 1750, the Scotch were the controlling spirits of this sect. They seemed to adhere as firmly to their faith in the wilderness of Monmouth, as they did among the heaths and mountains of Scotland. The names to the following paper show that as late as 1746, all the elders and deacons were Scotchmen or the children of the first Scotch settlers.

From "Memoirs of David Brainerd," a missionary to the Indians in Monmouth county.

"We, whose names are undersigned, being elders and deacons of the Presbyterian church in Freehold,§ do hereby testify, that in our humble opinion, God, even our Saviour, has brought a considerable number of the Indians of these parts, to a saving union with himself. Of this we are persuaded from a personal acquaintance with them; whom we not only hear speak of the great doctrine of the Gospel. with humility, affection and understanding, but we see as far as man can judge them, soberly, righteously and Godly. We have joined with them at the Lord's supper, and do from our hearts esteem, as our brethren in Jesus.

For those who were not God's people, may now be called the children of the living God. "It is the Lord's doing and is marvellous in our eyes," until he has subdued all things to himself this is and shall be the unfeigned desire and prayer of

Walter Ker,
Robert Cummins,
David Rhea,
John Henderson,
John Anderson,
Joseph Ker,
Elders.
William Ker,
Samuel Ker,
Samuel Craig,
Deacons.

Presbyterian church, Freehold, August 16th, 1746.

Book C. of Deeds.

At a Court held in Shrewsbury, June 26th, 1683, the following acts of the Assembly were read, and published by the Clerk:
1. An act for the more orderly keeping of swine.
2. An act that all processes and writts for actions, shall be issued by the Clerk of the Peace or the County Court.
3. An act for the due regulation of executions.
4. An act against trading with Negro Slaves.

Richard Gardiner is Clerk of the Court. Two writs issued and signed by Richard Gardiner, Clerk, to Eliakim Wardell, High Sheriff of the county of Monmouth or his deputy.

"These are in His Majesties name to will and require you forthwith, to arrest the body of Benjamin Deuell, *1 (or Devell) and him safely keep, or sufficient surety take, to answer Thomas Snawsell by his attorney, Richard Hartshorne, in an action of debt of twenty pounds, to be paid in good sheeps wool, at nine pence per pound, at the next County Court, to be held for the county of Monmouth, on the twenty-fifth day of September next, ensuing. Thereof you are not to faile, as you will answer the contrary, and make a true return. Dated the 25th of August, 1683.   RICHARD GARDINER,
                                Clerk.

"Summonds."

"Province of New East Jersey, September ye 22nd, 1683.
To the High Sheriff of the County of Monmouth, or his Deputy.

These are, in his Majesties name, to Will and Require you, forthwith, to summon Thomas Harbert, William Whitlock, James Bown, Henry Marsh and William Layton, all of Middletown, to appear at the next County Court to be holden in Middletown aforesaid, on the twenty-fifth of September, then and there to give in their evidence in the case depending betwixt Thomas Snawsell and Benjamin Devell. Whereof you are not to faile as you will answer to the contrary, and a true return make.
                RICHARD GARDINER, Clerk.

§ In old times, when Freehold is spoken of, the Township is generally meant. The present town of Freehold had no existence until 1715, when the Court House was built here; and even then and down until after the Revolutionary war, Freehold village was called "The Monmouth Court House." At the beginning of the present century, Freehold village was only a small place.

William Lloyd, (now seventy-seven years of age), can remember when there were only thirteen houses in Freehold, and two churches, viz., the Episcopal and Baptist.
*1. Duell afterward moved from Monmouth to Gloucester, in West Jersey. See Power of Attorney given by him to John Leonard.

OLD TIMES IN OLD MONMOUTH. 249

At next Court Richard Hartshorne, attorney for Thomas Snawseli, brings on the action against Benjamin Devell. The Jury go out and bring in their verdict:
"We, the jurors, taking things into serious consideration, find for the plain tiff with costs of Court. In behalf of the rest.
JOHN SLOCUM, Foreman."
Among the actions for the following December Court are:

1. "Nicholas Brown against Christopher Allmey for detaining a mare and her increase severall years." (This action is withdrawn in Court.)
2. "Christopher Allmy against Jacob Cole, Restore Lippincott and Nathaniel Slocum, in trespass for killing his neat cattle, to his damage 250 pounds."
3. Christopher Allmy against Richard Sadler for 18 pounds, in trespass for taking away and disposing of two cows and two calves which plaintiff's servant had in possession."
4. "Christopher Allmy against Jacob Cole, for debt of fifty pounds, due eight or nine years."

Allmy obtains a verdict against Sadler, but in his two other actions, as the defendants "account themselves is not legally summoned to appear at the Court, and therefore not capable to come to tryall this Court. Upon which the Court find they are not."

At a Court held in Middletown Village, March 25th and 26th, 1684, John Wilson, chosen constable by the inhabitants of Middletown, was "engaged for insuing year." Francis Jackson was "engaged Cryer of the Court. Ordered at the present Court, that from henceforth, the members of the Court shall be allowed 2 shillings and 6 pence for each action tryed," and the Cryer of the Court, 2 shillings an 3 pence for each action.

Ordered by this present Court, that John Throckmortion and the High Sheriff are the men appointed to agree with a Carpenter, to build a County Goal, at Middletown; and what agreement the said two men shall make with any such carpenter, the Court engages to stand by.

At next Court, June, 25 and 26th, Mary Oung, a single woman upon, oath charges John Slocum with being the father of her child. The Court send a letter to him to appear. Next day appears and denies the charge, is put on trial and jury find him guilty.

The Court sentence John Slocum "to pay Isaac Oung, father of Mary, for his charge and trouble, 50 shilling. 10 shillings to the Publique and Court Costs, and give sufficient security for good behaviour for six months, or go to common Goale and there remain for space of ten weeks."

Mary Oung is sentenced "to be taken to place of whipping, stripped to the waist and receive five lashes on the bare back with a rod or whip and give security for good behaviour for six months, or go to common Goale for ten weeks.

At a Court in September, 1684, they "order a rate (assessment) made for Building the Prison, and Remembrance Lippincott, of Shrewsbury, and James Bowne of Middletown to make it, and all persons are to give an account of their estates. That the "pay" is to be given to John Throckmorton and Eliakim Wardell, by Nov. 10."

"Subscription" of James Bowne "for commission to hold small Court."

I whose name is hereunto subscribed doe solemnly, in the presence of God, promise and declare, that I will bear true allegiance to the King of England, his heirs and successors, and be true and faithful to the Interest of the Lord Proprietors of the Province of East New Jersey; and their heirs executors and assigns; and that as a commissioned Minister of Justice by the authority of the Governor and Counsell of this Province of East New Jersey, for the determining of small causes in Court monthly, to be held in Middletown, according to commission granted to me by authority aforesaid, in all Articles and things in the Commission granted to me, according to the Laws and acts of the Generall Assembly of this Province, to poor and rich, I will to my power doe equall justice, in any matter depending before me, I will not be counsell in any matter depending before me. I will hold sessions in my County according to the act of the Generall Assembly. And will perform and doe the office or commission granted to me as aforesaid, to right and Justice, to the uttermost of my power and understanding and ability.

Witness my hand, Dated this 23d day of September, 1685.   JAMES BOWNE.

The above day mentioned, James Bowne did subscribe to the above engagement before us   JOHN HANCE,
  JOHN THROCKMORTON.
  PETER TILTON.

Benjamin Borden also took a similar oath, before Gawen Laurie.

The day, John Slocum appeared before me, John Throckmorton, and did engage to perform the place of a Ranger, duly and truly chosen between the Proprietors and Inhabitants of the County of Monmouth, as witness my hand, the third of March, 1685.   JOHN SLOCUM.

In 1687, an attachment was issued against the property of Richard Richardson, the first Clerk of the County. He had moved to the Island of Barbadoes, leaving some property in the hands of Lewis Morris.

Thomas Warne, of Middletown, did complain to the Court against his servants, Thomas Hankinson and Peter Hankinson, that said servants had absented themselves several times from his service, which was greatly to ye cost and damage of ye said Warne. The said servants pretending they were free by their time — Therefore the said Warne did humbly desire the court to be judge of their age, and also what time they should serve.

Book C of Deeds, Page 72.

At a Court of Sessions held at Middletown, June 25th, 1689, the Grand Jury present Ephraim Potter, Benjamin Hick, Stephen Cook, Richard Barnes, Joseph Hubbs, Thomas Carter, for horse racing, and playing at "nyne pins" on "ye sabbath day" also presented ———— for "selling rum to ye Indians." Nothing was proved against ———— and "he had no tryall."

The Court fined the persons for racing and playing nine pins on Sunday, five shillings each.

PAGE 73.

At the same Court, Benjamin Hick gave information against John Jenning, John West, Edward Williams, Lewis Morris, Caleb Allen, Clement Masters, John Lippencott, Jr., William Hulett, Peter Parker and Thomas Wainright, for "running of races" and "playing at nyne pins on the Sabbath day."

PAGE 86.

The following September, the Grand Jury presented, Thomas Wainright, Ephraim Potter, John West, Clement Masters, for "playing of nyne pins on ye First day," and Morgan Bryan for fighting.

Dec. 13, 1694. Richard Compton was married to Providence Usselton, by Lewis Morris.

PAGE 94.

At a Court of Sessions held at Shrewsbury, March 25th 1690.

Grand-jurymen.
Samuel Dennis, Foreman.
Francis Jackson.
Ephraim Allen.
Abraham Brown.
William Aston.
William Layton.
John Barcklay, (Barclay).
Caleb Shrieve.
John Baker.
William Stoutt.
John Williams.
Daniell Applegate.
Hanaiah Gifford.

The Court on examination, judged Thomas Hankinson to be eighteen, and should serve three years longer, and then six months for the costs and trouble he had put his master to.

Peter Hankinson is judged to be sixteen, and shall serve his master until twenty-one, and for the costs and trouble, six months after he comes of age. If either transgress again, they shall be punished at the whipping post.

Book B. of Deeds, page 105.

Deed from Robert Barclay of Ury, in Kingdom of Scotland, by his attorney John Reid to Thomas Warne of Monmouth county. Dated March 20, 1689.

Page 106.

Deed dated March 20th, 1689, from James Miller, of Carshore in Scotland, by his attorney John Reid of Hortencia, in Monmouth county, to Thomas Warne of Monmouth county.

Book B of Deeds, page 163.

Deed from Ilosehcote, Tapchalaway and Talinguanecan, Indian Sachems of Mecaponecks, dated August 10, 1690, to Lydia Bowne; conveys in consideration of seven pounds, five hundred acres known as Mowhingsunge, lying along Mowhingsunge and Matawan Creeks. Richard Salter, Richard James and John Bown are witnesses to this deed.

Page 178.

Deed dated March 29th, 1680, from Cherawas, Melileth, Cheslis, Puropa, Lendrick, Iraseef, Mestoa, Poruras, Petroas, Secpha, Secoes and Matopeck, conveys a tract of land on Swimming River to William Leeds.

Page 182.

Feb. 14, 1686, Shougham, sachem of Crosswicks Indian Town, sells a tract of land to Edward Webly.

Book C. of Deeds, Page I1.

Deed dated May 22, 1676, from Perropa, Emoroas, and Wawapa, chief Sachems of Ramesing, to Richard Hartshorne, conveys to him three Necks, called by the Indians Wacak, Arewenoe and Coneskunk, and beginning at the eastermost side of Wakecake Neck, by the Creek, and so up along the said Creek, called Wakecake Creek, about two miles or thereabouts, till you come about a quarter of a mile above, or to the southward of a piece of meadow called Walter Wall's meadow, which lies on the east side of Wakecake Creek, and from thence running westerly, upon a straight line, to a great rock that is a little to the southwest of the Indian path, that goes from Wakecake to the Indian Town, called Seapeckameck, etc., etc.

This deed is witnessed by James Dorsett and Gerard or Jarrett Wall. Each Indian has his own peculiar mark.

PAGE 17.

Deed dated July 16, 1684, from Iraseek, Sachem of Wickaton, to William Leeds and Daniel Applegate, conveys a tract of land in Middletown or Chawcosett,* called by the name of Climes Kake, which tract was marked out by Seahoppra, an uncle of Iraseek, in the presence of his brother. Necktoha and Powraas; consideration of the deed is four yards of Duffels, or equivalent in Rum, to be paid each year on the first of November, for three hundred and fifteen years from date, to Iraseek, his heirs or assign.

PAGE 33.

Deed dated Sept. 29th, 1676, from Peruppo, Penhoose, Irasecott and Myanick, the Chief Sachems of Wromasung and Machayis to John Bowne, of Middletown, conveys a tract beginning at Wropecketong, and so running along until it meets the marked trees that crosses the woods, from thence along the marked trees till it meets with the Hop River, and so along the Hop River till it meeteth with a certain small brook or runn that divideth between Memcokomeck and Tanganawamess, bounded by the most eastermost bank to a white oak tree, marked, which is the bound tree of Richard Stout's land, and from thence nearest east, along the marked trees, till it comes into a small runn by the path, which said runn falls into Mohorhes, and from thence along said Runn or Swamp westerly, till it meets

*This is sometimes spelled Choquasset, and sometimes hohassett.

with Memcokomek path, unto a white oak tree on the north side of the said path, marked, and from thence upon a direct line through the woods unto a certain branch of Changaroras River, and run nearest east into the woods near the mouth of the said Changaroras River, and so bounded by Conescong, Richard Hartshorne's former purchase, until it falls into the Bay, and then southwest unto the first station.

PAGE 35.

Deed dated October 8th, 1679, from Quahick, Jonatan, Perorack, Shenotape, Pandam, Chief Sachems of Wikatong to John Bowne, of Middletown, a tract described by marked trees.

PAGE 40.

Deed dated June 22d, 1678, from Checocus, Jonatan, Irasecutt, Wamaton, Chief Sachamachas or Sachems, inhabiting at Wicquatung to John Smith, late School Master of Middletown, in the Province of Eest New Jersey, conveys a tract called by the Indians, "Mengache," but hereafter to be called amongst our English, by the name of Smith's Field.

PAGE 45.

Deed dated August 12, 1677, from Jonatan, Perore, Quahuk, Merepoppe, Shenotape, Nemote, to Jonathan Holmes.

PAGE 92.

Deed dated June 25, 1689, from Aram aseek, Hougham, Wayanutan, of Mannu squam to Samuel Leonard, a tract of land at Mannusquam in the County of Monmouth, beginning at the land called Squamcum; thence running down Mannusquam River until it comes to land of William Worth, then running back in the woods from the River.

In 1688 Thomas Webly succeeded Robert Hamilton as Clerk of the Courts and Recorder of the County.

EXTRACTS FROM BOOK OF COURT MINUTES, No 1, 1688–1721, IN CLERK'S OFFICE AT FREEHOLD.

Second entry. Road laid out. "And from the King's Highway, that crosseth the brook—the bounds betwixt John Slocum and his brother Nathaniel—the breadth of the way lying eastward, the King's Highway is to run by the east side of the brook, the breadth of the Highway lying easterly, to a markt tree, at the head of the brook, and then crossing the Highway to the head of Thomas Huett's land, the breadth of the highway running westerly, then to a white oak markt, that is

Henry Chamberlin's southwesterly corner Tree, that is on the King's Highway; thence along the King's highway, formerly laid out, to a white oak tree markt, standing by the Whale Pond Brook. And from Thomas Eaton's southeast corner to a black oak markt, the King's Highway to run, as the road lyeth, to the Whale Pond Bridge, as Sam White's way goes to his House; the Highway to run over his brook westerly of his house, then the Highway running southerly of his house, to Horse Pound, standing by the sea, by his Little Water Pond; and it is to be noted, that the people of Dale are to have a passage way, through Francis Jeffrey's land and John Tucker's land to their meadows. And a Kings Highway is to run from Adam Channelhouse, his house, to the Whale Pond Bridge.

And from John Williams said corner to a white oak, being his most northerly and westerly corner, a King's Highway to run, as John Williams line runs, to Nathaniel Camocks south and westerly corner; thence to the King's highway, that goes to Whale Pond bridge, the breadth of the highway lying westerly. And from Henry Chamberlins south and westerly corner, the King's Highway to run, as his line runs to the sea, the breadth of the highway being southerly.

And beginning at a markt tree, a white oak, at the King's highway westerly of Thomas Eaton's Mill; thence running by markt trees, as the way now goes to the Falls of Shrewsbury, to a small red oak markt, lying northeast of Coll. Morris's house, the breadth of the way lying southerly. And from Nicholas Browne's said northwesterly corner, the King's High way, by markt trees to Edmund Laffetra's north and westerly corner; thence running by new markt trees, to the Falls, to the small red oak aforesaid, the breadth of the highway, all lying northerly.

It is to be noted that a Kings Highway runs betwixt John Lippingcott's great lot and Judah Allen, to Navesincks River, and another King's higuway to run from the King's highway that goes through Shrewsbury Town, betwixt Bryan Blackman and Peter Parker, to Navesincks River.

And another King's highway, running along by William Stout's line, to Glass maker's Landing, the breadth of the highway lying westerly.

And another King's Highway to run betwixt Robert West and Stephen West, to the the King's Highway that runs through Shrewsbury Neck.

And another King's Highway to run to James Grover's Landing, beginning at a little walnut tree markt, that goes through the town on Coll. Morris' land."

Just below this return is the following entry.

Att a Court of Sessions held at Shrewsbury for ye county aforesaid, the 26th day of December, 1693, the aforesaid record of highways was ordered, to be razed out of the records.

The next entry is as follows :

A record of a Certificate of Mr. Robert White's marriage. " These are to certifie all whom it may concern, that on this the last day of August, Anno one thousand six hundred ninety and four, Robert White, of the city of New York, and Frances Wales, of the Province aforesaid, was lawfully Joyned in holy-Wedlock, and this to be their sufficient Testimoniall.— Given from under my hand at Tinton Manors this day and date her,eof."

L. MORRIS.

A record of Mr. John French's marriage : Att Tinton Mannor in Shrewsbury, in the Province of East New Jersey, the last day of August. 1694. John French, of New York, and Mary White of the same Town, came before me, and did take each other in marriage, before several witnesses until death part. PETER TILTON.

East New Jersey.

A Record of John West's marriage. These are to certifie all to whom it may or shall concern, that on the day of the date hereof, John West and Jane ——— was lawfully Joyned in the holy estate of Wedlock, by me, and this shall be their sufficient testimonial. Given under my hand at Shrewsbury, in the county of Monmouth and Province aforesaid, the fifteenth day of October, Anno, 1694.

LEWIS MORRIS, Justice.

Following these certificates of marriage is a Power of Attorney, from Charles Haynes to Richard Hartshorne, then an inventory of the goods and chattels of Thomas Ingram, dec'd, of Middletown. Then " A record of Joseph West's certificate of marriage. These are to certifie all to whom it may concern, that Joseph West and Mary Webley were joyned together lawfully in wedlock by me, Peter Tilton, and before those persons who have hereto subscribed their hands. As wit-

OLD TIMES IN OLD MONMOUTH. 253

ness my hand and seal, this twelfth day of May, Anno, 1692. PETER TILTON."
Witnesses.
The mark of
Nicholas x Browne,
Mary Williams,
Audrey Webley,
John West,
Thomas Webley.

All the above entries were made in sheets separate, from the subsequent Court minutes, and afterwards, without regard to dates, bound together. From 1690 to 1715, there is considerable irregularity of this kind in this Book. For example, following above entires are some seven actions, with style, names of parties and amount involved, in the year 1692, then comes the Minutes of a Court in 1691:

Att a Court of Sessions held at Shrewsbury tne 23–24–25 of September 1691. The Court consisting off
John Johnston, Esq., President.
Peter Tilton, ⎫
John Hance,   ⎬ Justices.
Lewis Morris, ⎭
—Grand Jurymen—
Eliakim Wardell.
Ephraim Allen.
Samuel White.
John Tucker.
Abiah Edwards.
John Williams.
James Dorsett.
John Ruckman.
Francis Harbert.
Jacob Trewax.
John Crafford, Sr.
John Stout.
William Winter.

The Grand Jury above written, did all take their engagements and had their charge given them, from the President of the Court and so withdrew.

The Grand Jury came into Court again. They being cald over, every man answering to their names. Their Foreman delivered in the following indictments:
Imprimis.
That there was a woman called Mary Wright, inhumanly murthered by one negro Cesar, a servant of Mr. James Merling, of Middletown.
2d. That Stephen Cook and William Goodbody did unlawfully range the woods, and mark horsekine, contrary to law.
3d. That Mr. Anthony Pintar, (Pintard) did Deale very fraudulently, with his weights and measures.
4th. That Thomas Renshall was lately grievously abused, by Mr. Peter Jollis at or near the house of said Thomas Renshall, in Middletown. The abuse was with blows. The signs of these was made upon the body of Mr. Thomas Renshall.

The Grand Jury being dismissed, the Negro Cesars indictment was read off as followeth: "Cesar! hold up thy hand."
The which he did.
"Cesar, thou here stands indicted by the name of Cesar; having not the fear of God before thine eyes, but being moved and seduced by the instigation of the Devill, that thou, Cesar, on the twenty-fourth day of August, in the third year of the reign of our Lord and Lady, King William and Queen Mary, by the Grace of God, King and Queen of England; and that thou the said Cesar, at the Town of Middletown, in the County aforesaid, in and upon Mary Wright. in the peace of God and our Sovereign Lord, the King, then and there being, felloniously, volluntary and of thy Mallice afore-thought, did make an assault; and that thou, the aforesaid Cesar, with a knife of the value of sixpence, in and upon the body of the aforesaid Mary Wright, then and there fellioniously, wilfully and of thy mallice afore-thought, did then and there, her the said Mary Wright, stabb, and cutt, of which stabbs and cutts, her the said Mary Wright in manner and form aforesaid, she the said Mary Wright, Dyed. So thou, the said Cesar, in manner and form aforesaid, Mary Wright, feloniously wilfully and of mallice aforethought, did kill and Murder, against the Peace of our Sovereign Majesties, their Crown and Dignities.

The Prisoner's indictment being read over, the Clerk did demand of the said Prisoner, if he was "Guilty or not Guilty" of the Indictment."

The Prisoner said " he was guilty of the Fact."

Mr. Samuel Leonard was constituted by the Court, to be their Majesties Attorney.

The Pettit Jury was cald, and answered to their names as followeth:
Francis Jackson.
Thomas Hilborn.
William Case.
Charles Dennis.
Abraham Brown, Sr.
Jonathan Stout.
Thomas Huett.
John Vaughan.
John Woolley.
William Woolley.

Caleb Shrive.
George Curliss.
The Pettit Jury aforesaid, having all taken their engagement, the Kings Attorney pleaded to the bill of indictment against the said Negro Cesar. The said Jury withdrew out of Court

Then the Court and kings Attorney ordered the Clerk to issue outt, warrants against Stephen Cook, William Goodbody, Anthony Pinter, and Capt. John Slocum, to answer their Majesties, in the actions of which they did stand indicted off.

The Prisoner, Negro Cesar, being brought to the bar again, the Pettit Jury came into Court again, and being cald over, all answered to their names. The Clerk asked them "if they had agreed on their verdict." They all answered "yes," and that their Foreman should speak for them. Then he being asked "if he found the Prisoner, then at the bar, Guilty or not Guilty."

The Foreman of the said Jury answered "Guilty."

Our Soverign Lord the King,
                              Plaintiff.
STEPHEN COOK, Defendant.

The declaration being read over in Court, the Defendant was demanded to put in his plea. He being drunk, did swear four oaths and several idle words; the which the Court did take cognizance off. The case was delivered to the Jury, which said Jury did find the said Stephen Cook guilty of ranging the woods and marking of horse kine, contrary to law.

Our Sovereign Lord, the King,
                              Plaintiff.
WILLIAM GOODBODY, Defendant.

The declaration being read over, the Kings Attorney pleaded against the defendant for unlawfully ranging the woods and marking of horse kine, contrary to law.

The defendant by plea saith : "He is not guilty," in manner and form.

The case delivered to the Jury.

The jury brought in their verdict for the defendant.

Our Sovereign Lord, the King,
                              Plaintiff.
Mr. ANTHONY PINTAR, Defendant.

The Kings Attorney did plead to the declarations against the defendant, for being deceitful in weights and measures to the great damage of the public.

The defendant, by his attorney, Richard Hartshorne,[1] saith : "He is not guilty" in manner and form.

The case was delivered to the jury, and the said jury brought in their verdict for the defendant.

The judgment of the Court on the first action, that the defendant, Stephen Cook, shall pay for fines, for breech of several laws, viz :

1. Twenty pounds for unlawfully marking of horse kine.

2. Five pounds for being guilty of ranging the woods, contrary to law.

3. One pound for swearing four oaths in the presence of the Court.

4. Five shillings for being drunk, with costs of Court.

William Lawrence, Sr., and James Grover, Sr., are chosen and appointed overseers of the poor for the Town of Middletown for one whole year, from the date hereof.

The negro Cæsar was brought to the bar to receive his sentence, and the Clerk was ordered to read off his sentence, as followeth :

"Cesar ! Thou are found guilty by the country of those horrid crimes, that are laid to thy charge. Therefore the Court doth ajudg that thou, the said Cesar, shall return to the place [2] fromwhence thou camest, and from there to the place of execution, where *thy right hand shall be cut off, and thrown into a fire, and burnt before thine eyes.* Then thou shall be hanged up by thy neck, 'till thou are dead, dead, DEAD. Then thy body shall be cut down, and burnt to ashes in a fire.

And so the Lord have mercy on thy soul, Cesar !"

The Court adjourned 'till the fourth Tuesday of December, next ensuing.

At a court held at Middletown, 28th, 29th of June, 1692.

(Same Judges as before.)

---

[1]. Richard Hartshorne was the first citizen of Monmouth county, who practised law here. Whether he had studied law in England is unknown. He, however, was the first lawyer in this county.

[2]. This place was, doubtless, the jail in the Blockhouse, or Fort as sometimes called, in Middletown Village. This stood on the knoll where the Episcopal Church now stands. There is a dim tradition that this execution (the first in our county) together with three subsequent executions of negroes, which shortly followed, were carried out according to the sentence, on the high hill north of the village, and a little distance west of the present residence of Charles J. Hendrickson. The probabilities are, that they took place in the wide road, near or in front of the Blockhouse.

Grand Jurymen.
Eliakim Wardell,
Samuel Child,
James Dorsett,
Peter Stout,
Joseph West,
Charles Dennis,
Calieb Shrive,
John Vaughn,
John Whitlock,
John Stout,
Francis Usselton,
Thomas Whitlock,
Clement Masters.

1. This Grand Jury find a "bill against Elisha Allen, for feloniously stealing of swine."
2. A bill against Stephen Cook, "for violently abusing Alice Goodbody and Mary Chamberlin."
3. A bill against Sarah Reape, for a "Riott committed in carrying away grass from Ongs' meadow."

The following presentments were made:
Imprimis wee of the Grand Jury, do present Jedediah Allen, for threatening speeches to the widow Chamberlain, late deceased, which she did say, was the instrumental cause of her death, upon her death bed.

We, the Grand Jury, do present John Slocum for using threatening speeches to William Chamberlin, and for threatening to dash the said Chamberlin's brains out and to be the death of him, att the house of ———.

We of the Grand Jury do present Stephen Cook and George Hulett, for a violent assault of and upon William Goodbody, upon the King's Highway.

The Petit Jury consisted of
Robert Skelton.
Henry Mash.
Job Throckmorton.
William Layton.
Edward Taylor.
William West.
Edward Williams.
Nicholas Brown.
James Fullerton.
Moses Lippett.
Mordecai Gibbons.
James Grover.

Court of sessions held at Shrewsbury, December 27-28, 1692.

The Court consisted of
His Honor ye Governor, Coll. Andrew Hamilton.
Captain Andrew Brown.

Lewis Morris, of Tinton.
John Hance.
Peter Tilton.
Lewis Morris, of Passage Point.*
The Justices commissions were read by the Clerk.

Grand Jurymen.
Eliakim Wardell.
William Scott.
Francis Jackson.
Clement Masters.
Calieb Shrieve.
Thomas Vickard.
William Reape.
John Willson, Sr.
John Worthley.
John Williams.
John Tucker.
Charles Dennis.
John Lawrence.
Thomas Whitlock, Sr.
Samuel Chield.

John Starkey and William Goodbody were bound to answer at Sessions, for breaking the peace and fighting "on the Sabbath day."

The Court fined Starkey 20 shillings, and Goodbody 40 shillings with court costs, to be levied on their chattels.

At a court of Sessions at Middletown, 28-29th of March, 1693.
Andrew Bowne, President.
Lewis Morris of Tinton Manor.
John Hance.
Peter Tilton.
Lewis Morris of Passage Point.

Same Grand Jurors as at preceding Court, except two who did not appear.

The Court license Robert Hamilton to sell strong drink, and keep an inn at Middletown.

Quite a number of civil suits are tried. Lewis Morris of Tinton Manor is a party in several of them.

At a Court of Sessions at Middletown, 26th of September, 1693. Same judges as before.

Grand jurors.
James Ashton, Foreman.
Richard Davis.
William Whitlock.
James Reid.
Daniel Harber.
John Lippingcott, Sr.
Thomas Huett.
George Curliss.
John Whitlock.

* Passage Point was somewhere in Shrewsbury Township, on the Shrewsbury or South Shrewsbury River the exact location I have been unable to ascertain.

John Starkey.
James Bowne.
John Crafford, Jr.
The Grand Jury present several persons for selling "strong drink," in township of Shrewsbury, without license.†

THE PETIT JURY.
John Reid.
Nicholas Browne.
Abraham Brown, Sr.
Garrett Wall.
William West.
Gawen Drummond.
John Vaughan.
Robert Pattison.
James Dorsett.
Nathaniel Cammock.
Obadiah Holmes.
Obadiah Bowne.

A few civil suits are tried. This Court orders the Prison at Middletown to be repaired and enlarged.

At next Court, in Shrewsbury, ——— ——— is indicted for selling liquor without license, and Thomas Webley for "swearing four profane oaths."

At next Term, the Court sent to the Grand Jury, a bill against Jedediah Allen, of Shrewsbury, with instructions to indict him for "using threatening speeches to Ann Chamberlain, of same place, which she said *was the cause of her death.*" Which bill the said Grand Jury brought in "*ignoramus.*"

At a Court of Sessions held at Middletown, 25th, 26th, 27th days of September, 1694, Court consisted of Capt. Andrew Bowne, Lewis Morris, of Tinton Manor, John Hance, Peter Tilton, Lewis Morris, of Passage Point. The Grand Jury indicted Lewis Morris, of Passage Point, because he "with several of his negroes, did feloniously take away the hay of William Shattock." Lewis Morris, of Passage Point, removed this indictment by writ of Habeas Corpus to the Court, at Perth Amboy, Lewis Morris, of Tinton Manor, entered into bond for Lewis Morris, of Passage Point.

This independent Grand Jury which indicted one of the Judges, who sat on the bench, consisted of John Wilson, Jr., John Smith, Thomas Hilbourn, Eleazer Cottrell, Peter Stout, Henry Marsh, John Tilton, Sr., Peter Wilson, William Good-

---

† This was doubtless on account of the gross partiality shown to Lewis Morris, of Passage Point, by the Justices. They did not punish him for striking Nicholas Sarah, but let him go unwhipt of justice.

body, James Reid, Gershom Mott, Benjamin Stout.

They also presented another Judge, Lewis Morris, of Tinton Manor, as follows : "We, the Grand Jury, do present Lewis sued out against said Lewis Morris to answer the same.

At the next Court, held in Shrewsbury, Dec. 25th, 1694, the Grand Jury again indict Lewis Morris, of Passage Point, for striking Nicholas Sarah, of Freehold. The Court order a summons for him to appear at next Court. The next Court of Sessions was held at Middletown, March 27, 1695.

Judges—Lewis Morris, of Tinton Manor, John Hance, Peter Tilton, Lewis Morris, of Passage Point.

Grand Jurors—James Dorsett, Foreman, Thomas Morford, John Tilton, Sr., Moses Lippett, George Jobs, William Cheeseman, John Bray, Henry Mash, Samuel Willett, Thomas Usselton, John Ruckman, Sr., John Crafford, Jr., Richard Compton.

The aforesaid Grand Jury being all sworn and engaged, the President of the Court gave them their charge, and soe they withdrew out of Court. The Court adjourned 'till two of the clock in the afternoon. Att two of the clock in the afternoon the Court satt again. Capt. Andrew Bowne came into Court, and did sitt as President of ye said Court.

Morris, of Tinton Manor, for fencing in the Highway."

The Court orders a summons to be issued. Lewis Morris, of Passage Point, being presented at ye last Court of Sessions, for stricking of Nicholas Sarah several blows. The said Lewis Morris did inform the Court, how matters was, and submitted himself to the Bench ; and was by them dismist.

Lewis Morris, of Tinton Manor, and Lewis Morris, of Passage Point, by reason of their families were sick, did desire that they might withdraw and go home ; which was granted.

The Court then consisting of Capt. Andrew Bowne, John Hance and Peter Tilton, Esq'rs.

They brought in the following presentments : "We, the Grand Jury, do present ye overseers of the Highways of Middletown and Shrewsbury, for not repairing of the Highways, and for the great defect of them.

"We, the Grand Jury, do present Nicholas Sarah, of Freehold, for abusing Peter Tilton, one of the Majesties Justices of the Peace."†

At next Court Lewis Morris, of Tinton Manor, is again presented by the Grand Jury for stopping, and fencing in ye high way that goes to Freehold and Middletown. The Court avoid action by directing process for his appearance at next Court, although he was then sitting as one of the Justices. At this Court the following entry appears :

It is ordered by the Court that the negroes that are in the gaol, for the murdering of Lewis Morris, of Passage Point, shall be conveyed by the Sheriff to Perth Amboy, to attend the Court of Common Right, on the second Tusday of October next. And that a mittimus shall be directed to the Sheriff of Middlesex, to receive and keep said negroes.

MONMOUTH RECORDS—BOOK OF MINUTES No. 1, 1688—1721.

At a court of Sessions held at Middletown, 24, 25, 26 of March, 1695-6.

The Court, consisting of Capt. Andrew Bowne, President,

Lewis Morris,
Richard Hartshorne, } Esqrs.
John Hance,
Peter Tilton,

Grand Jury.

William Layton, Foreman,
Remembrance Lippincott,
Caleb Allen,
John Worthley,
James Bowne,
William Cheeseman,
Moses Lippett,
John Wilson, Jr.,
John Vaughan,
John Morford,
Eleazer Cottrell,
John Whitlock,
William Bowne.'

Thomas Gordon was, by the Court, constituted and appointed as King's Attorney. Lewis Morris, of Tinton Manor, Esqr., was presented for fencing in the King's Highway, that goes to Middletown and Freehold.

"The King's Attorney demanded a Fee of any one that would employ him, to plead to the indictment. There was no one that would prosecute ye said Morris, so that the presentment was Quasht."

The Grand Jury present "Samuel For-

man, High Sheriff of ye County of Monmouth, for letting Negro Jeremy, a murderer, make his escape out of the County Gaol, some time in February, 1695."

Evidence sworn in Court :

1. John Stout says on oath, that sometime after the Negro Jeremy was brought to the Gaole, the said Negroe's fetters was only Keyed with two or three shingle nails.

2. Eleazer Cottrell, upon oath, says that the said Sheriff took him, the said Cottrell, to assist him, the said Sheriff, to secure Jeremy in Gaole, and that with an axe hammer and a gimlet; that they did what they could with those Tooles; that the Sheriff thrust a long, thin piece of iron through the end of the bolt, but did not rivett it. Upon which, ye said Cottrell told him, he dident think it sufficient, but the Sheriff thought it would do.

3. Lewis Morris, Esq., sayed in open Court, he had advised and directed the Sheriff to secure the Fellon, and to iron him hand and foot, and rivitt ye irons ; but the Sheriff slighted his advice.

4. John Wilson, Jr.,*1 sayd on oath that he made two staples and two keys of good iron, as he thought, for the fettering of said negro.

Ordered by the Court, that Samuel Forman find four men, to give five hundred pounds security for his appearance, at the next court of Common Right, for the answering a negligent escape of ye Fellon, Negro Jeremy, committed to his charge, or be committed himself, and put in irons.

The Court adjourned to eight o'clock of the next morning.

Daniel Harker, Thomas Warne *2, Capt. Samuel Leonard, George Jobs, do acknowledge themselves to be indebted to our Soveraign Lord, the King, in the full and just sum of one hundred and twenty-five pounds, each person, for the appearance of Mr. Samuel Forman, at the next court of Common Right, to be held at Perth Amboy, the second Tewsday in May next ensuing; and that ye said Samuel Forman shall stand to the order, determination and arbitrament of ye Court, as they shall judge him, for ye escape of Negro Jeremy, who feloniously murdered his Master. Then this obligation to be void

---

† This offense seems to have been continued to this day Ocean Township was then part of Shrewsbury.

*1 Wilson's Blacksmith Shop stood on or near the present railroad cut, between the two railroad bridges over Middletown street and the turnpike to Keyport.

*2 Thomas Warne was one of the twenty four proprietors of East Jersey. He is buried at Topanemus.

and of no effect, or else to remain in full power and virtue.
Dated March 26, 1696.
The case referred to to be Tryed at Court of Common Right.
After some other business, Court adjourned until eight o'clock next morning. At eight of the clock ye next morning, Court sate again. About ten of clock news was brought that Negro Jeremy was catcht.
The Court adjourns until two o'clock in ye afternoon. At two of o'clock Court sat again.
The Negro Jeremy was brought to ye bar, and his indictment being read over, the prisoner was demanded, if he was guilty or not guilty, as he stood indicted.
The Prisoner owned himself guilty and all the facts, how and after what manner he killed his Master. The prisoner had his sentence pronounced as followeth:
"Jeremy:
You must goe to the place of execution, *when thy right hand shall be cut off, and burnt before thine eyes. Thou then shalt be hanged up by the neck, till thou art Dead, Dead, Dead. Then thy body shall be cut down, and thrown into a fire and burnt to ashes.*"
It is ordered by the Court, that William Goodbody, who did take the said Negro Jeremy, shall be paid twenty pieces of eight, out of the next County rate.
East New Jersey, Monmouth county, March 25, 1697.
————————, of Freehold, was bound over to answer at this Court of Sessions.
"————————, Thou stands indicted, by the name of ————, of Freehold, in the County and Province aforesaid, for that thou, being led by evil instigations did, sometime in the year 1695, take and carry away, and with premeditated intent and cunning, did steal ten swine of two years old, of the value of twenty pounds and ten shillings, the proper swine of William Davison, of the same place, where they were feeding in said Freehold, contrary to the peace of our Soverign Lord ye King, that now is, and ye laws of this Province, in that case made and provided. For all which thou stands indicted."
The Clerk askt said ————————, "if he was guilty or not guilty." The said ——————— says, "not guilty," and puts himself upon the County. Evidence being sworn, and they declared what they knew of the matter of fact.

The jury receiving their charge from ye Judge of the Court withdrew, with their officer charged to attend them.
The jury were out until late in the afternoon, when they came in, with following verdict.
"We the jurors find ———————— guilty of saying, that he knew what became of William Davison's hoggs. If that makes him guilty, then, Guilty. If not, then Not guilty."
The judgment of Court.
"That ———————— is guilty according to indictment, and that he pay to William Davison, fifty hoggs of ye value of sixty-two pounds ten shillings, or sixty-two pounds and ten shillings in money; and that he be committed to close Gaole 'till ye payment hereof."
Att a Court of Sessions and Court of Pleas, begun and held att Shrewsbury, for ye County of Monmouth, on ye twenty-eighth day of September, Anno Domini, one thousand six hundred ninety and seven; and then and there held by several adjournments, until ye second day of October following.
The Courtt, consisting of
Lewis Morris, }
John Hance, } Esqrs.
Peter Tilton, }
The Courtt being cald, and then adjourned 'till ye Morrow morning at seven of ye clock.
Att seven of clock ye morrow morning, ye Court of Sessions was opened again.
Capt. Andrew Bowne came into Court and sate President.
Mr. John Reid was required to take upon him, ye office of kings Attorney*4 for this Courtt. The which he, ye said Reid, refused to take. Therefore ye Courtt, committed ye said Reid, to close Gaole, until he shall pay ye fine of fourty shillings.
Capt. Samuel Leonard was required to take upon him, ye office of kings Attorney, which ye said Leonard refused to take. Therefore the Courtt committed ye said Leonard to close Gaole, until he should pay ye price of forty shillings.
Ye Courtt doth appoint Mr. Richard Salter, of Freehold, to be ye King Attorney, for this present Court.
At a Court of Sessions and of Common Pleas, held at Shrewsbury, 26-27 day of Sept. 1698.
Lewis Morris, of Tinton Manor, is again presented by the Grand Jury, for fencing

*4 Now Prosecutor of the Pleas or State's Attorney.

in the highway between Tinton Falls and Swimming River Bridge.

At a Court begun and held at Middletown on ye 31st day of August, 1699, by virtue of an act of the Assembly, "Impow~ring for ye trying of all negro slaves." The Justices present were
Capt. Andrew Bowne, President.
Richard Hartshorne, Esq.
Thomas Warren (Warne.)
Peter Tilton.
"The Grand Jury Impaniled for ye present service was these."
Garret Wall, Foreman.
Mordecai Gibbons.
James Ashton, Jr.
Nichalas Stevens*5.
Henry Marsh.
David Stout.
John Vaughan.
William Cheeseman, Sr.
John Skank, (Schanck.)
Garret Skank, (Schanck.)
Peter Stout.
James Stout.
John Ruckman, Jr.
John Bray.
A negro named Tom is indicted, tried and convicted of rape on a white woman named Grace Wood. The Court sentence him to death.

A record of a Coroner's Jury.
John Stout, Sr., Foreman,
Jarret Wall,
Jonathan Stout,
Peter Stout,
Richard Stout, Jr.,
John Gabeson, (Guybertson, Dutch.)
George Cook,
William Williams,
William Merrill,
John Morford,
Hendrick Hendrickson, (Dutch.)
Samuel Hewlett,
John Tilton,
Moses Lippett,
William Estill.
Monmouth, August ye 9th, 1699.

We, the above named Jurors, met the Coroner of Monmouth upon Sandy Hook, ye day abovesaid, and went to ye body of a deadman, which we judged, had died aboard of ship, and shoved overboard. Signed by Foreman, in behalf of ye rest.

JOHN STOUT.

Guybertson, (now Giberson) and Hendrick Hendrickson with his brother, Daniel Hendrickson, were from Flatbush, or vicinity, on Long Island. They came over and settled in Monmouth about the same time, (between 1693 ; nd 1699.) The Schancks and some other Hollanders came about the same time. Daniel Hendrickson was the first Dutchman to hold the office of High Sheriff of Monmouth county. He was appointed Nov. 12th, in the 5th year of the reign of Queen Anne, for one year. See Book A, A. A, of Commissions, in Secretary of State's office, at Trenton. From this time (1699) onward, Dutch names appear more and more frequently on our County Records.

At a Court of Sessions held at Shrewsbury, Sept. 12, 1699, the following order was made:

Whereas, by proclamation issued out, by ye Honorable Jeremiah Basse, Esq., Governor of New Jersey, for the apprehending of several persons accused of piracie; †1 and, whereas, application is made unto us by Jacob Ong and Randolph Simons, authorized by the High Sheriff, of Burlington, upon warrant for seizing and apprehending of persons, granted by the said Governor Basse. That they have here apprehended James Halstead, one of the persons named in said warrant and proclamation. Desiring our assistance to convey the said James Halstead to Burlington, from whence he, having been their prisoner, is escaped.

These are therefore, to warrant and authorize said Jacob Ong and Randolph Simons to carry the said James Halstead back again to Burlington, and that the High Sheriff of this county do aid and assist them with such force as they think fit, to carry back the said James Halstead to Burlington.

The order of the Court is, that the Sheriff press a man to assist Randolph Simons and Jacob Onge to carry James Halstead back to Burlington, and deliver him to the Sheriff of Burlington.

Lewis Morris is again presented by the Grand Jury, for fencing in the highway.

Capt Leonard did inform, in open court, that on the 22nd of this instant, September, he was riding through Middletown, and seeing Cornelius Compton, who had been presented for a felon, did

---

*5 This Nicholas Stevens was the ancestor of the celebrated John Stevens, whose works on Egypt and the Holy Land was once so popular.

†1. Raritan Bay is said to have been quite a rendezvous for piratical vessels, between 1690 and 1720. According to tradition, Capt. Kidd had several natives of Monmouth County from the Bay shore people, among his crew. Other piratical vessels are said to have received supplies, and frequently trafficked with the people along our coast.

arrest him, and request Garret Wall, Saftie Grover, John Vaughn, Samuel Willet and George Cook, to assist him in apprehending and securing the said Compton; and having informed them that the said Compton was presented for a felony, and all of them *did refuse,* "notwithstanding that he' told them *they were accessary to the felony, by refusing to assist him.*"

Garret Wall, one of said company, being apprehended and brought before Court, was asked, "why he did refuse to assist, and suffer the said felon to escape," did confess, in open Court, "that he did refuse," but assigned no reason for it, but " at that time he thought fit to refuse." Ordered by the Court, that the said Garret Wall give security in the sum of one thousand pounds, to appear at next Court of Common Right, to be held at Perth Amboy, and in default thereof is committed to custody of the Sheriff. James Bollen is also bound over to appear at the same Court, and committed to Sheriff's custody in default of security.

At a special Court held at Shrewsbury for the county of Monmouth, the seventh day of July, 1700.

Lewis Morris, President.

Samuel Leonard,
Jedediah Allen, } Justices.
Samuel Dennis,*

At the Court, Mingo, a negro, is indicted for killing a negro named Nedd. The murder occurred at the Town of Middletown, May 29th, 1700, in the night between 2 and 4 o'clock, Mingo killed Nedd while asleep, with a broad axe. The Prisoner admitted he killed Nedd, but did it "because Nedd would have killed him."

James Seabrook was the principal witness against Mingo.

The jury found him guilty, and Court pronounced the following sentence.

" Thou Mingo, the negro, shalt be carried back to the place‡ from whence thou came; and from there carried to the place of execution and there hanged by the neck till thou be dead, and the Lord have mercy on thy soul."

---

*This Samuel Dennis lies buried in the graveyard of the Episcopal church at Shrewsbury village; on his headstone is this inscription:

" Here lies, in hopes of a joyful resurrection, the body of Samuel Dennis, who came from Great Britain to this place, A. D. 1675, and lived here to the day of his death, which was the 7th of June, 1723, aged 72 years and 6 months; leaving issue two sons and three daughters, by his only wife Increase, who departed this life 28 years before him."

‡The place was the jail. This was for the fourth execution within fifteen years, all of negroes.

At a Court of Sessions held at Middletown, March 26th, 1700.

Capt. Samuel Leonard, President.

Jedediah Allen,
Samuel Dennis, } Justices.
Anthony Pintard,

The Court being open, the Justices commissions were read and the panel returned by the Sheriff, for the Grand Inquest, was called over and Eliazar Cottrell, was called for a juryman, appeared and made *some objection against the authority of the Court.*

The Court commanded the Sheriff to take him into custody.

Richard Salter *refusing and denying the authority of this Court,* the Court commanded the Sheriff to take him into custody for his contempt. James Bollen, the former clerk of this Court, being called before the Court, to deliver up the books, papers and records of this Court to the present Clerk, *positively refuse to doe the same, unless the Court would give him bond to save him harmless for the sum of ten thousand pounds.*

Adjourned for two hours.

Post Meridin, just as above.

The Court being opened; the Court did dismiss all such persons, who were returned on the Grand Jury, and were willing to serve their king and country, and there being several, who refused to serve on the Grand Jury, and had denied the authority of the Court, among whom was William Cheeseman, who came before the Court, and begged pardon for his misbehavior; and said he was very willing to serve. The Court upon his humble submission, did forgive and discharge him.

Ordered by the Court that the Sheriff do discharge Eleazar Cottrell and Richard Salter out of his custody.

Ordered by the Court that the said Eleazer Cottrell, for his contempt and misbehaviour before this Court, be fined, and the Court doth hereby fine the said Cottrell in the sum of five pounds current money, of this Province, to be levied by the Sheriff upon their goods and chattels of the said Eleazer.

And the Sheriff to have the said money, by sale of the said goods and chattels at the next Court, to be held for this county the fourth Tuesday in September at Shrewsbury.

The Court impose a fine of fifteen pounds on Richard Salter, to be levied and collected in same way.

Ordered by the Court, that John Ruckman, Sr., John Bray, John Wilson, Jr.,

OLD TIMES IN OLD MONMOUTH. 261

Daniel Hendrickson, John Cox, Richard Davis, Mordecai Gibbons, Nicholas Stevens and Moses Lippet, be each and every one of them fined.

"And the Court doth hereby fyne each and every one of said persons, severallie, in the soume of fourty shillings, current money of this Province, each of them, for contempt and misbehaviour before the Court, to be levied by the Sheriff upon the goods and chattels of each and every of the said persons, And that the Sheriff have the said money by the sale of the said goods and chattels at the next Court, to be held at Shrewsbury, the fourth Tuesday in September next, for the said Countie."
Adjourned.

A Court of Inquiry held at Shrewsbury for the Countie of Monmouth, the 27th of August 1700.
Lewis Morris, President.
Samuel Leonard,
Jedediah Allen, } Justices.
Samuel Dennis,
Anthony Pintard,

The Grand Jurie of inquirie for the present service were these
John Reid,
Jeremiah Stillwell,
John Slocum,
Thomas Hewitt,
Abiah Edwards,
John West,
John Leonard,
Alexander Adam,
Thomas Webley,
Patrick Cannon,
James Melven,
Peter Embly,
Samuel Hopenge, (Hopping),
William Layton,
William Hoge.*

And having their engagement and their charge given them by the President, withdrew with a constable to attend them.

The said Jury being called again, gave in the following presentments:
August ye. 27th, 1700.

We, jurors, present Richard Salter, John Bray, James Stout, David Stout, Benjamin Stout, Cornelius Compton, William Bowne, Thomas Taylor, Thomas Hankinson, Jacob Van Dorn, Arian Bennett, Thomas Sharp, Benjamin Cook, Robert James, Thomas Estill and Samuel, a servant of Salter for riotously assembling, on the 17th of July, and assaulting John Stewart, High Sheriff, and Henry Leonard, in the path near the house of Alexander Adam, and beat and grievously wounded the said persons, took their swords from them, carried them away and kept them, to the value of five pounds money of this Province, in the breach of the peace and terror of the Kings liege people. Signed in behalf of the rest by
JOHN REID, Foreman.

A Court of Sessions begun and held at Shrewsbury, on the fourth Tuesday in September, 1700.
Lewis Morris, President.
Samuel Leonard, Samuel Dennis, Anthony Pintard, Justices.

The Court being opened, Alexander Forman being bound by recognizance to appear at this Court, and be of good behaviour, made his appearance, and nothing appearing against him, he was acquitted.

Eliezar Cottrell, being bound as above, made his appearance, and nothing appearing against him, he was acquitted.

Arian Bennett and John Reid being bound by recognizance, dated the 1st day of August, 1700, each in the sum of ten pounds, that Arian Bennett should appear at this Court, and in meantime to be of good behaviour.

Arian Bennett made his appearance. But since taking that recognizance, the Jury of Inquiry for the Connty, on the 7th of August, 1700, presented Richard Salter, John Bray, James Stout, David Stout, Benjamin Stout, Cornelius Compton, William Bowne, Thomas Taylor, Thomas Hankinson, Jacob Van Dorn, Arian Bennet, Thomas Estele and Samuel, a servant to the aforesaid Salter.

And the aforesaid Arian Bennett, for riotously assembling, on the 17th day of July, 1700, and assaulting John Stewart, the High Sheriff, and Henry Leonard, on he path near the house of Alexander Adams, and beat and grievously wounded the said persons, took their swords from them, and carried them away and kept them, to the value of five pounds, money of this Province, in breach of the peace, and terror of the King's liege people. The said Bennett, in open Court, confessed, that "he was in company with the above named persons, when they *beat the Sheriff.* That they did beat and wound them and cracked their swords, but that he, Arian Bennett, was not aiding or assisting them *with his own hands.*"

---
*The greater part of this Grand Jury are new men. Lewis Morris, no doubt, selected them through the Sheriff.

The Court order that he, said Arian Bennett, be committed to the Sheriff's custody, till he give security to the value of one hundred pounds to ———"

The rest of this record is gone. The Court minutes of 1699-1700-1701-1702 are very imperfect. Besides being irregularly bound,'some pages are entirely gone, and fragments of the record left, as in above case.

At a Court of Sessions held at Shrewsbury, Third Tuesday, Oct. 1700.
Lewis Morris, President.
Samuel Leonard, ⎫
Jedediah Allen, ⎬ Justices.
Samuel Dennis, ⎪
Anthonie Pintard, ⎭

John Tilton was called, and committed to the Sheriff's custody, for *subscribing a seditious paper.*

The Court being informed, that Mr. Thomas Gordon was to pay some money to Cornelius Compton, one of those rioters and "Fellons," who absented himself, so that he could not be apprehended and brought to tryal, for his joining in the committing of said riot and felony, they, (Court) gave him (Gordon), a charge not to pay any of the said money to the said Compton, until he was cleared by law.

George Allen being asked the reason, why he did not serve on the Jury of Inquirie to inquire of certain riots, did acknowledge in open Court, and said "that Salter was his friend, and had done him several kindnesses, and that was the cause he did not appear, and serve on the said jury of Inquiry."

Joseph Clark was brought before the Court for refusing to attend, and assist the Justices of the Peace to apprehend certain rioters, and for his said contempt, the Court ordered Joseph Clark to be put in Common Gaol, there to remain, without bail or mainprize, for the space of one month, and to pay as a fine, the sum of twenty shillings, current silver of the Province, for the use of our Sovereign Lord, the King, and to remain in gaol, till he pay the said 20 shillings.

Garret Boulles (Boel), being brought before the Court, and being demanded by them, whether he put his hand to a certain seditious paper, sent by the mob to the Justices, and delivered to Jedediah Allen, one of the Justices, by Capt. John Bowne, one of the said Mob. The paper being shewed him, he did say that he could not write, but confessed "he did consent that his name should be put to that paper,"

for which the Court ordered Garret Boulles, to be put in gaol, till he gave security in the sum of twenty pounds, current silver of this Province, to appear at the next County Court to be held at Middletown, the forth Tuesday of March next, and in the meantime to be of good behaviour.

Thomas Webly having spoke several contemptuous and reproachful words in the Court, and having otherwise misbehaved himself, in the presence of the Court the Court therefore order, that said Thomas Webly doe immediately pay the sum of five shillings for the use of the poor, or be put by the constable in the stocks, for the space of two hours. Thomas Webly paid the said five shillings for the use aforesaid.

COMPLAINT.

To the worshipful, the Majesties Justices of the Peace of the County Court of Sessions of the County of Monmouth, now sitting at Shrewsbury this 17th, of Oct. 1700.

The information and complaint of John Stewart, High Sheriff of the said County, humbly showeth ; that whereas, on the 24th of September last at the first sessions of this Court, by order of the Court, Garret Wall, James Bollen and Arian Bennett, was committed to my custody, to be by me safely kept until they should give security for their and each of their appearance, at the next Court of Common Right to be held at Perth Amboy, the second Tuesday of October, then next following, or else to have them and each of them, their bodyes before the said Court of Common Right.

And whereas, each of said persons did refuse to give such security, as was by order of said Court appointed, in pursuance of said rule of Court, I was intending to carry the said persons to the common gaol of the said County, but the said Garret Wall, James Bollen and Arian Bennett, did forcibly make their escape, and run away from me. By reason of which forcible escape against my will, I was disabled to have the bodyes of the said persons before the said Court of Common Right, according to the rule of said Court. Upon which complaint the Court ordered as followeth : "Whereas the Sheriff of this county hath made complaint to this Court, that Garret Wall, James Bollen and Arian Bennett, who by order of this Court were committed to his custody, have forcibly escaped out of his custody against his will."

"Ordered by the Court, that the said Sheriff or his Deputy doe take the body of the said Garret Wall, James Bollen and

Arian Bennett, if they shall be found in his bailwick, and them safely keep in the County gaol, or sufficient security take, according to the former order of Court, so as he have them and each of their bodyes, before the next Court of Common Right to be held at Perth Amboy, the second Tuesday of May next, according to the former order of Court. *

The Court having ordered the jury to withdraw, made the following order :— Whereas, by order of the Court of Sessions or County Court, held at Middletown the 26th day of March last, 1700, Richard Salter was fined in the sum of fifteen pounds, Eleazer Cottrell in the sum of five pounds, John Ruckman, Sr., John Bray, John Wilson, Jr., Daniel Hendrickson, John Coxe, Richard Davis, Mordecai Gibbons, Nicholas Stevens and Moses Lippet, each of them in the sum of forty shillings, for their contempt and misbehaviour before the said Court, by the Sheriff or his deputy, upon them and each of their respective goods and chattels, as by the record of said Court doth appear, And whereas, there is information given to this Court, that the said fines are not yet levied, according to the order of said Court. Ordered* by the Court that the Sheriff of the said county or his Deputy doe forthwith levy the said several and respective fines, upon the goods and chattels of the said several and respective persons, by sale of the goods and chattels, and retaining the overplus, if any there be, according to the order of said Court, and that he have the same before his Majesties Justices, at the next County Court of Sessions to be held at Middletown for the said County, the fourth Tuesday of March next, and he will answer to the contrary at his perill."

March 25th, 1701.

Monmouth ss—At a court of sessions held for the county of Monmouth, at Middletown, in the countie aforesaid, and Province of New East Jersie.

Being present :
Col. ANDREW HAMILTON, Governor.
LEWIS MORRIS, } Esq'rs of the
SAMUEL LEONARD. } Governor's Council.
JEDEDIAH ALLEN, } Justices.
SAMUEL DENNIS, }

The court being opened, one Moses Butterworth, who was accused of piracy, and had confessed that he had sailed with Capt. William Kidd, in his last voyage,

when he came from the East Indies, and went into Boston with him. He was bound to make his appearance at this Court, that he might be examined and disposed of, according to his Majesty's orders, the said Butterworth was called, and made his appearance. When the Court was examining him, one Samuel Willett, an Inn holder, †1 said, that the "Governor and Justices have no authority to hold Court, and that he would break it up."

He accordingly went down stairs to a company of men, then in arms, and sent up a drummer, one Thomas Johnson, into the Court, who beat upon his drum.

Several of the company came up, with their arms and clubs, which, together with the drum continually beating, made such a noise (notwithstanding often proclamations made to be silent and keep the peace) that the Court could not examine the prisoner at the bar.

And when there were (as the Court judged) betwixt thirty and forty men come up into the Court, some with their arms and some with clubs ; two persons, viz : Benjamin Borden and Richard Borden, attempted to rescue the prisoner at the bar ; and did take hold of him by the arms, and about the middle and forced him from the bar. The constable and under-sheriff, by the command of the court, apprehended the said Bordens, upon which several of the persons in the court room, assailed the constable and under-sheriff (*the drum still beating and the people thronging up stairs with their arms*) and rescued the two Bordens. Upon which, the Justices and Kings Attorney General of the Province, (then present) after commanding the King's peace to be kept, and no heed being given thereto, drew their swords, and endeavored to re-take the prisoner, and apprehend some of the persons concerned in the rescue, but were resisted and assaulted themselves; the examination of the prisoner was torn in pieces. In the scuffle, both Richard Borden and Benjamin Borden were wounded ; but the endeavor of the Court was not effectual in retaking the prisoner, for he was rescued and carried off, and made his escape. The people, viz, Captain Saftie Grover, Richard Borden, Benjamin Borden, Obadiah Holmes, Obadiah Bowne, Nicholas Stevens, George Cook, Benjamin Cook, Richard Osborne, Samuel Willett, Joseph

---

*It was very easy for the Court to give orders, but it was very hard on the poor Sheriff to execute these orders, when the whole community about Middletown were hostile to the Court and the Proprietors.

†1. According to tradition, Willett kept tavern at Waykake Landing, and, perhaps, this pirate spent his ill gotten gold in carousals at his house, and made friends with the shore people.

West, Garret Bowles, (Boels) Garret Wall, James Bollen, Samuel Forman, William Winter, Jonathan Stout, James Stout, William Hendricks, †2 John Bray, William Smith, Gershom Mott, Abner Heughs, George Allen, John Cox, John Vaughan, Elisha Lawrence, Zebulon Clayton, James Grover, Jr., Richard Davis, Jeremiah Curingam, Joseph Ashton, with others, to the number of about one hundred persons, did traitorously seize the Governor and Justices, and the Kings Attorney General, and Secretary, and the Clerk of the court, and the under-sheriff, and kept them under guard, close prisoners, from Tuesday the 25th of March, till the Saturday following, being the 29th of the same month, and then released them.

GAWEN DRUMMOND, Clerk.

After this there are no court records until after the surrender, although some Court minutes of preceding years have been irregularly bound, and follow in the book, this record. It will be seen that Hamilton and Drummond were both Scotch. The influence of the Scotch Proprietors had placed several Scotchmen like John Reid, John Stewart, the High Sheriff, Gordon, Gawen Drummond and others, in high positions. This was very objectionable to the English, who were the original settlers, not only because of the national antipathy which then existed, but because the Scotch sided with the Proprietors and represented their interests. Thus the two parties were called the Scotch Party and English Party. The stronghold of the English was at Middletown. The sympathy of the Waykake people for Butterworth, was the spark which kindled into flame the passions of the people. In view of these troubles, in all of which Lewis Morris was prominent, and between him and the people of Middletown there exisited a hearty hatred, it would not be out of place to quote from a certain letter, which he wrote a year before this time (1700), to the Bishop of London, concerning the state of religion in the Jerseys.

"Freehold was settled from Scotland. (Mr. Keith began the first settlement there, and owned a fine plantation, which he afterwards sold, and went into Pennsylvania.) About one-half of the Inhabitants there§1 are Scotch Presbyterians and a sober people. The other part was settled by people (some from New England, some from New York, and some from the forementioned Towns§2) who are, generally speaking, of no religion — There is in this Town, a Quaker Meeting house.§3 but most of the Quakers who built it, have followed the views of Mr. Keith. and have not fixt yet on any religion, but are most inclinable to the Church, and could Mr. Keith be persuaded to go into this Country, he would (with the blessing of God) not only bring to the Church, the Quakers that followed his views in East and West Jersey, which are numerous, but make many converts in that Country.§4

Middletown was settled from New York and New England. It is a large Township. There is no such thing as a church or religion amongst them. They are, perhaps, the most ignorant and wicked people in the world. Their meetings on Sundays, are at the Public House. where they get their fill of rum, and go to fighting and running of races, which are practices very common, all the Province over.§5

Shrewsbury settled from New England, Rhode Island and New York. There are in it about thirty Quakers of both sexes, and they have a Meeting House. The rest of the people are, generally, of no religion. The youth of the whole Province are very debauched, and very ignorant.— The Sabbath day seems there to be set apart, for rioting and drunkenness. In a word, a general ignorance and immorality runs through the youth of the whole Province. There was in the year 1697, some endeavors made to settle a maintenance in that County for Ministers, and the greater part of the House of Commons (Assembly) were for it, but one Richard Hartshorne, a Quaker, and Andrew Bowne, an Anabaptist, found means to defeat it that session, and before the Assembly

---

†2. William Hendricks had two grandsons, who, with some others from Monmouth, emigrated to and settled in one of the eastern counties of Pennsylvania, prior to the revolution. From one of these grandsons Thomas A. Hendricks, of Indiana, is said to have descended.

§1 By "there" he means the old Township of Freehold.
§2 Bergen, Elizabethtown, Newark, Woodbridge, Piscataway and Perth Amboy.
§3 Topanemus.
§4 The British church evidently followed this advice, as George Keith was sent out as a missionary in 1702, and succeeded in turning many of the Freehold and Shrewsbury people to Episcopacy. He may therefore be justly termed the father of this denomination in Monmouth. Keith was first a Presbyterian, then became a Quaker to secure the patronage of Robert Barclay, then an Episcopalian to secure friends in the British church.
§5 This statement that there was no such thing as religion or a church in Middletown, was a deliberate falsehood. The Baptist church then and some thirty three years before, had been in existence.

OLD TIMES IN OLD MONMOUTH. 265

could sit again, one Jeremiah Bass, an Anabaptist Preacher, arrived, with a commission from the Proprietors of East Jersey as their Governor, and with instructions from them, not to consent to any act to raise a maintenance for any Minister of any persuasion whatsoever, so there is no hope of doing anything of this kind, till the government is in other hands.—*Whitehead's Papers of Governor Lewis Morris, pages 8, 9.*

This account of Governor Lewis Morris should be received with considerable allowance, not alone because of his animosity to the Middletown people, who had so frequently presented him, and ignored his authority, but, at the time he wrote this letter, he was anxious to secure the appointment of Governor from the British Crown. He sought the influence of the Church of England, which would likely have some power. Andrew Bowne, who he styles an Anabaptist, resided in Middletown Township, as did Richard Hartshorne, whom he styles a Quaker.— Both of these men were prominently talked of as being likely to get the appointment. In this letter he adroitly poisons the minds of the great dignitaries of *the* Church in England against them, and parades his own zealous efforts in behalf of "The Church." He also gratifies his hatred of the people, by abusing them. Lewis Morris was an ambitious and crafty man, and would have put the yoke of priestly tithes on the people of Monmouth, without any scruples, if it would have advanced his own interests. The people of Middletown had as poor an opinion of him, as he did of them, and when they broke up his Court and arrested him, they treated him like a common malefactor, holding both him and his Court in the greatest contempt.

At a Court of Quarter Sessions held at Shrewsbury, Feb. 28, 1704, the following persons are Judges.

Capt. Andrew Bowne, Esq.
John Bowne,
Richard Salter,
Obadiah Bowne, } Justices.
George Allen,
Jeremiah Stillwell,

Nearly all these Justices were among the party which broke up the Court in 1701, and imprisoned the officers.

At a Court of General Quarter Sessions held at Shrewsbury, Augt. 20th, 1704, the Court consisted of

Lewis Morris, Judge.

Anthony Pintard,
Jeremiah Stillwell, } Justices.
John Bowne,

The following entry appears on the Minutes at this Court.

"Edward, Viscount Cornbury, Captain General and Governor in Chief of ye Province of New York, New Jersey and all ye Territories and tracts of land depending thereon in America, and Vice Admiral of ye same.

To all to whom these Presents shall come, greeting: Know ye, that I, said Lord Cornbury, have assigned, constituted and appointed, and by these Presents, do assign, constitute, and appoint, Lewis Morris, Esq , to be Judge of His Magisties Inferior Court of Common Pleas, to be holden in ye County of Monmouth, in ye Province of New Jersey, with authority to use and exercise all power and jurisdiction, belonging to ye said Court, which are specified in ye ordinance, intitled an ordinance for establishing Courts of Judicature for ye ease and benefit of such respective City, Town and County, within ye Province of New Jersey. And ye said Lewis Morris, assisted with Andrew Bowne, Anthony Paintard, John Reid and Jeremiah Stillwell, Justices of the Peace in ye said County, or with any two of them, to hear, try and determine all cases and matters of law, cognizable in ye said Court and to award executions thereon, accordingly, Given under my hand and seal at Perth Amboy in ye Province of New Jersey this sixth and twentieth day of August Anno Domini, 1703, and in ye second year of Her Majesties Reign. CORNBURY.

A record of ye return of Highwaies, New Jersey.

27th of September, 1705.

We the Commissioners of the Countie of Monmouth, appointed by act of Assembly, in the third year of Her Majesties Reigne, for laying out of Highways, have laid them, as follows:

Beginning below John Leonard, at the Landing, known by the name of the Cherry Tree Landing; thence along the south side of the house, as the road goes to Remembrance Lippencotts corner, of his fence ; thence upon a straight line to the Pear Tree in William Worth's field ; thence on the northside of the Pear Tree, to the Brook ; thence along the southside of the highway at the south end of Richard Lippincots corner ; thence as the road lies to Francis Bordens corner tree, by the highway (ye tree to stand in ye middle of ye road); thence upon a straight line to the Brook by Bickleys; thence as the road lies to the corner of William Astens (Ashton) orchard; thence to a white oak tree standing a little to the eastward of John Lippincotts, Jr.; thence as the Path is to the old Road; thence along the Road to the corner of Joseph Parkers land; thence turning the corner up the path as the old road did lye, to the corner of Nicholas Browns fence, by the Meeting House; thence as the road now lyes to near Woodmancys house; then leaving the road near Woodmancys house, to go the most direct and convenient way to the place where Lewis Morris made a bridge on the Fall run, a little above the Landing, known by the name of the Fall Landingso over that place, the most direct and convenient way, along the north side of the said Lewis Morris cleared field, to a place called Little Falls, in the old way to Freehold and Amboy, and thence the most direct and convenient way to the north corner of Morris' wheat field, and thence along the north side of said field, the most direct and convenient way to Hoping Bridge; thence to Peter Tiltons; thence along the new markt trees on Stony Brook, to the old road; thence along the markt trees on the south side of the path, till they come into the path again; 'thence by Job Throckmorton's; thence as the road lyes to Combs Brook; thence as the road lyes to the gully be tween Thomas Formans and the Scoole (school) House; thence as the old road was laid out to David Claytons gully by his fence; thence —— road within his fence, so into the path, then along the old road as it was laid out, that bound the tract of land, 'till it comes to Coales' Path; thence along the ridge between the two paths, to Coales' Bridge; thence along the new mark't trees to the same path, to a black oak tree mark't on two sides, so along to a black oak tree marked upon two sides; thence turning out, on the north side of the road running along the new mark't trees, 'till it comes to Holman's road against Thomas Estill's; so along the road 'till it comes to a black oak tree. marked on two sides; thence turning out on the south side of the path along the new mark't trees 'till it comes to Moses Robbins' corner tree standing under Cunny Hillside; thence running along Cunny Hillside; thence along the new mark't trees, 'till it comes to Robert

Huchason's corner tree; thence to a hickory tree mark't on two sides; thence to two whiteoaks mark't on both sides, standing in the Post Road, and all roads to be four rods in breadth

ELISHA LAWRENCE,
OBADIAH BOWNE,
BENJAMIN BORDEN,
JOHN WOOLLEY.

Another highway beginning at the Falls River Bridge, above the Landing aforesaid; then in the most direct and convenient way, to the old Swimming River Bridge in the road to Middletown; thence as the road went to Jumping Brook; thence to Crooked run, as the road formerly went to Nutswamp; thence to Mordecai Gibbons, his fence; thence along the fence, by the path, as the path now is, to the middle of the road, and so along the path, as it now goes to Poraica, the most convenient way over; thence as the road now lies, till it comes to Moses Lippett's new field; thence cross the field to the fence at the head of the gully, so along to a small walnut tree. standing in Wilkins' wheat field, so to the road, down the hill and over the brook, along as the path now goes, to the corner of Wilkins' fence, so up the line between Wilkins and Hartshorne, (the line to be in the middle of the road), till it comes over the gully; thence all into the highway; so along Wilkins' fence, 'till it comes into the street, which is to remain four rods wide.

Sept. 28, 1705.

ELISHA LAWRENCE,
BENJAMIN BORDEN,
OBADIAH BOWNE.

Record of a highway from Middletown to ye County line, towards Amboy.

Also another highway, beginning at James Grover's; thence along Waycake path to a red oak marked; thence to the brook called Cochowdes' Brook† to a marked tree; thence to William Hendrick's Mill; thence to the bottom of James Dorsett's bog; thence to Benet's old house; thence to Wigwam Point; thence

†This brook has its source at Cocowder Spring, among the Middletown hills, a spring famous among the Indians and first settlers for its medicinal properties. John Ruckman, Sr., was the first settler on and owner of the lands around this Spring. He was celebrated as a hunter, and for his influence with the Indians. He was buried at the foot of the hill, just northeast from this Spring; but all traces of his grave are now gone. This property passed to the Taylor's, and in 1792, was sold by Sheriff John Taylor to George Crawford, Esq., and Taylor, a few years after this sale, moved to Perth Amboy, where he died.

to Freehold Bridge by ye Rocks; thence the most convenient way to the bottom of Mohwhingsong bog; thence to ye brook at the Pound, so direct to the Point where ye Indian Path went, down below Thomas Smith's; thence crossing ye brook, so to Amboy Path; thence ye directest and best way to the County line.

This road laid out by us.
ELISHA LAWRENCE,
JOHN HEBRON,
OBADIAH BOWNE,
Commissioners.

March ye 21st, Anno Dom. 1705-6.

A Record of a driftway, by Thomas Boleses (Boels) March ye 14th, 170 5-6.

Layd out a driftway, in Freehold, beginning at Samuel Redford's fence, by ye highway, then running, ?s ye mark't trees goes, cross ye lots of Agustus Gordon and Thomas Boell; allowing to said Boell, two gates upon ye said way, to ye head of a gully up on the north side of ye said Boell lot; thence cross a branch of Holman's Bog to the bridge that lays by Lovelyell's lot, so cross Lovelyell's lot, as ye way goes, through the brook by Thomas Boell's Barn, so along to Stone Hill, and to Thomas Hankinson's land, along as the road goes, till it comes where ye old road went into ve field; thence where the old road went, till it comes out of the field at the head of the Spring by Hankison's house; thence as the road now goes, till it comes to Amboy road, allowing swinging gates upon this road, which are not to be hung within ye space of ten years, but to lye open.

OBADIAH BOWNE,
BENJAMIN BORDEN,
ELISHA LAWRENCE,
JOHN HEBRON,
Commissioners.

Entered March 21, Anno Dom. 1705 6.

April 2d, 1706.

Then laid out a highway of three rods, beginning at William Hendricks' Mill; thence as direct, as sircumstance will admit of, to Cowder's Brook, where Walter Wall's path went over; thence over along the path, 'till it comes to Ruckman's path that goes to Waycake; thence cross the bog that comes from John Smith; thence direct, crossing a brook to S:out's Bridge, so over ye Swamp; thence along ye mark't trees to Raile Bridge; thence direct cross ye corner of John Jobs field, to a dead white oak tree standing between ye fence and ye brook; thence along ye old marked trees, till it comes to the path that goes to John Jobs, from John Bowne's; thence along the marked trees till it comes to ye path; thence along ye path, till it comes to ye fence of Samuel Culvers; so cross the corner of Samuel Culver's field to the Brook, that parts Culver's land from Hartshorne's land.

Also, another road from the mouth of James Bowne's Creek; thence along ye marked trees and path as it now goes, till it comes to Henry Mashes; thence along ye path till it comes to the Brook below John Stout's, to be two rods wide.

Also, another road from Waycake, along ye new path, till it runs to ye path that goes to John Smith's; thence direct to the bog that comes from John Smith's, where ye path comes from —— bridge. To be two rods wide.

OBADIAH BOWNE,
ELISHA LAWRENCE,
BENJAMIN BORDEN,
Commissioners.

Entered April 29, Anno Dom. 1706.

Book of Minutes No. 1, 1688-1721.

At a Court held on Fourth Teusday of December, 1705.

John Bowne, President.

Richard Salter, Obadiah Bowne, Anthony Woodward, George Allen, Jeremiah Stillwell, Assistants.

At ye request of John Craig, Walter Ker, William Bennet, Patrick Imly, in behalf of themselves and their brethren, ye Protestant Desenters of Freehold called Presbeterians, that their publick meeting house may be recorded. Ordered by this Court, that it be recorded as followeth: "The meeting house for religious worship, belonging to the Protestant desenters, called ye Presbyterians of ye Town of Freehold, in ye County of Monmouth, is situate, built, lying and being at and upon a piece of rising ground,* commonly known and called by the name of "Freehill" in said Town. (Township.)

Mr. John Boyd, Minister of the D. Presbeterians of Freehold, did also personally appear, and desire that he might be admitted to qualify himself, as the law directs in that behalf.

Ordered, that further consideration thereof be referred until the next Court of Quarter Sessions.

At the next Court of Quarter Sessions held at Shrewsbury, May 28th, 1706, the following action was taken.

---

*The little knoll on John Van Kirk's farm in Marlborough township, near Gideon C. McDowell's residence.

"Whereas, Mr. John Boyd, Minister of ye Presbyterians of Freehold, made application to ye Court of Sessions, held last December, that he might be admitted to qualifie himself, as ye law directs in that behalf, and ye Court ordered that the further consideration thereof should be referred. And now ye said John Boyd appeared in open sessions, and was by the Court permitted to qualifie himself, and accordingly the said John Boyd hath qualified himself as ye law in that case directs, viz., did take ye oath made, in a statute, made in the first year of their Majesties Reign, entitled, "An act for removing and preventing all questions and disputes concerning ye assembling of ye Parliament; and did make and subscribe ye declaration mentioned in ye statute made in ye 30th year of ye reign of King Charles ye 2nd, intitled, 'An act to prevent Papists from sitting in either house of Parliament,' and did also declare his approbation of, and did subscribe ye articles of religion, mentioned in ye statute made in ye 30th year of the Reign of ye late Queen Elizabeth except ye 34, 35 and 36, and these words of ye 20th article, viz., '*The Church hath power to decree rites or ceremonys and authority in controversies of faith and etc.*'"

All which are entered here of record, according to ye directions of another Act of Parliament, entitled, "An act exempting his Majesties Protestant subjects, desenting from ye Church of England, from the penalties of certain laws.

BURLINGTON, 11th June, 1708.

Gentlemen:—I am commanded by order of his Excellency, in Council, to write to you, to take diligent care to call before you, or any two of your Quorum, all such persons who have not, as yet, taken the oaths appointed, instead of ye oaths of allegiance and supremacy, and subscribed the rest, and subscribed and taken the abjuration oath appointed in the first year of her present Majesties Reign. And you are, as the law directs, to return the names of all such persons as shall refuse ye same, that they may be prosecuted against according to law. And of this you are by no means to faile.

I am you humble servant,

J. BASS.

Superscription
" For Her Majesties Service,"
To Capt. JOHN BOWNE,
Capt. RICHARD SALTER,
OBADIAH BOWNE,
ANTHONY WOODWARD,
JEREMIAH STILLWELL,
GEORGE ALLEN, Esq'rs.
Justices of ye Peace for ye County of Monmouth.

"Record of God's judgment on Richard Combs, at Shrewsbury, in a Court of Sessions, Anno Dom. 1707.

"Richard Combes, being on his examination before the Court, on charge of stealing Edward Taylor's hogs; he was bold in declaring his innocency, and was told by the Justices to take care, how he did persist to deny, *that which all men did believe him guilty of.* He then again called upon God, and said *that God knew his innocency*," and that he *was clear of the charge of stealing hogs.* One or two of the Justices looking full in his face, prayed him to forbear appealing to the Great Being, who would one day meet with him for it, if he was guilty of the crime charged. He again began to call on God, saying that *God knew he was clear*, and suddenly fell down, like one struck dead. He was helped up, just opened his eyes, and fell down again, and looked like a dead man, and did not recover in a considerable time to be sensible. His tongue hung out of his mouth, and he did not wholly come to himself in some weeks.

By order of the Court,
JAMES BOLLEN, Clerk.

There seems to have been no proof of his guilt before the Court, as they were then examining the case, yet the Court assumes his guilt. This was enough to excite a person conscious of his innocence.

A charge of this kind, perhaps, maliciously preferred by some sly and crafty person, was sufficient to set him in a fever of excitement, and when in spite of his solemn protestations of his innocency, the very tribunal, which should have waited until all the facts were before it, persisted in the assumption of his guilt. That under such excitement, there should have been a rush of blood to the brain, and a fit, is not very surprising. This record is proof that the Dogberries of the bench were unfit for their positions, but no proof of the defendant's guilt.

At a Court of Sessions held at Middletown, in Sept., 1709, Joseph Morgan was qualified in the same way as John Boyd, as the Minister of the Presbyterians of Freehold Township.

At a Court of Quarter Sessions held at Shrewsbury, the fourth Tuesday of February, 1710. the Judges were:

Jeremiah Bass, Esq., President; John Anderson, Samuel Dennis, John Leonard, James Ashton, Esquires.

Alexander Griffith, Attorney General.

Benjamin Stout, High Sheriff.

At a Court of Quarter Sessions held at Middletown, the First Tuesday of December, 1711.

Justices present—John Reid,† President; John Anderson,† John Leonard, James Hubbard, Assistants.

Henry Leonard, High Sheriff of the County.

GRAND JURY.

Hugh Hartshorne, Foreman,
Richard James,
William Hunt,
Joseph Golden,
Andrew Wilson,
Cornelius Tomson,
John Okeson,
John Scank (Schanck),
William Wilkison,
Benjamin Coleman,
John Chamberlin,
Hendrick Hulan,
Johannes Polhemus,
John Scot,
George Allen Smith,
John Warring,
Richard Job.

At a Court of Quarter Sessions held at Freehold,‡ for the County of Monmouth, the Fourth Tuesday of November, Anno Domini, 1715.

Justices present—John Reid, President; James Ashton, Lawrence Van Hook,§ Joseph Wardell, Richard Chambers, John Wilson.

Thomas Gordon, Esq., Attorney General.

Gideon Crawford, High Sheriff of said County.

GRAND JURORS.

Peter Wilson, Foreman,
John Coks, (Cox),
Alexander Doue.‖

Albert Covenoven, (Conover),
Cornelius Lain,
John Giseberson,
John Van Mater,
John Remine,
Hendrick Werwey,
Johannes Smack, (Smock),
Alexander Clark,
James Crage, (Craig),
Johannes Polhemus,
Jacob Covenoven, (Conover),
John Hulet,
Nathan Allen,
William Juel, (Jewell),
Gawin Watson.

At a Court of General Quarter Sessions held at Freehold, Feb. 28th, 1720.

Justices—John Reid, James Hubbard, David Johnston, John Wilson, Lawrence Van Hook.

Gideon Crawford, High Sheriff of the County.

GRAND JURYMEN.

Richard Stout,
Garret Schenck,
John Schenck,
John Wall,
Charles Gordon,
Garvin Watson,
Daniel Ketcham,
Timothy Lloyd,
John West,
John Eaton,
Marmaduke Horseman,
John Throckmorton,
William Madock,
Benjamin Van Cleave, (Cleaf),
William Jones,
John Sutphen,
Aert Williams,
William Clark,
Obadiah Holmes,
John Okerson,
Charles Hubbs,
David Allen, of Squan,
Jacob Large,
John King.

The Sachem, Wequehela, brought the Indian, Welehalely and some others into Court, to answer the complaint of Robert Hubbs and others, for shooting at the said Hubbs. After hearing the allegation on both sides the Court ordered Welehalely's gun to be delivered to him and dismissed complaint on both sides.

Among the constables and overseers of the highways appointed by this Court, we find the following names:

Mindart Le Fever, Richard Horsefield, constables for Freehold; Thomas Van

---

† John Reid and John Anderson were both buried at Topanemus. Their tombstones may be seen there at this day.

‡ This was the first County Court held in Freehold village, and the County seat has been here ever since—one hundred and sixty-two years.

§ Lawrence Van Hook was the first Dutchman to hold a judicial position in Monmouth County.

‖ Alexander Doue was a Scotchman, as we are informed by his tombstone at Topanemus burying ground.

The presiding judge of the Court of Quarter Sessions, Mr. John Reid, was a Scotchman, and a prominent man in his day. His grave and tombstone may still be seen at Topanemus graveyard, near Marlborough village. The following is a copy of a paper found among private family papers, which purports to have been written by him:

"Mr. John Reid's observations on the laws of New Jersey, 1713."

"Some observations of our Laws, in a letter to one of our Representatives for the Eastern Division of New Jersey."

"Having revised and sorted our Laws, and made some remarks thereupon in another paper, I find that during the Proprietors administration, there was 7 Sessions of the General Assembly, and 107 Acts Past. Whereof 8 are Repealed, 8 Expired, 4 the Reason of 'em are ceased; 22 supplanted by new acts; 14 are become useless by the alteration of our circumstances, on the surrendering of the government; a clause of one disagreeable to English Law; a clause of one and 49 Acts in force, one of which Acts contains 32 heads called General Laws, of which there is a clause of one Repealed; one ceased; two supplanted; one become useless as above; a clause of one and 27 laws in force. There are two clauses and 76 laws of force in the Eastern Division, but how many in the Western Division I can't tell. That must be the work of another hand.

In meantime, since the Surrender, when East and West Jersey was united, there has been 6 sessions of General Assembly, and 32 Acts past; whereof 2 almost and 11 quite expired, 3 ceased, 2 disallowed, 3 not yet approved, and 17 of force in the whole Province. And because the Eastern and Western Divisions have their distinct laws (as they were two Provinces), and that the laws of each can't be of force in both, tho' now united; Her Majesty has directed that these laws (of the Proprietors), be revised, and such of 'em as shall be found fit, be reenacted to oblige the whole Province. This would be a good and necessary work. But I think most of our laws, old and new, want mending; and experience tells that patching and mending Acts upon Acts, has very much accumulated and confused our laws.—Therefore I would propose a new digest of our Laws, and out of all our Acts to extract the most useful, (repealing the rest), and by adding these unto from the statutes and neighboring acts, compared with our circumstances, complete a sound body of Laws. This would be a noble work. 'Tis a great work, but not unsupportable. Committees may be appointed for the interval of assemblies, to prepare materials for this building, and at any sitting of Assembly, a committee to polish and bring 'em in from time to time, until this goodly structure can be raised. In the meantime, you know, sir, how these Laws (by the Proprietors), have been set at naught by designing men, and counted of no force, since the Surrender. But that this conceit should be entertained by others, even against their own interest, is most unaccountable. But as it would reflect on the wisdom of this Colony to part with their law so easily, so I believe the General Assembly will take notice of 'em. For my part I have considered all this matter, and can find but these nine imaginable ways whereby these laws can be avoided:

First, If they are repugnant to fundamentals, as the constitution of English Law and Government; the Queen's Prerogative; her peoples rights.

Second, Contrary to a statute forbidding the Proprieters to make any law against such an act of Parliament, as that for regulating the Plantation Trade. 7 & 8 W. 3. Ca. 22.

Third, Contrary to the Queen's Instructions and not yet approved; as the 2nd Act, Jan'y, 1709, ('t was for future Assemblies to sit at Burlington), but here observe, that in all other cases, the Royal approbation is tacit, and our Acts are in force until her Majesties disallowance of 'em, be signified to our Governor here, under the Queen's sign manual.

Fourth. Or where they are disallowed by her Majesty, as the 5th and 7th Acts of 1704. One was contrary to the Queen's Royal Proclamation; 'Tother was disagreeable to English Law, in castrating Negroes, that entice or attempt to ravish any white woman.

Fifth, Or Repealed by an act here; as that clause (30th of 8th Act, 1682), dissolving the marriage for adultery, as by the Act of 1692.

Sixth, Or expired by their own limitation, as the 3d Act, June 1709.

Seventh, Or, when the reasons of 'em are ceased, as the 3d Act, 1682.

Eighth, Or because useless by the alteration of our circumstances on the Surrender, as are almost all our acts for settling of Courts, pursuant to the Proprietors Concessions. Because her Majesties commission and Royal instructions to our Governor here, are instead of said concessions, in relation to the Government, and our Courts are now established by an ordinance of the Governor and Council. The same is befallen our 17th Act, 1682, which contains the oaths and subscriptions of our public officers, pursuant to said Concessions. For now her Majesty directs the oaths and subscriptions appointed by Parliament to be taken. Stat. 1, W & M. ca. 8, and 24 C. 2 ca. 2, and 13 W. 3 ca. 6 1 Ann. Ca. 22.

Ninth Or supplanted by new acts, as the 12th, 13th, 14th and 15th acts, 1682, for the most part by the 3d Act, 1704, for an old law gives place to a new law, when contrary laws come in question. 2nd, *Noyes Grounds and Maxims"*

And now it follows, of course, that all other acts which fall not under any of these nine heads, are of force in the place in which they were enacted. And tho' 'tis common to speak slightingly of these our Laws, yet but one instance against any of 'em, viz.: that our Acts for the regulating of marriages are repugnant to the Laws of England, and therefore void.

But if this was true, it can't. Militat against the rest of those laws. Besides, I must here observe a little. Tho' these Acts differ from that part of the statute (by taking in the Justices, where the Minister is not, or will not solemnize the marriage, as in the case of unbaptized persons), it does not make 'em void. For if our circumstances were the same in all respects with theirs in England, we had no need to make these or any other acts here.

In that case we should only need to have some representatives in Parliament. But as our circumstances vary, so must our Laws from those of England, and no otherwise. This is plainly implyed and presupposed in these words of her Majesties directions, viz : that our Laws be not repugnant, but as nigh as may be agreeable to the Laws and statutes of England, whence by the way, it may be easily inferred, that so far as the Laws and statutes of England (made for the benefit of the subject), that can fit our circumstances, and have the same reason here, take place here. According to those maxims of the law, ubi eadem ratis, est ubi eadem lex, where there's the same reason, there's the same law, if circumstances agree, but "cessante ratione legis, cessat ipsa lex," where there is not the same reason, the law ceases, for " ratio legis est anima legis," the reason of the law is the life of the law. And by these rules we may know what statutes reach here and what not, when any statute or part of a statute is applicable to cases here and when not. But it would prevent disputes, and give great satisfaction, if our General Assembly would collect such statutes, enact and print 'em, for the use of this Colony.

And now to return to our old Laws; I find the only argument devised against them is this; the power by which these laws here made is extinct, therefore they are become void. But how can this be?— 'Twas no usurped power, but graciously granted by the Crown. Can the Queen's power be extinct? For unless the fountain fail, the stream will run. Her Majesty's power and goodness emanates as the heat and light of the sun. The Beams can't be divided from the sun, nor this derived power from the Queen.

The Proprietors may appoint their Governors, but Her Majesty has the approving of 'em.

The proprietary governments may make laws not repugnant to English law, yet if they do Her Majesty has the controlling of 'em. Of late an act of the General Assembly in Connecticut, and another in Carolina, were both repealed by her Majesty in Council. For one was against the liberty ; 'tother against the property of her subjects. And so appeals lie to the Queen from all the Proprietary governments. See the Charter to the Duke of York. All these acts of government are performed by the Queen's Power which never dies. 'Twas by virtue thereof in the Proprietors charter, that all these our Laws were made and enacted, therefore they are all the Queen's Laws; all executed in the Queen's name ; and all this among the Queen's subjects, for which we may all thank God, and pray God save the Queen.

And how do you think the people of South and North Britain would like the argument, viz.: their distinct Paliaments, therefore all their laws before the union are become void. If you say, 'twas one of the conditions of the union that these laws should remain. I say 'twas one of the conditions of the surrender that our rights should remain, and these laws are part of our rights and guard our estates. If you say, the British Parliament confirmed the peculiar laws of South and North Britain, I say the New Jersey General Assembly no doubt will confirm the peculiar laws of the Eastern and Western Divisions, tho' hitherto omitted.

Again, the laws of England and Scotland ceased not between the union and confirmation Act of Great Britain's Parliament, nor does the laws of East and West New Jersey cease between the surrender and confirmation Act of New Jersey's General Assembly.

And if these laws were not in force many inconveniences would follow in the mean time.

And "ab inconvenienti" is an argument in law Coke 1, Institute Ca. 11. For example. If it were not for our 4th act, 1693. we should be as much perplexed about our several Townships, as our neighbors of the Western division are, for want of such an Act, and how inconvenient that would be is only too visible.

If it were not for the 11th of the 8th Act of 1682, entries as well as pleadings could not be in the English Tongue here; which would be very inconvenient, notwithstanding 'tis against the Practice as well as the statutes of England.

If it were not for our 2d Act, May, 1683, (whereby all process shall issue out of the office of the Clerk of the Peace of each County), here would be cause of error in all actions tried since the surrender, (where no rule of Court for it), which would be inconvenient with a vengeance, for there's no law or practice of England for that, nor ordinance of Governor nor Council here, neither can we plead prescription for it. But I am told, Sir, 'tis some attornies at law, whose interests differ from ours, that opposes these our laws, because some of 'em help to secure our land titles, which they would disturb.—They say of our titles, we can't eject strangers that get possession of our lands. For that every one of the Proprietors being Tenants in common, have not sealed our deed. And, if they dare thus question our title, what will become of all the neighboring plantations? For East New Jersey land titles were ever considered the best and that upon good grounds.

Our lands were granted by Patent, signed by the Governor and Council, with the broad seal of the Province affixed, instead of the hands and seals of all the Proprietors. And this by virtue of the Proprietors Original Concessions, and upon which this Colony was first planted and ever since peopled.

Moreover when the Proprietors had divided New Jersey into two provinces, and the number of Proprietors were increased to twenty-four in East New Jersey, and to whom the Duke of York made a new grant of confirmation, both of soil and Government, in the year 1682, and this ratified by Proclamation of King Charles 2d, in the year 1683, here the same method of conveyance was continued and pursued, and that same year, 1683, 'twas enforced by Act of General Assembly, whereby all patents made or to be made as aforesaid, and declared good, which act amongst the rest was confirmed pursuant to said concessions by all the Proprietors or their proxies residing here or in Great Britain.

Again, this Act among others, was also confirmed by another Act of General Assembly in the year, 1692. So that had there been any omission of some Proprietors, at any time, I think, by the concessions and acts, confirmations and continual usage, 'twas maugre Monins. For 'tis a maxim of the Law omnis consensus tollit errorem, such consent taken away error, had there been any.

And as the Proprietors have been thus careful, so their proceedings were as orderly. For the committee of proprietors and proxies, whereof the Governor was President, directed what land and to whom; which being entered by the Secretary, a warrant thence issued, signed by the Governor, for the Surveyor to lay it out. whose return (containing the situation and boundaries of each tract) was certified to the Secretary's office, where the same is recorded, in a Book and the original kept on file; from which the patent was drawn, then executed as above and lastly registered.

And now, sir, where is there any Colony that ever came up to this most exact method? And yet, I say, without all this to do, the Governor and Counsellors hands, with the broad seal of the Province gave the sanction.

And even without the said Concessions, (which alone are enough), and without these acts of the General Assembly, and confirmations of proprietors and proxies, this method is good; as 'twas all along the only and common way of conveyance here, according to that maxim of the Law, " communis error facit jus." A common error constitutes a right, as an acquiescence made by the majority alone, when there be a hundred proprietors, is good. Noys grounds and maxims of the Law, P. 9, Max. 27.

I'm also told, sir, that some of the same gentlemen, who have been suffered to go at this bold rate against our Laws and Land Titles, would also deprive us of the English statutes. Affirming that no statute reach here, unless the plantations are therein expressed, or by general words included, whereby they would confound these colonies with conquered countries.

For 'tis true, that to places conquered, (as the Island of Jamaica), the statutes extend not where not named, or generally included; but to places first discovered or possessed by the English (as these Colonies), all the Laws and Statutes, that can agree with our circumstances, and have the same reason here, came along with 'em, and all others of like nature made since or to be made, are and will be in force here, without any act of General Assembly. This is evident from the rules and maxims above mentioned. And here's a manifest difference, whether these gentlemen know it or not. But the goodness of our King and Queen causes English Law in another manner, to extend to these conquered countries, in granting 'em power to hold Parliaments or General Assemblies, example King Henry 2d, after he had conquered Ireland, at the instance of the Irish, sent thither the Modus tenendi Parliamentum. And by an act of Parliament in Ireland, they took in Magna Charta, and all the Antient Statutes of England. Anno 10. H. 7, which before that did not extend to Ireland, Coke 4, Insti 349-351. But the like was never said of Colonies first discovered or possessed by the English.

And when Jamaica was conquered from the Spaniards, 'twas the opinion of all the judges of England, that the Spanish Laws only were of force there, until the English should enact laws of their own. But was it ever said, that the Indian and not the English laws were in force here?

I mean in these 12 colonies on the Main Continent of America, besides several Islands in the West Indies, that were first discovered or possessed by the English.

Therefore, these gentlemen finding us possessed of and governed by English Laws, and seeing her Majesty will not suffer us the use of any other, by disallowing our 7th act, 1704, are forced to confess, that the Common Law of England extends to the Plantations. Well, but even this includes the principal statutes. For as the Common Law is the most General and Antient Law of England, so it appears and is to be found in the statutes of Magna Charta and other Antient Statutes, (which for the most part are affirmations of common law), in the original writs or judicial records, and in the books of terms and years, Coke's Institutes. And 'tis proved already, that none of these extend to conquered countries.

Moreover, in a late tryal had on an appeal home from Jamaica, concerning a devise not pursuing the statute, 29, C 2, ca. 3. It was resolved, that these statutes do not extend to Jamaica, whence these Gentlemen infer that the statutes extend not to any of the Plantations, when not named or by general words included, as to say "within any of the Queen's dominions." Which, if no indication of ignorance, it certainly discovered their design, as may be seen by what follows: For by the common law we can't convey our lands from one to another, without solemn livery of seizin or by Fine and Recovery. Coke 1st Inst. And if they can persuade us out of the help of the statutes, 27 H.'s, ca. 10, whereby the use is transferred into possession. thousands in these parts of the world wanting Livery of Seizin, have no possession in Law by consequence stranger may enter, and *these Gentlemen for a fee will defend 'em*. If joint tenants or tenants in common refuse to make partition, they can't be compelled by the Common Law, Lit 299. 318. And if they can keep off the statute 31 H. 8 ca., and 81 H, 8 ca, 32, those familes, whose lands have been so parted are to sue, and *these gentlemen must settle 'em*.

Nor can we devise our lands by the Common Law, Inst. 111 C. And if they can bar us the benefit of the statutes 32 H 8 ca. 1, and 34 II, 8 ca. 5, all the last wills in these parts of the world are null, (having no act here for 'em). And then, 'tis but for every respective heir to enter, and *these gentlemen may find imployment*.

But perhaps, sir, the extent of the statute may be, according to the clyant's cases. As if a man is disseized and the Disseisor made a feoffment to defraud the Plaintiff, he shall recover triple damages by the statnte 8, H. 6, ca. 9, if they be for the plaintiff, else the statute affects us not; or in an action for slanderous words, if the Jury find the damages under 40 shillings, the plaintiff shall recover no more costs than damages by the statute 21 : Jac. ca : 16, and when they be for the defendant, otherwise the statute concerns us not.

And now Sir, 'tis time for the Legislators, not the Advocates, to tell us what laws to take place here, which brings me to what I hinted at before, viz: If our General Assembly would extract the most beneficial statutes or parts of 'em, which can fit our circumstances, and that have the same reason here, 'twould prevent the trouble and charge of making many Acts Those that shall then be wanting because of our different circumstances from England, may be taken from our own and neighboring Acts, compared to complete our body of Laws.

But let all our temporary acts be stitched by themselves from time to time, that the bound books of our lasting laws may be intire; and copies of all sorts kept in the clerk's office of each County, that we be no more tossed with the precarious breath of *mercenary men.*

And remember, that no man be suffered to practice as an Attorney at Law, who is not an inhabitant of this Province.

And for shortening Law Suits and lessening costs, let these rules of Court (established in Monmouth county).* take place in all the Courts of this Colony, viz:

(1) That every man be allowed to appear in Court, and plead his own cause himself, or by his Attorney, or both.

(2) That all process be signed by the Clerk.

(3) That all writs of capias be signed underneath on the right hand by the clerk, and underneath on the left hand by the Plaintiff or his Attorney, or the writ abatable.

(4) Every plaintiff shall file his declaration in the Clerk's office, before or at sitting of the Court to which the capias is returnable, together with the original specialties or other instruments on which the action is grounded, or to be non-suited.

And every defendant shall put his plea into said office, with original papers, if any, within 30 days after said Court or judgment by default.

Where Replication is necessary, the plaintiff shall put his replication into said office within 20 days after the plea is put in, or be non-suited. And when Rejoinder is necessary, the defendant shall put in his rejoinder into said office, 30 days before next Court or judgment.

When other pleadings are necessary to

* See Book No. 1 of Minutes, 1688-1721, where these rules are entered. No doubt they were adopted by the Court of Common Pleas of Monmouth through John Reid's influence.

either side, they shall be put into said office and issue joined 14 days before the n Court, or be non-suited.

And if the defendant do not appear and stand tryal, the plain'iff shall take verdict by default.

(5) When the parties or their Attornies are present at the making any rule of Court, they are obliged to take notice of such rules without further service.

But when either party or Attorney are absent, the party or his attorney in whose favour the rule is made, shall serve the party absent or his attorney with a true copy thereof, at least eight days before the expiration of said Rule, or to take no benefit thereby.

(6) When any non-resident of the County takes out a writ against an inhabitant, he shall give bail into the Clerk's office to pay the costs, if non-suited, or he discontinues or withdraws his suit without consent of defendant.

(7) In all actions above the value of ten pounds, the defendant shall give special bail if required, except in actions of slander, *quare clausum fregit,* assault and battery, unless it be otherwise ordered by the Court.

(8) All persons being lawfully summoned to serve on juries, and not appearing shall be fined 13 shillings. 4 pence. unless they can give a satisfactory reason that they shall excuse 'em.

(9) Every Attorney at his first appearance in any case shall enter his warrant of attorney in the clerk's office.

(10) Every attorney having undertaken to plead a cause shall manage the same until it be fully determined, (unless discharged by his imployer), or the attorney shall pay all the costs and damages sustained by his imployer, if the case miscarry thro' his default.

Dated June 4th, 1713.
ic subscribetur,
AMICUS PATRIS.

OLD PAPERS BELONGING TO MR. JAMES
G. CRAWFORD.

LONDON, ye 9 of April, 1680.
Capt. Andrew Bowne.

Your orders are, that you take the first opportunity you see convenient, and sayle from Gravesend to the Downes, and from thence, make the best of your way you cann to New York, And there unload your ship and deliver your goods, According to your bills of Loading; And lay your ship in ther for London directly, and make what dispatch you cann from thence for London, And this is the orders of your friend.

William Antelby,
Phillip French,
And. Smithey,
Mrs. Eliz. Meriwether,

for myself and ye rest of ye trustees of ye Credits of John Parker and John Denham.
J. Cole,
Thomas Gibbs.

This paper is indorsed in the handwriting of Capt. Andrew Bowne, "my orders from my owners." This paper shows that prior to his settlement in Monmouth County, Capt Bowne was a sea captain.

Barbadoes,   Exchange for 25 0 0 £ s d
January 9th. 1684.

Therty days after sight, this my third bill of Exchange, my first and second not payd, pay unto John Haynes or his order the sum of twenty five pounds ster. for the like value rec'd here of ye said Haynes, make good payment and place it to ye acc't of your friend and servant,
JOSEPH COX.

To Mr John Hill,
Merch't,
In London.

New York, 7 Dec. 1685

I Thomas Rudyard, designed by Gods permission, on a voyage to Barbadoes and Jamaica, and having settled most of my affairs to my content and satisfaction, to assertain my mind and will as to what remains, in few lynes I make this my present last will and testament, viz: First, The deed of settlement made and executed the 5th instant, by me, to my sonnes in law, Mr. West and Mr. Winder, my will is yt, it stand and be kept firme in all ye parts thereof; somewhat I shall otherwise alter or dispose by this my last will. Item, I give and devise unto my naturall sonne, John Rudyard my land in West Jersey, viz: all my half propriety there. Item, I give to him, also all those eleven hundred acres of land lying on ye Raritan River, between Mr. Gyles and Mr. Codrington, to hold to him and his heires for ever. I also give him in money one hundred pounds sterling and to be maintained out of ye remainder of my estate to his age of 21 yeares, viz: my per sonal estate herein bequathed to pay one half and my reall estate to pay ye other moyety. All ye rest and remainder of my Land and propriety in East New Jersey, I give and bequath unto my daughter Anne. ye wife of Mr. John West, and Margaret, ye daughter of Mr. Sam'l Winder, equally to be devided between them and their heirs for ever. I give also to each of them one piece of plate, viz : the two largest I am possessed of, and they to cast lots for them. I give my said sonnes in law all my law books to be equally divided between them. I give Mr. Thomas Foullerton twenty pounds sterling moneys. I give my son, Ben Rudyard and my wife over and above ye estate they have settled on them, twenty pounds a piece, sterling money and my house and land at Rudyard town, in Stafford Shire. All the rest of my estate, reall and personall, goods and chattells, whatsoever. I give unto my servant, Hannah Beamont, as a reward for her faithfull service, sober and virtuous conversation. I make null and void all former wills by me made, and declaring this to be my last will therein, constituting and making and hereby declaring Capt. Andrew Bowne, my sonnes in law, John West and Samuel Winder, for matters, estate and things, being or to be in ye Provinces of New York, East and West Jerseys. to bee my executors. And for all matters estate or things being or to be in ye Barbadoes, Jamaica and Old England. I nominate and constitute the aforesaid Thomas Foullerton and Hannah Beaumont, the executors of this my last will and Tes'ament. In Testimony whereof I have hereunto set my hand and seal at New York, this seventh day of December Anno Dom , 1685.

THOMAS RUDYARD. (L S).

Signed, sealed, published and declared by ye Testator. to be his last will and Testatment in ye presence of
JOHN DELAVALL,
JOHN WHITE,
JOHN ROYSE.

Province of Pennsylvania 15th May, 1693. Personally appeared before me one of their Majestie's Justices of ye peace for ye said Province, ye above named John Delavall, who did solomnly attest and declare in ye presence of Almighty God, yt he did see ye above named Thomas Rudyard, sign, seal, publish and declare ye within and above to be his last will and Testament, and yt he was of a disposing mind at ye time of ye doing thereof to ye best of his understanding.

PAT. ROBINSON.

Mr. John White came before me this 19th day of June, 1693, and upon his oath did testify, yt he see ye above mentioned Thomas Rudyard, sign, seal and declare ye above mentioned to be his last Will aand Testament.

Samuel Dennis, Justice, East New Jersey.

Perth Amboy, 12th October, 1693. John White one of ye witnesses within written before ye Governor and Justices of ye Court of Common Right, in open Court deposed upon ye holy Evangelists of Almighty God yt he did see ye within written Thomas Rudyard, sign, seal and publish ye within written to be his last Will and Testament and and yt at ye time he was of sound mind and memory to be best of his understanding.

Jurat coram me.

ANDREW HAMILTON.

Memorandum (ye word) (Naturall) in ye 8th line these words (to hold to him and his heirs forever.) in ye 10th. and 11th lines are interlined in ye orginall or principall Will.

Peyth Amboy, 10th April, 1701. A true copy taken out of ve publick Records of ye said Province of East New Jersey, and therewith compared and examined by me.

THOMAS GORDON, D. Sec'y. and Reg.

This certified copy of tne Rudyard will and probate thereof, was found among the private papers of Capt. Andrew Bowne, who was one of the executors therein named. This Thomas Rudyard was a lawyer, and one of the twenty-four Proprietors. He came to New Jersey as Deputy Governor, and arriyed Nov. 13th, 1682. but not pleasing the Proprietors he was superseded by Governor Laurie, who arrived in New Jersey and assumed the office of Deputy Governor in the beginning of the year 1684. Rudyard held the office of Secretary and Register, until about the time the above will is dated Dec. 7, 1685. He then removed to the Island of Barbadoes, and died in the year 1692.

Original Lease and Release from Sir John Gordon to Thomas Pearson.

LEASE

" This Indenture made the twentieth third of april, Anno Dom. 1684, and in the thirtieth six year of the Reign of our Soveraign Lord, King Charles ye Second over England, etc., Between Sr. John Gordon, Advocate in ye Kingdom of Scotland of the one part. and Thomas Pearson, Mariner in the sd. Kingdom of the other part. Whereas, the said Sr. John Gordon is and standeth seised to him and his Heirs, of and in one full and equall fortyeight part, by virtue of Indenture of Lease and Release, bearing date the 11, and twelve days of December, 1683, conveyed from Thomas Cooper, one of the twenty-four Grantees, after mentioned, of all that Easterly part, share, and portion, and of all those Easterly parts, shares or portions of all that whole and intire Tract of Land in America, heretofore called New Caesaria, or New Jersey, extending Eastwards and Northwards along the Sea-Coast, and a certain River called Hudson's River. from the East side of a certain Place or Harbour, lying on the Southern part of the same Tract of Land, and commonly called or known in a Mapp of the said Tract of Land, by the name of Little-Egg-Harbonr, to that part of the said River called Hudson's River, which is in forty-one Degrees of Latitude, being the furthermost part of the said Tract of Land and Premises, which is bounded by the said River and crossing over from thence in a straight Line, extending from that part of Hudson's River aforesaid to the Northernmost branch of a certain River, called Delaware River. and to the most Northernly Point or Boundary of the said entire Tract of Land and Premises, now called the most Northernly Partition Point, extending Southward unto the most Southerly Point, by a strait and direct Line drawn through the said Tract of Land, from the said North Partition Point, unto the said South Partition Point, called the line of Partition, dividing the said Easterly Part, share and portion of the said Tract of Land, and of all and every the Isles, Islands, Rivers Mines, Minerals, oods. Fishings. Hawkings, Huntings, Fowling, and all other Royalties, Governments, Powers, Forts, Franchises, Harbors, Profits, Commodities and Hereditaments, whatsoever, unto the said Easternly part, share and portion, parts, shares and portion of the said Tract of Land and Premisses, belonging or in any wise appertaining, with their and every of their Appurtenances, and the Reversion ana R-ver-i-ns, Remainder and Remainders, Rents, Issues and Profits of the same, and of every part and parcel thereof. All which said Easterly part share and portion, parts shares and portions, are called by the name of East New Jersey, and were by several Conveyances. and Assurances in the Law, vested in the Right

Honorable James, Earl of Perth of the Kingdom of Scotland, John Drummond of Lundy, in the said Kingdom, Esq; Robert Barclay and David Barclay, Junior, of Ury, in the said Kingdom Esquires, Robert Gordon, of Clunny, in the said Kingdom, Esq; Arent Sonmans, in Wallyford, in the said Kingdom, Esq; William Penn, of Worminghurst, in the County of Sussex, Esq; Robert West, of the Middle-Temple, Esq; Thomas Rudyard, of London Gent.; Samuel Groome, of the Parish of Stepney, in the County of Middlesex, Marriner; Thomas Hart, of Enfield, in the said County of Middlesex, Merchant; Richard Mew, of Stepney, aforesaid Merchant; Ambrose Rigg, of Gatton-Place, in the County of Surry, Gent.; John Heywood and Hugh Hartshorne, Citizens and Skinners of London; Clement Plumstead, Citizen and Draper of London, Thomas Cooper, Citizen and Merchant Tayler of London; Gawen Laurie of London, Merchant; Edward Billing of the City of Westminster, in the County of Middlesex, Gent; James Brayn, of London, Merchant; William Gibson, Citizens and Haberdasher, of London; Thomas Barker, of London, Merchant; Robert Turner, of the City of Dublin, in the Kingdom of Ireland, Merchant; Thomas Warne, of ———, in the Kingdom of Ireland aforesaid, Merchant, their Heirs and Assign's. To whom his Royal Highnsss, James Duke of York, by his Indenture bearing Date the Fourteenth day of March one thousand six-hundred eighty and two, did amongst other things, Grant, Bargain, Sell, Release and Confirm all that part, share and portion, and all those parts, shares and portions of Land called or known by the name of East New Jersey in America, together with all the Islands, Bays, Rivers, Waters, Forts, Mines, Quarrys, Royalties, Franchises and Appurtenances, whatsoever to the same belonging or in any wise appertaining, as by the same Indenture, relation being thereunto had, may more fully and at large appear. Now these Presents witness that the said Sr. John Gordon, for and in consideration of five shillings of good and lawful money of England, to him in hand, paid by the said Thomas Pearson, at or before the sealing and delivery of these Presents. The Receipt whereof, he the said Sr. John Gorden, doth hereby acknowledge, hath bargained and sold, and by these presents doth bargain and sell unto the said Thomas Pearson, a full and equal tenth part of the said Sr. John Gordon, his forty-eighth part of all and singular the said Premises, called East New Jersey, to be Allotted and set out in such places or parts of the said Tract of Land or Province, and out of such parts or portions of Land in the said Province, as the said Sr. John Gordon, his executors and Assigns, his said forty-eight Part, or proportion, also to a lesser part shall be allotted and set out of. And of the said tenth part of all and singular his forty-eight part of the Isles, Islands, Rivers, Mines, Minerals, Woods, Fishings, Huntings, Haukings and Fowlings, and of all other Royalties, Forts, Harbors, Franchises, Profits Commodities and Hereditaments, whatever unto the said Province or Tract of Ground called East New Jersey, belonging, or in any wise appertaining, or to belong or appertain. To have and to hold the said Tenth part of the said Sir John Gordon, his forty eighth part, and other the premises having granted unto the said Thomas Pearson, his executors and assigns from the day next before the date hereof, for and during and unto the full end and Term of an whole year, from thence next ensuing and fully to be compleat and ended. To the intent and purpose, that by virtue of these presents and of the statute for transferring uses into possessions, the said Thomas Pearson may be in the actual possession of the said bargained premises, and be enabled to take and accept of a grant and release of the same premises, to him, to said Thomas Pearson, his heirs and assigns forever. In witness whereof the said parties have to these present indentures, interchangeably set their hands and seals. Dated the day and year first above written."

JOHN GORDON.

Sealed and delivered in the presence of
BARCLAY.
SANDILANDS.
PATRICK INNES

RELEASE.

"This indenture made the twenty fourth day of April Anno Dom., one thousand six hundred and eighty four and in the thirty-sixth year of the reign of our Sovereign Lord, King Charles the Second over England, &c. Between Sir John Gordon, in ye Kingdom of Scotland, Advocat of the one part, and Thomas Pearson, Mariner in ye said Kingdom of the other part. Whereas, His Royal Highness, James, Duke of York, by two several indentures of lease and release, Dated the three and twentieth, and four and twentieth of June, one thousand six hundred sixty and four, made between his Royal Highness of the one part, and John, Lord Barclay," (Berkeley), " and Sir George Cartwright " (Cartaret) "of the other part, did grant, convey and assure to them, the said John, Lord Barclay, and Sir George Cartwright, their heirs and assigns, all that tract of land in America, called Nova Caesarea, or New Jersey, limited and bounded, as in the said indentures is more particularly expressed, as being a part of certain tracts of land granted by the King to the said James, Duke of York, as by his Patent dated the twelfth day of March in the sixteenth year of His Majesties Reign, and renewed by other letters patents, Dated the nine and twentieth day of June, in the six and twentieth year of His said Majesties Reign, relation thereunto being had doth more at large appear. And whereas, Dame Elizabeth Cartwright, as sole executrix to the said Sir George Cartwright, and the Earl of Bath and the other Executors and Trustees of the said Sir George Cartwright have by their indentures of lease and release, Dated the first and second day of February, one thousand six hundred eighty and one, granted, bargained and sold to twelve persons (to wit), William Penn, of Worminghurst, in the County of Sussex, Esq.; Robert West of the Middle Temple, London, Esq.; Thomas Rudyard of London, Gent.; Samuel Groom, of the Parish of Stepney in the county of Middlesex, Mariner ; Thomas Hart, of Enfield, in the said county of Middlesex, Merchant; Richard Mew, of Stepney aforesaid, Merchant; Thomas Wilcox of London, Goldsmith; Ambrose Riggs, of Gatton Place in the county of Surrey. Gent.; John Heywood and Hugh Hartshorne, Citzens and Skinners of London ; Clement Plumsted, Citizen and Draper of London, and Thomas Cooper, Citizen and Merchant Tayler of London, all that part of the said New Jersey called or known by the name of East New Jersey, which by his said Royal Highness, by his indenture of lease and release, bearing date the ——— days of July in the six and twentieth year of His Majesties Reign to the said George Cartwright, his heirs and assigns were again conveyed, and which were bounded and limited as in the said lease and release of the first and second of February, one thousand six hundred eighty and one, is more particularly expressed, as relation being thereunto had, may more fully appear, and whereas, each of those twelve persons have sold the just half of their undivided twelve parts to twelve others, so that the Number of the Proprietors of the said Province, now called East New Jersey is now increased to the number of four and twenty, And whereas, his Royal Highness James, Duke of York, by his indenture Dated the fourteenth of March, one thousand six hundred and eighty-two, hath granted, bargained, sold, released and confirmed the said tract of land called East New Jersey, hereafter more particularly expressed unto the said Four and Twenty Proprietors, viz : The Right Honorable James, Earl of Perth of the kingdom of Scotland ; John Drummond of Lundy, in the said kingdom of Scotland, Esq.; Robert Barclay of Ury, in the said kingdom of Scotland, Esq.; David Barclay, Junior, of Ury, in the same kingdom of Scotland, Esq.; Robert Gordon of Cluny, in the said kingdom of Scotland, Esq.; Arent Sonmans, in Walliford, in the kingdom of Scotland, Esq.; William Penn, of Worminghurst, in the County of Sussex. Esq.; Robert West, of the Middle Temple, London, Esq.; Thomas Rudyard, of London, Gent.; Samuel Groom. Thomas Hart, Richard Mew, Ambrose Rigg, John Heywood, Hugh Hartshorne, Clement Plumsted, Thomas Cooper, Gawen Lawry, of London, Merchants ; Edward Billing, of the City of Westminster, in the County of Middlesexf Gent.; James Brayne, of London, Merchant ; William Gibson, Citizen and Haberdasher, of London ; Thomas Barker, of London, Merchant; Robert Turner of the City of Dublin, In the kingdom of Ireland, Merchant, and Thomas Warne, of Dublin aforesaid, Merchant, their heirs and assigns, as in the grant of the fourteenth of March, one thousand six hundred eighty and two, relation being thereunto had, may more fully appear.

Now this indenture witnesseth, that the said Sir John Gordon, being lawfully seized of, and in one full and equall forth-eighth part of the said Province of East New Jersey, by virtue of the several Letters Patents and Indentures before recited, and by virtue of indentures of lease and release bearing date the eleventh and twelve days of December, 1683, conveyed from Thomas Cooper, one of the twenty-four Grantees before mentioned, for and in consideration of a competent sum of good and lawful money of England to him, the said, Sir John Gordon by the said Thomas Pearson at or before the ensealing and delivering of these presents in hand, paid, the receipt whereof he doth hereby acknowledge, and thereof and therefore doth clearly and absolutely acquit, exonerate and discharge the said Thomas Pearson, his heirs, executors and assigns, and every of them; hath granted, bargained and sold, released and confirmed, and by these presents, doth grant, bargain, sell, release and confirm into the said Thomas Pearson, (in his actual possession now being by virtue of an indenture of bargain and sale for one year, bearing date the day before the date of their presents to him, thereof made by the said Sir John Gordon, and of the statute for transferring uses into possession), and to his heirs and assigns one full and equall tenth part of the s'd Sir John Gordon, his said forty eight part of all, and singular, that easterly part, share and portion of all that whole and Intire Tract of land in America, now called East New Jersey, as the same is and now are by the said indenture of bargain and sale, bearing date the day before the date of these presents, particularly bounded and described, and one full and equall tenth part of his said forty-eight part of all and sir gular, the Isles, Islands, Rivers, Mines, Minerals, Woods, Fishing, Hunting. Hawking, Fowlings and all other Royalties. Forts, Harbors, Franchises, Profits, Commodities, and Hereditaments, whatsoever unto the said Province or tract of ground called East New Jersey, belonging or in wise appertaining, or to belong or appertain, and the Reversion and Reversions, Rents, Issues and Profits of all, and singular, the premises hereby granted or intended to be granted. And all the Estate, Right, Title, Interest, Claim and Demand whatsoever of him, the said Sir John Gordon of and into the same and every part and parcel thereof. To have and to hold the said equall tenth part of the said Sir John Gordon, his forty-eighth part, and all and every other, the premises before granted and released with their and every of their appurtenances, unto the said Thomas Pearson, his heirs and assigns forever. To the only use and behoof of him, the said Thomas Pearson, his heirs and assigns, forever.

And the said Sir John Gordon for himself, his heirs, executors, administrators, doth covenant, promise, grant and agree to and with the said Thomas Pearson, his heirs and assigns, by these presents, that he the said Sir John Gordon for and notwithstanding any Acts, Matter or Thing whatsoever made, done, committed or wittingly or willingly suffered by him, to the contrary at the time of the sealing and delivery hereof, is and standeth lawfully and rightfully seized of, and in one full and quall forty-eight part of all and singular, the said premises, called East New Jersey, and all and singular, the said premises having granted of a good, sure perfect, lawful and absolute estate of inheritance in Fee Simple, without any manner of condition, trust or limitation of any use or uses, power of revocation, or other matter or thing whatsoever, to al er, change, determine, defeat and make void the same estate, and that for and notwithstanding any such acts, matter and thing as aforesaid, he, the said Sir John Gordon hath in himself good, rightful p wer, lawful and absolute authority to grant, convey one full and equall tenth part of his forty-eight part unto the said Thomas Pearson, his heirs and assigns, according to the true intent and meaning of these presents, and that the same and all, every the before hereby bargained premises are now and from time to time, and all times hereafter shall continue and be unto the said Thomas Pearson his heirs and assigns, free and clear or freely and clearly acquitted and discharged of and from all former and other grants, estates, titles, incumbrances and demands, whatsoever had made, done or wittingly suffered by the said Sir John Gordon or any other person or persons whatsoever lawfully claiming or to claim by, from or under him, or his estate. And further that the said Sir John Gordon, and all and every other person or persons lawfully claiming by, from. under or in trust, for him, shall and will from time to time, and at all times hereafter during the space of ten years now next ensuing, at or upon the reasonable request, cost and charges in the law of the same Thomas Pearson, his heirs and assigns make, do and execute, or cause and procure to be made, done, and executed all and every such further and other act and acts, thing and things, assurance and assurances, in law whatsoever, for the better and more absolute assuring and confirming these presents and the premises hereby granted and every part thereof, with their and every of their appurtenances unto the said Thomas Pearson his heirs and assigns, as by him or them, his or their counsel learned in the law shall be reasonably devised, or advised and required, so as such further assurance do not contain any further or other warrant or covenant save only against the person or persons who shall make the same, and all claiming under him or them.

And so as the person or persons who shall make the same be not compelled or compellable to travel from the place of his her or their abode and residence for the doing or executing thereof, further than the space of seven miles. And whereas the said Sir John Gordon is possessed and interested in one equall forty-eight part of a joynt stock in goods and effects, to the value of one thousand two hundred pounds sterling, employed or to be employed for the use, benefit and improvement of the said province of East New Jersey. Now this indenture witnesseth that for the consideration aforesaid, he the said Sir John Gordon hath granted, bargained, sold assigned and set over, and by those presents doth grant, bargain, sell, assign and set over to the said Thomas Pearson the tenth of his forty-eight part of the said stock. To have and to hold the said tenth of his forty-eight part of the said stock to the said Thomas Pearson, his executors and assigns for ever. In witness whereof the said parties have to these present indentures interchangeably set their hands and seals. Dated the Day and year first above written.

JOHN [L. S.] Gordon.

Sealed and delivered in the presence of
Barclay.
Sandilands.
Patrick Innes.

The above lease and release are printed on parchment, with blank spaces for the writing. John Gordon's signature is in a plain, round hand. His private seal is affixed between his christian and surname; the impression on the wax is as distinct as though made yesterday. There are no endorsements on these documents. of recording or registering.

PRIVATE DOCUMENTS AND PAPERS OF JAS G. CRAWFORD, ESQ.

"Know all men by these presents, yt I, John Stout, of Middletown, in the county of Monmouth, in the Province of East New Jersey, farmer, for and in consideration of a competent sum of money to me, in hand, paid by John Bowne, of Middletown, aforesaid, the receipt whereof I do hereby acknowledge, and myself therewith fully satisfied and contented, and thereof and of and from every part and parcel thereof, do freely and clearly aquit, exonerate and discharge ye s'd John Bowne, his heirs and assigns forever, have granted, bargained and sold, and by these presents doe grant, bargain and sell unto the s'd John Bowne, his heirs and assigns, all that lot of meadow or salt marsh situate, lying and being at Shole harbor, within the bounds of Middletown aforesaid, containing six acres in breadth, four in length, fifteen chains, bounded on ye east by Edward Tart, west by meadow formerly John Throckmorton's, south by ye land and north by a small creek, together with all the liberties, privileges and appurtenances to the same, belonging or appertaining to have, and to hold the same lott of meadow or salt marsh and premises with their and every of their appurtenances unto him, the sd John Bowne, his heirs and assigns forever, &c., to &c., for ye only, in and behoof of him the sd John Bowne, his heirs and assigns forever, under ye yearly charge of quit rent, due and payable, or which shall become due and payable to the Lords Proprietors of the said province; and further I, the said John Stout, doe covenant and agree to and with the said John Bowne or his heirs, to make any further assurance that the said John Bowne or his heirs, or any man learned in the law shall advise be, the said John Bowne, being at all the charges within the term of ten years to come. In witness whereof, I, the said John Stout, have hereunto set my hand and seal ye twenty-fifth day of March, one thousand six hundred and eighty-nine, and in the fifth year of our Sovereign Lord, James ye Second of England King's. JOHN STOUT, [L. S.]

Signed, sealed and
delivered in presents
of   JAMES BOWNE,
       THO. WEBLEY,

June 25th, 1689. There appeared before us John Stout, and did acknowledge this above wrighten instrument to be his acte and deed.   JOHN JOHNSTON,
                                   PETER TILTON,
                                   JOHN HAASE.
Endorsed,
John Stont to John Bowne, entered up on the publick Records of East New Jersie in lib d. in fol. 69.   JAS EMOTT,
                                   Copia Vera, Reg'st.

Then in handwriting of Capt. Andrew Bowne, "Copy of Deed Jno. Reid, Esq., sent me.

Letter direeted to
    Mr. John Bowne, Merchant,
        at Middletown, in East Jersey.
            BOSTON, the 25th Oct., 1697.
Mr. John Bowne:
    Sir—Here inclosed you have Messrs.

I. Bernards and L—— Bill on Moses Van Swieton and Cruger, Merchants in New York, which is made payable to myself or order. I have made it payable unto yourself or order. When the money is paid please to advise me of the receipt thereof. The sum being one hundred and twelve pounds, ten shillings. By the last post I wrote you the needful to which refer you and desire you will not faile to furnish with the forty barrels of pork, therein advised for to be sent Mr. Alexander Pygan at New London, there its to be put abord a vessell of mine bound thence to Barbadoes. soe that I doe request you will take care that it be well salted. Goe two barrills of mackrill one on board John Pains in a slope, who I have desired to take in the forty barrills of pork to carry to New London. He is a suitable person for you to agree with to take in anything you design to send for this place. It will be necessary your order be at New York to meet him. Since my last I have not been favored with any of yours. Which with respect I rest.

   Yor most humble ser't;
     AND'R. BELCHER.

This goeth inclosed to Mr. John Barclay, at Amboy, for speedy conveyance. Pray take care to pay him the postage, and charge it to my account. As yet no shipps from England. Yors,
       A. B.

Original commission from Jeremiah Basse to Capt. Andrew Bowne as Deputy Governor.

"Jeremiah Basse, Esq., Governor of the Province of East New Jersey in America, to our Trusty and well beloved Captain, Andrew Bowne, Esq., Greeting, whereas the Proprietors of the said Province have, by their commissions, under their hand the public seal of the said Province, nominated, constituted and appointed me Governor and Commander-in-Chief of the said Province, with full power and authority to nominate, constitute and appoint a Deputy Governor under me, to serve in my necessary absence therefrom and no longer, as in and by the said commission bearing date the fifteenth day of July, Ano Dom 1697, reference being thereunto had, it doth and may more fully appear, and having great confidence in the ability, prudence and integrity of you, the said Captain Andrew Bowne, have nominated, constituted and appointed, and by these presents do nominate, constitute and appoint you Deputy Governor of the said Province, giving you my full power and authority to command over and govern the same, and all persons therein, and to do and perform all and everything which to the charge and office of Deputy Governor doth belong and appertain, during my necessary abscence from the said Province, and no longer hereby requiring and commanding all Inferior officers to give due respect and obedience to you as Deputy Governor of the said Province, you allways following and observing all such instructions and orders as are or shall be made, given or sent you by the Proprietors or the committee of Proprietors of the said Province in London, or the major part of them for the time being, under the public seal of the said province, and governing according to the laws and constitutions of the said Province. Given under my hand and the public seal of the said Province att Perth Amboy, in the county of Middlesex, in the said Province, this tenth day of May, in the eleventh year of the Reign of our Sovereign Lord, William the Third over England, Scotland, France and Ireland, King, Defender of the faith, &c., Anoq Dom 1698.

JERE. { Province Seal. } BASSE.

Endorsed,

"Perth Amboy, 11th May, Anno Dom. 1699, entered upon ye public records of the said province in Lib C, fol. 292, by me,
    THOMAS GORDON,
    D. Sec'y and Reg'r.

This commission is on parchment and well preserved. The signature of Gov. Basse is very large and sprawling. He evidently intended that his name should not be overlooked, and covers more paper than the great seal of the Province.

Under this commission Capt. Andrew Bowne, was sworn in as Deputy Governor May 15, 1699. See "Record of Governor and Council of East Jersey. 1682, 1703," page 221.

A letter from the Proprietors,
   London, 25th March, 1701.
THOMAS GORDON.

The General neglect of yor duty in the imployment of Attorney Generall, of our Province of East New Jersie, giving the Proprietors no manner of account of their concerns in the execution of that office, but concealing yor proceedings therein from the Proprietors, from time to time, whereby you have abetted and suffered many Frauds to be put upon them, who placed you in that station. And having seen good testimony of yor misbehavior and factious doings, in promoting confusions and disorders in the Province to the great disturbance of the Planters and Inhabitants and dishonour of the Proprietors and their Government, together with your notorious injustice to others who had intrusthed you, has rendered you utterly unfit to be any longet continued in their service. Wherefore these are to let you know that the Committee of Proprietors had signed another commission for the said office of Attorney Generall, dated the 25 March, 1701, and sent it over under the publick seal of the said Province, upon arrivall whereof, we do dismiss you from the said office forever.

    Peter Sonmans,
    for myself and all
    the interest of Ar-
    ent Sonmans de-
    ceased.
    Thos. Barker,
    Wm. Dockwra,
    Tho. Hart,
    Tho. Cooper,
    Clem't. Plumsted.

The signatures of the Proprietors to this letter are all very clear and distinct, and the letter is well preserved.

ANDREW BOWNE'S COMMISSION AS GOVERNOR.

The Committee of Proprietors of the Province of East New Jersey in America, Residing in or about London on behalf of themselves and the rest of ye Proprietors of the said Province.

To our Trusty and Weil beloved Friend, Andrew Bowne of ye sd Province of East New Jersey, Esqr.

{ English } Greeting.
{ Stamp } Whereas, the Power of
{ 12 Pence } Government of the said Province of East New Jersey, is devolved upon us and assigned to us, by the late king James, the Second, by the name of James, Duke of York &c., with authority to nominate, Constitute and appoint such Commissioner, or Commissioners, Governor, Governors, Commander or Commanders in Chief, for the well ordering and Governing of the said Province as we or our assigns shall see meet, and having great confidence in the ability, Prudence and Integrity of you the said Andrew Bowne, we have nominated, constituted and appointed, And do hereby Nominate, constitute and appoint You Governor and Commander in Chief, of ye said Province. upon ye Receipt hereof, Giving you full power and Authority to Command, Order and Governe, the same and all persons therein, together with all Isles, Islands, Harbours, Ports, Rivers and Seas, within the Boundaries of the said Province, or belonging there unto, And to doe and Perform all and everything and things which to ye Charge and Office of a Governor or Commander in Chief, does Appertain for the space and Term of one whole year, from the day of Your receipt of these presents, and for so long after, until some other Per-on be nominated, Constituted and appointed Governor and Commander in Chief in your Room, by another Commission sent from London, under ye Publick seal of ye sd Province and there Produced and Published, on which this present commission to be immediately Null and Void, Commanding all Inferior Officers. (which we hereby Commissionate you to Constitute and appoint for so long as you Continue Governour,) Except our Secretary and Register which we have already Established, And except our Surveyour Generall and Receiver Generall, which we resreve to ourselves to Constitute and appoint by Patent under the Publick Seal of our Province. To give due respect and Obedience to you the said Andrew Bowne, as Governor and Commander in Chief of the sd Province, according to this our Commission and ye Powers thereby given to you, and according to ye Laws and Constitutions of ye sd Province, which are already confirmed or shall be confirmed by us, Which you ye sd Governor, are yourself also to observe and follow, as to your Duty and office doth appertain, as also to observe and fulfill all such Instructions and Order as are or shall be made and given or sent you by us or ye Committee of the Proprietors in London, or ye Major part of ym for ye time being, under ye public seal of ye said Province. And we do also commissionate and Impower by sd Andrew Bowne, to nominate, constitute and appoint by commission under your hands and seal of ye said Province, A Deputy Governor under you to serve in the said Province during your necessary absence therefrom, and no longer (he being by you obligated to observe and perform all such orders and instructions as shall be made and sent undr ye Publick Seal, of ye Province, by us or the Committee of Proprietors in London, or ye major part of them for the time being and Governing according to ye Laws and Constitution of ye sd Province, Given at London, under ye Public seal of ye sd

OLD TIMES IN OLD MONMOUTH.

Province of East New Jersey, this 25 day of March, and in the Thirteenth year of ye Reign of our Soveraign Lord, William the Third, by the Grace of God, King of England and Scotland, France and Ireland, Defender of the Faith and Annoq Domini, one thousand seven hunred and one.

W^M. DOCKWRA,
  Peter Ponmans,
   for himself and all the interest of Aront Jonman's dec'd.
  Tho. Cooper,
  Clemt. Plumsted,
  Thos. Barker,
  Thos. Hart.

Endorsed,
 Province of }
 New Jersey. }

"Recorded in the Secretarys, at the City of Perth Amboy, in the Book of Commissions in Libe C No 2 Fo 65 66."

This commission is on parchment, and the writing and the signatures of the six Proprietors who have signed it, very plain.

This is the identical document which caused such a commotion when Andrew Bowne, Esq., produced it before a Council held at Perth Amboy, Jan. 17, 1701. (See Record of Governor and Council of East New Jersey, 1682-1703, Pages 231, etc.) The then acting Governor, Andrew Hamilton, refused to recognize this commission.

This old Document is of considerable historical importance, and now belongs to Mr. James G. Crawford, of Holmdel township, who is a great-great-grandson of Capt. Andrew Bowne. Those interested in the early history of the State will feel under obligations to Mr. Crawford for his careful preservation of these old documents and letters. I am indebted to Mr. Crawford for all these private letters and papers, which once belonged to Capt. Andrew Bowne and John Bowne.

Letter directed to
 "The Honoured
  Andrew Bowne, Esq.
  Governor of East New Jersey.
   at Amboy,
    In America.
 LONDON, 28 November, 1701.

Honored Sir :

This friggot—the Jersie friggot halting still at Portsmouth, I kept the enclosed, a coppie of my letter of the 6th of September, sent Mr. Slater with the postscript of the 18th of October to send in company with this, as also have enclosed another commission for an Attorney General, with a blank, and another deputation for Secretary and Register also in blank, lest Mr. White should be dead or Mr. Slater has miscarried, which God forbid. Likewise, I have sent you a coppie of the Bill (which must needs heard of) that was brought into last Parliament, and begun in the House of Lords for Reuniting to the Crown, the Governments of all the Proprietary Collonyes and Plantations in America, to all which I referre you, adding no more now, because we have not our matters in pursuit, ripe enough to transmit to East Jersie as yet. But to close this, Give me leave to tell you, that notwithstanding Sr Tho. Lane and all his party, with their champion Goliah, L. M. who have boasted incredibly of their bringing in Coll. Hamilton again, over your heades in East Jersey, and those his opponents in West Jersie too, and such mighty powerful friends at Court with such a vigilant agent to attend and improve their great interest for Coll. Hamilton to be nominated the first Governor, according to their petition, which, no doubt he took care long since, should sail over in print to Jersey and New York, to proclaim victory before ye battle was half done, and so uppish they were as to crow, "Who will take upp 50 to one that Coll. Hamilton will be the King's Governor of New Jersie." I say notwithstanding all their noise and boasting, their 50 to one sank to 20 lately, and this last week to ten, and sunk to parr at last.— And for a welcome intimation to you, which, I pray communicate to Mr. Hartshorne, Mr. Royse, Capt. Bowne and the rest of your friends. We have found such ways and means to let His Majesty be well informed, and so ——these Lords whose proper stations are fittest for our assistance, and having gained already such previous points against Coll. Hamilton, that surely I do believe it is already determined to reject him, tho' it will not be made publeck untill the commission and instructions for a King's Governor, and the surrender, be finished and signed, and then it will soon be known that we that have said less, has struck the mark and done the more to rid you of a Scotch yoak, and you be sure we have not laboured in vain. but publick dispatches are so dilitory that I cannot see less than two months yet will run out before the preliminaries will be settled, and the surrender signed; And till that be done the King will not name

any person to be Governor, tho' there be severall candidates, (Englishmen to be sure), who are preparing to make interest by friends, etc., to get the imploymt, and I have seen their papers, petitions, etc., but they are not advised to give the King any petition untill we have the Government in ye Crown. I'll not write their names now for that will stretch out more room about, than is left in this margin, to which I resolve to co fine myself to night, and in my next I will tell you who they are. One of them you must know better than I, but whether he or ye others I shall be pleased with exchange for an English gentleman, to govern an English collony, soe comitt you to ye divine Protector, and rest, Sr. Yo'r M. H. S.
Wm. Dockwra.

An Old Time Bond.

Know all Men by these Presents, that I, John Bowne of New Jersey, am held and firmly bound unto Abraham De Lucena in the sum of thirty-one pounds, one shilling and three pence, lawful money of the Province of New York, To be paid to the said Abraham De Lucena or certain attorney executors, administrators or assigns. For which payment well and truly to be made and done, I do bind myself, my heirs, executors, administrators and every of these, jointly and singularly, firmly by these presents, sealed with my seal, dated the second day of May, in the fourth year of His Majestys Reign, Annoq Domini, 1705.

The condition of this obligation is such that if the above bounden John Bowne, of New Jersey, Merchant, heirs, executors or administrators shall, do well and truly pay or cause to be paid unto the above named Abraham De Lucena, merch't, or his certain attorney, executors, administrators or assigns, the just and full sum of fifteen pounds tenn shillings and seven pence half penny lawful money aforesaid to be paid to the said Abraham De Lucena at his dwelling house two months after ye date hereof, without any fraud or farther delay. Then this present obligation to be void and of none effect, otherwise to remain, abide, and be in full force and virtue.

Sealed and Delivered
in the Presence of us,
Mordecai Grover,
John Ellison.
} Jno. Bowne [l. s.]

Endorsed,

"Obligation of Capt. John Bowne of New Jersey, for £15, 10, 7½."

Then below in a strange hand,

" This bond paid Lucena, October the 19th, 1716."

Old Documents and Papers, of Receiver General's Commission.

"The Committee of Proprietors of the province of East New Jersey, in America, residing in and about London, on behalf of themselves and the rest of the Proprietors of the said Province.

To our trusty and well beloved friend John Bowne, of the said Province of East New Jersey, Merchant.

{ English } Greeting.
{ Stamp } Wee the said proprietors,
{ 12 Pence. } having good opinion of your diligence, industry, prudence and integrity, have nominated, constituted and appointed, ard do by these presents name, note, constitute and appoint you, the said John Bowne, Receiver Generall, of the said Province of East New Jersey, authorizing you by yourself or sufficient Deputy (for whom you must be answerable,) to collect and receive for the use of all ye Proprietors of ye said Province, All such quitt rents, as are or may become due to us within the said Province. As also to receive the effects of all wrecks at sea or elsewhere, and all strays at land, all fines and forfitures to us the Proprietors, and all payments, profits, dues and incomes of what nature or kind soever, which of right, is or may hereafter become due to us, our heirs and assigns within the said Province. Giving your receipt for the same, which wee confirm and allow, shall be a sufficient discharge to ye respective persons, and you are to pay and dispose of what you shall receive from time to time, according to such orders and directions as shall be made by us the Proprietors or the major part of us, the proprietors here in London, and sent under ye publick seal of ye said Province, and signed by William Dockwra, Secretary and Register of the Province, or ye Secretary and Register for the time being, And of what money or eff cts you receive or pay you are to keep a true and exact accompt and enter them in some book or books of the proprietors, for that purpose to be kept and to send a coppy or transcript once a year, of your accompt of Receipts and Payments ending every Lady Day, And if any Corporation, Township or Plantation, person or persons, refuse or neglect to pay in their quitt rents, whether arrears or growing rent at the time and place appointed to pay and receive them. Or if any person or persons

shall neglect or refuse to deliver in unto you any wrecks by water or strays by land, or pay ye true value thereof or neglect or refuse to pay any fines or forfitures or any profits, dues or incomes of what nature or kind soever, which may appear to be due to ye proprietors. You are to address yourself to the Governor or Deputy Governor for the time being who is to issue out his warrant to the Marshall Generall, Constable or other officers, to seize, distrain or levy the same, and if no effects or distress can be found, than to cause such persons so offending to be proceeded against according to ye laws of ye said Province, and wee, the said Proprietors, do hereby give and grant to you our Receiver Generall, tenn pounds per cent of what you shall receive in goods, in consideration of your greater trouble, and ye Proprietors to be freed from all charges and other deductions; and five pounds per cent out of what shall come to your hands. This patent or commission to continue and be in force for one whole year from ye date hereof, and so long after until the Committe of Proprietors residing in and about London, or the Major part of them shall appoint some other person to be Receiver Generall in the room of the said John Bowne, by a new pattent or commission sent from London under the seal of the said Province and signed by William Dockwra, Secretary and Register of the said Province, or by the Secretary and Register for the time being, upon the arrivall of which Pattent and Commission to ye hands of the Governors and provinciall counsell, or counsell of the Proprietors and Proxies and by the Governor and any of them published this patent or commission to be null and void

Given in London under the seal of the said Province, this five and twentieth day of March, in the thirteenth year of the Reign of William the Third, of England, &c., King, Annoq Domini, one thousand seven hundred and one.

   PETER SONMANS.
  WILL DOCKWRA, for myself
   and all the interest of
 ARENT SONMANS, deceased.
Tho. Cooper, Tho. Barker,
Clemt. Plumsted, Tho. Hart.

This commission is a thick, heavy parchment. The signatures of the six proprietors begin with William Dockwra on the letf hand side at bottom, then Peter Sonmans, Tho. Cooper and Tho. Barker running over to the right side on the same line, Clement Plumsted and Thomas Hart's are under Tho. Cooper and Thomas Barker on right hand.

Deputation of Secretary and Register.

{ Stamp 12 Pence. } "I, William Dockwra of London, Merchant, by virtue of my office of Secretary and Register of the Province of East New Jersey, in America, granted and confirmed to me by the Proprietors of the sd Province, reposing trust and confidence in the diligence, ability and fidelity of you, Charles Goodman, of the town of Amboy, in the County of Middl, in the Province of East New Jersey, Gent. Doe nominate, constitute and appoint you my lawful Deputy and Clerk for officiating and executing the service of the Secretary and Register office. Authorizing you for so long time as the sd William Dockwra see fitt and convenient, in generall to doe and perform all things relating to my sd office more particularly to keep the Provinciall seal and to be Clerk to the Provinciall Councill, and Councill of Proprietors and their Proxies, to make fair entries of all Acts of S ate, and all orders and instruments from the Provinciall Councill and Councill of Proprietors and their Proxies, to make all Warrants of State, Commissions, Recommendatory Letters, and provinciall passes, to take care of all addresses, petitions and answers to and from the Governor and provinciall Councill and Councill of Proprietors and their Proxies. Also to make all patents, assurances, leases and conveyances of land from the Proprietors and their Grantees And that you shall upon Record enroll the laws and statutes of the said Province, and Register all patents and grants, charts and rights, and all manner of Deeds. Assurances, lease or any other matter or thing from the Proprietors or Governor, and Councill of Proprietors and their Proxies, that shall be passed to any person whatsoever, likewise to Register all Wills, Letters of Administration, Marriages, Births and Burialls, Mortgages, Settlements, Statutes, Judgments, Bonds and all other obligations for money or goods that shall require registering, likewise servant indentures, and all other matters or things, and, or that shall in any case whatsoever, be appointed or required to be registered, that recourse may be had by all people and on all occasions to the said office of Secretary and Register, and to doe all other Act and Actes, thing and things which doe already or shall hereafter belong to the

sd office of Secretary and Register. For all which duty and service you, the said Charles Goodman are hereby authorized and impowered as my Deputy and Clerk, to take and receive for my account and use, all such Fees, Perquisites and Allowances, as doe or shall belong to the sd office of Secretary and Register, Injoyning you to keep a just and true account thereof, by entring the name of every person in a book or books, to be kept for that purpose, and how much you receive of each of them and when and for what, from time to time, not concealing or reserving any thing but honestly discharging the trust reposed in you, and for defraing the incident charges and expenses you may be at in the execution of the said office and for your care and pains therein as my Deputy and Clerk you are to retain one third part of all that be received, provided you keep true and faithfull accounts, ready at all times to be examined by my Attorney or Attorneys, and making oath to the truth thereof (if required) and that also you doe well and truly pay or cause to be paid half yearly to my Attorney or Attorneys for my proper account, and use the other two full third parts free and clear of all charges, expenses and deductions whatsoever, and all persons concerned are hereby required to give you the respect due to the said office, Given in London under my hand and seale the five and twentieth day of March, in the thirteenth year of the Reign of our Sovereign Lord, William the Third, by the Grace of God, of England, Scotland, France and Ireland, King, Defender of the Faith, &c., Annoq Domini one thousand seven hundred and one. WM. DOCKWRA, [L. S.]
Sec'y and Reg'r.

Signed sealed and executed (after Parliament stamp affixed) in the presence of RICHARD SLATER,
C. WOLLEY,
RICHARD SALTER.

There are no endorsements on this or the Receiver General's Commission to show thy were registered or recorded.— The three subscribing witnesses must have witnessed this last document in England. Richard Salter writes a kind of back hand, and the signature of C. Wolley, is large and compact.

COMMISSION AS JUDGE.

Anne By the Grace of God, of Engla'pu Scotland, France and Ireland, Queen, Defender of the Faith, &c. To our Trusty and well beloved Andrew Bowne, Esquire, Sendeth Greeting. We reposing speciall trust and confidence in your Integrity and ability have assigned, constituted and appointed and by these Presents assign, constitute and appoint you, the said Andrew Bowne, to be third Judge and Assistant to our Chief Justice of our Supreme Court of Judicature for our Province of New Jersey, in America, Giving and by these Presents Granting unto you full power and lawful authority to hear, try, and Determine all Pleas, whatsoever Civil Criminall and Mixt according to the Laws Statutes and customs of England, and the Laws and usages of our said Province, not being repugnant thereunto, and execution of all Judgments of the said Court to award and to make such rules and orders for the benefit of the said Province as may be found convenient and useful, and as near as may be ——— to the rules and orders of our Courts of Queen Bench Common Pleas and Exchequer in England, To have and hold and Enjoy the said office or place of third Judge and assistant to our Chief Justice in our said Province, and in all and singular the rights, Priveleges, profits, sallarys, fees and perquisite unto the said place belonging unto the said Andrew Bowne, during our Will and Pleasure. In Testimony whereof, we have caused the Great Seal of our said Province to be hereunto affixed. Witness our Right, Trusty and well beloved cousin, Edward Viscount Cornbury, Captain Generall and Governor in Chieff, and over our Province of New Jersey and New York and all the Territories and tracts of Land depending thereon in America and Vice Admirall of the same at Perth Amboy, in our Province of New Jersey, this sixth day of November, in the fourth year of our Reign.
By His Exellencys
commands
I BASS,.
Sec'y.

The great seal is appended, No endorsement.

Capt. ANDREW BOWNE'S
Commission as Judge,
from Lord CORNBURY.

(s s). Edward Viscount Cornbury, Captain Generall and Governor in Chief and over the Province of New York, New Jersey and and all the Territories and Tracts of Land depending thereon, in America, and Vice Admirall of the same, &c. To all to whom these presents shall come or may concern, Greeting. Know ye that I the said Lord Cornbury, have Assigned constituted and Appointed and by these Presents Andrew Bowne, Esquire, to be Judge of His Majesties Inferier Court of Common Pleas to be holdin in the County of Monmouth in the Province of New Jersey, with authority to use and exercise all power and jurisdiction pertaining to the said Court, which are specified in an ordinance intittled an Ordinance of his Excellency in Councill, for establishing Courts of Judicature for the care and benefitt of each respective City, Towne and County, within the Province of New Jersey, and the said Andrew Bowne, Assisted with John Bowne, Richard Salter, Obadiah Bowne and Anthony Woodward, Justices of the Peace of the said County, or with any two of them to hear, try and determine all causes and matters Civill by Law Cognizable in the said Court, and to award execution thereon Accordingly, Given under my hand and seale at Burlington, this eleventh day of December, in the third year of the Reign, of her most Sacred Majesty Queen Ann over England. etc., Defender of the faith, Annoq Dom. 1704.

By His Exccllencys Council, CORNBUBY, I. BASS.

This commission is on an oblong piece of fine parchment and very neatly and plainly written, although the writing is somewhat faded. The signature of Cornbury is very large, and peculiar. There is no endorsement on the back.

THE WILL OF CAPTAIN ANDREW BOWNE.

Know all whom it may concern that I, Andrew Bowne, of Middletown, in the County of Monmouth, in New Jersey, being sick and weak of body, but of a sound and disposing Memory, do make and ordain this to be my last will and testament as followeth. My will is all my debts be paid. My will is, if my negro man Robin behave himself well, he shall be free at the expiration of six years commencing from the twenty-fifth day of December next ensuing; and my will is if my negroman Jacob, behave himself well, he shall be free at the expiration of Seven years, commencing from the fifth day of December next ensuing. I give and bequath unto my loving wife all my personal estate, whatsoever and wheresoever, for her maintenance, and for the bringing up of my two grand daughters, Ann and Lidia Bowne. I give and devise unto my loving wife all my houseing and land wheresoever during her naturall life and after my wifes death, my will is and I do order, give and devise unto my three grand children, John, Ann and Lidia, all my housing and land wheresoever equally to be divided between them and to their heirs forever, and my true intent and meaning is, my three grand children shall not hold in joynt Tenancy and of this my last will and Testament. I make my loving wife sole executrix This sixth day of May, one thousand seven hundred and seven.

ANDREW BOWNE, (L S).

Signed sealed and published in the presence of, JOHN WHITE, RICHARD HARTSHORNE, JOHN BRAY, GEORGE MORLETT, ELIZABETH WHITE.

This is a straight forward sensible will, and deals justly with his wife and grand children, while it leaves her in full control for life. There is no parade of religious sentiment, but by his actual disposition of his property, showing the religious principle of his mind.

Andrew Bowne's will was proved June 26th, 1708, and letters Testamentary granted to his widow, Elizabeth Bowne.

Private letter directed
to Capt. JOHN BOWNE, Merchant,
In Amboy, in East New Jersey,
Barbadoes, May 11th, 1707.

Capt. JOHN BOWNE,

Sir: The above is what I wrote you in my last, Have little to inlarge, but to tell you that I could not get any fraight in any of those vessells to have sent you the ballance of your account Current, but you may depend of having your acct. with the ballance the first opportunity. Flower now at 30c to 32c a hundred. If any of these Commodities arrive before the London Fleet, they will meet a saveing Markett.

I wish you health and am
    Your Humble Serv't.,
(Following on same page.)   J. S.
                  June 23, 1707.

J. B. The above is what I wrote you in my last, and then did expect before this day I should have had the honner of seeing your sloop in company with Miss Bonow and Parker, but none appearing, makes me somewhat doubtfull, but hope thee may be well and I a happy sight of her in a few days.

Enclosed you have bill of loading and Invoyce for three hhd moll'a laden on bord the ship *Industry*, Phillip Joanes

Commander. As also your acc't sales and acc't currant by which you will see I have overshipt you one pound, seven shillings, 5½ pence, which (if no errors appear) I beg that you will creditt me for; flower at 25 p hundred, Brown Bread 20 p C, Midling 25 to 27½ p hundred Lamp oyle 4£ p. basile. I am with due respects to you, Mr. Parker, and all present, &c.
                    Your humble Servant,
                                JOHN SMITH.

An unrecorded Deed of Trust.
1714.

To all Christian People to whom these Presents shall come, I, John Bowne, of tne Township of Middletown, in the county of Monmouth and Eastern division of the Province of New Jersey, Merch, Send Greeting. Whereas Robert Barclay, of the Township of Freehold, in the County of Monmouth aforesaid, Yeoman. By one certain deed of Bargain and sale bearing even date with these presents did convey and confirme unto me all that tract of land situate, lying and being near a Branch of Matchiponix River. Begining at a white oak Tree on the Northeast side of Wemakoake Brook ; thence running west and by south, twenty-five chains ; thence southeast twenty-eight chains ; thence east and by north, twenty chains ; thence northwest to William Davison's lower corner at the Brook, and so along the Brook to where it began. And also another tract adjoining on the aforesaid tract. Beginning at John Kerr's lower corner, about twenty chains down the Brook from William Davidson's lower corner aforesaid, at a white oak tree standing on the north side of the Brook ; thence running Northeast, and by North to another white oak tree marked on four sides ; thence North, Northwest sixty-one chains to a small black oak tree standing on Spaotswood North Brook ; thence along the said Brook to where it meets Wemakoake Brook and so up Wemakoake Brook to where it began, the which two tracts containing, by estimation, one hundred and sixty acres, together with all the premises and appurtenances to the said tracts of land belonging as by the said deed may appear, relation thereunto being had. Now know ye If the said John Bowne doe hereby confess, acknowledge, testifie and declare that the said deed or Bargain and Sale was made to me in pure and special trust and confidence, and to the intent that if the said Robert Barclay or his heirs, executors or administrators shall and do pay, or cause to be well, truly and faithfully paid unto me, the said John Bowne, or my heirs, executors, and administrators, the full sum of eighty-five pounds, fifteen shillings current money, of the Eastern Division of the Province of New Jersey aforesaid, on or before the first day of August, that shall be in the year of our Lord one thousand seven hundred and seventeen. And that upon the payment of the said sum of money to me, in manner aforesaid, I, the said John Bowne, shall and will, at the request of the said Robert Barclay, his heirs or assigns, reassign and convey the said deed with all the granted and bargained premises therein mentioned, to the said Robert Barclay, his heirs and assigns forever Or to such other person or persons as he or they, in that behalf, shall name or appoint. And, therefore, in accomplishment and full performance of the trust and confidence I, the said John Bowne, for me, my heirs, executors and administrators, doe covenant, promise and grant to and with him, the said Robert Barclay, his heirs and assigns, by these presents, that I, the said John Bowne and my heirs, executors or administrators, shall and will, from time to time, and at any time after the payment of the money to me in manner aforesaid, at the request, cost and charge of the said Robert Barclay. his heirs, executors, administrators or assigns, assure, convey, confirme the above mentioned tracts of land, and all the Premises and appurtenances to them belonging, granted to me by said Deed and all the estate, Right, title, Interest and claim of me, the said John Bowne and my heirs, in and to the same and to any part or parcel thereof, clear and discharged of all incumbrances whatsoever, by us or any of us committed or done to the same, to him the said Robert Barclay, his heirs and assigns forever. In witness whereof I, the said John Bowne, have hereunto set my hand and seal this twenty-fifth day of February, in the thirteenth year of the Reign of our Sovereign Lady Anne over Great Brittain, France and Ireland, Queen, Annoq Dom. one thousand seven hundred and fourteen.
                        JOHN BOWNE, [L. S.]
Signed, sealed and
delivered in the presence of
   JOSEPH DENNES,
   JEREMIAH WHITE.

"Isabrant Van Cliff," (Van Cleaf or Cleve) his liberty to retail strong liquor in his house in Middletown and one mile around.

"Know all men by these Presents that we, Isabrant Van Cliff, of Middletown, in the County of Monmouth, Inn-holder, and Obediah Brown. of the said County, Gent. are held and firmly bound unto David Lyell and William Bradford, Esq'rs, Farmers of the Duty of Excise, laid on strong liquors retailed in the Province of New Jersey, in the sum of four pounds lawful silver money of America, (according to her late Majesty Queen Anne's Proclamation,) dated the 18th of June, 1704, and Act of Parliament passed in the sixth year of her said Majesty's R..ign, "For ascertaining the rates of Forreign coyns in the Plantations." To be paid to the said David Lyell and William Bradford, or either of them, their or either of their certain Attorney's, Executors, administrators or assigns. For the which payment well and truly to be made and done, we do bind ourselves and each of our heirs, executors and administrators, Joyntly and severally, firmly by these Presents, sealed with our seal, dated the first day of March, in the third year of his Majesties Reign, Annoq Domini 1716.

The condition of this obligation is such that if the above bounden Isabrant, or his heirs, executors or administrator, do well and truly pay or cause to be paid unto the above named David Lyell and William Bradford. or either of them, their or either of their certain Attorneys, Executors, administrators or assigns, the just and full sum of two pounds for the excise of ye places expressed and mentioned on the backside current money aforesaid, on or before the first day of June next ensuing the date hereof in the year of our Lord one thousand seven hundred and seventeen. And also well, truly and duly, immediately upon the receipt of any strong liquor into his house or any other place, make entry from time to time of all such wine, Brandy, Rum or Spirit Methiglin, Syder Royal, Bear and Syder which he shall so receive, the full quantity of each sort of liquor received. by what conveyance it came, and of whom bought and purchased, according to the true intent and meaning of an Act of Assembly entitled "An act laying an excise on all strong liquors retailed within this colony of New Jersey. And that without Fraud, cover or Further delay, then this obligation to be void and of none effect, or else to stand and remain in full force and virtue. ISABRANT VAN CLEEF.

Sealed and delivered in the presence of Joos. SOOY, (JOSEPH SOOY.) Endorsed,

Received this 28th of June, 1728, of Mr. John Bowne, one of the executors of Obediah Bowne, dec., the principal of the written bond in proclamation money and the interest in money at eight shillings ye oz. Rec'd in full by DAVID LYELL.

OLD DOCUMENTS AND PAPERS OF JAMES G. CRAWFORD, DEC'D.

This indenture made the third day of March, in the second year of the reigne of our Sovereigne Lord, King George, Anno Domini 1715-16, between Capt. John Bowne, of the Town of Middletown, in the County of Monmouth and Province of New Jersey, Mercht of the one part, and John Bowne, son of Obadiah Bowne, of the other part, witnesseth the said John Bowne first named, for and in consideration of the sum of three hundred and twenty-two pounds and one penny farthing, current money of the aforesaid Province to the said Capt. John Bowne already in hand paid by the said John Bowne, the receipt whereof the said John Bowne doth hereby acknowledge and himself therewith fully satisfyed contented and paid and of and from every part and parcell thereof, doth fully, clearly and absolutely aquit, exonerate and discharge him, the said John Bowne, his heirs, executors, administrators and assigns, and every of them forever, by these presents hath given, granted, bargained; sold, aliened, enfeoffed, released and confirmed, and by these presents doth give, grant, bargain, sell, alien, enfeoff, release and confirm unto him, the said John Bowne, son of Obadiah Bowne, all them tracts of land, situate, lying and being in the Town of Freehold, County and Province aforesaid. The first of the said tracts being that which is now in the use and occupation of Thomas Parker, Jun'r, is bounded northwest by Thomas Parker, Sen'r, northeast by Richard Borden's land, and southeast by the Pines, and southwest by Phillip Smith's land, lying on both sides of Burlington ould road, and is the southeasterly part of a tract of land formerly John Stout's. The other tract being in the present possession and tenure of Thomas Fenton of said Freehold, begins at Thomas Edwards, his southeast corner on Welch Brook, from thence running down the said brook to where the new road from Crosswicks to Capt Bowne crosses the said Brook. From thence southwesterly, along the said road to where the line of ye tract of land, formerly Benjamin Allen's, crosses the said road; thence directly northeast along the said line of said Allen's land to ye said Brook where it began. Together with all and all manner of housings, edifices, structures, buildings, barns, stables, orchards, fencings, floodings, pastures, meadows, woods, trees, waters, brooks, springs, ponds, pools, pitts, easements, profits, commodities, liberties, advantages, imolluments, hereditaments and appertenances to the same belonging, or in any manner of ways to the same tracts of land appertaining, and also all the estate, right, interest, possession, property, claim and demand, whatsoever of him the said Capt. John Bowne, as well in law as in equity, of, in or unto, the said tracts of land and premises as fully and amply to all interests, purposes and constructions as the same was granted, released and confirmed by deed of sale and conveyance from the said Thomas Parker, Jun'r, to Thomas Fenton, as may more fully appear by the deed of sale, relating thereunto, being had, to have and to hold the same tracts of land, and granted and bargained premises, with the appurtenances unto him, the said John Bowne, his heirs and assigns forever. And to the only proper use, benefit and behoof of him, the said John Bowne, his heirs and assigns forever. And he, the said Capt. John Bowne, doth for himself, his heirs, executors, administrators, and every one of them forever, covenants, promise, grant and agree to and with ye said John Bowne, his heirs and assigns by their presents in manner following, viz: That at the time of the ensealing and delivery of these presents, the said Capt. John Bowne is lawfully and rightfully seized of the said tracts of land and premises of a good title in ye law, and hath in himself good right, full power, lawfull and absolute authority to grant, bargain, sell and confirm the said tracts of land and premises, to him the said John Bowne in manner aforesaid, and yt the same is now free, and from time to time, and att all times forever, hereafter, shall remain free and clear of him, the said John Bowne, his heirs and assigns of and from, all and all manner of former gifts, grants, sales, leases, wills, intailes. troubles and incumbrances whatsoever, in the law had made done, committed or suffered to be done by the said Capt. John Bowne, or by any person or persons whatsover by, from or under him to alter, change, charge, defeat or make void the same estate or any part thereof. In witness whereof, the same John Bowne hath hereunto sett his hand and seale, the day and year first above written.

JNO. BOWNE, L. S.

Written, signed, sealed and delivered. in the presence of

JOSEPH DENNIS,
JOHN SALTER.

John Salter, one of the subscribing evidences, declared upon oath that the above named John Bowne, sealed and delivered this instrument as his act and deed before me.   JOHN REID.

Recorded in the Secretary's office, at Perth Amboy, in Book E, No. 3, page 336, &c., and examined by

JOHN MACKAY, D. Sec'y.

Letter directed to Mr. Obadiah Bowne, in Middletowne.

April 25th, 1716.

Hon'r Uncle Bowne—I have sent to my father, such writings as were in my hands and appertaining to the estate of my deceased uncle, Capt. John Bowne, near fifty pounds in them, my uncle had given to me, not many weeks before he dyed, and time failing the property of the debt was not altered in my name, see because I cannot fairly pretend to proceed to secure myself, without you having I thought fit to remitt ye same to ye estate, having only an order to take security for the same to my own use, from under his hand, and soe expect yt you will be favourable to me on yt score; I depend on your curtesy yt which was given to me is not in ye inventory. I have also sent a bond from John Chenoath to my uncle, under such like circumstances for ten pounds, and not altered as was ordered and intended to my brother, Lincon—the whole that is given and secured to my brothers, Thomas, Mordecaay and myself, amounts in all to about four hundred and twenty pounds or therabouts, which is secured in three deeds of gift to my brother, Thomas, and one to myself, and some debts transferred in my uncle's life-time, none of which are in the inventory. These are several of the aforesaid bonds indorsed. viz, which was given to myself and Mordecay. I hope you will appeare a kynd and generous uncle. Ye debt from the two Kirbys per bond is in lieu of Thomas Douglass, his bond, which was fifteen pounds, but interest and all amounts to nineteen pounds nine shillings. I have also sent several amounts for sundry people, which were remaining in my hands, I still keepe a deed for your son John in my hands for Thomas Parker, Jun'r, his farm and the Fentons deed to my uncle, I have, I shall also inform ye yt I took a pair of oxen of William Jewell, which are now at my father's for ten pounds, ten shillings and believe they are not in the inventory. I have been faithfull to my dec'd uncle and to yourself to my power. I hope I shall not be unkyndly rewarded by you, and I shall always be ready to do the best I can for you. I desire a few lines in answer, if your son shall chose some person to keep his deed, I shall readily discharge myself of that, and which other concerns I know of in relation to that business of my uncle in which I have been att all concerned This being the needfull yt all present offers, being in haste I bid ye adue, from Your ever faithfull and obedient nephew,

JOHN SALTAR.

This bond from ―― is in lieu of a bond of Robt. Killum.

AFFIDAVITS.

Richard Hartshorn, of ye County of Monmouth, aged 75 years or thereabouts, being affirmed, says yt on or about ye first of June, he heard Richard Saltar and Obadiah Bowne agree, to put ye papers and instruments belonging to ye estate of John Bowne, deceased, into ye hands of Gershom Mott to ye intent, both of them might have a free recourse to them as they pleased, providing that Gershom should be willing to take them into his keeping, and further saith, they appoynted a day, some few days after to meet at said Obadiah's, to carry ye papers to said Gershom, if he was willing to receive them.

Sometime afterwards, ye Affirmer, at his son's house, in Middletown, heard Saltar say to ye said Bowne, that ye method he took with ye estate of ye said deceased would never do. Instancing several particulars wherein he thought said Bowne acted amiss, and proposed to ye said Bowne, that they should take ye best of ye bonds and mortgages, and apply them first to ye payment of ye debts, and then to ye payment of ye widow and legacies, and what should remain they might divide among themselves. Bowne making no answer, said Saltar made the further proposal, to make an equal devision of ye estate betwixt them, and that he would give sufficient security to pay ye one half of ye debts and legacies if Bowne would give ye like for ye other half. To this proposal he remembered not ye answer and further saith not.

RICHARD HARTSHORNE.

Perth Amboy, July 16th, 1716.
Affirmed before us,
JAS. SMITH, Surrogate.
THO. FARMER.

Hugh Hartshorn of ye County of Monmouth, aged thirty-one years or thereabouts, being sworn, deposeth that sometime in ye first week of June last, Richard Saltar and Obadiah Bowne was in his house, and there he heard ye said Saltar say to ye said Bowne, that these practices of his about ye estate of John Bowne, deceased, would never doe. And proposed to said Bowne yt they should take ye best of ye bonds and apply them to ye payment of ye debts of ye deceased, and ye next best to ye payment of ye widdow and ye legacies, and if he did not like yt proposal, Saltar further proposed that they should divide ye estate of ye deceased betwixt them, and that if ye said Bowne would give security for ye payment of those, ye debts and legacies, he would give ye like for ye other half, and if you won't do so, says Saltar, I'll take ye regular steps of ye law to ye best of my knowledge. And Bowne answered, "Doe, and so will I." And deposeth further that sometime in ye said first week of June last, in his house he heard one ―― Johnston say to ye said Bowne, if he would give him up his bond, he would than pay ye money he had been owing to ye said deceased, to which ye said Bowne agreed that if you'll come to my house, and if I can get ye key from Capt. Saltar of ye scritore wherein ye papers lie, I'll give you up your bond. The deponent further sayth yt ye said Bowne told him yt he and Saltar had agreed to meet ye creditors at ye deponent's house to make up with them and to settle accounts with ye debtors and further say'th not.

HUGH HARTSHORNE.

Perth Amboy,
July 16th, 1716.
Sworn before us,
JA. SMITH,   THO. FARMER.
Surrogate,   A true copy by me
BARCLAY,
Dpt. Sec'y.

William Lawrence, Junior, aged twenty

seven years or thereabouts, being sworn, deposeth that he heard John Cannor and Albert Williamson demand their bond (which they had given to John Bowne, deceased) of his Executor, saying they had their receipts with them from Capt. Bowne, and then, too, when he had ordered payment for ye full satisfaction of ye bond.— To which they were answered by the Executor, that they could not have it, the bond not being there. And further saith, that when Mr. Bowne was askt why he did not bring ye bond, His reply, was he thought them safe enough where they were. All which was at ye house of Hugh Hartshorne, about the beginning of June last, and further saith not.
WILLIAM LAWRENCE, Jr.
Perth Amboy,
July 26th, 1716.
Sworn before us
JA. SMITH, Surrogate,
THO. FARMAR.
A true copy by me,
BARCLAY,
Dept. Sec'y.

Letter directed to
"James Paul, to be found in Middletown in the County of Monmouth, in East Jersey in America.
EDINBURGH, Feb. 9th, 1721.
Loveing and Dear Brother:
Having the present occasion of Mr. Watson's voyadge to that part of America where you stay. I thought it my duty to write to you, that I and my wife and children are all in good health, blessed be God for it. And wishes the happy news of your welfare and all belonging to you, to prosper. I received yours of the 19th of August, 1717, wherein you tell me of your being lame in the hand, and a stop put to receiving your money, or else you would have come home. These are indeed two sad disappointments, but Dear Brother, tho' this misfortune has befallen you, yet the most Righteous and just God, who orders all according to his blessed will, in his own tyme will bring matters to a happy issue with you, let your trust be in him, as the Psalmist David, and let your patience be as Job, for both of them had greater misfortunes than you, and yet made a happy end. I am glad that Mr. Watson has met with me, who tells me you are well and in good circumstances. I can do no more than wish you better and better, and would be glad you return home as soon as possible, for I long to see you and I am sure you should be very wellcome to me and all your other friends. If extraordinary business detains you, I trust you will send a letter to me on the first occasion. I add no more but that I and my wife and children (being two young lads) and your sisters has their service to you as all other friends, and my youngest son aged 18 years, has a great desire to come to you. I desire you send word in your letter if you have any need for him, and if you be coming home.
I am your
Dear and affectionate
Brother, till death,
THOMAS PAULL.
When this comes to your hands, see you go to Mr. John Watson, altho' it is some distance, and speak with him, because he and I spake together."

James Paul never got back to Scotland. By his will, dated Oct. 10, 1730, he devised all his property to the four youngest children of Obadiah Bowne, dec'd, viz: Mary, Cornelius, Obadiah and Thomas, in consideration of "manifold faviours and kindnesses received from Obadiah Bowne, in his life time, as my diet and entertainment for several yeais; with other provision for me by him made, both in my sickness and health."

The will was proved at Perth Amboy, March 16th, 1732.

Obadiah Bowne, the father of the children named in Paul's will, made his will in 1725, and died prior to 1730.

He devises to his four sons, John, Cornelius, Obadiah and Thomas, the following tracts of land.

(1). The tract of land called Westfield, in Monmouth county, whereon he then lived.

(2). A tract of land and meadow at Chinqueroras, in Monmouth, conveyed to him by his brother John, by deed dated Jan. 13th, 1715, All his share or moiety of a tract of land adjoining the west side of Westfield, which was granted and conveyed to his brother John, amongst other tracts, by patent from the Proprietors, dated the 16th July, 1700. These three tracts to be equally divided, and in case of the death of Cornelius, Obadiah and Thomas, without issue and before they arrive at the age of twenty-one, their survivors to take equally. He bequeaths to each of his three daughters fifty pounds, and all the rest of his personal estate to be equally divided between his seven children. In case his Brother John's estate, set apart to him (by act of Assembly, entitled, an act to enforce the due administration of the estate of Capt. John Bowne, dec'd, late of the county of Monmouth and Province of New Jersey, charging me one of the executors, with the payment of the moyety of my said brother's debts, and legacies) fall short, then in order to indemnify my securities from the penalty of the bond they entered into, pursuant to that act of Assembly, which bond is dated the 8th of Aprill, 1719, in the penalty of ten thousand pounds, he enjoined his executors or any two of them or the survivors, after payment of his own debts, to apply the residuary estate for their indemnity and discharge in paying his share of the debts and legacies.

He appoints his son John Bowne, Garrett Schanck and Daniel Hendrickson, executors. By codicil, he revokes the devise of the lands at Chinqueroras, and leaves this tract to his three daughters, to be equally divided between them.

LETTER.
New York, May 10th, 1725,
Mr. Obadiah Bowne.

Sir : The above is the estate account, what will bee due the 12th of the next month, which have also sent to your brother executor. I pray you will not between you, keep me any longer out of my just due. I pray you answer,
and am yr servant.
The Estate of Capt. John Bowne, Dr.
1715
May, To ye bond payable this
day, £51 : 7 : 8½
To interest thereof to ye 12th
Dec., 1722 31 4 : 6
To Court charges, pd on ye
Judgment to Witeman 5 16, 3
———
88, 8, 5½
Cr.
1722
Dec. 12. By Charles Morgan,
give bond for £55 5, 5½
Bal. due the 12th, Dec. 1722. £33, 3, 0
———
£88, 8, 5½
1722
12 Dec. To Ball. due this day £38, 4, —
To interest thereon to ye
12th June, 1725, £45, 15, 6
SAM'L BAYARD.

Letter to
Mr. John Bowne, of
Middletown.
Rockyhill, May 10th, 1735.
Mr. John Bowne :

I have but lately rec'd yours, dated the 1st of April last, wherein you intimate you are using your utmost endeavours to get me money, which you hope will be in a short time procured. I am oweing Mr. Isaac Van Dam nigh £5, which I formerly requested you to pay, which I now find you have not complyed with, by a letter I received from Mr. John Kelly lately, who has orders from Mr. Van Dam to prosecute me. I think it hard you have not complyed with that request, when your debt to me being £19, 4, 0 procl. money and so many years past has been due.

This is my last request to you, forthwith to pay Mr. John Kelly as attorney to Mr. Isaac Van Dam five pounds, this currency and take his receipt, and for the remainder due to me execute a bond I have left in the hands of Mr. Lawrence Smith to produce to you, he giving a receipt on the back of it in my name for the £5.— You are to pay as above desired, to be accepted as part payment of the Bond you are to sign, in which I shall acknowledge a satisfaction done to
Your humble servant,
J. STEVENS.
P. S. I hope you will prevent me being put to charges

COMMISSION.
By the Hon'ble Robert Hunter Morris, Esq., Chief Justice of the Province of New Jersey, and Joseph Bonnell Esq., one of the Justices of the Supreme Court of said Province.
To John Bowne, Esq.
Greeting.

We, reposing especial trust and confidence in your fidelity, ability and prudence, have thought fit to empower, authorize and appoint, and by these presents by virtue of the powers and authorities to us given by an Act of the General Assembly of this Province, passed in this present fifteenth year of his Majesty's reign, do empower, authorize and appoint you, the said John Bowne, Esq., to take and receive in ye County of Monmouth, all and every such recognizance or recognizances of Bail or Bails, as any person or persons shall be willing or desirous to acknowledge or make before you, in any action of suit depending or hereafter to be depending in the Supreme Court aforesaid, in such manner and form, and by such recognizance of bail pieces as the Justices of the said Supreme Court have used to take the same. And to do all other things, which by the said Act, we are empowered to authorize you to do, and that during our pleasure.— Given under our hands and the seal of the Supreme Court, at Perth Amboy, the twenfourth day of March in the fifteenth year of the reign of our Sovereign Lord, George the second, King of Great Britain, etc., Annoq. Dom., 1741-2.

ROBT. H. MORRIS.
JOSEPH BONNEL.
OLD DEED.

This Indenture, made the twenty-fourth day of August, in the twenty-first year of the Reign of our Sovereign Lord George the Second, by the grace of God, over Great Brittain, France and Ireland King, Defender of the Faith, annoq, Domini one thousand seven hundred forty and seven, by and between Obadiah Bowne, of Philadelphia, in the Province of Pennsylvania and Thomas Bowne, of the City of New York, in the Province of New York, Mariners of the one part, and John Bowne, of Middletown, in the County of Monmouth, Province of New Jersey, Esq., of the other part, Witnesseth that they, the said Obadiah Bowne and Thomas Bowne, for divers good causes and considerations them thereunto moving, Have given, granted, Bargained, sold, aliened, enfeoffed, released, conveyed and confirmed, and by these Presents do give, grant, bargain, sell, alien, enfeoff, Release, convey and confirm unto him, the said John Bowne, his heirs and assigns forever, the one moiety or full and equal half part of all that Tract of Land, called and known by the name of Mattawan, lying and being in the County of Monmouth, aforesaid, which was conveyed and confirmed unto them, the said Obadiah Bowne and Thomas Bowne, by deed of bargain and sale, under the hand and seal of him, the said John Bowne, and Anne, his wife, bearing date the twenty-second day of August instant, which said tract of land begins at a Spanish oak marked on four sides, and with the letters J. B., standing on the east side of Long Neck Creek, about thirty chains above the place, where it meets with Whale Creek, and thence running South, twenty-four degrees westerly about sixty-eight chains to a Birch Tree marked on four sides, standing by a fresh brook ; thence down the same about forty chains to Mattawan Creek and following Mattawan Creek to the Bay and along the edge of the Bay till it comes to the mouth of Whale Creek, and up Whale Creek to the mouth of Long Neck Creek, and up Long Neck Creek to the Spanish Oak, where it began. The whole tract containing, by estimation, Five hundred and thirteen acres. Also the one Moiety or full and equal half part of six acres of meadows out of the great piece of meadow on Mattawan Creek opposite to that part of Whingson called Oyster Shell Point, the said six acres of Meadow, Beginning at a stake standing by the side of said Creek, five chains fourteen links from the edge of the point of upland, where the Creek comes to the Point, and running North, twenty-eight degrees and a half easterly, four chains and a half to a small Creek, and following down the said small Creek as it runs to Mattawan Creek, about eleven chains on a straight line and following up Mattawan Creek to where it began. To have and to hold the said moiety or one full and equal half part of the above recited tracts of land and meadow, with all and singular, the appurtenances, Privileges and commodities to the same belonging or in any wise appertaining. to him, the said John Bowne, his heirs and assigns forever. To his and their own proper use, benefit and behoof forever. And they, the said Obadiah Bowne and Thomas Bowne, for themselves, their heirs, executors or administrators, and each of them do covenant, and Grant to and with the said John Bowne, his heirs and assigns, that before the ensealing hereof they are the true, sole and lawful owners of the hereby granted and Bargained Premises, and are fully seized and possessed of the same in their own proper right, as of a good, perfect and absolute Inheritance, in fee simple. And have in themselves good right, full power and absolute lawful authority to grant, bargain, sell, convey and confirm the hereby granted Premises in manner aforesaid. And that he, the said John Bowne, his heirs and assigns, shall and may, from time to time, and at all times forever, hereafter by force and virtue of these Presents, lawfully, peaceably, quietly, have, hold, use, occupy, possess, and enjoy the hereby granted and bargained Premises with the appurtenances, free and clear, and freely and clearly exonerated, acquitted and discharged of and from all and all manner of former and other gifts, grants, Bargains, sales, leases, mortgages, will, entails, jointures, Dowrys, judgments, executions, extents, troubles, and maintenances whatsoever, heretofore had made, done or suffered to be done by them, the said Obadiah Bowne or Thomas Bowne, or either of them.

Furthermore they, the said Obadiah Bowne and Thomas Bowne, for themselves, their heirs, executors and administrators, do covenant and Promise at and upon the reasonable request, and at the proper cost and charges in the law, of him, the said John Bowne, his heirs, etc., to make, do, perform and execute any further or lawful and reasonable acts, or act, Device or devices, in the law needful or requsite for the more perfect assurance, setling and sure making of the premises aforesaid.

Now, whereas they, the said Obadiah Bowne and Thomas Bowne, by a certain instrument in writing under their hands and seals, (as also under the hand and seal of Cornelius Bowne and his wife) bearing date the twentieth day of instant August, have released, conveyed and confirmed unto him, the said John Bowne, his heirs and assigns forever, all that their right, title, interest, property, claim and demand of his in or to a certain tract or parcell of land lying and being in Middletown aforesaid, which was formerly the residence and dwelling place of their father, Obadiah Bowne, and now is and has been for years past, the dwelling place of him, the said John Bowne, butted. Bounded, as in said instrument at large, is expressed, and contains six hundred and thirty-two acres English measure, which said tract of land, with other tracts of land, was given and devised in and by the last will and Testament of the said Obadiah Bowne unto his four sons, John Bowne, Cornelius Bowne, Obadiah Bowne and Thomas Bowne. But the said Obadiah Bowne having ordered in his last will and Testament that in case the moiety or part of the estate of his Brother, John Bowne, deceased, as ordered, set apart and appointed to him, the said Obadiah Bowne, shall not prove sufficient for the paying and discharging of his moiety or part of the Debts and Legacies as appointed by Act of General Assembly of the Province of New Jersey, entitled an act to enforce the due administration of the estate of Capt. John Bowne, deceased, late of Middletown, in the County of Monmouth and Province of New Jersey, that such deficiency should be made up by selling his then residuary estate for the saving harmless and indemnifying those Persons who were security for and bound with him in and by a certain writing obligatory, bearing date the eighth day of April, Annoq Domini 1719, conditioned for the well and true administering the estate of the said Capt. John Bowne, pursuant to the said Act of Assembly, the Penalty in said writing obligatory being ten thousand pounds. And he, the said John Bowne, having by deed of Bargain and Sale, bearing date the twenty-second day of instant August, conveyed and confirmed unto the above named Obadiah Bowne and Thomas Bowne, their heirs and assigns forever, the above mentioned tract of land at Matawan, being five hundred and thirteen acres, Bounded as above, and that as in exchange partly for the place or tract of land, whereon he, the said John Bowne, now dwells. It is agreed upon, by and between Grantors and Grantee, in these presents, anything herein before, or to the contrary notwithstanding, that if it should so happen at any time or times hereafter, that the place whereon he, the said John Bowne now dwells, and formerly was the residence of their father, Obadiah Bowne, should be obliged to be sold for the saving harmless and indemnifying the Persons or any of them who were security for and bound with the said Obadiah Bowne, deceased, by the writing obligatory, that then they the said Obadiah Bowne and Thomas Bowne, their heirs, executors, administrators, or some of them, shall pay or cause to be paid unto him, the said John Bowne, his heirs, executors, administrators or assigns, the just and full sum of one thousand Pounds, money, according to the late Queen's Proclamation, in lieu of said land if sold, which if they or either of them, their or either of their heirs, executors, administrators, shall do upon reasonable request or proper notice given them thereof (that is to say of said land being sold) then this Present deed and every claim and article contained, to be null, void and of none effect or else to remain, abide and be in full force and virtue.

      OBADIAH BOWNE, [L. S.]
      THO' BOWNE, [L. S.]

Sealed and delivered
in presents of
 MICHAEL WARD,
   his
 JOHN x NITE.
   mark.

(Third name is written in German, and cannot make it out.

Michael Ward swears to an affidavit on the back of the deed, before John Little, a judge of the Court of Common Pleas, of Monmouth county, that the said Obadiah and Thomas Bowne, sign, seal, and deliver it as their voluntary act and deed.

Recorded in Secretary office at Perth Amboy, in Book E, No. 3, page 101, &c., and examined by JOHN MACKAY,
Pro. Sec'ry.

Obadiah Bowne was a son of Capt Andrew Bowne, and prior to his father's death, had three children by his first wife, a son John and two daughters. By his second wife, he had three sons, Obadiah, Cornelius, and Thomas, and one daughter. One of his daughters married a Kearny and inherited the Bowne property at Keyport, or Chinqueroras, as then called.

LETTER FROM JOHN PINTARD.
NEW YORK, December 7th, 1751.
Brother Bowne:—

Yours of ye 27th November received by Capt. Burrowes. By him I now send you note and account with the money, which is £19, 19, 11, I wish safe to your hands. I send it in Jersey money, thinking it would best answere. Also send you proceeds of your butter and eggs. I had made up your account, the ginger at 1 shilling a pound, but when we got it, it cost 20d, which I think is very dear. As to a riddle, I can not find any smaller than what I send you. In case I should get sight of any I shall get you one.

I flatered meself to have had the pleasure of seeing you hear, this fall, I now give it over the season is so advanced. I have had a good deal of busness this fall, having two Snows,* one I built which is now laden with flax seed, the other which is called the Marsdin, she is now laden and ready to sail for Dublin, boath with flax seed, as I have too buy what chances, of them two snows cargoes takes me time up constantly. I hope, by Chrismas, the new Snow will be dispatched for Dublin. Also my wife is in a poor state of health, and gets no better. Lidia is very well in health. I am clear of the gout yet and hope I shant get it as long as I have this Snow in hand. My wife and self joynes with best respects to you and sister,
Your loving Brother,
JOHN PINTARD.

*A two masted vessel—See Webster's Dictionary.

I am glad to hear of Brother Thomas, safe arrival. I am fearful he has made a poor voyage, when you see him give me sarvice to him. This letter is directed to
JOHN BOWNE, Esq.,
at Middletown.
per Capt. JOHN BURROWS with Kear.

Letter from Obadiah Bowne, directed to John Bowne, at his farm.
Brother,
I have never heard or seen my fathers will, and Thomas sais Mr. Moore tuck them with him to N. York, and for your other letters, I don't know what other answer to give than I have. If you had a told me you expected me to pay my brothers debts, for what I never had, when you new I had cash by me, should, but as you said nothing, I did not expect such letters full of Reflections. I dont know that I ever gave you any Reason for it.
Your loving brother,
OBADIAH BOWNE.

July ye 17th, 1753.
Letter from Lewis Pintard, directed to John Bowne, Esq.
By favour of
Capt. BURROWES.
New York 6th May, 1758.
Dr. Sir:—

The handkerchief was left out when the Basket was sew'd up last trip, but I now send it to you, together with the returns of your cargo of eggs and pork, and the newspaper. We begin to very impatient to hear of the arrival of Admiral Boscawen at Halifax, by the acc't we get people begin to much afraid that the French Fleet will get into Louisbourg, before ours arrive. We are daily expecting to hear of a battle between the two fleets, tor 'tis thought they will meet, By a vessell arrived at Philadelphia from Liverpool, we hear that in February the King of Prussia beat the French army, under Richelieu all to pieces. He is a great hero. Wish we had such another here only for one campain. We would drive away all our bad neighbours. The fleet sail'd for Halifax the 3d Inst., and the provincials go to Albany in a day or two, but their arms and tents are not yet come from England. I think it high time they were here. Sister joins me in love to you all, being
Yr very humble serv't,
LEWIS PINTARD.

New York, 6th Nov. 1760.
Dr Sir:—
I rec'd yours Jan. 7th, last month, when I was sick abed which is the reason I did not answer it by the Boat. I really thought our butter Tub had been sent you long ago, I sent it by this boat, but it is so late that I don't expect it can be fill'd, and it happens lucky enough for us, as I have bought a parcel of choice Irish Butter very cheap, so that if 'tis inconvenient for your spouse to fill our Tub so late in the year, she can put just as much as she can spare in, and another year I will take care to send it early. I send you the newspaper by this Boat, enclose a letter for my sister who I hope will like the Country better, when she comes to be more used to it. My wife joins me in love and service to you and family, being in much esteem   Yr most hum, Ser't.

L. PINTARD.

Letter from Mary Taylor, directed to Mr. John Bowne, in Middletown, in East Jersey, by favor of Mary Whiley.

Middletown on Rhode Island, October ye 21st, 1765.

Respected Coz'n, John Bowne, Your favour of the eight of July 1765, I received by Capt. Andrew Brown, and was glad to hear from you and your family, that you was in so good a state of health as you were. And am glad to hear from uncle Jonathan that he is so good a state of health as he is, and should be glad to hear whether Uncle Jonathans wife is living or not. My uncle Samuel is still living and as well as can be expected of a man of his advanced age. Our Coz John and his daughters are both still living, but are both widows, Lydia hath lately lost her husband. My sister Freelove Pope, departed this life on the seventh of June last, after a long lingering disorder, as I have wrote to you.

My husband and I send our respects to you and all Enquiring friends. My Husband is in as good a state of health as can be expected for a man of his advanced years, and for myself I have been in but a poor state of health this summer past, and remain so still. I have had two sons and three daughters. My sons both died young. My daughters are all still living, the oldest is now a widow and hath three children, and now live with me. My second daughter hath Fits, followed her from a child, which hath much Impared her senses and my youngest is Married, hath seven children. My Uncle Joseph Holmes' son John and his family are well at this present time. My Brother Jonathan and my sisters are all well. I should be glad to hear from you by all opportunities and whereas, you wrote to me that your wife had some acquaintance with me one evening. I would be glad to hear who you married, having forgot the people I was acquainted with in that country. And so no more at Present, but that I remain

Your respected Couzen,
to serve
MARY TAYLOR.

SECOND LETTER.

Middletown, Rhode Island, November 14th, 1766.

Loving kinsman, JOHN BOWNE.

These few lines are come to let you know that we are all well in health at this present time, Hoping they may find you and your family in the same state.— I received yours of the 23d of October last, for which I am much obliged to you and hope you will write to me by all opportunity. I likewise inform you that my Uncle Samuel Holmes is as well as can be expected for a man of his advanced years. He is so well as to ride in his Shaes to Meeting, every first Day. My uncle Joseph Holmes widow, hath been dead about a year. My Brother and my sisters are all well at this present time. I would have writ to you by Capt. Andrew, last May, but we being distant from the Town and he being removed from Newport to Nantucket, we missed that opportunity. I have nothing of news to write unto you and so no more at present, but that I remain your loving Cozin.

MARY TAYLOR.

THIRD LETTER.

Middletown, Rhoads Island.

May 16th, 1769.

Respected Kinsman,
JOHN BOWNE.

I received your exceptable favours by Capt. Norris, and am glad to hear from you and your family, Hoping these may finde you and your family in health, as my family injoys the same Blessing. I have had a very poor winter, and am in a poor state of health as yet. My husband injoys his health as well as can be expected for so old a person. I am sorry to hear of Cozn Jonathan Holmes death. I have had the misfortune to loos my oldest sister Elizabeth Coggshall, she was taken in a fit in the night and expired immediately. She has been dec'd abote two months.

Unkle Samuel Holmes is in as good a state of health as can be expected. Our cozzen John Holmes, Josephs son, is gone to London, His wife has received a letter of his safe arrival there. My husband joyns with me in love to you, your wife and family, and all relations. I shall be glad to hear from you when opportunity serves.

J remain your loving friend,
MARY TAYLOR.

FOURTH LETTER.

Middletown in Rhoads Island.
December 5th, 1769.

Respected friend, JOHN BOWNE.

I write to let you know that I received your letter the third of December. and am glad to hear from you and family.— Hoping these may find you in health as mine are at present. I am as well as can be expected for so old a woman. I am sorry to hear of the death of Henry Green, he being a relation of ours. My husband went to visit Unkle Samuel Holmes the day I Received your letter, and he is as well as can be expected for so old a man. He is now in the Ninety-third year of his age, and walks about the house. I am sorry to acquant you with the Deth of Peleg Smith. He has been dead between nine and ten years. His wife was buried a few months after. He left but one son, who has now living, thirteen children.

My brothers and sisters are all well at present. I should have rit before, but our living out of Town, I have not so good an opportunity, as not knowing when the vessell goes. I shall be glad to hear from you when an opportunity serves. My husband joins with me in love to you, your wife and family, and all enquiring relations. So I conclude,

Your friend and well wisher,
MARY TAYLOR.

The following letter is from Peter Remsen, then a merchant in New York, to Roelef Schanck, who then lived near what is now the Brick church, in the Township of Marlborough.

Nieu York, augt-22nd 1754.

Cozyn Roelef Schenck.

Dese wynige zvn om u te laten weten dat wy noch alle door. Gods Genade Gezont zyn en hope het zelfde van u te hooren. Ick heb Volgens u Wyse Verzoeck het Volgen de Goet apgeshiest.

1 Stuck Bont £4 ,, 8 ,, 0
2 Gert Gestreept Bont, 0 ,, 9 ,, 0
25 Gert warendorps Linnen, ⅜ ,, 7 ,, 3 ,, 9

£ 12 ,, 0 ,, 0

Ick had Geen ander Stuk van warendorps diefyn Genoegh was en daarom stuerde ick dise 25 Gert Zynde al dat daer over Gebleeven was van het Stuk hoopende het sal u wel diener. Niet meer als de Hertelyke Groetnis aan u en u Vrow ende alle de rest vande Vriende en Verblys u onderdernize Vrient,

PETER REMSEN.

This letter is directed
Mr. Roelef Schenck,
att Naversinks,
near Freehold Church.

The above is a specimen of the language used, among a portion of our population a century ago. The Hollanders in Monmouth came in the first place from New York and the western towns of Long Island, principally between 1690 and 1720. Since then there has been some influx from Middlesex and Somerset Counties of this State. The original settlers were generally the younger sons, and left the crowded homesteads of their fathers on Long Island, to make new ones for themselves. Agriculture was their chief business, and the ownership of a large unincumbered farm, with a substantial house, large, well filled barns, and choice stock, their highest desire.

From Monmouth county, in the same way, the younger sons of the Dutch farmers have at different periods, emigrated and settled in one or two of the eastern counties of Pennsylvania, along the Mohawk River in New York. the Miami River in Ohio, the Jersey settlement in Illinois, and elsewhere. Wherever they have gone, the same industry, energy, honesty and hospitality have characterized them. As farmers, they have no superiors in the world. As citizens, they have been conservative and peaceable, and more apt to do, than to talk about what they have done. As patriots, they have ever been true to our Republican instioutions.

They were the descendants of the only people who were free, when they colonized New York and New Jersey. The Dutch are the original Republicans of America. During the Revolution the descendants of the Hollanders in Monmouth, with but few exceptions were sturdy and indomitable patriots. When the British army marched through Monmouth, and in the various raids by the Tories, the descendants of the Dutch, were generally the sufferers. It is greatly to be desired that the valuable historical materials, which the Rev. G. C. Schenck has collected, concerning this element of the population of Monmouth should be published. Without it the history of our county will be incomplete

At this time, (1878), the intermarriages of the past century and a half, have welded together the descendants of the English, Scotch, French Huguenots, and Dutch settlers of Monmouth. The blood of the Batavians now flow through the veins of nearly all our native population, and all may claim as their Fatherland the "little Republic of Holland." All may point with just pride, using the words of another, " to a people daring, enterprising, persevering, born almost in the sea which they had mastered, descendants of the ancient Norsemen, whose hardihood they inherited, nurtured amid morass and fen—exposed to icy blasts from the North Sea and humid exhalations from canal and dyke, taught early and ever to battle with nature or to perish ; where the face of the sea, land and sky—pale, sad and leaden, gives seriousness to the mind and resolve to the character. With a State but little larger than New Jersey, this people in 1579 had made a nation whose character had been formed amid peril and tears and blood. For over forty years they had battled with the fierce legions of Spain in defence of home and life. They did not run away from their native land, but by their own sturdy arms and faith in God, won their civil and religious freedom ; and when won, generously shared it with the world. For over forty years they had shown a constancy and perseverance under trial, and affliction, and defeat, almost unparalleled in human history. Now the seven United Provinces of the Netherlands, having established their liberties and consolidated their State, were vying with the other nations of Europe in schemes of exploration and dominion.

Their naval power was rapidly augmented. They wrested from Spain and Portugal a large portion of their Indian trade. They planted colonies in the Islands of the East, they visited realms of sun and snow, in furtherance of commerce and discovery, and became the factors and carriers of Europe. They built up a navy, that at one time checked the Spanish Armada, and at another drove the English fleets from the sea and triumphantly sailed up the Thames." For them, as a reward for their faithful struggle in the cause of true religion and human freedom, against the gigantic power of Popery and Spanish Empire, Providence reserved the the fairest portion of the American Hemisphere, the region bordering on the New York and Raritan Bays, and the various rivers which flow thereon, from the mighty Hudson to the placid Shrewsbury.

In searching the shores of the Western Continent for the fabled passage to Cathay, the Dutch discovered the Highlands of Navesinck, and the magnificent harbour of New York.

There on Manhattan Island, they planted the germ of the Empire City. "They builded, too, better than they knew."— They unwittingly found the true passage to the Indies, through the American continent. That passage which has been made from Jersey City to San Francisco by the iron rail. A passage by which, to-day, the rich fabrics of far Cathay, are carried through the Western Continent, faster than ship ever sailed. What was a wild dream in 1609 has become a practical reality in 1878.

The attempt to discover this passage, which subsequent generations have made, led to the settlement of New York and vicinity by Hollanders. From this source we get those people in Monmouth county, whe bear such names as Smock, Statsir, Schanck, Strycker, Suydam, Spader, Van Kirk, Sutphen, Lefferts and Leffertson, Hyer, Quackenbush, Polhemus, Conover, Vanderveer, Barkalow and Barricklo, Antonides, Marcellus, Wyckoff, Hoff and Hoffman, Neafie or Nevius, Hendricks and Hendrickson, Probasco, Terhune, Cortelyou, Gulick, Van Sickelen or Sickles, Tunis, Van Dyke, Denise, Bergen, Brinckerhoff, Remsen, Du Bois, Voorhees, Vredenburgh, Vought, Veghte, Truax, Schuyler, Hageman, Honce, Van Brunt, Van Dorn, Ten Eyck, Luyster, Van Mater, Van Schoick, Van Deventer, Van Cleaf, Van Hise, Van Pelt, and all the rest of the Vans.

It was the forefathers of many of these persons, who built, those substantial farm houses, which still exist here and there, through parts of Monmouth County. The roof running almost to the ground and projecting over, both in front and rear, and under them the "stoep." The outbuildings large and massive and often painted red. The old Dutch farmers of Monmouth delighted in large barns well filled, and with their stock, including negro slaves, sleek, fat and contented. Their hospitality was as solid and wide as the great doors which led into their dwellings and the open hearth, on which blazed and crackled a load of wood at a time.

The houses of the old time, well-to-do Dutch People have been well described by another, as follows: "The Bulls-eye in the door and the small size of the lower windows, indicated a residence amid perils and apprehensions of a savage foe. Within, the well scrubbed, snow white floor, is covered with the finest sand, and drawn in figures and festoons. Above, the polished oaken rafters, are cut in quaint device and motto.

Through the glass doors of the nut-wood cupboard, shine glittering in the sunlight, or by the blaze from the cheerful hearth, the generous pewter tankard and two-eared cup, and portly dram mug, and silver porringer and ladle,—relics, brought from the old sea home, and Delft ware, teapot and bowl and a few tiny cups. wherein the social bohea is often dealt out to appreciative guests, who knit and gossip between the frequent sips.

At one end in the alcove is the great four-posted family bedstead, the pride of the house, the family heirloom, endeared through associations with the past; on which rests its two beds of down, and chintz flowered curtains, and intricate patchwork quilt and silken coverlid, triumphs of domestic thrift and handicraft. In another place is the great cedar chest, where reposes the valued store of house hold linen, snow white and substantial, the good housewife's hereditary dowry, increased by industry, and destined to be apportioned among the blooming maidens of the household, when some Jan, Pieter or Jacobus can muster courage to ask them to leave the paternal roof. Extending almost along the breadth of the room is the great fireplace of those days, in whose ample embrasure, would gather the children, and the cats and dogs and the old negro slave, droning out his weird stories on the long winter's eve.

Brass mounted irons support the blazing pile of solid logs. In front is a brazen fender of intricate design, sent over by Holland friends. Scenes of Scriptural History are illustrated there by the little blue tiles, that line the chimney piece. Jonah's adventures and Toby's travels and Sampson's exploits. While on the lofty mantle, covered with flowered tabby chimney cloth, stands the hour glass; the old Bible with its brazen ends and clasps; the best pipe of the Master of the house, his trusty sword and fire-piece. In one corner stands the fire screen with its gay designs; in another the best spinning wheel, curiously inlaid. Against the wainscoted wall is the round tea table, with its turned up leaf, the benches in the window, and in prim array, each in its accustomed place, are the high backed chairs of Russia leather, adorned with double rows of brass headed nails, and one or two covered perhaps by embroidered back and seat, and trimmed with lace, the work of the dextrous fingers of the good housewife herself, in earlier days.

Hanging from the ceiling might be seen an ostrich egg; on the wall a little mirror in a narrow ebony frame, also a few framed engravings of Holland social life, portraits of some Dutch Magnate, or scenes of a naval fight, the taking of a galleon from hated Spain, or a broadside conflict between two high pooped frigates.

There too was the loom from which was made the homespun cloth, that clad the goodman and his boys, and made stout petticoats for the girls. No artificial pleasures lured them from the domestic circle. The family formed a tie of strength, where all were occupied and happy.— Such was the indoor life of many a Smock, Schenck, Vanderveer, Conover, etc., in Monmouth County, a century ago. There were also a few large land owners with numerous slaves, who lived like kings on their farms. The leading characteristics of this class is happily described by Edmund G. Stedman in his poem called " Alice of Monmouth," by the following lines :

Hendrick Van Ghelt, of Monmouth Shore,
His fame still rings the County o,er;
The Stock he raised, the stallion he rode,
The fertile acres his farmers sowed,
The dinners he gave; the yacht which lay
At his fishing dock in the Lower Bay;
The suits which he waged, thro' many a year,
For a rood of land behind his pier.
Of this, the chronicles yet remain
From Navesink Heights to Freehold Plain,
The Shrewsbury people in autumn help
Their Sandy topland with marl and kelp,
And their peach and apple orchard fill
The gurgling vats of the crossroad Mill.
They tell, as each twirls his tavern can,
Wonderful tales of that staunch old man,
And they boast of the draught, they have tasted and smelt,
'Tis good as the still of Hendrick Van Ghelt.

Some of our oldest citizens can remember how well these lines describe certain characteristics of several farmers in Monmouth, who were famous in the latter part of the last century and the beginning of the present. Men like Joseph H. Van Mater, Col. Barnes Smock, Hendrick Schanck, Capt. John Schanck, Capt. Daniel Hendrickson, "Farmer," Jacob Conover and others.

PAPER FOUND BY HON. WILLIAM P. FORMAN. AMONG THE PRIVATE PAPERS OF HIS GREAT-GRAND FATHER, PETER FORMAN, SON OF JONATHAN FORMAN.

To the Committee of the Township of Freehold, in the county of Monmouth :

Gentlemen : In answer to the several questions proposed by you on the 3rd of this instant, it is the sense of the people :

1st. That as the Province arms were purchased with our money, and expressly for our use, we think ourselves properly authorized to apply them to service in any emergency. We therefore request you to call on the Justices and Freeholders, in whose hands they now are, for liberty to have them immediately collected together and put in good repair. The expense of repairing them, to be defrayed out of the money to be raised as hereinafter expressed. We do, moreover, think it absolutely necessary that a magazine should be immediately established, lest, on emergency, we should be unable to supply ourselves with ammunition. To effect this grand point we do request you, as speedily as possible, to prepare and send a petition to our General Assembly. praying them to pass an act for raising a sum of money, as well for the support of a detachment of men, that it may be necessary to send from this Colony in defence of your liberties, as for the purpose of establishing a magazine. And should the Assembly be prevented from making this provision by a dissolution, or the want of the assent of the Governor and Council, or by any other cause, we do request you, will immediately make us acquainted therewith, and we will cheerfully subscribe a competent sum of money for these purposes.

2nd. We do fully concur with you in thinking the Military ought to be put upon a proper footing, for speedy improvement, as we are constrained to fear the melancholy time is near at hand, when the American Militia will, under God, be the only bulwark of our religion and property.

The mode that appears to us most proper to be adopted for our becoming a well regulated militia is as follows, viz : that you do immediately write, in the name of the people, to our Captains, and require them to call a general meeting of the Inhabitants of Freehold, on the thirtieth day of this instant, at Monmouth Court House, where, unless some more eligible method be adopted, we will by agreement, constitute companies for every neighborhood, each containing from 40 to 60 men, from 16 to 60 years of age, and appoint stated times, for calling the respective companies together, for Grand Muster. By these measures we shall meet together with little expense, and we hope raise a spirit of emulation in the several companies to excell each other.

(3d). We do request, you will call on every merchant in your district, without favour or affection, and demand of them upon honor. and if necessary, upon oath, to inform you of the average advance, they have had in their goods, from the 5th of Nov. 1773, to the 5th of Nov. 1774, and that they give up to your inspection their original invoices of the goods they purchased this Fall, and permit you to examine the advance they now sell at. By these steps, you will easily discover whether they have infringed the 9th article of the Association of the General Congress.

In case any of them, have transgressed, we do request you immediately to advertise it to the Public. The like inquiry we desire may be repeatedly made, and on the second offense, We do declare we will immediately break off all commerce with him or her so offending, or with his or her agents or factors and hold them up, as enemies to their country. We do further entreat this enquiry, may be made speedily without information or complaint lodged.

4th. Those persons who shall persist in extravagance, dissipation, gaming, etc., we will view as enemies to our country, and if after application made to them by you, they do persist in open violation of the continental resolves, We will on information from you, wait on the offenders, in such a manner, as will for the future convince them of the evil consequence of running counter to the sense of the people.

5th, As there are many evil minded people, among us, who for lucrative prospects would betray this country, and are daily endeavoring to sow the seeds of Dis-

302 OLD TIMES IN OLD MONMOUTH.

cord around them, by condemning the measures of Congress, calling our Meetings unlawful and rebellious, and declaring the right of taxing America to be in the British Patliament, We do insist that on you being acquainted with any such person, you will publickly advertise their names and places of abode, and we will treat them as rebels against their Country.

6th, We do request that you may have stated times of Meeting, that we may attend, as well to lay any new matter before you, as to be imformed of your proceedings.

7th, We desire these instructions may be entered on the Records or in the Town Book, and aknowledged by you, as your instructions from us."

This paper is not dated or signed by anybody. It was probably written in the month of November or December of 1774, as the words "this fall" occur after the date Nov. 5th, 1774, and in the same connection.

EXTRACTS FROM BOOK "B" OF MISCELLANEOUS RECORDS, 1780—1816, IN MONMOUTH CLERK'S OFFICE.

Page 1.

New Jersey, Monmouth County, January 27, 1780.

These do certify that Mathias Rue, a Militiaman of Capt. Hankinson's Company, of the first Regm't of Monmouth Militia, commanded by @oll. Nathaniel Scudder, was taken prisoner by the Enemies of the United States of America, in an engagement on the Highlands of Neversink, on the thirteenth day of February, 1777, and was carried to New York and, as I am told, there died, and left a widow and one child, born four and one-half months after his death, and that she yet remains the widow of said Rue. Witness my hand the day and year above written. JOHN WALTON, Ensign.

William Johnson being duly sworn, deposeth and sayeth, that he was taken prisoner in company with above mentioned Mathias Rue, and that the said Rue dyed the 28th day of February, 1777, and further saith not. WILLIAM JOHNSON.

Sworn before me this
21st day of January,
1780. P. SCHENCK,
Justice.

These do certify that we do verily believe that Elizabeth, the above named widow, was the lawful wife of said Mathias Rue, decd., and that his child was born in lawful wedlock. Witness our hands this 21st day of January, 1780.

JOHN ANDERSON, } Justices.
P. SCHENCK. }

1780, April.

These are to certify that we have examined the within certificate, and allow the same to be registered, and the within named Elizabeth Rue allowed half pay, due to her husband, as the law directs. Witness our hands.

JOHN ANDERSON, }
JOHN LONGSTREET, } Justices.
PETER FORMAN. }

Registered 13th June, 1780.

Page 21-3.

New Jersey, Monmouth County, October 27, 1779.

These do certify that James Crawford, a Militiaman belonging to my company in the first Batallion of Monmouth Militia, commanded by Coll. Nathaniel Scudder, was killed in an engagement (on the Highlands of Neversink) with the enemies of the United States, on the thirteenth day of February, one thousand seven hundred and seventy-seven, and left a widow named Margaret, and seven children, the youngest being five years old at this time. Witness my hand the day above written.

SAMUEL CARHART,
Capt,

These do certify we verily believe that the above named Margaret was the lawful wife of James Crawford, dec'd., and that the said Margaret Crawford, yet remains the widow of said James, witness our hand this 27th day of October, 1779.

PETER COVENHOVEN, } Justices.
P. SCHENCK. }

1780, April 27th. These are to certify that we have examined the within certificate and we do allow, that the same be registered, and also that the within named widow, Margaret Crawford, be allowed the half pay due her husband, as the Law directs. Witness our hands.

JOHN ANDERSON, }
JOHN LONGSTREET, } Justices.
PETER FORMAN. }

Registered 17th June, 1780.

Entries similar to above and pensions granted, appear in the following cases :

Alexander Clark, killed Feb. 13, 1777, in the Engagement on the Navesinck Highlands. John Whitlock, 2nd Lieut., killed in same fight, left a widow Lydia, and a child five months old.

Obadiah Stillwell, militia man of Capt. Joseph Stillwell's Co., taken prisoner in same fight.

Joseph Goodenough swears he was also taken prisoner, with Obadiah Stillwell, and saw him die in prison, in New York, April 13th, 1777. His widow's name was Mary Stillwell.

William Cole, taken prisoner in same fight. Joseph Goodenough swears he saw him die in prison in New York, about March 15th, 1778. His widow's name was Elizabeth.

James Winter, taken prisoner in same fight, died in prison in New York, March 4th, 1777, and Joseph Davis, likewise taken prisoner, died in prison in New York, March 11, 1777, and James Hibbet's, also taken prisoner, died in prison in New York.

Capt. Barnes Smock certifies that Lambert Johnson was taken prisoner in the engagement on the Highlands, Feb. 13th, 1777, and Jonathan Reid swears that said Johnson died in captivity at New York, March 25th, 1777.

Asher Holmes, Colonel 1st Regiment Monmouth Militia, certifies that Lieut. Garret Hendrickson, of his regiment, was wounded in an engagement with the enemy, Jan. 21, 1780, and thereby lost use of his right arm.

This certifies that I, the subscriber was called in as a surgeon to consult with Doctor Barber, on the above case of Lieut. Hendrickson, at several different times; that notwithstanding every endeavour was made to preserve the use of the arm, still they proved ineffectual and that the said Lieut. Hendrickson has lost almost entirely the use of the arm, and in my opinion, has no prospect of ever recovering the use thereof. THOS. HENDERSON.

The Court allow Lieut. Hendrickson $5 per month from 12th day of June, 1780.

This is to certify that John Farr, an inhabitant of the State of New Jersey, Monmouth County, was a listed soldier under the command of Capt. Joshua Huddy, in February, 1782, in the twelve-month service, and was killed in the Block house at Toms River, on the 24th day of March, 1782, and left a wife, who since his death has been delivered of a child which is now living, as witness my hand, the 24th day of April, 1783. JOHN WALTON, Capt.

John Eldreth swears he was with Huddy at the time, and when enemy made the attack in the morning, when Farr was killed, and that he helped bury him.

Thomas Barber swears that he attended as a Doctor, Walter Hier,* who was wounded while fighting the common enemy, June 21st, 1781, in right fore arm, by a sword or cutlass. By which wound he lost part of the bone, and his hand is rendered almost entirely useless.

Samuel Carhart, Capt., certifies that Walter Hier, son of Peter Hier, a militia soldier of his command on 21st day of June, 1781, at Pleasant Valley, in Monmouth county, in an engagement with the common enemy, while boldly fighting, received a wound in right wrist or forearm, from a sword or cutlass from the enemy.

Thomas Chadwick, Capt., certifies that on May 24, 1781 in township of Shrewsbury, Frances Jeffers was wounded by a musket bullet while fighting common enemy, in his right hand, by which he has become incapable of getting his living.

James English, Doctor, certifies that he has examined the wound and it has rendered him incapable of getting his livelhood.

Daniel Hendrickson, Col. 3d Regt. Monmouth Militia, and Asher Holmes, Col. of 1st Regt. Monmouth Militia, certifies that Capt. John Dennis, of 3d Regt. M. M., while on duty in Shrewsbury, Oct. 3d, 1777, in an engagement with a party of Refugees, received a wound and was made prisoner of war, and carried to New York, and continued there in confinement until January 16, 1778, at which time he died of his wounds.

Personally came before the subscriber, one of the Justices of the Peace of the county of Monmouth, Mathias Mount, who being duly sworn, upon his oath, saith: that the Deponent was a prisoner in New York in the year 1778, and was well acquainted with Capt. John Dennis, of the 3d Regt. of Militia of Monmouth county, and saith that the said John Dennis died in said prison in cold weather, and that said Dennis' wounds were not cured, and that said Dennis after his death, lay several days in the corner of the yard, before he was buried, and further saith not.

MATHIAS MOUNT.

Sworn this 24th April, 1787, before

JOSEPH STILLWELL.

To the Honorable Court of Quarter Ses-

*Note. Should be Hyer.

sions, to be holden in and for the county of Monmouth. Whereas L. Pangborn, a Militiaman, an inhabitant of Stafford, under command of Capt. Joseph Randolph, who was shot dead as he stood on guard, by a party of Refugees, on the 31st day of December, 1780, in the presence of Sylvester Tilton, (who was shot through with a bullet at the same time), and Reuben Randolph. Both being sworn and affirmed before me, Amos Pharo, say the above facts are true. SILVESTER TILTON,
REUBEN RANDOLPH.
AMOS PHARO.

Now the widow of him the deceased, by the name of Ann Pangborn, prays that your Honors may give her some aid for her support, as she is blind and in low circumstances.

The Court allow her half pay.

Page 30–31.

This is to certify that Joseph Murray, a Militia soldier, belonging to Col. Asher Holmes, Reg't of Monmouth Militia, under command of Lieut. Garret Hendrickson, then in service, was ordered to reconnoitre on the Bay shore, near Sandy Hook, on the 7th of June, 1780, and on the eighth, in the morning, had leave from me for his return to quarters, to visit his family. After being at home a few hours was killed by three Refugees, near his barn, and left a wife with four small children, as witness my hand this 25th day of April, 1788. GARRET HENDRICKSON,
Lieut.

Thomas Hill, being duly sworn, upon his oath saith, that the deponent and the above said Joseph Murray, with some other persons, had been on the lines on the Bay, on the night of the 7th of June, 1780, and in the morning went home with said Murray, and after a short time was going to a neighbor, not far distant, when deponent heard the report of a gun at the aforesaid Murray's house, and in a short time after he was alarmed with news, that said Murray was killed by three Refugees. Deponent saith he went immediately back where he came. He saw said Murray lay dead with his wounds bleeding. He had been shot and bayonetted in several places and deponent further saith that Joseph Murray left a wife with four small children, and that he had leave of absence from his officer. Sworn before me this 25th day of April, 1788.
THOMAS HILL.

JOSEPH STILLWELL,
Justice.

Joseph Murray was of Scotch descent. He was a farmer and lived in the house where John Hedden now resides, near the deep railroad cut in the township of Middletown. He was a bold and active patriot, during the revolution. He had detected and prevented several attempts to supply the British fleet in Sandy Hook Bay, with provisions. He had also caused the arrest of one or two of the leading Tories of Middletown, for communicating with the enemy, and likewise had seized their horses for the use of the light Horse of the American Army. He had thus aroused the fear and hatred of the Tories, and it was strongly suspected that some of the leading loyalists of Middletown had instigated or hired the three refugees to waylay and murder him.

They had concealed themselves in tall indian grass, adjoining a field he was about to harrow, for he had a family and was obliged to work for their support, as he could find time. On his return from his service as patrolman during the night, on the bay shore, he had hitched his horse to a harrow, and after placing his musket against a tree, started to harrow across the field. When he had reached the opposite side near the indian grass, he turned and started back. Two of the refugees rose up and fired at him and slightly wounded him, and then rushed on him with fixed bayonets. Murray was a very active and strong man, and succeeded in wresting a musket from one of his assailants and was making a desperate defence, when the third refugee who had not fired came up and shot him in the groin. This last wound brought him to the ground, where his assassins repeatedly drove their bayonets through his body, although with his last breath, the sturdy patriot grimly defied his murderers. Joseph Murray was married to Rebecca Morris, by Rev. Abel Morgan, the famous pastor of the Middletown Baptist Church. and he lies buried a little to the east of this church, with the brief inscription on his tombstone, " Died in the service of his Country." One of his sons, William, superintended and built the cells and other masonry of the Court House erected in Freehold, in 1808. The substantial nature of this work was shown by the way the walls stood the test of the great fire in 1873. The foundation walls and the front wall of the first story of our present Court House, in front of the Sheriff's office, the hall and Grand Jury room, remain the same to-day, as

OLD TIMES IN OLD MONMOUTH. 805

when put up by William Murray, seventy years ago and bid fair to outlast the new mason work of 1874, above and on each side of it.

William W. Murray, for a long time engaged in the merchantile business at Middletown Village and Postmaster there under many Democratic administrations, was a son of this William Murray. He was a trustee and treasurer of the old Baptist Church, at Middletown, a great many years and noted for his strict business habits and integrity of character. His son George C. Murray, now occupies the homestead in the village of Middletown.

John Imlay, and Denise Denise, Judges, allow Rebecca Murray, widow of said Joseph Murray, half pay of her deceased husband from June 8th, 1780.

PAGE 31.

Joseph Parker swears he was a listed soldier in Capt. Huddy's Company, and while at Toms River Block House, James Kinsly, a private soldier of same company, was shot through the head by British soldiers, about March 22d, 1782, as near as he can remember.

I do certify that a certain Abell Ivins, soldier in the fourth Reg't of New Jersey, was in the Platoon under my immediate command at the Battle of Brandywine on the eleventh day of September, one thousand seven hundred and seventy-seven, and was there killed.

Allentown.
Monmouth, June 5th, 1792.
WESSEL T. STOUT,
late Lieut., Jersey Line.

Abell Ivins, married Veleriah Compton, to whom Court allowed half pay as his widow.

Elihu Chadwick, Lieut., certifies that John Russel, a soldier in his Company, was March 13, 1780, wounded while in actual service, in an engagement with British troops, with a ball and buckshot in his right hip and shoulder.

Col. Asher Holmes of 1st Reg't, M. M., certifies to same.

David Rhea and Robert Laird swear to same facts.

The Sessions allow him $3 per month
PAGE 39.

We the subcribers, Ministers, Elders and Deacons for the time being of the First United Dutch Reformed congregation of Freehold and Middletown* in the County of Monmouth, and State of New

*Freehold and Middletown townships are meant.—They then joined each other.

Jersey, do hereby certify that we take the name, and are hereafter to be known as a corporate body by the name of Minister, Elders and Deacons of the First United Dutch Reformed congregation, of Freehold and Middletown, in the County of Monmouth and State of New Jersey. Done under our hands and seals this eleventh day of April, 1791.

Minister. Benjamin DuBois, [L. S.]
Elders.
Denise Denice, [L. S.]
Hendrick Smock, [L. S.]
Garret Hendrickson, [L. S.]
Tobias Polhemus, [L. S.]
Deacons.
Garret Schenck, [L. S.]
George Smock, [R. S.]
Auky Lefferson, [L. S.]
Cyrenius B. VanMater, [L. S.]

Recorded 14th day of May, 1791.

PAGES 43—44.

Association of the Baptist society of Middletown, in the county of Monmouth and State of New Jersey. Whereas it hath pleased Almighty God in his Divine goodness to plant and establish Gospel church, for His glory and the good of fallen men throughout the Christian world, whereby man is instructed in the way of true Religion, and the Gospel of Jesus, and his duty to God ; and as it is necessary while in this militant state to be concerned in the things of this world, as conducive to promote the cause of Christ; and do think it necessary to incorporate ourselves as a church and Body Politick, to be known in fact and in law ; and whereas, we the subscribers, being the supporters of said Society, agreeably to law in that case made and provided, passed at Trenton, March ye 16, 1786, to be called and known by the name of the Baptist Church of Middletown. And we do hereby associate ourselves for this purpose, and agree as soon as thirty or more persons have subscribed this association, any three or more of the associated members, may by advertisement of at least ten days notice, assemble the said associators, and others who may incline to associate, at the Baptist Meeting House, in said Township, and by plurality of voices of those met to choose and elect of those associated, not more than seven persons to be Trustees of the same, to incorporate the said Baptist society, and to constitute a Body Politick and corporate, agreeably to said law, and to transact all the temporal concerns of said society. In witness whereof we have hereunto set our hands this twentieth day of July, in the year of our Lord one thousand seven hundred and ninety three.

Richard Crawford,
John Stillwell,
Samuel Ogborne,
William Blair,
Rebeccah Stillwell,
Anna Chasey,
Sarah Bostwick,
Samuel Bray,
James Patterson,
Daniel Ketcham,
Jonathan Stout,
Asher Holmes,
Cornelius Hulshart,
William Green,
James Grover,
Jehu Patterson,
George Hunt,
Thomas Burrows,
David Burdge,
Daniel Hill,
Phillip Walling,
John Taylor,
Anthony Smith.

John Smock,
John Walling,
Joseph Stillwell,
James Bowne,
Cornelia Dennis,
Mary Holmes,
Obadiah Holmes,
Jacob Covenhoven,
Phœbe Ketcham,
James Walling,
Joseph Brown,
William Morford,
Cornel's Hulshart, Jr.,
Thomas Jeffreys,
Thomas Stillwell,
Benjamin Hulshart,
Benjamin Bennett,*
Jehu Patterson,
John Bowne,
Silvester Applegate,
John Wall,
Daniel Hendrickson,

This is to certify that at a meeting of a number of signers for the incorporating the Baptist church at Middletown, of which Benjamin Bennet is pastor, we the following persons, were chosen as Trustees for said Church, to-wit: John Smock, Jacob Covenhoven, Joseph Stillwell, Wm. Blair, John Stillwell, Jonathan Stout, and Daniel Ketcham, of whom, Joseph Stillwell was by the others chosen president; and having taken the oaths necessary as the law directs, and taken upon us the name of the Trustees for the Baptist church of Middletown, with the seal marked MN. B. C., do request the same to be recorded as the law in that case directs. As witness our hands and seals the 16th day of December, 1793.
Signed,

John Smock, [L. S.]
Jacob Covenhoven, [L. S.]
Jos. Stillwell, [L. S.]
William Blair, [L. S.]
John Stillwell, [L. S.]
Jonathan Stout, [L. S.]
Daniel Ketcham, [L S.]

*Benjamin Bennett, at one time was the Pastor of the Middletown Baptist church. He owned and occupied the farm where John B. Story now lives, and was one of the most progressive and foremost farmers in the county. He was also a Representative in Congress from 1815 to 1819. He was born in 1762, and died on his farm near Middletown village, Oct. 8th, 1840.

PAGE 65.
To the Honorable Court of Quarter Sessions, held in Monmouth on the fourth Tuesday in January, 1801.

May it please your Honors, that on the twentyeth day of this Present month, February 1801, I surveyed for the Prisoners, the Court House Lott and part of the street, as follows: Beginning about six foot to the southward of Merchant John Craig's peaazer, at the southeast corner from his dwelling house, and running (1) south, fifty one degrees west, one chain and thirty-two links to the southeast corner of the Court House Lott; thence the several courses as the Court House Lott now runs, untill it comes to a stone plant ed in the northerly edge of the street, a few feet from the southwest corner of the new brick office House; thence along the northerly edge of the street, south, fifty-one degrees west, six chains and eighty links to the southwest corner of the Church Lott; and thence south, thirty-one degrees east, eighty-six links, crossing the street to the south side of said street; thence along the southerly side of the said street, north, fifty degrees east, five chains and a half to Mr. Coward's Peaazer; thence North, sixty-one degrees east, four chains and a half, along the south side of said street to the easterly end of Major James Craig's Peaazer; thence crossing said street to the Beginning, containing two acres and a half, strict measure. Surveyed by me the 20th Day of Jan'y, 1801.
JOHN FORMAN.

DANIEL CRAIG, } Chain Bearers.
DAVID CRAIG.

January Term, 1801.
The Court agree that the above survey shall be recorded by the Clerk of the said Court as the Bounds of the Prisoners.

HENDRICK HENDRICKSON,
JOHN LLOYD,
JOHN FORMAN,   } Judges.
JONATHAN FORMAN,
JAMES ALLEN.

The rest of this book is nearly all taken up, with entries of deeds manumitting slaves. The following are fair specimens of these entries.

PAGE 97-98.

To all men unto whom these presents shall come, I Benjamin Bennet, Minister of the Gospel of the Township of Middletown, County of Monmouth and State of New Jersey, do by these presents manumit and set free my negro slave named Nanna, she being sound in mind and not under any bodily incapacity of obtaining a support, and not under the age of twenty-one years, nor above the age of forty years; and having previously complied with the provision of the law for the manumission of slaves in that case made.

In witness whereof I have unto these present, set my hand and seal this twenty-eighth day of March, one thousand eight hundred and five.

BENJAMIN BENNET, [L. S.]

Signed, sealed and delivered in the presence of
JOHN C. LUYSTER, }
HENDRICK BREWER, }

PAGE 124.

State of New Jersey, }
Monmouth S.S. }

To all to whom these presents shall come greeting.

It is hereby made known, that on this thirteenth day of March, in the year of our Lord one thousand eight hundred and ten, I, George Crawford, of the township of Middletown, in said county of Monmouth, have liberated, manumitted and set free, my negro slave called Betty, of the age of thirty-five years or thereabouts, and I do hereby liberate, manumit and set free my said negro slave, and discharge her from all services to be hereafter made, either by me or any person claiming by, from or under me.

In testimony whereof I have hereunto set my hand and seal the day and year aforesaid. GEORGE CRAWFORD.

Sealed and delivered in the presence of
WILLIAM, MURRAY,
WM. W. MURRAY.

State of New Jersey, }
Monmouth County, ss. }

Be it remembered that on the nineteenth day of March, one thousand eight hundred and ten, before me James Frost, one of the Justices of the peace in and for the County of Monmouth, personally appeared George Crawford, the within Grantor and did acknowledge the within instrument to be his voluntary act and deed by him signed sealed and and delivered for the purposes therein mentioned.

Acknowledged before me,
JAMES FROST.
Justice.

Monmouth County Court.

We do hereby certify that on the thirteenth day of March, in the year of our Lord one thousand eight hundred and ten, George Crawford of the Township of Middletown, in said County of Monmouth, brought before us, two of the overseers of the poor of the said Township, and two of the justices of the peace of the said County, his slave named Betty, who on view and examination, appears to us to be sound in mind, and not under any bodily incapacity of obtaining a support and also is not under the age of twenty-one years nor above the age of forty years. In witness whereof we have hereunto set our hands the Day and year above written.

CHRINEYONCE SCHENCK,
WM. STILLWELL.

Overseers of the poor of the said Township, Middletown.

JAMES FROST,
JEHU PATTERSON.

Justices of the peace in and for the said County of Monmouth.

Received and Recorded 25th of April, 1810. J. PHILLIP,
Clerk.

OLD PAPERS BELONGING TO RULIFF E. CONOVER ESQ., OF MARLBOROUGH TOWNSHIP.

OLD TIME BOND.

Know all men by these presents, that we, Samuel Holmes of Freehold and Obadiah Holmes and John Holmes of Middletown, and all of the county of Monmouth, in the Eastern Division of the Colony of New Jersey, Yeomen, are held and firmly bound unto Roelef Schenck, of Freehold aforesaid. yeoman, in the sum of one thousand pounds, current money of the colony of New York, to be paid unto the said Roelef Schenck, or to his certain attorney, executors, administrators or assigns, for the which payment well and truly to be made and done, we bind ourselves and each of us by himself, our and each and every of our heirs. executors and administrators, jointly and severally, firmly by these presents, sealed with our seals and dated the sixth day of July, in the twenty-sixth year of the reign of his Majesty, George the Second, King over Great Brittain, &c., one thousand seven hundred and fifty-two.

The condition of the above written obligation is such, that whereas the above named Roelef Schenck, together with the above named Obadiah Holmes, John Holmes, and Samuel Holmes, of Staten Island aforesaid, became security and bound in a bond bearing even date with this bond, with the first named Samuel Holmes, for the payment of five hundred pounds, current lawfull money of the Colony of New York aforesaid. unto John Chambers, Esq., of the City and Colony of New York aforesaid. Now, if the above bounden Samuel Holmes or Obadiah Holmes or John Holmes, or either of them or either of their heirs, executors or administrators shall save and keep harmless and indemnifie the said Roelef Schenck, his heirs, executors and administrators from paying the above said sum of five hundred pounds, or any part thereof, and from all charge or sum or sums of money that shall accrue thereby or therefrom, that then this above written obligation is to be null, void and of none effect, otherwise to stand and remain in full power, force and virtue.

SAMUEL HOLMES, [L.S.]
OBADIAH HOLMES, [L.S.]
JOHN HOLMES, [L.S.]

Sealed and delivered in the presence of
JOHN BURROWES,
JOHN RHEA.

ACCOUNT OF EXECUTORS.
1760.

Accompt per contrary of all the goods, chattels, and credit of Captain Daniel Hendrickson, of Middletown, deceased, that was inventoryed by his executors, also an accompt of the several tracts of land sold by his executors, pursuant to the testators will.

To a tract of land laying at Cnascung sold to William Willet,	£ 150	0 0
To 140 acres of propriety right sold to John Sutphen for	45	0 0
To meadow at Barnegat sold to Mr. Weils for	12	0 0
To the testators share of propriety right sold to Thomas Lawrence for	3 10	0
To £1130 8 0 apprised and inventoryed, taken of Captain Hendrickson's personal estate by his executors	1130 8	0
	£1340 18	0

There was a horse and two cows given by the testator to his nephew Daniel Hendrickson, and a horse to his son William, £13 0 0.   13 0 0
                                           £1327 18 0

The £392 1 0 which I have substracted is the testators personal estate that was left to his widow and her use, and in her possession   392 01 0
                                           £935 17 0

The £980 11 7 is the testators debts paid by Hendrick Hendrickson, one of the executor of testators'   980 11 7
                                           £ 44 14 7

The £44 14 7 is what we have paid more than we had of the testator's personal estate to pay his debts, accounting for the money the land was sold, as if in our hands, without allowing one shilling for the bad book debts, but if £47 0 0 is added for bad debts not paid, to the £44 74 7 there is   47 0 0

£91 14 7 paid by us more than we had, of the testators personal estate to pay his debts 91 14 7
There was £5 19 0 paid by John Sutphen for interest which I substract from the 05 19 0
£91 14 7 remains £85 15 7
The interest computed from the time that the inventory was taken will be double £85 15 7

85 14 7
———————
£171 10 2

That what is paid more than we had personal to pay the debts £71 10 2

JONATHAN HOLMES, } Executors.
ROELEF SCHENCK,

Errors excepted by us May 20th, 1760.

(Endorsed)
The accompts of the surviving executors of Captain Daniel Hendrickson.

ROELEF SCHENCK,
 and } Executors.
JONATHAN HOLMES,

LETTER FROM JONATHAN HOLMES TO ROELEF SCHENCK CONCERNING THIS ESTATE.

Brother Schenck:

I forgot to give my opinion to you in writing, concerning the personal estate of father Hendrickson, in brother Daniel's possession. First, the testator gives his widdow the use of his personal estate, during her natterall life or widdowhood, then to his son Daniel, if his widdow dies, or is remarried. But if she continues a widdow, the testator gives Daniel half of the lands given to his widow, and the half of his personal estate, as I remember; when the widow dies or ceases to be the testator's widow, then he gives his son Daniel all the lands which he gave his widow the use of. All the personal estate and lands given to the testator's widow's use is intended for Daniel. It is my opinion that the testator did not intend, that his son Daniel should be obliged to pay £350 legacy, to begin att 22 years of age or any age, to pay his sister's legacies, and have none of the testators personall estate, but only the land he gave his widow the use of, appears to me was not the testators intent, because, if the widow dies or is remarried before Daniel is 21 years old, he is obliged to pay the legacies one year after 21 years of age.— My second reason is, because, at his wid-

ow's decease, the testator gives all his land to his son Daniel, which he gave to his widow, therefore, as the testator gave his son Daniel the use of half his real and personal estate att 21 years of age, so I think that at the widow's decease, when the testator gives all his lands, that he gave his widow the use off, to his son Daniel, the whole personal estate that was left to the widow's use, is as much given to the testator's son Daniel, as the use of half was att 21 years of age. It appears to me, and I am of opinion that the personal estate of the testator, that his widow left upon the homestead, belongs to the testator's son Daniel, except what was mother's, exclusive of the testator's personal estate. I also except those that paid off, testators debts, if they demand the sum of money which they paid more than they had of the testator's personal estate, in their hands to pay his debts, I hope they, not paid, will not demand any of personal estate, but what Daniel will part with freely. As mother has left something considerable upon the homestead at her decease, of the testators personal estate, we the executors of the testator's last will and testament are obliged to see it executed according to his will, for he has appointed us his executors to execute his will, and we are sworn to execute his will and render an accompt when thereunto required, therefore it is our duty to order and dispose of the testators personal estate left upon the homestead by the testators widow, at her decease, according to his will; that was reason I told you last winter, that as they was about to proceed I would protest against it, becuuse I could not save my oath, without executing the testators will; I hope you and they will excuse me, if I differ in opinion from the rest of my brothers and sisters, when you and they consider, that I am an executor of the testator's will, and sworn to execute it. My thoughts are so crude and what I have written so indigested, I did not intend what I have written to be made publick, but to inform you what opinions I have concerning the personal estate left to Mother's use, but if you think it for the better, you may let them see it, but take no copy because my disorder affects my head very much, and much more by being so much swelled, and obliged to stop in preparing the method and order, and wrighting the accompt; that I can scarse see what I have written. Be sure to let William and Daniel see this paper before any others see it, and take their opinion about it. JONATHAN HOLMES. May the 21st, 1760.

The Captain Daniel Hendrickson above mentioned, lived where the Hon. Wm. H. Hendrickson now lives, in the Township of Holmdel, and was his great-great-grandfather. Jonathan Holmes, above, married one of his daughters, Tuniche, and the other executor, Ruliff Schanck, married another daughter, Ghesie. The two executors were therefore sons-in-law of the deceased.

Ruliff Schenck had a son named Hendrick, who married the the daughter of Jonathan Holmes aforesaid, his cousin; her name was Catharine.

Hendrick Schanck lived near the Brick church in the township of Marlborough, and owned the property there now occupied by his descendants, the Schancks, Conovers and VanKirks

The following paper alludes to this Hendrick Schanck, who died September 1, 1766. He had a son Ruliff who was the father of John, Jonathan, Tylee and Jacob Schanck:

Received this seventeenth day of June, in the year of our Lord one thousand seven hundred and seventy six, by us, Peter Covenhoven, Geashea Barrigan (Bergen), Jacob Cowenhoven, Rulif Cowenhoven and Mary Cowenhoven, of Rulift Schanck, son of Hendrick Schanck, deceased, as heirs of said Hendrick Schanck, the sum of one hundred and seventy pounds, light money. In part of a legesey left us by Ruliff Schenck, late of Freehold, deceased, by his last will and testament. We say it being in full of what has already become due, but not for what shall hereafter become due for one year to come, we say received by us, as witness our hands and seals, the day and year aforesaid.

GESHEA BERGEN, [L. S.]
PETER COVENHOVEN, [L. S.]
JACOB COVENHOVEN, [L. S.]
RALPH CONNOVER, [L. S.]
MARY COVENHOVEN, [L. S.]

Witness present
SIMON BERGEN,
WILLIAM SCHENCK,
SAM'L DENNIS.

BOND.

Know all men by these presents that I, Garret Covenhoven, Yeoman, of Freehold, in the County of Monmouth and Province of East New Jersey, am held and firmly bound unto Hendrick Schanck and Peter Covenhoven, executors of ye last will and testament of Ruliff Schanck, deceased, of ye County and province aforesaid, in the sum of seven hundred pounds, current money of the province of New Jersey, at eight shillings per oz., to be paid to the executors or to their certain attorney or assigns, to the which payment well and truly to be made, I bind myself, my heirs, executors, administrators and every of them, firmly by these presents, sealed with my seal, dated the fourth day of March in the year of our Lord one thousand seven hundred and sixty-six. 1766.

The condition of this present obligation is such, that if the above bounded Garret Covenhoven, hath had of Hendrick Schanck and Peter Covenhoven, executors of the last will and testament of Rulif Schanck, deceased, the sum of five hundred pounds, agreeable to the last will and testament of Ruliff Schanck, deceased, be the same more or less, as ye said will shall testify, as legisy given and bequeathed by the said Ruliff Schanck to Garret Covenhoven, if there be any debt or damage hereafter, of the said Ruliff Schanck, deceased, shall happen or be paid by the executors of sd Ruliff Schanck, the above sd Garret Covenhoven, shall pay back a ratable part of his legacy bequeathed above sd, then this present obligation to be void and of none affect, else to stand and remain in full force and virtue.

GARRET COVENHOVEN, [L. S.]

Sealed and delivered
ye presence of
DANIEL HOLMES, }
JOHN TICE. }

ENDORSEMENT.

Rec'd May the 8th, 1773, of the executors of Hendrick Schanck, deceased, by the hands of John Schanck, the sum of one hundred and twenty-eight pounds, six shillings and eight pence, being the first payment of a legacy given my wife, Nelly Covenhoven, by her father, Ruliff Schanck, as by the said will may appear.
GARRET COVENHOVEN.

OLD-TIME INVENTORY.

The goods and chattels of Hendrick Schanck, late of Freehold, deceased, taken by ye exec'trs and inventoried by Isaac Van Dorn, John Tice and Samuel Holmes, this third day of March, 1767. Taken in the currency of New York as it now Passeth.

Item. £ s d
Apparel, £18, Purse, £47, s12 65 12

To land rent that will be due from Cornelius Honce, in May, 1767.	40	
To notes of hand £14-12-6. Book debts £16-13 10.	31 6 4	
The Negroes aprized, to Brom, £70; Mork, £65; to Sare, £3, s10.	138 10	
To Aaron, £41, s10; to Mat, £35.	92 10	
To Lis £15.		
To a silver tankard, nine silver table and 5 silver tea spoons	20	
To clock and large looking glass and chest of drawers.	30	
To one large mahogany table and 2 old tables.	6	
To a large Dutch Bible and one English Bible, with some other books.	1 10	
To 1 beadstead and bead in an upper room, with its furniture.	20	
To a bead and beadstead with its furniture.	19	
To a bead and beadstead Sacken bottom, with its furniture	12	
To a bead and beadstead with its furniture.	7	
To a bead and beadstead @ £1, s10, to 1 great and 6 high back chears, @ £1, s10.	3	
To 1 boarded bedstead and Wind Mill.	6	
To a beadspread and 16 old chears.	1 12	
To 4 linnen wheels and 2 woolen wheels, reel and cradle @	2 15	
To a perch of Cheyney Boles and cups and saucers.	1 10	
To 15 stone and earthen plates, 3 tea cannesters, 3 small earthen boles and drinking glasses, 1 coffee pot, 4 earthen pots.	1	
To 2 small looking glasses and 4 pad irons and coals iron.	1 10	
To a pare of small stilliards with some lead weights.	10	
To a gun, 2 hatchets, trevit and sundries of pictures.	2 10	
To 7 pewter platters, six basins, 19 plaits, funel and some old puter.	3	
To bleaching pot lanterne, 6 patty pans, 2 chafing dishes, a skimer.	10	
To 3 old saddles, 2 stove irons, 4 old bells.	2	
To chease press, safe, 3 old tables and coffe mill.	1 5	
To 5 iron pots and kettles, copper pye pan, 2 copper tea kettles and brass skillet.	5 5	
To 3 tramels, 1 gridiron, 2 driping pans, 1 iron ladle, old iron and frying pan.	1 2	
To 1 pare of hand irens, 3 pare of tongues, iron shovel, 4 iron candle sticks.	1 10	
To a chest, trunk and small chest, case and bottles, a small table.	1 4	
To 2 negroes beads and a window curtain.	1 15	
To 7 horses and mares @ £45, to 4 two year old colts, @ £15.	60	
To 1 old horse, 2 old mares and a colt.	4	
To 17 cows and heafers, with calf @ £3, s5, per beast to 1 bull @ £4.	59 5	
To 3 four year old stears @ £3 per stear, to 11 calves @ £1-5 per calf.	22 15	
To 12 two and 3 year old heifers and stears, @ £1 s15 per beast.	21	
To 21 sheep @ s15 per sheep, and 10 hogs @ £6.	21 15	
To about 60 bushels of rye in sheaf s3 d3.	9 15	
To about 35 acres of standing corn @ 18 per acre.	31 10	
To about 23 acres of standing Rye, @ £11 to about 200 bushels of ingen corn in the ears @ 3-6, per bushell, and some oats in sheaf.	46 8	
To 406 bushels of wheat @ 6-3 per bushel.	126 17 6	
To about 90 bushels of wheat in the sheaf @ 6-3 per bushel.	28 2 6	
To 2 old waggons and 2 old sleads.	8	
To the whole of the horse gears, cleavises and pins.	2 10	
To forks, rakes, and the whole of the barn utensils.	1	
To 8 syths, 1 cradle with the tacle.	18	
To 1 brake, 1 cart hook @ 6, a grind stone @ 5	11	
To 43 old casks and tubs @ £2 s10, to 3 plows, 4 harrows.	10 10	
To part of a barl of tar and two tar tubs.	6	

To 6 axes, 2 broad hoes, beetle and weages, 1 spade, 1 shovel	1	10
To sider mill, 1 oister tonges, and 3 seader bolts.		16
To the carpenters' tools.		1
To 9 kelars, 7 pails, cheese tub, 2 chirns, and new tray, and meal box.		3
To 10 grain bags @ 15.		15
	£933 10	4

AGREEMENT.
1725.

Articles of agreement had, made, consented unto, and fully agreed upon, this eighteenth day of October, in the twelfth year of his Majesties Reigne, George over Great Brittain &c., King, anno dom. one thousand seven hundred and twenty-five, between Alice Van Kirk, of Freehold, in the county of Monmouth and Eastern Division of the Province of New Jersey, the widow, and one of the legatees of John Van Kirk, of the same place, (late deceased,) of the one part, and John Van Kirk, the son of the said John and Alice Van Kirk, of the other part, whereas the said deceased John Van Kirk, in and by his last will and testament, among several other gifts and bequests therein mentioned, did give unto the said Alice Van Kirk, his loving wife, the sole use of all his lands during her natural life. Now, these articles wittnesses, that the said Alice Van Kirk designing a marriage, which is intended to be had and solemnized between her and Thomas Hankison, of Freehold aforesaid, before the consummating thereof, assigns over her interest in the real estate of her deceased husband John Van Kirk to the above mentioned John Van Kirk, her son, on the conditions and with the provisoes hereinafter mentioned, viz: to have and to hold all her right, tytle, interest and claim in and to the said lands, (that were the deceased John Van Kirk) to him the said son, John Van Kirk and his heirs, for and during the term of twelve years, to commence from the date hereof, on condition that the said John Van Kirk shall and doe well and truly pay, and satisfye and discharge all such debts, that are now due from or by the said estate to be paid, either that were due by the testator at his decease, or since by the said Alice Van Kirk, contracted and unpaid; and after the expiration of the twelve years, for and during the term of his natural life, on condition that the said John Van Kirk shall pay and allow to his brothers and sisters, the rent that shall be reasonably adjudged by indifferent men, to be the value, that the said lands may yearly be rented att.—Provided allways, and it is fully agreed upon, and it is the true intent and meaning of both partys in these presents, That if the said Alice Van Kirk, after the marriage, as above mentioned shall be consummated, shall happen to be a widow, that then immediately, the said John Van Kirk shall and will deliver to her, all the first and former estate in the land, that was the said deceased, John Van Kirk's. In as full and ample manner as though this writing had never been made, and this writing is to be utterly void and of none effect, touching any thing or matter by either party after such re entry to be performed. In witness whereof, the said party to these presents have set their hands and seals, the day and year first above written. ELLICE VAN KIRK, [L S.]
JOHN VAN KIRK, [L.S.]

Witnesses.
ALEXANDER CLARK.
ROELEF SCHANCK.

DEED OF 1737. NEVER RECORDED.

This indenture made the twenty-second day of December, in the eleventh year of the Reign of our Sovereign Lord, George the second, by the grace of God, of Great Brittain, France and Ireland, King, Annog Domini, one thousand seven hundred and thirty-seven, Between Peter Tyssen of Freehold, in the county of Monmouth and Eastern Division of the Province of New Jersey, Yeoman, of the one part, and Roelef Schanck, of the same place, Carpenter, of the other part, witnesseth that the said Peter Tyssen for and in consideration of the sum of six pounds and ten shillings in money, to him allready in hand paid by him, the said Roelef Schanck, the receipt whereof, he, the said Peter Tyssen, doth hereby acknowledge, and himself to be therewith fully satisfied, contented and paid, and hereof and of and from every part and parcel thereof, Doth fully, clearly and absolutely, acquit exonerate and discharge him, the said Roelef Schanck, his heirs, executors, administrators and every of them forever, by these presents, hath granted, bargained, sold, aliened, enfeofed and confirmed, and by these presents doth fully, clearly and absolutely grant, bargain, sell, alien, enfeoff, release and confirm unto him, the said Roelef

OLD TIMES IN OLD MONMOUTH. 313

Schanck, his heirs and assigns forever, all that slip of land scituate, lying and being at Wequatunk, in the county of Monmouth aforesaid, twenty-one chains long and one and a half broad. Bounded, southerly, by said Roelef Schanck's land, called Brushneck; easterly, by Peter Schanck's land; northerly, by John Bennett's lott; westerly, by land now in the possession of John Bunnel, the which slip of land was conveyed and confirmed to him, the said Peter Tyssen, by deed of sale from John Bowne, bearing date, the sixth day of October, Annog Domini, one thousand seven hundred and nine, relation thereunto being had, may at large appear. Together with all and all housings, buildings, edifices, structures, barns, stables, orchards, fencings, feedings, pastures, meadows, woods, trees, waters, brooks, springs, ponds, pools, pits, easements, profits, commodities, libertys, fishings, fowlings, hawkings, huntings, advantages, privileges, emoluments, hereditaments and appurtenances whatsoever, to the said tract of land, belonging, or in any manner of ways thereunto appertaing. And also all the estate, right, tytle, interest, possession, property, claim and demand whatsoever of him, the said Peter Tyssen, as well in law as in equity of, in or unto the said slip of land, and granted and bargained premises and appurtenances thereof, to have and to hold the said tract of land as above butted and bounded and described, with all and singular and ever, the rights, liberties, privileges, profits and appurtenances to the same belonging, or on any manner of ways to any part or parcel thereof, appertaining, unto him the said Roelef Schanck, his heirs and assigns forever, to the only proper use and uses, benefit and behoof of him, the said Roelef Schanck, his heirs and assigns forever, and he, the said Peter Tyssen, Doth for himself, his heirs, executors and administrators, covenant, promise, grant and agree to and with him, the said Roelef Schanck, his heirs and assigns, by these presents, in manner and form following, viz: That at the time of the sealing and delivering hereof, he, the said Peter Tyssen, hath in himself good, rightfull power and absolute, lawful authority, to grant, bargain, sell, alien, enfeof, release and confirm the said slip of land, and all the premises and appurtenances thereof, unto him, the said Roelef Schanck, his heirs and assigns forever, in manner aforesaid, and that the same now is from time to time and at all times hereafter, shall remain free and clear to him, the said Roelef Schanck, his heirs and assigns forever, from all and all manner of former and other gifts, grants, bargains, sales, leases, mortgages, and of and from all other titles, troubles, charges, demands and incumbrances whatsoever, had made, committed, done or suffered to be done by him, the said Peter Tysen, or any other person or persons, whatsoever by him or under him, to alter, change, charge, defeat, determine or make voyd the same. In witness whereof, the said Peter Tysen hath hereunto set his band and seal, the day and year first above written, 1737.

his
Pieter x Tysen.
mark.

Signed, sealed and
delivered in the
presence of us,
John Van Vleek,
David Williamson,
Peter Schanck.

ENDORSED.

Be it remembered, that on ye twenty-eigth day of January, 1745-6, David Williamson, one of ye within subscribing evidences, came before me, Jonathan Forman, one of his majesties judges of ye Court of Common Pleas, for ye County of Monmouth, and being sworn on the holy evangelist of Almighty God, declared that he saw ye within named Peter Tysen, seal and deliver ye within instrument as his volluntary act and deed.

Jon'n Forman.

OLD DOCUMENTS IN POSSESSION
OF RICHARD AND GEORGE W.
CRAWFORD, OF MIDDLE-
TOWN TOWNSHIP.

An old Deed of 1687.

This Indenture made this third day of December, Anno Domini, one thousand six hundred and eighty-seven, and in the third year of the reign of our Sovereign Lord, James the second over England, etc. King. Between the Proprietors of the Province of East New Jersey, of the one part, and John Crawford of Middletown, in the County of Monmouth in the said Province, Gentleman, of the other part, witnesseth that the said Proprietors, as well for and in consideration of the Rent Services hereinafter reserved, as also for divers good causes, and lawfull considerations, them thereunto at present especially moving, have aliened, granted, bargained, sold, and by these presents do alien, grant, bargain and sell unto the said John Crawford, his heirs and assigns, all that tract of land, situate, lying and being within the bounds of Middletown aforesaid, containing two hundred acres, Beginning at a white oak marked on four sides, near the pathway from Middletown to the Falls, being John Wilson, Elder, Corner Tree, and running due south, sixty chains to a white oak marked on four sides, near the same path; thence running due east, thirty-three chains and a half to a black oak, marked on four sides; thence running due north, sixty chains to John Wilson's lines along Richard Gibbons line to a white oak marked on four sides; thence due west, thirty-three chains and a half to the place where it began. Bounded on the north, with John Wilson, Elder; on the east, with Richard Gibbons; on the south and west, with land unsurveyed. The which tract of land above mentioned, contains two hundred acres. Together with and all manner of feedings, pastures, woods, underwoods, trees, waters, water-courses, water-falls, ponds, pools, pitts, profits, easements, libertys, advantages, emoluments, hereditaments and appurtenances, whatsoever to the same belonging, or in any manner of ways appertaining. To have and to hold the said tract of land and premises, with their and every of their appurtenances, unto him, the said John Crawford, his heirs and assigns forever, to the only proper use benefit and behoof of him, the said John Crawford, his heirs and assigns forever, to be holden in free and common socage of them, the said Proprietors, their heirs and assigns, as in the seignory of East Greenwich, yielding and paying therefor yearly and every year, for the said two hundred acres, twenty pence, sterling, money of England, or the value thereof, being six pence, for every hundred acres thereof, unto the said proprietors, their heirs or assigns, at or upon every five and twentieth day of March, every year, forever hereafter, in lieu and stead of all other services and demands whatsoever. Provided always, that if the said yearly chief or quitt rent should be behind and unpaid in part or in all, at any of the said days or times, upon which the same is to be paid as aforesaid, that then and so often, it shall and may be lawful to and for the said proprietors and their heirs by any of their servants, agents or assigns, ten days after such neglect or non-payment of the said yearly chief or quitt rent, into the aforesaid lands, with the appurtenances, or into any part or parcel thereof, to enter, and then to distrain or the distress or distresses there taken to lead, drive, carry away, impound, and in their custody to detain, untill the said yearly chief or quitt rent, so being behind and unpaid, together with all costs and charges of such distress and impounding, shall be fully paid and contented, unto the said Proprietors, their heirs or assigns.

In witness whereof the Deputy Governor of this Province, and the major part of the council for the time being, to one part have subscribed their names, and affixed the common seal of the said Province, and to the other part thereof, the said John Crawford hath interchangeably set his hand and seal, the day and year first above written.

    Andrew Hamilton,
    John Johnston,
    Richafd Townly,
    James Emmett,
    Samuel Winder.

Recorded in Liber B. Folio 211 & 212. Copia Vera. Examined by
    Mich. Kearney,
    D. Sec'y.

This old paper is quite well preserved, and the writing very distinct, although nearly two hundred years has passed, since it was written. The land described is still in the possession of the descendants of John Crawford, Esq., being part of a tract known as the Crawford Homestead at Nut Swamp, and occupied now by George W. & Richard Crawford, sons of John B. Crawford, dec'd. The John Crawford named in above deed was the first settler of the name in Monmouth county. He was a Scotchman, from Ayrshire, and came to America about 1672. He first lived in Massachusetts, but afterwards went to Long Island, where he heard of the settlement at Middletown, and there he settled permanently. An old deed for a lot and house in Middletown Village to John Crawford from Richard Gibbons and wife, shows by the date that he was there as early as 1678. When he died is not known, but he was buried in the grave yard in the rear of the farm house, now occupied by Richard Crawford. The following deed shows that his oldest son, George, inherited his property.

DEED FROM JAMES HUTCHINS,
TO GEORGE CRAWFORD.

To all to whom these presents shall come, James Hutchins, of Middletown in the county of Monmouth and Eastern Division of the Province of New Jersey, Esq'r, sends greeting. Know ye, that the said James Hutchins, for divers good causes and valuable considerations him thereunto especially moving, hath remised, released and forever quit claimed, and by these presents for himself and his heirs, doth fully, clearly and absolutely remise, release and forever quit claim, unto George Crawford of Middletown, aforesaid, Yeoman, eldest son and heir at law to John Crawford, deceased, in his full and peaceble possession and seizen, and to his heirs and assigns forever. All such right, estate, tytle, interest and demand whatsoever, as he, the said James Hutchins now hath, ever had or ought to have, of, in or to all that land that lyes to the northard of a line, Beginning at a black oak tree marked on four sides, standing by the road that goes from Skunk Hill to the Falls; thence running east, forty-three chains to a white oak tree marked on four sides, standing in Nutswamp by the brook; thence running down the said Nutswamp Brook, as the brook runs, to Mordecai Gibbons line.

Together with all and singular, and every the rights, members and appurtenances to the land, to the northard of the said line and Nutswamp brook, belonging by any ways or means whatsoever.

To have and to hold the said land that lyes to the northard of the said east line and said Nutswamp Brook, and all and singular and every, the appurtenances and premises thereof, unto him, the said George Crawford, his heirs and assigns forever, to the only proper use and uses, benefit and behoof of him, the said George Crawford, his heirs and assigns forever, so that neither he, the said James Hutchins, nor his heirs, nor any other person or persons whatsoever, for him or them or in his or their names, or in the name, right or stead of them, shall or will, by any ways or means hereafter, have, claim, challenge or demand, any estate, right, tytle or interest of, in or to the land and premises thereof, that lyes to the northard of the said east line and Nutswamp brook, or to any part or parcel thereof, but from all and every, action, right, estate, tytle, interest and demand of, in or to the same, or any part or parcel thereof, they and every of them, shall be utterly excluded and barred forever by these presents, and also he, the said James Hutchins, doth for himself, his heirs, executors and administrators, covenant, promise, grant and agree, to and with him, the same George Crawford, his heirs and assigns, that the said James Hutchins and his heir, the said land that lyes to the northard of the said line and Nutswamp brook as above described, for the division and the premises and the appurtenances thereof, unto him, the said George Crawford, his heirs and assigns, to his and their own proper use and uses, against the said James Hutchins and his heirs, and all others claiming by, from or under him, shall and will warrant and forever defend by these presents.

In witness whereof, he, the said James Hutchins, hath hereunto set his hand and seal, this third day of April, in the fourth year of the reign of our Sovereign Lord, George the Second, over Great Brittain, &c., King, Annog Dom. one thousand seven hundred and thirty-one.

JAMES HUTCHINS, [L.S.]

Signed, sealed and
delivered in the
presence of

FRANCIS LOVE,
ANDREW CRAWFORD.

This deed appears never to have been recorded.

George Crawford, named in above deed, married one Esther Scott, of the Scott family in Shrewsbury, and lived on the homestead until his death. The following is a copy of his Will.

"In the name of God, Amen, the fifteenth day of March, one thousand seven hundred and forty five, coming six, I, George Crawford, of Middletown, in the County of Monmouth and Eastern Division of the Province of New Jersey, Farmer, very sick and weak in body, but of perfect mind and memory, thanks be given unto God. Therefore, calling unto mind the mortality of my body, and knowing that is appointed for all men once to dye, do make and ordain this, my last will and testament, that is to say, principally and first of all, I give and recommend my soul into the hands of God that gave it, and for my body, I recommend it to the earth to be buried in a christian like and decent manner, at the discretion of my executors, nothing doubting, but at the general resurrection I shall receive the same again, by the mighty power of God. And as touching such wordly estate, wherewith it hath pleased God in this life, to bless me with, I give, devise and dispose of the same, in the following manner and form.

Imprimus.—I give and bequeath unto Ester, my dearly beloved wife, her choice of my beds, and the furniture thereunto belonging, and the use of all my plantation as long as she remains my widow, and all her wearing apparell.

Item, I give to my well beloved sons, George Crawford and Richard, all my lands with the improvements thereon, after my said wife's decease, to be equally divided between them, to them, their heirs and assigns forever, they paying the legacy hereinafter mentioned, that is to say, to my son William, one hundred and fifty pounds. To my son Joshua, one hundred and fifty pounds. To my son Job, one hundred and fifty pounds, the said sums to be paid to my said sons, and to each of them, when they come to age of twenty-one years, and if any of them, my said sons should chance to dye, before they arrive to that age, then the said sums of one hundred and fifty pounds to be paid to the next in heirship. Item.—I give to my well beloved daughter Lydia, the sum of eighty pounds, to be paid to her when she arrives at the age of eighteen years. Item, I give to the child whereof my wife is now big, if it should prove a son, the sum of one hundred and fifty pounds, to be paid at the age of twenty-one years, and if it proves a daughter, the sum of eighty pounds, to be paid her at the age of eighteen years. Item, all my moveable estate I leave towards the maintainance of my family. Item, I give unto my son George Crawford, over and above the one equal half of my lands and tenaments, one two year old brown mare, whom, together with my loving friends, Joseph Stillwell and James Mott, I constitute, make, and ordain, executors of this my last will and testament, and I do hereby, utterly disallow, revoke and disanul, all and every other former testaments, wills, legacies and executors by me, in any ways before this time, named, willed and bequeathed, ratifying and confirming this and no other, to be my last will and testament.

In witness whereof I have hereunto set my hand and seal, the day and year above written.   GEORGE CRAWFORD, [L.S.]
Signed, sealed, published and pronounced by the said George Crawford, as his last will and testa-ment in the presence of us, the subscribers,
SAMUEL OGBORNE,
JOSEPH SHEPHERD,
WILLIAM CRADDOCK,

This will is written on parchment; annexed is a certificate, that the will was proved at Perth Amboy, May 10th, 1745, before Thomas Bartow, and administration granted to George Crawford, Joseph Stillwell and James Mott, the executors.

The anticipated child proved to be a daughter, and was named Elizabeth. Of the sons, George died young and unmarried, Joshua and Job a short time after they arrived of age, left the State; one settled in Pennsylvania, the other in Georgia. Their posterity are said to be numerous at this day in both States. William followed the sea, and became a sea captain. He married Catherine Bowne and had two sons and one daughter, of whom more hereafter.

Richard Crawford at the death of his brother George, became the owner of the whole of the real estate of his father, George Crawford. He married Catherine Shepherd, and lived on the old homestead until his death, which occurred Sept. 20, 1798, aged sixty years; his wife died Jan. 13, 1807, aged seventy two years. He was an active and leading member of the Baptist church of Middletown, and contributed much toward its support. After the battle of Monmouth, his house for one or two days was occupied by Gen'l Clinton, as headquarters. Seven valuable horses were stolen from his stable by the Hessians, and seven broken down army horses left in their place. He complained to General Clinton about it, but got no satisfaction.

The following is a copy of Richard Crawford's will:

In the name of God, Amen. I, Richard Crawford, of Middletown, in the county of Monmouth, being weak in body, but of sound and disposing memory, do make and ordain this to be my last will and testament, in manner and form following.—First, it is my will that all my just debts and funeral charges be paid out of my estate. Secondly, my will is and I do hereby give and bequeath unto my son, Richard Crawford, all my lands and meadows wheresoever lying, to him, his heirs and assigns, forever. Thirdly, I give unto my loving wife Catherine Crawford, the choice of the best bed and furniture, and the cnoice of the best room belonging to my house. My will and desire also is that my son, Richard Crawford, do support his mother decently out of my estate, as long as she remains my widow, but in case of remarriage, then my will and desire is, she have best bed and furniture belonging to my house, and fifty pounds to be paid in lieu of her third or dower, by my son, Richard Crawford. I also give unto my son Richard, my two young sorrels, the one a horse, the other a mare, and all the remaining part of my moveable estate, except such part as shall be hereafter otherwise disposed.

My will and desire is, that my son Richard, do pay unto my son George, the sum of two hundred and fifty pounds, as his legacy out of my estate. My will further is that my son George, have the one equal half of my apple nursery, he being at equal expense in pruning and keeping the same. Also that my son George have one small brown colt, called Liberty; and my will and is that my son Richard, do pay unto my daughter Catherine Leonard, the sum of one hundred and twenty pounds. Also to my daughter Ester, the sum of one hundred and twenty pounds, and to my daughter Hannah; one hundred and twenty pounds, my daughters Catherine and Ester's legacies to be paid in two years, after the date of these presents, and my daughter Hannah's to be paid, when she arrives at the age of eighteen, and my son George's legacy to be paid one year and a half after the date hereof. And my will and desire is that my son Richard, do give unto my grand daughter, Polly Leonard, one cow and calf, if she lives to the age of twenty-one. The whole of the legacies herein mentioned, to be paid in Spanish milled dollars at eight shillings, or in money to the value thereof. And I do hereby nominate, constitute and appoint my two sons, Richard and George Crawford, and my brother, William Crawford, executors of this my last will and testament. ratifying and confirming this, and making null and void all other wills by me heretofore made.

In witness whereof, I have hereunto set my hand and seal, this fourth day of May, in the year one thousand seven hundred and eighty one.

    RICHARD CRAWFORD, [L.S.]

Signed, sealed, published, pronounced and declared to be the last will and testament of the testa- tor, in the presence of us,

WILLIAM VANCLEEF, }
SAMUEL OGBORNE, }
JOSEPH MEXSON. }

Of the daughters named in this will, (1) Catherine married Nathaniel Leonard and had one daughter, who married Samuel C. Mott, and had the following children: Leonard and Samuel Mott, Ann Maria Mott, Jerusha Mott, Clementina Mott and Catherine Mott.

(2.) Ester married Thomas Burrowes, and had two sons and two daughters, (I,) Edward, who married his cousin Catherine, daughter of George Crawford by his first wife, Mary Seabrook. II. Richard, who married a daughter of Joseph Taylor, at Middletown. III. Catherine Burrowes married William Tilton. IV. Deborah married Richard Walling.

(3.) Hannah Crawford married Timothy White, and had two daughters, Catharine and Jemima. Jemima died young, and Catherine married Garret Morford, of Red Bank.

OF THE SONS OF RICHARD CRAWFORD,

(1.) George Crawford married as his first wife, Mary, daughter of Major Thomas Seabrook, and had one daughter, Catherine, who married Edward Burrowes, as above stated. After death of his wife, George Crawford married a second wife, Eleanor, a daughter of Hendrick Schanck by his wife Catherine Holmes, daughter of Jonathan Holmes; by his last wife he had four daughters. I. Mary, who married William W. Murray, II. Adaline, who married John Lloyd Hendrickson. III. Ann, who married Rev. Jacob TenBroeck Beekman. IV. Eleanor, who died young. Mary Seabrook, first wife of George Crawford, died Jan. 9, 1795, aged 28 years. Eleanor Schanck, second wife of George Crawford, died May 17, 1850, aged 86 years. George Crawford died July 11th, 1834, in his 76th year. They are all buried in the grave yard on the old Crawford homestead, in the rear of the mansion house, where John B. Crawford lived until his death, now occupied by his son Richard.

(2.) Richard, the son of Richard, who inherited the homestead, married Rebecca Stillwell, and lived on the old homestead until his death, which occurred Nov. 12, 1837, aged 81 years; during the war he was an efficient friend to the country. The following paper is still possessed and in the hands of his grandson. George W. Crawford.

This may certify that the bearer hereof, Mr. Richard Crawford, Jr., an inhabitant of Monmouth, has during this contest with Great Brittain, distinguished himself both as a citizen and a soldier, a firm and steady friend to the United States of America.

ASHER HOLMES.
Col. of first Reg't. M. M.
Monmouth County, April 19, 1783.

Richard Crawford by his wife, Rebecca, Stillwell, had one son, Richard, who died unmarried and comparitively young, and one daughter, Catherine, who married her second cousin, John Bowne Crawford, a grandson of William Crawford and his wife Catherine Bowne, of whom more hereafter. Catherine Crawford and her husband, John Bowne Crawford, had the following children : George W. Crawford and Richard Crawford, who occupy the old Crawford homestead; Rebecca S., who married Robert Allen, Jr., the well known lawyer at Red Bank. Catherine E., who married John D. Buckelew, of Jamesburg, formerly Sheriff of Middlesex County, and lately U. S. Consul at Stettin, in Germany. These are the descendants of Richard Crawford, son of George Crawford, William Crawford, brother of the first Richard, and son of George, married as before stated Catherine Bowne, and had one daughter, Ester, and two sons, John and William.

(1.) John married Caroline, daughter of Elnathan Fields, and had five sons, Andrew, William, John, Elnathan and James G. Andrew, Elnathan and John died young and unmarried. William married Elizabeth Fields and died childless. James G. married Elizabeth Smith and had two sons William and John J., both of whom now live in Holmdel township, and are amongst the first farmers of the county, and four daughters, Caroline, Ann, Mary and Elizabeth. Caroline married Sheriff Holmes Conover, and Ann married Joseph Holmes, now a leading farmer in the township of Holmdel.

(2.) William, the other son of William Crawford and Catherine Bowne, married Rebecca Patterson and had four sons. 1, John Bowne ; 2, William ; 3, Willfam H. 4. James P., and two daughters, Ann B. and Catherine.

(1.) John Bowne Crawford married his second cousin, Catherine, daughter of Richard Crawford, as before stated. (2.) William died young. (3.) William H. married Leah Conover, sister of Sheriff Holmes Conover, and had five sons and four daughters. (4.) James P. married Margaretta Bowne and had five children. (6) Ann B., the daughter married Hendrick Conover and had two sons, William and Jacob Conover, and four daughters. William Conover died young, and Jacob Conover, known as " Farmer Jacob," married Ellen Vanderveer and had three daughters, one of whom married a Scudder, of the celebrated missionary Scudders, and lately deceased. Rebecca Conover, a daughter of Hendrick Conover and Ann B. Crawford, married Tunis Conover.— Mary, second daughter of Hendrick Conover and Ann B. Crawford, married Judge James S. Lawrence. Ann, third daughter, married Charles Belden, and Catherine, the fourth daughter, married Dr. Wm. Johnson Conover.

THE Battle of Monmouth.

Compiled for the MONMOUTH DEMOCRAT from Contemporaneous History and designed to include everything of interest relating to that event.

The approach of the centennial anniversary of the Battle of Monmouth, which took place on the 28th of June, 1778, has awakened a renewed interest in that event, the result of which, in favor of the American arms, revived the drooping hopes of the people, and lent new energy to WASHINGTON and the brave and patriotic officers and soldiers of his army. In the lapse of time the details of the battle, and of the events connected with it, have long ceased to be subjects of discussion, and are fading from the memory of the survivors of the generation immediately succeeding that which participated in its scenes.— Much of it has never been brought to the notice of the present generation, but lies buried in long forgotten volumes, and in files of old newspapers, not easily accessible to the general public. These details at this time have a fascinating interest to the student of history, and will be eagerly perused by ordinary readers.

Over a year ago we began to collect from old publications the accounts of this battle. At first the results were meagre, and were principally confined to the American and British accounts written and published at the time. These accounts referred to matters that required further research to elucidate, and the result has been the accumulation of a very much larger amount of interesting matter than was at first anticipated. Instead of using these materials to construct a connected narrative which should embrace all the points of interest contained therein, we have determined, under the advice of friends to whom we have submitted them, to publish them entire, and by so doing put them in a shape to be preserved, and easily accessible to the future historian.

With this introduction we commence the publication; first, however, pausing to give a synopsis of events immediately preceding the battle, that our readers may understand the state of public sentiment at that time, the condition of the opposing armies, and the spirit which animated each of them.

EVENTS PRECEDING THE BATTLE.

At the close of the campaign of 1777 the British had complete possession of the Delaware river from Philadelphia to the sea, and of the country lying adjacent on both sides of the river, which afforded ample means of 'subsistence to the army quartered in Philadelphia, where Sir WILLIAM HOWE and his officers spent the winter in a round of balls, revelry and dissipation, winding up in the Spring with a grand ovation to Sir WILLIAM upon the eve of his departure for England. This was an entertainment devised and carried out by Major ANDRE, and was participated in by many of the ladies of Philadelphia, representatives of some of the aristocratic families still extant there. The entertainment was called "The Mischianza." It began at four o'clock in the afternoon of the 18th of May, and ended at four the next morning. It consisted of a variety of parts, including a grand procession of boats on the Delaware, a mock tournament, a grand ball on the shore under pavilions constructed for the purpose, and concluded with a costly display of fireworks.

In the meantime WASHINGTON and his devoted army were starving for food and almost destitute of clothing at Valley Forge, about sixteen miles from Philadelphia, where they built themselves huts and threw up strong earthworks for their defense. The weather was severely cold, and their sufferings were terrible. Gen. GREENE, on the 4th of December said :— "One half of our troops are without breeches, shoes and stockings, and some thousands without blankets. Last winter's campaign will confirm this truth, that unless men are well clothed, they must fall a sacrifice to the severity of the weather, when exposed to the hardships of a winter's campaign." Gen. WASHINGTON said to a friend : "Through the want of shoes and stockings, and the hard frozen ground, you might have tracked the army from White Marsh to Valley Forge by the blood of their feet." Again, in writing to the President of Congress, he said: "I would beg leave to mention that we are in great distress for want of money." In another letter he refers to a proposition to seize and force supplies from the people, and objects to it, that it would "embitter the minds of the people, and excite perhaps, a hurtful jealousy against the army." Notwithstanding their dire necessities, he preferred to endure them rather than endanger the cause of American liberty. He took up his position at Valley Forge that he might watch the enemy, and be ready to strike, should opportunity offer, any blow that might encourage the people to hope for the success of the cause.

What tended to aggravate the feelings of the army in this condition of affairs, was the fact that supplies of shoes, stockings and clothing were at different places and in the woods, lying and perishing for want of teams, and money to pay for the transportation. Gen. MIFFLIN was Quarter-Master General, but his health was so much impaired as to unfit him for duty, and he had resigned his commission some time before. At one time in December the army was four days without bread, and on the fifth day two regiments refused to do duty on that account, and only the prudence and persuasions of WASHINGTON prevented a mutiny and restored order. GORDON, in his history, quotes from a letter of WASHINGTON on the 23d of the same month, referring to a similar event, as follows : "This brought forth the only commissary in the purchasing line in this camp, and with him the melancholy alarming truth, that he had not a single hoof of any kind to slaughter, and not more than twenty five barrels of flour, and could not tell when to expect any. The present commissaries are by no means equal to the execution of the office, or the disaffection of the people is past all belief. * * Since the month of July we have had no assistance from the quarter-master General, and to want of assistance from this department the commissary General charges great part of his deficiency."— There were then nearly three thousand men in camp unfit for duty, because they were barefooted or otherwise deficient in clothing. For want of blankets numbers were obliged to sit up all night by fires, and yet WASHINGTON felt obliged to conceal the destitution and sufferings of his army, in order to support the confidence of the public, and exposed himself to detraction and calumny thereby.

New York was also in the possession of the British, under Lord HOWE. From here they made incursions into the country and committed depredations upon the property of prominent persons identified with the American cause. Our readers may form some idea of the feeling existing, from the following instance related in *Gordon's History :* "On the 18th of No-

OLD TIMES IN OLD MONMOUTH.

vember, Gen. TRYON sent about one hundred men under Capt. EMMERICK to burn some houses on PHILLIP'S manor, within about four miles of Gen. PARSON'S guard They effected it with circumstances of barbarity, stripping the clothing off the women and children, and turning them almost naked into the streets in a most severely cold night. The men were then made prisoners, and led with halters about their necks, with no other clothes than their shirts and breeches, in triumph to the British lines. A few days after PARSONS wrote to TRYON upon the occasion expostulating with him upon the business, and told him that he could destroy the houses and buildings of Colonel PHILLIPS and those belonging to the DELANCY family, each as near their lines as the buildings destroyed were to his guards; that not withstanding all their vigilance the destruction could not be prevented, and that it was not fear or want of opportunity, but a sense of the injustice and savageness of such a line of conduct, that had hitherto saved the buildings. TRYON answered from Kings Bridge on the 23d, and said, among other things, "Sir, could I possibly conceive myself accountable to any revolted subjects of the King of Great Britain, I might answer your letter of yesterday respecting the conduct of Capt. EMMERICK'S party upon the taking of PETER and CORNELIUS VANTASSEL. As much as I abhor every principle of inhumanity or ungenerous conduct, I should, were I in more authority, burn every committee-man's house within my reach, as I deem them the wicked instruments of the continued calamities of this country; and in order the sooner to purge the colony of them, I am willing to give twenty silver dollars for every acting committee-man, who shall be delivered up to the King's troops."— The stinging repartee made to this letter was contained in an expedition undertaken immediately after to Greenwich, about three miles from New York, where a small party arrived in the evening, advanced to Mr. OLIVER DELANCY'S house, secured the sentry, dismissed a few ladies in peace, though rather hastily, made a few men prisoners, burnt the house, occasioned the firing of the alarm gun in New York, then crossed the river and got safe off."

Another depressing feature of the times was the barbarous treatment of prisoners in the hands of the British. In Philadelphia they were confined in loathsome jails, and in New York in Sugar Houses and Prison Ships. It was a common practice when they were first taken to keep them several days without a morsel of food, and then to tempt them to join the British army. There were numerous instances of prisoners perishing from hunger. The general allowance of food did not exceed four ounces of meat and as much bread per day, and this often so damaged as to be uneatable.

On the 15th of November Congress adopted the first constitution, or "Articles of Confederation and Perpetual Union," and the confederacy then assumed the name of 'The United States of America." In December the "Conway Cabal," an intrigue to remove WASHINGTON from the command of the army, made its appearance in Congress. CONWAY was a French officer of Irish descent, who at the recommendation of SILAS DEAN, American representative to France, was appointed a Brigadier General. He was ambitious of further promotion, to which WASHINGTON was opposed. Learning that Congress was likely to grant CONWAY'S wish. WASHINGTON wrote to RICHARD HENRY LEE, then in Congress, warning him that the appointment would give a fatal blow to the existence of the army. That "General CONWAY'S merit as an officer and his importance in this army exists more in his own imagination than in reality.— For it is a maxim with him to leave no service of his own untold, nor to want anything which is to be obtained by importunity." CONWAY was the youngest brigadier in the service, and his effort was for a major-general's commission over the heads of the oldest officers in the service. A sentence in a letter from CONWAY to GATES, who hoped to supercede WASHINGTON, as Commander in Chief, was exposed by Gen. WILKINSON, when under the influence of liquor, and this led to the explosion of the conspiracy. CONWAY subsequently was wounded in a duel with General CADWALADER, and supposing himself to be dying, sent an humble apology to WASHINGTON for the part he had taken in it.

General LEE was a prisoner of war in New York, and was writing letters to friends in Philadelphia for his dogs to be sent to keep him company, and to Congress and to WASHINGTON, relative to his exchange. In December of 1776, LEE with an army of 3,000, instead of joining WASHINGTON as he had been repeatedly ordered to do, hung on the rear of the British army, which under CORNWALLIS had crossed the Hudson into New Jersey, and were supposed to be marching for Philadelphia. LEE'S object, in neglecting to obey WASHINGTON'S orders, appeared to be the hope of an opportunity to make some happy stroke that would raise him in popular estimation, and lead to the prize he so much coveted, that of Commander in Chief. On Dec. 12th, he had moved from Morristown to Vealtown, where he left the troops, and took up his quarters three miles off, at a tavern at Baskingridge. A tory who had learned where LEE was to lodge and breakfast, went immediately to New Brunswick, eighteen miles distant, and gave the information to the British. It was ten o'clock next morning, when LEE took breakfast, and after breakfast while he was writing a letter, a company of dragoons surprised the guard, surrounded the house, took LEE just as he was, in slippers and without a hat, mounted him on a horse, and hurried him off. *Irving*, speaking of this affair, says: "The loss of LEE was a severe shock to the Americans; many of whom, as we have shown, looked to him as the man who was to rescue them from their critical, and well-nigh desperate situation. With their regrets, however, were mingled painful doubts, caused by his delay in obeying the repeated summons of his commander-in-chief, when the latter was in peril; and by his exposing himself so unguardedly in the very neighborhood of the enemy. Some at first suspected that he had done so designedly and with collusion; but this was soon disproved by the indignities attending his capture, and his rigorous treatment subsequently by the British; who affected to consider him a deserter, from his having formerly served in their army." It may be well to remark here that when LEE joined the American army, he was a Major or Lieutenant-Colonel in the British Army. He had not been in active service, but was on half-pay; and had been in this country several years before the war broke out. As LEE will play a very prominent part in the history of the battle of Monmouth, these details in regard to his connection with the army, are necessary to a clear understanding of his conduct on that occasion, as will be fully shown hereafter.

And here we insert a document which was first brought to light in this country, in 1858, by Mr. GEORGE H. MOORE, librarian of the New York Historical Society, and published by him in a paper read before that society, and sub equently in a printed volume, accompanied by a sketch of LEE's history. The document had been surreptitiously obtained from a connection of LEE'S family in England, who had possession of his papers. and brought to this country and offered for sale. Mr. MOORE, after writing to England, and satisfying himself of the authenticity of the document, purchased it, and was afterwards permitted to retain it by the gentleman from whose custody it had been unlawfully obtained. It goes a great way in clearing up the mystery that surrounded LEE's conduct at the Battle of Monmouth. and leads inevitably, we think, to the conclusion that he was in sympathy with the British cause, and that he meant to betray the Americans on that occasion. The document is endorsed as "Mr. LEE'S Plan," and was written at the time he was a prisoner in the hands of the British in New York, and was submitted to Lord HOWE, who was then in command there. In the condition of the American cause at that time, struggling with drooping spirits of the people. and a very large portion of them looking for a reconciliation with the mother country, this " Plan," it must be admitted, was very shrewdly devised. It was accepted by Lord HOWE, but the attempt to carry it into effect was unsuccessful. Its success was only prevented, in the opinion of some of our leading men at that time, "by the interposition of Divine Providence." The following is a literal copy of the document, as published by Mr. MOORE:

"Mr. LEE's PLAN—*29th March*, 1777.

"As on the one hand it appears to me that by the continuance of the War America has no chance of obtaining the ends She proposes to herself; that altho by struggling She may put the Mother Country to very serious expense both in blood and Money, yet She must in the end, after great desolation, havock and slaughter. be reduc'd to submit to terms much harder than might probably be granted at present—and as on the other hand Great Britain tho' ultimately victorious, must suffer very heavily even in the process of her victories, evry life lost and evry guinea spent being in fact worse than thrown away: it is only wasting her own property, shedding her own blood and destroying her own strength; and as I am not only persuaded from the high opinion I have of the humanity and good sense of Lord and General Howe that the terms of accommodation will be as moderate as their powers will admit, but that their powers are more ample than their Successors (shoud any accident happen) wou'd be vested with, I think myself not only justifiable but bound in conscience to furnish all the lights, I can, to enable 'em to bring matters to a conclusion in the most compendious manner and consequently the least expensive to both Parties—I do this with the more readiness as I know the most generous use will be made of it in all respects—their humanity will incline 'em to have consideration for Individuals who have acted from principle and their good sense will tell 'em that the more moderate are the general conditions; the more solid and permanent will be the union, for if the conditions were extremely repugnant to the general way of thinking, it wou'd be only the mere patchwork of a day which the first breath of wind will discompose and the first symptoms of a rupture betwixt the Bourbon Powers and Great Britain absolutely overturn—but I really have no apprehensions of this kind whilst Lord and General Howe have the direction of affairs, and flatter myself that under their auspices an accommodation may be built on so solid a foundation as not to be shaken by any such incident—in this persuasion and on these principles I shall most sincerely and zealously contribute all in my power to so desirable an end, and if no untoward accidents fall out which no human foresight can guard against I will answer with my lips for the success.

"From my present situation and ignorance of certain facts, I am sensible that I hazard proposing things which cannot without difficulties be comply'd with; I can only act from surmise, therefore hope allowances will be made for my circumstances. I will suppose then that (exclusive of the Troops requisite for the security of Rhode Island and N. York) General Howe's Army (comprehending every species, British, Hessians and Provincials) amounts to twenty thousand men capable to take the field and act offensively; by which I mean to move to any part of the Continent where occasion requires—I will suppose that the General's design with this force is to clear the Jersey's and take possession of Philadelphia—but in my opinion the taking possession of Philadelphia will not have any decisive consequences—the Congress and People adhering to the Congress have already made up their minds for the event; already They have turn'd their eyes to other places where They can fix their seat of residence, carry on in some measure their Government; in short expecting this event They have devis'd measures for protracting the War in hopes of some favourable turn of affairs in Europe—the taking possession therefore of Philadelphia or any one or two Towns more, which the General may have in view, will not be decisive –to bring matters to a conclusion, it is necessary to unhinge or dissolve, if I may so express myself, the whole system or machine of resistance, or in other terms, Congress Government—this system or machine, as affairs now stand, depends entirely on the circumstances and disposition of the People of Maryland Virginia and Pennsylvania—if the Province of Maryland or the greater part of it is reduc'd or submits, and the People of Virginia are prevented or intimidated from marching aid to the Pennsylvania Army the whole machine is dissolv'd and a period put to the War, to accomplish which, is, the object of the scheme which I now take the liberty of offering to the consideration of his Lordship and the General, and if it is adopted in full I am so confident of the success that I wou'd stake my life on the issue—I have at the same time the comfort to reflect, that in pointing out measures which I know to be the most effectual I point out those which will be attended with no bloodshed or desolation to the Colonies. As the difficulty of passing and of re-passing the North River and the apprehensions from General Carlton's Army will I am confident keep the New Englanders at home, or at least confine 'em to the East side the River; and as their Provinces are at present neither the seat of Government strength nor Politicks, I cannot see that any offensive operations against these Provinces wou'd answer any sort of Purpose—to secure N. York and Rhode Island against their attacks will be sufficient. On the supposition then, that General Howe's Army (including every species of Troops) amounts to twenty or even eighteen thousand men at liberty to move to any part of the continent; as fourteen thoushand will be more than sufficient to clear the Jersey's and take possession of Philadelphia, I wou'd propose that four thoushand men be immediately embark'd in transports, one half of which shou'd proceed up the Potomac and take part at Alexandria, the other half up Chesepeak Bay and possess themselves of Annapolis. They will most probably meet with no opposition in taking possession of these Ports, and when possess'd they are so very strong by nature that a few hours work and some trifling artillery will secure them against the attacks of a much greater force than can possibly be brought down against them—their communications with the shipping will be constant and sure—for at Alexandria Vessels of a very con siderable burthen (of five or six hundred Tons for instance) can lie in close to the shore, and at Annapolis within musket shot—all the necessaries and refreshments for an Army are near at hand, and in the greatest abundance –Kent Island will supply that of Annapolis and every part on both banks of the Patomac that of Alexandria. These Ports may with ease support each other, as it is but two easy days march from one to the other, and if occasion requires by a single days march, They may join a and conjointly carry on their operations wherever it may be thought eligible to direct 'em; whether to take possession of Baltimore or post themselves on some spot on the Westward bank of the Susquehanna which is a point of the utmost importance—but here I must beg leave to observe that there is a measure which if the General assents to and adopts will be attended with momentous and the most happy consequences—I mean that from these Posts proclamations of pardon shou'd be issued to all those who come in at a given day, and I will answer for it with my life—that all the Inhabitants of that great tract southward of the Patapsico and lying betwixt the Patomac and Chesepeak Bay and those on the Eastern Shore of Maryland will immediately lay down their arms—but this is not all, I am much mistaken if those potent and populous German districts, Frederic County in Maryland and York

in Pennsylvania do not follow their example—These Germans are extremely numerous, and to a Man have hitherto been the most staunch Assertors of the American cause; but at the same time are so remarkably tenacious of their property and apprehensive of the least injury being done to their fine farms that I have no doubt when They see a probability of their Country becoming the seat of War They will give up all opposition but if contrary to my expectations a force should be assembled at Alexandria sufficient to prevent the Corps detach'd thither from taking possession immediately of the place, it will make no disadvantageous alteration, but rather the reverse—a variety of spots near Alexandria on either bank of the Patomac may be chosen for Ports equally well calculated for all the great purposes I have mentioned—viz—for the reduction or compulsion to submission of the whole Province of Maryland for the preventing or intimidating Virginia from sending aids to Pennsylvania—for in fact if any force is assembled at Alexandria sufficient to oppose the Troops sent against it, getting possession of it, it must be at the expence of the more Northern Army, as they must be compos'd of those Troops which were otherwise destin'd for Pennsylvania—to say all in a word, it will unhinge and dissolve the whole system of defence. I am so confident of the event that I will venture to assert with the penalty of my life if the plan is fully adopted, and no accidents (such as a rupture between the Powers of Europe) intervenes that in less than two months from the date of the proclamation not a spark of this desolating war remains unextinguished in any part of the Continent.

From Gordon's History of New Jersey.*

About the time the command of the army devolved upon Sir Henry Clinton, orders were received for the evacuation of Philadelphia. The part which France was about to take in the war, with the naval force she had prepared, rendered this city a dangerous position, and determined the administration, entirely, to abandon the Delaware. Preparations to this end were actively pursued, but it was some time uncertain to what point the army was destined. At length the intention was apparent to reach New York through the Jerseys. Upon this pre-

"A On the Road from Annapolis to Queen Ann there is one considerable River to be pass'd, but as the ships boats can easily be brought round from the Bay to the usual place of passage or Ferry, this is no impediment if the Two Corps chuse to unite They may by a single days march either at Queen Anns or Marlborough."

* The History of New Jersey from its Discovery by Europeans to the adoption of the Federal Constitution. By Thomas F. Gordon, Trenton. Published by Daniel Fenton, 1834.

sumption General Washington conducted his operations.

General Maxwell, with the Jersey Brigade, was ordered to take post about Mount Holly and to unite with Majorgeneral Dickenson, who was assembling the militia for the purpose of breaking down bridges, falling trees in the roads, and otherwise embarassing the march of the British general. Instructions were given to these officers to guard carefully against a *coup de main*, and to keep the militia in small light parties on his flanks.

When Washington learned that the greater proportion of the British army had crossed the Delaware,† he convened a council of general officers to determine on his course. The force of the armies was nearly equal, the numerical advantage being with the Americans; the British having ten, and the Americans between ten and eleven thousand. Of seventeen general officers, Wayne and Cadwalader alone were decidedly in favor of attacking the enemy. LaFayette inclined to that opinion without openly embracing it. Consequently it was resolved not to risk a battle.

Sir Henry Clinton moved with great deliberation, seeming to await the approach of his adversary. He proceeded through Haddonfield,‡ Mount Holly, Slabtown and Crosswicks, to Allentown and Imlaystown, which he reached on the twenty-fourth.

Dickenson and Maxwell retired before him, unable to obstruct his march otherwise than by destroying the bridges. As his route, until he passed Crosswicks, lay directly up the Delaware, and at no great distance from it, General Washington found it necessary to make an extensive circuit to pass the river at Coryell's Ferry. Pursuant to the settled plan of avoiding an engagement he kept the high grounds, directing his army so as to cover the important passes of the Highlands. He crossed the river on the twenty-second, and remained the twenty-third at Hopewell, in elevated country, adjacent to the river.

General Arnold, whose wounds yet unfitted him for service, was directed to possess himself of Philadelphia, and to detach four hundred continental troops and such militia as could be collected, to harass the rear of the enemy.

† June 18, 1778.
‡ The night that the British encamped at Haddonfield, Captain McLane, by order from General Arnold, passed through their camp, and reported their situation to the general.

This service, by the order of the commander-in-chief, was confided to General Cadwalader, who could only add to his continental force fifty volunteers and forty militia, commanded by General Lacy. From Hopewell, Morgan, with six hundred riflemen, was detatched to annoy his right flank; Dickenson, with about one thousand Jersey militia, and Maxwell's brigade, hung on his left.

In this position of the armies General Washington, who had rather acquiesced in than approved the decision of the late council of war, and was disposed to seek battle, again submitted the proposal to the consideration of the general officers, by whom it was again negatived. By their advice a chosen body of fifteen hundred men, under Brigadier-general Scott, was added to the corps on the left flank of the enemy. But Washington being supported by the wishes of some officers whom he highly valued, determined, on his own responsibility, to bring on a general engagement. The enemy being on his march to Monmouth Court-House, he resolved to strengthen the force on his lines by despatching General Wayne with an additional corps of one thousand men. The continental troops, now thrown in front of the army, amounted to four thousand men, a force sufficient to require the direction of a major-general. The tour of duty was General Lee's, but he having declared strongly against hazarding, even a partial engagement, and supposing that, in conformity with the advice signed by all the generals in camp, save one, nothing would be attempted beyond reconnoitering the enemy and restraining the plundering parties, showed no disposition to assert his claim, but yielded the command to General LaFayette. All the continental parties on the lines were placed under his direction, with orders to take measures in concert with General Dickenson, to impede the march of the British and to occasion them the greatest loss.— These measures demonstrated the wishes of the commander-in-chief, tending almost inevitably to a general battle.— Wayne had earnestly advised it, and La-Fayette inclined towards a partial engagement. Colonel Hamilton, who accompanied him, had the strongest desire to signalize the detachment, and to accomplish all the wishes of Washington. These dispositions having been made the main army was moved to Cranberry on the 26th, to support the advance. The intense heat of the weather, a heavy storm, and a temporary want of provisions, prevented it from proceeding further next day. The advanced corps had pressed forward and taken a position on the Monmouth road, about five miles in the rear of the enemy, with the intention of attacking him on the next morning. It was now, however, too remote and too far on the right to be supported in case of action; and, pursuant to orders, the Marquis filed off by his left towards Englishtown, early in the morning of the 27th.

General Lee had declined the command of the advance party, under the opinion that it was not designed for effective service; but perceiving soon after its march that much importance was attached to it, and dreading lest his reputation might suffer, he earnestly solicited to be placed at its head. To relieve his feelings, without wounding those of LaFayette, Washington detached the former with two other brigades to support the Marquis. Lee would, of course, have the direction of the whole front division, amounting now to five thousand men; but he stipulated that if any enterprise had been formed by LaFayette, it should be executed as if the commanding officer had not been changed.

Sir Henry Clinton had taken a strong position on the high grounds about Monmouth Court House; having his right flank in the skirt of a small wood, his left secured by a thick one, and a morass towards his rear. His whole front was also covered by a wood, and for a considerable distance toward his left, by a morass, and he was within twelve miles of the high grounds about Middletown; after reaching which he would be perfectly secure.

Under these circumstances, General Washington determined to attack their rear, the moment they should move from their ground. This determination was communicated to Lee, with orders to make his disposition and to keep his troops constantly lying on their arms, that he might be in readiness to take advantage of the first movement. Corresponding orders were also given to the rear division.

About five in the morning of the twenty-eighth, intelligence was received from General Dickenson, that the front of the enemy was in motion. The troops were immediately under arms, and Lee was directed to move on and attack the rear,

" unless there should be powerful reasons to the contrary." He was at the same time informed, that the main army would march to support him.

Sir Henry Clinton, perceiving that the Americans were in his neighborhood, changed the order of his march. The baggage was placed under the care of General Knyphausen, while the flower of this army, unincumbered, formed the rear division commanded by Lord Cornwalis; who, to avoid pressing upon Knyphausen, remained on his ground until about eight, and then descending from the heights of Freehold, into a plain of about three miles in extent, took up his line of march in rear of the front division.*

General Lee made the dispositions necessary for executing his orders; and, soon after the rear of the enemy was in motion, prepared to attack it General Dickenson had been directed to detach some of his best troops, to co-operate with him, and Morgan to act on the enemy's right flank, but with so much caution as to be able readily to extricate himself and to form a junction with the main body.

Lee appeared on the heights of Freehold, soon after the enemy had left them, and following the British into the plain gave orders to General Wayne to attack their covering party so as to halt them, but not to press them sufficiently to force them up to the main body, or to draw reinforcements from thence to their aid. In the meantime, he proposed to gain their front by a shorter road on their left, and entirely intercepting their communication with the line to bear them off before they could be assisted.

While in the execution of this design, a gentleman of General Washington's suite came up to gain intelligence, and to him Lee communicated his present object.

Sir Henry Clinton, soon after the rear division was in full march, observed a column of the Americans on his left flank.— This being militia, was soon dispersed. When his rear guard had descended from the hill, it was followed by a corps; soon after which a cannonade upon it was commenced from some pieces commanded by Colonel Oswald, and at the same time, he received intelligence that a respectable force had shown itself on both his flanks. Believing a design to have been formed

---

* Letter of Sir Henry Clinton.

OLD TIMES IN OLD MONMOUTH. 9

on his baggage, which in the defiles would be exposed, he determined in order to secure it to attack the troops in his rear so vigorously as to compel them to call off those on his flanks. This induced him to march back his whole rear division, which movement was making as Lee advanced for the purpose of reconnoitring to the front of the wood, adjoining the plain.— He soon perceived himself to have mis taken the force which formed the rear of the British, but he yet proposed to engage on that ground, although his judgment, as was afterwards stated by himself on an inquiry into his conduct, disapproved of it; there being a morass immediately in his rear, which could not be passed without difficulty, and which would necessarily impede the arrival of reinforcements to his aid and embarass his retreat should he be finally overpowered. This was about ten o'clock. While both armies were preparing for action General Scott (as stated by General Lee,) mistook an oblique march of an American column for a retreat, and in the apprehension of being abandoned left his position and repassed the ravine in his rear. Being himself of opinion that the ground on which the army was drawn up was by no means favourable to them, Lee did not correct the error Scott had committed, but directed the whole detachment to regain the heights they had passed. He was pressed by the enemy and the same slight skirmishing ensued during this retrograde movement, in which not much loss was sustained on either side.

When the first firing announced the commencement of the action, the rear division threw off their packs and advanced rapidly to support the front. As they approached the scene of action, Washington, who had received no intelligence from Lee notifying his retreat, rode forward, and about noon, after the army had marched five miles, to his utter astonishment and mortification, met the advanced corps retiring before the enemy with but having made a single effort to maintain their ground. Those whom he first fell in with, neither understood the motives which had governed General Lee nor his present design, and could give no other information than that by his orders, they had fled without fighting

Washington rode to the rear of the division, which was closely pressed. There he met Lee, to whom he spoke in terms of some warmth, implying disapprobation of his conduct. He also gave immediate orders to the regiments commanded by Colonel Stewart and Lieutenant-Colonel Ramsay, to form on a piece of ground which he deemed proper for the purpose of checking the enemy, who were advancing rapidly on them. General Lee was then directed to take proper measure with the residue of his force to stop the British column on that ground, and the Commander-in-Chief rode back himself to arrange the rear division of the army.— These orders were executed with firmness. A sharp conflict ensued, and when forced from the ground on which he had been placed, Lee brought off his troops in good order, and was then directed to form in the rear of Englishtown.

The check thus given the enemy, afforded time to draw up the left wing and second line of the American army on an eminence, partly in a wood, and partly in an open field, covered by a morass in front. Lord Sterling, who commanded the wing, brought up a detachment of artillery, under Lieut-colonel Carrington, with some field pieces, which played with considerable effect upon the enemy, who had passed the morass, and were pressing on to the charge. The pieces, with the aid of several parties of infantry detached for the purpose, effectually put a stop to their advance.

The American artillery were drawn up in the open field, and maintained their ground with admirable firmness, under a heavy and persevering fire from the British.

The right wing was for the day, commanded by General Greene. To expedite the march, and to prevent the enemy from turning the right flank, he had been ordered to file off by the new church, two miles from Englishtown, and to fall into the Monmouth road, a small distance in the rear of the court-house, while the residue of the army proceeded directly to that place. He had advanced on this road considerably to the right of, and rather beyond the ground on which the armies were now engaged, when he was informed of the retreat of Lee, and of the new disposition of the troops. He immediately changed his route, and took an advantageous position on the right.

Warmly opposed in front the enemy attempted to turn the left flank of the American army, but were repulsed, and driven back by parties of infantry. They then attempted the right, with as little success.—

General Greene had advanced a body of troops, with artillery, to a commanding piece of ground in his front, which not only marred their design of turning the right, but severely enfiladed the party which yet remained in front of the left wing. At this moment, General Wayne advanced with a body of infantry in front, who kept up so hot and well directed a fire of musketry, that the British soon gave way and withdrew behind the ravine, to the ground on which the first halt had been made. Here the British line was formed on very strong ground. Both flanks were secured by thick woods and morasses, while their front could be reached only through a narrow pass. The day had been intensely hot, and the troops were much fatigued. Still Washington resolved to renew the engagement. For this purpose, Brigadier-general Poor, with his own and the Carolina brigade, gained the enemy's right flank, while Woodford, with his brigade, turned their left, and the artillery advanced on them in front. But the impediments on the flanks of the enemy were so considerable, that before they could be overcome, and the troops approach near enough to commence the attack it was nearly dark. Under these circumstances, further operations were deferred until morning. The brigades on the flanks kept their ground through the night and the other troops lay on their arms in the field of battle in order to be in perfect readiness to support them.— General Washington, who had, through the day, been extremely active, passed the night in his cloak in the midst of his soldiers.

In the mean time, the British were employed in removing their wounded. About midnight they marched away in such silence, that their retreat was without the knowledge of General Poor, who lay very near them.

As it was perfectly certain that they would gain the high grounds about Middletown before they could be overtaken, where they could not be attacked with advantage, as the face of the country afforded no prospect of opposing their embarkation; and as the battle, already fought, had terminated favourably to the reputation of the American arms, it was thought advisable to relinquish the pursuit. Leaving the Jersey brigade, Morgan's corps and M'Lane's command* to hover about them, to countenance desertion, and protect the country from their depredations, it was resolved to move the main body of the army to the Hudson, and take a position which should effectually cover the important passes in the Highlands.

The loss of the Americans was eight officers and sixty-one privates killed, and about one hundred and sixty wounded. Among the slain were Lieut.-Colonel Bonner, of Pennsylvania, and Major Dickenson, of Virginia, both much regretted. One hundred and thirty were missing; of whom many afterwards joined their regiments.

Sir Henry Clinton stated his dead and missing at four officers, and one hundred and eighty-four privates; his wounded at sixteen officers, and one hundred and fifty-four privates. This account, so far as respects the dead, cannot be correct, as four officers and two hundred and forty-five privates were buried on the field, and some few were afterwards found and buried, so as to increase the number to nearly three hundred. The uncommon heat of the day was fatal to several on both sides.

As usual when a battle has not been decisive, both parties claimed the victory. In the early part of the day, the advantage was certainly with the British; in the latter part, it may be pronounced with equal certainty to have been with the Americans. They maintained their ground, repulsed the enemy by whom they were attacked, were prevented only by the night, and the retreat of Sir Henry Clinton from renewing the action, and suffered in killed and wounded less than their adversaries.

Independent of the loss sustained in action the British army was considerably weakened in its way from Philadelphia to New York. About one hundred prisoners were made, and near a thousand soldiers, principally foreigners, many of whom had married in Philadelphia, deserted the British standard during the march.

Whilst the armies were traversing the Jerseys, Gates, who commanded on the North river, by a well-timed and judicious movement down the Hudson, threatened New York, for the purpose of restraining the garrison of that place from reinforcing Sir Henry Clinton, should such a measure be contemplated.

The conduct of Lee was generally disapproved. As, however, he had possessed

---

*The militia had returned to their homes immediately after the action.

a large share of the confidence of the commander-in chief, it is probable that explanations might have been made, which would have rescued him from the imputations cast on him, and have restored him to the esteem of the army, could his haughty temper have brooked the indignity he believed to have been offered him on the field of battle. General Washington had taken no measures in consequence of the events of that day, and probably, would have come to no resolution concerning them, without an amicable explanation, had he not received from Lee a letter, in very unbecoming terms, in which he manifestly assumed the station of a superior, and required reparation for the in jury sustained from the very singular expressions said to have been used, on the day of the action, by the commander-in-chief.

This letter was answered by an assurance, that so soon as circumstances would admit of an inquiry, he should have an opportunity of justifying himself to the army, to America, and to the world in general, or of convincing them that he had been guilty of disobedience of orders, and misbehavior before the enemy. On the same day, on Lee's expressing a wish for a speedy investigation of his conduct, and for a court-martial rather than a court of inquiry, he was arrested:

First. For disobedience of orders in not attacking the enemy on the 28th of June, agreeably to repeated instructions. Secondly. For misbehavior before the enemy on the same day, in making an unnecessary, disorderly and shameful retreat.— Thirdly. For disrespect to the commander-in-chief in two letters. Before this correspondence had taken place, strong and specific charges of misconduct had been made against General Lee by several officers of his detachment, and particularly by Generals Wayne and Scott. In these the transactions of the day, not being well understood, were represented in colors much more unfavorable to Lee than facts would justify. These representations, most probably produced the strength of the expressions contained in the second article of the charge. A court-martial was soon called, over which Lord Stirling presided; and after a full investigation, Lee was found guilty of all the charges exhibited against him, and sentenced to be suspended for one year. This sentence was afterwards, though with some hesitation, approved, almost unanimously, by Congress. The court softened, in some degree, the severity of the second charge by finding him guilty, not in its very words, but of misbehavior before the enemy, by making an unnecessary, and, in some few instances, a disorderly retreat.

Lee defended himself with his accustomed ability. He suggested a variety of reasons justifying his retreat, which, if they do not absolutely establish its propriety, give it so questionable a form as to render it probable that a public examination never would have taken place, could his proud spirit have stooped to offer explanation, instead of outrage, to the commander-in-chief.

The attention of General Washington was now turned, principally to the North river, towards which the march of his army was directed, with the intention of continuing some time about Haverstraw. And soon after he crossed North river to the White Plains.

After remaining a few days on the high grounds of Middletown, Sir Henry Clinton proceeded to Sandy Hook, whence he passed his army over to New York. This transit was effected by means of a fleet under Lord Howe, which had arrived off the Hook on the 28th of June.

Upon the day of battle the French fleet, under Count D'Estaing, having on board a respectable body of land forces, made the coast off Chincoteague inlet. Had it arrived a few days earlier its superior force would have shut Lord Howe and the British fleet in the Delaware, and the capture of the army under Sir Henry Clinton would, probably, have followed. The Count proceeded to Sandy Hook for the purpose of attacking the British fleet in port, and should this be found impracticable, to make an attempt on Rhode Island. The first was defeated by the shoalness of the bar at the mouth of the harbors.

THE BRITISH ACCOUNT OF THE BATTLE.

From the Annual Register for 1778.*

Evacuation of Philadelphia.—Difficulties encountered by the British Army in their march across the Jersies.—General Washington crosses the Delaware.—-Battle near Monmouth.—-Gen. Lee tried by a court martial and suspended.—British army pass over to Sandy Hook Island, and are conveyed by the fleet to New York.—Toulon squadron arrive on the coast of America.—Appear before Sandy Hook where they cast anchor.—Alarm and preparation at Sandy Hook and New York.—Departure of the French fleet.—Arrival of reinforcements to Lord Howe.

[After reciting " the joy and exultation of the Americans" at the news of the ratification of the treaties between the Confederate States of America and the Government of France, the account goes on to recite as follows :]

May 8, 1778.—About the same time Sir Henry Clinton arrived to take the command of the army at Philadelphia, in the room of Sir William Howe, who returned to England, to the great regret of both officers and soldiery in general. In the beginning of June the three commissioners from England, being the Earl of Carlisle, Mr. Eden, and Governor Johnstone, (with whom were joined in the commission the Commander-in-Chief, Sir Henry Clinton) arrived in the Delaware.

[Here follows an account of the propositions made by the commissioners for a treaty of peace with the Colonies, making numerous concessions, including the assumption of the public debt and a representation in the British Parliament, and their rejection by the Continental Congress. The narrative then continues:]

If any strong hope of success in the negotiation had remained, the evacuation of Philadelphia, and the consequent retreat of the army to the northward, just at the arrival of the Commissioners, would have completely frustrated them. Commissioners accompanying a retreating army, which was in the act of abandoning the principal advantage of two years war, could not promise themselves a great superiority in any treaty; and the more advantageous

* The Annual Register; or a View of the History, Politics and Literature for the year 1778. London. Printed for J. Dodsley, in Pall Mall, 1779.

the offers which they should make in such circumstances, the more their concessions would be considered as proofs of weakness, not of good-will. This measure was carried into execution on the 18th of June, and the whole British army passed the Delaware on the same day without interruption or danger, under the excellent dispositions made by the Admiral, Lord Howe, for the purpose.

Washington, having penetrated into the intention of abandoning Philadelphia, had already sent General Maxwell with his brigade to reinforce the Jersey militia, in order to throw every possible obstruction in the way of the British army, so that by impeding their progress he might himself be enabled to bring up his force in such time, as to profit of those opportunities, which, it was well to be supposed, so long a march through so dangerous a country would have afforded, of attacking them with great advantage. This detached corps and the militia did not, however, effect anything more of importance than the breaking down of the bridges; the great superiority of the British force having obliged them to abandon the strong pass at Mount Holly without venturing an opposition.

The British army, notwithstanding, encountered much toil, difficulty, and numberless impediments in their march.— They were encumbered with an enormous baggage, including provisions; the number of loaded horses and wheel carriages being so great as to cover an extent of twelve miles in the narrow line of march which the nature of the country and roads afforded. This incumbrance, so far as related to the provision, proceeded, however, from the foresight and wisdom of the General, Sir Henry Clinton; who being well aware that the hostility of the country would cut off every source of subsistence from the troops, which was not within their own immediate comprehension, and being also uncertain as to the delays and obstructions which might occur on his march, was too prudent to put the fate of a whole army in any degree of hazard, for the trouble or difficulty that attended the conveyance of a certain and sufficient supply. The heat of the weather, which was then excessive, with the closeness of the narrow roads through the woods, and the constant labor of renewing or repairing bridges, in a country everywhere intersected with creeks and marshy brooks, were, altogether, severely felt by the army.

From all these causes, its progress was exceedingly slow; and nothing less than these could have accounted for its spending so many days in traversing so narrow a country. When the army had advanced to Allen's Town, it became a matter of consideration with the General whether to keep the direct course toward Staten Island, across the Rariton, or whether, by taking the road to his right, and drawing towards the sea-coast, he should push on to Sandy Hook. He knew that Generals Washington and Lee, with the whole continental force on that side, had already passed the Delaware; and he had heard that General Gates, with the northern army, was advancing to join them on the Rariton. The difficulty of passing the Rariton, and the circumstances with which it might have been attended, under his incumbrances, in the face of an enemy, with other concurring causes, determined him to the right-hand course, as much the more eligible.

On the other hand, General Washington, who had crossed the Delaware far above Philadelphia, at Coryel's Ferry, attributed, with his usual foresight and caution, the slow movements of the British army to a design of decoying him into the low country, where, by a rapid movement on the right, they might gain possession of the strong grounds above him, and so enclosing his army to the river, force him to a general engagement under every disadvantage. Under this persuasion, in which it is possible his sagacity deceived him, as the peculiar circumstances of the British army rendered it totally incapable of any such rapid movements as he apprehended, the slowness on the one side retarded the motions on the other. It is, however, likewise probable, that Washington reserved himself entire for the passage of the Rariton; which he concluded would have been their course, and which he knew would have afforded him great advantage in an attack.

But when he discovered that the British army had departed from its expected line of direction, and was bending its way on the other side towards the sea-coast, he immediately changed his system and sent several detachments of chosen troops, under the general conduct of the Marquis de Fayette, to harrass the army in its march, himself following at a suitable distance, with the whole force. As affairs grew more critical upon the near approach of the van of one army to the rear of the other, General Lee was dispatched with two brigades, to reinforce, and to take command of the advanced corps; which, by Washington's account, amounted then to about 5,000 men, although from the several detachments which he specifies, it would seem to have been stronger.

Sir Henry Clinton, on the march to a place called Freehold, judging from the number of the enemy's light troops which hovered on his rear, that their main body was at no great distance, judiciously determined to free that part of the army from the incumbrance and impediment of the baggage, which he accordingly placed under the conduct of General Knyphausen, who led the first column of the army. The other, which covered the line of march, being now disengaged and free for action, formed a body of troops which could not easily be equalled, and was under the immediate command of the General. It was composed of the 3d, 4th and 5th brigades of British, two battalions of British, and the Hessian grenadiers, a battalion of light infantry, the guards, and the 16th regiment of light dragoons.

June 28th. On the morning after this arrangement, General Knyphausen, with the first division and the carriages, began at the break of day to move, directing their march toward Middletown, which lay ten or twelve miles on their way, in a high and strong country. The second division, under the Commander in Chief, continued for some hours on their ground in the neighborhood of Freehold, both to cover the line of march, and to afford time for the chain of carriages to get clear on their way.

Having begun to march about eight o'clock, some parties of the enemy which appeared in the woods on their left flank, were engaged and dispersed by the light troops; but as the rear guard descended from the heights above Freehold into a valley about three miles in length and one in breadth, several columns of the enemy appeared likewise descending into the plain, who, about 10 o'clock began to cannonade the rear. The General at the same instant received intelligence that the enemy were discovered marching in force on both his flanks. He was immediately struck that an attack on the baggage was their principal object; and as the carriages were then entangled in defiles which continued for some miles, it seemed a matter of no small difficulty to obviate the danger.

In this critical situation the General, with great quickness and presence of mind judged that a vigorous attack and great pressure upon that body of the enemy which harrassed his rear would recall the detatchments on his flanks to its assistance, and seemed to be the only probable means of saving the convoy. For although he had good information that General Washington was at hand with his whole army, which he heard was estimated at 20,000 men, yet, as he knew that his main body was separated from that corps which attached Lord Cornwallis, in the rear, by two considerable defiles, he was not apprehensive that he could pass a greater body of troops through them, during the execution of the measure which he intended, than what the force along with him was well able to oppose; whilst on the other hand, even with that division of the army, Washington's situation would not be a little critical, if he should chance to come upon him, when he was struggling in his passage through the defiles.

Guarding, however, against every possible result of the measure, and to be in preparation for the event of a general engagement, he recalled a brigade of the British Infantry, and the 17th regiment of light dragoons, from Knyphausen's division, and left directions for them to take a position which would effectually cover his right flank, being the side on which he was most jealous of the design of the enemy. In the meantime the Queen's light dragoons had, with their usual spirit, attacked and routed the enemy's cavalry, under the Marquis de Fayette, and drove them back in confusion on their own infantry. The General then made dispositions to attack the enemy in the plain; but before he could advance they fell unexpectedly back, and took a strong position on the heights above Monmouth Court House.

The heat of the weather was in that season always intense; but upon that particular day was so excessive as to be seldom equalled, even in the sultry summers of that continent; so that the troops were already greatly fatigued. The situation of the army, however, rendered the most vigorous exertion necessary. The British grenadiers, with their left to the village of Freehold, and the guards on their right, began the attack with such spirit, that the enemy soon gave way. But their second line preserved a better countenance and resisted a fierce and eager attack with great obstinacy. They were, however, at length, completely routed; but in this exigency, with a very unusual degree of re collection, as well as resolution, took a third position with so much judgment, that their front was covered with a marshy hollow, which scarcely admitted of an attack by that way.

Sir Henry Clinton brought up part of the second line, and made some other dispositions to attack the enemy in this post and the light Infantry and Rangers had already turned their left for that purpose, but the army in general was now so overpowered by heat and fatigue, that upon consideration he thought it better not to press the affair any farther. He was also by this time confident that the purpose which had induced him to the attack was gained in the preservation of the convoy. A bold attempt of the enemy, to cut off the retreat of the light Infantry, rendered some new movements, notwithstanding the excessive toils of the day, still necessary. The army at length returned to that position, from whence they had at first driven the enemy, after their quitting the plain.

The General's opinion with respect to the design upon the baggage was justified in the event, and the propriety of his subsequent conduct in attacking the enemy on that principle confirmed. Two brigades of the enemy's light troops had passed the army, one on each flank, in that view, and had actually made the attempt, but by the good dispositions made by the commanders, the firmness of the 40th regiment, and the ready service of the light Horse, they were repulsed at the first onset, and the engagement in the plain then commencing, were immediately recalled.

Sir Henry Clinton having now fully attained his object, for the Generals Knyphausen and Grant, with the first division and baggage, were arrived at Nut Swamp, near Middletown, could have no inducement for continuing in his present situation. The troops had already gained sufficient honor, in forcing successively, from two strong positions a corps of the enemy, which he was informed, amounted to near 12 000 men ; and the merit of the service was much enhanced by the unequalled circumstances of heat and fatigue under which it was performed. The enemy were much superior in force to the division immediately under his command; and if the equality had been even nearer, it would still seem imprudent to have hazarded an engagement, at such a distance from the rest of his army, in a country not only entirely hostile, but which from its nature must have been ruinous to strangers under any circumstance of defeat. And as the heat of the day rendered marching by day intolerable, so the moonlight added much to the eligibility of the night for that purpose. Upon some or all of these troops having reposed till ten o'clock, the army was again put in motion, and they marched forward to join their fellows.

Such was the detail of the action at Freehold, or Monmouth, as it is otherwise called, as given on our side. The loss was not considerable in point of number, but rendered grievous by that of the brave Colonel Monckton. That gallant officer, who had frevuently encountered death in all its forms, had the fortune of being more than once grievously wounded, both in the last war and the present; and after the hair-breadth escape of a recovery, when left among the dead on the field, was only reserved to be killed on this day, at the head of the second battalion of grenadiers. This day and action were also rendered remarkable by the singular circumstance, unparalleled in the history of the New World, of 59 soldiers perishing! without receiving a wound, merely through the excessive heat and fatigue, Several of the Americans also, inured as they were to the climate, died through the same cause.

The Americans claim great honor to that part of their troops which had an opportunity to be engaged in this action.— They likewise claim, though without any apparent ground, the advantage as the affair now stands; but pretend that they should have gained a complete and decisive victory, if it had not been for the misconduct and disobedience of orders of General Lee. That officer had, some time before, by an exchange, obtained a release from his long confinement at New York; and we have already seen, was appointed to take the command of those different bodies of troops, which had been detached to harass the British army and to impede its march.

It appears from General Washington's account of the matter that he being well informed, that if the British army once gained the high and strong country near Middletown, no attempt could afterwards be made upon them, with the smallest prospect of success, he accordingly determined to fall upon their rear immediately upon their departure from the strong grounds in the neighborhood of Freehold, on which they had encamped during the night of the 27th. He communicated this intention to General Lee, with orders to make his dispositions for the attack, and to keep the troops lying upon their arms in constant preparation; which he also practised himself in the main body.

Washington having received an express at five in the morning, that the British army had begun their march, immediately dispatched an order to Lee to attack them; acquainting him, at the same time, that he was marching directly to his support, and that for the greater expedition, he should cause his men to disincumber themselves of that part of their baggage, which (it appears from hence) they carried upon their backs. To his great surprise and mortification, however, when he had marched above five miles, he met the whole advanced corps retreating, which they informed him was by General Lee's orders, without their making the smallest opposition, excepting the single fire of one detachment, to repulse the British light Horse.

The General found the rear of the retreating corps hard pressed by the enemy; but by forming them anew, under the brave and spirited exertions of their officers, (as he says,) he soon checked the advance of the British forces; and having by this means gained time to plant some batteries of cannon, and to bring up fresh forces, the engagement hung in an equal poize. In this situation (he continues) the enemy finding themselves warmly opposed in front, made an attempt to turn his left flank, but were bravely repulsed and driven back by some detached parties of Infantry. A similar attempt on the right was repelled by General Green, who afterwards, in conjunction with General Wayne, took such positions and kept up so severe and so well directed a fire, as compelled the British forces to retire behind that defile, where the first stand had been made in the beginning of the action.

In that situation, in which their flanks were secured by thick woods and morasses, and their front only assailable through a narrow defile, he notwithstanding made his dispositions (he says) for attacking them; but the darkness came on so fast as not to afford time for their surmounting the impediments in their way. The main body, however, lay all night upon their arms on the place of action, as the detached parties did in the several positions which they had been ordered to take, under a full determination of attacking the British army when the day appeared; but they retreated in such profound silence in the night, that the most advanced post, and those very near them, knew nothing of their departure until morning.

Washington represents the number of British buried by the Americans to be about four times greater than the loss acknowledged by our Gazette; and his own as much under that state. He says they carried off their wounded, excepting four officers, and about forty soldiers. He gives high and unusual praise, and expresses himself under the greatest obligation to the zeal, bravery, and conduct of his officers; and says, the behavior of the troops in general, after they had recovered from the surprise occasioned by the retreat of the advanced corps, was such as could not be surpassed. The public acknowledgments of the Congress were very flattering to the army but particularly so to the General and to his officers; in which they affected to consider this action as a battle, and the result as a great and important victory, obtained over the grand British army, under the immediate command of their General.

Washington took care to inform the Congress that the nature of the country rendered any further pursuit of the British army fruitless, and all attempts to disturb their embarkation at Sandy Hook equally impracticable and dangerous. He accordingly detached some light troops to observe and attend their motions, and drew off the main body of the army to the borders of the North River. The Americans lost some officers of name in this action; particularly a Colonel Bonner, of Pennsylvania, and a Major Dickenson, of Virginia, both of whom were much regretted.

[Here follows an account of the Court Martial of LEE, ordered by Washington to be held at New Brunswick on the 4th of July, and the action thereof, by which he was found guilty of part of the charges, and sentenced to be suspended from command for twelve months. Upon this action the writer comments as follows:

"It is impossible for us to enter into the merits of this sentence, in which party might have had a great share. When a dispute had been carried to so great an height between an officer on whom the Americans reposed their chief consequence and one subordinate and less popular, it is not difficult to divine where the blame will be laid."

The narrative then continues:]

In the meantime the British army arrived at the high lands of Navesink, in the neighborhood of Sandy Hook, on the last of June; at which latter place the fleet from the Delaware, under Lord Howe, after being detained in that river by calms, had most fortunately arrived on the preceding day. It had happened in the preceding winter that the peninsula of Sandy Hook had been cut off from the continent, and converted to an absolute island, by a violent breach of the sea; a circumstance then of little moment, but which now might have been attended with the most fatal consequences. By the happy arrival of the fleet at the instant when its assistance was so critically necessary, the ability of the noble commander and the extraordinary efforts of the seamen this impediment was speedily removed; a bridge of boats being completed with such expedition that the whole army was passed over this new channel on the 5th of July, and were afterwards conveyed with ease to New York; neither army nor navy yet knowing the circumstances of danger and ruin in which they had been so nearly involved.

For an unexpected enemy had now arrived on the coast of North America, who was to give a new and a strange turn to the circumstances of the war. On the second day after the conveyance of the army from Sandy Hook, Lord Howe received intelligence by his cruisers that D'Estaing's fleet had been seen on the coast of Virginia on the very day that the army had passed the bridge at Sandy Hook. If D'Estaing had met the transports either in the Delaware, or on the passage from thence, loaded and encumbered as they were, and convoyed by only two ships of the line, with a number of frigates, the consequence with respect to the fleet is obvious. But it may not so immediately appear that the fate of the army was so intimately combined with that of the fleet that the destruction of the one would have been the inevitable loss of the other. For as the army could not then, by any possible means, have prosecuted its way to New York, and would have been enclosed on one side by the American Army and on the other by the French fleet, cut off from all supply of provision, and destitute of every resource, a repetition of the Saratoga catastrophe must have been the certain consequence.

Although the fatal event was prevented by the bad weather, and unexpected impediments which D'Estaing met with on his voyage, yet if he had directed his course directly to New York, instead of the Chesapeake or Delaware, things could scarcely have been better, as he would then have come upon the fleet and army when they were entangled either with the laying or passing of the bridge at Sandy Hook. In either circumstance destruction would have been inevitable, and would have been of an amount and magnitude with respect both to the marine and land service, and the consequences hanging upon it, which, perhaps, has not been equalled of late ages. But D'Estaing's great object was the surprise of the fleet in the Delaware, and the consequent enclosure of the army at Philadelphia; fortunately the winds and weather frustrated his designs. Upon the whole, it may not be easy to point out a more signal or providential deliverance.

The danger, though lessened, was not, however, immediately removed; and it still required the most consummate ability and fortitude to render the kindness of fortune effective. On the 4th day after the account received of his arrival on the coast and subsequent advice of his having anchored at the Delaware being also received D'Estaing appeared suddenly (July 11) and rather unexpectedly at Sandy Hook. His force was great and in good condition, consisting of twelve ships of the line and three frigates of superior size. Among the former were several ships of great force and weight of metal; one carrying 90 another 80, and six carrying 74 guns each; and the squadron was said to have no less than eleven thousand men on board. On the other side the British fleet under Lord Howe consisted of six sixty-four gun ships, three of fifty, and two of forty guns, with some frigates and sloops. Most of the former had been long on service, were accordingly in bad condition, and were also wretchedly manned. If anything, however, could remedy such essential defects, it might have been hoped for from the superior abilities of their Commander and the excellency of his officers.

They had, however, the advantage of being in possession of that port or harbor which is formed by Sandy Hook; the entrance of which is covered by a bar and from whence the inlet passes to New York. The expected and avowed object of D'Estaing was to force that passage, and to attack the English squadron in the harbor. Notwithstanding the utmost exertions of preparation made by Lord Howe, that the time could possibly admit, yet from contrary winds, and other unavoidable incidents, the ships were not completely arrived in their respective situations of defence, nor had there been time to chose those situations with the judgment which was afterwards exercised, when D'Estaing appeared without the Hook. Under these circumstances, which, with respect to the effect, might be considered, in some degree, as affording the advantages of a surprise, if he had pushed on directly to pass the bar and force the passage, it would seem, that neither the advantage of situation, nor any eminence of ability or virtue on the other side, could be capable of counteracting the vast superiority of his force. The conflict would have been undoubtedly dreadful; and perhaps, in that respect, might have exceeded anything known in naval history; but the greatest portion of human spirit must recognize some adequate degree of strength to render its exertions effective.

A diversity of opinion seems to prevail on the practicability of the great ships of the French fleet passing in force through the strait and over the bar. Some are of opinion that it might have been attempted with prudence. If so, it may be considered as a happiness on all sides, that D'Estaing was not possessed of that spirit of enterprise which would have been equal to so arduous an attempt; that the terror of the British flag was yet in no degree weakened; and that the name of the noble commander who opposed him added some weight to that effect. D'Estaing accordingly cast anchor on the Jersey side, about four miles without the Hook, and in the vicinity of the small town of Shrewsbury.

The spirit that was displayed on this occasion, not only in the fleet and army, but through every order and denomination of seamen, was never exceeded and will not often be equalled. A thousand volunteers were immediatly dispatched from the transports to the fleet. The remainder of the crews could not restrain their indignation at being left behind, and sought every possible means by hiding in boats or otherwise, to escape on ¿oard the men of war, so that the agents could scarcely keep by force a sufficient number of hands for the watch of their respective ships. The masters and mates of the merchantmen and traders at New York solicited employment with the greatest earnestness, and took their stations at the guns with the common sailors. Others hazarded everything, by putting to sea in light vessels, to watch the motions of the enemy, and perform other necessary services. One in particular, with a noble disinterestedness and gallantry, which may be compared with anything known in history, offered to convert his vessel (in which his whole hope and fortune lay) into a fire-ship, to be conducted by himself, and spurned with disdain every proposal of indemnification or reward.

It will afford no surprise that this spirit should shine out in the army with equal lustre; and that the light infantry and grenadiers, who had scarcely recovered the fatigue of a most toilsome and dangerous march, and with many of the officers wounds still green and sore, should notwithstanding, contend with such eagerness, to serve on board the men of war as marines, that the point of honor was obliged to be decided by lots. In a word, the public spirit, zeal, bravery and magnanimity, displayed upon this occasion, would have stamped a character upon a nation that before had none; and is an honor even to this country. It must, however, be acknowledged, that the popularity of the noble commander, and the confidence founded on his great qualities, contributed not a little to these exertions.

The French fleet continued at anchor in the position we have mentioned, and taking in wood and water and provisions for eleven days. It may be well supposed that as D'Estaing did not profit of the first opportunity that offered, that any attempt made by him, after the exertions on the other side had taken their full effect, and the judicious defensive dispositions made by the British Admiral were completed, would have been not only ineffectual, but probably (notwithstanding the superiority of his force) ruinous. Neither the confidence arising from D'Estaing's hesitation, or from their own courage, was, however, any allay to the mixed passions of grief and indignation which now agitated the British seamen. They endured the mortification, for the first time, of seeing a British fleet blocked up and insulted in their own harbor, and the French flag flying triumphant without; and this was still more deeply embittered and aggravated by beholding every day vesssels under English colors (who had still been ignorant of the loss of their usual protection), captured under their eyes by the enemy. They looked out every hour with the utmost anxiety, and in the most eager expectation, for the arrival of Byron's squadron.

D'Estaing's fleet at length appeared July 22, under way; and as the wind was favorable, and the spring tides at the highest (the water rising that afternoon thirty feet on the bar) it was expected that he intended to carry his long delayed menace into execution; and that day would have afforded one of the hottest and most desperate engagements that had ever been fought, during the long enmity and rivalship that had subsisted between the two nations. Everything was at stake on the British side. If the naval force was destroyed, (and nothing less than destruction or victory could have ended the conflict) the vast fleets of transports and victuallers, with the army, must all have fallen along with it. D'Estaing, however, thought the attempt too dangerous; and shaping his course another way, was in a few hours out of sight.

Nothing was ever more critical than the Commander's stay at Sandy Hook; and few things could be more fortunate in the present circumstances than his departure at the exact period that he did. For if the whole, or any part of Admiral Byron's fleet had arrived during his stay, considering the ruined state in which it reached the coasts of America, there could scarcely have been a hope of its not falling almost a defenceless prey into his hands. That unfortunate squadron is said to have been, in many respects, badly equipped and provided. In this state they had the fortune of meeting unusually bad weather for the season; and being separated in different storms, and lingering through a tedious passage, arrived, scattered, broken, sickly, dismasted, or otherwise damaged, in various degrees of distress, upon different and remote parts of the coast of America. Between the departure of D'Estaing on the 22d and the 30th of July, the Renown, of 50 guns, from the West Indies, the Raisonable and Centurion, of

64 and 50, from Halifax, and the Cornwall, (one of Admiral Byron's squadron). of 74 guns, all arrived singly at Sandy Hook. The joy arising from this reinforcement could scarcely be superior to that excited by a sense of the imminent danger which they had so fortunately escaped. It seemed no less an instance of good fortune that the Cornwall was in better condition than most of the other ships of that squadron.

THE AMERICAN ACCOUNT OF THE BATTLE.

From Gordon's History of the United States, 1794.*

[The following extract from WILLIAM GORDON's *History of the United States*, published in 1794, but written soon after the events occurred, gives an account of the Battle of Monmouth, with some account of public affairs immediately preceding that event. We are indebted to Mrs. Judge McLEAN for the use of this work, which is a very rare one, and formerly belonged to her father, the late Judge HULL, of this town.]—ED. DEM.

1778—

Lieutenant Colonel Ethan Allen was at length exchanged; and congress granted him a brevet commission of Colonel [May 14] in reward of his fortitude and zeal in the cause of his country.

General Sullivan being sent to command at Providence, Gen. Pigot, who was at Newport, inferred that there was a design of attacking Rhode Island whenever an opportunity offered; the latter therefore concluded upon an expedition that might delay or frustrate the event. Lieutenant Col. Campbell, with about 500 British and Hessians, was sent off in the night of the 24th, passed up the river, and landed from the ships, tenders, and boats before day, between Warren and Poppasquash-point. At daylight [May 25.] they marched in two bodies, one for Warren, and the other for the head of the Kickemut river, where they destroyed about seventy flat-bottomed boats, and set fire to one of the State gallies, which was extinguished without doing much injury.— They burnt also a quantity of pitch, tar, plank, &c. They then fired the meetinghouse at Warren, and several dwelling houses; and retreated towards Bristol, where their ships and boats had fallen down to receive them. In Bristol they burnt two and twenty houses, and through mistake the church instead of the meeting house. The destruction of houses and places of worship was afterward attributed chiefly to the licentiousness of the soldiers, who treated both friends and foes with cruelty, plundering houses and robbing women of their shoe-buckles, gold rings and handkerchiefs. They carried off with them a state galley. A few days after, a party of 150 men were sent from Newport to burn the saw-mills and contiguous houses at Tiverton. They fired an old mill and old house near the place of landing; and then proceeded for the town to execute the business they were sent upon; but the bridge leading to it being defended by five and twenty men, they could not cross though they attempted it repeatedly. The advancing season will close these small excursions by bringing forward more capital operations; and for the counteracting of which, the Americans must depend much upon supplies from France.——This reminds me, that that on the 28th, a French 50 gun ship with 350 men, a brig and a schooner, bringing arms and dry goods, arrived in James river, Virginia, from Rochford. Congress the next day, to commemorate the agreeable event which has taken place between France and the United States, resolved that a new continental frigate, built in the Massachusetts, and lately launched, should be called the *Alliance*. Within three weeks after, the command of her was bestowed upon Capt. Peter Landais.

In the beginning of June, the Trident arrived in the Delaware with the earl of Carlisle, Mr. Eden and gov. Johnstone, three of the commissioners for restoring peace between Great Britian and America. On the 9th Sir Henry Clinton informed gen. Washington of their being at Philadelphia, and requested a passport for doctor Ferguson, their secretary, with a letter from them to congress. The general declined granting a passport, which was unanimously approved by congress. The

---

* The History of the Rise, Progress, and Establishment of the Independence of the United States of America: Including an Account of the Late War; and of the Thirteen Colonies, from their origin to that period. By WILLIAM GORDON, D. D. Second American Edition. New York: printed and sold by Samuel Campbell, No. 37 Hanover Square.—M. DCC. XCIV.

refusal made it necessary to forward the letter, with the acts, a copy of their commission and other papers by the common intercourse. They were received by an express from Washington on the 13th, and the letter was read till some offensive language against his most Christian Majesty offered, on which the further reading of it was suspended till the 16th; when the reading of that and the other papers was finished. They were referred to a committee, who drew up a letter to be sent by the president in answer to the letter and papers from the commissioners, which was unanimously agreed to by the delegates on the 17th, and was as follows—"I have received the letter from your excellencies of the 9th instant, with the enclosures, and laid them before congress. Nothing but an earnest desire to spare the further effusion of human blood could have induced them to read a paper containing expressions so disrespectful to his most Christian majesty, the good and great ally of these states, or to consider propositions so derogatory to the honor of an independent nation. The acts of the British parliament, the commission from your sovereign, and your letter, suppose the people of these States to be subjects to the crown of Great Britian, and are founded on the idea of independence, which is utterly inadmissible. I am further directed to inform your excellencies, that congress are inclined to peace notwithstanding the unjust claims from which this war originated, and the savage manner in which it hath been conducted. They will therefore be ready to enter upon the consideration of a treaty of peace and commerce, not inconsistent with treaties already subsisting, when the King of Great Britian shall demonstrate a sincere disposition for that purpose. The only solid proof of this disposition will be an explicit acknowledgement of the independence of these States, or the withdrawing his fleets and armies.—I have the honor to be, your excellencies most obedient and humble servant." Before this letter could be received by the commissioners, a movement took place at Philadelphia, which must have completely frustrated all negotiation, had the same been even in a train, answering to the wishes of the British agents; for it indicated an apprehension of great danger to the royal forces should they continue in the city.

Mr. Eden brought with him secret orders for the speedy evacuation of Philadelphia: they were so secret as not to be made known either to himself or Governor Johnstone. Whether the earl of Carlisle met with the like treatment is not yet ascertained. It has been publicly asserted, that the orders were dated exactly three weeks before the commissioners sailed from England, which carries the date back to the last of March. On their delivery Sir Henry Clinton immediately applied himself to the putting of them into execution. By the eighteenth everything being ready, the British army evacuated the city at three o'clock in the morning. They proceeded to Gloucester Point three miles down the river, and before ten the whole had passed in safety across the Delaware into New Jersey. At ten they began their march to Haddonfield, which they reached the same day. Your curiosity may make you desirous of knowing in what condition the British left Philadelphia. An American son of liberty, who visited it in the beginning of July, wrote to his friend—"The whole north side of the city, before you enter, is a promiscuous scene of ruin. Upon getting into the city I was surprised to find it had suffered so little. I question whether it would have fared better, had our own troops been in possession of it, that is, as to the buildings." The necessary preparations for its evacuation could not be concealed from general Washington; when the appearance of their intending to march through Jersey became serious, he detached general Maxwell's brigade, in conjunction with the militia of that State, to impede the progress of the royal troops, so as to give the American army time to come up with them, and to take advantage of any favorable circumstances that might offer. Some time before, gen. Lee having been exchanged, had joined the army at Valley forge. The evening preceding the evacuation, the principles of the operations proper to be adopted were taken up and fully discussed by his excellency and the general officers, when it appeared to be the common sentiment, that it would be highly criminal to hazard a general action with the enemy at present, as by it they might lose every advantage which a three years war, combined with many fortunate circumstances, had given to America. The next day his excellency after observing "near 11,000 men would be able to march off the ground in a condition for service," proposed in writing a set of queries to the several general officers, in order to learn the particular opinion of each, as to "what is to be done?" which was to be returned on paper. The answers were in common the same with the prevailing sentiment of the council on the preceding day. Gen. Mifflin was not of the number consulted. He would have gloried in being present to have taken an active part upon this occasion; but by some secret manoeuvres was thrown at a distance. He desired and obtained leave of Congress, on the 4th of May, to join the army, and repaired to Valley Forge. Some of the general officers were disgusted at the thought of his returning to his command, now the campaign was opening, to share in the honors it might yield, when he had not shared with them in the peculiar distresses of their winter quarters. When their sentiments came to be known to certain members of congress, measures were taken to produce and perfect the following motion on June 11th, "That gen. Washington be directed to order an inquiry to be made into the conduct of major general Mifflin, late quarter-master-general, and the other officers who acted under him in that department; and if it shall appear that the extraordinary deficiencies thereof, and the consequent distresses of the army, were chargeable to the misconduct of the quarter-master-general, or any of the said officers, that a court martial be held on the delinquents." When this enquiry was ordered to be made, he was with the army, and in a fair way of obtaining a just proportion of his countrymen's confidence. He clearly saw the meaning of the stroke; but the order made it necessary for him to obtain leave of absence for some weeks to collect materials for his justification.

When intelligence of Sir Henry Clinton's having evacuated Philadelphia and marched to Haddonfield, reached the American head quarters, the next measure to be taken by General Washington was apparent. Gen. Green, by his conduct and industry, as quarter-master-general, had effected such a happy change in the line of his department, as enabled his excellency with great facility to move with the whole army and baggage from Valley forge in pursuit of the enemy. The troops proceeded to and crossed the Delaware at Corriel's ferry; when a select corps of 600 men were immediately detached under Col. Morgan to reinforce gen. Maxwell. The slow advance of Sir Henry led his excellency to suspect, that he had a design of bringing on a general action, could he draw the Americans into the lower country. This consideration and a desire of refreshing the troops after the fatigues they had endured from rainy and excessive hot weather, determined the American General to halt about five miles from Princeton. While there he stated to the general officers [June 24.] the following facts—"the enemy's force is between 9 and 10,000 rank and file—the American army on the ground is 10,684 rank and file, beside the advanced brigade under General Maxwell of about 1,200, and about 1,200 militia"—on which he proposed the question, "Will it be advisable to hazard a general action?" The answer was—"Not advisable, but a detachment of 1,500 to be immediately sent to act as occasion may serve, on the enemy's left flank and rear, in conjunction with the other continental troops and militia already hanging about them, and the main body to preserve a relative position, to act as circumstances may require—Lee, Stirling, Green, Fayette, Steuben, Poor, Paterson, Woodward, Scott, Portial." The detachment was immediately made under gen. Scott. The same day Sir Henry concluding that general Washington, who had alway hitherto avoided a general action, would not now give into it against every dictate of policy, and that the American views were directed against his baggage, in which part he was indeed vulnerable, determined to take the right hand road leading to Sandy Hook, instead of making for the Rariton, where he suspected gen. Gates with the northern army might join that under gen. Washington. Gates arrived at Fishkill about the middle of May to take the command in that quarter. The troops under him were so few, that he could not answer for the defence of that pass through the highlands with which he was intrusted; and was persuaded, that if the enemy made a sudden and determined push to carry it, the militia would not come in time to save it. On the 17th of June draughts arrived, and militia were hourly expected; after mentioning this in a letter to congress, he exclaims—"Thank heaven for the precious time the enemy have so foolishly lost!" He had no idea of marching for the Rariton; but his cavalry, and a considerable body of infantry, was at this period so posted, as to give the alarm of an attack upon New York: and he proposed moving the main body of his army to White Plains, and taking a strong camp in that neighborhood, to keep up the alarm: which was highly approved of by gen. Washington, and procured his thanks. On the 25th his excellency moved his army to Kingston. Upon receiving intelligence that Sir Henry was prosecuting his route towards Monmouth court-house, he dispatched 1,000 select men under brigadier gen. Wayne, and sent the Marquis de la Fayette to take the command of the whole advanced corps, with orders to seize the first fair opportunity of attacking the enemy's rear. Gen. Lee declined the command, as he was against attacking, on which it was offered to the marquis, who accepted it with pleasure. In the evening of the same day, the whole army marched from Kingston, intending to preserve a proper distance for supporting the advanced corps, and arrived at Cranberry early the next morning. The intense heat of the weather, and a storm coming on, made it impossible to resume the march that day without great injury to the troops. The advanced corps being in consequence hereof too remote from the main body, and too far on the right to be supported, the marquis had orders sent him to file off by his left toward English-town, which he executed early in the morning of the 27th. Sir Henry being sensible of the approach of the American army, changed the disposition of his troops; and placed in the rear what were deemed the best, consisting of all the grenadiers, light infantry and chasseurs of the line; at the same time gen. Knyphausen was requested to take the baggage of the whole army under the charge of his division, which made the first column. Under the head of baggage was comprised, not only all the wheel carriages of every department, but also all the bat horses*—a train which, as the country admitted but of one route for carriages, extended near twelve miles. The alteration made by Sir Henry laid gen. Washington under the necessity of increasing the number of the advanced corps. His excellency embraced this opportunity of gratifying gen. Lee, with the consent of the marquis. Lee observed that his having declined the command of the advanced corps had lessened him in the opinion of officers and soldiers, wished

* A pack-horse belonging to an officer or to the baggage train.—*See Webster.*

to be appointed afresh. Washington would not consent to remove the marquis; but a reinforcement being wanted, he detached Lee with two brigades to join the marquis at English-town, and of course to take upon him the command of the whole. The main body marched the same day, encamped within three miles of that place. Morgan's corps was left hovering on Sir Henry's right flank, and the Jersey militia, amounting to about 700, under Gen. Dickenson, on his left. The royal army was strongly encamped in the neighborhood of Monmouth court-house, where they halted till the morning of the 28th. When once arrived at the heights of Middletown, about twelve miles in advance, there would have been no possibility of attempting any thing against them with a prospect of success, the American general therefore determined to attack their rear the moment they moved from their present ground, and communicated his intention to Lee, who was ordered to make the necessary disposition, and to keep his troops in readiness for the shortest notice. The like was done with respect to the troops under his own immediate command.

[June 28.] General Knyphausen moved at daybreak: Sir Henry, that he might not press upon him, did not follow till near eight o'clock, with the other division, composed of the 3d, 4th, and 5th brigades of British, two battalions of British grenadiers, the Hessian grenadiers, a batallion of light infantry, the guards, and the 16th regiment of light dragoons, a body of troops not easily to be equalled.

About one o'clock in the morning gen. Lee received a letter from gen. Washington, and in pursuance of the directions it contained, wrote to gen. Dickinson to select some hundreds of his best men, and detach them as nigh to the British rear as he could. These troops were to act as a corps of observation, and to forward the earliest intelligence respecting the enemy. He also ordered col. Morgan to advance with the men under his command so near as to attack them on their first movement: but it was left to him how to act. only he was to take care and not expose his troops, in that manner as to disable him from acting in conjunction with Lee, should there be a necessity for it. Orders were likewise sent to Grayson, as the commanding officer (of Scott and Varnum, consisting of about 600 men, to get them

OLD TIMES IN OLD MONMOUTH.

instantly in readiness to march. By day light they entered English-town; but it was not until between five and six that they marched from thence toward Monmouth court-house, having been detained for want of guides. Nearly at the same time, Lee gave orders to the several detachments and Maxwell's brigade to prepare for marching immediately, leaving their packs behind under proper guard: they followed the two just mentioned brigades about seven o'clock. About five Dickinson sent an express to general Washington, informing that the front of the enemy had began their march. His excellency instantly put the army in motion and sent orders to Lee to move on and attack them, unless there should be *very powerful reasons to the contrary*†; and acquainted him that he was marching to support him, and for doing it with the greater expedition and convenience, should make the men disencumber themselves of their packs and blankets. The exceptive clause in the orders rendered them discretionary; they manifested the earnest desire of the commander in chief, that an important blow might be struck which the enemy should feel; but Lee could not consider them as requiring him to risk a general engagement, in direct repugnancy to the spirit of those councils of war that had been repeatedly held upon the subject. While Lee was advancing with his column, he sent foward an aid to order Grayson to push on as fast as possible and attack the enemy. Before the aid overtook him he had passed Freehold meeting house with the two brigades. The aid delivered Lee's orders: but gave it as his opinion, that Grayson had better not move on, for that he had been informed that the main body of the enemy was near Monmouth court house, and was thought to be marching to attack them, of which circumstance he supposed Lee was ignorant. The aid on his return fell in with Dickenson, who gave him the same information, and charged him with a message to Lee. Lee conformed to it on its delivery, and gave orders for posting two militia regiments upon a hill for the securing of a particular road, and then pushed forward over a morass or ravine, by the bridge or causeway, to a height where Dickenson was with a few militia. During his stay on this height, intelligence of the most extraordinary nature was continually brought him. Some asserted, that the enemy had moved off with precipitation, and that it was only a covering party which remained; others averred, that the main force was still on the ground, and filing off in columns to the right and left—one while the enemy's troops were turning the flanks of the American's—at another, pushing in front. These opposite reports occasioned Varnum's brigade, and part of Scott's, and col. Durgee's brigade of Lee's column, to pass and repass the bridge over the morass several times, as it was universally agreed to be by no means warrantable to risk an action with a ravine in the rear, over which there was only one good passage. While these marchings and counter-marchings took place, the marquis de la Fayette arrived at the head of the main body of Lee's troops; when the general having reconnoitered a wood, into which it had been reported a battalion or two of the enemy had thrown themselves, and being satisfied that it was groundless, determined to march on, and ascertain with his own eyes, the number, order and disposition of the enemy, and then to conduct himself accordingly. His whole command amounted to about 4,0C0 men, exclusive of Morgan's corps and the Jersey militia: and consisted of gen. Scott's detachment, gen. Wayne's, gen. Maxwell's brigade, gen. Varnum's, gen. Scott's and col. Jackson's regiment. When they had nearly passed through the woods, with which the country abounds, and were arrived at a point facing the court-house, and on the edge of a plain about three miles in length and one in breadth, they were formed, but within the skirt of a wood, that the enemy might not discover them. Here they remained while generals Lee and Wayne, and a few others, went out upon the right and rode forward to reconnoitre. From the observations Lee made, and the intelligence he obtained, he concluded that the forces he saw, were no other than the enemy's covering party, and entertained hopes of an interval between them and the main body, sufficient to afford him the opportunity of cutting them off. That he might perfect this business, Wayne was appointed to command 700 men, to whom were attached pieces of artillery. Wayne was to attack the covering party in the rear faintly, so as to halt them, but not with vigor lest that should occasion their retreating with celerity to the main body, or drawing from it so powerful a reinforcement as to defeat the principal design. Meantime Lee was to endeavour, by a short road leading to the left, to gain the front of the party. While marching on this road, one of gen. Washington's suite came up to procure intelligence. Lee, with a fixed firm tone of voice and countenance which suggested confidence of success, desired him to inform his excellency, that the enemy did not appear well to understand the roads; that the route he was on cut off two mlles; that the rear of the enemy was composed of 1,500 or 2,000; that he expected to fall in with them, and had great certainty of cutting them off; and that gen. Wayne and col. Butler were amusing them with a few loose shot while he was performing the route. Wayne's command was advanced to the right and drawn up. The enemy appeared just in the edge of the wood upon an eminence with their light dragoons. A few of the American light horsemen were advanced upon the right, at a very considerable distance. One of Lee's aids de camp observed the queen's light dragoons parading as though they meant to charge these American light horsemen, who had no officer of eminence to head them: he therefore rode up and advised them to let the British dragoons come as near as could be done with safety, and then to retreat off to where gen. Wayne was and let him receive them. The British horse pursued till they came near the general, when receiving a fire from col. Butler's regiment posted on the skirt of a wood, they wheeled and galloped off in great haste to their own body: as they were retiring the two pieces of artillery fired a few shot at them Wayne then advanced, and encouraged his men to follow on, and charge the enemy with bayonets. The aid rode back to Lee, who immediately sent him forward to Wayne, with orders that he should only feign an attack, and not push on too precipitately, as that would subvert his plan, and disappoint his intentions. Lieut. col. Oswald, who commanded the artillery, supposed that the enemy were retreating, and so passed the morass in front over a causeway into a grain field, and began to cannonade. This happened after ten o'clock. About the same time a part of Lee's troop's issued out of a wood, on the left of and about a mile below the court-house, in small columns, and in an oblique direction with respect to the royal forces, rather toward their right and within cannon shot. These were drawn up ready to face the Americans, with their right near a wood; and their left on open ground covered by their cavalry and forming an obtuse angle with the court house. The cavalry filed off to the left, as if with design to attempt something on the right of Lee's troops, which occasioned an order to the marquis de la Fayette to wheel his column by his right, and to gain and attack the enemy's left flank. Lee having also ordered to the right the three regiments in Wayne's detachment, Wesson's, Stewart's and Livingston's, rode toward Oswald's artillery and reconnoitred the enemy, who appeared in full view marching back again toward the court-house, and in greater numbers than was expected, so that Lee said, he believed he was mistaken in their strength.

Let us now advert to the manœuvres of Sir Henry Clinton. Soon after he had begun with his column to follow gen. Knyphausen, reconnoitring parties of the Jersey militia appeared on his left flank. The queen's rangers fell in with, and dispersed some detachments among the woods in the same quarter. His rear guard having descended from the heights above Freehold into the plain, some American columns appeared likewise descending into it, and began the cannonade on his rear, which was returned by a superior fire. At this instant, intelligence was brought to Sir Henry, that the enemy were discovered marching in force on both his flanks. He conjectured, that the object of the Americans was the baggage, which at that juncture was engaged in defiles that continued for miles. He conceived that the only means of parrying the apprehended blow was by facing about, attacking the corps which harrassed his rear, and pressing it so hard, as to oblige the detachments to return from his flanks to its assistance. Thinking that the measure might possibly draw on a general action, he sent for a brigade of British, and the 17th light dragoons from Knyphausen's division, and at the same time gave gave directions, that on their arrival they should take a position for covering his right flank. He then made a disposition, and advanced in a direction toward the right of the Americans.

This happened while Lee was reconnoitering. The American column to the left of him under gen. Scott quitted the wood, crossed a morass, and formed in the plain field about a hundred yards in front of Maxwell; who expected an opportunity to form his brigade, by Scott's

OLD TIMES IN OLD MONMOUTH. 25

moving to the right as there was a vacancy between the latter and the troops with Lee. These were at that moment moving to the right, and every step they gained came nearer to the royal forces, who were also pushing to the right of the Americans. Lee's discernment led him immediately to send off one of his aids, with orders to Scott, whom he supposed to be in the wood on the other side of the morass, to halt his column in the wood, and continue there till further orders: that there might be no possible misconception, another aid was speedily dispatched with similar orders. Before these could be delivered, Scott had mistaken the movement on his right for a retreat; and apprehended danger to his own column in case of its remaining where he was, notwithstanding his detachment, and Maxwell's brigade with the other troops to the left made full two-thirds of Lee's whole command, and though the enemy appeared to bend their course from the left to the right of the Americans. Under such apprehension, Scott recrossed the morass, re-entered the wood, and retreated: Maxwell and the others did the like, of course. When the first aid reached that part of the wood to which he had been directed, and found that Scott had marched off the ground, he rode back: while returning, he met the second aid, and acquainted him with what had taken place: upon their coming to Lee, and communicating their information, the general discovered much surprise, and expressed his disapprobation of Scott's conduct in strong terms; but immediately upon the intelligence, directed a light horse officer to carry orders to the marquis de la Fayette to return to the Court-house. A general retreat now commenced on the right, till the troops reached Freehold and a neighboring wood. When these were quitted, the British pursued as far as the village, where they halted, Meanwhile the Americans marched on and passed the next morass in front of Carr's house, about half a mile from the village. The retreats and advances which took place were attended with cannonadings on each side. The halt of the British, on account of the intense heat of the weather, and their having suffered severely from fatigue, admitted of the Americans halting also for a considerable space, which heat and fatigue had rendered equally necessary for them. But upon the advance of the British from Freehold, and Lee's discerning that the position he at first meant to occupy with the design of receiving the enemy and baffling their attack, was not suitable; the whole of his command, Scott, Maxwell, and the others having now joined the corps which before formed the right, were ordered to retreat from the neighborhood of Carr's house toward a wood and eminence behind the morass they had crossed in the morning, which had been pointed out to him as a desirable and proper spot. Before they had wholly left the ground about Carr's house, the British cavalry made a sudden and rapid charge upon some parties of the American horse, who were in the rear reconnoitring. It was expected they would have attempted a charge on the whole rear, but they did not venture upon it.

Soon after Lee with his columns issued out of the woods, below the Court-house into the plain, gen. Washington was advancing with the main body of the army between Englishtown and Freehold meeting. Expecting from the information brought him that the van of Lee's command and the rear of the British would ere long engage, he ordered the right wing under gen. Greene to go to the right to prevent the enemy's turning his right flank; and then prepared to follow with the left wing directly in Lee's rear to support him. While this disposition was making, he learned, to his great surprise, from a countryman, that the continental troops were retreating. Though the account was confirmed by two or three persons whom he met on the road, after moving a few paces forward, yet he appeared to discredit it, having not heard any firing except a few cannon a considerable time before. He rode on, and between Freehold meeting and the morass, which he had just crossed, met the retreating troops marching towards the same, as Lee meant that they should repass it and then occupy the ground behind it, where he proposed making a stand against the enemy. Washington was exceedingly alarmed at finding the advanced corps falling back upon the main body, without the least notice given him. He desired one of the retreating colonels to march his men over the morass, halt them on the eminence, and refresh them. Seeing Lee at the head of the next column, he rode up to him with a degree of astonishment and indignation, and proposed certain questions that implied censure. Lee felt it, and answered with warmth and unsuitable language. Hard and irritating words passed between them for a short space, when Washington rode on toward the rear of the retreating troops. He had not gone many yards before he met his secretary, who told him that the British army were within fifteen minutes march of that place, which was the first intelligence he received of their pushing on so briskly. He remained there till the extreme rear of the retreating troops got up, when looking about, and judging the ground to be an advantageous spot for giving the enemy the first check, he ordered col. Stewart's and lieut. col. Ramsay's battalions to form and incline to their left, that they might be under cover of a corner of woods, and not be exposed to the enemy's cannon in front. Lee having been told by one of his aids, that Washington had taken the command, answered, "Then I have nothing further to do;" turned his horse and rode after his excellency in front. Washington on his coming up asked, "Will you command on this ground or not? If you will, I will return to the main body and have them formed upon the next height." Lee replied, "It is equal with me where I command." Washington then told him, "I expect you will take proper measures for checking the enemy." Lee said, "Your orders shall be obeyed, and I will not be the first to leave the field." Washington then rode to the main army, which was formed with the utmost expedition on the eminence with the moross in front. Immediately upon his riding off a warm cannonade commenced between the British and American artillery on the right of Steward and Ramsey; between whom and the advanced troops of the British army a heavy fire began soon after in the skirt of the woods before mentioned. The British pressed on close, their light horse charged upon the right of the Americans, and the latter were obliged to give way in such haste, that the British horse and infantry came out of the woods seemingly mixed with them. The action then commenced between the British and col. Livingston's regiment together with Varnum's brigade, which had been drawn up by Lee's order, and lined the fence that stretched across the open field in front of the bridge over the morass, with the view of covering the retreat of the artillery and the troops advanced with them. The artillery had timely retired to the rear of the fence, and from an eminence discharged several grapes of shot at the British, engaged with Livingston's and Varnum's troops; these were soon broken by a charge of the former and retired. The artillery were then ordered off. Prior to the commencement of the last action, Lee sent orders to col. Ogden, who had drawn up in the wood nearest the bridge, to defend that post to the last extremity, thereby to cover the retreat of the whole over the bridge. Lee was one of the last that remained on the field, and brought off the rear of the retreating troops. Upon his addressing general Washington after passing the morass with—" Sir, here are my troops, how is it your pleasure that I should dispose of them?" he was ordered to arrange them in the rear of English-town.

The check the British received, gave time to make a disposition of the left wing, and second line of the main army in the wood, and on the eminence to which Lee had been directed and was retreating. On this were placed some batteries of cannon by lord Stirling, who commanded the left wing, which played upon the British with great effect, and seconded by parties of infantry, detached to oppose them, effectually put a stop to their advance. Gen. Greene, who had early filed off to the right, on intelligence of the retreat of the advanced corps, marched up and took a very advantageous position on the right of Stirling. The British, finding themselves warmly opposed in front, attempted to turn the American left flank, but were repulsed. They also made a movement to the American right with as little success. Greene having advanced a body of troops with artillery to a commanding piece of ground, which not only disappointed their design, but severely infiladed those in the front of the left wing. In addition to this, Wayne advanced with a body of troops, and kept up so severe and well directed a fire, that the British were soon compelled to give way. They retired and took the position about Carr's house, which Lee had before occupied. Here their flanks were secured by thick woods and morasses, while their front could be approached only through a narrow pass. Washington, however, resolved to attack them; and for that purpose ordered gen Poor with his own, and the Carolina brigade, to move round upon their right; and gen. Woodward to their left; and the artillery to gall them in front; but they were prevented getting within reach before dark. They remained upon the ground which they had been directed to occupy, during the night, with an intention to begin the attack early the next morning, and the main body continued lying upon their arms in the field of action, to be in readiness for supporting them. During the action, Washington animated his forces by his gallant example; and by exposing his person to every danger common to the meanest soldier, taught them to hold nothing too dear for the good of their country. At night he laid down, and reposed himself in his cloak under a tree, in hope, as may be supposed, of a general action the ensuing day; for it appeared from several circumstances, that he was all along rather desirous of that event, notwithstanding the prevailing contrary opinion of the general officers whom he consulted. In the meantime Sir Henry Clinton's troops were employed in removing their wounded; and about twelve o'clock† at night they marched away in such silence, that though Poor lay extremely near them their retreat was effected without his knowledge. They left behind them four officers and about forty privates, whose wounds were too dangerous to permit their removal.

The extreme heat of the weather, the distance Sir Henry had gained by marching in the night, and the fatigue of the Americans, made a pursuit on the part of gen. Washington impracticable and fruitless. It would only have been fatal to numbers of the men, several of whom died on the day of action through the excessive heat; for Farenheit's thermometer was at 96 degrees in the Jerseys, and is said to have been 112 at Philadelphia. It was a deep sandy country through which they marched almost destitute of water; but had there been a plenty, many more would probably have perished by unguarded drinking to allay their thirst; some were

† In the London Gasette extraordinary, Aug. 24, 177⁸ Sir Henry Clinton is represented as writing in h s official letter—" Having reposed the troops till ter at night, to avoid the excessive heat of the day, I took advantage of the moonlight to rejoin lieut. gen Knyphausen." Poor Will's Almanack, printed at Philadelphia by Joseph Cruikshank, tells the public, that the new moon was on June 24th, at ten in the morning, and that on the 28th of June it set 55 minutes after ten at night. Sir Henry could have had little advantage from the light of the moon but four days old, and that was to set in an hours time had he marched off his troops precisely at ten; but if at about twelve as gen. Washington writes, and which is most likely to have been the case, the moonlight below the horizon could not have been of any advantage.

lost in that way. Sir Henry, without having been joined by the brigade of British and the 17th light dragoons from Knyphausen's division, secured by his manoeuvres the arrival of the royal army in the neighborhood of Sandy Hook on the 30th of June, without the loss of either the covering party or the baggage: but not without a considerable diminution of troops; for by a moderate calculation, from the evacuation of Philadelphia down to that day about eight hundred deserted, a great number of whom were Hessians. By the returns of the officers who had the charge of the burying parties, they left 245 non commissioned and privates on the field, and four officers. There were also besides these, several fresh graves and burying holes found near the field, in which they had put their dead before they had quitted it.‡ Fifty-nine of their soldiers perished without receiving a wound, in the same manner as several of the Americans, merely through fatigue and heat. The loss of lieut. col. Monckton, who was slain, was much lamented by the British. Upward of a hundred were made prisoners, including the officers and privates left upon the field. On the part of the Americans, lieut. col. Bonner and major Dickinson, officers of distinguished merit, were slain; beside six o.hers of inferior rank, and 61 non-commissioned and privates. The wounded were 24 officers and 136 non-commissioned and privates. The missing amounted to 130, but many of them, having only dropped through fatigue soon joined the army. Gen. Washington commended the zeal and bravery of the officers in general, but particularized Wayne as deserving special commendation. The behaviour of the troops in general, after recovering from the first surprise occasioned by the retreat of the advanced corps, was mentioned as what could not be surpassed. The public acknowledgements of congress were very flattering to the army, and particularly so to the general and his officers. The general having declined all further pursuit, detached only some light troops to attend the motions of the royal forces, and drew off the main body of his army to the borders of the North river.

The general, on his second interview with Lee upon the day of action, intimated by his reinstating and leaving him in the command of the advanced corps, that he

‡ Gen. Washton's letters.

meant to pass by what had happened, without further notice; but the latter could not brook the expressions used by the the former at their first meeting, and therefore wrote him two passionate letters, which occasioned his being put under an arrest, and brought to trial four days after the action, on the following charges exhibited against him by his excellency —1st, For disobedience of orders in not attacking the enemy on the 28th of June, agreeable to repeated instructions :—2dly, For misbehaviour before the enemy on the same day, by making an *unnecessary, disorderly, and shameful retreat :*—3dly, For disrespect to the commander-in-chief in two letters dated the 1st of July and the 28th of June. The letter dated 1st of July, was so dated through mistake, being written on the 28th of June. On the 13th of August, the court martial at which Lord Stirling presided, found him guilty upon every charge, and sentenced him to be suspended from any command in the armies of the United States of America for the term of twelve months. The terms of the second charge were softened down, as he was only found guilty of misbehaviour before the enemy, by making an unnecessary, and in some few instances, a disorderly retreat. Many were displeased with the conduct of the court martial, and thought he ought not to have been found guilty; except upon the last charge. They argued "It appears from Washington's own letter and other circumstances, that it was submitted to Lee's judgment whether to attack, in what manner, and when. There was manifest proof of Lee's intending to attack, in hope of cutting off the enemy's covering party; but he altered his opinion as to the promising prospect he had of doing it, on his coming into the plain, reconnoitring the enemy, and concluding that they were more numerous than before supposed: and upon finding Scott had quitted the point of wood where he meant to order him to remain, he judged an immediate retreat necessary. The detachment with which Lee was, amounted to no more than one third of his whole command, Scott's column, Maxwell's brigade, and the other troops to his left being full two thirds. When he began to retire, the main body was more than six miles distant, though advancing. The enemy's force was rendered the more formidable by their great superiority in cavalry, which was thought to be between four and five hundred. The ground being open was by no means advantageous to the Americans, as the British cavalry could have turned their flank. Would then an immediate attack under these circumstances, though it might have distressed the enemy's rear on the first outset, have been advisable, as it might probably have involved a general action before the detachment could have received support?— Did not prudence dictate falling back and taking a new position, rather than hazarding an action in the plain ? If Lee's judgment determined for the affirmative, how could he be declared guilty of disobeying orders? The circumstances already noted are in favor of the retreat's being necessary in the first instance : and when commenced, the prosecution of it was absolutely necessary till a good position could be taken for making an effectual stand against the enemy, to which position Lee was marching when met by Washington. The strenuous efforts of the British, after the main army was drawn up in that position, before they retired three miles from the scene of action, tend also to justify the commencement of the retreat. No mention should have been made of its being in a few instances, unless such instances were really chargeable to Lee's misconduct; whereas of these few it is certain, that some were owing to fatigue and the enormous heat of the weather. The very sentence of the court martial is in favor of Lee's innocence as to the two first charges; for a year's suspension from command is in no wise proportioned to his crimes, if guilty. Several are of opinion that he would not have been condemned on these two, had it not been for his disrespectful conduct toward Washington. On the other hand, some have surmised, that his manoeuvers were owing either to treachery or want of courage; but they who have the opportunity of knowing him most, will be furthest from such apprehensions.*

No sooner had Sir Henry Clinton with the army evacuated Philadelphia, than Lord Howe prepared to sail with the fleet to New York. Repeated calms retarded his passage down the Delaware, so that he could not quit the river till the evening of June the 28th : however he anchored off Sandy Hook the next day, followed by the transports. The succeeding day Sir Henry arrived, and the artillery, baggage, and part of the troops were removed from

*In compiling several of the preceding pages recourse has been had to the public letters of Sir Henry Clinton and Gen. Washington, to various private letters and information, and to gen. Lee's trial.—*Author's note,*

the main, as the weather permitted; the rest of the army passed, on the 5th of July, over a bridge of boats across a narrow channel to Sandy Hook. They were afterwards carried up to New York. On the 7th, lord Howe received advice that the Toulon squadron was arrived on the coast of Virginia. Count d'Estaing anchored at night on the 8th at the entrance of the Delaware, after being 87 days at sea. On that day the count wrote to Congress: on the receipt of his letter they sent word to gen. Washington, that it was their desire he would co-operate with the count, in the execution of such offensive operations as they should mutually approve. The same day the congress resolved that a suitable house should be provided for Monsieur Gerard,† and chose a committee of five to wait upon him on his arrival, and conduct him to his lodgings. The next morning d'Estaing weighed and sailed toward the Hook,‡ and in the evening of the 11th anchored without it. Had not bad weather and unexpected impediments prevented the count must have surprised Howe's fleet in the Delaware, as the latter would not have had time to escape after being apprised of his danger. The destruction of the fleet must have been the consequence of such surprisal; and that must have occasioned the inevitable loss of the royal army, which would have been so enclosed by the French squadron on the one side, and the American forces on the other, that the Saratoga catastrophe§ must have been repeated. This fatal stroke would have been of an amount and magnitude (with respect to both the marine and land service, and the consequence hanging upon it) not easily to be conceived. The prevention of it, by the various hindrances that d'Estaing met with on his voyage, ought to be considered by Great Britain as a signally providential deliverance.

Lord Howe's fleet consisted only of six 64 gun ships, three of 50 and two of 40, with some frigates and sloops. Count d'Estaing had 12 ships of the line, several of which were of great force and weight of metal, one carrying 90, another 80, and six 74 guns each; he had beside present with him three of the four stout large frigates that had attended him on his voyage. He anchored on the Jersey side, about four miles without the Hook;* and American pilots of the first abilities, provided for the purpose, went on board the fleet; among them were persons whose circumstances placed them above the rank of common pilots. Lord Howe had the advantage of possessing the harbour formed by Sandy Hook; the entrance of which is covered by a bar, and from whence the inlet passes to New York. As it could not be known whether the French would not attempt passing in force over the bar, it was necessary that the British should be prepared to oppose them. On this occasion a spirit displayed itself not only in the fleet and army, but through every order and denomination of seamen that is not often equalled. The crews of the transports hastened with eagerness to the fleet, tnat it might be completely manned: masters and mates solicited employment, and took their stations at the guns with the common sailors, the light infantry, grenadiers, and even wounded officers so contended to serve as mariners on board the men-of-war, that the point of honor was obliged to be decided by lot! In a word, the patriotism, zeal, bravery and magnanimity which appeared at this juncture, was a credit even to Great Britain. It must however be acknowledged, that the popularity of lord Howe, and the confidence founded on his abilities, contributed not a little to these exertions. But the American pilots declaring it impossible to carry the large ships of d'Estaing's squadron over the bar, into the Hook, on account of their draught of water, and Gen. Washington pressing him to sail to Newport, he left the Hook after eleven days tarriance, [July 22] and in a few hours was out of sight. Nothing could be more providential. While he remained, about twenty sail of vessels bound to New York fell into his possession; they were chiefly prizes taken from the Americans: but had he stayed a few days longer, admiral Bryon's fleet must have fallen a defenceless prey into his hands.† That squadron had met with unusual bad weather: and being separated in different storms, and lingering through a tedious passage, arrived,

† French minister to Congress, in recognition of the independence of the United States of America.

‡ His fleet consisted of 12 ships of the line and four frigates of a superior size. It sailed from Toulon April 13.

§ The surrender of Gen. Burgoyne's army at Saratoga, Oct. 16, 1777.

* Near Shrewsbury—*Irving*.

† This fleet, embraced 12 ships of the line, and sails from Portsmouth May 20th, but was stopped by an express and detained at Plymouth until June 5th.

scattered, broken, sickly, dismasted, or otherwise damaged, in various degrees of distress, upon different and remote parts of the American coast. Between the de parture of d'Estaing and the thirtieth of July, the Renown of 50 guns from the West Indies, the Raisonable and Centurion of 64 and 50 from Halifax and the Cornwall of 74 guns, all arrived singly at Sandy Hook. By his speedy departure a number of provision ships from Cork escaped also, together with their convoy.—They went up the Delaware within fifty miles of Philadelphia after lord Howe had quitted the river, not having obtained any information of what had happened. The British ministry had neglected countermanding their destination, though orders for the evacuation of Philadelphia had been sent off so early as to have admitted of their receiving fresh directions where to have steered, before sailing. Great rejoicings were made at New York upon their safe arrival, especially as provisions were much wanted by both the fleet and army.

Short Description of the Battle, Occuring in the Centennial Novel, the "Spur of Monmouth," Published by Claxton, Remsen & Haffelfinger, Phila., 1876, and alleged to be founded on Official Documents and Personal Information of Importance. The Book since acknowledged to have been Edited by Mr. Henry Morford, formerly of Monmouth County.

THE STORY OF MONMOUTH FIGHT.

The history of the Battle of Monmouth has been so often written and rehearsed, the earlier part of that eight-and-ninety years which have elapsed since it occurred, that any attempt to re-write it would be performing a work of great difficulty without a corresponding necessity to warrant it. It was but a trifling conflict, in the numbers engaged or the loss sustained by either combatant, in comparison with many that followed it at no great distance, and those which have still later succeeded it, at home and abroad. What new interest, then, in this combat of 1778 ?

And yet, what the Men of the Revolution, who had shared in it or the conflicts preceding or following, always designated as "Monmouth Fight," had peculiarities of surrounding and effect, making it of much more importance than the great average of battles that have had less than a thousand and slain on either side of the opposing forces. It has been already said that it had in it some of the features of the "turning point;" and it is well known that it was the carrying out of one of Washington's well-considered plans, the driving of the British forces from New Jersey, of which he had said some months earlier: "If we can oblige them to evacuate the Jerseys, we must drive them to the utmost distress; for they have depended upon the supplies from that State for their winter's support." Again, the battle was fought on a Sunday—something judged of more importance, at that less distant remove than the present from the Puritan period, and when neither the fact had been so well illustrated nor the adage made so broadly known in literature and the world, that: "There are no Sundays in war-time." Still again, the heat of the June weather was inordinate, and the additional suffering as well as greater mortality thus entailed, something likely to linger in tradition, long after other events of even more importance should grow dim in recollection. And yet again, it was at Monmouth Fight that the master-hand of the struggle came into collision with one who had before found few superiors and acknowledged none, in the meeting of Washington and Lee on the field, and the utterance of those words destined to slay a career as effectually as the sword could have ended life.

Under such circumstances, it is not strange that around this battle of June 28th, 1778, should have been woven much more of romance than really belonged to it, and that to the event should have been attributed something more of effect upon the patriot cause than it really exercised. It is not strange that more than one local ballad, dealing with Washington, Lee, Forman, and others immediately connected with the movements and fortunes of the day, came early from the lips or the pens of rural poets, and were trolled in cracked treble, long after, by the old soldiers who survived it. Of these, scarcely a couplet now remains, worth recalling; and it is to a rhyme of a much later period, called "The Battle of Monmouth—a Ballad of 'After the War,'" that we must recur, for all the poetry at present within memory, connected with this conflict.—Picked up, floating about in the newspapers of that period, many a long year ago, and unclaimed as some similar waif might be, discovered drifting aimlessly at sea,—

it yet seems to demand a place here, before entering upon a rapid resume of the events bringing on, accompanying, and following the battle. In the ballad, one of the veterans of '78, a few a years after, is telling the story, in other words but with the same spirit and the same effect as it was often told, many years later, to the present writer by the pensioners of of his charge:

"'Tis good ten years since Mercer fell,
  Borne down at Princeton fight;
'Tis good ten years since hill and dell
  With battle were alight.
The Hessians have gone back, to smoke
  Their long Dutch pipes at home;
The sword of war is bent and broke,
  And peaceful days have come.

"Earl Moria, on his Irish land,
  Forgets how Rawdon fought,
And Clinton holds no more command
  Where daring deeds are wrought.
Old 'seventy-six has glided by,
  And 'seventy-eight passed on;
And under freedom's happy sky
  We till the fields we won.

"The harvest waves on Monmouth ground;
  But I have seen the day
A bloodier harvest might be found,
  Stretched ou' in grim array:
When patrot men and hireling men
  Lay quiet, side by side,
With ghastly wounds, scarce counted then
  To tell how each had died.

"Oh, friends! it was bitter a day,
  As e'er in summer came
To drive all cooling breath away
  And heat the air to flame.
Beneath our light and scanty dress
  We bowed, as it were steel:
The very sand like burning brass
  Seemed all the day to feel.

"The water-springs were parched and dry,
  And dry the meadows-green:
The muddy ooze we carried by
  Grew hot in our canteens;
Yet well we bore the scorching day,
  And bore the battle's brunt;
And not a soldier slunk away,
  While brave men led our front.

"But once we trembled—when we stood
  Beneath the cannon's beat,
The foe on-rolling like a flood
  And Lee in full retreat;
But Burr dashed in beneath the shot,
  And Washington came on,
And bade our columns waver not,
  For yet no chance was gone.

"Oh, friends! ye've seen that great, good man,
  Whose glory makes our pride,
Borne onward in a people's van,
  With triumph at his side;
But nobler looked he in the fray,
  And prouder was his face,
As there he bade us wash away
  In victory our disgrace.

"Lee lives, his day of honor done,
  Because he dared, that day,
To speak hard words to Washington;
  And well, oh friends, he may!—
For sad defeat had rested long
  Upon old Monmouth's name,
Had Washington not curbed his wrong
  And showed us all our shame.

"We pressed them backward, foot by foot,
  Still fighting like brave men,—
Till long ere sunset we had put
  The foe to route again;
But warily did Clinton draw
  His broken troops away,
And with two armies, at nightfa',
  Upon the field we lay.

"The evening wind came fresh and cool
  Over the clover-farms,
As all that night, so worn and dull,
  We rested on our arms:
The fires were bright in Clinton's camp;
  But long ere morning's dawn
His beaten host was on the tramp,
  And all our foes were gone.

"I ween he thinks of Monmouth ground
  With less delight than we,
And seldom tells the check he found
  To those beyond the sea;
But ne'er again may cannon sweep
  Where waves the golden grain,—
And ne'er again an army sleep
  Upon old Monmouth's plain!"

Thus much of the poetical, in connection with this battle, which without doubt saw some of the keenest fighting of the whole struggle. In plain prose, the story of the conflict, so far as it may be deduced from already-written history and the still-remembered relations of those who took part in it, may be almost as briefly told. It can only be guessed that Sir Henry Clinton, who had originally intended to to leave Philadelphia by sea for New York, changed his plans in that regard, partially in apprehension of the French fleet, and partially under the fear that Washington might move more rapidly by land than he could do by sea, reach New York in advance of him, and possibly recapture that most important hold before his arrival. How well advised and ready for movement the Americans were, is shown by the fact that while Clinton did not leave Philadelphia until the 18th June, on the evening of the same day Washington commenced breaking up his camp at Valley Forge and prepared to push forward in pursuit.

What was really the force in this instance carried by Washington into the Jerseys, has been variously stated. His whole effective muster is known to have been twelve and fifteen thousand. A small detachment was sent, under the crippled Arnold, to take possession of Philadelphia; and other necessary details somewhat reduced the effective force, which was, however, more numerous than it had been when encamping at Valley Forge, and with the additions of a strong body of New Jersey militia under General Dickinson, and a considerable corps of Pennsylvania volunteers under General Cadwallader. At no previous time of the Revolution had the personal hands of Washington been so strengthened as at this moment, as appeared; for with Charles Lee second in command, and the presence of Greene, Wayne, Lafayette, Steuben, Maxwell, Hamilton, Morgan, and others only inferior to them in reputation as warriors, even that small army must have seemed incalculably stronger than indicated by its mere numbers.— Somewhat too late it afterwards became evident that this array of leaders rather weakened than strengthened the army, the counsels of so many being opposed to the opinions of the Commander, with other evils of partizanship necessarily involved.

Any attempt to measure the force with which Clinton left Philadelphia, for his march across the Jerseys, must be even more futile. The patriot relators, after the war, habitually set his numbers at eighteen to twenty thousand—fifty to seventy per cent. above those of Washington; but later developements made it doubtful whether the Americans were really at all outnumbered, while there was a certain supposed demoralization in the British force, already alluded to, considered inevitable from their winter in Philadelphia, but by no means shown in their combined dash and steadiness on the day of battle.

Clinton crossed the Delaware, to Gloucester Point, a short distance below Camden, on the New Jersey side, on the 18th.

Washington followed, crossing the Delaware at Coryell's Ferry, a little above Trenton, two days later, on the 20th. Sir Henry pursued his course across the State, nearly in a direct line for the Raritan at New Brunswick, by Haddonfield and Mount Holly, to some extent harrassed by the New Jersey militia and irregular bodies, but not seriously troubled through that agency. Washington pushed forward at some distance on his left, by the Somerset region, only bending southward when he found himself as far advanced as his foe—Clinton then halting at Allentown and changing his own line of march also to the southward, by Monmouth Court-House, (Freehold) for Middletown, Sandy Hook and the sea, evidently to avoid an engagement.

From the moment of discovering that disposition on the part of Clinton, Washington, who had so far been overruled by his leading officers as to the advisability of hazarding an attack in force, determined to adhere to his first resolution—to overtake Clinton, partially pass him, and attack him in flank at the earliest possible moment. With this object in view, he diverged southward, then also tending towards Monmouth Court-House, rightly divining the second line of march of the enemy. The result of all this was that on the 27th June, Sir Henry Clinton encamped his forces in the immediate neighborhood of Freehold, with his line extended some three miles beyond that town to the west, towards Allentown, and about half that distance to the east, towards Middletown and Shrewsbury. Washington formed his camp, the same night, at and near Englishtown, three or four miles westward, with Morgan's corps of riflemen thrown forward on the right, and the New Jersey militia, under Dickinson, similarly advanced on the left. It has long been well known that the American commander intended to force an engagement on the following day, and that the British commander, though anxious to avoid the combat, had yet made all preparations to repel any attack, in whatever force.

The onset of the Americans, to command any hope of success, required to be made at once, as the patriot general well understood—as another day's march of the British would bring them within shelter of the hills below Freehold, towards Middletown, where any assault must be made at a marked disadvantage. The division intended for the attack was thrown forward to Englishtown under Lafayette; but at that place, on the 27th, Lee was ordered to join him with two brigades, and as senior officer both in years and command, to assume charge of the whole attacking division. Those familiar with the late past events of this narration, cannot choose but to admire the action of Washington towards his jealous subordinate, in this instance; and yet little doubt remains that this generosity was an error, and that the young French general, then in the hot blood of his youth, and possessing military talents afterwards destined to display themselves so preeminently, should have been allowed to remain in command, for an enterprise peculiarly requiring dash and vigor. As if to make the error more disastrous in its effects, the Commander-in-chief (as was afterwards known) gave to Lee discretionary power as to the time and mode of making the attack, little warranted by the after-conduct of that officer.

Washington's intention, as already indicated, was to attack in force, early in the morning of the 28th, at the moment when the royal army should resume their line of march eastward for the seaboard. In the beginning, this programme was vigorously carried out, Lee ordering Morgan and Dickinson very near to the British as corps of observation, long before daylight, and himself moving to the attack at the moment when the first movement of the enemy was in progress. With him were the brigades of Wayne and Maxwell, while Grayson, with two picked brigades, was ordered forward to attack the British pickets and create confusion in the rear. So far, all had gone well for the patriots, and the success of their operations seemed literally assured.

The Americans had pressed forward to some miles beyond or eastward of Monmouth Court House, when that occurred, marring the fortunes of the day if not altogether changing them. Clinton, with a spirit he did not always manifest, changed front with great celerity, and signified his intention of making a return attack in force, instead of allowing his rear to be possibly cut off through inaction. Lee, unprepared for this counter-movement, and deceived as to the real intention halted his force at the critical moment, and began to give ground, to the infinite chagrin and mortification of Wayne, commanding under him. Lafayette, coming up with the main body of the advanced corps, believed the moment a favorable one for gaining the rear of that division of the enemy moving against them; but the caution of Lee prevailed, the previously-attacking force fell back before the advancing British, thus driven beyond the Court House, in the direction of the old Tennant Church, some four miles northwestward of Freehold. Here it was that the tide of reverse was at last stemmed, through the coming up of Washington at the head of the main body, pressing on to what he believed was victory in advance; and here it is that in all the years which have since gone by, the " battle-ground of Monmouth " has been located, in the numberless relations of the events of that day.

Here it was that the battle really became general, both combatants displaying bravery and determination never elsewhere excelled during the war. Here it was, that, around the Tennant Parsonage, and over fields and behind woods and hedgerows in the neighborhood, bush-fighting mingled with the ordinary tactics of civilized war, and the deadly aim of the sharp-shooter came into destructive prominence. Here it was that Wayne, half-crazed by the reverse which he believed the result of a blunder, raged in arms, in a manner to strengthen his soubriquet of " Mad Anthony." Here it was that the brave British Colonel Monckton fell, leading his grenadiers against Wayne with a steadiness worthy of his grave in the Tennant Churchyard and the admiration ever since expressed for him by his foes. Here it was that beneath the heat of the burning day, and in the fierce excitement of the battle, scores fell and died without the touch of bullet or blade, while scores of others perished in the morass then intersecting a part of the battle-field lying between the Tennant Church and the Parsonage.

Here it was—most notable of all single events of the day—that Washington met Lee in retreat, a mile eastward of the Parsonage, on the Freehold road, and hurled at him, in his surprise and indignation, words much more natural and much more forcible than so-called propriety has attributed to him, in the traditional formula: " Sir, I desire to know the reason of this unseemly retreat, and whence arises this disorder and confusion!" No such words formed the first greeting of the Commander-in-chief to his subordinate, in that moment of inevitable grief and anger : if the real words even involved profanity and insult, as the sharers in that memorable scene heard and oft repeated them, who shall blame the man on whose shoulders lay the destinies of a nation ?— and who shall recall them at this day, for that carping and critical dissection to which every expression of human feeling seems of late amenable ? How they were answered by "Boiling Water" of this chronicle, and what effect the after-conduct of Charles Lee with reference to them had upon his position and closing life,— this has been too often and too accurately told to need repetition.

Enough that thereafter Lee, however much he had erred, bore himself with great though boastful gallantry throughout the remainder of the action. Enough that from the moment of Washington's coming, however hard to undo the error of an hour, the tide of battle remained at a standstill, if it did not at once flow in favor of the patriots. When the night fell, the palm of assured victory was almost within the grasp of the patriot commander, and only the one question remained whether Clinton was or was not too much crippled to resume his march towards Sandy Hook. Only the broken character of the ground thwarted Washington's intention of testing his strength, by yet another attack after nightfall ; with such impediments, and in the exhausted state of his troops, the second attack was deferred until morning. Both forces lay on their arms, very near each other, but a little west of Monmouth Court House, when the night came on ; but when the morning broke, the British camp was deserted, and the harrassed hosts of Clinton were beyond the Court House and out of reach, having left so silently that even General Poor, in command of the American advanced corps, had no suspicion of the intention or its fulfilment. With this departure and virtual escape of the British, necessarily the combat was at an end. Clinton pursued his way, by the hills of Middletown, to Sandy Hook and the fleet of Lord Howe, which bore his troops away to New York ; and Washington, his enemy driven from the Jerseys if no more, marched northward with his army to New Brunswick, and thence to the Hudson and to White Plains in Westchester, destined to be so notable in the later conflicts preceding the close.

Thus ended Monmouth Fight, a drawn battle in some regards, and yet by no means so in its effect, already more than once stated. So far as human opinion can be final, it would have proved a decisive victory, but for the one error of Washington in entrusting so much of discretion to Lee, who, with a thousand desirable qualities, of this had *none ;* for the one error of Lee, in believing that Clinton dared an attack in force, instead of a mere effort to save his baggage ; and for the one additional error, for which no responsible agent has ever yet been found, which held Morgan, the hero of the Carolinian Cowpens and chief of the terrible riflemen bearing his name, within three or four miles of the place of conflict during all that memorable day, hearing the sounds of the battle, waiting orders to fall on the flank of the enemy, receiving none, and fuming out his ardent soul in wonder and rage, while remembering the one instance in which he had gone beyond the commands of Washington, with its bitter finale,—and thus not daring to place himself and his hunting-shirts where the aid of all was so sorely needed.

There have been scores of legendary incidents attached to the battle of Monmouth, with which, in this relation, we have no more to do than merely to pay them the respect of recognition. The world has heard, and heard again, the story of Moll Pitcher, who fought the gun of her dead cannonier husband and afterwards wore the uniform and received the half-pay of a sergeant in the service.— Many hearts have sorrowed over the fate of the poor young British officer, whose blood yet to day stains one of the seats of the old Tennant Church, where he was carried to die, and where he died with such touching last words on his lips. Though the incident has often been related as of another Forman—General David of that name—not all know how nearly Bessie Wayne-Forman came that day to being a widow, when Lewis Forman, serving with his Light Horse, and with his pistols emptied and his sword splintered in his hand, was chased through the open door of a harvest-barn by a British trooper intent on a blow at him, and only escaped by the matchless horsemanship which could hold his horse steady while that of his foe went down on the slippery oaken surface.

Not all know that Susan Allardyce that met her fate—being rescued from momentary danger by Major Robert Pomeroy, a young officer of the Maryland brigade,

OLD TIMES IN OLD MONMOUTH. 35

quite the equal of her lost idol in size and stature, while much more refined in bearing,—with whom she fell her whole moderate length in love, at once, the Major reciprocating, and the daughter of Captain John Allardyce becoming at a later day at once a bride and a Marylander, rather glad than the reverse that she had failed to capture the fancy of Lewis Forman. Not all know how Marc Antony, who had the preceding day served up a hive of bees as dessert to some foraging British officers who forced themselves on the hospitality of the Wayne-Forman mansion in the absence of its master,—on the day of the battle armed himself with the old king's-piece belonging to " de family, sah !" and went out shooting from behind hedges, his game, if any, remaining where it fell. Nor how Bessie Forman, jestingly called upon for a blessing by the same officers as they set foot in stirrup to ride away, blessed them with the hope " that Morgan's riflemen might catch them before they reached Sandy Hook."

These, though they naturally come back to mind in recalling the relations of the time and the event by the men who bore part in it, are little more than shadows floating around tne event itself. *
* *

The Following Account of the Battle of Monmouth is from Lossing, who visited the Battle Ground in 1850, and spared no pains to make it correct and complete.

Sir Henry Clinton intended to march from Haddonfield directly to Brunswick, and embark his troops on the Raritan River. He moved on slowly, by the way of Mount Holly to Crosswicks and Allentown. There being but a single road, his long train of baggage wagons and bat horses, (horses allowed to each company of the British army on foreign service, to carry cooking utensils, &c.,) together with his troops made
A line nearly twelve miles in extent.

He was obliged to build bridges and causeways over the streams and marshes, and his progress consequently was very tardy. When at Allentown, perceiving Washington almost on his front, Clinton changed his course, rather than risk a general action with all his encumbrances. Turning to the right he took the road leading to Monmouth Court House and Sandy Hook, with the determination of embarking his troops at the latter place. The American Army had now reached Kingston, on the Millstone River. General Lee was still strongly opposed to any interference with the movements of the enemy, and being next in command to Washington, his opinion had considerable weight with the other officers. Yet six general officers were in favor of continued annoyances by detachments and three of them (Greene, LaFayette and Wayne,) declared in favor of a general action. Washington was at first embarrassed by these divided opinions; but, relying upon his own judgment, which was strongly in favor of an engagement, he asked no further advice, but proceeded to make arrangements for battle He immediately ordered a detachment of one thousand men under General Wayne, to join the troops nearest the enemy ; gave General LaFayette the command of all the advanced parties, amounting to almost four thousand men, including the militia, and moved forward with the main body to Cranberry. The weather was intensely hot, which circumstance in connection with a heavy storm that commenced about nine in the morning, made it impossible to resume the march without injury to the troops.

Early on the morning of the 27th, LaFayette, with the advanced forces, proceeded to Englishtown, a hamlet about five miles westward of Monmouth Court House. Sir Henry Clinton was advised of the movements of the Americans, and properly apprehending an attack upon his flanks and rear changed the disposition of his line. He placed the baggage train in front, and his best troops consisting of the grenadiers, light infantry, and chasseurs of the line, in the rear. The baggage of the whole army (in which term were included the bat-horses and wheel carriages of every department) was placed under the charge of General Knyphausen. With his army thus arranged, Clinton encamped in a strong position near Monmouth Court House, secured on nearly all sides by woods and marshy grounds. His line extended on the right about a mile and a half beyond the Court House to the parting of the roads leading to Shrewsbury and Middletown, and on the left along the road from Monmouth to Allentown, about three miles.

The alteration in the disposition of his line of march made by Sir Henry Clinton obliged Washington to increase the number of his advanced corps, and accordingly he sent Major General Lee with two brigades to join LaFayette at Englishtown, and as senior officer, to take command of the whole division designed for making the first attack. The main army marched the same day and encamped within three miles of Englishtown. Morgan's corps was left hovering on the British right, and about seven hundred militia, under Dickinson, menaced their left. Washington foresaw the increased strength the enemy would gain by reaching the heights of Middletown, which were about three miles in advance. To prevent them from obtaining the advantage he determined to attack their rear the moment they should attempt to move. For this purpose he ordered General Lee to make the necessary disposition and to keep his troops in readiness to move at the shortest notice. Sir Henry Clinton, perceiving that an immediate action was inevitable, made preparations accordingly. The night of the 27th was one of great anxiety to both parties.

A Memorable Sabbath Day.

The 28th of June, 1778, a day memorable in the annals of the Revolution, was the christian Sabbath. The sky was cloudless over the plains of Monmouth when the morning dawned, and the sun came up with all the fervor of the summer solstice. It was the sultriest day of the year, not a zephyr moved the leaves; nature smiled in her beautiful garments of flowers and foliage, and the birds carolled with delight in the fullness of love and harmony. Man alone was the discordant note in the universal melody. He alone, the proud "lord of creation" claiming for his race the sole mundane possession of the Divine image, disturbed the chaste worship of the hour which ascended audibly from the groves, the streams, the meadows, and the woodlands. On that calm Sabbath morning, in the midst of paradisal beauty, twenty thousand men girded on the implements of hellish war to maim and destroy each other, to sully the green grass and fragrant flowers with human blood.

At about one o'clock in the morning, Lee sent an order to General Dickinson to detach several hundred men as near the British lines as possible, as a corps of observation. Colonel Morgan was also directed to approach near enough to attack them on their first movement. Orders were likewise given to the other divisions of the advanced forces to make immediate preparations to march, and, before daylight, Colonel Grayson, with his regiment, leading the brigades of Scott and Varnum, was in the saddle and moving slowly in the direction of Monmouth Court House.

General Knyphausen, with the first division of the British troops, among which was the chief body of the Hessians and the Pennsylvania and Maryland Loyalists, moved forward at daybreak. Sir Henry Clinton, with the other division consisting of the flower of his army, did not follow until eight o'clock. Dickinson observed the earliest movement and sent an express to Lee, and the Commander-in-Chief, the moment Knyphausen began his march. Washington immediately put the army in motion and sent orders to General Lee to press forward and attack the enemy, unless there should be very powerful reasons to the contrary. This discretionary clause in the order eventuated in trouble. Lee advanced immediately with the brigades of Wayne and Maxwell, and sent an order to Grayson to press forward and attack the pickets of the enemy as speedily as possible, while he himself pushed forward to overtake and support him. Grayson, with the two brigades had passed the Freehold meeting-house, two miles and a half from Monmouth, when he received the order. Lee's aid, who bore it, gave it as his opinion that he had better halt, for he had learned on the way that the main body of the British were moving to attack the Americans. This information was erroneous, but it caused Grayson to tarry. General Dickinson, who was posted on a height on the eastern side of the morass, received the same intelligence and communicated it to Lee, through the aid, on his return. Lee conformed to the reports, and after posting two regiments of militia upon a hill southeast of the meeting-house, to secure a particular road, he pushed forward with his staff, across the morass, at a narrow causeway, and joined Dickinson upon the height. There conflicting intelligence was brought to him. At one moment it was asserted that the enemy had moved off with precipitation, leaving only a covering party behind; at another, that the whole army was filing off to right and left to attack the Americans. While he was endeavoring to obtain reliable information on which to predicate orders, LaFayette arrived at the head of the main body of the advanced corps.

Having satisfied himself that no important force of the enemy was upon either flank, Lee determined to march on. His whole command now amounted to about four thousand troops exclusive of Morgan's corps and the Jersey militia. The broken country was heavily wooded to the verge of the plain of Monmouth. Under the cover of the forest, Lee pressed forward until near the open fields when he formed a part of his line for action, and with Wayne and others rode forward to reconnoitre.

Beginning of the Battle.

From observations and intelligence, he concluded that the column of the British army which he saw deploying on the left were only a covering party of about two thousand men; and entertaining hopes that he might succeed in cutting them off from the main army manœvered accordingly. Wayne was detached with seven hundred men and two pieces of artillery, to attack the covering party on the rear, not however, with sufficient vigor to cause them to retreat to the main body. Meanwhile Lee, with a stronger force endeavored by a short road leading to the left to gain the front of the party. Small detachments were concealed in the woods, at different points on the enemy's flanks, to annoy them.

At about nine in the morning, just as Wayne was prepared to make a descent upon the enemy, a party of American light-horse, advancing on the right observed the Queen's Dragoons upon an eminence in the edge of the wood, parading as if they intended to make an attack.— Lee ordered his light-horse to allow the dragoons to approach as near as could be done with safety, and then to retreat to where Wayne was posted, and let him receive them. The manœver was partially successful, the dragoons followed the retreating light-horse until fired upon by a party under Colonel Butler, ambushed in the edge of the woods when they wheeled and galloped off toward the main column. Wayne ordered Colonel Oswald to bring his two pieces of artillery to bear upon them, and then pushed forward himself his whole force to charge the enemy with bayonets. Colonel Oswald crossed a morass, planted his guns on a small eminence, and opened a cannonade at the same time. Wayne was prosecuting his attack with vigor, and with every prospect of full success, when he received an order from Lee to make only a feigned attack, and not to push on too precipitately, as that would subvert his plan of cutting off the covering party. Wayne was disappointed, chagrined, irritated. He felt that his commander had plucked the palm of sure victory from his hand, but like a true soldier, he instantly obeyed, and withheld his troops, hoping that Lee himself would recover what his untimely order had lost. In this, too, the brave Wayne was disappointed; for only a portion of the troops on the right, under Lee, issued out of the woods in small detachments, about a mile below the court house, and within cannon shot of the royal forces. At that instant Sir Henry Clinton was informed that the Americans were marching in force on both his flanks, with the evident design of capturing his baggage, then making a line of several miles in the direction of Middletown. To avert the blow he changed the front of his army by facing about, and prepared to attack Wayne with so much vigor, that the Americans on his flanks would be obliged to fly to the succor of that officer. This movement was speedily made by Clinton, and a large body of cavalry soon approached cautiously towards the right of Lee's troops.

The Retreat of General Lee.

LaFayette perceiving this, and believing it to be a good opportunity to gain the rear of the division of the enemy marching against them, rode quickly up to Lee, and asked permission to make the attempt.— "Sir," replied Lee, "you do not know British soldiers; we cannot stand against them, we shall certainly be driven back at first, and we must be cautious." LaFayette replied, "It may be so, general, but British soldiers have been beaten, and they may be again; at any rate I am disposed to make the trial." Lee so far complied as to order the marquis to wheel his column by his right, and gain and attack the enemy's left. At the same time he weakened Wayne's detachment on the left, by ordering the regiments of Wesson, Stewart, and Livingston to the support of the right. He then rode toward Oswald's battery to reconnoitre. At that moment, to his great astonishment, as he said, Lee saw a large portion of the British army marching back on the Middletown road toward the Court House. Apparently disconcerted, he immediately ordered his right to fall back. The brigades of Scott and Maxwell, on the left, were already moving forward and approaching the right of the royal forces, who were pressing steadily on in solid phalanx toward the position occupied by Lee, with the apparent design of gaining Wayne's rear and attacking the American right at the same moment. General Scott had left the wood, crossed a morass, and was forming for action on the plain, and Maxwell was preparing to do the same, when Lee ordered the former to re-enter the wood, arrange his column there and await further directions. Perceiving the retrograde movement on the right, and perhaps mjstaking the spirit of Lee's order, Scott recrossed the morass, retreated through the woods towards the Freehold meeting-house, followed by Maxwell. As soon as intelligence of this movement reached Lee, he sent an order to LaFayette to fall back to the Court House. The marquis obeyed, but with reluctance. As he approached the Court House he learned with surprise and deep mortification, that a general retreat had begun on the right, under the immediate command of Lee, and he was obliged to follow. The British pursued them as far as the court house, where they halted, while the Americans pressed onward across the morass above Carr's house to the broken eminence called the heights of Freehold, where they also halted. The heat was intense and both parties suffered terribly from thirst and fatigue. In many places they sank ankle deep in the loose, sandy soil. Their rest was of short duration. The royal troops pressed forward, and Lee, instead of making a bold stand in his advantageous position. resumed his retreat toward the Freehold meetinghouse. A panic seized the Republican troops, and over the broken country they fled precipitately and in great confusion, a large portion of them passing toward the causeway over a broad morass, where many perished ; while others, overpowered by the heat, fell upon the earth and were trampled to death in the sand by those pressing on behind them. In the first retreat a desultory cannonade had been kept up by both parties, but now nothing was heard but a few musket shots and loud shouts of the pursuing enemy.

While these manœuvres in the vicinity of Monmouth court house were occurring, Washington, with the reserve, was pressing forward to the support of Lee. ׆hen the latter made the discovery that a large covering party was in the rear of the royal army, and formed his plan to cut them off, he sent a messenger to the commander-in-chief, assuring him that success must follow. On the reception of this intelligence, Washington ordered the right wing, under General Green, to march to the right, " by the new church," or Freehold meeting house, to prevent the turning of that flank by the enemy, and to " fall into the Monmouth road a small distance in the rear of the court house," while he prepared to follow with the left wing, directly in Lee's rear, to support him. To facilitate the march of the men, and to contribute to their comfort on that sultry morning, they were ordered to disencumber themselves of their packs and blankets. Many laid aside their coats, and thus relieved, prepared for battle.

WASHINGTON TO THE FRONT.

While the chief was making this disposition near the Freehold meeting-house. a countryman, mounted on a fleet horse, came in hot haste from the direction of the contending forces. He brought the astounding intelligence that the continental troops were retreating, with the enemy in close pursuit. The commander-in-chief could not credit the report, for he had heard only a few cannon peals in the direction of the court house, and he did not conceive it possible that Lee would retreat without first giving battle. He spurred forward, and when about half way between the meeting house and the morass, he met the head of the first retreating column.— He was greatly alarmed on finding the advanced corps falling back upon the main army without notice, thereby endangering the order of the whole. Giving a hasty order to the commander of the first retreating division to halt upon an eminence, Washington, with his staff, pushed across the causeway to the rear of the flying column, where he met Lee, at the head of the second division of the retreating forces. The commander-in-chief was fearfully aroused by the conduct of that officer, and as he rode up to Lee he exclaimed in words of bitter anger, and tone of withering rebuke, "Sir, I desire to know what is the reason, and whence arises this disorder and confusion." Stung, not so much by these *words* as by the *manner* of Washington, Lee retorted harshly, and a few angry words passed between them. It was no time for dispute as the enemy was within fifteen minutes march of them. Wheeling his horse, Washington hastened to Ramsey and Stewart, in the rear, rallied a large portion of their regiments, and ordered Oswald, with his two pieces of cannon, to take post upon an eminence. By a well directed fire from his battery, Oswald checked the pursuing enemy. The presence of the chief inspired the fugitives with courage, and within ten minutes after he appeared the retreat was suspended, the troops rallied and soon order came out of the midst of the utmost confusion. - Stewart and Ramsey formed under cover of the wood, and co-operated with Oswald in keeping the enemy at bay. While the British grenadiers were pouring their destructive fire upon the broken ranks of the Americans, the voice of Washington seemed omnipotent with the inspiration of courage ; it was a voice of faith to the despairing soldiers. Fearlessly he rode in the face of the iron storm, and gave his orders. The whole patriot army, which half an hour before seemed on the verge of destruction, panic stricken and without order, was now drawn up in battle array, and prepared to meet the enemy with a bold and well-arranged front. This effected, Washington rode back to Lee, and pointing to the rallied troops, said :— " Will you, sir, command in that place?" " I will," eagerly exclaimed Lee. " Then," said Washington, " I expect you to check the enemy immediately." " Your command shall be obeyed," replied Lee, " and I will not be the first to leave the field."

Back to the main army Washington now hurried, and with wondrous expedition formed their confused ranks into battle order on the eminences on the western side of the morass. Lord Stirling was placed in command of the left wing ; while General Greene on receiving intelligence of Lee's retreat, had marched back and now took an advantageous position on the right of Stirling.

General Lee displayed all his skill and courage in obedience to the chief's order to " check the enemy." A warm cannonade had commenced between the American and British artillery on the right of Stewart and Ramsey when Washington recrossed the morass to form the main army, while the royal light horse charged furiously upon the right of Lee's division. At that moment Hamilton rode up to the chief and said : " I will stay with you, my dear general, and die with you. Let us all die rather than retreat." But the enemy pressed so closely upon them with an overwhelming force, that the Americans were obliged to give way. As they emerged from the woods, the belligerents seemed completely intermingled.

The enemy next attacked Livingston's regiment and Varnum's brigade, which lined a hedgerow that stretched across the open field in front of the causeway over the morass. Here the conflict raged severely for some time. Some American artillery took post on an eminence in the rear of the fence, and played with power; but the Btitish cavalry, and a large body of infantry, skillful in the use of the bayonet, charging simultaneously upon the Americans, broke their ranks. Lee immediately ordered Varnum and Livingston, together with the artillery, to retreat across the morass, while Colonel Ogden, with his men drawn up in a wood near the causeway, gallantly covered the whole as they crossed. Lee was the last to leave the field and brought off Ogden's corps, the rear of the retreating troops, in admirable order. Instantly forming them in line upon the slope on the western side of the morass, he rode to Washington and said, " Sir, here are my troops ; how is it your pleasure that I should dispose of them?" The poor fellows had thus far borne the whole brunt of the battles and retreats of the day ; Washington, therefore, ordered him to arrange them in the rear of Englishtown, while he prepared to engage the enemy himself with the fresh troops of the second and main divisions of the army.

THE GENERAL ACTION.

The action now became general. The second line of the main army was speedily formed in the wood which covered the eminence on the western side of the morass, the left commanded by Lord Stirling, the right by General Greene, and the center by Washington himself. Wayne, with an advanced corps, was stationed upon an eminence, in an orchard, a few rods south of the parsonage, while a park of artillery was placed in battery on Comb's Hill, beyond a marsh, on his right. The battery commanded the height upon which the enemy was stationed, and did great service. The British, finding themselves warmly opposed in front, attempted to turn the American flank, but were repulsed. They also moved toward the American right, but, being enfilaed by a severe cannonade from a battery under Knox, upon a commanding piece of ground occupied by General Greene, they fell back. Wayne, in the meantime, kept up a brisk fire upon the British center from his position in the orchard, and repeatedly repulsed the royal grenadiers, who several times crossed the hedgerow and advanced upon him. Colonel Monckton, their commander, perceiving that success depended upon driving Wayne from his position, harraunged his men, and, forming them in solid column, advanced to the charge with all the regularity of a corps on parade. Wayne's troops were partially sheltered by a barn, situated very near the one now standing a few rods from the parsonage. He ordered them to reserve their fire until the enemy approached very near, and then with sure aim, pick out the officers. Silently the British advanced until within a few rods of the Americans, when Monckton waved his sword, with a shout ordered his grenadiers to charge. At the same moment Wayne gave a signal; a terrible volley poured destruction upon the assailants, and almost every British officer fell.— Among them was their brave leader, Colonel Monckton. Over his body the warriors fought desperately, hand to hand, until the Americans secured it, and carried it to their rear. Hotly the conflict raged, not only at the center of the enemy's line, but at various other points. Wayne finally repulsed the grenadiers, and the whole British army soon gave way and fell back to the heights above Carr's house occupied by General Lee in the morning. It was a strong position, flanked by thick woods and morasses, with only a narrow way of approach on their front.

It was now almost sunset, yet Washington resolved to follow up his advantage, and attack them in their new and strong position. For that purpose, he ordered General Poor, with his own and the Carolina brigade, to move around to their right; General Woodford to gain their left, and the artillery to gall them in front.

There were so many impediments, owing to the broken character of the ground, that twilight came on before a proper disposition for battle could be made, and the attack was postponed until morning. The army reposed that night upon their arms upon the battle field, ready to spring upon their prey at the first gleam of light.

THE RETREAT OF THE BRITISH.

Wrapped in his cloak, the chief overpowered with fatigue, slumbered, with his suite, beneath a broad oak, around which many of the slain slept their last sleep. He felt certain of victory when his troops, refreshed, should rise to battle; but the morning light brought disappointment. At midnight, under cover of darkness, Sir Henry Clinton put his weary host in motion. With silent steps column after column left the camp and hurried toward Sandy Hook. So secret was the movement and so deep the sleep of the patriots, that the troops of Poor, lying close by the enemy, were ignorant of their departure until at dawn, they saw the deserted camp of the enemy. They had been gone more than three hours. Washington, considering the distance they had gained, the fatigue of his men, the extreme heat of the weather, and the deep, sandy country, with but little water, deemed pursuit fruitless, and Sir Henry Clinton escaped. Washington marched with his army to Brunswick, and thence, to the Hudson River, which he crossed at King's Ferry, and encamped near White Plains, in Westchester county. The Jersey brigade and Morgans corps were left to hover on the enemy's rear, but they performed no essential service. The British army reached Sandy Hook on the 30th, where Lord Howe's fleet, having come round from the Delaware, was in readiness to convey them to New York.

The Battle of Monmouth was one of the most severely contested during the war. Remarkable skill and bravery were displayed on both sides, after the shameful retreat of Lee, and the events of the day were highly creditable to the military genius of both commanders. Victory for the Americans was twice denied them during the day, first by the retreat of Lee in the morning and secondly, by the unaccountable detention of Morgan and his brave riflemen at a distance from the field. For hours the latter was at Richmond Mills (Shumars Mills, near Blue Ball) three miles below Monmouth Court House, awaiting orders, in an agony of desire to engage in the battle, for he was within sound of its fearful tumult. To and fro he strode, uncertain what course to pursue, and like a hound in the leash, panting to be away to action. Why he was not allowed to participate in the conflict, we have no means of determining.— It appears probable that had he fallen upon the British rear, with his fresh troops, at the close of the day, Sir Henry Clinton and his army might have shared the fate of the British at Saratoga.

The hottest of the conflict occurred near the spot where Monckton fell. Very few of the Americans were killed, on the west side of the morass, but many were slain in the field with Monckton, and lay among the slaughtered grenadiers of the enemy. The Americans lost in killed, six officers and sixty-one non-commissioned officers and privates. The wounded were twenty-four officers and one hundred and thirty-six non-commissioned officers and privates, in all two hundred and twenty-eight. The missing amounted to one hundred and thirty; but many of them having dropped down through fatigue, soon joined the army. Among the slain were Liuet. Colonel Bonner, of Pennsylvania, and Major Dickinson, of Virginia. The British left four officers and two hundred and forty-five non-commissioned officers and privates on the field. They buried some, and took many of their wounded with them. Fifty-nine of their soldiers perished by the heat, without receiving a wound; they lay under the trees, and by rivulets, wither they had crawled for shade and water.

(The official report of General Washington states that of the Americans eight officers and sixty-one non-commissioned officers and privates were killed; wounded eighteen officers and one hundred and forty-two non-commissioned officers and privates; missing five sergeants and one hundred and twenty-six rank and file, some of whom dropped from fatigue and heat afterwards reported for duty.

The official report of General Clinton says that of the British four officers and sixty-one non commissioned officers were killed and fifty-nine died from fatigue; fifteen officers and one hundred and fifty-five non-commissioned officers and privates were wounded and sixty eight missing)..

From Marshall's Life of Washington.*

About the time the command of the army devolved on sir Henry Clinton, orders were received for the evacuation of Philadelphia. The part it was now evident France was about to take in the war, the naval force which had been prepared by that power before she declared herself, and which was now ready to act, rendered Philadelphia a dangerous position, and determined the administration entirely to abandon the Delaware.

The preparations for this movement could not be made unobserved. The design was scon penetrated by the commander in chief, and had constituted one motive for detaching the marquis de Lafayette over the Schuykill.

It was, however, not easy, absolutely to determine the precise object, or course of the enemy. The preparations making in Philadelphia, were such as equally denoted an expedition to the south, an embarkation of the whole army for New York, or elsewhere, or an intention of marching to that city through New Jersey. The latter was, in the opinion of the commander in chief, the plan contemplated; but those were not wanting who were sanguine enough to hope that the war in the United States was no longer to be prosecuted.

In the meantime, every exertion was made by General Washington to strengthen his army. The detatchments were called in, and the state governments pressed to expedite the march of their new levies.

This subject had been taken up immediately after going into winter quarters, and an army of forty thousand men for the campaign had been required by Congress. The strongest representations were made to the states, of the importance of bringing their quotas into the field early in the spring, and of the dangers to which America had already been exposed from their delaying to furnish their recruits by the time the season would admit of action. But such were the real difficulties to be encountered by the states in raising men; and such the waste of time unavoidable in a system where the essential powers of government were vested in so many distinct bodies, that the spring was far advanced before the ranks were strengthened by any new levies; and in some instances, when the soldiers should have been in camp, the legislature was deliberating on the means of raising them.

Sensible of the difficulty of recruiting infantry, as well as of the vast importance of a superiority in point of cavalry; and calculating on the patriotism of the young, and the wealthy, if the means should be furnished them of serving their country in a character which would be compatible with their feelings, and with that pride of station which exists everywhere; it was earnestly recommended by congress to the young gentlemen of property and spirit in the several states, to embody themselves into troops of cavalry, to serve without pay until the close of the year.— Provisions were to be found for themselves and horses, and compensation to be made

* The Life of George Washington, Commander in Chief of the American Forces during the War which established the Independence of his Country, and First President of the United States. Complied under the inspection of the Honorable Bushrod Washington, from Original Papers bequeathed to him by his deceased relative and now in possession of the author. To which is prefixed, an Introduction, containing a compendious view of the Colonies planted by the English on the Continent of North America, from their settlement to the commencement of that war which terminated in their Independence. By John Marshall, Philadelphia. Printed und Published by C. P. Wayne, 1805.

for any horses which might be lost in service. This resolution did not produce the effect expected from it. The volunteers were few, and late in joining the army.

In the meantime, sir Henry Clinton hastened his preparations for the evacuation of Philadelphia; and the opinion that he intended to reach New York through the Jerseys, gained ground.

General Maxwell, with the Jersey Brigade, was ordered over the Delaware to take post about Mount Holly, and to join major general Dickenson, who was beginning to assemble the militia of that State, for the purpose of co-operating with the continental troops, in breaking down the bridges, falling trees in the roads, and otherwise embarrassing the march of the British general, should he attempt to reach New York by land. These troops were ordered to be careful not to expose themselves to a coup-de-main, and general Dickenson was advised to keep his militia in small light parties, hovering on the flanks of the enemy, so as to gall them on their march, without exhibiting an object of sufficient magnitude to induce any concerted plan against him.

A stronger detachment was requested, and general Gates, who now again commanded in the northern department, called earnestly for a re-enforcement to enable him to guard the highlands on the Hudson: but the state of the army did not admit of such a division. A report prevailed in Philadelphia that Sir Henry Clinton designed a visit to Valley Forge, before he took leave of Pennsylvania; and although this threat was not to be regarded while the army was kept entire, it was probable that such a distribution of the troops as was solicited would induce them to realize it. The determination, therefore, to keep the army in force, and in its present station, until Philadelphia should be absolutely evacuated, was rigidly adhered to; and while the means to that end were taking, magazines were laid up to support it in its march either to Fishkill or toward the lower parts of the Hudson.

In this state of things, authentic intelligence was received that great part of the British army had crossed the Delaware, and that the residue would undoubtedly soon pass that river.

The opinion of all the general officers was required on the course now proper to be pursued. As it was an event which had been for some time expected, the subject had of course been naturately considered. There were no advocates for an attempt to cut of the rear of the enemy while crossing the Delaware. All concurred in deeming it unadvisable to attempt entering the works about Philadelphia until they should be entirely abandoned.

On the system to be pursued after crossing the Delaware, there was not so much unanimity. General Lee, who had lately been exchanged, and whose military experience gave great weight to his opinions, was vehement against risking either a general or partial engagement. According to the best estimate which could be formed of the strength of the British army, it was computed at ten thousand effectives; that of the Americans amounted to between ten and eleven thousand. General Lee was decisively of the opinion that, with such an equality of force, it would " be criminal " to hazard an action. He relied much on the advantageous ground on which their late foreign connexions had placed the United States, and strongly contended that only a defeat of their army could now endanger their independence. To this, he said, the army ought not to be exposed. It would be impossible, he thought, to bring on a partial action, without risking its being made general, if such should be the choice of the enemy; since the detachment which should engage must be supported, or be cut to pieces. A general action ought not to be fought unless the advantage was manifestly with the American army. This at present was by no means the case. He attributed so much to the superiority of of the enemy in point of discipline, as to be of opinion that the issue of the engagement would almost certainly be unfavorable.

General Du Portail, a French officer of considerable military reputation, maintained the same opinions; and the baron De Steuben also thought an action ought carefully to be avoided. The American officers seem to have been influenced by the councils of the Europeans, and of seventeen generals, only Wayne and Cadwalader were decidedly in favor of attacking the enemy. Fayette appeared inclined to that opinion, without openly embracing it. General Greene also was disposed to hazard more than the councils of the majority would sanction. The country he thought must be protected; and if in doing so an engagement should become unadvoidable, it would be necessary to fight.

In the morning of the 18th of June, Philadelphia was evacuated,* and by two in the afternoon, all the British troops were encamped on the Jersey shore, from Cooper's creek to Red-bank. Although they availed themselves to a great extent of the facility of transporting their effects by water, yet their line of march was so lengthened and incumbered by baggage, and the weather was so intensely hot, that they were under the necessity of proceeding very slowly. Indeed their movements wore the appearance of purposed delay, and were well calculated to favor the opinion, that Sir Henry Clinton was willing to be overtaken, and wished for a general engagement.

He proceeded slowly through Haddonfield,† Mount Holly, Slabtown, and Crosswicks, to Allentown, and Imlaystown, which places he reached on the 24th.— General Maxwell who had been posted at Mount Holly, retired on his approach, and joined General Dickenson, who was collecting the Jersey militia; but they were able to give very little other interruption to the march of the enemy, than was produced by breaking up the bridges in his route.

Thus far the road taken by sir Henry Clinton left his future destination entirely uncertain. Admitting New York to be his immediate object, he might either take the direct course to Amboy, or pursue the lower and rather more circuitous route to Sandy-hook. It was believed by some that he designed to occupy the high country, and to bring on a general engagement, or to seize the passes through the highlands of the Hudson. He had not yet diverged from the course proper for the attainment of either of these objects.

As his line of march, until he passed Crosswicks, lay directly upon the Delaware, and at no great distance from it, general Washington, who was in motion the day on which Philadelphia was evacuated, found it necessary to make an extensive circuit, and cross that river higher up, at Coryell's ferry. The movements of the British general were so very slow, as

*While the British army were moving down Second street captain M'Lane, with a few light horse and an hundred infantry, entered the the city, and cut off and captured one captain, one provost marshall, one guide to the army, and 30 privates, without sustaining any loss.—Author's note

†The night that the British encamped at Haddonfield, M'Lane, by orders from general Arnold, passed through their camp, and reported their situation to the general.

to strengthen the opinion that he wished a general engagement, and as this, according to the plan settled in council, was to be avoided by the American army, Washington kept possession of the high ground, in Jersey, which enabled him to retain a choice, either of coming to, or avoiding an action ; and at the same time, to continue in the direct course to cover the important passes in the highlands, if there should be any indications of an intention to make a rapid movement against them. He crossed the river on the 22d, and remained the 23d at Hopewell, in the high country, adjacent to the ferry.

General Arnold. whose wounds were not sufficiently healed to fit him for active service, was appointed to take possession of Philadelphia. He was directed to detach about four hundred continental troops, and as many militia as could be collected in the city, and the adjacent country, to advance on the rear of the enemy. If general Cadwalader could be prevailed on to command them, he was named by Washington for that service, as an officer in whom full confidence might be placed. Cadwalader engaged in it with alacrity, but could only add to his continental force about fifty volunteers from Philadelphia, and about forty militia from the neighborhood, who were commanded by general Lacy.

While at Hopewell, Morgan was detached with orders to gain the right flank of the enemy, and use his utmost endeavors to annoy it.

Sir Henry Clinton was now encamped at and about Allentown. The main body of the American army was in Hopewell township, about five miles from Princeton.— Major general Dickenson with the Jersey militia, consisting of about one thousand men, and a brigade of continental troops commanded by Maxwell hung on the left flank of the enemy, towards his rear. General Cadwalader with Jackson's regiment, and a very few militia, was entirely in his rear ; and colonel Morgan with a regiment of six hundred men, was on his right. These detachments were furnished with guides by general Dickenson, and were ordered to harass the enemy as much as possible and to keep up a constant communication with the commander in chief, who proposed to regulate his movements by those of the hostile army.

Notwithstanding the almost concurrent opinion of the general officers against risking an action, Washington appears to have been strongly inclined to that measure. With a mind of uncommon firmness, he possessed a temper enterprising, as well as cautious, and could not readily be persuaded that, with an army which he believed to be rather superior in point of numbers to the enemy, he put too much in hazard by fighting him. The situation of the two armies therefore was once more submitted to the consideration of the general officers. His own, exclusive of Maxwell's brigade, was stated to amount, according to a field return received a few days before, to ten thousand six hundred and eighty-four effective rank and file.— The force of the enemy could not be so accurately stated, but was believed to be rather less than ten thousand. This was the seventh day since the evacuation of Philadelphia, and in that time, the British army had marched less than forty miles. They were by the latest advices in two columns, the one on the Allentown and the other on the Bordentown road.

Under these circumstances, he asked, whether it would be advisable, of choice, to hazard a general action? and if it would, whether it should be brought on by an immediate general attack, by a partial attack, or by taking such a position as must compel the enemy to become the assailants?

If the council should be of opinion that it was unadvisable to hazard an engagement, then he asked what measures could be taken, with safety to the army, to annoy the enemy in his march, should he proceed through the Jerseys?

The same opinion respecting a general action which had been given the day before the movement from Valley-forge, was repeated. The proposition was peremptorily and decidedly negatived. But it was proposed to strengthen the corps on the left flank of the enemy, with a re-enforcement of fifteen hundred men, to act as occasion might serve; and that the main body of the army should preserve such a relative position, as would enable it to act as circumstances should require.

In pursuance of this opinion of his military council, a detachment of fifteen hundred select men, under brigadier general Scott, was immediately formed, and marched to the lines; and the next day the army moved forward to Kingston.

Though every general officer except Wayne had signed the opinion given on the 24th, respecting the strength of his detachment, yet the council had on that point been nearly equally divided. Those who were decidedly against hazarding a serious action, either general or partial, thought the number agreed on competent to every purpose which ought to be contemplated; while others, who privately wished to bring on something more than light skirmishing, but had not sufficient confidence in themselves to hazard the responsibility of openly advising the measure, were desirous of augmenting it to two thousand or two thousand five hundred men.

General Washington still retained his inclination to engage the enemy, and finding himself supported by the private wishes of some officers whom he highly valued, he determined to take his measures on his own responsibility, and without calling another council. Hearing that the enemy were on their march towards Monmouth court-house, he resolved still further to strengthen the forces on the lines; and, in pursuance of this resolution, dispatched brigadier general Wayne with a further detachment of one thousand select men.

As the continental troops now in front of the main army amounted to at least four thousand men, a number believed to be capable of rendering the service expected from them, he deemed it proper to employ a major general to collect and command them.

This tour of duty, major general Lee had a right to claim. But as he had declared himself openly and strongly against hazarding even a partial engagement, and expected that, in conformity with the advice signed by all the general officers then in camp, with one single exception, nothing would be attempted further than merely to reconnoitre the enemy, and restrain plundering parties, he showed no disposition to assert his claim. Unintentionally promoting the private wishes of general Washington, that the command should be given to an officer whose view of the service comported more with his own, Lee yielded this important tour of duty to La Fayette. The orders given this general were, to proceed immediately with the detachment, and to form a junction as expeditiously as possible with that under general Scott; to use the most effectual means for gaining the enemy's left flank, and rear, and giving them every degree of annoyance. All the continental parties on the lines were placed under his command, and he was directed to take such measures in concert with general Dickenson, as would most impede the march of the British army, and occasion them the greatest loss. For these purposes, he was to attack them as opportunities might offer, by detachment, and, if a proper opening should be given, he was to act against them with the whole force under command.

A letter was at the same time addressed to general Dickenson, placing the militia under the orders of LaFayette.

The dispositions and orders manifest conclusively the intention and wish of the commander in chief. They could scarcely fail to bring on an engagement.— Wayne had openly espoused that measure, and LaFayette, although against seeking a general action, had been in favor of a partial one. Of consequence, if any proper occasion offered, he would certainly attack with his whole force, which would as certainly produce such measures on the part of the enemy, as would render it proper to support him with the whole army. He was accompanied too by colonel Hamilton, who felt the strongest desire to signalize the detachment, and to accomplish all the wishes of the commander-in chief.

Immediately after detaching this additional body of troops, general Washington moved to Cranberry, in order to be sufficiently near to support them. He reached that place about nine next morning, (June 26.)

The intense heat of the weather, a heavy storm, and a temporary want of provisions, prevented the army from resuming its march that day. The advanced corps being differently circumstanced, had pressed forward, and taken a position on the Monmouth road, about five miles in rear of the enemy, with the intention of attacking them next morning on their march.— It was found too remote, and too far on the right, to be supported in case of action, and orders were therefore sent to the marquis, to file off by his left towards Englishtown. These orders were executed early in the morning of the 27th.

Although general Lee had at first been disposed to yield the advanced party to LaFayette, from an opinion that no effective service was intended, and that his station in the army was more honorable, that officer had scarcely marched, when Lee began to regret this decision. He perceived that, in the opinion of all the general officers, a greater importance was attached to this command, than he had allowed to it; and that his reputation was in danger of being in some degree impaired by connecting his strenuous opposition to even a partial action, with his afterwards declining the command of a very strong detachment, which it was expected would fall in with, and engage the rear of the enemy. He therefore now solicited earnestly for the command he had before declined accepting.

To relieve the feelings of Lee without wounding those of LaFayette, general Washington detached him with two other brigades to Englishtown, to support the Marquis. He would of course, have the direction of the whole front division, which would now amount to five thousand men; but it was expressly stipulated, that if any enterprise had been already formed by La Fayette, it should be carried into execution as if the commanding officer had not been changed. To this condition Lee acceded, and with two additional brigades joined the front division of the army, the whole of which encamped at Englishtown. The main army also moved forward, and encamped about three miles in his rear.— Morgan's corps still hovered on the right flank of the British, and general Dickenson on their left.

Sir Henry Clinton had taken a very strong position. He lay on the high grounds about Monmouth court-house, having his right flank in the skirt of a small wood, while his left was secured by a very thick one, and a morass running towards his rear. His whole front was also covered by a wood, and, for a considerable distance towards his left, by a morass.

This position seemed unassailable; and the British were within twelve miles of the high grounds about Middletown, after reaching which, they would be perfectly secure.

Under these circumstances, general Washington determined to attack their rear the moment they should move from their ground. This determination was immediately communicated to general Lee, who was ordered to make his dispositions for the attack, and to keep his troops constantly lying on their arms, that he might be in readiness to take advantage of the first movement of the enemy. Corresponding orders were also given to the rear division of the army.

About five in the morning of the 28th, intelligence was received from general Dickenson, that the front of the enemy was in motion. The troops were immediately put under arms, and orders were dispatched to general Lee, directing him to move on and attack the rear, "unless there should be powerful reasons to the contrary." He was at the same time informed, that the main army would be on its march to support him.

Sir Henry Clinton had perceived from the appearances on his flanks and rear on the 27th, that the American army was in his nighborhood, and had therefore changed the order of his march. The whole baggage was placed under the care of general Knyphausen, while the strength and flower of his army, entirely unincumbered, formed the rear division, under the particular command of lord Cornwallis, which he accompanied in person.

To avoid pressing on general Knyphausen, Cornwallis remained on his ground until about eight, and then descending from the heights of Freehold, into a plain of about three miles in extent, took up his line of march in rear of the front division.*

On receiving the orders which had been given in the preceding evening, and repeated in the morning, general Lee had made the dispositions necessary for their execution; and, soon after the rear of the enemy was in motion, he prepared to attack it. General Dickenson had been directed to detach some of his best troops, to take such a position as to co-operate with him; and Morgan was ordered to act on their right flank, but with so much caution, as to be able readily to extricate himself, and to form a junction with the main body, should it be necessary.

Lee appeared on the heights of Freehold soon after the enemy had left them, and following the British into the plain, gave directions to general Wayne to attack their covering party in the rear so as to halt them, but not to press them sufficiently either to force them up to the main body, or to draw re-enforcements from thence to their aid. In the meantime, he proposed to gain their front by a shorter road on their left, and entirely intercepting their communication with the line, to bear them off before they could be assisted.

While in the execution of this design, a gentleman of general Washington's suite came up to gain intelligence, and to him, Lee communicated his present object.

Before he reached the point of destination, there was reason to believe that the enemy were in much greater force than

* Letter of Sir Henry Clinton.

had been expected. The intelligence on this subject was contradictory, and the face of the country, which was a good deal covered with woods, was well calculated to conceal the truth. He, therefore, deemed it advisable to reconnoitre them in person, and to satisfy himself, from his own view, of their numbers.

Sir Henry Clinton, soon after the rear division was in full march, had received intelligence that a column of the Americans was on his left flank. This being a corps of militia, was soon dispersed, and the march continued. When his rear guard had descended from the hills, he saw it followed by a strong corps, soon after which, a cannonade upon it was commenced from some pieces of artillery commanded by colonel Oswald, and at the same time, he received intelligence that a respectable force had shown itself on both his flanks. Believing a design to have been formed on his baggage, which in the defiles through which it was to pass, would be considerably exposed, he determined, in order to secure it from the danger with which it was threatened, to attack the troops in his rear with all his force, so vigorously, as to compel them to call off those on his flanks. This induced him to march back his whole rear division, which movement was making, as Lee advanced for the purpose of reconnoitring, to the front of the wood which adjoined the plain that has been mentioned. He soon perceived himself to have been mistaken in the force which formed the rear of the British; but he yet proposed to engage on that ground, although his judgment, as was afterwards stated by himself, on an inquiry into his conduct, disapproved of it; there being a morass immediately in his rear, which could not be passed without difficulty, and which would necessarily impede the arrival of re-enforcements to his aid, and embarrass his retreat should he be finally overpowered.

This was about ten. While both armies were preparing for action, and performing those previous manœuvres which each deemd necessary, general Scott (as stated by general Lee) mistook an oblique march of an American column for a retreat; and, in the apprehension of being abandoned, left his position, and repassed the ravine in his rear.

Being himself of opinion, that the ground on which the army was drawn up was by no means favorable to them, Lee did not correct the error Scott had committed, but directed the whole detachment to regain the heights they had passed. He was pressed by the enemy, and some slight skirmishing ensued during this retrograde movement, in which not much loss was sustained on either side.

When the first firing announced the commencement of the action, the rear division of the army threw off their packs, and advanced rapidly the support of the front. As they approached the scene of action, general Washington, who had received no intelligence from Lee notifying his retreat, rode forward; and about noon, after the army had marched about five miles, to his utter astonishment and mortification, met the advanced corps retiring before the enemy, without having made a single effort to maintain their ground. Those whom he first fell in with, neither understood the motives which had governed general Lee, nor his present design; and could give no other information than that, by his orders, they had fled without fighting.

General Washington rode to the rear of the division, which he found closely pressed. There he met Lee, to whom he spoke in terms of same warmth, implying disapprobation of his conduct. He also gave immediate orders to the regiments, commanded by colonel Stewart, and lieutenant-colonel Ramsay, to form on a piece of ground which he deemed proper for the purpose of checking the enemy, who were advancing rapidly on them. General Lee was then ordered to take proper measures with the residue of his force to stop the British column on that ground, and the commander-in-chief rode back himself to arrange the rear division of the army.

These orders were executed with firmness. A sharp conflict ensued, and when forced from the ground on which he had been placed, Lee brought off his troops in good order, and was then directed to form in the rear of Englishtown.

The check thus given the enemy afforded time to draw up the left wing and second line of the American army on an eminence, partly in a wood, and partly in an open field, covered by a morass in front. Lord Stirling, who commanded the left wing, brought up a detachment of artillery commanded by lieutenant-colonel Carrington, with some field pieces which played with considerable effect on the enemy, who had passed the morass, and were pressing on to the charge. These pieces, with the aid of several parties of infantry detached for the purpose, effectually put a stop to their advance. The American artillery were drawn up in the open field, and maintained their ground with admirable firmness, under a heavy and persevering fire from the British field artillery.

The right wing of the army was for the day commanded by general Greene. To expedite the march, and to prevent the enemy from turning the right flank, he had been ordered to file off by the new church, two miles from Englishtown, and to fall into the Monmouth road, a small distance in the rear of the court-house, while the residue of the army proceeded directly to that place. He had advanced on this road considerably to the right, and rather beyond the ground on which the armies were now engaged, when he was informed of the retreat of the party commanded by Lee, and of the new disposition of the troops occasioned by that circumstance. He immediately changed his route, and marching up with the wing he commanded, took an advantageous position on the right.

Finding themselves warmly opposed in front, the enemy attempted to turn the left flank of the American army, but were repulsed, and driven back by parties of infantry detached to oppose them. They then attempted the right with as little success.

General Greene had advanced a body of troops with artillery to a commanding piece of ground in his front, which not only disappointed their design of turning the right, but severely enfiladed the party which yet remained in front of the left wing. At this moment, general Wayne was advanced with a body of infantry to engage them in front, who kept up so hot and well directed a fire of musketry, that they soon gave way, and withdrew behind the ravine, to the ground on which the first halt had been made, where the action had commenced immediately after the arrival of general Washington.

Here the British line was formed on very strong ground. Both flanks were secured thick woods, and morasses, while their front could only be reached through a narrow pass. The day had been intensely hot, and the troops were very much fatigued. Notwithstanding this circumstance, and the difficulty with which the enemy could be approached, general Washington resolved to renew the engagement. For this purpose he ordered brigadier general Poor, with his own and the Carolina brigade, to gain their right flank, while Woodford with his brigade, should turn their left. At the same time the artillery were ordered to advance and play on them in front. These orders were obeyed with alacrity, but the impediments on the flanks of the enemy were so considerable that before they could be overcome, and the troops could approach them near enough to commence the attack, it was nearly dark. Under these circumstances it was thought most advisable to defer further operations until next morning.— For the purpose of commencing them with the return of light, the brigades which had been detached to the flanks of the enemy, continued on their ground through the night, and the other troops lay on their arms in the field of battle, in order to be in perfect readiness to support them.— General Washington, who had through the day been extremely active, and entirely regardless of personal danger, passed the night in his cloak in the midst of his soldiers. In the meantime, the British were employed in removing their wounded. About midnight, they marched away in such silence, that their retreat was affected without the knowledge of general Poor, though he lay very near them.

As it was perfectly certain that they would gain the high grounds about Middletown before it would be practicable to overtake them, in which position they could not be attacked with any advantage; as the face of the country afforded no prospect of opposing their embarkation; and as the battle already fought had terminated in such a manner as to make a general impression favorable to the reputation of the American arms; it was thought advisable to relinquish the pursuit. Leaving the Jersey brigade, Morgan's corps, and M'Lane's command* to hover about them, to countenance desertion, and protect the country from their depredations. it was resolved to move the main body of the army to the Hudson, and take a position which should effectually cover the important passes in the Highlands.

The commander-in-chief was highly gratified with the conduct of his troops in this action. Their behavior, he said, after

*The militia had returned to their homes immediately after the action.—*Author's note*.

they recovered from the first surprise occasioned by the unexpected retreat of the advanced corps, could not be surpassed. General Wayne was particularly mentioned. His conduct and bravery, it was declared merited peculiar commendation. The artillery too were spoken of in terms of high praise. Both the officers and men of that corps who were engaged were said to have distinguished themselves in a remarkable manner.

The loss of the Americans in the battle of Monmouth was eight officers and sixty-one privates killed, and about one hundred and sixty wounded. Among the slain were lieutenant-colonel Bonner, of Pennsylvania, and major Dickenson of Virginia, both of whom were much regretted. One hundred and thirty were missing; but of these, a considerable number afterwards rejoined their regiments.

In his official letter, Sir Henry Clinton states his dead and missing at four officers and one hundred and eighty-four privates; his wounded, at sixteen officers, and one hundred and fifty-four privates. This account, so far as respects the dead, cannot be correct, as four officers, and two hundred and forty-five privates were buried on the field by persons appointed for that purpose, who made their report to the commander-in-chief, and some few were afterwards found and buried, so as to increase the number to nearly three hundred. The uncommon heat of the day was fatal to several on both sides.

As usual, when a battle has not been decisive, both parties claimed the victory. In the early part of the day, the advantage was certainly with the British; in the latter part, it may be pronounced with equal certainty, to have been with the Americans. They maintained their ground, repulsed the enemy by whom they were attacked, were prevented only by the night and the retreat of Sir Henry Clinton from renewing the action, and suffered in killed and wounded less than their adversaries.

It is true, that Sir Henry Clinton effected what he states to have been his principal object. which was to save his baggage. But when it is recollected, that the general officers of the American army had decided against hazarding an action, that this advice must. of necessity, have trammeled the conduct, and circumscribed the views of the commander-in-chief he will be admitted to have effected no inconsiderable object, in giving the American arms the appearance of superiority which was certainly acquired by this engagement.

Independent of the loss sustained in this action, the British army was considerably weakened in its way from Philadelphia to New York. About one hundred prisoners were made, and near a thousand soldiers, principally foreigners, many of whom had married in Philadelphia, deserted the British standard during the march.

Whilst the armies were traversing the Jerseys, Gates, who commanded on the North river, by a well-timed and judicious movement down the Hudson, which was highly approved by general Washington, threatened New York, for the purpose of restraining the garrison of that place from re-enforcing sir Henry Clinton, should such a measure be contemplated.

The conduct of Lee was generally disapproved. As, however, he had possessed a large share of the confidence and good opinion of the commander-in chief, it is probable that explanations might have been made, which would have rescued him from the imputations cast on him, and have restored him to the esteem of the army, could his haughty temper have brooked the indignity he believed to have been offered him on the field of battle.— Gen. Washington had taken no measures in consequence of the events of that day and probably would have come to no resolution concerning them, without an amicable explanation, when he received from Lee a letter, expressed in very unbecoming terms, in which he manifestly assumed the station of a superior, and required reparation for the injury sustained from the very singular expressions said to have been used on the day of the action by the commander-in-chief.

This letter was answered after due deliberation by an assurance that so soon as circumstances would admit of an inquiry, he should have an opportunity of justifying himself to the army, to America, and to the world in general, or of convincing them that he had been guilty of disobedience of orders, and misbehavior before the enemy. On the same day, on Lee's expressing a wish for a speedy investigation of his conduct, and for a court-martial, rather than a court of inquiry, he was arrested.

First. For disobedience of orders in not attacking the enemy on the 28th of June. agreeably to repeated instructions.

Secondly. For misbehavior before the enemy on the same day, in making an unnecessary, disorderly, and shameful retreat.

Thirdly. For disrespect to the commander-in-chief in two letters.

Before this correspondence had taken place, strong and specific charges of misconduct had been made against general Lee, by several officers of his detatchment, and particularly by generals Wayne and Scott. In these the transactions of the day, not being well understood, were represented in colors much more unfavorable to Lee, than facts when properly explained would seem to justify. These representations, most probably, produced the strength of the expressions contained in the second article of the charge. A court martial was soon called, over which lord Stirling presided ; and, after a tedious investigation, Lee was found guilty of all the charges exhibited against him and sentenced to be suspended for one year. This sentence was afterwards, though with some hesitation, approved almost unanimously by congress. The court softened in some degree the severity of the second charge, by finding him guilty, not in its very words, but of misbehavior before the enemy by making an unnecessary, and, in some few instances, a disorderly retreat.

Lee defended himself with his accustomed ability. He proved that, after the retreat had commenced in consequence of general Scott's repassing the ravine on the approach of the enemy, he had designed to form on the first advantageous ground he should find, and that in his own opinion, and in the opinion of some other officers, no safe and advantageous position had presented itself until he met general Washington ; at which time it was his intention, to fight the enemy on the very ground afterwards taken by that officer.

He suggested a variety of reasons justifying his retreat, which, if they do not absolutely establish its propriety, give it so questionable a form, as to render it probable that a public examination never would have taken place, could his proud spirit have stooped to offer explanation instead of outrage to the commander-in-chief.

His suspension gave general satisfaction through the army. Without being masters of his conduct as a military man in making the retreat, they perfectly understood the insult offered to their general by his letters, and, whether rightly or not, believed his object to have been to disgrace Washington and to obtain for himself the supreme command. So devotedly were all ranks attached to their general, that the mere suspicion of such a design, would have rendered his further continuance in the army extremely difficult.

Whatever judgment may be formed on the propriety of retreating before the enemy, it seems difficult to justifiy either the omission to keep the commander-in-chief continually informed of his situation and intentions, or the very rude letters written after the action was over.

Congress was highly gratified with the success which attended their arms at Monmouth. In a resolution which passed unanimously, their thanks were given to general Washington, for the activity with which he marched from the camp at Valley forge, in pursuit of the enemy; for his distinguished exertions in forming the line of battle; and for his great good conduct in the action; and he was requested to signifying the thanks of congress to the officers and men under his command, who distinguished themselves by their conduct and valor in the battle.

The attention of general Washington was now turned principally to the North river, toward which the march of his army was directed, with the intention of continuing some time about Haverstraw.

After remaining a few days on the high grounds of Middletown, sir Henry Clinton proceeded to Sandy hook, where he passed his army over to New York.

From Col. Willett's Narrative.*

PRELIMINARY SKETCH.

Colonel Marinus Willett was born July 31 (O. S.) 1740, in Jamaica, Long Island. At the age of 18 he became lieutenant of a company to defend the frontiers of New York state from the French and Indians and was in the disastrous attempt upon Fort Ticonderoga, under Lord Howe, in 1758. He was one of the earliest to espouse the patriot cause at the outbreak of the Revolution, was captain of a company in 1775, and took part in Gen. Schuyler's campaign. In 1776 he was commissioned Lieut. Colonel, and took an active part in all the operations against the British in the neighborhood of Albany, until the close of that year, when

*A Narrative of the Military Actions of Colonel Marinus Willett, taken chiefly from his own manuscript. Prepared by his Son, William M. Willett. New York: Published by G. & C. & H. Carvill. 1831.

he was left in command of Fort Stanwix. The fall of Burgoyne having rid that section of the presence of the enemy, he led a life of comparative inactivity.

BATTLE OF MONMOUTH.

Wearied with the inactive life he ledt and seeing no prospect of more brillian, service in that remote section at that period, Colonel Willett once more, with the approbation of Colonel Gansevort, set out to visit the commander-in chief, with the view of endeavouring to have the regiment relieved and of joining the main army; objects which he was extremely desirous of effecting. At Peekskill he found Gen. Gates, and happened to be at his quarters on the night of the 21st of June, when an express from Gen. Washington brought advice of the evacuation of Philadelphia by the enemy. Gen. Gates, having suggested his intention of sending a confidential messenger to Gen. Washington, with a statement of the force and magazines under his command, which, as the army under Washington would probably move that way, it was necessary he should be well acquainted with, Colonel Willett was pleased with the opportunity of offering his services on that occasion. Having accordingly been furnished with a fresh horse, which the quarter-master was ordered to procure for the purpose, he crossed the river the next morning, and arrived at head-quarters the evening of the same day. Having finished his business with the commander-in-chief, he obtained from him permission to remain with the army. On Wednesday the 23d of June, being the morning after his arrival, he was informed that a detachment of light troops under the command of general Scott, of Virginia, was ordered to march towards the enemy, with the intention of harassing them on their retreat. Having obtained an introduction to general Scott, Colonel Willett offered himself as a volunteer aid, and his offer being cordially accepted, he had the satisfaction of remaining with him until after the battle of Monmouth, which took place the Sunday following.

General Scott's detachment of light troops marched the first day to within a few miles of the enemy's rear; in the evening of the same day it was joined by the Jersey brigade. Early the next morning they got upon the enemy's track, which they followed; but as their columns were kept close and their line of march was compact, no opportunities of an advantageous attack presented itself. A few prisoners and deserters were all that fell into their hands. As the weather was very warm and the country through which they passed barren and sandy, the troops suffered for want of water; the more so as the enemy had taken care to fill up the wells. In the evening general Scott was re-inforced with upwards of one thousand men under General Wayne, and the command of the whole detachment was put under the Marquis DeLaFayette.

Early on the morning of the 27th, an attempt was made to impede the march of the enemy by an attack upon their rear; but it was ineffectual and they continued their route to Monmouth Court House. In the course of the day the detachment was increased to five thousand, and the command conferred on general Lee. Early on Sunday morning, being the 28th of June, a smart fire was commenced, just as the enemy began to march. This attack became so serious that the enemy found it necessary to halt their line and turn the whole of their force upon us.— The light infantry to which Colonel Willett was attached, were formed on the edge of the wood, when the Marquis De LaFayette galloping up to them, told them that the British grenadiers were advancing to gain their right, and ordered them to march with a quick step to oppose them. This order was obeyed with alacrity; but as the enemy had halted beyond a marshy piece of ground, and by their last movement the light infantry had become separated from the rest of the troops, General Scott took an advantageous position, which he had just gained when he was ordered to retire.— General Scott conceiving that the order would be countermanded, if General Lee were once made acquainted with the excellence of his position, sent Colonel Willett to give him a particular account of its advantages in case the enemy should advance to attack them. Before Colonel Willett could find the General, he observed that all the troops were retiring; when near the Court-House, he fell in with General Wayne, and at the same time General Scott rode up and informed him that he had received a second order, and that the troops had of course left their position and were retiring. Both these gentlemen expressed great mortification at the measures adopted, and pointed out several important advantages which might be gained by waiting the attack of the enemy, who were then advancing pretty rapidly towards them.

While Colonel Willett, with Generals Scott and Wayne, were conversing together they discovered General Lee, for the first time, since the troops commenced retreating, on a pretty conspicuous piece of ground, and, anxious to learn the cause of the retreat, rode fast toward him. It appears that some person had already suggested to the General, some doubts as to the propriety of the movements the troops were making; for just as Colonel Willett got within reach of hearing, the first words that struck his ears, from General Lee, were, "It does not signify, the enemy have too much cavalry for us."

The enemy, perceiving that a retreat had commenced, moved forward more rapidly. The fire from their artillery had become brisk.

The enemy had brought cavalry in front, and the only clever thing Colonel Willett witnessed, on the part of General Lee, was, that on observing the cavalry advancing he ordered some troops to a good position to check them; when, calling his dog he left the spot where he was and joined the troops he had stationed to oppose the enemy's cavalry. These, advancing on a canter, received so severe a fire, as completely broke and dispersed them. Here a horse was to be seen galloping away without its rider, and there a horseman rising from the dust.

A brisk fire of musketry, as well as artillery, had now commenced in different parts of the line. The weather was extremely warm. Some of the troops, especially such as had charge of field-pieces, were obliged to break their columns, in order to avoid a marsh, across which they could not carry the artillery.

This was the case with some of General Scott's detachment of light infantry, who had charge of two field-pieces. This being observed by the enemy, they detached a regiment of Highlanders, to attack General Scott's detachment. The Highlanders briskly advanced across an orchard to the attack, but were received by a well-directed fire, which killed upwards of thirty of them in a few minutes.

By this time General Washington had arrived on the field, and put a stop to the retrograde movement; such a line was formed as effectually checked the advance of the enemy. Two formidable lines were formed in front of each other, to a considerable extent. The fire of artillery from both lines was severe and not without execution. It was doubtful on which side the artillery was best served; but, in every instance where our musketry was opposed to the enemy's, the advantage was, evidently, on our side.

General Washington, who never to Colonel Willett appeared so great as he did on that day,* (though to him he always appeared greater than anybody else) was mounted on a fine large sorrel horse; he had a spy-glass in his hand, and from a commanding situation, within the line of the enemy's fire, he seemed to observe and know everything. Firmness, composure and dignity, sat on his brow. His presence inspired universal ardour along the line, and in the poetical description of Mr. Addison,

"He taught the doubtful battle where to rage."

General Washington's situation within the line of fire, with a number of officers about him, appeared to attract the attention of the enemy, so as to induce them to direct their fire on that more than any part of the line. Colonel Willett happened to be near him when this was evidently the case, and directed one of his aides to ride around among the officers and request them to withdraw, as they offered a mark for the enemy's fire. Upon this intimation a number of them withdrew, and Colonel Willett then retired to that part of the line where the light infantry was formed. He had been there but a few minutes when two gentlemen riding slowly along, he heard one of them exclaim, "Poor Lee." As General Lee was near General Washington at the time Colonel Willett left the spot where he was, on hearing the exclamation of "Poor Lee," he concluded he was killed, and, turning to the person who made the exclamation, enquired if Lee was shot, to which he replied "No, but he is a great deal worse off, for the General has given him a most severe reprimand, and ordered him to English Town, (which was four miles in the rear,) with orders to collect such scattered troops as he might find, and assemble them at that place."

In the meanwhile, by a well timed order, General Green and Lord Stirling, took possession of commanding ground, from whence a heavy fire so enfiladed the enemy's line, as to compel them to retreat. The position they left was instantly occupied by the American troops and so hot a fire poured in upon the enemy, as compelled them to retreat. The late hour of the day necessarily prevented any further operations, except placing such part of the army as had experienced the the least fatigue, in such positions as would enable them to commence another attack early the next morning. But this was prevented by the retreat of the enemy in the night leaving their wounded behind them.† They had taken the road toward Sandy Hook, and when it was discovered they had retreated, were so far ahead, as not to render it advisable to pursue them with the army. Some light troops were ordered to follow at a distance, with a view of picking up any deserters or stragglers from the enemy, while the main army filed off towards Brunswick; but, learning that the enemy had landed at New York, they marched toward the Hudson, which they crossed at Stony Point.

The remainder of the campaign, of the year '78, after the Battle of Monmouth, Colonel Willett spent with the main army, which encamped in West Chester County.

FROM THE LIFE OF HENRY KNOX.*

"Mrs. Knox arrived in camp at Valley Forge on May 20, 1778, soon after the news of the alliance with France had been received. She was attended from New Haven by General Arnold, who was of great service to her during her journey, and remained with the army until it disbanded.

---

* The appearance of General Washington, says Colonel Willett, was such, as to excite admiration and respect. I recollect feeling these sentiments the first time I ever saw him, which was the year after the memorable defeat of General Braddock. He was then only twenty-three years of age. His manly, sedate countenance and deportment, together with the fineness of his person, forcibly attracted attention and respect, even in those, his youthful days. Nineteen years had elapsed from that period to the time of my seeing him again, which was a few days after he was appointed to command the American Army. His greatness appeared to have increased with his years. His noble countenance displayed the greatness of his mind; and his whole demeanour was calculated to command veneration. I have seen him in a variety of situations and none in which he did not appear great; but never did I see him when he exhibited such greatness as on this day.

† As General Washington had ordered Colonel Morgan, with his rifle corps, which was reinforced by some other troops, by a circuitous march to attack the enemy's baggage, the victory would have been much more complete, if the attack had not been prevented by the retrograde movement of General Lee.

*Life and Correspondence of Henry Knox, Major General in the American Revolutionary Army. By Francis S. Drake, Boston: Samuel G. Drake, 17 Bromfield street. 1873. (Memorials of the Massachusetts Cincinnati Society.)

"At the battle of Monmouth, which occurred on June 28th, and of which he ever after spoke with much pride, Knox reconnoitred in front, rallying the retreat, and bringing up the rear with a brisk fire from a battery planted in the night, directed by his brigade adjutant, the chevalier Mauduit, Duplessis. Of the services of this arm, Washington in general orders, says he 'can with pleasure inform Gen. Knox and the officers of the artillery that the enemy has done them the justice to acknowledge that no artillery could have been better served than ours.'

"To his brother and to his wife, Knox wrote the particulars of this battle, and of the events which preceded it:—

To his Brother William.

Hopewell Township, New Jersey, 4 o'clock A. M., 25th June, 1778.

"The enemy evacuated Philadelphia on the 19th. Lucy and I went in, but it stunk so abominably that it was impossible to stay there, as was her first design. The enemy are now at Allen Town, about ten miles southeast of Princeton, and we are about six miles north [of] Princeton, so that the two armies are now about nineteen or twenty miles apart. We are now on the march towards them, and their movements this day will determine whether we shall come in close contact with each other. We have now very numerous parties harassing and teasing them on all quarters. Desertion prevails exceedingly in their army, especially among the Germans. Above three hundred German and English have deserted since they left Philadelphia. Had we a sufficiency of numbers, we should be able to force them to a similar treaty with Burgoyne; but, at present, have not quite such sanguine hopes. If general actions had no other consequences than merely the killed and wounded, we should attack them in twenty-four hours. But the fate of posterity, and not the illusive brilliancy of military glory, governs our Fabian commander, the man [to whom], under God, America owes her present prospects of peace and happiness.

To Mrs. Knox.

June 29, near Monmouth Court House.

"My dearest Love.—I wrote you some few days ago that a day or two would determine whether we should have an engagement with the Britons. Yesterday, at about nine o'clock A. M., our advanced parties under General Lee attacked their rear while on the move towards Shrewsbury, upon which their whole army, except the Hessians, came to the right about; and after some fighting, obliged him to retire to the main army, which was about two miles distant. The enemy advanced with great spirit to the attack, and began a very brisk cannonade on us, who were found to receive them.

"The cannonade lasted from about eleven until six o'clock, at which time the enemy began to retire on all quarters, and left us in possession of the field. We have had several field officers killed, and a considerable number of others. Colonel Ramsay, Mrs. Ramsay's husband, was taken prisoner, and this morning released on his parole. I have had several officers killed and wounded. My brave lads behaved with their usual intrepidity, and the army gave the corps of artillery their full proportion of the glory of the day.

"Indeed, upon the whole, it is very splendid. The capital army of Britain defeated and obliged to retreat before the Americans, whom they despised so much! I cannot ascertain either our or the enemy's loss, but I really think they have lost three times the number we have. I judge from the field of battle, which to be sure, is a field of carnage and blood: three to one of the British forces lie there.— The Britons confess they have never received so severe a check. The enemy took a strong post, about a mile from the place of action, to dislodge them from which as it was dark would cost too many men, and by which they covered the retreat of their army. After having been fighting all day, and one of the hottest I ever felt, they decamped in the night and marched off with the utmost precipitation, leaving a great number of their wounded, both officers and men, in our hands. We have sent out large bodies in pursuit, but I believe they will not be able to come up with the main body...... The number of deserters since they left Philadelphia must exceed eight hundred. The march has proved to them a most destructive one, and is very ill calculated to give Sir H. Clinton any elect. He may storm Fort Montgomery, but is very ill calculated, in my opinion, to be at the head of a large army.

"My friend, Harry [Jackson], crossed over from Philadelphia, and was in the unfortunate [i. e., early] part of the day. I saw him once on the field, for a moment: he appeared much fatigued. His regiment had a few killed and wounded and is reported to have behaved well."

To His Brother William.

Camp Brunswick, 3d July, 1778,

......" The enemy inclined more to their right' than we expected, and took the road to Sandy Hook, instead of the supposed one to South Amboy.

"A body of Jersey militia, amounting to near 2,000, had endeavored to retard them, by taking up the bridges, felling trees, and harrassing their flanks and rear. Beside these his Excellency General Washington had detatched several large bodies for the same purpose, all of which except Colonel Morgan, were, on the 28th ult., united under General Lee, who early on that morning advanced to Monmouth Court House with the intention of attacking the covering party by left flank, the main army moving on at the same time, to support him, although it was some miles in the rear. The parties under General Lee, instead of finding a covering party as was expected, found their whole army or the greater part of it. After some manœuvring, cannonading, and some other circumstances, which are not yet sufficiently explained, it was thought proper by General Lee to retire until it met the main army, which it effected without much loss. The army was drawn up on advantageous ground to receive the enemy, who advanced to the attack with considerable impetuosity, and began a brisk cannonade, which was returned with becoming spirit. The action of the musketry was various, and with intermissions until about six o'clock, when we pushed the enemy off the field.. ... Their whole loss may amount to about ten or twelve hundred killed, wounded and prisoners. His Excellency, the General, has done the corps of artillery, and me the honor to notice us in General orders in very pointed and flattering terms. Indeed, I was highly delighted with their coolness, bravery, and good conduct. The effects of the *Battle of Monmouth* will be great and lasting. It will convince the enemy and the world that nothing but a good constitution is wanting to render our army equal to any in the world."

[Moore's Diary of the American Revolution, V 2, p. 66.]

June 19.—* * * * *

The British army, early yesterday morning, completed their evacuation of Phila-

delphia, having before transported their stores and most of their artillery into Jersey, where they had thrown up some works, and several of their regiments were encamped. They manned the lines the preceding night, and retreating over the commons, crossed at Gloucester Point.*— It is supposed they will endeavor to go to New York. A party of the American light horse pursued them very close, and took a great number of prisoners, some of whom were refugees. Soon after the evacuation, the Honorable Major-General Arnold took possession of Philadelphia, with Colonel Jackson's Massachusetts Regiment.
—*Pennsylvania Evening Post*, June 20.

June 29.—His Excellency General Washington, having early intelligence of the intended movement of the enemy from Philadelphia, detached a considerable body of troops under the command of Major-General Lee, in order to support General Maxwell's brigade of continental troops already in New Jersey, and the militia under Generals Dickinson and Heard. These troops were intended to harass the enemy on their march through the State to Amboy, and retard them till General Washington, with the main body, could get up. In the mean time several small skirmishes happened between the enemy and General Maxwell's troops, joined by the militia, but without any considerable execution on either side.

The march of the enemy being by this means impeded, and the main army having crossed the Delaware at Coryell's Ferry.† on the 20th and 21st ultimo, proceeded by way of Hopewell, Rocky Hill, Kingston and Cranbury, and on the 27th overtook the enemy at Monmouth Court House, whither they retired from Allentown on the approach of our troops, leaving their intended route to Amboy.

It having been previously determined to attack the enemy on their march, a suitable disposition was made the same evening. General Lee, with a detachment of picked men, consisting of about fifteen hundred, and reinforced by a strong body of Jersey militia, advanced to English Town, (about six miles from Monmouth Court House ;) the militia then proceeded to the meeting house, the main army, under General Washington being about four miles in the rear of English Town. In this

*Gloucester Point is in New Jersey, on the Delaware, about three miles below Camden.
†Now Taylorsville, opposite "Washington's Crossing," a station on the Belvidere Delaware Railroad.

OLD TIMES IN OLD MONMOUTH. 55

position the whole halted until advice could be received of the enemy's motion.

At three o'clock yesterday (Sunday) morning, their first division under General Knyphausen, began their march, of which we had intelligence in about two hours, when General Lee had orders to advance and begin the attack, the main army at the same time advancing to support him. About half a mile beyond the Court House, General Lee began his attack, and drove the enemy for some time, when they being reinforced, he was obliged to retreat in turn, till met by General Washington with the main army, which formed on the first advantageous ground. In the mean time two field-pieces, covered by two regiments of the detachment, and commanded by Colonels Livingston and Stewart, were advanced to check the enemy's approach, which they performed with great spirit and considerable loss on both sides. This service being performed, they retired with the pieces to the front line, then completely formed, when the severest cannonading began that it is thought ever happened in America. In the mean time, strong detachments marched and attacked the enemy with small arms, with various success. The enemy were finally obliged to give way, and we took possession of the field, covered with dead and wounded. The intense heat of the weather, and the preceding fatigue of the troops, made it necessary to halt then to rest for some time;‡ the enemy, in the meantime, presenting a front about one mile advanced beyond the seat of action. As soon as the troops had recovered breath, General Washington ordered two brigades to advance upon each of their flanks, intending to move on in front at a proper time to support them, but before they could reach their destination, night came on, and made any further movements impracticable.

The British left on the field the Honorable Colonel Monckton with several other officers, and a great number of privates, which cannot yet be ascertained with precision. About twelve o'clock last night they moved off with great precipitation, towards Middletown, leaving at the Court House five wounded officers, and above forty privates. They began the attack with their veteran grenadiers and light infantry, which renders their loss still more important. On our side Lieutenant-Colonel Bonner, of Pennsylvania, and Major Dickinson, of Virginia, are slain. Colonel Barber,§ of New Jersey, is wounded by a musket ball, which passed through the right of his body : but it is hoped will not prove mortal. Our troops behaved with the greatest bravery, and opposed the flower of the British army. Our artillery was well served, and did amazing execution. Before, during and after the action, deserters came over to us in great numbers, and still continue so to do. Of. the enemy's dead many have been found without any wound, but being heavily clothed, they sank under the heat and fatigue. We are well assured the Hessians absolutely refused to engage, declaring it was too hot. Their line of march from the Court House was strewed with dead, with arms, knapsacks, and accoutrements, which they had dropped on their retreat. They had the day before taken about fifteen prisoners, whom, in their haste they left behind.— Had we been possessed of a powerful body of cavalry on the field, there is no doubt the success would have been much more complete, but they had been employed in harassing the enemy during the march, and were so detached, as to give the enemy a great superiority in number, much to their advantage. Our success, under Heaven, is to be wholly ascribed to the good disposition made by his excellency, supported by the firmness and bravery of both officers and men,.who were emulous to distinguish themselves on this occasion.. The great advance of the enemy on their way, their possession of the strong grounds at Middletown, added to the exhausted state of our troops, made an immediate pursuit ineligible ; and the American army now remains about one mile advanced from the field of battle, having been since employed in collecting the dead and wounded, and burying the former;‖—*New*

---

‡The heat of the weather proved fatal to many in both armies. A correspondent in a letter to London, says, "A major-general, high in command, lost three horses during the engagement from the intense heat of the weather, the thermometer having been at the astonishing height of ninety-two."—*Upcott*, V. 143.

§Francis Barber.

‖Gaine gives the following account of this action:— On Sunday morning the 28th instant, the rear of the royal army, under the command of General Sir Henry Clinton, was attacked by the rebel army, commanded by Generals Washington, Lee, Wayne and LaFayette, about one mile and a half west of Freehold Court House, in Monmouth county, New Jersey, when the grenadiers, light infantry, and Queen's Rangers distinguished themselves in a particular manner, having opposed the whole of Mr. Washington's army and pursued them several miles. Their loss we know not, but it is said to be great.

"The following officers are amongst the killed in the royal army:—Lieutenant Colonel Monckton and Captain John Gore of the 5th.* The wounded are Lieutenant-Colonel Trelawney of the Guards ; Lieutenant-Colo-

RETREAT FROM MONMOUTH.

JUNE 30.—This evening, the party despatched yesterday by his excellency to observe the motions of the enemy, returned to camp. They report that the enemy have continued their march very precipitately. The roads are strewn with knapsacks, firelocks, and other implements of war. On the night of their retreat, they moved off the field so silently, that our outposts did not discover their absence until late in the morning. To-day they are at Sandy Hook, from whence it is expected they will remove to New York.*

Thus, (says a correspondent) the enemy have had two campaigns to march from New York to Philadelphia, and back again, with the diminution of at least half his army. How much cheaper might his Brittannic Majesty buy sheep and oxen in England, in the usual manner, than he now gets them, by employing an army to steal them in America!—*New York Journal, July 13.*

COL. JOHN LAURENS' ACCOUNT.

HEADQUARTERS, ENGLISHTOWN,
30TH JUNE 1778.

MY DEAR FATHER :

I was exceedingly chagrined that public business prevented my writing to you

nel Abercrombie, 37th ; Major William Gardner, 10th; Captain Andrew Cathcart, 15th ; Captain William Brereton, 17th ; Captain Harry Ditmass, 15th ; Captain Baildwin Leighton, 46th; Lieutenant Mungo Paumier, do.; Lieutenant Disborough of the marines ; Captain John Powell, 52d ; Captain Thomas Wills, 23d ; Lieutenant Patrick Belley, Guards ; Captain Stephenson, Queen's Rangers, (before the action ;) Lieutenant-Colonel Simcoe, Queen's Rangers ; Captain Lloyd, 46th ; Lieutenant Kennedy, 44th. We are informed that the following is an exact return of the loss of the royal army: killed, 101 ; wounded, 172; missing, 56 ; total 338.

† It is certain the rebels have not suffered so heavy a loss as on this occasion, in any engagement since their defeat on Long Island."—*New York Gazette,* July 6.

* A private letter from an officer in the guards to his friend in London, mentions, that in the affair between the American rebels and the royal army on the 28th of June, General Clinton behaved with the greatest coolness and intrepidity; that his manœvres were highly capital, but that he narrowly missed being killed by a musket ball, which passed within a few inches of his head and knocked down a sergeant who stood near him.—*Upcott,* V. 143.

* Carver ii. 31. Smythe, in his diary, November 8, says : " This afternoon a party of our horse brought in two rebel privates from Powles Hook. One of them is very intelligent and communicative: but the other is the most whimsical tory I ever have seen. Wherever he goes he carries with him a large grey cat, which he says came into the rebel camp on the night after the battle at Freehold Meeting House, and which he first discovered lapping a spot of dry blood on his sleeve, as he lay on his arms expecting another dash at the British. His affection for the cat is as wonderful as hers is for him, for they are inseparable He says if we do'nt allow him extra rations for his cat, he will be obliged to allow them out of his own.

from the field of battle, when the General sent his despatches to Congress. The delay, however, will be attended with this advantage, that I will be better able ‡to give you an account of the enemy's loss ; tho' I must now content myself with a very succinct relation of this affair. The situation of the two armies on Sunday was as follows : Genl. Washington, with the main body of our army, was at 4 miles distant from English Town. Genl. Lee, with a chosen advanced corps, was *at* that town. The enemy were retreating down the road which leads to Middletown ; their flying army composed (as it was said), of 2 battalions of British grenadiers, 1 Hessian grend'rs, 1 battalion of light infantry, 1 regiment of guards, 2 brigades of foot, 1 regt. of dragoons and a number of mounted and dismounted Jagers. The enemy's rear was preparing to leave Monmouth village, which is 6 miles from this place, when our advanced corps was marching towards them. The militia of the country kept up a random running fire with the Hessian Jagers ; no mischief was done on either side. I was with a small party on horse, reconnoitring the enemy, in an open space before Monmouth, when I perceived two parties of the enemy advancing by files in the woods on our right and left, with a view as I imagined, of enveloping our small party or preparing a way for a skirmish of their horse. I immediately wrote an account of what I had seen to the General, and expressed my anxiety on account of the languid appearance of the continental troops under General Lee. Some person in the meantime reported to Genl. Lee that the enemy were advancing upon us in two columns, and I was informed that he had, in consequence, ordered Varnum's brigade, which was in front, to repass a bridge which it had passed. I went myself and assured him of the real state of the case ; his reply to me was, that his accounts had been so contradictory, that he was utterly at a loss what part to take. I repeated my account to him in positive, distinct terms, and returned to make further discoveries. I found that the two parties had been withdrawn from the wood, and that the enemy were preparing to leave Monmouth. I wrote a second time to Genl. Washington. Genl. Lee at length gave orders to advance. The enemy were forming themselves on the Middle Town road, with their Light infantry in front, and cavalry on the left flank, while a scattering distant fire was commenced between our flanking parties and theirs. I was impatient and uneasy at seeing that no disposition was made, and endeavored to find Genl. Lee to inform him of what was doing, and to know what was his disposition. He told me that he was going to order some troops to march below the enemy and cut off their retreat. Two pieces of artillery were posted on our right without a single foot soldier to support them. Our men were formed piecemeal in front of the enemy, and there appeared to be no general plan or disposition calculated on that of the enemy; the nature of the ground, or any of the other principles which gen erallly govern in these cases.

The enemy began a cannonade from two parts of their line; their whole body of horse made a furious charge upon a small party of our cavalry and dispirited them, and drove until the appearance of our infantry and a judicious discharge or two of artillery made them retire precipitately. Three regiments of ours that had advanced in a plain open country towards the enemy's left flank, were ordered by Genl. Lee to retire and occupy the village of Monmouth. They were no sooner formed there than they were ordered to quit that post and gain the woods. One order succeeded another with a rapidity and indecision calculated to ruin us. The enemy had changed their front and were advancing in full march toward us; our men were fatigued with the excessive heat. The artillery horses were not in condition to make a brisk retreat. A new position was ordered, but not generally communicated, for part of the troops were forming on the right of the ground, while others were marching away, and all the artillery driving off. The enemy after a short halt resumed their pursuit; no cannon was left to check their progress. A regiment was ordered to form behind a fence, and as speedily commanded to retire. All this disgraceful retreating passed without the firing of a musket, over ground which might have been disputed inch by inch. We passed a defile and arrived at an eminence beyond, which was defended on one hand by an impracticable fen, on the other by a thick woods where our men would have fought to advantage. Here, fourtunately for the honor of the army, and the welfare of America, Genl. Washington met the troops retreating in disorder, and without any plan to make an opposition. He ordered some pieces of artillery to be brought up to defend the pass, and some troops to form and defend the pieces. The artillery was too distant to be brought up readily, so that there was but little opposition given here. A few shot though and a little skirmishing in the wood checked the enemy's career. The Genl. expressed his astonishment at this unaccountable retreat. Mr. Lee indecently replied that the attack was contrary to his advice and opinion in council. We were obliged to retire to a position, which, though hastily reconnoitred proved an excellent one. Two regiments were formed behind a fence in front of the position. The enemy's horse advanced in full charge with admirable bravery to the distance of forty paces, when a general discharge from these two regiments did execution among them, and made them fly with the greatest precipitation. The grenadiers succeeded to the attack. At this time my horse was killed under me. In this spot the action was hottest, and there was considerable slaughter of British grenadiers. The General ordered Woodford's brigade with some artillery to take possession of an eminence on the enemy's left, and cannonade from thence. This produced an excellent effect. The enemy were prevented from advancing on us, and confined themselves to cannonad, with a show of turning our left flank. Our artillery answered theirs with the greatest vigor. The General seeing that our left flank was secure, as the ground was open and commanded by us, so that the enemy could not attempt to turn it without ex. posing their own flank to a heavy fire from our artillery, and causing to pass in review before us, the force employed in turning us. In the meantime, Genl. Lee continued retreating. Baron Steuben was ordered to form the broken troops in the rear. The cannonade was incessant and the General ordered parties to advance from time to time, to engage the British grenadiers and guards. The horse shewed themselves no more. The grenadiers shewed their backs and retreated eyerywhere with precipitation. They returned, however, again to charge, and were again repulsed. They finally retreated and got over the strong pass, where, as I mentioned before, Genl. Washington first rallied the troops. We advanced in force, and continued masters of the ground; the standards of liberty were planted in triumph on the field of battle. We remained looking at each other with the defile between us, till dark, and they stole off in silence at midnight. We have buried of the enemy's slain, 233, principally of grenadiers; forty odd of their wounded whom they left at Monmouth, fell into our hands. Several officers are our prisoners. Among their killed are Col. Moncton, a captain of the guards, and several captains of the grenadiers. We have taken a very inconsiderable number of prisoners, for want of a good body of horse. Deserters are coming in as usual. Our officers and men behaved with that bravery which becomes freemen, and have convinced the world that they can beat British grenadiers. To name any one in particular wd. be a kind of injustice to the rest. There are some, however, who came more immediately under my view, whom I can mention that you may know them. B. Genl. Wayne, Col. Barber, Col. Stewart, Col. Livingston, Col. Oswald, ef the artillery, Capt. Doughty, deserve well of their country, and distinguished themselves nobly.

The enemy buried many of their dead that are not accounted for above, and carried off a great number of wounded. I have written diffusely, and yet I have not told you all. Genl. Lee, I think, must be tried for misconduct. However, this is a matter not generally known, tho' it seems almost universally wished for. I would beg you, my dear father, to say nothing of it. You will oblige me much by excusing me to Mr. Drayton for not writing to him. I congratulate you, my dear father, upon this seasonable victory, and am ever,

Your most dutiful and affectionate,
JOHN LAURENS.
The Honorable Henry Laurens, Esqr.

We have no returns of our loss as yet. The proportion on the field of battle appeared but small. We have many good officers wounded.

GENERALS WAYNE AND SCOTT TO
GENERAL WASHINGTON.

ENGLISHTOWN, 30th June, 1778.

SIR:—We esteem it a duty, which we owe to our country, ourselves and the officers and soldiers under our command, to state the following facts to your Excellency:

On the 28th instant, at five o'clock in the morning we received orders to march with the following detachments, namely, Scott's and Varnum's brigades, Colonels Butler and Jackson in front, amounting to seventeen hundred men; Colonels Wesson, Livingston, and Stewart, with one thousand men, commanded by General Wayne; a select detachment of fourteen hundred men, rank and file, under General Scott, with ten pieces of Artillery properly distributed among the whole.

About eight o clock, the van under Col Butler arrived on the left of Monmouth Court House, on the rear of the left flank of the enemy, who were in full march, moving in great haste and confusion. At this time our main body under General Lee, were formed at the edge of a wood about half a mile distant from the Court House. General Wayne, who was in front reconnoitring the enemy, perceiving that they had made a halt and were preparing to push Colonel Butler with their horse and a few foot, gave direction for him to form and receive them and at the same time sent Major Ryles to General Lee, requesting that those troops might be advanced to support those in front, and for the whole to form on the edge of a deep morass, which extends from the east of the Court House on the right a very considerable distance to the left. The troops did arrive in about an hour after the requisition, and were generally formed in this position.

About the same time General Scott's detachment had passed the morrass on the left, and the enemy's horse and foot that had charged Colonel Butler, were repulsed. The number of the enemy now in view might be near two thousand, though at first not more than five hundred exclusive of their horse. The ground we now occupied was the best formed by nature for defence of any, perhaps in the country. The enemy advanced with caution, keeping at a considerable distance in front. General Scott, having viewed the position of the enemy, as well as the ground where about twenty-five hundred of our troops were formed, repassed the morass and took post on the left, in a fine open wood, covered by said morass in front.

Whilst this was doing, General Wayne perceiving that the troops on the right from the wood to the Court House, were retreating, sent General Fishbourn to General Lee, requesting that the troops might return to support him. In the interim General Wayne repassed the morass, leaving Colonel Butler's regiment to keep post on the right flank of the enemy. Generals Scott and Wayne then went together along the morass to the Court House, when Major Fishbourn returned, and said that General Lee gave no other answer, than that he would see General Wayne himself, which he never did. The enemy having now an opening on the right of General Scott began to move on, when General Wayne and General Scott sent to General Lee to request him at least to form, to favor General Scott's retreat, but this requisition met with the same fate as the last. The troops kept still retreating, when General Scott perceiving that he would not be supported, filed off to the left. General Wayne ordered Colonel Butler to fall back also. Thus were these several select detachments unaccountably drawn off without being suffered to come to action, although we had the most pleasing prospect from our number and position, of obtaining the most glorious and decisive victory. After this we fortunately fell in with your Excellency. You ordered us to form part of those troops, whose conduct and bravery kept the enemy in play until you had restored order.

We have taken the liberty of stating these facts, in order to convince the world that our retreat from the Court House was not occasioned by the want of numbers, position, or wishes of both officers and men to maintain that post. We also beg leave to mention that no plan of attack was ever communicated to us, or notice of a retreat, until it had taken place in our rear, as we supposed by General Lee's order. We are &c.,
ANTHONY WAYNE.
CHARLES SCOTT.

FROM GENERAL WASHINGTON.

HEAD QUARTERS, 30 May, 1778.

SIR. Poor's, Varnum's, and Huntington's brigades are to march in one division under your command to the North River. The quartermaster-general will give you the route, encampment, and halting days, to which you will conform as strictly as possible, to prevent interfering with other troops, and that I may know precisely your situation every day. Leave as few sick and lame on the road as possible.—Such as are absolutely incapable of marching with you are to be committed to the care of proper officers, with directions to follow as fast as their condition will allow.

Be strict in your discipline, suffer no rambling, keep the men in their ranks and the officers with their divisions, avoid pressing horses as much as possible, and punish severely every officer or soldier, who shall presume to press without proper authority. Prohibit the burning of fences In a word you are to protect the persons and property of the inhabitants from every kind of insult and abuse.

Begin your march at four o'clock in the morning at the latest, that it may be over before the heat of the day, and that the soldiers may have time to cook, refresh, and prepare for the ensuing day—I am, &c., Go. WASHINGTON.

P. S.—June 18th.—The foregoing instructions may serve you for general directions, but circumstances have varied since they were written. You are to halt on the the first strong ground after passing the Delaware at Coryell's Ferry, till further orders, unless you should receive authentic intelligence, that the enemy have proceeded by a direct route to South Amboy, or still lower. In this case you will continue your march to the North River, agreeably to former orders, and by the route already given you. If my memory does not deceive me, there is an advantageous spot of ground at the ferry to the right of the road leading from the water.

ORDER OF MARCH AND ROUTE OF THE ARMY FROM CAMP VALLEY FORGE TO NEWBURG ON THE NORTH RIVER OPPOSITE FISHKILL.

Poor Varnum Huntington	1st	Lee	Coryells
1st Pennsa 2d do Late Conway	2nd	Mifflin	Sherard
Woodford Scott No. Carolina	3d	Marquis	Coryells
Glover Patterson Larned	4	deKalb	Easton
Weedon Muhlenberg 1s Maryld 2d do	5	Stirling	Coryells

The Detachmt under Colo. Jackson to move to and take possession of Philadelphia and prevent plundering & any abuse of Persons. Van Scoicks Regiment to replace the 8th Pennsylvania Regt in the Pennsylvania Brigade—The 2d State Regment of Virginia to replace the 13th Regiment in Scott's Brigade—Park of Artillery to be attached to the Several Divisions Equally and march with them.

The 1st & 2d Divisions to move the morning after Intelligence is received of the Enemy's Evacuation of the City.

The 3rd & 4th Divisions the morning after these, & the 5th Division the morning succeeding—every day's march to begin at 4 o'clock, A. M. at furthest.

      Go. WASHINGTON.

1st 3d & 5th Divisions by Coryell's Ferry & thro the Clove by Smiths.

To Coryell's and Cross ....3 days
Halt.. 1
White House............................. 1
3 miles beyond the Cross Roads......1
4 miles beyond Morristown............1
Halt..1
Pompton Bridge.......... 1
Sufferans......................................1
Near Smith's Tavern.....................1
Halt if necessary..........................1
Newborough................................1
        — 13

2d Division by Sherard's Ferry and Sussex Court House.

To Sherard's Ferry and Cross.........3
Halt........ 1
Union Iron Works.........................1
Halket's Town...............................1
Sussex Court House......................1
Halt. 1
4 M. beyond Col. Martin's 1
Warwick.......................................1
5 M. beyond Chester.....................1
Halt if necessary...... 1
Newborough................................1
        — 13

4th Division by Easton and Sussex Court House.

To Easton 3
Halt............................. 1
Crossing..1
6 miles beyond Carrs.....................1
Sussex Court House......................1
Halt................... 1
Then as in 2d Division..................5
        — 13

Regard to be had to the convenience of Water as well as distance.

ORDERS RELATIVE TO THE MARCH FROM VALLEY FORGE, JUNE 1778, AFTER GEN. LEE'S AND GEN. MIFFLIN'S DIVISNS HAD MARCHED.

The Army is to March to Morrow & till further Orders in the following Order.

The Marquis De ⎫ Woodford's ⎫
LaFayette is to ⎬ Scotts ⎬ Brigades.
lead with   ⎭ N'th Car'a ⎭

The Baron ⎫ Glovers ⎫
De Kalb ⎬ Pattersons ⎬ Brigades.
next with ⎭ Learneds ⎭

The Artillery Park and spare Ammunition.

Lord Sterling with ⎰ Weedons, ⎱
       ⎱ Muhlenbergs ⎰
       ⎰ 1st Maryland, ⎱
       ⎱ 2d Maryland. ⎰

The disposition for the baggage of the army to be as follows:

The Commander in Chief's Baggage is to march in the front of the column of Waggons—The Adjutant General's, Paymaster General's Engineers Muster Master General Auditor of Accounts The Baggage of the Marquis De La Fayettes DeKalbs Division the Baggage of Lord Stirlings Division and then the Waggons of the Quarter Master Generals Department Flying Hospital & lastly the Comy & Forage Master General's Waggons—The whole Baggage to fall in the Rear of the Column of Troops. The Genl officers commanding the Grand Division to appoint such guards upon the baggage as shall be necessary for the Security thereof—They will also, appoint a party of Pioneers to move in front of the Columns, to assist the Artificers in repairing Bridges and bad places in the roads.

There will be a party of Artificers to go in front & rear of the whole, to mend Bridges and repair the Broken Carriages; which will take their Orders from the Q. M. Genl.

The sub Inspectors are to assist the Quarter Master General in regulating the order of March, encampment and planting of Guards and to accompany and follow his Directions accordingly.

      Go. WASHINGTON.

Note, the Light Horse is to March in front and upon the Right flank a days and encamp in the Rear of the Troops o Nights.

The new guards will form the advanced guards of the army and the old guards the rear guard. Each regiment will send out a flank guard on the right flank in the proportion of a sergeant and 12 men to every 200 men.

CURIOUS INCIDENT IN THE LIFE OF CHAS. LEE.

Sparks, in a note, Vol. 5—p 532, mentions a curious incident in the life of General Lee. "By an order of Congress, while the army was at Valley Forge, Washington was directed to administer the oath of allegiance to the general officers. The major-generals stood around Washington, and took hold of a Bible, according to the usual custom; but Lee, just as the oath was about to be administered deliberately withdrew his hand twice. The movement was so singular and performed in so odd a manner that the officers smiled and Washington inquired the meaning of his hesitancy. Lee replied: "As to King George, I am ready enough to absolve myself from all allegiance to him, but I have some scruples about the Prince of Wales." The strangeness of this reply was such that the officers burst into a laugh, and even Washington could not refrain from a smile. The ceremony was of course interrupted. It was renewed as soon as composure was restored proper for the solemnity of the occasion, and Lee took the oath with the other officers.—Connected with the subsequent conduct of Gen. Lee, this incident was thought by some to have a deeper meaning than at first appeared, and to indicate a less ardent and fixed patriotism toward the United States, than was consistent with the rank and professions of the second officer in the command of the American forces."

INSTRUCTIONS OF GENERAL WASHINGTON TO BRIGADIER GENERAL WAYNE.

SIR: You are to proceed with the first and second Pennsylvania regiments, and the brigade, late Conway's, by the direct route to Coryell's Ferry, leaving a proper interval between your division and General Lee's, so as to prevent their interfering with each other. The instructions given to General Lee, are to halt on the first strong ground after passing the Delaware at the said ferry, until further orders, unless he should receive authentic intelligence, that the enemy have proceeded by the direct road to South Amboy, or still lower. In this case he is to continue his march to the North River. Given at Headquarters, this 18th day of June, 1778.

LETTER OF GENERAL WASHINGTON TO MAJOR GENERAL GATES.

Four o'clock, 20 June, 1778.

SIR: I think it necessary to inform you by the return of the express, who brought your packet by Congress, that I am now with the main body of the army within ten miles of Coryell's Ferry, General Lee is advanced with six brigades. and will cross to-night or to-morrow morning. By the last intelligence the enemy were near Mount Holly, and moving very slowly; but as there are so many roads open to them, their route could no be ascertained. I shall enter the Jerseys to-morrow and give you the earliest notice of their movements and whatever may affect you. As the supplies of forage and provision in your quarter will be objects of the utmost importance, they will therefore claim your attention.

I am, Sir, &c.

From Dawson's Battles of the United States.

The hardships to which the troops had been exposed at Valley Forge had tried their fiedelity, as well as their powers of endurance; and they gathered around their illustrious chief, in his dreary quarters, to cheer his solitary moments and to make new resolves for their future government. The machinations of his enemies, in their attempts to destroy the confidence which his country had reposed in him, by forging letters in his name, and in producing distress among the troops, by secretly interfering with his quartermaster's and commissary's department had failed to withdraw from him the affections of the army; and, although the sufferings of the troops were extreme, the Cabal received no accessions to its numbers from that source. They were true to their chief and their country; and Gates, at the head of the Board of War, Lee, in nominal captivity; and Mifflin, Conway, and Reed, in more comfortable quarters, were left to concoct new schemes, and to create new discontents.

The enemy, amply provided for in Philadelphia, had passed the winter gayly and in comparative inactivity; the celebrated *Conciliatory Bills*, introduced by Lord North, had been published in the United States, and their proffered conciliation had been rejected by the Congress; three commissioners, sent over from England, to negotiate with that body, had extended the olivebranch to the country in vain; and the formal alliance of France with the infant republic had been consummated and proclaimed, infusing fresh hopes and more determined activity among the people.

With thanksgivings to the Almighty Disposer of events for the increased strength which this alliance had brought to the cause of freedom, the army and the people entered on the active duties of the campaign of 1778 with increased confidence, while the enemy, numbering more than twice the force of the Americans, was preparing to open the operations of the campaign by *a retreat*, and to expose himself—with nineteen thousand five hundred men in Philadelphia, and ten thousand four hundred at New York, within supporting distance—to the public shame of being *pursued* by eleven thousand eight hundred half-starved and half-clad Americans, from the huts of Valley Forge. His experienced commanders-in-chief, Gage, Burgoyne, and the Howes, with their well-laid plans, their extensive supplies, and their powerful armies, and no less powerful fleets, in magnificent procession, had appeared before the world, displayed their emptiness, and disappeared; and another, who had seen much service, and who understood the character of the contest, was about to take the place which they had occupied, and, ultimately, to share with them the animosity of an unwise ministry and the censure of a despoiled nation.

The treaty between France and America had compelled the enemy to change his proposed plan of operations; and the expected co-operation of a powerful fleet with the allies rendered a farther occupation of the Delaware and the city of Philadelphia impossible, without jeopardizing the safety, both of the army and the fleet. General Sir Henry Clinton, who had succeeded General Howe in the command of the British forces, saw his danger, and made immediate, although secret, preparations to withdraw to New York. A scarcity of transports prevented him from proceeding by water; and he determined to ship his cavalry, the provision train and heavy baggage, many of the loyalists of Philadelphia, and part of the German troops,* while, with the main body, he would march through the Jerseys, and risk an action with the feeble force under General Washington.

Although General Clinton was thus actively engaged, the greatest secrecy was observed; and, while it was known to the Americans that an enterprise of some kind was intended, it was a matter of doubt what was to be its character and object. General Gates had expressed his belief that the Hudson River and the Eastern States would be the objects of attack. Elias Boudinot had suggested a different view; and General Charles Lee, who had been exchanged and returned to his post in the army, supposed the enemy would either "march directly and rapidly towards Lancaster," and force the army into a general engagement on disadvantageous terms, or that he would march down and occupy the lower parts of the Susquehannah, from whence, supported by his shipping, he could foster the Indian disaffections, and at the same time, act advantageously against the American. General Lee "had *particular reasons* to think" the latter was their object,† but General Washington thought differently, and the desires of the traitor, in attempting to open a free course for the escape of Sir Henry Clinton, were disregarded.

The commander in-chief, probably from intelligence which had been communicated by his secret correspondents in the city, was convinced that a retreat through the Jerseys was intended, and all his energies were directed in that direction. General Dickinson, the energetic commander of the militia of New Jersey, was already in the field, and General Maxwell, also a Jerseyman, was ordered to cross the Delaware with a brigade of Jersey troops, to take post in the neighborhood of Mount Holly, and to co-operate with General Dickinson in breaking up the bridges, felling trees in the roads, and in harassing the enemy should he attempt to march in that direction. Particular instructions were given to avoid every possibility of being surprised, and to keep small parties on the enemy's flanks in order to annoy him, without being too much exposed themselves.

On the evening of the seventeenth of June, the enemy's arrangements being nearly completed, General Washington asked the advice of his Generals on the question of attacking the enemy in case he retreated through the Jerseys, and he requested them to submit their answers, in writing, on the following morning. The events of that evening and the following morning rendered these answers of great interest to the General and to the student of the history of our country, with the transactions of the succeed-

---

* Sparks, p 270; Irving, iii p 416; Duer's Life of Lord Stirling, p 156. Notwithstanding this determination, it appears that all the troops, except the Anspach regiment of German mercenaries, were taken across the Jerseys. "*They were afraid to trust*" the Anspachers on this route, and some of our well known citizens have sprung from those who deserted from the ranks of the Hessians, whose desertion showed that they, too, could not be relied on.

† Gen Lee to Gen Washington, June 15.
Gen Lee, in his celebrated "*Plan*," communicated by him to Gen Howe, had advised this very step, as the one best calculated to suppress the revolt; and, as was shown by G H Moore, Esq, in his paper on "The Treason of Gen Lee," read before the N Y Historical Society, June, 1858, it is quite evident that he understood what were the views and intentions of Gen Sir Henry Clinton.

ing week before him, they are not less important. General Lee, the second in command—evidently with the same motives which influenced him in his attempted diversion of the Generals' attention towards Lancaster and the Susquehannah on the fifteenth—with great vehemence, opposed all offensive operations, and maintained that it would " be criminal" to hazard an engagement. General Duportail, the Baron Steuben, and a large majority of the general officers, were influenced by General Lee's arguments, and by his high reputation as an officer, and reported against the proposed engagement, Generals Greene, Lafayette, Wayne, and Cadwalader, alone sustaining the views of the commander in chief.

While this important question was pending in the American camp, near Valley Forge, about three thousand of the enemy's troops were embarked on the transports, and, about nine o'clock on Wednesday evening, June 17th, his baggage, and a portion of his troops crossed the Delaware by way of Cooper's Ferry, the grenadiers and light-infantry occupying the lines, and lying on their arms during the whole night. At an early hour on the following morning (Thursday, June 18th,) General Clinton and the remainder of the troops left the city by way of Gloucester Point, three miles below Camden; when the entire force, led by the Hessians under General Knyphausen, marched five miles, to Haddonfield, and halted.

Some of the American scouting-parties and light-horse, discovering the movement, pushed into the city and captured some sixty or seventy prisoners among whom were six officers. The joyful inlligence was immediately conveyed to Valley Forge, reaching the camp at half-past eleven in the morning, when six brigades—those of Generals Hunterdon, Poor, and Varnum, under General Lee; and that of General Conway, and the First and Second Pennsylvania brigades under General Wayne—were put in motion, the former moving at three o'clock and the latter at five o'clock the same day. They were directed to cross the Delaware at Coryell's Ferry (now the site of the New Hope and Lambertsville Bridge), with orders " to halt on the first strong ground after passing the Delaware, until farther orders; unless they should receive authentic intelligence that the enemy had proceeded, by direct road, to South Amboy, or still lower: in this case they were to continue their march to the North River." At five o'clock the next morning (Friday, June 19th,) the main body of the army moved towards Coryell's Ferry, but its progress, as well as that of Generals Lee and Wayne's commands, was much impeded by heavy rains—the latter crossing the Delaware on Saturday night (June 20th), and the former on Monday (June 22d.)

In the meantime the movements of the enemy had been marked with unusual deliberation and caution. On Friday (June 19th), General Knyphausen, with the Hessians and two brigades of British troops, remaining at Haddonfield, Generals Clinton and the main body of his army moved about eight miles, to Evesham, and encamped. On his march thither, General Leslie, who commanded the enemy's advanced guard, fell in with a reconnoitering party, and wounded and captured Captain Jonathan Beesley of the Cumberland county militia, one of the number. He refused to give any information of the movements of the American army, and died on the same afternoon, when he was buried with the honors of war, the General remarking, that " he was a braveman, and should not be treated with indignity."

At four o'clock, on the following morning (Saturday, June 20th), the line of march was again resumed, and at eleven, having reached Mount Holly, about seven miles from Evesham, the column again halted, and remained until Monday.

At nine o'clock on Sunday morning (June 21st), General Knyphausen, with his command, who had been left at Haddonfield on the preceding Friday, joined the main body, having marched from that place by way of Moorestown; and, on Monday morning (June 22d), the entire force marched to the Black Horse (now Columbus), seven miles from Mount Holly, where it halted.

At five o'clock on Tuesday morning (June 23d), the enemy was again in motion. General Leslie, with the Yagers and Fifth brigade of British troops, took the Bordentown road; General Clinton, with the First and Second battalions of grenadiers, the First and Second light-infantry, two battalions of Hessian grenadiers, and the First, Second, and Third brigades of British troops, advanced to Crosswicks (four miles east from Bordentown, on the road to Freehold), and General Grant, with the Fourth brigade of British troops, and General Knyphausen, with the remainder of the Hessians, brought up the rear. As General Leslie approached Bordentown, he was advised of the occupation of that place by a portion of the troops commanded by General Dickinson, the main body of which had been withdrawn and posted in other positions, where it was supposed the enemy might approach. This small party was commanded by Colonels Frelinghuysen, Van Dyke, and Webster, and when the approach of the enemy was discovered, they took up the planks from, and raised the draw of the bridge which here crossed Crosswick's Creek, preventing his passage, and forcing him to seek a more eligible crossing-place. General Clinton, also, met with some opposition as he approached Crosswick's. About five hundred men appeared to oppose his passage across the creek at that place, by felling trees across the road which approached it, but when the advanced party, under Lieutenant-colonel Simcoe, appeared, they prudently retired, taking up the planks of the bridge occupying a wood on the opposite bank, and making an appearance of contesting the passage. The most formidable demonstrations were immediately made,—troops formed in order of battle, flanked by dismounted dragoons, and supported by several pieces of artillery,—when the little party retired, and the Rangers, after the danger had ceased to exist, " behaved with their usual spirit," crossing over on the timbers of the bridge, and gallantly pursuing, without catching, the retreating militia.

On Wednesday (June 24th) Generals Clinton and Knyphausen, in the same order, crossed the creek, and resumed their march—the former halting at Allentown, in Monmouth county, and the latter in Imlaystown, three miles nearer Freehold. General Leslie, who had been sent towards Bordentown on the preceding day, joined the main body, with the detachment under his command, at this place.

On Thursday (June 25th) the forces were put in motion at an early hour.— General Clinton, until he reached Allentown, had not determined what route he would pursue. At this place, through the sagacity of Lieutenant-colonel Simcoe, he received information of the movements of General Washington and the different portions of the American army and he was no longer left in doubt respecting the proper course for him to pursue. The passage to the Raritan River was too difficult and hazardous, and he resolved, instead of that, to take the road to Sandy Hook, by way of Freehold, hoping, thereby, to "outwit" the Americans, and secure his baggage and provision-train, the possession of which, he supposed, was the principal object of General Washington's movements. His rear and flanks were also harassed by the Ameican light troops,—the gallant Morgan being on his right flank, General Maxwell's brigade on his left, and Generals Scott and Cadwalader in his rear— while General Dickinson, in his front, destroyed the bridges and opposed his progress with remarkable energy. With a clear understanding of his danger, General Clinton "requested" General Knyphausen, who commanded the advance, to take the baggage of the whole army under his charge, and move forward at an early hour the the next morning, while he, in person, would cover the retreat. In accordance with this request, the veteran Hessian, with an immense train, extending nearly twelve miles, moved from Imlaystown early on the morning of the twenty-fifth, and, at five o'clock, Generals Leslie and Clinton followed, with their respective divisions. General Knyphausen, sensible of the importance of his charge, notwithstanding the intense heat, marched to the borders of Freehold, thirteen miles distant, while the main body halted at the Rising Sun, seven miles from Allentown.

On Friday (June 26th,) General Knyphausen moved four miles, to Freehold, and foraged, where, at 10 A. M., the main body also arrived, having marched nineteen miles that morning, and remained during that and the following day.

During this series of deliberate movements,—which was probably caused more by the intense heat, the frequent and heavy showers, and the extreme activity of the American light troops in obstructing the enemy's march, than by any feeling of security on his part,—General Washington, and those who were under his command, were not disinterested or idle spectators. Generals Lee and Wayne had been pushed forward to harass the retreating enemy; General Arnold had been sent to Philadelphia to take the command in that city, with orders to detach some four hundred Continental troops and as many volunteers as he could obtain, under General Cadwalader, for the same purpose; and the commander in-chief, with the main body of the army, had passed the Delaware, detached Colonel Morgan, with six hundred men, to strengthen the advance, and on Tuesday, the twenty-third of June, taken post at Hopewell township, about five miles from Princeton.

The extreme heat, rendered still more oppressive by frequent and heavy showers, added to the labors of the march, had greatly fatigued the troops, and they remained in camp during that and the following day (June 24th.) While at Hopewell, it is said that a second council of war was held, at which, after presenting the relative positions and strength of the two armies, General Washington asked, "Will it be advisable to hazard a general engagement?" Again General Charles Lee, the second in command, interposed, and, with his usual impetuosity and brilliant declamation influenced the council to answer that it was not advisable to do more than detach fifteen hundred men to strengthen the forces which were already hanging on the enemy's left flank and rear, while the main body should preserve a relative position, to act as circumstances might require. It appears that General Wayne did not sympathize with this decision at all; and that Generals Greene, Lafayette, Steuben Duportail, and Patterson, desired to send forward twenty-five hundred, or, at least, two thousand men; while "it was clearly the wish of these officers," unlike those of General Lee and his friends, to draw the enemy into a general engagement, if it could be done under favorable circumstances. It is equally clear that the commander-in-chief was disposed to hazard the risks of a battle, on almost any terms, and that disposition was strengthened by the fearless dissent of General Wayne, and the subsequent privately expressed opinions of Generals Greene and Lafayette. With apparent deference to the decision of the council, therefore, he immediately dispatched General Scott, with fifteen hundred men, "to gall the enemy's left flank and rear," but it is quite evident that he had not been convinced of his error by the action of the council, and that he had determined to adopt such measures—and to employ such instrumentalities as would, probably, accomplish the result which he desired.

On Thursday (June 25th), the army advanced to Kingston, about three miles east from Princeton; and, having learned that General Clinton had given evidences of alarm by taking the lower road, towards Freehold, instead of the upper road, leading towards New Brunswick, General Washington no longer hesitated to fulfil the expectations of his country in attacking her fugitive enemy. With this intention, passing by those whose opinions differed from his own, and placing the enterprise in the hands of those who were its friends and the friends of its originator, he ordered General Wayne, with one thousand picked men, and General Lafayette, with orders to take the command of the entire advance of the army, including General Maxwell's brigade and Colonel Morgan's riflemen, who were on the enemy's flanks, and General Poor's brigade, which he took, with him, to move forward and "take the first fair opportunity of attacking the enemy's rear." On the evening of the same day (June 25th), leaving his baggage at Kingston, the whole army approached still nearer the enemy's line of march by moving to Cranberry, where it arrived early the next morning (June 26th.)

A heavy storm coming on, the army was compelled to remain at Cranberry during the entire day, but the advanced corps before referred to, moved forward and occupied a position on the Freehold road, within five miles of the enemy's rear. At this time General Lee, perceiving the effect which the detachment under General Lafayette would produce in overthrowing his treasonable designs and in preventing the safe retreat of General Clinton, manifested considerable uneasiness, and requested permission to take the command of it. General Lafayette, having been advised of this trouble, had expressed a wish "to ease him of it;" and General Lee was directed to take with him the brigades of Generals Scott and Varnum, and support "the several detachments then under the command of the Marquis." This, without apparent indignity to General Lafayette, vested the command in General Lee, the senior officer, although he was instructed to allow the Marquis to carry out any plan which he might have began to execute. During the same day, the army being still at Cranberry, it was found that the advanced corps was too remote to be properly supported, and too far to the right either for efficient offensive or defensive movements. General Lafayette was, therefore, ordered to file off by his left towards Englishtown, which was done on Saturday morning (June 27th); and, during the same day, the main body, under General Washington, moved from Cranberry, and encamped within three miles of the same place. The two armies were thus brought within eight miles of each other, while the American advanced guard, under General Lee, some five thousand strong, exclusive of Colonel Morgan's corps and the New Jersey militia, were three miles nearer; and thus they passed the night of Saturday, the twenty-seventh of June. The enemy had now reached a point within ten or twelve miles from the Heights of Middletown, on reaching which it would be impossible to attempt anything against him with any prospect of success, and General Washington resolved to attack his rear the moment he moved from the position he then occupied. Orders were accordingly issued to General Lee, without incumbering him with details, and he was expected to arrange the plan of operations in such a manner as would secure that object. In addition to that order, the commander-in-chief, through Colonel Hamilton, late on Saturday night, directed General Lee to detach a party of observation to watch the enemy's movements, to prevent a sudden retreat in the night, and to keep up a communication with the main body. With a singular disregard of the spirit and object of this order it was three o'clock before it was promulgated, and it was sunrise before the detachment which embraced the brigades of Generals Scott and Varnum, numbering about three hundred men in each, commanded by Col. Grayson, was put in motion.

As has been stated, it was near sunrise before this party of observation marched from the camp, and when it reached the ground between the church and the court-house the enemy was found to be engaged with a portion of General Dickinson's troops, whose presence had become obnoxious to him; and, soon afterwards, he retired.

At about five o'clock, General Washington had received intelligence from General Dickinson that the enemy's advance was moving from his position near Freehold, and orders were immediately issued to General Lee to move forward with the advance and attack the enemy, unless some powerful reason prevented. At the same time the main body was put in motion to sustain him, the men leaving behind them their packs, and, in some cases, their coats, to enable them to move forward with greater expedition and comfort, the morning being an intensely hot one, and both men and officers feeling confident that some severe work was to be done. The right wing of the army in the absence of General Lee, was commanded by General Greene, and the left by General Lord Stirling. The former to expedite the march, and to counteract any attempt which might be made to turn the right flank, was ordered to file off near the "new" meeting-house,—now so well known to all who have attempted to unravel the tangled thread of occurrences at Monmouth,—and to fall into the road again a short distance in the rear of the court-house; while Lord Stirling, with the left wing, was to move directly on towards the same spot.

In the mean time, the advanced corps, under General Lee, had moved from Englishtown towards the enemy—Colonel Richard Butler, at the head of the column, with two hundred men; followed by General Scott's and part of General Woodford's brigades, about six hundred in number, with two pieces of artillery; General Varnum's brigade, of about the same strength, with two pieces of artillery; General Wayne's command, a thousand strong, with two pieces of artillery; General Scott's "detachment" of fourteen hundred men, with four pieces of artillery; and General Maxwell's detachment of a thousand men, with two pieces of artillery, in all, exclusive of Colonel Grayson's command of six hundred men, and of the flanking parties under General Dickinson and Colonel Morgan, five thousand men and twelve pieces of artillery. During their progress they were occasionally halted, in consequence of the contradictory and imperfect intelligence which was conveyed to General Lee; and during one of these halts, General Wayne was ordered to leave his detachment, which was some distance back in the column, and to take command of the troops which had been sent out in the morning under Colonel Grayson. Advancing towards Freehold, the column soon afterwards came in sight of a small body of the enemy's troops, cavalry and infantry, when it was immediately halted, and, by "wheeling to the right, it was reduced to a proper front to the enemy's horse," and Generals Lee and Wayne rode forward to reconnoitre. General Wayne soon perceived that it was merely a small covering party, and ordered Colonels Butler and Jackson, with their detachments, to dislodge them, which was done, amidst which it was seen that "the enemy was moving from them in very great disorder and confusion."

While these movements were being made by the advance under General Lee the main body under Generals Greene and Lord Stirling, was moving forward to support it, and to share in the perils and glories of the contest; and General Sir Henry Clinton was urging onward his plans for securing his army and its baggage, which he supposed to be the primary object of attack, General Knyphausen had moved forward, at an early hour, with the baggage-train; and, at eight o'clock, Sir Henry took up his line of march. He had collected in his rear the very *elite* of his army, evidently under the supposition that an attack would be made at some time during the day. With the Third, Fourth, and Fifth brigades of British troops, the First and Second battalions of British grenadiers, the entire bodies of the Hessian grenadiers and of the British Guards, the First battalion of light-infantry, and the Sixteenth regiment of light dragoons, he descended from the heights, on which he had encamped, to the plains of Monmouth, and took the route which General Knyphausen had taken at an earlier hour in the morning.

It was this movement which General Wayne had seen, and he immediately dispatched a messenger to General Lee, asking that "the troops might be pushed on." No such order was issued, however, until it was evident that the enemy (or a small party in his rear apparently from eight to nine hundred in number) had halted, and appeared to invite an attack. Orders were then issued to General Wayne to take about four hundred men from the detachments of Colonels Butler and Jackson, and to advance towards him. With his wonted gallantry, General Wayne did so, when the Queen's light-dragoons were sent back by General Clinton to check the movement. Forming his troops to receive the charge, Colonel Butler, with great gallantry, repulsed the enemy, driving the horse back upon a body of foot which had been sent out to support them, and following it up with a rapid pursuit. A larger body of troops soon afterwards appeared to be moving towards General Wayne's right, when he ordered his two pieces of artillery to open a fire on them, asked a reinforcement, and prepared for battle.

While General Wayne was thus employed, General Lee appears to have determined to cut off the party with which the former was engaged, and, for this purpose, he made a *detour* on the left, with the intention of falling on the line of Sir Henry Clinton's march, between the rear of the main body and this detachment.

This movement, with those of Colonel Morgan, and Generals Dickinson and Wayne, appears to have confirmed the suspicion of General Clinton, that the capture of the baggage was the object of General Washington, and he determined to return to the plains near Freehold, and take measures for its protection. With great good judgment he reasoned, that while this immense train, which was comparatively unprotected, was in the defiles through which it had to pass, it would be in great danger, and the most certain way to protect it, and insure its safety, was to attack the corps which harassed his rear, and to press it so hard as to oblige the detachments to return from his flanks to the assistance of their friends. He supposed General Washington was too far in the rear to support the advanced corps, and he immediately, by a retrograde movement, proceeded to carry out his design.

The first step taken was to attack the command of General Wayne, of which notice has been already taken; the next was the detachment of the Seventeenth light-dragoons and a brigade of British troops from General Knyphausen's command, to strengthen General Clinton's right flank; and finally, a disposition of the main body, under Lord Cornwallis, was made on the plain, to attack General Lee and the several detachments of the advance corps, under his command.

Perceiving these movements before they had been fully accomplished, General Lee had given orders to the several corps of his detachment to retreat, and they fell back towards the meeting-house, in some cases in great confusion, and in all without knowing either the object of the retreat—the great body of the troops having seen nobody, and except General Wayne's small detachment, none having fired a shot—or the ground on which they were to reform. All were indignant, but General Wayne, whose position and opportunity corresponded with his wishes, was peculiarly so, and gave vent to his feelings in the severest terms.

While this series of misfortunes was attending the movements of General Lee, the main body of the army, under General Washington, was hastening on towards Freehold—the left wing, led by David Forman and Peter Wikoff, as guides, marched on the road, the right, by a *detour*, marched at same distance from the left—wholly unconscious of the retreat of the advance, and unprepared to counteract its evil effects. The commander-in chief, with the left wing, was passing down the road, between the meeting-house and the parsonage, when he met a fifer, "who appeared to be a good deal frightened. The General asked him whether he was a soldier belonging to the army, and the cause of his returning that way; he answered that he was a soldier, and that the Continental troops that had been advanced were retreating." It is said "the General seemed to be exceedingly surprised, and rather more exasperated, appearing to discredit the account, and threatened the man, if he mentioned a thing of the sort, he would have him whipped." He passed on "a few paces," when a similar scene ensued between the General and two or three others whom he met; but, as he had heard no firing except a few cannon, a considerable time before, he still appeared to discredit the statements. It was considered prudent however, to send forward some trusty officers to gain information, and Colonel Harrison (the General's "old secretary") and Colonel Fitzgerald having volunteered for that purpose, rode forward towards Freehold. At the bridge these officers met Colonel Grayson's regiment; a little farther on, Colonel Parke's; and farther still, Colonel William Smith's. Colonel Ogden was next met, and, in a towering passion, informed the anxious inquirers, "By God! they were flying from a shadow." Colonel Rhea and General Maxwell were next encountered, but all were alike "agitated, expressive of their disapprobation, and concerned that they had no place assigned to go where the troops were to halt." They were all ignorant of the cause of the retreat, and each appeared to feel that *he* had been robbed of the laurels which had been providentially placed within his reach.— General Lee was the next person seen by Colonel Harrison, but he was silent; and, in the post of danger, next to the enemy,—who was "pressing very hard upon them at two, or three, or four hundred yards distance,"—were Colonel Stewart, General Scott, and General Wayne.— Having "no other concern than at the retreat itself," the latter saw no difficulty in checking the enemy "provided any effort or exertion was made for the purpose, alleging that a very select body of men had been that day *drawn off* from a body far inferior in number;" and he sent some suggestions to General Washington for the disposition of the troops. Leaving the gallant Pennsylvanian in the post of danger—where he remained during the day—Colonel Harrison galloped back, and reported the situation of affairs—the first intimation which the General had received of the position and movements of the enemy.

While his faithful and intelligent secretary was thus engaged in the front, General Washington was not less active in seeking information and in checking the retreat. Riding forward, and accosting the several commandants of regiments as he met them, he received the same negative answers and the same evidences of dissatisfaction that his secretary had received until, in the rear of the retreating column, he met the commands of Colonels Ramsay and Stewart. Calling these officers to him and telling them that he "should depend upon them that day to give the enemy a check," he directed General Wayne to form them with two pieces of artillery on their right, and hold the enemy in check. At this instant the guilty author of the mischief, General Lee, rode up, and the commander-in-chief demanded, in the sternest manner, "What is the meaning of all this, sir ?"— Disconcerted and crushed under the tone and terrible appearance of his chief, General Lee could do nothing more than stammer, "Sir, sir ?" When, with more vehemence, and with a still more indignant expression, the question was repeated. A hurried explanation was attempted—his troops had been misled by contradictory intelligence, his officers had disobeyed his orders, and he had not felt it his duty to oppose the whole force of the enemy with the detachment under his command.— Farther remarks were made on both sides, and closing the interview with calling General Lee "a dammed poltroon,"* the comder-in-chief hastened back to the high ground, between the meeting-house and the bridge, where he formed the regiments of Colonels Shreve, Patterson, Grayson, Livingston, Cilley and Ogden, and the left wing under Lord Stirling. When the first line of troops had been formed on the heights, General Washington rode up to General Lee, and inquired in a calmer tone, "Will you retain the command on this height, or not? If you will, I will return to the main body, and have it formed on the next height." General Lee accepted the command, when, giving up the command, General Washington remarked, "I expect you will take proper means for checking the enemy," and General Lee promised, "Your orders shall be obeyed; and I shall not be the first to leave the ground."

In the mean time, General Clinton was not inactive. Sending forward to the division under General Knyphausen, who was hurrying off with the baggage, he ordered back a brigade of British troops and the Seventeenth light-dragoons, for the purpose of strengthening his left, and made vigorous attempts against the American forces. The British grenadiers, with their left on the village of Freehold, and the Guards on their right, had driven General Lee's advance, and they approached the position, near the parsonage, which General Wayne occupied, with great spirit. The confidence which General Washington had reposed in Colonels Stewart and Ramsay, and in General Wayne, their commander, was not misplaced. The grenadiers crossed a fence, which passed in front of his position, and were driven back with great slaughter. A second time they advanced, and were repulsed in like manner; and here, and along the entire line, the battle raged with great fury. At length Lieutenant-colonel Monckton, of the Second grenadiers, harangued his men, and placing himself at their head, led them to the charge. As they approached General Wayne's position a deadly fire was opened upon them, in which their gallant leader and several other officers were killed, and—after a desperate hand-to-hand struggle for the possession of Colonel Monckton's body, in which the Americans succeeded—they were repulsed, and it was not attacked again during the day.

Sir Henry Clinton moved the main body of the British army against the left of the American lines, where Lord Stirling commanded, but the batteries were so well served that he was glad to seek an inglorious retreat. He then moved towards the right of the American position, but General Greene. with the right wing, opposed him, and Chevalier Plessis De Mauduit (one of the heroes of Red Bank) took him in the flank with six pieces of cannon, and he was equally unsuccessful in that direction.

At this moment General Wayne "advanced with a body of troops, and kept up so severe and well-directed a fire that the enemy was soon compelled to retire behind the defile where the first stand was made, in the beginning of the action." In this charge by General Wayne a characteristic incident occurred, which was not without its effect on the enemy. His dispositions had been made for the charge, and his men—who were mostly without their coats—seeing the character of the intended movement, and knowing the peculiarities of their leader, were impressed with the idea that a struggle of unusual determination was about to be commenced. For the purpose of rendering themselves as free as possible, some of the troops *rolled up their shirt sleeves*, which was immediately imitated by their associates, and when the trying moment arrived the detachment rushed forward with a shout, and handled their weapons with so much vigor that the enemy, astonished and overpowered, hastily retired.†

In this new position the enemy was comparatively secure. His flanks were secured by thick woods and morasses, while his front could only be approached through a narrow pass. Notwithstanding these advantages, General Washington resolved to attack him; and, for this purpose, ordered General Poor, with his own and the Carolina brigades, to move round upon his right, while General Woodford was to move, in a like manner, upon his left, and the artillery was to gall his front. Before these detachments reached the ground they had been directed to occupy, night overtook them, and they bivouaced for the night within

---

* This statement is made on the authority of Gen. Lafayette, who gave it on the piazza of the residence of Vice-president Daniel D. Tompkins, Sunday morning, August 15, 1824. Gen. Lafayette referred to it as the only instance wherein he had heard the General swear.

† This statement is made on the authority of the late John Orolius, Esq., of this city, who was one of the first of those who rolled up their shirt-sleeves.

a very short distance of the enemy's lines. The entire army, worn out with fatigue, threw itself on the ground and slept soundly until morning, when it awoke to learn that the prize which, on the evening before, was considered within its reach, was no longer in the neighborhood.

Sir Henry Clinton "having reposed the troops until ten at night, to avoid the excessive heat of the day, took advantage of the moonlight to rejoin General Knyphausen, who had advanced to Nut Swamp, near Middletown," taking with him his wounded, except about forty, who could not be removed; and, on the following morning, the extreme heat, the fatigue of the men, and the distance the enemy had gained, rendering a pursuit "impracticable and fruitless," it was not attempted.

"The battle of Monmouth"—for such is the title by which it was designated— was attended with many circumstances of peculiar interest. The day was unusually hot, and many of the troops, in both armies, died from its effects; while the tongues of hundreds of others were swollen so as to render them incapable of speaking.‡

Here, also, the well-known Molly Pitcher gained her commission and epaulette, as a reward for her energetic conduct in supplying her husband's place at the cannon to which he had been attached.

But, above all, here the treason of General Charles Lee received its final check. Opposing the commander-in-chief, in his proposition to the council of general officers, he determined to oppose him in the field, also; and thus secure the retreat of the British army, and the stores and baggage which retarded its march. With this intent he secured the command of the advance—superseding those who were known to favor an attack on the fugitive enemy,—received the orders to bring on a general action, by attacking the main body of the enemy; and sent back messages of confidence in the result, in order to mislead the commander-in-chief and to retard his movements. Instead of carrying out the expectations of the army and the orders of his chief, he attacked the rear-guard only, instead of the main body; and instead of bringing on a general engagement, he attempted nothing more than the carrying off a covering party. It is true the result was different from that which he expected and desired, but it is equally true that it was also dif-

‡ Dr Sam Forman's statement.

ferent from that which Sir Henry Clinton anticipated. Both these officers appear to have manœuvred for the same end— the safety of the baggage and stores; and both supposed General Washington was beyond supporting distance, and therefore beyond the distance where he could control the movements of either army.

In the retreat of General Lee, *per se*, there can, probably, be but little to condemn, beyond its disorderly character.— It is, doubtless, true that the detachment was in great danger; and that a retreat (or, as General Lee termed it, "a retrograde movement") was as necessary to secure it from actual capture by Sir Henry Clinton, as to secure the safety of General Knyphausen's division. It is equally true, however, that General Lee's disobedience of orders was the cause of Sir Henry Clinton's "retrograde movement," which produced the danger spoken of; and that an attack on the enemy's main body by the five thousand picked troops, which General Lee commanded, would have secured the co operation of the detachments under Colonel Morgan and General Dickinson, which, under existing circumstances, were rendered entirely inefficient from want of orders.

The enemy's loss, it is said, was Lieutenant-colonel Hon. H. Monckton, Captain Gore, Lieutenants Vaughan and Kennedy, four sergeants, and fifty-seven rank and file killed; three sergeants and fifty-six rank and file died from fatigue; Colonel Trelawney, Lieutenant-colonel Simcoe, Major Gardner, Captains Cathcart, Bereton, Willis, Leighton, Powell, Bellue, and Ditmas, and Lieutenants Kelly, Paumier, Goroffe, Desborough, and Gilchrist, seven sergeants, one hundred and forty-eight rank and file wounded; and seven sergeants and sixty-one rank and file missing.* The American army lost Lieutenant-colonel Bonner, Major Dickinson, three captains, three lieutenants, one sergeant, seven matrosses, one bombardier, and fifty-two rank and file killed; two colonels, nine captains, six lieutenants, one ensign, one adjutant, nine sergeants, one gunner, ten matrosses, and one hundred and twenty-two rank and file wounded; five sergeants, one matross, and one

* It is evident that a great error was made in the report of Sir Henry Clinton to the government, from which this statement is copied, as four officers and 245 privates were buried by the Americans, besides those who had been buried by the enemy.—Gen. Washington to Pres. of Cong., July 1, and Jos. Clarke's Diary, June 28.

hundred and twenty-six rank and file missing, many of whom, who had been overcome by the heat, afterwards came in.

CORRESPONDENCE.

LETTER OF COLONEL ALEXANDER HAMILTON BY THE ORDERS OF GENERAL WASHTON TO GENERAL CADWALADER.

HOPEWELL, 23d June, 1778.

DEAR SIR:—I have just received yours this day from the Draw Bridge. The army marched this morning to this place. Is was my intention to have taken post near Princeton, but finding the enemy are dilatory in advancing, I am doubtful of the propriety of proceeding any farther, till their intention is ascertained. I wish you to inform me more particularly of the obstructions which have been thrown in their way that I may be better able to judge whether their delay is owing to necessity or choice. Any circumstance that may serve to throw light upon this question, I shall be obliged to you for, as it is of very great importance. If their delay is voluntary, it argues a design to draw us into a general action, and proves that they consider this to be a desirable event. They may, perhaps, wish to draw us from the Delaware, far to the left, and then by a rapid movement gain our right flank and rear.

I should be glad of your sentiments fully as to their probable designs, and the conduct which it will be most proper for us to observe in consequence. You will be pleased to continue to advise me punctually of every movement and appearance of the enemy.

Let me remind you of mentioning always the hour at which you write, which is of the greatest moment.

LETTER OF GENERAL WASHINGTON TO MAJOR GENERAL PHILEMON DICKINSON, COMMANDING THE NEW JERSEY MILITIA.

HEAD-QUARTERS, HOPEWELL, 24 June, 1778.

SIR:—As the several detachments of Continental troops, employed in harassing the enemy on their march, will have the greatest need of intelligent guides, not only for their own safety, but to enable them to direct their offensive operations with greater precision, it will be necessary that among the militia, which you shall think proper to annex to each party, there be persons perfectly acquainted with the roads and communications, which it is most interesting to the different commanding officers to know. The disposition for these detachments is as follows. Morgan's corps is to gain the enemy's right flank : Maxwell's brigade to hang on their left : Brigadier General Scott is now marching with a very respectable detachment destined to gall the enemy's left flank and rear. Two or three hundred Continentals, and such volunteers as General Cadwalader has been able to collect, have crossed the Delaware, and are now marching to the enemy's rear. Colonel White's detachment of horse is to join Genl. Scott. Enclosed is a letter for Colonel Morgan, which you will forward.

I am &c.

DISPOSITION OF THE MILITIA BELONGING TO THE STATE OF NEW JERSEY, MADE BY MAJOR GEN'L DICKINSON, VIZ :

Head-Quarters, Chamber's Tavern,
June 25, 1778.

Colonels Furman, Haight & Holmes, with their respective Battalions, are ordered to gain the Enemies Right Flank & join Col. Morgan's detachment, who are to annoy the Enemy in that Quarter as much as in their power. They will consist of 3 Col—1 Lt. Col—3 Maj—7 Cap—15 Subs—13 Serg't—12 Corp—163 Priv.

Colonels Neilson & Webster with their Battalions will take Post in Front of the Enemy, throw every possible obstruction in their Rout, impede their march & harass them, whenever opportunity presents. This Detachment will consist of 2 Col—1 Lt Col—1 Maj—6 Capt.—16 Subs—19 Serj'ts—13 Corps—218 Privates.

Capt. Lane & 25 of his Company of Axmen to attend Col. Neilson.

Col. Scudder with his Battalion will join Brig'r Genl Scott on the left flank of the Enemy consisting of 150 Privates.

The whole of the remaining Militia, are to be equally divided & to do duty on the lines alternately, Officers as well as privates.

INSTRUCTIONS OF GENERAL WASHINGTON TO THE MARQUIS DE LAFAYETTE.

Sir :—You are immediately to proceed with the detachment commanded by General Poor, and form a junction as expeditiously as possible with that under the command of General Scott. You are to use the most effectual means for gaining the enemy's left flank and rear, and giv-

ing them every degree of annoyance.—
All Continental parties, that are already
on the lines, will be under your command,
and you will take such measures, in concert with General Dickinson, as will cause
the enemy the greatest impediment and
loss in their march. For these purposes
you will attack them as occasion may require by detachment, and, if a proper
opening should be given, by operating
against them with the whole force of your
command. You will naturally take such
precautions, as will secure you against surprise, and maintain your communication
with this army. Given at Kingston, this
25th day of June, 1778.

Monmouth's Centennial.

From the Monmouth Democrat, July 4th, 1878.

An eminent English statesman has wisely said that "A people which takes no pride in the noble achievements of remote ancestors, will never achieve anything worthy to be remembered with pride by remote descendants." However great may be the sins of the United States as a nation, never can it, with truth, be said that her citizens of to day have forgotten the historic past, and neglect to honor the memories of those heroic men, who waded through seas of privation and bloodshed to break the chains of English despotism, and found a nation of freemen. Within the past few months celebration after celebration has caused the great heart of the nation to throb with patriotic pride. One of the grandest, most interesting, and most important of these celebrations occurred at Freehold, on Friday, June 28th. It was in commemoration of the one hundredth anniversary of the Battle of Monmouth, that battle so justly famous in the annals of our infant republic, so glorious in the magnificent achievements of the American hosts, still more glorious in the grand results which followed those achievements. For weeks previous to the day of celebration, faithful committees had been patiently, unceasingly and untiringly at work, making every preparation which human ingenuity and labor could devise, in order to make the affair a success. Their efforts were crowned with signal success, for never was a celebration of such magnitude, planned and carried out in a more felicitous manner, and with such perfect harmony of opinion and action. At length the long expected anniversary day arrived. The booming of cannon on Briar Hill and the Englishtown pike ushered in its birth, and soon the joyous peals of bells rung out on the morning air. The sun rose in regal splendor. A century before the same old sun cast his golden rays from heaven's firmament upon a land distracted with internal dissensions, torn and bleeding with the cruel wounds of war, while on Monmouth soil two hostile armies were about engaging in deadly conflict, the one contending for arbitrary power, the other for precious liberty.—What stupendous changes are wrought in a single century ! On this 28th of June, 1878, the same sun scatters his splendrous beams upon a land smiling with cultivation, rich in ripening harvests, watched over and guarded by the angel of Peace. On the battle field which one hundred years before echoed and re-echoed with the notes of war, to-day, a solemn silence reigns, broken only by the notes of feathered songsters, while gentle breezes kiss the forest trees, as if afraid to disturb the sacred stillness of the scene. Instead of hostile armies in glittering array, a mighty throng of 20,000 peaceful citizens, all aglow with patriotism, gather in the leaf embowered streets of Freehold. The flag of our country floats in the breeze from every house, while the public buildings and many a splendid private mansion are gorgeously decked with starry banners and tri-colored bunting.

A great event like the battle of Monmouth needs a great celebration, and in the present instance the people of old Monmouth were fully equal to the emergency. The procession was a magnificent one. As it passed down Main street, the horsemen mounted on gaily prancing, richly caparisoned steeds, the white plumed Knights Templar, the white aproned Masons, the sun-browned Soldiers with their glittering muskets, the Zouaves with their bright red costumes, the elegant carriages filled with civilians, made a gorgeous and brilliant spectacle. The masonic ceremonies at the laying of the corner-stone of the battle monument, were of a deeply solemn nature, and were eminently suitable at the founding of a monument to honor the heroes

"Who read their history in a nation s eyes."

The orators at both stands were filled with the importance of the occasion, and, as they spoke in grand and glowing language of the thrilling events of a century ago, the vestal fire of patriotism burning in the breasts of their auditors, found expression in frequent hearty applause.— The 28th of June, 1878, with its commemorative exercises, will be long affectionately cherished in the memory of thousands of citizens of New Jersey and other states. Though it should fade from memory may the event it celebrated never sink into oblivion, but may it ever be a flaming beacon, lighting the pathway of Columbia's hosts to future victories in freedom's cause. The following is a full report of the proceedings, and all the scenes and incidents of the celebration :

The Decorations.

The way in which Freehold was decorated reflected great credit upon its patriotic citizens. One could not turn his eyes in any direction without having them greeted with a sight of the stars and stripes. It would be an impossibility to mention each private residence and place of business which was particularly noticable for the beauty of its decorations and we shall therefore mention only a very few. The homelike, hospitable mansion of Mrs. Daniel S. Schanck—from whose hands the Monument Association has received that splendid gift, Monument Park—was elegantly and tastefully decorated. At Ex-Gov. Parker's residence lines of flags adorned the cornices and the verandah, while a fine engraving of Washington at Monmouth was suspended over the entrance door. Mr. Acton C. Hartshorne's large Knight Templar flags and other handsome decorations attracted considerable attention. Mr. Jacob B. Rue had a rich display of flags, signals, &c. At the Seminary there was displayed among other decorations, a flag made by the pupils in 1861, and a large British flag reversed beneath a small American flag. The decorations at Mr. James A. Perrine's were very pretty and were artistically arranged. On the portico were five chairs belonging to the family, each over one hundred years old. Ferris Lockwood displayed the flag presented to him by Col. E E. Ellsworth. Elaborate decorations were also displayed by Hon. A. R. Throckmorton, Dr. D. M. Forman, Charles A. Bennett, John H. Ellis, Freehold Fire Department, Joseph W. Hulse, W. W. Cannon (and others ad infinitum). The immense labor of adorning the Court House was magnificently executed under the skillful direction of Messrs. David S. Crater, John L. Conover and Aaron R. Throckmorton. Four lines of flags extended from the top of the belfry to each corner of the building, while four large flags hung from staffs run out from the top windows of the same. A wide band of golden starred bunting ran along the top of the front, while the pillars were tastefully wrapped with a like material, so that the whole presented a strikingly beautiful appearance. Several large flags hung in the middle of Main street, in the centre of the town, and the red, white and blue made a pleasing contrast with the rich green trees bordering the sidewalk.

Arrivals.

The first body of visitors to arrive was the McKnight Rifles, from Asbury Park, and, not long after them, came the Vredenburgh Rifles, of Blue Ball. By nine o'clock twenty car loads of people had been landed at the F. & J. station from the eastern parts of the county. Soon train after came in and before noon, not less than twenty thousand people were in town. The Freehold and New York road reported sixty car loads of people, and some of the cars were more than comfortably filled.

The arrangements for receiving visitors were admirable. The invited guests reported immediately at Seminary Hall, where they were received by Ex-Gov. Joel Parker. Among the distinguished gentlemen from abroad who attended the celebration, were Gov. McClellan, Ex-Gov Bedle, Ex-Gov. Price, Ex-Gov. Newell, Brig. Gen. H. B. Carrington, U. S. A., who had come from Indiana expressly for the occasion, Capt. Jos. A. Yard, Col. J. C. Clark, U. S. A., Capt. Chauncey Harris, of Elizabeth, Speaker John Egan. Gen. Wm. S. Truex, Hon. A. R. Van Cleaf, Ohio, Hon. C. Holywarth, Newark. Hon. G. O. Vanderbilt, Senator Crowell Marsh, of Mercer, Senator Kirk, of Essex. Hon. V. W. Mount, Gen'l Judson Kilpatrick, Hon. Amos Clark, Hon. T. B Peddie. Dr. C. S. Stockton, Newark, Hon. S. S. Cox, Prof. H C. Cameron, Princeton, Elwood E. Thorne, P. G. Master of Masons of N. Y. The representatives of the press met at the Engine House where they found a committee to care for them.

Dr. Freeman's parlor, where Washington held a Masonic Lodge the night after the battle, had been arranged for a meeting of the Grand Lodge, but it was found necessary to forego anything more than a visit, as individuals.

At 10 o'clock, Gov. McClellan and staff were received by Ex.-Gov. Parker and the other dignitaries under the shade of Seminary Hall. By this time the troops, bands and societies from the northern and southern portions of the State had arrived and were falling into line on Broad Street. This occupied an hour, but shortly after eleven the procession began to move down Yard avenue, headed by Grand Marshal Major James S. Yard and his aids. The following is a list in the order in which they marched, of the component parts of

The Procession.

GRAND MARSHALL, MAJOR JAMES S. YARD.
Aids:
John B Conover, J Hull McLean, James J Conover, John T Rosell, Henry Campbell, John V N Willis, James L Shinn, Peter Conover, W S Throckmorton, Grenville B Little, D McLean Forman.

Committee of the Day:
Hon. G. W. Shinn, Hon. A. R. Throckmorton,
Col. E. F. Applegate.

GEN. W. J. SEWELL AND STAFF,
Commanding Second Brigade, N. G. of N. J.,
in the following order:
Peterman's band, Trenton, 16 pieces.
Winkler's Drum Corps of Trenton.
COL. A. W. ANGEL,
Commanding Seventh Regiment, N. G. of N. J.,
in the following order:
Staff officers:
Lieutenant Colonel James C Manning, Major, C M Sloan, Surgeon, C H Larison, Judge Advocate, B F Chambers, Adjutant, C M Van Sciver, Quartermaster, Geo. T. Crammer, Chaplain, Rev.
H. H. Baum,
Companies:
Co A, Trenton, Capt W H Skirm, 50 men; Co B, Trenton, Capt W H Bilbee, 40 men: Co C, Capt Chas W. Kitchen, Lambert-ville, 60 men ; Co D, of Trenton, Capt M Hurley, 40 men; Co. E., of Turkey, Capt. John C. Patterson, 55 men;
Co. F, of Mount Holly, Capt W. A.
Barrows, 60 men ;
COL. E. B. GRUBB, AND STAFF,
Commanding Sixth Regiment, N. G. of N. J.,
in the following order :
Sixth Regiment Band and Drum Corps, Joseph Jennings, leader.
Companies :
Co A, Burlington, Capt Samuel Phillips, 58 men ; Co. B, Camden. Capt J. H. Austin, 48 men ; Co. C, Camden, Capt Jos Lee, 50 men ; Co. D, Camden, Capt C S Benard, 42 men; Co E, Camden, Capt Sandman, 50 men; Co F, Beverly, Capt R R Eckendorf, 51 men; Co G, Cape May, Capt C M Magra h, 42 men; Co K, Vineland, Capt
C H Cheever, 58 men.
Governors Island Band of New York, 25 pieces, Amiel Steiger, Leader.

4 OLD TIMES IN OLD MONMOUTH.

Third Regiment Drum Corps, 15 men, E R Trimble, Leader.
COLONEL W. A. MORELL AND STAFF.
Commanding Third Regiment, N G of N J, in the following order:
Companies:
Co B, Elizabeth, Capt B P Holmes, 57 men ;Co C, Elizabeth, Capt W H DeHart, 45 men; Co D, New Brunswick, Capt M N Oviatt, 58 men; Co E, Plainfield, Capt C B Sherring, 60 men; Co F Rahway, Capt Wm Bloodgood,53 men ; Co G, Keyport, Capt B A Lee, 85 men ; Co I, Asbury Park, Capt Rainier, 45 men ;
Drake's Boy Brass Band of Elizabeth,
Elizabeth Veteran Zouaves with two Gatling Guns, Gen J Madison Drake, Commanding, 60 men.
THE MASONIC ORGANIZATION.
Vogel's band of Newark, with drum and fife corps, 50 men, Drum Major MacVeagor, Leader.
Damascus Commandery, No 5, Knights Templar, of Newark, St. John's Commandery, of Elizabeth, Cour De Leon Commandery of New Brunswick, 100 men.
The M W Grand Lodge of Free Masons of New Jersey, Wall Lodge No 73 F A M of Squan; Olive Branch Lodge, No 16, F A M of Freehold, and visiting members from other Lodges.
Carriages
Containing the General Committee of Arrangements, officers, of the Monmouth Battle Monument Association, Gov. McClellan and Staff, Executive and Judicial officers of the State, and members of the Legislature.
Executive and Judicial officers of Monmouth County, Board of Commissioners of the Town of Freehold, and Clergy.
Capt. Enoch L Cowart, David M Rue, Major Henry Bennett, Capt Joseph A Yard, Ex-Sheriff Samuel Conover, Ex-Judge Wm D Oliphant, survivors of the Committee of celebration arrangements of 1854.
(Major James S Yard, Grand Marshall, was also a member of the above committee.)
Veterans the War of 1812 and Mexican war.
Newing's Drum Corps of Long Branch, and Band.
Washington Continental Guards of Princeton, Capt A L Green, 50 men.
The First Regiment band, of Newark, 20 pieces.
The Joel Parker Association of Newark, 120 men.
Bordentown Drum Corps.
Delaware Hose Co. of Bordentown, with Hose Carriage.

Drake's Zouaves carried four tattered battle flags, among which was Gen Phil Kearney's and the flag which Gen Drake unfurled in Virginia, May 24, 1861, when the army crossed the Long Bridge. Each Gatling Gun is capable of discharging 1,100 shots per minute, was drawn by one horse, and was under the charge of three men. One of the color bearers was immense, weighing 325 pounds, but he did not seem to fall away any notwithstanding the excessive heat of the day.
The Masonic display was new to most people in town and was heartily applauded, Newing's Drum Corps of Long Branch with Band, and the Princeton Continentals, whose real old time soldier clothes, well represented the dress of the patriots of the Revolution
The Joel Parker Association of Newark, was dressed in black suits and white high hats, and wore a handsome purple badge emblazoned with the portrait of the Ex-Governor. They carried with them a handsome silk banner appropriately inscribed, and likewise bearing on its front a large picture of Gov Parker.

The procession paraded the principal streets of Freehold for about an hour and was attended by a full sidewalk escort throughout. Frequent applause greeted the various organizations as they marched along in beautiful ranks with a step of clock work regularity. The horsemen, mounted on their spirited steeds, which danced and curveted at sound of the martial music, presented a remarkably fine appearance. The magnificent horses bestrode by Brigadier General W. J. Sewell and Grand Marshal Major James S Yard elicited universal admiration. They were loaned for the occasion by Rev. F. Kivelitz, of the Catholic church. The procession was a most splendid display, and as it passed through the town, the Knights Templar and soldiers executing their evolutions in perfect order, and the various bands playing our grand national airs, it was indeed a scene calculated to fill the heart of every beholder with pratriotic pride.

When the line reached Monument Park, the noon salute of thirty-eight guns thundered forth, the bands were all playing and the scene was one long to be remembered. The military filed to the left and entered the spacious and well shaded grounds of "Larchwood," the residence of Mrs. D. S. Schenck, who has already been mentioned as the generous donor of Monument Park. Here they rested, while the Knights Templar opened order and the Masonic brethren marched through in inverse order and ascended upon the stand erected in the Park, around the corner-stone of the prospective monument.

At Larchwood

the dignitaries were entertained in a splendid manner by Mrs. SCHENCK and the ladies of her family. Through the courtesy of Col. JOHN A. HALL many were introduced to a young lady who wished to see them, and many bore away centennial medals of the battle of Monmouth as mementoes of their pleasant meeting.

At Shinn's Hall,

the military were given a hearty dinner at 1.30 P. M. The dinner was under the general management of Hon. GEO. W. SHINN, assisted by 75 of the patriotic ladies and gentlemen of the town. The walls of the hall were destitute of any decorations with the exception of the pictures which usually ornament it, but what they lacked in bunting was made up in eatables with which the tables were tastefully and bounteously laden. The hall was filled with five tables running the full length of the building, while the annex to the hall was also provided with tables, both buildings being so arranged as to seat with

OLD TIMES IN OLD MONMOUTH.

comfort 900 people. As the large gates at the end of the hall were thrown open the men filed in two by two, some passing through the main building into the annex, and all taking their places at the tables remained standing. The tables being all filled in both buildings, Rev. Mr. BOND, of Easton, Pa., asked a blessing, after which the guests were seated and at once began satisfying the cravings of nature. The meal being over one of the officers proposed three cheers for the ladies, to which the boys ably responded. The Knights Templar, not willing to be behind the military in gallantry, also proposed and gave three ringing cheers in honor of the ladies. The hall was three times filled by the invited guests, and all being fed and plenty to spare being left, aids were sent out to ask in the people who had not eaten. This was repeated until, as the aids rode through the crowd requesting others to eat and be filled, the response became general, "We've all had enough." Over 3,000 people were fed at these tables and still there was enough provisions left to feed 1,000 more, all of which was raised by public contribution.

The ladies are deserving of great credit and of the heartfelt thanks of all who shared their hospitality, for their indefatigable efforts to handsomely entertain their guests. From what we were told by some of the visitors we judge that they were successful in their praiseworthy undertaking, for we were told by a number that they had been at several entertainments of this kind, and that they had never been entertained more hospitably than by the ladies of Freehold.

EXERCISES AT MONUMENT PARK.

The procession arrived at the stand on Monument Park, at 1 P. M. The audience in attendance was not so large as might have been expected from the vast throng which filled the streets, but this may be explained by the fact that there is no shade in the immediate vicinity of the stand and large numbers were afraid of sunstroke should they stand out under the blazing rays of the sun, without the grateful protection of shade trees. The canvass canopied stand was filled with distinguished guests, both ladies and gentlemen, while a formidable army of reporters were seated at the long table which had been erected exclusively for their benefit.

Presentation of Monument Park.

It was a few minutes past 1 o'clock when Theodore W. Morris, Esq., son-in-law of Mrs. Daniel S. Schanck, in behalf of that generous and public spirited lady, presented the deed for Monument Park to Ex-Gov. Parker, President of the Monument Association, in the following neat speech :

Mr. President—It is my agreeable duty, as the representative of the executrix and heirs of the estate of Daniel S. Schanck, to present to you, as President of the Monmouth Battle Monument Assaciation, the document pertaining to the transfer of this ground to the possession and ownership of that society.

The gift has no reservation beyond the requirement that the property shall not be diverted from the purposes of the association.

The pleasure of this duty is enhanced by the circumstance that the ancestors of the family I have the honor to represent, were no more laggard in the patriotic service of that memorable Sabbath in 1778, than their descendants are this day in the spirit that prompts this gift.

Many of our family names were called on this battle field one hundred years ago, and the record of what they did bears no taint of hesitancy, cowardice or treachery.

The impartial pen of history has left no trace of dishonor, and one—a maternal great grandfather—was an ensign on this field, and rose to the rank of a colonel in the Continental army.*

The only desire expressed by the donors of this property is that there shall be expeditiously reared here a memorial shaft to remind the generations that shall gaze upon it of the grand fortitude, self-sacrifice, and courage of those who then so heroically fought and suffered, that we, with all their descendants, might enjoy the heritage of freedom in a Union of States " one and inseparable forever."

Ex-Gov. PARKER, Pesident of the Association, in accepting the document replied to Mr. MORRIS as follows :

On behalf of the Monument Association I accept this agreement for transfer of this valuable property, to be used forever as a site for a monument to commemorate the Battle of Monmouth.

No more beautiful location and none more appropriate could have been selected.

* Col. Ephram Whitlock.

I know the history of the family you represent on this occasion. Many of them were in the American army during the war of the revolution, and some were at the Battle of Monmouth.

You truly say that no stain of dishonor rests upon the memory of any of them.

Convey to Mrs. SCHANCK and the others for whom you speak the thanks of the Monument Association for their most liberal gift. It will be our aim speedily to rear upon this spot a monument worthy of the great event. This we can do, if in addition to what has already been contributed, the people continue to manifest the same liberality that has characterized them for the last few days.

Laying the Corner Stone of the Monument.

The corner stone of the Monmouth monument was then laid with solemn and impressive Masonic ceremonies, as follows:

Rev. Marshall B. Smith, Grand Master of Masons of New Jersey, having called the assembly to order announced the object of the occasion. He said: Brethren of the Masonic fraternity, friends and fellow citizens: We are here to-day at the invitation of the Monmouth Monument Association, for the purpose of laying the corner stone of a monument to commemorate the battle of Monmouth. The Masonic fraternity is a patriotic body and it is hence with the deepest pleasure and with a high sense of the honor conferred upon us that we lay the corner-stone of this monument. In every great and important undertaking it is eminently fitting that we should invoke the presence and blessing of our heavenly Father; I therefore call upon the Grand Chaplain to offer prayer.

Prayer by Rev. Nathaniel Petit.

Almighty and everlasting God, we would praise and bless Thy holy name. When Thou dids't lead Thy children over Jordan, Thou dids't cause twelve stones to be set up as a monument in memorial of the deliverance of Thy children from Egyptian bondage. In like manner we are now to erect a stone in commemoration of the victory achieved by our fathers at Monmouth. Our fathers trusted in Thee, and when they were sorely pressed and held in bondage by their British foes, Thou, Oh! God, dids't rise in Thy might and burst their bonds asunder. Thou dids't cast their enemies out of the land. For all Thy mercies we bless Thee. We praise Thee, Oh! God, for Thy wondrous works. Before Thee the angels bow and cherubim and seraphim veil their faces. And now, O God of our fathers, we ask Thy blessing upon this solemn act in which we are now to engage. Let Thy protection rest upon the workmen who shall be employed in the construction of this monument, and when this offering of our gratitude shall have been completed may it tell our children and our children's children of the noble deeds of our ancestors. All of which blessing we humbly ask for the sake of Him who brought "immortality to light through the Gospel" and who has taught us to pray, "Our Father which art in Heaven, hallowed be Thy name. Thy kingdom come. Thy will be done in earth, as it is in heaven. Give us this day our daily bread. And forgive us our debts, as we forgive our debtors. And lead us not into temptation, but deliver us from evil; for Thine is the kingdom, and the power, and the glory, for ever. Amen."

The Masonic Ceremonies.

The Grand Treasurer, CHARLES BECHTEL, then placed the box into the cavity beneath the stone, and WILLIAM SEGOINE, Grand Secretary, *pro. tem.*, read the following list of articles deposited therein:

Copy of the Holy Bible.
Constitution of the State of New Jersey.
Journal of the Proceedings of the Constitutional Convention of New Jersey, 1844.
Governor McClellan's Inaugural Address.
List of Judicial and Executive officers of New Jersey, 1878.
Battles of the Revolution, by Gen. Carrington, presented by the author.
Monmouth County Directory, including a list of County Officials, Officials of Incorporated Towns, Banks, Insurance Companies, Lodges, and Benevolent Organizations, &c., for 1878.
Copies of the Medals struck in commemoration of this event.
Copy of the Early History of Monmouth, by Hon. Edwin Salter. The Boundaries of the County of Monmouth, by Hon. G. C. Beekman; and the History of the Battle of Monmouth, including all the early accounts of that event, reprinted from the MONMOUTH DEMOCRAT. Presented by James S. Yard.
List of Officers and Men in the Revolutionary War. Presented by Adjutant-General Stryker.
Constitution and By-Laws of the Grand Lodge F. & A. M.; Portrait of Col. David Cox, First Grand Master of New Jersey; Proceedings of Grand Lodge of New Jersey, 1878. Presented by M. W. Grand Master Smith.
Maps of New Jersey, 1777 and 1877. Presented by John O. Raum, Esq., of Trenton.
Public Ledger Almanac, 1878.
Programme of the Exercises of the Day.
List of Officers of the Monmouth Battle Monument Association.
Newspapers of the County.
Copy of the *Daily Graphic*, with illustrations of the Town of Freehold.
The box was of copper, made by Charles Lounsberry.

The massive stone weighing two tons, was then gradually lowered upon its foundation, there to remain for centuries to come, "a memorial of the past, a monitor to the present and all succeeding generations."

Mr. JAMES T. BURTIS, a member of Olive Branch Lodge of Free Masons of Freehold, who had been chosen to represent the Architect, then presented the working tools to the Grand Master, who handed the Square to the Deputy Grand Master (HAMILTON WALLIS, of Elizabeth), the Level to the Senior Grand Warden (JOSEPH W. MARTIN, of Rahway), and the Plumb to the Junior Grand Warden (WM. HARDACRE, of Camden), and the ceremony then proceeded as follows:

Grand Master.—R. W. Deputy Grand Master, test this corner-stone by the Square.

After this had been done, the Deputy said: Most Worshipful Grand Master, the stone is square.

Grand Master.—R. W. Senior Grand Warden, prove this corner-stone by the Level.

Senior Grand Warden—Most Worshipful Grand Master, the corner-stone is level.

Grand Master—R. W. Junior Grand Warden, try this corner-stone by the Plumb.

Junior Grand Warden—Most Worshipful Grand Master, the corner-stone is plumb

The Grand Master then advanced to the corner-stone, attended by the Grand Deacons, and said:

This corner-stone having been tested by the Square, Level, and Plumb, I find that the workmen have faithfully performed their duty, and that this stone is well formed and correctly laid, according to the rules of our Ancient Art; and I so declare, as Grand Master of Masons of New Jersey. (The Grand Master then struck the stone three times with his gavel, and with a silver trowel spread cement upon it. He then said): Let the elements of consecration be presented.

The Deputy Grand Master then advanced, and pouring corn from a silver pitcher upon the stone, said:

May the blessing of the Great Architect of the Universe rest upon the rulers and people of this Commonwealth, and may the corn of nourishment abound within our borders.

To which the brethren responded—So mote it be.

The Senior Grand Warden then advanced, and pouring wine upon the stone, said:

May the Great Architect of the Universe watch over and protect those who erect this monument, and bless them, and all men, with the wine of refreshment and peace.

Response—So mote it be.

The Junior Grand Warden then advanced, and pouring oil upon the stone, said:

May the Great Architect of the Universe, the God of our fathers, preserve our heritage and grant unto us, now and ever, the oil of joy.

Response—So mote it be.

The Grand Marshal then presented the Architect to the Grand Master, who returned to him the working tools.

The Grand Master, attended by the Grand Deacons, then advanced to the corner-stone, and made a short prayer; after which came

The Grand Master's Address.

MEN AND BRETHREN HERE ASSEMBLED: Be it known unto you, that we are lawful Masons, true and faithful to the laws of our country, and engaged by solemn obligations to erect buildings for the craft, to lay the foundations of Monumental structures at the call of the civil authority, to be serviceable to the Brotherhood of Man, and above all to fear and honor God, the Great Architect of the Universe.

We have among us, concealed from the eyes of all men, secrets which cannot be divulged, but these secrets are lawful and honorable, and not repugnant to the laws of God or man They were entrusted, in peace and honor to the Masons of ancient times, and having been faithfully transmitted to us, it is our duty to convey them unimpaired to the latest posterity. Unless our craft were good and our calling honorable, we should not have lasted for so many centuries, nor should we have been honored with the patronage of so many illustrious men in all ages, who have ever shewn themselves ready to promote our interests and defend us from all adversaries.

We are assembled here to-day—as Free and Accepted Masons—to lay the corner-stone of a Monument, which we trust shall commemorate to the latest generations, the valor of those who on this historic soil—one hundred years ago—determined, under God, the destiny of a nation, and sealed the charter of our liberty with deeds that a great confederation of sovereign states will not willingly forget. May our patriotism be anew enkindled on this spot made sacred by such associations; and may none of us ever allow the torch of the social incendiary to kindle the fire that would reduce to ashes the temple of our freedom and the charter of our blood-bought rights.

Especially as Masons have we a right to honor this day and its associations. Our institution planted on the soil of New Jersey, in 1730, have, for nearly one hundred and fifty years, embraced within its number great and brave and good men of this commonwealth. Every Mason—so far as known—in the historic Battle at Monmouth Court House, was a craftsman tried and true; one of them was afterward Governor of New Jersey and Grand Master of Masons, and two others were also Grand Masters of New Jersey. Of the twenty-seven Governors New Jersey has had, fourteen have been or are members of our Fraternity, and seven of them, beginning with Governor RICHARD HOWELL, active officers or members of our Grand Lodge.

The first Grand Master of New Jersey after the Revolution was the Hon. DAVID BEASLEY, Chief Justice of the State, who, with distinguished ability, governed the craft as Grand Master for four years, (from 1786 to 1790 inclusive).

In Olive Branch Lodge, St. John's Lodge, and in many other old historic Lodges of this jurisdiction, soldiers and officers of the revolution held the gavel and ruled the labors of the craft.

Thus the history of Freemasonry in New Jersey is linked with the patriotic record of the commonwealth; and to-day we weld another link as in the presence of our honored Chief Magistrate and his immediate predecessors—true craftsmen all—we symbolize our loyalty to the State, and our reverence for the heroic dead, in this perfect ashlar, that bedded in the courses laid by the hands of operative Masons, shall be a memorial, to the centuries yet unborn, of the undimmed patriotism of New Jersey, and of the loyalty of our time-honored Institution.

Amid the booming of artillery, the measured tread of soldiery, and the gathering host of historic associations, we as the great Masonic Brotherhood, can hear the voice of the God who rules in the camp as by the fireside, in the State as in the family, proclaiming " Peace on earth;" and even at this hour, on this old historic battle field, we look forward joyously to the day

"When forever
Man's dread banners shall be furled,
And the angel Peace be welcomed
As Regent of the world."

At the conclusion of the above address, the Grand Chaplain pronounced the Benediction, and the Grand Marshal proclaimed as follows :

Silence—silence—silence !

In the name of the Grand Lodge of the Most Ancient and Honorable Society of Free and Accepted Masons for the State of New Jersey, I proclaim that this corner-stone has this day been laid by the Most Worshipful Grand Master of Masons of New Jersey, in ample form.

This closed the Masonic ceremonies.

Literary Exercises.

At the close of the ceremony of laying the corner stone, Mr. John J. Ely advanced upon the stage and announced that the meeting would now organize with the following gentlemen as officers: President, Ex-Gov. Parker; Vice Presidents—Dr. Robert Laird, Thomas Burrows, John H. Laird, Judge Chillion Robbins, K. W. Dayton, G. H. Van Mater, John A. Morford; Secretaries—John B. Conover, John J. Ely.

Ex-Gov. Parker, as President, then called upon the Rev. Frank Chandler to open the exercises with prayer.

Prayer by Rev. Frank Chandler.

Oh Lord God of providence, Supreme Ruler of the universe, we worship Thee.— Under the bright light of this June sun, and beneath these beautiful skies once blackened by the clouds of war, we thank Thee for thy goodness to us. Thou art King of kings and Lord of lords. We bless Thee that Thou hast given this land to us as our goodly heritage, and because Thou hast proclaimed to all the earth that man, of right, should be free. We thank Thee that Thou didst give success to our fathers in their grand struggle for liberty. We thank Thee for the blessings we have enjoyed in the past and for those we now enjoy, as descendants of those brave ancestors. Make this land, we beseech Thee, a noble land of freedom, where the final battle shall be fought for human rights. – We thank Thee that we to-day lay the corner-stone of a monument, in commemoration of the Battle of Monmouth. May we lay it with reverent hands. Grant that the whole nation may be inspired with the spirit of true patriotism, when the people hear and read of the celebration of this one hundredth anniversary of the battle of Monmouth. Deliver us, O Lord, from all the evils which threaten us as a nation and grant that the time may speedily come when Thy name shall be known, and Thy rule recognized, over the whole earth. And unto Thee, the ever living God, unto Father, Son and Holy Ghost, be glory and honor, forever and ever. Amen.

Ex-Gov. JOEL PARKER, as President of the meeting and of the Monument Association, next addressed the meeting as follows :

Gov. Parker's Speech.

FELLOW CITIZENS :—We are assembled on a battle field of the American revolution. Here, one hundred years ago, our forefathers struck a blow for liberty.— Near the spot where we now stand, on that quiet Sabbath morning in June, the first gun of the battle of Monmouth was fired and the first blood shed. Here the Continental troops emerged from the woods and yonder (pointing to an eminence where the other meeting was in progress) the Queen's Rangers received the first volley, fled through the village and joined the main army of the British, then slowly retiring over the plain beyond. The American advance, under Lee, quickly crossed the ravine, which forms the eastern boundary of this farm, descended into the plain and engaged the British rear.

In and around the village of Monmouth Court House the hostile forces manoeuvered for position, and fought, both with artillery and musketry, for more than three hours, when the Americans, having been ordered to retreat towards the main army, retired over the very ground we now occupy. Checked in their retreat, rallied and re-formed by Washington, in person, they turned upon the pursuing foe and before night drove him discomfited from the field of conflict.

Notwithstanding the perfidious conduct of the general who commanded the advance, impending defeat was changed into victory.

It is not my purpose to detain you by a recital of the causes which led to the American Revolution, nor by a detailed account of the battle, the centennial anniversary of which we this day celebrate; nor will I comment upon the consequences which resulted therefrom. These subjects will be left for the eloquent gentlemen whom I will presently introduce to you.— It is proper however that I should allude to some of the incidents of the battle and briefly notice its general features.

The Battle of Monmouth was one of the most important of the War and its result gave great encouragment to the Americans. Remarkable bravery and endurance were exhibited on both sides. The ability of the continental troops to stand before British Grenadiers, re-form their broken lines while in retreat in the presence of the enemy, when commanded by an officer in whom they had confidence—to renew the fight—dispute every inch of ground—and finally put to flight the flower of Sir Henry Clinton's army—was here demonstrated.

The battle of Monmouth was the last and almost the only field engagement of that war between the main armies of the contending powers. More officers of distinction participated in it than in any other battle of the Revolution.— On the side of the British were Sir Henry Clinton, Lord Cornwallis, Sir William Erskine, Leslie, Knyphausen and others; while with the Americans were Washington—the greatest of all—Lafayette, the young enthusiast for liberty, Greene, upon whose wisdom Washington much relied, the intrepid Wayne, and Knox the artillery general, in speaking of whom Sir Henry Clinton said, that "no artillery could have been better served than his, on the field of Monmouth." Here also was Baron Steuben, who, in the long cold dreary winter at Valley Forge, had organized and disciplined the American army for the summer campaign. Lord Sterling, Maxwell, Dickinson and Forman, commanding New Jersey troops, were also here. There were some here of inferior military rank who subsequently held exalted civil positions. James Monroe, fifth President of the United States, and John Marshall, who became chief justice, served at Monmouth, in Virginia Regiments; and the great statesman, Alexander Hamilton, was attached to the military family of the Commander-in-Chief. On what battlefield did there ever appear such a galaxy of talent, patriotism, bravery, integrity and historic renown?

There were many incidents of a dramatic character connected with the battle of Monmouth which give it peculiar interest and much prominence in history. The meeting of Washington and Lee, the Godlike form and countenance of the Commander-in-chief, as with terrible energy he rode almost into the jaws of death and by his very presence stopped the retreat; and the bravery of that patriotic woman of humble origin, who, when her husband, serving with the artillery, was shot down, seized the rammer and helped to work the gun until victory was assured and his death avenged—all these have formed subjects for the pencil of the artist, have inspired the orator to eloquence and aroused poetic genius.

Is not then the field of Monmouth hallowed ground? Should not some memorial worthy of the event, commemorate the heroic deeds and perpetuate the memory of those who on this soil aided in securing liberty and establishing the free institutions we now enjoy?

On this beautiful and appropriate site, the generous gift of a public spirited lady, whose paternal as well as maternal ancestors were in the battle— in the presence of this vast multitude— with most solemn and fitting ceremonies, we have laid the corner-stone of a monument. The work is auspiciously begun and the monument will be built. The honor of the county of Monmouth is pledged to its completion.

When all here assembled shall have passed from earth, the granite shaft to rise on this spot will still point toward heaven, and in after centuries will speak to the generations who follow us of the heroic deeds and virtues of those noble men who on these fields one hundred years ago achieved a victory which helped to make our country free.

Letters from Distinguished Men.

At the close of his address, the Governor read letters expressing regrets on account of inability to attend the exercises, from Gens. Sherman and Hancock, Post Master Gen. Key, Attorney Gen. Devens, Ex-Gov. Samuel J. Tilden, Ex-Gov. Horatio Seymour, G. W. Childs, A. J. Drexel, Wm. Cullen Bryant and others. The letters of Messrs. Drexel and Childs, each contained a check for $100 for the Monument. The letter from Wm. Cullen Bryant was written only the day before he was stricken down with his last illness. Mr. Bryant had been invited to write an ode for the occasion and in his letter he expressed his appreciation of the honor conferred upon him, and likewise his inability to accept the invitation on account of other engagements. The President announced that Henry Armitt Brown, who was to have delivered an oration, would not be able to do so, as he had been stricken down with bilious fever and his physicians considered it utterly impracticable for him to leave home.

The following are copies of some of the letters read:

FROM WILLIAM CULLEN BRYANT.

NEW YORK, May 18, 1878.

MY DEAR SIR: I did not get your letter until last evening, or it would have been answered sooner.

Your Committee have done me honor in applying to me for an ode on the occasion of commemorating one of the most important events of our Revolution, the Battle of Monmouth. But I have so many engagements of a literary nature, and otherwise, on hand that I have no time to spare for such a task, and these must plead my excuse for declining the request.

I am, sir, faithfully yours,
W. C. BRYANT.
Hon. Joel Parker.

FROM GEN. SHERMAN.

WASHINGTON, D. C., June 4, 1878.
Hon Joel Parker, Freehold, N. J.:

MY DEAR SIR: I recognize fully the extreme politeness and kindness of your note of yesterday, just received, but regret that I must inform you that I have already made as many engagements of this kind as I can possibly fulfill this summer.

Wishing you the realization of all you indicate, I am, with great respect, your obedient servant,
W. T. SHERMAN,
General.

FROM W. L. STONE, SECRETARY OF THE SARATOGA MONUMENT ASSOCIATION.

NEW YORK CITY, June 14, 1878.
Hon. Joel Parker:

MY DEAR SIR: I sincerely regret that circumstances will prevent my accepting your polite invitation to be present at the Centennial of the Battle of Monmouth. I can fully sympathize with you in your arduous labors, having recently passed through a similar ordeal. I cannot but believe that, under your able management, the celebration will be a most grand success, and I remain, cordially yours,
WM. L. STONE.

FROM THE POSTMASTER-GENERAL.

WASHINGTON, June 15th, 1878.
Hon. Joel Parker, et al., Committee:

GENTLEMEN: It will afford me much pleasure to accept your invitation to be present at the celebration of the centennial anniversary of the Battle of Monmouth, if my official engagements will permit, but I fear that they will require my constant presence here.

Very respectfully,
D. M. KEY,
Postmaster-General.

FROM U. S. ATTORNEY-GENERAL DEVENS.

WASHINGTON, June 22, 1878.

GENTLEMEN: I am extremely sorry that my engagements compel me to decline your polite invitation to attend the celebration of the Centennial of the Battle of Monmouth. Your obedient servant,
CHARLES DEVENS,
Attorney-General.
To Messrs. Joel Parker and others, Freehold, N. J.

FROM GEN. HANCOCK.

NEW YORK, June 22, 1878.

MY DEAR SIR: Yours of the 1st inst., inviting me to be present at the Centennial Celebration of the Battle of Monmouth, on the 28th inst., was duly received, and has been kept by me, without reply, until this time, in the hope that I might be able to properly recognize your courtesy by my presence at the ceremonies; but to my sincere regret, I now find it impossible to leave New York at that time.

Orders just received by me requiring a change of my headquarters, and other important official matters which cannot be set aside, prevent my making any engagement which would take me away from this city between this and the 1st proximo.

With many thanks for your courteous invitation, I am, dear sir, very truly yours,
WINFIELD S. HANCOCK,
Major-General U. S. Army.
To the Hon. Joel Parker, Chairman of Committee, Freehold, N. J.

FROM HON. WM. M. EVARTS.

DEPARTMENT OF STATE, }
WASHINGTON, D. C., June 24, 1878. }

GENTLEMEN: I am in receipt of your polite invitation to be present at the Centennial anniversary of the Battle of Monmouth, at Freehold, N. J., on the 28th inst., and regret extremely that it will not be in my power to take part upon so interesting an occasion.

Very truly yours,
WM. M. EVARTS.
To Messrs. Joel Parker, James S. Yard, Theo. W. Morris, Committee.

FROM EX-GOVERNOR SEYMOUR.

UTICA, June 25th, 1878.

MY DEAR SIR: It is a matter of great regret to me that I am not able to go to Freehold and to take part in the celebration of the Battle of Monmouth. I have felt a deep interest in all such efforts to remind the American people of their obligations to the men who fought out the war of the Revolution. Their acts laid the foundation of our Union. Their struggles and sacrifices made the paternal feelings between all those living in different sections of our country, which must ever be our reliance for the maintenance of our government and the glory and prosperity of our country. Beyond these general motives there were some personal to myself which made me anxious to take part in the proceedings at Freehold. I was very much gratified with the invitation of your committee. I attach great value to it; nevertheless, I felt a pride in the fact that I had the right to be upon the ground on this occasion by virtue of a still higher claim. I love to feel that I had an ancestor who took a part in the Battle of Monmouth, who bore an honorable commission from the State of New Jersey, who served faithfully and well through the whole course of the Revolution, and who was one of those who was at the surrender of Cornwallis and saw the close of a bloody struggle which established the independence of the Colonies. I love to look upon his commission that made him a lieutenant-colonel in a New Jersey regiment, and also upon his certificate of membership in the Cincinnatti Society, signed by George Washington. My grandfather's name was Jonathan Forman. He was a native of Monmouth county. After the Revolution he moved to the interior of this State.

Not only patriotic sentiments but filial piety make me anxious to take part in your celebration, and deepen the regret that I cannot do so. I am yours, &c.,

HORATIO SEYMOUR.

HON. JOEL PARKER.

FROM HENRY ARMITT BROWN.

PHILADELPHIA, June 26—Evening.

MY DEAR SIR: I write you by an amanuensis,and from my bed. I have been sick since Sunday, and am not able to stand up; but I am better this evening, slightly, and hope that the next twenty-four hours will make a decided change.

I shall come to you on Friday if I have to be carried to the cars, or, to speak more sensibly, if there be any chance that I can endure the journey and make the speech.

* * * * * * *

Very truly yours,

HENRY ARMITT BROWN, per J. L. B.

To Hon JOEL PARKER.

FROM CHANCELLOR RUNYON,

NEWARK, June 27, 1878.

GENTLEMEN: I return my sincere acknowledgments for the invitation which you have extended to me to be present at the ceremonies which are to take place tomorrow in commemoration of the Battle of Monmouth. My official engagements will prevent me from availing myself of it. I need not assure you of my interest in the occasion, or of my best wishes for the success of the patriotic undertaking with which the ceremonies are immediately connected. Yours very truly, &c.,

THEODORE RUNYON.

Messrs. Joel Parker, James S. Yard, and Theo. Morris, Committee.

FROM EX-SENATOR TEN EYCK.

MOUNT HOLLY, June 27, 1878.

Hon. Joel Parker, James S. Yard, and Theo. Morris, Committee:

DEAR SIRS: I had the honor to receive your invitation to attend the Centennial anniversary at Freehold, to-morrow, and had hoped to be present, but circumstances have arisen to deprive me of that pleasure. I trust the celebration will be a success, and make the erection of the monument a sure and certain thing.

Very truly yours, &c.,

J. C. TEN EYCK.

The following telegrams were also read:

FROM EX-GOVERNOR TILDEN.

NEW YORK, June 27, 1878.

To Hon. Joel Parker:

I regret that engagements here deprive me the pleasure of accepting your kind invitation to be present to-morrow at the celebration of the Centennial anniversary of the Battle of Monmouth and the commemoration of the heroic struggle of our forefathers at an important crisis in our national history.

SAMUEL J. TILDEN.

FROM HENRY ARMITT BROWN, ESQ.

PHILADELPHIA, June 28, 1878.

To Hon. Joel Parker:

Mr. Henry Armitt Brown is ill. Doctor utterly forbids his going to-day.
J. S. BROWN.

FROM EX-GOVERNOR WARD.

NEWARK, N. J., June 28, 1878.

To Hon. Joel Parker:

Regret that 'unexpected and imperative demands upon me deprive me the pleasure of participating as contemplated in anniversary exercises.

MARCUS L. WARD.

Gov. PARKER then said: l now have the pleasure of introducing the Hon. SAMUEL S. Cox, of New York, a gentleman through whose veins courses patriotic blood, whose grandfather fought in the revolution, whose father and mother were born in Monmouth county, who is one of the orators of the day and will now address you.

Address by Samuel S. Cox.

Congressman Cox advancing, spoke substantially to the following effect:

Mr. President, Sons and Daughters of New Jersey: It is the ancient and beautiful custom to recall, by such celebrations as this, ancestral and historic renown.— The Greeks began it by their battle celebrations. Thus Greece preserved her martial spirit and patriotic ardor; while the arts found congenial subjects and the Muse her lofty inspiration. Casting our eye back through the vista of 2,000 years, from this heroic ground of vantage and under the light of a better civilization, we can add but little by our observances to the elegance and grace of those customs. These customs were continued in Greece for many generations after the heroes were dead and they only ceased when the State became corrupt. Our country has imitated these customs upon every yearly occurrence of our independence anniversary. You of New Jersey have your heroes. Their remains lie under mossy stones in your old grave yards, but from their dust they speak with their wonted fire. Since they fought, one hundred years have bridged the abyss between us and them, yet still do they not speak from this cherished spot? It was the passionate hatred of arbitrary methods and despotic power that led them to devote themselves to their patriotic work. They seem to say to us this day "You have had a century of the blessings we secured for you. Pay us, your fathers, the debt of gratitude you owe, for the trials of Valley Forge and the struggles of Monmouth.— Our battles were for peace, home, self government and true liberty. We preferred death with that living to life without it.

True we did not fight to acquire liberty.— No, we never lost that, but we fought to defend what was already ours. We fought those who would deprive us of it, for independence of them forever. We require from you no lament. Our bodies are dissolved but our immortal felicities will only continue when you, our children, continue to remember us by preserving what we bequeathed." Sons of New Jersey, is it not a part of our heritage to remember with filial and pious gratitude the very death volleys which closed the lives of our ancestors on yonder field, to regenerate our liberties? The blood which moistened the sods of Monmouth or mingled with its rivulets was, and is, ours forever. This is holy ground! For a hundred years it has not been profaned. It has helped to give New Jersey its high name on the roll of honor, as the battle ground of the Revolution. Whatever may be said of other states who have vaunted their service with literary circumstance and superlative art, it is undoubtedly true that New Jersey was the battle-ground of the Revolution. The contest here was much more sanguinary and vindictive than in the other provinces. The "Pine Robbers" and other Tory desperadoes, kept the people of this county in perpetual alarm. Farmers worked in their fields with loaded guns at hand, and many a pine fiend bit the dust for his audacious crimes. Burning houses; hanging men and outraging women; insecurity and terror at every hearth, this was the condition of your state, until Clinton, with his crowd of wretched allies and camp followers, was driven from your shores. Thank God, our fathers not only whipped the foreign foe but also crushed the domestic traitors. I would not do injustice to the other states, but yet it must be admitted as an historical fact that it was New Jersey, more than all combined, which made most sacrifice upon this crucial test of the Revolution. True, at Monmouth, every province was represented.— Leading spirits of the Revolution were there assembled to fight for the common cause. But it was New Jersey's "embattled farmers" who withstood the main shock of the contest. Other localities have celebrated their Concord and Lexington, Bennington, Oriskany and Saratoga. These battles represented crises in our fate. Concord has been called one of the fifteen decisive battles of the world.— It was significant; for it led to the alliance with France, and our recognition in Europe. But Monmouth was the first military result of that alliance. It was the turning point in the Revolution. It marks a great epoch in American history and Washington was its hero. The speaker then described in his own peculiarly vigorous and graphic style the compromise efforts of England, the timely help of France, the condition of the British and American armies just prior to the battle of Monmouth, and then referring to the battle he said : Whether we consider the skirmishes before, or the actors in the battle; or the dramatic scenes between its actors, which occurred during its progress, or the intense personalities between Washington and Lee and the august persons engaged in it; or the military game of death and retreat, recovery and slaughter, which made its vicissitudes; certainly no battle has a higher claim upon our romantic and patriotic susceptibility. Whether we regard the varying conflict of the day and the quiet retreat of the night, it was a battle of rare strategic skill and desperate intrepidity. No one denies that the British fought resolutely and desperately and the Americans with a courage rarely, if ever, equalled. Whatever may be claimed by historians, as to the decisiveness of the battle, it may undoubtedly be said that in the early part of the day the advantage was with the British, in the latter portion, was with the Americans. The Americans maintained their ground, and when at tacked repulsed the enemy. They suffered less than their adversaries and were only prevented by the sudden retreat of Clinton from making their victory still more signally glorious. Few battles have more authentic and satisfactory descriptions in history. This is owing to the fact that Gen. LEE was tried and convicted upon testimony before a court, out of which a clear unvarnished narrative has been deduced. It is not, however, in the brief notes of the court that we can gather the limning or the pigments for a battle scene like that of Monmouth. Every battle, like a picture, has its design and its unity.— The etchings or details for the design are but faintly delineated by the ordinary historic annals. One should go to the minutiæ of the preparations for the march and its convincing result. Mr. Cox here gave some interesting extracts from Washington's original orderly book for the year 1778, used at Valley Forge and Monmouth Court House. These orders have never yet been printed. Before the army crosses the Delaware orders are issued for cooking. When they reach Coryell's ferry "no man is permitted to bathe until sunset." When they cross the ferry earth is ordered instead of rails for the repair of the roads, " to prevent crippling the horses." Damage to fruit trees is sternly prohibited; drinking cold water, when heated, is forbidden. The order of march for the brigades is carefully noted, guides are provided and the paroles and countersigns registered. When Cranberry is reached on the 24th, Washington is nearing the enemy. Mark the parole! "Look out!" and the countersigns, "Sharp" and "Keen." On the 25th, at Penslopen, vigilance and precaution are "essentially necessary." " Officers at the posts and soldiers on picket must be ready to march at a moment's notice." This was the last order before the battle. From Freehold, after the battle, the parole is " Monckton," the countersign " Bonner " and " Dickenson." Then follows the Chief's congratulations and sincere thanks to his officers and men who distinguished themselves in the action by their gallant conduct. Dickenson and the militia of New Jersey are especially thanked for the noble spirit they displayed in opposing the enemy.— Next come other orders and among them an order of thanksgiving to the Supreme Dispenser of human events for the victory obtained at sunset over the flower of the British troops. These, said the speaker, but faintly outline the immense details which this consummate soldier supervised for this march through Jersey, and the battle that ensued, and yet we know that this Commander-in-Chief was looking toward the Hudson and sweeping the horizon with prudent care for all the armies of the Republic. History may dismiss with few pages these pains-taking details by a few generalizations. It has however taken note of other less significant facts which make up the outlines of this famous march and battle. Mr. Cox pictured the battle in the following terse and eloquent description: To obtain a picturesque view of the scene, one must look down upon the contest from a height, where the diversity of detail may be grouped in the unity of another art than that of speaking or even photographing. It is a Sabbath morning, calm and cloudless. The leafy month of June covers the hills and valleys with the garniture of green. The heat is intense, the thermometer at 96° in the shade. A more sultry day never glowed with the fervor of the summer solstice. The arrows of Apollo wound more than the bayonet or sabre. The British in their woolen dress suffer more than the thinly clad Americans.— The Sabbath quietude is at length broken not by the song of birds, or the voices of nature, but by the long roll of the various camps. You may see Knyphausen's men mounting their horses or buckling on their knapsacks and grasping their muskets, while the motley crowd of followers and refugees crowd after the moving train of baggage wagons. The ear takes in the confused sounds of the British camp; but there is an earnest silence among the Americans. The eye perceives the quiet movement of the regiments. There is a cleaning of guns and a stealthy movement of aids; when, hark to a fresh stir among the Americans. They become alert. Clinton is moving upon them. The note of preparation is hushed. All wait on Lee's orders. Dickenson reconnoitres the enemy and exchanges fire. La Fayette arrives and with Maxwell's light horse dashes into the plain. Then the British dragoons charge. Along with them are the grenadiers in their bear skin caps, the guards in their red coats, and the kilted Highlanders. Lee is confused and orders a retreat. Washington appears upon the scene mounted on his white charger. "Suspicion flashed across his mind," says Irving, " of warm-headed conduct on the part of Lee to mar the plan of attack adopted contrary to his counsels." He sternly demands the meaning of the retreat. Lee is disconcerted and stammers out some excuse. A disdainful reply from Washington follows, but there is little time for parley. Lee is ordered to the rear. The retreat must be retrieved. The place is favorable. The routed troops form. Batteries are stationed. Even Lee is called again to his command, and is ordered to check the enemy. The cannonading begins. The enemy halts. Washington takes a secure position placing Stirling on the left, Greene on the right. The artillery serves its batteries with stupendous effect. Knox is there, the chief of artillerists of the union. He enfilades whole platoons by one shot. This is on the enemy's left wing. His fire is continued and kept up on the enemy's centre. Stirling's guns give back from the left their thunder in response to Green's batteries. Grenadier and guard fall back. They return. Then "Mad Anthony" meets them with his fine soldierly frenzy and the slaughter is reversed. Moncton falls, and our standards are planted in the field. Night closes the scene. Evening fell upon the uncompleted victory, and Washington lay upon his cloak taking with his soldiers the rest so much needed. Call this a partial or a complete victory, or call it otherwise, the morning sun revealed no enemy in sight. Silently they had stolen away in the night for the heights of Middletown and Sandy Hook.— One more gallant struggle thus marked the progress of our fathers toward American independence. The speaker after describing the noble valor of Washington, and the officers who distinguished themselves in that day, closed thus: I have said that a picture is incomplete unless it has a higher design than that which appears upon its surface, either in form, delineation or color. There is also an inner meaning to each battle. It is not the mere victory, the numbers killed or wounded, nor the heavy battalions, and the thundering artillery which give significance to the battles of mankind. It is for philoscphy, aided sometimes by the muses and graces, to give to heroism its true meed of glory and honor. The iconoclast may not appear for centuries, but the statues which should have no niche will surely fall before his hand. That which makes human struggle immortal is the unselfish idea of achieving something for the hereafter. This is what ennobles and dignifies the battle fields of our earth. What, then, is the meaning of this Monmouth battle? Was it not the contest of a people for liberty and union? It was said in the aforetime "Liberty first, union afterwards." I say it should be as our history teaches us, liberty for and with union, union for and with liberty. Dissociate never, but hand in hand they move on to establish, protect and defend for ourselves and posterity, the rights of mankind. In this was the ideal grandeur of the conflict. This is the divine genius behind the picture. In this was the cause commended to all people. This was the consummate flower of the declaration of Independence, and the ripe fruitage of the constitution. Indissoluble as a federation, through the covenants contained in our charter of national, state and individual rights, our nation has sustained itself against the corrosion of time and the shock of embattled armies. Through this paternal union and indossoluble covenant, a code more perfect than that of Rome and more comprehensive than that of England has been developed and maintained. Nor is our flag less typical of this unity of the states than the constitutional fasces in which they are imbound. On its folds is the streaming blazoning of the original 13 states, symbolled in its stripes, and the name of each and all are written on the radiant lustre and beauty of a night of stars; while the staff, from which our ensign floats, lifts stars and stripes as one—unsullied and high advanced amidst the smoke of battle or the tempest of civil strife. Finally let me say to you, that so long as Monmouth's hills remain, so long as these fields smile with cultivation, so long as the ocean waves leap in liberty upon your shores, so long as your ministers of justice hold its scales with equal poise and the spires of your churches point with silent emphasis to God; so long as Washington's name is revered for his military service and his civic wisdom; so long will Monmouth be a vestal flame, watched with unwinking vigilance, upon the patriotic altar of America. Under such inspirations may our future wipe out the wrongs of the past, and cast our institutions in a better mold! "Let the new cycle shame the old;" and spread over our spacious plains and grand mountains, from sea to sea, the purer lustre of a better polity and a civilization instinct with liberty and justice.

Oration by B. W. Throckmorton.

B. Wood Throckmorton, Esq., of Jersey City, was introduced as the next speaker, by Judge Robbins, one of the Vice Presidents of the meeting. He delivered a brilliant and scholarly address, of which the following is a synopsis: Friends and Fellow Patriots: Should a stranger, forgetful of the day we honor, ask why the early morning quiet was broken by the booming of cannon; why in this usually peaceful city, unwonted bustle, even before daybreak, was apparent; why starry banners float upon the breeze, while processions of citizens and soldiers, with showy uniforms and gleaming bayonets, wind through the streets; why distinguished men of this and other states are present; why ordinary avocations are stopped and the people assemble in thousands; why upon this spot the cornerstone of a monument is laid with impressive Musonic ceremonies. The answer is that to-day is the centennial of the battle of Monmouth and the voice of our fathers' blood cries to us from beneath the soil, which it moistened fittingly, to honor it. Upon grand occasions like this the individual is as nothing. The time, the place, the associations are everything. Yet some few must be selected to tell the story forever old, yet ever new, of this day 100 years ago. Never did feet of pilgrim bear him to some sacred shrine more willingly and proudly, than mine have borne me to this my native town, to participate in these memorial services. How inadequate seems all speech upon an anniversary so memorable as this! But I beg, even at the risk of needless repetition, to touch upon the story, so thrilling that whenever told, it holdeth children from play and old men from the chimney corner. The speaker now gave an elaborate and detailed account of the battle after which he proceeded as follows: West Point had its Arnold, Monmouth its Charles Lee. Better for Arnold that he had died at Saratoga. Better for Lee that he had remained a prisoner of war in the hands of the British. If Charles Lee was true at heart to the American cause, why, during the war, did he correspond with Burgoyne, and secretly forward letters to Clinton before the latter's evacuation of Philadelphia? Why, when a prisoner at New York, did he prepare for the British commander, in his own hand-writing, a plan, still in existence, and endorsed by the commissioner, "Mr. Lee's plan," a plan which, to use Lee's own words, "would unhinge and dissolve the whole system of defense," and put an end to the war on terms of *moderate accommodation?* Why, when Washington administered the oath, under direction of Congress, to the officers at Valley Forge, did Lee, when his turn came, twice withdraw his hand from the Bible and give as a reason, that he was ready to absolve his allegiance to King George, but that he had some scruples about the Prince of Wales? Why did he so strenuously oppose Washington's taking the offensive against Clinton, at Monmouth? Why did he at first refuse to lead the advance sent forward to harass the enemy as soon as they should move from Freehold? Why, when he did assume command, was it only to compel a disorderly retreat? Why did he send no messenger to Washington that he was retreating? Why did he disobey specific and definite instructions? Why did he imperil the safety of a whole army and the cause of independence? In the light of these questions the language of Moore, the historian, applied to Lee, has a startling emphasis, "The pages upon which Lee recorded his own condemnation, indicate his high place upon the list of traitors, of whom—to the sorrow and shame of humanity be it spoken—Judas was not the first nor Benedict Arnold the last." In contrast, as marked as day is from night, against the dark background of Lee's incompetency, perverted purposes and defection, stands Washington.— Throughout the whole of that dreary winter at Valley Forge he shared the trials of his troops, who were naked, without coats to their backs, shoeless, starving and tortured by diseases, and the agony of the knowledge that their families were suffering at home; maligned and conspired against himself by a cabal, he had yet been calm, patient, prayerful, caring nothing for himself, so long as his country's cause was preserved.— Reaching this spot he saw that here a glorious victory might be won, that would in some degree compensate for the suffering that had been undergone. He laid his plans and issued his orders accordingly. While pressing forward to Lee's support he learned that that General was retreating. He could not believe it and, hastening on to ascertain the truth, met Lee face to face. "No words can paint the Titan sculpture of the moment." Washington's form towered like a giant's. Righteous indignation and scorn flashed from the eyes that rooted to the spot the "poltroon," who had well nigh sacrificed an army and its holy cause. In words of terrible condemnation he visited his mighty wrath upon the head of the offender, so utterly paralyzing the culprit's utterance that he can only stammer out a weak and deprecating Sir, Sir! The Chief's passion spent, again behold him. Here, then, everywhere, the inspiring, energizing, directing, controlling master power; unmindful of the heat, so intense, that his white charger drops under him and soldiers of both armies fall dead without a wound, and the tongues of the living are swollen so they cannot speak. Fearlessly facing the storm of shot and shell falling like hail from heaven, shaking from his hat the leaves and twigs cut by the bullets from the trees, resting never till night closes the contest, with the enemy in retreat.

Judged by its results the battle of Monmouth was a great victory for the patriot army. EDMUND BURKE had said "The Americans have done much, but it is evident they cannot look standing armies in the face," but here upon these plains "occurred the new birth of the American soldier." 700 negroes formed part of the American forces engaged. The victory here achieved restored confidence to the Continental Congress, reinvigorated the determination of the colonists everywhere, cheered our troops, brought comfort to the ever courageous Washington, broke the cabal that sought his ruin, and forever strike off the nightmare of Lee. Complete, then, fellow citizens of Monmouth, the glorious work of erecting here a monument that shall last while the earth revolves around the sun and "stars hold their festival about the midnight throne," until time shall be swallowed up in eternity.

Let us this day consecrate anew, at this shrine, our lives to duty. Holding before our gaze the mirror memory, each for himself can see therein reflected his past life. Some of it, perchance, beautiful as nature in June; melodious as the ripple of rivulets, the play of fountains, the song of birds; some of it, perchance, sad as the sighing of winds through cypress groves, as the moaning of the waves on lonely nights; the dull thud of the sod falling upon the coffin; as the words, "Earth to earth, ashes to ashes, dust to dust." Some of it, active, eager, expectant as the leap of the forest stream over obstructions. Some of it calm, contented, restful as the inland lake, slumbering under the benediction of the moonlight; some of it, turbulent, disturbed, wrathful, as the waves of the sea lashed into fury by the tempest; some of it, depressed as the pit that opens into the earth; dark, dismal, and filled with discordant sounds; some of it rare in its exaltation as the mountain peak illumined by the sun! If in that past we behold with pain (pain that brings its lesson with its avenging sequel), that for any cause we have allowed our individual standards to trail in the dust, and have fallen far below the ideals, the contemplation of the great characters and events such as we honor to-day, inspires us to form, let us here resolve to lift those standards up! And when we shall go down into the valley of the shadow of death, may all stains have been washed out by the dews of heaven, that, like baptismal tears, will fall upon and redeem them.

Here on the field of Monmouth was fought the last great battle of the revolution. Marathon, Leuctra, Arbela, Tours, Hastings, Waterloo, Lexington, Bunker Hill, Oriskanny, Saratoga, are immortal, and Monmouth is immortal, too. Its name shines with fadeless lustre upon the "battle roll" of the revolution. By the memory of that bloody fight, by the memory of Washington, by the warning of Lee's example, by all the associations of the past, by all the hopes of the future, and "in the name of God," let us swear devotion that can never falter to the nation Washington founded and Lincoln saved!

Relics of Monmouth.

When Mr. THROCKMORTON had finished his oration, some relics of the battle of Monmouth, picked up in the field of conflict, were exhibited to the audience by Mr. THENFORD WOODHULL, of New York city. The relics consisted of a sword and two bayonets. The sword was presented in 1825 to Dr. GILBERT WOODHULL. It is the sword of a British officer. One of the bayonets was plowed up on the battle field about the year 1825. The other was picked up on the day of the battle by Rev. Dr. JOHN WOODHULL, for many years pastor of the Tennent Church.

The Exercises Closed

with the benediction, pronounced by Rev. A. M NORTH, pastor of the Freehold M. E. church.— The throng of auditors, who had shown almost as much endurance as their heroic ancestors, by standing for three hours under a burning sun, observing the interesting, solemn, and impressive exercises, only assuaging their thirst by drinking in the eloquence of the orators as they recounted the glorious deeds of yore, then sought the maple and elm tree shade of Freehold, and the other comforts of that good old hospitable town.

EXERCISES IN THROCKMORTON'S FIELD.

The attendance at the stand in Throckmorton's field was not large. The few, however, that attended here, enjoyed the cool breezes which played under the tent, and the able addresses by Ex-Gov. NEWELL and Gen. CARRINGTON. The latter gentleman is author of an admirable book on the Battles of the Revolution, and his address on this occasion showed a depth of research as to details of the battle, and an erudition as to motives of those engaged on either side, which is only gained by a most careful study of all the historical papers extant, both English and American. Gen. CARRINGTON had prepared a map at least 15 feet long and 10 feet wide, showing the whole topography of the battle-field of Monmouth, the positions of both armies on the day previous to the battle, the exact location of the different commands on the day of the battle, the spot where Washington met Lee on his retreat, and many other details. This map had been suspended at the stand sometime before the speaking began, and was generally studied and admired. Ex-Gov. NEWELL presided, and about 2 o'clock introduced Rev. T. H. CULLEN, Rector of St. Peter's Church, Freehold.

Prayer by Rev. Mr. Cullen.

Mr. CULLEN invoked the blessing of the Almighty God, King of Kings, and ruler supreme of the armies of heaven and the inhabitants of earth. Thanks were offered for the light and knowledge of the present age, and that we live in a time of peace, with none to molest and make afraid. The Rev. gentleman prayed for God's blessing on the undertaking of building a monument to the memory of those who fell on Monmouth's battle-field, that we may enjoy the blessed heritage of freedom and liberty, also for the furtherance of sound learning and religion.

Ex-Gov. Newell's Address.

The Ex-Governor predicated his speech by saying that the mail of the evening previous had brought him the first intelligence that he was expected to preside at one of the stands and give an address. Hence, what he was to say, had been written after midnight.

More than one hundred years ago, said he, our forefathers resolved to leave their own country, and turn their faces toward the new world. Among the chief causes that brought this exodus, was the desire to rid themselves of the persecutions of the aristocracy. Always subservient, they brought with them few ideas of real liberty. As the years rolled on, and as prosperity was assured, they became more and more restless of restraint, until finally they resolved to uphold a better and freer form of government, and thereby secure the alleviation of the evils with which they were afflicted. Each maintained the right to be governed by the dictates of his own conscience, and with a high sense of the justice of their cause, they entered into the war for independence. It was a weary war of eight long years, and step after step was sternly contested. Among all the battles fought during that war, none were more important than Monmouth. Here were engaged the most distinguished officers in the American Army. Washington, Lee, LaFayette, Wayne, Morgan, Butler and others, and nowhere did some of them show more ability and valor. Here Gov. NEWELL made a strong appeal for the battle monument. He thought it was a worthy object, and should receive the support of every citizen who honored val or and loved liberty. He closed by drawing a picture of what our aim of the future should be. Gen. CARRINGTON was now introduced.

Gen. Carrington's Address.

The battle of Monmouth formed a dividing point between the battles of the north and the south. The number engaged in it has often been overestimated. It is probable that over 20,000 men were engaged on both sides. The retreat of the British from Philadelphia was forced by Admiral Howe's hearing that a French fleet was coming to aid the Americans. He knew that he could not re-

OLD TIMES IN OLD MONMOUTH. 17

sist without imperilling New York. Its abandonment therefore was a forced necessity, and the reaching of New York of prime importance. The plan of Howe was to reduce the province as a whole. This plan had sacrificed the army of Burgoyne in '77. General Howe acted substantially as Lee had told him. Washington took the offensive at Germantown, which although indeterminate in its results ended previous to Monmouth the offensive in the north. Lee was opposed to acting in the offensive at Monmouth. He had no faith in American success. On the 15th of June he expressed the opinion that if an attack was made it would result in failure. And this was based upon the wish of the safe arrival of Clinton in New York. Gen. Lee had no attachments of home, and little of country. He was the open rival of Washington, and Monmouth was the first place where he confronted the British openly. It has often been asserted that the evacuation of Philadelphia by the British was a surprise to Washington.— This is not true. For after the arrival of Steuben at Valley Forge, the preparations for offensive warfare began. The strength of the British army had been vastly overrated by Lee, when it was well known that it was weak. When an army, whose fancied security becomes suddenly weak and evacuation a necessity, is tested in point of strength it is soon seen to be a sham. The whole British army became demoralized at Philadelphia, while Washington never lost confidence in the manhood or valor of his men, and could not be swayed from his purpose of making an attack during the retreat of the British. Trenton and Princeton as well as Germantown determined his judgment. Wayne, LaFayette and Steuben favored the same plan, and were sent to attack in advance with the chosen and select men of the American army. The speaker here gave a succinct account of how Clinton was delayed on his march by the advance of the Americans, and the reason of Washington's taking the route by Allentown. After referring to Lee's being relieved of command and his assuring it a gain, Gen. CARRINGTON continued as follows : No matter what excuses may be offered for Lee's misconduct, the prime difficulty was not in want of support, but the failure of General Lee to direct and control the army. The British army was spread over 12 miles of road, and in such a condition, that if struck fairly there was no doubt of success. It has been asked why Washington remained so far behind. It was because he was afraid of being attacked. The speaker here related the conversation which took place between LaFayette and Lee, upon the latter's again resuming command, after which he said : On the evening of the 27th, Washington went to the camp of Lee,

and ordered him to draw up his troops and be in readiness, to run no risk, and when he had concerted methods of attack to immediately send orders to Morgan and other officers to send up their troops and join in the action.— These orders were never executed. Hence there was sluggishness in the attack, because there were no preparations, not even any reconnoitering. Lee with 5,000 soldiers attacked the rear of the British, consisting of 1,500 men. The speaker here drew a picture of the retreat, the appearance of Washingto as he met the first fugitives, as he afterwards met officer after officer conveying the direful news, as he met Lee, and finally, how he brought order out of chaos, and rallied a not discouraged but panic stricken army. Gen. CARRINGTON now explained from l is large map of the topography of the battle field, dwelling on the fact that the map of the field by Sparks, the one usually used by historians, and which appeared in a recent number of Harpers, has the rivers running north instead of east and west. In the battle the British lost 235 men, the Americans 230. About 1,000 men deserted from the English army. The General concluded by referring to the patriotic spirit manifested by the people of New Jersey in erecting a monument to perpetuate the valorous deeds of their ancestors.

Governor NEWELL then offered a resolution of thanks to Gen. CARRINGTON, who he believed knew more of the battle of Monmouth than any other living man. This closed the exercises at this stand. The large map was presented to Prof. LOCKWOOD, who had it folded and sent to his home.

After the Literary Exercises

All the bands which were in attendance upon the celebration, gave a serenade in front of the residence of Mrs. D. S. SCHENCK, in honor of that estimable lady and her family. Each band played two of their choicest selections, and for more than half an hour the ambient air was laden with lovely strains of sweetest harmony.

When the exercises at Monument Park had been concluded, the Knights Templar returned to the Seminary Grounds, where they enjoyed the cool shade and pure cold water. Their band found some music stands in the basement of the school building, and organized an open air concert that delighted their large audience. The party were enthusiastic over their reception, and expressed their appreciation of the courtesies extended to them. On their way home they serenaded the ladies at Ex-Gov. PARKER'S, A. C. HARTSHORNE'S and Dr. FREEMAN'S.

Military Review.

Before the soldiers left for their homes, they passed in review before Gov. McCLELLAN at Ex-Gov. PARKER'S. They proceeded down Main street from Yard avenue, to their railroad stations. Marching by company front, they filled the street from curb to curb.— Though Gov. McCLELLAN has reviewed thousands of our nation's troops, we are confident that he never witnessed finer marching than on the present occasion.

Reception at Gov. Parker's.

During the afternoon Ex-Gov. Parker gave a reception at his residence. Among those present were : Hon. S. S. Cox and Mrs. Cox ; Gov. McClellan and staff; Hon. John A. Hall, Gov. McClellan's Private Secretary ; Quartermaster General Perrine ; Gen. Mott and Adjutant General Stryker ; Ex-Governors Bedle and Price; Ex-Congressman Amos Clark ; Colonel Zulick, of Newark ; Prof Cameron, of Princeton; Judge Woodruff, of Trenton ; Dr. John Vought and Rev. F. Chandler, of Freehold ; Mrs. Sewell; the Misses Gummere ; Samuel R. Gummere, Esq ; Hugh and Samuel Hammill, and many others. Also, the "Joel Parker Association," of Newark, serenaded Ex-Gov. Parker at his residence, and partook of his hospitality. Probably two hundred and fifty persons were entertained by the Ex-Governor. The Joel Parker Club also serenaded Ex-Gov. BEDLE, who was the guest of Dr. VOUGHT.

The Delaware Hose Company

were disappointed at not finding our department in line, but were fully satisfied when the state of affairs was explained to them. Their carriage was housed at the Department headquarters when not on parade, and the members were cared for by those on duty there.

The Game of Polo.

Among the many attractions of the day we should not lose sight of the game which took place on the Fair Ground at 3.30 P. M. Gov. Parker having secured the attendance of some members of the Long Branch Polo club, an exhibition was given of that novel and interesting game by Messrs. Arthur Dewell, Howard Stokes, Henry Herbert, and George Elders. The grounds were under the management of Doctor D. M. Forman. The first heat resulted in a score for the men dressed in red, it being well contested. After a few moments rest for the men and horses the ball was again thrown in the field, and after a few raps of the ball the second heat was won by the boys in blue. The third and last heat was the most hotly contested of the three, each party eing desirous of gaining the score. Several times the ball was near each goal, but by a dexterous stroke of the opposite party would be sent to the centre of the field again only to be closely pursued by its tormentors. After several moments exertion a rest was taken, both parties and their horses being nearly exhausted. The heat was finally declared in favor °of the men in red. This was a very fine heat, and called forth several rounds of applause from the spectators.

After this game was finished three of the four young men took part in a hurdle race. Three hurdles were erected in the half-mile track about 20 inches high. This was a single heat which was won by Fox, ridden by Howard Stokes.

The attendance at the Fair Ground was small, owing to the fact that the majority of the people were looking at the military review, which came off while the Polo match was in progress. The want of conveyances by which to reach the grounds was also a serious drawback, as it prevented many from attending who might otherwise have done so.

The Celebration Ended.

By half-past four crowds of people began to seek the stations, and train after train bore away the thousands who had visited us. As the setting sun painted the western skies with gorgeous rainbow tints, his lurid glare fell upon Monmouth's battle plains, not as a century before steeped in human blood, but clothed in their " daisy sprinkled" garments of sweet scented clover. The very clouds which strove in vain to obscure the glories of the sinking sun seemed a foreshadowing of America's future. They seemed to prophesy that though storms of foreign war and fierce internecine conflict might sweep over our land, still the great Republic would proudly stand, her banner of civilization uplifted high and pressing far in advance of any other nation on the globe. By 8 o'clock the town of Freehold had reassumed its wonted quiet. Had a stranger entered the place he would have learned of the day's celebration only from the stars and stripes which still floated on the evening breeze—only from the hugh stone, which slumbered in Monument Park, the base of a noble monument destined to lift its summit unto the blue heavens and speak to us, to our children, and to our children's children, " of patriotism and courage, of free government, of the moral improvement and elevation of mankind, and of the immortal memory of those who, with heroic devotion, sacrificed their lives for their country."

Casualties.

No great event is entirely unaccompanied by accidents and misfortunes, and our celebration was no exception to the general rule.

At the corner of Main and Throckmorton streets, a carryall wagon drawn by two mules, belonging to Pat Donahay, of Hillsdale, and filled with a party of young people, backed into a one-horse vehicle belonging to Wm. Francis, of Francis Mills. Both wagons had their right hind wheels broken. Mr. Francis and his daughter were violently thrown out upon the ground, the former sustaining severe though not dangerous bruises. The carryall party escaped unhurt.

Two, if not three, soldiers were overcome by the heat One was cared for by Dr James S Conover, and went home with his comrades. Another was more seriously affected, and was cared for by Mr T W Morris, aided by Dr D M Forman. Mr Morris spent the night with the sick man, doing all in his power to render him comfortable, and sent him safely home on Saturday night.

For the Thirsty Ones

Ample provision had been made through the suggestion of Mr John H Bawden. The railroad stations had barrels filled with ice-water, the F. & J. station consuming nearly a ton of ice. Ten men were employed by the committee in charge and equipped with badges reading, "cold water free," who passed to and fro giving to all who were thirsty a cup of cold water. Similar placards were posted throughout the town. Result, less intoxication than ever before known on a similar occasion. The various stands for the sale of lemonade were forced to sell at a low rate, some losing much by stock left on hand.

The Old Curiosity Shop Museum,

Which was situated on South street, was well worth the admission. The curiosities were carefully selected from various portions of the county by Prof Samuel Lockwood, and most of them were in some way connected with the Battle. The attention of the visitors was called to the Museum by one of the country's best relics, which was the old Court-House bell which was used in 1756. This was hung in front of the building, and could be heard at almost any moment during the entire day.

Among the curiosities were: An old bayonet which was found on the Monmouth battle ground; an oration on the Death of Washington, by Samuel Stanhope Smith, D D, dated M D C C C; a chair which was frequently used by Washington at the house of Sheriff David Forman, father of Lewis and grandfather of J Conover Forman; flint-lock musket used in the Battle of Monmouth; a large cannon ball shot from the French man-of-war off Long Branch during the French and English war; a copy of *The True American*, published by James J Wilson, dated Sept 7, 1812; a copy of the *Boston Gazette and Country Journal* of March 12, 1770; several cannon balls found on Monmouth battle ground; a gridiron used by Molly Pitcher; sword-hilt and a screw used for spiking cannon, from Monmouth battle ground; pictures of Molly Pitcher, Thomas Paine, Dr Livingstone, Col Monkton; a Dutch Bible, printed in 1773; a pocketbook used by Lawrence Ryder 1777 ; oye glasses used before the Revolution; five-dollar note used in Philadelphia in 1775; seal used in the Province of Georgia in 1772; scales used before the Revolution; whalebone corset stays 300 years old; British stirrup from battle ground. Besides these were some old furniture, spinning wheels, crockery, photographs Chinese relics, &c, many of which were loaned by Thomas W Ryall.

Police Items.

Thieves and pickpockets were plentiful in Freehold and vicinity, and notwithstanding the admirable police arrangements, many persons were relieved of watches and many dwellings were robbed of their valuable contents while the owners were occupied with the pleasures of the celebration. Superintendent Walling, of the New York City police force, was in town, with De ective James Irving and four assistants, and they did all in their power to keep "the light-fingered" in order. While walking in the street, Mr Jacob S Wyckoff, of Freehold, had his gold watch picked from his pocket, as did also Dr Beam of New Egypt. "Aunt Betsy Osborn" and Mr. Curtis, both of Manasquan, were robbed, the former of a valuable gold watch and chain, and the latter of a pocketbook containing $300. At Marlborough, the residence of Ex-Judge Charles H. Conover was broken into and thoroughly ransacked during the absence of the family, who were all at Freehold except the hired men, who were at work in the field gathering hay. The thieves carried off two gold watches, a quantity of valuable old family silver, an amethyst bracelet, some gold coin, several other articles of jewelry, silk dresses, &c. On Henry street, Freehold, the residence of Mrs Andrew Gasner, sister-in-law of Col Applegate, was broken open, and a $200 velvet cloak, several silk dresses, some jewelry, a satchel, a number of silver teaspoons, and several smaller articles were stolen therefrom.

Perrine Voorhees' house also suffered. After getting into his house the thieves kicked in and broke through the doors that were locked. They stole a lot of jewelry and silverware. They tested all the plated ware by breaking it and then casting it aside. Edwin Bawden's house was robbed of a gold ring.

The residence of A S Lokerson was likewise visited. Mr Lokerson reports that when he went home, shortly after noon, he found the kitchen door open, and upon entering, discovered the doors leading to the hall, dining room, pantry, &c., open, and everything in confusion. Passing up-stairs, he found that all the rooms had been visited. His own and his wife's clothing had been piled on a bed and the contents of bureau-drawers strewn upon the floor. On the dining-room floor were two of his best coats, which had been dropped by the thief while passing out. The only articles carried off were a gold locket and a gold pen and case, the whole valued at $10. In one of the bureau drawers was a gold watch chain, and in another some silver spoons, which the thief overlooked. Previous to leaving the house, Mrs Lokerson removed the silverware to a chest in the attic.

The following communication will explain itself:

FREEHOLD, N. J., June 28, 1878.
To the Members of the Committee on Press:
GENTLEMEN : For myself and all other members of the Press of New York, I hereby express our earnest and grateful thanks for the courtesies extended to us by your committee to day, and hope that it may be our pleasure, on some day or days in the near future, to return to each and all of you our personal marks of the reciprocation of your graceful compliments.
Very respectfully,
WM. A. H. WRITE,
Agent New York Associated Press.

Centennial Poems.

On the 30th of May last Mr. HENRY MORFORD, a native of Monmouth, and well known to many of our people, sailed for Europe to meet literary engagements connected with the great Exposition. On the day before he enclosed to us the following poem, one of the best of his composition, which he desired to have read at the Celebration. As other arrangements had already been made for a poem, the committee could not accept it. We copy it, however, as the contribution of a Monmouth poet to the literary fund of Monmouth's Centennial year.—ED. DEM.

MONMOUTH'S CENTENNIAL.

An hundred years since battling armies stood
In deadly conflict on old Monmouth's plain—
Since been and flower were wet with patriot blood
As freely shed as e'er fell summer rain.
An hundred years ! So long · and yet so small
In that great roll, 'neath God's all-seeing eye
Displayed, as nations rise and peoples fall,
And the long march of centuries goes by.

An hundred years—of growth, and loss, and change ;
Of morning clouds, and noonday suns, and eves
Full fraught with glories wondrous, rare and strange—
Such as in air the Mighty Master weaves.
The old tone passed away ; the young grown old
And gone to death's deep quiet in their turn;
And yet a third in birth and death enrolled,
While still undimmed their watching planets burn.

What history for the world, within that space !—
What miracles, misfortunes, errors, deeds !
What wondrous quickening in that rapid pace
With which the finite to th' eternal spreads !

What widening of all bounds, in earth and wave,
What gain and loss of wonders, since man's brain
The great steam-giant's strength to labor gave
And shaped to words the fierce electric chain!
Why this, for Monmouth? Only that to-day
One link which binds the Present with the Past
Is brightened by fair Freedom's holiest ray,
And here that sacred radiance is cast—
That here, to-day, within a grand old book
We read one chapter writ in veriest flame,
And see unroll before us, as we look,
One agency through which the great change came.

Here patriots stood, to drive a foreign foe
From fields his foot polluted, or to die!
No grander task does centuried history know;
No nobler deed o'erlooks the wide blue sky.
Here, at his proudest, stood the Man of Men,
The Washington of record's noblest page—
Defied the foe's assault, and turned again
To pour on faltering Lee his godlike rage.

And so the elements were blended here,
That form a great free people, at the end :
The leader bold—the followers dead to fear—
The cause to which all thoughts and motives bend.
And so to Monmouth's battle-field is given
To stand with Cannae and with Waterloo—
No spot more sacred, underneath the heaven
Than where our fathers came to die or do!

An hundred years. Are they forgotten? No!
They sleep in honored graves, who gave the boon
Of freedom through their red blood's deadly flow
In the hot blaze of that long-perished June.
We honor what they did—we honor *them*,
If words and thoughts of ours can go beyond
The mere leaf's tribute to the parent stem—
Mere whispering words, however true and fond.

Thank God that once they lived—that so they died!
Thank God for Monmouth, as for Bunker Hill!
True tides may join, although the land is wide,
And State to State the honoring cup may fill.
Who did, that day, his work of peril best?
Ah, they are gone who knew, if any knew;
But one true record stands by all confessed—
No second honor holds the Jersey Blue!

And when another hundred years have gone—
Nay, when *one year* is added to the train—
Here let a column of enduring stone
Monmouth's Centennial tribute proud remain!
The free sun, rising o'er free Monmouth fields,
Touch it, and gild it, as the centuries die,
To crown the tribute free New Jersey yields
To those who saved her in the days gone by!

Dr. English's Poem.

The following poem was written by
Thomas Dunn English, in 1867, and published originally in the *Northern Monthly Magazine* of that year. It was copied into the Monmouth Democrat of June 27, 1867. It is understood that this poem would have been read by Dr. English at the celebration last week, if he had not been prevented from attending :

The Battle of Monmouth, June 28, 1778.

Four and-eighty years are o'er me, great-grand-children sit before me ;
These my locks are white and scanty, and my limbs are weak and worn ;
Yet I've been where cannon roaring, firelocks rattling, blood outpouring,
Stirred the souls of patriot soldiers, on the tide of battle borne—
Where they told me I was bolder far than many a comrade older,
Though a stripling at that fight for the right.

All that sultry day in Summer beat his sullen march the drummer,

Where the Briton strode the dusty road until the sun went down ;
Then on Monmouth plain encamping, tired and footsore with the tramping,
Lay all wearily and drearily the forces of the crown,
With their resting horses neighing, and their evening bugles playing,
And their sentries pacing slow to and fro.

Ere the day to night had shifted, camp was broken,
knapsacks lifted,
And in motion was the vanguard of our swift retreating foes;
Grim Knyphausen rode before his brutal Hessians, bloody Tories—
They were fit companions, truly, hirelings these, and traitors those—
While the careless jest and laughter of the teamsters coming after,
Rang round each creaking wain of the train.

'Twas a quiet Sabbath morning, nature gave no sign of warning
Of the struggle that would follow when we met the Briton's might ;
Of the horseman fiercely spurring, of the bullets shrilly whirring,
Of the bayonets brightly gleaming through the smoke that wrapt the fight ;
Of the cannon thunder-pealing, and the wounded wretches reeling,
And the corses gory red of the dead.

Quiet nature had no prescience, but the Tories and the Hessians
Heard the baying of the bugles that were hanging on their track—
Heard the cries of eager ravens soaring high above the cravens—
And they hurried worn and worried, casting startled glances back,
Leaving Clinton there to meet us, with his bull-dogs fierce to greet us,
And the veterans of the crown scarred and brown.

For the fight our souls were eager, and each Continental leaguer,
As he gripped his fire-lock firmly, scarce could wait the word to fire ;
For his country rose such fervor, in his heart of hearts to serve her,
That it gladdened him and maddened him and kindled raging ire ;
Never panther from his fastness, through the forest's gloomy vastness
Coursed more grimly night or day for his prey.

I was in the main force posted—Lee of whom his minions boasted,
Was commander of the vanguard, and with him were Scott and Wayne ;
What they did I knew not, cared not—in their march of shame I shared not—
But it startled me to see them, panic-stricken, back again,
At the black Morass's border, all in headlong, fierce disorder,
With the Briton plying steel at their heel.

Outward cool when combat waging, howsoever inward raging,
Never Washington showed feeling when his forces fled the foe ;
But to-day his forehead lowered, and we shrank his wrath untoward,
As on Lee his bitter speech was hurled in hissing tones and low—
"Sir, what means this wild co fusion ? Is it cowardice or collision !
Is it treachery or fear brings you here ?"

Lee grew crimson in his anger—rung his curses o'er the clangor,
O'er the roaring din of battle, as he wrathfully replied ;

But his raging was unheeded, fastly on our chieftain
speeded,
Rallied quick the fleeing forces, stayed the dark re-
treating tide;
Then, on foaming steed returning, said to Lee, with
wrath still burning—
"Will you now strike a blow at the foe?"
At the words Lee drew up proudly, curled his lip and
answered loudly:
"Aye!" his voice rang out, "and will not be the first
to leave the field;"
And, his word redeeming fairly, with a skill surpassed
but rarely,
Struck the Briton with such ardor, that the scarlet
column reeled;
Then, again, but with good order, past the black
Morass's border,
Brought his forces rent and torn, spent and worn.

As we turned on flanks and centre, in the path of death
to enter,
One of Knox's brass six-pounders lost its Irish cannoneer;
And his wife who, 'mid the slaughter, had been bearing
pails of water
For the gun and for the gunner, o'er his body shed
no tear—
"Move the piece!"—but there they found her loading,
firing that six-pounder,
And she gayly till we won worked the gun.

Loud we cheered as Captain Molly waved the rammer—
then a volley
Pouring in upon the grenadiers, we sternly drove
them back;
Though like tigers fierce they fought us, to such zeal
had Molly brought us,
That though struck with heat and thirsting, yet of
drink we felt no lack—
There she stood amid the clamor, busily handling
sponge and rammer,
While we swept with wrath condign on their line.

From our centre backward driven, with his forces rent
and riven,
Soon the foe reformed in order, dressed again his
shattered ranks;
In a column firm advancing; from his bayonets hot
rays glancing,
Showed in waving lines of brilliance as he fell upon
our flanks,
Charging bravely for his master—thus he met renewed
disaster
From the stronghold that we held back repelled.

Monckton, gallant, cool and fearless, 'mid his bravest
comrades fearless,
Brought his grenadiers to action but to fall amid the
slain;
Everywhere their ruin found them; red destruction
rained around them
From the mouth of Proctor's cannon, from the musketry of Wayne;
While our sturdy continentals, in their dusty regimen-
tals
Drove their plumed and scarlet force, man and horse.

Beamed the sunlight fierce and torrid, o'er the battle
raging horrid,
Till in faint exhaustion sinking, death was looked on
as a boon;
Heat, and not a drop of water—heat that won the race
of slaughter—
Fewer far with bullets dying than beneath the sun of
June—
Only ceased a terrible firing, with the Briton sl w re-
tiring,
As the sunbeams in the west sank to rest.

On our arms so heavily sleeping, careless watch our
sentries keeping,
Ready to renew the contest when the dawning day
should show;

Worn with toil and heat, in slumber soon were wrapt
our greatest number,
Seeking strength to rise again and fall upon the
wearied foe—
For we felt his power was broken; but what rage was
ours outspoken,
When on waking at the dawn, he had gone.

In the midnight still and sombre, while our force was
wrapt in slumber,
Clinton set his train in motion, sweeping fast to
Sandy Hook;
Safely from our blows he bore his mingled Britons,
Hessians, Tories—
Bore away his wounded soldiers, but his useless dead
forsook;
Fleeing from a worse undoing, and too far for our pur-
suing—
So we found the field our own, and alone.

KEYPORT, June, 29th, '78.
To the Editor of the Monmouth Democrat:

I was in Freehold yesterday, and deposited in the
box, that is now in the corner stone of the Battle
Monument, a poem on the Monument, and by request
of the gentleman in charge of the Box, send you a copy
of the same, for publication, should you decide that its
merits are worthy of a place in your columns.
Yours Resp'tly,
FRANK P. HOLMES.

MONMOUTH BATTLE MONUMENT.

A hundred year have been our lot
Since our brave fathers fought and bled,
Still no monument marks the spot
To tell where their life blood was shed.

With love of country uppermost,
And love for fathers dead and gone,
We'll sound the praises of that host,
In all our walks, in all our song.

'Midst fire and smoke, despair and woe,
Brave men gave up their lives to save
Our country from a foreign foe,
That our flag in triumph might wave.

Through the heat and fire of that day,
Many a man lay down his life;
But thanks to God they broke the sway,
And freed themselves from foreign strife.

Good Washington—the firm and just,
Was in the fight through thick and thin;
In Peace and War he was the first,
And in the hearts of countrymen.

Some there are who would mar his fame
And from him take his fair even seat;
Who say in vain he took God's name,
When meeting Lee in full retreat.

Mollie Pitcher carried water
To the men who fought that day;
Her husband fell in the slaughter,
She took his place without delay.

Nobly and well she did her part,
And at the cannon bravely stood;
With steady hand, and her true heart,
And yet a woman, kind and good.

With reverence we hold the ground
Where our fathers so bravely fought;
On Monmouth's field we hope to found
A Tribute, not to be forgot.

Though many years have past and gone,
Still will we hold those mem'ries dear;
In thought and deed, in prose and song,
To our hearts, keep them ever near.

The shaft of stone we'll raise to them,
Who gave us what we now enjoy;

We'll sound the praises of those men,
Who added to our earthly joy.

Their deeds deserve all we can do
To mark the spot where they were slain;
Their love of home and country, too,
Has been our everlasting gain.

The following poem was written for the Celebration by Capt. E. L. COWART, Quartermaster of the 14th regiment in the late war, and one of the survivors of the celebration committee of 1854:

CENTENNIAL OF THE BATTLE OF MONMOUTH.

Come let us rejoice with a right good cheer,
That we live to see this Centennial year,
And enjoy the fruits of a goodly land,
Once wrung from the grasp of a tyrant's hand.

Now o'er the fields where we joyfully stray,
Two armies were met in martial array;
And as the Historians all relate
Fought Monmouth's Battle, June, seventy-eight.

The treacherous Lee there made a retreat,
Resulting almost in fatal defeat;
But the troops were rallied and victory won
By commander-in-chief, our Washington.

Here Hamilton, and Wayne, and Knox, and Green,
Dashed on with warrior's armor and sheen

Through the clashing of arms, and smoke and shell
The day was ours when the brave Monckton fell.

While generations yet unborn
Shall tune their harps to freedom's song,
Columbia's sons shall ne'er forget
That champion patriot, Lafayette.

We render our fathers and mothers, too,
The gratitude we owe, so justly due.
And honor the soldier and all the brave
Who gallantly fought their country to save.

These quiet hills so rich in lore,
Which echoed to the cannon's roar,
Now clad in all their choice array,
Combine to celebrate this day.

With hands united devoutly we'll spread
Sweet garlands over the graves of the dead,
While freedom's broad banner shall ever wave
In memory of all the true and the brave.

We are now at peace, and our homes are free,
And all men enjoy equal liberty.
We will render to God our grateful praise
For all we enjoy these bright happy days.

Then let this Monument tower up high,
'Till its fair summit shall kiss the blue sky;
Where sons of freemen shall ever combine
To pledge holy vows at its sacred shrine.

Comments of the Press.

From the New York Herald.

Yesterday was the hundredth anniversary of the battle and the men of Monmouth made the most possible out of the occasion—celebrated it with a spirit and a unanimity of feeling worthy alike of the event and of the memory of our valorous forefathers who sacrificed their lives in the cause of American freedom. Between twenty and thirty thousand people, or as many British and Americans as were present at the battle itself, participated in the centennial celebration. People from every part of the county and State were present. The town of Freehold, within the limits of which is the battle ground, never witnessed such a sight, such an effervescence of patriotic feeling. This broke out in various forms, but principally in a brilliant display of bunting. Not a house in town but had some display, and many were dotted with flags from base to attic. The Court House was especially gorgeous in starry banners. * * * The procession took a march altogether of about eight miles*—hot work with the thermometer at 94 degrees.

From the New Brunswick Daily Fredonian.

FRIDAY, June 28th, 1878, was a great day in the town of Freehold. * * * Nearly all the residences, business houses and public buildings were most profusely decorated with flags and bunting, many of them in an extremely handsome manner. We never saw before so much decoration in a village as was to be seen on this occasion. Most of the business places were closed during the entire day, and everybody gave themselves up to the celebration. All the arrangements were ample, and the people of the town did themselves great credit for the thorough and generous manner in which they carried out the programme, and in taking care of the crowds in attendance. The houses of the citizens were thrown open, and the most generous hospitality was shown on every hand. The soldiers and invited guests were gratuitously fed at Shinn's Hall, to the number of nearly three thousand, a committee of ladies and young men, devoting their energies the entire day for that purpose, and right royally did they perform their duty. Plates were set for eight hundred persons at once, and all were promptly served by the volunteer committee. A kettle holding four hundred gallons of coffee was among the curiosities of this great dining-room, it taking one hundred and twenty-five pounds of coffee to charge it at one time. Ample arrangements at the hotels and temporary restaurants scattered through the town provided for the thousands at moderate charges. Cold ice water was placed in tanks and barrels throughout the town, and placards posted everywhere that it was free to all. No one therefore suffered from hunger and thirst this hot day. * * * The crowd was probably greater than ever before seen in that village. The railroads brought in twelve thousand and thousands came in carriages from the surrounding country, some of them coming from over twenty miles distant. It was estimated that there were at least twenty thousand strangers in the town during the day. Many of them arrived the day previous, and nearly or quite every bed in the hotels and private residences were filled the night before to say nothing of

* This is an error—the entire route traversed by the rocession did not exceed two miles.—ED. DEM.

the cots and all sorts of temporary contrivances resorted to for the occasion. * * * The procession was very promptly placed in line, and started within a few minutes after eleven o'clock, and marched through the main streets of the village to Monument Park. The procession was a beautiful one, and occupied nearly half an hour passing a given point. * * There were many noteworthy incidents connected with this celebration which time and space forbid us to mention today. Suffice it to say it was a grand celebration of one of the grandest events in our early National history.

From the Jersey City Argus.
"Glorious Monmouth."

From the Toms River Courier.
Last Friday was a glorious day for Old Monmouth.

From the Woodbridge Independent Hour.
The celebration was a grand success and the sun of Friday set upon the grandest day old Freehold has ever seen.

From the Matawan Journal.
We can only say, to conclude, that the whole affair reflected credit upon those who had its management in charge.

From the Rahway Democrat.
Everything passed off in order, there appearing very little of the rowdyism and disturbance frequently prevalent on such occasions.

From the Elizabeth Journal.
Great credit is due the citizens of the town and county for the way they managed the celebration. There was very little intemperance, not over half a dozen persons were seen under the influence of liquor.

From the Hightstown Gazette.
The houses of all the prominent men of the town were thrown open and lunch served to their friends in a lavish manner. To much praise cannot be given to the committees and citizens generally for their hospitality and hearty welcome.

From the Daily Graphic, July 1.
These centennials have their penalty.— At the Freehold, N. J.. celebration a document turned up which revealed the fact that six of our heroic sires on that glorious day received forty lashes on the bare back for swapping their cartridges for cider!

From the Newark Journal.
If there was no blood spilled on the "sacred soil of the field of Monmouth" to-day, it is still safe to say that there was quite as much bustle and excitement, and more, than there was this day a century ago. * * Passing from rhetoric to facts, the celebration was a grand success. * * Patriotism glowed everywhere here to-day at white heat.

From the Bricksburg Times.
* * It is good to know that there was no patriotism wanting; that the weather was oppressively hot and the dust choking; that the celebration was a grand success, and that the corner-stone of a monument that is to commemorate the decisive struggle of the Revolution and perpetuate the memory of heroic patriotism was laid with impressive and appropriate ceremonies.

From the Newark Register.
Every house was gaily decorated, and all legitimate business except that for the sale of refreshments, was suspended for the day. * * * At noon when the heat was almost unbearable, the sky being cloudless, the surging mass, exposed to the rays of a merciless sun, must have numbered 20,000 souls. * * * The procession which was about twenty-five minutes in passing a given point, was one of the grand events of the day, and was witnessed by at least 15,000 people. It formed and moved about 11 o'clock. * * * An excellent collation was provided, and enough for five thousand people.

From the Philadelphia Ledger.
The one hundredth anniversary of the Battle of Monmouth was celebrated to-day with much ceremony and enthusiasm.— The people of New Jersey, and more particularly of Monmouth county, showed their patriotism by visiting this place to the number, as estimated, of between 30,000 and 40,000. * * From 9 o'clock in the morning until 6 o'clock in the evening, the streets of the village were thronged with visitors. The court house was tastefully decorated with flags and bunting, as was also nearly every dwelling in the village. The various points of interest in connection with the battle of Monmouth were marked with sign boards and flags.

From the Ocean Grove Record.

* * The centennial celebration of the Battle of Monmouth exceded the highest anticipations of all charged with the responsibility of making the occasion one of the grandest events known in that vicinity. The turnout was simply amazing. * * The beautiful town was decorated with lavish taste. The speeches were appropriate, and although the day was one of the hottest of the year, comparatively little discomfort was experienced, and no serious mishap, except those resulting from the operations of a gang of pickpockets, marred the pleasure or checked the enthusiasm of the day.

Col. I. S. BUCKELEW never had a better chance to display his administrative capacity as a railroad man than in the management and dispatch of the immense trains which arrived and departed from Freehold during the day.

From the Bordentown Register.

The people of Freehold deserve no little praise for the hearty manner in which they entertained the visitors. On every street corner and even between squares, barrels of ice water were to be found, to slake people's thirst, which was uncommonly keen on account of the great heat of the day. Ebony-colored individuals were also very numerous, and from buckets supplied a cooling draught to those who couldn't get to the barrels. The representatives of the press couldn't have been cared for better than they were by Mr. CHAS. F. RICHARDSON, a careful reporter and a practical young man. About two dozen of the press gang found him to be the right man in the right place. Col. BUCKELEW, with coat off and prespiration running down his cheeks, saw to the arrival and departure of those from a distance; ex-Gov. PARKER extended the hospitality of his fine house; Major YARD had an eye over things generally, and indeed the citizens seemed to vie with each other to make the day the memorable one it is and will remain as long as the United States exist.

From the Mount Holly Herald.

Just before lunch time at Freehold on Friday, Col. ANGEL turned over the command of the Seventh regiment to Major SLOAN, under whose orders the troops marched to the big feed. It was a splendid collation and did great credit to the big-hearted people who so bountifully prepared it. When the soldiers had satisfied their appetites, Major SLOAN arose and after praising the repast, proposed three cheers for the same, which were given heartily; after which was done, with his usual galiantry, he came to his feet, and with a smile playing over his handsome countenance, suggested three cheers for the ladies of Freehold. It is needless to say they were given with a will. The Major smiled outwardly and no doubt, inwardly too, conscious that he had performed a duty which was deservedly owing to the handsome, zealous, patriotic, charming and attentive ladies of Monmouth Court House.

From the Seaside.

* * The affair was one of those grand successes of which any county may well be proud. The weather, true to historic precedents, was clear and terribly warm. Freehold was decorated as it never was before, and the first impression upon arrival was that it was intended to give everybody a chance to enjoy and participate in the exercises. The committee of the Day, with Major E. F. APPLEGATE as chief had made every preparation necessary for, the comfort of invited guests and the public. Col. I. S. BUCKELEW gave his personal supervision to the railroad movements, which worked like a charm. Col. JAMES S. YARD. Grand Marshal, with his competent aids, was every where, but always in the very place where his skill was most needed. One of the most striking and effective "signs of the times" was that of "Cold Water Free" which was posted on every public and private pump and on innumerable barrels of ice water placed along the streets. In fact the people of Freehold and their committee gave evidence on all sides of a liberal and thoughtful hospitality. The impressive Masonic ceremonies, the splendid marching of the troops under Gen. SEWELL, the grand review by Gen. McCLELLAN, the songs, music, addresses, and in fact everything that had been announced, was successfully carried out, and all the exercises were enjoyed by a host of people that could not be numbered.

From the New York Times.

Not since the armies of WASHINGTON and CLINTON met in Monmouth county on this day 100 years ago, has Freehold contained so many persons at one time as it did to-day. The centennial anniversary of that decisive conflict was a great success in that respect. But it was also largely a success in interesting many people anew in local history. For weeks nothing has been talked about but the coming celeination; old books and papers have been ransacked for information; the memories of the oldest inhabitant have been shaken up for recollections of the battle; and the many excellent discourses heard to-day have imparted much knowledge to many, and refreshed the remembrances of many who had time to recall interesting stories concerning the stirring scenes of Sunday, June 28, 1778. * * * The streets were even more densely crowded during the afternoon than in the morning, and there could not have been less than 20,000 persons in the little town. * * The crowd began to leave for their homes late in the afternoon, and the good people of Monmouth returned to their accustomed routine of life, thoroughly satisfied with their celebration, declaring unanimously that it had been for them a "day of days."

From the Long Branch News.

* * * The warmest and most patriotic of Monmouth's citizens could not have wished a better day, or a grander demonstration. Though the day was oppressive, and scarcely a breeze ruffled the leaves of the surrounding trees, Freehold presented an appearance which it will hardly wear again for another hundred years. Business was absolutely suspended, and the streets from early morning were crowded by a happy, joyously disposed crowd. * * * The scene was wonderfully sublime. To a spectator witnessing it [the procession] as it filed up the gaily decorated street, with the flare of bayonets, the bright colors of the uniforms, the music of the bands, it will be a day and an occasion never forgotten. * * In summing up the events of so memorable a day, as citizens of Monmouth county we are proud. The celebration was a genuine burst of the right kind of patriotism, and a magnificent success.—Well may those who have devoted time, energy and means to make it a day bright in the chronicles to come, feel proud; they have triumphed, and old Monmouth County takes her place in the history of our country first in gratitude and patriotic pride. The entire arrangements reflected the generous nature of our people, and in the days to come when those now but young in years recall the Centennial Anniversary of the famed Battle of Monmouth aud the monument to be raised in its commemoration, joy shall be theirs to know that their fathers aided in its erection and added lustre to the cause it is designed to make immortal.

From the New York Tribune.

And worthily was it commemorated.— The program was a good one, and fairly carried out. Crowds wandered over all the miles through which the battle drifted. Even Monckton's grave in the old Tennent church-yard was not too far away, and as the pilgrims gazed at the blood stains in the old church, there was no irreverent suggestion that perhaps the Monmouth farmers imitate the example of the prudent Scots, who are slyly accused of brightening up with red paint, at least once a year, the traces left by Rizzio's blood in Holyrood palace.

So many people and so much stir and excitement have not been seen in this ordinarily quiet town since June 28, 1778, as yesterday, when apparently all the inhabitants of Monmouth county turned out to celebrate the one hundredth anniversary of that eventful day. * * The morning was beautiful, but gave promise of an exceedingly warm day. Nature seemed determined to do her part by furnishing a day as nearly as possible like that experienced by the Revolutionary soldiers on the same spot. * * The town was decorated from one end to the other. It was a very poor house or store that did not burst forth into a glory of flags. The court house particularly, was a mass of bunting. * * The audiences which listened to the speeches were small, but no shadow of a failure rested on the celebration. People went about it in their own way and in the shade. The greatest hilarity and enjoyment were noticed on all sides.

From the Somerset Messenger.

The celebration was a most worthy one and highly creditable to the people of Monmouth and the citizens of Freehold in particular. The arrangements were elaborate and so successfully carried out that it left nothing wanting.
* * * * * * * *
This was a very spirited celebration and one to be remembered with pleasure by all present. We cannot but express our admiration of the citizens of Freehold for

the exceedingly handsome manner in which they carried out this project and for their liberali:y in making provision for the occasion. Friend and stranger were treated with unbounded hospitality at the private residences of her leading citizens who threw their houses open and spread generous collations for all.— The soldiers also were handsomely entertained by the voluntary contributions of the citizens in a large hall at four or five long tables well loaded down, and waited upon by the first young ladies of the town. The present citizens of Monmouth are worthy of their spirited ancestors of Revolutionary fame. Their hospitality was as generous as it was hearty, and they seemed only fearful lest they should come short in anything demanded by the occasion. We were never more pleasantly, generously, nor heartily received than we were by some of Monmouth's leading citizens, among which we particularly notice Mr. JAMES A. PERRINE and Surrogate THROCKMORTON, whose acquaintance we are happy to have made.

From the Newark Daily Advertiser.

The celebration of the centenary of the Battle of Monmouth at Freehold, Friday, was a success. Had the American troops in 1778 been as numerous as those who celebrated their deeds, Sir Henry Clinton's Regulars, Mercenaries and Tories would have been annihilated; had they been as well entertained they would have gone into the fight with better spirits, had the arrangements been as excellent, and as fully executed, the treason of Lee would not have been an historical fact; and had they been as cordially welcomed, there would have been no opportunity for thousands of Jerseymen to enjoy themselves Friday, for there would have been no fight. * * * There was much dust, and there were some other trifling annoyances. But on the whole everything went off smoothly. * * Considerable money was subscribed for the monument, and taken altogether the number of those who were sorry they went was exceedingly small. * * Load after load of people arrived and the streets were soon crammed with a handsome, healthy, well-dressed crowd, many of them bearing baskets filled with edibles for themselves, and part for their guests, for such any one outside of Monmouth was considered to be. By 11 o'clock the incoming tide slackened, and at 12 it stopped. At that time good estimates placed the number of people in town at 20,-000, and it was more probably greater than less.

The notes of bugle and fife and taps of drum nt 11.30 indicated the start of the procession and the expectant thousands lined the streets. It was a beautiful display, worthy of all praise. * * Nothing but praise of their reception and of the event was heard from the departing multitude. The townspeople, to whom the event was of unparalleled importance, were elated at its result and grudged not their exertions. They deserve all sorts of praise.— There was little drunkenness, and no cases of disorder worth noticing.

From the True American.

One hundred years ago on yesterday the beautiful fields of Monmouth were the scene of a dreadful carnage, and American blood stained the verdant emerald of the waving grass. The air was filled with the smoke of battle—and the music of the birds, the peaceful quiet of the plain—was drowned in the din of war. Yet the day, notwithstanding all this, was a glorious one in the annals of American history—a victory had been won that loosened, as it were, the last foothold of unjust tyranny upon American soil. That victory was celebrated by the good people of Monmouth yesterday in a style worthy of the occasion.

About five o'clock a section of artillery * * arrived in Freehold and at once proceeded out into the country, one gun being posted on Briar Hill and the other on Combs' Hill. The artillery men went into bivouac, and were visited by hundreds of people who were anxious to see what kind of men were those who were to celebrate the doings of a century past.

* * * * * * *

There were about twenty thousand persons in Freehold. They came frem New York, Philadelphia, Trenton, in fact from all parts of the country. Farmers from miles around drove into the town with their wives and children to see the centennial, and the greatest enthusiasm and patriotism prevailed. The weather was excessively warm, and both troops and spectators suffered extensively from the the heat.

The celebration was a grand success in every respect, and did great credit to those who had the matter in charge. The arrangements were perfect, and were carried out with the nicest exactness under the direction of the Marshal of the Day. The people were delighted and the citizens of Monmouth county may well feel proud of the celebration.

From the Vineland Independent.

· · · Several miles before reaching the scene of action, we were reminded that there was "somethng in the wind" by the display of flags and bunting and the general holiday appearance of the country. The hay and cornfields were minus their accustomed laborers, while the grain cut the day before was still in the swath; the farmers had all gone to "enthuse" at the celebration. Arriving at Freehold, we found the town fully occupied. Look in whatever direction and you saw plumes and epaulettes, and to really see the town was an impossibility—there were so many people. Traverse any street, and the jostling crowd was there; take to the open field, and you would find that an army of pilgrims to this Revolutionary Mecca had preceded you. The amount of flags and bunting displayed, together with patriotic pictures, was immense; buildings were completely coverwith these patriotic emblems, so that the composition of the buildings was a thing of doubt.

Freehold is a beautiful old town.— The Court House is the chief building, and is really a creditable structure. The streets are nicely shaded by large trees, and the visiting soldiery had occasion during their long march, to say, "blessed be he who planted these trees. · · The "press gang" were kindly taken in custody by Mr. RICHARDSON, and given the most favourable position to see the procession go by. · · Too much cannot be said of the arrangements of the day, and the liberal patriotism of the people of Freehold. · · To cap the climax, the ladies of Freehold dispensed free lunch to the multitude in Shinn's Hall, a good, substantial farmer's bill of fare being furnished without money and without price. · · So liberal and wholesome a spirit, such open hospitality has been exercised by few towns, as that displayed by the citizens of Freehold on this day of rejoicing. · ·

· Freehold is proud of her celebration, and well may she be. It will be many a day before her streets are again trod by 25,000 people, as they were on this occasion.

From the Camden Press.

The one hundredth anniversary of the battle of Monmouth was celebrated in an imposing manner on Friday last. Freehold was in holiday attire, and the citizens of that beautiful town proved themselves thoroughly patriotic and none the less hospitable.

* * * * * * * * *

The military review concluded the festivities of the day, which were brilliant and successful, and were creditable in the highest degree to all concerned. Throughout the day the entire military and the guests of the occasion were furnished with a bounteous repast at Shinn's Hall, as many as nine hundred sitting down to the tables at one time. There was full and plenty, and none were permitted to leave dissatisfied. Such hospitality has rarely been equalled, and the ladies, of whom there were many, were unremitting in their attentions in waiting upon the men who had come to Freehold to help swell the throng, and to add to the interest of the great centennial celebration of the battle of Monmouth.

The committee of arrangements understood their business perfectly. We never saw an entertainment more admirably managed. Hundreds of soldiers and other guests were profusely entertained without unnecessary noise or confusion, and the quality and quantity of the provisions were universally extolled. Much was expected of old Monmouth at this celebration, but she came gallantly up and beyond all that the most critical could anticipate.

Freehold is really a very pretty place!— There must be considerable wealth there, if so many handsome houses surrounded by neat, well-kept grounds be a criterion. The surrounding country, too, is just such as one would expect from so handsome and wide-a-wake a village—gently rolling hills and verdant vales form the rich setting off, and these extend for miles in every direction. A Jerseyman who is of Monmouth, "old Monmouth," may well be proud of his State,—a State which was the battle ground of the Revolution, whose soil has been moistened with the blood of heroes.

The special thanks of the newspaper fraternity are due to Mr. RICHARDSON, of Freehold, for the careful manner in which he looked after their comforts at the Monmouth Centennial. Mr. RICHARDSON being a newspaper man himself, understood the characteristic diffidence of the fraternity, and very kindly cared for them.— The manner in which he did it proved him to be the right sort of a man for so important a duty.

OLD TIMES IN OLD MONMOUTH.

From the State Gazette.

Yesterday was a proud and notable day for Freehold and Monmouth county. The chief significance of the Centennial celebration of the Battle of Monmouth lies not so much in the important and decisive character of the results of that revolutionary struggle, as in the celebration. We have lived as a nation, as a Republic, for a hundred years since the day which struck a powerful blow for liberty—this is the great and glorious fact which filled the hearts of Jerseyman with pride on Monmouth's battle ground yesterday and inspired the enthusiastic celebration of a day glorious in the annals of humanity's heroes.

* * * * * * * *

Monmouth county and New Jersey have great reason to take pride in that glorious day.

[Here followed a concise review of the Battle and its results.]

Thus it is that New Jersey justly and honestly takes such a laudable pride in that battle of a hundred years ago—first, because it aided materially in establishing liberty on this continent, and, second, because her own sons bore such an honorable and conspicuous part in the fight.

If there had been a choice of days granted to the managers of the Monmouth celebration, they could not, perhaps, have chosen a brighter or more beautiful day in which to make famous the anniversary of the renowned battle of Monmouth Cou t House.

There was not a cloud in the blue sky that beamed on the face of nature below, and not a grumble from the voice of thunder to keep back the surging throng of nearly thirty thousand people who had gathered there to witness the splendid scene. * * Every face was joyous with that genuine enthusiasm which made this last Centennial celebration a most glorious success. This spirit of to-day is in full accord with the letter and spirit of those resolutions passed on the 6th day of June, 1774, when the inhabitants of Lower Freehold resolved to stand firmly against the forces of King George's minions.

* * * * * * * *

Ten o'clock rolled around, and the throngs of visitors, soldiers and civilians, began to pour in from all quarters of the State, and the procession fell into line on Broad street. At eleven o'clock the line was ready to move, and the "press gang," with the cedar in one hand and note book in the other, filed out of the Firemen's Hall down on Main street to witness the passing of the grandest turnout that has ever graced the streets of Freehold.

* * * * * * * *

While the speech making was going on at the stand the troops were marched down to Shinn's Hall where they made a glorious attack upon a collation which was most generously served by the ladies of Freehold, who, after the soldiers and invited guests had been fed, threw open the doors of the hall and invited the visiting thousands to partake of their providing. They were truly types of the good Lady Bountiful.

* * * * * * * *

Who shall say that the people of Monmouth county do not know how to get up a celebration?

From the Elizabeth Herald.

* * A complete success in every particular. * * The noble and historic old county of Monmouth did itself great credit yesterday.

From the Perth Amboy Democrat.

It was a grand and picturesque sight. Every house was gayly decorated with bunting, and a happy, joyous, rollicking kind of smile, pervaded almost every countenance.

From the Asbury Park Journal.

The occasion was celebrated in a manner befitting its historic importance. * * Everything passed off smoothly and all expressed themselves well satisfied with the celebration.

From the Red Bank Standard.

The celebration of the centennial of the Battle of Monmouth, and the laying of the corner stone of the monument commemorating the same, last Friday, the 28th, was a grand success.

From the Keyport Weekly.

Grandly and fittingly the people of old Monmouth prepared for the great event. * * All things united to make the 100th anniversary an occasion long to be talked of. * * The day passed without any serious accidents, and with the exceptions noted was a great success. The celebration was worthy of the occasion and speaks well for the enthusiasm of old Monmouth.

From the Red Bank Register.

The celebration of the Battle of Monmouth was a grand success. * * Ample preparations had been made to entertain visitors, and the proverbial hospitality of the people of Freehold was outdone on this occasion in their efforts to entertain their guests.

Although the celebration was by the entire county, still the brunt of the preparation fell upon the people of Freehold and the neighboring townships, and great praise should be given to the men and women who made it successful by their untiring and patriotic efforts.

From the Hightstown Gazette.

The celebration of the one hundredth anniversary of the battle of Monmouth, at Freehold, on Friday, June 28th, was a grand success, and too much credit cannot be given to the people of Monmouth, the citizens of Freehold, and the committee of arrangements for that success. * * We do not believe that as large a number of people ever gathered under similar circumstances, and went away better satisfied than did the twenty or more thousands who were in Freehold last Friday. * * The streets were cleaner than we ever saw the streets of that town before, and it almost seemed as if the dust had been removed for the occasion. * * The hotels and saloons were open, but we can honestly say that we saw fewer drunken men in Freehold on Friday than on any other day that we remember having spent in the town. * * It would take a "square" or two if we merely named the different persons who invited us to their houses for lunch. * * Before the celebration we heard it sneeringly remarked that it "was to be a Freehold affair entirely." If this was in any sense true then Freehold may put a feather in her cap, for a more pleasant welcome, a more substantial hospitality, and a more successful carrying out of grand preparations was never displayed by a place of its size.

From the Sussex Independent.

The MONMOUTH DEMOCRAT devotes 13 columns to the celebration of Monmouth's Centennial. The affair was one of the most notable that ever occurred in this State. Over 20,000 people gathered from all parts of the State and of the Union, witnessed the grand display. * * The people of Monmouth deserve great praise for their liberality and enterprise in carrying to a successful issue the celebration of the anniversary of the important historical battle fought in 1778.

From the Vineland Weekly.

The people of Freehold have reason to be proud of the success of their celebration. In the more important and in the minor details it was all that could be asked. The day was a perfect one, and the grateful shade of the trees and groves of this beautifully situated county seat made it cool and comfortable. Their invited guests turned out in full force, and the military display, and that of the Masonic and other fraternities, was unusually brilliant. For creature comforts they provided lavishly. Refreshments in abundance were furnished for both military and civilians, and everything was of the best. For the editorial fraternity they provided a guide to see that they should see everything, excellent seats on the platform, a sumptuous lunch, and a cozy, comfortable room for those wishing to write out their reports. All the editors and reporters, at least, will retain most pleasant recollections of the good people of Freehold, one and all.

From the Vineland Advertiser.

Everything that could be done for the comfort of every visitor was done. Mr. RICHARDSON of the committee of arrangements, taking every care of the members of the press, and showing them every attention—caring only that the guests lacked nothing that was necessary. The hearty thanks of all concerned are due to the committee, and especially to Mr. RICHARDSON, for the efficient manner in which these arrangements were carried out.

* * * * * * *

During the speeches the militia boys were taken down to Shinn's hall to be fed by the noble women of Freehold. It was an enormous task to attempt, but their patriotic spirit showed itself, and one could no longer wonder that Monmouth should occupy a marked position in the old times, when the same spirit showed itself as strongly here. We saw frail ladies hard at work, intent only on attending to the wants of the boys, who confessed to have been hard at it, without intermission since early morning, and yet kept at it. To say that the boys appreciated it would hardly be an adequate expression. As each relay rose from the tables, cheer upon cheer for the " ladies of Freehold" went up. For devotion and determination to carry out their plans, the ladies of Freehold certainly deserve the highest praise, and their memory will be cherished by the many they fed on that day. Some of the Company K boys recognized old comrades of Philipsburg, in the knives, forks and plates. Capt. CHEEVER got hold of a knife he was sure he had seen before.

Oration of Hon. S. S. Cox.

It is an ancient and beautiful custom to recall, by such celebrations as this, ancestral and historic renown. The Greeks began it by their battle celebrations. The memorable defeat of her Persian invaders was not merely pronounced by the eloquent panegyrist, but architecture, music, painting and poetry gave their graces to the eulogy. Thus was preserved her martial spirit and patriotic ardor; while the arts found congenial subjects and the muse her lofty inspiration.

These ceremonies were thought to be as gratifying to the dead as they were ennobling to the living. On such occasions the bones of the dead were produced in chests of cypress, and an empty bier with a pall over it, for the missing. Coming forth from the monuments where these emblems and offerings were laid and ascending the tribunal, the orator graced the noble fervor of his hour by recounting the valor of the dead, and bestowing encomiums upon the sacred cause in which they died. Thus came down to us the renowned exploits of Marathon, Salamis, Mycale and Plataea, forever embalmed in classic eloquence.

Casting our eye back through the vista of two thousand years, from this heroic ground of vantage and under the light of a better civilization, we can add but little by our observances, to the elegance and grace of those ancient customs. We seem to see the broken column green with laurel, while around lie spear, shield, sword, helmet, cuirass, trumpet and torso, insignia and instruments of that triumphant life which gave to battle its signal and prowess and sanctified its success forever in the achievements of home-independence against alien rule!

These customs were continued long after the children of the heroes were sleeping with their fathers, even until the latest generation. They only ceased when the state became corrupt and the people pusillanimous.

It is a custom which our country has imitated upon every yearly occurrence of our independence anniversary; and since the hundred years have chimed, with its procession of heroic battles, the custom has brought with it signal memories.

Long years or cycles after the wounds of sorrow are closed over our brave countrymen fallen in battle, these memories are renewed, without social poignacy and with patriotic pride. Fresh wreaths are added to the bright chaplet of heroic endeavor; the unwritten remembrance of it is perpetuated in distant and barbarous climes, and thus the whole earth becomes vocal with its renown.

You of New Jersey have your heroes. They are mingled with your dust, or their remains lie under mossy stones in your old grave yards; but from their dust do they not speak with their wonted fire? Since they fought, one hundred years have bridged the abyss between us and them; but still they speak from this cherished spot: "Hearken to us!" they seem to say: "Are ye not children of valiant, free and honest men? Will ye desert the rank above all crowns and coronets, which we won, held and transmitted? We might have preserved our lives and fortunes at the expense of our manhood; but we chose rather to risk all, hunger, freezing, privations from home, and safety, than plunge you, our descendents, into abasement before a foreign master. All pursuits are vain and all possessions fleeting, without that spirit of independence which makes the pursuit noble and the possession opulent. All knowledge is craft, and all display meretricious, all public honors badges of disgrace, when you forget the elder glory, which we learned from the Hollandish heroes who contended against Philip II and Alva, and from the Hampdens and Sidneys of our ancestral isle! It was not ambition, nor desire of promotion, nor greed of earthly gain that kindled our patriotism. It was not even revenge, except when forgetful of Washington's advice and Christ's mercy, we saw British and Tory, Hessian, and savage allies. outrage the laws of civilized warfare, that led us to devote ours and ourselves to th:s patriotic work. It was the passionate hatred of arbitrary methods and despotic power. To remember the lessons of unrepresented tax, and the subjected victims, is to remember why we fought and why we never yielded. You have had a century of the blessings we secured for you. Pay us, your fathers, the debt of gratitude for the trials of Valley Forge and the struggles of Monmouth, and thus vindicate the great declaration at Philadelphia. Did we not risk exile, prision and scaffold, and the exposure of our rebel heads on Temple Bar, the scorn of Tory and, Briton, the sarcasm which follows failure of all enterprizes, tor what? For you, that military despotism and illegal exactions should not be fixed, neither upon the inhabitants of this grand country nor upon any who should come to it as an asylum. Our battles were for peace, home, equity, self-government and true liberty

—" which always with right reason dwells
Twin'nd and from her bath no dividual being."

We have preferred death with that liberty, to life without it; death in our own land rather than life and dependence upon another land. True, we did not fight to acquire liberty. No! We never lost that, but we fought to defend what was already ours. We fought those who would deprive us of it, for independence of them. We require from you no lament: our bodies are dissolved, but our immortal felicities will only continue when you, our children, continue to remember us by preserving what we bequeathed."

It is true that every year, that every century, nay, that every day and hour turn islres such lessons ; for each has its event. The sun in its revolution and the stars in their courses, give us epochs, which are the mark, association and stimulus of memory. A hundred years! It is but a sand grain upon the shore of time. It is scarcely heeded, when we undertake to comprehend eternity. But in human vicssitudes a hundred years may be to man what a thousand is said to be to God: as one day! For us, that day is here! It is thronged with memories that are associated with our proudest patriotic devotion. It is this we celebrate, and to this we raise this monument.

Whatever may be the result of these celebrations, whether they reproach England or her ministry, glorify France and her alliance or encourage and dignify rebellion for any cause however light or grevious, it is our duty to recall the sacrifices and retouch the features of these heroic men and times. We cannot rely on classic models or mystic legends to gratify the pride of ancestry or glorify the exploits of Washington, Knox, Gieene and Wayne. These heroes and their cause are all our own.

Let us remember and record the facts, local and general, which led to the British march over Jersey, before they are veiled behind the gilded cloud of tradition. Is it no incentive to present patriotism, to recall 1774, with its stamp act, and its fifth of March massacre at Boston ; or 1775, which ushered in Burke's great plea for conciliation, and Gen. Gage's inglorious attempt against the stone walls of Eastern Massachusetts, with Concord, Lexington, Bunker Hill, and the beacon that flew like a living torch to the extremes of our thirteen provinces?

Is it no incentive to love our land, to know that Virginia lifted that torch, and passed it to New Jersey, and so along the line of States upon our sea-board, until it was ablaze with patriotic fire? Is it not a cement to union, to recall hard, upon the 1st of August, 1774, Virginia declared that " an attack on one of our sister colonies, to compel submission to arbitrary taxes, was an attack on all British North America, and threatens ruin to the rights of all, unless the united wisdom of the whole should be applied?" Is it nothing to recall how New Jersey disposed of her subservient and over-loyal Governor, Franklin, and her old institutions, because they were conducted by him with perfidy to her chartered priviliges, and how she reinstated a better government, with Livingston at its head? Is it nothing to recall his defiance of British presumption in his first message to the

Assembly, when he set his voice and will as a flint against arbitrary rule from a distant power?* What Jerseymen does not feel fresh fervor in the cause of liberty, when he recalls the struggles of her delegates at Philadelphia, with Richard Stockton, and Francis Hopkinson, the author of "Hail Columbia," at their head? Did they give an uncertain sound in preparation for the battle, with civil as well as military sagacity and prudence? Is there no pride of statehood or kinship, in knowing that New Jersey furnished some of the most cultivated and courageous Barons of our Runymede, in spite of local disaffection, thus giving an impulse to popular sentiment, which emphasized our Magna Charta of Human Rights? It is well that as time rolls on, and the seasons come and go, having with them such memories, that they should be made monumental.

Fifty years ago the heroic sentiment began to languish with sectional asperities and to die, with the heroes of the Revolution. The centennial of the Great Charter gave it glad renewal. The very events of our civil strife, and our temporary alienation, with its heart burnings, fused into us a new love of the historic days of the Republic, when north and south were united as at Monmouth, in sentiment and in battle, against a common enemy.

Is it not a part of our heritage, sons of New Jersey, to remember with filial and pious gratitude the very death volleys which closed the lives of our ancestors on yonder field, to regenerate our liberties? The blood which moistened the sod of Monmouth, or mingled with its rivulets under the shadow of its alders, was, and is, ours forever! It is holy ground! For a hundred years it has not been profaned. It has helped to give New Jersey its high name on the roll of honor—as the battle

---

* "Let us, gentlemen," so closes this earnest call for their warmest sympathy, and most vigorous exertions in the American cause, "both by precept and practice, encourage a spirit of economy, industry and patriotism, and that public integrity and righteousness which cannot fail to exalt a nation; setting our faces at the same time, *like a flint* against that dissoluteness of manners and political corruption which will ever be the reproach of any people. May the foundation of our infant State be laid in virtue and the fear of God, and the superstructure will rise glorious, and endure for ages. Then may we humbly expect the blessing of the Most High, who divides to the nations their inheritance, and separates the sons of Adam. In the fine, gentlemen, whilst we are applauded by the whole world for the old fabric, rotten and ruinous as it is, let us unitedly strive to prove ourselves master builders, by giving beauty, strength and stability to the new."—*Extract from Gen, Livingston's Address, Aug.* 3, 1776. See Gordon's History of New Jersey, p. 238.

ground of the revolution !—a ground where the Tory pursued his Whig neighbor and kinsman all too relentlessly, but where foreign and domestic foes retreated before native valor, and where the upstarts of HOWE and CLINTON, who had revelled the winter and spring in Philadelphia, made fleet footsteps hence to the safe hills of Middletown and the hospitable shore of Sandy Hook.

It was a fitting tribute to the heroic men of the Revolutionary period, when your Governor RANDOLPH, in June, 1870, gave present interest to the annals of your State, by perpetuating the names and rank of the soldiers who fought in the early struggle. I have seen a volume of nearly nine hundred pages, containing this compilation. Whether it be the officers of the "Jersey line," or the minute men, or the privates, teamsters, hostlers, armorers, artificers, barrack masters, or boatmen, on land or sea, the official roster of the Continental army and the militia, their names are registered as the pride and glory of New Jersey.! From the base to the top of the column their names are inscribed in golden recollections. Many of these are to me as familiar as household names. I am almost tempted to rehearse them.— In my youth I heard them from my father's lips, as he had heard them from his father, who was their associate in war and friend in peace.

Whatever may be said of other States who have vaunted their service with literary circumstanse and superlative art, it is neverthele s true that New Jersey was the battle ground of the Revolution. The contest here was much more sanguinary, perilous, critical and vindictive than in the other provinces. It was aggravated by the Tories and Loyalists, some of them the meanest of mankind, and others timid men of wealth and respect. The former haunted the forests and shores of Monmouth, and the mountains of Morris and Essex. They did more harm and provoked fiercer resentment than the regular enemy. Being almost a frontier province, over which were so many marches and struggles, New Jersey suffered more losses and distresses from the marauding and disaffected, than any other province, except, perhaps, South Carolina. She was the Belgium of our Continental struggle.

Again and again, under the advice of Congress and especially of WASHINGTON, and from the best motives of humanity, New Jersey was lenient toward what was called these "bosom traitors," who were too savage to be humanized by the practice of forbearance, or the laws of decent warfare. Pillage, slaughter and murder made New Jersey the dark and bloody ground of the Revolution. The pine robbers and other Tory desperadoes of the time, kept the people of this county in perpetual alarm. Farmers worked in their fields with loaded guns at hand, and many a pine fiend bit the dust for his audacity and crimes. Burning houses, hanging men and outraging women; insecurity and terror at every hearth, especially of the families of those absent with the patriot army, this was the condition of your State until CLINTON, with his crowd of wretched allies and camp followers, fled from it with their ill-gotten possessions, misbegotten persons and worse characters.

It is said that at the battle of Platæa, dissension was so rife, and factions so formidable, that all external enemies were as riends in comparison, and that when a disaffected body of Greeks joined the Persians as auxillaries, the place of honor in the fight, opposite the Hellenic renegades —the "bosom traitors"—was given to the Theban troops. Well they earned it, by routing and slaying the domestic enemy! Well bestowed upon them was the guerdon, known among the Greeks as *Aristeia*, being the first among military decorations. New Jersey won this renown by suppressing her home foes.

True, at Monmouth, every section and province was represented. Leading spirits of the Revolution were there assembled to fight for the common cause—the Carolinas, Virginia, Pennsylvania, New York, New England—each and all by most conspicuous men. Rhode Island gave us GREENE, the Quaker boy, all familiar with Jersey soil and its previous conflicts; Pennsylvania gave WAYNE, than whom no more impetuous and faithful soldier ever served a good cause, beside giving us CADWALLADER, and BRUNNER; New Hampshire gave us Col. DEARBORN, who commanded a regiment of "full-blooded Yankees," as he said, with some little profanity; New York gave STIRLING, the hero of Long Island, the friend of WASHINGTON and ALEXANDER HAMILTON, greater in peace than war; Massachusetts gave KNOX, chief of artillerists, large, generous and buoyant, as well as trustworthy and trusted; Virginia, GRAYSON, SCOTT, DICKINSON and WOODFORD; Ireland, Captain MOLLY; France, LAFAYETTE; Germany, STEUBEN, and the United Colonies gave us WASHINGTON, the leader of them all, whose fame has no equal, and whose courage on Jersey soil, no parallel, even in his own achievements.

But it was New Jersey more than all combined, which made most sacrifice upon this crucial test of the Revolution. It was her "embattled farmers," who withstood the shock of the contest.

Other localities have celebrated their Concord and Lexington, Bennington, Oriskany and Saratoga. These battles represent crises in our fate.

Concord, it is said, fired the first shot— heard round the world. New England has had her apotheosis to WARREN and those who ushered in that epoch. Saratoga, too, has been called one of the fifteen decisive battles of the world. It was significant; for it led to the alliance of France and our recognition in Europe.— Thanks were given by Congress, and medals were struck; and Gates received the honors of the young nation. But Monmouth was the first great military result of that French alliance, and of the abject f ilure of the Peace Commissioners. Monmouth, too, marks an epoch, and Washington was its hero!

Hitherto our successes for the year 1777 had so resulted that New England and Northern New York were rescued from the enemy. Saratoga was the closing scene of one act of our seven years drama; but New York was still held. Philadelphia had succumbed to an overwhelming force; and the capital of the country had been removed from thence to York. Washington had failed at Brandywine and at Germantown, and nothing was left for the defeated army but the wintry terrors of Valley Forge.

It is needless to rehearse the long agony upon the Schuylkill, nor how our army lived in huts, wet, hungry and freezing, depending upon forced contributions for scanty food, until Washington countermanded the arbitrary authority by which they had forced supplies. What tongue can tell how sickness, wretchedness and death. dissensions and jealouises, Canadian diversions and intrigues for Gates and Conway "cabals" for Lee in Congress and in the army, and against the great commander, discouraged the patriots and their patriot chief? Nor how they encouraged the loyal and disaffected, and the debauchees of Howe's army rioting in Philadelphia? Is it not written in blood-

OLD TIMES IN OLD MONMOUTH. 35

prints upon the snows of that dreary winter? To add to the discouragement England, through Lord North, proposed conciliatory bills, and sent them as olive branches to the disheartened colonies.— From the effect of these, more than from desertion and mutiny, Washington apprehended a "malignant influence on the Republic in America." Besides, English commissioners were proposed, who should accompany these bills. They landed in the spring at Philadelphia. They were considered more dangerous at that perilous time to our cause, than ten thousand of their men. The history of their failure, their attempt to reach Congress by bribery, and finally, when failing, to reach the people, by threats of vengeance and savage desolation, is a part of our well authenticated annals, for which we, at least, have no cause to blush. It was the touchstone of our undeviating faith, for at once an answer sprung from the pen of one of our patriot scholars, stigmatizing the project as that of "an enemy faithless, fraudulent and barbarous."

Meanwhile, the army of Howe was luxuriating in Philadelphia. The Quaker city was in strange contrast with Valley Forge. While our suffering army had insufficient food and fuel, still they were daily drilling under Steuben. While their enemy in the city of Brotherly Love was enjoying the dance house, the theatre, and the gaming table, the unwasting spirit of the American army kept its patriotic fealty to its commander and the country.— The commissioners, on their arrival, found no encouragement there for their mission. The hilarity of Howe's troops went on, under the eye of their sluggish, dilatory, pleasure-loving chief. He had allowed the winter to pass away in dalliance with the dames and deviltry of the city, without attempting to break up the American camp.

The English commissioners expected, on their arrival, to receive the submission of the colonies, and to pardon rebellion. They were as sanguine as George III, in 1774, when he said that four regiments could conquer America. They even communicated to Congress the views of England as that of a fond mother willing to caress her wayward children. With what dignified scorn Congress received their condescending impertinence !

Close upon these events came the rescript of France, which acknowledged American independence. She dated it *nunc pro tunc*, on the 4th of July, 1776, thus recognizing the fact that "Nationality, by its own declaration, could speak itself into being !" On the 4th of May the treaties of commerce and alliance with the King of France were ratified. France became our friend. Nay, she was proclaimed the "protector of the rights of mankind."

Here was a rift in the wintry cloud at Valley Forge. A herald from France had landed from a French frigate at Portland, Maine. It is on the 7th day of May, at 9 o'clock in the morning, when the American army is on parade, that the news is communicated to them. The brigades are in order. True, their uniforms are not as gay as those in Philadelphia, and the feet and bodies of many are bare.— Some wear the remnants of their winter blankets. The treaty of alliance is read to them. The chaplain gives thanks to Almighty God that France is our friend. Huzzas for France, Washington, and the Republic follow. Musketry rattles through the whole line, and in jubilant thunder thirteen rounds from big guns are fired for thirteen States ! Ah ! Too late ! ye Commissioners of Peace ! too late your tender of *quasi* independence ; too late your measure to discharge the debts of America, and raise its credit and pay off its money ; too late your reciprocal deputation of agents in Parliament, and too late your concession of the power of legislatures in each State to settle its own revenue and internal government. Congress will not hearken to ye ! But still the revelry goes on in the Quaker city. The pleasure seeking army is about to lose its roystering general. His field officers would signalize his departure by an entertainment. They give to it the Italian name of *Mischianza* or *Medley*. It was the first tournament of knights ever seen in our unfeudal land. Each knight is attended by a squire like Don Quixote, appearing in honor of some peerless damsel. He enters the list while ladies in Turkish attire look on to bestow the prize of valor on the victor. A rare device this medley shows for General Howe. It is significant in several senses. It was a sign with the motto :

"Luceo discendens, aucto splendore resurgam."

That army of his descended on the soil of Jersey, and never rose to the heights of Monmouth again. That sunset of Howe gave him no mystical lore, for he discerned none of the shadows before the coming events. There was no discernment of the prophecy written upon the wall at this feast of loyalty. On goes the revel on shore and river! The hautboys upon the Delaware make their music while their galley's glittered with colors and streamers, and the transport vessels are tricked in holiday attire. "God save the Queen," reverberates upon the air till midnight, while the shore is illumined with thousands of lights. Another sort of shout goes up among the huts of Valley Forge, "Long live the King of France!" Privations are forgotten and the least garment gives warmth, the poorest food is a luxury. France, the land of the sun, the home of Lafayette, was with us—and when the movement began by which Pennsylvania and New Jersey were enfranchised, the effect in Paris, as Dr. Franklin described it, was thrilling, electrical, overwhelming and indescribable. Its effect here was to change the war to the southern States and prepare the way for Yorktown and peace. What added to the general joy was the fact that the French Toulon squadron had sailed, bearing an accredited minister for the United States, and troops as our allies for the future. This precipitated the retreat of Clinton from Philadelphia.

How shall he reach New York in safety? It was a serious question. To go by water might bring him in conflict with the French fleet upon the Delaware. He had but one alternative—to cross the Jerseys, and, if possible, to convoy the ragged route of ragged rascals who followed, and protect the *impedimenta* which had accumulated during the winter, from the detachments which were sure to harass his march. What a dilemma was this for the loyalists! Well might they look back with regret upon their revelry. Their papers of protection were now sources of peril, their possessions a temptation to the enemy, and their honors a odium to themselves. How should he reach New York where the British fleet was stationed? Should he cross the Raritan or move towards Sandy Hook? He pauses and decides at Allentown. He concludes to move upon the Monmouth road. Washington, wary, prudent and sagacious, finds out the design and prepares to follow, harass, and if possible, destroy him. Call it what you may, fate or design, or prescience, the battle of Monmouth is preparing.

Whether we consider the skirmishes before or the actors in the battle, or the dramatic scenes between its actors which occurred during its progress, or the intense personalities between Washington and Lee, and the august persons engaged in it, or the military game of death and retreat, recovery and slaughter, which made its vicissitudes, certainly no battle has a higher claim upon our romantic and patriotic susceptibility. Whether we regard the varying conflicts of the day and the quiet retreat of the night, it was a battle of rare strategic skill and desperate intrepidity. No one denies that the British fought resolutely and desperately, and the Americans with a courage rarely, if ever, equalled. It was no slight compliment that the King of Prussia paid on reading the account of this action, when he declared that it displayed more military knowledge than any during the war. But he showed nice discernment when he said, "Clinton reaches New York with the wreck of an army, and America is lost to England." (Cheers.) Whatever may be claimed by historians as to the decisiveness of the battle, it may be said that in the early part of the day the advantage was with the British—in the latter portion was with the Americans. The Americans maintained their ground, and, when attacked, repulsed the enemy. They suffered less than their adversaries, and were only prevented by the sudden retreat of Clinton from consummating the victory.

Few battles have more authentic and satisfactory descriptions. This is owing to the fact that General Lee was arrested, tried and convicted, upon testimony before a court, out of which a clear and unvarnished narrative has been deduced.

But it is not in the brief notes of the court that we can gather the limning or the pigments for a battle scene like that of Monmouth. Every battle, like a picture, has its design and its unity.

Notwithstanding the diversity of opinion among the seventeen officers with whom Washington advised; notwithstanding the fact that six of the general officers were in favor of the annoyance of the foe by detachments and opposed to a general engagement, and that Generals Greene, Lafayette and Wayne only were in favor of general action, Washington relied upon his own judgment—asked no further advice, and proceeded to design the battle. The etchings or details for the design are but faintly delineated by the ordinary historic annals. One should go to the minutiæ of the preparations for the march and its crowning result. I have seen in the Library of Congress, at Washington city, the original Orderly Book of Washington for the year 1778, from Valley Forge to Monmouth Court House. This volume was purchased from the Lewis family of Virginia, where it had remained for fifty years. It begins at Valley Forge on the first of January, 1778. Its first words are, "Now begins a new year. The General orders a gill of spirits to each man."

I see a friend yonder who smiles at this order; but it may be interesting to know that not merely at Valley Forge, but at other points, the Revolution received some of " the spirit of 1776," from corn whiskey and applejack. (Laughter.)

The exactitude of the directions is marvellous—the moderation of his character shines through them; while the providence which he exhibits and the plans which he forms can be gathered from the least detail. *Ex pede Herculem.* These orders have not yet been printed. I have extracts of them before me.* Before the army crosses the Delaware orders are issued for cooking. When they reach Coryell's ferry "no man is permitted to bathe until sunset." When they cross the ferry, earth is ordered instead of rails for the repair of the roads, " to prevent crippling the horses." Damage to fruit trees is sternly prohibited, while drinking cold water when heated is forbidden.— The order of march for the brigades is carefully noted; guides are provided and the parades and countersigns registered. When Cranberry is reached, on the 24th, he is nearing the enemy. Mark the parole! " Lookout!" and the countersigns "Sharp" and "Keen." On the 25th, at Penslopen, vigilance and precaution are " essentially necessary." Officers at their posts, and soldiers on picket must be ready to form and march at a moment's warning. This was the last order before the battle. From Freehold the parole is Monckton, the British officer, who had been killed while gallantly fighting; the countersigns Bonner and Dickinson, who had fallen upon our side so honorably. Then a high note of congratulation for the ' victory obtained over the armies of his Britannic Majesty, and sincere thanks to the gallant officers and men who dis-

EXTRACTS FROM WASHINGTON'S ORDERLY BOOK, 1778, AT VALLEY FORGE, MONMOUTH COURT HOUSE, &c.

HEADQUARTERS, DOCTOR SHERMAN'S, }
FRIDAY, June 19, '78. }

" If any of the troops have marched without the proper quantity of cooked Provisions, they are to cook enough this afternoon to serve them to-morrow and the next day, provided their rations are of salt meat. The old and new guards will parade in the road opposite Mr. Sherman's, precisely at half-past three o'clock in the morning.'

HEADQUARTERS, BUCKINGHAM, }
SATURDAY, June 20, 1778. }

" If the Commissariers are provided, the men are to have each a Gill of spirits served to them this afternoon."

HEADQUARTERS, CORYELL'S FERRY, June 21st, 1778.
" No men are to be permitted to bathe till sunset."

HEADQUARTERS, CORYELL'S FERRY, }
MONDAY, June 22d, 1778. }

" When circumstances will permit, the Artillery and Pioneers are to advance before the Van Guard of the Army, and repair the road with earth instead of rails, which serve to cripple the horses.

The Brigadier of the day with officers ordered to remain in the Rear, will see that everything is properly conducted there—the Guards kept to their duty and all damage to the fruit trees prevented, of which the whole road hitherto exhibits such shameful proofs.

Commanding officers of companies will see that their men fill their canteens before they begin the march, that they may not be under the necessity of running to every spring and injuring themselves by drinking cold water when heated with marching.

The General will beat at three o'clock in the morning, and the army march at four o'clock precisely.

AFTER ORDERS.

The following Brigades during the march are to compose the Right Wing of the Army and be commanded by Major General Lee. Woodford's, Scott's, No. Carolina; Poor's, Varnum's and Huntington's, 1st Pennsylvania, 2nd Pennsylvania; Late. Conway's, Glover's, Larned's and Paterson's are to comprise the Left Wing, and be commanded by Major General Lord Stirling.

The Second Line is to consist of 1st and 2nd Maryland, Muhlenberg's, Weedon's, and Maxwell's, (when it joins) and be commanded by Major General, the Marquis De la Fayette; the army to march from the left.— The Quarter Master General will furnish guides.

HEADQUARTERS, HUNT'S HOUSE, }
TUESDAY, June 23d, 1778. }

Parole, Philadelphia. C. Signs { Brunswick, Boston.

The troops will cook their Provisions, and in every respect be in the greatest readiness possible for a march or action very early in the morning.

HEADQUARTERS, KINGSTOWN. }
THURSDAY, June 25th, '78. }

Parole, Monmouth. C. Signs, { Minden, Mexico.

HEADQUARTERS, CRANBURY, FRIDAY, June 26th, 1778.
Parole, Lookout. C. Signs, { Sharp. Keen.

HEADQUARTERS, PENSLOPEN, SATURDAY, June 27, 1778,
Parole, ——— C. Signs, {

" As we are now near the Enemy and of consequence Vigilance and Precaution more essentially necessary, the Commander in Chief desires and enjoins it upon all officers to keep their Posts and the several soldiers compact, so as to be ready to form and marchat a moment's warning, as circumstances may require.

HEADQUARTERS, FREEHOLD, (MONMOUTH COUNTY, }
June 29th, 1778. }

Parole Monckton. C. Signs, { Bonner, Dickinson.

The Commander in Chief congratulates the Army on

tinguished themselves in the action, and such others, who by their good orders and coolness gave the happiest presage of what might have been expected had they come to action." Dickinson and the militia of New Jersey are thanked for the noble spirit which they have shown in opposing the enemy, for the aid which they have given by harassing and impeding their motions so as to allow the continental troops time to come up with them. Then an order for a burial party, the officers to be buried with military honors due to men who have fought nobly and died in the cause of liberty and their country, and that the wounded and sick be removed to Princeton hospital. "It is with an expression of peculiar pleasure that the Commander-in-chief can inform General Knox and the officers of artillery, that the enemy have done them the justice to acknowledge that no artillery could be better served than theirs." Following this, is an order for the men to wash themselves and to appear as clean and decent as possible. Then, an order of thanksgiving to the Supreme Dispenser of Human Events for the victory obtained at sunset over the flower of the British troops.—

Next, returns of the missing and provisions for the morrow, and then an order for a movement, and for the righting of wrongs done upon the march, by a strict search of the soldier's packs at parade and the recovery of property to be sent to the owner, with the admonition that the detestable crime of marauding shall be henceforward punished with instant death.— Closing these orders, in so far as I have copied them, is one for the march, requiring that as much sleep and refreshment as possible be taken, that all may be better prepared ; while a general court martial, with Lord Stirling as President, shall sit in Brunswick to-morrow for the trial of General Lee. These but faintly outline the numerous details which this consummate soldier supervised for this march through Jersey, and the battle that ensued. Yet we know that this Commander-in-chief was looking toward the Hudson, and sweeping the horizon with prudent care for all the armies of the Republic. History may dismiss with a few pages these painstaking details by a few generalizations. It has, however, taken note of other less significant facts, which make up the outlines of this famous march and battle.

---

the Victory obtained over the Arms of his British majesty yesterday, and thanks most sincerely the gallant officers and men who distinguished themselves upon the occasion, and such others as by their good order and coolness gave the happiest presages of what might have been expected had they come to action.
General Dickinson and the Militia of this State, are also thanked for the noble spirit which they have shown in opposing the enemy on their march from Philadelphia, and for the aid which they have given by harrassing and impeding their motions so as to allow the Continental troops time to come up with them.
A Party consisting of two hundred men to parade immediately, to bury the slain of both armies: Genl. Woodford's Brigade is to cover this party
The officers of the American Army are to be buried with military honors, due to men who have nobly fought and died in the cause of Liberty and their Country
Doctor Cochran will direct what is to be done with the wounded and sick. He is to apply to the Quartermaster and Adjutant General for necessary assistance. The several detachments (except those under Col. Morgan) are to join their respective Brigades immediately, and the lines to be formed agreeable to the order of the 22nd instant. The army is to march from the left, the second line in front, the cavalry in the rear, the march to begin at five o'clock this afternoon.
A Sergeant, Corporal and twelve men from General Maxwell's Brigade to parade immediately to guard the sick to Princetown Hospitals Doctor Conik will give directions to the guard.
Col. Martin is appointed to superintend collecting the sick and wounded on the Army-route through Jersey between Coryell's and Monmouth and send them to Princetown Hospitals—he will call immediately at the order office for further orders.
It is with peculiar pleasure in addition to the above that the Commander in-Chief can inform General Knox and the officers of Artillery that the enemy have done them the justice to acknowledge that no artillery could be better served than ours.

HEADQUARTERS, ENGLISHTOWN, June 30th, 1778.
The men are to wash themselves this afternoon and appear as clean and decent as possible.
Seven o'clock this evening is appointed that we may publickly unite in thanksgiving to the Supreme Disposer of human events for the victory which was obtained on Sunday over the Flower of the British Troops.
Accurate returns of the killed, wounded and missing in the Battle of Monmouth, are immediately to be made to the Adjutant General's Office.
The troops are to be completed with provisions for to-morrow and have it cooked to-day.
The whole army, except Maxwell's Brigade, is to move at two o'clock to-morrow morning,—and everything is to be in the most perfect readiness to-night.
General Maxwell will apply at Headquarters for particular orders.
Complaint having been made to the Commander-in-Chief that certain persons belonging to the army have seized the property of inhabitants which had been concealed in order to escape the ravages of the enemy. He calls upon the commanding officers of corps to order a strict search of the soldiers packs at parade time, that the offender may be discovered and brought to condign punishment, such articles as may be found agreeable, to a list left at the Adjutant General's, are to be sent to his office that they may be sent to the owners.
The General further gives notice that the detestable crime of marauding, will henceforward be punished with instant death.

HEADQUARTERS, SPOTTSWOOD,
Wednesday, July 1st, 1778.
The General will beat at twelve o'clock, troop at half past twelve and the march begins at one. The troops are in the meantime to take as much sleep and refreshment as possible that they may be the better prepared.
A general Court Martial, whereof Lord Stirling is appointed President, will set in Brunswick to-morrow (the hour and place to be appointed by the President) for the trial of Major General Lee.

OLD TIMES IN OLD MONMOUTH.

Washington made his first dispositions to harass the enemy by detachments.

The slow movements of Clinton induced the belief that he was manoeuvreing for a general action, and Lee was opposed to this. But with Morgan's riflemen on the enemy's right flank, Maxwell's brigade on their left and Scott, with fifteen hundred chosen men on their rear and flanks, the militia of New Jersey under Dickinson, and the Pennsylvania volunteers under Cadwallader,—Clinton was harassed from the time he crossed the Delaware. His long twelve mile train was a target for the militia. The destruction of bridges and causeways rendered his movement tardy. When he reaches Allentown, Lee is placed in command of five thousand as an advance. Clinton encamps in strong position at Monmouth Court House, secure on all sides by woods and marshy grounds.—His line extends on the right a mile and a half beyond the Court House to the parting of the roads leading to Shrewsbury and Middletown; and on the left, along the road from Monmouth to Allentown, about three miles.

To make a brief resume of the situation, it is sufficient to say, that on the 24th the main body of the American army was encamped about five miles from Princeton, and that of the British at Allentown.—Their effective rank and file were not unequal, and at that time it was absolutely determined to bring on the general engagement. Without calling another council. Washington took the responsibility.—On the 26th Lafayette took position on the Monmouth road five miles in the rear of the British camp. The main army was not then sufficiently advanced and his corps was called, on the morning of the 27th, to Englishtown. Lafayette was kindly relieved of his command to gratify Lee and the five thousand troops under Lee encamped at Englishtown, with the main army of Americans three miles in his rear. Clinton meanwhile takes a strong position near Monmouth, seven miles in advance of Lee, with Morgan on his right and Dickinson on the left. The order is given to attack should the British move.

Let it be remembered that Clinton had selected his best troops for his rear—grenadiers, light infantry, and chasseurs. They were commanded by Cornwallis,—albeit familiar with Jersey and her soil and people. Knyphausen with his Hessians and Tories were properly designated to take care of the baggage.

It is impossible to photograph, at this day, the lights and shades of these Monmouth hills, woods, and morasses. The scenery is greatly changed with time.—Scarcely a monument remains as it was, except the meeting-house.

However, the relations I have given was the situation on the night of the 27th.—These constitute the details of the picture, which were marked into definite outline and color the next day. Let it be remembered that the advance detachments were powerially reinforced; that it was understood the British march was a real retreat and not a feint; that orders had been sent to Lee to begin the attack as soon as the British should be in motion. When, therefore, the German troops moved on, at day break on the 28th, Clinton wisely held the rear till near eight o'clock. The rear of the British army descended from the heights of Freehold into the plains below, when behold! the advancing Americans are seen approaching in pursuit. Then Clinton finds it necessary to relieve his baggage, ascend the heights, and attack the enemy. It cannot be denied that his men showed ardor and intrepidity. At this critical moment Washington is moving with his main body, and courier after courier, officer after officer comes to him with information of the inexplicable retreat of the Americans under Lee, which led to the final battle.

To obtain a picturesque view of the scene, one should look down upon the contest from a heighth, where the diversity of detail may be grouped in the unity of another Art than that of speaking or even photographing.

It is a Sabbath morning, calm and cloudless. The leafy month of June covers the hills and valleys with the garniture of green. The heat is intense, the thermometer at 96° in the shade. A more sultry day never glowed with the fervor of the summer solstice. The arrows of Apollo wound more than the bayonet or sabre.—The British are dressed in their woollens and suffer more than the thinly clad Americans. The army are aweary with the long march over the deep sand and in the heavy rains. The Sabbath quietude is at length broken, not by the song of birds, or the voices of nature, but by the "long roll" of the various camps. The bugles begin their blare—signals for the arousal and departure of the van under Knyphausen. You may see his men mounting their horses or buckling on their knapsacks and grasping their muskets; while the motley crowd of followers and refugees crowd after the moving train of baggage wagons. The noise of teamsters, the commands of officers and clank of sabres fill the air around the British camp; while in groups, the officers stand, and in hot haste aides and orderlies come and go. The ear takes in the confused sounds of the British camp; but there is an earnest silence among the Americans. The eye perceives the quiet movement of the battalions and regiments; there is a picking of flints, a cleaning of guns and a stealthy movement of aids, when, hark to a fresh murmur and stir among the Americans!— They become alert! Clinton is moving upon them! There can be no doubt of it.— The Hessians are on their march in one direction with the baggage, but Clinton moves in another direction toward them! So quickly is it done that the eye has scarcely caught the red cap, green coat, brown breeches and red boots of the Germans, before they are dimmed by distance. Still on yonder flank are our riflemen, in green uniform, red sash and skin cap, tufted with feathers. Here and there are groups of Americans in anxious council. The cocked hat, blue coat, with buff facings and trousers, plainly indicate the provincial officers, while around them are the patriot soldiers in blanket coats, buckskin breeches and rustic wamusses. The note of preparation is hushed. All wait on Lee's orders.— Dickinson reconnoitres the enemy on the hill and exchanges fire. Lafayette arrives and with Maxwell's light horse dashes into the plain. Then the British dragoons charge. Look! Two cavalry regiments dash from Clinton's lines towards Lee.— Along with them are the grenadiers, in their bear-skin caps, the guards in red coats, and the kilted Highlanders! Lee is confused. Is the whole British army upon him? Lafayette sends hurriedly to Washington. Washington himself appears upon his " fine, large sorrel " charger,* surrounded by his staff. Words follow as hot as the day itself.

"Suspicion flashed across his mind," says IRVING, "of wrongheaded conduct on the part of LEE, to mar the plan of attack adopted contrary to his counsels." When he beholds LEE approaching with his command in retreat, he sternly de-

*See Col. Willetts' Narrative, Pub. N. Y. 1831, by G. & C. H. Carville. It is generally thought that Washington rode his familiar white horse on that day. This is a mistake, as Col. Willetts' narrative shows.

mands its meaning: LEE is disconcerted. WASHINGTON'S aspect is terrible. "I desire to know the meaning of this!" he exclaims. Some excuse is rendered; a disdainful reply from WASHINGTON; some flashes of anger from our demi-god of the Revolution—an oath, it may be, for there are occasions when common language fails. There is little time for parley. LEE is ordered to the rear. The retreat must be retrieved. The routed troops form. Batteries are stationed. Even LEE is called again in command to check the enemy. The cannonading begins. The enemy halts. WASHINGTON gallops to the main body, forms a secure position, placing STIRLING on the left, and GREENE on the right. The artillery serves its batteries with stupendous effect. KNOX is there —the chief of artillerists of the Union. He enfilades whole platoons by one shot. This is on the enemy's left wing. His fire is continued and kept up on the enemy's centre. STIRLING'S guns give back from the left their thunder in response to Greene's batteries! Grenadier and guard fall back. They return. Then "Mad Anthony" meets them with his fine soldiery frenzy and the slaughter is renewed. (Cheers.) Monckton falls, and our standards are planted on the field. Night closes the scene. Evening fell upon the uncompleted victory, and Washington lay upon his cloak amid his soldiers, taking with them the rest so needed after the fatigue and heat of the day. Call this a partial or full victory, or call it otherwise, the morning's sun revealed no enemy in sight. (Cheers.) They had hurried off. Silently, they stole away in the night for the secure heights of Middletown. The work of burying began with the morning. This was one more gallant struggle to mark the progress of our fathers toward American Independence.

It is impossible to make a picture of this battle-field under the cloudless, burning sky, of one of the last days of June, without filling it with the portraits of the heroes who achieved the victory. Dickinson, with his Jersey militia, Sterling with his artillery, Steuben with his discipline, Maxwell with his Jerseymen, Morgan with his riflemen, Cadwallader with his brigades, should not be forgotten because overtopped by such Generals as Mercer, Greene, Lafayette, Wayne and Knox, each filling in the after time large places in the American heart. Nathaniel Greene was the source and controller of operations South, which made a part of our empire—Nathaniel Greene—the quartermaster of the army, without whom little could have been achieved, where it was so difficult to obtain provisions for an army. Ever in the saddle upon this march, marking out the route and the encampments, urging the fight, until the battle was over, and not disdaining at the end of the conflict to present the wife of the bold cannoneer, who had so gallantly taken the place of her slaughtered husband. Alas! for the gratitude of Republics! He fills an unknown grave, without a monument.

Nor can we omit the picture of Lafayette—never to be forgotton, while Republican Liberty makes more lustrous his achievements and example in his native France. Anthony Wayne, —as he rises before the fancy in his continental uniform, the image of a broad, active officer, prompt and ready, impatient of restraint, careless of scabbard and eager to attack the enemy, sword in hand. His name is a part of the history of the Republic. He was especially commended to Congress in the dispatches of Washington for good conduct and bravery throughout the whole action. Knox, the bookseller boy of Boston, the skillful artillerist, the friend of Washington and his first Secretary of War, he, too, was here as one of the heroes of Monmouth. How shall the pen of impartial history describe the marplot in these battle-councils and manœuvres? It is enough to drop over the name of Charles Lee the pall of forgetfulness. At this day his attempt to sully the name of Washington seems like the whim of disappointed ambition, or the frenzy of maddened jealousy. But towering above them all, like Jove, "by his great power and looks imperial," is George Washington; best beloved by New Jersey—aye, even more than by Virginia. (Cheers.) The triumphal arch, under which she received him after her institutions were secured by his courage, faintly expressed the lasting love of Jerseymen for this saviour of their State. In other States his prudence was most conspicuous. He was their Fabius—but in New Jersey he was the Cæsar of the contest; skillful, impetuous, daring and successful, illustrating his valor, alacrity, and courage, so as to astonish the zealous, confound the timid, and disarm the criticism of his most malignant foes. (Cheers.)

I have said that a picture is incomplete unless it has a higher design than that which appears upon its surface either in form, delineation, or color. There is an inner meaning to each battle. An English dramatist has said, in speaking of his love for books: " Give me the place that does contain my books, my best companions, where hourly I converse with sages and philosophers, and soldiers too, calling their victories, if unjustly got, to a strict account, and in my fancy, displace their ill-placed statues." It is not, therefore, the mere victory, the numbers killed or wounded, nor the heavy battalions and the thundering artillery which give significance to the battles of mankind. It is for philosophy, aided sometimes by the muses and graces, to give to heroism its true meed of glory and honor; to bestow them upon the vanquished who have contended for peace, security and liberty, although in vain. The iconoclast may not appear for centuries, but the statues which should have no niche, will surely fall before his hand. That which makes human struggle immortal, is the unselfish idea of achieving something for the hereafter, something grand for the children and their children forever. This, and this only, is what ennobles and dignifies the battle fields of our earth.

What, then, is the meaning of this Monmouth battle? Was it not the contest of a people for Liberty and Union? It was said in the aforetime: "Liberty first,—Union afterwards." I say, it should be as our history teaches us,—Liberty for and with Union and Union for and with Liberty!! (Cheers.) Dissociate, never, but hand in hand they move on to establish, protect and defend for ourselves and posterity the rights of mankind. In this was the ideal grandeur of the conflict. This is the divine genius behind the battle picture. In this was the cause commended to all peoples. This was the consummate flower of the Declaration of Independence and the ripe fruitage of the Constitution. Indissoluble as a federation, through the covenants contained in our charter of national, state and individual rights—our nation has sustained itself against the corrosion of time and the shock of embattled armies.

Through this fraternal Union and indissoluble covenant,—a code more perfect than that of Rome and more comprehensive than that of England has been developed and maintained. It is the Supreme law of the land; an altar raised to which may fly for safety the people of this and every other country

Our flag is as typical of this unity of the States, as the constitutional fasces in which they are imbound! On its folds is the streaming blazonry of the original thirteen States, symbolled in its stripes; and the names of each and all are written in the radiant lustre and beauty of a night of stars; while the staff from which our ensign floats, lifts stars and stripes as one—unsullied and high advanced amidst the smoke of battle or the tempest of civil strife! (Cheers.)

While the fields of your State smile with cultivation, or the ocean waves leap in liberty upon your shores; so long as your ministers of justice hold its scales with equal poise, and the spires of your churches point with silent emphasis to God; so long as Washington's name is revered for his military service and his civic wisdom, so long will Monmouth be a vestal flame, watched with unwinking vigilance, upon the patriotic altar of America! (Cheers.)

Under such inspirations, let our future wipe out the wrongs and profligacies of the past, and cast our institutions in a better mold! "Let the new cycle shame the old;" and spread over our spacious plains and grand mountains, from sea to sea. the fairer lustre of a better polity and civilization, instinct with Liberty and Justice.

CONSIDERATION OF THE CASE
OF
MAJOR GENERAL CHARLES LEE,
AT MONMOUTH, JUNE 28, 1878.
From the Monmouth Democrat, August 15th, 1878.

One of the difficulties which attend the study of the Battle of Monmouth is the *unresolved* question as to the conduct of Maj. Gen. Charles Lee. Whether Lee, elsewhere or otherwise, was a traitor to the American cause has nothing to do with the consideration of his conduct at Monmouth. The case must be confined to an investigation of his motives and actions from the time that Washington moved from Valley Forge to pursue Clinton on the 18th of June, 1778, down to the period when Lee was relieved of his command, and a General Court Martial was called upon his conduct on the 1st, 2d, &c., July, 1778. The decision of this Court is very unsatisfactory. *If guilty*, Lee's punishment was altogether too mild for the offenses charged; and if *innocent*, it was totally unjustified. Lee unfortunately placed himself in a false position after the battle by writing—to which he was too prone—although in one of his letters, he intimates a truth, that whoever undertook to collide with Washington would be sure to be condemned whether he was right or wrong, because the majority of the army and of the people had by this time worked themselves up to believe that Washington could not err. (L. P. ii, 479.)

If Lee had been in sympathy with Washington he would have received no censure.

Lee's guilt or innocence can never be set forth clearly until some unprejudiced and careful critic compares the contemporaneous detailed maps and plans, the original reports, correspondence, letters written before and at as well as after the occurrence, evidence, &c., and topographical treatises, and divests himself of all bias either in favor of Washington or against Lee. The finding and sentence of the Court Martial upon Lee demonstrates that he was not nearly as much to blame *as a soldier* as he has been made to appear; nor did all the American troops behave as well as those who had immediately felt, experienced, and proved the effect of Steuben's instructions on the drill ground and carried it into practice on the actual battle field.

It would appear that Lee undertook with discordant elements, to fight in accordance with his own will and mental purpose, and to regulate as to how the battle should develop itself and when and where it should determine. This is something which the greatest generals in the world have not as a rule, been able to do, even with the most thoroughly trained veteran armies, and only can be done with accidents and everything requisite entirely concurring.

This investigation was undertaken with the intention of going into the minutest details of the action, but, after examining the testimony given before the Lee Court Martial, as well as after studying the British, German, and the

American statements of occurrences, the original idea has been abandoned. It is impossible to reconcile the antagonisms; and very often to express an independent opinion involves the inconveniences which induced General Berthezene and many others to postpone the publication of their memoirs until they were safe from the explosion which they expected would result therefrom.

General Greene writes to Sullivan, 23d August, 1778, "that to attack 6,000 regular troops in redoubts, with an expectation of carrying them, would require 15,000 troops of equal or superior quality." Lee, against his own judgment, was sent to engage about 6,500 to 7,000 veteran troops which had no superiors in the world, with equal numbers, partly militia, partly new levies, all green to grand tactics or evolutions of the line, and commanded by officers antagonistic to him in their views. (Compare L. P. iii, 186.)

The result of the operations on the morning of the Monmouth fight completely justifies the opinion of Greene.

Lee undertook an attack upon superior numbers of veterans and soon found his aggressive checked and reversed by the return-offensive of a smaller force than his own.

Bear this in mind; not a single witness at the Lee trial estimates the force of the British actually engaged with the Americans in the morning (L. P. iii, 199, &c.,) as anything like equal to the latter whether under Lee or subsequently. To discover the truth it is necessary to wade through pages of dry testimony but the search will reveal it.

The falling back of the troops, the abandoning of the highly defensible positions to the east and west of the Court House, etc., has all been charged upon Lee.

There is no use here attempting to enter into the discussion of the actions of individuals or the apparent causes of movements.—Certain fixed facts are incontestible, localities, distances, &c. The rare individuals who feel a conviction that Lee has been over severely dealt with will find it really worth their while to examine the proceedings, &c., &c. They will discover more than one explanation of what has been made to seem so heinous and yet may be and is susceptible of the very contrary elucidation.

To attempt to reconcile the American and British reports, the patriot and loyal representations, the testimony recorded in the proceedings of the court martial on Lee, republished among the "Lee Papers," in the N. Y. Historical Society Collections, Vols. II. and III, 1872—1873; the correspondence relating to this event, note books, journals, and published facts, is almost impossible. It is but natural that those who were the most open to censure should seek to throw the blame on Lee, who by his intemperance of procedure prepared himself to be made a scapegoat. To express an honest and adequate judgment on the action of individuals concerned and their faults, would require an independence of thought and of expression which few individuals possess, and a courage which rises superior to policy.

The testimony on the Lee trial, and in fact the whole evidence in regard to the battle, of all kinds, and on both sides, are often irreconcilable either with each other, or with maps, with results, with the observation of experience and with any fair estimate of personal character.

Throughout a series of articles in regard to the Revolutionary Campaigns in the Jerseys, constant efforts have been made to impress upon the reader's mind that it is impossible to judge of the character of the country fought over, from any examination of it in its present condition and aspect. One hundred years ago there were dense woods where there are now mere holts, extensive marshes, and vast thickets, which are now arable land; ugly streams which have left scarcely any traces of their channels, and wastes of brambles and alders, which are now smiling fields, metamorphosed by cultivation and the labors through a century of a dense and denser population. The very physical condition of Monmouth county at the period of the Revolution may account for Lee's not being able to follow, direct and combine, the movements of his morning command.

Lee was no traitor to the Americans on this, the 28th of June, 1778. At Monmouth, he was simply unequal to the situation. His own plan was excellent.

This his plan, was exactly that of Barclay de Tolly for the Russians against Napoleon in 1812. "He was desirous while apparently inviting attack, of falling back before the enemy, with his own force entire; well furnished with supplies and continually strengthened by supports, Barclay de Tolly hoped thus to allure the assailants on, upon a path where every step in advance was a loss to them of men, horses, and material, until their gradual wasting away, and his increase restored the equality of numbers and gave them an opportunity of fighting upon equal terms."

Such is their similarity that this exposition by Sir Robert Wilson seems nothing more than a paraphrase or explanation of Lee's conception of what he intended to do at Monmouth.

Nevertheless Lee set out to execute a plan to which his experienced judgment was opposed. He assumed command under the most disadvantageous circumstances; his subordinates were as a rule strangers to him—and it is to be feared, prejudiced against him. La-

Fayette, whom he superseded, continued with him as a volunteer, and exercised an influence injurious to Lee's intended development of the affair. La Fayette, of whom General Greene remarked : " The Marquis's great thirst for glory and national attachment often run him into errors." Wayne, again, was not a proper instrument, or rather piece of machinery for the execution of such a project as that of Lee. Wayne was always spoiling for a fight under any circumstances. His constitutional battle fever was too ardent to render him a reliable subordinate in a delicate operation which depended much more upon calm manoeuvring without fighting, than upon hot fighting. (L P. iii, 96-'7.)

As Lee justly observed on his trial, he did not have positive orders to bring on a battle. His orders to attack decidedly were not peremptory. His instructions gave him great latitude to exercise his judgment, and in degree were simply advisory. (L. P. iii, 175.) As he remarked to his aide-de-camp, Captain Mercer, he was in a shocking condition, as he hardly knew a single man or officer under his command or his rank. (L. P. iii, 119.) Lee, moreover, had no maps, no information, no personal knowledge of the country and no reliable guides. (L. P. iii, 177-'8.)

Consequently, as he again emphasised, if the country is unreconnoitered, and the force, disposition, and situation of the enemy doubtful, I must profess that I cannot persuade myself that a precise plan can be attended with any good consequences, but that it must distract, lead astray, and in effect, be ruinous.— The writer made just such an observation in 1861, to one of our most distinguished Major Generals who called upon him for a plan, and the latter acknowledged the absolute correctness of the reply. Moreover, worst of all for Lee, when the firing began he did not happen to be in the proper place to develop the action—the extreme central front, whence he could observe everything, direct, or lead everything.

Nevertheless, whether Lee was or was not in his proper place has nothing to do with the question of his being a traitor, it simply affects his personal ability.

While Lee was forming his first line of battle, the British Cavalry the Queen's Light Dragoons, were deploying to charge. At this juncture La Fayette, young, ardent, inexperienced, was desirous, it is said, of permission to turn the enemy. Lee refused "You do not know British soldiers" he remarked, " we can not stand against them, we shall certainly be driven back at *first*, and we must be *cautious.*"

Mark these words "*at first*" and "*cautious.*" They are both the expression of discretion and observation. No sensible man can put an evil construction upon them. The young French Marquis thereupon replied : "It may be so, General, but British soldiers have been beaten and may be beaten again." Yes, they might be beaten by Americans and have been, but they have never been worsted *but in one* great battle by La Fayette's countrymen, and then under the most exceptional circumstances.

Now in regard to the panic among these troops, a great many works have been examined and all agree, in degree, as to their condition either directly or by implication. Stedman, who was on the field with Cornwallis, says " that Lee's troops fled on all sides, and that Washington probably saved his advance corps from total ruin " Gordon, the great American historian, states that " Washington was exceedingly alarmed at what he saw when he came up." Dawson says "they fell back * * in great confusion." Botta, (ii, 134) speaks of "the retreat or rather flight." Laurens wrote " Washington met the troops retreating and in disorder," (L. P. ii, 433.)— Tomes, (iv. 123) a very conscientious writer, uses the terms "full retreat," " British were rapidly pressing forward in pursuit of the fugitives "

Washington stigmatizes these retreats as "disorder and confusion." Cust, a very fair man, speaks of "rout" when American writers say "repulse." One fact is susceptible of only a single explanation : Steuben, (Kapp, 162-163), says, that he saw Lee's division " retreating in great disorder," and that he assembled part of General Maxwell's Brigade and part of General Scott's detachment, and formed them behind the creek at Englishtown. Now, from the spot where Maxwell and Scott deployed for action, about 10 A. M , to Englishtown, according to Barber's plan and scale, without considering the sinuosities of the road, is between six and seven miles — According to Carrington's plan and scale, over 5 miles in an air line. Steuben does not mention the hour, but it must have been early in the afternoon. Sifting out all the evidence, the battle was regulated by heat and fatigue, and not by firearms.

Major Ogden is credited with the justest expression of all ; " By ——, they (the Americans) are flying from a shadow."

Colonels and Generals are reported as appearing with broken commands. There was a panic for a time or something very like it. " Those that have often been in action," writes Greene, on the 6th September, 1778, " can only judge what is to be expected of good, bad, and indifferent troops *Men are often struck with panics* and they are generally subject to that passion in a greater or lesser degree, according as the force of discipline has formed the mind by *habit*, to meet danger and death."

Lossing mentions "a panic among the American troops, and they fled in great confusion."

In extenuation Carrington (424) observes that "some of these troops, first engaged, were new and in want of cartouch boxes," &c., &c.

According to von Eelking, the British attack, principally with the bayonet, was so impetuous tl at the enemy [Americans] were quickly put to flight."

Now, if Lee's troops were affected by a panic, was Lee responsible for this ; if they retreated in disorder, was it not rather the fault of their immediate Brigadiers and Colonels than of the General of Division Chief-in-command.

To render Lee responsible it must be proved that Lee himself was demoralized and the preponderance of the testimony shows that he was not. On the contrary it appears that he was brave, self-possessed, judicious and competent to comprehend the situation and if duly supported provide a remedy.

In all that occurred there is nothing to show that Lee was false to his trust, to the Colonies, or to his superior ; nothing to prove that he presented any indications of incapacity or cowardice.

Washington's popularity, Lee's own impolitic virulence, public clamor, and personal prejudices condemned Lee He could make himself intensely disagreeable at times and in this connection he succeeding in outdoing himself.

Lee was an excellent professional soldier.— Considering Monmouth, according to circumstances within all ordinary human calculations, he judged correctly that no decided success could reward an attack upon Clinton— that is success from a military point of view. He was not sufficiently American perhaps to consider the matter from a political or a popular standpoint as Washington did. Attacking against his better judgment, he engaged about 6,500 veterans and the veterans were mostly English troops which have never been defeated, standing on the defensive, except by Anglo-Saxons, from Hastings to Inkerman.

Moreover the British light Infantry at this time were unsurpassed and unsurpassable.— Wayne—a host in himself—it is true was there with 700 to 1,000 excellent troops. Still even American vanity cannot suppose that such a comparatively small number in the days of flint-locks, smoothbores and short ranges could hold their own, one against three, when the best of infantry were backed by excellent Cavalry and Artillery.

Lee it is true fought in violation of the first rule of grand tactics. This, however, was a professional error, not treason or cowardice.— He engaged contrary to his own professional experience, he fought fractions against a unit. He was defeated as he expected to be and as he had reason to believe that he would be, but he was beaten in obedience to orders. Washington appeared at the exact point when the ground favored the defensive. He brought up forces " fresh and unfatigued" (L P iii 260) which converted the one to three, into numerically three to two, physically six to two.

No one has ever questioned Washington's superlative influence and his own was buttressed by that of Steuben. Washington exposed himself recklessly, more so than commanding generals are expected to do, and as they seldom do. Nevertheless he did not deem it it necessary or proper to deprive Lee of his command and Lee at the crisis displayed great abilities. Lee had been desirous to draw the British into a trap from which worn out and fought out they had no escape. This nearly occurred. Let justice be done to a man however criminal in any other respects. He did all that a man could to redeem himself and fortunately he was wonderfully assisted by Steuben's vigorous discipline.

Botta the Italian historian of the American War ii. xi. 137 passed a capital judgment upon this incident of the Revolution:

" Lee was arrested and brought before a Court Martial to make answer to the three following charges ; for dis obedience in not attacking the enemy on the 28th June, agreeably to his instructions ; for having made an unnecessary, disorderly and shameful retreat ; and for disrespect to the commander-in-chief in his two letters.— He defended himself with great ingenuity and with a sor. of eloquence, so that impartial and military men remained in doubt whether he was really culpable or not. Nevertheless the Court Martial found him guilty of all the charges bating the epithet of "Shameful," which was expunged, and *sentenced him to be suspended for one year. a judgment certainly either too mild if Lee was guilty, or too severe if innocent.* This a dair occasioned much conversation, some approving, others blaming the sentence. The Congress, *though with some hesitation*, confirmed it.

The fact is Maj. Gen. Lee has been so consistently abused that in these days to lift up a voice to excuse or even to endeavor to diminish the odium cast upon him, is almost considered in the light of a collusion with the crime imputed to him.

Under these circumstances and in this world where it is regarded excusable if not justifiable to join the " hue and cry," and to trample upon the fallen, it is pleasant to come suddenly upon a few clear sentences in vindication of the helpless.

Charles Smith, in his rare work " The American War from 1775 to 1783," N. Y., Printed for C Smith, Bookseller and Publisher, No.

51 Maiden Lane, 1797*, appends the following criticism as a note to page 72 in connection with his narrative of the Battle of Monmouth. This note reads thus:

"The conduct of General Lee on this day, which was so severely arraigned by the Americans, was worthy of applause. He had been betrayed across some narrow passes of a marsh, by the persuasion that he had to deal with a rear guard of only two or three battalions, when he suddenly perceived 6,000 men forming to receive him. He retired with such quickness and decision, though not attacked, that he repassed the marsh before the British line was in readiness to move. Had he, in expectation of support, maintained his ground on the plain, until the enemy had attacked him, he must have been overpowered, and would not have had any retreat."

That Lee bore himself on the field bravely and with self possession, there is not the slightest question. Examine the records of the trial. Colonel Stewart (L. P. iii. 42) testifies as to his care to care to protect the men against the overpowering heat. Colonel Hamilton (Ibid, 62) to his personal intrepidity. Colonel Mead (Ibid 64) as to the distinctness and clearness of his method of expressing himself. Colonel William Smith, (Ibid 86) himself a very gallant fellow, corroborates Meade with "perfectly so." General Maxwell (Ibid, 94) goes into an explanation and then adds that "all that appeared to disturb Lee was the situation of the men from the heat of the day." Captain Mercer (Ibid, 114) considered him "exceedingly composed." Lt. Col. Only (Ibid, 128) says "he never saw an officer in action to possess or exhibit more coolness and calmness." Lieut. Col. Oswald (Ibid. 137) one of the bravest of the brave, who made the brilliant artillery charge, not only excuses Lee, but says "that the general was in as great danger as his own pieces," and that he "appeared calm and intrepid and seemed fully self-possessed through the whole process of the day, and upon all occasions." Lt. Col Brooks, (Ibid, 151) Lee's Adjutant General, testified, "You appeared through the whole course of the day to be as cool and deliberate, and thoroughly to possess yourself, as I can have any idea of" General Knox, (Ibid, 158) who was one of Washington's personal friends and favorites, is the strongest witness to Lee's high professional conduct, his perfect comprehension of the ground and concluded by saying "I thought you (Lee) perfectly master of yourself; the circumstances of pointing out the knoll," [on which the most important battery was posted.] "I thought a very good proof of it, though not the only one." Peter Wikoff, (Ibid 172-3) a sort of guide, showed Lee Combs' Hill on which the six pieces which decided the day were afterward posted. He

*[Here let it be remarked that a bookdealer of peculiar acuteness, in his search for old works which would command high prices, stated that he had never seen a copy of this Charles Smith's History.]

swore that Lee "approved of the position and begged me to lead his troops on and show them the place, which I did. The eminence was the very piece of ground His Excellency, General Washington afterwards formed his army on. But previous to General Lee sending any troops to the last mentioned place, he threw a number of troops into a skirt of the woods on the right of the enemy and on the left, where Colonels Stewart and Ramsey first formed their regiments, and where, as I believe, the first heavy fire of musketry began."

So much for the testimony before the Court Martial, although many more pertinent extracts might have been made.

Washington met Lee at the most unfortunate moment for the latter. George Washington Greene, in the Life of his Grandfather, Maj. Gen. Nathaniel Greene, (i 94) remarks: "It is well known though not generally acknowledged, that Washington had a very quick temper, and was often led to sudden and violent manifestations of it. Few of those who lived on an intimate footing with him were with him long without witnessing, even when they did not draw it upon themselves, some hasty expression of his irritation; and the more thoughtful of them, adopted for themselves from the beginning a method of dealing with it, suited to their individual character and position." It is not politic to pursue this subject.

Washington was a miracle of common sense, but still he was only a mortal and subject to like passions with other men.

There is quite an interesting anecdote in this connection in Mason's " Newport Illustrated" (37), which shows that he did not exalt himself as modern writers have striven to transcendentalize nim.

When Washington visited Newport in 1780 to confer with Rochambeau, there was a public reception and procession. "A little boy had heard so much of Washington that he conceived a strong desire to see him. His father, to gratify his wish, lifted him in his arms and approached an open window, near which Washington stood, whom he pointed out. The child was amazed, and exclaimed aloud: Why, father, General Washington is a man!", It reached the ear of the hero, who turned 'round and said as he patted the boy on the head: "Yes, my lad, *and nothing but a man.*"

All histories concur in representing that Washington accosted Lee with great severity, without waiting for any explanation of the condition of things which in themselves justified uneasiness and even indignation.— Still, his warmest admirers must admit that he spoke unadvisedly unless he was assured that the disorder which excited his wrath was attributable directly to Lee, because it was not possible for any one to have arrived at this conclusion intuitively, under the circumstances.

Major Ogden expressed the truth in a few words, "By God! they (the Americans) *are flying from a shadow.*"

No good can result from a discussion of whether the Americans were "routed," or "flying," or "abandoning position after position," under the influence of a "panic." There is no doubt that they were retreating in disorder. Conceding that Lee was an unprincipled man, there is no proof at any moment of this battle, that he showed himself a traitor or that he "misbehaved himself in the presence of the enemy."

On the authority of General LaFayette, who gave it on the piazza of the residence of Vice President, Daniel B. Tompkins, Sunday Morning, August 15th, 1824; General Washington closed the interview (on the field) with calling General Lee "a damned poltroon."

This statement of LaFayette is reported by G. W. P. Custis in his "Recollections" page 218, who says, moreover, that Brigadier General Charles Scott declared that Washington "swore on that occasion until the leaves shook on the trees, charming, delightfully." Custis also reports "Captain Thomas Washington, who commanded the leading platoon of General Grayson's troops, as saying, that when Lee observed to Washington that his (Lee's) troops were not able to meet British Grenadiers, Washington, much excited, replied "By God, they should do it."

* * * * * * *

Let Lee be charged with every crime under heaven, still there never was the slightest indication of his being a physical coward. Besides being personally a brave man, he (as repeatedly remarked for *emphasis*) was a fair, experienced, professional soldier. Weems, referring to this meeting, tones down Washington's language. He says Washington asked with great warmth "what's the cause of this ill timed prudence," and that Lee, quite convulsed with rage, replied: "No man sir can boast a larger portion of that rascally virtue than Your Excellency." Fancy such words were uttered, they were nothing more than the expression, under an access of fury, of the covert sneers of Jefferson (G. W. P. C. 213), the Adamses and others in referring to Washington's Fabian, or delaying, policy which saved the country.

Under the excitement of the moment, Lee may have given way to his temper and made a most insulting answer to his superior, but this is no evidence of want of courage or of military ability. Had he been a poltroon, he would have cowed before the reproof of his superior and slunk away.

With these preliminary reflections let us consider the theory now advanced in regard to this conflict.

Lee, likewise the majority, of the American Generals were opposed to bringing on an action.

Professional pride urged Charles Lee, when an attack was ordered, by Washington, to assert his right as Senior Major General to the command at first confided to LaFayette.— His dispositions, when first he set out to attack Clinton, were by no means deficient. He appears to have intended, in case he could not alarm and disorder the British at once, by threatening their baggage, by flanking, or turning manoeuvres, as well as by direct attacks,—to feign a retreat, fall back gradually and orderly, entice the enemy to follow him, draw them on and away from their supports, weary them out and finally, when enfeebled by fighting and marching under the terriffic heat, by thirst, by their very cumbrous equipments and heavy clothing,—when they were exhausted, physically, and equally so in ammunition, to make a stand on the very spot where Washington finally drew up his main army and overwhelmed the exhausted enemy with "fresh and unfatigued troops."

This is Lee's explanation of his plan. It is very plausible that—as an old soldier—he knew enough to devise it. He wanted to draw the British through and across obstacle after obstacle, until they had to break as a wave bursts against a breakwater—the eligible positions, absolutely indicated beforehand by Lee, as testified by Knox and sworn to by Wykoff, exactly the eminence whereon Washington posted his "fresh and unfatigued" troops Knox and Wykoff the latter in a different way, certified to this. Thus the English, exhausted in every sense of the word, were to be caught, as Napoleon expressed it, "*en flagrant delit.*" It was to the misunderstanding of his orders and to the faults of others, that he attributes the failure of an excellent plan, which required officers more experienced in evolutions of the line and troops more accustomed to deadly or close fire than those which he commanded, to insure its faithful execution.

Let us see how Lee was obeyed. Not to quote too extensively, one example will suffice. It is conceded that Gordon is the most reliable American authority. He shall be the Cæsar to whom this article will appeal.

While Lee was reconnoitring, say 10 A. M., the British advanced towards the right of Lee's development.

"The American column to the left of him under General Scott, quitted the woods, crossed a morass, and formed in the plain field about a hundred yards in front of Maxwell who expected an opportunity to form his

OLD TIMES IN OLD MONMOUTH. 49

brigade, by Scott's moving to the right as there was a vacancy between the latter and the troops with Lee.— These were at that moment moving to the right and every step they gained came nearer to the royal forces, who were also pushing to the right of the Americans. Lee's discernment led him immediately to send off one of his aids, with orders to Scott, whom he supposed to be in the wood on the other side of the morass, to halt his column in the wood, and continue there till further orders; that there might be no possible misconception, another aid was speedily dispatched with similar orders. Before these could be delivered, Scott had mistaken the movements on his right for a retreat; and apprehended danger to his own column in case of its remaining where he was, notwithstanding his detachment, and Maxwell's brigade with the other troops to the left made *full two-thirds of Lee's whole command*, and though the enemy appeared to bend their course from the left to the right of the Americans. Under such apprehension, Scott recrossed the morass, re-entered the wood, and retreated: Maxwell and the others did the like of course. When the first aid reached that part of the wood to which he had been directed, and found that Scott had marched off the ground, he rode back; while returning he met the second aid, and acquainted him with what had taken place: upon their coming to Lee and communicating their information, the general discovered much surprise and expressed his disapprobation of Scott's conduct in strong terms; but immediately upon the intelligence, directed a light-horse officer to carry orders to the Marquis de La Fayette to retreat to the Court-House. A general retreat now commenced on the right till the troops reached Freehold and a neighboring wood. When these were quitted the British pursued as far *as the Village where they halted."—Gordon's American Revolution, Vol. III, p,* 143-4.

Does this throw the slightest blame upon Lee for the disorder? Does it not prove how badly he was seconded and obeyed.

* * * * * * * *

The position which Lee selected beforehand for the final stand was an admirable one ; on a range of heights, sloping like a glacis to Wemrock brook and a marsh, " the west ravine," the last representing a difficult wet ditch. The approaches to this ditch and glacis could be enfiladed from the very height on which Green, or Steuben, or Plessis Mauduit posted the batteries which decided the repulse of the British.

To make an orderly retreat in the face of an audacious enemy, is one of the most ticklish operations in war. To make it with new troops, however brave, under commanders likewise new to their trade—like LaFayette—however gallant, is to tempt the very forbearance of fortune. To make it in a broken country and amid woods, marshes, and the most trying diversities of ground, would have tasked a Frederic and his perfect military machines constructed and worked under a discipline of fire and of iron.

It has been observed that even Washington could not command as a Ferdinand of Brunswick, but had almost to disguise his *orders* under the form of *requests*. (Ctn, 422.) If Washington was compelled to use policy how much more compulsory was such a course to Lee.

Lee failed to grasp the situation and equally failed in observing the *suaviter in modo* however er *fortiter in re.*

The retreat which he intended as a feint, through the inevitable circumstances of the situation, degenerated into whatever it may please our people to style it—" disorder," " flight," " panic," " rout," all of which terms are used by different American writers. In the midst of this Washington arrived.—He saw what he supposed defeat imminent. He regarded Lee as the guilty cause—most likely Lee was already prejudged—and believed that it was necessary for himself to assume the task of arresting disorder, disaster, and decided defeat.

Notwithstanding, he did not remove Lee from the command. Lee's troops appeared to be disordered but not Lee himself. The latter fact was clearly established before the Court Martial.

Washington did not immediately relieve Lee of his command and it was Lee who made the dispositions which first checked, if they did not completely arrest and repulse the British,

With *this* and these facts before us, is there no possibility in the theory hereon advanced, viz: that Lee failed from inability to make the most of defective or inefficient material, both of which Washimgton could render available. This reduces the matter simply to the fact that Washington was, as Hamilton expressed it, a " MASTER WORKMAN " (L. P. 11, 470), and a better general than Lee, which nobody will deny.

Washington appeared, converted chaos into order, and achieved whatever was accomplished toward a happy result.

This fact is undeniable. But if Lee's intentions had been carried out, might not the result have been at least equally satisfactorily, if not immensely more important.

This whole Lee problem is now insoluble. Lee's intemperance of reply and subsequent conduct rendered it insoluble at the time and after events, intensified by passion and prejudice, have rendered it unsusceptible of solution for all time.

Who, now living, has the right of judgment to stand forth, without a full examination of the complete evidence, and accuse Lee of want of competency and of integrity at Monmouth ?

Reflect upon this !

Is it reasonable to suppose that Washington after he met Lee would have left the latter for a moment in command if he had considered him in the faintest degree in the light of a traitor to his military duties or regarded him as a man deficient in ability or wanting in manhood ?

As Lee intimated, such was Washington's

influence and popularity it is unquestionable that if any one even the stainless Schuyler, had come into absolute collision with him, the result would most likely have been the same as it was in the case of Charles Lee.

Colonel Carrington sums the matter up concisely and with justice, p. 445. "If he (Lee) had been in sympathy with Washington, he would have received no censure. If he had exercised reasonable self-control at the close of the action, he would have saved his commission. He contended indeed with many difficulties. He " knew few of the officers," the country was unknown, the guides were few and his staff seem to have been inefficient even in executing his restricted orders, but he had earnestly solicited the command and thus fatally closed his military career at Monmouth.

Summing up : Lee was not a traitor nor a betrayer in any sense of the word. He was not a coward nor deficient in any single simple soldierly quality. He was the victim of circumstances. Through pride of place he sought a command which involved the execution of a military operation which his judgment condemned. Nevertheless his orders while *apparently* imperative were certainly sufficiently conditional or discretionary so as to allow the exercise of his judgment. He undertook to accomplish one of the finest pieces of work in the Art and Science of War, a *simulated* retreat in the face of an enterprising enemy, and to do this with inadequate means ; with officers he did not know personally—neither their stations, relative rank, faces, nor professional capacity for movements requiring the precision and impassiveness of clockwork—evolutions of the line under fire—and with a force in which the regiments had no uniforms nor distinguishing colors. Worse than all for Lee his subordinates were in an army in which even Washington had to temper his own imperative directions into something resembling pressing request. Lee also allowed LaFayette, (his equal in rank) whom he had superseded, to remain with him as a volunteer —the inexperienced LaFayette—the Major General of 21 years of age—the soldier of less than a year's practice.

Another prominent subordinate was Wayne, who, although the most proper man for a fight was the least so when a fight was to be avoided, especially when opposed to Cornwallis, of whom Schlosser justly remarks that " he never hesitated a moment to accept a battle when the opportunity was given him."

Lee planned admirably but his execution, through no fault of his own, was execrable. The magic power to make the Americans beat the British Guards, Grenadiers, and Light Infantry at Monmouth, lay in Washington alone : Lee did not possess it. The only fault to be found with him is that knowing the insufficiency of the material of which the American army was, as a whole, composed—for fine work not mere fighting—he sought the command of the vanguard on such a day as this, the political as well as military field of decision —Monmouth. He knowingly undertook the great risk of performing an important military operation with troops unequal to the task. He placed his neck under the guillotine to see how it worked and Fate touched the spring—the blade fell and chopped his head off.

(ANCHOR.) J. W. De P.

Representatives of Monmouth County.

From the Monmouth Democrat, September 5, 1878.

IN THE PROVINCIAL ASSEMBLY.

I, 1703.—Obadiah Bowne, Jedadiah Allen, Michael Howden, Peter Van Este, John Reid, John Harrison, Cornelius Tunison and Richard Hartshorne.

II, 1704.—Capt. John Bowne, Richard Hartshorne, Richard Salter, Obadiah Bowne, Anthony Woodward, John Tunison, John Lawrence, Jasper Crane, Peter Van Este, Thos. Gordon, John Barclay, John Royse.

III, 1707.—John Harrison, Lewis Morris, Elisha Parker, Tho. Farmer, Jasper Crane, Dan'l Price, John Bowne, Wm. Lawrence, Wm. Morris, and Enoch Mackelson.

IV, 1708.—Gershom Mott, Elisha Lawrence.
V, 1709.—Gershom Mott, Elisha Lawrence.
VI, 1710.—Gershom Mott, William Lawrence.
VII, 1716.—William Lawrence, Elisha Lawrence.
VIII, 1721—William Lawrence, Gerrit Scanck.
IX, 1727.—John Eaton, James Grover.
X, 1732.—John Eaton, James Grover.
XI, 1738.—John Eaton, Cornelius Van Der Veer.
XII, 1740.—John Eaton, Cornelius Van Der Veer.
XIII, 1743.—John Eaton, Robert Lawrence.
XIV, 1744.—John Eaton, Robert Lawrence.
XV, 1745.—John Eaton, Robert Lawrence.
XVI, 1746.—John Eaton, Robert Lawrence, (speaker).
XVII, 1749.—John Eaton, Robert Lawrence.
XVIII, 1751.—Robert Lawrence, (speaker), James Holmes.*
XIX, 1754.—Robert Lawrence, James Holmes.
XX, 1761.—James Holmes, Richard Lawrence.
XXI, 1769.—Robert Hartshorne, Edward Taylor.
XXII, 1772.—Edward Taylor, Richard Lawrence.

IN THE LEGISLATIVE COUNCIL.

1776.—Nathaniel Scudder.
1777.—Joseph Holmes.
'78 '79 do
1780.—Elisha Lawrence.
'81, '82, '83. do.
1784.—John Imlay.
1785.—David Forman.
1786.—Asher Holmes.
'87, '88. do
1789.—Elisha Lawrence (Vice President).
'90, '91, '92. do do
1793.—Thomas Henderson, (Vice President).
1794.—Thomas Henderson, (Vice President).
1795.—Elisha Lawrence, (Vice President).
1796.—Elisha Walton.
'97, '98. do
1800.—John Lloyd.
1801.—Thomas Little.
1808.—William Lloyd.
1810.—James Schureman.
1811.—Silas Crane.
1812.—James Schureman.
1814.—Silas Crane.
1822.—William Andrews.
1823.—William J. Bowne.
1825.—William I. Emley.
1826.—Henry D. Polhemus.
1828.—William I. Emley.
1830.—Samuel G. Wright.
1831.—Jehu Patterson.
1832.—Daniel Holmes.
1835.—Thomas Arrowsmith.
1837 —William L. Dayton.
1838.—Benjamin Oliphant.
1840.—Peter Vredenburgh, Jr.
1841.—James Patterson, (Vice Pres't 1843-4.)

---

* James Holmes of Monmouth, and James Wetherill, of Middlesex, were expelled at a session held at Elizabethtown, March 31st, 1757, for " having left this House, after being requested by the members to stay, as without their assistance the public business would be retarded." A warrant was issued for a new election, and they were again returned, and appeared and took their seats on the 25th of May, following.

52   OLD TIMES IN OLD MONMOUTH.

IN THE STATE SENATE.
Under the Constitution of 1844.
1845.—Thomas E. Combs.*
1846.—George F. Fort.
1849.—John A. Morford.
1852.—William D. Davis.
1855.—Robert Laird.
1858.—William H. Hendrickson.
1861.—Anthony Reckless.
1864.—Henry S. Little.
1867.—Henry S. Little.
1870.—Henry S. Little.
1872.—William H. Conover, Jr.†
1873.—William H. Hendrickson.
1876.—William H. Hendrickson.

IN THE GENERAL ASSEMBLY.
Under the Constitution adopted July 3, 1776.
1776, John Covenhoven, Joseph Holmes, Jr., James Mott, Jr.
1777, James Mott, Jr., Peter Schenck, Hendrick Smock.
1778, James Mott, Jr., Peter Schenck, Hendrick Smock.
1779, James Mott, Jr., Hendrick Smock, Thomas Seabrook.
1780, Thomas Seabrook, Nathaniel Scudder, Thomas Henderson.
1781, Thomas Seabrook, Thomas Henderson, John Covenhoven.
1782, Thomas Henderson, John Covenhoven, Daniel Hendrickson.
1783, Thomas Henderson, Daniel Hendrickson, Peter Covenhoven.
1784, Thomas Henderson, Daniel Hendrickson§, Elisha Walton.
1785, Daniel Hendrickson, Elisha Walton¶,

* Under the new constitution, the first Senate was divided into three classes of one-third each, their seats to be vacated at the expiration of one, two and three years, respectively, so that one-third of the members should thereafter be elected every year. Mr. Combs drew his lot in the first class, and retired after one year's service.
† To fill the unexpired term of Mr. Little, who vacated the office by accepting the appointment of Clerk in Chancery.
§ Speaker.
¶ Oct. 26, 1785. Charles Gordon, John [Covenhoven, and others presented a petition to the Assembly for leave to set forth certain illegal proceedings held at the late annual election in Monmouth. Subsequently the Assembly resolved : " That the election of Messrs. Walton, Hendrickson and Henderson was illegal, and that the same thereupon be void." Also resolved, "That in the opinion of this House the late annual election in the county of Monmouth was illegal as well in the choice of a Sheriff as of the members of this House, and no Coroners having been chosen at said election, and doubts arising whether there is any other officer in said county to whom a writ for a new election can be properly directed, a law ought to be passed for a new election in said county." On the same day a petition was read praying for a division of the county and that a new county be set off. Subsequently a bill was introduced and passed for a new election. At the second session, on 26 February, 1786, Elisha Walton and Joseph Stillwell presented a certificate of election, and were admitted. The same day a petition was presented from citizens of Monmouth asking for a law enabling them to vote by ballot, and recommending a general law to apply to the whole State, for the same purpose. On the 17th Peter Schenck appeared and took his seat.

(Thomas Henderson did not claim his seat).
1786, Elisha Walton, Joseph Stillwell, Peter Schenck.
1787, Joseph Stillwell, Thomas Little, James Rogers.
1788, '89, Joseph Stillwell, Thomas Little, James Rogers.
1790, Joseph Stillwell, Thomas Little, John Imlay.
1791, Joseph Stillwell, Thomas Little, John Imlay.
1792, Joseph Stillwell, Thomas Little, John Covenhoven.
1793, Joseph Stillwell, Thomas Little, James H. Imlay.
1794, Joseph Stillwell, James H. Imlay, Elisha Walton.
1795, Joseph Stillwell, James H. Imlay, Elisha Walton.
1796, Joseph Stillwell, James H. Imlay, (speaker,) William Wickoff.
1797, Joseph Stillwell, Robert Montgomery, William Lloyd.
1798, Joseph Stillwell, William Lloyd, Jonathan Forman.‡
1799, Joseph Stillwell, William Lloyd, Edward Taylor.
1800, Joseph Stillwell, William Lloyd, David Gordon.
1801, John A. Scudder, Peter Knott, James Cox.
1802, '3, Jonn A. Scudder, Peter Knott, James Cox.
1804, John A. Scudder, James Cox, Henry Tiebout.
1805, '6, '7, John A. Scudder, James Cox, Henry Tiebout.
1808, Robert Montgomery, Tylee Williams, David Gordon.
1809, Robert Montgomery, Tylee Williams, David Gordon.
1810, Peter Knott, John S. Holmes, Thomas Cox.
1811, John S. Holmes, Thomas Cox, James Anderson.
1812, Tylee Williams, John Stillwell, James Lloyd.
1813, John S. Holmes, Thomas Cox, James Anderson.
1814, John S. Holmes, Thomas Cox, James Anderson.
1815, George Holcombe, Matthias VanBrakle, Reuben Shreve.
1816, George Holcombe, Matthias VanBrakle, Reuben Shreve.
1817, Matthias VanBrakle, Reuben Shreve, Charles Parker.
1818, Charles Parker, Matthias VanBrakle, Reuben Shreve.
1819, Charles Parker, William TenEyck, Thomas Cox, Jacob Butcher.

‡ Forman declined to serve.

OLD TIMES IN OLD MONMOUTH. 53

1820, Thomas Cox, Matthias VahBrakle, Samuel F. Allen, Isaac Hance.
1821, Charles Parker, William I. Conover, Corlies Lloyd, John T. Woodhull.
1822, William I. Conover, Corlies Lloyd, John T. Woodhull, John J. Ely.
1823, William I. Conover, John T. Woodhull, Cornelius Walling, James Lloyd.
1824, William I. Conover, John T. Woodhull, James West, Joseph Conover.
1825, John T. Woodhull, James West, Joseph Conover, James Lloyd.
1826, John T. Woodhull, James West, Joseph Conover, James Lloyd.
1827, John T. Woodhull, James West, James Lloyd, James Hopping.
1828, James West, James Lloyd, Daniel H. Ellis, Leonard Walling.
1829, James West, Daniel H. Ellis. Augustus W. Bennett, Ivins Davis.
1830, James West, Daniel H. Ellis. Augustus W. Bennett, Ivins Davis.
1831, Benjamin Woodward, Thomas G. Haight, Daniel B. Ryall, Annaniah Gifford.
1832, Annaniah Gifford, Elisha Lippincott, James S. Lawrence, Nicholas VanWickle.
1833, Annaniah Gifford, Daniel B. Ryall, Thomas G. Haight. Benjamin Woodward.
1834, Annaniah Gifford, Daniel B. Ryall, Thomas G. Haight, William Burtis.
1835, Annaniah Gifford, Daniel B. Ryall, Thomas G. Haight, William Burtis.
1836, Annaniah Gifford, Thomas G. Haight, William Burtis, Arthur V. Conover.
1837, Samuel Mairs. Edmund T. Williams, Thomas Miller, James Gulick.
1838, James Craig, Thomas E. Combs, William P. Forman, Garret Hires.
1839, James Craig, Thomas E. Combs, William P. Forman, Garret Hires.
1840, John Mairs, Henry W. Wolcott, James Grover, Charles Morris.
1841, Thomas C. Throckmorton, John R. Conover, Joseph Brinley, Samuel M. Oliphant, Benjamin L. Irons.
1842, '3, Thomas C. Throckmorton, John R. Conover, Joseph Brinley, Samuel M. Oliphant, Benjamin L. Irons.

Under the Constitution of 1844.†

1845, George F. Fort, Hartshorne Tantum, Andrew Simpson, Joseph B. Coward, James M. Hartshorne.‡
1846, William VanDoren, Hartshorne Tantum, Joseph B. Coward, Andrew Simpson, John Borden.
1847, William VanDoren, Hartshorne Tantum, Joseph B. Coward, Andrew Simpson, John Borden.
1848, William W. Bennett, Joel Parker, Ferdinand Woodward, Samuel Bennett,§ Joel W. Ayres.
1849, Alfred Walling, George W. Sutphin, John B. Williams, James D. Hall, William G. Hooper.
1850, Alfred Walling, George W. Sutphin, William G. Hooper, James D. Hall, Charles Butcher.
1851, William H. Conover, Bernard Connolly, Samuel W. Jones, Garret S. Smock.
1852, William H. Conover, Samuel W. Jones, Garret S. Smock, Charles Butcher.

Under the District System. ¶

1853, Charles Allen, Daniel P. VanDorn, Samuel W. Jones, Robert Allen.
1854, Forman Hendrickson, John L. Corlies, Henry E. Lafetra, Robert Allen.
1855, Henry E. Lafetra, Thomas B. Stout, William H. Johnston, John Vandorn.
1856, Samuel Vaughn, John R. Barriclo, Henry E. Lafetra, Samuel Beers.
1857, Jacob Herbert, John R. Barriclo, John V. Conover, Samuel Beers.
1858, George Middleton, Austin H. Patterson, John V. Conover, Richard B. Walling.
1859, George Middleton, Austin H. Patterson, John V. Conover, Richard B. Walling.
1860, William H. Mount, A. H. Patterson, James J. McNinny, James Patterson.
1861, William H. Mount, William V. Ward, Charles Haight, James Patterson.
1862, William V. Ward, Charles Haight, George C. Murray.
1863, Michael Taylor, Osborn Curtis, David H. Wyckoff.
1864, Michael Taylor, Osborn Curtis, David H. Wyckoff.
1865, Michael Taylor, Daniel A. Holmes, George Schenck.
1866, William C. Bowne, Daniel A. Holmes, George Schenck.
1867, Charles Allen, Francis Corlies, Thomas S. R. Brown.
1868, Charles Allen, Francis Corlies, Thomas S. R. Brown.
1869, William H. Conover, Jr., Daniel H. VanMater, Andrew Brown.
1870, Austin H. Patterson, Daniel H. Van Mater, Andrew Brown.
1871, Austin H. Patterson, John T. Haight, William S. Hornor.
1872, Austin H. Patterson, John T. Haight, William B. Hendrickson.

---

† Previous to 1844 the Legislature met in October of each year. Under the new constitution (of 1844) the Legislature meets in January of each year.
‡ Mr. Hartshorne died before he took his seat.

§ Mr. Bennett died before he took his seat.
¶ Previous to the election in the fall of 1852, members of the Assembly were elected on a general ticket.

1873, George W. Patterson, John B. Gifford, John S. Sproul.
1874, George W. Patterson, John B. Gifford, Andrew Brown.
1875, George W. Patterson, Charles D. Hendrickson, William V. Conover.
1876, James L. Rue, Charles D. Hendrickson, William V. Conover.
1877, James L. Rue, William H. Bennett, James H. Leonard.
1878, George J. Ely, William H. Bennett, Arthur Wilson.

The Affair of Freehold,

or BATTLE OF MONMOUTH; or, as BETTER KNOWN, OF MONMOUTH COURT HOUSE.

SUNDAY, 28TH JUNE, 1778.

From the Monmouth Democrat of October 17, 1878.

"*C'est la solide pierre ou S'asseoit* * * * *le Siecle.*"—MICHELET.

The Winter and Spring of 1778, produced three almost inestimable results for the Americans. First, with the opening of the year, 6th February, came the Recognition of American Independence by France, and the French Alliance, with its fleets and further promise of an army. Second, the sufferings and privations of Valley Forge, and the drill of Steuben evolved an American army of Regulars worthy to cope with the best troops that could be brought against them. Third, the approaching French fleet showed to the British the necessity of evacuating Philadelphia and of transferring the centre of British operations from a city—separated from the sea by a hundred miles of difficult navigation—to one, New York, immediately upon the ocean, from which expeditions conveying troops could sail to any point and at every season of the year. As to the French Alliance, little do the Americans dream to whom it was immediately due. Not to the "ex-workman," "good-man Richard," the astute philosopher Franklin, nor to any diplomat or statesman can this inestimable result be attributed. No! Michelet says to "Figaro" Beaumarchais, reckless speculator, agent of one king's mistress and courier of another's queen;" to a Doctor Dubourg, intimate with the French Minister Vergennes. Others had a hand in it, but Beaumarchais was the *Deus ex machina*, the controlling spirit, the power behind the throne, the "*kleine Ursache*" of Zschockke. He held the hesitating King and vacillating Minister to the idea of récognition and assistance, by the threat that, whichever way they decided, war was inevitable; that if they refused to assist the Colonies to free themselves, these would make up their quarrel with the mother country, and both united fall upon France. To casual readers this may seem ridiculous. Martin, quoting Droz, who was behind the scenes, nevertheless corroborates it. He says that many Americans were inclined to this course through the remembrance of their origin; that Gates, after Burgoyne's Surrender, wrote to this purport to influential Englishmen.— Gates, who gloried in being an Englishman, even after he had become the phantasm idol of the victorious Americans through the preparations of the grievously wronged and superseded Schuyler. Lord Mahon likewise produces clear evidence to this effect. Garden, in his "Revolutionary Anecdotes," pp. 89-90, states that Col. Laurens, in defiance of the vehement protest of Franklin, threatened Louis XVI, face to face, with active hostilities in case of further delays in extending assistance to the Colonies. Colonel Laurens, walking directly up to the King, delivered a memorial, to which he solicited his most serious attention, and said—"Should the favor asked be denied, or even delayed, there is cause to fear that the sword which I wear may no longer be drawn in defence of the liberties of my country, but be wielded as a *British subject* against the monarchy of France."

Moreover, in corroboration of this view, witness the affray between the Colonists and French seamen at Charlestown, S. C., on the 6th September, 1778, in which small arms and even cannon were used, several lives lost and many wounded. Again, on the 8th of the same months, a collision occurred at Boston, in which a French naval officer was killed. Gordon half admits "it may be feared that Americans were concerned in the riot," although attempts were made to shift it on British deserters. Gordon [iii. 200] likewise concedes a certain coolness on the part of the better class of Bostonians toward the French, which was imputed to a continuance of the cordiality still entertained toward Great Britain. Botta, a foreigner, most cordially inclined to our country is very manifest on this subject; and Book X, of his 2d Volume, is worthy of examination. The excitable French would not have stood so much from Sullivan and others in words, and from the people in acts, if their interests had not regulated their feelings, since the efforts of the Colonies against England, an hereditary enemy, constituted a sufficient antidote. Severe language and a few lives were nothing in comparison to the certain advantages to France of the recently arranged Alliance.

There is no doubt but that without the "Convention" or "Capitulation of Saratoga," neither the author of the "Barber of Seville," nor of "Poor Richard's Almanack" would have won their, (the new world's), stupendous little game. It happened most opportunely. The certainty of the surrender and the magnitude of the achievement became known in Paris on the 4th, [16th, Michelet,] December, 1777. France, which had hitherto looked askance upon the Colonies, regarding them as a doubtful weapon to assist in wreaking its vengeance upon England, now learned to regard them as an effective instrument. On the 6th of February, 1778, the Treaty of Recognition and Alliance was signed. The news was brought by a swift-sailing French frigate, the *Sensible*, to what is now Portland, Maine, on the 13th April. Congress at Yorktown, [York, Pa.] received the welcome intelligence on the 2d May; thence it was communicated to Washington at Valley Forge, on the 3d May; and there it was celebrated on the 6th or 7th of May—accounts differ (?) as to the exact latter date.

During the Winter, Sir William Howe had notified the British government, that, if it expected him to accomplish the desired results, he must be strongly re inforced.

Lord Amherst, the conqueror of Crown Point and Ticonderoga, in 1759, the King's military adviser, urged George III to send out 40,000 additional fresh troops to America.—Both the request and the counsel were ignored. Lord Germaine, the Secretary for the Colonies, completed the mismanagement. As Lord George Sackville, he had been cashiered for robbing Prince Ferdinand of the fruits of his victory at Minden. Politics and family influence restored him to the opportunity of ruining a Crown as he had already paralyzed a Commander. With such concurrent imbecility Fortune herself became disgusted.—Howe, the idol of his army—to critical investigation, incomprehensibly so—asked to be relieved.

To the military student, the observation of the German historian, Becker, [xi. 360] seems concisely conclusive. From 11th September, 1777, to 21st May, 1778, Howe had done nothing worthy of his reputation, of his opportunities, nor of his means. "Howe," says Becker, "remained faithful to his original plan, to venture nothing, [not to run the slightest risk,] down to the last moment of his command-in-chief." Too late for its own interests the British government appeared to awaken to this fact, and his assumed or actual wishes for the appointment of his successor were no sooner received than his request was promptly and gladly complied with.

On the 8th of May, Sir Henry Clinton reached Philadelphia to assume the command of an army which did not desire him; and on the 24th May, Howe left the city amid the regrets of all ranks, and even the tears of many. Sir Henry Clinton knew at once that for strategic reasons, Philadelphia must be abandoned.

At this juncture it cannot be otherwise than interesting to present brief notices of the British Generals who played such important parts in the American "First War for Independence." Although Sir William Howe is about to disappear from the stage, he is entitled to the first consideration, in view of his supreme influence on the occurrences of 1776 and 1777. There is no doubt that Howe's personal advantages in connection with his demeanor, had a great deal to do with his popularity; but as a general his abilities and courage were almost completely neutralized by his indolence. He stood fully six feet high, and had a fine figure, which was admirably proportioned. In appearance he was not unlike Washington, but he was a better made and a better looking man. He had a good face and a pleasant expression; and his manners were polished, graceful, and dignified.—His successor, Sir Henry Clinton, presented a contrast in almost every particular. He was short and fat; and although he had an animated countenance and intelligent expression, his face was too full and his nose too prominent. In comparison with Sir William, he was rather punctillious in his intercourse with subordinates, and not inclined to intimacy. Moreover, although polite and courtly in his manners, he was more formal and distant than Howe. Both were voluptuaries in the refined sense of the word; but Howe was the more graceful of the two, even in this.—Washington had so little an opinion of Clinton's generalship, that when he had an opportunity of kidnapping him, in the Kennedy House, No. 1 Broadway, N. Y., (built by the way, by the writer's grand-uncle) he deemed it more wise to leave things as they were than, by Clinton's capture, to make way, perhaps for a far abler man—Carleton for instance, or Cornwallis—whose course of action would be less patent and more liable to miscomprehension. Belsham, in his "George III," sums up Clinton in two pregnant sentences: "Though uniformly in a certain degree, successful in his enterprises, this officer acquired little accession of military reputation in America. Brave as a soldier, but in the capacity of General, slow, cautious, and indecisive, he deviated into an extreme, the opposite of General Burgoyne, who was censured as rash, presumptious and romantic."

Although the Loyalists, who lost everything,—country, property, consideration, all a man holds dear—had much cause to blame Burgoyne and the ill-advised efforts of the British Crown to retrieve the Colonies, and did so justly—the real cause after all of Royal unsuccess, was the pleasant " ne'er-do-weel," Sir Henry Clinton. Even the timid Gates exclaimed on the 17th June, 1778—" Thank heaven for the precious time the enemy have so foolishly lost." Clinton's slowness might have found some compensation in his bravery had not the latter been hampered by a caution which sometimes amounted, in appearance, to timidity under certain circumstances, while both caution and courage in crises were neutralized by indecision. His failure to support Burgoyne in time in September—October, 1777, was inexcusable, and his depleting Cornwallis in October, 1781, and planting him in a position whence there was no escape—when the latter needed all the support which the Crown officers could afford him—were superlatively fatal to the Royal and Loyal causes. Clinton had two courses to pursue. The first, von Bulow's plan, inevitably successful in the long run, was inapplicable after the arrival of the French; the second, Cæsar's—all great generals'—was incompatible with sloth or self-indulgence. The descendants of the American Loyalists must in their hearts treat the memory of Sir Henry Clinton at this day as even do the Jews that of Haman. At the feast of Purim, in commemoration of their escape, the Jews exhibit the strongest evidences of undying execration of the man who simply *planned* their destruction.

The two next in command were Cornwallis and Knyphausen. The former was certainly the best soldier the Crown had in the revolted American Colonies. More than once, especially in 1776-'77, Washington only escaped his prevision and precision through the cold and dilatory action and orders of Howe. The chivalrous Carleton was undoubtedly better fitted for the command-in-chief, because his military character was exceeded by his marvellous administrative power, and both of these by his magnanimity, but he was out of favor, and his jurisdiction was restricted to Canada. Like all honest men, he was too independent and outspoken; whereas Cornwallis, who never came in direct contact with the ministry, kept the favor which he might have lost if he collided, as did others, with Mr. Secretary Germaine, or if he had experienced the treatment of Carleton, of Burgoyne, and of Howe. Moreover, Cornwallis enjoyed the advantages of high rank, which exerts such an influence in Great Britain. The Marquis, although short and thick set, was not corpulent in the same degree as Clinton; his features were very regular; his nose aquiline and handsome; his expression agreeable; this last would have been positively fine if he had not been affected by a nervous twitching of the left eye-lid. When young, his hair had been light, and somewhat inclined to sandy, but it became rather gray before he left America. He was greatly beloved because he always was accessible, even to the humblest of his soldiers; and towards all, his manners were unusually easy and affable.

Knyphausen, who commanded the contingent of his countrymen, was a fine looking German, a trifle under six feet in height, straight and martial in appearance, although slender. He was greatly beloved by his superiors, perhaps for the reason that he was no more indulgent to the faults of his own people than he was to those of the English. The British Crown had no better division commander than himself. He could get all out of his soldiers that it was possible for them to accomplish, because he was one of the commanders who say " Come " rather than " Go," and he was willing to share the sufferings as well as the dangers of his troops.

Lieutenant Gen. Sir William Howe, by blood was uncle of George III, (although not legitimately), and a younger brother of " Black Dick," the British Admiral, Lord, afterwards Earl, Howe, who commanded the British fleet in American waters at this time. In 1778, General Howe was forty-nine; Clinton, forty; Cornwallis, thirty-nine; Washington, forty-six; Greene, thirty-six; Wayne, thirty-three; Lord Stirling, fifty-two.— Among the foreigners, LaFayette was twenty-one; Pulaski was thirty-one; Kosciusko about the same age; " the traitor," (unjustly so styled) Charles Lee, forty-seven; the date of the birth and death of the intriguing Irish Conway, does not appear; and the honest Steuben, forty-eight. The last named officer was, by all odds, the most practical, tactical officer in the Colonial service, and although he is scarcely ever mentioned, personally, in connection with the Battle of Monmouth, influentially he was everywhere at the point of danger and success. Whatever glory accrued to his adopted country from this collision, was and is due immediately and remotely to him, always conceding the first place to Washington.

Stedman, the only truly military, and the

truthful historian of the Revolution, develops this necessity of the evacuation of Philadelphia in a few pregnant sentences, clear even to laymen. Arrangements were at once begun to extricate the British fleet before the French navy could blockade it in the Delaware. To the Loyalists of Philadelphia, which included so much of the best and the most valuable portion of the population, this determination was the assurance of ruin, exile, life-long misery. Washington—miracle of common sense—counseled forbearance, charity to these unfortunates. Politicians and the populace carried out then as they are fulfilling now, their own vicious tendencies. Von Eelking, concisely but pathetically, describes the scenes which preceded the British evacuation. " As to the maiority, the citizens contemplated the arrival of the Colonists with terror or stupefaction.* Property was sacrificed ; and with what they could gather up, all hastened to take refuge on ship-board—that is, as many as the vessels could receive. With these, embarked in fifty-seven transports, convoyed by a squadron of frigates, Clinton sent off at least 3,000 of his troops ; a Franconian [Ansbach and Bayreuth] infantry regiment which had been tampered with, and his " cavalry,"—he retained his dragoons.

To dismiss a painful subject, the Loyalists who remained behind, received the treatment they feared ; many were roughly handled ; others were imprisoned ; two very respectable Quakers, Roberts and Carlisle, were hung. Thus, as too often, were Washington's counsels and wishes disregarded.

Clinton's army was not the unit, or such, indeed, that it is generally represented. Desertions were numerous, the majority, Germans. Washington writes " they are chiefly foreigners," *i. e.* not English. Many hid themselves to avoid marching with their comrades. It is said that Clinton lost from 1,000 to 2,000 by desertion, between Philadelphia and Sandy Hook. Of these, 600 returned to wives, sweethearts or other connections with whom alliances had been formed during the Winter of 1777-1778, in the City of Brotherly—and in this case—Sisterly Love.

Clinton was a good soldier, using the term in contradistinction to a General and proficient in strategy. He understood a soldier's business. He was a hero in action. He had learned his profession under the best of masters—Ferdinand of Brunswick, to whom he had been aide-de-camp, in the greatest war of these times, the German " Seven Years War." But he could not stand responsibility where the scope was grand. It made him nervous,

*[Greene, [*G. W. G. II*, 207] refers to "horrid acts of plunder by some of the Pennsylvania Line," [Regulars] as " equal to anything committed by the Hessians," the *betes noirs* of the Colonists.]

it might be said morally timid. He could not stand what our Scott called "a fire in the rear." He had sacrificed the boasting Burgoyne ; he was to sacrifice the capable Cornwallis. If there is a man living in the United States, whose ancestors lost home, happiness, fortune, all men hold dear, through adherence to principle and the Crown, he can point to Sir Henry Clinton and anathematize him as the factor of fatality.

Still, Sir Henry Clinton was " a grand good soldier " in the face of an enemy. He carried out his evacuation faultlessly ; and his retreat through the Jerseys has been pronounced by a German military critic of high rank, as almost a miracle of generalship—as even finer than that of Moreau (of just about as many days) through the Black Forest in 1796, the latter extolled to the skies as something unsurpassed and unsurpassable in its line.

Two Brigades and a large amount of baggage were ferried over from Philadelphia into Jersey, on the 15th of June. On the 17th, other troops followed. At 3 A. M. of the 18th, the bulk of the army and its enormous trains commenced to cross. By 10 o'clock everything was safely over on Gloucester Point, and ready to start for this British " March to the Sea." Unlike Sherman's peaceable military promenade, it was to be accomplished at the expense of a battle. In the case of Clinton, he paid the bloody ransom himself. In the case of Sherman, Washingtonian Thomas met the sanguinary draft which relieved his superior of all pressure.

Washington was perfectly well aware of what was going on. It is claimed that the American leaders were certainly all in accord as to the intentions of the enemy.

That Washington did not annoy or impede Clinton's movements justifies the criticism of a German eye-witness, " that he deemed it more wise to build a bridge of gold for a flying enemy." Once that the British were off, he was all activity. He detached Maxwell— and subsequently, (after the main army was across the Delaware at Coryell's Ferry) Morgan, the latter the best commander of riflemen in the world—to harass the enemy on their march.

Morgan, finally, was to the right and according to one or more histories, Maxwell continued on the left as well as Dickinson, the latter subordinate to the former, not independent of direction.

Arnold was the first into Philadelphia. He captured a few stragglers or a small portion of the British rear-guard, and was made commander of the city. Fatal appointment! It was " the direful spring " of all his after misery.

Clinton's line of march was almost due north-east, for he was aiming directly for New

OLD TIMES IN OLD MONMOUTH. 59

York. Superficial writers say that he moved slowly. Considering the vast trains he had to convoy, the extraordinary sultriness of the weather—alternating heat of unusual intensity and tropical showers, succeeded by stifling humidity—strategic and logistic difficulties, deep, "thirsty," sandy roads, constantly recurring streams whose bridges the Americans did or sought to destroy—considering all this he got over this difficult ground very quickly. It was natural obstacles and not opposing forces that occasioned any detention. Moreover, despite the encumbrance of his enormous *impedimenta*, he pushed forward more quickly than the Americans who were comparatively in light marching order.

NOTE.

A correspondent signing himself TRENTON, in the Magazine of American History, Vol. ii, (1878) No. 9, (September) page 569, seeks to disparage my account of the battle of Monmouth, by the comparison of a paragraph from my statement and the citation of another paragraph from Sir Henry Clinton's report. If official military reports are not open to investigation and are to be received as unanswerable or infallible history, what need then, is there for a subsequent writer to attempt to sift out the truth. If such a rule is adopted, it would simply be necessary to stereotype the reports on one side or the other, and rest the case, on the principle of the Dutch justice who invariably decided after hearing the plaintiff, because he said if he listened to both parties "it bothered his head." If all the official reports on both sides were published without comment, it would be impossible to reconcile the contradictious, as was absolute by the case in regard to Monmouth. For instance, contrast the following statements: Sir Henry Clinton says he marched from Monmouth, at 10 P. M., by the light of the moon, and to take advantage of this. I believe him .Washington says,' he. [Clinton,] moved about 12 P. M.," when the moon had set. I think Washington's informants were mistaken. On the other hand I believe Washington is more correct when he says, "The slow advance of the enemy had greatly the *air of design*, and led me, with many others, to suspect that General Clinton, desirous of a general action, was endeavoring to draw us down into the lower country. In order by a rapid movement to gain our right, and take possession of the strong grounds above us. This consideration, and to give the troops time to repose and refresh themselves from the fatigues they had experienced from rainy and excessively hot weather, determined me to halt at Hopewell township, about five miles from Princeton, where we remained till the morning of the 25th " Greene, second alone to Washington as a strategist, corroborates the latter's view, (Caldwell, pp. 76), and pretty m ich all the testimony establishes the idea by implication that Clinton moved slowly to invite an attack on ground favorable to the admirable organization of his " three arms."

The following reconciles every seeming contradiction. Sir Henry Clinton moved *slowly* when *deception* was intended, and he moved with promptness and celerity when these qualities were the requisites of the occasion. This writer referred to important bridges, not mere spans which a few farmers could tear down and remove in a few minutes.

Reports are very often written with the sole intention of deceiving, as for instance, Napoleon's bulletins.— Even if the Americans did destroy some of the small bridges, they made no effectual stand. They abandoned the important pass at Mount Holly, and bridge over Rancocas creek, a d von kelkuig only mentions a single attempt to break down, completely, one *important* bridge, (at Crosswicks) which was frustrated by the Hessian Jagers. If one clause of Sir Henry's report is extracted as incontrovertible evidence against the writer's' deductio is, on the same principle, the whole report should be accepted *verbatim*. This is the only fair alternative. The writer read from fifty to seventy-five authorities and judged for, himself. It is very likely there were two reasons for Sir Henry's slow advance.— First, his desire to court a fight; second, his determination to bring off in safety his trains of all kinds, his army's "loot," and the vast impedimenta which embarrassed his movements. An army encumbered with a superabundance of v hicles, moves very slowly over the best of roads, and under the most favorable circumstances. General de Wimpffen, writing as late as the 2d of September, '78, speaking of the French army at home, marching on the finest possible "routes" at the most propitious season of the year, when speed was the *desideratum* of the hour, says : " We accomplished in some (*quelques*) days scarcely a distance of six to eight leagues," 18 to 24 miles. As a set off to this, Clinton, in a new country, amid very heavy showers of rain, alternating with fatal heat, on very bad roads, mostly deep, heavy sand, although kept back by a train which stretched out twelve to fourteen miles, in spite of his enemies and their efforts to destroy the bridges, etc., accomplished 18 to 23 leagues, 54 to 70 miles (according to the roads as then or now laid out), in 8 or 9 days.— Calculate this. He left Philadelphia on the 18th, and was at Monmouth on the night of the 26th June, according to his own engineer's map, of which a copy is in the N. Y. Historical Society.

Clinton moved on the hypothenuse of a right angled triangle, and Washington on the two other sides. Thus, from Philadelphia to Monmouth, the former marched, according to the roads, between 60 and 70 miles; the latter, the Americans, 80 to 90 and very likely 100 miles.

On the night of the 18th of June, the British lay at Haddonfield. On the 19th, they moved off in two divisions; Knyphausen's in the rear, Cornwallis's leading off. The British expected to meet with difficulty in forcing what was termed the "Mount Holly* Pass," but did not. There was a sharp little skirmish at Crosswicks, at the Bridge and Mill over and on the creek of the same name.

On the 24th of June, the British reached Allentown and Imlay or Imalytown, three miles apart. The line, N & S, between " the Jersies," (i. e. East and West Jersey) runs between these villages. Here the Order of March was reversed and here a change of plan occurred. Cornwallis, with his division, assumed the more dangerous duty of covering the withdrawal, and Knyphausen that of protecting the trains.

As to Clinton's change of plan, some explanation is necessary. Clinton at first intended to cross from Amboy to Staten Island, and so on to New York. He now perceived that this involved the perilous operation of forcing the passage of the Raritan at New Brunswick. His cavalry had proved to him what these always should be to a general— " the eyes and ears of our army." The Loyalist, Simcoe, with his "Queen's Rangers," had brought him certain information of the

---

* Mount Holly is so styled from a hill rising 200 feet above the sea level. It is at the head of navigation about 20 miles E. N. E. of Philadelphia, 19 miles S. Trenton ; and 30 miles S. W. of Monmouth Court House, on the north branch of Rancocas Creek.

movements of Washington. The American commander had moved up the right or West bank of the Delaware, and crossed to the left between the 20th and 22d of June, at Coryell's Ferry—his stereotyped route in all his Jersey campaigns. On the 25th, (24th?) while Clinton lay at Allentown, Washington was at Princeton. Take a map, and at once the advantages of the latter's position become perceptible.— Washington was nearer to (New) Brunswick, could move on interior lines through a denser, friendly population, where he could find supplies. If Clinton (who had to carry his food with him) still prosecuted his march to (New) Brunswick, he might find himself in a *cul-de-sac* with the Raritan in front; the South river, and extensive and impassable marshes extending for miles, southward ; to his right, Lawrence Brook, then a much more important stream, embarrassing his immediate communications; while Washington could come in on his left flank and rear, and catch him as "old* Frederick " used to delight in surprising his adversaries under most disadvantageous circumstances to the latter. In this position, Washington expected to hold him until the Northern Army, under Gates, could be brought down from the Hudson, to prevent the escape of the British, until the militia could be assembled from every quarter. Thus, between his own army, that of Gates, and the Militia, Saratoga might be repeated, and Clinton be swarmed out—" Burgoyned." This is no after-thought. The danger is alluded to in publications of the year. It is doubtful if Gates had generosity enough to smother his jealousy, and constitute himself a subordinate portion of the smashing machinery of his rival—rival, but his superior in everything which goes to constitute a patriot, a hero, and a man.

Clinton was too intelligent a commander to be caught in any such a trap. Americans love to deceive themselves into the idea that Clinton was afraid of Washington; that he was flying before him; even the sensible Greene indulges in such slurring remarks.— (G. W. G ii, 131, 142). Washington does not countenance any such idea. This is sheer delusion. Clinton was anxious for a battle if he could bring it on in a position in which the chances were in his favor. Washington knew this, and had no idea of allowing himself to be enticed into a battle in the flat or "lower country" (G. W. G. ii, 87) where Clinton's cavalry and thoroughly veteran army would enjoy so many advantages.

Nor did he intend to engage Clinton among the hills where the natural positions were unfavorable to himself. He did want to bring on an engagement because for the Americans a battle was a political necessity. France had already done so much, America had now to do something. Washington longed to try his new regulars against the British. The country demanded it. Now was the opportunity. It is well known Washington's Fabian policy, although hitherto so successful, had excited great animadversion among the politicians; likewise among the discontented officers who composed or clung to the skirts of the Conway "Cabal." The cross-grained Samuel Adams, had exactly expressed the opinion of numbers and John Adams (not to mention Lovell and others) had growled out something to the same purport.

Above all this, Washington's force as to that of Clinton was over three to two. How many did each have ? No question of the kind has ever excited greater controversy.— Von Eelking, writing, in Germany—he published eighty-five years after the event—with no object to misrepresent, says that Clinton had "scarcely 13,000" and Washington about 20,000.†

The writer of this article arrived at exactly these aggregates by a long, careful, and curious calculation, and they were in print before he saw von Eelking's statement. Lossing (in his "Field Book of the Revolution," Vol. ii, pages 146, '7, note 2), says: "At a Council of War, held on the 18th of May, it was thought reasonable to anticipate that, when all the re-inforcements were brought in, the whole army, fit for duty, would amount to about 20,000 men." Washington, according to Gordon, (iii, 133) stated on the 24th of June, while at Princeton, within 7 to 8 miles of Clinton, who lay at Allentown, " the enemy's force is between 9,000 and 10,000 rank and file—the American army on the ground is 10,684 rank and file, besides the advance brigade under General Maxwell of about 1,200, and about 1,200 militia." "The militia of New Jersey were in the highest spirits, and *almost to a man* in arms." (N. Y. H. S. Coll., ii, 429.)

Basing a calculation on this language and taking rank and file in its unqualified sense, and adding the due proportion of officers, non-commissioned officers, etc., etc., in accordance with the strength of the British and American battalions or regiments, the latter's

† Washington had five divisions, [Lee, Mifflin, La Fayette, DeKalb, Stirling,] the 1st, 2d, 3d and 4th each of three Brigades, and the 5th of four Brigades. This does not appear to include Horse or Artillery. (*Lee Papers, N. Y. Hist. Soc. Colls. II*. 408, &c.) Lee, on the 28th, had under him over 5,000, one-third of the army, (regular line infantry) besides Morgan's riflemen, 600, and the militia under Generals Dickinson and Heard, and, mark this, the New Jersey militia " were in arms almost to a man."

OLD TIMES IN OLD MONMOUTH. 61

Regulars.‡ Militia, etc., just about von Eelking's estimate will be reached.

It is the fashion to make out Clinton's force as greatly superior to Washington's, but Washington claims nothing like this.— He concedes his numerical superiority about 4 to 3, and on this founds the question, " will it be advisable to hazard a general action ?" Of the Council of war to which it was submitted, the only officer who gave an unqualified for vote fighting, was Wayne, [Except (?) Cadwallader]. Wayne was unquestionably the most unmitigated advocate for fighting " in season and out of season," in the American Army; and he was not a man to express in words what he was not ready to endorse with deeds. Wayne had what church members style a "realizing sense" of fighting. It is well known what he wrote to Washington on the 10th of July, 1779, when the latter proposed for him to storm Stony Point. " General, if *you* will only plan it, I will storm *Hell !*" ₴

Returning to the question of numbers, this account of Monmouth is predicated on the opinion that Washington had "about 20,000, and Clinton scarcely 13,000 men."

According to the Engineer Map of Clinton's Army, (copy in collection N. Y. Historical Society), it reached the hamlet of Freehold—generally known as Monmouth Court House—in the course of P. M. Saturday, 26th June. To people who deceive themselves into the idea that Clinton was afraid of a fight, all that is necessary to disprove this would be to read the internal evidence. Spies and reconnoissances found his troops perfectly at their ease, tents pitched, horses at pasture, pickets and videttes well out, taking it comfortably.

According to different maps, the location of the British is apparently contradictory, but still very reconcilable. The main body of their army lay stretched out nearly five miles along the road from Allentown to Shrewsbury, from W. S. W. to E. N. E. with its centre about at Freehold; but there was certainly a detachment to the West of the Court

‡ Greene, for instance, mentions an American Continental regiment which numbered only 130 men. If this means privates, the officers, non-commissioned officers, musicians, etc., must have numbered 100 more.— On the 27th July, 1778, [*G. W. G. II.* 106], he alludes to an undue number of officers. During the Rebellion there were Union regiments which, after long service, did not have all told more than 120 effectives. At Five Forks the 6th N. Y. Cavalry could only put in line 45 carbines and 17 officers, total 62. (Citizen 268, 3 12:70.) Numbers on paper are no indications of valid force. At Valley Forge, Washington's army drew 32,000 rations with only 7,500 men fit for duty. [*G. W. G. i–ii.* 138.]

₴ Wayne, however, was not the first or last man to make such a speech. Napoleon said of Vandamme: "If ever I have to make war against the devil, it is him, [Vandamme] I will send to carry it on." Alexander of Russia made about the same remark of Platoff, Hetman of the Cossacks, to Napoleon: "If I were to order Platoff to march against Hell, he would set off at once with whatever troops I gave him, simply requesting some indications of the road."

House, in fact with fractions all around it, except, perhaps, to the northward.

The writer makes out that the British encamped N. W., S. W., S.S.E., and E. of Freehold.

Clinton slept on the night of the 27th, at a farm house on the Mount Holly road, i. e. nearest to the point where he expected the enemy. The same night, Washington's main army was within 8 miles; Lee, with the advanced guard 3 miles nearer; within 5 miles. Morgan lay at the present hamlet or village of Blue Ball, 3 miles south of Monmouth Court House; Dickinson, with the New Jersey militia somewhere to the north-westward of Freehold.

The Americans could not have been feeling "very strongly toward Clinton." Colonel John Laurens (L. P. ii, 431), wrote : " The militia of the country kept up a random running fire with the Hessian Jagers (Riflemen) ; no mischief was done on either side." Moreover, on the night of the 27th, 28th, or morning of the 28th, Steuben, undertaking to reconnoitre closely, lost his hat and would have lost his life, except for Knyphausen, who recognized him ; and the American general came near being taken prisoner.

The fact of the matter is, Clinton's great concern was to save his baggage. His trains, if captured, would have excited as much surprise among the innocent American troops as the booty taken by Frederick the Great's " Monks of the Flag " from the French, after Rosbach.

According to the notebook of a German officer present at Monmouth, this train stretched out from 12 to 14 miles along a single road which it was compelled to follow, because there was none other practicable for carriages.

The rich British officers had with them coaches, draught and saddle horses in abundance; servants of all kinds; baggage of all sorts ; *mistresses*, and a mass of such trifles or rubbish. Von Eelking says : " That a soldier of the present day could have no conception of such a procession." Over and above all this, there were the military trains proper; bat, baw, or pack horses in great numbers.— It was almost a repetition of the train of Xerxes ; of Napoleon, in Russia ; and of Louis Napoleon, in 1870, always basing any parallel on the numerical disproportion of these different armies.

Washington knew the time had come when he must attack Clinton, if he expected to fight him at all. If Clinton could reach the defiles or heights of Middletown now only a few miles distant—he was beyond the hopes of a successful aggressive. On the other hand, Clinton appeared to have no nervousness, except for the safety of his baggage ; " baggage," in more than one sense of the word, and he considered that this was the " objective " of the Americans who were hovering all about him.

Having thus brought the two armies together—" Washington's, about 20,000 ; Clinton's, scarcely 13,000"—(Gen. Cust. B. A. in his " Annals of the Wars," 1, iii, 207, says Clinton had 10,000)—the next duty in order is to describe the country which constituted the stage of their action, and the field of the impending battle.

Monmouth County, N. J., presents a level surface, except in its north-east triangular-shaped township of Middletown, which is broken and hilly. The noted Highlands of Navesink are in its eastern angle. These extend about five miles along the coast, and rise to the height of 300 feet above the sea.

Monmouth Court-House, or the hamlet of Freehold, is on what might be termed a plateau, 191 feet above the sea level. The expression, the "Heights of Freehold," so frequently used, is a mere figure of speech, and is very delusive. There are no apparent heights The ground descends in every direction from the settlement, and from its site the rain sheds into the whole surrounding district, finding its way, north, into the Raritan, east, into the Navesink, and south-east, into the ocean.

Although it is a general opinion that the line of the British encampment on the night of the 27th of June, 1778, stretched out from four to five miles along the road from Allentown and Imlaystown, through Freehold toward Middletown, from S. W. to N. E., with its centre at the Court-house. Knyphausen lay farthest away—say about a mile to the Eastward. It would appear from Steuben's letters, as well as other contemporary authorities, that the British must have lain in confident security all around Freehold on the night of the 27th—utterly defiant, tents pitched and horses at pasture.

When promptness and decision were the requisites of the hour and occasion, Clinton was too quick for the Americans and equal to every emergency ; otherwise he moved leisurely, taking things as easily and comfortably as if he was in a friendly country. His whole army was at Freehold, (30 miles east of Trenton, Cr'tn) by 10 A. M., of 26th June. (Dw'sn, I., 400, (1,) notes 4, 5 : Simcoe 67-'9) and he lay there foraging with his horses at pasture until the morning of the 28th. He was, indeed, so completely at his ease, that things looked very much as if he wasted these two days to court an attack, and felt perfectly certain of his complete ability to punish it. The forty-six hours thus lost, had Clinton been actually afraid of pursuit, would have placed him beyond the possibility of a collision. The position assumed by Clinton, if be held to his original intention of forcing the battle, was almost impregnable. Washington, Greene, Lee, (" Light Horse Harry," no

relation to Charles, the victim of the coming fray)---as well as others, the best judges, all agree that the British general seemed to court rather than to avoid a battle. The conduct of the Americans after the battle (especially if Stedman is correct) serves to substantiate the idea that they were willing, as Doubleday said of Meade, to let the enemy "*severely* alone." Washington only fought at Monmouth as a political necessity.

Steuben, reconnoitering (night-morning of the 27th-28th) to the west of the village, was recognized by Gen. Knyphausen, and would have been killed if the latter had not given orders to take him, if possible, without harming him. He escaped capture, but lost his hat. Dickinson also had a skirmish next morning, 28th, still further to the west of Freehold.

According to Major-Gen. Stryker, THE authority on New Jersey military matters of all kinds, the face of the country is so changed that it would be almost impossible at this date to recognize the distribution of the scenery and stage arrangements of the action in 1778, and a mere casual visit to the field would not assist the student. A prolonged stay of a week or so, devoted to an examination of the vicinity and a comparison of personal observations with records and traditions of the people, might throw some little light upon the subject, but scarcely enough to repay the expense and the trouble. Col. Carrington, in his *Battles of the American Revolution*, (Barnes & Co., New York, publishers,) has furnished an excellent battle-plan. But, after all, as clear a plan as any was published at Brussels and Paris, in 1782, in connection with his *Historical and Political Essays on the American Revolution*, by M. Hilliard d'Auberteuil. It was reproduced in Barber and Howe's *Historical Collections of the State of New Jersey*, 1860, page 338. There is another plan at page 340 of the same work. These two, with the explanatory text and indices, will furnish about as good an idea of the movements of the troops as any ordinary reader would desire. The stage of action comprises an area of about seven miles, from Englishtown, west, to the ridge east of Briar Hill and Freehold (the ridge on which Clinton faced about to fight) to the east, and some three and a half miles from north to south.

Thanks to the uniform kindness and courtesy of Major-Gen. William S. Stryker, Adjutant-General of New Jersey, an opportunity has likewise been afforded of examining the Map of the County of Monmouth, made under the act authorizing a State geological survey, bearing date 20th January, 1857.— According to this map the east marsh, (or " ravine," as it is sometimes styled,) which the Americans crossed to make their first attack upon the British, lies at the foot of the "Heights of Freehold," so termed, and directly to north-east by east of the village. It is drained north by a small affluent of the Swimming River, which empties into the North or Navesink. This marsh, or the hollow in continuation of it, was apparently drained likewise to the southward by little feeders of the Manasquan River, which finds its way southeast into the Atlantic. The middle and west marshes or "ravines" feed branches of the Machiponix River—(Carrington styles the most important Wemrock Brook)—which, through the South River, finds its way into the Raritan.

The battle-ground proper---that is, the scene of the only real hard fighting--- was between the middle and west marshes, but much nearer to the latter. It lies north and south of a point where the dirt road from Englishtown joins the Freehold and Jamesburg Agricultural Railroad, about two and one-eighth miles west-north-west of Monmouth Court-house. The hedgerow, (hedge, or living fence,) where Wayne effectually stopped Clinton's attacks, and finally repulsed the British, is between the middle and west marshes or ravines, closer to the latter. Col. Monckton was killed in front of this hedge, and Washington met Lee at the north end of it. Comb's Hill, on which Greene posted the batteries which decided the battle, is about five-eighths of a mile directly south of the south end of this hedge. The central point of the battle-field---the hedge---is two miles and a quarter west-north west of Freehold, and fully three miles and a half west of the spot where the first skirmishing of the morning occurred at the time that the British faced about and deployed. The British camp or bivouac after the battle was about a mile east of the hedge; just east of the middle marsh. This, their position on the evening of the 28th, was about two and a half miles west of where they were deployed between 8 and 9 A. M. Consequently Clinton drove the Americans before him from three and a half to four miles, and he himself did not fall back over a mile and a half from the furthest point to which he pushed his incomparable Light Infantry, and about a mile from where Wayne repulsed the English Coldstream Guards and Grenadiers. The American brigades of Poor and Woodford lay on their arms all night, just west of the middle marsh, within a quarter of a mile of the British bivouacs, the pickets on both sides much closer together. Englishtown is five miles and a half west-north-west of Monmouth Court-house, or Freehold, and over six miles west by north of the scene of the first collision. The old-fashioned "double-decker" Freehold meeting-house, so often alluded to, where the rude and only

memorial of Hon. Col. H. Monckton, brother of the Earl Galway, was set up, is a mile and a quarter north-west of the centre of the battle-ground, and a mile and a half south-west of Englishtown.

The following are the relative positions of the opposing forces when the fighting began between 8 and 9 o'clock on the morning of Sunday, the 28th. Knyphausen commenced to break camp at daybreak, between 3 and 4 A. M., (the sun rose at 4.31 A. M,) and thus his long procession of carriages had gained a good start. The last of his division—principally Germans, in the rear of the British baggage train, moving on the Middletown road, was two and a half to three miles northeast of Freehold. Sir Henry Clinton, with the division of Cornwallis, did not quit his camping-ground until 8 A. M., crossed a plain or flat about a mile wide and three miles long, north and south, ascended the ridge beyond, and thus interposed his choice British troops between Knyphausen and the Court-house. Dickinson, with the New Jersey Militia, soon after issued from the woods on a spur of the ridge east of the eastern marsh (about two miles north northeast of Freehold) known as Briar Hill, and began to tease the British flank facing east and to cut in upon Knyphausen. Not to recur to Knyphausen again, it is sufficient to say that Dickinson's objective was the British baggage. The Germano-British General repelled this attack at once and with ease, and according to plan moved on in perfect order, without any further molestation worthy of remark.

By 9 A. M. Lee and the American vanguard, over 5,000 strong, were already east of the road to Amboy, which ran directly north from Freehold, with their left on Briar Hill and their right at the Court house, and Washington with his main army was coming up through Englishtown. As the Americans gained the brow of the elevation [the Heights of Freehold] they beheld the splendid grenadiers of the enemy, moving in compact masses, along the valley below; while further on was visible the long line of baggage wagons, toiling like some huge serpent through the dusty plain, here lost in the woods, there reappearing in the open country, until finally vanishing in the obscure distance. This magnificent spectacle was seen only for a moment, for, descending into the level ground, Lee prepared to attack the foe."

An even better way perhaps to furnish an idea of the relative position of the English and the American troops, when the firing began, will be to suggest a simile incapable of being misunderstood, and always ready to a reader. Extend the little finger of the left hand, (palm downward), close the other three, and stretch out the thumb at a right angle.—

The nail of the little finger represents Dickinson's division—American extreme advanced left—with the New-Jersey Militia, almost in the right rear of Clinton's first division, (under Cornwallis), facing toward the hand, and threatening Clinton's second division (under Knyphausen) moving off from the hand parallel to the little finger.

Clinton, with the division of Cornwallis, comprising about half of his army, at first ployed in columns to move off, *deployed* to the right and left, *now* facing W. on the road to Middletown, as soon as the American demonstrations developed themselves and showed they meant "fight." He also detached the Queen's Light Dragoons to take up a position on the American right (i. e. to the South) as it issued from the woods. Carrington, who devoted so much attention to this engagement, said in his speech delivered on the very stage of the first collision, at the Centennial Anniversary of the battle, " The number [of British] reported as moving from the woods [in delivering this their *counter-blow*] was stated by different [American] officers to be from 1,400 to 1,500 men. Some place the ultimate number at 2,500." A comparison of the testimony given at the Lee Court Martial demonstrates that the British forces engaged, throughout the day, were far inferior in numbers to the Americans actively confronting them. It is very doubtful if 3,000 at most were actively or actually "engaged" in the strict or technical sense of the word.

The thumb-nail indicates the relative position of Morgan with his 600 riflemen, about three miles south of Freehold, at a locality known a century since as "the Richmond Mills;" within the last 25 years as Shumar's Mills. These, although they are now the property of new owners, are still called Shumar's Mills. They are just on the outskirt west of "Blue Ball," a little village or hamlet in Howell township. Bear in mind, Morgan was destined to fall on the British right while Dickinson and others assailed their left. For some reason never explained—although in direct communication both with Lee and with Wayne—Morgan took no part whatever in the fight, nor did he "feel to it," although he distinctly heard the firing. In fact, on such a quiet day he could not have failed to hear it—both the crash of the musketry and the roar of the artillery—for the cannonade at Monmouth, according to the report of a German officer, was to the Seven Years War, known as "the Revolution," what that of Torgau was to the "Seven Years' War" in Germany, 1756–1763, the heaviest recorded on either side in the course of both of those seven years' struggles.

Again, what the heat of Monmouth was to our First War for Independence, the heat of Kunersdorf, 12th August, 1759, was to Prussia's great war for National integrity.

There may be, however, a somewhat satisfactory explanation of Morgan's inaction, in the anecdote introduced by G. W. P. Custis in his "Recollections, etc., of Washington," xii. 310–320. " *Si non e vero e ben trovato.*"

A night or two before the battle of Monmouth, Morgan, contrary to the express orders of Washington, personally given,—" not to fire a single shot, or bring on any skirmishing with the enemy,"—disobeyed both. For this, he being temporarily confined to his tent or put under arrest.

Next day, after this disregard of orders, and subsequent fright occasioned by Washington's reproof, he was restored to favor. If this story is true, it may serve to account for his inaction, although it is impossible to conceive how he could have been deaf to the appeals of Wayne, backed by the invitations " aux canons!" of the explosions of the near-at-hand battle. Morgan was undoubtedly in communication with Lee's grand division during the engagement of the morning (Lee Papers, N. Y. H. C. iii. 23, 120, impt.) If so why did he not do something. He had the requisite authority. Wayne sent him word " *the enemy are advancing and Colonel Morgan should govern himself accordingly.*" Could any message, from a soldier to a soldier, have been more significant or less susceptible of miscomprehension.

Graham, Morgan's biographer (210–'11), furnishes the following weak excuse for his hero's absence. " They [Morgan and Dickinson] had already partially engaged the enemy, when the latter were observed retracing their steps towards Monmouth. Soon after, and while the din of the conflict that ensued was heard in the distance, Morgan received orders to join the army. Unfortunately, he took a route on his return which diverged somewhat from that leading to the field of battle ; and from this cause, with the late hour of the day at which he commenced a march of some miles through a broken country, he did not reach the American army until night. Excessive was his mortification, and that of his corps, upon being informed of the events of the day, and of the opportunities which, from want of information, they had lost, of attacking the enemy in rear during the engagement."

Returning to the simile of the hand, the four knuckles represent the four (or five, and eventually more numerous) columns or detachments which obliqued to the left, or advanced directly to the front and deployed to support Dickinson in the flanking movement to the left and fill out Lee's line to the right. These five columns were commanded respectively by Brig-Gens. Maxwell, Wayne, Varnum and Scott, and Cols. Jackson and Grayson.— Some of these troops with their commanders had retreated so far by early afternoon that Steuben was ordered to stop them and assemble them behind the creek at Englishtown.— According to the clearest maps, this was over six miles, by the route followed, from the locality of their first meeting with the British, near Briar Hill, in the morning. In extenuation of this, a large portion of these troops were new levies and absolutely deficient in equipments. The two subordinate commanders, according to Gordon, who first withdrew, carried off with them over two thirds of his force, say about 3,500 to 4,000 men. Perhaps one half of Lee's grand division went off without doing anything, either through his own mismanagement or the errors of their immediate chiefs. The German Gosch (300- '2) does not blame Lee. Lossing places Greene in the fore-front, but he was not there. He was miles away, and had nothing to do with the preliminary work.

Lee was drawn partly across the eastern marsh and partly into the plain by the idea, or rather the reports, that the British were absolutely making off. He speedily realized his mistake. His five columns, N of Freehold, were deploying into line of battle when they were struck by the British, "a body of troops not equaled if to be surpassed by any in the world." These were in light fighting order, having divested themselves of their packs or knapsacks and encumbrances and they attacked as none but British Infantry, at this date, could charge with the bayonet. They drove the mass of the Americans in "confusion, worse confounded," nearly four miles.

Wayne was by far the most prominent, both as to will, audacity, and fighting power, in this the morning encounter, as he was in the afternoon's bloody work. He performed gallant service in the first phase of the battle, and might have done even better, but he could not act independently, or as he felt he ought, and as he intended. Wayne was the great fighting factor throughout, and Washington, by the special mention he makes of him in his report, acknowledges his preponderating influence upon the fortunate result. From opposite the knuckle of the middle finger, Col. Oswald threw himself forward, with a section of artillery, and, "alone and unsupported," opened a memorably vigorous cannonade at short range upon the British infantry and against their guns on the right of Clinton's first deployment, now facing west, i. e., toward Freehold. This was a dashing artillery manœuvre, and corresponds to the audacity of a rebel battery which darted out in advance of the rebel skirmish line, and poured in such a deadly fire of canister upon the right flank of Humphrey's Second Division of the Third Corps (Army of the Potomac) on the second day of Gettysburg.

Freehold, or Monmouth Court-house, lay a little back of the knuckle of the index finger, and the severest fighting of the first phase of this battle occurred between the nail of the little finger, (Dickinson's position toward the right and at Briar Hill,) and the Court-house to the left, where Simcoe's Queen's Rangers made so gallant a charge.— About the same time, the Seventeenth Light Dragoons scattered the American horse about the centre of Lee's line, and were in turn thrown back in disorder by Butler's American infantry regiment. Between Briar Hill north-east and Freehold south west there were woods on either side, a depression of the ground, a morass, "the east marsh," and a large pond drained north by sluggish streams —all these to the east of the road to Amboy. Clinton's return upon Lee drove the Americans not only across this first easterly marsh and the Amboy road, but likewise over the second central and worse morass. This (the middle) marsh was impassable for artillery or even horsemen without corduroying. In fact it could be only traversed with safety by a single causeway, about a mile and three-eights west of Monmouth Court-house, and was such a dangerous slough that a number of soldiers on both sides were suffocated in its treacherous depths. It was situated relatively to the other localities indicated very much as the wrist is to the knuckles of the hand, and was about central to the arena of the fighting. The Wemrock brook flowed out of it northward, and then bent round southward through a third wet bottom, (Carrington's "west ravine.") Beyond this rose the ridge (originally selected by Lee) on which Washington formed his main army, and the British, according to different plans, actually followed these troops across this brook, until they were rallied by Washington.

This ended the operations of the morning which have been indicated by the parallel of a left hand, palm down, pointing east. The operations of the afternoon of this day may be likewise represented by the disposition of a left hand, palm down, pointing west, with the fore and little finger alone extended, as the Italians make the demonstration (la Gettatura) against the effects of the evil eye. A coral charms of a hand, thus disposed, is very common. The nail of the forefinger would then indicate the position of the British Light Infantry and Queen's Rangers, which were repulsed by the American left in their bold attempt at a flanking or turning manœuvre. All the detailed narratives are very much involved. Botta says the British "endeavored to surround" the American main body. It is very likely that such was Clinton's intention, but the movement was so quickly frustrated that it scarcely amounted to anything except to exhibit British boldness, endurance, and discipline. This proves that, notwithstanding the exhausted condition of his troops, Clinton had such confidence in them that he did not hesitate to undertake the most audacious manœuvring. The column or detachment of Light Infantry which he shot out to the right actually collided with the left of Washington's main army. It called forth the best exertions of Lord Stirling, assisted by Steuben, to repulse these daring fellows. The nail of the little finger points out the direction of the furthest advance of the British left ---a second flanking attempt or demonstration of Clinton's second line. This, however, was after the British had fallen back across the Wemrock Brook and "the hedge." It must have been simultaneous with the dashing assault of Col. Monckton with the British grenadiers upon Wayne at the hedge row, a prominent feature in all the plans of this battle. This attack, thrice gallantly made, and finally so bloodily repulsed by "Mad Anthony," ended the battle proper.

Here it was Bunker Hill over again, and heavy artillery to render the defence more formidable, with trained regulars behind the hedge fence instead of green hands and new levies without bayonets. Monckton's assault was almost as desperate, in proportion to the number hurled upon his opponents, as that of Sherman upon the rebel lines at Kenesaw. The English troops were overloaded with woolen clothes and the heaviest accoutrements ; had been under arms at least 10 hours ; some of them had marched almost as many miles, and others even a greater distance, on the hottest or most overpowering day : ecorded in our history. They had been allowed to divest themselves of their uniforms—coats as well as their packs, &c., at Bunker Hill, 17 June, 1776, because they were at home, as it were, in Boston. Here the troops had to keep everything on because they were on the march, and what was put down even for a moment, was not likely to be ever recovered or replaced in an enemy's country. In regard to the heat of this day there is something inexplicable. It is claimed to have been the hottest, in the sense of unbearable, ever known in the Colonies. It must have been superlatively phenomenal, for the thermometer was only at 96° in the field, 112° in Philadelphia. European troops have fought with the thermometer many degrees higher both in the East and West Indies, and in Africa. General Kearny, while with the French army in Africa, speaks of active operations under an African tropical sun which struck down soldiers every hundred yards. In Egypt, both English and French fought right through the hot season, and there the thermometer sometimes rises to 120 in the shade in the daytime, and does not fall to the severest summer heat of New Jersey even during the night. It is said that the German troops positively refused to fight at Monmouth on account of the excessive heat. No wonder; poor devils! Their uniforms, arms, equipments and ordinary loads, and horribly stiff "getting-up" and "setting-up" were sufficient in themselves to exhaust any human being simply standing still under such a tropical heat. Nevertheless, nearly two hundred men on both sides were killed by the heat. The horses suffered even more. Shortly after the battle, Greene (*G. W. G. ii*. 91) who was Quarter Master General, had to busy himself to obtain a new supply of horses to make up for the heavy losses which the army had sustained in the field and on the march, [to and at Monmouth] in both of which large numbers had dropped dead from the heat." It is extraordinary, but horses are more sensible to the vicissitudes of the weather than human beings. Writing of the cold storm which assailed Sullivan's army in Rhode Island on the 12th-13th August, 1778, an eye witness says, "I saw for the first time that men were more hardy than horses, for a great many horses sank down and died." (*Cowell's Spirit of '76 in Rhode Island*, p. 167.) As will be seen, 50 English and 11 Germans perished without a wound, merely through the excessive heat and fatigue. Surgeon Thatcher attributes an equal loss from the same cause to the Americans. In many cases their tongues were so swollen from heat and thirst that officers and men were rendered speechless. The horses fell dead in troops. One Major-General lost three horses in succession, and Washington's splendid donated white charger dropped dead under him.* The Americans, who were at home, fought in their shirt-sleeves, which gave them immense advantages at a period of such terrific heat.

* When Washington first appeared on the battlefield and had the famous interview with Lee, he was mounted on a magnificent WHITE horse which had been presented to him by the then popular Governor of New Jersey, within a week, and since he crossed the Delaware. G. W. P. Custis says that this was the only occasion during the war that Washington rode a white horse. This is doubtful ; if memory serves, one of the horses he rode on the day of the Braddock Disaster, was white. When the donated charger sank down and died, Washington mounted a "CHESTNUT blood mare, with a long mane and tail," which Will Lee, or Billy, his favorite body servant, led up at once. This beautiful animal soon became covered with foam from excitement and hard galloping from point to point while its rider was disposing his main army.

To prevent any discussion about color in horses it may be well to state that "Chestnut" and "Sorrel" are often confounded in this country, both signifying "a reddish brown." The French draw a marked distinction between the two colors. Sorrel is *Alezan* or *Saure*, whereas Chestnut is Chataine.

In regard to Monckton's death the American and British testimony is irreconcilable. "On account of his singular merit" (says Lendrum, Boston, 1795, ii 221,) " he was universally lamented. The facts in regard to an individual of such note must have been best known to his comrades and followers. Stedman reads that "his men paid the most marked tribute of respect to his memory. During the confusion of a dangerous cannonade the battalion, in parties, relieved each other, until, with their bayonets, (being destitute of more proper tools), they perfected a grave, where they laid the body of their beloved commanding officer, placing over it with their hands the earth they had moistened with their tears." On the other hand, the American historians declare that Monckton's corpse remained in the hands of our troops, and was interred by them. Stedman (who was with Cornwallis at this time) is the most reliable witness.

If Clinton had acted as did Frederic the Great at Sohr, and sacrificed his baggage, he might have achieved as great a triumph on the 28th June, 1778, as Prussia's hero on the 30th September, 1745— a result which decided the fate of 33 years of war and uncertain peace or armistice, in favor of the Black Eagle of Brandenburg. Instances of such sagacious sacrificing of the lesser to the greater, of the immaterial to material interests, might be multiplied *ad nauseam*. Arbela, Larissa, Fornova, Janikau, Mollwitz, Chotusgst, &c. Clinton was not great enough in zeal to discriminate justly. He saved his bougage and he lost (abandoned) the field. Thereupon Frederic the Great, greatest living judge, gave as his decision upon the reports of the English themselves: " Clinton gained no advantage except to reach New York. * * America is probably lost to England."

Monmouth was no victory in the " Field of Mars," but in the Field of Political and Moral Results it was a Waterloo, a Sadowa, and a Gettysburg.

Charles de Mazade (1877), in his Life of Count Cavour (199) uses some expressions which are not inapplicable to Monmouth, 28th June, 1778. "But already, before this *more bloody* than decisive battle of June 24th, [Solferino, 1859], there had been some clouds in the camp of the Allies With the progress of events the situation grew more complicated." Exactly so with the Allies, British and Germans. The complication arose from Clinton's incomprehension of the situation. A decided victory would have dissolved the American forces. Notwithstanding, the short-sighted Clinton was hindering of his baggage when England's supremacy in the New World was at stake. All that Great Britain had battled for, for nearly a century, was in the scales balancing a twelve-miles-long baggage train.

The American born Major-General, Henry Lee, sums up the whole matter with a soldier's judgment. " It must be admitted, on a full view of the action, that the palm of victory clearly belonged to Washington,although it was not decisive, nor susceptible of improvement."

☞ Military, and immediately, all that was accomplished by the Americans was to delay Clinton about fourteen hours, and kill and disable two or three hundred of his men. Morally, and remotely, the results were of almost incalculable importance.

From the hedge in front of which Monckton, whom (our) Heath styles " a brave and experienced officer," was killed, the British did not fall back much more than 50 rods to their bivouac for the night. Consequently, measuring from the furthest point to which Clinton pushed his Light Infantry to the west to the farthest point to which Lee's troops advanced to the east, the Americans did not win back more than a third of the ground from which they had been driven during the earlier part of the day. It would appear by comparison and harmonizing of testimony that the American defense at this time was rendered effectual by a battery on Comb's Hill, far to the right and in advance of the American main line of battle. This battery will receive a special notice. The movement of Clinton's right is positively defined on the French plan in Barber, as elsewhere, but that of his left is not so clear, although it is established by Washington's as well as by his own report, and by concurrent circumstances. Meanwhile the knuckles of the two intervening fingers, closed, will not inaptly represent Clinton's main line of battle, opposed at the hedge, or living fence, to Wayne, where the grand fight and repulse occurred, [Brevet] Lieut.-Col. [Local Brig: Gen :?] Hon. H. Monckton having been killed at the knuckle of the middle finger:—Freehold, as in the former case, would occupy about the position of the left prominent wrist bone.

The final repulse or arrest of Clinton's vigorous counter w s achieved by a battery of six guns posted on Comb's Hill, about a quarter of a mile south-west of Monckton's deployment, which poured in such a terrific enfilading fire upon the British line that nothing human could stand it. It is asserted as a fact that a single round shot from one of these guns, passing just over the heads of the grenadiers knocked the muskets out of the hands of a whole platoon—something almost incredible, even conceding the precision of British drill and tactics. These six guns, commanded by the French Chevalier Plessis-Mauduit, played the same part in determining the success of the Americans as the 12 pieces gathered into battery by Marmont at Marengo, which he claims as the decisive incident that turned the vibrating scales of victory in favor of Bonaparte. Or, to bring the simile nearer home, Plessis-Mauduit's battery exercised the saving influence of the little crescent of artilery hastily disposed by Pleasanton, with which he stopped the hitherto victorious onset of Stonewall Jackson on Hooker's right at Chancelorsville. The contradictory evidence as to who buried Moncton† is only the beginning of the difficulties which becloud the conclusion of the story of Monmouth.

Washington, who slept or rested, under a wide-spreading oak tree on the battle-field, states in his report to Congress that his troops lay extremely close to the British during the night, and that the latter marched away about 12 P. M. in such silence that they effected their retreat without the knowledge of the American troops in closest vicinity. This statement could not be from Washington's own knowledge, but must have been founded on the report of these very same troops. On the other hand, Clinton says that he commenced to move at 10 P. M. He likewise reposed, wrapped in his cloak, upon the field among his troops, ready for any emergency. There is not a line in Clinton's report which emanates directly from himself, and depends upon his own knowledge, (i. e. is "first hand," not prompted by *ruse* or based on the reports of subordinates) which does not carry with it internal evidence of its truthfulness; not a sentence which will not impress upon an unprejudiced reader a conviction of its correctness and sincerity. Nevertheless, Clinton's statement that he moved at 10 P. M. is disputed, and his taking advantage of the moonlight derided, because the moon set at 10.59 P. M. If Clinton did move at 10 P. M., as he said, (and the writer believes he did,) he then did have 59 minutes of moonlight; besides the shimmering or twilight subsequent to the setting, which might be calculated at

*The following striking anecdote must be credited to F. D Stone, Esq., Librarian of the Pennsylvania Historical Society, who was kind enough to transcribe it from the " Historical Record of the 52d Regiment, B. A."
" On the 28th June, [1778] as the last division descended from the heights above Freehold, in New Jersey, the Americans appeared in their rear and on both flanks, when some sharp fighting took place. The grenadier company of the 52d, had Captain John Powell killed, and Lieutenant Francis Grose, wounded."—General Hunter says that Captain Powell made the fourth captain of grenadiers that the 52d had lost during the American War, and it was on this occasion that the Drummer of his company was heard to exclaim, " Well, I wonder who they'll get to accept of our grenadier company now. I'll be d——d if I would."

†How aptly Scott's lines apply to his case:
" Dread then to speak, presumptuous doom,
On noble Marmion's lowly tomb ;"
(" They dug his grave e'en where he lay,")
" But say ; he died a gallant knight,
With sword in hand for England's right."

15 minutes more. A moon four days old is almost a quarter moon, and would shed a great deal of light in a level country. This is the opinion of experts who have been consulted—-persons—-particularly county physicians—whose business compels them to move about the country at night.— The writer heard and read enough of the arguments about moonlight, in connection with Gettysburg, to become satisfied that the opinions of very few people, who did not note down their own observations at the time, are worthy of any confidence. This brings us to the next point, whether or not the British marched off in silence. Stedman, one of the most reliable of historians, and a member of the staff of Cornwallis, traverses the American account and records that "just as the British were beginning to move, some horses or cattle were straggling through a wood, and a battalion of Light Infantry, taking them for the enemy, began a fire upon them, which continued for five minutes." In one of our histories there is an allusion to dropping shots even after the moon rose. This may refer to the firing cited by Stedman, when the British were already leaving their bivouacs. Gen. William Irvine distinctly states that the battle, proper, ended at 4.30 P. M.

It is very strange how events repeat themselves. Such straggling of animals has more than once precipitated a battle, and the fighting on the second day of Gettysburg was brought on to the left by a contest between Berdan's Sharpshooters and the nearest rebel skirmishers, for the possession of some cattle which strayed on and across their fronts.

The idea that the British decamped so noiselessly that they failed to attract the attention of the American pickets is almost incredible. On a warm Summer night in the country the slightest sharp sound will be heard for miles. It is conceded that the British removed the majority of their wounded. Some of these sufferers must have yelled with pain, even if stirred after fever had set in, and their groans could have been heard for a long distance on a quiet night. What is more, there is always a great deal of rattling connected with the rolling of artillery over uneven ground, and sufficient noise is inseparable from the movements, of army wagons and even ambulances, to have alarmed the American sentries, just across the Middle Marsh, if these had been awake, or alert, or anxious to bring on a renewal of the fighting. Something very much like such lassitude and inattention, if not worse, occurred after the third day's struggle at Gettysburg.

The fact is, Washington could not have attacked the British with any hope of success if Clinton had chosen to stop and try it out, and had sufficient food for guns and men.—

Clinton lay behind a marsh almost impassable, a slough which had swallowed up a number of the retreating Americans, crossed only by a single narrow causeway. The British were beaten by the heat of the day, and the Germans, more or less disaffected, would not fight from the same cause. This is the true solution of the problem. Washington's army was certainly unanimous ; Clinton's certainly was not so ; the Germans had been tampered with. That he did not deem them all reliable was demonstrated by his action before evacuating Philadelphia. Sold by despotic Princes to be slaughtered in foreign shambles, it could hardly be expected that their hearts would be strongly enlisted in the work. The majority of what the Germans accomplished was the result of natural courage and discipline. In other words, they were constitutionally brave, and were driven, as a rule, into action as cattle are forced into the abattoirs. Clinton's fighting, proper, as a whole at Monmouth was done by the pick of the British, and they did it as well as it could have been done. No exception can be taken to the conduct of the regular Americans disciplined by Steuben; but Militia are Militia, and New Levies unreliable ; such they always have been, are, and ever will be. Washington did not deem the ordinary Militia worthy to rank as effectives ; did not include them in his estimates of force ; and certainly disparaged them.

Lamb (English service) in his noted Journal, sums up the case about as justly as possible and as follows : " The total disagreement between the British and American accounts of this action is not a little perplexing to the impartial narrator. Both parties claim the advantage, but the Americans particularly, at that time, had their reasons for their misrepresentations—reasons which did not at all influence the report of the British commander."

The American-born Major-General, Henry Lee, presents the gist of the whole matter with a soldier's judgment and conciseness :— " It must be admitted, on a full view of the action, that the palm of victory clearly belonged to Washington, *although it was not decisive, nor susceptible of improvement.*"

Major General Heath, in his " Memoirs " which often breathe a charming spirit of candor (185-188) after alluding to Clinton's being " encumbered with an immense train of stores and baggage," adds " these are the greatest incumbrance to a General, on a march of danger from an attack of his opponent to which he can be exposed." He applauds Clinton's " wise resolution to make a stand with a part of his best troops, while he pushed on his baggage," etc.

" Gen. Washington, acting with equal skill, and equal bravery, made every arrangement which the moment called for. * * * *

Here was Gen. Washington seen in all his splendor ; for this critical situation is the orb in which he shines the brighest. He rallied the retreating troops ; he inspired them by precept and by example ; and the misfortune of the morning was considerably retrieved." * * * Both Generals undoubtedly have much credit for their conduct in this action. Gen. Clinton's object being to reach New York with his baggage, &c., obtained this victory, with the loss which he sustained.— Gen. Washington's conduct was well calculated for victory on his side ; and *how far he would have succeeded*, had it not been for the misfortune of the morning, *none can tell.* This misfortune began by exposing the American advanced troops, in line, on the side of the field where they were cannonaded by the British, who at the same time wisely exposed only their artillery to that of the Americans. * * * * It was here that the firm Col. Wesson had his back peeled of its muscles, almost from shoulder to shoulder, by a cannon ball. The confidence of the troops could not be fully recovered, until they saw the presence of their beloved General Washington !

We Americans are so much accustomed to view everything in the light of our own glory that we are willing to receive as an undoubted truth the statement that Washington was anxious to renew the struggle on the morning of the 29th, and disappointed to find that the enemy had vanished. As it is impossible to decide whether this is so or not, it may be worthy of consideration to recall what the imperial Field Marshall Dunn said to his superior, the Archduke Charles, just before the opening of the battle of Lissa, or Leuthen.— The Austrians occupied a strong position, and were from 80,000 (von Kausler) to 90,000 strong. When the Prussians, about 30,000, commenced their oblique movement toward the Austrian left, Daun supposed that instead of advancing to the attack they were moving off, and said : " Let them go, we are well rid of them." After such a fight as that of the 28th some such idea may have occurred to the American commander.

It has been previously observed that a regular pitched battle requires a heavy butcher's bill ; there was none such at Monmouth. Washington reported only 8 officers, 1 sergeant, and 60 privates ; total, 69 (of whom according to the American Surgeon Thatcher) about 60 perished through the heat of the day) killed ; 19 officers, 9 Sergeants, and 133 privates wounded. There is no use of considering the 132 missing, because a majority afterward turned up. Conceding that Washington only had 15,000 men, this total of casualites is only 1½ per cent. Clinton, on the other hand, reported only 147 British and

Germans as dead—of these, 70 victims to the heat, so that only 77 were killed, 170 wounded, and 68 missing. The killed in battle and wounded were not 2½ per cent. of his aggregate force. Comparing such losses with those sustained on both sides during the Slaveholders' Rebellion and they furnish no evidence of hard fighting. Concede, however, that the American account is true, and that the Americans buried 217 British dead,‡ or the highest amount claimed---249---besides those previously interred by the British themselves, then Clinton lost in killed by round shot and bullets, 10 per cent. of his troops actually under fire, and the Americans from the same cause not one-quarter per cent.

One fact in connection with Monmouth Court House should never be forgotten—of the "Revolutionary patriots who on that day [Monmouth] periled life for their country, more than 700 black Americans [negroes, or colored men] fought side by side with the white."

MARVELOUS INFLUENCE OF WASHINGTON.

When Washington appeared upon the field it is impossible to recognize anything like an orderly retreat on the part of the Americans. Charles Smith, who published a very rare *History of the American War from 1775 to 1783*, in 1797, and is very favorable to Lee, nevertheless remarks that " the arrival of Washington with the main army" and Washington's dispositions " probably saved his advanced corps from total ruin." Lossing, who examined the battle-field more than 25 years ago, says : " A panic seized the republican

‡ The official returns of the American burial parties give 217 British interred, but, as an unbiased American writer observes, due allowance must be made for the ordinary errors of such reports. Clinton had no incentive to falsify in this regard, and his report carries conviction of no intention to deceive. The English never seem to care much for removing their dead at the time. High or low, they are wrapped in their blankets and interred where they fall, as for instance, Lt. Col. Willington, who was killed at Plattsburg, 12 September, 1814. Lamb, in his Journal, (so often referred to) makes a very pertinent comment and entry He says: "The total disagreement between the British and American accounts of this action is not a little perplexing to the impartial narrator; both parties claim the advantage; but the Americans, particularly at that time, had their reasons for their misrepresentations—reasons which did not at all influence the reports of the British commanders." (Page 242.) Major-Gen. (then Lieutenant) Philip Kearny, in his account of his experiences with the French Army in Algiers, says that Marshal Vallee regulated his reports to suit the Parisian clamor for bloodless victories — The Swiss authorities, it is said, never dared to make public the Federal losses in putting down their Secession movement—*Sonderbund*—for fear they could never get their Militia out again in force, if the truth were told ; and Washington, it is very likely, may have had to formulate his reports on this republican principle. It would seem as if the Colonists were not particularly anxious to enlist, for Major Shaw wrote in April, 1780, " 'Tis really abominable that we should send to France for soldiers, when there are so many sons of America die." See Chotteau in this connection.

troops, and over the broken country they fled precipitately and in great confusion, a large portion of them pressing toward the causeway over a broad morass, (the 'middle ravine,') where many perished; while others, overpowered by the heat, fell upon the earth and were trampled to death in the sand by those pressing on behind them." Col. John Laurens wrote, on the 30th of June, 1778 : " All this disgraceful retreating passed, without the firing of a musket, over ground which might have been disputed inch by inch. * * * Here, fortunately for the honor of the Army and the welfare of America, Gen. Washington met the troops retreating in disorder, and without any plan to make an opposition." Col. Hamilton, in his letter, 5th of July, 1778, remarks : " After changing their position two or three times by retrograde movements, our advanced corps got into a general confused retreat, and even rout would hardly be too strong an expression. * * * I never saw the General to so much advantage. His coolness and firmness were admirable. He instantly took measures for checking the enemy's advance, and giving time to the Army, which was very near, to form and make a proper disposition. * * * America owes a great deal to Gen. Washington for this day's work. A general rout, dismay and disgrace would have attended the whole in any other hands but his. By his own good sense and fortitude he turned the fate of the day. Other officers have great merit in performing their parts well, but he directed the whole with the skill of a Master Workman. He did nothing himself at a distance [referring to Gates at Saratoga] and leave an Arnold to win laurels for him ; but by his own presence he brought order out of confusion, animated his troops, and led them to success."

Under any circumstances Washington was right in fighting, since (to quote " Military Ends and Moral means ") " However avrricious a General may be of the blood of his men, *it may sometimes be good policy to fight, in order to establish amongst the troops a feeling of confidence in their commander*; that feeling which is the fundamental basis of an army, and which can only exist when soldiers and officers have a mutual knowledge of each other, founded on experience in war."

If it is true that Washington exposed himself as recklessly as he is represented to have done, then was Monmouth the acme of his glory. Riding fearlessly in the face of the iron storm vomited by the enemy's artillery, and amid the more destructive volleys of the British grenadiers, he restored confidence with words of cheer, " a voice of faith to the despairing soldiers," " a voice omnipotent with the inspiration of courage " to the broken Americans; and Monmouth was for Washington what Munda (modern Marbella) was for Cæsar. Hirtius, one of Cæsar's friends, seems to be describing Monmouth when he dilates upon "the plain and the bright sun which shone out as if the gods had made it a day for triumph," such a sun as that which Napoleon often cited to inspire enthusiasm, the "*Soleil d' Austerlitz.*" The day of Munda was won, not by the soldiers, but by the General—Cæsar! Whatever glory accrues to America from Monmouth glows like a never-fading aureola about the head of Washington. ¶

CONCLUSION.

The battle of Monmouth has always been looked upon as a sort of military conundrum; the problem unsolved and insoluble.‖ Conflicting interests have made it so, but such was not in reality the fact. Still it was a *tohu bohu* of fighting, just as the testimony is a *tohu bohu* of words. It would not be pleasant, perhaps, for every one engaged if the testimony was winnowed and only the pure grain of truth presented. For Washington the battle was a moral or political necessity, and all that he did could not have been better done. Lee is not responsible for what occurred in the morning, but a scape-goat was requisite, and the indulgence of his acrimonious temper afforded an opportunity of throwing the blame upon him.₰ It was equally a matter of absolute necessity that no doubt should be permitted to get abroad that the Americans had not been unquestionably victorious. Clinton's unnecessary retreat—(like Bennington's withdrawal from his victorious field of Preuss-Eylau, thus conceding the triumph to Napoleon which the latter had not won by fighting)—gave to the Thirteen Colo-

¶ Jefferson, in endeavoring to portray Washington's military capacity, doubtless arrived at a very just conclusion. He said that give Washington sufficient time to plan a campaign or a battle, and no general that ever lived could do it better; but that to do so he required time. He could not improve if anything traversed or disordered a plan of his; his mind did not work quickly enough to accommodate itself to sudden changes of circumstances. What always saved Washington was his excellent common sense. No man better understood the relations of cause and effect. For this reason he was so successful in his Trenton-Princeton triumph.— This, the great tactical writer, von Bulow, declares was sufficient to elevate him to the Temple of Immortality, and it was carried out in exact accordance with the plan, the very enemy assisting rather than thwarting it was reserved for Monmouth to put the seal to the preamble on the Monongahela (Braddock's Defeat, 9th July, 1755), that Washington was a hero as far as exposing his person was concerned in battle as well as a general. What might have occurred if Lord North's "one wise thought"—the sending of Lord Clive to command in America—had been carried into effect, is among the unresolved and insoluble questions. The opportune suicide of Lord Clive, prevented the opposing of a real genius to "the long head" of Washington, who, in Clive, would have encountered "a general, who, in vigor of will and fertility of resources, was unequalled by any European commander since the death of Marlborough." This must exclude Frederic the Great, or else the author does not know what he is writing about; otherwise it is pertinent.

Nevertheless, Washington erred in allowing Lee to supersede LaFayette and Wayne, and thereby *violated* one of the "Maxims of War," as quoted in "Military Ends and Moral Means" by the author of the "Art of War." His words exactly portray the position mentally, morally, and militarily occupied by Lee.

"The idiosyncrasy of individual officers and soldiers [is] to be studied." "To commit the execution of a purpose to one who disapproves of the plan of it, is to employ but one-third of the man; his heart and his head are against you; you have command only of his hands."

"An unwilling commander. it is said, is half beaten before the battle begins, therefore, an officer [like Wayne] who is in favor of the measure, is to be preferred for the execution of it, to one [Lee] who disapproves of the plan, and one who volunteers to carry it out [even like LaFayette] is to be preferred to either, supposing the qualifications of all three to be on a par in other respects."

‖ Dr Ludwig Gosch published at Giessen (Hesse-Darmstadt), in 1817, a work entitled "Washington and the North American Revolution."

Wherever he obtained the particulars, he furnishes more clearly than any other historian examined, the votes and opinions of the American Generals composing the Councils of War during the movements prior to Monmouth. He says, "not a single general officer was in favor of attempting any hindrance to the British passage of the Delaware, or any attack upon them before they evacuated Philadelphia."

Lee was opposed to bringing on either a battle or any sort of collision. (Gosch, strange to say, seems to agree with General Cust. B. A. that the British army was only 10,000 strong.) Lee thought that it would be criminal to risk a battle, on account of the equal numbers in either army of which each was about 10,000 strong, more or less. (This must mean rank and file of Regulars; for including militia, &c., no candid critic can pretend that Washington had less than 15,000.) Gen. du Portail, a French officer of great military reputation, likewise Baron von Steuben, endorsed Lee's views. Out of seventeen American generals, only two—Wayne and Cadwallader—*were decided for a fight.* LaFayette appeared to incline to the counsels of the last two, without expressing himself clearly to this effect. General Greene, while agreeing, felt that more should be undertaken than the majority of the Council of War held to be advisable; that the country must be protected, and, if, in consequence, an engagement should become necessary, he was for fighting the enemy. Washington coincided with Wayne and Cadwallader. These three were unconditionally for a battle: Washington through his extraordinary decision of character, no less than through his spirit of enterprise and foresight. (In a word, Washington saw that to keep up not only the spirit of the people but the spirit and reputation of the army itself, and the faith of all classes in an army, a battle was—from every possible point of view—an unavoidable necessity.) Providence, not man, so regulated circumstances (as during the Slaveholders Rebellion) that Monmouth, like Antietam, was not decisive, nor any battle determinately decisive until events had matured, and then came NASHVILLE and Appomattox Court House.

Gosch may have derived these facts from Marshall's Life of Washington, or from original papers, although the writer has never seen Marshall's work in the vernacular, but only in a French translation, and the German writer is more significant in the turn of his sentences.

LEE.

₰ As the writer has already published an elaborate consideration of the case of Major General Charles Lee, in the MONMOUTH DEMOCRAT. 15th August, 1878, there is no need of repeating what appeared in this issue. Still, there are other testimonies in his favor which it is but fair to present. These were passed over when the defense was prepared and published.

The American-born Major General, (Provisional Army, 1798) Henry Lee—(Colonel, Revolutionary Army)— no relative of the English born Charles Lee—in his Menies all the advantages of a victory—although Clinton certainly was not beaten, and he could not have been beaten in the very strong position which he assumed, if he had not allowed his ammunition and provision trains to get beyond his reach. His abandonment of the field could scarcely be explained away, although as a professional soldier his reputation did not suffer under the scrutiny of the severest critics.

The story of this conflict has been seasoned to suit the palate of our people. There is a perfect parallel to this course of procedure in the case of Marengo. Marengo in its results was a great victory for the French; but it was by no means so clear that Bonaparte was the grand hero of it. The battle had certainly been lost by him, as Monmouth is said to have been by Lee, when Dessaix came up. Fortunately for the First Consul, Dessaix was killed, and Kellerman, who played the part of Wayne, and Marmont of Greene, Steuben, or Plessis Mauduit, could be comparatively ignored. What was the result?

"The confusion of events at Marengo," says Lanfrey, the French historian, "had been so extraordinary, that, although Bonaparte was accustomed to rectify on paper his military operations, by arrangements which were *after-thoughts* that often gave to them an order and a perspicuity which they did not intrinsically possess, it was impossible for him to write of this victory anything else but an informal account, in which there was neither plan nor instant. * * No attack it seems can be made on Gen. Washington but it must recoil on the assailant."

Alexander Gorden, a Continental officer, in his "Anecdotes of the Revolutionary War," etc., (353) uses these emphatic words while criticising Lee's manœuvres, "acquitting him thoroughly of the infamous motives that have been alleged against him."

Lendrum, in his "History of the American Revolution," Boston, 1795, (ii. 221) takes the same favorable view of the circumstances.

"In this action General Lee was charged by General Washington with disobedience and misconduct in retreating before the British army. He was tried by a court martial, and sentenced to be suspended from his command in the American army for a twelve-month. Many were displeased with this sentence, because it had been submitted to his discretion whether to attack or not, and likewise when and in what manner, and they thought that suspension from command was not a sufficient punishment for his crimes, if guilty. *They therefore inferred his innocence from the lenient sentence of his judges.*"

Finally, W. Belsham in his George III ii. 306-7, has a curious and pertinent paragraph: "It was suspected that the Commander-in-Chief was not displeased at the dismissal of a man so haughty and impracticable; nor did the army in whose estimation he had been visibly lessened since the disaster which had befallen him, appear much to regret his loss. For though the capture of General Lee was merely fortuitous, misfortune is in the minds of men nearly allied to disgrace, disgrace produces contempt, and contempt verges towards alienation and hatred."

As compa isons have often been instituted between the conductors on this day, of the experienced professional, LEE, and the amateur tyro LAFAYETTE, it is but fair to present what Chotteau in his "War for Independence." (prefaced by Laboulaye). 185-9 says, that he proposed to Rochambeau even in 1780, when he had enjoyed a three years apprenticeship in the art of war, "extravagant plans" and that his project showed "the influence of unwise counsels." The French commander replies "like an aged father to a young, tender son, whom he greatly loves and esteems. Lord Mahon is worthy of examination in this connection, (vi. 152-156). He likewise quotes Napoleon and the noted M. de St Priest, both of whom had no opinion of LaFayette's judgment. These, as well as other French writers, justify theremark of Gen. Greene, "The Marquis's thirst for glory and national attachment often run him into errors." (G. W. G., ii. 127.) Reflect upon the following paragraph from Lord Mahon's pages, "That zeal, favored as it was by fortune, adapted to the times that came upon him, and urged forward by great personal vanity, laid the foundations of his fame far more, as I conceive, than any strength of mind or talents of his own. Few men have ever been so conspicuous from afar with so little, when closely viewed, of real weight or dimension. As a General, it can scarcely be pretended that his exploits were either many or considerable."

---

moirs of the War, etc., devotes chapter ix, page 37, and appendix 423, to the consideration of Monmouth and unhappy case of his namesake.

"Major General Lee" "possessed a sublime genius, highly improved by books and travel; but was eccentric from freedom of thought, which he uttered without reserve; sarcastic without malignity of heart, but with asperity of tongue; and imprudent from an indisposition to guard himself by cramping mental independences." "He was arrested upon sundry charges, tried, found guilty, and sentenced to be suspended from his command in the army for one year. The effect of which was, that the veteran soldier who had relinquished his native country to support a cause dear to his heart, became lost to that of his adoption, and soon after lost to himself; as the few years he survived seem to have been passed in devotion to the sway of those human tormentors, envy and hate. The records of the court-martial *manifest on their face the error of the sentence;* and it is wonderful how men of honor and of sense could thus commit themselves to the censures of the independent and impartial. If General Lee had been guilty of all the charges as affirmed by their decision, his life was forfeited; and its sacrifice only could have atoned for his criminality. He ought to have been cashiered and shot; instead of which the mild sentence of suspension, for a short time, was the punishment inflicted. The truth is, the unfortunate general was only guilty of neglect in not making timely communication of his departure from orders, *subject to his discretion*, to the commander-in-chief, which constituted no part of the charges against him. This was certainly a very culpable omission; to which was afterwards added personal disrespect, where the utmost respect was not only due, but enjoined by martial law, and enforced by the state of things; two armies upon the very brink of battle, himself intrusted with the direction of an important portion of one of them, for the very purpose of leading into action, to withhold the necessary explanations from his chief, and to set the example of insubordination by his mode of reply to an interrogatory, indispensably, though warmly, put to him, merited punishment. But this offence was different, far different, from "disobedience to orders," or "a shameful retreat;" neither of which charges were supported by testimony; and both of which were contradicted by fact."

The Annual Register, 1778, has likewise several pertinent paragraphs, of which one, the most important, reads as follows, 226*: "It is impossible for us to enter into the merits of this sentence; in which *Party* might have had a great share. When a dispute had been carried to so great an height, between an officer (Washington) on whom the Americans reposed their chief consequence, and one (Lee) subordinate and less popular, *it is not difficult to divine where the blame will be laid.*" No wonder the unfortunate Lee wrote, July 22d, to Gen. Reed: "I am conscious that nothing but cabal, artifice, power and iniquity can tarnish my name for an

consequences. This had to be remedied, and the attempts and methods adopted to straighten out the story were not abandoned as long as he lived.

"During his reign he revised his bulletin or report three times, so as to modify it for effect in history. In these three narratives, which have been preserved in the *Memorial de la Guerre*, the reader perceives that he contradicts and falsifies himself every instant." Jomini called Marengo an *echauffouree, i. e.*, a rash, headlong, or blundering enterprise; technically a skirmish. Such was Monmouth, and nothing more.

The world must judge of results; and according to this rule Monmouth counts as a most resultive victory for America. Frederick the Great—than whom no better critic could be cited—viewed it in this light. The court of appeals of events has confirmed his decision. France may lament over the loss of Lorraine and Alsace, but all the scribbling in the world will not reverse the accomplished fact decided by the "wager of battle." The South, in like manner, may pour rivers of ink upon steppes of paper to prove that they were not conquered, without altering the decision of blood—not ink—at Appomattox Court-house.

American historians have endeavored to demonstrate that Monmouth was a "pitched battle," and cite Lord Mahon to prove it. But his language is very qualified. He says: "Thus, on the whole, it was a pitched battle; the advantage, if any, being rather on the side of the British, who had fought only to secure their retreat, and who had succeeded in that object. The Americans ascribe their disappointment to the fault of Gen. Lee." *

The sober truth is, it was nothing but a rearguard fight. Unprejudiced scrutiny cannot discover that 3,000 British troops were under even cannon fire at any period of the day, whereas, first and last, the majority of the American forces were brought into action. Clinton fought for nothing else but to

---

* Surgeon Thatcher, in his *Journal* (136), writes: "This contest was conducted with military ardor and spirit on the side of both armies, but *was not on so broad a scale* as to prove very decisive in its consequences. Each side, it is said, claims the victory; but, allowing the honor to be equally divided, the enemy is incomparably the greatest sufferer. If reports are accurate. the loss of the Royalists consists of 4 officers and 245 rank and file killed and left on the field buried by our people; (of these, 70 victims to the heat,) 1,245 wounded, 107 prisoners, and 1,572 deserted during the march; total of their loss after they left Philadelphia, according to accounts circulated, 3,189. Of the Continentals, according to returns, 69 were killed, 142 wounded, and about 160 missing. The intense heat of the weather, great fatigue, and drinking cold water proved fatal to about 60 or 80 men of *each party*." (How inconsistent! According to this, only 9 Americans could have been killed by the British at most, which is simply conceding the Americans were not under even a moderate fire or within ordinary battle range.)

save his baggage and to secure his retreat. He did not see the effect of his course upon the future.

To elevate any conflict between armies to the dignity of a pitched battle requires a grand object or objective and corresponding results, likewise—"a heavy butcher's bill." Of all the battles of the "Slaveholder's Rebellion," it approaches nearest to Perryville or Chaplin Hills, 8th October, 1862, where Bragg made a return upon Buell, or rather McCook—in the same way as Clinton did upon Lee—to save his baggage and his plunder of Kentucky. In other respects again it bears some resemblance to Williamsburg, 5th May, and to South Mountain, 14th September, 1862—although there is no similarity in the severity of the fighting—to Malvern Hill, to Antietam, and to Cumberland Church, the last fight of the Army of the Potomac, 7th April, 1865. All these belong to the same class, which includes Monmouth, likewise Busaco, where Wellington turned on Massena, 27th September, 1810. (Study Seneffe, 1 August, 1674, for some curious parity of circumstances, in the "Field of Mars.")

Charles Lee, with all his faults, was an experienced professional soldier, and knew the exact meaning of military terms. In a letter of the 3d of July, 1778, he says: "To call the affair a complete victory would be a dishonorable gasconade. It was, indeed, a very handsome check, which did the Americans honor. No affair can be more convincing of what they are equal to; in a retrograde manœuvre of near four miles, no confusion was observable but what arose, and ever will arise, from a monstrous abuse, which, if tolerated, will be one day fatal---I mean the liberty which individuals, without authority, take to direct and give their opinions. The behavior of the whole, both men and officers, was so equally good that it would be unjust to make distinctions, though I confess it is difficult to refrain from paying compliments to the artillery, from Gen. Knox and Col. Oswald down to the very driver. It is difficult to say which was the decisive point—it was *a battle in pieces*, and by dint of fighting in a variety of places—in the plain and in the woods—by advancing and retreating, the enemy were at last fairly worn down." Just so, *worn down!*

Now let us see what foreigners have to say. The French were certainly our friends. According to their account, "Clinton availed himself of the darkness, not choosing to wait for the hazards of the to-morrow. * * * Yet the objects aimed at by Washington were still unaccomplished, his victory still uncertain. He wished to prevent Clinton from passing beyond Monmouth and re-embarking, but his intentions were frustrated, and, although he had gained the victory, he could not reap from it any advantage. On the other hand, Clinton, although vanquished and flying, had secured all that he had promised to himself."

Botta, the champion of America, reads:— "Clinton, besides, had not to blush for this day, since with his rear guard he had repulsed the American van, and had finally arrested the whole army of the enemy. His troops were greatly inferior in numbers to those of Washington ; but it would have been an imprudence even for an army of equal force to risk a new engagement when so great a part of it was at such a distance and in a country whose inhabitants and whose surface presented little else but opposition and obstacles. The loss of the battle would have been followed by the total ruin of the army. On all these considerations he decided for retreat."

Schlosser, the prominent German historian of the eighteenth century, concludes his remarks, (v. 200) on these movements thus :— "The Americans not only harassed them [the British] on their march through the Jerseys, but even ventured upon a formal attack, from which, however, they derived but little advantage. On this march Cornwallis and Knyphausen gained as great reputation as Washington."

Never was British discipline, courage, fortitude and endurance more resplendently displayed ; never were British troops more elegantly handled and manœuvred and fought than upon the field of Monmouth. Clinton's native army comprised a body of soldiers which could scarcely be equaled in the world. The Coldstream Guards had, and have, a world-wide renown ; Britain's Grenadiers have always stood at the head of the infantry of civilized military organizations ; its Light Infantry at this time was unsurpassed and unsurpassable, and its Cavalry was excellent. That the American troops met such veterans as these, led by two such heroes in battle as Clinton and Cornwallis—the latter, like Wayne, always " spoiling for a fight,"—not to forget Grant and " No—flint," or " Bayonet " Grey, and others less known to fame but equally efficient, on equal terms, indeed, was a triumph of Steuben's discipline and Washington's marvelous influence.

There is no question that the Continentals, (Congress—soldiers or Regulars drilled by Steuben), behaved in a manner to reflect absolute glory on the American militarily constituted Army. No exception can be taken to their behavior.

But as to the new levies and militia, what Moeller in his *Eclaircissements* terms *le Rebut* (riff-raff) of armies ; they behaved in the open field as they always have done, always do, and always will do when opposed to veteran regulars. Washington did not deem them worthy to count as "effectives." and did not willingly include them in his estimates of absolute fighting force. He certainly disparged them, and has left his testimony against them as a reliable element of national military strength. They gave way, scattered, and (pardon the plain Saxon word) they must have run. Col. Cleveland perfectly understood this when he attacked " Bull-dog" Ferguson at King's Mountain. "If you *will* retreat," he said, "don't run away or quite off; when you can do no better, take to the trees." His men did this, and Ferguson's regulars, who drove the Americans with the bayonet, were shot down like wild beasts in a *battu*.† Regulars have their tactics adapted to open ground, and upon this must always be victorious over what is generically Militia. These, again, have their tactics under cover, and if they have courage enough and ammunition and numbers sufficient they will swarm out regulars, unless the latter likewise understand "bushwacking." This is a sort of tactics in which few regulars except Americans are instructed. The rebels got the better of the Union troops in the woods because they "bushwhacked" better " on a big scale," and our officers say the Union troops whipped the rebels in the open because the Northern discipline, proper, was better.

Monmouth proved that a disciplined American could become as perfect a soldier as any in the world ; that Wayne was as reliable to defend as to attack, and that Washington was equal to any emergency. Still, all these were no fresh discoveries. These were problems long since solved and known in certain circles. Monmouth simply revealed them to the world. Monmouth was the last field in America whereon 10,000 men on each side contended for victory, or were even present.— After this date the war was made up of comparative skirmishes or actions whose objectives alone gave to them the dignity of battles. In one respect, however, it was THE battle of the Revolution, for upon its parched, deep, sandy field occurred the "new birth " of the American regular soldier. Hereon, he showed himself the first-class manœuvring as well as fighting power, substantiated subsequently in a thousand fields—in Canada, in Florida, in Mexico, on the Prairies, among the " Bad Grounds " mountains and " Lava Beds " of the West, and on the gory checker-boards of the "great American Conflict " waged to crush or to sustain the mightiest rebellion which ever convulsed a nation.

ANCHOR, (J. W. DE P.)

SHARPSHOOTERS.
†The American sharpshooters knew no influence of magnanimity, whereas British chivalry often spared

gallant officers. LaFayette owed his escape at Monmouth to the generosity of Clinton. Washington must credit his life, at Germantown, to the nobility of soul of "Bull-Dog" Ferguson—a marksman, accompanied by two others of skill, who never missed his or their aim. Morgan ordered his riflemen to deliberately murder (as the writer esteems it) Fraser, at Saratoga. Col. Hanger tells us that when the Southern Riflemen had picked off the noble Ferguson, they left his body to the Scavenger birds of the region, the filthy turkey buzzards. (Life of Col. George Hanger, ii. 406.)

THE END.

INDEX.

The following index contains the names of all Persons mentioned on the preceding pages—not including, however, the "Battle of Monmouth," and the celebration of its "Centennial." An asterisk following a number indicates that the name is mentioned on that page more than once.

Aaron—a black boy, 142*, 143, 311-
Abbott, 70.
Abbott, Benjamin, 17, 70, 100*, 101, 128.
Adam, Alexander, 261*.
Aikens, Abiel, 17, 18, 70.
Alexander, 54. 69. 139, 141*.
Allen, Ben., 170, 290*.
Allen, Caleb, 250, 257.
Allen, David, 269,
Allen, Elisha, 255.
Allen Ephraim, 250, 253.
Allen, George, 203*, 204, 262, 264, 265, 267, 268.
Allen, Henry, 170.
Allen, Isaac, 15, 51.
Allen, James, 306.
Allen, Jedediah, 255, 256, 260*, 261, 262*, 263.
Allen, John, 148, 187, 207*.
Allen, Joseph, 169.
Allen. Judd, 105, 170, 252.
Allen, Nathan, 269.
Allen, Robert, 318.
Allinson, 173.
Allmy, Christopher, 176, 186, 199, 204, 206*, 207, 208, 239*, 241*, 242,*, 243*, 249*.
Allmy. Job, 186, 206, 207.
Alricks, Jacob, 13, 14.
Alricks, Peter, 41*, 42*.
Anderson, 86, 108.
Anderson, Capt. 68, 169.
Anderson, John, 28, 31, 32, 93*, 238°, 248, 269*, 302*.
Anderson, Joshua, 91. 92*.
Anderson, Kenneth, 71.
Andre, Major, 67.
Andress, Lawrence, 920.
Andress, Lordue, 3, 210.
Andrews, 35.
Andros. Gov. 42, 43, 223, 243*, 244*.
Antelby, Wm. 275.
Antonides, 299.
Applegate, Bartholomew, 5*. 226*.
Applegate, Daniel, 2-0, 251.
Applegate, Silvester, 306.
Applegate. Thomas, 5*, 226*, 241*.
Aramaseek, 251,
Argyle, 245.
Arlington, 214.
Arnold, 157*.
Arnold, Benedict, 59*.
Arnold, Stephen, 107*. 186. 187, 199, 206, 207.
Arnold, Wm., 186.
Arrowsmith, 185.
Arrowsmith, George, 183.
Arrowsmith, Thomas, 183
Asbury, Bishop Francis, 100*, 101*, 128.

Asgill, Capt. Charles, 76*, 82*, 83*, 84*, 85*, 86* 87. 89, 90*, 138, 142.
Asgill, Madame, 76, 83*, 84*, 85*, 86*
Ashfield, Mary, 49, 150.
Ashton, 53, 106.
Ashton, Jam s, 2, 106, 167*, 199, 201*, 202, 207, 208, 210, 216, 241, 243, 255, 259, 269*,
Ashton, Joseph, 264
Ashton, Rev. Thomas, 106*.
Ashton, Wm., 250, 266.
Atkinson, Rev. John, 100.
Ausley, Ozias, 51.
Aylmer, Brab, 56.
Bacho, Theophilus, 127.
Backus, 186.
Backus. Isaac, 186, 189, 190, 191*, 192.
Bacon, Capt. John, 17, 34. 43* 44*, 45*, 4*, 69*, 124*, 123*, 124.
Bailey, Francis, 108, 109*,
Bainbridge, Absalom, 107*, 51.
Bainbridge, Joseph, 48.
Bainbridge, Wm., 48*.
Baker, John, 211, 250
Baley, Joseph, 14.
Ball, 299.
Ballaguier, John, 234.
Bancroft, 94.
Barbara, John, 51.
Barber, Dr. 303.
Barber, Thomas, 71, 303.
Barclay, 100, 172, 259*, 277, 280, 291, 292.
Barclay, David, 277, 278.
Barclay, John, 55, 237, 245, 250, 278*, 281.
Barclay, Robert, 19, 37*, 55, 215, 234. 245, 250, 264, 277, 278. 288*.
Barkalow, (variously spelled), 24, 183, 238, 299*
Barker, Thomas, 277, 278, 282, 283, 285*.
Barnes, John, 51.
Barnes, Richard, 250.
Barnes, Thomas, 241*.
Barrigan,(Bergen)Ge shea, 310*.
Barrowes, Rev. John, 106*.
Bartow, Thomas, 316.
Bash, (Indian), 22.
Bashan, 208,
Bassa, Jeremiah, 259* 264 268, 269 281*, 286, 287.
Bathsheba, (Indian Queen), 22*.
Bayard, Nicholas, 226, 227.
Bayard, Samuel, 293.
Beak, John, 3
Bearcroft, Rev. Dr, 100.

Beaumont, Hannah, 275*
Beckwith, Capt. 125.
Bee, Mr. 81.
Beecher, Henry Ward, 177,
Beekman, Garnardus, 15
Beekman, Geo. C. 155*, 197.
Beekman, J. TenBroeck, 168, 317.
Beers. Samuel, 155*.
BeHell, (Binckes) Jacob, 227.
Belcher, Andrew, 281.
Belcher, Jonathan, 100, 173
Belden, Charles, 318.
Bell, Andrew, 48.
Bell, Jeremiah, 61, 116.
Bell, Tom. 90*. 91*, 92.
Benckes, Jacob, 4*.
Bendal, Mr., 192.
Benedict, 51, 52*.
Benedict, David, 105.
Benet, 266.
Bennett, 153,
Bennett, Arian, 261*, 262*, 263.
Bennett, Benjamin, 107, 163, 306*, 307.
Bennett, David, 45.
Benrett. Henry, 193.
Bennett, Jeremiah, 167.
Bennett, John, 313.
Bennett. Wm., 267.
Bergen, 299.
Bergen, S mon, 310.
Berkeley, 198*, 222.
Berkley, Lord John, 210*, 211*, 213*, 215*, 216, 217
Berkley, Thomas, 61, 117.
Bernards J., 281.
Berry, Capt. John, 220, 227*.
Besse, 226
Bettridge, Wm., 106.
Betty, (Negro), 307*.
Beveridge, Dr., 97.
Bickley, 233, 266.
Bigelow, Capt., 18, 67.
Bill, L. 281.
Billing. Edward, 277, 278.
Bills, Thomas. 14.
Binckes, Jacob, 223*, 224*.
Bird, John 208.
Bird, Richard, 34*, 39, 40*
Birdsall, Capt. Amos, 149*.
Bishop, John, 3, 210.
Blackman, Bryan, 252.
Blair, Wm., 306*
Blanchard, Lieut. 16*, 17.
Blauvelt, Abraham, 180.
Blossome, Elizabeth. 151.*
Blowers, S. S.,75, 135*, 136*.
Boels, 57.
Bowls, (Bowels, Boulles, &c.) Garret, 262*, 264.
Boels, Thomas, 56, 57*, 98, 169, 267.

Boggs, Commodore, 49, 150.
Boggs, James, 14.
Boice, 246.
Bollen, 213.
Bollen, James, 170, 217*. 260*, 262*, 264, 268.
Bonnell, Joseph, 293, 294.
Bonnett, Alex., 69*.
Bonow, Miss, 287,
Borden, 169. 170*, 171, 187, 207*, 208, 249, 263*. 266*, 267*.
Borden, Francis, 240*, 215.
Borden, Richard. 187, 206, 207*, 239. 265*, 289,
Borden, Wm., 62*, 63*, 64*, 78.
Boscawen, Admiral, 296.
Bostwick, Sarah, 306.
Boudinot, 81, 84, 162.
Bowne, (sometimes Bound), 53, 72, 114, 146.
Bowne, Capt. Andrew, 32, 171*, 177, 222, 255*, 256*, 257, 258, 259. 264, 265*. 274. 275*, 276, 2 0, 281*, 282*, 283*, 286*, 287*, 296, 297.
Bowne. Ann, 287*, 294.
Bowne Catharine, 316 318*.
Bowne, Cornelius, 292*, 295*, 298.
Bowne, Elizabeth, 287.
Bowne, George. 177.
Bowne, Gerrard, 207*.
Bowne, James. 199, 201*, 202, 204. 205, 206, 207, 208, 241, 244*, 248, 249*, 256, 257, 306.
Bowne, John, 1, 2, 5, 14, 92*, 104*. 105*, 106, 165, 166*, 168. 177*, 210, 201, 202*. 204*, 206*, 207*, 208, 209*, 210, 214, 216, 220*, 221*, 222*, 223, 226*, 227*, 229*, 241*, 243, 244*, 250, 251*, 262, 265*, 267*, 268, 286*, 283, 284*, 285, 287*, 288*, 289*, 290*, 291*, 292*.
293*. 294*, 295*, 296*, 297*, 298, 306, 313.
Bowne, Lydia, 168*, 223. 250, 287*.
Bowne, Margaretta, 318.
Bowne, Mary, 292.
Bowne, Obadiah. 92*, 169*, 170*, 171*, 256. 263, 265, 266*, 267*, 268, 287, 289, 290. 291*, 292*, 293. 294*, 295*, 296*.
Bowne, Samuel, 73. 114,
Bowne, Thomas, 292*, 294*, 295*. 296*.
Bowne, W m., 201, 202, 206, 207, 208, 257, 261*.
Boyd, 24

INDEX.

Boyd, John, 267, 268*.
Boyer, Joseph, 207.
Brackenridge, Hugh Henry, 108*.
Bradford, Gov, Wm., 187.
Bradford, Wm., 289*.
Bradley, James, A. 196.
Brainerd, Rev. David, 152, 248.
Branson, Jonathan, 175
Bray, John. 106*, 167, 256, 259, 260, 261*, 263, 264, 287.
Brayn, James, 277, 278.
Brearley, David, 71.
Breese, Samuel, 33*, 71.
Brevoort, Henry, 111*.
Brewer, 44*. 45*.
Brewer, Hendrick, 307.
Bridges, Robert, 187, 188.
Brinckerhoff, 299.
Brindley, 170*.
Brindley, Geo., 61, 64*. 117.
Brinley, Francis W., 41, 186, 206, 207.
Britton, 181.
Brittain, James, 51.
Brittain, Joseph, 51.
Britton, Israel, 14.
Brom, (Negro), 311.
Bromfield, 70*, 145*.
Brooks, Timothy, 106, 137.
Brown. 179, 185.
Brown, Abraham, 250. 253, 256.
Brown, John, 106, 122, 246.
Brown, Jonathan, 106.
Brown, Joseph, 306.
Brown, Nicholas; there were two persons of this name, an uncle and nephew, the latter being son of Abraham Brown; 5, 166, 169, 177, 204, 206, 207, 209*, 225, 249, 252, 253, 256, 266.
Brown, Samuel, 39*, 101.
Bryan, Morgan, 250.
Buchanan, 87.
Buck, Aaron. 17*, 18*.
Buck, John, 112.
Buckelew, John D., 318.
Buckman, John, 106.
Bull, Henry, 186, 203, 206, 207.
Bullen, 53.
Bunnel, John, 313
Bunnell, Thomas, 149*.
Burdge, David, 306.
Burge, 38*.
Burke. 35*. 36*, 68, 140.
Burke, Stephen. 34, 35, 37*, 38
Burke, Thomas, 34, 35, 38*.
Burnyeate, John, 11*, 12*, 13.
Burrows, 72, 113, 296, 308.
Burroughs, Edward, 56, 317*.
Burrowes, John, 31, 71, 93, 106, 113, 296*.
Burrows, Thomas, 306, 317.
Butterworth, 264
Butterworth, Moses, 263*.
Buttolph, Thomas, 192*.
Calvin, Bartholomew S., 21*.
Calvin, James, 53.
Calvin, Stephen, 54*.
Calvin, Peter, 53.
Calviri, Stephen, 53.
Camden, 117.

Cameron, 246. 247*.
Camocks, Nathaniel, 252, 256.
Campbell (Poet), 111*.
Campbell, John, 71.
Campbell, Peter, 51.
Campton, Wm., 167.
Cann, Robert, 101.
Cannon, Patrick, 261.
Cannor, John, 292.
Cantwell, Capt. 42.
Capoose, (Indian), 53.
Carey, Matthew, 109, 161.
Carhart, Samuel, 302, 303.
Carleton, Sir Guy, 50, 81, 86*, 138, 140, 142.
Carman, 147.
Carr, Robert, 41*, 187, 206, 207*, 239.
Carter, Thomas, 150.
Carteret, 2, 3, 198*, 222.
Carteret, Sir George, 166, 210*, 211*, 213*, 214*, 215*, 216, 217, 220, 241, 243.
Carteret, Philip, 209, 210, 217, 219, 241*, 243.
Cartwright, (Carterett) Elizabeth, 278.
Cartwright, (Carterett) Sir George, 278*.
Cartwright, Thomas, 95.
Case, Wm., 253.
Castler, Peter, 183.
Cayford, Richard, 51.
Cæsar, 253*. 254*.
Chadwick, 59*, 72, 78, 114.
Chadwick, Elihu, 305.
Chadwick, Thomas, 303.
Challoner, 75, 135*.
Chamberlain. 265.
Chamberlain, Ann, 256.
Chamberlain, Thomas, 102.
Chamberlin, Henry, 25*.
Chamberlin, John, 269.
Chamberlin, Mary, 255.
Chamberlin, Wm. 255*.
Chambers, Mrs., 72.
Chambers, Col. James, 159.
Chambers, John, 308.
Chambers, Richard, 269
Chandler, Asael, 14.
Chandler, Wm. 51.
Channelhouse, Adam, 252.
Chasey, Anna, 306.
Checocus, 261.
Cheesemen, 168*.
Cheeseman, Wm 106, 256, 257, 259, 260.
Chenaoth, John 290.
Cherawas, 250.
Cheslis, 250.
Chield, Samuel, 255.
Child, Samuel, 255.
Church, Edward, 106.
Chute, Geo., 206, 207, 241.
Clark, 69, 239.
Clark, Alexander, 14, 269, 302, 312.
Clark, Amos, Jr., 162
Clarke, John, 187*, 188*, 191*.
Clark, Joseph, 262*.
Clark, Richard, 246.
Clark, Walter, 1, 165, 186, 203*, 206, 207*, 239.
Clark, William, 269.
Claus Benjamin, 53, 54.
Clayton. David, 266.
Clayton, Hannah, 180.
Clayton, Joseph, 14.
Clayton, Zebulon, 264.

Clifton, Thomas, 206, 207*.
Clinton, DeWitt. 109.
Clinton, Gen., 316*.
Clinton, Sir Henry, 48, 50*, 76, 77, 79*, 80, 81,* 83, 87, 89, 138*, 141, 142*.
Coales, 266*.
Cockburn, Admiral, 148, 149
Cocker, 42.
Codington, Wm., 186, 206, 207.
Coddington, Nathaniel, 240.
Codrington, 275.
Coggehall, 206.
Coggshall, Elizabeth, 297.
Coggshall, John, 186, 207.
Coggshall, Joshua, 186, 203*, 207*.
Cole, 192.
Cole, Edward, 187. 207.
Cole, Elizabeth, 303.
Cole, J., 192, 275.
Cole, Jacob, 249*.
Cole, Richard, 14.
Cole, Robert, 187.
Cole, Wm., 303.
Coleman, Benjamin, 269.
Coleman, Joseph, 206, 207.
Collins, 43.
Collins, Ebenezer, 39.
Collins, Eli, 22.
Collyare, Wm., 187,
Colman, John, 6*, 10*.
Colve, Anthony, 223*, 224, 225*, 226*, 227.
Colver, (or Culver), John, 147, 148.
Colver, (or Culver), Thomas, 147.
Combes, Richard, 268.
Combs, John, 51.
Combs, Joseph, 193.
Compton, Cornelius, 259, 260*, 261*. 262*.
Compton, Richard. 250, 256.
Compton, Veleriah, 305.
Compton, Wm., 106.
Connelly, Stephen, 142*, 143*.
Conover, 25, 113, 299, 300, 310.
Conover, (Covenhoven), Albert, 269.
Conover, Ann, 318.
Conover, Catharine, 318.
Conover, Col. Elias, 112.
Conover, Hendrick, 318*.
Conover, Hendrick E., 238.
Conover, Holmes, 318*.
Conover, Ira, 246.
Conover, (Covenhoven), Jacob, 182, 269, 301, 318*.
Conover, Jas. P., 318
Conover, Joseph, 183.
Conover, Leah, 318.
Conover, Mary, 318.
Conover, Rebecca, 348.
Conover, Ruliff E., 308.
Conover, Tunis, 318.
Conover, Tylee, 193.
Conover, Wm., 318*.
Conover, Wm. H., 112.
Conover, Wm. Johnson, 318.
Cooke and Cooke, 69.
Cock, Benjamin, 261, 263.
Cook, David, 113.
Cook, George, 259, 260, 263
Cook, Joel, 122*, 123*.
Cook, John, 17*, 71, 79*, 206, 207.
Cook, Sam'l, 14, 48*, 50, 100

Cook, Stephen, 250, 253, 254*, 255*.
Cook, Thomas, 26*, 27*.
Cooper, Ezekiel, 100, 101.
Cooper, Thomas, 276, 277, 278*, 282, 283, 285.
Corlies, (Curliss, Courlies, &c.) 195.
Corlies, George, 254, 255.
Corlies, James, 14.
Corlies, John, 72, 114.
Corlies, John L., 184.
Corlies, Wm. 37*. 66*.
Cernbury, Lord, 265*, 286*, 287*.
Cornelius, Francis, 45.
Cortelyou, 229, 299.
Cortelyou, Jacques, 228.
Cortland, Philip, 51*.
Coryel, Mrs. Amelia, 36*.
Cotton, Mr. 191.
Cottrell, 114, 169.
Cottrell, Eleazer, 168*, 256, 257*, 260*, 261*, 263.
Cottrell, John, 14.
Cottrell, Wm., 73.
Couchee, Zeb. 53.
Courtney, 55.
Covenhoven, 72, 113, 114.
Covenhoven, Benj., 175.
Covenhoven, Cornelius, 171, 174*.
Covenhoven, Garret, 310*.
Covenhoven, Jacob, 228, 306*, 310*.
Covenhoven, Capt. Jno., 28, 31, 32, 78.
Covenhoven, Joseph, 71, 113.
Cowenhoven, Mary, 310*.
Covenhoven, Nelly, 310.
Covenhoven, Peter, 73, 114, 302, 310*.
Cavenhoven, Ralph. 310.
Cowenhoven, Rulif, 310.
Coventry, Henry, 213.
Coward, 306.
Coward, Capt. Joseph, 24*.
Cowder, 267.
Cowgill, Isaac, 175.
Cox, (and Coxe) 4, 139.
Cox, James, 113, 163*.
Cox, John, 92, 106, 261, 263, 264, 269.
Cox, John C., 193.
Cox, Joseph, 275.
Cox, Richard, 78.
Cox, Thomas, 167*, 174, 206, 208, 241*, 243.
Cozens, Daniel, 51, 70*, 136.
Craddock, Wm., 316.
Crafford, John, 253, 254*.
Craig. Archibald, 246.
Craig, Daniel, 306.
Craig, David, 306.
Craig, James, 269, 306
Craig, John, 267, 306.
Craig, Mary, 246.
Craig, Samuel, 248.
Crandall, John, 187*, 188.
Crane, Stephen, 29, 93.
Crawford, 53.
Crawford, Adaline, 317.
Crawford, Andrew, 315, 318*.
Crawford, Ann, 317, 318*.
Crawford, Ann B., 318*.
Crawford, Caroline, 318*.
Crawford, Catharine, 316, 317*. 318*.
Crawford, Cath. E., 318.
Crawford, Deborah, 317.

INDEX. iii.

Crawford, Eleanor, 317.
Crawford, Eliz., 316, 318.
Crawford, Elnathan, 318*.
Crawford, Ester, 315, 317*, 318.
Crawford, George, 266, 307*, 314, 315*, 316*, 317*, 318*.
Crawford, Geo. W., 313, 314, 318*.
Crawford, Gideon, 269*.
Crawford, Hannah, 317*.
Crawford, James, 177, 302*.
Crawford, James G., 274, 280, 283*, 289, 318*.
Crawford, Jas. P., 318.
Crawford, Job, 316*.
Crawford, John, 313, 314,* 315, 318*.
Crawford, John Bowne, 117, 314, 317, 318*.
Crawford, John J., 177, 318.
Crawford, Joshua, 316*
Crawford, Lydia, 316.
Crawford, Marg't, 302*.
Crawford, Mary, 317, 318.
Crawford, Rebecca, 318.
Crawford, Richard, 306, 313, 314*, 316*. 317*, 318*.
Crawford, Samuel. 246.
Crawford, Wm. 246, 316*, 317, 318*.
Crawford, Wm. H., 168*. 318*.
Cregier, Capt. Martin, 228.
Crocheron, 231.
Crowell, Joseph, 51.
Crowell, Thomas, 14, 48, 136. 137.
Cruger, 281.
Cuish, Joseph, 53.
Culver, Samuel, 267.
Cummins, Robert, 248.
Cunklin, John, 206.
Cunningham, Capt Wm., 15*, 16, 66*, 138, 139*.
Curingam, Jeremiah, 264.
Danker and Sluyter, 288.
Dankers, Jasper, 230.
Darwin, 111.
Davenport, 17, 34*, 39*, 69, 124.
Davidson, Josiah, 54*.
Davis, Joseph, 303.
Davis, Nichollas, 1, 165, 206, 207.
Davis, Richard, 167*, 255, 261, 263, 264.
Davison, Wm., 170, 258*, 288*.
Dayton, Wm. L., 163*.
DeBow, 34, 35*.
DeFoe, 178.
DeKalb, Baron, 179*.
Delancey, Stephen, Lieut. Col, 51.
Delavale, John, 275*.
DeLucena, Abraham, 284*.
Denham, John, 275.
Denise, 299.
Denise, Dennis, 71, 305*.
Denise, James, 114.
Denise, Jaques, 73.
Dennis, Capt. Major Benjamin, 33, 36*, 37*.
Dennis, Mrs. Benj., 36*.
Dennis, Charles, 253, 255*.
Dennis, Cornelia, 306.
Dennis, John, 303*.
Dennis, Joseph, 288, 290
Dennis, Samuel, 57, 250, 260*, 261*, 262, 263, 269, 276, 310.
Dennis, (Increase), wife of Samuel Dennis, 260.

Dennison, George Taylor, 50*.
DeRuyter, 211.
Devell, 187.
Devell, Wm., 187*.
Devill, 187.
Devill, Benjamin, 167*, 248*, 249.
DeVries, David Peterson, 2-7.
DeWitt, Jan 211.
Dickenson, Gov. Philemon, 74*.
Dier, (Dyer) Henry, 241.
Dilleu, (and Dillon), Wm., 17*, 18. 35*, 68*.
Dillon. 18.
Disborough, 181.
Dobie, 174.
Dockura, Wm., 4, 282, 283, 284*, 285*, 286.
Dod, Benjamin, 95.
Dougan, Gov., 226.
Dorn, Cornelius, 171.
Dorsett, James, 241*. 243, 251, 253, 255, 256*, 266.
Dorsey, Benedict, 175*.
Doue, 239.
Doue, Alexander, 269*.
Douglas, Thomas, 290.
Downing, Joseph, 56.
Drummond, Gawen, 256, 264*.
Drummond, John, 215, 277, 278.
DuBois, 299.
Duane, 60, 84, 116.
DuBois, Benj., 305.
DuBois, Charles, 167.
Duke, William, 100.
Dungan, Thomas, 207.
Dunlap, 179, 226.
Dunmore, Lord, 73.
Dunstan, 54.
Duyckinck, E A., 111, 113.
Dyckman, Hugh, 5, 224.
Eaglesfield, Geo., 106.
Easson, Peter, 207.
Easton, John, 239.
Easton, Nicholas, Jr., 204.
Eaton, 25*.
Eaton, John, 93*, 170, 269.
Eaton, Thomas, 252*.
Eccles, Charles, 243.
Edsall, Samuel, 3, 210.
Edward, 147.
Edwards. Abiah, 253, 261.
Edwards. Morgan, 105, 107.
Edwards, Mrs. 67.
Edwards, Stephen, 38, 48, 50, 66*, 67*, 86, 140.
Edwards, Thos., 290.
Eldreth, John, 303.
Ellis, 206
Ellis, Roger. .06, 207.
Ellison, John. 284
Elmore, Mr., 87.
Elsworth, Christopher, 228, 229*, 230.
Ely, Isaac, 181.
Ely, James, 135,
Ely, John J., 182.
Ely, Joseph I., 181.
Ember, John, 150.
Embly, Peter, 261.
Emley, 101.
Emmett, James, 314.
Emmons, 34, 37*, 38*.
Emmons, Jacob, 15
Emmons, Lucretia, 72.
Emmons, Thomas, (alias Burke), 68.
Emorons, 251.
Emott, Jas., 280.

Empson, Ephraim P., 69.
Endicott, 236.
Endicott, Gov., John, 188, 191, 192.
English, James, 303.
Esson, Petter, 206.
Estells, John, 53.
Estill, Daniel, 208.
Estill, Thomas, 261*, 266.
Estill, Wm., 259.
Estrees, Count de, 223.
Estrees, M. de, 223.
Evans, Lewis, 143.
Evans, Rev. Thos., 106.
Evans, Tom, 53.
Everitt, 100.
Evertson, Admiral, 223,
Evertson, Cornelis, 4*, 223, 224*, 227.
Everson, Cornelis de Joyce, 227.
Fagan, 140.
Fagan, Jacob, 34, 36*, 37, 38*.
Falkinburgh, Capt. Timothy, 22.
Falkner, 54.
Farmer. A. W., 33.
Farmer, Thomas, 291*, 292.
Farnham, 38*.
Fa-nham, John, 34, 65*, 66, 115*.
Farr, John, 17, 303*
Farr, Thomas, 34*, 35*.
Farrier, (Farmer). Col., 223.
Fennimore, John, 61*, 78, 116, 117.
Fenton, 140.
Fenton, Lewis, 34*, 35*, 36.
Fenton. Thos., 289, 290.
Fenwick, John, 41, 42*, 241, 242.
Field, Richard S., 90
Fields, Caroline, 318.
Fields, Eliz., 318.
Fields, Elnathan, 318.
Finley, Rev. Dr. Samuel, 107.
Fish, John, 69.
Fisk, col. James, 194.
Fitz Randolph, 51.
Fitz Randolph, Edward, 151*.
Fitz Randolph, Hannah, 151.
Fitz Randolph, John, 151.
Fitz Randolph, Margaret, 151.
Fitz Randolph, Mary, 151*.
Fitz Randolph, Nathaniel, 151*
Fleming. 16.
Fleming, Jacob, 17, 64, 75*, 79, 80, 135*, 136*, 137*.
Fleming, Stephen, 78.
Flint, Thomas, 190*.
Fontaine John, 232.
Forker, Samuel C., 162.
Forman, 14, 16*, 73, 78, 136, 138, 140*, 145, 259.
Forman, Alexander, 261*.
Forman, David, 23, 24*, 32, 62, 63, 64*, 65*, 94, 112, 117, 162*, 175.
Forman, Denise, 112.
Forman, Eleanor, 112.
Forman, Ezekiel, 38*.
Forman, John, 28, 82, 306*, 145*. 301, 306, 313*.
Forman, Mary, 112.
Forman, Miss, 145.
Forman, Mrs. 73.
Forman, Peter, 28, 32, 78, 301, 302*.
Forman, Samuel, 15, 23, 24,

38, 71, 75,* 78, 94, 112, 159, 160, 257*, 264.
Forman, Sam'l S., 145.
Forman, Thomas, 266.
Forman, Tunis, 23*, 24.
Forman, Wm. P., 301.
Forster, Miles, 20, 55*.
Fort, Governor, 123*.
Foster, Wm., 53.
Foullerton, Thomas, 275*.
Fourier, 177*.
Fowler, 176, 184.
Fowler, John, 54.
Fox. Geo., 11, 12*, 13*, 225, 226.
Francis, John W., 110*.
Franck, (negro woman), 244.
Franklin. Benjamin, 70, 113, 178.
Franklin, Gov. Wm., 48, 49, 64, 70, 86*, 88, 113 124. 136*, 137*, 138*, 139*, 140*, 141. 142*.
Freeborn, Gideon, 207.
French, John, 252*.
Freuch, Philip, 275.
Freneau, 234.
Freneau. Peter, 107*, 109, 111.
Freneau, Philip, 107*, 108, 109*, 110*. 111*, 112*, 145, 178.
Freneau, Mrs. Philip, 112*.
Freneau, Philip, L, 111.
Frost, James, 307*.
Fullerton, 54.
Fullerton, James, 255.
Furman, 54.
Gage, Gen., 15.
Gaines, Hugh, 108, 111.
Galleway, 70.
Gant, (or Gaunt), Aunias, 239.
Gant, (or Gaunt), Israel, 239.
Gant, (or Gaunt,) Zachary, 187, 206, 207, 239.
Gapee, Hockan, 54.
Gardner, Richard, 104, 167, 177. 248*.
Gardinier, Pierre C., 232*.
Garretson, Freeborn, 100, 101.
Garretson, Rev. Richard, 100.
Gatch, Rev. Philip, 180.
Genet, 109, 231.
George. 180.
Gibbons, Mordecai, 255, 259, 261, 263, 266, 316.
Gibbons, Richard, 1, 165, 177. 199, 200, 202, 204*, 206, 207, 208*, 209, 216, 229, 314*.
Gibbs, Joshua 174, 175*.
Gibbs, Thomas, 275.
Giberson, 240.
Giberson, Benjamin, 15, 14.
Giberson, Gisbert, 15.
Giberson. John, 34*, 172, 259*, 269.
Giberson, Mallakeath, 15.
Giberson, Wm., Jr., 15.
Gibson, Wm., 277, 278.
Gifford, Hanaiah, 250.
Gifford, Wm., 207.
Gilian, 65*. 66.
Gilian. Wm, 115*.
Golden, John, 177, 183.
Golden, Joseph, 171, 269.
Goodbody, 170.
Goodbody, Alice, 255.
Goodbody, Wm., 253, 254*, 255*, 256, 258.

iv. INDEX.

Goodenough, Joseph, 303*.
Goodman, Charles, 286.
Gooteleck, 54.
Gordon, 10, 264.
Gordon, Augustus, 267.
Gordon, Charles, 269.
Gordon, John E., 183, 276*, 277*, 278*, 279*, 280*.
Gordon, Major, 83*, 86*.
Gordon, Robert. 215, 234, 257, 262*, 269, 276, 277, 278, 281*.
Gosling, Samuel, 53.
Gould, Daniel 186, 203*, 207*.
Gould, Jay, 194*.
Goulding, 228.
Goulding, Wm., 146, 165, 199, 204, 205*, 206, 208*, 211.
Goldsmith, Ralph, 206, 267.
Graham, 82.
Graham, Gen., 83.
Graham, John, 216*
Graudin, Daniel, 61, 62, 63, 117.
Grant, Capt. Asa, 149.
Gray, Capt. Wm, 69*.
Greeley, Horace, 177.
Green, Elizabeth, 75.
Green, Henry. 293.
Green, Capt. James, 65, 75, 77, 80 115.
Green, Thomas. 49.
Green, Wm., 306.
Green. Gen, 156, 159*.
Greville, Col., 9.9*.
Grey, 110.
Griffith, Alexander, 269
Griggs, John, 183.
Grimm, Baron de, 76, 82, 83, 84
Groome, Sam'l, 104, 220, 277, 278*.
Grose, Capt., 160.
Grover, Barzilla, 15.
Grover, James, 1, 2, 31. 93*, 104, 105, 106*, 165, 167*, 169, 177, 198, 200, 201, 202, 204*, 205*, 206*, 207, 208*, 209*, 210, 216*, 220, 227, 241*, 242, 252, 254, 255, 264, 266, 306.
Grover, Joseph. 15, 243.
Grover, Mordecai, 284
Grover, Safety, 105, 260, 263.
Grover, Samuel, 15.
Grover, Thomas, 15.
Grover, William, 15, 38*.
Gulick, 299.
Gulick, Aaron, 193.
Gurlding, Wm., 1.
Guthrie, 161.
Gytes, Mr. 275.
Hageman, 299.
Haggerty, 182.
Haige, Wm, 20*.
Haight, Charles, 152*.
Haight, Thomas G., 72.
Haight, Wm, 193.
Hall, John, 113, 208
Hall, Walter, 106.
Halstead, James, 259*.
Halstead, Jesiah, 32.
Hamilton, 54, 109, 264
Hamilton, Andrew, 255, 263, 276. 283*, 314.
Hamilton, Geo., 94.
Hamilton, Mrs. Gen., 156.
Hamilton, John, 54.
Hamilton, Robert, 167*, 243, 244, 251, 255.

Hampton, John, 15, 167*, 168.
Hance, George, 195.
Hance, James, 166.
Hance, John, 2, 5, 104*, 105, 169, 202*, 204*, 205, 206, 207, 208, 209. 210, 224. 241, 244*, 249, 253. 255*, 256*, 257, 258, 280.
Handley, Richard, 203.
Hankins, John, 171.
Hankinson, 302.
Hankinson, John, 15.
Hankinson, Kenneth, 15.
Hankinson, Peter, 250*.
Hankinson. Thomas, 250*, 261*, 267*, 312.
Harber, Daniel, 255.
Harber, Jacob, 15.
Harbert, Francis, 255.
Harbert, Thomas, 167, 218.
Hardan, Mr. 87.
Hardy, Commodore, 148*, 149*,
Harker, Daniel, 257.
Harker, Samuel, 107.
Harrison, Charles, 51.
Hart, Thomas, 171, 207.
Hartshorne, 184*, 266, 267, 283.
Hartshorne, Hugh, 12, 269, 277, 278*, 291, 292*.
Hartshorne, Lawrence, 48.
Hartshorne, Mary, 150.
Hartshorne, Rich'd, 2, 5, 12*, 21*. 22*, 71, 92*. 104*, 166*, 167*, 169, 170, 204, 210, 226*, 221*, 222, 226*, 243, 248, 251*, 252, 254*, 257, 259, 264*, 287, 291*.
Hartshorne, Robert, 93.
Hart, Thos., 282, 283, 285*, 277, 278*.
Hartshorne, Wm., 150.
Harvey, 180,
Haudson, Tobias, 206, 207.
Hanndell, John, 207.
Have, 16.
Havens, John, 169, 170.
Haynes, Charles, 252.
Haynes, John, 275*.
Hazard, Robert. 187, 207.
Hazell, John, 187, 189, 191*, 192*.
Heard, James, 202*.
Heath, Gen., 80*.
Hebron, John, 170, 171, 267*.
Heckwelder, 8.
Hedden, John, 384.
Henderson, Hendrick 73.,
Henderson, John, 246, 248.
Henderson, Michael, 246.
Henderson, Dr. T., 32.
Hendricks, 21, 299.
Hendricks, Conrad, 14.
Hendricks, Thomas A., 264
Hendricks, Wm., 264*, 266, 267.
Hendrickson. 59*, 60, 61, 72, 114, 116, 178, 299.
Hendrickson, Alfred, 151.
Hendrickson, Charles J., 254.
Hendrickson, Cornelis, 150*.
Hendrickson, Daniel, 33*, 71, 171*, 183, 240*, 259*, 261, 263, 291, 301, 303, 306, 308*, 309, 310.
Hendrickson, Capt. Denise, 113.
Hendrickson, Garret, 73*, 114*, 151, 303*, 304*. 305.
Hondrickson, G. C., 167.
Hendrickson. Ghesie, 310.

Hendrickson, Haus, 233*.
Hendrickson, Hendrick Capt., 113. 114, 151, 171*, 213, 240*, 259*, 306, 308.
Hendrickson, John Lloyd, 317.
Hendrickson, Legar, 150.
Hendrickson, Rutger, 150.
Hendrickson, Thomas, 303.
Hendrickson, Tuniche, 310.
Hendrickson, Wm., 308.
Hendrickson, Wm. H., 183, 240, 310.
Hepburn, John, 171*.
Hetfield, 123, 124.
Hetherly, Timothy, 187.
Heughs, Abner, 264.
Hewitt, Thomas, 261.
Hewlett, Samuel, 259.
Hewlett, Wm, 73.
Heywood, John, 277, 278*.
Hibbets, James, 303
Hick, Benjamin, 250*
Hier, Peter, 303.
Hier, (Hyer) Walter, 303*.
Higgs, John, 177.
Hilborn, Thomas, 253, 256.
Hildreth, George, 157.
Hill, Daniel, 306.
Hill, John, 275.
Hill, Thomas, 304*.
Hillyer, (Hilliard) 231.
Hinkson, Benzeor, 14.
Hoff, 299.
Hoffman, 299.
Hoffmire. Isaiah, 174*.
Hogan, Gen., 82*.
Hoge, Wm., 261.
Holbert, James, 220.
Holliman, Ezekiel, 187.
Holliman, Samuel, 187, 206.
Hollingshead, 64
Holman, 266, 267.
Holman, Samuel, 207.
Holmes, 39, 146, 169, 186*, 187.
Holmes, Asher. 28, 32, 71*, 78. 303*, 304, 305, 306, 318.
Holmes, Catharine, 310, 317.
Holmes, Col., 43, 72, 73, 74, 78, 113, 138.
Holmes, Daniel, 310.
Holmes, James, 9, 9*, 150.
Holmes, John, 36*, 45*, 72, 114, 297, 298, 308*.
Holmes. Mrs. John, 45.
Holmes, Jonathan, 2, 5, 106, 167, 168, 177. 157*, 199. 201*, 202, 206, 207, 208, 241, 251, 297, 309*, 310*, 317.
Holmes, Joseph, 31, 48, 93, 297*, 298, 318.
Holmes, Josiah, 31, 33*, 93.
Holmes, Mary, 306.
Holmes, Obadiah, 1, 106, 165, 185, 187*, 188*, 189*, 191*, 192*, 206, 207, 239, 256, 263, 269, 306, 308*.
Holmes, Samuel, 297, 293*, 308*, 310
Holmes, Wm., 45.
Honce, 299.
Honce, Cornelius, 311.
Hook, Lawrence, 269.
Hopnycock, Geo., 3.
Hopenge, (Hopping) Samuel, 261.
Horabin, John, 206, 207, 208.
Horner, Fuller, 15.
Horner, John, 15.
Horsefield, Richard, 269

Horsman, Marmaduke, 54 169, 269.
Hosack's, Dr., 111.
Houdin, Michael, 96
Hougham, 251.
Howard, Alexander. 175.
Howe, 34*, 35, 48, 58, 60, 61 65*, 67, 72, 73, 76, 114, 115* 116, 152, 154*, 159.
Howe, Henry, 24, 25, 158.
Howell, Richard, 18 ?.
Howell, Robert, 61, 116.
Hubbard, 171, 177*.
Hubbard, Jacob, 71.
Hubbard, James, 171, 269*.
Hubbs, Charles, 269.
Hubbs, Joseph, 256.
Hubbs, Robert, 269*.
Hnchason, Robert, 266.
Huddy, Elizabeth, 75*.
Huddy. Capt Joshua, 15 16*, 17*, 18, 49, 50*, 60, 61*, 62*, 63*, 64*, 65, 66*, 67*, 72*, 73*, 74*, 75*, 76*, 77* 78*, 79*. 80*, 81*, 82*, 83. 84. 86*, 87*, 88*, 89*, 90*, 114*, 115, 116*, 117*, 126 135*, 136*, 137*, 138*, 139*, 140*, 141*, 142. 303*, 305.
Huddy, Martha, 75*.
Huddy, Mrs., 73.
Hudson, Sir Henry, 6*, 8*, 10*, 11, 162.
Huett, Joseph, 243.
Huett, Rendell, 201, 204 208*, 239.
Huett, Thomas, 242, 251, 253, 255.
Hughes, John, 102.
Hulan, Hendrick, 269.
Hulett, 154.
Hulett, George, 241, 255.
Hulett, John, 269.
Hulett, Joseph, 242.
Hulett, Wm., 250.
Hull 109.
Hull, Wm., 170.
Hulshart, Benj., 306.
Hulshart, Cornelius, 306*.
Hulse, 182.
Hume, 55.
Humphrey, 97.
Hunlock, Thomas, 51.
Hunn, Thomas. 71.
Hunt, Geo, 306.
Hunt, Wm., 169, 269.
Hutchins, James, 315*.
Hutchinson, 58*.
Hutchinson, Wm., 51.
Hyler, 17.
Hnyler, Adam, Capt., 82*, 124*, 125*, 126*, 127*, 144.
Hyde, Col., 72, 113.
Hyer, 299,
Iloseheote, 250.
Imlay, David, 17.
Imlay, James H., 163.
Imlay, John, 305.
Imly, Patrick, 267.
Ingoldsby, Col. Richard, 171.
Innes, Patrick, 277.
Innes, Rev. Mr., 55, 57*.
Inslee, Lieut., 17.
Ingram, Thomas, 252.
Irasecutt, 251*.
Iraseek, 251*.
Iredell, Lieut., 17.
Irons, John, 15.
Ironig, Washington, —
Isaac, 78.
Irin, Moses, 182*, 184.
Ivins, Abell, 305*.
Ivins, Anthony, Jr., 144.

INDEX.

v.

Jackson, Capt., 127.
Jackson, Francis, 249, 250, 253, 255.
Jackson, James, 175.
Jacob, (Indian) 25, 26*.
Jacob. (negro) 287.
James, Earl of Perth, 215.
James, James, 106.
James. Richard, 169, 250, 269.
James, Robert, 261.
James, Thomas, 187.
James, Wm., 187, 206, 207.
Jarvis, 110.
Jay, John, 12, 239.
Jeffers, Frances, 303.
Jefferson, Thos., 109*, 113.
Jeffrey, 110, 143.
Jeffrey, Francis, 252.
Jeffreys, Thos.. 306.
Jenckes, Joseph, 191.
Jenkins, Capt. Ephraim,17*, 18*, 43, 45, 67.
Jenkins, John, 202*, 207*.
Jenks, Gov., 147*.
Jening, John, 203, 250.
Jeremy, (negro) 257*, 258*.
Jewell, Wm., 269 291
Joanes, Philip, 287.
Job, Richard, 269.
Jobs, George, 256, 257
Jobs, John, 267*.
John, Capt., 53, 54.
John. (Indian), 228*. 229.
Johnson, 54, 57*, 135. 233 246*, 291.
Johnson, David, 169, 269.
Johnson, Rev. Jettus, 101.
Johnson, John, 168, 253, 280, 314.
Johnson, Johnson, 53.
Johnson, Lambert, 303*.
Johnson, Nicholas, 106.
Johnson, Peter, 113. 253
Johnson, Thomas, 263.
Johnson, Wm., 302*.
Jouatan, 251*.
Jones, 39.
Jones, John, 122.
Jones, S. W., 177, 193.
Jones, Rev. Thomas, 134*.
Jones, Wm., 172, 269.
Journeay, 231.
Jube, (negro) 74*, 115*.
Juet, Alfred, 6.
Just, Alfred, 162.
Karr, Elisha, 181.
Kearney, 112, 233*, 296.
Kearney, Major, 71, 73, 74*, 113, 114*.
Kearney, Mich., 314.
Keating, 51.
Keith, 176.
Keith, Geo, 13, 19*, 20* 21, 55*, 56, 57, 98, 166, 167, 172, 173*, 174*, 234, 238, 264*.
Kekott, Robert. 53.
Kelly. John, 293*.
Kelly, Samuel, 175.
Kenny. John, 3, 210.
Ker, Joseph, 248.
Ker, Samuel, 248.
Ker. Walter, 248, 267.
Ker, Wm., 248.
Kerr, John, 288
Ketcham, Daniel, 269, 306*
Ketcham, Phoebe, 306
Kidd, Capt., 25*, 259, 263.
Kiffen, Wm. 188.
Kiker, Tobias, 15.
Killingsworth, Rev. Thos. 106.
Killum, Robert, 291

King, John, 100, 269.
King, Mrs., 146.
Kinsey, John, 92.
Kinsley, James, 17, 305.
Kirby, John. 169.
Kirkpatrick, Chief Justice, 143.
Knott, David, 33*.
Knox, Geo., 159*.
Knyff, Captain, 5*, 225*.
Lacques, Abraham, 53.
Lafayette, Marquis de, 93*. 159.
Lafetter, (Lafetra), 15.
Lain, Cornelius, 269.
Laird, Robert, 305.
Lane, Tho., 285.
Laphitra, Edmund, 206, 208, 241*, 252.
Lamb, Joseph. 175.
Lambert, John. Gov, 36.
Lane, 195.
Laue, Cornelius, 33.
Large, Jacob, 269.
Lawrence, Commodore, 49, 150.
Lawrence, Elisha, 14*, 15, 29, 34, 49*, 51, 71, 92, 93, 150*, 169*, 170*, 171*, 264, 266*, 267*
Lawrence, Elizabeth, 150*.
Lawrence, Hannah, 150.
Lawrence, Helena, 150.
Lawrence, Sir James, 150.
Lawrence, James, 172*.
Lewrence, James S., 318.
Lawrence, John, 15*, 31, 34, 48, 49*, 93, 150*, 170, 172, 255.
Lawrence, John Brown, 49 150
Lawrence. Joseph, 15, 150, 170*, 175.
Lawrence, Lucy, 150
Lawrence, Mary, 150*.
Lawrence, Rebecca, 150.
Lawrence, Richard, 29, 93*.
Lawrence, Robert, 150.
Lawrence, Sir Robert, 150*.
Lawrence, Sarah, 150*.
Lawrence, T., 150.
Lawrence, Thomas, 61, 150, 308.
Lawrence. Wm., 15, 92, 93*. 150*, 167, 168*, 169, 170*, 199, 268, 216, 254, 292.
Lawrenson, Peter, 228.
Lawrie, Gawen, 215, 244. 249, 276, 277, 278.
Lawrie, Thomas, 237, 244
Layton, 156.
Layton, Samuel 15*
Layton, Wm., 106, 167*, 208 248, 250, 255, 257, 261
Leadbeaker. Mrs., 111.
Leads, Mary, 57.
Leaming, 103*.
Leaming & Spicer, 166*. 197*, 209, 210*.
LeChaudronnier, 232.
LeCompte Wm., 150.
Ledyard, Col, 70*. 145*
Lee Gen. Chas. 93*, 94*. 159*.
Lee, John 51.
Lee, Major, 35.
Leeds, Wm, 57, 97, 167, 183, 250, 251
LeFever, Mindart. 269.
Leffers, Ouka. 170*.
Lefferson, Auky, 305.
Lefferts, 299
Leffertson, 299.
Lendick, 250.

Leonard, 101*, 167*, 259.
Leonard, Catharine. 317*.
Leonard, Henry. 170, 171, 261*, 269.
Leonard, James, 207.
Leonard, John, 15, 169*, 170*, 171, 248, 261, 265, 269*.
Leonard, Nath'l, 317.
Leonard, Polly, 317.
Leonard, Samuel, 61*, 62*. 63*, 117*. 251, 253, 257, 258*, 260*, 261*, 262, 263
Leonard, Thomas, 14, 48, 170.
Leverson, 156.
Levey, John, 195.
Lewis, Commodore, 149.
Lippincott, 38, 65*, 66. 102*
Lippincott, Barth., 208.
Lippincott, Elisha, 195.
Lippincott, Esther Borden, 50
Lippincott, John, 250, 252, 255, 266.
Lippincott, R., 204.
Lippincott, Remembrance, 249. 257, 265
Lippincott, Restore, 170. 249.
Lippincott, Richard, 15, 18, 48, 49*, 50*, 62, 64*, 65. 66, 75*, 76*, 77*, 78, 81*. 82*, 84*, 86*, 87, 88, 104, 115*. 124*, 126*, 135*. 136*, 137*, 138*, 139*, 140*, 141*, 142*. 202, 204, 206, 207*, 209*, 214, 265.
Lippitt, Henry, 206, 207.
Lippitt, Moses, 255, 256, 257, 259, 261, 263, 266
Lippitt, Nathaniel, 241*, 242*.
Lis, (negro) 311.
Little, Christopher, Capt., 71, 113.
Little, Henry S., 196
Littles, John, 33, 296.
Livingston, Dr., 59.
Livingston, Edward, 109.
Livingston, Gov., 35, 70*.
Lloyd, 193.
Lloyd, John, 306.
Lloyd, Timothy, 269.
Lloyd, Wm, 248.
Lockhart, Mr. 55.
Longstreet, Derrick, 25*, 102.
Longstreet, Garret, 33.
Longstreet, John, Jr., 14, 225, 302*.
Longstreet. Samuel, 33
Longstreet, Stoffel, 171, 174
Loulax, Wm., 53.
Loockermans, Govert, 228. 229*.
Losing, Benj. J., 156. 158*, 160.
Lothrop, Rev John, 151.
Loochyell, 267*.
Love, Francis, 315
Lovelace, Gov., 41*, 42*, 43, 211*, 212.
Lucer, M., 206, 207.
Luyster, 178, 299.
Luyster, David, 193.
Luyster, Hendrick V. 183.
Luyster, John C., 307.
Luyster, John P., 183.
Lyell, David, 289*.
Lyon, Henry, 105.
Macdonough, 110.
Mackry, 296.
Mackay, John, 290.

Madison, James, 107, 110, 113.
Madock. Wm., 269.
Magie, Richard, 183.
Man, James, 187.
Manitto, 8*, 9*.
Manu, Sarah, 147.
Manners, John, 106.
Manning, Capt., 4.
Mapes, David, 144.
Marcellus, 10, 11, 299.
Marcy, Samuel S., 193.
Marlet, Doore, 54.
Maro, James, 69.
Marpole, George, 54.
Marriner, Capt. Wm., 127*.
Marsh, Henry, 243, 248, 256, 259.
Marshall, 94.
Mash, Henry, 255, 256.
Mashes, Henry, 267.
Masters, Clement, 250*, 255*.
Masters, Francis, 206, 208, 241, 242.
Mat, (negro) 311.
Mater, Joseph H., 301.
Matopeck, 250.
Mattage, Thomas, 169.
Matthews, Daniel, 127*.
Mattison, 170.
Mattix, Lewis, 239.
McDowell, Gideon C., 246, 267.
McDowell, Richard, 193.
McGee, 54.
McHenry, Geo., 193.
McKean, Washington, 193.
McKnight, 59, 72, 114, 152, 153.
McMullen, Robert, 38*, 68*.
Melag, Thomas, 171.
Melveu, James, 261.
Merepoppe, 251.
Meriwether, Mrs. Eliz., 275.
Merling, James, 253.
Merrick, Rev. John, 101.
Merrill, Wm, 259.
Mersereau, 231.
Meston, 250.
Mew, Richard, 277, 278*.
Mexson, Joseph, 317.
Meg, Capt., 144.
Micheau, 231.
Middleton, Amos, 175.
Middleton, Geo., 162.
Middleton. W. J., 108, 113.
Milileth, 250.
Miller James, 250.
Millery, Michael, 38, 68.
Millidge, Thomas, 51.
Mills, Griffith, 106.
Mills, Nathaniel B., 161.
Mills, Wm., 102*, 103.
Mingo, (negro) 260*
Minturn, E., 168.
Milop, Gauriel, 53.
Molass. Charles, 22*.
Moncrieff, Major, 127.
Moncton, Col., 159*, 160, 161*.
Monmouth, Duke of, 104.
Monteeth, Mrs. A. Stuart, 246,
Montgomery, 84.
Montgomery, Wm., 71.
Montigncy, Capt. de, 224.
Moody, 124.
Moody, Lady Debora, 145, 146*.
Moody, Bonnell, 58*.
Moody, James, 43, 51*, 58*, 59*, 60*.
Moor, Richard, 207.
Moor, Thomas, 206

vi.   INDEX.

Moore, 213, 296.
Moore, George H., 94.
Moore, Samuel, 210*, 216, 217*.
Moore, Thomas, 239*, 240.
Morford, 168.
Morford, Charles, 193.
Morford, Garret, 317.
Morford, John, 257, 259.
Morford, Thomas, 33, 167, 256.
Morford, Wm., 193, 306.
Morgan, Atei, 106*, 107, 304.
Morgan, Charles, 228, 229*. 293.
Morgan, Joseph, 268.
Morgin, Major, 82.
Morgan, Samuel, 107.
Mork, (negro) 311.
Morlett, Geo., 287.
Morrell. Thomas, 101.
Morris, 57*, 123, 137*, 170.
Morris, H., 149*.
Morris, John, 15, 50, 51, 65, 115.
Morris, Lewis, 3, 25, 37*, 57, 92, 96, 97, 100, 103*. 104*, 105*, 154, 166*, 169*. 225*, 226*, 233, 239, 244*, 250*, 252*, 253, 255*, 256*, 257*, 258*, 259, 260, 261*, 262, 263, 264, 265*, 266*.
Morris, Rebecca, 304.
Morris, Richard, 225*.
Morris, Robert, 15.
Morris, Robert Hunter, 90, 91, 293, 294.
Morris, Wm., 195.
Morrison, Elisha J., 195.
Morse, 161.
Morse, Prof., 161
Moses, (negro), 61*, 78*, 116, 117*.
Mott, Ann Maria, 317.
Mott, Catharine, 317.
Mott, Clementina, 317.
Mott, Gershom, 92, 93*, 256, 264, 291*.
Mott, James, 18, 67*, 71 113, 316*.
Mott, Jerusha, 317.
Mott, Leonard, 317.
Mott. Samuel, 317.
Mott, Sam'l C, 317.
Mount. Geo, 106, 207*, 241, 243.
Mount, Jas., 14.
Mount, John, 14.
Mount, Mathias, 303*.
Mullis, Jabob, 53,
Mullis, Jacob, 54.
Mundy, 157*.
Murat, Prince, 155.
Murphy, 185.
Murphy, Francis, 185.
Murphy, Henry C., 185, 227. 230, 231, 239.
Murphy. John G., 185.
Murphy, Joseph, 185.
Murphy, Timothy. 185.
Murray, Geo. C., 193, 305
Murray, Rev. John, 128*, 129*, 130*, 131*, 132*, 133* 134*, 135.
Murray, Joseph, 304*, 305.
Murray, Rebecca. 305.
Murray, Wm., 304, 305*, 307.
Murray. Wm. W., 305, 307 317.
Myanick, 251.
Myer, Peter, 51.
Nabby, 111.
Nauny, 111.

Neafie, 299.
Neaper, Alexander, 57.
Necktoha, 251.
Nedd, (negro), 260*.
Neill, Mr., 99.
Nemote, 251.
Nevins, 299.
Newell, Wm. A., 162*.
Newlin, 39.
Newman, 102.
Newman, Wm., 5, 225.
News, Bill, 53.
Nicolls, Matthias, 2, 244.
Nicolls, Richard, 1, 2*, 41*, 43, 104, 146, 145, 186, 197, 198*, 202, 208, 209*, 210.
211*, 212, 213, 215*, 217, 221, 222.
Nightingale, 69.
Nive, John, 295.
Noah, Major, 126.
Norris, Capt., 297.
North, John, 62*, 63*, 64*, 78.
Norton, Richard, 135.
Nowel, 191*.
Nowell, Increase, 189, 192*.
Oakerson, Samuel, 15.
O'Callaghan, E. B., 223*, 224, 226, 240.
Ogborne, Samuel, 306, 316, 317.
Ogden, 177.
Ogden, Colonel, 49.
Okeson, John, 14, 166*, 269*.
Oldmixon, 3*, 4.
Ong, Jacob, 259*.
Ongs, 205.
Ogborn, Ann, 183.
Orange, Prince, 232*.
Osborne, Richard, 263.
Osborne, Samuel, 14, 99
Osborne, Wm., 180.
Osgood, Mr. 84.
Ortley, Michael, 144*.
Oung, Isaac, 244*, 249.
Oung, Mary, 249*.
Page, 208.
Pains, John, 281.
Painter, John, 146.
Pangborn, 131*
Pangborn, Ann, 304.
Pangborn, L., 304
Pangborn, Lines, 44, 131*.
Par, 182.
Parke, John, 109.
Parker, 154, 287, 288.
Parker, Charles, 23, 149.
Parker, Gov.. 4*, 23.
Parker, Joel, 149.
Parker, John, 275.
Parker, Joseph, 73, 104*, 105. 166*, 177. 220*, 221, 241*, 242, 244, 266, 305.
Parker, Nathaniel, 15.
Parker, Peter, 199, 241, 250, 252.
Parker, Thos. 289*, 290, 291.
Patison, Geo., 11.
Patterson, 38*.
Patterson, Jas., 64, 306.
Patterson, John, 113, 306,* 307.
Patterson, Rebecca, 318.
Patterson, Wm., 180.
Pattison, Edward, 199, 204, 206, 207, 208.
Pattison, Robert, 256.
Paul, James, 292*.
Paul, Thomas, 292*.
Peale, Rembrandt, 111.
Pearce, 71, 113.
Pearson, Robert, 54.
Pearson, Thomas, 276*, 277*,

279*, 280.
Pedeu, Alexander, 246.
Pedicord, Caleb B., 100.
Pedler, Mary, 167.
Peepy, (Indian), 53.
Pembolus, John, 53.
Penhoose, 251.
Penn, 4.
Penn Admiral, 226.
Penn, Granville, 226.
Penn, Wm., 147, 277, 278*.
Penver. Capt.. 176.
Percy, Henry, 199, 208.
Percival, Commodore, 149*, 150.
Percy. James, 242.
Perez, Samuel, 234.
Perine, (or Perrine), 231.
Perine, John, 15.
Perorack, 251.
Perore, 251*.
Perot, Elliston, 152*.
Perropa, 251.
Peruppo, 251.
Peter, (Indian), 22*, 23*.
Petrous, 250.
Pew, James, 14, 38*.
Pharo, Amos, 304.
Pharo, Jarvis, 54.
Pharo, Joseph W., 182.
Pharo, Samuel, 182.
Philip, (Indian), 53.
Phillip, J., 307.
Phillips, John, 175.
Pratt, Martha, 75. 87*, 88.
Pidgeon, Wm., 54.
Pike, 53.
Pike, John, 3, 210.
Pintard, Anthony, 253, 254*, 260, 261*, 262, 265.
Pintard, Jeremiah, 265.
Pintard, John, 14, 296*.
Pintard, Lewis, 296*, 297.
Pintard, Thos., 296
Pitcher, Capt. Molly, 155*, 156*.
Pitlochie, 245*, 246*.
Pitney. Jonathan, 173.
Platt, Wm., 149.
Plumstead, Clement, 277, 278*, 282, 283, 285.
Polhemus, 102, 299.
Polhemus, Johannes, 170*, 269*,
Polhemus, John, 15, 38*,
Polhemus, Tobias, 305.
Pompshire, 54.
Pompshire, John, 53*, 54.
Poole, Gen. Richard, 113.
Poor, Gen., 159.
Popamora, (Indian), 205*.
Pope, 111.
Pope, Freelove, 297.
Porter, 109.
Porurus, 250,
Potter, Ephraim, 250*
Potter, Gen. James, 158.
Potter, Joseph, 180, 185.
Potter, Thomas, 101*, 128*, 129*, 130*, 131*, 132*, 133* 134*, 135*, 187, 206*, 207.
Potter, William Wilson, 158
Powrnas, 251.
Preston, 180.
Price, 46.
Price, Benj., 220.
Price, James, 15.
Price, John, 45*, 175.
Price, Michael, 14.
Price, W., 149*, 150.
Prince, Thomas, 187.
Probasco, 246, 299.
Prund, 21.

Pulaski, Count, 46.
Puropa, 250.
Pye, John E ,, 197.
Pygan, Alexander, 281.
Pyie, Simon, 101, 180*.
Quackenbush, 246, 299.
Quahick, 251.
Quahuk, 251.
Quaquahela, 53.
Quaquag, Derrick, 53.
Quay, John, 113.
Quicksels, John, 175*.
Quikems. (Indian), 229.
Rambo. Peter, 42.
Randolph, 16, 88, 151*, 148.
Randolph, Bennington, F. 151.
Randolph. Daniel, 17, 18* 49, 64, 75*, 78, 79*, 80,135* 136*, 137*.
Randolph, James, 69
Randolph, Joseph, 304.
Randolph, Jeseph F., 151.
Randolph, Reuben, 304*.
Randolph, Capt. Reuben F 44*, 45, 67.
Randolph, Theodore F, 151
Rawson. 236.
Ray, Robert, 57.
Raybold, Rev. Geo A., 102
Read, 57.
Read, Charles, 53.
Read, John, 57*.
Read, Stacy B., 184.
Reape, Sarah, 167*, 171, 255
Reape. William, 165, 186 203, 204*, 207, 208, 209* 255.
Redford, Margaret. 246.
Redford, Samuel, 267.
Redford, Wm., 246*.
Reed, Daniel D., 180.
Reed, Gov., 162.
Reeder, Elizabeth, 246.
Reeder, Jeremiah, 246.
Reid, James, 255, 256.
Reid, John, 168. 170*, 171*, 234, 238*, 246*, 250*, 256, 258*, 261*, 264, 265, 269*, 270*, 274, 280, 290.
Reid, Jonathan, 303.
Reid, Margaret, 238.
Relly, Rev. James, 133*, 134.
Remine, John, 269.
Remsen, 299.
Remsen, Peter, 295*,
Reushall, Thomas, 253.*
Renshaw, 152*.
Reynold, Peter, 195.
Reynolds, Christopher Robert, 99.
Reynolds. Wm., 113.
Rezeau, (Rezo), 231.
Rhea, David, 71, 248, 305.
Rhea, J., 174.
Rhea, John, 308.
Rhea, Lieut., 61, 117.
Rhodes, Capt. Wm., 69.
Richard, John, 13*.
Richards, Thomas H., 193.
Richardson, 178.
Richardson, R., 201*, 204, 205, 208, 209*.
Richardson, Richard, 199, 200, 202, 206, 207, 208, 244, 250.
Richardson, Wm., 203.
Rigg (or Riggs) Ambrose, 277, 278*.
Ritchies, Polly, 54.
Rittenhouse, 109.
Rivington, 141*.
Roberts, Lieut., 16, 17.
Robertson, Capt., 68.

INDEX. vii.

Robertson, Gen., 81.
Robin, (negro), 287.
Robin, M. Abbe, 109.
Robins, Aaron, 172*.
Robbins, Elijah, 16.
Robbins, George R. 162.
Robbins, Miles, 162
Robbins, Moses, 17, 266.
Robinson, Patrick, 275
Robinson, Thomas, 187.
Robyn, 231.
Rochembeau, Count de 83.
Rockhed, 239.
Rogers, Capt. Jesse, 148.
Rogers, John, 18, 147*.
Rogers, Michael, 175*
Rose, Mrs 156.
Rose, Wm. 122.
Ross, Miles, 162
Ross, Capt. Stewart, 16.
Rowland, Rev. Mr. 90*, 91*, 92*.
Royse, 283.
Royse, John, 275.
Ruckman, 267.
Ruckman, John, 166, 168, 171*. 202, 206, 207, 208*, 253, 256, 259, 260, 263, 266.
Ruckman, Jonathan, 169.
Ruckman, Samuel, 171*,
Ruckmau, Thomas, 172.
Rudyard, 20,
Rudyard, Ben, 275.
Rudyard, John, 275.
Rudyard, Thomas, 275*,276*, 277, 278*.
Rue, Elizabeth 302*.
Rue, Mathias 302*.
Ruff, Daniel, 100.
Russell, 38, 115*.
Russell, John, 61, 62*, 63*, 64*, 65*, 66, 78, 115*, 116*, 305.
Rutledge. Mr., 84*,
Ryall, Daniel B , 163.
Sabine, 48, 50,
Saddler, Richard, 5*. 208, 226*, 240, 242*, 243. 249.
Salter, John, 290*, 291.
Salter, Joseph, 71, 150.
Salter, Lincon, 290.
Salter, Mordecai, 290*.
Salter, Richard, 53, 92, 150, 168, 250, 258, 260*, 261*, 262, 263, 265, 267, 268, 286*, 287, 290*, 291*.
Saltonstall, Gov., 148.
Samuel, (a servant,) 261*.
Sandam. 251.
Sandford, 220.
Sandford. Wm., 243*.
Sandilands, 277, 280.
Sarah, Nicholas, 256* 257.
Sare, (Negro,) 311.
Sargent, 162.
Sargent, Jonathan, D. 93.
Sauvigny, de., 84, 86.
Schenck (Schanck, &c.) 73*, 87, 114*, 259, 299. 300,
Schenck, Chrineyouce, 307.
Schenck, Eleanor, 317*.
Schenck, Garre , 93, 259. 269, 293, 305
Schanck, G. C., 299.
Schenck, Hendrick, 301, 310*. 317.
Scheuck, Jacob, 310.
Schenck, John, 73, 78, 127, 259, 269*, 301. 310*.
Schenck, Jonathan, 310.
Schenck, Peter, 302*, 313*.
Schenck, Roelof. 298*, 308*, 309*. 310*, 312*, 313*.
Schenck. Tylee, 310.
Schenck, Wm., 310.

Schuyler, 299.
Scobey, Timothy, 15.
Scott, 81, 146.
Scott, Gen. Chas., 93.
Scott, Esther, 315.
Scott, George, 246.
Scott, Sir John, 245*.
Scott, John, 269,
Scott Joseph, W., 142.
Scott, Wm,, 255.
Scudder, 318.
Scudder, Col. Jacob, 162, 163.
Scudder, John, 71.
Scudder, John Anderson, 163.
Scudder, Dr. Nathaniel, 28*, 31, 32, 71*. 73*, 93, 114*, 182*, 163, 302*.
Seabrook, James, 260.
Seabrook, Mary, 317*.
Seabrook, Thomas, 71, 78, 317.
Seahoppra, 251,
Secoes, 250.
Secphu, 250.
Seguine (or Seguine,) 231.
Servauier, James, 51.
Seymour, Henry, 145*.
Seymour, Horatio 112, 145.
Seymour, Mary Ledyard, 145*.
Shaak, Capt., 125.
Shaberly, Wm., 206, 207.
Shaddock, Tom, 206.
Shaddock, Wm., 204*, 207*, 208, 256.
Sharp Thomas, 261,
Shatlock, Wm., 214.
Shearman, Wm , 208.
Shenotape, 251*.
Shepherd, 156.
Shepherd, Catharine, 316, 235.
Shepherd, Jack, 90.
Shepherd, Joseph, 316.
Shongham, 250.
Shrieve, Caleb, 250, 254. 255*.
Sickles, 299.
Sickles, Wm., I., 183.
Silvester, Nathaniel, 165. 206, 207.
Simons, Randolph, 259*.
Sims, Lancaster, 233.
Sissell, Richard, 207.
Skelton, 53.
Skelton, Charles, 162.
Skelton, Robert, 255.
Skinner, 98
Skinner, B. G., 51.
Skinner, Gen. Cortlandt, 37, 50, 70*, 113.
Skinner, Elisha, 51.
Skullthorp, 184.
Slater, 283*.
Slater, Richard, 286.
Slender, Robert, 109.
Slidell, John, 163.
Slocum, 154.
Slocum, Gyles, 239.
Slocum, John, 105*, 154*, 166, 177, 214*, 239*, 249* 250*, 251, 254, 255, 261.
Slocum, Nathaniel, 249, 251.
Sluyter, Peter, 230.
Smith, 36*.
Smith, Anthony, 306.
Smith, Asher, 180*, 183.
Smith, David, 15.
Smith, Derrick, 205
Smith, Edward, 186, 187*, 201*, 202, 206, 207, 239*.
Smith, Eliz, 318.
Smith, George Allen, 269.

Smith, J., 55.
Smith, Ja, 291, 292.
Smith, James, 90*, 291.
Smith, John, 5, 23, 187, 207, 208, 225, 241, 251, 256, 267*, 288.
Smith, John P., 185.
Smith, Laurence, 293.
Smith, Peleg, 298.
Smith, Philip, 289.
Smith, Robert, 23.
Smith, Samuel, 14.
Smith, Thomas, 122*, 171, 172, 267.
Smith, Wm., 14, 92, 264.
Smithey, And., 275.
Smock, 48, 113, 137*, 299, 300.
Smock, Capt. Barney 72.
Smock, Denise H., 177.
Smock, George, 305,
Smock, Hendrick, 28, 32, 305.
Smock, Henry, 137.
Smock, Johannes, 269.
Smock, John, 71. 78. 306.
Smock, R. P., 177.
Snawsell, Thomas, 248*, 249.
Snell, 5*, 225*.
Snowden, Ross, 151.
Snozell, Thomas, 243, 244.
Sonmans, Arent, 182, 277, 278, 282, 283, 285.
Sonmans, Peter, 182, 282, 283, 284, 285.
Sooy, Joseph, 289.
Soper, Hezekiah, 46. 148.
Soper, Joseph, 45*, 46*.
Soper, Reuben, 45*, 46*.
Soper, Timothy, 148.
Southard, Samuel L., 21, 153.
Southwick, Cassandra, 234, 235.
Sowden, Thomas, 54.
Spader, 299.
Sparks, 50, 194.
Sparks, Robert, 101.
Spicer, 103*, 146.
Spicer, Benjamin, 207.
Spicer, Jacob, 53.
Spicer, Samuel, 1, 146*, 165, 167*, 200, 202, 206, 207, 208, 229.
Spilsbury, John, 188.
Spinning, Asel, 183.
Spragg, Jeremiah, 148.
Springer, Benjamin, 54.
Spar, John, 191*, 192*.
Standish, Capt. Miles, 187.
Starkey, John, 255*, 256.
Statsir, 299.
Stratton, J. L. N., 162.
Stedman, Edmund G., 300.
Steelman, 46*, 73, 114.
Stephensen, Henry, 141*.
Sterling, James, 128.
Stevens, Benjamin 91, 92*.
Stevens, J., 293.
Stevens, John, 53.
Stevens, Nicholas, 259, 261, 263*
Stevenson, 73, 114.
Stewart, Abner, 175.
Stewart. John, 122*, 123*, 261*, 262, 264.
Still, Isaac, 53, 54.
Stillwell, James, 14.
Stillwell, Col.. Jarrett, 113, 265*, 267, 268.
Stillwell, Jeremiah, 261, 264, 306*, 315, 316.
Stillwell, John, 71, 174, 306*.
Stillwell, Joseph, 78, 303*, 304, 306*, 315, 316.

Stillwell, Mary, 303.
Stillwell, Obadiah, 303*.
Stillwell, Rebecca, 306, 317, 318.
Stillwell, Samuel, 15.
Stillwell, Thos., 306.
Stillwell, Wm., 307
Stirling, Lord, 159*.
Stockton, John, 91*, 92.
Stockton, L. H., 142.
Stockton, R. Jr., 142*.
Stockton, R., 142.
Stockton, Richard, 91.
Stockton, R. V., 51.
Stokes, 194.
Stokes, John, 68.
Store, Josiah, 51. 53,
Store, Sarah, 53, 54.
Store, Thomas, 53, 54*, 152*.
Storer. 87, 127*.
Story, Capt , 125.
Story, John, 54.
Story, John B., 306.
Story, Robert, 207*, 239.
Story, Wm., 172.
Stout, Alice, 53.
Stout, Benjamin, 52, 135, 171, 256. 261*, 269.
Stout, David, 52, 169*, 259, 261*.
Stout, James, 52, 67*, 259, 261*, 264.
Stout, John, 18, 22, 52, 53, 106, 167*, 169, 208, 241*. 243, 253, 255, 257*, 259*, 267, 280*, 289.
Stout, Jonathan, 252, 253, 259, 264, 306*.
Stout, Lucy, 150.
Stout, Mary, 53.
Stout, Penelope, 51*, 52, 53.
Stout, Peter, 52, 255, 256, 259*.
Stout, Richard, 1, 51, 52*, 53, 106, 113, 165, 168*, 17 , 171, 200, 201*, 202*, 204*, 206, 207, 208, 209*, 216, 241, 243, 251, 259, 269.
Stout, Robert, 15.
Stout, Sarah, 53.
Stout, Wessel T., 305.
Stout, Wm., 250, 252.
Stowlett, Geo., 105,
Strong, Dr., 10.
Strycker, 299.
Stuart, 233*.
Studson, Lieut. Joshua, 17, 43*, 44*, 69.
Studson, Mrs., 17*.
Stuyvesant, Gov. Peter, 146*, 229.
Suke, (Indian), 22.
Sullivan, Gen., 49.
Sunderland. 215.
Sutphen, 299.
Sutphen, John, 269, 308, 309.
Sutphen, Wm. T., 160, 183.
Suydam, 299.
Swauelea, Isaac, 52. 53.
Swart, Cornelius, 14, 48.
Sykes, Geo., 162.
Sylvester, Nathaniel 1.
Symonds, Mr., 192.
Talbot, Rev. John, 55*, 56*, 57*.
Talinguanecan, 250.
Talman, Christopher, 14.
Talman, Oliver, 15.
Tauner, 167, 171, 176, 183.
Tanners, 185.
Tapchalaway, 250.
Tartt, Edward, 206, 207, 208, 209, 216*, 220, 280.
Tawlayenum, 54.

viii. INDEX.

Taylor, 167, 266*.
Taylor, Col. Geo., 48, 67*, 71*.
Taylor, Edward, 29, 31*, 32, 93*, 175, 193, 255, 268.
Taylor, Geo., Jr. 14.
Taylor, John, 14, 15, 29, 31, 48*, 93, 266, 306
Taylor, Jonathan, 297.
Taylor, Joseph, 14, 317.
Taylor, Mary, 48, 297*, 298*.
Taylor, Morford, 15, 137.
Taylor, Robert, 207*.
Taylor, Samuel, 136, 137*.
Taylor, Samuel I., 193.
Taylor, Thomas, 157*, 261*.
Taylor, Wm., 48.
Teedyescunk, (Indian), 53, 54.
Telamen, (Indian), 53.
TenEyck, 299.
TenEyck, John C., 163.
Tennent, Gilbert, 92.
Tennent, Rev. John, 246.
Tennent, Rev. Wm., 90*, 91*, 92*, 101*, 16C*.
Terhune, 299.
Tessemaker, Dominie, 231.
Thatcher, Dr., 82.
Thomas, Rev. A. C., 133*, 134, 135.
Thomas, Capt., 16.
Thomas, Elisha, 106.
Thomas, Gabriel, 95, 181.
Thomas, Wm. 187.
Thomson, Cornelius, 171.
Thompson, John, 14.
Thompson, Thomas, 46, 95*.
Thompson, Wm., 73*, 114.
Thorne, Thomas, 14, 175*.
Throckmorton, 53, 101, 160, 214.
Throckmorton, Job, 100, 167, 176, 208, 255, 266.
Throckmorton, John, 14, 102, 104, 105, 166, 176, 186, 187, 206, 207, 239*, 244*, 249*, 250, 269, 280.
Throckmorton, Jos., 33.
Thurston, Edward, 186, 207*.
Tice, John, 310*.
Tiebout, 156.
Tilley, James, 38, 39.
Tilton, Abigail, 146.
Tilton, Abraham, 175*.
Tilton, Clayton, 14, 18, 49*, 64, 75*, 135*, 136*, 137, 139*, 140*.
Tilton, Daniel, 170, 171*.
Tilton, Esther, 146.
Tilton, Ezekiel, 14.
Tilton, John, 1, 14, 66, 77, 79, 85, 137*, 138, 145*, 146*, 165, 200, 201, 204*, 206, 239, 256*, 259, 262.
Tilton, John, P. L., 184.
Tilton, Jonathan, 177.
Tilton, Mary, 146*.
Tilton, Peter, 104, 105, 167, 204, 244*, 240, 252*, 253*, 255*, 256*, 257*, 258, 259, 266, 280.
Tilton, Farah, 146.
Tilton, Sylvester, 44*, 45*, 304*.
Tilton, Thomas, 146, 171.
Tilton, Wm., 1-5, 317.
Timpany, Robert, 51.
Toby, Sir, 108.
Tocus, (Indian), 22.
Tohokenum, 54.
Tom, Capt. Wm., 40*, 41*, 42*, 43*.

Tom, (negro), 259.
Tomkins, Nathan, 207.
Tompkins, Gov. 93.
Tompkins, Nathaniel, 207.
Tomson, Cornelius, 269.
Tomson, Henry, 187.
Tomson, John, 207.
Torrey, 194.
Torrington, Admiral, 223.
Torry, Wm., 193.
Tory, Joseph, 187.
Totamy, (Indian), 53, 54*.
Totamy, Moses, 53*, 54.
Totman, (Tilton), John, 229.
Townly, R.ch'd, 314.
Townsend, 146.
Townsend, John, 206, 207.
Trewax, Jacob, 253.
Truax, 53, 299.
Truex, John, 174*.
Troup, Lieut. 51.
Tucker. Ebenezer, 18.
Tucker, John, 252, 253, 255.
Tunis, 299.
Tunison, Derrick, 239, 242.
Turner, Robert, 277, 278.
Tye, Col. (a slave), 72, 73, 114*.
Tyssen, Peter, 312*, 313*.
Unami. Great, (Chief) 10.
Upham, Rev. C. W., 94.
Usselton, Francis, 255.
Uzselton, Providence, 250.
Usselton, Thomas, 256.
VanBrunt, 299.
VarBuskirk, Jacob, 51.
VanBrackle, Anna, 185.
VanBrockle, 72, 113.
VanBrunt, Hendrick, 71.
VanBrunt, Nicholas, 33*.
VauBuskirk, Abraham, 51.
Vance, 54.
VanCleaf, (variously spelled) 299.
VanCleaf, Benjamin. 269.
VanCleaf, Isabrant, 289*.
VanCleaf, Wm., 317.
VanDame, Isaac, 293*.
Vanderbilt, Commodore, 179, 180.
Vanderhoef, Cornelius P., 113.
Van lerveer, 299, 300.
Van Ierveer, Cornelius, 33, 93*.
Vanderveer. David R., 183.
Vanderveer, Ellen, 318.
Vanderveer, Garret, 195*.
Vanderveer, John G., 197.
VanLeventer, 299.
VanDorn, 299.
VanDoen, Isaac, 113, 310.
VanDor. Jacob, 261*.
VanDyke, 299.
VanEmburg, Major, 69*.
VanGhelt, Hendrick, 300*
Van Hise, 299.
VanHook, Lawrence, 269*
VanKirk. 299, 310.
VanKirk, Alice, 312*.
VauKirk, John, 37*, 245, 267, 312*.
VanMater, 35*, 36, 177, 299.
VanMater, Aaron, 183
VanMater, Cyrenius B., 305.
VanMater. Daniel, 14.
VanMater, Gilbert, 72, 114.
VanMater, Hendrick, 14.
VanMater, John, 269.
Vannote, 54.
Vannote. Peter, 15.
VanOrden, John. 51.
VanPatten, Aart Theunissen, 229.

VanPelt, 299.
VanPelt, John, 113.
Vanprincis, 52.
VanSchaick, 299.
VanSickelen, 299.
VanSwieton, Moses, 281.
VanVleek, John, 313.
Vaughan, John, 253, 255, 256, 257, 259, 260, 264.
Veghte, 299.
Verazzano, 6*.
Vergennes, Count de, 76, 83*, 84*, 85*. 86, 87.
Vesey, Rev. Mr. 96.
Vickard, Thomas, 255.
Vincent, Ensign, 73.
Voorhees, 299.
Vought, 299.
Vowavapon, (Indian), 21, 22.
Vredenburgh, 299.
Waddell, Henry, 29, 150.
Waeir, Abraham, 148.
Wainwright, John, 17.
Wainwright, Nicholas, 99.
Wainwright, Thomas, 250*.
Wales, Edmund L B., 193.
Wales, Frances, 252.
Walker, George, 174.
Wall, Garrett, 251, 256, 259*, 260*, 262*, 264.
Wall, Garret D., 142, 163*, 184, 185.
Wall, Gerard, 251.
Wall, James, 54
Wall, Col. James W., 163.
Wall, John, 171*, 206, 269, 386.
Wall, Joseph, 71, 113.
Wall, Walter, 206, 207, 208*, 251, 267.
Walling, James, 306.
Walling, John, 306.
Walling, Philip, 306.
Waln, Richard, 175, 317.
Walters, Anthony, 240.
Walton, 73.
Walton, Elisha, 71, 78
Walton. John, 62, 63, 64, 302, 303.
Walton. Wm., 14, 113.
Wamaton, 251.
Ward, Anthony, 246
Ward, Marmaduke, 207.
Ward, Michael, 295, 296.
Wardell, 154.
Wardell, Ebenezer, 15.
Wardell, Eliakim, 5, 104, 199, 201, 204*, 205, 206, 207, 208, 224, 248, 249, 253, 255*.
Wardell, John, 14, 49, 50.
Wardell, Joseph, 269.
Wardell, Peter, 15.
Wardell, Solomon, 144.
Ware, 100.
Warn, 172.
Warne, Thomas, 20, 220, 237*, 250*, 257*, 259, 277, 278.
Warner, Capt., 65, 115
War:en, Admiral, 129.
Warring, John, 269.
Washington, Gen., 14, 37, 44, 49, 59, 61, 62*, 66, 74, 75, 76*, 77, 78*, 79*, 80*, 81*, 82*, 83*, 84*, 85*, 86, 87, 89*, 90, 93*, 94, 95, 119, 110, 126, 138* 142, 152, 156*, 159*.
Washington, Lawrence, 150.
Washington, Matilda, 150.
Watemar, 293.
Watson, 50, 152*, 153, 154, 162, 29 !*.

Watson, Gawin, 54, 269*.
Watson, John, 292.
Watson, Luke, 210*, 21 217*.
Watters, Wm., 100*.
Wawapn, 251.
Wayana'am, 251.
Wayne, Gen., 59, 158*, 159
Webb, George, 206, 267*.
Webb, Thomas, 100.
Webley, Audrey, 253.
Webley, Edward, 250.
Webley, Mary, 252.
Webley, Thomas, 249, 25 253, 256, 261, 262*, 280.
Webley, Walter, 225*, 243.
Webster, 43.
Weenis, 93.
Welehaiely, 269*.
Wells, 308.
Wequehela, 269.
Werwey, Hendrick, 269.
West, 38, 275.
West, Mrs. Anne, 275.
West, Bartholomew, 19! 204, 206, 207, 208.
West, John, 250*, 252*, 25; 261, 269, 275*.
West, Jonathan, 34, 38.
West, Joseph, 96, 252*, 256 264.
West, Robert, 206, 207, 25; 277, 278*.
West, Stephen, 34, 37*, 24(252.
Westcott, Geo. C., 74.
Wetherill, John, 54.
Wharton, Edward, 202*, 206 207.
Wheelwright, Geo., 53.
Whiley, Mary, 297.
White, 135*, 283.
White, Aaron, 60, 61,* 62* 63, 64*, 75, 78*, 135*, 137 139*, 152.
White. Britton, 15.
White, Catharine, 317*.
White, Col. 152*.
White, Elizabeth, 287.
White, Gordon, D., 196.
White, Jacob, 183*.
White, Jemima, 317*.
White Jeremiah, 195*, 288.
White, John, 152, 275*, 276, 287.
White, Josiah, 15, 152.
White, Mary, 252.
White. P., 102.
White, Phil, 49, 50*, 60, 61*, 62*, 63*, 64*, 65*, 66*, 76* 77*, 78*, 80*, 116*, 117*, 135*, 136*, 137, 138, 139*, 140, 152*.
White, Robert, 252*.
White, Sam., 252, 253.
White, Timothy, 317.
White, Wm., 243.
Whitehead, Wm. A., 19, 104, 226, 265.
Whitfield, 90, 91.
Whitlock, John, 255*, 257, 302
Whitlock, Lydia, 303.
Whitlock, Thomas, 5, 106, 167, 206, 207, 208, 229, 255*.
Whitlock, Wm., 240, 248, 255.
Willocks, George, 172*.
Wilcocks, Wm., 78.
Wilcox, Thomas, 478.
Wild, Jonathan, 90.
Wilgus, Richard, 114.
Wilkins, 266*.

INDEX. ix.

Wilkison, Wm., 269.
Will, Indian, 25*, 26*, 154.
Willett. Samuel, 256, 260, 263*.
Willett, Wm., 308
Willetts, James, 44*.
Williams, 37, 38, 55.
Williams, Aert, 269.
Williams, Edward, 31, 93 250, 255.
Williams, Ezekiel, 34, 37*.
Williams, John, 14, 225, 241, 250, 252*, 253, 255.
Williams, Mary, 253.
Williams, Roger, 147, 186.
Williams, Wm., 100, 259
Williamson, 84, 178.
Williamson, Albert, 292.
Williamson, David, 177, 313.
Williamson, John, 5.
Willockins, 53.

Wilson, Andrew, 171*, 269
Wilson, James, 54.
Wilson, John, 106, 188*, 204 206, 207, 208*, 249, 255, 256, 257*, 260, 263, 269*, 314*.
Wilson, Peter, 256, 269.
Wilson, Wm., 46* 47, 158*, 159.
Wilson, Wm. R., 158*.
Winder, 275.
Winder, Margaret, 275.
Winder, Sam'l, 275*, 314.
Winner, Capt. Jonathan, 148.
Winter, James. 303.
Winter, Wm., 253, 264.
Winterbottom, 161.
Winterton, 204.
Winterton, Thomas, 206, 207, 208, 209.

Withers, Robert, 11.
Witherspoon, John. 107.
Witter, Wm., 187, 189*
Wood Grace, 259.
Wood, John, 34, 38*, 68, 207*.
Wood, Joseph, 106.
Woodhull, Anna Maria, 112, 163.
Woodhull, Dr. John, 75, 101*, 160*.
Woodmansee, 39, 43, 266*.
Woodmansee, David. 102.
Woodmansee, Gabriel, 175.
Woodward, Anthony, 169, 267, 268, 287.
Woodward, George, 175.
Woodward, John, 51
Woodward, Joseph, 184.
Woolley, Andrew, 53, 54*, 152.

Woolley, Benjamin, 15.
Woolley, C., 286*.
Woolley, Eben-zer, 53.
Woolley, Emanuel, 206, 207.
Woolley, James T., 195.
Woolley, John, 170, 171, 253, 266.
Woolley, Joseph. 53.
Woolley Wm., 253.
Worth, Mrs. Mercy, 40.
Worth, Wm,, 251, 265.
Worthley, John, 78, 255, 257.
Wright, Caleb, 39.
Wright, Mary. 253*.
Wright, Nathan, 175*.
Wright, Samuel G., 162.
Wyckoff, 299.
Wyckoff, Anke, 71.
Wyckoff, Col. 59, 72, 114.
Wyckoff, Peter, 94, 171, 180.
Zevel, Peter, 228.